**Property of**
Charlotte County
Public Schools

# Florida
# Biology

Stephen Nowicki

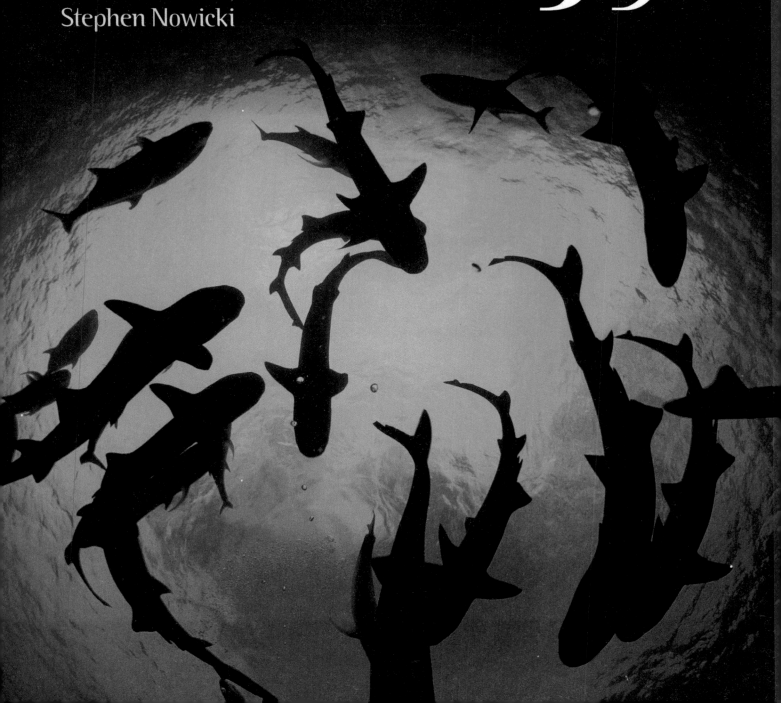

# Stephen Nowicki, Ph.D.

Stephen Nowicki grew up with a strong interest in music and at one time wanted to be a classical musician. A biology course in college sparked his excitement for biology, leading him to major in both biology and music. Nowicki obtained his bachelor's and master's degrees from Tufts University. He received his doctorate in neurobiology and behavior from Cornell University in 1985.

Nowicki is now Dean and Vice Provost for Undergraduate Education, as well as Bass Fellow and Professor in the departments of Biology, Psychology, and Neurobiology at Duke University. He has taught at Duke since 1989, where he directed a complete redesign of the introductory biology program. Nowicki's research explores animal communication and sexual selection from an integrative perspective that includes a wide range of behavioral, ecological, neuroethological, developmental, genetic, and evolutionary approaches. Birds are a common model system for his work, but he and his students also have worked with insects, spiders, shrimp, lobsters, lizards, and primates.

Nowicki's research has been published in more than 95 articles in scientific journals, including *Science, Nature,* and *Proceedings of the National Academy of Sciences.* He coauthored the book *The Evolution of Animal Communication: Reliability and Deception in Signaling Systems* and is the author of a video lecture series based on the introductory biology course he taught at Duke. In 2010, he was elected a Fellow of the American Association for the Advancement of Science.

Outside of his professional interests, Nowicki continues to enjoy music. He has played the trombone since the fourth grade, and he plays both trombone and tuba with the Duke University Pep Band at basketball games. Juggling and cooking are other hobbies that he enjoys in his free time. Nowicki is married to Susan Peters, who also studies animal communication, and they have one son, Schuyler. Nowicki and his wife live in Durham, North Carolina.

## Cover Photo Credits

*Sharks* ©Jeffrey L. Rotman/Corbis; *beetle* ©Ocean/Corbis

2019 Edition
Copyright © by Houghton Mifflin Harcourt Publishing Company

Florida Standards courtesy of the Florida Department of Education.

Printed in the U.S.A.

ISBN   978-1-328-79284-6

3 4 5 6 7 8 9 10   0868   26 25 24 23 22 21 20 19 18

4500709493           B C D E F G

# Online Edition

 **HMHScience.com**

 **SELF-CHECK Online**
HMHScience.com
**GO ONLINE**

Check your progress and get immediate feedback.

 **INTERACTIVE Review**
HMHScience.com
**GO ONLINE**

Prepare for upcoming tests in a fun format.

 **WEBLINKS**
HMHScience.com
**GO ONLINE**

Extend and enrich each chapter's content with hand-selected resource links.

 **Web Quest**
HMHScience.com
**GO ONLINE**

Explore the Web to answer scientific questions.

 **Smart Grapher**
HMHScience.com
**GO ONLINE**

Analyze your data and visualize experimental results.

**Human Growth Hormone**

Growth Ho...

| 1 | 5 | 6 | 7 | 8 | 9 | 10 | 11 | 12 | 13 | 14 | 15 | 16 | 17 | 18 | 19 | 20 |

Age (years)

☐ Growth Hormone, girls     ☐ Growth Hormone, boys

 **BIOZINE**

Connect to current events with features such as science news feeds, updates on current biology research, careers, and in-depth detail about unit features.

# Look for

# Labs ↗ Online

↗ HMHScience.com

## Standard Labs

Focus on experimental skills and the application of chapter concepts through the use of scientific methods.

## Open Inquiry Labs

Drive the lab activity—you make decisions about what to research and how to do it.

## STEM Labs

Explore the engineering design process through hands-on inquiry projects.

## QuickLabs

Encounter key concepts in your classroom with QuickLabs. They're right in your book.

## Biotechnology Labs

Experience the intersection of technology and biology.

## Forensics Labs

Investigate practical applications of biology, such as crime-scene analysis.

## Challenge Labs

Extend your understanding and lab expertise with advanced techniques, equipment, and content.

## Probeware Labs

Integrate electronic data-collection technology into exciting activities that enhance hands-on biology.

## Video Labs

Enjoy professionally produced demonstrations of labs and activities.

## Virtual Labs

Conduct meaningful experiments with tools, instruments, and techniques that take you beyond your classroom.

VIRTUAL Lab

# Content Reviewers

**Mark Baustian, Ph.D.**
President
West Hill Biological Resources
Spencer, NY

**John Beaver, Ph.D.**
Professor Emeritus
College of Education and Human Services
Western Illinois University
Macomb, IL

**Elizabeth A. De Stasio, Ph.D.**
Associate Professor and Raymond H. Herzog
   Professor of Science
Department of Biology
Lawrence University
Appleton, WI

**Dan Franck, Ph.D.**
Botany Education Consultant
Chatham, NY

**Francine Galko, M.A.**
Science Consultant
Austin, TX

**Linda Graham, Ph.D.**
Professor of Botany
Department of Botany
University of Wisconsin
Madison, WI

**David Harbster, M.A. in Biology Education**
Professor of Biology
Paradise Valley Community College
Phoenix, AZ

**Anthony Ippolito, Ph.D.**
Visiting Assistant Professor
Department of Biological Sciences
DePaul University
Chicago, IL

**Sönke Johnsen, Ph.D.**
Assistant Professor
Department of Biology
Duke University
Durham, NC

**Paula Lemons, Ph.D.**
Assistant Professor of the Practice
Department of Biology
Duke University
Durham, NC

**Lori Marino, Ph.D.**
Senior Lecturer
Neuroscience and Behavioral Biology Program
Emory University
Atlanta, GA

**Louise McCullough, M.D./Ph.D.**
Director of Stroke Research
Department of Neurology
University of Connecticut Health Center
Farmington, CT

**Elizabeth Panter, R.D.**
Dietitian
Clinical Nutrition Department
Johns Hopkins Bayview Medical Center
Baltimore, MD

**Sheila Patek, Ph.D.**
Assistant Professor
Department of Integrative Biology
University of California
Berkeley, CA

**Adam Savage, B.S., M.F.A.**
Science Consultant
Chicago, IL

**F. Daniel Vogt, Ph.D.**
Professor
Department of Biological Sciences
State University of New York at Plattsburgh
Plattsburgh, NY

**Jerry Waldvogel, Ph.D.**
Associate Professor
Department of Biological Sciences
Clemson University
Clemson, SC

## Safety Reviewer

**Juliana Texley, Ph.D.**
Former K–12 Science Teacher and School
   Superintendent
Boca Raton, FL

## Program Consultant

**Laine Gurley, Ph.D.**
Biology Teacher
Rolling Meadows High School
Rolling Meadows, IL

# Teacher Reviewers and Lab Evaluators

**Elaine Armstrong**
Battle Ground High School
Battle Ground, WA

**Amy Bell**
Arcadia High School
Phoenix, AZ

**Jerry Bell**
Desert Vista High School
Phoenix, AZ

**Tracey Boyd, M.Ed.**
West Brook HIgh School
Beaumont, TX

**Bonnie Brenner**
Niles West High School
Niles, IL

**Shirley Bryant**
Granada Hills Charter High School
Granada Hills, CA

**Jason Campbell**
Schaumburg High School
Schaumburg, IL

**Christopher Dignam**
Lane Tech High School
Chicago, IL

**Jennifer Ellberg**
Maine West High School
Des Plaines, IL

**Charles Ellwood**
Pebblebrook High School
Mableton, GA

**Barry Feldman**
Corona del Sol High School
Tempe, AZ

**Gerry Foster**
Desert Vista High School
Phoenix, AZ

**Riley Greenwood**
Valley Center High School
Valley Center, KS

**Michelle Hadden**
La Joya High School
Avondale, AZ

**Randy Hein**
Floyd Central High School
Floyds Knobs, IN

**Stephen Hobbs**
Seton Catholic High School
Chandler, AZ

**Jason Hook**
Manor ISD
Manor, TX

**Janet Jones**
Sullivan High School
Chicago, IL

**Karen Klafeta**
Morton East High School
Cicero, IL

**Robert Kolenda**
Neshaminy High School
Langhorne, PA

**Tina Lanquist**
Moorpark High School
Moorpark, CA

**Michael McDowell**
Napa New Technology High School
Napa, CA

**Wanda Miller**
Martinsburg High School
Martinsburg, WV

**Birgit Musheno**
Desert Vista High School
Phoenix, AZ

**Kenneth Nealy**
Windsor Public Schools
Windsor, CT

**Lonnie Newton**
Arvada West Senior High
Arvada, CO

**Palak Patel**
Wheaton North High School
Wheaton, IL

**Heather Pereira**
Amador Valley High School
Pleasanton, CA

**Yvonne Perry**
Douglas County High School
Douglasville, GA

**Tracy Rader**
Fulton Jr-Sr High School
Indianapolis, IN

**Kathey Roberts**
Lakeside High School
Hot Springs, AR

**Tomas M. Rodriguez III**
United South High School
Laredo, TX

**Cassandra Ross**
Redan High School
Stone Mountain, GA

**Lori Ruter**
Lake Norman High School
Mooresville, NC

**James Rutkowski**
Erie School District
Erie, PA

**Sara Sagmeister**
Maine South High School
Park Ridge, IL

**Patricia Smith (retired)**
Clear Brook HIgh School
League City, TX

**Jackie Snow**
Lee's Summit North High School
Lee's Summit, MO

**Laura Spitznogle**
Williamsville East High School
East Amherst, NY

**George Wandiko**
Rialto High School
Rialto, CA

**Jason Wikman**
Charlotte High School
Punta Gorda, FL

# Contents in Brief

# Introducing Biology

## Unit Focus

Unit 1 gives you a general understanding of what modern biology is all about and reviews and explains the chemistry of living systems. You will explore scientific thinking, methods, equipment, and experimentation.

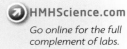
HMHScience.com
*Go online for the full complement of labs.*

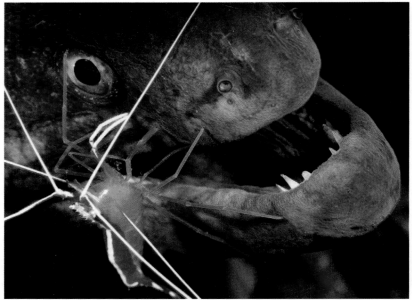
Moray eel and cleaner shrimp

©Carlos Villoch/MagicSea.com/Alamy Images

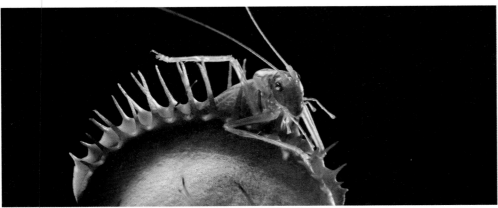
Venus flytrap and grasshopper

 **ONLINE BIOLOGY**
HMHScience.com

**VIRTUAL Lab**

Chapter 2 Calorimetry

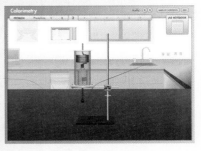

**Animated BIOLOGY**

**Chapter 1** Cells Through Different Microscopes, Experimental Design

**Chapter 2** Hydrogen Bonding, Energy and Chemical Reactions, Atoms and Bonding

**WebQuest**

**Chapter 1** Bioethics

**Chapter 2** Prions and Public Health

**INTERACTIVE Review**

Key Concepts, Vocabulary Games, Concept Maps, Animated Biology, Section Self-Checks

**BIOZINE**

**INTERNET MAGAZINE**
**Continually updated articles and the latest biology news**

Additional labs and a variety of online activities are available in Student Resources at
HMHScience.com.

©Maximilian Weinzierl/Alamy

## Unit Focus

In Unit 2, you will learn about different types of cells, the structures and functions of their specialized parts, energy use in cells, and cell division.

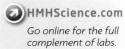
HMHScience.com
*Go online for the full complement of labs.*

HMHScience.com
*Go online for the full complement of labs.*

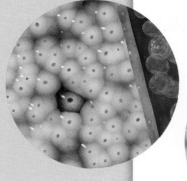
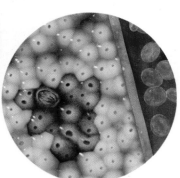
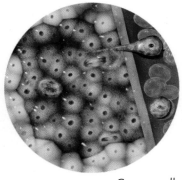

Cancer cells

**ONLINE BIOLOGY**
HMHScience.com

**VIRTUAL Lab**

**Chapter 12**  Comparing Hominoid Skulls

***Animated* BIOLOGY**

**Chapter 10**  Principles of Natural Selection, Natural Selection

**Chapter 11**  Mechanisms of Evolution, Founder Effect

**Chapter 12**  Endosymbiosis, Geologic Time Scale

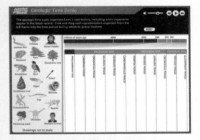

**Web*Quest***

**Chapter 10**  Dinosaur Descendants
**Chapter 11**  Speciation in Action
**Chapter 12**  Geologic Dating

**INTERACTIVE Review**

Key Concepts, Vocabulary Games, Concept Maps, Animated Biology, Section Self-Checks

**BIOZINE**

**INTERNET MAGAZINE**
Continually updated articles and the latest biology news

Additional labs and a variety of online activities are available in Student Resources at
HMHScience.com.

Tarsiers

©Per-Andre Hoffmann/LOOK Die Bildagentur der Fotografen GmbH/Alamy Images

## Unit Focus

In Unit 5, ecology is defined as "the study of interactions among living and nonliving things in an ecosystem." You will learn about various types of interactions and how scientists study them, how Earth is divided into biomes, and how humans can impact ecosystems within these biomes.

**ONLINE BIOLOGY**
HMHScience.com

**VIRTUAL Lab**

Chapter 13 Estimating
Population Size

*Animated* BIOLOGY

**Chapter 13** Build a Food Web

**Chapter 14** Survive Within a
Niche, What Limits Population
Growth?

**Chapter 15** Lake Turnover,
Where Do They Live?

**Chapter 16** Human Effects on a
Food Web

**Chapter 17** Pavlov's Dog, Behavioral Costs and Benefits

**Web Quest**

Chapter 13 Keystone Species
Chapter 14 Environmental Stress
Chapter 15 Explore an Ecosystem
Chapter 16 Invasive Species
Chapter 17 Animal Cognition

**INTERACTIVE Review**

Key Concepts, Vocabulary Games,
Concept Maps, Animated Biology,
Section Self-Checks

**BIOZINE**

**INTERNET MAGAZINE**
Continually updated articles
and the latest biology news

Additional labs and a variety
of online activities are available
in Student Resources at
HMHScience.com.

# UNIT 6

# Diversity of Life

## Unit Focus

Unit 6 first introduces the way in which scientists classify living things. Next, it begins the exploration of diversity of living things with viruses and prokaryotes and then protists and fungi.

*Euplotes,* an animal-like protist

©Steve Gschmeissner/Photo Researchers, Inc.

White oak (*Quercus alba*)

**ONLINE BIOLOGY**
HMHScience.com

**VIRTUAL Lab**

Chapter 19  Testing Antibacterial Products

***Animated* BIOLOGY**

Chapter 18  Molecular Clock, Build a Cladogram

Chapter 19  What Would You Prescribe?

Chapter 20  Protist and Fungus Life Cycles

Chapter 21  Plant and Pollinator Matching Game

**Web*Quest***

Chapter 18  Classify a Sea Cucumber

Chapter 19  Antibiotics in Agriculture

Chapter 20  Sickening Protists

Chapter 21  Endangered Plants

**INTERACTIVE Review**

Key Concepts, Vocabulary Games, Concept Maps, Animated Biology, Section Self-Checks

Additional labs and a variety of online activities are available in Student Resources at
HMHScience.com.

# Diversity of Life continued

©Larry Michael/Nature Picture Library

**ONLINE BIOLOGY**
HMHScience.com

***Animated* BIOLOGY**

**Chapter 23** Digestive Tract Formation, Shared Body Structures

**Chapter 24** Gas Exchange in Gills, Frog Metamorphosis, What Type of Fish Is It?

**Web*Quest***

**Chapter 23** Parasites

**Chapter 24** Fisheries on the Brink

**INTERACTIVE Review**

**Key Concepts, Vocabulary Games, Concept Maps, Animated Biology, Section Self-Checks**

Additional labs and a variety of online activities are available in Student Resources at
HMHScience.com.

# UNIT 7

# Human Biology

## Unit Focus

In Unit 7, you will learn about how your body systems work together to maintain a stable internal environment. Structures and functions of all the major body systems are addressed.

**ONLINE BIOLOGY**
HMHScience.com

**VIRTUAL Lab**

**Chapter 27** Blood Typing

**Animated BIOLOGY**

**Chapter 25** Human Organ Systems, Keep an Athlete Running

**Chapter 26** Nerve Impulse Transmission, Reflex Arc, Diagnose a Hormone Disorder

**Chapter 27** How You Breathe, Heart Pumping Blood, Build the Circulatory and Respiratory Systems

**Chapter 28** Vaccines and Active Immunity, Destroy the Invaders

**Web Quest**

**Chapter 25** Hypothermia
**Chapter 26** Drug Addiction
**Chapter 27** Asthma
**Chapter 28** HIV and AIDS

**INTERACTIVE Review**

Key Concepts, Vocabulary Games, Concept Maps, Animated Biology, Section Self-Checks

Additional labs and a variety of online activities are available in Student Resources at
HMDScience.com.

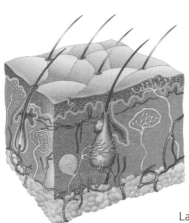

Layers of skin

# Human Biology continued

*Animated* BIOLOGY
**Chapter 29** Developmental Timeline

**Web***Quest*
**Chapter 29** Healthy Diet, Healthy Baby

**INTERACTIVE Review**
Key Concepts, Vocabulary Games, Concept Maps, Animated Biology, Section Self-Checks

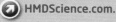
**BIOZINE**
**INTERNET MAGAZINE**
**Continually updated articles and the latest biology news**

Additional labs and a variety of online activities are available in Student Resources at
HMDScience.com.

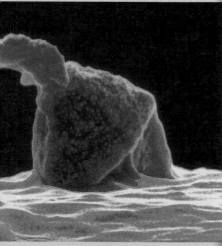
*Sperm and egg*

©Thierry Berrod, Mona Lisa Production/Science Source

# Data Analysis

**Smart Grapher**
HMHScience.com

**PREMIUM CONTENT**
Use Smart Grapher to create animated charts and graphs.

The Data Analysis activity in each chapter helps you develop skills you need to analyze data from scientific investigations.

Jane Goodall and chimpanzees

# QuickLabs

Explore key concepts and develop basic lab skills using these QuickLabs.

(b) ©age fotostock/SuperStock; (inset) © HMH

Are you learning English? You can learn science and English at the same time. You already know a lot about science from the world around you. You can also learn English from the world around you. Your teacher will help you. Other students will be happy to help. But there are things you can do too.

Below are some ideas that will help you get ready to learn English. Other ideas will help you learn better in class and while you read. There are also some ideas to help you remember and use what you learn.

## GET READY TO LEARN

You can do these things before you go to science class.

| GET READY TO LEARN STRATEGIES | |
| --- | --- |
| **Visit Your Classroom and Teacher** | Go with other students if you can. Look carefully around the room. What things are there?<br><br>• Ask your teacher to tell you the names of things you do not know. You can ask, "What is this?" or "Will we use this in class?" or "What does it do?"<br>• Learn how to say and read the names of things you will use to learn science.<br>• Are there signs on the wall? What do they say? If you do not know, ask your teacher or other students, "What does this sign say? What does it mean?"<br>• Remember the words on signs. Signs in many places can have the same words. |
| **Learn Some Science Words** | You will learn a lot of new words in your science class. It is easier to learn them if you already know a few science words.<br><br>• Ask your teacher to say and write some words you need to know.<br>• Ask what the words mean. Then learn the words very well.<br>• Learn how to say and read the words. Learn what they mean. |
| **Ask Your Teacher for Help with Reading** | Your teacher can help you read your science book. He or she can help you learn new words that you need to know before you read.<br><br>• Your teacher might give you a list of the important words or ideas you will read or a list of questions to answer when you read.<br>• He or she might give you a graphic organizer to help you understand what you read. A graphic organizer is a drawing that helps you learn and remember. |
| **Read Before Class** | Your teacher tells you what he or she will talk about tomorrow. If part of your book tells about the same thing, read the book today.<br><br>When you are done reading, you already know some of what the teacher will say. Then it is easier for you to understand when the teacher talks. |

| GET READY TO LEARN STRATEGIES | |
|---|---|
| **Look at Pictures Before You Read** | You need to read some pages in your science book.<br><br>• What should you do first? Look at the pictures. Use what you already know.<br>• If there are words with the pictures, read the words. Try to figure out what the pictures show.<br>• It will be easier to read the pages if you already know a little bit from looking at the pictures. |
| **Get Ready to Ask Questions** | You might have a question about what you read before class.<br><br>• First, write down your question. If you are worried about how to say the question, practice it.<br>• Bring your question to class. Listen carefully when the teacher talks about the same thing as your question. Maybe the teacher will answer the question.<br>• If you still do not have an answer, raise your hand. Ask the question you wrote and practiced.<br>• Listen carefully to the answer. |
| **Start Taking Notes Before Class** | Taking notes means writing something to help you remember what you read or hear.<br><br>• You do not write all the words you read or hear. Write just a few important words or make drawings.<br>• It can be hard to take notes when you listen. It is easier if you start your notes before class, when you read your book. Write down important words that you read. Write your own words or draw something to help you remember important ideas. Leave lots of space on your paper.<br>• Then, take your notes to class. Use the same paper to take notes when you listen in class. Write more notes in the space you left. |
| **Get Ready to Answer Questions** | Science teachers ask a lot of questions. Learn these question words: *what, where, when, who, why, how much, is it, will it*. Learn how to answer questions that use each word.<br><br>• *What:* Tell the name of a thing.<br>• *What will happen, what happened, what happens when we:* Tell how something changes or stays the same.<br>• *Where:* Tell a place.<br>• *When:* Tell a time (you can also say before or after something).<br>• *Who:* Tell a person. Your teacher might ask, "Who can tell me . . .?" That means, "Do you know the answer?" If you do, raise your hand.<br>• *How much:* Tell an amount.<br>• *Why:* Tell what made something happen or explain a reason.<br>• *Is it or Will it:* Answer yes or no. You can also give a reason for your answer. |

# WHILE YOU LEARN

You can do these things in your science class.

| WHILE YOU LEARN STRATEGIES | |
|---|---|
| **Use What You Know** | When you hear or read about something new, think about what you already know.<br><br>If a new word sounds like a word you already know, maybe the two words mean close to the same thing. Maybe you already know something about a new idea.<br><br>Use what you know to help you understand the new word or idea. |
| **Get Help If You Do Not Understand** | If you don't understand something, get help.<br><br>• Ask your teacher or another student. Raise your hand and ask in class or wait until the teacher is done talking.<br>• If you do not understand a word, try to say the word. Then ask, "What does that word mean?"<br>• If you do not know how to do something, you can ask, "How do I do this?"<br>• If you do not understand an idea or picture, tell what you do know. Then ask about the part you do not understand. |
| **Understand Instructions** | Instructions tell you how to do something. They are sometimes called directions.<br><br>You need to follow instructions many times in science class. Sometimes your teacher says the instructions. Sometimes you need to read the instructions.<br><br>Most instructions have many parts, called steps. Sometimes the teacher or book will use numbers (1, 2, 3 . . .) to tell you when to do each step.<br><br>Other times, instructions use words. Learn the words that tell you when to do things:<br><br>• *first*<br>• *then*<br>• *next*<br>• *before*<br>• *after*<br>• *while*<br>• *last*<br><br>Listen and look for these words in instructions. Use them to help you know when to do things.<br><br>You can also use these words to give other people instructions. You can use them when you write or tell about something you did. |

| WHILE YOU LEARN STRATEGIES | |
|---|---|
| **Answer Questions** | When your teacher asks you a question, you need to answer. Here are some things that can help you:<br><br>• Listen carefully to the question. If you do not understand the words, you can ask, "Could you repeat the question?" or "Can you say that more slowly?"<br>• Listen for the question word. It tells you what kind of answer to give.<br>• Look to see if the teacher is pointing at something. The question is probably about that thing. You can talk about that thing in your answer.<br>• Remember what the teacher said before the question. The question might be about what the teacher said. Maybe you can use some of the teacher's words in your answer.<br>• If you do not know an answer, tell the teacher you do not know. You can say, "I don't know" or "I did not understand that very well" or "I don't remember that." |
| **Talk in Groups** | In science class, you often work with other students. You need to understand what your group should do.<br><br>• Read instructions if you have them. You can ask, "Can I have some more time to read?"<br>• If you do not understand the instructions, you can ask, "Do you understand Step 4?" or "Can you help me understand this step?"<br>• Talk about the instructions after you read. You can ask, "Who should . . .?" or "What should we do first?"<br>• Tell what you can do. Ask the other students what they will do.<br>• As you work, you can ask your partner for help. You can say, "Can you hold this?" or "What do we do next?"<br>• Be sure to help your partner. You can say, "Do you need me to pour that?"<br>• If you have an idea, you can say, "I think we should do this" or "What if we do it this way?" or "I have an idea." |

# REMEMBER AND USE WHAT YOU LEARN

You can do these things to help you learn important science words and ideas. Do them before class, in class, or after class.

| REMEMBER AND USE WHAT YOU LEARN STRATEGIES | |
|---|---|
| **Say It Again (and Again and Again)** | One way to learn new words is to repeat them, or say them many times.<br><br>• First, make sure that you can say the word correctly.<br>• Be sure you know what it means too. Ask a friend or your teacher. Have the person tell you if you need to say the word differently or if you do not have the right meaning.<br>• When you can say the word correctly and know what it means, say the word several times. This is more fun with a partner. Take turns saying the word and telling each other the meaning.<br>• You will remember better if you say the meaning in your own words. You will remember even better if you say your own sentence that uses the word. Try to say a different sentence each time you repeat. |
| **Use Flash Cards** | Flash cards help you learn new words.<br><br>• To make flash cards, use some pieces of paper that are all the same size. Get the words you need to learn.<br>• Write one word on a piece of paper. Turn the paper over. Write the meaning of the word.<br>• Use your own words or draw pictures to help you remember.<br>• Write the other words on other pieces of paper. Write the meaning of each word on the back of the paper.<br><br>To use flash cards, look at a word. Say what you think it means. Check the back of the paper.<br><br>• If you got the meaning right, do not look at that card again. Do this with all your words.<br>• If you get some wrong, look at them again and again.<br><br>You can use flash cards alone or with a partner. |
| **Tell Somebody** | Ask a friend or a person in your family to help you learn. Have the person ask you a question. If you need to learn some science words, have him or her ask you what the words mean.<br><br>If you need to remember how something in science works, have the person ask you. Then use your own words to tell what you know from your book or class. Tell the person what the words mean or how something works.<br><br>Answer all the person's questions. Helping that person understand helps you understand and remember too. |

| REMEMBER AND USE WHAT YOU LEARN STRATEGIES | |
|---|---|
| **Make a Picture** | Sometimes a picture can help you remember better than words can. |
| | You can draw pictures when you take notes. Draw your own picture or use a graphic organizer. |
| | A graphic organizer is a drawing that helps you learn and remember. There are many different graphic organizers. |

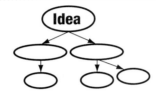

A concept map shows how information is connected. Write one word or idea in the large circle. Write and draw lines to other words to show how they explain or are like the thing in the large circle.

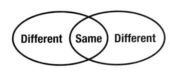

Use a Venn diagram to show how two things are the same and how they are different. Write how they are different in the two circles. Write how they are the same where the two circles come together.

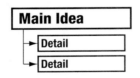

Use a drawing like this to show a main idea and some important details to remember about the idea.

| **Summarize** | When you use your own words to tell the most important parts of something, you summarize it. |
|---|---|
| | • You can summarize what your teacher says in class. |
| | • You can summarize what you read. |
| | Write or say in your own words what you learned in class or from your reading. Do not tell everything. Tell only the most important parts. |
| | Summarizing can help you understand and remember better. |

# NEXT GENERATION SUNSHINE STATE STANDARDS: BIOLOGY

The HMH Biology program provides a full year of interactive experiences that address the Next Generation Sunshine State Standards: Biology. As you read, experiment, and interact with print and digital content, you will be learning what you need to know and be able to do to complete this course. The Florida standards explain the content, concept, and principles of major themes in Biology. The standards are listed here for your convenience. You will also see them referenced throughout this book.

## Nature of Science
## SC.912.N.1: The Practice of Science

**SC.912.N.1.1** Define a problem based on a specific body of knowledge, for example: biology, chemistry, physics, and earth/space science, and do the following:

1. pose questions about the natural world,
2. conduct systematic observations,
3. examine books and other sources of information to see what is already known,
4. review what is known in light of empirical evidence,
5. plan investigations,
6. use tools to gather, analyze, and interpret data (this includes the use of measurement in metric and other systems, and also the generation and interpretation of graphical representations of data, including data tables and graphs),
7. pose answers, explanations, or descriptions of events,
8. generate explanations that explicate or describe natural phenomena (inferences),
9. use appropriate evidence and reasoning to justify these explanations to others,
10. communicate results of scientific investigations, and
11. evaluate the merits of the explanations produced by others.

**SC.912.N.1.3** Recognize that the strength or usefulness of a scientific claim is evaluated through scientific argumentation, which depends on critical and logical thinking, and the active consideration of alternative scientific explanations to explain the data presented.

**SC.912.N.1.4** Identify sources of information and assess their reliability according to the strict standards of scientific investigation.

**SC.912.N.1.6** Describe how scientific inferences are drawn from scientific observations and provide examples from the content being studied.

## SC.912.N.2: The Characteristics of Scientific Knowledge

**SC.912.N.2.1** Identify what is science, what clearly is not science, and what superficially resembles science (but fails to meet the criteria for science).

**SC.912.N.2.2** Identify which questions can be answered through science and which questions are outside the boundaries of scientific investigation, such as questions addressed by other ways of knowing, such as art, philosophy, and religion.

# NEXT GENERATION SUNSHINE STATE STANDARDS: BIOLOGY (CONTINUED)

## SC.912.N.3: The Role of Theories, Laws, Hypotheses, and Model

**SC.912.N.3.1** Explain that a scientific theory is the culmination of many scientific investigations drawing together all the current evidence concerning a substantial range of phenomena; thus, a scientific theory represents the most powerful explanation scientists have to offer.

**SC.912.N.3.4** Recognize that theories do not become laws, nor do laws become theories; theories are well supported explanations and laws are well supported descriptions.

### Earth Science
## SC.912.E.7: Earth Systems and Patterns

**SC.912.E.7.1** Analyze the movement of matter and energy through the different biogeochemical cycles, including water and carbon.

### Life Science
## SC.912.L.14: Organization and Development of Living Organisms

**SC.912.L.14.1** Describe the scientific theory of cells (cell theory) and relate the history of its discovery to the process of science.

**SC.912.L.14.2** Relate structure to function for the components of plant and animal cells. Explain the role of cell membranes as a highly selective barrier (passive and active transport).

**SC.912.L.14.3** Compare and contrast the general structures of plant and animal cells. Compare and contrast the general structures of prokaryotic and eukaryotic cells.

**SC.912.L.14.4** Compare and contrast structure and function of various types of microscopes.

**SC.912.L.14.6** Explain the significance of genetic factors, environmental factors, and pathogenic agents to health from the perspectives of both individual and public health.

**SC.912.L.14.7** Relate the structure of each of the major plant organs and tissues to physiological processes.

**SC.912.L.14.26** Identify the major parts of the brain on diagrams or models.

**SC.912.L.14.36** Describe the factors affecting blood flow through the cardiovascular system.

**SC.912.L.14.52** Explain the basic functions of the human immune system, including specific and nonspecific immune response, vaccines, and antibiotics.

## SC.912.L.15: Diversity and Evolution of Living Organisms

**SC.912.L.15.1** Explain how the scientific theory of evolution is supported by the fossil record, comparative anatomy, comparative embryology, biogeography, molecular biology, and observed evolutionary change.

**SC.912.L.15.4** Describe how and why organisms are hierarchically classified and based on evolutionary relationships.

**SC.912.L.15.5** Explain the reasons for changes in how organisms are classified.

**SC.912.L.15.6** Discuss distinguishing characteristics of the domains and kingdoms of living organisms.

**SC.912.L.15.8** Describe the scientific explanations of the origin of life on Earth.

**SC.912.L.15.10** Identify basic trends in hominid evolution from early ancestors six million years ago to modern humans, including brain size, jaw size, language, and manufacture of tools.

**SC.912.L.15.13** Describe the conditions required for natural selection, including: overproduction of offspring, inherited variation, and the struggle to survive, which result in differential reproductive success.

**SC.912.L.15.14** Discuss mechanisms of evolutionary change other than natural selection such as genetic drift and gene flow.

**SC.912.L.15.15** Describe how mutation and genetic recombination increase genetic variation.

## SC.912.L.16: Heredity and Reproduction

**SC.912.L.16.1** Use Mendel's laws of segregation and independent assortment to analyze patterns of inheritance.

**SC.912.L.16.2** Discuss observed inheritance patterns caused by various modes of inheritance, including dominant, recessive, codominant, sex-linked, polygenic, and multiple alleles

**SC.912.L.16.3** Describe the basic process of DNA replication and how it relates to the transmission and conservation of the genetic information.

**SC.912.L.16.4** Explain how mutations in the DNA sequence may or may not result in phenotypic change. Explain how mutations in gametes may result in phenotypic changes in offspring.

**SC.912.L.16.5** Explain the basic processes of transcription and translation, and how they result in the expression of genes.

**SC.912.L.16.8** Explain the relationship between mutation, cell cycle, and uncontrolled cell growth potentially resulting in cancer.

**SC.912.L.16.9** Explain how and why the genetic code is universal and is common to almost all organisms.

**SC.912.L.16.10** Evaluate the impact of biotechnology on the individual, society and the environment, including medical and ethical issues.

**SC.912.L.16.13** Describe the basic anatomy and physiology of the human reproductive system. Describe the process of human development from fertilization to birth and major changes that occur in each trimester of pregnancy.

# NEXT GENERATION SUNSHINE STATE STANDARDS: BIOLOGY (CONTINUED)

**SC.912.L.16.14** Describe the cell cycle, including the process of mitosis. Explain the role of mitosis in the formation of new cells and its importance in maintaining chromosome number during asexual reproduction.

**SC.912.L.16.16** Describe the process of meiosis, including independent assortment and crossing over. Explain how reduction division results in the formation of haploid gametes or spores.

**SC.912.L.16.17** Compare and contrast mitosis and meiosis and relate to the processes of sexual and asexual reproduction and their consequences for genetic variation.

## SC.912.L.17: Interdependence

**SC.912.L.17.2** Explain the general distribution of life in aquatic systems as a function of chemistry, geography, light, depth, salinity, and temperature.

**SC.912.L.17.4** Describe changes in ecosystems resulting from seasonal variations, climate change and succession.

**SC.912.L.17.5** Analyze how population size is determined by births, deaths, immigration, emigration, and limiting factors (biotic and abiotic) that determine carrying capacity.

**SC.912.L.17.8** Recognize the consequences of the losses of biodiversity due to catastrophic events, climate changes, human activity, and the introduction of invasive, non-native species.

**SC.912.L.17.9** Use a food web to identify and distinguish producers, consumers, and decomposers. Explain the pathway of energy transfer through trophic levels and the reduction of available energy at successive trophic levels.

**SC.912.L.17.11** Evaluate the costs and benefits of renewable and nonrenewable resources, such as water, energy, fossil fuels, wildlife, and forests.

**SC.912.L.17.13** Discuss the need for adequate monitoring of environmental parameters when making policy decisions.

**SC.912.L.17.20** Predict the impact of individuals on environmental systems and examine how human lifestyles affect sustainability.

## SC.912.L.18: Matter and Energy Transformations

**SC.912.L.18.1** Describe the basic molecular structures and primary functions of the four major categories of biological macromolecules.

**SC.912.L.18.7** Identify the reactants, products, and basic functions of photosynthesis.

**SC.912.L.18.8** Identify the reactants, products, and basic functions of aerobic and anaerobic cellular respiration.

**SC.912.L.18.9** Explain the interrelated nature of photosynthesis and cellular respiration.

**SC.912.L.18.10** Connect the role of adenosine triphosphate (ATP) to energy transfers within a cell.

**SC.912.L.18.11** Explain the role of enzymes as catalysts that lower the activation energy of biochemical reactions. Identify factors, such as pH and temperature, and their effect on enzyme activity.

**SC.912.L.18.12** Discuss the special properties of water that contribute to Earth's suitability as an environment for life: cohesive behavior, ability to moderate temperature, expansion upon freezing, and versatility as a solvent.

## HE.912.C: Health Literacy Concepts
## HE.912.C.1: Core Concepts – Comprehend concepts related to health promotion and disease prevention to enhance health.

**HE.912.C.1.3** Evaluate how environment and personal health are interrelated.

**HE.912.C.1.5** Analyze strategies for prevention, detection, and treatment of communicable and chronic diseases.

**HE.912.C.1.7** Analyze how heredity and family history can impact personal health.

## LA.910.2: Literary Analysis
## LA.910.2.2: Nonfiction

**LA.910.2.2.3** The student will organize information to show understanding or relationships among facts, ideas, and events (e.g., representing key points within text through charting, mapping, paraphrasing, summarizing, comparing, contrasting, or outlining).

## LA.910.4: Writing Applications
## LA.910.4.2: Informative

**LA.910.4.2.2** The student will record information and ideas from primary and/or secondary sources accurately and coherently, noting the validity and reliability of these sources and attributing sources of information;

## MA.912.S.3: Summarizing Data

**MA.912.S.3.2** Collect, organize, and analyze data sets, determine the best format for the data and present visual summaries from the following:
- bar graphs
- line graphs
- stem and leaf plots
- circle graphs
- histograms
- box and whisker plots
- scatter plots
- cumulative frequency (ogive) graphs

# NEXT GENERATION SUNSHINE STATE STANDARDS: BIOLOGY (CONTINUED)

## Language Arts Florida Standards: Reading in Science and Technical Subjects

**LAFS.910.RST.1.1** Cite specific textual evidence to support analysis of science and technical texts, attending to the precise details of explanations or descriptions.

**LAFS.910.RST.1.2** Determine the central ideas or conclusions of a text; trace the text's explanation or depiction of a complex process, phenomenon, or concept; provide an accurate summary of the text.

**LAFS.910.RST.1.3** Follow precisely a complex multistep procedure when carrying out experiments, taking measurements, or performing technical tasks, attending to special cases or exceptions defined in the text.

**LAFS.910.RST.2.4** Determine the meaning of symbols, key terms, and other domain-specific words and phrases as they are used in a specific scientific or technical context relevant to grades 9–10 texts and topics.

**LAFS.910.RST.2.5** Analyze the structure of the relationships among concepts in a text, including relationships among key terms (e.g., force, friction, reaction force, energy).

**LAFS.910.RST.2.6** Analyze the author's purpose in providing an explanation, describing a procedure, or discussing an experiment in a text, defining the question the author seeks to address.

**LAFS.910.RST.3.7** Translate quantitative or technical information expressed in words in a text into visual form (e.g., a table or chart) and translate information expressed visually or mathematically (e.g., in an equation) into words.

**LAFS.910.RST.3.8** Assess the extent to which the reasoning and evidence in a text support the author's claim or a recommendation for solving a scientific or technical problem.

**LAFS.910.RST.3.9** Compare and contrast findings presented in a text to those from other sources (including their own experiments), noting when the findings support or contradict previous explanations or accounts.

**LAFS.910.RST.4.10** By the end of grade 10, read and comprehend science/technical texts in the grades 9–10 text complexity band independently and proficiently.

## Language Arts Florida Standards: Speaking and Listening

**LAFS.910.SL.1.1** Initiate and participate effectively in a range of collaborative discussions (one-on-one, in groups, and teacher-led) with diverse partners on grades 9–10 topics, texts, and issues, building on others' ideas and expressing their own clearly and persuasively.

   **a.** Come to discussions prepared, having read and researched material under study; explicitly draw on that preparation by referring to evidence from texts and other research on the topic or issue to stimulate a thoughtful, well-reasoned exchange of ideas.

**b.** Work with peers to set rules for collegial discussions and decision-making (e.g., informal consensus, taking votes on key issues, presentation of alternate views), clear goals and deadlines, and individual roles as needed.

**c.** Propel conversations by posing and responding to questions that relate the current discussion to broader themes or larger ideas; actively incorporate others into the discussion; and clarify, verify, or challenge ideas and conclusions.

**d.** Respond thoughtfully to diverse perspectives, summarize points of agreement and disagreement, and, when warranted, qualify or justify their own views and understanding and make new connections in light of the evidence and reasoning presented.

**LAFS.910.SL.1.2** Integrate multiple sources of information presented in diverse media or formats (e.g., visually, quantitatively, orally) evaluating the credibility and accuracy of each source.

**LAFS.910.SL.1.3** Evaluate a speaker's point of view, reasoning, and use of evidence and rhetoric, identifying any fallacious reasoning or exaggerated or distorted evidence.

**LAFS.910.SL.2.4** Present information, findings, and supporting evidence clearly, concisely, and logically such that listeners can follow the line of reasoning and the organization, development, substance, and style are appropriate to purpose, audience, and task.

**LAFS.910.SL.2.5** Make strategic use of digital media (e.g., textual, graphical, audio, visual, and interactive elements) in presentations to enhance understanding of findings, reasoning, and evidence and to add interest.

## Language Arts Florida Standards: Writing in Science and Technical Subjects

**LAFS.910.WHST.1.1** Write arguments focused on *discipline-specific* content.

- Introduce precise, knowledgeable claim(s), establish the significance of the claim(s), distinguish the claim(s) from alternate or opposing claims, and create an organization that logically sequences the claim(s), counterclaims, reasons, and evidence.

- Develop claim(s) and counterclaims fairly and thoroughly, supplying the most relevant data and evidence for each while pointing out the strengths and limitations of both claim(s) and counterclaims in a discipline-appropriate form that anticipates the audience's knowledge level, concerns, values, and possible biases.

- Use words, phrases, and clauses as well as varied syntax to link the major sections of the text, create cohesion, and clarify the relationships between claim(s) and reasons, between reasons and evidence, and between claim(s) and counterclaims.

- Establish and maintain a formal style and objective tone while attending to the norms and conventions of the discipline in which they are writing.

- Provide a concluding statement or section that follows from or supports the argument presented.

**LAFS.910.WHST.1.2** Write informative/explanatory texts, including the narration of historical events, scientific procedures/experiments, or technical processes.

- Introduce a topic and organize complex ideas, concepts, and information so that each new element builds on that which precedes it to create a unified whole; include formatting

# NEXT GENERATION SUNSHINE STATE STANDARDS: BIOLOGY (CONTINUED)

(e.g., headings), graphics (e.g., figures, tables), and multimedia when useful to aiding comprehension.

• Develop the topic thoroughly by selecting the most significant and relevant facts, extended definitions, concrete details, quotations, or other information and examples appropriate to the audience's knowledge of the topic.

• Use varied transitions and sentence structures to link the major sections of the text, create cohesion, and clarify the relationships among complex ideas and concepts.

• Use precise language, domain-specific vocabulary and techniques such as metaphor, simile, and analogy to manage the complexity of the topic; convey a knowledgeable stance in a style that responds to the discipline and context as well as to the expertise of likely readers.

• Establish and maintain a formal style and objective tone while attending to the norms and conventions of the discipline in which they are writing.

• Provide a concluding statement or section that follows from and supports the information or explanation presented (e.g., articulating implications or the significance of the topic.)

**LAFS.910.WHST.2.4** Produce clear and coherent writing in which the development, organization, and style are appropriate to task, purpose, and audience.

**LAFS.910.WHST.2.5** Develop and strengthen writing as needed by planning, revising, editing, rewriting, or trying a new approach, focusing on addressing what is most significant for a specific purpose and audience.

**LAFS.910.WHST.2.6** Use technology, including the Internet, to produce, publish, and update individual or shared writing products, taking advantage of technology's capacity to link to other information and to display information flexibly and dynamically.

**LAFS.910.WHST.3.7** Conduct short as well as more sustained research projects to answer a question (including a self-generated question) or solve a problem; narrow or broaden the inquiry when appropriate; synthesize multiple sources on the subject, demonstrating understanding of the subject under investigation.

**LAFS.910.WHST.3.8** Gather relevant information from multiple authoritative print and digital sources, using advanced searches effectively; assess the usefulness of each source in answering the research question; integrate information into the text selectively to maintain the flow of ideas, avoiding plagiarism and following a standard format for citation.

**LAFS.910.WHST.3.9** Draw evidence from informational texts to support analysis, reflection, and research.

**LAFS.910.WHST.4.10** Write routinely over extended time frames (time for reflection and revision) and shorter time frames (a single sitting or a day or two) for a range of discipline-specific tasks, purposes, and audiences.

## English Language Development

**ELD.K12.ELL.SC.1** English language learners communicate information, ideas and concepts necessary for academic success in the content area of Science.

**ELD.K12.ELL.SI.1** English language learners communicate for social and instructional purposes within the school setting.

## Mathematics Florida Standards

**MAFS.K12.MP.1.1** Make sense of problems and persevere in solving them.

**MAFS.K12.MP.2.1** Reason abstractly and quantitatively.

**MAFS.K12.MP.3.1** Construct viable arguments and critique the reasoning of others.

**MAFS.K12.MP.4.1** Model with mathematics.

**MAFS.K12.MP.5.1** Use appropriate tools strategically.

**MAFS.K12.MP.6.1** Attend to precision.

**MAFS.K12.MP.7.1** Look for and make use of structure.

**MAFS.K12.MP.8.1** Look for and express regularity in repeated reasoning.

**MAFS.912.N-Q.1.1** Use units as a way to understand problems and to guide the solution of multi-step problems; choose and interpret units consistently in formulas; choose and interpret the scale and the origin in graphs and data displays.

**MAFS.912.N-Q.1.3** Choose a level of accuracy appropriate to limitations on measurement when reporting quantities.

(➔) **BIOZINE**
HMHScience.com

**When Knowledge
and Ethics Collide**
**TECHNOLOGY** Genetic Testing
**CAREER** Geneticist

**BIG IDEA** Biology is the scientific study of all aspects of living things, and it shapes our understanding of our world, from human health to biotechnology to environmental preservation.

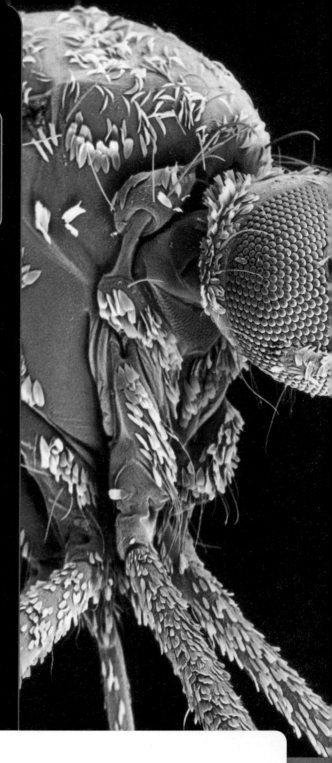

## ⊘ ONLINE BIOLOGY    HMHScience.com

**ONLINE** Labs
- Manipulating Independent Variables
- **QuickLab** Life Under a Microscope
- Manipulating Plant Growth
- Biology in the News
- Measuring Microscopic Objects
- Biotechnology and Food Products

- Fruit Preservation
- **Video Lab** SI Units
- **Video Lab** Microbe Growth
- **Video Lab** The Counterfeit Drug
- **Open Inquiry Lab** The Study of Life
- **S.T.E.M. Lab** Biomimicry in Engineering

(t) © Eye of Science/Photo Researchers, Inc.

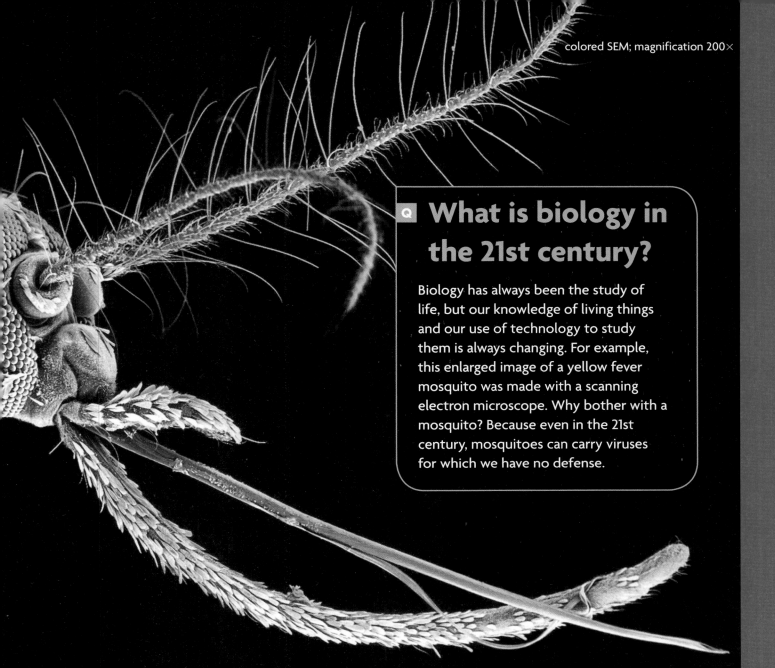

## Q What is biology in the 21st century?

Biology has always been the study of life, but our knowledge of living things and our use of technology to study them is always changing. For example, this enlarged image of a yellow fever mosquito was made with a scanning electron microscope. Why bother with a mosquito? Because even in the 21st century, mosquitoes can carry viruses for which we have no defense.

 **READING** TOOLBOX — **This reading tool can help you learn the material in the following pages.**

### USING LANGUAGE

**Hypothesis or Theory?** In everyday language, there is little difference between a hypothesis and a theory. But in science, the meanings of these words are more distinct. A hypothesis is a specific, testable prediction for a limited set of conditions. A theory is a general explanation for a broad range of data. A theory can include hypotheses that have been tested, and it can also be used to generate new hypotheses. The strongest scientific theories explain the broadest range of data and incorporate many well-tested hypotheses.

### YOUR TURN

Use what you have learned in this paragraph to answer the following questions.

1. What is the difference between a hypothesis and a theory?
2. Propose a testable hypothesis to explain why the chicken crossed the road.

# 1.1 The Study of Life

| KEY CONCEPT **Biologists study life in all its forms.**

**MAIN IDEAS**

- Earth is home to an incredible diversity of life.
- Biology is the scientific study of all forms of life.
- Humans have studied living things throughout history.

**VOCABULARY**

biosphere
biodiversity
species
biology
science

## Connect to Your World

It's a warm, summer evening. Maybe you're laughing and joking while waiting to eat at a family barbecue. As you sit down for dinner, mosquitoes flying around have the same idea. But their dinner is you, not the barbecue. Probably the most attention that you pay to mosquitoes is when you take careful aim before smacking them. Biologists have a somewhat different view of mosquitoes, unless of course they are the ones being bitten. But from a less emotional perspective, a biologist can see a mosquito as just one example of the great diversity of life found on Earth.

## ▶ MAIN IDEA

## Earth is home to an incredible diversity of life.

In Yellowstone National Park, there are pools of hot water as acidic as vinegar. It might be difficult to believe, but those pools are also full of life. Life is found in the darkness of the deepest ocean floors and in thousands-of-years-old ice in Antarctica. Not only are living things found just about anywhere on Earth, but they also come in a huge variety of shapes and sizes. Plants, for example, include tiny mosses and giant redwood trees on which moss can grow. There are massive animals such as the blue whale, which is the largest animal living on Earth. There are tiny animals such as the honeypot ant in **FIGURE 1.1,** which can store so much food for other ants that it swells to the size of a grape.

### The Biosphere

All living things and all the places they are found on Earth make up the **biosphere.** Every part of the biosphere is connected, however distantly, with every other part of the biosphere. The biosphere includes land environments such as deserts, grasslands, and different types of forests. The biosphere also includes saltwater and freshwater environments, as well as portions of the atmosphere. And different types of plants, animals, and other living things are found in different areas of the biosphere. Even the inside of your nose, which is home to bacteria and fungi, is a part of the biosphere.

**FIGURE 1.1** Honeypot ants live in deserts where food and water are scarce. Some of the ants in the colony act as storage tanks for other ants in the colony.

(b) ©Leo Meier/Australian Picture Library/Corbis; (l) ©John Brown/Oxford Scientific/Getty Images

## Biodiversity

The variety of organisms in a given area is called biological diversity, or **biodiversity.** Biodiversity generally increases from Earth's poles to the equator. More living things are able to survive in consistently warm temperatures than in areas that have large temperature changes during the year. Because more living things, especially plants, can survive in warm areas, those areas provide a larger, more consistent food supply for many different species.

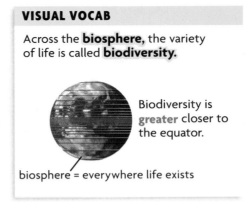
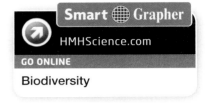
Smart ⊕ Grapher
HMHScience.com
**GO ONLINE**
Biodiversity

There are several different ways the term *species* can be defined. One definition of **species** is a group of organisms that are closely related and can produce fertile offspring. About 2 million different living species have been identified, but biologists estimate that tens of millions of species remain to be discovered. Over half of the known species are insects, but no one knows how many insect species actually exist.

Every year, biologists discover more than 10,000 new species. In contrast, some scientists estimate that over 50,000 species die out, or become extinct, every year. Occasionally, however, a species thought to be extinct is found again. For example, the ivory-billed woodpecker was thought to have become extinct in 1944, but a team of scientists reported seeing it in Arkansas in 2004.

**Apply** Describe biodiversity in terms of species.

### ▶ MAIN IDEA
# Biology is the scientific study of all forms of life.

The diverse organisms that live on Earth relate and interact with other organisms and their environments. **FIGURE 1.2** shows a bee collecting pollen from a flower, an interaction that benefits both the bee and the plant. When a bee collects pollen to use as food, the pollen sticks to the bee's body. Then, as the bee flies from plant to plant, the pollen from one plant is left behind on other plants. This interaction pollinates the plants and allows them to reproduce. **Biology,** or life science, is the scientific study of living things and their interactions with their environment.

The study of living things sheds new light on our understanding of humans and our world. For example, until chimpanzees were observed to use sticks and other tools to hunt insects and other organisms, high intelligence and the ability to make and use tools were considered strictly human characteristics. **Science** is the knowledge obtained by observing natural events and conditions in order to discover facts and formulate laws or principles that can be verified or tested. People who contribute to science come from all backgrounds and different fields of interest. Biology is one of three basic areas of science: life science, earth science, and physical science.

**FIGURE 1.2** Life science is the study of the interaction of organisms, such as this bee and the flowering plant from which it collects pollen.

**FIGURE 1.3** Prehistoric cave paintings indicate that early humans observed and studied the living things around them.

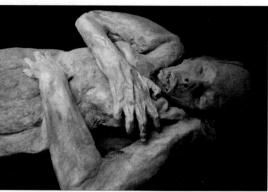

**FIGURE 1.4** Mummification, a process of preserving bodies, requires precise understanding of processes and materials. Ancient Egyptian civilizations studied and improved mummification over many centuries.

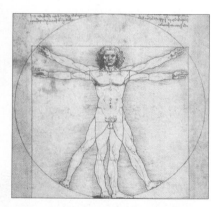

**FIGURE 1.5** Leonardo da Vinci's study of many areas of science, including anatomy, were part of a renaissance of scientific learning in Europe. Leonardo's drawing *Vitruvian Man* shows a relationship of anatomy and geometry.

## ● MAIN IDEA

# Humans have studied living things throughout history.

The study of living things began long before the invention of computers, microscopes, or other scientific tools and techniques. Early records, such as the prehistoric cave painting in **FIGURE 1.3**, show that prehistoric people were interested in the animals they observed and used as food. Other art, carvings, and papyri show how early humans began to understand basic biological concepts such as anatomy, medicinal use of herbs, and embalming. Evidence shows that some human populations began domesticating animals as early as 8500 BCE. Even without knowing it, these early humans were using genetics to select for characteristics that were most valuable in the organism, such as high milk production and taste or high yield in crops.

## Science in Ancient Civilizations

Many ancient civilizations studied biology. Just as we do now, they learned about natural processes and used this knowledge to address the needs of society. Asian civilizations used herbal medicines. South American civilizations developed agricultural techniques, such as crop domestication and irrigation. Ancient Egyptian civilizations practiced mummification of royalty, nobility, and the wealthy, as shown in **FIGURE 1.4**.

Greek civilization made significant contributions to the development of life science. They are credited with originating the basic principles of modern science. Around 400 BCE, Greek physician Hippocrates established a school of medicine. He taught that all living bodies were made up of four humours or fluids: blood, black bile, phlegm, and yellow bile. Imbalances in the four humours were thought to cause most illnesses.

The first classification system for living organisms is attributed to the Greek philosopher Aristotle and dates back to 330 BCE. Aristotle's system divided animals up into those with red blood, such as wolves and rabbits, and those without blood, such as mollusks and arthropods. Aristotle is also credited with developing a system of logic and a dependence on empirical evidence in science.

## The Scientific Revolution

Scientists of any era are limited by the demands and rules of society. The ancient Greek and Roman societies are known for their milestones in science and philosophy, but changes in politics and governance also influenced the progress of science. The Middle Ages of European history (500s–1450s CE) are marked by little scientific development, though scientific knowledge continued to grow in other parts of the world, such as India and China.

Fifteenth-century European societies gave rise to a renewal of interest in art and science and the beginning of the Scientific Revolution (1450s–1700). Early in this time period, Italian artist and scientist Leonardo da Vinci began close studies of the anatomy of both animals and humans. The drawing *Vitruvian Man,* shown in **FIGURE 1.5**, gives evidence of Leonardo's detailed understanding of anatomy and movement. His legacy includes the introduction of systematic observation and documentation methods that are still in use today. Andreas Vesalius, a Flemish physician, published a book of anatomy in the mid-1500s. Vesalius challenged anatomical concepts made from limited observations by the ancient Greeks. Vesalius practiced dissection of corpses, so his descriptions of anatomy were based on repeated explorations of the insides of bodies, whereas the Greeks based their descriptions only on external observation and philosophy.

Scientific understanding is always limited by available technology. Many of the advances in biology and other areas of science that occurred during the Scientific Revolution were made possible by new technologies. For example, the invention of the microscope around the start of the 1600s allowed for the discovery of cells and microorganisms.

## Science from the Industrial Revolution to Today

The Industrial Revolution, which began in the last half of the 18th century, brought about significant advances in science. Travel and communication allowed for the exchange of ideas, universities developed robust science programs, and technology enabled scientists to explore the natural world with greater accuracy and precision. Such explorations led to new knowledge and built upon or replaced old knowledge.

For example, the development of cell theory replaced the notion of spontaneous generation, a belief that some life forms arose from nonliving matter. Experiments by Louis Pasteur in 1859, using broth in the equipment shown in **FIGURE 1.6**, demonstrated that living things did not come from nonliving matter but were the result of reproduction by other living things. As a result of this and other studies, three German scientists, Theodor Schwann, Matthias Schleiden, and Rudolph Virchow, proposed a theory summarizing the basic properties of living organisms. These basic concepts are collectively known as the cell theory. You will read more about cell theory in the chapter Cell Structure and Function. Other important advances in biology are also discussed throughout the book.

**FIGURE 1.6** The development of technology, tools, and equipment such as the swan-neck flasks used by Louis Pasteur, enable new scientific knowledge.

**Apply** **Why has scientific knowledge changed throughout history?**

(cr) ©Musée Pasteur de Dole

---

**SELF-CHECK Online**
HMHScience.com
**GO ONLINE**

## 1.1 Formative Assessment

### REVIEWING ▶ MAIN IDEAS

1. How are **species** related to the concept of **biodiversity**?

2. How does technology affect the advancement of **science?**

3. What societal needs were addressed by science in the ancient world?

### CRITICAL THINKING

4. **Support** Explain how the history of biology demonstrates that new knowledge can change established knowledge.

5. **Synthesize** How does biodiversity depend on a species' ability to reproduce?

### CONNECT TO

#### HUMAN BIOLOGY

6. The development of the microscope requires an understanding of physics concepts such as light and reflection. How else might an understanding of physics impact biology?

# Unifying Themes of Biology

**KEY CONCEPT** **Unifying themes connect concepts from many fields of biology.**

**MAIN IDEAS**

- ◗ All organisms share certain characteristics.
- ◗ All levels of life have systems of related parts.
- ◗ Structure and function are related in biology.
- ◗ Organisms must maintain homeostasis to survive in diverse environments.
- ◗ Evolution explains the unity and diversity of life.

## ☀ Connect to Your World

What do you think about when you hear the term *theme*? Maybe you think about the music at the start of your favorite TV show or the colors and organization of a computer desktop. In both cases, that theme shows up over and over again. In biology, you will see something similar. That is, some concepts come up time after time, even in topics that might seem to be completely unrelated. Understanding these themes, or concepts, can help you to connect the different areas of biology.

## ◗ MAIN IDEA

## All organisms share certain characteristics.

An **organism** is any individual living thing. All organisms on Earth share certain characteristics, but an actual definition of life is not simple. Why? The categories of living and nonliving are constructed by humans, and they are not perfect. For example, viruses fall into a middle range between living and nonliving. They show some, but not all, of the characteristics of living things.

**Cells** All organisms are made up of one or more cells. A **cell** is the basic unit of life. In fact, microscopic, single-celled organisms are the most common forms of life on Earth. A single-celled, or unicellular, organism carries out all of the functions of life, just as you do. Larger organisms that you see every day are made of many cells and are called multicellular organisms. Different types of cells in a multicellular organism have specialized functions, as shown in **FIGURE 2.1**. Your muscle cells contract and relax, your stomach cells secrete digestive juices, and your brain cells interpret sensory information. Together, specialized cells make you a complete organism.

**Need for energy** All organisms need a source of energy to carry out life processes. Energy is the ability to cause a change or to do work. All living things, from bacteria to ferrets to ferns, use chemical energy. Some organisms use chemicals from their environment to make their own source of chemical energy. Some organisms, such as plants,

**FIGURE 2.1** Cells can work together in specialized structures, such as these leaf hairs that protect a leaf from insects. (LM; magnification 700×)

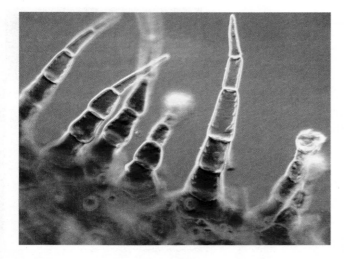

algae, and some bacteria, absorb energy from sunlight and store some of it in chemicals that can be used later as a source of energy. Animals obtain energy by eating other organisms. In all organisms, energy is important for **metabolism,** or all of the chemical processes that build up or break down materials.

**Response to environment** All organisms must react to their environment to survive. Light, temperature, and touch are just a few of the physical factors, called stimuli, to which organisms must respond. Think about how you respond to light when you leave a dimly lit room and go into bright sunlight. One of your body's responses is to contract the pupils of your eyes. Your behavior might also change. You might put on sunglasses or raise your hand to shade your eyes. Other organisms also respond to changes in light. For example, plants grow toward light. Some fungi need light to form the structures that you know as mushrooms.

**Reproduction and development** Members of a species must have the ability to produce new individuals, or reproduce. When organisms reproduce, they pass their genetic material to their offspring. In all organisms, the genetic material that contains the information that determines inherited characteristics is a molecule called deoxyribonucleic acid (dee-AHK-see-RY-boh-noo-KLEE-ihk), or **DNA.**

**FIGURE 2.2** Reproductive strategies differ among species. The male gold-specs jawfish protects unhatched eggs by holding them in his mouth.

Single-celled organisms can reproduce when one cell divides into two cells. Both new cells have genetic information that is identical to the original cell. Many multicellular organisms, such as the gold-specs jawfish in **FIGURE 2.2**, reproduce by combining the genetic information from two parents. In both cases, the instructions for growth and development of organisms, from bacteria to people, are carried by the same chemicals—DNA and ribonucleic acid (RNA). The process of development allows organisms to mature and gain the ability to reproduce.

**Summarize** **What characteristics are shared by all living things?**

## ▶ MAIN IDEA
# All levels of life have systems of related parts.

Think about the separate parts of a car—tires, engine, seats, and so on. Even if you have a complete set of car parts, you might not have a functioning car. Only when all of the parts that make up a car are put together in the correct way do you have a working car. A car is a system. A **system** is an organized group of related parts that interact to form a whole. Like any other system, a car's characteristics come from the arrangement and interaction of its parts.

Systems exist on all scales in biology, from molecules that cannot be seen, to cells that can be seen only with a microscope, to the biosphere. In just one heart muscle cell, for example, chemicals and processes interact in a precise way so that the cell has energy to do its work. Moving up a level, heart muscle, valves, arteries, and veins form a system in your body—the circulatory system.

FIGURE 2.3 The moray eel and the cleaner shrimp are parts of a system in which both organisms benefit. The shrimp cleans the eel's mouth and gets food and protection in return.

Two organisms that interact can also be a system, as you can see in **FIGURE 2.3**. On a larger scale, you are a part of a biological system—an ecosystem—that has living and nonliving parts. An **ecosystem** is a community of organisms and their physical environment. When you hear the term *ecosystem*, you might think about a large region, such as a desert, a coral reef, or a forest. But an ecosystem can also be a very small area, such as an individual tree.

Often, different biologists study different systems. For example, a person studying DNA might focus on very specific chemical interactions that take place in a cell. A person studying behavior in birds might focus on predator–prey relationships in an ecosystem. However, more and more biologists are working across different system levels. For example, some scientists study how chemicals in the brain affect social interactions.

## ▶ MAIN IDEA
# Structure and function are related in biology.

Think about a car again. In a car, different parts have different structures. The structure of a car part gives the part a specific function. For example, a tire's function is directly related to its structure. No other part of the car can perform that function. Structure and function are also related in living things. What something does in an organism is directly related to its shape or form. For example, when you eat, you probably bite into food with your sharp front teeth. Then you probably chew it mostly with your grinding molars. All of your teeth help you eat, but different types of teeth have different functions.

Structure and function are related at the level of chemicals in cells. For example, membrane channels and enzymes are both proteins, but they have very different structures and functions. A channel is a protein molecule that extends through the membrane, or outer layer, of a cell. It has a structure like a tube that allows specific chemicals to pass into and out of a cell. Enzymes are protein molecules that make chemical processes possible in living things. These proteins have shapes that allow them to attach to only certain chemicals and then cause the chemicals to react with each other.

FIGURE 2.4 The snout beetle (below) has specialized prongs and pads on its tarsi (right) that allow it to easily walk on both smooth and rough surfaces. (colored SEMs; magnifications: beetle 20×; tarsus 100×)

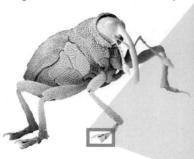

Different types of cells also have different functions that depend on their specialized structures. For example, cells in your brain process information. They have many branches that receive information from other cells. They also have long extensions that allow them to send messages to other cells. Red blood cells are very different. They are much smaller, disk shaped, and are specialized to carry oxygen. Their structure allows them to fit through even the smallest blood vessels to deliver oxygen through-out your body. Of course, a brain cell cannot take the place of a red blood cell.

Structure and function are also related on the level of the organism. For example, your foot structure allows you to walk easily on rough, fairly level surfaces. Walking on a surface such as ice is more difficult, and walking up a wall is impossible for you. The beetle in **FIGURE 2.4** is different. Its tarsi, or feet, have sharp prongs that can grip smooth or vertical surfaces, as well as soft pads for walking on rough surfaces. The beetle's tarsus has a different structure and function than your foot has, but both are specialized for walking.

**Infer** **Do you think heart muscle has the same structure as arm muscle? Explain.**

## ▶ MAIN IDEA
# Organisms must maintain homeostasis to survive in diverse environments.

Temperature and other environmental conditions are always changing, but the conditions inside organisms usually stay quite stable. How does the polar bear in **FIGURE 2.5** live in the Arctic? How can people be outside when the tempera-ture is below freezing, but still have a stable body temperature around 37°C (98.6°F)? Why do you shiver when you are cold, sweat when you are hot, and feel thirsty when you need water?

**Homeostasis** (HOH-mee-oh-STAY-sihs) is the maintenance of constant internal conditions in an organism. Homeostasis is important because cells function best within a limited range of conditions. Temperature, blood sugar, acidity, and other conditions must be controlled. Breakdowns in homeostasis are often life threatening.

Homeostasis is usually maintained through a process called negative feedback. In negative feedback, a change in a system causes a response that tends to return that system to its original state. For example, think about how a car's cruise control keeps a car moving at a constant set speed. A cruise control system has sensors that monitor the car's speed and then send that information to a computer. If the car begins to go faster than the set speed, the computer tells the car to slow down. If the car slows below the set speed, the computer tells the car to speed up. Similarly, if your body temperature drops below normal, systems in your body act to return your temperature to normal. Your muscles cause you to shiver, and blood vessels near your skin's surface constrict. If your body temperature rises above normal, different responses cool your body.

Behavior is also involved in homeostasis. For example, animals regulate their temperature through behavior. If you feel cold, you may put on a jacket. Reptiles sit on a warm rock in sunlight if they get too cold, and they move into shade if they get too warm.

**Summarize** **What is homeostasis, and why is it important?**

**FIGURE 2.5** The polar bear can maintain homeostasis in very cold climates. Its hollow hair is one adaptation that helps the bear retain its body heat. (SEM; magnification 450×)

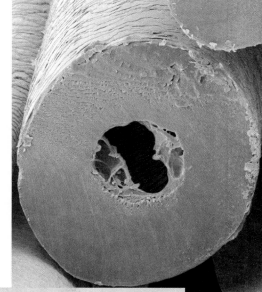

# Evolution explains the unity and diversity of life.

**⁂ CONNECT TO**

**EVOLUTION**

The processes of evolution, natural selection, and adaptation are described in more detail in the **Evolution** unit.

**Evolution** is the change in living things over time. More specifically, evolution is a change in the genetic makeup of a subgroup, or population, of a species. The concept of evolution links observations from all levels of biology, from cells to the biosphere. A wide range of scientific evidence, including the fossil record and genetic comparisons of species, shows that evolution is continuing today.

## Adaptation

One way evolution occurs is through natural selection of adaptations. In natural selection, a genetic, or inherited, trait helps some individuals of a species survive and reproduce more successfully than other individuals in a particular environment. An inherited trait that gives an advantage to individual organisms and is passed on to future generations is an **adaptation.** Over time, the makeup of a population changes because more individuals have the adaptation. Two different populations of the same species might have different adaptations in different environments. The two populations may continue to evolve to the point at which they are different species.

Consider the orchid and the thorn bug in **FIGURE 2.6.** Both organisms have adapted in ways that make them resemble other organisms. The orchid that looks like an insect lures other insects to it. The insects that are attracted to the orchid can pollinate the flower, helping the orchid to reproduce. The thorn bug's appearance is an adaptation that makes predators less likely to see and eat it. This adaptation allows the thorn bug to survive and reproduce.

**FIGURE 2.6** Through evolution, some orchids (left) have flowers that look like insects, and some insects, such as the thorn bug (right), look like parts of plants.

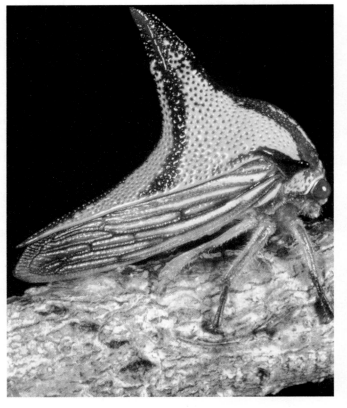

In different environments, however, you would find other orchid and insect species that have different adaptations.

Adaptation in evolution is different from the common meaning of adaptation. For example, if you say that you are adapting to a new classroom or to a new town, you are not talking about evolution. Instead, you are talking about consciously getting used to something new. Evolutionary adaptations are changes in a species that occur over many generations due to environmental pressures, not through choices made by organisms. Evolution is simply a long-term response to the environment. The process does not necessarily lead to more complex organisms, and it does not have any special end point. Evolution continues today, and it will continue as long as life exists on Earth.

## Unity and Diversity

Evolution is a unifying theme of biology because it accounts for both the diversity and the similarities, or the unity, of life. As you study biology, you will see time after time that organisms are related to one another. When you read about cells and genetics, you will see that all organisms have similar cell structures and chemical processes. These shared characteristics result from a common evolutionary descent.

Humans and bacteria have much more in common than you may think. Both human and bacterial genetics are based on the same molecules—DNA and RNA. Both human and bacterial cells rely upon the same sources of energy, and they have similar cell structures. Both human and bacterial cells have membranes made mostly of fats that protect the inside of the cell from the environment outside the cell.

Now think about the vast number of different types of organisms. All of the species alive now are the result of billions of years of evolution and adaptation to the environment. How? Natural selection of genetic traits can lead to the evolution of a new species. In the end, this genetic diversity is responsible for the diversity of life on Earth.

**Analyze** **How does evolution lead to both the diversity and the unity of life?**

**SELF-CHECK Online**
HMHScience.com
**GO ONLINE**

## 1.2 Formative Assessment

### REVIEWING ⊙ MAIN IDEAS

1. Describe a biological **system.**
2. Why is **homeostasis** essential for living things?
3. What is the relationship between **adaptation** and natural selection?

### CRITICAL THINKING

4. **Analyze** How are structure and function related to adaptation?
5. **Apply** How is the process of natural selection involved in **evolution**?
6. **Apply** Describe the relationship between **cells** and **organisms**.

### ⚡ CONNECT TO

#### CELLS

7. Do you think homeostasis is necessary at the level of a single cell? Explain.

# Qualitative and Quantitative

**Smart Grapher**
HMHScience.com
**GO ONLINE**
Biodiversity

Scientists collect two different types of data: qualitative data and quantitative data.

**Qualitative data** Qualitative data are descriptions in words of what is being observed. They are based on some quality of an observation, such as color, odor, or texture.

**Quantitative data** Quantitative data are numeric measurements. The data are objective—they are the same no matter who measures them. They include measurements such as mass, volume, temperature, distance, concentration, time, or frequency.

## Model

Suppose that a marine biologist observes the behavior and activities of dolphins. She identifies different dolphins within the group and observes them every day for a month. She records detailed observations about their behaviors. Some of her observations are qualitative data, and some are quantitative data.

### Qualitative data examples

- Dolphin colors range from gray to white.
- Dolphins in a pod engage in play behavior.
- Dolphins have smooth skin.

### Quantitative data examples

- There are nine dolphins in this pod.
- Dolphins eat the equivalent of 4–5% of their body mass each day.
- The sonar frequency most often used by the dolphins is around 100 kHz.

Notice that the qualitative data are descriptions. The quantitative data are objective, numerical measurements.

## Practice  Identify Data Types

Suppose that you are a biologist studying jackals in their natural habitat in Africa. You observe their behaviors and interactions and take photographs of their interactions to study later. Examine the photograph of the jackals shown to the right.

1. **Analyze**  Give three examples of qualitative data that could be obtained from the photograph of the jackals.

2. **Analyze**  Give three examples of quantitative data that could be obtained from the photograph of the jackals.

# 1.3 Scientific Thinking and Processes

SC.912.N.2.1,
SC.912.N.3.1

**SC.912.N.2.1** Identify what is science, what clearly is not science, and what superficially resembles science (but fails to meet the criteria for science).

**SC.912.N.3.1** Explain that a scientific theory is the culmination of many scientific investigations drawing together all the current evidence concerning a substantial range of phenomena; thus, a scientific theory represents the most powerful explanation scientists have to offer.

## VOCABULARY

observation
data
hypothesis
experiment
independent variable
dependent variable
constant
theory

**KEY CONCEPT** **Science is a way of thinking, questioning, and gathering evidence.**

### MAIN IDEAS

- Like all science, biology is a process of inquiry.
- Biologists use experiments to test hypotheses.
- A theory explains a wide range of observations.
- Scientists communicate information in many different ways.

### Connect to Your World

What does the study of fungus have in common with the study of human heart disease? How is research in a laboratory similar to research in a rain forest? Biologists, like all scientists, ask questions about the world and try to find answers through observation and experimentation. How do your daily observations help answer questions that you have about the world?

### ● MAIN IDEA

## Like all science, biology is a process of inquiry.

Science is a human process of trying to understand the world around us. There is no one method used by all scientists, but all scientific inquiry is based on the same principles. Scientific thinking is based on curiosity, skepticism, and logical thinking.

- Curiosity is what drives scientists to ask questions about the world around them.
- Skepticism is the use of critical thinking to question results and conclusions.
- Logical thinking is the use of reasoning through information to make conclusions that are supported by evidence.

One of the most important points of science is that scientific evidence may support or even overturn long-standing ideas. Scientists depend on empirical evidence as the basis for scientific knowledge. Empirical evidence is evidence that is observed directly through research and investigation. Such evidence is used to construct testable explanations and predictions of natural phenomena. The written descriptions and drawings of the gorilla in **FIGURE 3.1** are examples of observations and empirical evidence from a field investigation of gorillas. To improve our understanding of the world, scientists share their findings with each other. The open and honest exchange of data is extremely important in science.

**FIGURE 3.1** Biology, like other areas of science, depends on observations.

**CONNECT TO**

**DATA ANALYSIS**

Biology relies on the analysis of scientific data. Use the Data Analysis activities in each chapter in this book to build your data analysis skills.

**That's Amazing!**

**Video Inquiry**
HMHScience.com

**GO ONLINE**

Poison Frogs

## Observations, Data, and Hypotheses

All scientific inquiry begins with careful and systematic observations. Of course, **observation** includes using our senses to study the world, but it may also involve other tools. For example, scientists use computers to collect measurements or to examine past research results. Empirical evidence is gathered through observation.

Observations are often recorded as **data** that can be analyzed. Scientists collect two general types of data: qualitative data and quantitative data. Qualitative data are descriptions of a phenomenon that can include sights, sounds, and smells. This type of data is often useful to report what happens but not how it happens. In contrast, quantitative data are characteristics that can be measured or counted, such as mass, volume, and temperature. Anything that is expressed as a number is quantitative data that can be used to explore how something happens.

Scientists use observations, data, and scientific literature to form a hypothesis. A **hypothesis** (plural, *hypotheses*) is a proposed answer for a scientific question. A hypothesis must be specific and testable. You probably form and test many hypotheses every day, even though you may not be aware of it. Suppose you oversleep, for example. You needed to get up at 7 a.m., but when you wake up you observe that it is 8 a.m. What happened? Did the alarm not go off? Was it set for the wrong time? Did it go off, but you slept through it? You just made three hypotheses to explain why you overslept—the alarm did not go off, the alarm was set for the wrong time, or the alarm went off, but you did not hear it.

## Hypotheses, Results, and Conclusions

A hypothesis leads to testable predictions of what would happen if the hypothesis is valid. How could you use scientific thinking to test a hypothesis about oversleeping? If you slept late because the alarm was set for the wrong time, you could check the alarm to find out the time for which it was set. Suppose you check, and the alarm was actually set for 7 p.m. In this case, your hypothesis would be supported by your data.

For scientists, just one test of a hypothesis is usually not enough. Most of the time, it is only by repeating tests that scientists can be more certain that their results are not mistaken or due to chance. Why? Biological systems are highly variable. By repeating tests, scientists take this variability into account and try to decrease its effects on the experimental results. After scientists collect data, they use statistics to mathematically analyze whether a hypothesis is supported. Analyzed data are the results of the experiment. There are two possible outcomes or results.

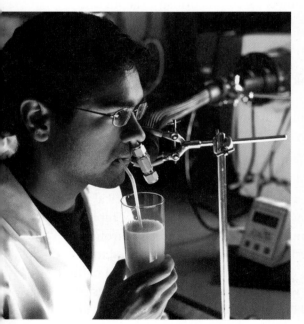

**FIGURE 3.2** In this experiment, a scientist studies how chemicals are detected in the mouth and nose to produce taste.

- **Nonsignificant** The data show no effect, or an effect so small that the results could have happened by chance.
- **Statistically significant** The data show an effect that is likely not due to chance. When data do not support a hypothesis, the hypothesis is rejected. But these data are still useful because they often lead to new hypotheses.

## FIGURE 3.3  Scientific Thinking

**Science is a cycle. The steps are shown in a certain order, but the cycle does not begin or end at any one point, and the steps may take place in various orders.**

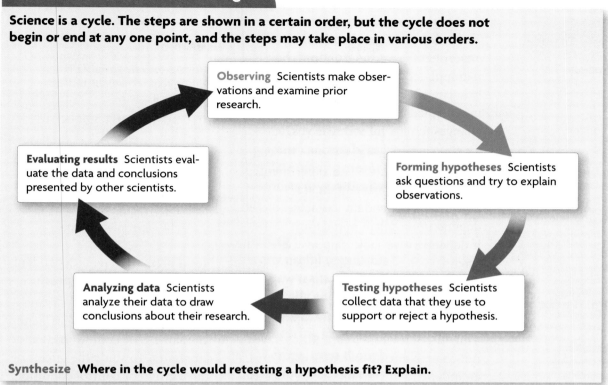

**Observing** Scientists make observations and examine prior research.

**Forming hypotheses** Scientists ask questions and try to explain observations.

**Evaluating results** Scientists evaluate the data and conclusions presented by other scientists.

**Analyzing data** Scientists analyze their data to draw conclusions about their research.

**Testing hypotheses** Scientists collect data that they use to support or reject a hypothesis.

**Synthesize** **Where in the cycle would retesting a hypothesis fit? Explain.**

Experimental methods and results are evaluated by other scientists in a process called peer review. Only after this review process is complete are research results accepted. Whether the results support an existing theory or disagree with earlier research, they are often used as a starting point for new questions. In **FIGURE 3.3,** you see the cycle of observing, forming hypotheses, testing hypotheses, analyzing data, and evaluating results that keeps scientific inquiry going.

**Synthesize** **Why is there no one correct process of scientific investigation?**

## ▶ MAIN IDEA

# Biologists use experiments to test hypotheses.

Observational studies help biologists describe and explain something in the world. But in observational studies, scientists try not to interfere with what happens. They try to simply observe a phenomenon. One example involves the endangered white stork. The number of white storks had decreased sharply by 1950, even becoming extinct in some countries. To help protect the storks, biologists studied the migration patterns of the birds. Observational studies can tell a biologist about changes in migration path and distance. They told scientists where the storks were breeding and how many eggs they would lay. Because of these efforts, stork populations have rebounded by 20% worldwide. Observational studies can provide much information and answer many questions. But there is one question that observations cannot answer: What causes any changes that might be observed? The only way to answer that question is through an experiment.

*Animated*
**Biology**
HMHScience.com
**GO ONLINE**
Experimental Design

Virtual
**INVESTIGATION**
HMHScience.com

GO ONLINE

The Scientific Process

**READING TOOLBOX**

**VOCABULARY**

In common usage, the term *constant* means "unchanging." In experimental research, a constant is a condition or factor that is controlled so that it does not change.

Scientific experiments allow scientists to test hypotheses and find out how something happens. In **experiments.** scientists study factors called independent variables and dependent variables to find cause-and-effect relationships. The **independent variable** in an experiment is a condition that is manipulated, or changed, by a scientist. The effects of manipulating an independent variable are measured by changes in dependent variables.

**Dependent variables** are observed and measured during an experiment; they are the experimental data. Changes in dependent variables depend upon the manipulation of the independent variable. Suppose a scientist is testing medications to treat high blood pressure. The independent variable is the dose of medication. The dependent variable is blood pressure, as shown in **FIGURE 3.4**.

Ideally, only one independent variable should be tested in an experiment. Thus, all of the other conditions have to stay the same. The conditions that do not change during an experiment are called **constants.** To study the effects of an independent variable, a scientist uses a control group or control condition. Subjects in a control group are treated exactly like experimental subjects except for the independent variable being studied. The independent variable is manipulated in experimental groups or experimental conditions.

Constants in the blood pressure medication experiment include how often the medication is given and how the medication is taken. To control the experiment, these factors must remain the same, or be held constant. For example, the medication could be tested with 0, 25, 50, or 100 milligram doses, twice a day, taken by swallowing a pill. By changing only one variable at a time—the amount of medication—a scientist can be more confident that the results are due to that variable.

**Infer  How do experiments show cause-and-effect relationships?**

**VISUAL VOCAB**

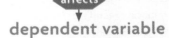

The **independent variable** is a condition that is manipulated, or changed, by a scientist.

in**dependent variable**

affects

**dependent variable**

**Dependent variables** are observed and measured during an experiment; they are the experimental data.

**FIGURE 3.4  COMPARING VARIABLES**

This graph compares the effects of the same dosage of two different medications on blood pressure. The independent variable (dosage) stayed the same for each type of medication tested.

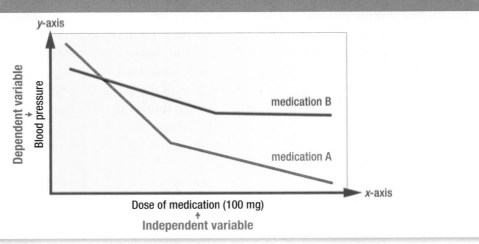

# A theory explains a wide range of observations.

The meaning of a word may change depending on the context in which it is used. The word *theory* has different meanings. In everyday conversation, the word *theory* means a guess or a hunch. In science, the meaning of the word *theory* is very different. A **theory** is a proposed explanation for a wide range of observations and experimental results that is supported by a wide range of evidence. Recall that a hypothesis is a proposed answer to a scientific question. Hypotheses about natural and physical phenomena that have been tested over a wide variety of conditions are incorporated into theories. For example, natural selection is a scientific theory. It is supported by a large amount of data, and it explains how populations can evolve.

Hypotheses propose answers to scientific questions. Scientific theories provide explanations of phenomena. In contrast to hypotheses and theories, a scientific *law* defines relationships that are valid everywhere in the universe. For example, the law of conservation of energy states that energy may change form, but it cannot be created or destroyed. A law describes without providing any explanations.

Theories are not easily accepted in science, and by definition they are never proved. Eventually, a theory may be broadly accepted by the scientific community. Scientific hypotheses and theories may be supported or refuted, and they are always subject to change. New theories that better explain observations and experimental results can replace older theories. Scientists must always be willing to revise theories and conclusions as new evidence about the living world is gathered. Science is an ongoing process. New experiments and observations refine and expand scientific knowledge.

One example of how scientific understanding can change involves the cause of disease. Until the mid-1800s, illnesses were thought to be related to supernatural causes or to imbalances of the body's humours, or fluids. Then scientific research suggested that diseases were caused by microscopic organisms, such as bacteria. This is the basis of the germ theory of disease, which is still accepted today. However, the germ theory has changed over time. For example, the germ theory has been expanded due to the discoveries of viruses and prions. Viruses and prions are not living organisms, but they do cause disease. The link between prions and disease was not even suggested until the early 1980s when evidence pointed to prions as the cause of mad cow disease and, in humans, both classic and variant Creutzfeldt–Jakob disease.

Scientific inquiry is important to understanding nature, but there are limitations to the kinds of questions that scientific inquiry can answer. For example, observations must be testable and verifiable. Observations that cannot be verified or replicated cannot count as evidence in scientific inquiry. Some phenomena that are not scientifically testable now may become testable with new or better technology. Other phenomena, such as supernatural phenomena, may never be testable or scientific.

**Compare** **Distinguish between a hypothesis, a theory, and a law.**

**FIGURE 3.5** For many years, scientific evidence indicated that stomach ulcers (top) were caused by stress. Then new evidence showed that the ulcers are actually caused by a type of bacteria called *Helicobacter pylori* (bottom). (colored SEM; magnification 4000×)

**FIGURE 3.6** Professional scientists present research and discuss implications at a science symposium.

**FIGURE 3.7** Doppler images, like this one of Hurricane Claudette in 2003, are models of weather data. In a television report, forecasters may use a Doppler image to summarize and predict future weather patterns and advise viewers about safety.

▶ MAIN IDEA

# Scientists communicate information in many different ways.

You may have seen written sources that include scientific information, such as product advertisements, magazine articles, or webpages. Scientific information may be presented at science fairs and symposia, which are forums for professional scientists to present and discuss new research, as in **FIGURE 3.6**. Because there are so many ways to communicate scientific information, it is important to know how to evaluate different methods of communication.

## Primary and Secondary Sources

Recall that new scientific research is reviewed by other scientists through the peer review process. During peer review, scientists consider many things. How was an experiment done? How were the data analyzed? Do the data support the conclusions? Is there bias in the experimental design or in the conclusions? Peer-reviewed scientific information is published in scientific journals. Scientific journals are primary sources of scientific information and include results and conclusions, along with experimental methods, data, and details that other scientists would need to recreate the investigation.

Almost all scientific knowledge presented to the public comes from secondary sources. Secondary sources summarize or report only portions of primary information. Magazine articles, news reports, textbooks, and advertisements are examples of secondary sources of information. Secondary sources may contain pieces of data that are most relevant to the source.

## Evaluating Scientific Information

Not all information that is presented as scientific is reliable. Reliable sources of scientific information are based on empirical evidence, logical reasoning, and testing. When evaluating scientific information, consider the evidence that supports the scientific claim, the purpose of the source, and whether any bias is present. Use critical thinking skills to evaluate the information.

**List** What are four sources that might include scientific information?

(tl) ©Oliver Morin/AFP/Getty Images; (c) ©National Weather Service (NOAA)/ National Weather Bureau

**SELF-CHECK** Online
HMHScience.com
**GO ONLINE**

## 1.3 Formative Assessment

### REVIEWING ▶ MAIN IDEAS

1. What role do **hypotheses** play in scientific inquiry?

2. Explain why a hypothesis must be testable.

3. Why would a scientific **theory** be revised over time?

### CRITICAL THINKING

4. **Compare and Contrast** How are hypotheses and theories similar? How do they differ?

5. **Criticize** What are two characteristics of a scientific information source that may indicate the information is unreliable?

### CONNECT TO

**SCIENTIFIC PROCESS**

6. Why is the statement "All life is made of cells" an example of a theory? Explain.

# Importance of Basic Research

In high school, students are usually required to take a variety of classes with the idea that the variety will ensure a well-rounded education. Later, students can pursue a career that allows them to focus their attention on a field where their talents and interests intersect. A foundation in basic scientific research can help set the stage for many careers. Through the collaborative nature of science, basic research contributes to a broad base of knowledge that scientists in specific research fields rely on heavily.

Basic scientific research has been compared to fishing, because it requires patience, persistence, and a bit of luck for success. It also has been compared to drilling for oil, because both money and time are required to drill many wells, but the payoff can be big once the right place is found. There is a creative element to basic research too. Scientists who pursue basic research are often simply curious about a subject and develop a method to find the answer. Sometimes the research can have very useful results.

In 1966, Indiana University professor Thomas Brock and undergraduate student Hudson Freeze were studying heat-loving microbes in the hot springs of Yellowstone National Park when they discovered a kind of bacteria that could thrive in water temperatures as warm as 50°C to 80°C. They named this bacterium *Thermus aquaticus*. Brock and Freeze did not realize at the time that their discovery would accelerate the scientific progress of everything from disease diagnosis to forensics.

Samples of *Thermus aquaticus* cultures were placed in the American Type Culture Collection in Washington D.C., where, a few years later, they were found by a biotechnology researcher who was looking for a heat-stable enzyme for polymerase chain reaction, or PCR. PCR is a technology that can make millions of copies of a DNA fragment in a short time, which is extremely useful in DNA research. The work of Brock and Freeze not only benefitted DNA research and science in general, but also indirectly benefitted society in unintended ways, such as improved healthcare. The later discovery of thermophilic, or heat-loving, microbes in deep-ocean hydrothermal vents means that other scientists now use culture methods developed by Dr. Brock.

Basic research has taught scientists so much about the bacteria *Escherichia coli*, the fruit fly *Drosophila melanogaster*, and the microscopic roundworm *Caenorhabditis elegans* that these organisms are now routinely used as model organisms for scientific studies around the world. Basic research also provides baseline data that may become important decades later when changes occur. Even when the benefits of scientific research are not immediately apparent, the sometimes-routine observations or unusual subjects of basic research can lead to a deeper understanding of current ideas and possibly even a scientific breakthrough.

Lower Geyser Basin, Yellowstone National Park, Wyoming

# 1.4 Biologists' Tools and Technology

**SC.912.L.14.4**

**KEY CONCEPT** Technology continually changes the way biologists work.

**MAIN IDEAS**

- Observations include making measurements.
- Technology contributes to the progress of science.
- Complex systems are modeled on computers.
- The tools of molecular genetics give rise to new biological studies.

## VOCABULARY

measurement
accuracy
precision
microscope
gene
molecular genetics
genomics

SC.912.L.14.4 Compare and contrast structure and function of various types of microscopes.

### Connect to Your World

Can you imagine life without cars, computers, or cell phones? Technology changes the way we live and work. Technology also plays a major part in the rapid increase of biological knowledge. In the early days of biology, scientists were limited to making measurements and observations with simple tools. Today, technology allows biologists to view tiny structures within cells and activity within a human brain. Technology even allows biologists to study and change genes. What will technology allow next?

### ▶ MAIN IDEA

## Observations include making measurements.

A wildlife biologist records a description of the alligator mating rituals she observes in her field journal. A pharmaceutical researcher uses probes and computers to measure and calculate the pH of stomach acids. Though very different, these situations are both examples of observation and the use of tools in scientific investigations. Tools serve a variety of purposes. Some tools, such as laboratory glassware and hot plates, allow scientists to set up experiments. Tools such as microscopes and hand lenses are used to enhance senses. Rulers, balances, and timing devices enable the gathering of quantitative data. Computer software is a tool that enables scientists to analyze and report data.

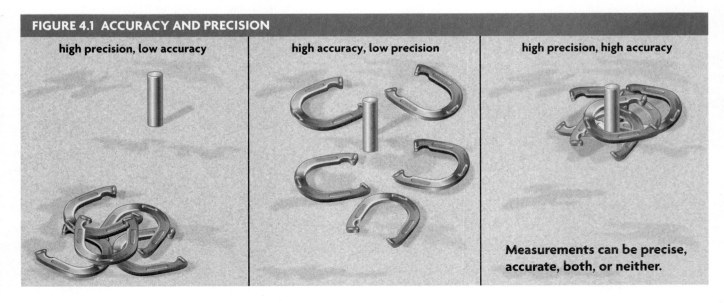

**FIGURE 4.1 ACCURACY AND PRECISION**

high precision, low accuracy

high accuracy, low precision

high precision, high accuracy

Measurements can be precise, accurate, both, or neither.

Quantitative data are gathered through **measurement,** the determination of the dimensions of something using a standard unit. The modern metric system, called the International System of Units, or SI, is the language for all scientific measurement. The quality of measurements can be described by their accuracy and precision. **Accuracy** is a description of how close a measurement is to the true value of the quantity measured. **Precision** is the exactness of a measurement. Accuracy and precision are demonstrated by the results of horseshoe tosses in **FIGURE 4.1.** When the horseshoes are close to each other, even if they are not near the goalpost, the results are precise. When the horseshoes are centered around the goalpost, even if they are not near each other, the results are accurate. When the horseshoes are centered around the goalpost and close to each other, the results are both precise and accurate.

▶ MAIN IDEA

## Technology contributes to the progress of science.

Until the late 1600s, no one knew about cells or single-celled organisms. Then the microscope was invented. Scientists suddenly had the ability to study living things at a level they never knew existed. Thus, the microscope was the first in a long line of technologies that changed the study of biology.

### Microscopes

A **microscope** provides an enlarged image of an object. Some of the most basic concepts of biology—such as the fact that cells make up all organisms—were not even imaginable before microscopes. The first microscopes magnified objects but did not produce clear images. By the 1800s, most microscopes had combinations of lenses that provided clearer images. Today's light microscopes, such as the one in **FIGURE 4.2** that you might use, are still based on the same principles. They are used to see living or preserved specimens, and they provide clear images of cells as small as bacteria. Light microscopes clearly magnify specimens up to about 1500 times their actual size, and samples are often stained with chemicals to make details stand out.

Electron microscopes, first developed in the 1930s, use beams of electrons instead of light to magnify objects. These microscopes can be used to see cells, but they produce much higher magnifications so they can also show much smaller things. Electron microscopes can clearly magnify specimens as much as 1,000,000 times their actual size. They can even be used to directly study individual protein molecules. However, electron microscopes, unlike light microscopes, cannot be used to study living organisms because the specimens being studied have to be in a vacuum.

**Explain Describe why newer technology may not make older technology obsolete.**

**FIGURE 4.2** Biologists use microscopes to study cells which are generally too small to be seen with the naked eye.

**OBSERVING**

## Life Under a Microscope

Using a microscope properly is an important skill for many biologists. In this lab, you will review microscope skills by examining a drop of water from the surface of a local pond.

**PROBLEM** What types of organisms can be found in pond water?

**PROCEDURE**

1. Make a wet mount slide. Place a drop of pond water in the center of a microscope slide, and carefully put a cover slip over the water. Learn how to make a wet mount by reading the Lab Handbook.

2. View the pond water sample under low power on the microscope. Use the coarse focus knob to bring the sample into focus. Draw and label any organisms that you see in the sample.

3. View the slide under high power. Use the fine focus knob to bring portions of the sample into focus. Draw and label any organisms, including details of their structures, that you see in the sample.

**ANALYZE AND CONCLUDE**

1. **Connect** Describe how organisms in the sample exhibit the characteristics of living things.

2. **Compare and Contrast** Make a table to compare and contrast the characteristics of organisms in the sample of pond water.

**MATERIALS**
- 1 drop pond water
- eyedropper
- microscope slide
- cover slip
- microscope

There are two main types of electron microscopes.

- A scanning electron microscope (SEM) scans the surface of a specimen with a beam of electrons. Usually, the specimen's surface is coated with a very thin layer of a metal that deflects the electrons. A computer forms a three-dimensional image from measurements of the deflected electrons.

- A transmission electron microscope (TEM) transmits electrons through a thin slice of a specimen. The TEM makes a two-dimensional image similar to that of a light microscope, but a TEM has a much higher magnification.

SEM and TEM images are artificially colorized with computers so that tiny details, such as the leaf pores, or stoma, shown in **FIGURE 4.3,** are easier to see.

**Animated Biology**
HMHScience.com

**GO ONLINE**

**Cells Through Different Microscopes**

## FIGURE 4.3 Comparing Micrographs

| LIGHT MICROGRAPH (LM) | SCANNING ELECTRON MICROGRAPH (SEM) | TRANSMISSION ELECTRON MICROGRAPH (TEM) |

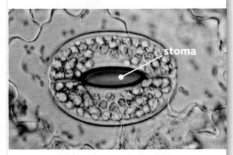

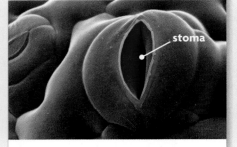

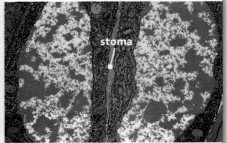

A light micrograph shows a two-dimensional image of a specimen. This light micrograph shows the actual color of the specimen.

An SEM shows a three-dimensional image of a specimen's surface. (colored SEM; magnification 1500×)

A TEM shows a two-dimensional image of a thin slice of a specimen. (colored TEM; magnification 5000×)

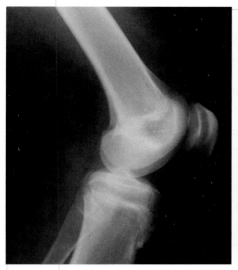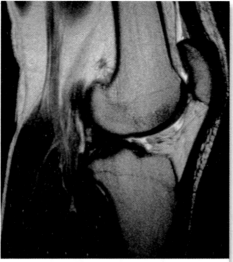

**FIGURE 4.4** An x-ray of the human knee (left) shows dense tissues, such as bone, in detail. An MRI of the human knee (right) shows both soft and dense tissues in detail.

## Medical Imaging

Imaging technology is not limited to microscopes. For example, doctors or dentists have probably taken x-ray images of you several times. An x-ray image is formed by x-rays, which pass through soft tissues, such as skin and muscle, but are absorbed by bones and teeth. Thus, x-ray images are very useful for looking at the skeleton but not so useful for examining soft tissues such as ligaments, cartilage, or the brain.

To image soft tissues, another imaging technology called magnetic resonance imaging (MRI) is used. MRI uses a strong magnetic field to produce a cross-section image of a part of the body. A series of MRI images can be put together to give a complete view of all of the tissues in that area, as you can see in **FIGURE 4.4.** Advances in technology have led to new uses for MRI. For example, a technique called functional MRI (fMRI) can show which areas of the brain are active while a person is doing a particular task.

## Computers and Probeware

The first digital, electronic computers were invented in the 1940s. They were expensive and so large that one computer filled an entire room. As technology improved, computers, computer software, and hardware, such as probeware, have become invaluable to the practice of biology. Word processing software is used to generate reports. Spreadsheet software is used to quickly and accurately calculate, analyze, and display data in charts, graphs, and other visual representations. The use of probeware in conjunction with computers allows both data collection and analysis. Probeware are measuring tools that can take constant readings of data such as temperature and pH. When probeware is connected to a computer, the data can be calculated and analyzed instantly.

**Infer  How might probeware be used by a biologist studying the decline of fish in a certain lake?**

# Complex systems are modeled on computers.

**Normal heartbeat**

**Heart attack**

**FIGURE 4.5** This computer-generated model shows that heart activity (red) is tightly regulated during a normal heartbeat. During a heart attack, heart activity is widespread and disorganized.

Computer-based technology has greatly expanded biological research. As computers have become faster and more powerful, biologists have found ways to use them to model living systems that cannot be studied directly. A computer model simulates the interactions among many different variables to provide scientists with a general idea of how a biological system may work.

Computers can model complex systems within organisms. For example, computer models are used to study how medicines might affect the body or, as you can see in **FIGURE 4.5,** the effects of a heart attack. Scientists have even used computer models to find out how water molecules travel into and out of cells. The scientists made a computer program that took into account more than 50,000 virtual atoms in a virtual cell. The computer model showed that water molecules must spin around in the middle of a channel, or a passage into the cell, to fit through the channel. Water molecules had a specific fit that other molecules could not match.

Computer models can also help biologists study complex systems on a much larger scale. Epidemiology, which is the study of how diseases spread, depends on computer models. For example, the computer model in **FIGURE 4.6** can predict how fast and how far a disease might spread through a herd of cattle. A model can calculate the number of cattle who might get sick and suggest where the disease could be spread to humans through eating contaminated meat or other sources. This study cannot be done with real cattle and people. Computer models are used when actual experiments are not safe, ethical, or practical. However, all models have limitations, and they are not able to replicate exactly all aspects of the system they are showing.

**Conclude** What are some reasons why biologists use computer models?

## FIGURE 4.6  Computer Simulation

Computer simulations can help epidemiologists to predict the spread of disease and to develop a response plan.

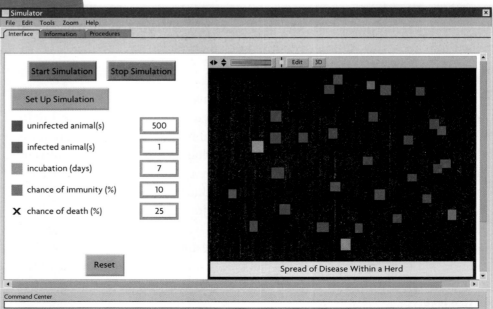

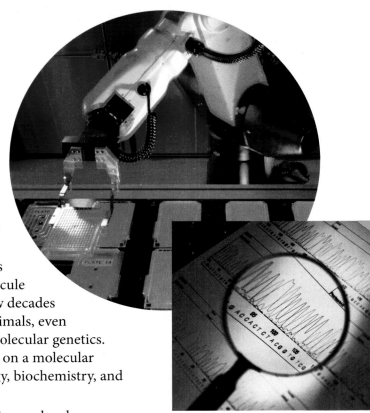

FIGURE 4.7 Robots are used to speed up research into the human genome (top). Computers are used to sequence human DNA (bottom).

## ● MAIN IDEA

# The tools of molecular genetics give rise to new biological studies.

Computer-based technologies, such as those shown in **FIGURE 4.7**, have led to major changes in biology. But perhaps the greatest leap forward in our knowledge of life has happened in genetics. In just 40 years, we have gone from learning how the genetic code works, to changing genes, to implanting genes from one species into another.

What is a gene? A **gene** is a segment of DNA that stores genetic information. Our understanding of the DNA molecule has led to many technologies that were unimaginable a few decades ago—genetically modified foods, transgenic plants and animals, even replacement of faulty genes. These advances come from molecular genetics. **Molecular genetics** is the study and manipulation of DNA on a molecular level. Molecular genetics is used to study evolution, ecology, biochemistry, and many other areas of biology.

Entirely new areas of biology have arisen from combining molecular genetics with computer technology. For example, computers are used to quickly find DNA sequences. Through the use of computers, the entire DNA sequences, or genomes, of humans and other organisms have been found. **Genomics** (juh-NOH-mihks) is the study and comparison of genomes both within and across species.

All of the information from genomics is managed by computer databases. By searching computer databases, a process called data mining, a biologist can find patterns, similarities, and differences in biological data. Suppose a biologist identifies a molecule that prevents the growth of cancerous tumors. The biologist could use computer databases to search for similar molecules.

This is the cutting edge of biology today. Where will biology be when your children are in high school?

**Connect** **What does the term *genetics* mean to you? Why?**

> ⚡ **CONNECT TO**
> ## GENETICS
> You will learn much more about these and other genetics topics in the **Genetics** unit.

---

## 1.4  Formative Assessment

**SELF-CHECK Online**
HMHScience.com
**GO ONLINE**

### REVIEWING ● MAIN IDEAS

1. What are two ways scientists can describe the quality of **measurements**?

2. Why is computer modeling used in biological studies?

3. Why do computer models have limitations?

### CRITICAL THINKING

4. **Apply**  Viruses are smaller than cells. What types of microscopes could be used to study them? Explain.

5. **Synthesize**  Provide an example of how technology has helped biologists gain a better understanding of life.

> ⚡ **CONNECT TO**
> ## EVOLUTION
> 6. **Genomics** can be used to study the *genetic* relationships among species. Why might genomics be important for research on evolution? Explain.

(t) ©David Parker/Photo Researchers, Inc.; (r) ©Kevin Curtis/Photo Researchers, Inc.

# 1.5 Biology and Your Future

HE.912.C.1.3,
SC.912.L.16.10

**KEY CONCEPT** **Understanding biology can help you make informed decisions.**

**HE.912.C.1.3** Evaluate how environment and personal health are interrelated.

**SC.912.L.16.10** Evaluate the impact of biotechnology on the individual, society and the environment, including medical and ethical issues.

### VOCABULARY
biotechnology
transgenic

### MAIN IDEAS
- Your health and the health of the environment depend on your knowledge of biology.
- Biotechnology offers great promise but also raises many issues.
- Biology presents many unanswered questions.

### Connect to Your World

Should brain imaging technology be used to tell if someone is lying? Is an endangered moth's habitat more important than a new highway? Would you vote for or against the pursuit of stem cell research? An informed answer to any of these questions requires an understanding of biology and scientific thinking. And although science alone cannot answer these questions, gathering evidence and analyzing data can help every decision maker.

## MAIN IDEA

# Your health and the health of the environment depend on your knowledge of biology.

Decisions are based on opinions, emotions, education, experiences, values, and logic. Many of your decisions, now and in the future, at both personal and societal levels, involve biology. Your knowledge of biology can help you make informed decisions about issues involving endangered species, biotechnology, medical research, and pollution control, to name a few. How will your decisions affect the future of yourself and others?

### Biology and Your Health

What you eat and drink is directly related to your health. But you may not think twice about the possibility of contaminated food or water, or a lack of vitamins in your diet. Not long ago, diseases caused by vitamin deficiencies were still fairly common. The first vitamins were identified less than 100 years ago, but today the vitamins found in foods are printed on labels.

Even today we still face food-related causes of illness. For example, you might hear about an outbreak of food poisoning, and mad cow disease was only recognized in the late 1980s. Of perhaps greater concern to you are food allergies. Many people suffer from severe, even life-threatening, allergies to foods such as peanuts and shellfish. Beyond questions about the sources of food are questions and concerns about what people eat and how much they eat. For example, scientists estimate that more than 69% of adults in the United States are overweight or obese. The health consequences of obesity include increased risks of diabetes, stroke, heart disease, breast cancer, colon cancer, and other health problems. Biology can help you to better understand all of these health-related issues.

### READING TOOLBOX

**TAKING NOTES**
Use a mind map to take notes about the importance of studying biology.

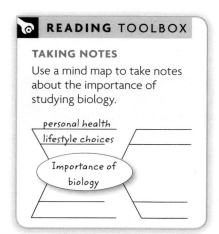

An understanding of biology on many different levels—genetic, chemical, and cellular, for example—can help you make any number of lifestyle choices that affect your health. Why is it important to use sunscreen? What are the benefits of exercise? What are the effects of using alcohol, illegal drugs, and tobacco? Cigarette smoke does not just affect the lungs, as shown in **FIGURE 5.1**; it can also change a person's body chemistry. Lower levels of monoamine oxidase in the brain can affect mood, and lower levels in the liver could contribute to high blood pressure.

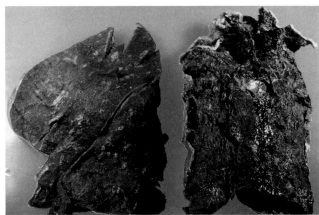

**FIGURE 5.1** As compared with nonsmokers, smokers have visibly damaged lung tissue that is blackened by tar deposits.

## Biology and the World Around You

In 1995, some middle school students from Minnesota were walking through a wetland and collecting frogs for a school project. The students stopped to look at the frogs, and what they saw shocked them. Many of the frogs had deformities, including missing legs, extra legs, and missing eyes. What caused the deformities? Scientists investigated that question by testing several hypotheses. They studied whether the deformities could have been caused by factors such as a chemical in the water, ultraviolet radiation, or some type of infection.

Why would frog deformities such as that in **FIGURE 5.2** provoke such scientific interest? The frogs are a part of an ecosystem, so whatever affected them could affect other species in the area. If the deformities were caused by a chemical in the water, might the chemical pose a risk to people living in the area? In other regions of the United States, parasites caused similar deformities in frogs. Might that parasite also be present in Minnesota? If so, did it pose a risk to other species?

At first, parasites were not found in the frogs. However, scientists now suggest that the frog deformities were due to a combination of infection by parasites, called trematodes, and predation by dragonfly nymphs. Science has answered some questions about the cause of the leg deformities. However, scientists now think that a chemical may be connected to the increased number of parasite infections.

Suppose that the chemical comes from a factory in the area. Is it reasonable to ban the chemical? Should the factory be closed or fined? In any instance like this, political, legal, economic, and biological concerns have to be considered. What is the economic impact of the factory on the area? Is there any evidence of human health problems in the area? Is there a different chemical that could be used? Without an understanding of biology, how could you make an informed decision related to any of these questions?

These are the types of questions that people try to answer every day. Biologists and other scientists research environmental issues such as pollution, biodiversity, habitat preservation, land conservation, and natural resource use, but decisions about the future are not in the hands of scientists. It is up to everyone to make decisions based on evidence and conclusions from many different sources.

**FIGURE 5.2** Deformities in frogs can be an indication of chemical pollution in an ecosystem.

**Connect  How might biology help you to better understand environmental issues?**

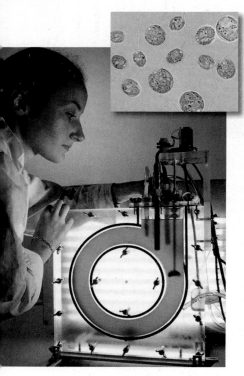

**FIGURE 5.3** Biotechnology is being used in the search for alternative energy sources, as shown in this bioreactor that uses algae (inset) to produce hydrogen gas. (LM; magnification 400×)

## CONNECT TO

### GENETICS

You will learn more about genetic screening and how it is used in the chapter **Frontiers of Biotechnology.**

> **MAIN IDEA**

# Biotechnology offers great promise but also raises many issues.

**Biotechnology** is the use and application of living things and biological processes. Biotechnology includes a very broad range of products, processes, and techniques. In fact, some forms of biotechnology have been around for centuries, such as the use of microorganisms to make bread and cheese. Today, biotechnology is used in medicine, agriculture, forensic science, and many other fields. For example, people wrongly convicted of crimes have been freed from prison when DNA testing has shown that their DNA did not match DNA found at crime scenes. Biotechnology has great potential to help solve a variety of modern problems, such as the search for alternative energy sources using algae, as shown in **FIGURE 5.3**. However, along with the advances in biotechnology come questions about its uses.

## Benefits and Biological Risks

All domestic plants and animals are the result of centuries of genetic manipulation through selective breeding. Today, genetic manipulation can mean the transfer of genetic information from one organism to a very different organism. Organisms that have genes from more than one species, or have altered copies of their own genes, are called **transgenic** organisms. Transgenic bacteria can make human insulin to treat people with diabetes. Transgenic sheep and cows can make human antibodies and proteins. When you hear about genetically modified foods, you are hearing about transgenic organisms.

Genetically modified foods have many potential benefits. Crop plants are changed to increase the nutrients and yield of the plants and to resist insects. Insect-resistant crops could reduce or end the need for chemical pesticides. However, the long-term effects of genetically modified crops are not fully known. Is it safe to eat foods with genetically modified insect resistance? What if genetically modified plants spread undesirable genes, such as those for herbicide resistance, to wild plants? Around the world, the benefits and risks of biotechnology are debated. Understanding these benefits and risks requires knowledge of ecosystems, genetic principles, and even the functions of genes.

## Benefits and Ethical Considerations

Another form of biotechnology is human genetic screening, which is the analysis of a person's genes to identify genetic variations. Genetic screening can indicate whether individuals or their potential offspring may be at risk for certain diseases or genetic disorders. Genetic screening has the potential for early diagnosis of conditions that can be treated before an illness occurs.

Genetic screening also raises ethical concerns. For example, who should have access to a person's genetic information? Some people are concerned that insurance companies might refuse health insurance to someone with a gene that might cause a disease. Suppose genetic screening reveals that a child might have a genetic disorder. How should that information be used? Genetic screening has the potential to eliminate some disorders, but what should be

(t) ©Pascal Goetgheluck/Photo Researchers, Inc.; (cl) ©Pascal Goetgheluck/Photo Researchers, Inc.

considered a disorder? Of greater concern is the possibility that people might use genetic screening to choose the characteristics of their children. Is it ethical to allow people to choose to have only brown-eyed male children who would be at least 6 feet (ft) tall?

**Predict** **How might genetically modified crops affect biodiversity?**

## ▶ MAIN IDEA
# Biology presents many unanswered questions.

The structure of DNA was described in 1953. By 2003, the entire human DNA sequence was known. Since 1953, our biological knowledge has exploded. But even today there are more questions than answers. Can cancer be prevented or cured? How do viruses mutate? How are memories stored in the brain? One of the most interesting questions is whether life exists on planets other than Earth. Extreme environments on Earth are home to living things like the methane worms in **FIGURE 5.4**. Thus, it is logical to suspect that other planets may also support life. But even if life exists elsewhere in the universe, it may be completely different from life on Earth. How might biological theories change to take into account the characteristics of those organisms?

**FIGURE 5.4** Methane hydrate ice worms live in frozen methane gas at the bottom of the Gulf of Mexico. Because some organisms can live in such extreme environments, some scientists hypothesize that life exists, or once existed, on the planet Mars.

A large number of questions in biology are not just unanswered—they are unasked. Before the microscope was developed, no one investigated anything microscopic. Before the middle of the 20th century, biologists did not know for sure what the genetic material in organisms was made of. As technology and biology advance, who knows what will be discovered in the next 20 years?

**Evaluate** **Do you think technology can help answer all biological questions? Explain your views.**

# 1.5 Formative Assessment

### REVIEWING ▶ MAIN IDEAS

1. Give three examples of ways in which biology can help inform everyday decisions.

2. What are some of the potential benefits and potential risks of **biotechnology**?

3. What are some of the unanswered questions in biology?

### CRITICAL THINKING

4. **Synthesize** Scientists disagree on whether genetically modified foods are safe to eat. What type of scientific evidence would be needed to show that a genetically modified food is unsafe?

5. **Connect** How might your study of biology help inform you about your lifestyle choices?

### CONNECT TO

**ECOLOGY**

6. What effects might genetically modified plants and animals have on an ecosystem if they breed with wild plants and animals?

# 1 Summary

Biology is the scientific study of all aspects of living things and it shapes our understanding of our world, from human health to biotechnology to environmental preservation.

## KEY CONCEPTS

### 1.1 The Study of Life

**Science is the knowledge obtained through observation of natural events and conditions in order to discover facts and formulate laws or principles that can be verified or tested.** Biology is the study of all forms of life and their interactions with each other and the environment. Everywhere that organisms are found on Earth is considered to be the biosphere. Biology has been studied throughout history.

### 1.2 Unifying Themes of Biology

**Unifying themes connect concepts from many fields of biology.** Organisms are made of one or more cells, need energy for all of their functions, respond to their environment, and reproduce by passing their genetic information to offspring. Interactions occur at various levels, from chemical processes within cells to interactions between species within an ecosystem. Individual organisms depend on the relationship between structure and function, and on the ability to maintain homeostasis. Over billions of years, evolution and adaptation have given rise to all of the species on Earth.

 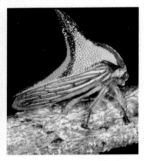

### 1.3 Scientific Thinking and Processes

**Science is a way of thinking, questioning, and gathering evidence.** Scientists test hypotheses, or proposed explanations, through observation and experimentation. In a scientific experiment, a scientist controls constants, manipulates independent variables, and measures dependent variables. A scientific theory explains a wide range of observations and experimental results. A theory is supported by a wide range of evidence, and it is widely accepted by the scientific community.

### 1.4 Biologists' Tools and Technology

**Technology continually changes the way biologists work.** Observation and measurement result in the data that are analyzed in scientific study. Tools for observation and measurement improve as technology improves. The development of fast, powerful computers and probeware has given scientists the ability to quickly and accurately analyze data and model aspects of life that cannot be studied directly.

### 1.5 Biology and Your Future

**Understanding biology can help you make informed decisions.** An understanding of biology can help you to make important decisions about your own health and lifestyle, as well as decisions that will shape the world around you. The development of biotechnology and genetic manipulation is just one issue in biology that will affect you and the rest of society in the coming years.

---

### READING TOOLBOX    SYNTHESIZE YOUR NOTES

**Content Frame** Identify relationships between the characteristics of living things and the unifying themes of biology. Use your notes to make content frame organizers like the one below to summarize the relationships.

| Characteristic | Theme | Example |
|---|---|---|
| Cells | Systems | Cells work together in multicellular organisms. |
| | Structure and Function | |
| | | |

**Concept Map** Use concept maps like the one below to visualize general relationships among topics in biology.

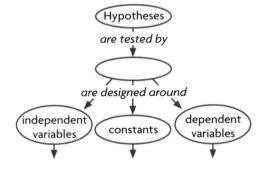

# 1 Review

**INTERACTIVE Review**
HMHScience.com
**GO ONLINE**
Review Games • Concept Map • Section Self-Checks

## CHAPTER VOCABULARY

**1.1**
biosphere
biodiversity
species
biology
science

**1.2**
organism
cell
metabolism
DNA
system
ecosystem

homeostasis
evolution
adaptation

**1.3**
observation
data
hypothesis
experiment
independent variable
dependent variable
constant
theory

**1.4**
measurement
accuracy
precision
microscope
gene
molecular genetics
genomics

**1.5**
biotechnology
transgenic

## Reviewing Vocabulary

### Compare and Contrast

Describe one similarity and one difference between the two terms in each of the following pairs.

1. biosphere, ecosystem
2. hypothesis, theory
3. accuracy, precision

### Write Your Own Questions

Think about the relationship between each word pair below. Then write a question about the first term that uses the second term as the answer. For the terms *organism, cell,* the question could be "What is the basic building block of all organisms?" Answer: the cell

4. evolution, adaptation
5. observation, data
6. DNA, gene

### READING TOOLBOX · GREEK AND LATIN WORD ORIGINS

7. The prefix *bio-* means "life." How does this meaning relate to the definitions of terms in the chapter that contain the prefix *bio-*?

8. The prefix *homeo-* comes from a Greek word that means "same." The suffix *-stasis* comes from a Greek word that means "stoppage," or "standstill." How are these definitions related to the meaning of the word *homeostasis*?

## Reviewing MAIN IDEAS

9. Why is it important that biology studies the interactions of organisms with both their environments and other organisms?

10. Explain why domestication of plants and animals was likely one of the first areas of biology.

11. Briefly describe the basic characteristics that all living things on Earth have in common.

12. Give an example of how structure and function are related in an organism.

13. How does negative feedback act to maintain homeostasis in living things?

14. Explain how scientists use observations and data to develop a hypothesis.

15. What is the difference between a scientific hypothesis and a scientific theory?

16. Explain the difference between tools that enhance senses and tools that are used for measurements.

17. Briefly describe why the development of the microscope was important in biology.

18. How can an understanding of biology play a role in your health? in the health of your environment?

19. Describe an example of biotechnology, including its benefits and risks.

# Critical Thinking

**20. Synthesize** In 1973, the insecticide called DDT was banned in the United States due to scientific research showing it was toxic to fish and that it may have affected birds. There is little scientific evidence that DDT is directly harmful to humans. How could banning DDT be beneficial to human health and society?

**21. Apply** A student is trying to predict the effects on wildlife of a proposed construction project in an undeveloped area nearby. Describe how the student can evaluate scientific information extracted from news reports, marketing materials, and online resources.

**22. Evaluate** Discuss the impact of scientific research on society and the environment. Consider the benefits and risks of scientific research and the challenges that unanswered questions leave for biologists and other scientists to wrestle with.

**23. Evaluate** Suppose a scientist is investigating plant growth. During the experiment, both the type of light and the type of plant are manipulated. The scientist concludes that the results are caused only by changes in the light. Is this an appropriate conclusion? Why or why not?

**24. Justify** Why is science limited to studying phenomena that are scientifically testable? Give two examples of questions that are outside the realm of science.

## Interpreting Visuals

Use the diagram below to answer the next two questions.

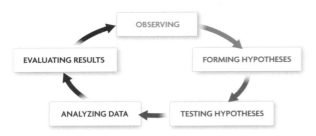

**25. Apply** Observing is shown at only one point during the cycle. At what other points during the cycle is observing necessary? Explain.

**26. Distinguish** Where in the process are scientists most likely to make inferences and predict trends from data?

## Analyzing Data    Identify Data Types

Use the information below to answer the next three questions.

Suppose a team of scientists is studying the migration of animal species in Africa. One of the scientists takes the photograph below.

**27. Apply** Give three examples each of quantitative and qualitative data that could be collected during this research.

**28. Identify** What are four tools that the team of scientists likely used while conducting, analyzing, and communicating their work? Explain your answer.

**29. Evaluate** Suppose the scientists wanted to change the number of species present in this study. What are some limitations and advantages of using a computer model to simulate the change?

## Making Connections

**30. Defend** Much of the work and ideas of early scientists, such as Hippocrates's four humours and Aristotle's classification system for animals, were shown to be incorrect and have been discarded or replaced. Why, then, are early Greeks credited as the fathers or inventors of science?

**31. Analyze** The yellow fever mosquito shown on the Chapter Opener is just one type of mosquito that can pass disease-causing viruses to people. Mosquitoes can also carry other diseases such as malaria, Dengue fever, and West Nile virus. And even if mosquitoes do not carry dangerous viruses, they are certainly pests. On the other hand, mosquitoes are a source of food for many types of animals. Suppose you developed a way to rid Earth of mosquitoes. Do you think it should be used? Why or why not?

# Standards-Based Assessment

Record your answers on a separate piece of paper.

## MULTIPLE CHOICE

1 Finch species in the Galapagos Islands have a wide variety of beak shapes. The theory of natural selection suggests that these differences arose because —

A changes occurred over a short period of time

B finches with certain beak shapes survived in greater numbers

C conscious decisions allowed certain finches to survive

D individual finches adapted to their environment

2

Which of the following *best* completes this concept map?

A biodiversity

B homeostasis

C evolution

D adaptation

3 Based on their limitations, which of the following models is the *best* representation of how the human skeletal and muscular systems work together to produce motion?

A a detailed illustration in a textbook

B a skeleton made up of human bones that can be manually manipulated

C a computer simulation of the skeletal and muscular systems in motion

D a human running on a treadmill

4 A student is provided with a sample of pond water that contains a variety of single-celled organisms. How might the student determine if any of the organisms in the sample are in the process of reproducing?

A Examine the pond water with a hand lens to determine if the water in the sample is moving.

B Examine a sample of the pond water with a compound microscope to determine if any of the cells are dividing into two cells.

C Observe a drop of pond water with a compound microscope, return the drop back to the larger sample, and then repeat the process every hour for three hours to see if the population size changes.

D Examine the pond water with a compound microscope to determine whether the single-celled organisms it contains are moving.

5 Students hypothesized that water pollution affects the growth of fish. In an experiment, they added the same amount of food to ponds polluted by fertilizers and industrial waste. They measured fish growth and found that most fish grow slowly in each of these environments. Why is their conclusion not reliable?

A They did not have a control.

B They did not have a clear hypothesis.

C They only tested one independent variable.

D They did not have a dependent variable.

### THINK THROUGH THE QUESTION

When scientists study how one thing affects another, the investigation generally has a control, a testable hypothesis, one manipulated (independent) variable, and one measured (dependent) variable. Are these components present in the student's experiment?

CHAPTER

# 2 Chemistry of Life

**BIG IDEA** Living things depend on chemical reactions that require water, carbon-based molecules, and other molecules including enzymes to regulate chemical reactions.

**2.1** **Atoms, Ions, and Molecules**

**2.2** **Properties of Water**

**2.3** **Carbon-Based Molecules**

**Data Analysis**
**IDENTIFYING VARIABLES**

**2.4** **Chemical Reactions**

**2.5** **Enzymes**

---

## ⊘ ONLINE BIOLOGY    HMHScience.com

**ONLINE** Labs
- **QuickLab** Chemical Bonding
- Enzymatic Activity
- Testing pH
- Enzymes
- Modeling Biochemical Compounds
- The Biochemistry of Compost Bins

- Action of Yeast
- Acids and Bases
- Enzyme Action: Testing Catalase Activity
- **Virtual Lab** Calorimetry
- **Video Lab** Enzymes in Detergents
- **Open Inquiry Lab** Chemical Reactions

©Maximilian Weinzierl/Alamy

**How can this plant digest a grasshopper?**

Like other carnivores, the Venus flytrap eats animals to get nutrients that it needs to make molecules such as proteins and nucleic acids. Other chemical compounds made by the plant's cells enable the Venus flytrap to digest the animals that it eats. These chemicals are similar to the chemicals that allow you to digest the food that you eat.

## READING TOOLBOX    This reading tool can help you learn the material in the following pages.

### USING LANGUAGE

**Quantifiers** Quantifiers are words that describe how much, how large, and how often. Quantifiers can also describe the order in which things occur. Words that describe an order include first, second, third, fourth, primary, secondary, tertiary, and quaternary.

### YOUR TURN

Use what you have learned about quantifiers to answer the following questions.

1. Place the following months in order of fourth, third, second, and first: January, March, April, February.
2. Would a student attending primary school be younger or older than a student attending secondary school?

# 2.1 Atoms, Ions, and Molecules

SC.912.L.18.1

**KEY CONCEPT** **All living things are based on atoms and their interactions.**

**MAIN IDEAS**
- Living things consist of atoms of different elements.
- Ions form when atoms gain or lose electrons.
- Atoms share pairs of electrons in covalent bonds.

**VOCABULARY**

atom
element
compound
ion
ionic bond
covalent bond
molecule

**SC.912.L.18.1** Describe the basic molecular structures and primary functions of the four major categories of biological macromolecules.

### Connect to Your World

The Venus flytrap produces chemicals that allow it to consume and digest insects and other small animals, including an unlucky frog. Frogs also produce specialized chemicals that allow them to consume and digest their prey. In fact, all organisms depend on many chemicals and chemical reactions. For this reason, the study of living things also involves the study of chemistry.

## MAIN IDEA

# Living things consist of atoms of different elements.

**READING TOOLBOX**

**TAKING NOTES**
Use a main idea web to help you make connections among elements, atoms, ions, compounds, and molecules.

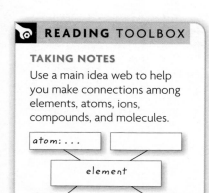

What do a frog, a skyscraper, a car, and your body all have in common? Every physical thing you can think of, living or not, is made of incredibly small particles called atoms. An **atom** is the smallest basic unit of matter. Millions of atoms could fit in a space the size of the period at the end of this sentence. And it would take you more than 1 trillion (1,000,000,000,000, or $10^{12}$) years to count the number of atoms in a single grain of sand.

### Atoms and Elements

Although there is a huge variety of matter on Earth, all atoms share the same basic structure. Atoms consist of three types of smaller particles: protons, neutrons, and electrons. Protons and neutrons form the dense center of an atom—the atomic nucleus. Electrons are much smaller particles outside of the nucleus. Protons have a positive electrical charge, and electrons have a negative electrical charge. Neutrons, as their name implies, are neutral—they have no charge. Because an atom has equal numbers of positively charged protons and negatively charged electrons, it is electrically neutral.

An **element** is one particular type of atom, and it cannot be broken down into a simpler substance by ordinary chemical means. An element can also refer to a group of atoms of the same type. A few familiar elements include the gases hydrogen and oxygen and the metals aluminum and gold. Because all atoms are made of the same types of particles, what difference among atoms makes one element different from other elements? Atoms of different elements differ in the number of protons they have. All atoms of a given element have a specific number of protons that never varies. For example, all hydrogen atoms have one proton, and all oxygen atoms have eight protons.

The electrons in the atoms of each element determine the properties of that element. As **FIGURE 1.1** shows, electrons are considered to be in a cloud around the nucleus. The simplified models of a hydrogen atom and an oxygen atom on the left side of **FIGURE 1.2** illustrate how electrons move around the nucleus in regions called energy levels. Different energy levels can hold different numbers of electrons. For example, the first energy level can hold two electrons, and the second energy level can hold eight electrons. Atoms are most stable when they have a full valence, or outermost energy level.

Of the 91 elements that naturally occur on Earth, only about 25 are found in organisms. Just 4 elements—carbon (C), oxygen (O), nitrogen (N), and hydrogen (H)—make up 96% of the human body's mass. The other 4% consists of calcium (Ca), phosphorus (P), potassium (K), sulfur (S), sodium (Na), and several other trace elements. Trace elements are found in very small amounts in your body, but you need them to survive. For example, iron (Fe) is needed to transport oxygen in your blood. Chromium (Cr) is needed for your cells to break down sugars for usable energy.

**FIGURE 1.1** The exact position of electrons cannot be known. They are somewhere in a three-dimensional electron cloud around the nucleus.

## FIGURE 1.2 Representing Atoms

### BOHR'S ATOMIC MODEL

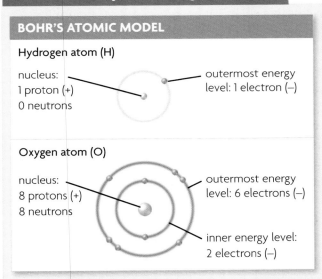

Hydrogen atom (H)

nucleus:
1 proton (+)
0 neutrons

outermost energy level: 1 electron (−)

Oxygen atom (O)

nucleus:
8 protons (+)
8 neutrons

outermost energy level: 6 electrons (−)

inner energy level: 2 electrons (−)

### SIMPLIFIED MODEL

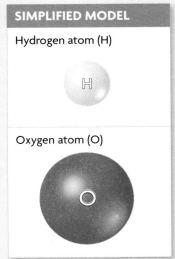

Hydrogen atom (H)

Oxygen atom (O)

The model of the atom developed by Niels Bohr (left) shows that an atom's electrons are located outside the nucleus in regions called energy levels. Different types of atoms have different numbers of electrons and energy levels.

Often, atoms are shown as simplified spheres (right). Different types of atoms are shown in different sizes and colors.

**Evaluate** What information does the Bohr atomic model provide that the simplified model does not provide? What is a limitation of both models?

## Compounds

The atoms of elements found in organisms are often linked, or bonded, to other atoms. A **compound** is a substance made of atoms of different elements bonded together in a certain ratio. Common compounds in living things include water ($H_2O$) and carbon dioxide ($CO_2$). A compound's properties are often different from the properties of the elements that make up the compound. At temperatures on Earth, for example, hydrogen and oxygen are both gases. Together, though, they can form water. Similarly, a diamond is pure carbon, but carbon atoms are also the basis of sugars, proteins, and millions of other compounds.

**Contrast** How are elements different from compounds?

# Ions form when atoms gain or lose electrons.

**Atoms and Bonding**

An **ion** is an atom that has gained or lost one or more electrons. An ion forms because an atom is more stable when its outermost energy level is full; the gain or loss of electrons results in a full outermost energy level. An atom becomes an ion when its number of electrons changes, and it gains an electrical charge. This charge gives ions certain properties. For example, compounds consisting only of ions—ionic compounds—easily dissolve in water.

Some ions are positively charged, and other ions are negatively charged. The type of ion that forms depends on the number of electrons in an atom's outer energy level. An atom with few electrons in its outer energy level tends to lose those electrons. An atom that loses one or more electrons becomes a positively charged ion because it has more protons than electrons. In contrast, an atom with a nearly full outer energy level tends to gain electrons. An atom that gains one or more electrons becomes a negatively charged ion because it has more electrons than protons.

Ions play large roles in organisms. For example, hydrogen ions ($H^+$) are needed for the production of usable chemical energy in cells. Calcium ions ($Ca^{2+}$) are necessary for every muscle movement in your body. And chloride ions ($Cl^-$) are important for a certain type of chemical signal in the brain.

Ions usually form when electrons are transferred from one atom to another. For example, **FIGURE 1.3** shows the transfer of an electron from a sodium atom (Na) to a chlorine atom (Cl). When it loses its one outer electron, the sodium atom becomes a positively charged sodium ion ($Na^+$). Its second energy level, which has eight electrons, is now a full outermost energy level. The transferred electron fills chlorine's outermost energy level, forming a negatively charged chloride ion ($Cl^-$). Positive ions, such as $Na^+$, are attracted to negative ions, such as $Cl^-$. An **ionic bond** forms through the electrical force between oppositely charged ions. Salt, or sodium chloride (NaCl), is an ionic compound of $Na^+$ and $Cl^-$. Sodium chloride is held together by ionic bonds.

**Apply** **What determines whether an atom becomes a positive ion or a negative ion?**

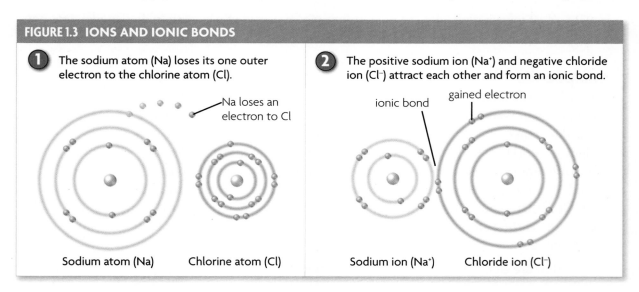

**FIGURE 1.3 IONS AND IONIC BONDS**

**1** The sodium atom (Na) loses its one outer electron to the chlorine atom (Cl).

Na loses an electron to Cl

Sodium atom (Na)    Chlorine atom (Cl)

**2** The positive sodium ion ($Na^+$) and negative chloride ion ($Cl^-$) attract each other and form an ionic bond.

ionic bond    gained electron

Sodium ion ($Na^+$)    Chloride ion ($Cl^-$)

## ▶ MAIN IDEA
# Atoms share pairs of electrons in covalent bonds.

Not all atoms easily gain or lose electrons. Rather, the atoms of many elements share pairs of electrons. The shared pairs of electrons fill the outermost energy levels of the bonded atoms. A **covalent bond** forms when atoms share a pair of electrons. Covalent bonds are generally very strong, and depending on how many electrons an atom has, two atoms may form several covalent bonds to share several pairs of electrons. **FIGURE 1.4** illustrates how atoms of carbon and oxygen share pairs of electrons in covalent bonds. All three atoms in a molecule of carbon dioxide ($CO_2$) have full outer energy levels.

### 🔲 READING TOOLBOX
**VOCABULARY**
The prefix *co-* means "together," and the term *valent* comes from a Latin word that means "power" or "strength."

### FIGURE 1.4  COVALENT BONDS

A carbon atom needs four electrons to fill its outer energy level. An oxygen atom needs two electrons to fill its outer energy level. In carbon dioxide, carbon makes a double bond, or shares two pairs of electrons, with each oxygen atom.

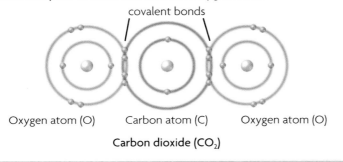

covalent bonds

Oxygen atom (O)     Carbon atom (C)     Oxygen atom (O)

Carbon dioxide ($CO_2$)

A **molecule** is two or more atoms held together by covalent bonds. In the compound carbon dioxide, each oxygen atom shares two pairs of electrons (four electrons) with the carbon atom. Some elements occur naturally in the form of diatomic, or "two-atom," molecules. For example, a molecule of oxygen ($O_2$) consists of two oxygen atoms that share two pairs of electrons. Almost all of the substances that make up organisms, from lipids to nucleic acids to water, are molecules held together by covalent bonds.

**Summarize** What happens to electrons in outer energy levels when two atoms form a covalent bond?

## 2.1   Formative Assessment

### 🔁 SELF-CHECK Online
HMHScience.com
**GO ONLINE**

### REVIEWING ▶ MAIN IDEAS

1. What distinguishes one **element** from another?

2. Describe the formation of an **ionic compound.**

3. What is the difference between an **ionic bond** and a **covalent bond**?

### CRITICAL THINKING

4. **Compare and Contrast** How does a **molecule** differ from an **atom**?

5. **Apply** Explain why a hydrogen atom can become either an **ion** or a part of a molecule.

6. **Evaluate** Explain the benefits and limitations of atomic models.

### ⸬ CONNECT TO

### CHEMISTRY

7. A sodium atom has one outer electron, and a carbon atom has four outer electrons. How might this difference be related to the types of compounds formed by atoms of these two elements?

# 2.2 Properties of Water

SC.912.L.18.12

SC.912.L.18.12 Discuss the special properties of water that contribute to Earth's suitability as an environment for life: cohesive behavior, ability to moderate temperature, expansion upon freezing, and versatility as a solvent.

## VOCABULARY

hydrogen bond
cohesion
adhesion
solution
solvent
solute
acid
base
pH

**KEY CONCEPT** Water's unique properties allow life to exist on Earth.

### MAIN IDEAS

- Life depends on hydrogen bonds in water.
- Many compounds dissolve in water.
- Some compounds form acids or bases.

### Connect to Your World

When you are thirsty, you need to drink something that is mostly water. Why is the water you drink absolutely necessary? Your cells, and the cells of every other living thing on Earth, are mostly water. Water gives cells structure and transports materials within organisms. All of the processes necessary for life take place in that watery environment. Water's unique properties, which are related to the structure of the water molecule, are important for living things.

## MAIN IDEA

# Life depends on hydrogen bonds in water.

How do fish survive a cold winter if their pond freezes? Unlike most substances, water expands when it freezes. Water is less dense as a solid (ice) than as a liquid. In a pond, ice floats and covers the water's surface. The ice acts as an insulator that allows the water underneath to remain a liquid. Ice's low density is related to the structure of the water molecule.

### Water and Hydrogen Bonds

Water is a polar molecule. You can think about polar molecules in the same way that you can think about a magnet's poles. That is, polar molecules have a region with a slight positive charge and a region with a slight negative charge. Polar molecules, such as the water molecule shown in **FIGURE 2.1,** form when atoms in a molecule have unequal pulls on the electrons they share. In a molecule of water, the oxygen nucleus, with its eight protons, attracts the shared electrons

**FIGURE 2.1** In water molecules, the oxygen atom has a slightly negative charge, and the hydrogen atoms have slightly positive charges.

more strongly than do the hydrogen nuclei, with only one proton each. The oxygen atom gains a small negative charge, and the hydrogen atoms gain small positive charges. Other molecules, called nonpolar molecules, do not have these charged regions. The atoms in nonpolar molecules share electrons more equally.

Opposite charges of polar molecules can interact to form hydrogen bonds. A **hydrogen bond** is an attraction between a slightly positive hydrogen atom and a slightly negative atom, often oxygen or nitrogen. Hydrogen bonding is shown among water molecules in **FIGURE 2.2**, but these bonds are also found in many other molecules. For example, hydrogen bonds are part of the structures of proteins and of DNA, which is the genetic material for all organisms.

Animated Biology
HMHScience.com
GO ONLINE
Hydrogen Bonding

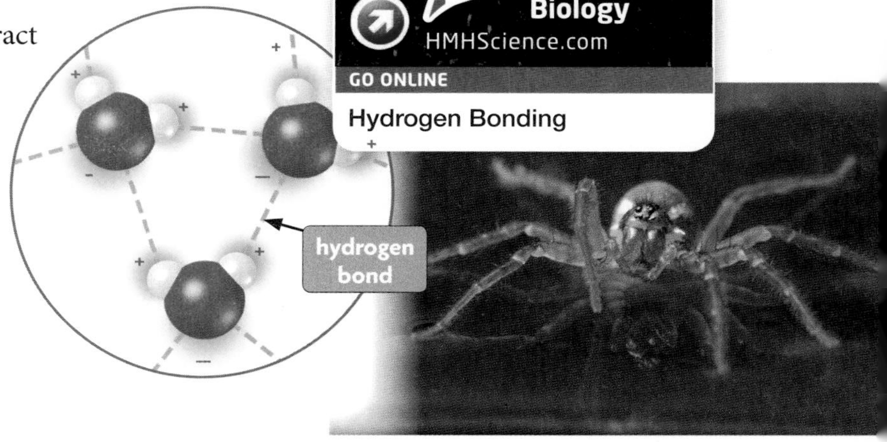


**FIGURE 2.2** Water's surface tension comes from hydrogen bonds (left) that cause water molecules to stick together.

## Properties Related to Hydrogen Bonds

Individual hydrogen bonds are about 20 times weaker than typical covalent bonds, but they are relatively strong among water molecules. As a result, a large amount of energy is needed to overcome the attractions among water molecules. Without hydrogen bonds, water would boil at a much lower temperature than it does because less energy would be needed to change liquid water into water vapor. Water is a liquid at the temperatures that support most life on Earth only because of hydrogen bonds in water. Hydrogen bonds are responsible for three important properties of water.

- **High specific heat** Hydrogen bonds give water an abnormally high specific heat. This means that water resists changes in temperature. Compared to many other compounds, water must absorb more heat energy to increase in temperature. This property is very important in cells. The processes that produce usable chemical energy in cells release a great deal of heat. Water absorbs the heat, which helps to regulate cell temperatures.
- **Cohesion** The attraction among molecules of a substance is **cohesion.** Cohesion from hydrogen bonds makes water molecules stick to each other. You can see this when water forms beads, such as on a recently washed car. Cohesion also produces surface tension, which makes a kind of skin on water. Surface tension keeps the spider in **FIGURE 2.2** from sinking.
- **Adhesion** The attraction among molecules of different substances is called **adhesion.** In other words, water molecules stick to other things. Adhesion is responsible for the upward curve on the surface of the water in **FIGURE 2.3** because water molecules are attracted to the glass of the test tube. Adhesion helps plants transport water from their roots to their leaves because water molecules stick to the sides of the vessels that carry water.

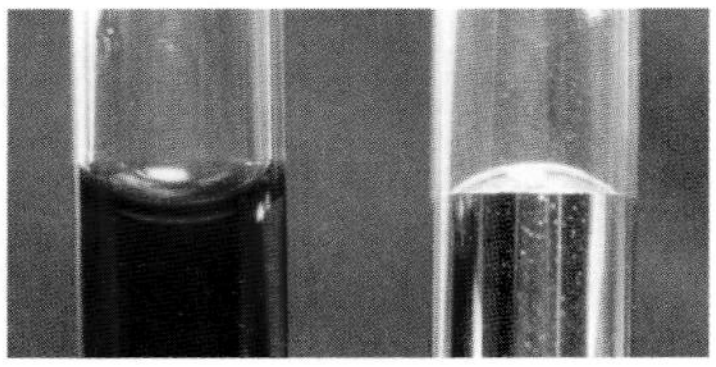

**FIGURE 2.3** The water's surface (left, dyed red) is curved down because water has greater adhesion than cohesion. The surface of the mercury (right) is curved up because mercury has greater cohesion than adhesion.

**Compare How are hydrogen bonds similar to ionic bonds?**

MAIN IDEA

## Many compounds dissolve in water.

Molecules and ions cannot take part in chemical processes inside cells unless they dissolve in water. Important materials such as sugars and oxygen cannot be transported from one part of an organism to another unless they are dissolved in blood, plant sap, or other water-based fluids.

Many substances dissolve in the water in your body. When one substance dissolves in another, a solution forms. A **solution** is a mixture of substances that is the same throughout—it is a homogeneous mixture. A solution has two parts. The **solvent** is the substance that is present in the greater amount and that dissolves another substance. A **solute** is a substance that dissolves in a solvent.

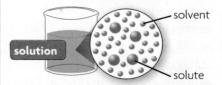
The amount of solute dissolved in a certain amount of solvent is a solution's concentration. One spoonful of a drink mix in water has little flavor because it has a low concentration. But a solution with four spoonfuls in the same amount of water tastes stronger because it has a higher concentration.

The liquid part of your blood, called plasma, is about 95% water. Therefore, the solvent in plasma is water, and all of the substances dissolved in it are solutes. Most of these solutes, such as sugars and proteins, dissolve in the water of blood plasma because they are polar. Polar molecules dissolve in water because the attraction between the water molecules and the solute molecules is greater than the attraction among the molecules of the solute. Similarly, ionic compounds, such as sodium chloride, dissolve in water because the charges of the water molecules attract the charges of the ions. The water molecules surround each ion and pull the compound apart.

Nonpolar substances, such as fats and oils, rarely dissolve in water. Nonpolar molecules do not have charged regions, so they are not attracted to polar molecules. Polar molecules and nonpolar molecules tend to remain separate, which is why we say, "Oil and water don't mix." But nonpolar molecules will dissolve in nonpolar solvents. For example, some vitamins, such as vitamin E, are nonpolar and dissolve in fat in your body.

**Connect** What are the solvent and solutes in a beverage you drink?

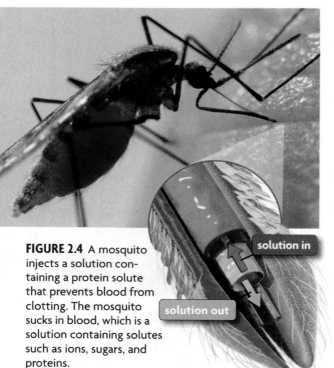

solution in

solution out

**FIGURE 2.4** A mosquito injects a solution containing a protein solute that prevents blood from clotting. The mosquito sucks in blood, which is a solution containing solutes such as ions, sugars, and proteins.

## ▶ MAIN IDEA
# Some compounds form acids or bases.

Some compounds break up into ions when they dissolve in water. An **acid** is a compound that releases a proton—a hydrogen ion ($H^+$)—when it dissolves in water. An acid increases the concentration of $H^+$ ions in a solution. **Bases** are compounds that remove $H^+$ ions from a solution. When a base dissolves in water, the solution has a low $H^+$ concentration. A solution's acidity, or $H^+$ ion concentration, is measured by the **pH** scale. In **FIGURE 2.5**, you can see that pH is usually between 0 and 14. A solution with a pH of 0 is very acidic, with a high $H^+$ concentration. A solution with a pH of 14 is very basic, with a low $H^+$ concentration. Solutions with a pH of 7 are neutral—neither acidic nor basic.

©Roger Eritja/Alamy

## FIGURE 2.5  Understanding pH

**The pH of a solution depends on the concentration of H⁺ ions.**

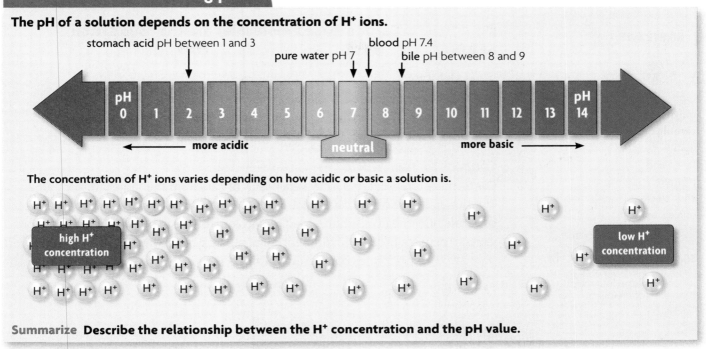

stomach acid pH between 1 and 3

blood pH 7.4

pure water pH 7

bile pH between 8 and 9

pH 0  1  2  3  4  5  6  7  8  9  10  11  12  13  pH 14

← more acidic        neutral        more basic →

The concentration of H⁺ ions varies depending on how acidic or basic a solution is.

high H⁺ concentration

low H⁺ concentration

**Summarize** Describe the relationship between the H⁺ concentration and the pH value.

Most organisms, including humans, need to keep their pH within a very narrow range around neutral (pH 7.0). However, some organisms need a very different pH range. The azalea plant thrives in acidic (pH 4.5) soil, and a microorganism called *Picrophilus* survives best at an extremely acidic pH of 0.7. For all of these different organisms, pH must be tightly controlled.

One way pH is regulated in organisms is by substances called buffers. A buffer is a compound that can bind to an H⁺ ion when the H⁺ concentration increases, and can release an H⁺ ion when the H⁺ concentration decreases. In other words, a buffer "locks up" H⁺ ions and helps to maintain homeostasis. For example, the normal pH of human blood is between 7.35 and 7.45, so it is slightly basic. Just a small change in pH can disrupt processes in your cells, and a blood pH greater than 7.8 or less than 6.8, for even a short time, is deadly. Buffers in your blood help prevent any large changes in blood pH.

**Apply** Cells have higher H⁺ concentrations than blood. Which has a higher pH? Why?

### CONNECT TO
**HUMAN BIOLOGY**

In the human body, both the respiratory system and the excretory system help regulate pH. You will learn about human systems and homeostasis in the chapter **Human Systems and Homeostasis.**

**SELF-CHECK Online**
HMHScience.com
GO ONLINE

## 2.2  Formative Assessment

### REVIEWING ▸ MAIN IDEAS

1. How do polar molecules form **hydrogen bonds**?

2. What determines whether a compound will dissolve in water?

3. Make a chart that compares **acids** and **bases.**

### CRITICAL THINKING

4. **Compare and Contrast** How do polar molecules differ from nonpolar molecules? How does this difference affect their interactions?

5. **Connect** Describe an example of **cohesion** or **adhesion** that you might observe during your daily life.

### CONNECT TO
**CELLULAR RESPIRATION**

6. When sugars are broken down to produce usable energy for cells, a large amount of heat is released. Explain how the water inside a cell helps to keep the cell's temperature constant.

## 2.3 Carbon-Based Molecules

SC.912.L.18.1

**KEY CONCEPT** Carbon-based molecules are the foundation of life.

### MAIN IDEAS
- Carbon atoms have unique bonding properties.
- Four main types of carbon-based molecules are found in living things.

**VOCABULARY**

monomer
polymer
carbohydrate
lipid
fatty acid
protein
amino acid
nucleic acid

**SC.912.L.18.1** Describe the basic molecular structures and primary functions of the four major categories of biological macromolecules.

### Connect to Your World
Car manufacturers often build several types of cars from the same internal frame. The size and style of the cars might differ on the outside, but they have the same structure underneath. Carbon-based molecules are similar, but they are much more varied. There are millions of different carbon-based molecules, but they form around only a few simple frames composed of carbon atoms.

### ▶ MAIN IDEA
## Carbon atoms have unique bonding properties.

Carbon is often called the building block of life because carbon atoms are the basis of most molecules that make up living things. These molecules form the structure of living things and carry out most of the processes that keep organisms alive. Carbon is so important because its atomic structure gives it bonding properties that are unique among elements. Each carbon atom has four unpaired electrons in its outer energy level. Therefore, carbon atoms can form covalent bonds with up to four other atoms, including other carbon atoms.

As **FIGURE 3.1** shows, carbon-based molecules have three fundamental structures—straight chains, branched chains, and rings. All three types of molecules are the result of carbon's ability to form four covalent bonds. Carbon chains can bond with carbon rings to form very large, complex molecules. These large molecules can be made of many small molecules that are bonded together. In a sense, the way these molecules form is similar to the way in which individual links of metal come together to make a bicycle chain.

---

**FIGURE 3.1 CARBON CHAINS AND RINGS**

| Straight chain | Branched chain | Ring |
|---|---|---|

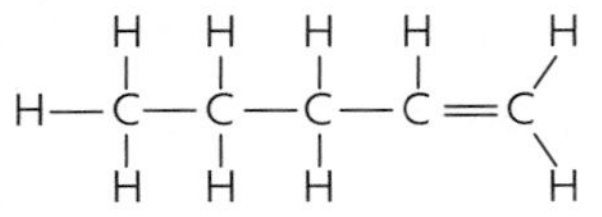

**Straight chain**

A simplified structure can also be shown as:

$CH_3-CH_2-CH_2-CH=CH_2$

Pentene

**Branched chain**

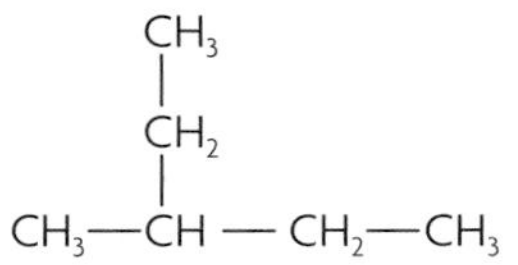

$CH_3-CH-CH_2-CH_3$

Hexane

**Ring**

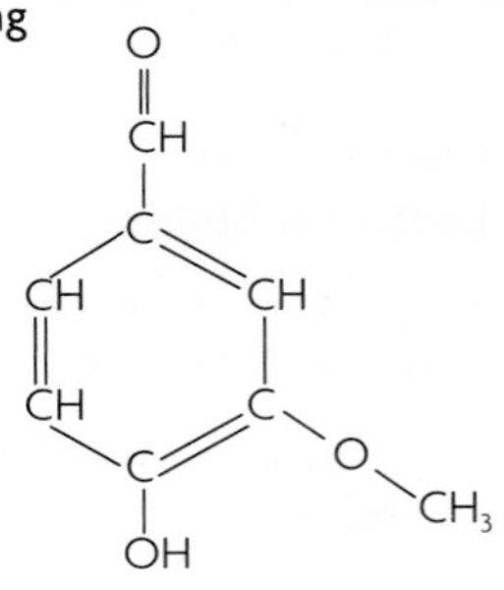

Vanillin

---

In many carbon-based molecules, small molecules are subunits of an entire molecule, like links in a chain. Each subunit in the complete molecule is called a **monomer.** When monomers are linked, they form molecules called polymers. A **polymer** is a large molecule, or macromolecule, made of many monomers bonded together. All of the monomers in a polymer may be the same, as they are in starches, or they may be different, as they are in proteins.

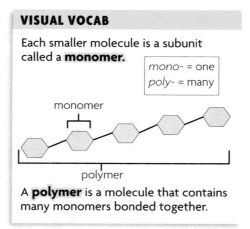

**VISUAL VOCAB**

Each smaller molecule is a subunit called a **monomer.**

mono- = one
poly- = many

monomer

polymer

A **polymer** is a molecule that contains many monomers bonded together.

**Synthesize** **Write your own analogy for the formation of a polymer from monomers.**

● MAIN IDEA

# Four main types of carbon-based molecules are found in living things.

All organisms are made of four types of carbon-based molecules: carbohydrates, lipids, proteins, and nucleic acids. These molecules have different structures and functions, but all are formed around carbon chains and rings.

## Carbohydrates

Fruits and grains are in different food groups, but they both contain large amounts of carbohydrates. **Carbohydrates** are molecules composed of carbon, hydrogen, and oxygen, and they include sugars and starches. Carbohydrates can be broken down to provide a source of usable chemical energy for cells. Carbohydrates are also a major part of plant cell structure.

The most basic carbohydrates are simple sugars, or monosaccharides (MAHN-uh-SAK-uh-RYDZ). Many simple sugars have either five or six carbon atoms. Fruits contain a six-carbon sugar called fructose. Glucose, one of the sugars made by plant cells during photosynthesis, is another six-carbon sugar. Simple sugars can be bonded to make larger carbohydrates. For example, two sugars bonded together make the disaccharide table sugar, shown in **FIGURE 3.2.** Many glucose molecules can be linked to make polysaccharides (PAHL-ee-SAK-uh-RYDZ), which are polymers of monosaccharides.

Starches, glycogen, and cellulose are polysaccharides. Most starches are branched chains of glucose molecules. Starches are made and stored by plants, and they can be broken down as a source of energy by plant and animal cells. Glycogen, which is made and stored in animals, is more highly branched than plant starches.

**READING TOOLBOX**

**TAKING NOTES**

Use a content frame to help you understand monomers and polymers in carbon-based molecules.

| Monomer | Polymer | Example | Function |
|---|---|---|---|
|  |  |  |  |
|  |  |  |  |

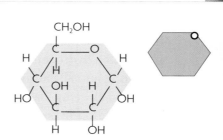

$CH_2OH$

Glucose ($C_6H_{12}O_6$) can be ring shaped and is often shown as a simplified hexagon. During photosynthesis, six molecules of $CO_2$ combine with six molecules of $H_2O$ to form one molecule of glucose and six molecules of $O_2$.

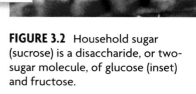

**FIGURE 3.2** Household sugar (sucrose) is a disaccharide, or two-sugar molecule, of glucose (inset) and fructose.

GO ONLINE

**Macromolecules of Life**

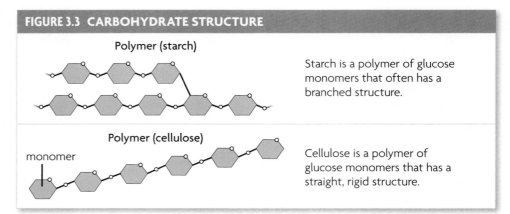

**FIGURE 3.3 CARBOHYDRATE STRUCTURE**

Polymer (starch)

Starch is a polymer of glucose monomers that often has a branched structure.

Polymer (cellulose)

monomer

Cellulose is a polymer of glucose monomers that has a straight, rigid structure.

**CONNECT TO**

**CELL STRUCTURE**

A cell wall made of cellulose surrounds the membrane of plant cells. You will learn more about cell walls in the chapter **Cell Structure and Function.**

Cellulose is somewhat different from starch and glycogen. Its straight, rigid structure, shown in **FIGURE 3.3**, makes the cellulose molecule a major building block in plant cell structure. Cellulose makes up the cell wall that is the tough, outer covering of plant cells. You have eaten cellulose in the stringy fibers of vegetables such as celery, so you know that it is tough to chew and break up.

## Lipids

**Lipids** are nonpolar molecules that include fats, oils, and cholesterol. Like carbohydrates, most lipids contain chains of carbon atoms bonded to oxygen and hydrogen atoms. Some lipids are broken down as a source of usable energy for cells. Other lipids are parts of a cell's structure.

Fats and oils are two familiar types of lipids. They store large amounts of chemical energy in organisms. Animal fats are found in foods such as meat and butter. You know plant fats as oils, such as olive oil and peanut oil. The structures of fats and oils are similar. They both consist of a molecule called glycerol (GLIHS-uh-RAWL) bonded to molecules called fatty acids. **Fatty acids** are chains of carbon atoms bonded to hydrogen atoms. Two different types of fatty acids are shown in **FIGURE 3.4**.

Many lipids, both fats and oils, contain three fatty acids bonded to glycerol. They are called triglycerides. Most animal fats are saturated fats, which means they have the maximum number of hydrogen atoms possible. That is, every place that a hydrogen atom can bond to a carbon atom is filled with a hydrogen atom, and all carbon–carbon bonds are single bonds. You can think of the fatty acid as being "saturated" with hydrogen atoms. In contrast, fatty acids in oils have fewer hydrogen atoms because there is at least one double bond between carbon atoms. These lipids are called unsaturated fats because the fatty acids are not saturated with hydrogen atoms. Fats and oils are very similar, but why are animal fats solid and plant oils liquid? The double bonds in unsaturated fats make kinks in the fatty acids. As a result, the molecules cannot pack together tightly enough to form a solid.

**FIGURE 3.4** Fatty acids can be either saturated or unsaturated.

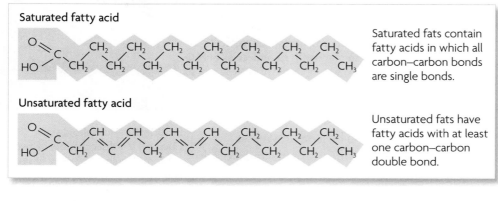

Saturated fatty acid

Saturated fats contain fatty acids in which all carbon–carbon bonds are single bonds.

Unsaturated fatty acid

Unsaturated fats have fatty acids with at least one carbon–carbon double bond.

First, energy is added to break bonds in molecules of oxygen and glucose. **Bond energy** is the amount of energy that will break a bond between two atoms. Bonds between different types of atoms have different bond energies. Energy is released when bonds form, such as when molecules of water and carbon dioxide are made. When a bond forms, the amount of energy released is equal to the amount of energy that breaks the same bond. For example, energy is released when hydrogen and oxygen atoms bond to form a water molecule. The same amount of energy is needed to break apart a water molecule.

## Chemical Equilibrium

Some reactions go from reactants to products until the reactants are used up. However, many reactions in living things are reversible. They move in both directions at the same time. These reactions tend to go in one direction or the other depending on the concentrations of the reactants and products. One such reaction lets blood, shown in **FIGURE 4.2,** carry carbon dioxide. Carbon dioxide reacts with water in blood to form a compound called carbonic acid ($H_2CO_3$). Your body needs this reaction to get rid of carbon dioxide waste from your cells.

$$CO_2 + H_2O \rightleftharpoons H_2CO_3$$

The arrows in the equation above show that the reaction goes in both directions. When the carbon dioxide concentration is high, as it is around your cells, the reaction moves toward the right and carbonic acid forms. In your lungs, the carbon dioxide concentration is low. The reaction goes in the other direction, and carbonic acid breaks down.

When a reaction takes place at an equal rate in both directions, the reactant and product concentrations stay the same. This state is called equilibrium. **Equilibrium** (EE-kwuh-LIHB-ree-uhm) is reached when both the reactants and products are made at the same rate.

**Apply** **Explain why concentration is important in a chemical reaction.**

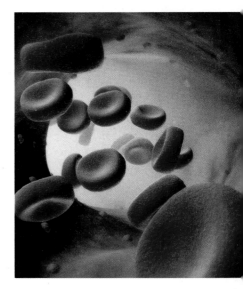

**FIGURE 4.2** Blood cells and plasma transport materials throughout the body. Carbonic acid dissolves in the blood so that carbon dioxide can be transported to the lungs.

(tr) © HMH; (br) ©MedicalRF.com/Alamy Images

## FIGURE 4.3 Energy and Chemical Reactions

Energy is required to break bonds in reactants, and energy is released when bonds form in products. Overall, a chemical reaction either absorbs or releases energy.

**Animated Biology**
HMHScience.com
GO ONLINE
Energy and Chemical Reactions

### ACTIVATION ENERGY

When enough activation energy is added to the reactants, bonds in the reactants break and the reaction begins.

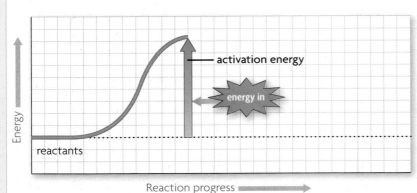

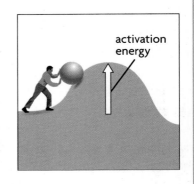

### EXOTHERMIC REACTION  Energy Released

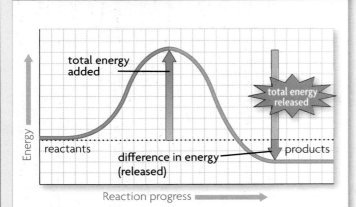

The products in an exothermic reaction have a higher bond energy than the reactants, and the difference in energy is released to the surroundings.

### ENDOTHERMIC REACTION  Energy Absorbed

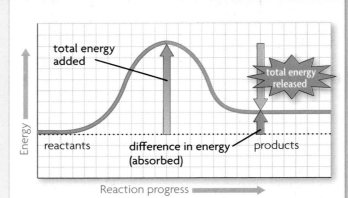

The products in an endothermic reaction have a lower bond energy than the reactants, and the difference in energy is absorbed from the surroundings.

**CRITICAL VIEWING**  Is the amount of activation energy related to whether a reaction is exothermic or endothermic? Why or why not?

## ► MAIN IDEA
# Chemical reactions release or absorb energy.

All chemical reactions involve changes in energy. Energy that is added to the reactants breaks their chemical bonds. When new bonds form in the products, energy is released. This means that energy is both absorbed and released during a chemical reaction. Some chemical reactions release more energy than they absorb. Other chemical reactions absorb more energy than they release. Whether a reaction releases or absorbs energy depends on bond energy.

Some energy must be absorbed by the reactants in any chemical reaction. **Activation energy** is the amount of energy that needs to be absorbed for a chemical reaction to start. Activation energy is like the energy you would need to push a rock up a hill. Once the rock is at the top of the hill, it rolls down the other side by itself. A graph of the activation energy that is added to start a chemical reaction is shown at the top of **FIGURE 4.3**.

An **exothermic** chemical reaction releases more energy than it absorbs. If the products have a higher bond energy than the reactants, the reaction is exothermic. The excess energy—the difference in energy between the reactants and products—is often given off as heat or light. Some animals, such as squids and fireflies, give off light that comes from exothermic reactions, as shown in **FIGURE 4.4**. Cellular respiration, the process that uses glucose and oxygen to provide usable energy for cells, is also exothermic. Cellular respiration releases not only usable energy for your cells but also heat that keeps your body warm.

An **endothermic** chemical reaction absorbs more energy than it releases. If products have a lower bond energy than reactants, the reaction is endothermic. Energy must be absorbed to make up the difference. One of the most important processes for life on Earth, photosynthesis, is endothermic. During photosynthesis, plants absorb energy from sunlight and use that energy to make simple sugars and complex carbohydrates.

**Analyze** How is activation energy related to bond energy?

**READING** TOOLBOX

**VOCABULARY**
The prefix *exo-* means "out," and the prefix *endo-* means "in." Energy moves out of an exothermic reaction, and energy moves into an endothermic reaction.

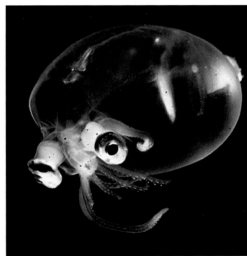

**FIGURE 4.4** The glow of the bugeye squid comes from an exothermic reaction that releases light.

**SELF-CHECK** Online
HMHScience.com
**GO ONLINE**

## 2.4 Formative Assessment

### REVIEWING ► MAIN IDEAS

1. Hydrogen peroxide ($H_2O_2$) breaks down into water ($H_2O$) and oxygen ($O_2$). Explain why this is a **chemical reaction**. What are the **reactants** and the **products** in the reaction?

2. How do **endothermic** and **exothermic** reactions differ?

### CRITICAL THINKING

3. **Infer** The process below is exothermic. What must be true about the **bond energies** of the reactants and the products? Explain.

$$6O_2 + C_6H_{12}O_6 \longrightarrow 6CO_2 + 6H_2O$$

4. **Evaluate** Why might it not always be possible to determine the reactants and the products in a reaction? Explain your answer in terms of chemical **equilibrium.**

### CONNECT TO

**BIOCHEMISTRY**

5. A chemical reaction can start when enough **activation energy** is added to the reactants. Do you think the activation energy for chemical reactions in living things is high or low? Explain your answer.

©Peter Batson/ExploreTheAbyss.com

## 2.5 Enzymes

SC.912.L.18.11

**KEY CONCEPT** **Enzymes are catalysts for chemical reactions in living things.**

SC.912.L.18.11 Explain the role of enzymes as catalysts that lower the activation energy of biochemical reactions. Identify factors, such as pH and temperature, and their effect on enzyme activity.

**VOCABULARY**

catalyst
enzyme
substrate

**MAIN IDEAS**

◐ A catalyst lowers activation energy.
◐ Enzymes allow chemical reactions to occur under tightly controlled conditions.

### ⋆ Connect to Your World

How can a Venus flytrap digest a frog? It happens through the action of proteins called enzymes. Enzymes help to start and run chemical reactions in living things. For example, enzymes are needed to break down food into smaller molecules that cells can use. Without enzymes, a Venus flytrap couldn't break down its food, and neither could you.

### ▶ MAIN IDEA

## A catalyst lowers activation energy.

Remember what you learned about activation energy in Section 4. Activation energy for a chemical reaction is like the energy that is needed to push a rock up a hill. When enough energy is added to get the rock to the top of a hill, the rock can roll down the other side by itself. Activation energy gives a similar push to a chemical reaction. Once a chemical reaction starts, it can continue by itself, and it will go at a certain rate.

Often, the activation energy for a chemical reaction comes from an increase in temperature. But even after a chemical reaction starts, it may happen very slowly. The reactants may not interact enough, or they may not be at a high enough concentration, to quickly form the products of the reaction. However, both the activation energy and rate of a chemical reaction can be changed by a chemical catalyst, as shown in **FIGURE 5.1**. A **catalyst** (KAT-l-ihst) is a substance that decreases the activation energy needed to start a chemical reaction and, as a result, also increases the rate of the chemical reaction.

### FIGURE 5.1 CATALYSTS AND ACTIVATION ENERGY

Under normal conditions, a certain amount of activation energy is needed to start a chemical reaction. A catalyst decreases the activation energy needed.

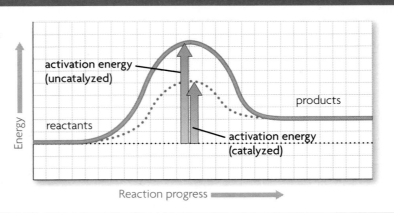

# 2 Review

INTERACTIVE Review
HMHScience.com
GO ONLINE
Review Games • Concept Map • Section Self-Checks

## CHAPTER VOCABULARY

**2.1**
atom
element
compound
ion
ionic bond
covalent bond
molecule

**2.2**
hydrogen bond
cohesion
adhesion
solution
solvent

solute
acid
base
pH

**2.3**
monomer
polymer
carbohydrate
lipid
fatty acid
protein
amino acid
nucleic acid

**2.4**
chemical reaction
reactant
product
bond energy
equilibrium
activation energy
exothermic
endothermic

**2.5**
catalyst
enzyme
substrate

## Reviewing Vocabulary

### Vocabulary Connections

The vocabulary terms in this chapter are related to each other in various ways. For each group of words below, write a sentence or two to clearly explain how the terms are connected. For example, for the terms *covalent bond* and *molecule,* you could write "A molecule is made of atoms connected by covalent bonds."

1. atom, ion
2. hydrogen bond, cohesion
3. solution, solvent
4. acid, base, pH
5. exothermic, endothermic
6. catalyst, enzyme

### READING TOOLBOX  WORD ORIGINS

7. The word *atom* comes from the Greek word *atomos,* which means "indivisible." Describe the relationship between the Greek term and your understanding of atoms.

8. The letter *p* in the term *pH* stands for the German word *Potenz,* which means "power" or "potential." The letter *H* represents hydrogen ions ($H^+$). How are these related to the definition of pH?

9. The prefix *mono-* means "one" and the prefix *poly-* means "many." Some lipids are monounsaturated, and others are polyunsaturated. Explain the difference between the fatty acids in these different types of lipids.

## Reviewing MAIN IDEAS

10. Explain how the combination of electrons, protons, and neutrons results in the neutral charge of an atom.

11. Potassium ions ($K^+$) have a positive charge. What happens to a potassium atom's electrons when it becomes an ion?

12. Some types of atoms form more than one covalent bond with another atom. What determines how many covalent bonds two atoms can make? Explain.

13. How is hydrogen bonding related to the structure of the water molecule?

14. Explain the difference between solvents and solutes.

15. Describe the relationship between hydrogen ions ($H^+$) and pH. How is pH related to a solution's acidity?

16. Carbon forms a very large number of compounds. What characteristic of carbon atoms allows the formation of all of these compounds? Explain.

17. Describe examples of monomers and polymers in carbohydrates, proteins, and nucleic acids.

18. Explain the relationship between a protein's structure and its ability to function.

19. What are the components of a chemical reaction?

20. Explain the difference between exothermic and endothermic reactions.

21. Describe the effect of a catalyst on activation energy and reaction rate.

22. What is the role of enzymes in organisms?

# Critical Thinking

23. **Compare and Contrast** How are phospholipids similar to lipids such as triglycerides? How are they different?

24. **Compare and Contrast** Briefly describe the similarities and differences between hydrogen bonds and ionic bonds. Which type of bond do you think is stronger? Why?

25. **Infer** Suppose that you have a cold. What characteristics must cold medicine have that allow it to be transported throughout your body? Explain.

26. **Predict** Homeostasis involves the maintenance of constant conditions in an organism. What might happen to a protein if homeostasis is disrupted? Why?

27. **Compare and Contrast** Describe the structures and functions of starch and cellulose. How are the molecules similar? How are they different?

28. **Apply** Suppose you had a friend who wanted to entirely avoid eating fats. What functions of lipids could you describe to convince that person of the importance of fats to his or her health?

29. **Infer** The human body can reuse some of the enzymes found in raw fruits and vegetables. Why is this not the case for cooked fruits and vegetables?

## Interpreting Visuals

The diagram below shows the lock-and-key model of enzyme function. Use it to answer the next three questions.

30. **Summarize** Briefly explain what is happening at each step of the process. Be sure to identify each of the substances (A–D) shown in each step of the process.

31. **Apply** How does Substance A affect the amount of activation energy needed by the process? Explain.

32. **Synthesize** Describe the importance of buffers in solutions in allowing the process shown above to take place.

## Analyzing Data  Identify Variables

Use the graph below to answer the next three questions.

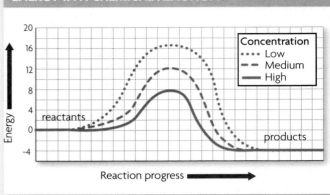

33. **Apply** Suppose the graph was constructed from data collected during an experiment. What were the independent and dependent variables in the experiment? Explain.

34. **Analyze** How much activation energy is needed to start the chemical reaction represented by each line on the graph? How much energy is released from each reaction?

35. **Apply** Explain whether each of the chemical reactions shown on the graph is endothermic or exothermic.

## Making Connections

36. **Write About Chemical Equilibrium** Carbon dioxide reacts with water in blood plasma to form carbonic acid. The equation for this reaction is shown on the second page of Section 4. Imagine that you are a molecule of carbon dioxide. Describe the chemical reactions that take place when you enter the blood and when you leave the blood. Explain what determines how these reactions occur. Be sure to include all terms from the chapter that are related to the chemical reaction.

37. **Apply** The Venus flytrap shown in the photograph on the chapter opener uses enzymes to digest its prey. Describe how pH, solutions, and chemical reactions all play important roles inside the trap of this carnivorous plant.

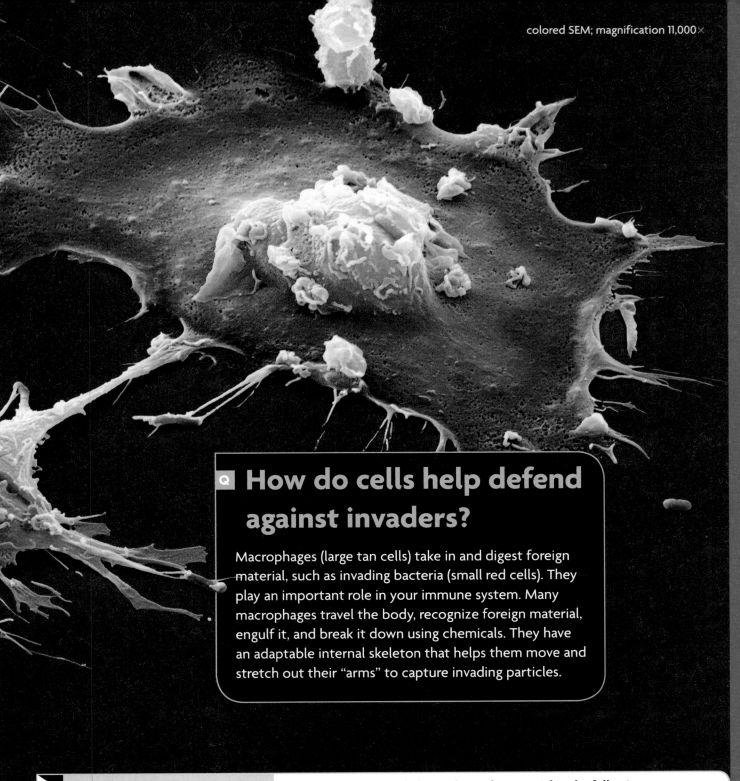

## Q How do cells help defend against invaders?

Macrophages (large tan cells) take in and digest foreign material, such as invading bacteria (small red cells). They play an important role in your immune system. Many macrophages travel the body, recognize foreign material, engulf it, and break it down using chemicals. They have an adaptable internal skeleton that helps them move and stretch out their "arms" to capture invading particles.

 **READING** TOOLBOX    **This reading tool can help you learn the material in the following pages.**

### USING LANGUAGE

**Similes** Similes help relate new ideas to ideas that you already know. Often, similes use the terms *like* or *as*. For example, if you were describing a motorcycle to someone who had never seen one, you might say that it is like a bicycle that has a motor.

### YOUR TURN

Use the information in the chapter to perform the following tasks.

1. Find a simile to describe the endoplasmic reticulum.
2. Write a simile to describe the function of a mitochondrion.

# 3.1 Cell Theory

| **KEY CONCEPT** **Cells are the basic unit of life.**

**MAIN IDEAS**

- Early studies led to the development of the cell theory.
- Prokaryotic cells lack a nucleus and most internal structures of eukaryotic cells.

## VOCABULARY

cell theory
cytoplasm
organelle
prokaryotic cell
eukaryotic cell

**SC.912.L.14.1** Describe the scientific theory of cells (cell theory) and relate the history of its discovery to the process of science.

### Connect to Your World

You and all other organisms are made of cells. As you saw on the previous page, a cell's structure is closely related to its function. Today, we know that cells are the smallest unit of living matter that can carry out all processes required for life. But before the 1600s, people had many other ideas about the basis of life. Like many breakthroughs, the discovery of cells was aided by the development of new technology—in this case, the microscope.

 **READING** TOOLBOX

**TAKING NOTES**

As you read, make an outline using the headings as topics. Summarize details that further explain those ideas.

I. Main Idea
  A. Supporting idea
    1. Detail
    2. Detail
  B. Supporting idea

## ▶ MAIN IDEA

# Early studies led to the development of the cell theory.

Almost all cells are too small to see without the aid of a microscope. Although glass lenses had been used to magnify images for hundreds of years, the early lenses were not powerful enough to reveal individual cells. The invention of the compound microscope in the late 1500s was an early step toward this discovery. The Dutch eyeglass maker Zacharias Janssen, who was probably assisted by his father, Hans, usually gets credit for this invention.

A compound microscope contains two or more lenses. Total magnification, the product of the magnifying power of each individual lens, is generally much more powerful with a compound microscope than with a single lens.

### Discovery of Cells

In 1665, the English scientist Robert Hooke used the three-lens compound microscope shown in **FIGURE 1.1** to examine thin slices of cork. Cork is the tough outer bark of a species of oak tree. He observed that cork is made of tiny, hollow compartments. The compartments reminded Hooke of small rooms found in a monastery, so he gave them the same name: cells. The plant cells he observed, shown in **FIGURE 1.2** (top), were dead. Hooke was looking only at cell walls and empty space.

Around the same time, Anton van Leeuwenhoek, a Dutch tradesman, was studying new methods for making lenses to examine cloth. As a result of his research, his single-lens microscopes were much more powerful than Hooke's crude compound microscope. In 1674, Leeuwenhoek became one of the first people to describe living cells when he observed numerous single-celled organisms swimming in a drop of pond water. Sketches of his "animalcules" are pictured in **FIGURE 1.2** (bottom).

**FIGURE 1.1** Hooke first identified cells using this microscope. Its crude lenses severely limited the amount of detail he could see.

©Science Museum London/HIP/The Image Works

As people continued to improve the microscope over the next century and a half, it became sturdier, easier to use, and capable of greater magnification. This combination of factors led people to examine even more organisms. They observed a wide variety of cell shapes, and they observed cells dividing. Scientists began to ask important questions: Is all living matter made of cells? Where do cells come from?

## Cell Theory

The German scientist Matthias Schleiden also used compound microscopes to study plant tissue. In 1838, he proposed that plants are made of cells. Schleiden discussed the results of his work with another German scientist, Theodor Schwann, who was struck by the structural similarities between plant cells and the animal cells he had been studying. Schwann concluded that all animals are made of cells. Shortly thereafter, in 1839, he published the first statement of the cell theory, concluding that all living things are made of cells and cell products. This theory helped lay the groundwork for all biological research that followed. However, it had to be refined over the years as additional data led to new conclusions. For example, Schwann stated in his publication that cells form spontaneously by free-cell formation. As later scientists studied the process of cell division, they realized that this part of Schwann's idea was wrong. In 1855, Rudolf Virchow, another German scientist, reported that all cells come from preexisting cells. These early contributors are shown in **FIGURE 1.3**.

This accumulated research can be summarized in the cell theory, one of the first unifying concepts developed in biology. The major principles of the **cell theory** are the following:

- All organisms are made of cells.
- All existing cells are produced by other living cells.
- The cell is the most basic unit of life.

**Summarize  Explain the three major principles of cell theory in your own words.**

**FIGURE 1.2**  Hooke observed the cell walls of dead plant cells (top). In contrast, Leeuwenhoek observed and drew microscopic life, which he called "animalcules," in pond water (bottom).

## FIGURE 1.3 Contributors to Cell Theory

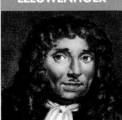
**HOOKE**
**1665** Hooke was the first to identify cells, and he named them.

**LEEUWENHOEK**
**1674** Because he made better lenses, Leeuwenhoek observed cells in greater detail.

**SCHLEIDEN**
**1838** Schleiden was the first to note that plants are made of cells.

**SCHWANN**
**1839** Schwann concluded that all living things are made of cells.

**VIRCHOW**
**1855** Virchow proposed that all cells come from other cells.

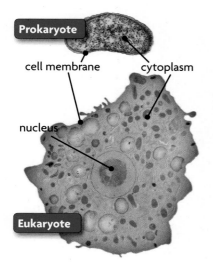

Prokaryote

cell membrane    cytoplasm

nucleus

Eukaryote

**FIGURE 1.4** In prokaryotic cells, such as this bacterium (top), DNA is suspended in the cytoplasm. In eukaryotic cells, such as this protozoan (bottom), the nuclear envelope separates DNA from the cytoplasm. (colored TEMs; magnifications: protozoan 3200×; bacterium 19,000×)

✦ **CONNECT TO**

**PROKARYOTES**

You will learn more about prokaryotes in the chapter **Viruses and Prokaryotes,** which discusses their requirements to sustain life, their role in the ecosystem, and their role in human disease.

▶ **MAIN IDEA**

# Prokaryotic cells lack a nucleus and most internal structures of eukaryotic cells.

The variety of cell types found in living things is staggering. Your body alone is made of trillions of cells of many different shapes, sizes, and functions. They include long, thin, nerve cells that transmit sensory information, as well as short, blocky, skin cells that cover and protect the body. Despite this variety, the cells in your body share many characteristics with one another and with the cells that make up every other organism. In general, cells tend to be microscopic in size and have similar building blocks. They are also enclosed by a membrane that controls the movement of materials into and out of the cell.

Within the membrane, a cell is filled with cytoplasm. **Cytoplasm** is a jellylike substance that contains dissolved molecular building blocks—such as proteins, nucleic acids, minerals, and ions. Cytoplasm also contains ribosomes—molecules where proteins are assembled. In some types of cells, the cytoplasm also contains **organelles,** which are structures specialized to perform distinct processes within a cell. Most organelles are surrounded by a membrane. In many cells, the largest and most visible organelle is the nucleus.

As shown in **FIGURE 1.4,** cells can be separated into two broad categories based on their internal structures: prokaryotic cells and eukaryotic cells.

- **Prokaryotic cells** (pro-KAR-ee-AHT-ihk) do not have a nucleus or other membrane-bound organelles. Instead, the cell's DNA is suspended in the cytoplasm. Most prokaryotes are microscopic, single-celled organisms.

- **Eukaryotic cells** (yoo-KAR-ee-AHT-ihk) have a nucleus and other membrane-bound organelles. The nucleus, the largest organelle, encloses the genetic information. Eukaryotes may be multicellular or single-celled organisms.

**VISUAL VOCAB**

**Prokaryotic cells** do not have a nucleus or other membrane-bound organelles.

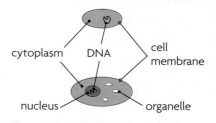

cytoplasm    DNA    cell membrane

nucleus    organelle

**Eukaryotic cells** have a nucleus and other membrane-bound organelles.

**Compare** What characteristics are shared by most cells?

---

## 3.1 Formative Assessment

**SELF-CHECK** Online
HMHScience.com
**GO ONLINE**

### REVIEWING ▶ MAIN IDEAS

1. How did improvements in the microscope help scientists form the **cell theory**?

2. How do **prokaryotic** and **eukaryotic cells** differ?

### CRITICAL THINKING

3. **Analyze** Today, scientists can study human cells grown in petri dishes. Explain how this technique builds on the work of early scientists.

4. **Compare** In what way are cells similar to atoms?

✦ **CONNECT TO**

**MEDICINE**

5. Suppose a certain poison kills human cells by blocking pores in the nuclear membrane. Explain why it would or would not kill bacteria.

# 3.2 Cell Organelles

SC.912.L.14.2,
SC.912.L.14.3

SC.912.L.14.2 Relate structure to function for the components of plant and animal cells. Explain the role of cell membranes as a highly selective barrier (passive and active transport).

SC.912.L.14.3 Compare and contrast the general structures of plant and animal cells. Compare and contrast the general structures of prokaryotic and eukaryotic cells.

## VOCABULARY

cytoskeleton
nucleus
endoplasmic reticulum
ribosome
Golgi apparatus
vesicle
mitochondrion
vacuole
lysosome
centriole
cell wall
chloroplast

| KEY CONCEPT   Eukaryotic cells share many similarities.

### MAIN IDEAS

- Cells have an internal structure.
- Several organelles are involved in making and processing proteins.
- Other organelles have various functions.
- Plant cells have cell walls and chloroplasts.

### Connect to Your World

Your body is highly organized. It contains organs that are specialized to perform particular tasks. For example, your skin receives sensory information and helps prevent infection. Your intestines digest food, your kidneys filter wastes, and your bones protect and support other organs. On a much smaller scale, your cells have a similar division of labor. They contain specialized structures that work together to respond to stimuli and efficiently carry out other necessary processes.

### MAIN IDEA

## Cells have an internal structure.

Like your body, eukaryotic cells are highly organized structures. They are surrounded by a protective membrane that receives messages from other cells. They contain membrane-bound organelles that perform specific cellular processes, divide certain molecules into compartments, and help regulate the timing of key events. But the cell is not a random jumble of suspended organelles and molecules. Rather, certain organelles and molecules are anchored to specific sites, which vary by cell type. If the membrane were removed from a cell, the contents wouldn't collapse and ooze out in a big puddle. How does a cell maintain this framework?

Each eukaryotic cell has a **cytoskeleton,** which is a flexible network of proteins that provide structural support for the cell. It is made of small protein subunits that form long threads, or fibers, that crisscross the entire cell, as shown in **FIGURE 2.1.** Three main types of fibers make up the cytoskeleton and allow it to serve a wide range of functions.

- Microtubules are long, hollow tubes. They give the cell its shape and act as "tracks" for the movement of organelles. When cells divide, microtubules form fibers that pull half of the DNA into each new cell.
- Intermediate filaments, which are somewhat smaller than microtubules, give a cell its strength.
- Microfilaments, the smallest of the three, are tiny threads that enable cells to move and divide. They play an important role in muscle cells, where they help the muscle contract and relax.

**FIGURE 2.1** The cytoskeleton supports and shapes the cell. The cytoskeleton includes microtubules (green) and microfilaments (red).
(epifluorescence microscopy; magnification 750×)

components of
the cytoskeleton

©Albert Tousson/Phototake

FIGURE 2.2 Cell Structure

**GO ONLINE**

Cell Structures

Eukaryotic cells have highly organized structures, including membrane-bound organelles. Plant and animal cells share many of the same types of organelles, but both also have organelles that are unique to their needs.

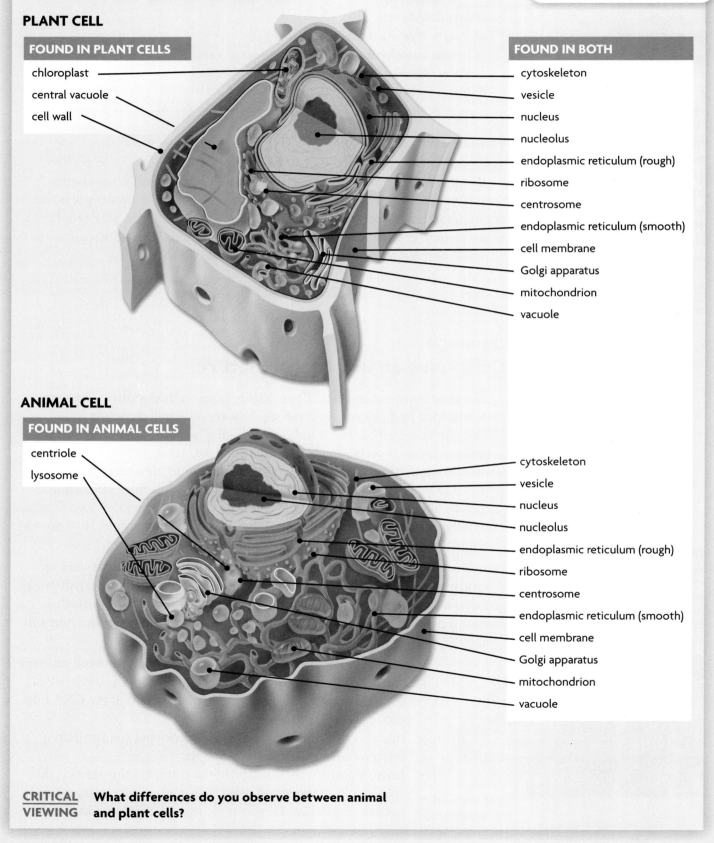

## PLANT CELL

**FOUND IN PLANT CELLS**

- chloroplast
- central vacuole
- cell wall

**FOUND IN BOTH**

- cytoskeleton
- vesicle
- nucleus
- nucleolus
- endoplasmic reticulum (rough)
- ribosome
- centrosome
- endoplasmic reticulum (smooth)
- cell membrane
- Golgi apparatus
- mitochondrion
- vacuole

## ANIMAL CELL

**FOUND IN ANIMAL CELLS**

- centriole
- lysosome

- cytoskeleton
- vesicle
- nucleus
- nucleolus
- endoplasmic reticulum (rough)
- ribosome
- centrosome
- endoplasmic reticulum (smooth)
- cell membrane
- Golgi apparatus
- mitochondrion
- vacuole

**CRITICAL VIEWING** What differences do you observe between animal and plant cells?

Cytoplasm, which you read about in Section 1, is itself an important contributor to cell structure. In eukaryotes, it fills the space between the nucleus and the cell membrane. The fluid portion, excluding the organelles, is called cytosol and consists mostly of water. The makeup of cytoplasm shows that water is necessary for maintaining cell structure. This is only one of many reasons that water is an essential component for life, however. Many chemical reactions occur in the cytoplasm, where water acts as an important solvent.

The remainder of this chapter highlights the structure and function of the organelles found in eukaryotic cells. As **FIGURE 2.2** shows, plant and animal cells use many of the same types of organelles to carry out basic functions. Both cell types also have organelles that are unique to their needs.

**Infer** **What problems might a cell experience if it had no cytoskeleton?**

## ⊙ MAIN IDEA

# Several organelles are involved in making and processing proteins.

Much of the cell is devoted to making proteins. Proteins are made of 20 types of amino acids that have unique characteristics of size, polarity, and acidity. They can form very long or very short protein chains that fold into different shapes. And multiple protein chains can interact with each other. This almost limitless variety of shapes and interactions makes proteins very powerful. Proteins carry out many critical functions, so they need to be made correctly.

## Nucleus

The **nucleus** (NOO-klee-uhs) is the storehouse for most of the genetic information, or DNA (deoxyribonucleic acid), in your cells. DNA contains genes that are instructions for making proteins. There are two major demands on the nucleus: (1) DNA must be carefully protected, and (2) DNA must be available for use at the proper times. Molecules that would damage DNA need to be kept out of the nucleus. But many proteins are involved in turning genes on and off, and they need to access the DNA at certain times. The special structure of the nucleus helps it meet both demands.

The nucleus is composed of the cell's DNA enclosed in a double membrane called the nuclear envelope. Each membrane in the nuclear envelope is similar to the membrane surrounding the entire cell. As **FIGURE 2.3** shows, the nuclear envelope is pierced with holes called pores that allow large molecules to pass between the nucleus and cytoplasm.

The nucleus also contains the nucleolus. The nucleolus is a dense region where tiny organelles essential for making proteins are assembled. These organelles, called ribosomes, are a combination of proteins and RNA molecules. They are discussed on the next page, and a more complete description of their structure and function is given in the chapter From DNA to Proteins.

### READING TOOLBOX

**TAKING NOTES**

Make a chart to correlate each organelle with its function.

| Organelle | Function |
|-----------|----------|
| Nucleus | stores DNA |
| Ribosome | |

### CONNECT TO

**BIOCHEMISTRY**

Recall from the chapter **Chemistry of Life** that certain amino acids within a protein molecule may form hydrogen bonds with other amino acids. These bonds cause the protein to form a specific shape.

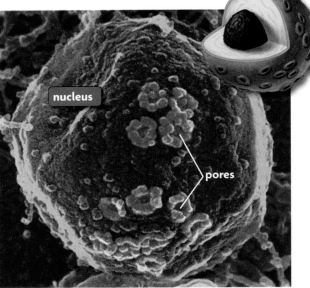

**FIGURE 2.3** The nucleus stores and protects DNA. (colored SEM; magnification 90,000×)

nucleus

pores

©Dr. Elena Kiseleva/Photo Researchers, Inc.

## Endoplasmic Reticulum and Ribosomes

A large part of the cytoplasm of most eukaryotic cells is filled by the endoplasmic reticulum, shown in **FIGURE 2.4**. The **endoplasmic reticulum** (EHN-duh-PLAZ-mihk rih-TIHK-yuh-luhm), or the ER, is an interconnected network of thin, folded membranes. The composition is very similar to that of the cell membrane and nuclear membranes. The ER membranes form a maze of enclosed spaces. The interior of this maze is called the lumen. Numerous processes, including the production of proteins and lipids, occur both on the surface of the ER and inside the lumen. The ER must be large enough to accommodate all these processes. How does it fit inside a cell?

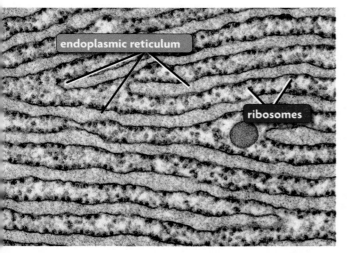

**FIGURE 2.4** The endoplasmic reticulum aids in the production of proteins and lipids.

The ER membrane has many creases and folds. If you have ever gone camping, you probably slept in a sleeping bag that covered you from head to foot. The next morning, you stuffed it back into a tiny little sack. How does the entire sleeping bag fit inside such a small sack? The surface area of the sleeping bag does not change, but the folds allow it to take up less space. Likewise, the ER's many folds enable it to fit within the cell.

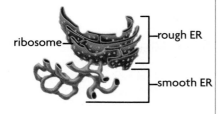

In some regions, the ER is studded with **ribosomes** (RY-buh-SOHMZ), tiny organelles that link amino acids together to form proteins. Ribosomes are both the site of protein synthesis and active participants in the process. Ribosomes are themselves made of proteins and RNA. After assembly in the nucleolus, ribosomes pass through the nuclear pores into the cytoplasm, where most protein synthesis occurs.

Surfaces of the ER that are covered with ribosomes are called rough ER because they look bumpy when viewed with an electron microscope. As a protein is being made on these ribosomes, it enters the lumen. Inside the lumen, the protein may be modified by having sugar chains added to it, which can help the protein fold or give it stability.

Not all ribosomes are bound to the ER; some are suspended in the cytoplasm. In general, proteins made on the ER are either incorporated into the cell membrane or secreted. In contrast, proteins made on suspended ribosomes are typically used in chemical reactions occurring within the cytoplasm.

Surfaces of the ER that do not contain ribosomes are called smooth ER. Smooth ER makes lipids and performs a variety of other specialized functions, such as breaking down drugs and alcohol.

## Golgi Apparatus

From the ER, proteins generally move to the Golgi apparatus, shown in **FIGURE 2.5**. The **Golgi apparatus** (GOHL-jee) consists of closely layered stacks of membrane-enclosed spaces that process, sort, and deliver proteins. Its membranes contain enzymes that make additional changes to proteins. The Golgi apparatus also packages proteins. Some of the packaged proteins are stored within the Golgi apparatus for later use. Some are transported to other organelles within the cell. Still others are carried to the membrane and secreted outside the cell.

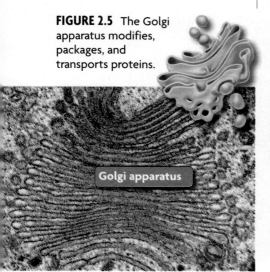

**FIGURE 2.5** The Golgi apparatus modifies, packages, and transports proteins.

## Vesicles

Cells need to separate reactants for various chemical reactions until it is time for them to be used. **Vesicles** (VEHS-ih-kuhlz), shown in **FIGURE 2.6,** are a general name used to describe small, membrane-bound sacs that divide some materials from the rest of the cytoplasm and transport these materials from place to place within the cell. Vesicles are generally short-lived and are formed and recycled as needed.

After a protein has been made, part of the ER pinches off to form a vesicle surrounding the protein. Protected by the vesicle, the protein can be safely transported to the Golgi apparatus. There, any necessary modifications are made, and the protein is packaged inside a new vesicle for storage, transport, or secretion.

**Compare and Contrast  How are the nucleus and a vesicle similar and different in structure and function?**

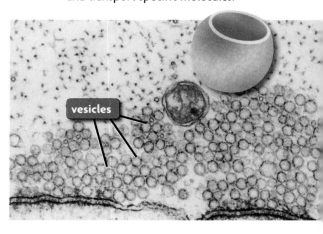

**FIGURE 2.6**  Vesicles isolate and transport specific molecules.

 **MAIN IDEA**

# Other organelles have various functions.

## Mitochondria

**Mitochondria** (MY-tuh-KAHN-dree-uh) supply energy to the cell. Mitochondria (singular, *mitochondrion*) are bean shaped and have two membranes, as shown in **FIGURE 2.7.** The inner membrane has many folds that greatly increase its surface area. Within these inner folds and compartments, a series of chemical reactions converts molecules from the food you eat into usable energy. You will learn more about this process in Cells and Energy.

Unlike most organelles, mitochondria have their own ribosomes and DNA. This fact suggests that mitochondria were originally free-living prokaryotes that were taken in by larger cells. The relationship must have helped both organisms to survive.

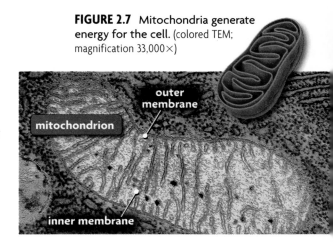

**FIGURE 2.7**  Mitochondria generate energy for the cell. (colored TEM; magnification 33,000×)

## Vacuole

A **vacuole** (VAK-yoo-OHL) is a fluid-filled sac used for the storage of materials needed by a cell. These materials may include water, food molecules, inorganic ions, and enzymes. Most animal cells contain many small vacuoles. The central vacuole, shown in **FIGURE 2.8,** is a structure unique to plant cells. It is a single, large vacuole that usually takes up most of the space inside a plant cell. It is filled with a watery fluid that strengthens the cell and helps to support the entire plant. When a plant wilts, its leaves shrivel because there is not enough water in each cell's central vacuole to support the leaf's normal structure. The central vacuole may also contain other substances, including toxins that would harm predators, waste products that would harm the cell itself, and pigments that give color to cells—such as those in the petals of a flower.

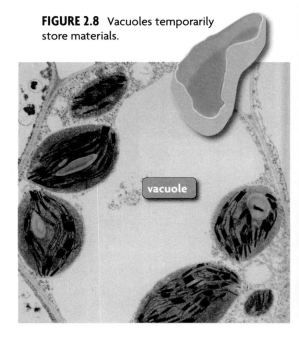

**FIGURE 2.8**  Vacuoles temporarily store materials.

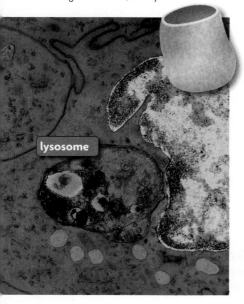

**FIGURE 2.9** Lysosomes digest and recycle foreign materials or worn-out parts. (colored TEM; magnification 21,000×)

lysosome

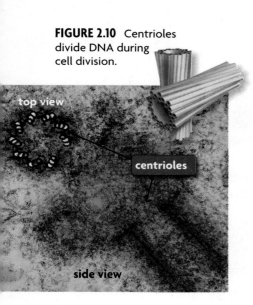

**FIGURE 2.10** Centrioles divide DNA during cell division.

top view

centrioles

side view

## Lysosomes

**Lysosomes** (LY-suh-SOHMZ), shown in **FIGURE 2.9**, are membrane-bound organelles that contain enzymes. They defend a cell from invading bacteria and viruses. They also break down damaged or worn-out cell parts. Lysosomes tend to be numerous in animal cells. Their presence in plant cells is still questioned by some scientists, but others assert that plant cells do have lysosomes, though fewer than are found in animal cells.

Recall that all enzymes are proteins. Initially, lysosomal enzymes are made in the rough ER in an inactive form. Vesicles pinch off from the ER membrane, carry the enzymes, and then fuse with the Golgi apparatus. There, the enzymes are activated and packaged as lysosomes that pinch off from the Golgi membrane. The lysosomes can then engulf and digest targeted molecules. When a molecule is broken down, the products pass through the lysosomal membrane and into the cytoplasm, where they are used again.

Lysosomes provide an example of the importance of membrane-bound structures in the eukaryotic cell. Because lysosomal enzymes can destroy cell components, they must be surrounded by a membrane that prevents them from destroying necessary structures. However, the cell also uses other methods to protect itself from these destructive enzymes. For example, the enzymes do not work as well in the cytoplasm as they do inside the lysosome.

## Centrosome and Centrioles

The centrosome is a small region of cytoplasm that produces microtubules. In animal cells, it contains two small structures called centrioles. **Centrioles** (SEHN-tree-OHLZ) are cylinder-shaped organelles made of short microtubules arranged in a circle. The two centrioles are perpendicular to each other, as shown in **FIGURE 2.10**. Before an animal cell divides, the centrosome, including the centrioles, doubles and the two new centrosomes move to opposite ends of the cell. Microtubules grow from each centrosome, forming spindle fibers. These fibers attach to the DNA and appear to help divide it between the two cells.

Centrioles were once thought to play a critical role in animal cell division. However, experiments have shown that animal cells can divide even if the centrioles are removed, making their role questionable. In addition, although centrioles are found in some algae, they are not found in plants.

Centrioles also organize microtubules to form cilia and flagella. Cilia look like little hairs; flagella look like a whip or a tail. Their motion forces liquids past a cell. For single cells, this movement results in swimming. For cells anchored in tissue, this motion sweeps liquid across the cell surface.

**Compare** In what ways are lysosomes, vesicles, and the central vacuole similar?

## ▶ MAIN IDEA

# Plant cells have cell walls and chloroplasts.

Plant cells have two features not shared by animal cells: cell walls and chloroplasts. Cell walls are structures that provide rigid support. Chloroplasts are organelles that help a plant convert solar energy to chemical energy.

## Modeling the Cell Membrane

The cell membrane regulates what moves into and out of the cell.

**PROBLEM** How does the cell membrane regulate what moves into and out of the cells?

### PROCEDURE

1. Bundle the swabs as shown.
2. Make a receptor from one pipe cleaner. It should extend through the bunch of swabs and have a region that would bind to a signal molecule. Use the other pipe cleaner to make a carbohydrate chain. Insert the chain into the "membrane" of the bunch of swabs.
3. Cut the drinking straw in half and insert both halves into the bunch of swabs.

### ANALYZE AND CONCLUDE

1. **Explain** How do the swabs represent the polar and nonpolar characteristics of the cell membrane?
2. **Evaluate** In this model, the swabs and proteins can be moved around. Explain whether this is an accurate representation of actual cell membranes.

### MATERIALS

- 50 cotton swabs
- 1 thick, medium-sized rubber band
- 2 pipe cleaners, each a different color
- 1 drinking straw
- scissors

## Selective Permeability

The cell membrane has the property of **selective permeability,** which means it allows some, but not all, materials to cross. Selective permeability is illustrated in **FIGURE 3.2.** The terms *semipermeable* and *selectively permeable* also refer to this property. As an example, outdoor clothing is often made of semipermeable fabric. The material is waterproof yet breathable. Molecules of water vapor from sweat are small enough to exit the fabric, but water droplets are too large to enter.

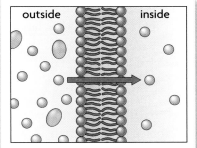

**FIGURE 3.2** A selectively permeable membrane allows some, but not all, molecules to cross.

Selective permeability enables a cell to maintain homeostasis in spite of unpredictable, changing conditions outside the cell. Because a cell needs to maintain certain conditions to carry out its functions, it must control the import and export of certain molecules and ions. Thus, even if ion concentrations change drastically outside a cell, these ions won't necessarily interfere with vital chemical reactions inside a cell.

Molecules cross the membrane in several ways. Some of these methods require the cell to expend energy; others do not. How a particular molecule crosses the membrane depends on the molecule's size, polarity, and concentration inside versus outside the cell. In general, small nonpolar molecules easily pass through the cell membrane, small polar molecules are transported via proteins, and large molecules are moved in vesicles.

**Connect** **Describe a semipermeable membrane with which you are already familiar.**

### CONNECT TO

#### HOMEOSTASIS

Recall from the chapter **Biology in the 21st Century** that homeostasis must be maintained in all organisms because vital chemical reactions can take place only within a limited range of conditions.

## ▶ MAIN IDEA

# Chemical signals are transmitted across the cell membrane.

Recall that cell membranes may secrete molecules and may contain identifying molecules, such as carbohydrates. All these molecules can act as signals to communicate with other cells. How are these signals recognized?

A **receptor** is a protein that detects a signal molecule and performs an action in response. It recognizes and binds to only certain molecules, ensuring that the right cell gets the right signal at the right time. The molecule a receptor binds to is called a ligand. When a receptor and a ligand bind, they change shape. This change is critical because it affects how a receptor interacts with other molecules. Two major types of receptors are present in your cells.

## Intracellular Receptor

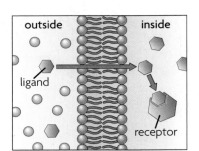

**FIGURE 3.3** Intracellular receptors are located inside the cell. They are bound by molecules that can cross the membrane.

A molecule may cross the cell membrane and bind to an intracellular receptor, as shown in **FIGURE 3.3**. The word *intracellular* means "within, or inside, a cell." Molecules that cross the membrane are generally nonpolar and may be relatively small. Many hormones fit within this category. For example, aldosterone can cross most cell membranes. However, it produces an effect only in cells that have the right type of receptor, such as kidney cells. When aldosterone enters a kidney cell, it binds to an intracellular receptor. The receptor-ligand complex enters the nucleus, interacts with the DNA, and turns on certain genes. As a result, specific proteins are made that help the kidneys absorb sodium ions and retain water, both of which are important for maintaining normal blood pressure.

## Membrane Receptor

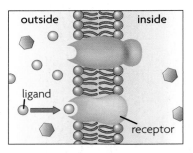

**FIGURE 3.4** Membrane receptors bind to molecules that cannot enter the cell. When bound, the receptor transmits the signal inside the cell by changing shape.

A molecule that cannot cross the membrane may bind to a receptor in the cell membrane, as shown in **FIGURE 3.4**. The receptor then sends the message to the cell interior. Although the receptor binds to a signal molecule outside the cell, the entire receptor changes shape—even the part inside the cell. As a result, it causes molecules inside the cell to respond. These molecules, in turn, start a complicated chain of events inside the cell that tells the cell what to do. For instance, band 3 protein is a membrane receptor in red blood cells. When activated, it triggers processes that carry carbon dioxide from body tissues to the lungs.

**Contrast** How do intracellular receptors differ from membrane receptors?

SELF-CHECK Online
HMHScience.com
GO ONLINE

## 3.3 Formative Assessment

### REVIEWING ▶ MAIN IDEAS

1. Why do **phospholipids** form a double layer?

2. Explain how membrane **receptors** transmit messages across the **cell membrane.**

### CRITICAL THINKING

3. **Compare** Describe the similarities between enzymes and receptors.

4. **Infer** If proteins were rigid, why would they make poor receptors?

### ▶ CONNECT TO

**HUMAN BIOLOGY**

5. Insulin helps cells take up sugar from the blood. Explain the effect on blood sugar levels if insulin receptors stopped working.

# 3.4 Diffusion and Osmosis

SC.912.L.14.2


## VOCABULARY

passive transport
diffusion
concentration gradient
osmosis
isotonic
hypertonic
hypotonic
facilitated diffusion

**SC.912.L.14.2** Relate structure to function for the components of plant and animal cells. Explain the role of cell membranes as a highly selective barrier (passive and active transport).

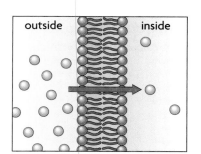

**FIGURE 4.1** Passive transport is the movement of molecules across the membrane from areas of higher concentration to areas of lower concentration. It does not require energy input from the cell.

**CONNECT TO**

## HUMAN BIOLOGY

As you will learn in the chapter **Respiratory and Circulatory Systems,** diffusion plays a key role in gas exchange in the lungs and other body tissues.


**KEY CONCEPT** Materials move across membranes because of concentration differences.

## MAIN IDEAS

- Diffusion and osmosis are types of passive transport.
- Some molecules diffuse through membrane proteins.

### Connect to Your World

If you have ever been stuck in traffic behind a truck full of pigs, you know that "unpleasant" fails to fully describe the situation. That is because molecules travel from the pigs to receptors in your nose, and your brain interprets those molecules to be a really bad odor. Or, perhaps you have tie-dyed a T-shirt and have seen dye molecules spread throughout the pot of water, turning it neon green or electric blue. Why does that happen? Why don't the molecules stay in one place?

### ⬤ MAIN IDEA

## Diffusion and osmosis are types of passive transport.

Cells almost continually import and export substances. If they had to expend energy to move every molecule, cells would require an enormous amount of energy to stay alive. Fortunately, some molecules enter and exit a cell without requiring the cell to work. As **FIGURE 4.1** shows, **passive transport** is the movement of molecules across a cell membrane without energy input from the cell. It may also be described as the diffusion of molecules across a membrane.

### Diffusion

**Diffusion** is the movement of molecules in a fluid or gas from a region of higher concentration to a region of lower concentration. It results from the natural motion of particles, which causes molecules to collide and scatter. Concentration is the number of molecules of a substance in a given volume, and it can vary from one region to another. A **concentration gradient** is the difference in the concentration of a substance from one location to another. Molecules diffuse down their concentration gradient—that is, from a region of higher concentration to a region of lower concentration.

In the tie-dye example, dye molecules are initially at a high concentration in the area where they are added to the water. Random movements of the dye and water molecules cause them to bump into each other and mix. Thus, the dye molecules move from an area of higher concentration to an area of lower concentration. Eventually, they are evenly spread throughout the solution. This means the molecules have reached a dynamic equilibrium. The concentration of dye molecules is the same throughout the solution (equilibrium), but the molecules continue to move (dynamic).

In cells, diffusion plays an important role in moving substances across the membrane. Small lipids and other nonpolar molecules, such as carbon dioxide and oxygen, easily diffuse across the membrane. For example, most of your cells continually consume oxygen, which means that the oxygen concentration is almost always higher outside a cell than it is inside a cell. As a result, oxygen generally diffuses into a cell without the cell expending any energy.

## Osmosis

Water molecules, of course, also diffuse. They move across a semipermeable membrane from an area of higher water concentration to an area of lower water concentration. This process is called **osmosis.** It is important to recognize that the higher the concentration of dissolved particles in a solution, the lower the concentration of water molecules in the same solution. So, if you put 1 teaspoon of salt in a cup of water and 10 teaspoons of salt in a different cup of water, the first cup would have the higher water concentration.

A solution may be described as isotonic, hypertonic, or hypotonic relative to another solution. Note that these terms are comparisons; they require a point of reference, as shown in **FIGURE 4.3**. An **isotonic** solution has a solute concentration equal to the solute concentration inside a cell. A **hypertonic** solution has a solute concentration higher than the solute concentration inside a cell. A **hypotonic** solution has a solute concentration lower than the solute concentration inside a cell.

Some animals and single-celled organisms can survive in hypotonic environments. Their cells have adaptations for removing excess water. In plants, the rigid cell wall prevents the membrane from expanding too much.

**FIGURE 4.2** Diffusion results from the natural motion of particles.

## FIGURE 4.3  Effects of Osmosis

**Osmosis is the diffusion of water across a semipermeable membrane from an area of higher water concentration to an area of lower water concentration.**

| ISOTONIC SOLUTION | HYPERTONIC SOLUTION | HYPOTONIC SOLUTION |
| --- | --- | --- |
| 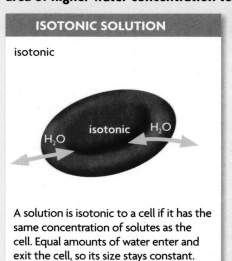 | 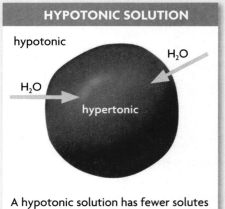 | |
| A solution is isotonic to a cell if it has the same concentration of solutes as the cell. Equal amounts of water enter and exit the cell, so its size stays constant. | A hypertonic solution has more solutes than a cell. Overall, more water exits a cell in a hypertonic solution, causing the cell to shrivel or even die. | A hypotonic solution has fewer solutes than a cell. Overall, more water enters a cell in a hypotonic solution, causing the cell to expand or even burst. |

**Apply**  How would adding salt to the isotonic solution above affect the cell?

(tl) ©HMH; (bl), (bc), (br) ©Monica Schroeder/Science Source

Remember from Section 2 that pressure exerted on the cell wall by fluid inside the central vacuole provides structural support for each cell and for the plant as a whole.

**Apply** **What will happen to a houseplant if you water it with salt water (a hypertonic solution)?**

## ▶ MAIN IDEA
## Some molecules diffuse through membrane proteins.

Biologists have long known that osmosis alone cannot account for the rapid movement of water into and out of cells, especially cells such as red blood cells and certain kidney cells. More recent research has revealed that a group of membrane proteins called aquaporins also play an important role in the transport of water into and out of these cells. Aquaporin molecules form channels, or tunnels, through the cell membrane. The structure of these channels allows water molecules to pass through in a single file. However, no charged particles, not even hydrogen ions, can pass through.

The transport of water by aquaporins is one example of **facilitated diffusion,** the diffusion of molecules across a membrane through transport proteins. The word *facilitate* means "to make easier." Transport proteins make it easier for molecules to enter or exit a cell. But the process is still a form of passive transport. The molecules move down a concentration gradient, requiring no energy expenditure by the cell.

There are many types of transport proteins. Like aquaporins, most types allow only a certain type of molecule or ion to pass. As **FIGURE 4.4** shows, some transport proteins are simple channels through which particles such as ions can pass. Others act more like enzymes. When a specific molecule binds with the protein, the protein changes shape in a way that allows the molecule to travel the rest of the way into the cell.

**Explain** **What role do transport proteins play in the cell membrane?**

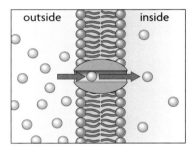

**FIGURE 4.4** Facilitated diffusion enables molecules that cannot directly cross the phospholipid bilayer to diffuse through transport proteins in the membrane.

## 3.4 **Formative Assessment**

**REVIEWING ▶ MAIN IDEAS**

1. Explain what a **concentration gradient** is and what it means for a molecule to diffuse down its concentration gradient.

2. Explain why **facilitated diffusion** does not require energy from a cell.

**CRITICAL THINKING**

3. **Apply** A cell is bathed in fluid. However, you notice that water is flowing out of the cell. In what kind of solution is this cell immersed: **isotonic, hypotonic,** or **hypertonic**?

4. **Compare** How are receptors and transport proteins similar?

**CONNECT TO**

**HEALTH**

5. When a person becomes dehydrated due to the loss of fluids and solutes, saline solution (water and salts) is infused into the bloodstream by medical personnel. Why is saline solution used instead of pure water?

# Biomimicry

People have looked to the natural world to help solve problems for centuries. The dream of building airplanes likely came from watching birds in flight. In the mid-1900s, the hook-and-loop fastener, commonly called by its brand name, Velcro®, was invented after a Swiss engineer noticed how burs have little hooks that stick to fur and clothing. Over time, using nature as a guide for solving human problems has moved from an occasional or accidental occurrence to an intentional practice called biomimicry, from the Greek words *bio* ("life") and *mimesis* ("to imitate"). The growing field of biomimicry recognizes that humans are grappling with problems that nature has been solving for millions of years.

Today, examples of biomimicry can be found in almost every industry—even in sports. At the 2008 Summer Olympic Games in Beijing, the vast majority of swimmers who broke world records were wearing suits modeled after sharkskin. The technology proved to be such an advantage that the material has been banned, at least in its full-length version, from future competitions. It turns out that sharks are not just fast, they are microbe-free. Researchers are developing plastic films that mimic sharkskin—made of tiny denticles, or teethlike scales. This type of material can be used to keep bacteria off surfaces in restaurants and hospitals.

The health-care industry has looked to biomimicry for other solutions as well. Water purification once was limited to pushing water through a membrane, a process that required a lot of energy and frequently required membranes to be unclogged or replaced. New technology looks to our own cells for solutions to these problems, using aquaporin proteins to escort water molecules across a membrane and leaving contaminants behind.

Because natural processes are inherently sustainable, some industries are using biomimicry in efforts to be more environmentally friendly. One manufacturer of carpets has looked to nature to solve several issues. Inspiration from the forest floor has led to carpet colors and patterns that are purposely less uniform than traditional designs, leading to less waste during manufacturing and fewer quality-control checks. Instead of using conventional glues that release toxic chemicals into the air, manufacturers use Earth's gravity to hold the carpets down. Creating carpet pieces that hook to each other with tiny hairs, similar to the hairs that allow a gecko to cling to a wall, provides enough weight to hold carpets in place. Reducing the use of glue has the additional benefit of allowing the carpet to be more easily recycled at the end of its use.

Considering how products can be used and then broken down into their components and reused is not only sustainable, but it is also more evidence of biomimicry in action. Nature's cycling of matter ensures that nothing goes to waste, and the field of life-cycle engineering looks not only at the development of a product and how it will be used but also at how waste can be reduced or eliminated after the product is no longer useful. From engineering to design to waste management, taking the time to explore the natural world can provide inspiration for the next innovative solution in virtually any field you choose to pursue.

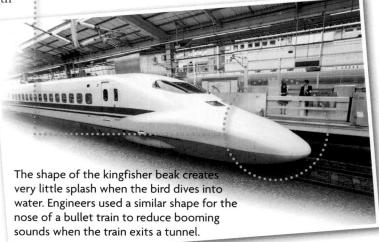

The shape of the kingfisher beak creates very little splash when the bird dives into water. Engineers used a similar shape for the nose of a bullet train to reduce booming sounds when the train exits a tunnel.

# 3.5 Active Transport, Endocytosis, and Exocytosis

**SC.912.L.14.2**

**SC.912.L.14.2** Relate structure to function for the components of plant and animal cells. Explain the role of cell membranes as a highly selective barrier (passive and active transport).

**KEY CONCEPT** Cells use energy to transport materials that cannot diffuse across a membrane.

### MAIN IDEAS

- Proteins can transport materials against a concentration gradient.
- Endocytosis and exocytosis transport materials across the membrane in vesicles.

### Connect to Your World

If you want to go up to the second floor of the mall, you're going to need help beating gravity. You could take an escalator, which uses energy to move you against gravity, much like transport proteins involved in active transport use energy to move molecules against a gradient. Alternatively, you might take the elevator, entering on the first floor and hopping out when the doors open on the second. In endocytosis and exocytosis, vesicles act like that elevator, surrounding molecules on one side of a membrane and releasing them into the other.

### ▶ MAIN IDEA

## Proteins can transport materials against a concentration gradient.

You just learned that some transport proteins let materials diffuse into and out of a cell down a concentration gradient. Many other transport proteins, often called pumps, move materials against a concentration gradient. **Active transport** drives molecules across a membrane from a region of lower concentration to a region of higher concentration. This process, shown in **FIGURE 5.1,** uses transport proteins powered by chemical energy. Cells use active transport to get needed molecules regardless of the concentration gradient and to maintain homeostasis.

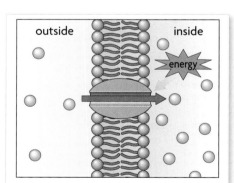

**FIGURE 5.1** During active transport, a cell uses energy to move substances against a concentration gradient—that is, from a lower to a higher concentration.

Before we discuss active transport proteins, let's look at transport proteins in general. All transport proteins span the membrane, and most change shape when they bind to a target molecule or molecules. Some transport proteins bind to only one type of molecule. Others bind to two different types. Some proteins that bind to two types of molecules move both types in the same direction. Others move the molecules in opposite directions.

**CONNECT TO**

### HUMAN BIOLOGY

As you will learn in the chapter **Digestive and Excretory Systems,** active transport is a necessary part of nutrient absorption.

FIGURE 5.2 Just as a cell uses energy in the process of active transport, this boy uses energy to pump air against a concentration gradient.

The key feature of active transport proteins is that they can use chemical energy to move a substance against its concentration gradient. Most use energy from a molecule called ATP, either directly or indirectly. For example, nerve cells, or neurons, need to have a higher concentration of potassium ions and a lower concentration of sodium ions than the fluid outside the cell. The sodium-potassium pump uses energy directly from the breakdown of ATP. It pumps three sodium ions out of the cell for every two potassium ions it pumps in. The proton pump, another transport protein, uses energy from the breakdown of ATP to move hydrogen ions (or protons) out of the cell. This action forms a concentration gradient of hydrogen ions ($H^+$), which makes the fluid outside the cell more positively charged than the fluid inside. In fact, this gradient is a form of stored energy that is used to power other active transport proteins. In plant cells, this gradient causes yet another protein to transport sucrose into the cell—an example of indirect active transport.

Synthesize  **In what ways are active transport proteins similar to enzymes?**

 **MAIN IDEA**

# Endocytosis and exocytosis transport materials across the membrane in vesicles.

A cell may also use energy to move a large substance or a large amount of a substance in vesicles. Transport in vesicles lets substances enter or exit a cell without crossing through the membrane.

## Endocytosis

**Endocytosis** (EN-doh-sy-TOH-sihs) is the process of taking liquids or fairly large molecules into a cell by engulfing them in a membrane. In this process, the cell membrane makes a pocket around a substance. The pocket breaks off inside the cell and forms a vesicle, which then fuses with a lysosome or a similar type of vesicle. Lysosomal enzymes break down the vesicle membrane and its contents (if necessary), which are then released into the cell.

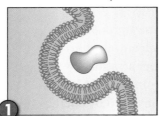
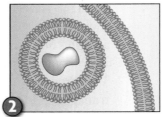
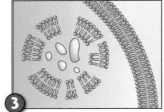

**1** During endocytosis, the cell membrane folds inward and fuses together, surrounding the substance in a pocket.

**2** The pocket pinches off inside the cell, forming a vesicle.

**3** The vesicle fuses with a lysosome or a similar vesicle, where enzymes break down the membrane and its contents.

**Phagocytosis** (FAG-uh-sy-TOH-sihs) is a type of endocytosis in which the cell membrane engulfs large particles. The word literally means "cell eating." Phagocytosis plays a key role in your immune system. Some white blood cells called macrophages help your body fight infection. They find foreign materials, such as bacteria, and engulf and destroy them.

## Exocytosis

**Exocytosis** (ЕНК-soh-sy-TOH-sihs), the opposite of endocytosis, is the release of substances out of a cell by the fusion of a vesicle with the membrane. During this process, a vesicle forms around materials to be sent out of the cell. The vesicle then moves toward the cell's surface, where it fuses with the membrane and releases its contents.

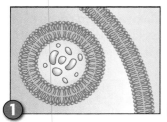

**1** The cell forms a vesicle around materials that need to be removed or secreted.

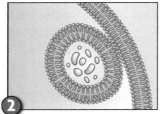

**2** The vesicle is transported to the cell membrane.

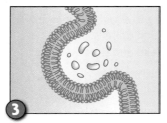

**3** The vesicle membrane fuses with the cell membrane and releases the contents.

Exocytosis happens all the time in your body. In fact, you couldn't think or move a muscle without it. When you want to move your big toe, for example, your brain sends a message that travels through a series of nerve cells to reach your toe. This message, or nerve impulse, travels along each nerve cell as an electrical signal, but it must be converted to a chemical signal to cross the tiny gap that separates one nerve cell from the next. These chemicals are stored in vesicles within the nerve cells. When a nerve impulse reaches the end of a cell, it causes the vesicles to fuse with the cell membrane and release the chemicals outside the cell. There they attach to the next nerve cell, which triggers a new electrical impulse in that cell.

**Hypothesize** What might happen if vesicles in your neurons were suddenly unable to fuse with the cell membrane?

## 3.5 Formative Assessment

### REVIEWING ▶ MAIN IDEAS

1. How do transport proteins that are pumps differ from those that are channels?

2. How do **endocytosis** and **exocytosis** differ from diffusion?

### CRITICAL THINKING

3. **Apply** Small lipid molecules are in high concentration outside a cell. They slowly cross the membrane into the cell. What term describes this action? Does it require energy?

4. **Apply** Ions are in low concentration outside a cell. They move rapidly into the cell via protein molecules. What term describes this action? Does it require energy?

# 3 Summary

## KEY CONCEPTS

### 3.1 Cell Theory

**Cells are the basic unit of life.** The contributions of many scientists led to the discovery of cells and the development of the cell theory. The cell theory states that all organisms are made of cells, all cells are produced by other living cells, and the cell is the most basic unit of life.

### 3.2 Cell Organelles

**Eukaryotic cells share many similarities.** They have a nucleus and other membrane-bound organelles that perform specialized tasks within the cell. Many of these organelles are involved in making proteins. Plant and animal cells share many of the same types of organelles, but both also have organelles that are specific to the cells' unique functions.

### 3.3 Cell Membrane

**The cell membrane is a barrier that separates a cell from the external environment.** It is made of a double layer of phospholipids and a variety of embedded molecules. Some of these molecules act as signals; others act as receptors. The membrane is selectively permeable, allowing some but not all materials to cross.

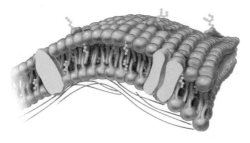

### 3.4 Diffusion and Osmosis

**Materials move across membranes because of concentration differences.** Diffusion is the movement of molecules in a fluid or gas from a region of higher concentration to a region of lower concentration. It does not require a cell to expend energy; it is a form of passive transport. Osmosis is the diffusion of water. Net water movement into or out of a cell depends on the concentration of the solution.

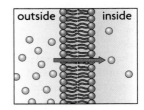

outside        inside

**Passive transport**

### 3.5 Active Transport, Endocytosis, and Exocytosis

**Cells use energy to transport materials that cannot diffuse across a membrane.** Active transport is the movement of molecules across a membrane from a region of lower concentration to a region of higher concentration—against a concentration gradient. The processes of endocytosis and exocytosis move substances in vesicles and also require energy.

**Endocytosis**

**Exocytosis**

---

## READING TOOLBOX   SYNTHESIZE YOUR NOTES

**Main Idea Web** Plant and animal cells, though similar, each have some unique features. Identify how these cell types differ by placing plant cell characteristics on the left side of the main idea web and animal cell characteristics on the right.

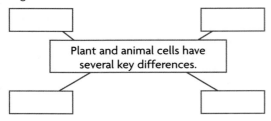

Plant and animal cells have several key differences.

**Concept Map** Fill in a concept map like the one below to summarize what you know about forms of transport.

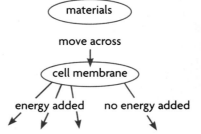

materials

move across

cell membrane

energy added        no energy added

active transport
passive transport
diffusion
endocytosis
materials
exocytosis
osmosis
cell membrane

# 3 Review

**INTERACTIVE** Review
HMHScience.com

**GO ONLINE**

Review Games • Concept Map • Section Self-Checks

## CHAPTER VOCABULARY

**3.1** cell theory
cytoplasm
organelle
prokaryotic cell
eukaryotic cell

**3.2** cytoskeleton
nucleus
endoplasmic reticulum
ribosome
Golgi apparatus
vesicle

mitochondrion
vacuole
lysosome
centriole
cell wall
chloroplast

**3.3** cell membrane
phospholipid
fluid mosaic model
selective permeability
receptor

**3.4** passive transport
diffusion
concentration gradient
osmosis
isotonic
hypertonic
hypotonic
facilitated diffusion

**3.5** active transport
endocytosis
phagocytosis
exocytosis

## Reviewing Vocabulary

**Labeling Diagrams**

In your science notebook, write the vocabulary term that matches each numbered item below.

1.
2.
3.
4.
5.
6.
7.
8.

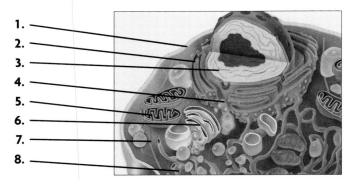

**Labeling Diagrams**

Describe one similarity and one difference between the two terms in each of the following pairs.

9. eukaryotic, prokaryotic

10. cell wall, cell membrane

11. diffusion, facilitated diffusion

**READING** TOOLBOX  **GREEK AND LATIN WORD ORIGINS**

12. The word *organelle* is the diminutive, or "tiny," form of the Latin word for organs of the body. How is an organelle like a tiny organ?

13. The Greek word *karuon* means "nut." The prefix *pro-* means "before," and the prefix *eu-* means "true." Thus, *prokaryote* means "before nut," and *eukaryote* means "true nut." How do these meanings relate to structural differences between these two cell types?

## Reviewing  MAIN IDEAS

14. According to the cell theory, what is required for an object to be considered alive?

15. What role do membranes play in prokaryotic cells? in eukaryotic cells?

16. How do the cytoskeleton and the cytoplasm contribute to a cell's shape?

17. You know that many organelles are involved in protein production. Briefly explain where proteins are made, modified, and packaged within a cell.

18. Explain what mitochondria do and why evidence suggests that they might have descended from free-living prokaryotes in the evolutionary past.

19. If you were looking through a microscope at an un-known cell, how might you determine whether it was a plant cell or an animal cell?

20. Cells are surrounded by a watery fluid, and they contain cytoplasm. Explain how the structure of the lipid bilayer is related to these two watery environments.

21. How are cells able to respond to signal molecules that are too large to enter the cytoplasm?

22. How do transport proteins make it easier for certain molecules to diffuse across a membrane?

23. Under what conditions would a molecule need to be actively transported across a membrane?

24. Do you think that endocytosis and exocytosis can occur within the same cell? Explain your reasoning.

# Critical Thinking

25. **Summarize** How was the development of cell theory closely tied to advancements in technology?

26. **Analyze** What structural features suggest that eukaryotic cells evolved from prokaryotic cells?

27. **Synthesize** If vesicles are almost constantly pinching off from the ER to carry proteins to the Golgi apparatus, why does the ER not shrink and finally disappear?

28. **Compare and Contrast** You know that both vesicles and vacuoles are hollow compartments used for storage. How do they differ in function?

29. **Infer** When cells release ligands, they are sent through the bloodstream to every area of the body. Why do you think that only certain types of cells will respond to a particular ligand?

30. **Provide Examples** What are two ways in which exocytosis might help a cell maintain homeostasis?

31. **Compare** How is facilitated diffusion similar to both passive transport and active transport?

## Interpreting Visuals
Use the diagram to answer the next three questions.

32. **Apply** What process is occurring in the diagram, and how do you know?

33. **Predict** If the transport proteins that carry amino acids into this cell stopped working, how might the process shown be affected?

34. **Infer** What might you conclude about the membrane structure of the final vesicle and the cell membrane?

## Analyzing Data   Form an Operational Definition
Use the text and table below to answer the next three questions. Reactive oxygen species, or ROS, are clusters of highly reactive oxygen atoms that can damage the body. As people age, the amount of ROS in the body increases, causing a condition called oxidative stress. In one study, researchers studied how the number of mitochondria might be involved in this situation.

- Muscle tissue was obtained from patients.
- Radioactive probes labeled the mitochondria.
- A machine counted the mitochondria per cell.

| AGE AND MUSCLE CELL MITOCHONDRIA | | |
|---|---|---|
| **Patient** | **Age** | **Mitochondria per Muscle Cell** |
| 1 | 47 | 2026 |
| 2 | 89 | 2987 |
| 3 | 65 | 2752 |
| 4 | 38 | 1989 |

35. **Apply** If the independent variable in this study is age, what is the operational definition of the dependent variable?

36. **Analyze** What do the data show about the relationship between age and number of mitochondria?

37. **Infer** What might the relationship between age and number of mitochondria indicate about the increase in ROS levels?

## Making Connections

38. **Write an Analogy** The cell membrane regulates what can enter and exit a cell. In eukaryotes, it encloses a complex group of organelles that carry out special jobs. Make an analogy to describe the cell membrane and the variety of organelles and processes that take place inside it. Explain any limitations of your analogy.

39. **Connect** On the chapter opener, you saw a picture of macrophages eating up bacteria. Identify the ways in which the cytoskeleton helps the macrophage carry out this job.

### EMPTY POCKETS

This part of the bag has pockets to hold stuff that it might need later. It also makes a few things.

One of the things it makes is that stuff that helps your arms and legs get stronger. Sometimes, people who want to run or ride fast will put bottles of that stuff into their body and then lie about it.

### CONTROL AREA

This area in the middle holds information about how to make the different parts of your body. It writes this information in notes and sends them out into the bag.

Bags make more bags by breaking in half. When this happens, the control area also breaks in half, and each half gets a full set of the bag's information.

Not all bags have these control areas. The bags in human blood don't (which means blood can't grow) but the bags in bird blood do.

This control area may have once been a living thing on its own, just like the green things in leaves.

### CONTROL AREA HOLES

Notes and workers go out through these openings.

### LITTLE BUILDERS

This area is covered in little building machines that build new parts for the bag. The builders sit just outside the control area, reading the notes from inside that tell them what to build.

After the builder makes a part, the part falls away into the bag. Each part has a job to do. Maybe its job is to tell another part it's time to stop working. Maybe its job is to turn one kind of part into another. Maybe it makes another part do something different. Or maybe it has a job, but waits until it sees *another* part before it starts working.

The strange thing is, no one tells the part where to go. It just falls out into the room with all the other parts, and hangs around until it runs into whatever part it's supposed to grab. (Or until another part grabs *it!*) This sounds strange, and it is! There are so many parts, and they're all grabbing each other and stopping each other and helping each other.

The insides of these bags are harder to understand than almost anything else in the world.

### THINGS THAT MAKE YOU SICK

These tiny things can get into your bags and take control of them. When they do that, they use the bag to build more of them.

When the kind shown here gets into you, your body gets hot, your legs hurt, and you have to lie down. Your whole body feels bad, and it makes you hate everything. You feel like you're going to die but usually don't.

We say all life is made of bags, but these things aren't. They also can't make more of themselves; they have to get a bag to make them. So we don't know if it makes sense to say they're "alive." They're more like an idea that spreads itself.

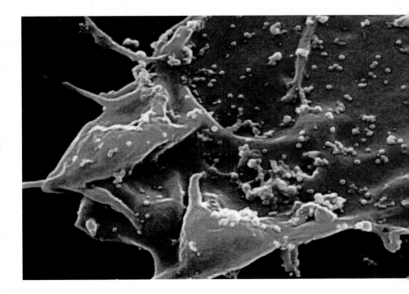

# CHAPTER 4 Cells and Energy

**BIG IDEA** All living things require energy in the form of ATP to carry on cell processes, and ATP is most often produced by the linked reactions of photosynthesis and respiration.

## ⊙ ONLINE BIOLOGY  HMHScience.com

**ONLINE** Labs
- Rates of Photosynthesis
- **QuickLab** Fermentation
- Cellular Respiration
- Investigate Fermentation in Foods
- Designing an Experiment to Test a Hypothesis
- Photosynthesis and Respiration

- The Effect of Temperature on Respiration
- **Virtual Lab** Carbon Dioxide Transfer Through Snails and *Elodea*
- **Video Lab** Cellular Respiration

(t) ©Andrew Syred/Photo Researchers, Inc.

**Q** **What makes these cells so important to many other organisms?**

These diatoms are single-celled algae that use the process of photosynthesis to store chemical energy in sugars. Animals eat photosynthetic organisms such as plants and algae to get this chemical energy. Photosynthetic organisms also produce the oxygen that is required to release much of the chemical energy in sugars.

colored SEM; magnification 1000×

---

 **READING** TOOLBOX     **This reading tool can help you learn the material in the following pages.**

**USING LANGUAGE**

**Describing Space** As you read the chapter, look for language clues that answer the question, Where does this process take place? Words such as *inside, outside,* and *between* can help you learn where these processes take place to help you better understand them.

**YOUR TURN**

Describe as precisely as you can where the following processes happen.

1. photosynthesis
2. cellular respiration

# 4.1 Chemical Energy and ATP

**SC.912.L.18.10**

| **KEY CONCEPT** **All cells need chemical energy.**

**MAIN IDEAS**

- ◗ The chemical energy used for most cell processes is carried by ATP.
- ◗ Organisms break down carbon-based molecules to produce ATP.
- ◗ A few types of organisms do not need sunlight and photosynthesis as a source of energy.

## VOCABULARY

ATP
ADP
chemosynthesis

**SC.912.L.18.10** Connect the role of adenosine triphosphate (ATP) to energy transfers within a cell.

✺ *Connect to Your World*

The cells of all organisms—from algae to whales to people—need chemical energy for all of their processes. Some organisms, such as diatoms and plants, absorb energy from sunlight. Some of that energy is stored in sugars. Cells break down sugars to produce usable chemical energy for their functions. Without organisms that make sugars, living things on Earth could not survive.

◗ **MAIN IDEA**

## The chemical energy used for most cell processes is carried by ATP.

Sometimes you may feel that you need energy, so you eat food that contains sugar. Does food, which contains sugar and other carbon-based molecules, give you energy? The answer to this question is yes and no. All of the carbon-based molecules in food store chemical energy in their bonds. Carbohydrates and lipids are the most important energy sources in foods you eat. However, this energy is only usable after these molecules are broken down by a series of chemical reactions. Your energy does come from food, but not directly.

All cells, like that in **FIGURE 1.1**, use chemical energy carried by ATP—adenosine triphosphate. **ATP** is a molecule that transfers energy from the breakdown of food molecules to cell processes. You can think of ATP as a wallet filled with money. Just as a wallet carries money that you can spend, ATP carries chemical energy that cells can use. Cells use ATP for functions such as building molecules and moving materials by active transport.

**VISUAL VOCAB**

**ATP** transfers energy to cell processes.

adenosine  **tri**phosphate

**tri** = 3

**ADP** is a lower-energy molecule that can be converted into ATP.

adenosine  **di**phosphate

**di** = 2

The energy carried by ATP is released when a phosphate group is removed from the molecule. ATP has three phosphate groups, but the bond holding the third phosphate group is unstable and is very easily broken. The removal of the third phosphate group usually involves a reaction that releases energy.

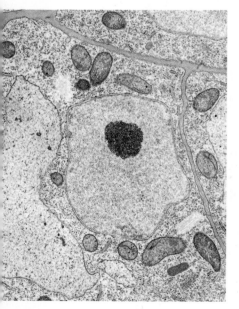

**FIGURE 1.1** All cells, including plant cells, use ATP for energy. (colored TEM; magnification 9000×)

©Biophoto Associates/Photo Researchers, Inc.

## FIGURE 1.2 ATP and ADP

**Adding a phosphate group to ADP forms ATP.**

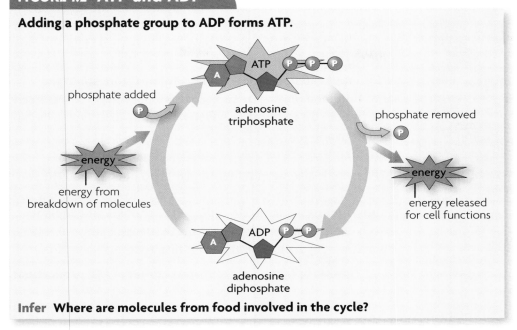

adenosine
triphosphate

phosphate added

energy

energy from
breakdown of molecules

phosphate removed

energy

energy released
for cell functions

ADP

adenosine
diphosphate

**Infer** **Where are molecules from food involved in the cycle?**

When the phosphate is removed, energy is released and ATP becomes ADP—adenosine diphosphate. **ADP** is a lower-energy molecule that can be converted into ATP by the addition of a phosphate group. If ATP is a wallet filled with money, ADP is a nearly empty wallet. The breakdown of ATP to ADP and the production of ATP from ADP can be represented by the cycle shown in **FIGURE 1.2**. However, adding a phosphate group to ADP to make ATP is not a simple process. A large, complex group of proteins is needed to do it. In fact, if just one of these proteins is faulty, ATP is not produced.

**Synthesize** **Describe the relationship between energy stored in food and ATP.**

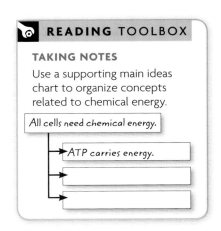

**CONNECT TO**

**BIOCHEMISTRY**

As you learned in the chapter **Chemistry of Life,** carbon-based molecules in living things—carbohydrates, lipids, proteins, and nucleic acids—have different structures and functions.

## ◯ MAIN IDEA
# Organisms break down carbon-based molecules to produce ATP.

Foods that you eat do not contain ATP that your cells can use. First, the food must be digested. One function of digestion is to break down food into smaller molecules that can be used to make ATP. You probably know that different foods have different amounts of calories, which are measures of energy. Different foods also provide different amounts of ATP. The number of ATP molecules that are made from the breakdown of food is related to the number of calories in food, but not directly.

The number of ATP molecules produced depends on the type of molecule that is broken down—carbohydrate, lipid, or protein. Carbohydrates are not stored in large amounts in your body, but they are the molecules most commonly broken down to make ATP. The breakdown of the simple sugar glucose yields about 36 molecules of ATP.

**READING TOOLBOX**

**TAKING NOTES**

Use a supporting main ideas chart to organize concepts related to chemical energy.

All cells need chemical energy.

ATP carries energy.

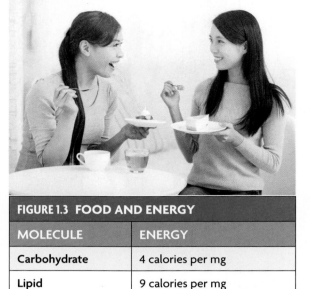

## FIGURE 1.3  FOOD AND ENERGY

| MOLECULE | ENERGY |
|---|---|
| Carbohydrate | 4 calories per mg |
| Lipid | 9 calories per mg |
| Protein | 4 calories per mg |

You might be surprised to learn that carbohydrates do not provide the largest amount of ATP. Lipids store the most energy, as **FIGURE 1.3** shows. In fact, fats store about 80% of the energy in your body. And, when fats are broken down, they yield the most ATP. For example, a typical triglyceride can be broken down to make about 146 molecules of ATP. Proteins store about the same amount of energy as carbohydrates, but they are less likely to be broken down to make ATP. The amino acids that cells can break down to make ATP are needed to build new proteins more than they are needed for energy.

Plant cells also need ATP, but plants do not eat food the way animals do. Plants make their own food. Through the process of photosynthesis, which is described in Sections 2 and 3, plants absorb energy from sunlight and make sugars. Plant cells break down these sugars to produce ATP, just as animal cells do.

**Compare and Contrast**  How do lipids and carbohydrates differ in ATP production?

⊙ MAIN IDEA

## A few types of organisms do not need sunlight and photosynthesis as a source of energy.

Most, but not all, organisms rely directly or indirectly on sunlight and photo-synthesis as their source of chemical energy. In places that never get sunlight, such as in the deep ocean, there are areas with living things. Some organisms live in very hot water near cracks in the ocean floor called hydrothermal vents. These vents release chemical compounds, such as sulfides, that can serve as an energy source. **Chemosynthesis** (KEE-mo-SIHN-thih-sihs) is a process by which some organisms use chemical energy to make energy-storing carbon-based molecules. These organisms still need ATP for energy. The processes that make their ATP are very similar to those in other organisms. Like plants, chemosynthetic organisms make their own food, but the raw materials differ.

**Compare**  How are chemosynthetic organisms and plants similar as energy sources?

©aslysun/Shutterstock

SELF-CHECK Online
HMHScience.com
GO ONLINE

## 4.1  Formative Assessment

### REVIEWING ⊙ MAIN IDEAS

1. How are **ATP** and **ADP** related?
2. What types of molecules are broken down to make ATP?
3. How are some organisms able to survive without sunlight and photo-synthesis?

### CRITICAL THINKING

4. **Apply**  Describe how you get energy indirectly from the food that you eat.
5. **Compare and Contrast**  How are the energy needs of plant cells similar to those of animal cells? How are they different?

### ⊹ CONNECT TO
### CHEMICAL REACTIONS

6. A water molecule is added to an ATP molecule to break ATP down into ADP and a phosphate group. Write the chemical equation for this reaction.

# 4.2 Overview of Photosynthesis

SC.912.L.18.7

**KEY CONCEPT** **The overall process of photosynthesis produces sugars that store chemical energy.**

## VOCABULARY

photosynthesis
chlorophyll
thylakoid
light-dependent reactions
light-independent reactions

**SC.912.L.18.7** Identify the reactants, products, and basic functions of photosynthesis.

### MAIN IDEAS

○ Photosynthetic organisms are producers.
○ Photosynthesis in plants occurs in chloroplasts.

### Connect to Your World

Solar-powered calculators, homes, and cars are just a few things that use energy from sunlight. In a way, you are also solar-powered. Of course, sunlight does not directly give you the energy you need to play a sport or read this page. That energy comes from ATP. Molecules of ATP are often made from the breakdown of sugars, but how are sugars made? Plants capture some of the energy in sunlight and change it into chemical energy stored in sugars.

### ○ MAIN IDEA

## Photosynthetic organisms are producers.

Some organisms are called producers because they produce the source of chemical energy for themselves and for other organisms. Plants, as well as some bacteria and protists, are the producers that are the main sources of chemical energy for most organisms on Earth. Certainly, animals that eat only plants obtain their chemical energy directly from plants. Animals that eat other animals, and bacteria and fungi that decompose other organisms, get their chemical energy indirectly from plants. When a wolf eats a rabbit, the tissues of the rabbit provide the wolf with a source of chemical energy. The rabbit's tissues are built from its food source—the sugars and other carbon-based molecules in plants. These sugars are made through photosynthesis.

**Photosynthesis** is a process that captures energy from sunlight to make sugars that store chemical energy. Therefore, directly or indirectly, the energy for almost all organisms begins as sunlight. Sunlight includes a wide range of radiant energy, such as ultraviolet radiation, microwaves, and the visible light that lets you see. Plants absorb visible light for photosynthesis. Visible light appears white, but it is made up of several colors, or wavelengths, of light.

**Chlorophyll** (KLAWR-uh-fihl) is a molecule in chloroplasts, shown in **FIGURE 2.1,** that absorbs some of the energy in visible light. Plants have two main types of chlorophyll, called chlorophyll *a* and chlorophyll *b*. Together, these two types of chlorophyll absorb mostly red and blue wavelengths of visible light. Neither type absorbs much green light. Plants have other light-absorbing molecules that absorb green light, but there are fewer of these molecules. As a result, the green color of plants comes from the reflection of light's green wavelengths by chlorophyll.

**Apply** **Describe the importance of producers and photosynthesis.**

**FIGURE 2.1** Chloroplasts in plant cells contain a light-absorbing molecule called chlorophyll. (leaf cell: colored TEM; magnification 4000×)

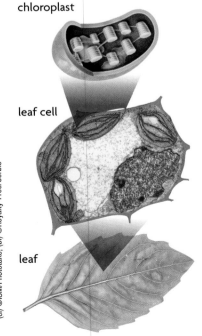

chloroplast

leaf cell

leaf

(cl) ©ISM/Phototake; (bl) ©Royalty-Free/Corbis

## ▶ MAIN IDEA

# Photosynthesis in plants occurs in chloroplasts.

Chloroplasts are the membrane-bound organelles where photosynthesis takes place in plants. Most of the chloroplasts are in leaf cells that are specialized for photosynthesis, which has two main stages as shown in **FIGURE 2.2**. The two main parts of chloroplasts needed for photosynthesis are the grana and the stroma. Grana (singular, *granum*) are stacks of coin-shaped, membrane-enclosed compartments called **thylakoids** (THY-luh-ĸoyDz). The membranes of the thylakoids contain chlorophyll, other light-absorbing molecules, and proteins. The stroma is the fluid that surrounds the grana inside a chloroplast.

## FIGURE 2.2 Photosynthesis Overview

Chloroplasts absorb energy from sunlight and produce sugars through the process of photosynthesis.

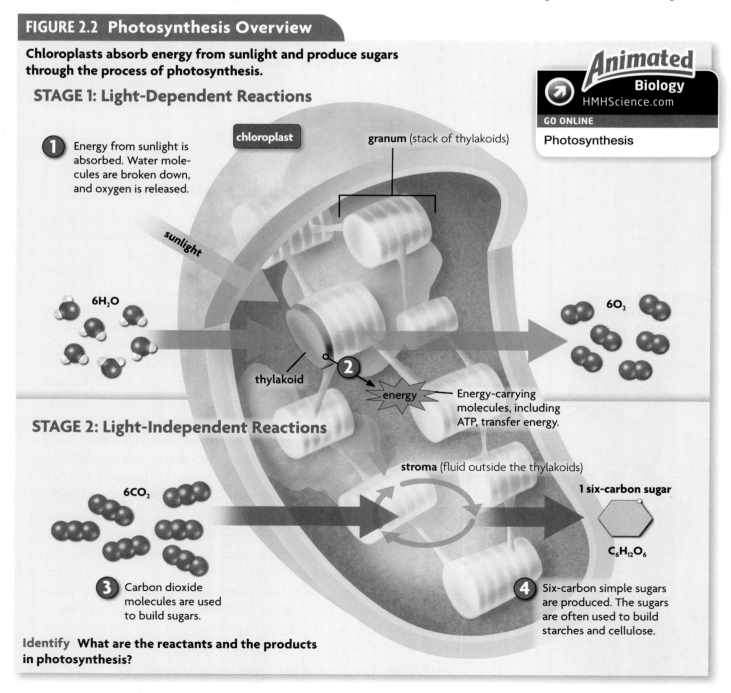

### STAGE 1: Light-Dependent Reactions

**Animated Biology**
HMHScience.com
GO ONLINE
Photosynthesis

chloroplast

**granum** (stack of thylakoids)

1 Energy from sunlight is absorbed. Water molecules are broken down, and oxygen is released.

sunlight

$6H_2O$

$6O_2$

thylakoid

2 energy — Energy-carrying molecules, including ATP, transfer energy.

### STAGE 2: Light-Independent Reactions

**stroma** (fluid outside the thylakoids)

**1 six-carbon sugar**

$6CO_2$

$C_6H_{12}O_6$

3 Carbon dioxide molecules are used to build sugars.

4 Six-carbon simple sugars are produced. The sugars are often used to build starches and cellulose.

**Identify** What are the reactants and the products in photosynthesis?

The **light-dependent reactions** capture energy from sunlight. These reactions take place within and across the membrane of the thylakoids. Water ($H_2O$) and sunlight are needed for this stage of photosynthesis.

**1** Chlorophyll absorbs energy from sunlight. The energy is transferred along the thylakoid membrane. Water molecules ($H_2O$) are broken down. Oxygen molecules ($O_2$) are released.

**2** Energy carried along the thylakoid membrane is transferred to molecules that carry energy, such as ATP.

The **light-independent reactions** use energy from the light-dependent reactions to make sugars. These reactions occur in the stroma of chloroplasts. Carbon dioxide molecules ($CO_2$) are needed during this stage of photosynthesis.

**3** $CO_2$ is added to a cycle of chemical reactions to build larger molecules. Energy from the light-dependent reactions is used in the reactions.

**4** A molecule of a simple sugar is formed. The sugar, usually glucose ($C_6H_{12}O_6$), stores some of the energy that was captured from sunlight.

The equation for the whole photosynthesis process is shown below. As you can see, there are many arrows between the reactants—$CO_2$ and $H_2O$—and the products—a six-carbon sugar and $O_2$. Those arrows tell you that photosynthesis has many steps. For example, the light-independent reactions need only one molecule of $CO_2$ at a time, and the six-carbon sugar comes from a reaction that combines two three-carbon sugars. Also, enzymes and other chemicals are needed, not just light, carbon dioxide, and water.

$$6CO_2 \;+\; 6H_2O \longrightarrow \rightarrow \rightarrow \rightarrow \rightarrow \rightarrow C_6H_{12}O_6 \;+\; 6O_2$$

| carbon dioxide | water | light, enzymes | a sugar | oxygen |

Glucose and other simple sugars, such as fructose, are not the only carbohydrates that come from photosynthesis. Plants need the simple sugars to build starch and cellulose molecules. In effect, plants need photosynthesis for their growth and development. You will learn more about the importance of another product of photosynthesis—oxygen—in Sections 4 and 5.

**Summarize**  **How is energy from sunlight used to make sugar molecules?**

> **CONNECT TO**
> **CALVIN CYCLE**
> The light-independent reactions include a series of chemical reactions called the Calvin cycle. You can read more about the Calvin cycle in **Section 3.**

## 4.2 Formative Assessment

**REVIEWING ▶ MAIN IDEAS**

1. What are the roles of chloroplasts and **chlorophyll** in **photosynthesis**?

2. Describe the stages of photosynthesis. Use the terms **thylakoid, light-dependent reactions,** and **light-independent reactions** in your answer.

**CRITICAL THINKING**

3. **Apply**  Suppose you wanted to develop a light to help increase plant growth. What characteristics should the light have? Why?

4. **Analyze**  Explain why photosynthesis is important for building the structure of plant cells.

> **CONNECT TO**
> **CHEMICAL REACTIONS**
> 5. Overall, do you think photosynthesis is endothermic or exothermic? Explain your answer.

# Artificial Photosynthesis

As the world population and demand for energy increase, the reserves of fossil fuels are being depleted. The development of power from alternative energy sources such as wind, water, and the sun has helped slow the depletion of fossil fuels. However, these renewable energy sources haven't replaced fossil fuels. And as coal, oil, and natural gas are burned to release needed energy, they also release carbon dioxide. Increasing amounts of carbon dioxide in the atmosphere are implicated in Earth's climate change.

To help address the twin problems of decreasing fossil fuel reserves and increasing carbon dioxide emissions, scientists are attempting to do what plants and other green organisms have been doing for billions of years—convert solar energy into chemical energy. In nature, plants capture energy from sunlight in chlorophyll molecules within the chloroplasts. The solar energy is used to transfer electrons from water molecules to carbon dioxide molecules, reducing the carbon dioxide and storing the energy in the chemical bonds of a fuel. In plant photosynthesis, that fuel is a carbohydrate, glucose. Oxygen also forms.

Researchers in Berkeley, California, have made important advances in the field of artificial photosynthesis using nanotechnology to mimic natural photosynthesis. Unlike the process in plants that uses chlorophyll, artificial photosynthesis uses a membrane of semiconducting nanowires to harness solar energy. Bacteria embedded in the membrane use this solar energy to convert carbon dioxide and water into acetate rather than glucose. Acetate is a chemical building block that scientists use to make more-complex molecules that make up biodegradable plastics, medicines, and even fuels. For example, the Berkeley scientists have produced methane, $CH_4$, the main component of natural gas.

The basis of their artificial photosynthesis system is an array of silicon and titanium oxide nanowires that functions much like a chloroplast. The structure of the wire array protects oxygen-sensitive bacteria that are embedded among the wires in the membrane. When the wires absorb solar energy, light-excited electrons are generated. The electrons are delivered to the bacteria, which use them to reduce carbon dioxide and combine it with water molecules to make acetate and oxygen. Once acetate has formed, other bacteria that have been genetically engineered for the process are used to synthesize desired chemical products such as fuels.

The same group of scientists has achieved a more recent breakthrough. They have now developed a new hybrid system with nanowires that are made of different materials. These materials also harness solar energy and use it to split water molecules into oxygen and hydrogen molecules. This process is called the hydrogen evolution reaction (HER). Then the hydrogen is passed to bacteria that use it to reduce carbon dioxide to methane. Since most of the methane currently used comes from natural gas, this new ability to generate methane from a renewable hydrogen source may decrease our reliance on fossil fuels in the future.

The diagram below summarizes the new process, a form of solar-to-chemical conversion similar to photosynthesis. After the membrane made of semiconductor nanowires absorbs solar energy, the energy is used to split water molecules, generating hydrogen gas. Then, bacteria in the membrane combine the hydrogen produced in the HER with carbon dioxide from the atmosphere to produce methane.

The new system has two advantages over the scientists' original system. First, hydrogen molecules, rather than electrons, are used as the energy carrier. This approach opens up the possibility that carbon dioxide fixation can use hydrogen from other sustainable sources, such as wind, hydrothermal, or nuclear energy. Second, now that scientists know that one species of bacteria can use renewable hydrogen, they can expand their search to find other organisms and use them in the production of other valuable chemical products.

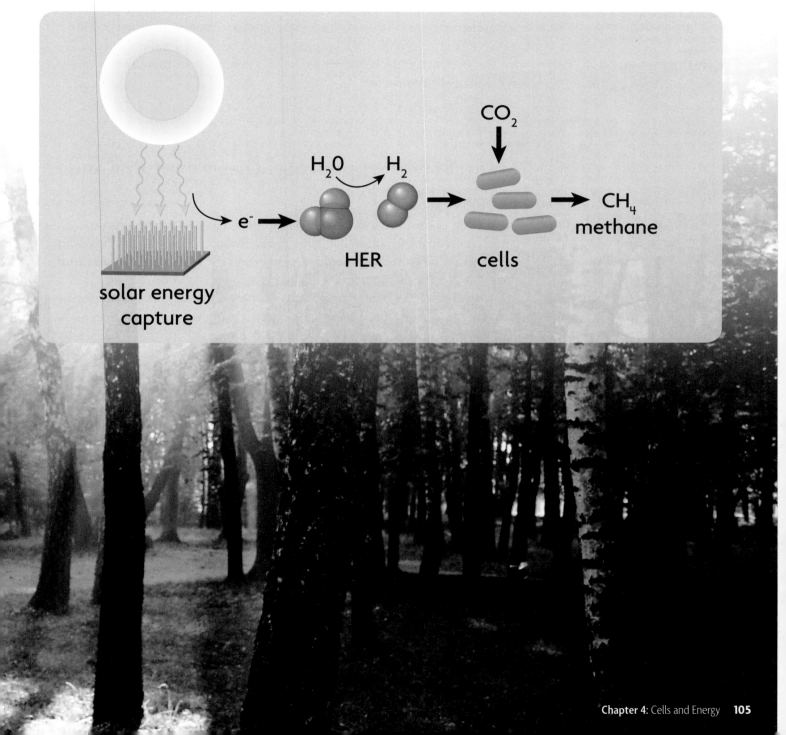

# 4.3 Photosynthesis in Detail

SC.912.L.14.7,
SC.912.L.18.7

SC.912.L.14.7 Relate the structure of each of the major plant organs and tissues to physiological processes.

SC.912.L.18.7 Identify the reactants, products, and basic functions of photosynthesis.

**VOCABULARY**

photosystem
electron transport chain
ATP synthase
Calvin cycle

**KEY CONCEPT** **Photosynthesis requires a series of chemical reactions.**

**MAIN IDEAS**

- The first stage of photosynthesis captures and transfers energy.
- The second stage of photosynthesis uses energy from the first stage to make sugars.

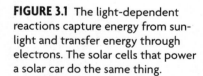 **Connect to Your World**

In a way, the sugar-producing cells in leaves are like tiny factories with assembly lines. In a factory, different workers with separate jobs have to work together to put together a finished product. Similarly, in photosynthesis many different chemical reactions, enzymes, and ions work together in a precise order to make the sugars that are the finished product.

## ▶ MAIN IDEA

# The first stage of photosynthesis captures and transfers energy.

In Section 2, you read a summary of photosynthesis. However, the process is much more involved than that general description might suggest. For example, during the light-dependent reactions, light energy is captured and transferred in the thylakoid membranes by two groups of molecules called **photosystems.** The two photosystems are called photosystem I and photosystem II.

### Overview of the Light-Dependent Reactions

The light-dependent reactions are the *photo-* part of photosynthesis. During the light-dependent reactions, chlorophyll and other light-absorbing molecules capture energy from sunlight. Water molecules are broken down into hydrogen ions, electrons, and oxygen gas. The oxygen is given off as a waste product. Sugars are not made during this part of photosynthesis.

The main functions of the light-dependent reactions are to capture and transfer energy. In these reactions, as in the solar car in **FIGURE 3.1,** energy is transferred to electrons. The electrons are only used for energy in a few specific processes. Recall a time when you went to an amusement park. To go on rides, you needed special tickets that could be used only there. Similarly, the electrons are used for energy during photosynthesis but not for the cell's general energy needs.

Energy from the electrons is used to make molecules that act as energy carriers. These energy carriers are ATP and another molecule called NADPH. The ATP from the light-dependent reactions is usually not used for a cell's general energy needs. In this case, ATP molecules, along with NADPH molecules, go on to later stages of photosynthesis.

**FIGURE 3.1** The light-dependent reactions capture energy from sunlight and transfer energy through electrons. The solar cells that power a solar car do the same thing.

©Stefano Paltera/North American Solar Challenge

## Photosystem II and Electron Transport

In photosystem II, chlorophyll and other light-absorbing molecules in the thylakoid membrane absorb energy from sunlight. The energy is transferred to electrons. As shown in **FIGURE 3.2**, photosystem II needs water to function.

**1** **Energy absorbed from sunlight** Chlorophyll and other light-absorbing molecules in the thylakoid membrane absorb energy from sunlight. The energy is transferred to electrons (e⁻). High-energy electrons leave the chlorophyll and enter an **electron transport chain,** which is a series of proteins in the membrane of the thylakoid.

**2** **Water molecules split** Enzymes break down water molecules. Oxygen, hydrogen ions (H⁺), and electrons are separated from each other. The oxygen is released as waste. The electrons from water replace those electrons that left chlorophyll when energy from sunlight was absorbed.

**3** **Hydrogen ions transported** Electrons move from protein to protein in the electron transport chain. Their energy is used to pump H⁺ ions from outside to inside the thylakoid against a concentration gradient. The H⁺ ions build up inside the thylakoid. Electrons move on to photosystem I.

## Photosystem I and Energy-Carrying Molecules

In photosystem I, chlorophyll and other light-absorbing molecules in the thylakoid membrane also absorb energy from sunlight. The energy is added to electrons, some of which enter photosystem I from photosystem II.

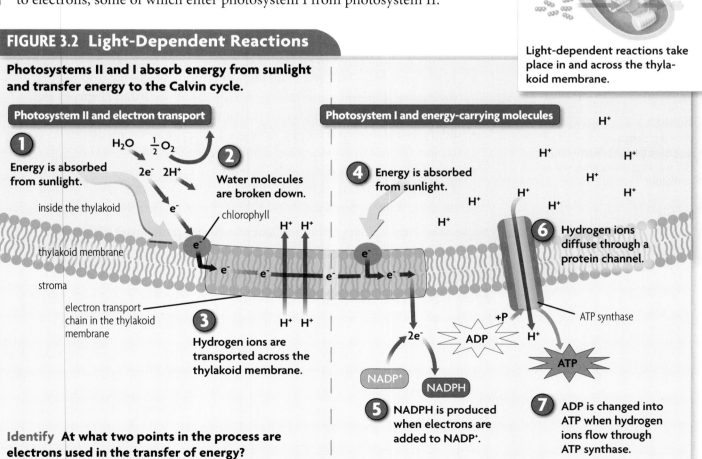

Light-dependent reactions take place in and across the thylakoid membrane.

## FIGURE 3.2 Light-Dependent Reactions

**Photosystems II and I absorb energy from sunlight and transfer energy to the Calvin cycle.**

**Photosystem II and electron transport**

**1** Energy is absorbed from sunlight.

$H_2O$  $\frac{1}{2}O_2$

$2e^-$  $2H^+$

**2** Water molecules are broken down.

inside the thylakoid

chlorophyll

thylakoid membrane

$e^-$

stroma

electron transport chain in the thylakoid membrane

$H^+$  $H^+$

**3** Hydrogen ions are transported across the thylakoid membrane.

$H^+$  $H^+$

**Photosystem I and energy-carrying molecules**

**4** Energy is absorbed from sunlight.

$H^+$  $H^+$  $H^+$  $H^+$  $H^+$  $H^+$  $H^+$  $H^+$  $H^+$

**6** Hydrogen ions diffuse through a protein channel.

ATP synthase

$2e^-$  ADP  +P  $H^+$

NADP⁺  NADPH

ATP

**5** NADPH is produced when electrons are added to NADP⁺.

**7** ADP is changed into ATP when hydrogen ions flow through ATP synthase.

**Identify** At what two points in the process are electrons used in the transfer of energy?

**4** **Energy absorbed from sunlight** As in photosystem II, chlorophyll and other light-absorbing molecules inside the thylakoid membrane absorb energy from sunlight. Electrons are energized and leave the molecules.

**5** **NADPH produced** The energized electrons are added to a molecule called NADP$^+$, forming a molecule called NADPH. In photosynthesis, NADP$^+$ functions like ADP, and NADPH functions like ATP. The molecules of NADPH go to the light-independent reactions.

### ATP Production

The final part of the light-dependent reactions makes ATP. The production of ATP depends on the H$^+$ ions that build up inside the thylakoid from photosystem II, and on a complex enzyme in the thylakoid membrane.

**6** **Hydrogen ion diffusion** Hydrogen ions flow through a protein channel in the thylakoid membrane. Recall that the concentration of H$^+$ ions is higher inside the thylakoid than it is outside. This difference in H$^+$ ion concentration is called a chemiosmotic gradient, which stores potential energy. Therefore, the ions flow through the channel by diffusion.

**7** **ATP produced** The protein channel in Step 6 is part of a complex enzyme called **ATP synthase,** shown in **FIGURE 3.3.** As the ions flow through the channel, ATP synthase makes ATP by adding phosphate groups to ADP.

### Summary of the Light-Dependent Reactions

- Energy is captured from sunlight by light-absorbing molecules. The energy is transferred to electrons that enter an electron transport chain.
- Water molecules are broken down into H$^+$ ions, electrons, and oxygen molecules. The water molecules provide the H$^+$ ions and electrons that are used in the light-dependent reactions.
- Energized electrons have two functions. They provide energy for H$^+$ ion transport, and they are added to NADP$^+$ to form NADPH.
- The flow of H$^+$ ions through ATP synthase makes ATP.
- The products are oxygen, NADPH, and ATP. Oxygen is given off as a waste product. Energy from ATP and NADPH is used later to make sugars.

**Summarize** **How is energy from sunlight transferred to ATP and NADPH?**

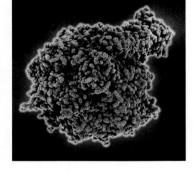

**FIGURE 3.3** Scientists have made detailed computer models of ATP synthase (above). Scientists are still working on viewing the actual molecule.

⊙ MAIN IDEA

# The second stage of photosynthesis uses energy from the first stage to make sugars.

The light-independent reactions, like the light-dependent reactions, take place inside chloroplasts. But as the name implies, the light-independent reactions do not need sunlight. These reactions can take place anytime that energy is available. The energy sources for the light-independent reactions are the molecules of ATP and NADPH formed during the light-dependent reactions. The energy is needed for a series of chemical reactions called the Calvin cycle, which is named for the scientist who discovered the process.

## The Calvin Cycle

The Calvin cycle cannot take place without the ATP and NADPH from the light-dependent reactions. The chemical reactions of the **Calvin cycle** use carbon dioxide ($CO_2$) gas from the atmosphere and the energy carried by ATP and NADPH to make simple sugars. Because the light-independent reactions build sugar molecules, they are the *synthesis* part of photosynthesis. Only one molecule of $CO_2$ is actually added to the Calvin cycle at a time. The simplified cycle in **FIGURE 3.4** shows three $CO_2$ molecules added at once.

**READING** TOOLBOX

**VOCABULARY**
The light-dependent reactions are the *photo-* part of photosynthesis. The light-independent reactions are the *synthesis* part of photosynthesis.

**1** **Carbon dioxide added** $CO_2$ molecules are added to five-carbon molecules already in the Calvin cycle. Six-carbon molecules are formed.

**2** **Three-carbon molecules formed** Energy—ATP and NADPH—from the light-dependent reactions is used by enzymes to split the six-carbon molecules. Three-carbon molecules are formed and rearranged.

**3** **Three-carbon molecules exit** Most of the three-carbon molecules stay in the Calvin cycle, but one high-energy three-carbon molecule leaves the cycle. After two three-carbon molecules have left the cycle, they are bonded together to build a six-carbon sugar molecule such as glucose.

**4** **Three-carbon molecules recycled** Energy from ATP molecules is used to change the three-carbon molecules back into five-carbon molecules. The five-carbon molecules stay in the Calvin cycle. These molecules are added to new $CO_2$ molecules that enter the cycle.

## FIGURE 3.4 Light-Independent Reactions (Calvin Cycle)

The Calvin cycle produces sugars.

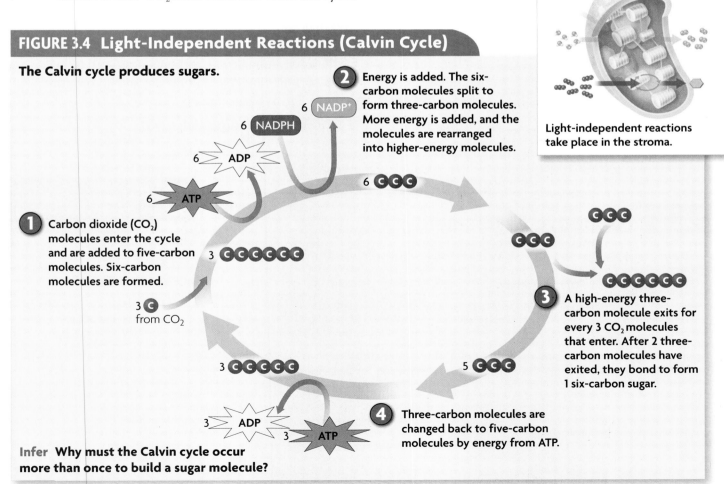

**2** Energy is added. The six-carbon molecules split to form three-carbon molecules. More energy is added, and the molecules are rearranged into higher-energy molecules.

Light-independent reactions take place in the stroma.

**1** Carbon dioxide ($CO_2$) molecules enter the cycle and are added to five-carbon molecules. Six-carbon molecules are formed.

**3** A high-energy three-carbon molecule exits for every 3 $CO_2$ molecules that enter. After 2 three-carbon molecules have exited, they bond to form 1 six-carbon sugar.

**4** Three-carbon molecules are changed back to five-carbon molecules by energy from ATP.

**Infer** Why must the Calvin cycle occur more than once to build a sugar molecule?

## Summary of the Light-Independent Reactions

- Carbon dioxide enters the Calvin cycle.
- ATP and NADPH from the light-dependent reactions transfer energy to the Calvin cycle and keep the cycle going.
- One high-energy three-carbon molecule is made for every three molecules of carbon dioxide that enter the cycle.
- Two high-energy three-carbon molecules are bonded together to make a sugar. Therefore, six molecules of carbon dioxide must be added to the Calvin cycle to make one six-carbon sugar.
- The products are a six-carbon sugar such as glucose, NADP⁺, and ADP. The NADP⁺ and ADP molecules return to the light-dependent reactions.

## Functions of Photosynthesis

Photosynthesis is much more than just a biochemical process. Photosynthesis is important to most organisms on Earth, as well as to Earth's environment. Recall that plants produce food for themselves and for other organisms through photosynthesis. Both plant cells and animal cells release the energy stored in sugars through cellular respiration. Cellular respiration, which uses the oxygen that is a waste product of photosynthesis, is the process that makes most of the ATP used by plant and animal cells.

Photosynthesis does more than make sugars. It also provides materials for plant growth and development. The simple sugars from photosynthesis are bonded together to form complex carbohydrates such as starch and cellulose. Starches store sugars until they are needed for energy. Cellulose is a major part of plant structure—it is the building block of plant cell walls. Photosynthesis also helps to regulate Earth's environment. The carbon atoms used to make sugar molecules come from carbon dioxide gas in the air, so photosynthesis removes carbon dioxide from Earth's atmosphere.

**Summarize**  How does the Calvin cycle build sugar molecules?

**That's Amazing!**
**Video Inquiry**
HMHScience.com
**GO ONLINE**
Lungs of the Planet

**CONNECT TO**
**ECOLOGY**
Photosynthesis is a major part of the carbon cycle. You will learn more about the carbon cycle in the chapter **Principles of Ecology.**

---

## 4.3  Formative Assessment

**SELF-CHECK Online**
HMHScience.com
**GO ONLINE**

### REVIEWING ▶ MAIN IDEAS

1. How do the two **photosystems** work together to capture energy from sunlight?

2. Explain the relationship between the light-dependent and the light-independent reactions.

### CRITICAL THINKING

3. **Connect**  Explain how the **Calvin cycle** is a bridge between carbon in the atmosphere and carbon-based molecules in the food you eat.

4. **Evaluate**  Explain why the chemical equation for photosynthesis is a simplified representation of the process. How is the equation accurate? How is it inaccurate?

### CONNECT TO
### CELL FUNCTIONS

5. Explain how both passive transport and active transport are necessary for photosynthesis to occur.

# 4.4 Overview of Cellular Respiration

SC.912.L.18.8

**KEY CONCEPT** The overall process of cellular respiration converts sugar into ATP using oxygen.

### VOCABULARY

cellular respiration
aerobic
glycolysis
anaerobic
Krebs cycle

**SC.912.L.18.8** Identify the reactants, products, and basic functions of aerobic and anaerobic cellular respiration.

**MAIN IDEAS**
- Cellular respiration makes ATP by breaking down sugars.
- Cellular respiration is like a mirror image of photosynthesis.

### Connect to Your World

The term *cellular respiration* may lead you to form a mental picture of cells breathing. This image is not correct, but it is useful to remember. Your cells need the oxygen that you take in when you breathe. That oxygen helps your body release the energy in sugars and other carbon-based molecules. Indirectly, your breathing is connected to the ATP that your cells need for everything you do.

### ▶ MAIN IDEA

## Cellular respiration makes ATP by breaking down sugars.

Plants use photosynthesis to make their own food. Animals eat other organisms as food. But food is not a direct source of energy. Instead, plants, animals, and other eukaryotes break down molecules from food to produce ATP. **Cellular respiration** releases chemical energy from sugars and other carbon-based molecules to make ATP when oxygen is present. Cellular respiration is an **aerobic** (air-OH-bihk) process, meaning that it needs oxygen to take place. Cellular respiration takes place in mitochondria, which are often called the cell's "powerhouses" because they make most of a cell's ATP.

A mitochondrion, shown in **FIGURE 4.1,** cannot directly make ATP from food. First, foods are broken down into smaller molecules such as glucose. Then, glucose is broken down, as shown below. **Glycolysis** (gly-KAHL-uh-sihs) splits glucose into two three-carbon molecules and makes two molecules of ATP. Glycolysis takes place in a cell's cytoplasm and does not need oxygen. Glycolysis is an **anaerobic** process because it does not need oxygen to take place. However, glycolysis is necessary for cellular respiration. The products of glycolysis are broken down in mitochondria to make many more ATP.

mitochondrion

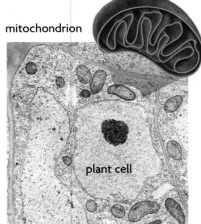

**FIGURE 4.1** Mitochondria, found in both plant and animal cells, produce ATP through cellular respiration. (colored TEM; magnification 7000×)

plant cell

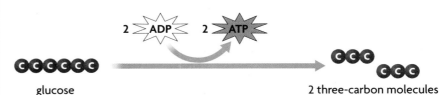

2 ADP      2 ATP

glucose          2 three-carbon molecules

**Explain** What is the function of cellular respiration?

> **MAIN IDEA**

# Cellular respiration is like a mirror image of photosynthesis.

**CONNECT TO**

**PHOTOSYNTHESIS**

Review the overall process of photosynthesis in **Section 2**, and compare photosynthesis to cellular respiration.

Photosynthesis and cellular respiration are not true opposites, but you can think about them in that way. For example, chloroplasts absorb energy from sunlight and build sugars. Mitochondria release chemical energy to make ATP. The chemical equation of cellular respiration is also basically the reverse of photosynthesis. But the structures of chloroplasts and mitochondria are similar. A mitochondrion is surrounded by a membrane. It has two parts that are involved in cellular respiration: the matrix and the inner mitochondrial membrane. In mitochondria, cellular respiration takes place in two main stages, as shown in **FIGURE 4.2**.

## FIGURE 4.2  Cellular Respiration Overview

**When oxygen is available, ATP is produced by cellular respiration in mitochondria.**

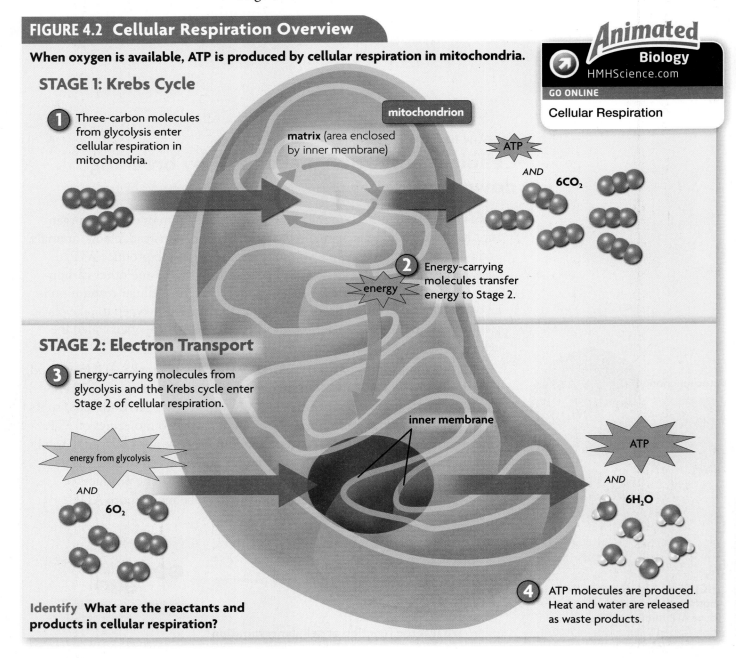

### STAGE 1: Krebs Cycle

**1** Three-carbon molecules from glycolysis enter cellular respiration in mitochondria.

**mitochondrion**

**matrix** (area enclosed by inner membrane)

ATP AND $6CO_2$

**2** Energy-carrying molecules transfer energy to Stage 2.

energy

### STAGE 2: Electron Transport

**3** Energy-carrying molecules from glycolysis and the Krebs cycle enter Stage 2 of cellular respiration.

energy from glycolysis AND $6O_2$

inner membrane

ATP AND $6H_2O$

**4** ATP molecules are produced. Heat and water are released as waste products.

**Identify** What are the reactants and products in cellular respiration?

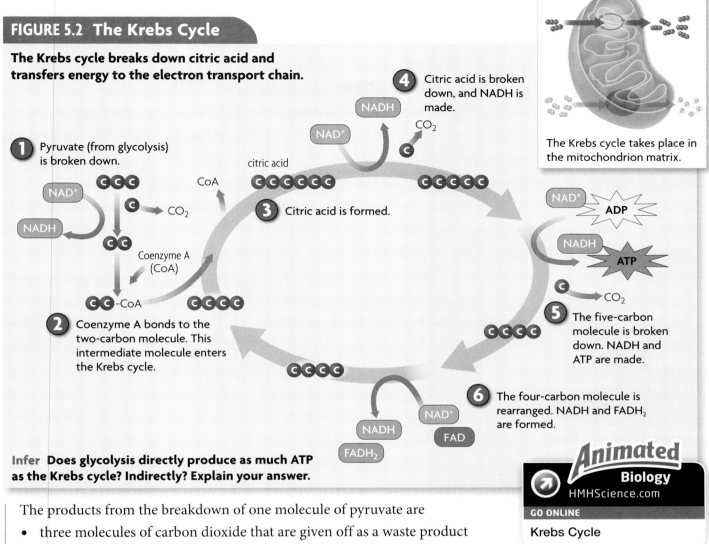

## FIGURE 5.2 The Krebs Cycle

**The Krebs cycle breaks down citric acid and transfers energy to the electron transport chain.**

**1** Pyruvate (from glycolysis) is broken down.

NAD⁺

NADH

CoA

$CO_2$

**2** Coenzyme A bonds to the two-carbon molecule. This intermediate molecule enters the Krebs cycle.

Coenzyme A (CoA)

-CoA

citric acid

**3** Citric acid is formed.

NAD⁺

NADH

**4** Citric acid is broken down, and NADH is made.

$CO_2$

The Krebs cycle takes place in the mitochondrion matrix.

NAD⁺    ADP

NADH    ATP

$CO_2$

**5** The five-carbon molecule is broken down. NADH and ATP are made.

**6** The four-carbon molecule is rearranged. NADH and $FADH_2$ are formed.

NADH

$FADH_2$

NAD⁺

FAD

**Infer** Does glycolysis directly produce as much ATP as the Krebs cycle? Indirectly? Explain your answer.

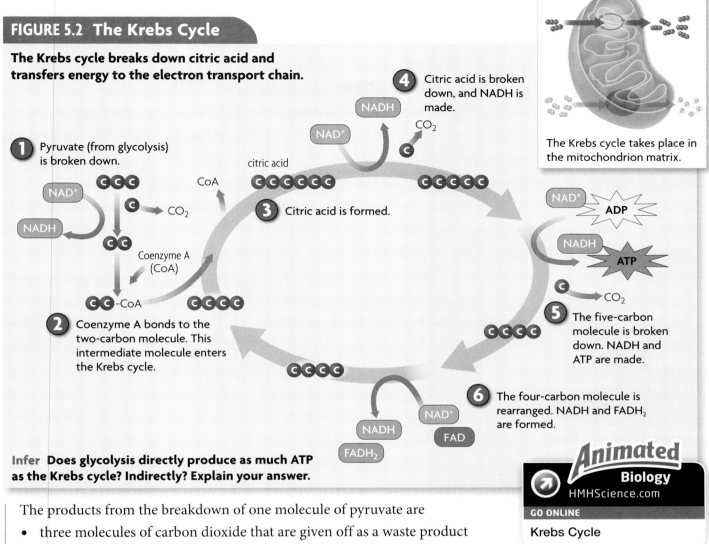

**Animated Biology**
HMHScience.com

**GO ONLINE**

Krebs Cycle

The products from the breakdown of one molecule of pyruvate are

- three molecules of carbon dioxide that are given off as a waste product
- one molecule of ATP
- four molecules of NADH to the electron transport chain
- one molecule of $FADH_2$ to the electron transport chain

Remember, glycolysis produces two pyruvate molecules. Therefore, the products above are half of what comes from one glucose molecule. The totals are six carbon dioxide, two ATP, eight NADH, and two $FADH_2$ molecules.

**Analyze** How are the products of the Krebs cycle important for making ATP?

**▶ MAIN IDEA**

# The electron transport chain is the second main part of cellular respiration.

The electron transport chain takes place in and across the inner membrane of a mitochondrion. As with electron transport in photosynthesis, proteins make up the electron transport chain in cellular respiration. The proteins use energy from the electrons supplied by NADH and $FADH_2$ to pump hydrogen ions against a concentration gradient and across the inner mitochondrial membrane.

The ions later flow back through the membrane to produce ATP. Oxygen is needed at the end of the process to pick up electrons that have gone through the chain. The electron transport chain is shown in **FIGURE 5.3.**

**1** **Electrons removed** Proteins inside the inner membrane of the mito-chondrion take high-energy electrons from NADH and FADH$_2$. Two molecules of NADH and one molecule of FADH$_2$ are used.

**2** **Hydrogen ions transported** High-energy electrons travel through the proteins in the electron transport chain. The proteins use energy from the electrons to pump hydrogen ions across the inner membrane to produce a chemiosmotic gradient, just as in photosynthesis. The hydro-gen ions build up outside of the inner mitochondrial membrane.

**3** **ATP produced** Just as in photosynthesis, the flow of hydrogen ions is used to make ATP. Hydrogen ions diffuse through a protein channel in the inner membrane of the mitochondrion. The channel is part of the ATP synthase enzyme. ATP synthase adds phosphate groups to ADP to make ATP molecules. For each pair of electrons that passes through the electron transport chain, an average of three ATP molecules are made.

**4** **Water formed** Oxygen finally enters the cellular respiration process. The oxygen picks up electrons and hydrogen ions to form water. The water molecules are given off as a waste product.

**Animated**
**Biology**
HMHScience.com
**GO ONLINE**
Electronic Transport Chain

## FIGURE 5.3  The Electron Transport Chain

**Energy from the Krebs cycle is used to produce ATP.**

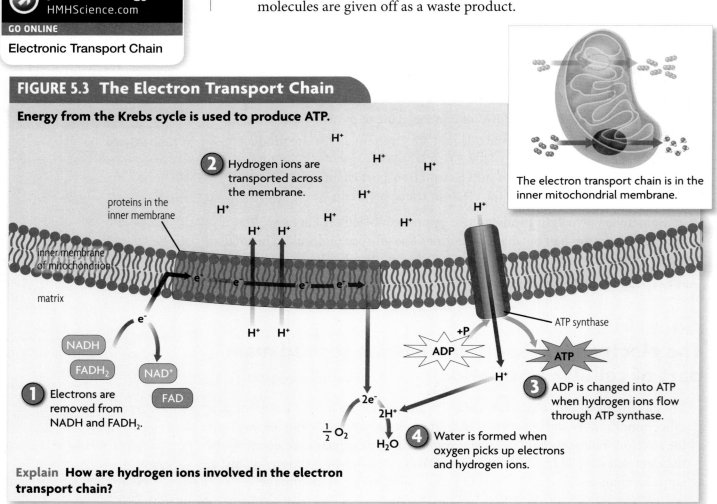

**2** Hydrogen ions are transported across the membrane.

proteins in the inner membrane

inner membrane of mitochondrion

matrix

NADH
FADH$_2$
NAD$^+$
FAD

**1** Electrons are removed from NADH and FADH$_2$.

$\frac{1}{2}$ O$_2$

2e$^-$
2H$^+$
H$_2$O

**4** Water is formed when oxygen picks up electrons and hydrogen ions.

+P
ADP
ATP

ATP synthase

**3** ADP is changed into ATP when hydrogen ions flow through ATP synthase.

The electron transport chain is in the inner mitochondrial membrane.

**Explain  How are hydrogen ions involved in the electron transport chain?**

The products of cellular respiration—including glycolysis—are

- Carbon dioxide from the Krebs cycle and from the breakdown of pyruvate before the Krebs cycle
- Water from the electron transport chain
- A net gain of up to 38 ATP molecules for every glucose molecule— 2 from glycolysis, 2 from the Krebs cycle, and up to 34 from the electron transport chain

## Comparing Cellular Respiration and Photosynthesis

Again, think about how photosynthesis and cellular respiration are approximately the reverse of each other. Photosynthesis stores energy from sunlight as chemical energy. In contrast, cellular respiration releases stored energy as ATP and heat. Look at **FIGURE 5.5**, and think about other similarities and differences between the processes.

| FIGURE 5.5 PHOTOSYNTHESIS AND CELLULAR RESPIRATION | | |
|---|---|---|
| | **PHOTOSYNTHESIS** | **CELLULAR RESPIRATION** |
| **Organelle for process** | chloroplast | mitochondrion |
| **Reactants** | $CO_2$ and $H_2O$ | sugars ($C_6H_{12}O_6$) and $O_2$ |
| **Electron transport chain** | proteins within thylakoid membrane | proteins within inner mitochondrial membrane |
| **Cycle of chemical reactions** | Calvin cycle in stroma of chloroplasts builds sugar molecules | Krebs cycle in matrix of mitochondria breaks down carbon-based molecules |
| **Products** | sugars ($C_6H_{12}O_6$) and $O_2$ | $CO_2$ and $H_2O$ |

**FIGURE 5.4** Like sandbags passed down a line of people, high-energy electrons are passed along a chain of proteins in the inner mitochondrial membrane.

Animated
**Biology**
HMHScience.com
GO ONLINE

**Mirror Processes**

Recall the roles of electrons, hydrogen ions, and ATP synthase. In both processes, high-energy electrons are transported through proteins. Their energy is used to pump hydrogen ions across a membrane. And the flow of hydrogen ions through ATP synthase produces ATP. As you can see, the parts of the processes are very similar, but their end points are very different.

**Analyze** How does the electron transport chain depend on the Krebs cycle?

SELF-CHECK Online
HMHScience.com
GO ONLINE

# 4.5 Formative Assessment

### REVIEWING ▶ MAIN IDEAS

1. What is the role of pyruvate in cellular respiration?
2. Describe in your own words the function of the Krebs cycle.
3. Explain the functions of electrons, hydrogen ions, and oxygen in the electron transport chain.

### CRITICAL THINKING

4. **Compare** Describe the relationship between cellular respiration and photosynthesis in terms of energy and matter.
5. **Evaluate** Is oxygen necessary for the production of all ATP in your cells? Why or why not?

### CONNECT TO

### COMMON ANCESTRY

6. Protein molecules called cytochromes are part of the electron transport chain. They are nearly identical in every known aerobic organism. How do these molecules show the unity of life on Earth?

©AP/Wide World Photos

# Fermentation

**VOCABULARY**

fermentation
lactic acid

**KEY CONCEPT** Fermentation allows the production of a small amount of ATP without oxygen.

**MAIN IDEAS**

- Fermentation allows glycolysis to continue.
- Fermentation and its products are important in several ways.

**SC.912.L.18.8** Identify the reactants, products, and basic functions of aerobic and anaerobic cellular respiration.

## Connect to Your World

Think about a time when you worked or exercised hard. Maybe you moved heavy boxes or furniture. Maybe, playing basketball, you found yourself repeatedly running up and down the court. Your arms and legs began to feel heavy, and they seemed to lose strength. Your muscles became sore, and even when you rested you kept breathing hard. Your muscles were using fermentation.

## ▶ MAIN IDEA

## Fermentation allows glycolysis to continue.

The cells in your body cannot store large amounts of oxygen for cellular respiration. The amount of oxygen that is provided by breathing is enough for your cells during normal activities. When you are reading or talking to friends, your body can maintain its oxygen levels. When you are doing high levels of activity, as the sprinter is in **FIGURE 6.1,** your body cannot bring in enough oxygen for your cells, even though you breathe faster. How do your cells function without enough oxygen to keep cellular respiration going?

Recall that glycolysis yields two ATP molecules when it splits glucose into two molecules of pyruvate. Glycolysis is always occurring and does not require oxygen. If oxygen is available, the products of glycolysis—pyruvate and the electron carrier NADH—are used in cellular respiration. Then, oxygen picks up electrons at the end of the electron transport chain in cellular respiration. But what happens when oxygen is not there to pick up electrons? The production of ATP without oxygen continues through the anaerobic processes of glycolysis and fermentation.

**Fermentation** does not make ATP, but it allows glycolysis to continue. Fermentation removes electrons from NADH molecules and recycles NAD$^+$ molecules for glycolysis. Why is this process important? Because glycolysis, just like cellular respiration, needs a molecule that picks up electrons. It needs molecules of NAD$^+$.

**FIGURE 6.1** Muscle cells use anaerobic processes during hard exercise.

**VISUAL VOCAB**

**Fermentation** is an anaerobic process that allows glycolysis to continue.

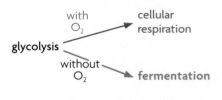

glycolysis

with O$_2$ → cellular respiration

without O$_2$ → fermentation

Without NAD⁺ to pick up high-energy electrons from the splitting of glucose, glycolysis would stop. When the high-energy electrons are picked up, though, a eukaryotic cell can continue breaking down glucose and other simple sugars to make a small amount of ATP.

Suppose that a molecule of glucose has just been split by glycolysis in one of your muscle cells, but oxygen is unavailable. A process called lactic acid fermentation takes place. Lactic acid fermentation occurs in your muscle cells, the cells of other vertebrates, and in some microorganisms. **Lactic acid,** $C_3H_6O_3$, is what causes your muscles to "burn" during hard exercise.

**1** Pyruvate and NADH from glycolysis enter the fermentation process. Two NADH molecules provide energy to convert pyruvate into lactic acid. As the NADH is used, it is converted back into NAD⁺.

**2** Two molecules of NAD⁺ are recycled back to glycolysis. The recycling of NAD⁺ allows glycolysis to continue.

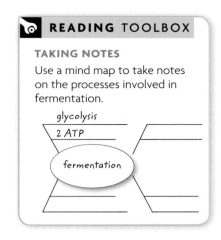
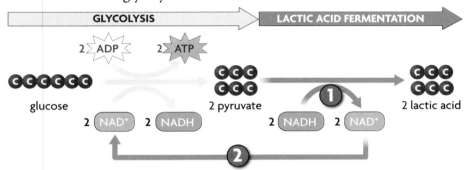

As you can see, the role of fermentation is simply to provide glycolysis with a steady supply of NAD⁺. By itself, fermentation does not produce ATP. Instead, it allows glycolysis to continue to produce ATP. However, fermentation does produce the lactic acid waste product that builds up in muscle cells and causes a burning feeling. Once oxygen is available again, your cells return to using cellular respiration. The lactic acid is quickly broken down and removed from the cells. This is why you continue to breathe hard for several minutes after you stop exercising. Your body is making up for the oxygen deficit in your cells, which allows the breakdown of lactic acid in your muscles.

**Sequence** Which process must happen first, fermentation or glycolysis? Explain.

**● MAIN IDEA**
## Fermentation and its products are important in several ways.

How would your diet change without cheese, bread, and yogurt? How would pizza exist without cheese and bread? Without fermentation, a pizza crust would not rise and there would be no mozzarella cheese as a pizza topping. Cheese, bread, and yogurt are just a few of the foods made by fermentation. Milk is changed into different cheeses by fermentation processes carried out by different types of bacteria and molds. Waste products of their fermentation processes give cheeses their different flavors and textures. Additionally, some types of bacteria that use lactic acid fermentation sour the milk in yogurt.

Lactic acid fermentation is not the only anaerobic process. Alcoholic fermentation occurs in many yeasts and in some types of plants. Alcoholic fermentation begins at the same point as lactic acid fermentation. That is, glycolysis splits a molecule of glucose and produces two net ATP molecules, two pyruvate molecules, and two NADH molecules. Pyruvate and NADH enter alcoholic fermentation.

**1** Pyruvate and NADH from glycolysis enter alcoholic fermentation. Two NADH molecules provide energy to break down pyruvate into an alcohol and carbon dioxide. As the NADH molecules are used, they are converted back into molecules of NAD⁺.

**2** The molecules of NAD⁺ are recycled back to glycolysis. The recycling of NAD⁺ allows glycolysis to continue.

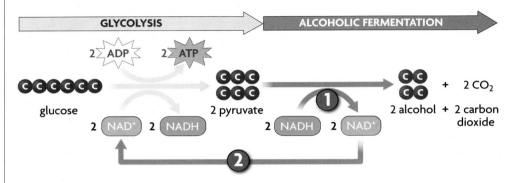

The products of this process are two molecules of an alcohol, often ethyl alcohol, two molecules of carbon dioxide, and two molecules of NAD⁺. Just like lactic acid fermentation, alcoholic fermentation recycles NAD⁺ and so allows glycolysis to keep making ATP.

## QUICKLAB    DESIGN YOUR OWN

### Fermentation

One waste product of alcoholic fermentation is carbon dioxide. In this lab, you will determine which beverage causes yeast to undergo a higher rate of fermentation.

**PROBLEM** What factors affect the rate of fermentation in yeast?

**PROCEDURE**

1. Write an operational definition for the dependent variable that you will use to measure the rate of fermentation.
2. Develop a technique using a balloon to measure fermentation rate.
3. Design your experiment. Have your teacher approve your experimental design. Write your experimental procedure and conduct your experiment.
4. Construct a data table to record your data. Construct a graph to display your data.

**ANALYZE AND CONCLUDE**

1. **Identify** What are the independent variable, dependent variable, and constants?
2. **Analyze** How did the independent variable affect the rate of fermentation? Why?
3. **Experimental Design** Identify possible reasons for any inconsistent results you observed.

**MATERIALS**

- 2 empty plastic bottles
- 1 package of yeast
- 2 100-mL graduated cylinders
- 2 250-mL beakers
- 2 beverages
- 2 round balloons
- 30 cm string
- metric ruler

**FIGURE 6.2** Fermentation by molds and bacteria produces the different flavors and textures of various cheeses.

Alcoholic fermentation in yeast is particularly useful. When bread or pizza crust is made, yeast is used to cause the dough to rise. The yeast breaks down sugars in the dough through glycolysis and alcohol fermentation. The carbon dioxide gas produced by alcoholic fermentation causes the dough to puff up and rise. When the dough is baked, the alcohol that is produced during fermentation evaporates into the air. The yeast in dough is killed by the heat of baking.

Bacteria that rely upon fermentation play a very important role in the digestive systems of animals. Microorganisms in the digestive tracts of animals, including humans, must obtain their ATP from anaerobic processes because oxygen is not available. Without them, neither you nor other animals would be able to fully digest food. Why? These bacteria continue the breakdown of molecules by taking in undigested material for their needs. The additional breakdown of materials by digestive bacteria allows the host animal to absorb more nutrients from food.

**Apply** Explain the importance of alcoholic fermentation in the production of bread's light, fluffy texture.

**Virtual INVESTIGATION**
HMHScience.com
**GO ONLINE**

Photosynthesis and Cellular Respiration

**SELF-CHECK Online**
HMHScience.com
**GO ONLINE**

## 4.6 Formative Assessment

### REVIEWING ▶ MAIN IDEAS

1. What is the relationship between glycolysis and **fermentation**?

2. Summarize the process of alcoholic fermentation in yeast.

### CRITICAL THINKING

3. **Compare and Contrast** How are **lactic acid** fermentation and alcoholic fermentation similar? How are they different?

4. **Compare and Contrast** Describe the similarities and differences between cellular respiration and fermentation.

### ☀ CONNECT TO

**CELLULAR RESPIRATION**

5. How is the role of oxygen in cellular respiration similar to the role of $NAD^+$ in fermentation ?

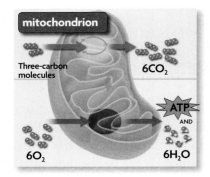

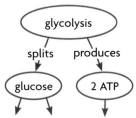

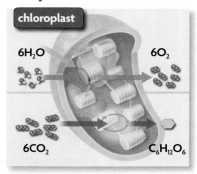

All living things require energy in the form of ATP to carry on cell processes, and ATP is most often produced by the linked reactions of photosynthesis and respiration.

## KEY CONCEPTS

### 4.1 Chemical Energy and ATP

**All cells need chemical energy.** Adenosine triphosphate (ATP) is the primary source of energy in all cells. ATP transfers energy for cell processes such as building new molecules and transporting materials.

### 4.2 Overview of Photosynthesis

**The overall process of photosynthesis produces sugars that store chemical energy.** Photosynthesis uses energy captured from sunlight to change carbon dioxide and water into oxygen and sugars. Sunlight is absorbed during the light-dependent reactions, and sugars are made during the light-independent reactions.

### 4.3 Photosynthesis in Detail

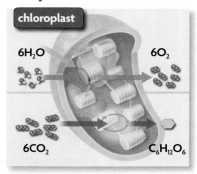

chloroplast

$6H_2O$     $6O_2$

$6CO_2$     $C_6H_{12}O_6$

**Photosynthesis requires a series of chemical reactions.** Energy from sunlight is absorbed in the thylakoid membrane by photosystems II and I in the light-dependent reactions. The energy is transferred to the Calvin cycle, which builds sugar molecules from carbon dioxide.

### 4.4 Overview of Cellular Respiration

**The overall process of cellular respiration converts sugar into ATP using oxygen.** Glycolysis splits glucose; the products of glycolysis are used in cellular respiration when oxygen is present. The Krebs cycle transfers energy to the electron transport chain, which produces most of the ATP in eukaryotic cells.

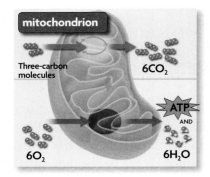

mitochondrion

Three-carbon molecules     $6CO_2$

ATP AND

$6O_2$     $6H_2O$

### 4.5 Cellular Respiration in Detail

**Cellular respiration is an aerobic process with two main stages.** The Krebs cycle breaks down carbon-based molecules and transfers energy to electron carriers. The electron carriers provide energy to the electron transport chain. ATP is produced by the electron transport chain when hydrogen ions flow through ATP synthase.

### 4.6 Fermentation

**Fermentation allows the production of a small amount of ATP without oxygen.** Fermentation allows glycolysis to continue producing ATP when oxygen is unavailable. Lactic acid fermentation occurs in many cells, including human muscle cells.

---

**READING** TOOLBOX     SYNTHESIZE YOUR NOTES

**Two-Column Chart** Compare and contrast photosynthesis and cellular respiration. Use your notes to make detailed charts that include details about both processes. Highlight important vocabulary and processes.

| Photosynthesis | Cellular Respiration |
|---|---|
| absorbs sunlight occurs in chloroplasts $6CO_2+6H_2O \rightarrow C_6H_{12}O_6+6O_2$ | produces ATP occurs in mitochondria $C_6H_{12}O_6+6O_2 \rightarrow 6CO_2+6H_2O$ |

**Concept Map** Use a concept map like the one below to summarize and organize the processes of photosynthesis, cellular respiration, and fermentation.

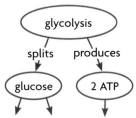

glycolysis

splits     produces

glucose     2 ATP

# 4 Review

**INTERACTIVE Review**
HMHScience.com

**GO ONLINE**

Review Games • Concept Map • Section Self-Checks

## CHAPTER VOCABULARY

**4.1**
ATP
ADP
chemosynthesis

**4.2**
photosynthesis
chlorophyll
thylakoid
light-dependent reactions
light-independent reactions

**4.3**
photosystem
electron transport chain
ATP synthase
Calvin cycle

**4.4**
cellular respiration
aerobic
glycolysis
anaerobic
Krebs cycle

**4.6**
fermentation
lactic acid

## Reviewing Vocabulary

**Keep It Short**

For each vocabulary term below, write a short, precise phrase that describes its meaning. For example, a short phrase to describe the term *ATP* could be "energy for cells."

1. photosynthesis
2. light-dependent reactions
3. cellular respiration
4. aerobic
5. Krebs cycle
6. fermentation

**READING TOOLBOX** GREEK AND LATIN WORD PARTS

Use the definitions of the word parts to answer the next three questions.

| Prefix or Root | Meaning |
|---|---|
| *photo-* | light |
| *syn-* | together |
| *aero-* | air |
| *spirare* | to breathe |

7. Describe how the meaning of the term *photosynthesis* is a combination of the meanings of the prefixes *photo-* and *syn-*.

8. Explain how the prefix *aero-* is related to the terms *aerobic* and *anaerobic*.

9. Why is the root *spirare* the basis of the term *cellular respiration*? Explain your answer.

## Reviewing MAIN IDEAS

10. Describe the roles of ADP and ATP in the transfer and use of energy in cells.

11. What types of carbon-based molecules are most often broken down to make ATP? Explain how ATP production differs depending on the type of carbon-based molecule that is broken down.

12. Describe how and where energy from light is absorbed during photosynthesis. What happens to the energy after it is absorbed?

13. Write the chemical equation for photosynthesis and explain what it represents.

14. What roles do electrons and hydrogen ions play in the light-dependent reactions of photosynthesis?

15. Describe how the light-independent reactions are the synthesis part of photosynthesis.

16. How does glycolysis contribute to the overall process of cellular respiration?

17. Write the chemical equation for cellular respiration and explain what it represents.

18. What is the function of the Krebs cycle? In your answer, describe the products of the Krebs cycle and what happens to them.

19. Explain the function of the electron transport chain in cellular respiration. Why is oxygen needed for the electron transport chain?

20. Fermentation does not produce ATP. Why is fermentation such an important process in cells?

21. How is alcoholic fermentation similar to lactic acid fermentation? How is it different?

# Critical Thinking

**22. Infer** Human brain cells do not use fermentation. Explain why a lack of oxygen for even a short period of time might result in the death of brain cells.

**23. Apply** Energy is transferred in several different ways during photosynthesis and cellular respiration. Give two examples of the way energy is transferred in the processes. Explain both examples.

**24. Analyze** How do photosynthesis and cellular respiration form a cycle of energy storage and use?

**25. Synthesize** How do cellular respiration and fermentation depend on glycolysis? How does glycolysis depend on aerobic and anaerobic processes?

**26. Analyze** Consider the following two groups of processes:
- light-dependent reactions and electron transport chain
- Calvin cycle and Krebs cycle

Which pair is nearly identical? Which is nearly opposite? Explain.

## Interpreting Visuals

Use the diagram to answer the next three questions.

**27. Apply** Which process stores energy? Which process releases energy? How do you know?

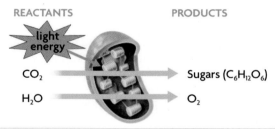

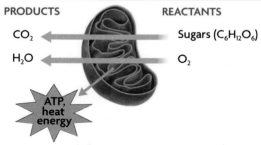

**28. Infer** Use information in the visual to explain how matter, in the form of reactants and products, is cycled through these processes.

**29. Infer** Which of the processes in the diagram is necessary for most living things to survive? Explain.

## Analyzing Data  Interpret a Graph

Use information in the text and the graph below to answer the next two questions.

Plants have several different molecules that together absorb all of the different wavelengths of visible light. Visible light ranges between the wavelengths of about 400 and 700 nanometers (nm).

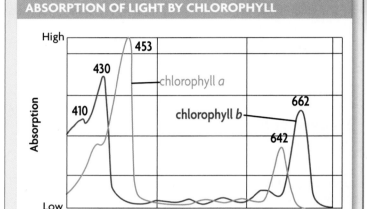

ABSORPTION OF LIGHT BY CHLOROPHYLL

**30. Analyze Data** What range of wavelengths is absorbed by chlorophyll *a*? chlorophyll *b*?

**31. Synthesize** Suppose a type of plant has only chlorophylls *a* and *b* and is exposed to different wavelengths of light. At which wavelengths would there be the greatest amounts of carbon dioxide in the air around the plants? the least? Explain your answers.

## Making Connections

**32. Write an Analogy** Suppose that photosynthesis and cellular respiration take place in a factory. You are a tour guide at the factory, explaining each step of the process to a group of visitors. Use analogies to describe what happens at each step. For example, you could describe the photosystems of photosynthesis as "the green machines next to windows to absorb light." Be sure to include important details of the process you select.

**33. Analyze** Look at the micrograph of diatoms on the chapter opener. Write a paragraph that explains the role of these single-celled organisms in a marine food web.

# Standards-Based Assessment

Record your answers on a separate piece of paper.

## MULTIPLE CHOICE

1 A group of students wants to find out how much carbon dioxide is used by plants during the daytime. What control could be used in this experiment?

   A the amount of water used during the daytime

   B the amount of oxygen released at night

   C the amount of carbon dioxide used at night

   D the amount of oxygen used during the daytime

2 The concept map below shows some of the carbon-based molecules in cells. Some of these molecules can be broken down to produce usable chemical energy.

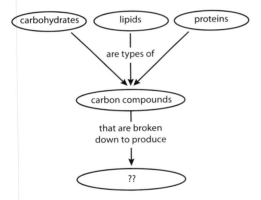

Which of the following terms **best** completes this concept map?

   A glucose

   B ATP

   C lactic acid

   D oxygen

3 Photosynthesis is a part of various cycles that help to move oxygen and carbon through the environment. What form of abiotic carbon do plants remove from the environment?

   A glucose

   B starch

   C carbon dioxide

   D ATP

> **THINK THROUGH THE QUESTION**
>
> Some terms in questions, such as biotic or abiotic, may be unfamiliar to you. Often, terms like these are used to present an example but are not necessary to answer the question. Find the important pieces of information in the question and focus on those points.

4

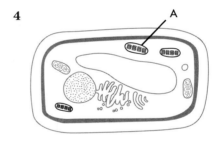

Which of the following **best** represent the final products of the chemical reactions that take place inside the organelle labeled A in the diagram above?

   A sugars, oxygen

   B ATP, electrons

   C ATP, sugars

   D carbon dioxide, water

5 Which process is represented by the following chemical equation?

$$6CO_2 + 6H_2O \longrightarrow C_6H_{12}O_6 + 6O_2$$

   A photosynthesis

   B fermentation

   C glycolysis

   D cellular respiration

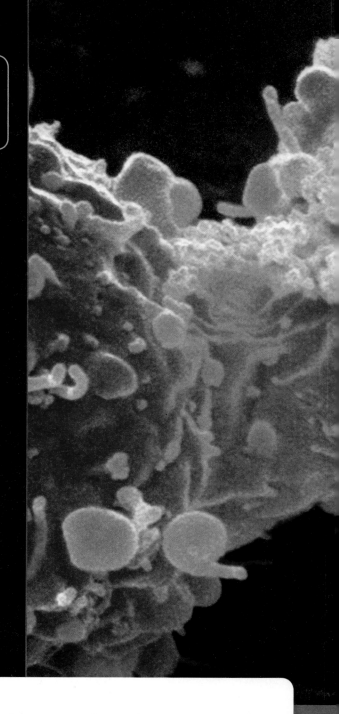

CHAPTER

# 5 Cell Growth and Division

**BIG IDEA** Cells have their own life cycle that includes reproduction, growth, and regulation, which allows organisms to carry out life functions and grow.

**5.1 The Cell Cycle**

**5.2 Mitosis and Cytokinesis**

**Data Analysis**
**CONSTRUCTING DATA TABLES**

**5.3 Regulation of the Cell Cycle**

**5.4 Asexual Reproduction**

**5.5 Multicellular Life**

---

⊘ **ONLINE BIOLOGY** HMHScience.com

**ONLINE** Labs
- Mitosis in Onion Root Cells
- **Quick Lab** Cancer
- Modeling Cell Surface Area–to-Volume Ratio
- Apoptosis
- Animating Mitosis
- **Virtual Lab** Investigating Bacterial Growth

- **Video Lab** Mitosis in Plant Cells
- **S.T.E.M. Lab** Modeling Induction in Embryos

(t) ©Photo Researchers, Inc.

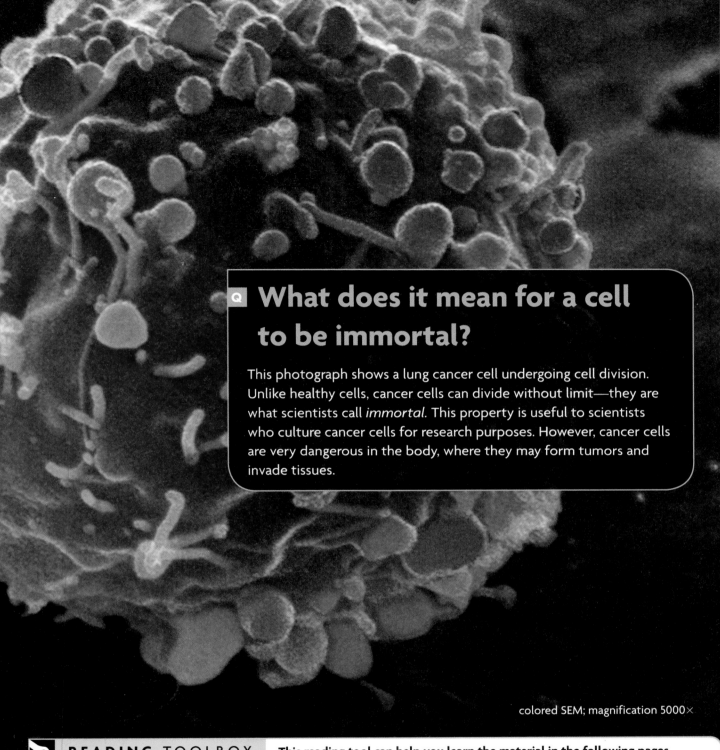

**What does it mean for a cell to be immortal?**

This photograph shows a lung cancer cell undergoing cell division. Unlike healthy cells, cancer cells can divide without limit—they are what scientists call *immortal*. This property is useful to scientists who culture cancer cells for research purposes. However, cancer cells are very dangerous in the body, where they may form tumors and invade tissues.

colored SEM; magnification 5000×

 **READING** TOOLBOX    **This reading tool can help you learn the material in the following pages.**

## USING LANGUAGE

**Cause and Effect** In biological processes, one step leads to another step. When reading, you can often recognize these cause-and-effect relationships by words that indicate a result, such as *so, consequently, if-then,* and *as a result.*

## YOUR TURN

Identify the cause and effect in the following sentences.

1. People often shiver as a result of being cold.
2. The light got brighter, so the pupil of the eye got smaller.
3. If the cell passes the $G_2$ checkpoint, then the cell may begin to divide.

# 5.1 The Cell Cycle

SC.912.L.16.14

**KEY CONCEPT** Cells have distinct phases of growth, reproduction, and normal functions.

**VOCABULARY**

cell cycle
mitosis
cytokinesis

**MAIN IDEAS**

- The cell cycle has four main stages.
- Cells divide at different rates.
- Cell size is limited.

**SC.912.L.16.14** Describe the cell cycle, including the process of mitosis. Explain the role of mitosis in the formation of new cells and its importance in maintaining chromosome number during asexual reproduction.

## Connect to Your World

Many of life's little chores can be quietly satisfying and rather fun. Washing dishes by hand, however, is not so fun, which is why some clever person made the dishwasher. This handy invention soaks, washes, and rinses your dishes to a spot-free, sanitary sparkle. You unload the dishes, and the machine is ready to start the cycle all over again. A cell goes through a cycle, too. This cycle of growth, DNA synthesis, and division is essential for an organism to grow and heal. If it goes out of control, abnormal cell growth may occur, resulting in cancer cells like those shown on the previous page.

## MAIN IDEA

# The cell cycle has four main stages.

Just as all species have life cycles, from tiny chihuahuas to massive beluga whales, cells also have a life cycle. The **cell cycle** is the regular pattern of growth, DNA duplication, and cell division that occurs in eukaryotic cells. **FIGURE 1.1** shows its four main stages: gap 1, synthesis, gap 2, and mitosis. Gap 1, synthesis, and gap 2 together make up what is called interphase.

The stages of the cell cycle get their names from early studies of cell division. Scientists' observations were limited by the microscopes of the time. When a cell was not actively dividing, they could not see activity in it. Thus, they originally divided the cell cycle into two parts: interphase, when the cell appeared to be at rest, and mitosis, when the cell was dividing. Improved techniques and tools later allowed scientists to detect the copying of DNA (DNA synthesis), and they changed their description of the cell cycle to include the synthesis stage. Since they still could not see anything happening during the other parts of interphase, scientists named the periods between mitosis and synthesis "gap 1" and "gap 2." Eventually scientists learned that, during interphase, cells carry out their normal functions and undergo critical growth and preparation for cell division.

**FIGURE 1.1** Cells grow and copy their DNA during interphase. They also carry out cell-specific functions in $G_1$ and $G_2$. During M stage, both the nucleus (in mitosis) and cytoplasm (in cytokinesis) are divided.

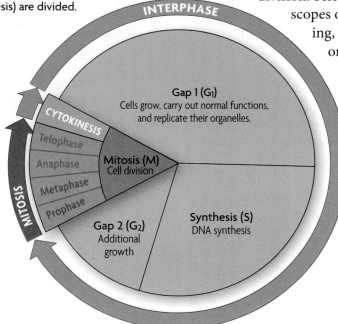

INTERPHASE

CYTOKINESIS

Telophase
Anaphase
Metaphase
Prophase

MITOSIS

**Gap 1 (G₁)**
Cells grow, carry out normal functions, and replicate their organelles.

**Mitosis (M)**
Cell division

**Gap 2 (G₂)**
Additional growth

**Synthesis (S)**
DNA synthesis

## Gap 1 (G₁)

The first stage of the cell cycle is gap 1 ($G_1$). During $G_1$, a cell carries out its normal functions. If it is a skeletal muscle cell, it contracts to move joints. If it is an adrenal cell, it secretes hormones such as adrenaline. If it is an intestinal cell, it absorbs nutrients. During $G_1$, cells also increase in size, and organelles increase in number. A cell spends most of its time in the $G_1$ stage, although the length of this stage varies by cell type.

During $G_1$, the cell must pass a critical checkpoint before it can proceed to the synthesis stage. Just as it would be dangerous for you to run a marathon if you had not slept or eaten for several days, it would also be dangerous for your cells to continue dividing if certain conditions were not met. For instance, most animal cells need enough nutrition, adequate size, and relatively un-damaged DNA to divide successfully. They also need specific signals from other cells, telling them whether more cell division is needed.

## Synthesis (S)

The second stage of the cell cycle is the synthesis (S) stage. *Synthesis* means "the combining of parts to make a whole." During the S stage, the cell makes a copy of its nuclear DNA. In eukaryotes, DNA is located in the nucleus. During interphase, it is loosely organized and appears grainy in photographs. By the end of the S stage, the cell nucleus contains two complete sets of DNA.

## Gap 2 (G₂)

Gap 2 ($G_2$) is the third stage of the cell cycle. During $G_2$, cells continue to carry out their normal functions, and additional growth occurs. Like $G_1$, this stage includes a critical checkpoint. Everything must be in order—adequate cell size, undamaged DNA—before the cell goes through mitosis and division.

## Mitosis (M)

Mitosis (M), the fourth stage of the cell cycle, includes two processes: mitosis and cytokinesis. **Mitosis** (my-TOH-sihs) is the division of the cell nucleus and its contents. During mitosis, the nuclear membrane dissolves, the duplicated DNA con-denses around proteins and separates, and two new nuclei form. Lastly, **cytokinesis** (sy-toh-kuh-NEE-sihs) is the process that divides the cell cytoplasm. The result is two daughter cells that are genetically identical to the original cell.

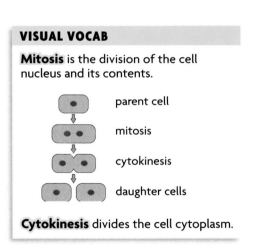

**VISUAL VOCAB**

**Mitosis** is the division of the cell nucleus and its contents.

parent cell

mitosis

cytokinesis

daughter cells

**Cytokinesis** divides the cell cytoplasm.

The stages of the cell cycle and the proteins that control it are similar in all eukaryotes. For example, scientists have demonstrated that some of the molecules that regulate checkpoints in the yeast cell cycle can work in human cells, too. Such similarities suggest that eukaryotes share a common ancestry.

**Predict** **What might happen if the G₂ checkpoint stopped working in cells?**

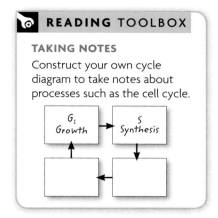

**READING TOOLBOX**

**TAKING NOTES**

Construct your own cycle diagram to take notes about processes such as the cell cycle.

**CONNECT TO**

**DNA REPLICATION**

As you will learn in the chapter **From DNA to Proteins**, DNA synthesis is also called DNA replication. During this process, the DNA molecule unzips and each strand is used as a pattern for a new DNA strand.

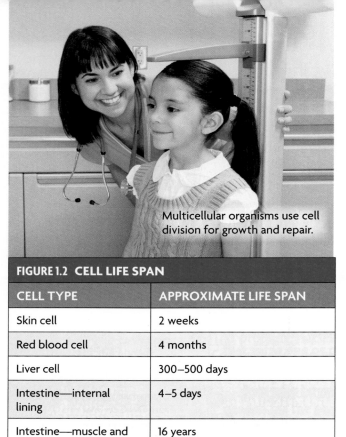

Multicellular organisms use cell division for growth and repair.

## FIGURE 1.2 CELL LIFE SPAN

| CELL TYPE | APPROXIMATE LIFE SPAN |
|---|---|
| Skin cell | 2 weeks |
| Red blood cell | 4 months |
| Liver cell | 300–500 days |
| Intestine—internal lining | 4–5 days |
| Intestine—muscle and other tissues | 16 years |

Source: Spaulding et al., *Cell* 122:1.

### CONNECT TO

**LYMPHOCYTES**

As you will learn in the chapter **Immune System and Disease,** lymphocytes are a part of your immune system. There are two major types of lymphocytes, B and T cells. Both types recognize specific antigens.

### ▶ MAIN IDEA

# Cells divide at different rates.

Rates of cell division vary widely, as shown in **FIGURE 1.2.** The prokaryotic cell cycle is similar but not identical to that of eukaryotic cells. Recall that prokaryotes do not have the membrane-bound organelles and cytoskeleton found in eukaryotes. Thus, prokaryotic cells typically divide much faster than do eukaryotic cells.

The rate at which your cells divide is linked to your body's need for those cells. In human cells, the S, $G_2$, and M stages together usually take about 12 hours. The length of the $G_1$ stage differs most from cell type to cell type. The rate of cell division is greater in embryos and children than it is in adults. Children have a shorter cell cycle, and many of their organs are still developing. But the rate of cell division also varies within different tissues of the adult body. The internal lining of your digestive tract receives a lot of wear and tear. As a result, cells that line your stomach and intestine are replaced every few days. In contrast, cells that make up the rest of your intestine (mainly smooth muscle) and many of your internal organs, such as lungs, kidneys, and liver, divide only occasionally, in response to injury or cell death.

Cells that divide only rarely are thought to enter a stage that some scientists call $G_0$. In $G_0$, cells are unlikely to divide, although they continue to carry out their normal functions. Some cells, such as neurons, appear to stay permanently in the $G_0$ stage. However, some data suggest that neurons actually can divide, and this question continues to be actively researched. Other cells, such as lymphocytes, a type of white blood cell, may remain in $G_0$ for years until they recognize an invader. Once the invader binds to a lymphocyte receptor, the lymphocyte goes through rapid cell divisions to help fight infection.

**Infer Do you think a skin cell would have a long or short $G_1$ stage? Explain why.**

### ▶ MAIN IDEA

# Cell size is limited.

Cells have upper and lower size limits. If cells were too small, they could not contain all of the necessary organelles and molecules. For instance, a cell with too few mitochondria would not have enough energy to live. However, cells cannot grow beyond a certain size, even if surrounded by plenty of nutrients. The upper limit on cell size is due to the ratio of cell surface area to volume. Recall that oxygen, nutrients, and wastes move across the cell membrane, or the surface of the cell. These materials must be transported in adequate amounts and with adequate speed to keep the inside of the cell functioning. But as a cell increases in size, its volume increases faster than its surface area, as shown in **FIGURE 1.3.** Therefore, a further increase in size could result in a surface area too small for the adequate exchange of materials.

## FIGURE 1.3 Ratio of Surface Area to Volume in Cells

As a cell grows, its volume increases more rapidly than its surface area. When the surface area–to-volume ratio is too small, the cell cannot move materials into and out of the cell at a sufficient rate or in sufficient quantities.

| Relative size | 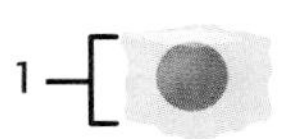 | 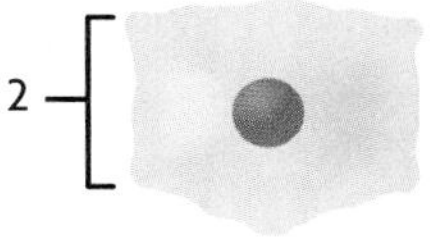 | 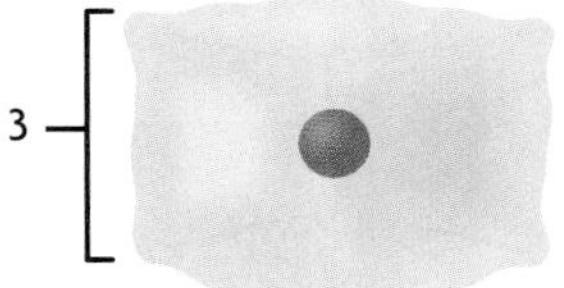 |
|---|---|---|---|
| Surface area (length × width × number of sides) | 6 | 24 | 54 |
| Volume (length × width × height) | 1 | 8 | 27 |
| Ratio of surface area to volume | $\frac{6}{1}$ = 6:1 | $\frac{24}{8}$ = 3:1 | $\frac{54}{27}$ = 2:1 |

**Compare** Which cell has the largest surface area? Which cell has the largest surface area–to-volume ratio?

Some cells, however, must be large. A neuron running down a giraffe's neck to its legs may be several meters long, for instance. But it is not shaped like a cube or a sphere. Instead, it is extremely long and thin. This structure gives the neuron a large surface area with a relatively small increase in volume.

To maintain a suitable cell size, growth and division must be coordinated. If a cell more than doubled its size before dividing, the daughter cells would be larger than the original cell. If this happened with each generation, cells would quickly become too large to live. Similarly, if a cell did not double its size before dividing, the daughter cells would be smaller than the original cell. If this happened with each generation, cells would become too small to live.

**Connect** Which has the larger ratio of surface area to volume, a tennis ball or a soccer ball? Explain your reasoning.

SELF-CHECK Online
HMHScience.com
GO ONLINE

## 5.1 Formative Assessment

### REVIEWING ▶ MAIN IDEAS

1. During which stage of the **cell cycle** is the DNA copied?

2. Which stages of the cell cycle generally require about the same amount of time in all human cells?

3. What limits the maximum size of a cell?

### CRITICAL THINKING

4. **Infer** Suppose you were to draw a diagram representing the cell cycle of a neuron. Explain where and how you would represent $G_0$.

5. **Predict** Suppose you treat cells with chemicals that block **cytokinesis.** Describe what you think the cells would look like.

### CONNECT TO

**SCIENTIFIC PROCESS**

6. Predict how the rate of cell division would differ between single-celled algae living in a sunny, nutrient-rich pond versus algae living in a shady, nutrient-poor pond. How could you test your prediction?

# 5.2 Mitosis and Cytokinesis

SC.912.L.16.14

**KEY CONCEPT** Cells divide during mitosis and cytokinesis.

**MAIN IDEAS**

- ◯ Chromosomes condense at the start of mitosis.
- ◯ Mitosis and cytokinesis produce two genetically identical daughter cells.

**VOCABULARY**

chromosome
histone
chromatin
chromatid
centromere
telomere
prophase
metaphase
anaphase
telophase

**SC.912.L.16.14** Describe the cell cycle, including the process of mitosis. Explain the role of mitosis in the formation of new cells and its importance in maintaining chromosome number during asexual reproduction.

**⟐ Connect to Your World**

When you were a child, perhaps you attended a birthday party where goody bags were handed out. Whoever stuffed the bags had to make sure that each bag had exactly the same number of erasers, candies, and stickers. Otherwise, some ill-mannered child (not you, of course) might have raised a fuss if an item was missing. In a similar way, your cells must receive a full set of DNA—no more, no less—to work properly. Dividing DNA is a complicated task because the DNA is so long and stringy. Mitosis is an amazing process that efficiently sorts two sets of DNA and divides them between two nuclei.

**▶ MAIN IDEA**

## Chromosomes condense at the start of mitosis.

DNA is a double-stranded molecule made of four different subunits called nucleotides. A **chromosome** is one long continuous thread of DNA that consists of numerous genes along with regulatory information. Your body cells have 46 chromosomes each. If stretched out straight and laid end to end, the DNA in just one of your cells would be about 3 meters (10 feet) long. How does it fit inside the nucleus of a microscopic cell?

DNA wraps around proteins that help organize and condense it. During interphase, or when a cell is not dividing, DNA is loosely organized—it looks a bit like spaghetti. During mitosis, however, your chromosomes are tightly condensed, as shown in **FIGURE 2.1**. These changes in DNA's organization allow a cell to carry out its necessary functions. During all of interphase, proteins must access specific genes for a cell to make specific proteins or to copy the entire DNA sequence. During mitosis, the duplicated chromosomes must condense to be divided between two nuclei. If chromosomes remained stringy during mitosis, they could become entangled.

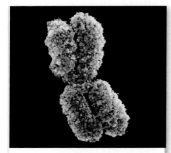

**FIGURE 2.1** This duplicated chromosome is tightly condensed. (colored SEM; magnification unknown)

Perhaps a cell would get two copies of one chromosome and no copies of a different one. **FIGURE 2.2** shows the process that converts a chromosome from a linear strand of DNA to its highly condensed form. The key to this process is the association between DNA and proteins.

**CONNECT TO**

**BIOCHEMISTRY**

As you will learn in the chapter **From DNA to Proteins,** a nucleotide is made of three parts: a sugar, a phosphate group, and a nitrogen-containing molecule called a base. When the sugars and phosphate groups bond, they form the backbones of the long chains called nucleic acids.

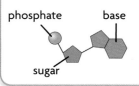

©Biophoto Associates/Photo Researchers, Inc.

# Exploring Elephants' Low Cancer Rates

More than eight million people around the globe succumb to cancer every year, including more than half a million deaths in the United States alone. Researchers have been working for decades to understand the disease better and to discover improved treatments, diagnosis, and prevention. One way to do this is to study cancer in other animals.

Recent genetic studies have shed light on one of science's long-standing questions: How can animals as large as elephants have such a low incidence of cancers? The answer potentially lies in a particular protein encoded in a gene called TP53.

In 1977, British epidemiologist and statistician Richard Peto pointed out that most animals, regardless of their size, have roughly the same rates of cancer occurrence. He found this surprising because of the way cancer spreads in the body. Basically, when a cell divides, a mutation that makes the cell grow more quickly may occur. The more times the cell divides, the more chances there are for more mutations to occur. Therefore, larger animals—which have more cells than smaller animals and whose cells have divided many more times than those of smaller animals—should have higher rates of cancer occurrence than smaller animals. Yet, they don't. This puzzle is known as Peto's paradox.

Elephants are one of the world's longest-lived animals, with an average lifespan of 60 to 70 years, depending on the species. They are also the world's largest land animals, with an average weight of 5,000 to 8,000 kg (~11,000 to 17,000 lbs) and an average height of 3 to 4 m (9 to 13 ft). Their size and age mean they have trillions of cells that have divided many times, so they would seem to be prime candidates

for cancer. Yet, only 5 percent of elephant deaths are caused by cancer, compared with a much higher cancer death rate in humans: 11 to 25 percent.

Several different teams of scientists recently set out to investigate Peto's paradox as it applies to African and Asian elephants. The teams independently found evidence that the secret of the elephant's resistance to cancer might lie in the TP53 gene, which makes proteins that work to suppress tumors. These proteins repair damage to a cell's DNA. If the damage is too great, the proteins can stop the cell from dividing or even trigger the death of the cell. Because cancer is caused by out-of-control cell division, the deaths of damaged cells are beneficial to the organism, because the cells are prevented from dividing further.

While humans (and some other animals) have only one copy of the TP53 gene, elephants have evolved to have 20 copies, which appears to multiply their cancer-fighting abilities. Damaged elephant cells self-destruct at a much higher rate than do those of humans, which further boosts elephants' resistance to cancer.

The findings of the recent studies must be replicated, and more research must be done, before scientists can say with any certainty what role TP53 plays in the low incidence of deaths from cancer in elephant populations. However, the initial evidence points to an intriguing evolutionary solution to the problem of cancer.

## 5.3 Regulation of the Cell Cycle

**SC.912.L.16.8**

**KEY CONCEPT** Cell cycle regulation is necessary for healthy growth.

### MAIN IDEAS
- Internal and external factors regulate cell division.
- Cell division is uncontrolled in cancer.

**SC.912.L.16.8** Explain the relationship between mutation, cell cycle, and uncontrolled cell growth potentially resulting in cancer.

#### Connect to Your World
Have you ever watched a movie in which people play with the elements of nature? They might bring back dinosaurs or make a newfangled robot. And have you noticed that these movies are always scary? That's because things go out of control. The robots take over, or the dinosaurs start eating humans. If cell growth goes out of control in your body, the result can be even scarier. Cancer is uncontrolled cell growth and results from many factors that affect the cell cycle. So how does your body regulate all the millions of cell divisions happening in your body?

### ▶ MAIN IDEA
## Internal and external factors regulate cell division.

Both external and internal factors regulate the cell cycle in eukaryotic cells. External factors come from outside the cell. They include messages from nearby cells and from distant parts of the organism's body.

Internal factors come from inside the cell and include several types of molecules found in the cytoplasm. Both types of factors work together to help your body control the process of cell division.

**FIGURE 3.1** Normal animal cells (top) respond to external factors and stop dividing when they touch each other. Cancer cells (bottom) fail to respond and form clumps.

**Normal cell growth**

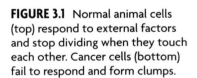

**Cancerous cell growth**

### External Factors
External factors that help regulate the cell cycle include physical and chemical signals. One example of a physical signal is cell-to-cell contact. Most mammal cells grown in the laboratory form a single layer on the bottom of a culture dish, as shown in **FIGURE 3.1**. Once a cell touches other cells, it stops dividing. The exact reason for this phenomenon is unknown. One hypothesis is that receptors on neighboring cells bind to each other and cause the cells' cytoskeletons to form structures that may block the signals that trigger growth.

Many cells also release chemical signals that tell other cells to grow. For example, **growth factors** are a broad group of proteins that stimulate cell division. Growth factors bind to receptors that activate specific genes to trigger cell growth. In general, cells grow and divide in response to a combination of different growth factors, not just one.

Some growth factors affect many types of cells. For example, platelets are sticky fragments of bone marrow cells. They form clots that help stop bleeding. Platelets store a type of growth factor that helps your body repair wounds by triggering the growth of many cell types. Other growth factors have more specific targets. For instance, erythropoietin (ih-RIHTH-roh-poy-EE-tihn) stimulates the production only of cells that will become red blood cells. Red blood cells carry oxygen. If you moved from the coast to the mountains, your blood oxygen levels would be lower because the air pressure is lower at higher altitudes. The decrease in blood oxygen levels would cause your body to produce more erythropoietin. That factor would increase the number of red blood cells and raise your blood oxygen levels.

Various hormones may also stimulate the growth of certain cell types. In particular, growth hormone results in bone growth and also affects your protein and fat metabolism.

## Internal Factors

When external factors bind to their receptors, they can trigger internal factors that affect the cell cycle. Two of the most important and well-studied internal factors involved in the eukaryotic cell cycle are kinases and cyclins. A kinase is an enzyme that, when activated, transfers a phosphate group from one molecule to a specific target molecule. This action typically increases the energy of the target molecule or changes its shape. Your cells have many types of kinases, and they are almost always present in the cell. Those kinases that help control the cell cycle are activated by cyclins. Cyclins are a group of proteins that are rapidly made and destroyed at certain points in the cell cycle. These two factors help a cell advance to different stages of the cell cycle when cells bind to each other.

## Apoptosis

Just as some cells need to grow and divide, other cells need to die. **Apoptosis** (AP-uhp-TOH-sihs) is programmed cell death. It occurs when internal or external signals activate genes that help produce self-destructive enzymes. Many questions remain about this process. What is known is that the nucleus of an apoptotic cell tends to shrink and break apart, and the cell is recognized by specialized cells in the immune system. These cells very tidily gobble up the apoptotic cell and recycle its chemical parts for use in building other molecules. **FIGURE 3.2** shows a classic example of apoptosis. In the early stages of development, human embryos have webbing between their fingers and toes, or digits. Before a baby is born, those cells typically go through apoptosis. Most babies are born with little unwebbed fingers and toes they love to put in their mouths.

**Predict** **Suppose a child was born with growth hormone receptors that did not work properly. How do you think this would affect the child's development?**

**FIGURE 3.2** Human embryos have webbed digits early in their development. The cells between the digits undergo apoptosis during later stages of development. As a result, the baby is born with unwebbed fingers and toes.

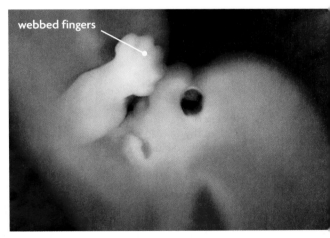
webbed fingers

## MAIN IDEA
# Cell division is uncontrolled in cancer.

**Cancer** is the common name for a class of diseases characterized by uncontrolled cell division. It arises when regulation of the cell cycle is disrupted. Unlike healthy cells, cancer cells grown in a culture dish continue to divide, even when surrounded by neighboring cells. Cancer cells can also continue to divide in the absence of many of the growth factors required for division in healthy cells. As a result, they divide much more often than do healthy cells.

Cancer cells form disorganized clumps called tumors. In a **benign** tumor, the cancer cells typically remain clustered together. This means the tumor may be relatively harmless and can probably be cured by removing it. However, if a tumor is **malignant,** some of the cancer cells can break away, or **metastasize** (mih-TAS-tuh-syz), from the tumor. These breakaway cells can be carried in the bloodstream or lymphatic system to other parts of the body, as shown in **FIGURE 3.3,** where they can form more tumors, called metastases. Once a tumor metastasizes, it is much more difficult to entirely rid the body of tumors.

But why are tumors harmful? Cancer cells do not perform the specialized functions needed by the body. In the lung, for example, cancer cells do not exchange oxygen and carbon dioxide. In the brain, they do not transmit the carefully ordered electrical messages needed to interpret information. Therefore, the body has large clumps of rapidly dividing cells that require lots of food and a hearty blood supply but that contribute nothing to the body's function. In addition, a growing tumor can exert great pressure on surrounding organs. For instance, a tumor growing inside the skull will cramp the brain for space, and some regions will be unable to function properly. If cancer cells continue to grow unchecked, they will eventually kill the organism.

Cancer cells come from normal cells that have suffered damage to the genes that help make proteins involved in cell-cycle regulation. Most cancer cells carry mutations, or errors, in two types of genes. One type, called oncogenes, accelerate the cell cycle. The second type act as cell-cycle brakes. Mutations in these genes can be inherited. For instance, some breast cancers appear to be caused by inherited errors in specific genes. Other mutations can be caused by exposure to radiation or chemicals. For example, some skin cancers are due to DNA damage caused by ultraviolet radiation from sunlight. Substances known to produce or promote the development of cancer are called **carcinogens** (kahr-SIHN-uh-juhnz). These include tobacco smoke and certain air pollutants, which are both associated with lung cancer. Some mutated forms of oncogenes are even carried by viruses; one such virus can cause cervical cancer.

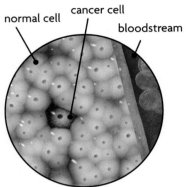
**FIGURE 3.3** Cancer cells form tumors that may metastasize to other parts of the body.

normal cell / cancer cell / bloodstream

1. A healthy cell may become a cancer cell if certain genes are damaged.

2. Cancer cells divide more often than do healthy cells and may form disorganized clumps called tumors.

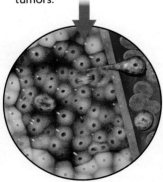

3. Sometimes, cancer cells break away from the tumor. They can be carried in the bloodstream to other parts of the body, where they form new tumors.

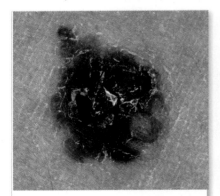
**FIGURE 3.4** This cancerous mole is an example of a skin cancer, which may metastasize quickly.

©CNRI/Photo Researchers, Inc.

## Cancer

In this lab, you will compare normal cells with cancerous cells and observe the differences between them.

**PROBLEM** How do normal and cancerous cells compare?

**PROCEDURE**

1. Examine the slides of normal cells under the microscope. Draw and describe your observations.

2. Repeat step 1 with slides of cancer cells.

**ANALYZE AND CONCLUDE**

1. **Compare** How does the structure of the normal cells compare with the structure of the cancerous cells for each of the slides you viewed?

2. **Infer** Cancer cells not only appear different from normal cells but they also divide more rapidly. Why do you think chemotherapy, a common treatment for cancer, results in the loss of hair?

**MATERIALS**

- microscope
- slides of normal cells
- slides of cancerous cells

Standard cancer treatment often involves both radiation and chemotherapy. Radiation therapy is the use of radiation to kill cancer cells and shrink tumors. It works by damaging a cell's DNA so much that the cell cannot divide. Radiation is usually localized—that is, its use is targeted to a specific region—because it can also hurt healthy cells. Chemotherapy uses certain drugs, often in combination, to kill actively dividing cells. Like radiation, it kills both cancerous and healthy cells. However, chemotherapy is systemic—drugs travel throughout the entire body.

Medical researchers use laboratory-grown cancer cells in their search for cancer treatments. Much of what is known about the cell cycle has come from studies that use cancer cells. The most famous cancer cells used for research are called HeLa cells. HeLa cells were originally obtained in 1951 from a cervical tumor removed from a woman named Henrietta Lacks. This cell line continues to be grown and studied in laboratories all over the world.

WebQuest
HMHScience.com
GO ONLINE
Skin Cancer

**Analyze** **HeLa cells are also used to study cell signaling processes. What might be a disadvantage of using cancer cells to study processes occurring in healthy cells?**

# 5.3 Formative Assessment

SELF-CHECK Online
HMHScience.com
GO ONLINE

## REVIEWING ▶ MAIN IDEAS

1. Describe what a **growth factor** is and how it influences the cell cycle.

2. Explain how **cancer** cells differ from healthy cells.

## CRITICAL THINKING

3. **Contrast** How do **benign** and **malignant** tumors differ?

4. **Hypothesize** Suppose chromosomes in a skin cell are damaged by ultraviolet radiation. If the damaged genes do not affect cell cycle regulation, do you think the cell will become cancerous? Explain.

## CONNECT TO

### CELL ORGANELLES

5. Some anticancer drugs prevent microtubules from forming spindle fibers. Why do you think these drugs might be effective treatments for cancer?

# 5.4 Asexual Reproduction

**SC.912.L.16.14**

# Asexual Reproduction

| KEY CONCEPT **Many organisms reproduce by cell division.**

**MAIN IDEAS**
- Binary fission is similar in function to mitosis.
- Some eukaryotes reproduce through mitosis.

**VOCABULARY**

asexual reproduction
binary fission

**SC.912.L.16.14** Describe the cell cycle, including the process of mitosis. Explain the role of mitosis in the formation of new cells and its importance in maintaining chromosome number during asexual reproduction.

### Connect to Your World

In this flashy world of ours, you may think that the humble bacterium would have little chance of finding a mate. No dazzling smile, no fancy hair products, no shiny car, and—if we are brutally honest—not even a brain. With all of these limitations, it may seem that our bacteria friends would be destined to die out. And yet, bacteria are found in abundance and live just about everywhere on Earth. How can there be so many bacteria?

## ▶ MAIN IDEA

# Binary fission is similar in function to mitosis.

Reproduction is a process that makes new organisms from one or more parent organisms. It happens in two ways—sexually and asexually. Sexual reproduction involves the joining of two specialized cells called gametes (eggs and sperm cells), one from each of two parents. The offspring that result are genetically unique; they have a mixture of genes from both parents. In contrast, **asexual reproduction** is the production of offspring from a single parent and does not involve the joining of gametes. The offspring that result are, for the most part, genetically identical to each other and to the single parent.

### Binary Fission and Mitosis

Most prokaryotes reproduce through **binary fission** (BY-nuh-ree FIHSH-uhn), the asexual reproduction of a single-celled organism by which the cell divides into two cells of the same size. Binary fission and mitosis have similar results. That is, both processes form two daughter cells that are genetically identical to the parent cell. However, the actual processes are different in several important ways.

As you already learned, prokaryotes such as bacteria do not have nuclei. They also do not have spindle fibers. And although they have DNA, prokaryotes have much less DNA than do most eukaryotes. The DNA of most bacteria is in the form of a single circular chromosome.

### CONNECT TO

**CELL STRUCTURE**

Recall from the chapter **Cell Structure and Function** that many scientists hypothesize that mitochondria and chloroplasts were originally free-living prokaryotes. One piece of evidence that supports this hypothesis is the fact that these two organelles replicate much as bacteria do, through fission.

**VISUAL VOCAB**

**Binary fission** is the asexual reproduction of a single-celled organism by division into two roughly equal parts.

parent cell

DNA duplicates

cell begins to divide

daughter cells

FIGURE 4.1 This micrograph shows three individual bacteria, each at a different stage of binary fission. First, a cell elongates (1), and the DNA is replicated. Next, the cell membrane pinches inward (2). Finally, the membrane meets, and a new cell wall forms, separating the two cells (3).

Binary fission, shown in **FIGURE 4.1,** starts when the bacterial chromosome is copied. Both chromosomes are attached to the cell membrane. As the cell grows and gets longer, the chromosomes move away from each other. When the cell is about twice its original size, it undergoes cytokinesis. The membrane pinches inward, and a new cell wall forms between the two chromosomes, which completes the separation into two daughter cells.

## Advantages and Disadvantages of Asexual Reproduction

Very often, whether something is helpful or harmful depends on the situation. In favorable environments that do not change much, asexual reproduction can be more efficient than sexual reproduction. Recall that asexual reproduction results in genetically identical offspring. If they are well suited to the environment, genetic variation could be more harmful than helpful. In other words, if it ain't broke, don't fix it.

However, asexual reproduction may be a disadvantage in changing conditions. Genetically identical offspring will respond to the environment in the same way. If population members lack traits that enable them to reproduce in a changed environment, the entire population could die off. In contrast, sexual reproduction increases genetic diversity, which raises the chance that some individuals will survive in changing conditions.

Keep in mind, however, that the act of asexual reproduction itself is not more efficient; rather, the associated costs of sexual reproduction are greater. For example, all asexually reproducing organisms can potentially reproduce. Suppose two organisms each have ten offspring. If one organism reproduces asexually, all ten offspring can have offspring of their own. If the other organism reproduces sexually, having five females and five males, only the five females can bear offspring. In addition, sexually reproducing organisms must attract a mate. This effort involves not only the time and energy needed to find a mate but also many structures, signals, and behaviors that have evolved to attract mates. Organisms that reproduce asexually do not have these costs.

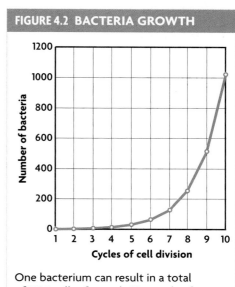

FIGURE 4.2 BACTERIA GROWTH

One bacterium can result in a total of 1024 cells after only 10 rounds of cell division.

**CONNECT TO**

**EVOLUTION**

As you will learn in the chapter **Viruses and Prokaryotes,** the misuse of antibiotics has resulted in multidrug-resistant bacteria. The bacteria not killed by antibiotics can reproduce quickly, passing the genes for antibiotic resistance on to their offspring.

**Summarize** **How is asexual reproduction an advantage in some conditions?**

# Some eukaryotes reproduce through mitosis.

Some eukaryotes also reproduce asexually, through mitosis. Have you ever grown a new plant from a stem cutting? Or seen a new sea star growing from the arm of another one? These new organisms are the result of mitotic reproduction and are therefore genetically the same as the parent organism. Mitotic reproduction is especially common in simpler plants and animals. It occurs in both multicellular and unicellular eukaryotes. It can take several forms, including budding, fragmentation, and vegetative reproduction.

In budding, a small projection grows on the surface of the parent organism, forming a separate new individual. The new organism may live independently or attached as part of a colony. For instance, hydras and some types of yeast reproduce by budding. Examples are shown in **FIGURE 4.3**.

In fragmentation, a parent organism splits into pieces, each of which can grow into a new organism. Flatworms and sea stars both reproduce by fragmentation. Many plants, including strawberries and potatoes, reproduce via vegetative reproduction. In general, vegetative reproduction involves the modification of a stem or underground structures of the parent organism. The offspring often stay connected to the original organism, through structures called runners, for example.

Many organisms can reproduce both asexually and sexually. The form of reproduction may depend on the current conditions. The sea anemone can reproduce in many ways. It can reproduce asexually by dividing in half, by breaking off small pieces from its base, or by budding. It can also reproduce sexually by making eggs and sperm. Some species of anemone have separate males and females. In other anemone species, the same organism can produce both eggs and sperm cells.

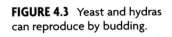

**FIGURE 4.3** Yeast and hydras can reproduce by budding.

Hydra

bud

Yeast

**Synthesize** How might the asexual reproduction of genetically identical plants be useful to humans? How could it prove harmful to our food supply?

---

## 5.4 Formative Assessment

### REVIEWING ⊙ MAIN IDEAS

1. Explain how mitosis differs from **binary fission.**

2. Briefly explain why cutting a flatworm into pieces would not kill it.

### CRITICAL THINKING

3. **Infer** How does an organism benefit by being able to reproduce both sexually and asexually?

4. **Apply** Yeasts are growing in two dishes. You treat one dish with a chemical that blocks DNA replication but forget to label it. How can you identify the treated dish?

**SELF-CHECK Online**
HMHScience.com
GO ONLINE

#### CONNECT TO
**ECOLOGY**

5. Two populations live in the same habitat and compete for food. The first group is larger and multiplies through **asexual reproduction;** the second reproduces sexually. What could happen to cause the second group to out-

SC.912.L.16.10

**KEY CONCEPT** **Cells work together to carry out complex functions.**

## MAIN IDEAS

- ▷ Multicellular organisms depend on interactions among different cell types.
- ▷ Specialized cells perform specific functions.
- ▷ Stem cells can develop into different cell types.

**SC.912.L.16.10** Evaluate the impact of biotechnology on the individual, society and the environment, including medical and ethical issues.

**VOCABULARY**

tissue
organ
organ system
cell differentiation
stem cell

### Connect to Your World

Each of us enters this world as a helpless infant. At first, your ability to eat solid foods or take your first steps elicits a great deal of praise. Over time, however, your development of normal skills gets far less attention. By the time you reach the age of 18, people want to know what you plan to do with your life. Will you build houses or design clothing or treat patients? What will your specialty be? Cells, too, undergo specialization to carry out the complex functions required by the body.

### ▷ MAIN IDEA

## Multicellular organisms depend on interactions among different cell types.

Within multicellular organisms, cells communicate and work together in groups that form increasingly larger, more complex structures. This arrangement progresses from cells to tissues to organs to organ systems, as shown in **FIGURE 5.1**. **Tissues** are groups of cells that work together to perform a similar function. Groups of tissues that work together to perform a specific function or related functions are called **organs.** For instance, plants have photosynthetic tissues made of chlorophyll-containing cells. Conductive tissues transport sugars, water, and minerals to and from other parts of the plant. Protective tissues help prevent water loss. Together, these and other tissues form a leaf, the plant's food-producing organ.

Organs that carry out similar functions are further grouped into **organ systems.** In plants, the shoot system is above the ground. It includes stems that support the plant, leaves that capture radiant energy, and flowers that aid reproduction. Beneath the ground, the root system has different types of roots and root hairs that anchor the plant and absorb water and minerals.

As organ systems work together, they help an organism maintain homeostasis. For example, plants need to maintain a certain level of water within their cells, otherwise they will wilt and die. They absorb water through their roots and expel it as water vapor through openings in their leaves called stomata. Stomata are controlled by special cells called guard cells, which close the stomata when a plant's water intake cannot keep up with its water loss.

**Apply** **Suppose your family goes out of town and forgets to ask your neighbor to water the plants. Do you think the plants' stomata will be open or closed? Explain.**

### CONNECT TO

### HOMEOSTASIS

As you learned in the chapter **Biology in the 21st Century,** homeostasis is the maintenance of a stable internal environment. Both an organism's physiology and its behavior help it achieve homeostasis.

## FIGURE 5.1 Levels of Organization

**Cells work together in groups that form larger, specialized structures.**

| CELL | TISSUE | ORGAN | SYSTEMS |
|---|---|---|---|
| Vessel elements are tube-shaped cells. | Vessel elements, tracheids, and parenchyma cells form xylem. (colored SEM; magnification 240×) | Xylem and other tissues form roots that absorb water and nutrients. | |

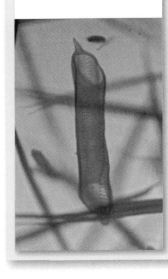
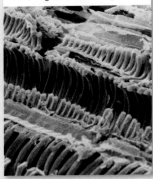
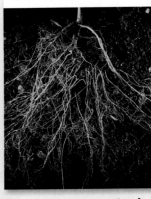
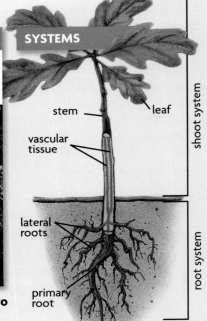

stem · leaf

vascular tissue

lateral roots

primary root

shoot system

root system

**Apply** How is the shape of this plant's roots suited to their function?

> ▶ **MAIN IDEA**
# Specialized cells perform specific functions.

**☀ CONNECT TO**

**GAMETOGENESIS**

As you will learn in the chapter **Meiosis and Mendel,** the egg is stocked with organelles and molecules that are necessary for an embryo to grow. Many of these molecules are not evenly distributed throughout the cell; they form gradients.

It is easy to see that a skin cell can divide to make a new skin cell, or that a single bacterium can generate another bacterium. But how does a complex organism like you develop? Your body began as a single fertilized egg. If the egg simply divided to make lots of identical cells, it would not form a baby. To form the intricate structures that make up your body and the bodies of countless organisms around you, cells must specialize.

**Cell differentiation** is the process by which a cell becomes specialized for a specific structure or function during multicellular development. While almost every cell in your body has a full set of DNA, each type of cell expresses only the specific genes it needs to carry out its function. That is, a cell differentiates among the genes and uses only certain ones. You can think of your DNA as a cookbook. When you want to make a specific dish, you select that recipe and carry out its instructions. If you need to make a dessert, you might choose brownies. If you need to make a main course, you might fix lentil stew. The dishes are very different, but they all come from the same cookbook.

A cell's location within the embryo helps determine how it will differentiate. In plant cells, the first division of a fertilized egg is unequal, or asymmetric, as shown in **FIGURE 5.2.** The apical cell forms most of the embryo, including the growth point for stems and leaves. The major role of the basal cell is to provide nutrients to the embryo; it also creates the growth point for the roots. Plant cells cannot easily migrate because of the cell wall, but they adapt to changing conditions and continue to develop throughout their lifetime.

As the plant grows, new cells continue to differentiate based on their location. For example, cells on the outer layer of a leaf may become epidermal cells that secrete a waxy substance that helps prevent water loss. Cells on the lower leaf surface may become guard cells that control the exchange of water, air, and carbon dioxide.

## FIGURE 5.2 Cell Differentiation in Seed Plants

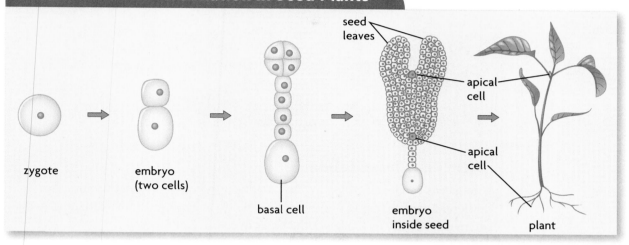

zygote — embryo (two cells) — basal cell — seed leaves / apical cell / apical cell / embryo inside seed — plant

In animals, an egg undergoes many rapid divisions after it is fertilized. The resulting cells can migrate to a specific area, and the cells quickly begin to differentiate. The early animal embryo generally takes the shape of a hollow ball. As the embryo develops, part of the ball folds inward, forming an inner layer and creating an opening in the outer cell layer. A middle layer of cells then forms. As shown in **FIGURE 5.3,** in vertebrates, the outer cell layer differentiates to form the outer layer of skin and elements of the nervous system, such as the brain and spinal cord. The middle cell layer forms bones, muscles, kidneys, and the inner layer of skin. The inner cell layer forms internal organs, such as the pancreas, lungs, and digestive system lining.

**Analyze**  **Why is regulation of the differentiation process during the early stages of development so critical?**

**Animal embryo cross section**

outer
middle
inner

## FIGURE 5.3 Cell Differentiation in Animals

**Cell differentiation in the developing animal embryo is based on location.**

**Outer**  Skin cells help prevent infection and dehydration.
(colored SEM; magnification 500×)

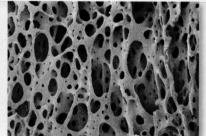

**Middle**  Bone cells form a hard matrix (shown) that supports and protects organs.
(colored SEM; magnification 15×)

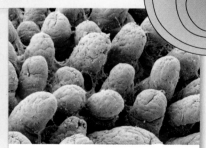

**Inner**  Intestinal epithelia have a large surface area that increases absorption.

**⁜ CONNECT TO**

## VOCABULARY

*Potent* comes from a Latin word meaning "to be able."
The addition of prefixes defines the level of power or ability.
*toti-* = all
*pluri-* = more, several
*multi-* = many

▶ MAIN IDEA

# Stem cells can develop into different cell types.

**Stem cells** are a unique type of body cell that can (1) divide and renew themselves for long periods of time, (2) remain undifferentiated in form, and (3) differentiate into a variety of specialized cell types. When a stem cell divides, it forms either two stem cells or one stem cell and one specialized cell.

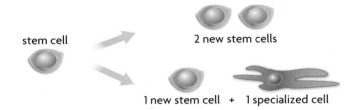

stem cell → 2 new stem cells

1 new stem cell + 1 specialized cell

## Stem Cell Classification

Stem cells can be classified by their ability, or potential, to develop into the differentiated cell types of different tissues. In general, the more differentiated a stem cell already is, the fewer the types of cells it can form.

- Totipotent stem cells can grow into any other cell type. Only a fertilized egg and the cells produced by the first few divisions of an embryo are totipotent.
- Pluripotent stem cells can grow into any cell type except for totipotent stem cells.
- Multipotent stem cells can grow only into cells of a closely related cell family.

Stem cells are also classified by their origin, as either adult or embryonic. Adult stem cells have been studied for decades, but the ability to grow human embryonic stem cells was not developed until 1998. Since that time, embryonic stem cells have attracted great attention because of their potential to form almost any cell type.

## Adult Stem Cells

Adult stem cells are partially undifferentiated cells located among the specialized cells of many organs and tissues. They are found all over the body, in the brain, liver, bone marrow, skeletal muscle, dental pulp, and even fat. These stem cells are also found in children and in umbilical cord blood, so the term *somatic stem cell* is more accurate although less frequently used.

A major advantage of adult stem cells is that they can be taken from a patient, grown in culture, and put back into the patient. Thus, the risk of transplant rejection by a patient's immune system is very low. This method also avoids many ethical issues associated with using embryonic stem cells.

Adult stem cells currently pose many disadvantages as well. They are few in number, difficult to isolate, and sometimes tricky to grow. They may also contain more DNA abnormalities than do embryonic stem cells. For years, much evidence suggested that adult stem cells were multipotent. This would mean that a stem cell from fat would produce only fat cells, never muscle cells.

Newer data suggest otherwise. Adult stem cells treated with the right combination of molecules may give rise to a completely different type of tissue. This process, called transdifferentiation, remains an active area of research.

## Embryonic Stem Cells

Most embryonic stem cells come from donated embryos grown in a clinic. These embryos are the result of in vitro fertilization, a process by which eggs are fertilized outside a woman's body. The stem cells are taken from a cluster of undifferentiated cells in the three-to-five-day-old embryo. These cells, called the inner cell mass, do not have the characteristics of any specific cell type. Because they are pluripotent, they can form any of the 200 cell types of the body. They can also be grown indefinitely in culture. These qualities offer hope that many diseases will be treatable or even curable. Stem cells have long been used to treat patients with leukemia and lymphoma, and people with diabetes might someday be cured if nonworking cells in the pancreas are replaced with healthy, growing cells. Even damaged organs might be strengthened by an injection of healthy cells.

Embryonic stem cells also have a downside. If these cells are used in treatment, a patient's body might reject them as foreign material. A different possibility is that the stem cells could grow unchecked in a patient's body and form a tumor. The use of embryonic stem cells also raises many ethical questions. **FIGURE 5.4** shows the most common method of obtaining embryonic stem cells. This method currently involves destruction of the embryo, which some people consider ethically unacceptable.

FIGURE 5.4 HARVESTING EMBRYONIC STEM CELLS

inner cell mass

fertilized egg

muscle cells

neurons

red blood cells

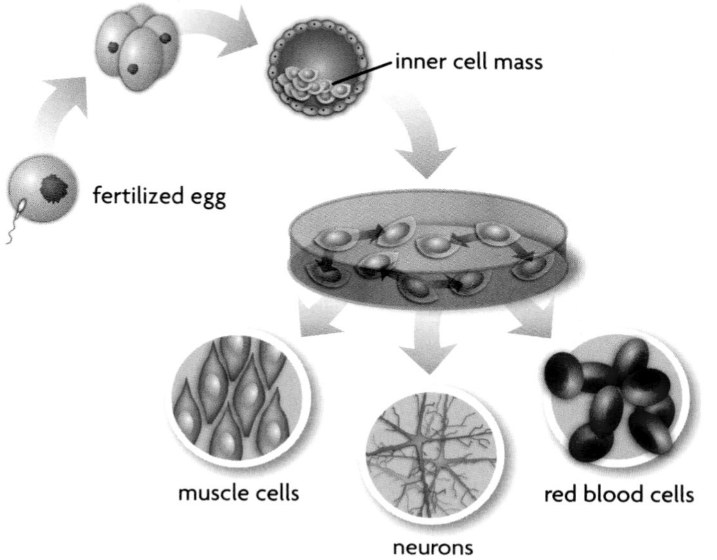

First, an egg is fertilized by a sperm cell in a petri dish. The egg divides, forming an inner cell mass. These cells are then removed and grown with nutrients. Scientists try to control how the cells specialize by adding or removing certain molecules.

**Compare and Contrast** **List treatment benefits and risks of both types of stem cells.**

## 5.5 Formative Assessment

SELF-CHECK Online
HMHScience.com
GO ONLINE

### REVIEWING ▶ MAIN IDEAS

1. How does communication between cells help maintain homeostasis?

2. Why is **cell differentiation** an important part of the development of a multicellular organism?

3. What are the defining characteristics of **stem cells**?

### CRITICAL THINKING

4. **Compare** Describe how cells, **tissues, organs,** and **organ systems** are related.

5. **Evaluate** What role does the location of a cell in a developing embryo play in cell differentiation?

### CONNECT TO

**ETHICS IN BIOLOGY**

6. Explain which factor you think is most important in deciding whether stem cell research should be legal and government-funded.

# 5 Summary

Cells have their own life cycle that includes reproduction, growth, and regulation, which allows organisms to carry out life functions and grow.

## KEY CONCEPTS

### 5.1 The Cell Cycle

**Cells have distinct phases of growth, reproduction, and normal functions.** The cell cycle has four main stages: $G_1$, S, $G_2$, and M. The length of the cell cycle can vary, resulting in different rates of cell division. This variability is based on the body's need for different cell types. Cells also divide because they need a sufficient surface area–to–volume ratio to move materials into and out of the cell.

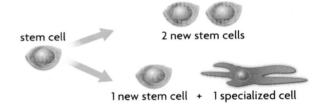

### 5.2 Mitosis and Cytokinesis

**Cells divide during mitosis and cytokinesis.** Mitosis divides the nucleus into two genetically identical nuclei in a four-phase process: prophase, metaphase, anaphase, and telophase. In prophase, the duplicated chromosomes condense tightly. Cytokinesis actually divides the cell cytoplasm.

### 5.3 Regulation of the Cell Cycle

**Cell cycle regulation is necessary for healthy growth.** Cell growth and division are regulated by both external factors, such as hormones and growth factors, and internal factors, such as cyclins and kinases. When proper regulation of cell growth is disrupted, a cell may become cancerous. Cancer cells grow more rapidly than do normal cells and form clumps called tumors that may metastasize to other regions of the body.

### 5.4 Asexual Reproduction

**Many organisms reproduce by cell division.** Most prokaryotes reproduce through a process called binary fission, in which a cell divides into two approximately equal parts. Some eukaryotes reproduce through mitosis. The offspring that result from asexual reproduction are genetically identical to the parent organism, except when mutations occur. Whether being identical is an advantage or a disadvantage depends on the environment.

### 5.5 Multicellular Life

**Cells work together to carry out complex functions.** Within multicellular organisms, cells form tissues, tissues form organs, and organs form organ systems. The cells differentiate to perform specific functions. Much of this specialization is determined by a cell's location within the developing embryo. Stem cells are a special type of cell that continue to divide and renew themselves for long periods of time.

stem cell → 2 new stem cells

1 new stem cell + 1 specialized cell

---

SYNTHESIZE YOUR NOTES

**Concept Map** Use a concept map like the one below to summarize what you know about mitosis.

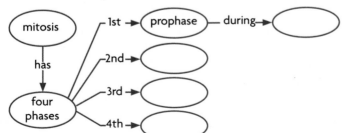

**Venn Diagram** Draw a Venn diagram like the one below to summarize the similarities and differences between embryonic and adult stem cells.

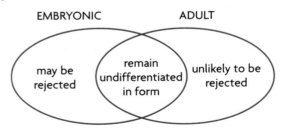

# 5 Review

**INTERACTIVE Review**
HMHScience.com
**GO ONLINE**
Review Games • Concept Map • Section Self-Checks

## CHAPTER VOCABULARY

**5.1** cell cycle
mitosis
cytokinesis
**5.2** chromosome
histone
chromatin
chromatid
centromere
telomere

prophase
metaphase
anaphase
telophase
**5.3** growth factor
apoptosis
cancer
benign
malignant

metastasize
carcinogen
**5.4** asexual reproduction
binary fission
**5.5** tissue
organ
organ system
cell differentiation
stem cell

## Reviewing Vocabulary

**Visualize Vocabulary**

For each term below, draw a simple picture that represents the meaning of the word. Here is an example for *mitosis*.

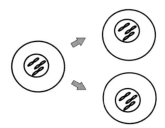

**1.** prophase
**2.** metaphase
**3.** anaphase
**4.** telophase
**5.** cytokinesis
**6.** centromere
**7.** telomere

### READING TOOLBOX    WORD ORIGINS

**8.** The prefix *pro-* means "earlier than" or "prior to." Explain how this meaning relates to the word *prophase*.

**9.** The prefix *telo-* means "distant, far, or end." How does this meaning relate to the words *telophase* and *telomere*?

**10.** The term *mitosis* comes from the Greek root *mitos*, which means "thread." How does this meaning relate to the process of mitosis?

## Reviewing MAIN IDEAS

**11.** The cell cycle has four main stages—$G_1$, S, $G_2$, and M. What occurs in the cell during each stage?

**12.** Compare the rates of cell division occurring in your neurons and your hair follicles.

**13.** What is the relationship between a cell's surface area and its volume?

**14.** You know that a chromosome is a very long, continuous strand of DNA. How do proteins help condense chromosomes?

**15.** Describe what happens in each main phase of mitosis—prophase, metaphase, anaphase, and telophase.

**16.** How does the process of cytokinesis differ from the process of mitosis?

**17.** Increased levels of cyclin help trigger a cell to divide. Do you think a growth factor would increase or decrease cyclin levels? Explain.

**18.** Describe how uncontrolled cell division is dangerous in organisms.

**19.** List one similarity and one difference between binary fission and mitosis.

**20.** You pull a leaf from a plant and place it in a cup of water. After a week, roots start to grow from the leaf. What type of reproduction has occurred, and what role does mitosis play in it?

**21.** Briefly describe how cell differentiation occurs in the developing animal embryo.

**22.** List three characteristics of all stem cells.

# Critical Thinking

**23. Synthesize** How do regulatory proteins of the cell cycle help maintain homeostasis?

**24. Describe** How is the location of a cell in an embryo related to differentiation of that cell?

**25. Analyze** A scientist wants to use asexually reproducing vegetables to increase crop yields. He plans to distribute budding potatoes and teach farmers how to separate them into new plants. What are some potential benefits and risks that could result from this situation?

**26. Analyze** The rates of DNA mutations in bacteria are known to increase when they are under stressed environmental conditions. Why do you think this is important for an organism that reproduces asexually?

**27. Apply** Suppose an organism usually has 24 chromosomes in its nucleus. How many chromatids would it have just after the S phase of the cell cycle?

**28. Predict** If a mutation made histone proteins bind less tightly to DNA, how might the cell cycle be affected?

## Interpreting Visuals

Use the picture of onion root cells shown below to answer the next three questions.

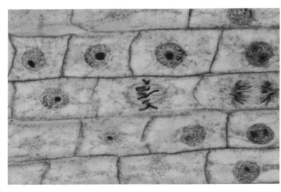

magnification 120×

**29. Apply** In what stage of the cell cycle are most of these cells? Explain.

**30. Apply** How can you visually distinguish between newly formed cells and older cells?

**31. Synthesize** If these cells were immersed in salt water, how would the cells undergoing mitosis be affected? (Hint: Think about the process of osmosis.)

## Analyzing Data  Construct a Data Table

The graph below shows the five-year survival rate, expressed as percentages, of patients diagnosed with cancer from 1985 through 1997. This data is for all types of invasive cancers and includes males and females of all races. Use the graph to answer the next two questions.

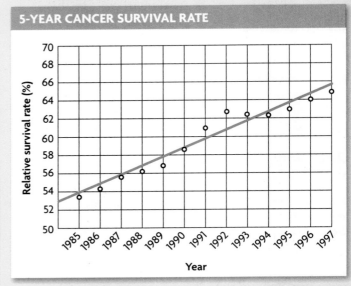

**5-YEAR CANCER SURVIVAL RATE**

**32. Analyze** Which points do not follow the best-fit line for the data?

**33. Interpret** What is the trend in the data of cancer survival during the span of time given?

## Making Connections

**34. Write a Narrative** Imagine that you are a single chromosome about to undergo replication and mitosis. Describe what will happen to you starting from the S phase through mitosis. Be creative. Use humor and a first-person point of view. Come up with sounds or perspectives that illustrate what is happening. Be sure to include all details of the process and related terms.

**35. Design an Experiment** Cancer cells, such as those shown on the chapter opener, are frequently grown in labs for research uses. Suppose you wanted to determine whether a certain substance was a carcinogen. Outline a plan for an experiment to describe what questions you would want to answer, what experiments you would perform, and what the different possible results would suggest.

# Standards-Based Assessment

Record your answers on a separate piece of paper.

## MULTIPLE CHOICE

1 Scientists researching anticancer drugs treat a cell culture with a compound. Following treatment, they notice that the culture stopped growing. Untreated cells from the same culture, however, have continued to grow. These results indicate that the compound blocks the normal cell cycle. What else could have caused these results?

A The compound had degraded.

B The compound prevented cells from mutating.

C The compound killed the treated cells.

D The compound had no effect.

### THINK THROUGH THE QUESTION

The untreated cells serve as a control in this experiment. Therefore, differences between the treated and untreated cells should be the result of the drug. If the drug has no effect, the two groups of cells should be the same.

2 Which describes the role of DNA in cell differentiation?

A It regulates cell differentiation.

B It carries the code from which each cell type expresses specific genes.

C It removes genes that are unneeded from differentiated cells.

D It prevents a full set of DNA from being passed on to stem cells.

3 One environmental factor that plays a key role in cell differentiation in multicellular organisms is the location of the developing cell with respect to other cells. In human development, from which cell layer in the embryo will a nerve cell develop?

A within the nucleus

B outer layer

C middle layer

D inner layer

4

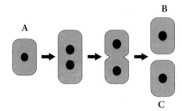

In the diagram above, cell A is undergoing mitosis. If cell A has 6 chromosomes, how many chromosomes will cells B and C have?

A none

B 3 each

C 6 each

D 12 each

5

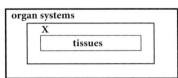

The figure above represents some levels of organization in multicellular organisms. Which term fits in the box marked "X"?

A cells

B organelles

C organs

D organisms

6 Unlike stem cells, most body cells cannot form different types of cells. For example, skin cells can only make skin cells, and nerve cells only make nerve cells. Which statement **best** explains why skin cells will never become nerve cells?

A Each type of cell gets a different message from the central DNA, which is stored in DNA cells.

B Each type of cell has only the part of the DNA necessary for making that type of cell.

C Each cell type is determined by messages sent from the brain, which directs development.

D Both types of cells have the same DNA, but each cell uses only part of the DNA message.

# BIOZINE

*at* **HMHSCIENCE.COM**

**INTERNET MAGAZINE**

*Go online for the latest biology news and updates on all BioZine articles.*

Expanding the Textbook

News Feeds

Science Daily

CNN

BBC

Careers

Bio Bytes

Opinion Poll

Strange Biology

**A group of embryonic stem cells**
(colored SEM, magnification 1,000×)

## Stem Cell Research— Potential Solutions, Practical Challenges

*A news program asks viewers to vote on-line: "Should stem cell research be banned? Yes or no?" Some people claim that stem cell therapy will revolutionize medicine. Others believe that some types of stem cell research violate ethical standards and are not justified by the potential benefits. Between these two positions exists a wide range of ideas about what is or is not acceptable. Would you know how to vote?*

## Using Stem Cells

Stem cells are undifferentiated cells that can regenerate themselves and develop into specialized types of cells. Stem cell research offers the hope of understanding basic cell processes and treating or even curing many diseases. However, many technical challenges must be overcome before stem cell therapy is a realistic option, and ethical issues continue to surround stem cell research.

## Potential Benefits

Stem cell research offers many potential benefits.

- Studying adult stem cells may help scientists better understand how tissues develop and what goes wrong when those tissues become diseased.

- A better understanding of the properties of stem cells may give scientists more information about how cancer cells replace themselves and thus help scientists develop more-targeted cancer therapies.

- Stem cells could be used to grow human tissues to test the effects of drugs and chemicals.

- Stem cells may be used to replace healthy cells that are killed by radiation treatment for cancer.

- Stem cells may be used to regenerate tissues. For example, chemotherapy kills blood-producing cells in bone marrow. To replace these cells, stem cells could be used instead of the patient's own marrow, which may contain cancer cells.

- Stem cells may be used to treat spinal cord injuries and neurodegenerative diseases, such as Parkinson's.

# TECHNOLOGY S.T.E.M.

## Somatic Cell Nuclear Transfer

Somatic cell nuclear transfer (SCNT), also called therapeutic cloning, is a method for obtaining stem cells that has been used to clone animals. The process is still under development, however, and it has not yet been used to produce stem cells for humans. SCNT offers the hope of using a patient's own DNA to produce stem cells that can form many types of specialized cells. Many SCNT studies have been done in mice and pigs; the diagram to the right shows how the SCNT process might be applied in human cells.

**1** An unfertilized egg is taken from a female's body, and the nucleus—containing the DNA—is removed. A cell is then taken from a patient's body. The nucleus is removed and inserted into the egg.

**2** The egg is given a mild electrical stimulation, which makes it divide. The DNA comes from the patient's nucleus, and the materials needed for division come from the egg.

**3** The stem cells could then be cultured and caused to differentiate into any tissue or organ needed by the patient.

Once a stem cell line is established, in theory it can continue to grow indefinitely. Researchers could use these cell lines without having to harvest more stem cells. The cell lines also could be frozen and shipped to other researchers around the world.

**Read More >>** *at* HMHScience.com

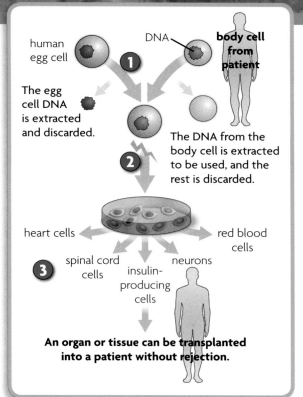

human egg cell · DNA · body cell from patient

**1**

The egg cell DNA is extracted and discarded.

The DNA from the body cell is extracted to be used, and the rest is discarded.

**2**

heart cells · red blood cells

spinal cord cells · insulin-producing cells · neurons

**3**

**An organ or tissue can be transplanted into a patient without rejection.**

## Technical Challenges

Adult stem cells have been used therapeutically for years in the form of bone marrow transplants. Nevertheless, many technical challenges must still be overcome before stem cells can be used to treat a wide range of disorders. Examples are highlighted below.

**Supply** Stem cells can be taken from a variety of sources, including an embryo, a patient in need of treatment, a patient's relative, or an established embryonic stem cell line. Embryonic stem cells are taken from embryos fertilized in an in vitro fertilization clinic, whereas established stem cell lines are cultures of embryonic stem cells used to grow additional stem cells that match the ones that came from

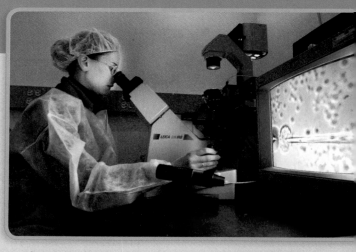

This researcher is micro-injecting mouse stem cells into fertilized mouse eggs to be used in drug research.

the original embryo. Each source presents its own special set of ethical considerations.

**Transplantation into the target area** The delivery of stem cells to targeted tissues can be complex, especially if the tissues are deep inside the body. And once delivered, stem cells must "learn" to work with other cells. For instance, inserted cardiac cells must contract in unison with a patient's heart cells.

**Prevention of rejection** Stem cells may be rejected if a patient's body sees them as foreign. This problem can remain even when certain identifying proteins are removed from the cells' membranes. The development of SCNT technology in humans could help solve this problem so that patients would not have to take drugs to suppress their immune system.

**Suppression of tumor formation** By their very nature, stem cells remain undifferentiated and continue to divide for long periods of time. When transplanted into an organism, many embryonic stem cells tend to form tumors. This risk must be removed before the cells can be used therapeutically.

## Unanswered Questions

Stem cell research and therapy do not only involve questions of what we can do. They also involve questions about what we should do, who should benefit, and who should pay.

- Should human embryos be a source of stem cells?
- How should stem cell research be funded?
- How can the benefits of stem cell research best be shared by all people, regardless of income?
- Should insurance cover costly stem cell procedures?

**Read More >>** *at* HMHScience.com

### CAREERS

## Cell Biologist in Action

| DR. GAIL MARTIN | |
|---|---|
| **TITLE** Professor, Anatomy, University of California, San Francisco | |
| **EDUCATION** Ph.D., Molecular Biology, University of California, Berkeley | |

In 1974 Dr. Gail Martin was working at the University College in London when she made a huge advance. She developed a way to grow stem cells in a petri dish. These fragile cells were hard to work with, so Dr. Martin's breakthrough removed a big obstacle to stem cell research. Seven years later, she made another key discovery while working in her own laboratory at the University of California, San Francisco, in her native United States—how to harvest stem cells from mouse embryos. Her work has helped other scientists develop ways to harvest stem cells from human embryos and explore their use in treating disorders.

Dr. Martin likes to point out that her work shows how small advances in basic biology can pay off years later in unexpected ways. She states that many people focus on cures for specific diseases, not realizing that these cures "may come from basic research in seemingly unrelated areas. What is really going to be important 20 years from now isn't clear."

**Read More >>** *at* HMHScience.com

(tr) ©Chris Stewart/San Francisco Chronicle/Corbis

# UNIT 3

# Genetics

## BIOZINE
HMHScience.com

**Medical Technology—
The Genetic Forefront**
**TECHNOLOGY** Biochips
**CAREER** Cancer Geneticist

**BIG IDEA** In meiosis, genetic material from two parent organisms results in offspring with traits that follow a pattern of inheritance.

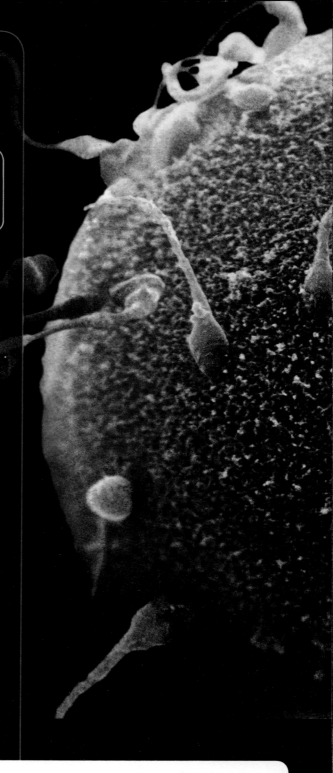

⊘ **ONLINE BIOLOGY**   HMHScience.com

**ONLINE** Labs
- **QuickLab** Using a Testcross
- Allele Combinations and Punnett Squares
- Modeling Meiosis
- **S.T.E.M. Lab** Modeling Chromosomes in Meiosis
- Probability Practice
- Modeling Monohybrid and Dihybrid Crosses

- **Virtual Lab** Breeding Mutations in Fruit Flies
- **Video Lab** Meiosis Model

(t) ©Photo Researchers/Getty Images

Q **What makes you who you are?**

The human egg and sperm cells (left) are the result of meiosis, a process that reduces a cell's chromosome number by half. Millions of sperm could potentially fertilize the egg, but only one actually succeeds. The fusion of egg and sperm triggers a series of events that lead to the development of a healthy new organism displaying features of both the mother and the father.

---

 **READING TOOLBOX**   This reading tool can help you learn the material in the following pages.

### USING LANGUAGE

**Comparisons**  Comparing is a way of looking for the similarities between different things. Contrasting is a way of looking for differences. Certain words and phrases can help you determine if things are being compared or contrasted. Comparison words include *and, like, just as,* and *in the same way.* Contrast words include *however, unlike, in contrast,* and *on the other hand.*

### YOUR TURN

In the following sentences, find the things that are being compared or contrasted.

1. Like mitosis, meiosis is a process that reproduces new cells.

2. In contrast to many other reptiles, the Burmese python does not reproduce sexually.

## 6.1 Chromosomes and Meiosis

SC.912.L.16.16

SC.912.L.16.16 Describe the process of meiosis, including independent assortment and crossing over. Explain how reduction division results in the formation of haploid gametes or spores.

**VOCABULARY**

somatic cell
gamete
homologous chromosome
autosome
sex chromosome
sexual reproduction
fertilization
diploid
haploid
meiosis

**KEY CONCEPT** **Gametes have half the number of chromosomes that body cells have.**

**MAIN IDEAS**

- You have body cells and gametes.
- Your cells have autosomes and sex chromosomes.
- Body cells are diploid; gametes are haploid.

### Connect to Your World

Perhaps you are familiar with the saying, "Everything old is new again." This phrase usually indicates that a past style is again current. However, it applies equally well to you. The fusion of a single egg and sperm cell resulted in the complex creature that is you. There's never been anyone quite like you. And yet the DNA that directs your cells came from your mother and father. And their DNA came from their mother and father, and so on and so on. In this chapter, you will examine the processes that went into making you who you are.

### ▶ MAIN IDEA

## You have body cells and gametes.

You have many types of specialized cells in your body, but they can be divided into two major groups: somatic cells and germ cells. **Somatic cells** (soh-MAT-ihk), also called body cells, make up most of your body tissues and organs. For example, your spleen, kidneys, and eyeballs are all made entirely of body cells. DNA in your body cells is not passed on to your children. Germ cells, in contrast, are cells in your reproductive organs, the ovaries or the testes, that develop into gametes. **Gametes** are sex cells—ova, or eggs, in the female, and spermatozoa, or sperm cells, in the male. DNA in your gametes can be passed on to your children.

Each species has a characteristic number of chromosomes per cell. This number is typically given for body cells, not for gametes. Chromosome number does not seem to be related to the complexity of an organism. For example, yeast have 32 chromosomes, which come in 16 pairs. The fruit flies commonly used in genetic experiments have 8 chromosomes, which come in 4 pairs. A fern holds the record for the most chromosomes—more than 1200. Each of your body cells contains a set of 46 chromosomes, which come in 23 pairs. These cells are genetically identical to each other unless mutations have occurred. As you have learned, cells within an organism differ from one another because different genes are expressed, not because they have different genes.

**Identify** Which cell type makes up the brain?

### ◉ READING TOOLBOX

**TAKING NOTES**

Make a two-column table to keep track of the vocabulary in this chapter.

| Term | Definition |
|------|------------|
| somatic cell | |
| gamete | |
| | |
| | |

## MAIN IDEA
# Your cells have autosomes and sex chromosomes.

Suppose you had 23 pairs of gloves. You would have a total of 46 gloves that you could divide into two sets, 23 right and 23 left. Similarly, your body cells have 23 pairs of chromosomes for a total of 46 that can be divided into two sets: 23 from your mother and 23 from your father. Just as you use both gloves when it's cold outside, your cells use both sets of chromosomes to function properly.

Together, each pair of chromosomes is referred to as a homologous pair. In this context, the word *homologous* means "having the same structure." **Homologous chromosomes** are two chromosomes—one inherited from the mother, one from the father—that have the same length and general appearance. More importantly, these chromosomes have copies of the same genes, although the two copies may differ. For example, if you have a gene that influences blood cholesterol levels on chromosome 8, you will have one copy from your mother and one copy from your father. It is possible that one of these copies is associated with high cholesterol levels, while the other is associated with low cholesterol levels. For convenience, scientists have assigned a number to each pair of homologous chromosomes, ordered from largest to smallest. As **FIGURE 1.1** shows, the largest pair of chromosomes is number 1, the next largest pair is number 2, and so forth.

Collectively, chromosome pairs 1 through 22 make up your **autosomes,** chromosomes that contain genes for characteristics not directly related to the sex of an organism. But what about the 23rd chromosome pair?

Most sexually reproducing species also have **sex chromosomes** that directly control the development of sexual characteristics. Humans have two very different sex chromosomes, X and Y. How sex is determined varies by species. In all mammals, including humans, an organism's sex is determined by the XY system. An organism with two X chromosomes is female. An organism with one X and one Y chromosome is male. Sex chromosomes make up your 23rd pair of chromosomes. Although the X and Y chromosomes pair with each other, they are not homologous. The X chromosome is the larger sex chromosome and contains numerous genes, including many that are unrelated to sexual characteristics. The Y chromosome is the sex chromosome that contains genes that direct the development of the testes and other male traits. It is the smallest chromosome and carries the fewest genes.

**Summarize** Are homologous chromosomes identical to each other? Explain.

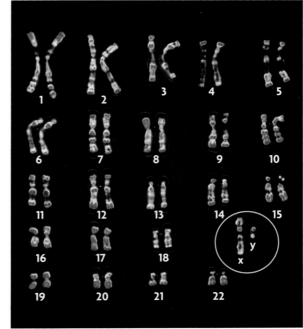

**FIGURE 1.1** Human DNA is organized into two sets of 23 chromosomes. Each set contains 22 autosomes and 1 sex chromosome. Females have two X chromosomes. Males have an X and a Y chromosome (circled). (colored LM; magnification 4400×)

"The parents are both geneticists."

(t) ©CNRI/Photo Researchers, Inc.; (b) Cartoon by Mick Stevens

# Body cells are diploid; gametes are haploid.

**Sexual reproduction** involves the fusion of two gametes, resulting in offspring that are a genetic mixture of both parents. The actual fusion of an egg and a sperm cell is called **fertilization.** When fertilization occurs, the nuclei of the egg and sperm cell fuse to form one nucleus. This new nucleus must have the correct number of chromosomes for a healthy new organism to develop. Therefore, both the egg and the sperm cell need only half the usual number of chromosomes—one chromosome from each homologous pair.

## Diploid and Haploid Cells

Body cells and gametes have different numbers of chromosomes. Your body cells are diploid. **Diploid** (DIHP-LOYD) means that a cell has two copies of each chromosome: one copy from the mother, and one copy from the father. Diploid cells can be represented as 2*n*. In humans, the diploid chromosome number is 46.

Gametes are not diploid cells; they are haploid cells, represented as *n*. **Haploid** (HAP-LOYD) means that a cell has only one copy of each chromosome. Each human egg or sperm cell has 22 autosomes and 1 sex chromosome. In the egg, the sex chromosome is always an X chromosome. In the sperm cell, the sex chromosome can be an X chromosome or a Y chromosome. The reason for this difference will be discussed in the following sections.

Maintaining the correct number of chromosomes is important to the survival of all organisms. Typically, a change in chromosome number is harmful. However, increasing the number of sets of chromosomes can, on occasion, give rise to a new species. The fertilization of nonhaploid gametes has played an important role in plant evolution by rapidly making new species with more than two sets of chromosomes. For example, some plants have four copies of each chromosome, a condition called tetraploidy (4*n*). This type of event has occurred in many groups of plants, but it is very rare in animals.

## Meiosis

Germ cells in your reproductive organs undergo the process of meiosis to form gametes. **Meiosis** (my-OH-sihs) is a form of nuclear division that divides a diploid cell into haploid cells. This process is essential for sexual reproduction. The details of meiosis will be presented in the next section. **FIGURE 1.2** highlights some differences between mitosis and meiosis in advance to help you keep these two processes clear in your mind.

## FIGURE 1.2 Comparing Mitosis and Meiosis

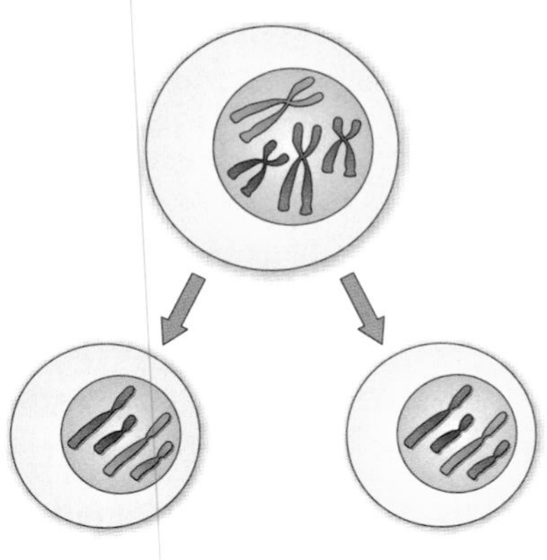

| MITOSIS | | | MEIOSIS |
|---|---|---|---|
| | Produces genetically identical cells | Produces genetically unique cells | |
| | Results in diploid cells | Results in haploid cells | |
| | Takes place throughout an organism's lifetime | Takes place only at certain times in an organism's life cycle | |
| | Involved in asexual reproduction | Involved in sexual reproduction | |

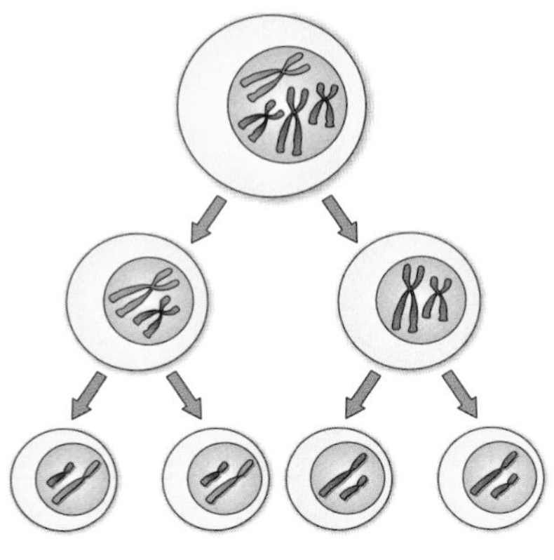

**Compare** Using the diagrams above, explain how you think the process of meiosis differs from mitosis.

You have already learned about mitosis, another form of nuclear division. Recall that mitosis is a process that occurs in body cells. It helps produce daughter cells that are genetically identical to the parent cell. In cells undergoing mitosis, DNA is copied once and divided once. Both the parent cell and the daughter cells are diploid. Mitosis is used for development, growth, and repair in all types of organisms. It is also used for reproduction in asexually reproducing eukaryotes.

In contrast, meiosis occurs in germ cells to produce gametes. This process is sometimes called a "reduction division" because it reduces a cell's chromosome number by half. In cells undergoing meiosis, DNA is copied once but divided twice. Meiosis makes genetically unique haploid cells from a diploid cell. These haploid cells then undergo more processing in the ovaries or testes, finally forming mature gametes.

**Apply** Why is it important that gametes are haploid cells?

**SELF-CHECK** Online
HMHScience.com
**GO ONLINE**

## 6.1 Formative Assessment

### REVIEWING ▶ MAIN IDEAS

1. Where are germ cells located in the human body?

2. What is the difference between an **autosome** and a **sex chromosome**?

3. Is the cell that results from **fertilization** a **haploid** or **diploid** cell? Explain.

### CRITICAL THINKING

4. **Infer** Does mitosis or **meiosis** occur more frequently in your body? Explain your answer.

5. **Analyze** Do you think that the Y chromosome contains genes that are critical for an organism's survival? Explain your reasoning.

### CONNECT TO

**TELOMERES**

6. The ends of DNA molecules form telomeres that help keep the ends of chromosomes from sticking to each other. Why might this be especially important in germ cells, which go through meiosis and make haploid **gametes**?

# Interpreting Bar Graphs

**Smart Grapher**
HMHScience.com
**GO ONLINE**
Create animated charts and graphs using Smart Grapher.

**Bar graphs** show data with bars. In a bar graph, the independent variable is usually graphed on the *x*-axis and the dependent variable is usually graphed on the *y*-axis. Both axes are labeled with the name and unit of the variable.

## Model

The bar graph below contains data about the frequency of some genetic disorders in the human population. Each of the disorders listed is the result of nondisjunction, the failure of two chromosomes to separate properly during meiosis. This results in one extra chromosome or one less chromosome being passed on to the offspring.

For each syndrome on the *x*-axis, the bar extends vertically on the *y*-axis to represent the incidence per 100,000 births. For example, out of 100,000 births, 111 children are born with Down syndrome.

In most cases, Down syndrome results from an extra chromosome 21.
(colored LM; magnification 2000×)

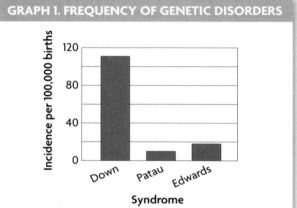

**GRAPH 1. FREQUENCY OF GENETIC DISORDERS**

Source: U.S. National Library of Medicine

## Practice   Interpret a Bar Graph

The bar graph below contains data about the diploid number of chromosomes in different organisms.

1. **Analyze**  Which organism has the greatest number of chromosomes? the least?

2. **Evaluate**  Does chromosome number appear to correlate to the type of organism? Explain.

3. **Hypothesize**  Do you think there is an upper limit to chromosome number? Explain.

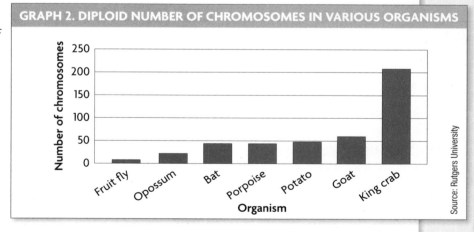

**GRAPH 2. DIPLOID NUMBER OF CHROMOSOMES IN VARIOUS ORGANISMS**

Source: Rutgers University

©CNRI/Photo Researchers, Inc.

# 6.2 Process of Meiosis

SC.912.L.16.16

KEY CONCEPT **During meiosis, diploid cells undergo two cell divisions that result in haploid cells.**

### MAIN IDEAS
- ⊙ Cells go through two rounds of division in meiosis.
- ⊙ Haploid cells develop into mature gametes.

### VOCABULARY
gametogenesis
sperm
egg
polar body

**SC.912.L.16.16** Describe the process of meiosis, including independent assortment and crossing over. Explain how reduction division results in the formation of haploid gametes or spores.

---

### ☀ *Connect to Your World*

Sometimes division, such as splitting the bill at a restaurant or dividing people into teams for basketball, is difficult. Luckily, understanding how meiosis divides chromosomes between cells is not that hard. Meiosis begins with a diploid cell that has already undergone DNA replication. The cell copies the chromosomes once and divides them twice, making four haploid cells.

### ⊙ MAIN IDEA

## Cells go through two rounds of division in meiosis.

Meiosis is a form of nuclear division that creates four haploid cells from one diploid cell. This process involves two rounds of cell division—meiosis I and meiosis II. Each round of cell division has four phases, which are similar to those in mitosis. To keep the two processes distinct in your mind, focus on the big picture. Pay attention to the way meiosis reduces chromosome number and creates genetic diversity.

### Homologous Chromosomes and Sister Chromatids

To understand meiosis, you need to distinguish between homologous chromosomes and sister chromatids. As **FIGURE 2.1** shows, homologous chromosomes are two separate chromosomes: one from your mother, one from your father. Homologous chromosomes are very similar to each other, since they have the same length and carry the same genes. But they are not copies of each other. In contrast, each half of a duplicated chromosome is called a chromatid. Together, the two chromatids are called sister chromatids. Thus, the term *sister chromatids* refers to the duplicated chromosomes that remain attached (by the centromere). Homologous chromosomes are divided in meiosis I. Sister chromatids are not divided until meiosis II.

### ☀ CONNECT TO

**MITOSIS**

As you learned in the chapter **Cell Growth and Division,** a condensed, duplicated chromosome is made of two chromatids. Sister chromatids separate during anaphase in mitosis.

### 🔍 READING TOOLBOX

**TAKING NOTES**

Draw a Venn diagram like the one below to summarize the similarities and differences between meiosis I and meiosis II.

Meiosis I — Meiosis II

divides homologous chromosomes | chromosomes condense | divides sister chromatids

---

**FIGURE 2.1** Homologous chromosomes (shown duplicated) are two separate chromosomes—one inherited from the mother, and one from the father.

homologous chromosomes

sister chromatids · sister chromatids

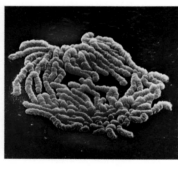

**FIGURE 2.2** Homologous chromosomes separate during anaphase I. (colored SEM; magnification 2200×)

## Meiosis I

Before meiosis begins, DNA has already been copied. Meiosis I divides homologous chromosomes, producing two haploid cells with duplicated chromosomes. Like mitosis, scientists describe meiosis in terms of phases, illustrated in **FIGURE 2.3** below. The figure is simplified, showing only four chromosomes.

**1** **Prophase I** Early in meiosis, the nuclear membrane breaks down, the centrosomes and centrioles move to opposite sides of the cell, and spindle fibers start to assemble. The duplicated chromosomes condense, and homologous chromosomes pair up. They appear to pair up precisely, gene for gene, down their entire length. The sex chromosomes also pair with each other, and some regions of their DNA appear to line up as well.

**2** **Metaphase I** The homologous chromosome pairs are randomly lined up along the middle of the cell by spindle fibers. The result is that 23 chromosomes—some from the father, some from the mother—are lined up along each side of the cell equator. This arrangement mixes up the chromosomal combinations and helps create and maintain genetic diversity. Since human cells have 23 pairs of chromosomes, meiosis may result in $2^{23}$, or 8,388,608, possible combinations of chromosomes.

**3** **Anaphase I** Next, the paired homologous chromosomes separate from each other and move toward opposite sides of the cell. The sister chromatids remain together during this step and throughout meiosis I.

**4** **Telophase I** The nuclear membrane forms again in some species, the spindle fibers disassemble, and the cell undergoes cytokinesis. The end result is two cells that each have a unique combination of 23 duplicated chromosomes coming from both parents.

## FIGURE 2.3 Meiosis

**Meiosis I divides homologous chromosomes.**

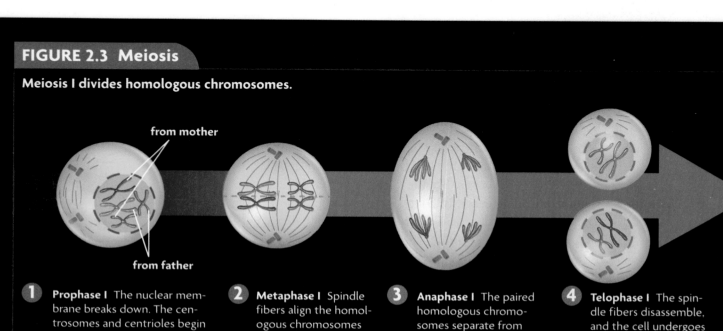

from mother

from father

**1** **Prophase I** The nuclear membrane breaks down. The centrosomes and centrioles begin to move, and spindle fibers start to assemble. The duplicated chromosomes condense, and homologous chromosomes

**2** **Metaphase I** Spindle fibers align the homologous chromosomes along the cell equator. Each side of the equator has chromosomes from both parents.

**3** **Anaphase I** The paired homologous chromosomes separate from each other and move toward opposite sides of the cell. Sister chromatids remain attached.

**4** **Telophase I** The spindle fibers disassemble, and the cell undergoes cytokinesis.

## Meiosis II

Meiosis II divides sister chromatids and results in undoubled chromosomes. The following description of this process applies to both of the cells produced in meiosis I. Note that DNA is not copied again between these two stages.

**(5)** **Prophase II** The nuclear membrane breaks down, centrosomes and centrioles move to opposite sides of the cell, and spindle fibers assemble.

**(6)** **Metaphase II** Spindle fibers align the 23 chromosomes at the cell equator. Each chromosome still has two sister chromatids at this stage.

**(7)** **Anaphase II** Next, the sister chromatids are pulled apart from each other and move to opposite sides of the cell.

**(8)** **Telophase II** Finally, nuclear membranes form around each set of chromosomes at opposite ends of the cell, the spindle fibers break apart, and the cell undergoes cytokinesis. The end result is four haploid cells with a combination of chromosomes from both the mother and father.

Now that you've seen how meiosis works, let's review some key differences between the processes of meiosis and mitosis.

- Meiosis has two cell divisions. Mitosis has only one cell division.
- During meiosis, homologous chromosomes pair up along the cell equator. During mitosis, homologous chromosomes never pair up.
- In anaphase I of meiosis, sister chromatids remain together. In anaphase of mitosis, sister chromatids separate.
- Meiosis results in haploid cells. Mitosis results in diploid cells.

**Contrast** **What is the major difference between metaphase I and metaphase II?**

**Virtual INVESTIGATION**
HMHScience.com
**GO ONLINE**
Phases of Meiosis

**CONNECT TO**

### CYTOKINESIS

As you learned in the chapter **Cell Growth and Division,** cytokinesis is the division of the cell cytoplasm. This process is the same in cells undergoing either mitosis or meiosis.

**Animated Biology**
HMHScience.com
**GO ONLINE**
Meiosis

**Meiosis II divides sister chromatids. The overall process produces haploid cells.**

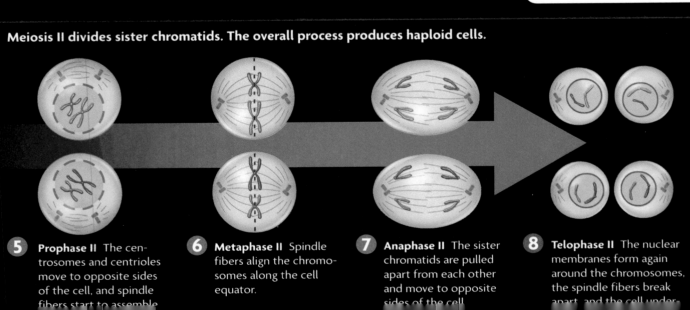

**(5)** **Prophase II** The centrosomes and centrioles move to opposite sides of the cell, and spindle fibers start to assemble.

**(6)** **Metaphase II** Spindle fibers align the chromosomes along the cell equator.

**(7)** **Anaphase II** The sister chromatids are pulled apart from each other and move to opposite sides of the cell.

**(8)** **Telophase II** The nuclear membranes form again around the chromosomes, the spindle fibers break apart, and the cell under-

# Haploid cells develop into mature gametes.

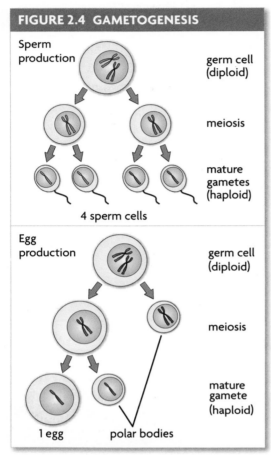

**FIGURE 2.4  GAMETOGENESIS**

Sperm production

germ cell (diploid)

meiosis

mature gametes (haploid)

4 sperm cells

Egg production

germ cell (diploid)

meiosis

mature gamete (haploid)

1 egg          polar bodies

Haploid cells are the end result of meiosis. Yet these cells are incapable of fertilization until they go through more changes to form mature gametes. **Gametogenesis** (guh-MEE-tuh-JEHN-ih-sihs) is the production of gametes. As **FIGURE 2.4** shows, gametogenesis includes both meiosis and other changes that produce a mature cell. The final stages of gametogenesis differ between the sexes.

The **sperm** cell, the male gamete, is much smaller than the **egg,** the female gamete. The sperm cell's main contribution to an embryo is DNA. Yet it must swim to an egg to fertilize it, so the ability to move is critical. Sperm formation starts with a round cell and ends by making a streamlined cell that can move rapidly. During this process, significant changes occur. DNA is tightly packed and much of the cytoplasm is lost, resulting in a compact head. The sperm cell develops a whiplike flagellum and connecting neck region packed with mitochondria that drive the cell. Other changes, such as the addition of new proteins to the cell membrane, also take place.

The formation of an egg is a complicated process. It begins before birth, inside the developing body of a female embryo, and is not finished until that egg is fertilized by a sperm many years later. The process includes periods of active development and long periods of inactivity.

An egg not only gives its share of DNA to an embryo, but also contributes the organelles, molecular building blocks, and other materials an embryo needs to begin life. Only one of the four cells produced by each round of meiosis actually makes an egg. One cell—the egg—receives most of the organelles, cytoplasm, and nutrients. Many molecules are not evenly distributed throughout the egg's cytoplasm. This unequal distribution of molecules helps cells in the developing embryo to specialize. The other cells produced by meiosis become **polar bodies,** cells with little more than DNA that are eventually broken down. In many species, including humans, the polar body produced by meiosis I does not undergo meiosis II.

**Apply**  Briefly explain how a sperm cell's structure is related to its function.

**SELF-CHECK Online**
HMHScience.com
**GO ONLINE**

## 6.2 Formative Assessment

### REVIEWING ◉ MAIN IDEAS

1. How do homologous chromosomes differ from sister chromatids?

2. Explain why an **egg** is so much larger than a **sperm** cell.

### CRITICAL THINKING

3. **Predict**  If, during metaphase I, all 23 maternal chromosomes lined up on one side of the cell, would genetic diversity increase? Explain.

4. **Contrast**  List the key differences between meiosis I and meiosis II.

### CONNECT TO

**CELL BIOLOGY**

5. Both mitosis and meiosis are types of nuclear division, but they result in different cell types. Describe how the steps of meiosis I differ from those of mitosis.

# Mendel and Heredity

SC.912.L.16.1

**SC.912.L.16.1** Use Mendel's laws of segregation and independent assortment to analyze patterns of inheritance.

**KEY CONCEPT** **Mendel's research showed that traits are inherited as discrete units.**

**MAIN IDEAS**

- Mendel laid the groundwork for genetics.
- Mendel's data revealed patterns of inheritance.

## Connect to Your World

When a magician makes a coin disappear, you know that the coin has not really vanished. You simply cannot see where it is. Maybe it is up a sleeve or in a pocket. When organisms reproduce, some traits seem to disappear, too. For centuries, no one could explain why. Then a careful, observant scientist showed that behind this phenomenon were inherited units, or genes.

### MAIN IDEA

## Mendel laid the groundwork for genetics.

When we think of how offspring resemble or differ from their parents, we typically refer to specific traits. **Traits** are distinguishing characteristics that are inherited, such as eye color, leaf shape, and tail length. Scientists recognized that traits are hereditary, or passed from one generation to the next, long before they understood how traits are passed on. **Genetics** is the study of biological inheritance patterns and variation in organisms.

The groundwork for much of our understanding of genetics was established in the middle of the 1800s by an Austrian monk named Gregor Mendel, shown in **FIGURE 3.1.** Scientists of the time commonly thought that parents' traits were blended in offspring, like mixing red and white paint to get pink paint. But this idea failed to explain how certain traits remained without being "diluted." Mendel, a shrewd mathematician, bred thousands of plants, carefully counting and recording his results. From his data, Mendel correctly predicted the results of meiosis long before chromosomes were discovered. He recognized that traits are inherited as discrete units from the parental generation, like different colored marbles mixed together that can still be picked out separately. By recognizing that organisms inherit two copies of each discrete unit, what we now call genes, Mendel described how traits were passed between generations.

**Connect** **Give two examples of traits not listed above.**

Gregor Mendel

**FIGURE 3.1** Gregor Mendel is called "the father of genetics" for discovering hereditary units. The significance of his work went unrecognized for almost 40 years.

### MAIN IDEA

## Mendel's data revealed patterns of inheritance.

Mendel studied plant variation in a monastery garden. He made three key choices about his experiments that played an important role in the development of his laws of inheritance: control over breeding, use of purebred plants, and observation of "either-or" traits that appeared in only two alternate forms.

©Bettmann/Corbis

FIGURE 3.2 MENDEL'S PROCESS

Mendel controlled the fertilization of his pea plants by removing the male parts, or stamens.

He then fertilized the female part, or pistil, with pollen from a different pea plant.

**READING TOOLBOX**

**VOCABULARY**

In Latin, the word *filius* means "son" and the word *filia* means "daughter."

## Experimental Design

Mendel chose pea plants for his experiments because they reproduce quickly, and he could easily control how they mate. The sex organs of a plant are in its flowers, and pea flowers contain both male and female reproductive organs. In nature, the pea flower typically self-pollinates; that is, the plant mates with itself. If a line of plants has self-pollinated for long enough, that line becomes genetically uniform, or **purebred.** As a result, the offspring of purebred parents inherit all of the parent organisms' characteristics. Mendel was able to mate plants with specific traits by interrupting the self-pollination process. As you can see in **FIGURE 3.2**, he removed the male parts of flowers and fertilized the female parts with pollen that contained sperm cells from a different plant. Because he started with purebred plants, Mendel knew that any variations in offspring resulted from his experiments.

Mendel chose seven traits to follow: pea shape, pea color, pod shape, pod color, plant height, flower color, and flower position. All of these traits are simple "either-or" characteristics; they do not show intermediate features. The plant is tall or short. Its peas are wrinkled or round. What Mendel did not know was that most of the traits he had selected were controlled by genes on separate chromosomes. The selection of these particular traits played a crucial role in enabling Mendel to identify the patterns he observed.

## Results

In genetics, the mating of two organisms is called a **cross.** An example of one of Mendel's crosses is highlighted in **FIGURE 3.3.** In this example, he crossed a purebred white-flowered pea plant with a purebred purple-flowered pea plant. These plants are the parental, or P, generation. The resulting offspring, called the first filial—or $F_1$—generation, all had purple flowers. The trait for white flowers seemed to disappear. When Mendel allowed the $F_1$ generation to self-fertilize, the resulting $F_2$ generation produced both plants with purple flowers and plants with white flowers. Therefore, the trait for white flowers had not disappeared; it had been hidden, or masked.

## FIGURE 3.3 Mendel's Experimental Cross

**Traits that were hidden when parental purebred flowers were crossed reappeared when the $F_1$ generation was allowed to self-pollinate.**

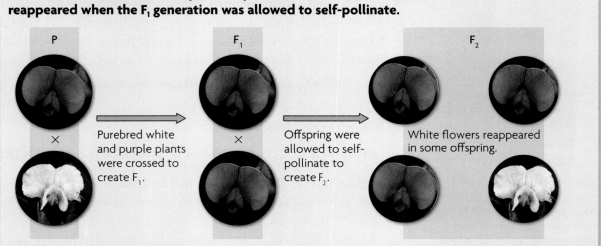

P

Purebred white and purple plants were crossed to create $F_1$.

$F_1$

Offspring were allowed to self-pollinate to create $F_2$.

$F_2$

White flowers reappeared in some offspring.

©George D. Lepp/Corbis

Mendel did not cross only two plants, however; he crossed many plants. As a result, he was able to observe patterns. He noticed that each cross yielded similar ratios in the $F_2$ generation: about three-fourths of the plants had purple flowers, and about one-fourth had white flowers. A ratio is a comparison that tells how two or more things relate. This ratio can be expressed as 3:1 (read "three to one") of purple:white flowers. As you can see in **FIGURE 3.4,** Mendel's data show this approximately 3:1 ratio for each of his crosses.

| FIGURE 3.4 MENDEL'S MONOHYBRID CROSS RESULTS | | | |
|---|---|---|---|
| $F_2$ TRAITS | DOMINANT | RECESSIVE | RATIO |
| Pea shape | 5474 round | 1850 wrinkled | 2.96:1 |
| Pea color | 6022 yellow | 2001 green | 3.01:1 |
| Flower color | 705 purple | 224 white | 3.15:1 |
| Pod shape | 882 smooth | 299 constricted | 2.95:1 |
| Pod color | 428 green | 152 yellow | 2.82:1 |
| Flower position | 651 axial | 207 terminal | 3.14:1 |
| Plant height | 787 tall | 277 short | 2.84:1 |

Source: Mendel, *Abhandlungen* (1865).

## Conclusions

From these observations, Mendel drew three important conclusions. He demonstrated that traits are inherited as discrete units, which provided an explanation for individual traits that persisted without being blended or diluted over successive generations. Mendel's two other key conclusions are collectively called the **law of segregation,** or Mendel's first law.

- Organisms inherit two copies of each gene, one from each parent.
- Organisms donate only one copy of each gene in their gametes. Thus, the two copies of each gene segregate, or separate, during gamete formation.

Section 5 covers Mendel's second law, the law of independent assortment.

**Infer** **Explain why Mendel's choice of either-or characteristics aided his research.**

**CONNECT TO**

**MEIOSIS**

As you learned in **Section 2,** homologous chromosomes pair up in prophase I and are separated in anaphase I of meiosis. The overall process produces haploid cells that have a random assortment of chromosomes.

**SELF-CHECK Online**
HMHScience.com
**GO ONLINE**

## 6.3 Formative Assessment

### REVIEWING ▶ MAIN IDEAS

1. Mendel had no understanding of DNA as the genetic material, yet he was able to correctly predict how **traits** were passed between generations. What does Mendel's work in **genetics** show about the value of scientific observation?

2. Why is it important that Mendel began with **purebred** plants?

### CRITICAL THINKING

3. **Analyze** Mendel saw purple flowers in the $F_1$ generation, but both purple and white flowers in $F_2$. How did this help him see that traits are inherited as discrete units?

4. **Evaluate** If Mendel had examined only one trait, do you think he would have developed the **law of segregation**? Explain.

**CONNECT TO**

**SCIENTIFIC PROCESS**

5. You have learned that scientific thinking involves observing, forming hypotheses, testing hypotheses, and analyzing data. Use examples from Mendel's scientific process to show how his work fit this pattern.

# 6.4 Traits, Genes, and Alleles

SC.912.L.16.1,
SC.912.L.16.2

**KEY CONCEPT** Genes encode proteins that produce a diverse range of traits.

**MAIN IDEAS**
- The same gene can have many versions.
- Genes influence the development of traits.

## VOCABULARY

gene
allele
homozygous
heterozygous
genome
genotype
phenotype
dominant
recessive

**SC.912.L.16.1** Use Mendel's laws of segregation and independent assortment to analyze patterns of inheritance.

**SC.912.L.16.2** Discuss observed inheritance patterns caused by various modes of inheritance, including dominant, recessive, codominant, sex-linked, polygenic, and multiple alleles.

### Connect to Your World

Most things come in many forms. Bread can be wheat, white, or rye. Cars can be two-door, four-door, hatchback, or convertible. Potatoes have more varieties than can be counted on two hands. Genes, too, come in many forms.

> **MAIN IDEA**
## The same gene can have many versions.

As you have learned, Mendel's discrete units of heredity are now called genes. But what are genes? You can think of a **gene** as a piece of DNA that provides a set of instructions to a cell to make a certain protein. This definition is not precise, but it gives you the main idea. Each gene has a locus, a specific position on a pair of homologous chromosomes. Just as a house is a physical structure and an address tells where that house is located, you can think of the locus as the "address" that tells where a gene is located on a chromosome.

Most genes exist in many forms. In Mendel's experiments, the effects of these different forms were easy to see: yellow or green, round or wrinkled. An **allele** (uh-LEEL) is any of the alternative forms of a gene that may occur at a specific locus. Your cells have two alleles for each gene, one on each of the homologous chromosomes on which the locus for that gene is found. Each parent gives one allele. The two alleles may be the same, or they may be different. The term **homozygous** (HOH-moh-ZY-guhs) describes two of the same alleles at a specific locus. For example, both might code for white flowers. The term **heterozygous** (HEHT-uhr-uh-ZY-guhs) describes two different alleles at a specific locus. Thus, one might code for white flowers, the other for purple flowers.

**Compare and Contrast** Distinguish between the terms *allele* and *locus*.

> **VISUAL VOCAB**
>
> **Homozygous** alleles are identical to each other.
>
> homozygous alleles
>
> heterozygous alleles
>
> wrinkled    wrinkled
>
> wrinkled    round
>
> **Heterozygous** alleles are different from each other.

## MAIN IDEA
# Genes influence the development of traits.

You may have heard about the Human Genome Project. Its goal was to find out the sequence of the 3 billion nucleotide pairs that make up a human's genome. A **genome** is all of an organism's genetic material. Unless you have an identical twin, you have a unique genome that determines all of your traits. Some of your traits, such as the color of your eyes, can be seen. Other traits, such as the exact chemical makeup of your eyeball, cannot be seen.

In genetics, we often focus on a single trait or set of traits. A genome is all of an organism's genes, but a **genotype** (JEHN-uh-TYP) typically refers to the genetic makeup of a specific set of genes. The genotype of a pea plant includes both of the genes that code for flower color, even if one of these genes is masked. In contrast, the physical characteristics, or traits, of an individual organism make up its **phenotype** (FEE-nuh-TYP). A pea plant with purple flowers has a phenotype for purple flowers. The plant might have a hidden gene for white flowers, but that does not matter to its phenotype.

## Dominant and Recessive Alleles

If an organism is heterozygous for a trait, which allele will be expressed? That is, if a plant has one allele for purple flowers and one for white flowers, what color will the flowers be? As Mendel learned, one allele may be dominant over another allele. A **dominant** allele is the allele that is expressed when two different alleles or two dominant alleles are present. A **recessive** allele is the allele that is expressed only when two copies are present. In Mendel's experiments, the allele for purple flowers was dominant to the allele for white flowers. All $F_1$ plants were purple even though they had only one allele for purple flowers.

**VISUAL VOCAB**

A **dominant** allele is expressed when two different alleles are present.

genotype      phenotype

wrinkled—recessive    round—dominant

genotype      phenotype

wrinkled—recessive    wrinkled—recessive

A **recessive** allele is expressed only when two copies are present.

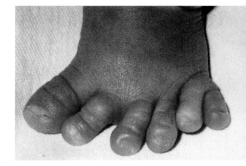

**FIGURE 4.1** Polydactyly is the condition of having more than the typical number of fingers or toes. The allele for polydactyly is dominant.

Sometimes the word *dominant* is misunderstood. A dominant allele is not necessarily better or stronger than a recessive allele. It does not necessarily occur most often in the population. An allele is dominant in a heterozygote simply because it is expressed and the other allele is not.

Alleles are often represented on paper with individual letters. An organism's genotype for a trait can be shown with two letters—one per allele. Uppercase letters are used for dominant alleles, and lowercase letters are used for recessive alleles. For example, the dominant allele for height in pea plants is written as *T*, for tall. The recessive allele for short plants is written as *t*.

### CONNECT TO

#### EXCEPTIONS TO MENDEL'S LAWS

Mendel's theory of inheritance cannot explain all patterns of inheritance. As you will learn in the chapter **Extending Mendelian Genetics,** incomplete dominance, codominance, polygenic traits, and environmental influences all provide exceptions.

©CNRI/Photo Researchers, Inc.

A plant's genotype might be homozygous dominant (*TT*), heterozygous (*Tt*), or homozygous recessive (*tt*).

## Alleles and Phenotype

Because some alleles are dominant over others, two genotypes can produce the dominant phenotype. For example, smooth pods and constricted pods in pea plants, shown in **FIGURE 4.2,** are phenotypes. A plant with smooth pods could have a homozygous dominant (*SS*) or heterozygous (*Ss*) genotype. In contrast, a plant with constricted, or compressed, pods could have only a homozygous recessive (*ss*) genotype.

What actually makes one allele dominant over another? The answer is very complicated. It depends on the nature of the protein that is, or is not, made. Let's look at a fairly simple example. Pigment gives cells color. If *P* directs flower cells to make pigment, the flower may look purple. If *p* directs the cells not to make pigment, the flower looks white. So *P* codes for pigment to be present, but *p* codes for nothing, the absence of pigment. As a result, *P* has to be dominant. Even if the flower has only one *P* allele (*Pp*), that one allele tells its cells to make pigment, and the flower has color. Flower pigment is only one example. Many factors make one allele dominant over another.

As you know, most plants are not simply tall or short. Most flowers are not just white or purple. Most traits occur in a range. Other factors also affect traits. A lack of sunshine or vital nutrients could stunt a plant's growth. How does genetics account for these issues? Mendel studied traits that follow simple dominant-recessive patterns of inheritance, and each trait was the result of a single gene. In general, however, inheritance is much more complex. Most alleles are not simply dominant or recessive; some are codominant. Many traits are influenced by multiple genes. The environment also interacts with genes and affects their expression.

**Contrast** **Explain the difference between genotype and phenotype.**

**FIGURE 4.2** Both the homozygous dominant and heterozygous genotypes result in smooth, or inflated, pods (top). Only the homozygous recessive genotype results in constricted pods (inset).

©Gilbert S. Grant/Photo Researchers, Inc.

## 6.4 Formative Assessment

**SELF-CHECK** Online
HMHScience.com
GO ONLINE

### REVIEWING ▶ MAIN IDEAS

1. How are the terms **gene,** locus, and **allele** related?

2. Explain why an organism's genotype may be **homozygous** dominant, homozygous recessive, or **heterozygous,** but never heterozygous recessive.

### CRITICAL THINKING

3. **Apply** Suppose you are studying a fruit fly's DNA, and you discover a gene for antenna length on chromosome 2. What word describes its location, and where would it be found in other fruit flies' DNA?

4. **Predict** If a **recessive** allele helps an organism reproduce, but the **dominant** allele hinders reproduction, which will be more common in a population?

### CONNECT TO

### HUMAN BIOLOGY

5. Cystic fibrosis is a recessive disease that causes the production of abnormally thick, life-threatening mucus secretions. What is the **genotype** of a person with cystic fibrosis: *CC, Cc,* or *cc*? Explain.

 **6.5**

# Traits and Probability

**SC.912.L.16.1**

**VOCABULARY**

Punnett square
monohybrid cross
testcross
dihybrid cross
law of independent
   assortment
probability

**KEY CONCEPT** The inheritance of traits follows the rules of probability.

**MAIN IDEAS**

- Punnett squares illustrate genetic crosses.
- A monohybrid cross involves one trait.
- A dihybrid cross involves two traits.
- Heredity patterns can be calculated with probability.

## Connect to Your World

If you have tried juggling, you know it can be a tricky thing. Keeping three flaming torches or clubs in motion at the same time is a challenge. Trying to keep track of what organism has which genotype and which gamete gets which allele can also be a lot to juggle. Fortunately, R. C. Punnett developed a method to keep track of all of the various combinations graphically.

## ▶ MAIN IDEA

## Punnett squares illustrate genetic crosses.

Shortly after Mendel's experiments became widely known among scientists, a poultry geneticist named R. C. Punnett, shown in **FIGURE 5.1**, developed the Punnett square. A **Punnett square** is a grid system for predicting all possible genotypes resulting from a cross. The axes of the grid represent the possible gamete genotypes of each parent. The grid boxes show all of the possible genotypes of offspring from those two parents. Because segregation and fertilization are random events, each combination of alleles is as likely to be produced as any other. By counting the number of squares with each genetic combination, we can find the ratio of genotypes in that generation. If we also know how the genotype corresponds to the phenotype, we can find the ratio of phenotypes in that generation as well.

Let's briefly review what you've learned about meiosis and segregation to examine why the Punnett square is effective. Both parents have two alleles for each gene. These alleles are represented on the axes of the Punnett square. During meiosis, the chromosomes—and, therefore, the alleles—are separated.

**VISUAL VOCAB**

The **Punnett square** is a grid system for predicting possible genotypes of offspring.

Parent 1 alleles

|  | *A* | *a* |
|---|---|---|
| *A* | *AA* | *Aa* |
| *a* | *Aa* | *aa* |

Parent 2 alleles

possible genotypes of offspring

Each gamete gets one of the alleles. Since each parent contributes only one allele to the offspring, only one allele from each parent is written inside each grid box. Fertilization restores the diploid number in the resulting offspring. This is why each grid box has two alleles, one from the mother and one from the father. Since any egg has the same chance of being fertilized by any sperm cell, each possible genetic combination is equally likely to occur.

**Explain** **What do the letters on the axes of the Punnett square represent?**

## ⊙ MAIN IDEA
# A monohybrid cross involves one trait.

Thus far, we have studied **monohybrid crosses,** crosses that examine the inheritance of only one specific trait. Three example crosses are used below and on the next page to illustrate how Punnett squares work and to highlight the resulting ratios—for both genotype and phenotype.

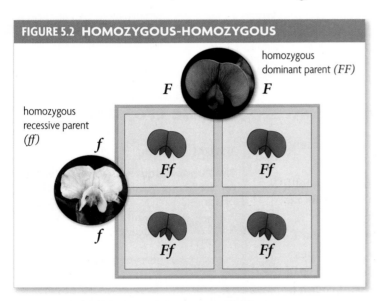

FIGURE 5.2  HOMOZYGOUS-HOMOZYGOUS

homozygous dominant parent *(FF)*

homozygous recessive parent *(ff)*

FIGURE 5.3  HETEROZYGOUS-HETEROZYGOUS

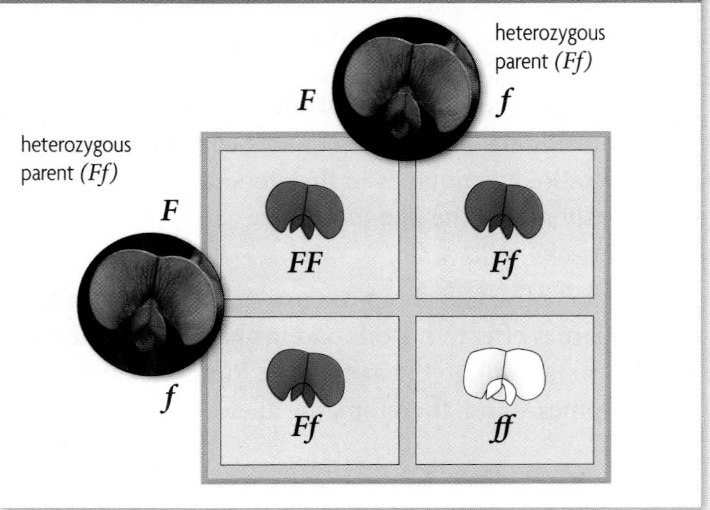

heterozygous parent *(Ff)*

heterozygous parent *(Ff)*

### Homozygous-Homozygous
Suppose you cross a pea plant that is homozygous dominant for purple flowers with a pea plant that is homozygous recessive for white flowers. To determine the genotypic and phenotypic ratios of the offspring, first write each parent's genotype on one axis: *FF* for the purple-flowered plant, *ff* for the white-flowered plant. Every gamete from the purple-flowered plant contains the dominant allele, *F*. Every gamete from the white-flowered plant contains the recessive allele, *f*. Therefore, 100% of the offspring have the heterozygous genotype, *Ff*. And 100% of the offspring have purple flowers because they all have a copy of the dominant allele, as shown in **FIGURE 5.2.**

### Heterozygous-Heterozygous
Next, in **FIGURE 5.3,** you can see a cross between two purple-flowered pea plants that are both heterozygous *(Ff)*. From each parent, half the offspring receive a dominant allele, *F*, and half receive a recessive allele, *f*. Therefore, one-fourth of the offspring have a homozygous dominant genotype, *FF*; half have a heterozygous genotype, *Ff*; and one-fourth have a homozygous recessive genotype, *ff*. Both the *FF* and the *Ff* genotypes result in purple flowers. Only the *ff* genotype results in white flowers. Thus, the genotypic ratio is 1:2:1 of homozygous dominant:heterozygous:homozygous recessive. The phenotypic ratio is 3:1 of purple:white flowers.

## Heterozygous-Homozygous

Finally, suppose you cross a pea plant that is heterozygous for purple flowers (*Ff*) with a pea plant that is homozygous recessive for white flowers (*ff*). As before, each parent's genotype is placed on an axis, as shown in **FIGURE 5.4**. From the homozygous parent with white flowers, the offspring each receive a recessive allele, *f*. From the heterozygous parent, half the offspring receive a dominant allele, *F*, and half receive a recessive allele, *f*. Half the offspring have a heterozygous genotype, *Ff*. Half have a homozygous recessive genotype, *ff*. Thus, half the offspring have purple flowers, and half have white flowers. The resulting genotypic ratio is 1:1 of heterozygous:homozygous recessive. The phenotypic ratio is 1:1 of purple:white.

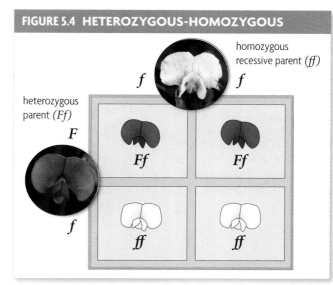

**FIGURE 5.4 HETEROZYGOUS-HOMOZYGOUS**

homozygous recessive parent (*ff*)

heterozygous parent (*Ff*)

Suppose we did not know the genotype of the purple flower in the cross above. This cross would allow us to determine that the purple flower is heterozygous, not homozygous dominant. A **testcross** is a cross between an organism with an unknown genotype and an organism with the recessive phenotype. The organism with the recessive phenotype must be homozygous recessive. The offspring will show whether the organism with the unknown genotype is heterozygous, as above, or homozygous dominant.

**Apply** From an *FF* × *Ff* cross, what percent of offspring would have purple flowers?

## QUICKLAB    INFERRING

### Using a Testcross

Suppose you work for a company that sells plant seeds. You are studying a plant species in which the dominant phenotype is pink flowers (*PP* or *Pp*). The recessive phenotype is white flowers (*pp*). Customers have been requesting more plants with pink flowers. To meet this demand, you need to determine the genotypes of some of the plants you are currently working with.

**PROBLEM** What is the genotype of each plant?

**PROCEDURE**

1. Suppose you are presented with Plant A of the species you are studying. It has pink flowers. You want to determine the genotype of the plant.

2. You cross Plant A with Plant B of the same species. This plant has white flowers and a known genotype of *pp*.

3. The resulting cross yields six plants with pink flowers and six plants with white flowers. Use Punnett squares to determine the genotype of Plant A.

**MATERIALS**
- pencil
- paper

**ANALYZE AND CONCLUDE**

1. **Apply** What is the genotype of Plant A? Explain how you arrived at your answer.

2. **Apply** What are the possible genotypes and phenotypes of offspring if Plant A is crossed with a plant that has a genotype of *PP*?

3. **Calculate** What ratio of dominant to recessive phenotypes would exist if Plant A were crossed with a plant that has a genotype of *Pp*?

4. **Evaluate** Is Plant A the best plant, in terms of genotype, that you can work with to produce as many of the requested seeds as possible? Why or why not? Which genotype would be best to work with?

## ▶ MAIN IDEA
# A dihybrid cross involves two traits.

**CONNECT TO**

**LAW OF SEGREGATION**

As you learned in **Section 3,** Mendel's first law of inheritance is the law of segregation. It states that organisms inherit two copies of each gene but donate only one copy to each gamete.

All of the crosses discussed so far have involved only a single trait. However, Mendel also conducted **dihybrid crosses,** crosses that examine the inheritance of two different traits. He wondered if both traits would always appear together or if they would be expressed independently of each other.

Mendel performed many dihybrid crosses and tested a variety of different combinations. For example, he would cross a plant with yellow round peas with a plant with green wrinkled peas. Remember that Mendel began his crosses with purebred plants. Thus, the first generation offspring ($F_1$) would all be heterozygous and would all look the same. In this example, the plants would all have yellow round peas. When Mendel allowed the $F_1$ plants to self-pollinate, he obtained the following results: 9 yellow/round, 3 yellow/wrinkled, 3 green/round, 1 green/wrinkled.

Mendel continued to find this approximately 9:3:3:1 phenotypic ratio in the $F_2$ generation, regardless of the combination of traits. From these results, he realized that the presence of one trait did not affect the presence of another trait. His second law of genetics, the **law of independent assortment,** states that allele pairs separate independently of each other during gamete formation, or meiosis. That is, different traits appear to be inherited separately.

The results of Mendel's dihybrid crosses can also be illustrated with a Punnett square, like the one in **FIGURE 5.5.** Drawing a Punnett square for a dihybrid cross is the same as drawing one for a monohybrid cross, except that the grid is bigger because two genes, or four alleles, are involved. For example, suppose you cross two plants with yellow, round peas that are heterozygous for both traits (*YyRr*). The four allele combinations possible in each gamete— *YR*, *Yr*, *yR*, and *yr*—are used to label each axis. Each grid box can be filled in using the same method as that used in the monohybrid cross. A total of nine different genotypes may result from the cross in this example. However, these nine genotypes produce only four different phenotypes. These phenotypes are yellow round, yellow wrinkled, green round, and green wrinkled, and they occur in the ratio of 9:3:3:1. Note that the 9:3:3:1 phenotypic ratio results from a cross between organisms that are heterozygous for both traits. The phenotypic ratio of the offspring will differ (from 9:3:3:1) if one or both of the parent organisms are homozygous for one or both traits.

**Analyze** In **FIGURE 5.5,** the boxes on the axes represent the possible gametes made by each parent plant. Why does each box have two alleles?

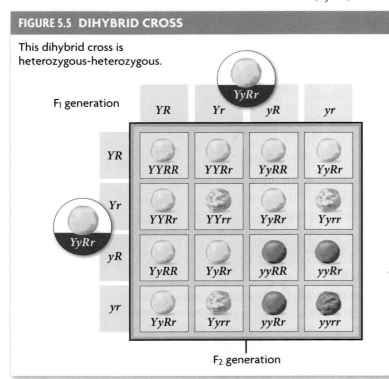

**FIGURE 5.5 DIHYBRID CROSS**

This dihybrid cross is heterozygous-heterozygous.

$F_1$ generation

*YyRr*

| | YR | Yr | yR | yr |
|---|---|---|---|---|
| **YR** | YYRR | YYRr | YyRR | YyRr |
| **Yr** | YYRr | YYrr | YyRr | Yyrr |
| **yR** | YyRR | YyRr | yyRR | yyRr |
| **yr** | YyRr | Yyrr | yyRr | yyrr |

*YyRr*

$F_2$ generation

## ► MAIN IDEA

# Heredity patterns can be calculated with probability.

**Probability** is the likelihood that a particular event will happen. It predicts the average number of occurrences, not the exact number of occurrences.

$$\text{Probability} = \frac{\text{number of ways a specific event can occur}}{\text{number of total possible outcomes}}$$

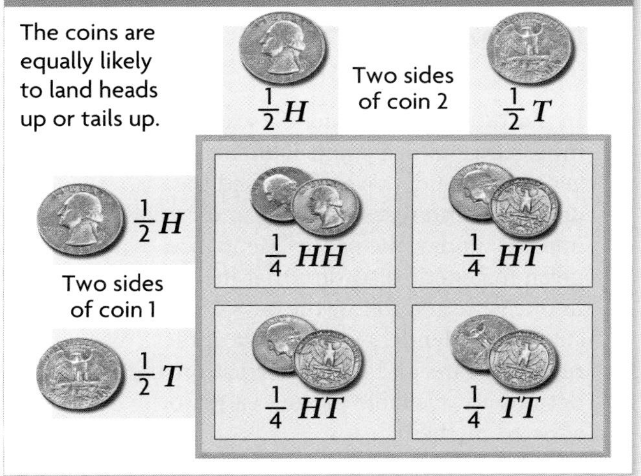

Suppose you flip a coin. The number of total possible outcomes is two: heads up or tails up. The probability that it would land heads up is 1/2, or one out of two. The probability that it would land tails up is also 1/2.

Next, suppose you flip two coins. How one coin lands does not affect how the other coin lands. To calculate the probability that two independent events will happen together, multiply the probability of each individual event. The probability that both coins will land heads up, for example, is $1/2 \times 1/2 = 1/4$.

These probabilities can be applied to meiosis. Suppose a germ cell undergoes meiosis in a plant that is heterozygous for purple flowers. The number of total possible outcomes is two because a gamete could get a dominant or a recessive allele. The probability that a gamete will get a dominant allele is 1/2. The probability that it will get a recessive allele is also 1/2.

If two plants that are heterozygous for purple flowers fertilize each other, the probability that both egg and sperm have a dominant allele is $1/2 \times 1/2 = 1/4$. So, too, the probability that both have a recessive allele is 1/4. There is also a 1/4 chance that a sperm cell with a dominant allele will fertilize an egg with a recessive allele, or that a sperm cell with a recessive allele will fertilize an egg with a dominant allele. These last two combinations are basically the same. In either case, the resulting plant will be heterozygous. Thus, the probability that a pea plant will be heterozygous for this trait is the sum of the probabilities: $1/4 + 1/4 = 1/2$.

**FIGURE 5.6  PROBABILITY AND HEREDITY**

The coins are equally likely to land heads up or tails up.

Two sides of coin 2

$\frac{1}{2}H$      $\frac{1}{2}T$

Two sides of coin 1

$\frac{1}{2}H$

$\frac{1}{2}T$

| $\frac{1}{4}$ HH | $\frac{1}{4}$ HT |
| $\frac{1}{4}$ HT | $\frac{1}{4}$ TT |

**Apply** Explain how Mendel's laws relate to probability.

---

## 6.5  Formative Assessment

### REVIEWING ► MAIN IDEAS

1. What do the grid boxes in a **Punnett square** represent?

2. Why does the expected genotypic ratio often differ from the expected phenotypic ratio resulting from a **monohybrid cross**?

3. How did Mendel's **dihybrid crosses** help him develop his second law?

### CRITICAL THINKING

4. **Calculate** What would be the phenotypic ratios of the offspring resulting from the following cross: *YYRr* × *YyRr*?

5. **Predict** If you are working with two tall pea plants and know that one is *Tt*, how could you determine the genotype of the other plant?

**SELF-CHECK Online**
HMHScience.com
**GO ONLINE**

### ⁂ CONNECT TO

#### ADAPTATION

6. You have seen that one-quarter of offspring resulting from two heterozygous parents are homozygous recessive. Yet for some genes, the recessive allele is more common in the population. Explain why this might be.

# Identifying Single-Gene Conditions

In the 1800s, Gregor Mendel's studies of patterns of inheritance in pea plants launched the scientific field of genetics. Mendel's work revealed the existence of dominant and recessive traits and explained how they interact. Today, the name "Mendelian conditions" is given to genetic disorders that involve a single mutation in one gene and follow the laws of inheritance demonstrated by Mendel's work. Most of these diseases are relatively rare, and little information and few therapy options are available to the vast majority of people affected by them.

To address this problem, in 2011 the National Human Genome Research Institute (NHGRI) and the National Heart, Lung, and Blood Institute (NHLBI) founded the Centers for Mendelian Genomics (CMG) program. Its mission is to uncover the genetic basis of all human Mendelian conditions in order to increase scientific knowledge of these diseases and to improve therapy options for affected patients.

The mission of CMG is a challenging one. Scientists estimate that there are at least 7,300 known Mendelian conditions, including well-known ones such as cystic fibrosis, muscular dystrophy, sickle cell disease, and Huntington's disease. Each disease may affect only a small number of people, but all Mendelian conditions together affect 20 million to 30 million people in the United States alone.

More than 500 scientists in 36 countries are working together on the CMG program, which is centered at four universities in the United States. People who have a known Mendelian condition—or whose physicians suspect they might—can submit DNA samples to the CMG program for whole genome sequencing, which includes protein-coding genes. Data collected from thousands of patients are shared with researchers so that important connections can be made.

In the years since the program was founded, CMG scientists have made connections between gene mutations and diseases that were not yet understood to be caused by gene mutations, suggesting possible therapies for affected people. Researchers have also:

- discovered that a single mutation in many different genes can cause the same or a similar disease;
- deduced that a gene can be mutated in more than one way, with each mutation causing a different disease;
- learned that a single mutation in one gene can have one effect on one family member and a similar, but weaker, effect on another family member; and
- realized that a person may inherit two different genetic changes that interact to cause one condition.

One of the more astounding findings of CMG research is that some Mendelian conditions are not inherited. Some affected people, researchers have found, are the only ones affected in their families. Researchers call these mutations *de novo*, or new, mutations.

So far scientists have identified the genomic causes for about half of the 7,300 conditions. The CMG research has led to more avenues of inquiry, such as whether exposure to chemicals or other environmental factors might cause an underlying Mendelian condition to be revealed. People affected by Mendelian conditions have reason to hope that CMG research will bring them even more information in the near future.

## S.T.E.M. Activity

Consider the mission of the CMG program. What resources are needed for scientists to continue their work in this program? What constraints do you think might hinder their work?

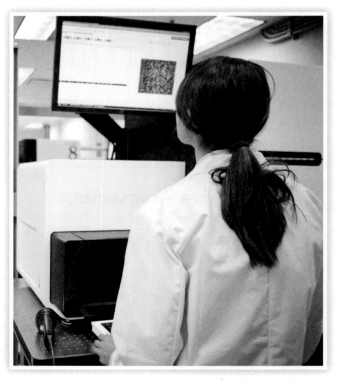

A scientist studies DNA sequencing.

©Assembly/Iconica/Getty Images

# 6.6 Meiosis and Genetic Variation

SC.912.L.15.15,
SC.912.L.16.16

**KEY CONCEPT** Independent assortment and crossing over during meiosis result in genetic diversity.

### VOCABULARY

crossing over
genetic linkage

### MAIN IDEAS

- ◯ Sexual reproduction creates unique gene combinations.
- ◯ Crossing over during meiosis increases genetic diversity.

**SC.912.L.15.15** Describe how mutation and genetic recombination increase genetic variation.

**SC.912.L.16.16** Describe the process of meiosis, including independent assortment and crossing over. Explain how reduction division results in the formation of haploid gametes or spores.

## ⌖ Connect to Your World

A surprising number of people make their living as Elvis impersonators. They wear slicked-up hairdos, large sunglasses, and big white jumpsuits. They mimic his voice, his dancing, and his phrases. They copy every possible detail, but they still do not come close to being the King. Elvis, like all people, was unique, or one of a kind. This uniqueness arises more from the events of meiosis—from the tiny shufflings of chromosomes and the crossing over of DNA segments—than from our hairstyles or our clothing.

### ◉ MAIN IDEA

## Sexual reproduction creates unique gene combinations.

**FIGURE 6.1** This photograph shows only a small sample of the great genetic potential for variety in the human population.

The major advantage of sexual reproduction is that it gives rise to a great deal of genetic variation within a species, as shown in **FIGURE 6.1.** This variation results largely from (1) the independent assortment of chromosomes during meiosis and (2) the mixing of alleles as gametes join during fertilization.

Recall that homologous chromosomes pair up randomly along the cell equator during meiosis I. In other words, it's a matter of chance which of the two chromosomes from any homologous pair ends up on a given side of the cell equator. As you've learned, human cells have 23 pairs of chromosomes, and each pair lines up independently. As a result, gametes with $2^{23}$, or about 8 million, different combinations of chromosomes can be produced through meiosis from one human cell.

Now think about the fact that sexual reproduction produces offspring through the combination of gametes. In humans, for example, a sperm cell with one of $2^{23}$ (about 8 million) chromosome combinations fertilizes an egg cell, which also has one out of $2^{23}$ chromosome combinations. If sperm cells and eggs were combined at random, the total number of possible combinations is the product of $2^{23} \times 2^{23}$, or more than 70 trillion. In other words, a human couple can produce a child with one of about 70 trillion different combinations of chromosomes.

**CONNECT TO**

**EVOLUTION**

As you will learn in the chapter **Principles of Evolution**, natural selection is a mechanism by which individuals that have inherited beneficial adaptations produce more offspring on average than do other individuals. The rabbit-eared bandicoot (below) has adaptations that enable it to survive and reproduce in regions of Australia.

Independent assortment and fertilization play key roles in creating and maintaining genetic diversity in all sexually reproducing organisms. However, the number of possible chromosome combinations varies by species. The probability that a bald eagle or a rabbit-eared bandicoot will inherit a specific allele is determined in the same way that it is for a pea plant.

Sexual reproduction creates unique combinations of genes. This results in organisms with unique phenotypes. The offspring of sexual reproduction have a mixture of both parents' traits. For example, rabbit-eared bandicoot offspring all share many traits for the things that make them bandicoots, but they may also differ in many ways. Some may be colored more like the mother, others more like the father. Some may dig deeper burrows or hunt more skillfully; others may in time produce more milk for their own offspring or have more litters. Having some of these traits may allow one bandicoot to reproduce in conditions where another bandicoot could not.

**Calculate** Fruit fly gametes each have four chromosomes, representing $2^4$, or 16, possible chromosome combinations. How many chromosome combinations could result from fertilization between a fruit fly egg and a sperm cell?

▶ **MAIN IDEA**

## Crossing over during meiosis increases genetic diversity.

It is clear that independent assortment creates a lot of variation within a species. Another process, called crossing over, occurs during meiosis and helps create even greater variation. **Crossing over** is the exchange of chromosome segments between homologous chromosomes during prophase I of meiosis I. At this stage, each chromosome has been duplicated, the sister chromatids are still connected to each other, and homologous chromosomes have paired with each other. When homologous chromosomes are in this position, some of the chromatids are very close to each other. Part of one chromatid from each chromosome breaks off and reattaches to the other chromosome, as shown in **FIGURE 6.2**. Crossing over happens any time a germ cell divides. In fact, it can occur many times within the same pair of homologous chromosomes.

## FIGURE 6.2  Crossing Over

Crossing over exchanges segments of DNA between homologous chromosomes.

**1** Two homologous chromosomes pair up with each other during prophase I in meiosis.

**2** In this position, some chromatids are very close to each other and segments cross.

**3** Some of these segments break off and reattach to the other homologous chromosome.

**Synthesize** Draw the four chromosomes that would result after the above chromosomes go through meiosis.

Because crossing over results in new combinations of genes, it is also called recombination. The term *recombination* generally refers to any mixing of parental alleles, including recombination events.

Now that you know about crossing over, let's look again at some of Mendel's results and conclusions. As you know from his research, genes located on separate chromosomes assort independently. This independence is caused by the random assortment of chromosomes during meiosis. But you also know that a single chromosome can have hundreds of genes. What happens when two genes are both on the same chromosome? Will they display independent assortment as well? Or will they travel together as a unit?

The answer to these questions is, "It depends." Recall that each gene has its own locus, or place on a chromosome. As **FIGURE 6.3** shows, some genes on the same chromosome are close together; others are far apart. The farther apart two genes are located, the more likely they are to be separated when crossing over happens. Thus, genes located close together tend to be inherited together, which is called **genetic linkage.** Linked genes will be inherited in the same predicted ratios as would a single gene. In contrast, genes that are far apart are more likely to assort independently. For example, the alleles for flower and seed color are located on the same chromosome in pea plants, but they are not near each other. Because they are so far apart, Mendel observed independent assortment for these traits.

Genetic linkage has let scientists calculate the physical distance between two genes. By exploring relationships between many genes, scientists have been able to build a linkage, or genetic, map of many species.

**Predict Suppose two genes are very close together on a chromosome. Are the genes likely to be separated by crossing over? Explain.**

**WebQuest**
HMHScience.com
GO ONLINE
Selective Breeding

## FIGURE 6.3 GENETIC LINKAGE

A and B are not linked to C and D because they are so far apart. Crossing over is likely to occur in the space between genes B and C, thereby separating A and B from C and D.

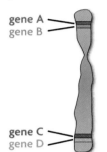

gene A
gene B

A and B are referred to as linked because they would likely be inherited together.

gene C
gene D

C and D are referred to as linked because they would likely be inherited together.

---

## 6.6 Formative Assessment

SELF-CHECK Online
HMHScience.com
GO ONLINE

### REVIEWING ▶ MAIN IDEAS

1. Briefly explain how sexual reproduction generates new allele combinations in offspring.

2. How does **crossing over** contribute to genetic diversity?

### CRITICAL THINKING

3. **Infer** You know that you get half your DNA from your mom, half from your dad. Does this mean you got one-quarter of your DNA from each of your grandparents? Explain your reasoning.

4. **Synthesize** Suppose you know that two genes exist on the same chromosome. How could you determine if they are located close to each other?

### CONNECT TO

#### MITOSIS

5. Mitosis creates daughter cells that are genetically identical to the parent cell. If crossing over occurred between sister chromatids during mitosis, would it increase genetic diversity? Explain.

# 6 Summary

## KEY CONCEPTS

### 6.1 Chromosomes and Meiosis

**Gametes have half the number of chromosomes that body cells have.** Your body cells have 23 pairs of homologous chromosomes, making 46 total chromosomes. Gametes have only 1 chromosome from each homologous pair—23 chromosomes in all.

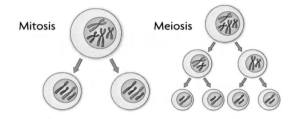

### 6.2 Process of Meiosis

**During meiosis, diploid cells undergo two cell divisions that result in haploid cells.** In meiosis I, homologous chromosomes pair up along the cell equator and are divided into separate cells. In meiosis II, sister chromatids are divided into separate cells, making a total of four haploid cells that are genetically unique.

### 6.3 Mendel and Heredity

**Mendel's research showed that traits are inherited as discrete units.** His large amount of data, control over breeding, use of purebred plants, and observation of "either-or" traits allowed him to see patterns in the inheritance of traits. He concluded that organisms inherit two copies of each gene and that organisms donate only one copy of each gene in their gametes.

### 6.4 Traits, Genes, and Alleles

**Genes encode proteins that produce a diverse range of traits.** Every diploid organism has two alleles for each gene: one from the mother, one from the father. These two alleles may be the same (homozygous) or different (heterozygous). One allele may be dominant over another.

### 6.5 Traits and Probability

**The inheritance of traits follows the rules of probability.** Punnett squares are a grid system for predicting all possible genotypes resulting from a cross. When Mendel performed two-trait crosses, he discovered that different traits appear to be inherited separately—the law of independent assortment. The patterns of inheritance that he observed can be predicted by using mathematical probabilities.

### 6.6 Meiosis and Genetic Variation

**Independent assortment and crossing over during meiosis result in genetic diversity.** Independent assortment produces unique combinations of parental chromosomes. Crossing over between homologous chromosomes creates a patchwork of genes from both parents. Genetic linkage describes genes that are close together and tend to be inherited as a unit.

---

**READING TOOLBOX** SYNTHESIZE YOUR NOTES

**"Y" Diagram** Use a "Y" diagram to summarize what you know about meiosis I and meiosis II.

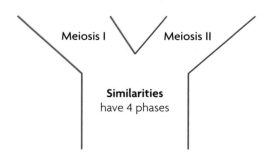

**Cycle Diagram** Fill in a cycle diagram like the one below to show the relationship between diploid and haploid cells.

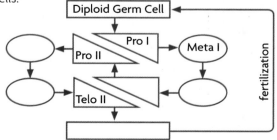

# 6 Review

**INTERACTIVE Review**
HMHScience.com

**GO ONLINE**

Review Games • Concept Map • Section Self-Checks

## CHAPTER VOCABULARY

**6.1**
somatic cell
gamete
homologous chromosome
autosome
sex chromosome
sexual reproduction
fertilization
diploid
haploid
meiosis

**6.2** gametogenesis
sperm

egg
polar body
**6.3** trait
genetics
purebred
cross
law of segregation
**6.4** gene
allele
homozygous
heterozygous
genome

genotype
phenotype
dominant
recessive
**6.5** Punnett square
monohybrid cross
testcross
dihybrid cross
law of independent assortment
probability
**6.6** crossing over
genetic linkage

## Reviewing Vocabulary

### Visualize Vocabulary

For each term below, use simple shapes, lines, or arrows to illustrate its meaning. Below each picture, write a short caption. Here's an example for the term *diploid*:

1. gene
2. fertilization
3. crossing over
4. genetic linkage
5. haploid

Diploid cells have two copies of each chromosome.

### READING TOOLBOX  GREEK WORD ORIGINS

6. The word *meiosis* comes from a Greek word meaning "to diminish," or make less. How does this word's origin relate to its meaning?

7. The word *haploid* comes from the Greek word *haplous,* which means "single." The word *diploid* comes from the Greek word *diplous,* which means "double." Explain how these two terms' meanings relate to their origins.

8. The Greek prefix *homo-* means "one and the same." How does this relate to the words *homologous* and *homozygous*?

### Compare and Contrast

Describe one similarity and one difference between the two terms in each of the following pairs.

9. monohybrid cross, dihybrid cross
10. heterozygous, homozygous
11. genotype, phenotype

## Reviewing  MAIN IDEAS

12. Each of your cells has a set of chromosomes, including autosomes and sex chromosomes. Explain the main differences between these two types of chromosomes.

13. A fruit fly has diploid cells with 8 chromosomes. Explain how many chromosomes are in its haploid gametes.

14. Meiosis is a continuous process, but we can think of it as taking place in two stages, meiosis I and meiosis II. How do the products of meiosis I differ from those of meiosis II?

15. The foundation for our modern study of genetics began with Gregor Mendel, who studied pea plants. What were Mendel's two main conclusions about how traits are passed between generations?

16. How did Mendel's use of purebred plants—for example, purebred white- and purebred purple-flowered peas—contribute to his understanding of inheritance?

17. How does the homozygous condition differ from the heterozygous condition? In your answer, use the terms *gene, homologous chromosome,* and *allele.*

18. What does each of the following parts of a Punnett square represent: (a) the entries on each axis of the grid and (b) the entries in the four squares within the grid?

19. How did the results of Mendel's dihybrid crosses lead him to formulate the law of independent assortment?

20. How does crossing over during meiosis I increase genetic diversity?

# Critical Thinking

**21. Hypothesize** Could a mutation in one of an individual's somatic cells be passed on to the individual's offspring? Explain your answer.

**22. Predict** Consider a species with a 2*n*, or diploid, chromosome number of 4. If gametes were formed by mitosis, rather than meiosis, what would happen to the chromosome number of the offspring of these organisms over generations? Explain.

**23. Contrast** Draw a pair of homologous chromosomes before and after duplication. Use your drawings to explain how homologous chromosomes and sister chromatids differ.

**24. Synthesize** Mendel's law of independent assortment states that allele pairs separate independently of each other during meiosis. How does this law relate to crossing over and genetic linkage?

**25. Infer** Imagine that you are studying the trait of flower petal shape in a species of plant. Petal shape is determined by a single gene with two alleles. You make a cross of two plants with unknown genotypes, both with smooth petals, and get the following $F_1$ offspring phenotypes: 23 wrinkled and 77 smooth. What conclusions can you draw about the inheritance of this trait? In your answer, include the probable genotypes of each parent, and indicate which allele is likely dominant.

**26. Analyze** In a particular species of butterfly, the genes for two different traits, antenna shape and antenna color, are located on the same chromosome. As a result, crosses between these butterflies do not obey one of Mendel's laws. Which law does not apply, and why?

## Interpreting Visuals

The drawing to the right shows a cell at a certain point during meiosis. Use the drawing to answer the next two questions.

**27. Identify** What stage of meiosis is shown above? Defend your answer.

**28. Apply** Is the above cell diploid or haploid? Explain.

## Analyzing Data   Interpret a Bar Graph

During meiosis, pairs of homologous chromosomes separate independently of the others, and gametes receive one of the two chromosomes from each pair. The number of possible chromosome combinations for a species is 2*n*, where *n* = the number of homologous pairs. The graph below shows the number of possible chromosome combinations for a variety of species. Use it to answer the next two questions.

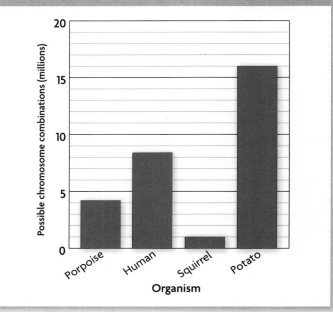

**POSSIBLE CHROMOSOME COMBINATIONS**

Source: Rutgers University

**29. Summarize** List the organisms in the above graph, in order, from least to most possible chromosome combinations.

**30. Infer** What can you infer from the graph about the number of homologous chromosomes in squirrels compared with potatoes?

## Making Connections

**31. Write a Diary Entry** Put yourself in Mendel's shoes. It is the mid-1800s. DNA and genes have not been identified, and the mechanisms of heritability are not understood. Write a diary entry (or letter) about one of Mendel's crosses from his perspective. Describe the results of the cross and ideas that may have come from the results.

**32. Synthesize** Look again at the picture of the egg and sperm cells on the chapter opener. Each of these sperm cells is genetically unique. What are the sources of variation that make each one different from the others?

## Disorders Caused by Recessive Alleles

Some human genetic disorders are caused by recessive alleles on autosomes. Two copies of the recessive allele must be present for a person to have the disorder. These disorders often appear in offspring of parents who are both heterozygotes. That is, each parent has one dominant, "normal" allele that masks the one disease-causing recessive allele.

For example, cystic fibrosis is a severe recessive disorder that mainly affects the sweat glands and the mucus glands. A person who is homozygous for the recessive allele will have the disease. Someone who is heterozygous for the alleles will not have the disease but is a carrier. A **carrier** does not show disease symptoms but can pass on the disease-causing allele to offspring. In this way, alleles that are lethal, or deadly, in a homozygous recessive individual can remain in a population's gene pool. This inheritance pattern is shown in **FIGURE 1.2**.

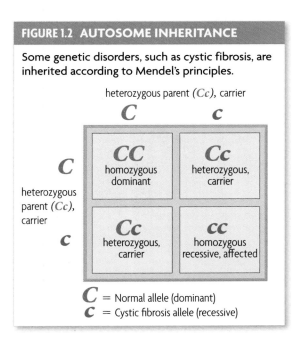

**FIGURE 1.2 AUTOSOME INHERITANCE**

Some genetic disorders, such as cystic fibrosis, are inherited according to Mendel's principles.

## Disorders Caused by Dominant Alleles

Dominant genetic disorders are far less common than recessive disorders. One example is Huntington's disease. Huntington's disease damages the nervous system and usually appears during adulthood. Because the disease is caused by a dominant allele, there is a 50% chance that a child will have it even if only one parent has one of the alleles. If both parents are heterozygous for the disease, there is a 75% chance that any of their children will inherit the disease. Because Huntington's disease strikes later in life, a person with the allele can have children before the disease appears. In that way, the allele is passed on in the population even though the disease is fatal.

**Connect** How are Mendel's observations related to genes on autosomes?

## ▶ MAIN IDEA
# Males and females can differ in sex-linked traits.

Mendel figured out much about heredity, but he did not know about chromosomes. As it turns out, he only studied traits produced by genes on autosomes. Now we know about sex chromosomes, and we know that the expression of genes on the sex chromosomes differs from the expression of autosomal genes.

### Sex-Linked Genes

Genes that are located on the sex chromosomes are called **sex-linked genes.** Recall that many species have specialized sex chromosomes called the X and Y chromosomes. In mammals and some other animals, individuals with two X chromosomes—an XX genotype—are female. Individuals with one X and one Y—an XY genotype—are male. As **FIGURE 1.3** shows, a female can pass on only an X chromosome to offspring, but a male can pass on an X or a Y chromosome.

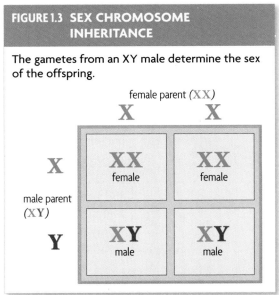

**FIGURE 1.3 SEX CHROMOSOME INHERITANCE**

The gametes from an XY male determine the sex of the offspring.

**TAKING NOTES**
Use a two-column chart to compare and contrast the expression of autosomal and sex-linked genes.

| autosomes | sex chromosomes |
|-----------|-----------------|
|           |                 |

Genes on the Y chromosome are responsible for the development of male offspring, but the X chromosome actually has much more influence over phenotype. The X chromosome has many genes that affect many traits. Scientists hypothesize that the Y chromosome may have genes for more than sex determination, but there is little evidence to support this idea.

In many organisms, including humans, the Y chromosome is much smaller and has many fewer genes than the X chromosome. Evidence suggests that over millions of years of evolution, the joining of the X and Y chromosomes during meiosis has resulted in segments of the Y chromosome being transferred to the X. You will read more about specific sex-linked genes and their locations on the human X and Y chromosomes in Section 4.

## Expression of Sex-Linked Genes

Because the X and Y chromosomes have different genes, sex-linked genes have a pattern of expression that is different from autosomal genes. Remember, two copies of an autosomal gene affect a trait. What happens when there is only one copy of a gene, as is the case in an XY male? Because males have only one copy of each type of sex chromosome, they express all of the alleles on both chromosomes. In males, there are no second copies of sex-linked genes to mask the effects of another allele. This means that even if all of the alleles of sex-linked genes in a male are recessive, they will be expressed.

## QUICKLAB    PREDICTING

### Sex-Linked Inheritance

The relationship between genotype and phenotype in sex-linked genes differs from that in autosomal genes. A female must have two recessive alleles of a sex-linked gene to express a recessive sex-linked trait. Just one recessive allele is needed for the same trait to be expressed in a male. In this lab, you will model the inheritance pattern of sex-linked genes.

**PROBLEM**  How does probability explain sex-linked inheritance?

**PROCEDURE**

1. Use the tape and marker to label two coins with the genetic cross shown on your group's index card. One coin represents the egg cell, and the other coin represents the sperm cell.

2. Flip the two coins and record the genotype of the "offspring."

3. Repeat Step 2 until you have modeled 50 genetic crosses. Make a data table to record each genetic cross that you model.

4. Calculate the genotype and phenotype probabilities for both males and females. Calculate the frequency of male offspring and female offspring.

**ANALYZE AND CONCLUDE**

1. **Analyze**  Do all of the females from the genetic cross show the recessive trait? Do all of the males show the recessive trait? Why or why not?

2. **Apply**  Make a Punnett square that shows the genetic cross. Do the results from your Punnett square agree with those from your experiment? Why or why not?

**MATERIALS**
- 2 coins
- masking tape
- marker
- index card with genetic cross

(br) © HMH

**FIGURE 1.4** The female calico cats have two X chromosomes with different alleles for fur color. Both alleles are expressed in a random pattern. The male cat has only one X chromosome, and its allele for fur color is expressed across the entire body.

$X^O$ = Orange fur allele
$X^o$ = Black fur allele

In mammals, the expression of sex-linked genes in females is also different from the way in which genes on other chromosomes are expressed. In each cell of female mammals, one of the two X chromosomes is randomly "turned off" by a process called **X chromosome inactivation.** Because of X chromosome inactivation, females are a patchwork of two types of cells—one type with an active X chromosome that came from the mother, and a second type with an active X chromosome that came from the father.

Colorful examples of X chromosome inactivation are seen in female tortoiseshell cats and female calico cats. The female calico cats shown in **FIGURE 1.4** have white fur, as well as alleles for black or orange fur on their X chromosomes. Those alleles are expressed randomly in cells across the cat's body. As a result, its coat is a mixture of color splotches. It is truly a patchwork of cells. Because male calico cats only have one X chromosome, they have white fur and one sex-linked gene for either orange or black fur.

**Infer  Why are males more likely than females to have sex-linked genetic disorders?**

**CONNECT TO**

**MITOSIS**

Recall from the chapter **Cell Growth and Division** that DNA coils to form chromosomes. In XX females, one of the two X chromosomes in each cell is "inactivated" by becoming even more tightly coiled.

**SELF-CHECK Online**
HMHScience.com
**GO ONLINE**

## 7.1 Formative Assessment

### REVIEWING ▶ MAIN IDEAS

1. How are autosomal traits, including recessive genetic disorders that are carried in a population, related to Mendel's observations of heredity?

2. Describe how **sex-linked genes** are expressed differently in males and in females.

### CRITICAL THINKING

3. **Apply**  How might a scientist determine whether a trait is sex-linked by observing the offspring of several genetic crosses?

4. **Compare and Contrast**  How is the expression of sex-linked genes both similar to and different from the expression of autosomal genes?

**CONNECT TO**

**MEIOSIS**

5. Scientists hypothesize that over millions of years, the Y chromosome has lost genes to the X chromosome. During what stages of meiosis might the Y chromosome have transferred genes to the X chromosome? Explain.

©John Daniels/Ardea

# Complex Patterns of Inheritance

**SC.912.L.16.2**

### VOCABULARY
incomplete dominance
codominance
polygenic trait

**SC.912.L.16.2** Discuss observed inheritance patterns caused by various modes of inheritance, including dominant, recessive, codominant, sex-linked, polygenic, and multiple alleles.

| KEY CONCEPT **Phenotype is affected by many different factors.**

**MAIN IDEAS**
- Phenotype can depend on interactions of alleles.
- Many genes may interact to produce one trait.
- The environment interacts with genotype.

○ *Connect to Your World*

Suppose you have blue and yellow paints to paint a room. You paint the walls yellow, let them dry, then paint the walls blue. The blue paint masks the yellow paint, so you could say that the blue paint is "dominant." You could also combine the paints in other ways. You could paint the room in blue and yellow stripes, or you could mix the colors and paint the room green. You can think of different alleles as different paint colors, but in genetics there are many more paint colors—alleles—and many more ways that they are combined.

### CONNECT TO

**PRINCIPLES OF GENETICS**

Recall from the chapter **Meiosis and Mendel** that a homozygote has two identical alleles of a gene, and a heterozygote has two different alleles of a gene.

**Virtual INVESTIGATION**

HMHScience.com

**GO ONLINE**

**Experiments and Models of Heredity**

○ MAIN IDEA

## Phenotype can depend on interactions of alleles.

Although Mendel's basic theory of heredity was correct, his research could not have explained all of the continuous variations for many traits. For example, many traits result from alleles with a range of dominance, rather than a strict dominant and recessive relationship.

The pea flowers that Mendel observed were either white or purple. One allele was dominant, but dominance does not mean that one allele "defeats" the other. Usually, it means that the dominant allele codes for a certain protein, and the recessive allele codes for a variation of the protein that has little or no effect. In Mendel's pea flowers, a heterozygous plant makes enough of the purple color that only one dominant allele is needed to give the flowers a purple color. But in many cases, a phenotype comes from more than just one gene, and many genes in a population have more than just two alleles.

### Incomplete Dominance

Sometimes, alleles show **incomplete dominance,** in which a heterozygous phenotype is somewhere between the two homozygous phenotypes. Neither allele is completely dominant nor completely recessive. One example of incomplete dominance is the four-o'clock plant. When plants that are homozygous for red flowers are crossed with plants that are homozygous for white flowers, the offspring have pink flowers. The pink color is a third, distinct phenotype. Neither of the original phenotypes of the plants in the parent's generation can be seen separately in the $F_1$ generation offspring.

## FIGURE 2.1 Incomplete Dominance

| PHENOTYPE | GENOTYPE | PHENOTYPE | GENOTYPE | PHENOTYPE | GENOTYPE |
|-----------|----------|-----------|----------|-----------|----------|
| green | $B_1B_1$ | steel blue | $B_2B_2$ | royal blue | $B_1B_2$ |

| The green betta fish is homozygous for the green color allele. | The steel blue betta fish is homozygous for the blue color allele. | The royal blue betta fish is heterozygous for the two color alleles. |
|---|---|---|

Another example of incomplete dominance is the color of betta fish shown in **FIGURE 2.1**. When a green fish ($B_1B_1$) is crossed with a steel blue fish ($B_2B_2$), all of the offspring have the heterozygous genotype ($B_1B_2$). These offspring will be a royal blue color that comes from the phenotypes from both alleles. The alleles of this gene follow a pattern of incomplete dominance. What happens when two royal blue betta fish are crossed? Some offspring (25%) will be green ($B_1B_1$), some (50%) will be royal blue ($B_1B_2$), and some (25%) will be steel blue ($B_2B_2$).

### READING TOOLBOX

**VOCABULARY**

When alleles are neither dominant nor recessive, such as with incomplete dominance, uppercase letters with either subscripts or superscripts are used to represent the different alleles.

## Codominance

Sometimes, both alleles of a gene are expressed completely—neither allele is dominant nor recessive. In this case, alleles show **codominance,** in which both traits are fully and separately expressed. Suppose a plant that is homozygous for red flowers is crossed with a plant that is homozygous for white flowers. In incomplete dominance, the offspring have pink flowers. Codominant alleles are different. Instead of what looks like an intermediate phenotype, both traits are expressed. The flowers will have some red areas and some white areas.

One trait that you likely know about—human ABO blood types—is an example of codominance. And, because the blood types come from three different alleles in the human population, this trait is also considered a multiple-allele trait. The multiple alleles, shown in **FIGURE 2.2**, are called $I^A$, $I^B$, and $i$. Both $I^A$ and $I^B$ result in a protein, called an antigen, on the surface of red blood cells. Allele $i$ is recessive and does not result in an antigen. Someone with a genotype of $I^Ai$ will have type A blood, and someone with a genotype of $I^Bi$ will have type B blood. But remember that the $I^A$ and $I^B$ alleles are codominant.

### FIGURE 2.2 CODOMINANCE

| PHENOTYPE (BLOOD TYPE) | | GENOTYPES |
|---|---|---|
| A | antigen A  | $I^AI^A$ or $I^Ai$ |
| B | antigen B  | $I^BI^B$ or $I^Bi$ |
| AB | both antigens  | $I^AI^B$ |
| O | no antigens  | $ii$ |

People with both codominant alleles ($I^A I^B$) have both antigens, so they have type AB blood. People with an *ii* genotype have red blood cells without either antigen, and they have type O blood. Two heterozygous people, one with type A blood ($I^A i$) and one with type B blood ($I^B i$), can have offspring with any of the four blood types, depending on the alleles that are passed on.

**Apply**  How can two people with type B blood have a child with type O blood?

▶ MAIN IDEA

# Many genes may interact to produce one trait.

As you have seen, some variations in phenotype are related to incomplete dominance, codominance, and multiple alleles. But most traits in plants and animals, including humans, are the result of several genes that interact.

### Polygenic Traits

Traits produced by two or more genes are called **polygenic traits.** Human skin color, for example, is the result of four genes that interact to produce a continuous range of colors. Similarly, human eye color, which is often thought of as a single gene trait, is polygenic. As **FIGURE 2.3** shows, at least three genes with complicated patterns of expression play roles in determining eye color. For example, the green allele is dominant to blue alleles, but it is recessive to all brown alleles. These genes do not account for all eye color variations, such as changes in eye color over time, the continuous range of eye colors, and patterns of colors in eyes. As a result, scientists hypothesize that still undiscovered genes affect eye color.

> **VISUAL VOCAB**
>
> Traits that are produced by two or more genes are called **polygenic traits.**
>
> many    genes
> **poly**   **genic**

### Epistasis

Another polygenic trait is fur color in mice and in other mammals. In mice, at least five different genes interact to produce the phenotype. Two genes give the mouse its general color, one gene affects the shading of the color, and one gene determines whether the mouse will have spots. But the fifth gene involved in mouse fur color can overshadow all of the others. In cases such as this, one gene, called an epistatic gene, can interfere with the expression of other genes.

## FIGURE 2.3  Eye Color

At least three different genes interact to produce the range of human eye colors, such as in the examples on the right.

| GENE NAME | DOMINANT ALLELE | RECESSIVE ALLELE |
|-----------|-----------------|------------------|
| BEY1 | brown | blue |
| BEY2 | brown | blue |
| GEY | green | blue |

Order of dominance: brown > green > blue.

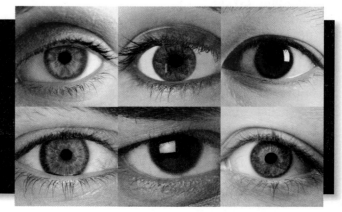

In albinism, a single epistatic gene interferes with the expression of other genes. Albinism, as you can see in **FIGURE 2.4**, is characterized by a lack of pigment in skin, hair, and eyes. A mouse that is homozygous for the alleles that prevent the coloration of fur will be white, regardless of the phenotypes that would normally come from the other four genes. A person with the alleles for albinism will have very light skin, hair, and eyes, regardless of the other genes he or she has inherited.

**Contrast** How do multiple-allele traits differ from polygenic traits?

**FIGURE 2.4** Albinism in mammals, such as this hedgehog, is caused by an epistatic gene that blocks the production of pigments.

### ● MAIN IDEA
## The environment interacts with genotype.

Phenotype is more than the sum of gene expression. For example, the sex of sea turtles depends both on genes and on environment. Female turtles make nests on beaches and bury their eggs in the sand. Eggs that mature in warmer temperatures develop into female turtles. Eggs that mature in cooler temperatures develop into male turtles.

Genes and environment also interact to determine human traits. Think about height. Genes give someone a tendency to be either short or tall, but they do not control everything. An interesting question for the interaction between genes and environment is "Are identical twins always identical?" Studies of identical twins have shown that the environment during early development can have long-lasting effects. One twin might get more nutrients than the other because of its position in the mother's uterus. This difference can result in height and size differences that last throughout the twins' lives. Also, twins raised in environments with different nutrition and health care often differ in height and other physical traits. In the end, phenotype is usually a mixture of genes and environment.

**Smart Grapher**
HMHScience.com
**GO ONLINE**
Average Height

**Connect** Sunlight can cause a person's hair to become lighter in color. Is this an example of an interaction between genes and the environment? Why or why not?

**SELF-CHECK Online**
HMHScience.com
**GO ONLINE**

## 7.2 Formative Assessment

### REVIEWING ● MAIN IDEAS

1. How is **incomplete dominance** expressed in a phenotype?

2. Why might **polygenic traits** vary more in phenotype than do single-gene traits?

3. Explain how interactions between genes and the environment can affect phenotype.

### CRITICAL THINKING

4. **Synthesize** How is **codominance** the same as having no dominant and recessive relationship at all between two alleles?

5. **Compare and Contrast** How are codominant alleles and incompletely dominant alleles similar? How are they different?

### CONNECT TO
**PRINCIPLES OF GENETICS**

6. Why can parents who are heterozygous for type A and type B blood have children with any of the four human blood types? Use a Punnett square to support your answer.

# The Genetics of Autism

Autism affects an estimated 1 in 68 people in the United States. The incidence has been rising since autism was first recognized as a disorder, in part because of better awareness and diagnosis, but perhaps also because of changes in the environment. In addition, researchers are

Scientists use fluorescence microscopes to look for copy number variants on fragments of DNA.

certain there is a genetic component to autism, but determining exactly what genes are involved is complicated.

Part of the difficulty in determining the causes of autism comes from the wide range of symptoms displayed by those with the disorder. Autism is more accurately called Autism Spectrum Disorder (ASD), which reflects that there is a wide range of effects, from barely detectable to severely disabling. To varying degrees, people who have been diagnosed with ASD have problems with communicating and relating to others. The disorder is often characterized by restrictive, repetitive patterns of behavior and interests. Early signs in young children include not making eye contact, not returning smiles, not asking to be picked up, and not playing games such as peek-a-boo. Sometimes, toddlers with ASD start developing these skills but then seem to lose them. Boys have a three to four times greater chance of being diagnosed with ASD than girls do.

Scientific interest in what causes ASD has been so great that large databases of DNA samples have been collected from families where at least one member has been diagnosed with ASD. Researchers who used one such database determined that if one child in a family has ASD, there is a two to six percent chance of a second child in that family having the disorder. If ASD were due to a mutation on a single gene, the probability of siblings having ASD would be close to either 25% or 50%. While most research has looked at small changes in genes, these researchers found that either duplications or deletions of entire sections of DNA are common in many ASD patients. Called copy number variants (CNVs), these differences were discovered using comparative genomic hybridization (CGH) arrays. Fragments of DNA, both from a person with ASD and a person without ASD, are separated into single strands and labeled with a fluorescent tag. The strands are then allowed to bind, and any differences can be observed with computer software and a fluorescence microscope. Twenty out of our twenty-three pairs of chromosomes appear to have regions that influence the onset of ASD, suggesting that there may be many different ways for this disorder to arise.

## Questions

1. Researchers have found that identical twins are much more likely to have ASD than are fraternal twins. Identical twins share the same genes, whereas fraternal twins are no more genetically related than any two siblings. What does this suggest about ASD?

2. Does the fact that identical twins share a likelihood of having ASD rule out environmental factors as a cause or trigger of the disorder? Explain.

3. How does the wide range of possible symptoms of ASD support the finding that multiple genes and biological pathways are involved in the disorder?

**SC.912.L.16.2**

**KEY CONCEPT** **Genes can be mapped to specific locations on chromosomes.**

**SC.912.L.16.2** Discuss observed inheritance patterns caused by various modes of inheritance, including dominant, recessive, codominant, sex-linked, polygenic, and multiple alleles.

**VOCABULARY**

linkage map

**MAIN IDEAS**

- Gene linkage was explained through fruit flies.
- Linkage maps estimate distances between genes.

**Connect to Your World**

If you leave a banana out on a table until it is very ripe, you might see some of the most useful organisms for genetic research—fruit flies—buzzing around it. In your kitchen, fruit flies are pests. In the laboratory, early experiments with fruit flies showed not only that genes are on chromosomes, but also that genes are found at specific places on chromosomes.

**MAIN IDEA**

## Gene linkage was explained through fruit flies.

Gene linkage, which you read about previously, was first described by William Bateson and R. C. Punnett, who invented the Punnett square. Punnett and Bateson, like Mendel, studied dihybrid crosses of pea plants. But their results differed from the 9:3:3:1 phenotype ratios that Mendel observed. The results suggested that some genes were linked together. But how could genes be linked and still follow Mendel's law of independent assortment?

American scientist Thomas Hunt Morgan, who worked with fruit flies (*Drosophila melanogaster*), found the answer. At first, Morgan was just looking for an organism to use in genetic research. He found fruit flies very useful because he could quickly and cheaply grow new generations of flies. He observed among fruit flies easily identifiable variations in eye color, body color, and wing shape. Knowing these variations, Morgan and his students set up experiments similar to Mendel's dihybrid crosses. They chose one type of fly with traits associated with the wild type, or most common phenotype. They crossed the wild type flies with mutant flies, or flies with a different, less common phenotype. You can see examples of fruit flies in **FIGURE 3.1**.

Morgan's results, like those of Punnett and Bateson, did not always follow the 9:3:3:1 ratio predicted by Mendel. But the results did differ in a noticeable pattern. Some traits appeared to be inherited together. Morgan called these traits linked traits, and they appeared to fall into four groups. As it turns out, fruit flies have four pairs of chromosomes. Each of the four groups of linked traits identified by Morgan matches one of the chromosome pairs. Morgan concluded that linked genes were on the same chromosome. The chromosomes, not the genes, assort independently during meiosis. Because the linked genes were not inherited together every time, Morgan also concluded that chromosomes must exchange homologous genes during meiosis.

**Wild type**

**Mutant**

**FIGURE 3.1** The wild type fruit fly (top) shows the most common phenotype. The mutant fruit fly (bottom) has a yellow body and curly wings.

**Synthesize** **How did Morgan's research build upon Mendel's observations?**

### CONSTRUCTING BAR GRAPHS

Scientists tested the reaction of fruit flies to stress by exposing them to bright light—a source of stress for *Drosophila*. The scientists recorded the time it took for half of the flies in each group to reach food, which they called a "half-time." Three strains of flies were tested—wild type 1, wild type 2, and a mutant eyeless type—under a controlled condition and with bright light. The data are shown in Table 1.

1. **Graph Data** Construct a bar graph that shows the data in the table. Recall that the independent variable is on the *x*-axis and the dependent variable is on the *y*-axis.

2. **Analyze** How did the condition of bright light affect the flies? Were all strains affected to the same degree? Why or why not?

| TABLE 1. *DROSOPHILA* RESPONSES TO LIGHT | | |
|---|---|---|
| **Strain** | **Condition** | **Half-Time (min)** |
| Wild type 1 | control | 4.0 |
| Wild type 1 | bright light | 12.5 |
| Wild type 2 | control | 4.5 |
| Wild type 2 | bright light | 12.0 |
| Eyeless | control | 4.5 |
| Eyeless | bright light | 5.0 |

Source: V. Min, B. Condron, *Journal of Neuroscience Methods*, 145.

▶ MAIN IDEA

## Linkage maps estimate distances between genes.

The probability that two genes on a chromosome will be inherited together is related to the distance between them. The closer together two genes are, the more likely it is that they will be inherited together. The farther apart two genes are, the more likely it is that they will be separated during meiosis.

One of Morgan's students, Alfred Sturtevant, hypothesized that the frequency of cross-overs during meiosis was related to the distance between genes. This meant that the closer together two genes were, the more likely they were to stay together when cross-overs took place. Sturtevant identified three linked traits in fruit flies—body color, eye color, and wing size—and then crossed the fruit flies. He recorded the percentage of times that the phenotypes did not appear together in the offspring. This percentage represented the frequency of cross-overs between chromosomes.

From the cross-over frequencies, Sturtevant made **linkage maps,** which are maps of the relative locations, or loci, of genes on a chromosome. On a linkage map, one map unit is equal to one cross-over for each 100 offspring, or one percentage point. You can see an example of a linkage map in **FIGURE 3.2.**

Making a linkage map is fairly easy if all of the cross-over frequencies for the genes being studied are known. Suppose the following data were collected.

- Gene A and gene B cross over 6.0% of the time.
- Gene B and gene C cross over 12.5% of the time.
- Gene A and gene C cross over 18.5% of the time.

According to Sturtevant's conclusions, genes A and B are 6 map units apart because they cross over 6% of the time. Similarly, genes B and C are 12.5 map units apart because they cross over 12.5% of the time. But where are the genes located in relation to each other on the chromosome?

### CONNECT TO

#### CROSSING OVER

Recall from the chapter **Meiosis and Mendel** that segments of non-sister chromatids can be exchanged during meiosis.

## FIGURE 3.2 Gene Linkage in *Drosophila*

**Linkage maps show the relative locations of genes.**

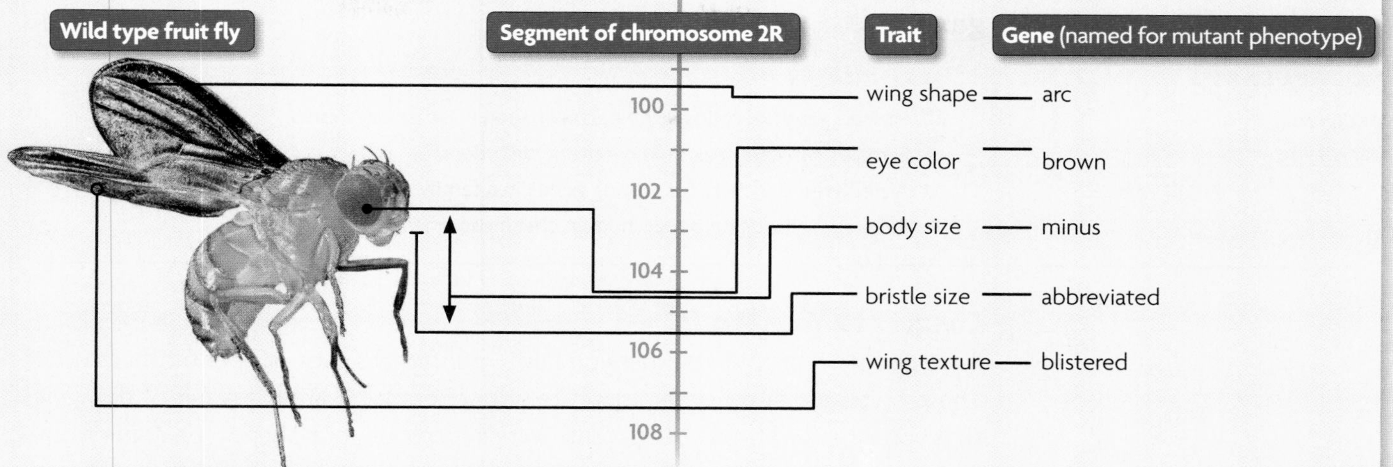

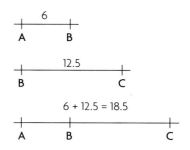

| Wild type fruit fly | Segment of chromosome 2R | Trait | Gene (named for mutant phenotype) |

| Position | Trait | Gene |
| --- | --- | --- |
| 100 | wing shape | arc |
| 102 | eye color | brown |
| 104 | body size | minus |
| | bristle size | abbreviated |
| 106 | wing texture | blistered |
| 108 | | |

**Apply** Which genes are most likely to cross over? least likely? Why?

Think about gene A as a point on a line. Gene B is either to the left or to the right of gene A. The same is true of the relationship between genes B and C. But if you only know the distances between genes A and B, and between genes B and C, you cannot determine the order of all three genes. You must also know the distance between genes A and C. As shown in **FIGURE 3.3**, the map distances between genes A and B and between genes B and C equal the map distance between genes A and C. Therefore, gene B must be located between genes A and C. If the map distance between genes A and C were 6.5 map units instead of 18.5 map units, then gene A would be between genes B and C.

Although linkage maps show the relative locations of linked genes, the maps do not show actual physical distances between genes. Linkage maps can give you a general idea about distances between genes, but many factors affect gene linkage. As a result, two pairs of genes may be the same number of map units apart, but they may not have the same physical distance between them.

**Summarize** How can a linkage map be used to analyze chromosomes?

**FIGURE 3.3** The order of genes on a chromosome can be determined if all of their cross-over frequencies are known.

---

**SELF-CHECK Online**
HMHScience.com
**GO ONLINE**

## 7.3 Formative Assessment

### REVIEWING ▶ MAIN IDEAS

1. Summarize the importance of comparing wild type and mutant fruit flies in genetic research.

2. How is a **linkage map** related to cross-overs that take place during meiosis?

### CRITICAL THINKING

3. **Compare and Contrast** How are linked genes similar to sex-linked genes? How are they different?

4. **Apply** Draw a linkage map based on the following cross-over percentages for three gene pairs: A – B = 8%, B – C = 10%, and A – C = 2%.

### CONNECT TO
**SCIENTIFIC PROCESS**

5. Punnett, Bateson, and Morgan found phenotype ratios that differed from Mendel's results. Explain how these differences led to new hypotheses and new investigations in genetics.

## 7.4 Human Genetics and Pedigrees

KEY CONCEPT **A combination of methods is used to study human genetics.**

**VOCABULARY**

pedigree
karyotype

**MAIN IDEAS**

- ◗ Human genetics follows the patterns seen in other organisms.
- ◗ Females can carry sex-linked genetic disorders.
- ◗ A pedigree is a chart for tracing genes in a family.
- ◗ Several methods help map human chromosomes.

 *Connect to Your World*

Have people ever told you that you have your father's eyes or your mother's nose? These traits, and every other aspect of your phenotype, are the result of the genes that you inherited from your parents. Which parts of your phenotype come from which parent? In some cases, such as hair color or eye color, it may be very easy to tell. Often, however, it is not so obvious.

◗ MAIN IDEA

# Human genetics follows the patterns seen in other organisms.

Fruit flies and pea plants may seem boring and simple, but the basic principles of genetics were worked out using those organisms. Humans follow the same patterns of heredity. First, meiosis independently assorts chromosomes when gametes are made for sexual reproduction. Second, human heredity involves the same relationships between alleles—dominant and recessive interactions, polygenic traits, and sex-linked genes, among others.

The inheritance of many traits is very complex. A single trait may be controlled by several genes that interact. As you read in Section 2, eye color is controlled by at least three different genes. And, although several genes affect height, a person's environment during growth and development plays a large role in his or her adult height. What might seem like an obvious phenotype is rarely as simple as it looks.

Nonetheless, single-gene traits are very helpful in understanding human genetics. One such trait is the shape of a person's hairline. A hairline with a downward point, such as a widow's peak shown in **FIGURE 4.1,** is a dominant trait. A straight hairline is a recessive trait. The inheritance of this trait follows the same dominant and recessive pattern as the traits in Mendel's pea plants. Many genetic disorders, such as Huntington's disease, hemophilia, and Duchenne's muscular dystrophy, are also caused by single genes that follow a dominant and recessive pattern. In fact, much of what is known about human genetics comes from studying genetic disorders.

**FIGURE 4.1** The widow's peak, or pointed hairline, is a phenotype produced by a dominant autosomal gene.

**Apply** **Why can the genetics of pea plants and fruit flies be applied to humans?**

© HMH

## ▶ MAIN IDEA

# Females can carry sex-linked genetic disorders.

Recall from Section 1 that some genetic disorders are caused by autosomal genes. A carrier of an autosomal disorder does not show the disease but can pass on the disease-causing allele. Both males and females can be carriers of an autosomal disorder.

In contrast, only females can be carriers of sex-linked disorders. Several genetic disorders are caused by genes on the X chromosome, as you can see in **FIGURE 4.2**. Recall that males have an XY genotype. A male who has a gene for a disorder located on the X chromosome will not have a second, normal allele to mask it. One copy of the allele is enough for males to have the disorder. There are no male carriers of sex-linked disorders because any male who has the gene displays the phenotype. Females can be carriers because they may have a normal allele that gives them a normal phenotype. The likelihood of inheriting a sex-linked disorder depends both on the sex of the child and on which parent carries the disorder-causing allele. If only the mother has the allele and is a carrier, a child has a 50% chance of inheriting the allele. A daughter who inherits it will not show the phenotype, but a son will.

The British royal family provides a historical example of a sex-linked disorder. Queen Victoria (1819–1901) was a carrier of a recessive sex-linked allele for a disorder called hemophilia, which is a lack of proteins needed for blood to clot. People with hemophilia do not stop bleeding easily. Queen Victoria passed the allele to her son, who had hemophilia. He passed it to his daughter, who was a carrier, and so on. Members of royal families tended to marry into royal families in other countries, and by the early 1900s the royal families of several countries, including Russia and Spain, also had the allele for hemophilia. The allele in all of these people is traced back to Queen Victoria.

**Contrast** How can carriers differ between autosomal and sex-linked disorders?

> ▶ **READING TOOLBOX**
>
> **VOCABULARY**
> The term *carrier* means "a person who transports something." In genetics, a carrier is a person who "transports" a recessive allele but does not express the recessive phenotype.

## FIGURE 4.2 Comparing the X and Y Chromosomes

The X chromosome has about 1100 known genes, including many that cause genetic disorders. The Y chromosome is about one-third the size of the X and has only about 250 known genes.

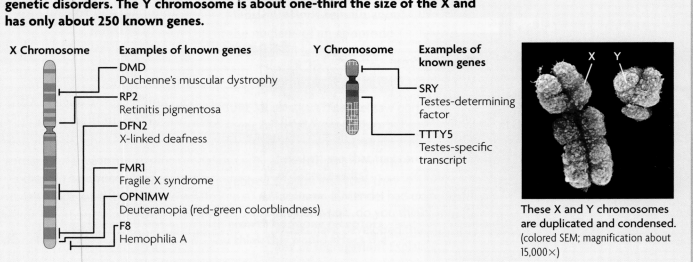

X Chromosome

Examples of known genes

DMD
Duchenne's muscular dystrophy

RP2
Retinitis pigmentosa

DFN2
X-linked deafness

FMR1
Fragile X syndrome

OPN1MW
Deuteranopia (red-green colorblindness)

F8
Hemophilia A

Y Chromosome

Examples of known genes

SRY
Testes-determining factor

TTTY5
Testes-specific transcript

These X and Y chromosomes are duplicated and condensed.
(colored SEM; magnification about 15,000×)

©Biophoto Associates/Photo Researchers, Inc.

**Chapter 7: Extending Mendelian Genetics** **205**

▶ MAIN IDEA

# A pedigree is a chart for tracing genes in a family.

If two people want to know their child's chances of having a certain genetic disorder, they cannot rely upon their phenotypes. The parents also need to know their genotypes. A **pedigree** chart can help trace the phenotypes and genotypes in a family to determine whether people carry recessive alleles. When enough family phenotypes are known, genotypes can often be inferred.

A human pedigree shows several types of information. Boxes represent males and circles represent females. A shaded shape means that a person shows the trait, a white shape means that the person does not, and a shape that is half-shaded and half-white means that a person is a carrier. Lines connect a person to his or her mate, and to their children.

Using phenotypes to figure out the possible genotypes in a family is like putting pieces of a puzzle together. You have to use clues and logic to narrow the possibilities for each person's genotype. One particular clue, for example, can tell you whether the gene is on an autosome or on a sex chromosome. If approximately the same number of males and females have the phenotype, then the gene is most likely on an autosome. If, however, the phenotype is much more common in males, then the gene is likely on the X chromosome.

## Tracing Autosomal Genes

It is fairly easy to trace genotypes through a pedigree when you know that you are dealing with a trait controlled by an autosomal gene. Why? A person who does not show the phenotype must have a homozygous recessive genotype. Any other genotype—either heterozygous or homozygous dominant—would produce the phenotype. Use the following steps to work your way through a pedigree for a gene on an autosome. The inheritance of an autosomal trait, such as the widow's peak described earlier, is shown on the top of **FIGURE 4.3.**

- People with a widow's peak have either homozygous dominant (*WW*) or heterozygous (*Ww*) genotypes.
- Two parents without a widow's peak are both homozygous recessive (*ww*) and cannot have children who have a widow's peak.
- Two parents who both have a widow's peak can have a child who does not (*ww*) if both parents are heterozygous for the dominant and recessive alleles (*Ww*).

## Tracing Sex-Linked Genes

When a gene is on the X chromosome, you have to think about the inheritance of the sex chromosomes as well as dominant and recessive alleles. Also, recall that more males than females show a sex-linked trait in their phenotype and that females can be carriers of the trait.

One example of a sex-linked trait is red-green colorblindness. Three genes for color vision are on the X chromosome, so a male with even one recessive allele of one of the three genes is partially colorblind. He will pass that allele to all of his daughters, but he cannot pass the allele to any sons. A pedigree for colorblindness, which is sex-linked, is shown on the bottom of **FIGURE 4.3.**

**Web Quest**

HMHScience.com

**GO ONLINE**

Genetic Heritage

# FIGURE 4.3 Interpreting Pedigree Charts

Figuring out genotypes from phenotypes requires you to use a process of elimination. You can often determine which genotypes are possible, and which ones are not.

□ Male without phenotype

▨ Male with phenotype

◩ Male carrier

○ Female without phenotype

● Female with phenotype

◓ Female carrier

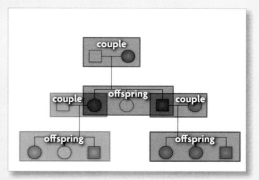

## TRACING AUTOSOMAL GENES: WIDOW'S PEAK

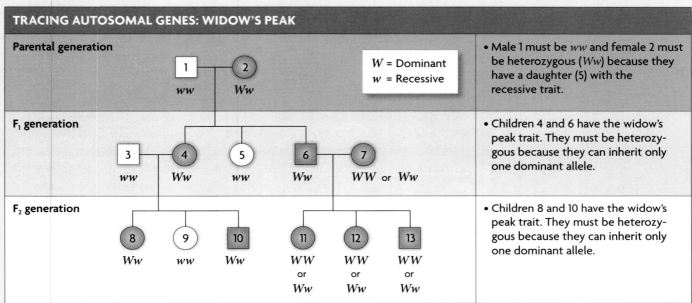

**Parental generation**

1 ♂ — 2 ♀
ww    Ww

$W$ = Dominant
$w$ = Recessive

• Male 1 must be $ww$ and female 2 must be heterozygous ($Ww$) because they have a daughter (5) with the recessive trait.

**F₁ generation**

3 — 4    5    6 — 7
ww   Ww  ww   Ww   WW or Ww

• Children 4 and 6 have the widow's peak trait. They must be heterozygous because they can inherit only one dominant allele.

**F₂ generation**

8    9    10    11    12    13
Ww   ww   Ww   WW    WW    WW
                or    or    or
                Ww    Ww    Ww

• Children 8 and 10 have the widow's peak trait. They must be heterozygous because they can inherit only one dominant allele.

## TRACING SEX-LINKED GENES: COLORBLINDNESS

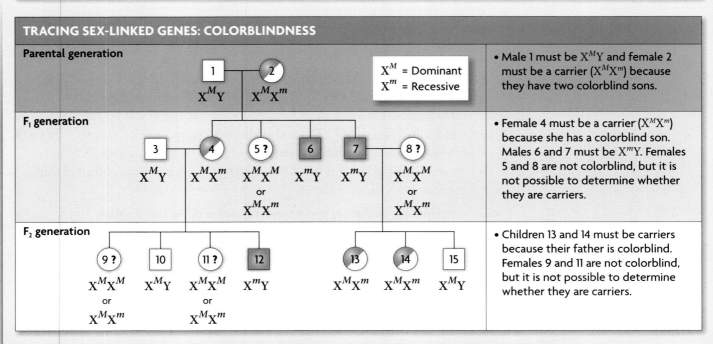

**Parental generation**

1 — 2
$X^M Y$   $X^M X^m$

$X^M$ = Dominant
$X^m$ = Recessive

• Male 1 must be $X^M Y$ and female 2 must be a carrier ($X^M X^m$) because they have two colorblind sons.

**F₁ generation**

3 — 4    5 ?    6    7 — 8 ?
$X^M Y$  $X^M X^m$  $X^M X^M$  $X^m Y$  $X^m Y$  $X^M X^M$
                   or                            or
                   $X^M X^m$                     $X^M X^m$

• Female 4 must be a carrier ($X^M X^m$) because she has a colorblind son. Males 6 and 7 must be $X^m Y$. Females 5 and 8 are not colorblind, but it is not possible to determine whether they are carriers.

**F₂ generation**

9 ?    10    11 ?    12    13    14    15
$X^M X^M$  $X^M Y$  $X^M X^M$  $X^m Y$  $X^M X^m$  $X^M X^m$  $X^M Y$
or                 or
$X^M X^m$          $X^M X^m$

• Children 13 and 14 must be carriers because their father is colorblind. Females 9 and 11 are not colorblind, but it is not possible to determine whether they are carriers.

---

**CRITICAL VIEWING**   Explain why it is not possible to identify all of the genotypes in the pedigree charts above. What information would you need to identify the genotypes of those people?

## FIGURE 4.4 RED-GREEN COLORBLINDNESS

A person with normal color vision can easily distinguish between different colors. A person who is red-green colorblind cannot.

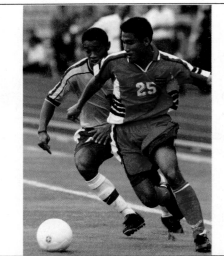

| PHENOTYPE | GENOTYPES | PHENOTYPE | GENOTYPES |
|---|---|---|---|
| normal vision | $X^MX^m$ or $X^MX^M$ or $X^MY$ | red-green colorblind | $X^mX^m$ or $X^mY$ |

The steps below can be applied to any sex-linked trait. By using a process of elimination, you can often figure out the possible genotypes for a given phenotype. First, think about the individuals shown in the pedigree chart.

- Colorblind females must be homozygous recessive ($X^mX^m$).
- Males who are colorblind must have the recessive allele ($X^mY$).
- Females who are heterozygous for the alleles ($X^MX^m$) do not show the phenotype, but they are carriers of the trait.

Then, think about the possible offspring of the people shown in the pedigree.

- A female carrier ($X^MX^m$) and a male with normal color vision ($X^MY$) have a 50% chance that a son would be colorblind ($X^mY$). The same couple has a 50% chance that a daughter would be a carrier ($X^MX^m$).
- Colorblind females ($X^mX^m$) and males with normal color vision ($X^MY$) will have daughters who are carriers ($X^MX^m$) and colorblind sons ($X^mY$).
- Two colorblind parents ($X^mX^m$ and $X^mY$) always have colorblind children because both parents always pass on the recessive allele.

**Contrast** How are pedigrees and Punnett squares different? Explain.

## ▶ MAIN IDEA
# Several methods help map human chromosomes.

The human genome, or all of the DNA in a human cell, is so large that mapping human genes is difficult. As a result, a combination of several methods is used. Pedigrees are useful for studying genetics in a family. Scientists can even gather a large number of pedigrees from people who are not related to look for inheritance patterns.

©Reuters/Corbis

Other methods more directly study human chromosomes. A **karyotype** (KAR-ee-uh-TYP), for example, is a picture of all of the chromosomes in a cell. In order to study the chromosomes, chemicals are used to stain them. The chemical stains produce a pattern of bands on the chromosomes, as shown in **FIGURE 4.5**. The sizes and locations of the bands are very consistent for each chromosome, but the bands differ greatly among different chromosomes. Therefore, different chromosomes can be easily identified in a karyotype.

Karyotypes can show changes in chromosomes. Chromosome changes can be dramatic, such as when a person has too many chromosomes. In Down syndrome, for example, a person has an extra copy of at least part of chromosome 21. In XYY syndrome, a male has an extra Y chromosome. Other times, a karyotype reveals the loss of part of a chromosome. In the figure, you can see a deletion of a large part of chromosome 1. Scientists also use karyotypes to estimate the distances between genes on a chromosome. A karyotype can help show the possible location of a gene on a chromosome.

Chromosome mapping can be done directly by searching for a particular gene. All of the chromosomes are cut apart into smaller pieces. Then this library of chromosome parts is searched to find the gene. Although many genes and their locations have been identified through this process, it is a slow and inefficient method. The large-scale mapping of all of the genes on human chromosomes truly began with the Human Genome Project, an international effort to map, sequence, and identify all of the genes in the human genome.

**Apply** **Why must a combination of methods be used to study human genetics?**

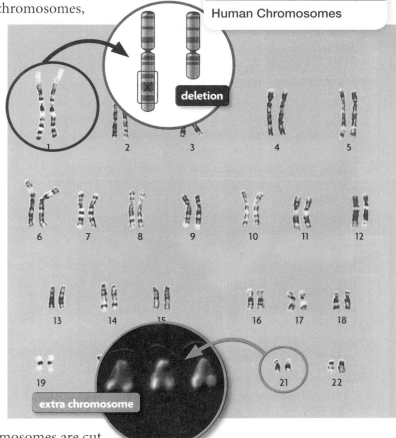

**FIGURE 4.5** A karyotype can help show chromosomal disorders, such as the deletion in chromosome 1 (top inset) and the extra chromosome 21 in Down syndrome (bottom inset). (LM; magnifications: deletion 8000×; colored LM, extra chromosome 11,000×)

# 7.4 Formative Assessment

**SELF-CHECK Online**
HMHScience.com
**GO ONLINE**

## REVIEWING ▶ MAIN IDEAS

1. How can Mendel's principles be used to study human traits?

2. Is a person who is homozygous recessive for a recessive genetic disease a carrier? Explain.

3. Describe how phenotypes can be used to predict genotypes in a **pedigree**.

4. How can a **karyotype** be used to study human chromosomes?

## CRITICAL THINKING

5. **Apply** Suppose a colorblind male and a female with no recessive alleles for colorblindness have children. What is the probability they will have a colorblind son or daughter?

6. **Contrast** How do pedigrees for autosomal genes differ from pedigrees for sex-linked genes?

## CONNECT TO
### PRINCIPLES OF GENETICS

7. Explain why Mendel's principles of inheritance can be applied to all sexually reproducing species.

# 7 Summary

## KEY CONCEPTS

### 7.1 Chromosomes and Phenotype

**The chromosomes on which genes are located can affect the expression of traits.** Two alleles of autosomal genes interact to produce phenotype. Genes on the sex chromosomes are expressed differently in males and females of many species. In humans, males are XY and females are XX. Males only have one copy of each gene found on the sex chromosomes, so all of those genes are expressed in their phenotype.

### 7.2 Complex Patterns of Inheritance

**Phenotype is affected by many different factors.** Phenotype is rarely the result of a simple dominant and recessive relationship between two alleles of a gene. Often, there are more than two possible alleles of a gene. Incomplete dominance produces an intermediate phenotype. Codominance results in both alleles being fully and separately expressed. Many traits are polygenic, or controlled by several genes. Interactions between genes and the environment also affect phenotype.

### 7.3 Gene Linkage and Mapping

**Genes can be mapped to specific locations on chromosomes.** Studies of wild type and mutant fruit flies led to a new understanding of genetics. Linked genes are often inherited together. During meiosis, linked genes can be separated from each other when parts of chromosomes are exchanged. By studying the frequency of cross-overs between chromosomes, it is possible to create a linkage map that shows the relative order of genes on a chromosome.

### 7.4 Human Genetics and Pedigrees

**A combination of methods is used to study human genetics.** Although most traits do not follow a simple dominant and recessive pattern, single-gene traits are important in the study of human genetics. Several genetic disorders are caused by a single gene with dominant and recessive alleles. Carriers are people who have an allele for a genetic disorder but do not express the allele in their phenotype. The patterns of genetic inheritance can be studied in families by pedigree analysis. Pedigree analysis is an indirect method of investigating human genotypes. Karyotypes can show large changes in chromosomes.

---

## READING TOOLBOX     SYNTHESIZE YOUR NOTES

**Main Idea Web** Use a main idea web like the one shown below to organize your notes. Make connections among the genetics concepts in the chapter, such as chromosomes and gene expression.

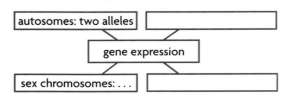

**Concept Map** Make a concept map like the one shown below to synthesize your knowledge of Mendelian genetics with more complex patterns of inheritance.

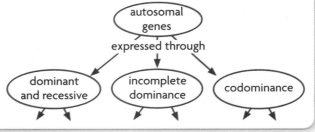

# 7 Review

**INTERACTIVE Review**
HMHScience.com

**GO ONLINE**

Review Games • Concept Map • Section Self-Checks

## CHAPTER VOCABULARY

**7.1**  carrier
sex-linked gene
X chromosome inactivation

**7.2**  incomplete dominance
codominance
polygenic trait

**7.3**  linkage map
**7.4**  pedigree
karyotype

## Reviewing Vocabulary

**Compare and Contrast**

Describe one similarity and one difference between the two terms in each of the following pairs.

1. sex-linked gene, carrier
2. incomplete dominance, codominance
3. linkage map, karyotype

**Visualize Vocabulary**

For each term below, use simple shapes, lines, or arrows to illustrate the meaning. Below each picture, write a short caption. Here's an example for the term *linkage map*.

B          A          C

A linkage map shows the order of genes on a chromosome.

4. polygenic trait
5. pedigree
6. X chromosome inactivation

### READING TOOLBOX    WORD ORIGINS

Use the definitions of the word parts to answer the next two questions.

| Word Part | Meaning |
|-----------|---------|
| *poly-* | many |
| *co-* | together; the same amount |
| *genic* | produced by genes |

7. How are the word parts *poly-* and *genic* related to the meaning of the term *polygenic trait*?

8. How is the prefix *co-* related to the meaning of the term *codominant*?

## Reviewing MAIN IDEAS

9. Explain why disorders caused by dominant alleles on autosomes are less common than those caused by recessive alleles on autosomes.

10. Describe how the expression of sex-linked genes can differ between males and females.

11. How do codominance and incomplete dominance differ from a simple dominant and recessive relationship between alleles?

12. Humans have a tremendous range of hair, eye, and skin color. How does the polygenic nature of these traits explain the wide range of phenotypes?

13. Give two examples that demonstrate how the environment can interact with genotype to affect an organism's phenotype.

14. How did Morgan's research with fruit flies help to explain Punnett's and Bateson's observations of pea plants?

15. Explain how linked genes and cross-over frequencies are used to make linkage maps.

16. What are two main ways in which human genetics follows the genetic patterns seen in other organisms?

17. Under what circumstances could two individuals with no symptoms of a recessive genetic disease have children that do have the disease?

18. What are one similarity and one difference between patterns for autosomal and sex-linked genes on a pedigree chart?

19. What is a karyotype, and how can it be used to study human chromosomes and to map human genes?

# Critical Thinking

20. **Analyze** Can a person be a carrier for a dominant genetic disorder? Explain.

21. **Apply** Both men and women can be colorblind, but there are approximately 100 times as many colorblind men as women in the world. Explain why men are more likely to be colorblind than women.

22. **Apply** Suppose two plants with light purple, or lavender, flowers are crossed. About 25% of the offspring have white flowers, 25% have purple flowers, and 50% have lavender flowers. Which of the following could explain these results: codominance, incomplete dominance, or multiple alleles? Explain.

23. **Apply** Copy the chart below into your science notebook. Following the provided example, fill in the chart to show the number of possible genotypes given 2, 3, or 4 alleles.

| Number of Alleles | Number of Possible Genotypes |
|---|---|
| 2 (A, B) | 3 (AA, AB, BB) |
| 3 (A, B, C) | |
| 4 (A, B, C, D) | |

24. **Apply** Some members of David's family have an autosomal recessive disease. David does not have the disease; neither do his parents, nor his two brothers. His maternal grandfather has the disease, his paternal grandmother has the disease, and his sister has the disease. Draw a pedigree chart to represent the genotypes of all grandparents, parents, and children. Next to each person, write his or her possible genotype.

25. **Synthesize** Why are studies of identical twins important in helping understand interactions between environment and genotype? Explain.

## Interpreting Visuals

Copy into your science notebook the pedigree chart on the right to answer the next two questions. Use *A* as the dominant allele, and use *a* as the recessive allele.

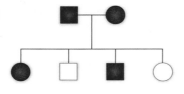

26. **Analyze** Is this trait most likely recessive or dominant? Explain.

27. **Analyze** What is the genotype of each individual in the pedigree chart? Explain your answers.

## Analyzing Data   Construct a Bar Graph

A scientist studies four linked traits in fruit flies and observes the frequency with which the traits cross over. The bar graph below shows the cross-over frequencies among genes A, B, C, and D. Use the graph to answer the next three questions.

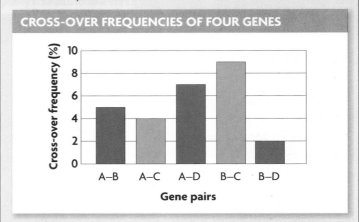

28. **Evaluate** Which two genes are least likely to be inherited together? How do you know?

29. **Evaluate** Which two genes are most likely to be inherited together? How do you know?

30. **Apply** Explain why a bar graph is an appropriate type of graph for displaying these data.

## Making Connections

31. **Write an Ad** Imagine that you are starting a business that will make pedigree charts for people who want to map particular family traits. Write an ad in simple language that all readers will understand. Your ad should demonstrate that you have the necessary understanding of human genetics for a successful pedigree chart-making business.

32. **Synthesize** Look again at the tremendous range of human phenotypes in the photographs on the chapter opener. How is human genetics similar to and different from the genetics of Mendel's pea plants?

# Standards-Based Assessment

Record your answers on a separate piece of paper.

## MULTIPLE CHOICE

1 A genotyped pedigree of 239 people shows evidence of an inheritable recessive disease. One female, however, doesn't fit the pattern of inheritance demonstrated by all of the other family members. What is *most likely* true of this individual?

   A She had been treated for the disease.

   B She accumulated additional mutations.

   C She is immune to the disorder.

   D She was genotyped incorrectly.

   ### THINK THROUGH THE QUESTION

   Consider both what a pedigree chart shows and what it doesn't show. Phenotypes are shown on a pedigree, but genotypes are inferred from the phenotypes.

2 Many animals, including humans, have sex chromosomes. Which of the following shows the sex chromosome genotype a normal human male would inherit from his parents?

   A XX

   B YY

   C XY

   D Y

3 A scientist studying two traits in mice knows that each trait is determined by one gene and that both genes are on the same chromosome. If the two traits are not always inherited together by the offspring of the mice, what is *most likely* true?

   A The genes are not on the same chromosome.

   B The genes are far enough apart to allow crossing over.

   C The inheritance of these genes leads to codominance.

   D One of the genes has a high rate of mutation.

4 Genes on a pair of chromosomes often cross over during meiosis, as shown in the diagram below.

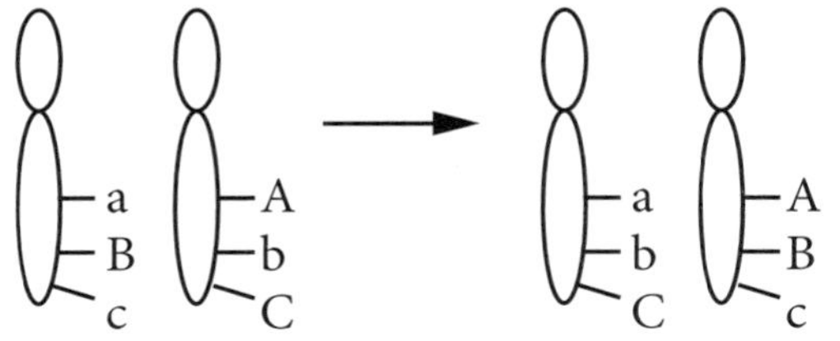

The discovery of crossing over added to Mendel's law of independent assortment, which states that genes assort independently of one another. What do crossovers indicate?

   A Crossing over allows for more than two alleles of a gene.

   B Independent assortment between genes depends on their locations.

   C Genes do not assort independently of one another.

   D Crossing over decreases genetic variation in populations.

5

| Fruit Fly Dihybrid Cross | | | | |
|---|---|---|---|---|
| Eeww\eeWw | eW | ew | eW | ew |
| Ew | | | | |
| Ew | | | | |
| ew | | | ■ | |
| ew | | | | |

Red eyes is dominant (*E*); white eyes is recessive (*e*).
Normal wings is dominant (*W*); short wings is recessive (*w*).

A fruit fly with red eyes and short wings is crossed with a fruit fly with white eyes and normal wings. According to the cross shown in the diagram above, what is the expected phenotype of fruit flies in the shaded box?

   A white eyes and normal wings

   B white eyes and short wings

   C red eyes and normal wings

   D red eyes and short wings

# 8 From DNA to Proteins

**BIG IDEA** DNA and RNA are the genetic material in all living things and provide the molecular basis for reproduction and development.

**ONLINE BIOLOGY** HMHScience.com

**ONLINE** Labs
- Extracting DNA
- **QuickLab** Replication
- UV Light and Skin Cancer
- Modeling Transcription
- Observing *Drosophila* Mutations
- Exploring Protein Crystallization

- **Video Lab** DNA Extraction from Wheat Germ

(t) © Eye of Science/Photo Researchers, Inc.

# Q Why is this mouse glowing?

This mouse's eerie green glow comes from green fluorescent protein (GFP), which glows under ultraviolet light. Scientists put a GFP gene from a glowing jellyfish into a virus that was then used to infect a mouse egg. The jellyfish gene became part of the mouse's genes. As a result, the mouse's cells produce the same jellyfish protein and make the mouse glow. Researchers hope to use GFP to track cancer cells.

---

 **READING TOOLBOX**   **This reading tool can help you learn the material in the following pages.**

### USING LANGUAGE

**Finding Examples** When you are reading scientific explanations, finding examples can help you put a concept into practical terms. Thinking of your own examples will help you remember what you read.

### YOUR TURN

For each category of items below, brainstorm as many examples as you can think of that could fit into the category.

1. hereditary traits
2. words that include the word part *–her–*

# 8.1 Identifying DNA as the Genetic Material

SC.912.N.1.3,
SC.912.L.16.9

**VOCABULARY**

bacteriophage

**KEY CONCEPT** DNA was identified as the genetic material through a series of experiments.

**MAIN IDEAS**

- Griffith finds a "transforming principle."
- Avery identifies DNA as the transforming principle.
- Hershey and Chase confirm that DNA is the genetic material.

**SC.912.N.1.3** Recognize that the strength or usefulness of a scientific claim is evaluated through scientific argumentation, which depends on critical and logical thinking, and the active consideration of alternative scientific explanations to explain the data presented.

**SC.912.L.16.9** Explain how and why the genetic code is universal and is common to almost all organisms.

## Connect to Your World

Some people think that a complicated answer is better than a simple one. In the early 1900's, for example, most scientists thought that DNA's chemical composition was too repetitive for it to be the genetic material. Proteins, which are more variable in structure, appeared to be a better candidate. Starting in the 1920s, experiments provided data that did not support this idea. By the 1950s, sufficient evidence showed that DNA—the same molecule that codes for GFP in the glowing mouse— carries genetic information.

## ▶ MAIN IDEA

# Griffith finds a "transforming principle."

In 1928 the British microbiologist Frederick Griffith was investigating two forms of the bacterium that causes pneumonia. One form is surrounded by a coating made of carbohydrates. This form is called the S form because its colonies look smooth. The second form of bacteria does not have a smooth coating and is called the R, or rough, form. As you can see in **FIGURE 1.1,** when Griffith injected the two types of bacteria into mice, only the S type killed the mice. When the S bacteria were killed with heat before injection, the mice were unaffected. Therefore, only live S bacteria would cause the mice to die.

### READING TOOLBOX

**TAKING NOTES**

Make a table to keep track of the experiments discussed in this section and to note how they contributed to our understanding of DNA.

| Experiment | Results |
|---|---|
| Griffith's mice | A transferable material changed harmless bacteria into disease-causing bacteria. |

## FIGURE 1.1 Griffith's Experiments

**The S form of the bacterium is deadly; the R form is not.**

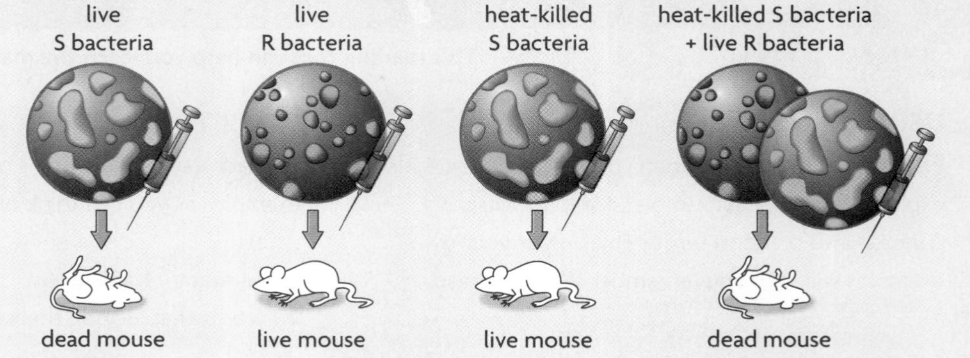

| live S bacteria | live R bacteria | heat-killed S bacteria | heat-killed S bacteria + live R bacteria |
|---|---|---|---|
| dead mouse | live mouse | live mouse | dead mouse |

Griffith next injected mice with a combination of heat-killed S bacteria and live R bacteria. To his surprise, the mice died. Even more surprising, he found live S bacteria in blood samples from the dead mice. Griffith concluded that some material must have been transferred from the heat-killed S bacteria to the live R bacteria. Whatever that material was, it contained information that changed harmless R bacteria into disease-causing S bacteria. Griffith called this mystery material the "transforming principle."

**Infer** What evidence suggested that there was a transforming principle?

**CONNECT TO**

**MICROBIOLOGY**
Much of our knowledge of the chemical basis of genetics has come from the study of bacteria. You will learn much more about bacteria in the chapter **Viruses and Prokaryotes.**

## ● MAIN IDEA
# Avery identifies DNA as the transforming principle.

What exactly is the transforming principle that Griffith discovered? That question puzzled Oswald Avery and his fellow biologists. They worked for more than ten years to find the answer. Avery's team began by combining living R bacteria with an extract made from S bacteria. This procedure allowed them to directly observe the transformation of R bacteria into S bacteria in a petri dish.

Avery's group next developed a process to purify their extract. They then performed a series of tests to find out if the transforming principle was DNA or protein.

- **Qualitative tests** Standard chemical tests showed that no protein was present. In contrast, tests revealed that DNA was present.
- **Chemical analysis** As you can see in **FIGURE 1.2**, the proportions of elements in the extract closely matched those found in DNA. Proteins contain almost no phosphorus.
- **Enzyme tests** When the team added to the extract enzymes known to break down proteins, the extract still transformed the R bacteria to the S form. Also, transformation occurred when researchers added an enzyme that breaks down RNA (another nucleic acid). Transformation failed to occur only when they added an enzyme that specifically destroys DNA.

### FIGURE 1.2 Avery's Discoveries

**CHEMICAL ANALYSIS OF TRANSFORMING PRINCIPLE**

|  | % Nitrogen (N) | % Phosphorus (P) | Ratio of N to P |
|---|---|---|---|
| Sample A | 14.21 | 8.57 | 1.66 |
| Sample B | 15.93 | 9.09 | 1.75 |
| Sample C | 15.36 | 9.04 | 1.69 |
| Sample D | 13.40 | 8.45 | 1.58 |
| Known value for DNA | 15.32 | 9.05 | 1.69 |

Source: Avery, O. T. et al., *The Journal of Experimental Medicine* 79:2.

**Analyze** How do the data support the hypothesis that DNA, not protein, is the transforming principle?

Oswald Avery

In 1944 Avery and his group presented this and other evidence to support their conclusion that DNA must be the transforming principle, or genetic material. The results created great interest. However, some scientists questioned whether the genetic material in bacteria was the same as that in other organisms. Despite Avery's evidence, some scientists insisted that his extract must have contained protein.

**Summarize** List the key steps in the process that Avery's team used to identify the transforming principle.

## ⊙ MAIN IDEA

# Hershey and Chase confirm that DNA is the genetic material.

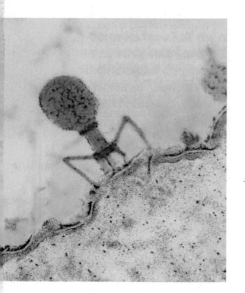

**FIGURE 1.3** This micrograph shows the protein coat of a bacteriophage (orange) after it has injected its DNA into an *E. coli* bacterium (blue). (colored TEM; magnification 115,000×)

Conclusive evidence for DNA as the genetic material came in 1952 from two American biologists, Alfred Hershey and Martha Chase. Hershey and Chase were studying viruses that infect bacteria. This type of virus, called a **bacteriophage** (bak-TIR-ee-uh-FAYJ), or "phage" for short, takes over a bacterium's genetic machinery and directs it to make more viruses.

Phages such as the ones Hershey and Chase studied are relatively simple—little more than a DNA molecule surrounded by a protein coat. This two-part structure of phages offered a perfect opportunity to answer the question, Is the genetic material made of DNA or protein? By discovering which part of a phage (DNA or protein) actually entered a bacterium, as shown in **FIGURE 1.3**, they could answer this question once and for all.

Hershey and Chase thought up a clever procedure that made use of the chemical elements found in protein and DNA. Protein contains sulfur but very little phosphorus, while DNA contains phosphorus but no sulfur. The researchers grew phages in cultures that contained radioactive isotopes of sulfur or phosphorus. Hershey and Chase then used these radioactively tagged phages in two experiments.

- **Experiment 1** In the first experiment, bacteria were infected with phages that had radioactive sulfur atoms in their protein molecules. Hershey and Chase then used a kitchen blender and a centrifuge to separate the bacteria from the parts of the phages that remained outside the bacteria. When they examined the bacteria, they found no significant radioactivity.
- **Experiment 2** Next, Hershey and Chase repeated the procedure with phages that had DNA tagged with radioactive phosphorus. This time, radioactivity was clearly present inside the bacteria.

From their results, Hershey and Chase concluded that the phages' DNA had entered the bacteria, but the protein had not. Their findings finally convinced scientists that the genetic material is DNA and not protein.

**Apply** **How did Hershey and Chase build upon Avery's chemical analysis results?**

©Biozentrum, University of Basel/Photo Researchers, Inc.

---

## 8.1 Formative Assessment

SELF-CHECK Online
HMHScience.com
GO ONLINE

### REVIEWING ⊙ MAIN IDEAS

1. What was "transformed" in Griffith's experiment?
2. How did Avery and his team identify the transforming principle?
3. Summarize how Hershey and Chase confirmed that DNA is the genetic material.

### CRITICAL THINKING

4. **Summarize** Why was the **bacteriophage** an excellent choice for research to determine whether genes are made of DNA or proteins?
5. **Analyze** Choose one experiment from this section and explain how the results support the conclusion.

### CONNECT TO

**MENDELIAN GENETICS**

6. Describe how Mendel's studies relate to the experiments discussed in this section.

# Epigenetics

Inheritance through the passing on of genes is well understood, but it is becoming increasingly clear that it is not the whole story when it comes to our DNA. Even if DNA is completely unchanged, how it is expressed can be controlled by "tags" on our genes, and those tags just might pass through to future generations. The branch of science that investigates how these tags affect genes is called epigenetics (*epi-* means "over, above"), and it can have implications for disease, nutrition, and many lifestyle choices people make.

Researchers have demonstrated the effects of epigenetic tags on cells by using bioengineered cells that express the GFP protein—the same protein that can be used to make mice glow—when the gene is switched on. Researchers then added a chemical that causes methyl ($-CH_3$) group tags to attach to genes. Methyl group tags are one of the ways that genes are controlled in living organisms. They attach to cytosine on DNA without disrupting the DNA double helix itself. Methyl and acetyl ($-COCH_3$) groups also can attach to histone proteins, controlling how tightly the DNA is wound around the histone spools and thereby controlling whether the segments of DNA are copied. The researchers found that methyl group tags added to the bioengineered cell culture prevented the cells from glowing, indicating that the genes were "silenced" by the tags. When another chemical was added to remove the tags, the cells began to glow brightly again.

Epigenetic tags are critical for our cell processes. They are responsible for much of how our cells differentiated—changing from stem cells into eye, liver, bone, or any other specialized cell type that organisms have. Epigenetic tags also are responsible for genetic imprinting, determining whether a father's or mother's copy of a gene is expressed.

Epigenetic tags play a role in more unlikely processes as well. Researchers have made the surprising discovery that high or low maternal care in mice may affect the number of methyl group epigenetic tags in offspring that is then passed down through generations and affects how the offspring handle stress. In Sweden, scientists looked at 200 years' worth of harvest records to determine that the amount of food that boys had when they were between the ages of nine and twelve, when immature sperm cells were first maturing in their bodies, may have affected the health of their future children and grandchildren.

While DNA remains fixed for a lifetime, epigenomes are flexible and able to respond to the environment, and can even be formed through food choices and exposure to toxins. This discovery has changed the way scientists are looking at how genes affect phenotypes and at the influence of our lifestyle choices on not only our health but also the health of generations to come.

©Jaromir Urbanek/Shutterstock

# 8.2 Structure of DNA

SC.912.L.16.9

| KEY CONCEPT **DNA structure is the same in all organisms.**

### MAIN IDEAS

- DNA is composed of four types of nucleotides.
- Watson and Crick developed an accurate model of DNA's three-dimensional structure.
- Nucleotides always pair in the same way.

**VOCABULARY**

nucleotide
double helix
base pairing rules

SC.912.L.16.9 Explain how and why the genetic code is universal and is common to almost all organisms.

## Connect to Your World

The experiments of Hershey and Chase confirmed that DNA carries the genetic information, but they left other big questions unanswered: What exactly is this genetic information? How does DNA store this information? Scientists in the early 1950s still had a limited knowledge of the structure of DNA, but that was about to change dramatically.

## MAIN IDEA

# DNA is composed of four types of nucleotides.

Since the 1920s, scientists have known that the DNA molecule is a very long polymer, or chain of repeating units. The small units, or monomers, that make up DNA are called **nucleotides** (NOO-klee-uh-TYDZ). Each nucleotide has three parts.

- A phosphate group (one phosphorus with four oxygens)
- A ring-shaped sugar called deoxyribose
- A nitrogen-containing base (a single or double ring built around nitrogen and carbon atoms)

One molecule of human DNA contains billions of nucleotides, but there are only four types of nucleotides in DNA. These nucleotides differ only in their nitrogen-containing bases.

**VISUAL VOCAB**

The small units, or monomers, that make up a strand of DNA are called **nucleotides.** Nucleotides have three parts.

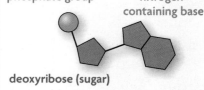

phosphate group

nitrogen-containing base

deoxyribose (sugar)

The four bases in DNA are shown in **FIGURE 2.1.** Notice that the bases cytosine (C) and thymine (T) have a single-ring structure. Adenine (A) and guanine (G) have a larger, double-ring structure. The letter abbreviations refer both to the bases and to the nucleotides that contain the bases.

For a long time, scientists hypothesized that DNA was made up of equal amounts of the four nucleotides, and so the DNA in all organisms was exactly the same. That hypothesis was a key reason that it was so hard to convince scientists that DNA was the genetic material. They reasoned that identical molecules could not carry different instructions across all organisms.

**CONNECT TO**

## BIOCHEMISTRY

The nucleotides in a strand of DNA all line up in the same direction. As a result, DNA has chemical polarity, which means that the two ends of the DNA strand are different. The 5' carbon is located at one end of the DNA strand, and the 3' carbon is located at the other end. When the two strands of DNA pair together, the 5' end of one strand aligns with the 3' end of the other strand.

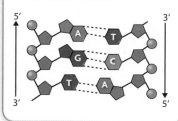

## FIGURE 2.1  The Four Nitrogen-Containing Bases of DNA

| PYRIMIDINES = SINGLE RING | | | PURINES = DOUBLE RING | | |
|---|---|---|---|---|---|
| Name of Base | Structural Formula | Model | Name of Base | Structural Formula | Model |
| thymine | 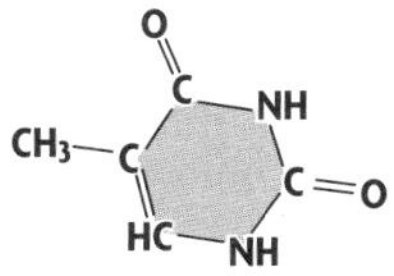 (structural formula) |  T | adenine | 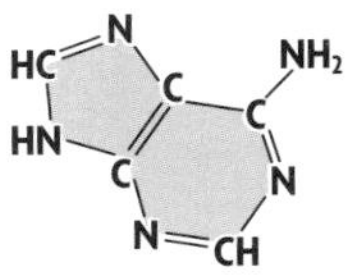 (structural formula) | 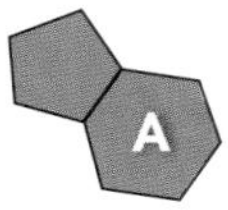 A |
| cytosine | 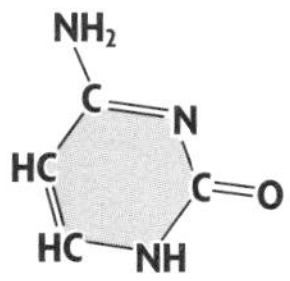 (structural formula) |  C | guanine | 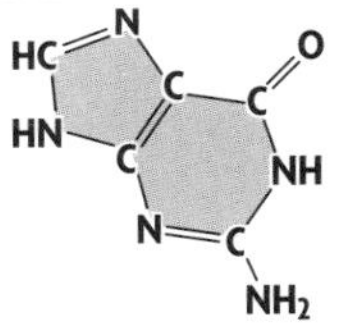 (structural formula) | 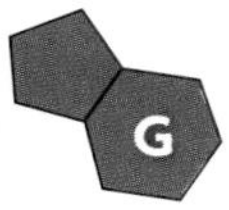 G |

**Compare** Which base is most similar in structure to thymine?

By 1950 Erwin Chargaff changed the thinking about DNA by analyzing the DNA of several organisms. Chargaff found that the same four bases are found in the DNA of all organisms, but the proportion of the four bases differs somewhat from organism to organism. In the DNA of each organism, the amount of adenine approximately equals the amount of thymine. Similarly, the amount of cytosine roughly equals the amount of guanine. These A = T and C = G relationships became known as Chargaff's rules.

**Summarize** How do the four DNA nucleotides differ in structure?

### ▶ MAIN IDEA

# Watson and Crick developed an accurate model of DNA's three-dimensional structure.

The breakthrough in understanding the structure of DNA came in the early 1950s through the teamwork of American geneticist James Watson and British physicist Francis Crick. Watson and Crick were supposed to be studying the structure of proteins. Both men, however, were more fascinated by the challenge of figuring out DNA's structure. Their interest was sparked not only by the findings of Hershey, Chase, and Chargaff but also by the work of the biochemist Linus Pauling. Pauling had found that the structure of some proteins was a helix, or spiral. Watson and Crick hypothesized that DNA might also be a helix.

## X-Ray Evidence

At the same time, Rosalind Franklin, shown in **FIGURE 2.2**, and Maurice Wilkins were studying DNA using a technique called x-ray crystallography. When DNA is bombarded with x-rays, the atoms in DNA diffract the x-rays in a pattern that can be captured on film. Franklin's x-ray photographs of DNA showed an X surrounded by a circle. Franklin's data gave Watson and Crick the clues they needed. The patterns and angle of the X suggested that DNA is a helix consisting of two strands that are a regular, consistent width apart.

*Rosalind Franklin*

**FIGURE 2.2** Rosalind Franklin (above) produced x-ray photographs of DNA that indicated it was a helix. Her coworker, Maurice Wilkins, showed the data without Franklin's consent to Watson and Crick, which helped them discover DNA's structure.

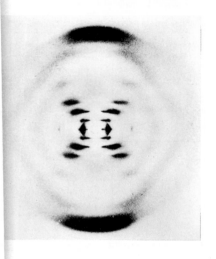

**FIGURE 2.3** James Watson (left) and Francis Crick (right) used a model to figure out DNA's structure. Their model was influenced by data from other researchers, including an x-ray image (far right) taken by Rosalind Franklin. When x-rays bounce through a sample of DNA, they form this characteristic x-shaped pattern.

James Watson and Francis Crick

### The Double Helix

Back in their own laboratory, Watson and Crick made models of metal and wood to figure out the structure of DNA. Their models placed the sugar-phosphate backbones on the outside and the bases on the inside. At first, Watson reasoned that A might pair with A, T with T, and so on. But the bases A and G are about twice as wide as C and T, so this produced a helix that varied in width. Finally, Watson and Crick found that if they paired double-ringed nucleotides with single-ringed nucleotides, the bases fit like a puzzle.

In April 1953 Watson and Crick published their DNA model in a paper in the journal *Nature*. **FIGURE 2.3** shows their **double helix** (DUB-uhl HEE-liks) model, in which two strands of DNA wind around each other like a twisted ladder. The strands are complementary—they fit together and are the opposite of each other. That is, if one strand is ACACAC, the other strand is TGTGTG. The pairing of bases in their model finally explained Chargaff's rules.

**Apply** How did the Watson and Crick model explain Chargaff's rules?

### ▶ MAIN IDEA
## Nucleotides always pair in the same way.

The DNA nucleotides of a single strand are joined together by covalent bonds that connect the sugar of one nucleotide to the phosphate of the next nucleotide. The alternating sugars and phosphates form the sides of a double helix, sort of like a twisted ladder. The DNA double helix is held together by hydrogen bonds between the bases in the middle. Individually, each hydrogen bond is weak, but together, they maintain DNA structure.

As shown in **FIGURE 2.4,** the bases of the two DNA strands always pair up in the same way. This is summarized in the **base pairing rules:** thymine (T) always pairs with adenine (A), and cytosine (C) always pairs with guanine (G). These pairings occur because of the sizes of the bases and the ability of the

## FIGURE 3.1 REPLICATION

When a cell's DNA is copied, or replicated, two complete and identical sets of genetic information are produced. Then cell division can occur.

**1** A DNA molecule unzips as nucleotide base pairs separate. Replication begins on both strands of the molecule at the same time.

nucleotide

The DNA molecule unzips in both directions.

nucleotide

Strand of DNA unzipping (colored TEM, magnification unknown)

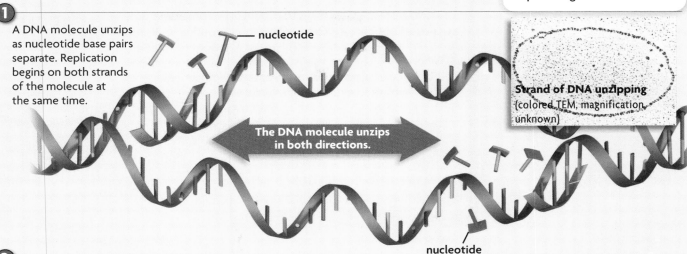

**2** Each existing strand of the DNA molecule is a template for a new strand. Free-floating nucleotides pair up with the exposed bases on each template strand. DNA polymerases bond these nucleotides together to form the new strands. The arrows show the directions in which new strands form.

DNA polymerase

new strands

nucleotide

DNA polymerase

**3** Two identical double-stranded DNA molecules result from replication. DNA replication is semiconservative. That is, each DNA molecule contains an original strand and one new strand.

original strand

new strand

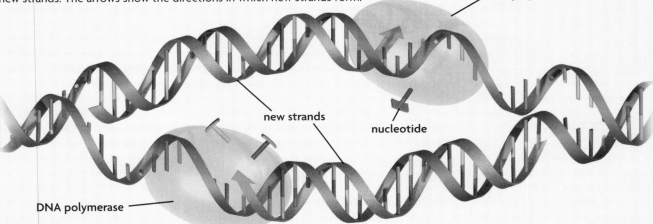

Two molecules of DNA

**CRITICAL VIEWING** How is each new molecule of DNA related to the original molecule?

▶ **MAIN IDEA**

# Replication is fast and accurate.

**FIGURE 3.2** Eukaryotic chromosomes have many origins of replication. The DNA helix is unzipped at many points along each chromosome. The replication "bubbles" grow larger as replication progresses in both directions, resulting in two complete copies.

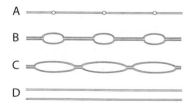

In every living thing, DNA replication happens over and over again, and it happens remarkably fast. In human cells, about 50 nucleotides are added every second to a new strand of DNA at an origin of replication. But even at this rate, it would take many days to replicate a molecule of DNA if the molecule were like a jacket zipper, unzipping one tooth at a time. Instead, replication proceeds from hundreds of origins of replication along the chromosome, as shown in **FIGURE 3.2**, so the process takes just a few hours.

Another amazing feature of replication is that it has a built-in "proofreading" function to correct errors. Occasionally, the wrong nucleotide is added to the new strand of DNA. However, DNA polymerase can detect the error, remove the incorrect nucleotide, and replace it with the correct one. In this way, errors in replication are limited to about one error per 1 billion nucleotides.

Replication is happening in your cells right now. Your DNA is replicated every time your cells turn over, or replicate themselves. Your DNA has replicated trillions of times since you grew from a single cell.

**Infer** Why does a cell need to replicate its DNA quickly?

## 8.3    Formative Assessment

**SELF-CHECK Online**
HMHScience.com
**GO ONLINE**

**REVIEWING ▶ MAIN IDEAS**

1. Explain the function of **replication**.

2. Explain how DNA serves as its own template during replication.

3. How do cells help ensure that DNA replication is accurate?

**CRITICAL THINKING**

4. **Summarize** Describe two major functions of **DNA polymerases.**

5. **Infer** Why is it important that human chromosomes have many origins of replication?

**CONNECT TO**

**CELL BIOLOGY**

6. DNA is replicated before both mitosis and meiosis. How does the amount of DNA produced in a cell during mitosis compare with that produced during meiosis?

# 8.4 Transcription

**KEY CONCEPT** **Transcription converts a gene into a single-stranded RNA molecule.**

**MAIN IDEAS**

- RNA carries DNA's instructions.
- Transcription makes three main types of RNA.
- The transcription process is similar to replication.

**SC.912.L.16.5** Explain the basic processes of transcription and translation, and how they result in the expression of genes.

### Connect to Your World

Suppose you want to play Skee-Ball® at a game center, but the Skee-Ball lane takes tokens and you only have quarters. Do you go home in defeat? Do you stand idly by as someone else becomes high scorer? No, you exchange your quarters for tokens and then proceed to show the other players how it's done. In a similar way, your cells cannot make proteins directly from DNA. They must convert the DNA into an intermediate molecule called RNA, or ribonucleic acid. That conversion process, called transcription, is the focus of this section.

#### ▶ MAIN IDEA

## RNA carries DNA's instructions.

Soon after his discovery of DNA structure, Francis Crick defined the **central dogma** of molecular biology, which states that information flows in one direction, from DNA to RNA to proteins. The central dogma involves three processes, as shown in **FIGURE 4.1**.

- Replication, as you just learned, copies DNA (blue arrow).
- Transcription converts a DNA message into an intermediate molecule, called RNA (red arrow).
- Translation interprets an RNA message into a string of amino acids, called a polypeptide. Either a single polypeptide or many polypeptides working together make up a protein (green arrow).

In prokaryotic cells, replication, transcription, and translation all occur in the cytoplasm at approximately the same time. In eukaryotic cells, where DNA is located inside the nuclear membrane, these processes are separated both in location and time. Replication and transcription occur in the nucleus, whereas translation occurs in the cytoplasm. In addition, the RNA in eukaryotic cells goes through a processing step before it can be transported out of the nucleus. Unless otherwise stated, the rest of this chapter describes how these processes work in eukaryotic cells.

RNA acts as an intermediate link between DNA in the nucleus and protein synthesis in the cytoplasm. Like DNA, **RNA,** or ribonucleic acid, is a chain of nucleotides, each made of a sugar, a phosphate group, and a nitrogen-containing base. You can think of RNA as a temporary copy of DNA that is used and then destroyed.

**FIGURE 4.1** The central dogma describes the flow of information from DNA to RNA to proteins. It involves three major processes, shown in a eukaryotic cell below.

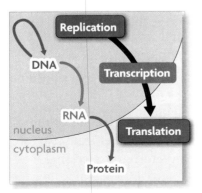

CONNECT TO

### DNA STRUCTURE

As you learned in **Section 2**, nucleotides are made of a phosphate group, a sugar, and a nitrogen-containing base. In DNA, the four bases are adenine, thymine, guanine, and cytocine. In RNA, uracil (below) replaces thymine and pairs with adenine.

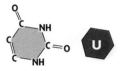

RNA differs from DNA in three significant ways. First, the sugar in RNA is ribose, which has one additional oxygen atom not present in DNA's sugar (deoxyribose). Second, RNA has the base uracil in place of thymine. Uracil, like thymine, forms base pairs with adenine. Third, RNA is a single strand of nucleotides, in contrast to the double-stranded structure of DNA. This single-stranded structure allows some types of RNA to form complex three-dimensional shapes. As a result, some RNA molecules can catalyze reactions much as enzymes do.

**Contrast  How do DNA and RNA differ?**

▶ MAIN IDEA

# Transcription makes three main types of RNA.

**Transcription** is the process of copying a sequence of DNA to produce a complementary strand of RNA. During the process of transcription, a gene—not an entire chromosome—is transferred into an RNA message. Just as replication is catalyzed by DNA polymerase, transcription is catalyzed by **RNA polymerases,** enzymes that bond nucleotides together in a chain to make a new RNA molecule. RNA polymerases are very large enzymes composed of many proteins that play a variety of roles in the transcription process. **FIGURE 4.2** shows the basic steps of transcription in eukaryotic cells.

1. With the help of other proteins and DNA sequences, RNA polymerase recognizes the transcription start site of a gene. A large transcription complex consisting of RNA polymerase and other proteins assembles on the DNA strand and begins to unwind a segment of the DNA molecule, until the two strands separate from each other.

2. RNA polymerase, using only one strand of DNA as a template, strings together a complementary strand of RNA nucleotides. RNA base pairing follows the same rules as DNA base pairing, except that uracil, not thymine, pairs with adenine. The growing RNA strand hangs freely as it is transcribed, and the DNA helix zips back together.

3. Once the entire gene has been transcribed, the RNA strand detaches completely from the DNA. Exactly how RNA polymerase recognizes the end of a transcription unit is complicated. It varies with the type of RNA.

Transcription produces three major types of RNA molecules. Not all RNA molecules code for proteins, but most play a role in the translation process. Each type of RNA molecule has a unique function.

- **Messenger RNA (mRNA)** is an intermediate message that is translated to form a protein.
- **Ribosomal RNA (rRNA)** forms part of ribosomes, a cell's protein factories.
- **Transfer RNA (tRNA)** brings amino acids from the cytoplasm to a ribosome to help make the growing protein.

Remember that the RNA strand must be processed before it can exit the nucleus of a eukaryotic cell. This step occurs during or just after transcription. However, we will next examine translation and then return to processing.

**Analyze  Explain why transcription occurs in the nucleus of eukaryotes.**

### READING TOOLBOX

#### VOCABULARY

The word *transcribe* means "to make a written copy of." *Transcription* is the process of transcribing. A *transcript* is the copy produced by transcription.

## FIGURE 4.2 Transcription

Transcription produces an RNA molecule from a DNA template. Like DNA replication, this process takes place in the nucleus in eukaryotic cells and involves both DNA unwinding and nucleotide base pairing.

**1**

A large transcription complex made of RNA polymerase and other proteins recognizes the start of a gene and begins to unwind the segment of DNA.

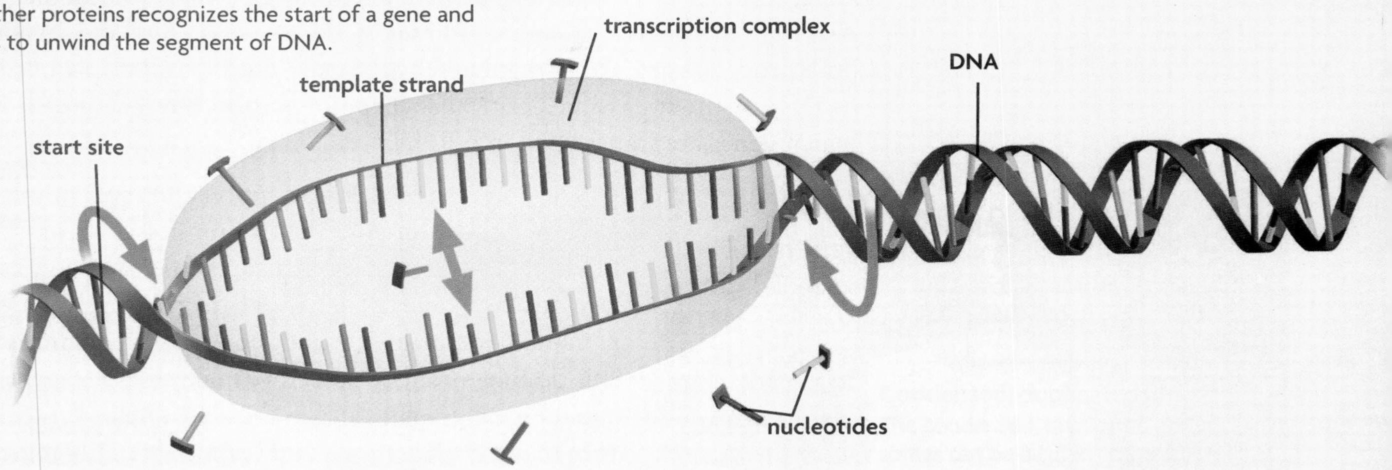

transcription complex

DNA

template strand

start site

nucleotides

**2**

RNA polymerase uses one strand of the DNA as a template. RNA nucleotides form complementary base pairs with the DNA template. G pairs with C, and A pairs with U. The growing RNA strand hangs freely as it is transcribed. Then the DNA strand closes back together.

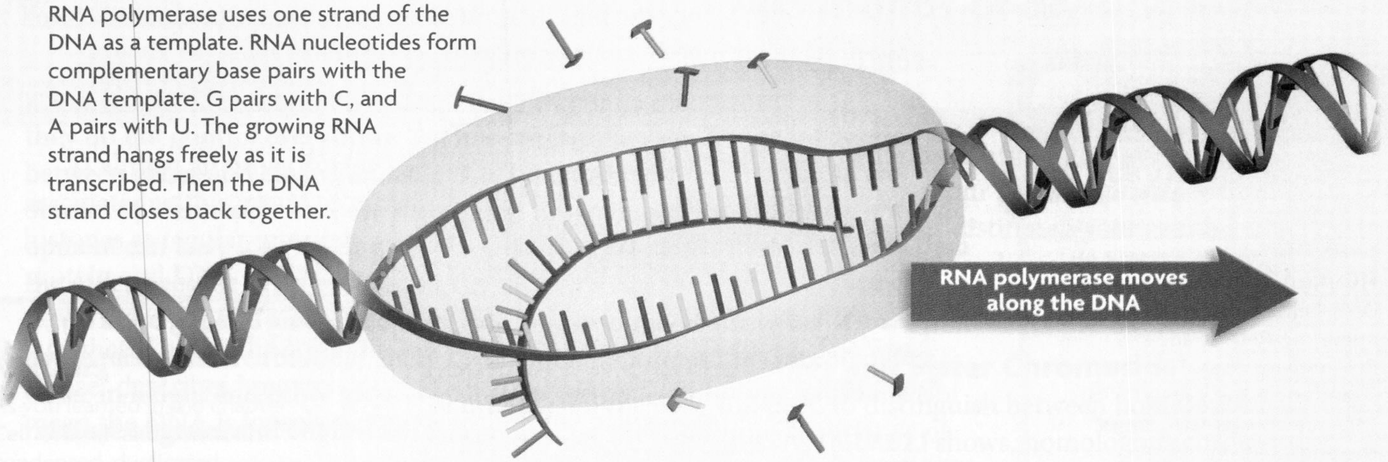

RNA polymerase moves along the DNA

**3**

The completed RNA strand separates from the DNA template, and the transcription complex falls apart.

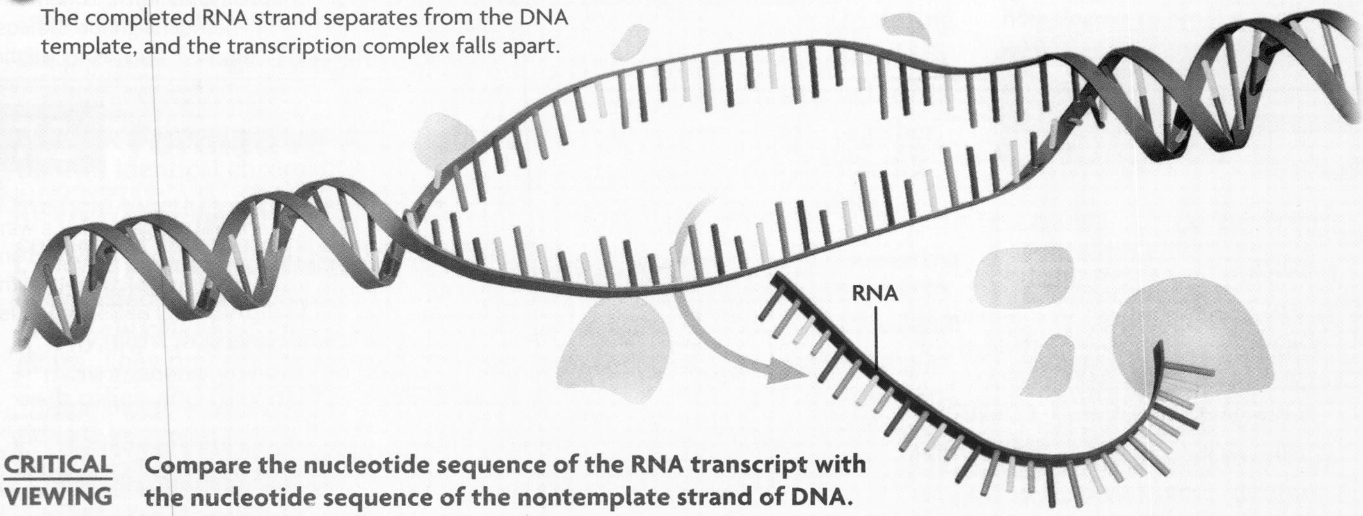

RNA

**CRITICAL VIEWING** Compare the nucleotide sequence of the RNA transcript with the nucleotide sequence of the nontemplate strand of DNA.

# The transcription process is similar to replication.

The processes of transcription and replication share many similarities. Both processes occur within the nucleus of eukaryotic cells. Both are catalyzed by large, complex enzymes. Both involve unwinding of the DNA double helix. And both involve complementary base pairing to the DNA strand. In addition, both processes are highly regulated by the cell. Just as a cell does not replicate its DNA without passing a critical checkpoint, so, too, a cell carefully regulates which genes are transcribed into RNA.

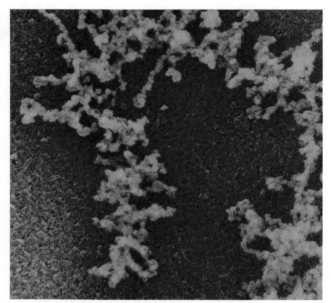

**FIGURE 4.3** This SEM shows DNA being transcribed into numerous RNA strands by many RNA polymerases. The RNA strands near the start of each gene are shorter than those near the end. (SEM; magnification unknown)

The end results of transcription and replication, however, are quite different. The two processes accomplish very different tasks. Replication ensures that each new cell will have one complete set of genetic instructions. It does this by making identical sets of double-stranded chromosomes. This double-stranded structure makes DNA especially well suited for long-term storage because it helps protect DNA from being broken down and from potentially harmful interactions with other molecules. Replication occurs only once during each round of the cell cycle because each cell needs to make only one copy of its DNA.

In contrast, a cell may need hundreds or thousands of copies of certain proteins, or the rRNA and tRNA molecules needed to make proteins. Transcription enables a cell to adjust to changing demands. It does so by making a single-stranded complement of only a segment of DNA and only when that particular segment is needed. In addition, many RNA molecules can be transcribed from a single gene at the same time to help produce more protein. Once RNA polymerase has transcribed one portion of a gene and has moved on, another RNA polymerase can attach itself to the beginning of the gene and start the transcription process again. This process can occur over and over again, as shown in **FIGURE 4.3**.

**Compare** How are the processes of transcription and replication similar?

©Biophoto Associates/Science Source

**SELF-CHECK Online**
HMHScience.com
GO ONLINE

## 8.4 Formative Assessment

### REVIEWING ▶ MAIN IDEAS

1. What is the **central dogma**?

2. Why can the **mRNA** strand made during **transcription** be thought of as a mirror image of the DNA strand from which it was made?

3. Why might a cell make lots of **rRNA** but only one copy of DNA?

### CRITICAL THINKING

4. **Apply** If a DNA segment has the nucleotides AGCCTAA, what would be the nucleotide sequence of the complementary **RNA** strand?

5. **Synthesize** What might geneticists learn about genes by studying RNA?

### ☼ CONNECT TO

#### CELL CYCLE

6. A healthy cell cannot pass the $G_2$ checkpoint until all of its DNA has been copied. Do you think that a cell must also transcribe all of its genes into RNA to pass this checkpoint? Explain.

# 8.5 Translation

SC.912.L.16.5

**KEY CONCEPT** **Translation converts an mRNA message into a polypeptide, or protein.**

**MAIN IDEAS**

- Amino acids are coded by mRNA base sequences.
- Amino acids are linked to become a protein.

## VOCABULARY

translation
codon
stop codon
start codon
anticodon

**SC.912.L.16.5** Explain the basic processes of transcription and translation, and how they result in the expression of genes.

### Connect to Your World

As you know, translation is a process that converts a message from one language into another. For example, English words can be translated into Spanish words, into Chinese characters, or into the hand shapes and gestures of sign language. Translation occurs in cells too. Cells translate an RNA message into amino acids, the building blocks of proteins. But unlike people who use many different languages, all cells use the same genetic code.

### ▶ MAIN IDEA

## Amino acids are coded by mRNA base sequences.

**Translation** is the process that converts, or translates, an mRNA message into a polypeptide. One or more polypeptides make up a protein. The "language" of nucleic acids uses four nucleotides—A, G, C, and T in DNA; or A, G, C, and U in RNA. The "language" of proteins, on the other hand, uses 20 amino acids. How can four nucleotides code for 20 amino acids? Just as letters are strung together in the English language to make words, nucleotides are strung together to code for amino acids.

### Triplet Code

Different words have different numbers of letters. In the genetic code, however, all of the "words," called codons, are made up of three letters. A **codon** is a three-nucleotide sequence that codes for an amino acid. Why is the genetic code read in units of three nucleotides? Well, we can't entirely answer that question, but consider the possibilities. If one nucleotide coded for one amino acid, RNA could code for only four amino acids. If two nucleotides coded for one amino acid, RNA could code for 16 ($4^2$) amino acids—still not enough. But if three nucleotides coded for one amino acid, RNA could code for 64 ($4^3$) amino acids, plenty to cover the 20 amino acids used to build proteins in the human body and most other organisms.

### CONNECT TO

#### BIOCHEMISTRY

Recall from the chapter **Chemistry of Life** that amino acids are the building blocks of proteins. Although there are many types of amino acids, only the same 20 types make up the proteins of almost all organisms.

**VISUAL VOCAB**

A **codon** is a sequence of three nucleotides that codes for an amino acid.

codon for methionine (Met)    codon for leucine (Leu)

A U G C U U

**Segment of mRNA**

FIGURE 5.1  Genetic Code: mRNA Codons

**The genetic code matches each mRNA codon with its amino acid or function.**

Suppose you want to determine which amino acid is encoded by the CAU codon.

**1** Find the first base, C, in the left column.

**2** Find the second base, A, in the top row. Find the box where these two intersect.

**3** Find the third base, U, in the right column. CAU codes for histidine, abbreviated as His.

| First base | Second base | | | | Third base |
|---|---|---|---|---|---|
| | **U** | **C** | **A** | **G** | |
| **U** | UUU / UUC phenylalanine(Phe) | UCU / UCC serine (Ser) | UAU / UAC tyrosine (Tyr) | UGU / UGC cysteine (Cys) | U / C |
| | UUA / UUG leucine (Leu) | UCA / UCG serine (Ser) | UAA STOP / UAG STOP | UGA STOP / UGG tryptophan (Trp) | A / G |
| **C** | CUU / CUC / CUA / CUG leucine (Leu) | CCU / CCC / CCA / CCG proline (Pro) | CAU / CAC histidine (His) | CGU / CGC / CGA / CGG arginine (Arg) | U / C |
| | | | CAA / CAG glutamine (Gln) | | A / G |
| **A** | AUU / AUC / AUA isoleucine (Ile) | ACU / ACC / ACA / ACG threonine (Thr) | AAU / AAC asparagine (Asn) | AGU / AGC serine (Ser) | U / C |
| | AUG methionine (Met) | | AAA / AAG lysine (Lys) | AGA / AGG arginine (Arg) | A / G |
| **G** | GUU / GUC / GUA / GUG valine (Val) | GCU / GCC / GCA / GCG alanine (Ala) | GAU / GAC aspartic acid (Asp) | GGU / GGC / GGA / GGG glycine (Gly) | U / C |
| | | | GAA / GAG glutamic acid (Glu) | | A / G |

**Apply** Which amino acid would be encoded by the mRNA codon CGA?

As you can see in **FIGURE 5.1,** many amino acids are coded for by more than one codon. The amino acid leucine, for example, is represented by six different codons: CUU, CUC, CUA, CUG, UUA, and UUG. There is a pattern to the codons. In most cases, codons that represent the same amino acid share the same first two nucleotides. For example, the four codons that code for alanine each begin with the nucleotides GC. Therefore, the first two nucleotides are generally the most important in coding for an amino acid. As you will learn in Section 7, this feature makes DNA more tolerant of many point mutations.

In addition to codons that code for amino acids, three **stop codons** signal the end of the amino acid chain. There is also one **start codon,** which signals the start of translation and the amino acid methionine. This means that translation always begins with methionine. However, in many cases, this methionine is removed from the protein later in the process.

For the mRNA code to be translated correctly, codons must be read in the right order. Codons are read, without spaces, as a series of three nonoverlapping nucleotides. This order is called the reading frame. Changing the reading frame completely changes the resulting protein. It may even keep a protein from being made if a stop codon turns up early in the translation process. Therefore, punctuation—such as a clear start codon—plays an important role in the genetic code. **FIGURE 5.2** shows how a change in reading frame changes

**FIGURE 5.2** Codons are read as a series of three nonoverlapping nucleotides. A change in the reading frame changes the resulting protein.

**Reading frame 1**

**Reading frame 2**

WebQuest
HMHScience.com
GO ONLINE
Transgenic Organisms

the resulting protein. When the mRNA strand is read starting from the first nucleotide, the resulting protein includes the amino acids arginine, tyrosine, and two serines. When the strand is read starting from the second nucleotide, the resulting protein includes aspartic acid, threonine, and valine.

## Common Language

The genetic code is shared by almost all organisms—and even viruses. That means, for example, that the codon UUU codes for phenylalanine when that codon occurs in an armadillo, a cactus, a yeast, or a human. With a few minor exceptions, almost all organisms follow this genetic code. As a result, the code is often called universal. The common nature of the genetic code suggests that almost all organisms arose from a common ancestor. It also means that scientists can insert a gene from one organism into another organism to make a functional protein.

**Calculate  Suppose an mRNA molecule in the cytoplasm had 300 nucleotides. How many amino acids would be in the resulting protein?**

## ▶ MAIN IDEA
# Amino acids are linked to become a protein.

Let's take a step back to look at where we are in the process of making proteins. You know mRNA is a short-lived molecule that carries instructions from DNA in the nucleus to the cytoplasm. And you know that this mRNA message is read in sets of three nucleotides, or codons. But how does a cell actually translate a codon into an amino acid? It uses two important tools: ribosomes and tRNA molecules, as illustrated in **FIGURE 5.3**.

Recall that ribosomes are the site of protein synthesis. Ribosomes are made of a combination of rRNA and proteins, and they catalyze the reaction that forms the bonds between amino acids. Ribosomes have a large and small subunit that fit together and pull the mRNA strand through. The small subunit holds onto the mRNA strand, and the large subunit holds onto the growing protein.

The tRNA acts as a sort of adaptor between mRNA and amino acids. You would need an adaptor to plug an appliance with a three-prong plug into an outlet with only two-prong openings. Similarly, cells need tRNA to carry free-floating amino acids from the cytoplasm to the ribosome. The tRNA molecules fold up in a characteristic L shape. One end of the L is attached to a specific amino acid. The other end of the L, called the anticodon, recognizes a specific codon. An **anticodon** is a set of three nucleotides that is complementary to an mRNA codon. For example, the anticodon CCC pairs with the mRNA codon GGG.

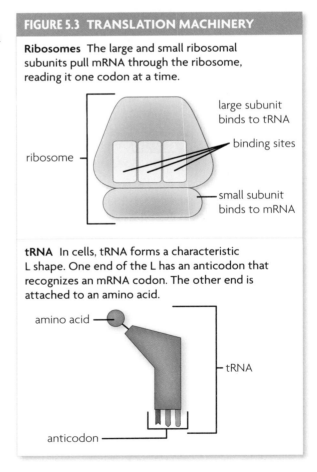

**FIGURE 5.3  TRANSLATION MACHINERY**

**Ribosomes**  The large and small ribosomal subunits pull mRNA through the ribosome, reading it one codon at a time.

large subunit binds to tRNA

binding sites

ribosome

small subunit binds to mRNA

**tRNA**  In cells, tRNA forms a characteristic L shape. One end of the L has an anticodon that recognizes an mRNA codon. The other end is attached to an amino acid.

amino acid

tRNA

anticodon

## FIGURE 5.4  Translation

**Translation converts an mRNA transcript into a polypeptide. The process consists of three repeating steps.**

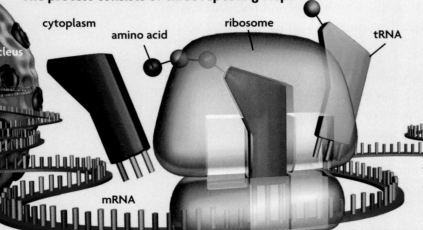

Translation occurs in the cytoplasm of both eukaryotic (illustrated) and prokaryotic cells. It starts when a tRNA carrying a methionine attaches to a start codon.

**1** The exposed codon in the first site attracts a complementary tRNA bearing an amino acid. The tRNA anticodon pairs with the mRNA codon, bringing it very close to the other tRNA molecule.

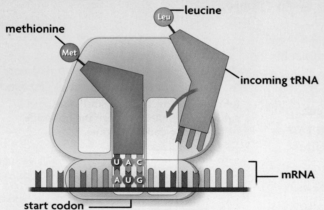

**2** The ribosome forms a peptide bond between the two amino acids and breaks the bond between the first tRNA and its amino acid.

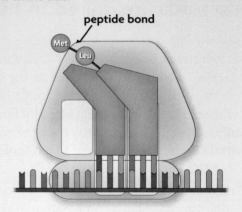

**3** The ribosome pulls the mRNA strand the length of one codon. The first tRNA is shifted into the exit site, where it leaves the ribosome and returns to the cytoplasm to recharge. The first site is again empty, exposing the next mRNA codon.

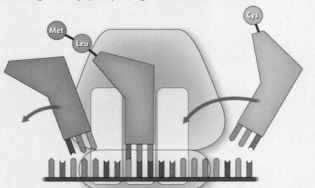

The ribosome continues to translate the mRNA strand until it reaches a stop codon. Then it releases the new protein and disassembles.

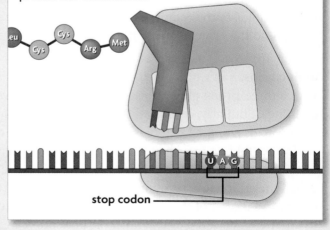

**CRITICAL VIEWING**  The figure above shows how the first two amino acids are added to a growing protein. Draw a series of sketches to show how the next two amino acids are added.

Translation, shown in **FIGURE 5.4**, has many steps and takes a lot of energy from a cell. It happens in the cytoplasm of both prokaryotic and eukaryotic cells. Before translation can begin, a small ribosomal subunit must bind to an mRNA strand in the cytoplasm. Next, a tRNA with methionine attached binds to the AUG start codon. This binding signals a large ribosomal subunit—which has three binding sites for tRNA molecules—to join. The ribosome pulls the mRNA strand through itself one codon at a time. As the strand moves, the start codon and its complementary tRNA molecule shift into the second site inside the large subunit. This shift leaves the first site empty, which exposes the next mRNA codon. The illustration shows the process in one ribosome, but in a cell many ribosomes may translate many mRNA molecules from the same gene at the same time.

**1** The exposed codon attracts a complementary tRNA molecule bearing an amino acid. The tRNA anticodon pairs with the mRNA codon. This action brings the new tRNA molecule very close to the tRNA molecule occupying the second site.

**2** Next, the ribosome helps form a peptide bond between the two amino acids. The ribosome then breaks the bond between the tRNA molecule in the second site and its amino acid.

**3** The ribosome pulls the mRNA strand the length of one codon. The tRNA molecule in the second site is shifted into the third site, which is the exit site. The tRNA leaves the ribosome and returns to the cytoplasm to be charged with another amino acid. The tRNA molecule that was in the first site shifts into the second site. The first site is again empty, exposing the next mRNA codon.

Another complementary tRNA molecule is attracted to the exposed mRNA codon, and the process continues. The ribosome moves down the mRNA strand, attaching new amino acids to the growing protein, until it reaches a stop codon. Then the ribosome lets go of the new protein and falls apart.

**Summarize** **Explain the different roles of the large and small ribosomal subunits.**

## 8.5 Formative Assessment

### REVIEWING ▶ MAIN IDEAS

1. Explain the connection between a **codon** and an amino acid.

2. Briefly describe how the process of **translation** is started.

### CRITICAL THINKING

3. **Synthesize** Suppose a tRNA molecule had the **anticodon** AGU. What amino acid would it carry?

4. **Hypothesize** The DNA of eukaryotic cells has many copies of genes that code for rRNA molecules. Suggest a hypothesis to explain why a cell needs so many copies of these genes.

### CONNECT TO

**BIOCHEMICAL REACTIONS**

5. Enzymes have shapes that allow them to bind to a substrate. Some types of RNA also form specific three-dimensional shapes. Why do you think RNA, but not DNA, catalyzes biochemical reactions?

# 8.6 Gene Expression and Regulation

**SC.912.L.16.5**

**KEY CONCEPT** Gene expression is carefully regulated in both prokaryotic and eukaryotic cells.

**MAIN IDEAS**
- Prokaryotic cells turn genes on and off by controlling transcription.
- Eukaryotic cells regulate gene expression at many points.
- Environmental factors influence gene expression, resulting in different cell types.

**SC.912.L.16.5** Explain the basic processes of transcription and translation, and how they result in the expression of genes.

### ☼ Connect to Your World

Ours is a world of marvels. So many, in fact, that we may overlook what seem like little ones, such as plumbing. The turn of a handle sends clean water to your sink or shower. One twist and the water trickles out; two twists and it gushes forth. Another turn of the handle and the water is off again. But think about the mess and waste that would result if you couldn't control its flow. In a similar way, your cells have ways to control gene expression. Depending on an organism's needs, a gene can make a lot of protein, a little protein, or none at all.

### ⊙ MAIN IDEA

## Prokaryotic cells turn genes on and off by controlling transcription.

The regulation of gene expression allows prokaryotic cells, such as bacteria, to better respond to stimuli and to conserve energy and materials. In general, this regulation is simpler in prokaryotic cells than in eukaryotic cells, such as those that make up your body. DNA in a prokaryotic cell is in the cytoplasm. Transcription and translation can happen at the same time. As a result, gene expression in prokaryotic cells is mainly regulated at the start of transcription.

A gene includes more than just a protein-coding sequence. It may have many other nucleotide sequences that play a part in controlling its expression. The start of transcription is largely controlled by these sequences, including promoters and operators. A **promoter** is a DNA segment that allows a gene to be transcribed. It helps RNA polymerase find where a gene starts. An operator is a DNA segment that turns a gene "on" or "off." It interacts with proteins that increase the rate of transcription or block transcription from occurring.

Bacteria have much less DNA than do eukaryotes, and their genes tend to be organized into operons. An **operon** is a region of DNA that includes a promoter, an operator, and one or more structural genes that code for all the proteins needed to do a specific task. Operons are most often found in prokaryotes and roundworms. The *lac* operon was one of the earliest examples of gene regulation discovered in bacteria. It will serve as our example. The *lac* operon has three genes, which all code for enzymes that play a role in breaking down the sugar lactose. These genes are transcribed as a single mRNA transcript and are all under the control of a single promoter and

### READING TOOLBOX

**VOCABULARY**
The word *promote* comes from the Latin prefix *pro-*, meaning "forward," and the Latin word *movere*, meaning "to move."

operator. This means that although we're dealing with several genes, they act together as a unit.

The *lac* operon is turned on and off like a switch. When lactose is absent from the environment, the *lac* operon is switched off to prevent transcription of the *lac* genes and save the cell's resources. When lactose is present, the *lac* operon is switched on to allow transcription. How does this happen?

Bacteria have a protein that can bind specifically to the operator. When lactose is absent, this protein binds to the operator, which blocks RNA polymerase from transcribing the genes. Because the protein blocks—or represses—transcription, it is called a repressor protein.

**Without lactose** (switched off)

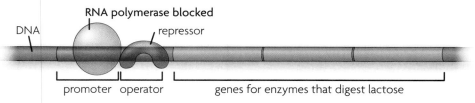

**RNA polymerase blocked**
DNA
repressor

promoter   operator         genes for enzymes that digest lactose

When lactose is present it binds to the repressor, which makes the repressor change shape and fall off the *lac* operon. RNA polymerase can then transcribe the genes in the *lac* operon. The resulting transcript is translated and forms three enzymes that work together to break down the lactose.

**With lactose** (switched on)

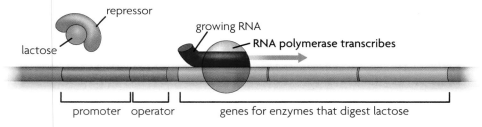

repressor
growing RNA
RNA polymerase transcribes
lactose

promoter   operator         genes for enzymes that digest lactose

**Analyze  Explain how the *lac* operon is turned on or off like a switch.**

## ▶ MAIN IDEA

# Eukaryotic cells regulate gene expression at many points.

You have already learned that every body cell in an organism has the same set of DNA. But your cells are not all the same. Cells differ from each other because different sets of genes are expressed in different types of cells. Eukaryotic cells can control the process of gene expression at many different points because of their internal compartments and chromosomal organization. As in prokaryotic cells, however, one of the most highly regulated steps is the start of transcription. In both cell types, RNA processing is a part of the transcription process. In eukaryotic cells, however, RNA processing also includes the removal of extra nucleotide segments from an mRNA transcript.

## FIGURE 6.1 Starting Transcription

Transcription factors that bind to promoters and other DNA sequences help RNA polymerase recognize the start of a gene in a eukaryotic cell.

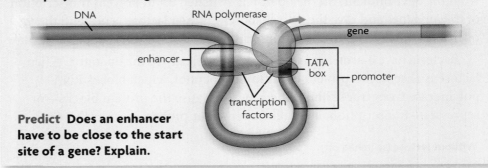

DNA RNA polymerase gene
enhancer TATA box promoter transcription factors

**Predict** Does an enhancer have to be close to the start site of a gene? Explain.

## Starting Transcription

The start of transcription in eukaryotic cells is controlled by many elements that work together in complex ways. These elements include regulatory DNA sequences and proteins called transcription factors, as shown in **FIGURE 6.1.** They occur in different combinations in different types of cells. The interplay between these elements results in specialized cells and cell responses.

Eukaryotes have many types of regulatory DNA sequences. These sequences are recognized by transcription factors that bind to the DNA strand and help RNA polymerase know where a gene starts. Some DNA sequences, such as promoters, are close to the start of a gene. Others are far away from the genes they affect. However, DNA can loop and bend, bringing these sequences with their transcription factors into close contact with their target sequences.

Each gene has a unique combination of regulatory sequences. Some are found in almost all eukaryotic cells. For example, most eukaryotic cells have a seven-nucleotide promoter (TATAAAA) called the TATA box. Eukaryotic cells also have other types of promoters that are more specific to an individual gene. DNA sequences called enhancers and silencers also play a role by speeding up or slowing down, respectively, the rate of transcription of a gene.

Some genes control the expression of many other genes. Regulation of these genes is very important because they can have a large effect on development. One such gene codes for a protein called sonic hedgehog. This protein was first found in fruit flies, but many other organisms have very similar proteins that serve a similar function. Sonic hedgehog helps establish body pattern. When sonic hedgehog is missing in fruit flies, the embryos are covered with little prickles and fail to form normal body segments.

## mRNA Processing

Another important part of gene regulation in eukaryotic cells is RNA processing, which is shown in **FIGURE 6.2.** The mRNA produced by transcription is similar to a rough cut of a film that needs a bit of editing. A specialized nucleotide is added to the beginning of each mRNA molecule, which forms a cap. It helps the mRNA strand bind to a ribosome and prevents the strand from being broken down too fast. The end of the mRNA molecule gets a string of nucleotides, called the tail, that helps the mRNA molecule exit the nucleus.

### CONNECT TO

**ANIMALS**

As you will learn in the chapter **Invertebrate Diversity,** most animals have homeobox genes. These genes are among the earliest that are expressed and play a key role in development. The illustration below shows the expression of homeobox genes in fruit fly and human embryos.

## FIGURE 6.2  mRNA Processing

**An mRNA molecule typically undergoes processing during or immediately after DNA transcription.**

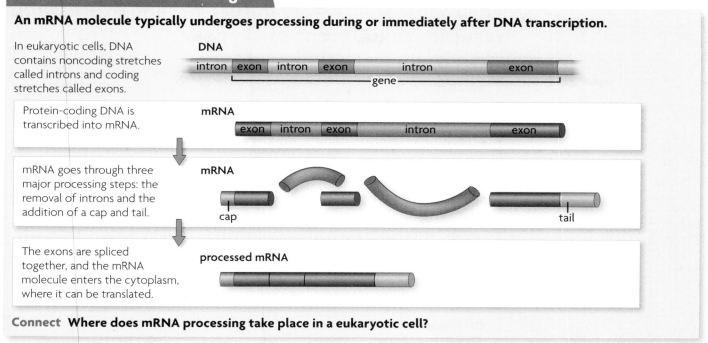

In eukaryotic cells, DNA contains noncoding stretches called introns and coding stretches called exons.

Protein-coding DNA is transcribed into mRNA.

mRNA goes through three major processing steps: the removal of introns and the addition of a cap and tail.

The exons are spliced together, and the mRNA molecule enters the cytoplasm, where it can be translated.

**Connect**  **Where does mRNA processing take place in a eukaryotic cell?**

The "extra footage" takes the form of nucleotide segments that are not included in the final protein. In eukaryotes, **exons** are nucleotide segments that code for parts of the protein. **Introns** are nucleotide segments that intervene, or occur, between exons. Introns are rare in prokaryotes. Introns are removed from mRNA before it leaves the nucleus. The cut ends of the exons are then joined together by a variety of molecular mechanisms.

The role of introns is not fully understood. They may regulate gene expression. In addition, some mRNA strands can be cut at various points, resulting in different proteins. As a result, introns increase genetic diversity without increasing the size of the genome.

## RNA Interference

RNA can also be stopped from translating the amino acids that build a protein. One way to interrupt the process is by cleaving a protein-coding mRNA transcript so that it cannot translate a full protein. Surprisingly, the molecules that perform this cleaving are other RNA molecules. These special types of RNA function not to code for proteins but instead to regulate mRNA in a process called **RNA interference** (RNAi).

RNAi is performed by naturally occurring small RNA molecules, known as small interfering RNAs (siRNAs) or microRNAs (miRNAs) depending on their cellular origin. miRNAs are formed from regions of RNA transcripts that fold back on themselves to form short hairpin loops, while siRNAs derive from longer regions of double-stranded RNA. In each case, an enzyme called Dicer chops up the larger molecules into either miRNA or siRNA. These small RNAs, spanning about 20 nucleotides, match part of the target mRNA sequence and, with the help of catalytic proteins, cause the mRNA molecules to be cleaved. By degrading mRNA and preventing translation, the expression of specific genes can be increased, decreased, or even silenced.

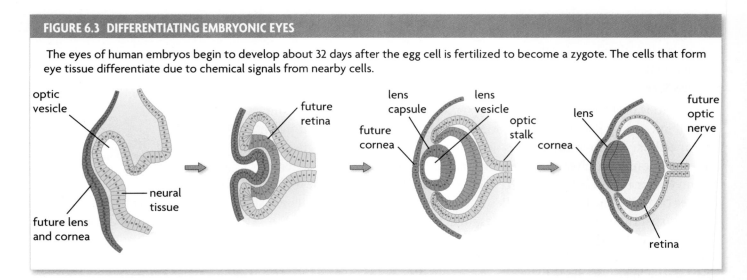

## MAIN IDEA

# Environmental factors influence gene expression, resulting in different cell types.

Most multicellular organisms begin as a single fertilized egg cell, or zygote, which grows and divides into two cells. This process of growth and division repeats over and over. Cell differentiation is the process by which unspecialized cells develop into their mature forms and functions. Gene expression is responsible for the differentiation of cells. Gene expression is affected by both the internal and external environment. An organism's internal environment includes all the factors within the organism and its cells. The external environment refers to any factors outside the organism.

As cells grow and divide, subtle differences become more evident as distinct cell types are formed. During embryonic development, cell differentiation and cell growth form tissues and organs in a process called morphogenesis. **FIGURE 6.3** shows the morphogenesis of embryonic eyes through the differentiation of cells.

### Internal Factors

The differentiation of embryonic cells is based on several internal factors. First, the genetic make-up of the zygote provides the organism with many instructions for differentiation. A zygote's genetic make-up includes all the genes that can be expressed within any cell of the organism, even after the organism has grown and developed. Genes that are expressed in the cells of a developing organism initiate cell differentiation.

Even before an egg cell is fertilized, the internal environment of the egg cell promotes differentiation. Proteins, mRNA, organelles, and other substances in the egg cell cytoplasm are not spread evenly throughout the egg cell. After fertilization, as the zygote divides, the molecules in the cytoplasm are distributed unevenly among the different cells of the developing embryo. These molecules regulate gene expression in each cell and help determine what type of cell it will become.

---

**FIGURE 6.3 DIFFERENTIATING EMBRYONIC EYES**

The eyes of human embryos begin to develop about 32 days after the egg cell is fertilized to become a zygote. The cells that form eye tissue differentiate due to chemical signals from nearby cells.

Each cell in a developing embryo is influenced by other cells around it. In the developing eyes, for example, cells close to the optic vesicle are influenced to thicken and fold inward. These changes eventually lead to the development of the lens and cornea. Cells influence and communicate with each other by sending and receiving molecules that act as signals. Signals may also come from molecules embedded in the cell membrane. Signal molecules are proteins that induce a cell to follow a specific developmental path by causing a change in its gene expression. Signal molecules cause the expression of certain genes to be turned on or off. Some signal molecules can affect genes by preventing a gene from transcribing genetic information to mRNA. Gene expression also can be controlled after translation has occurred. For example, a protein may be produced by translation and then broken down by enzymes.

## External Factors

Factors in an organism's external environment also can affect gene expression. For example, temperature can influence gene expression in some organisms. The *C* gene in Himalayan rabbits is involved in development of the black color of fur, skin, and eyes. When the external temperature is above 35°C, the central parts of the rabbit's body are over 30°C, and the gene is inactive. No pigments are produced, and the fur color is white. Below 20°C, the outer parts of the rabbit—such as the ears, tail, feet, and tip of the nose—are cooler, and the gene is expressed. These body parts are black.

The presence of drugs and chemicals in an organism's external environment can also affect gene expression and cell differentiation. When magnesium chloride is present in the environment of certain fish embryos, they develop one eye instead of two. In the 1960s, the drug thalidomide was found to cause severe arm and leg deformities in human embryos. Children born from mothers who took this drug often had shortened and malformed limbs.

Light affects gene expression in *Vanessa* butterflies. If the immature caterpillars are placed in red light, the wings that develop in the adult butterflies are brightly colored. When the caterpillars are placed in green light, the adults have dark wings. Under blue light or in darkness, the wings are a pale color.

**Identify** Name two internal and two external factors that affect gene expression.

**SELF-CHECK** Online
HMHScience.com
**GO ONLINE**

## 8.6 Formative Assessment

### REVIEWING ⊙ MAIN IDEAS

1. What is a **promoter**?
2. In eukaryotic cells, genes each have a specific combination of regulatory DNA sequences. How do these combinations help cells carry out specialized jobs?

### CRITICAL THINKING

3. **Predict** Suppose a bacterium had a mutated repressor protein that could not bind to the *lac* operator. How might this affect regulation of the **operon**?

4. **Summarize** What are the three major steps involved in mRNA processing?

**CONNECT TO**

**DNA**

5. DNA is loosely organized in areas where RNA polymerase is transcribing genes. What might you infer about a region of DNA that was loosely organized in muscle cells but tightly coiled in lung cells?

# Mutations

## VOCABULARY

mutation
point mutation
frameshift mutation
mutagen

**SC.912.L.15.15** Describe how mutation and genetic recombination increase genetic variation.

**SC.912.L.16.4** Explain how mutations in the DNA sequence may or may not result in phenotypic change. Explain how mutations in gametes may result in phenotypic changes in offspring.

**SC.912.L.16.8** Explain the relationship between mutation, cell cycle, and uncontrolled cell growth potentially resulting in cancer.

**KEY CONCEPT** Mutations are changes in DNA that may or may not affect phenotype.

### MAIN IDEAS

◯ Some mutations affect a single gene, while others affect an entire chromosome.

◯ Mutations may or may not affect phenotype.

◯ Mutations can be caused by several factors.

### ⚞ Connect to Your World

We all make mistakes. Some may be a bit embarrassing. Others become funny stories we tell our friends later. Still others, however, have far-reaching effects that we failed to see in our moment of decision. Cells make mistakes too. These mistakes, like our own, can have a range of effects. When they occur in DNA, they are called mutations, and cells have evolved a variety of methods for dealing with them.

### ▶ MAIN IDEA

## Some mutations affect a single gene, while others affect an entire chromosome.

You may already know the term *mutation* from popular culture, but it has a specific meaning in biology. A **mutation** is a change in an organism's DNA. Many types of mutations can occur, as shown in **FIGURE 7.2**. Typically, mutations that affect a single gene happen during replication, whereas mutations that affect a group of genes or an entire chromosome happen during meiosis.

### Gene Mutations

A **point mutation** is a mutation in which one nucleotide is substituted for another. That is, an incorrect nucleotide is put in the place of the correct nucleotide. Very often, such a mistake is caught and fixed by DNA polymerase. If it is not, the substitution may permanently change an organism's DNA.

A **frameshift mutation** involves the insertion or deletion of a nucleotide in the DNA sequence. It usually affects a polypeptide much more than does a substitution. Frameshift mutations are so named because they shift the entire sequence following them by one or more nucleotides. To understand how this affects an mRNA strand, imagine a short sentence of three-letter "codons":

**THE CAT ATE THE RAT**

If the letter *E* is removed, or deleted, from the first "THE," all the letters that follow shift to the left. The sentence now reads:

**THC ATA TET HER AT . . .**

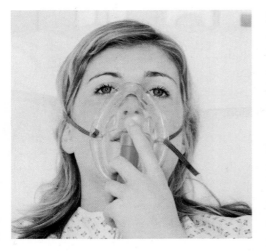

**FIGURE 7.1** Cystic fibrosis (CF) is a genetic disease that is most commonly caused by a specific deletion. It causes the overproduction of thick, sticky mucus. Although CF cannot be cured, it is treated in a number of ways, including oxygen therapy (above).

## FIGURE 7.2 Types of Mutations

**A mutation is a change in an organism's DNA.**

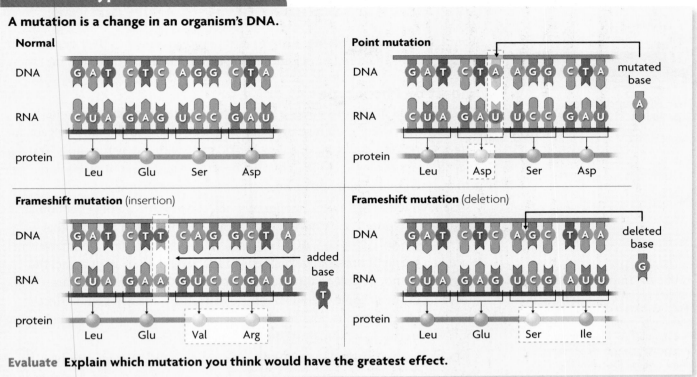

**Evaluate** Explain which mutation you think would have the greatest effect.

The sentence no longer makes sense. The same would be true if a nucleotide was added, or inserted, and all the letters shifted to the right. In the same way, a nucleotide sequence loses its meaning when an insertion or deletion shifts all the codons by one nucleotide. This change throws off the reading frame, which results in codons that code for different amino acids.

## Chromosomal Mutations

Recall that during meiosis, homologous chromosomes exchange DNA segments through crossing over. If the chromosomes do not align with each other, these segments may be different in size. As a result, one chromosome may have two copies of a gene or genes, which is called gene duplication. The other chromosome may have no copy of the gene or genes. Gene duplication has happened again and again throughout eukaryotic evolution.

Translocation is another type of chromosomal mutation. In translocation, a piece of one chromosome moves to a nonhomologous chromosome. Translocations are often reciprocal, which means that the two nonhomologous chromosomes exchange segments with each other.

**Explain** How does a frameshift mutation affect reading frame?

**Gene duplication**

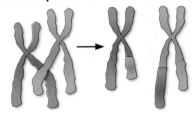

**Gene translocation**

1     17          1          17
  normal            translocated

**Virtual INVESTIGATION**

HMHScience.com

**GO ONLINE**

DNA, RNA, and Gene Expression

**▶ MAIN IDEA**

# Mutations may or may not affect phenotype.

A mutation can affect an organism to different degrees. The effect depends on factors such as the number of genes involved and the location of the mutation.

## Impact on Phenotype

Chromosomal mutations affect a lot of genes and tend to have a big effect on an organism. A mutation may break up a gene, which could make the gene no longer work, or it could make a new hybrid gene with a new function. Translocated genes may also come under the control of a new set of promoters, which could make many genes be more or less active than usual.

Gene mutations, though smaller in scale, can also have a big effect on an organism. Suppose a substitution occurs in a coding region of DNA that changes an AAG codon to CAG. The resulting protein will have a glutamine in place of a lysine. If this change happens in the active site of an enzyme, the enzyme may not be able to bind to its substrate. If the substituted amino acid differs from the original one in size or polarity, the mutation could affect protein folding and thus possibly destroy the protein's function. A substitution could also result in a premature stop codon.

Even a mutation that occurs in a noncoding region can cause problems. For example, such a mutation could disrupt an mRNA splice site and prevent an intron from being removed. A mutation in a noncoding region could also interfere with the regulation of gene expression, keeping a protein from being produced or causing it to be produced all the time.

Many gene mutations, however, do not affect an organism's phenotype. Remember that many codons code for the same amino acid. Therefore, some substitutions have no effect, especially those occurring in the third nucleotide of a codon. If AAG changes to AAA, the resulting protein still has the correct amino acid, lysine. A mutation that does not affect the resulting protein is called silent. Similarly, an incorrect amino acid might have little effect on a protein if it has about the same size or polarity as the original amino acid or if it is far from an active site. If a mutation occurs in a noncoding region, such as an intron, it may not affect the encoded protein at all.

## Impact on Offspring

Mutations happen both in body cells and in germ cells. Mutations in body cells affect only the organism in which they occur. In contrast, mutations in germ cells may be passed to offspring. They are the underlying source of genetic variation, which is the basis of natural selection. Mutations in the germ line affect the phenotype of offspring. Often, this effect is so harmful that offspring do not develop properly or die before they can reproduce. Other mutations, though less severe, still result in less adaptive phenotypes. In such cases, natural selection removes these mutant alleles from the population. More rarely, a mutation results in a more beneficial phenotype. These mutations are favored by natural selection and increase in a population.

**Apply** Why aren't mutations in body cells passed on to offspring?

**FIGURE 7.3** The coronary artery supplies blood to the heart. If it becomes blocked (top), a heart attack may result. Some people have a mutation that appears to help protect against coronary artery disease (bottom) by increasing their "good" cholesterol levels and decreasing their triglyceride levels. (colored LMs; magnifications: 15×)

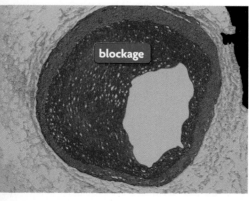

blockage

no blockage

# Mutations can be caused by several factors.

Mutations are not uncommon, and organisms have many tools to repair them. However, events and substances can make mutations happen faster than the body's repair system can handle.

## Replication Errors

As you have learned, DNA polymerase has a built-in proofreading function. Nevertheless, a small number of replication errors are not fixed. They build up over time, and eventually affect how the cell works. For example, many studies suggest that mutations are a significant cause of aging.

## Mutagens

**Mutagens** are agents in the environment that can change DNA. They speed up the rate of replication errors and, in some cases, even break DNA strands. Some mutagens occur naturally, such as ultraviolet (UV) rays in sunshine. Many others are industrial chemicals. Ecologists such as Rachel Carson, shown in **FIGURE 7.4,** warned the public about mutagens.

The human body has DNA repair enzymes that help find and fix mutations. For instance, UV light can cause neighboring thymine nucleotides to break their hydrogen bonds to adenine and bond with each other instead. Typically, one enzyme removes the bonded thymines, another replaces the damaged section, and a third bonds the new segment in place. Sometimes, these enzymes do not work. If these mistakes interfere with regulatory sites and control mechanisms, they may result in cancer. In rare cases, people inherit mutations that make their DNA repair systems less active, which makes these people very vulnerable to the damaging effects of sunlight.

Some cancer drugs take advantage of mutagenic properties by causing similar damage to cancer cells. One type of drug wedges its way between nucleotides, causing so many mutations that cancer cells can no longer function.

**Summarize** **Explain why mutagens can damage DNA in spite of repair enzymes.**

Rachel Carson

**FIGURE 7.4** Rachel Carson was one of the first ecologists to warn against the widespread use of pesticides and other potential mutagens and toxins.

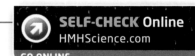

**SELF-CHECK Online**
HMHScience.com
GO ONLINE

## 8.7 Formative Assessment

### REVIEWING ▶ MAIN IDEAS

1. Explain why **frameshift mutations** have a greater effect than do **point mutations**.

2. If GUA is changed to GUU, will the resulting protein be affected? Explain.

3. Explain how **mutagens** can cause genetic **mutations** in spite of your body's DNA repair enzymes.

### CRITICAL THINKING

4. **Connect** Some genetic mutations are associated with increased risk for a particular disease. Tests exist for some of these genes. What might be the advantages and disadvantages of being tested?

5. **Illustrate** How could a mutated gene produce a shorter protein than that produced by the normal gene? Draw an example.

### CONNECT TO

**ECOLOGY**

6. How might the presence of a chemical mutagen in the environment affect the genetic makeup and size of a population over time?

# 8 Summary

DNA and RNA are the genetic material in all living things and provide the molecular basis for reproduction and development.

## KEY CONCEPTS

### 8.1 Identifying DNA as the Genetic Material

**DNA was identified as the genetic material through a series of experiments.** Griffith discovered a "transforming principle," which Avery later identified as DNA. Hershey and Chase's experiments with bacteriophages conclusively demonstrated that DNA is the genetic material.

### 8.2 Structure of DNA

**DNA structure is the same in all organisms.** DNA is a polymer made up of four types of nucleotides. Watson and Crick discovered that DNA consists of two strands of nucleotides bonded together into a double helix structure. Nucleotides always pair in the same way— C with G, and A with T.

### 8.3 DNA Replication

**DNA replication copies the genetic information of a cell.** During replication, a DNA molecule separates into two strands. Each strand serves as a template for building a new complementary strand through a rapid, accurate process involving DNA polymerase and other enzymes.

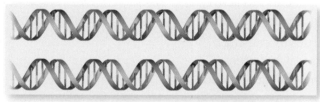

Two identical double-stranded DNA molecules result from replication.

### 8.4 Transcription

**Transcription converts a gene into a single-stranded RNA molecule.** The transcription process is similar to DNA replication and makes three types of RNA. Messenger RNA is an intermediate molecule that carries DNA's instructions to be translated.

### 8.5 Translation

**Translation converts an mRNA message into a polypeptide, or protein.** This process occurs on ribosomes, which are made of rRNA and proteins. Transfer RNA molecules bring amino acids to the growing protein by selectively pairing with mRNA codons.

### 8.6 Gene Expression and Regulation

**Gene expression is carefully regulated in both prokaryotic and eukaryotic cells.** In prokaryotes, transcription is the primary point of control. In eukaryotes, gene expression is controlled at many points, including RNA processing. Internal and external factors influence gene expression and cell differentiation.

### 8.7 Mutations

**Mutations are changes in DNA that may or may not affect phenotype.** Some mutations affect a single gene, and others affect an entire chromosome. Mutations may occur naturally, or they may be caused by mutagens. A mutation that does not affect phenotype is called a silent mutation. Mutations in sperm or egg cells can be passed to offspring.

---

## READING TOOLBOX   SYNTHESIZE YOUR NOTES

**Summarize** How can you summarize the process by which proteins are made? Use your notes to make a detailed version of the graphic organizer below. Include important details about the processes of transcription and translation. Mark important vocabulary terms.

From DNA to Proteins

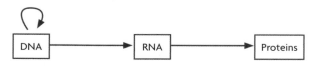

**Concept Map** Use a concept map like the one below to summarize what you know about mutations.

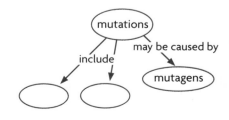

# 8 Review

**INTERACTIVE Review**
HMHScience.com
**GO ONLINE**
Review Games • Concept Map • Section Self-Checks

## CHAPTER VOCABULARY

**8.1** bacteriophage

**8.2** nucleotide
double helix
base pairing rules

**8.3** replication
DNA polymerase

**8.4** central dogma
RNA
transcription

RNA polymerase
messenger RNA (mRNA)
ribosomal RNA (rRNA)
transfer RNA (tRNA)

**8.5** translation
codon
stop codon
start codon
anticodon

**8.6** promoter
operon
exon
intron

**8.7** mutation
point mutation
frameshift mutation
mutagen

## Reviewing Vocabulary

### Compare and Contrast

Describe one similarity and one difference between the two terms in each of the following pairs.

**1.** translation, transcription

**2.** point mutation, frameshift mutation

**3.** messenger RNA (mRNA), transfer RNA (tRNA)

**4.** codon, anticodon

### READING TOOLBOX WORD ORIGINS

**5.** The word *codon* was coined in 1962 by putting together the word *code* with the suffix *-on,* which means "a hereditary unit." How do these word parts relate to the meaning of the term *codon*?

Use the word parts in this table to answer the next two questions.

| Part | Meaning |
|------|---------|
| *-gen* | to give birth |
| *muta-* | to change |
| *phago-* | eating |
| *poly-* | many |

**6.** Use the meaning of the word parts to write your own definitions for the following terms: *mutagen, bacteriophage, polypeptide.*

**7.** Suggest a likely definition for these biology terms: *polygenic, phagocyte.*

## Reviewing MAIN IDEAS

**8.** How did qualitative, chemical, and enzyme tests help Avery identify DNA as the transforming principle?

**9.** Hershey and Chase confirmed that DNA, not protein, was the genetic material. How do the results of their two experiments support this conclusion?

**10.** Describe Watson and Crick's double helix DNA model. Include a labeled drawing of the model.

**11.** One DNA strand has the nucleotide sequence AACGTA. What is the sequence of the other strand?

**12.** How do the base pairing rules explain how a strand of DNA acts as a template during replication?

**13.** What are three main steps in DNA replication?

**14.** What does it mean to say that there is a "proofreading" function in DNA replication?

**15.** Describe two differences between DNA and RNA.

**16.** List the main types of RNA and their functions.

**17.** Explain the process of mRNA codons and tRNA anticodons coding for a specific amino acid.

**18.** What role do ribosomes play in translation?

**19.** Where in the eukaryotic cell do replication, transcription, RNA processing, and translation each occur?

**20.** How do the promoter and operator work together to control gene expression?

**21.** Describe mRNA processing in eukaryotic cells.

**22.** Describe three ways mutations can occur.

# Critical Thinking

23. **Identify** Give one example of how a mutation may affect an organism's traits, and one example of how a mutation may not affect an organism's traits.

24. **Describe** Explain the roles of DNA, RNA, and environmental factors in gene expression and cell differentiation.

25. **Hypothesize** If the nucleus were surrounded by a membrane that had fewer pores than usual, how might the rate of protein synthesis be affected, and why?

26. **Illustrate** For the DNA sequence TACCAAGTGAAAATT, write the sequence of its RNA transcript and the sequence of amino acids for which it codes. Write the sequence of its RNA transcript to illustrate an example of a point mutation.

27. **Predict** Suppose you genetically altered a gene in a line of eukaryotic cells by inserting only the operator from the bacterial *lac* operon. Would adding lactose to the cell culture cause the cells to start transcribing the altered gene? Explain your reasoning.

28. **Contrast** What process did Watson and Crick use to develop their model of DNA, and how did it differ from the controlled experiments used by Griffith, Avery, and Hershey and Chase?

29. **Recognize** Why was it difficult for scientists to be convinced that DNA was the genetic material common to all organisms?

30. **Synthesize** Watson and Crick learned from Franklin's x-ray crystallography that the distance between the backbones of the DNA molecule was the same for the length of the molecule. How did this information, combined with what they knew about the four base sizes, lead to their model of DNA structure?

## Interpreting Visuals

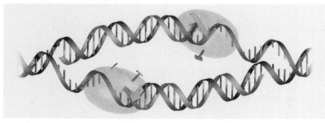

Use the diagram to answer the next three questions.

31. **Apply** What process is taking place in this diagram?

32. **Apply** What do the arrows on the yellow strands indicate?

33. **Predict** If you were to extend the diagram in both directions, what would you expect to see?

## Analyzing Data  Interpret a Histogram

Many factors contribute to breast cancer, including some that are genetic. For example, women with a mutation in the BRCA1 gene have an especially high risk of developing breast cancer. The histogram below shows the total estimated number of new breast cancer cases for women in the United States for 2003. Use the data in the histogram to answer the next two questions.

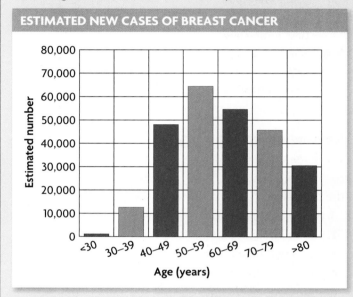

**ESTIMATED NEW CASES OF BREAST CANCER**

Source: American Cancer Society

34. **Analyze** In which age group was the incidence of new cases the lowest? the highest?

35. **Hypothesize** Using the data in this histogram, develop a hypothesis to explain why breast cancer genes are still present in the population.

## Making Connections

36. **Write an Analogy** This chapter includes an analogy about exchanging quarters for tokens at a game center to represent the process of transcription. Think of your own analogy for one of the processes you learned about in this chapter. Write a paragraph using that analogy to explain the process. Also, note any limitations of your analogy. (That is, in what ways does it not "fit" the process you're explaining?)

37. **Synthesize** Look again at the picture of the glowing mouse on the chapter opener. The gene for the protein GFP was inserted into a mouse egg, and then expressed in the mouse. What genetic processes are involved in the expression of this gene?

## MAIN IDEA
# Restriction enzymes cut DNA.

Why would scientists want to cut DNA? To answer that question, you have to remember that a gene is a sequence of DNA nucleotides, and that a chromosome is one long DNA molecule. A whole chromosome is too large for scientists to study a particular gene easily, so they had to find a way to get much smaller pieces of DNA. Of course, slicing a chromosome into pieces is not as simple as picking up the molecule and cutting it with a pair of scissors. Instead, scientists use enzymes that act as molecular "scissors." These enzymes, which slice apart DNA, come from many types of bacteria.

Bacterial cells, like your cells, can be infected by viruses. As protection against these invaders, bacteria produce enzymes that cut up the DNA of the viruses. As **FIGURE 1.1** shows, a DNA molecule can be cut apart in several places at once by several molecules of a restriction enzyme, or endonuclease. **Restriction enzymes** are enzymes that cut DNA molecules when they identify specific nucleotide sequences. In fact, any time the enzyme finds that exact DNA sequence, it cuts the DNA molecule. The sequence of nucleotides that is identified and cut by a restriction enzyme is called a restriction site. These enzymes are called restriction enzymes because they restrict, or decrease, the effect of the virus on the bacterial cell.

There are hundreds of known restriction enzymes. Different restriction enzymes will cut the same DNA molecule in a variety of ways. For example, one restriction enzyme may find three of its restriction sites in a segment of DNA. Another restriction enzyme might find six of its restriction sites in the same segment. Different numbers of fragments with different lengths result. As you can see below, two different restriction enzymes can cut the same strand of DNA in very different ways.

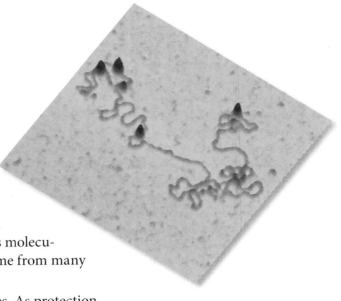

**FIGURE 1.1** A restriction enzyme (blue peaks) from an *E. coli* bacterium helps protect against viruses by cutting DNA (red). This cutting "restricts" the effect of a virus on a bacterium. (colored 3D atomic force micrograph; magnification 63,000×)

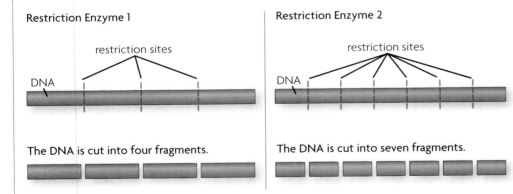

Restriction Enzyme 1

restriction sites

DNA

The DNA is cut into four fragments.

Restriction Enzyme 2

restriction sites

DNA

The DNA is cut into seven fragments.

Restriction enzymes recognize nucleotide sequences that are between four and eight base pairs long, and then cut the DNA. Some enzymes make cuts straight across the two strands of a DNA molecule. These cuts leave behind fragments of DNA that end in what are called "blunt ends."

© Torunn Berge/Photo Researchers, Inc.

## FIGURE 1.2  Restriction Enzymes Cut DNA

**Some restriction enzymes leave behind nucleotide tails, or "sticky ends," when they cut DNA.**

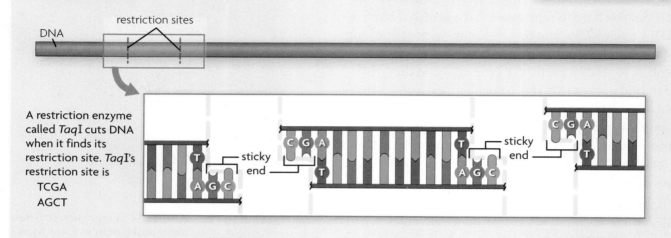

A restriction enzyme called *Taq*I cuts DNA when it finds its restriction site. *Taq*I's restriction site is
TCGA
AGCT

**Infer**  How would the above illustration change if *Taq*I left behind blunt ends rather than sticky ends when it cuts DNA?

### CONNECT TO

**DNA BASE PAIRS**

In the chapter **From DNA to Proteins** you learned that DNA nucleotides match up by complementary base pairing. A always pairs with T, and C always pairs with G.

Other restriction enzymes, as shown in **FIGURE 1.2**, make staggered cuts that leave tails of free DNA bases on each side of the cut. These nucleotide tails of the cut DNA strands are called "sticky ends." Sticky ends are like tiny pieces of Velcro® that are ready to hook on to their opposite sides. If two pieces of DNA with sticky ends and complementary base pairs come close to each other, the two segments of DNA will join by hydrogen bonding. Because of this characteristic of DNA, restriction enzymes that leave sticky ends when they cut DNA are often used in biotechnology, as you will learn in Section 4.

**Summarize  How do different restriction enzymes produce different DNA fragments from the same DNA molecule?**

▶ **MAIN IDEA**

## Restriction maps show the lengths of DNA fragments.

After a long DNA molecule has been cut by restriction enzymes into many smaller fragments, several things can be done with the DNA. For example, the DNA sequence of a gene can be studied, or a gene cut out from the DNA can be placed into the DNA of another organism. But before anything else can be done, the DNA fragments have to be separated from one another. The fragments are sorted according to their sizes by a technique called gel electrophoresis (ih-LEHK-troh-fuh-REE-sihs).

In **gel electrophoresis,** an electrical current is used to separate a mixture of DNA fragments from each other. A sample of DNA is loaded into a gel, which is like a thin slab of hard gelatin. A positive electrode is at one end of the gel. At the other end is a negative electrode. Because DNA has a negative charge,

VIRTUAL Lab
HMHScience.com
GO ONLINE
Gel Electrophoresis

the fragments move toward the positive electrode, or the positively charged pole. The gel also has tiny pores running through it. The pores allow small molecules to move quickly. Larger molecules cannot easily move through the gel and they travel more slowly. Therefore, the length of a DNA fragment can be estimated from the distance it travels through a gel in a certain period of time. As shown in **FIGURE 1.3**, DNA fragments of different sizes appear as different bands, or lines, on a gel. The pattern of bands on the gel can be thought of as a map of the original strand of DNA. **Restriction maps** show the lengths of DNA fragments between restriction sites in a strand of DNA.

The bands on a gel indicate only the lengths of DNA fragments. Alone, they do not give any information about the DNA sequences of the fragments. Even though restriction maps do not directly show the makeup of a fragment of DNA, the maps are very useful in genetic engineering, which you will read about in Section 4. They can also be used to study gene mutations. How? First, a mutation may add or delete bases between restriction sites, which would change the lengths of DNA fragments on a gel. Second, a mutation may change a restriction site, and the DNA would not be cut in the same places.

Suppose, for example, that when a normal allele of a gene is cut by a restriction enzyme, five DNA fragments appear as five different bands on a gel. Then, when a mutant allele of the same gene is cut with the same enzyme, only three bands appear. Comparisons of restriction maps can help diagnose genetic diseases, as you will see in Section 6. A restriction map from a person's DNA can be compared with a restriction map from DNA that is known to be normal. If the restriction maps differ, it is an indication that the person has inherited a disease-causing allele of the gene.

**Synthesize** How are restriction enzymes used in making restriction maps?

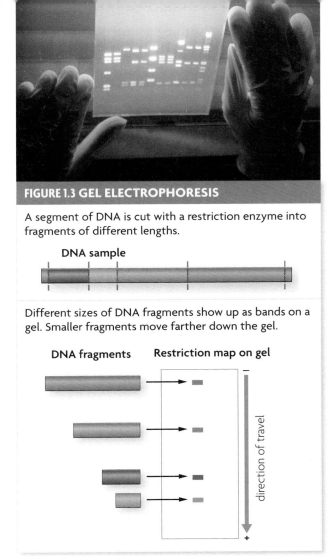

**FIGURE 1.3 GEL ELECTROPHORESIS**

A segment of DNA is cut with a restriction enzyme into fragments of different lengths.

DNA sample

Different sizes of DNA fragments show up as bands on a gel. Smaller fragments move farther down the gel.

DNA fragments    Restriction map on gel

direction of travel

©Explorer/Science Source

## 9.1 Formative Assessment

**SELF-CHECK Online**
HMHScience.com
**GO ONLINE**

### REVIEWING ▶ MAIN IDEAS

1. List four ways in which scientists can manipulate DNA.
2. What determines how DNA will be cut by a **restriction enzyme**?
3. How does **gel electrophoresis** separate DNA fragments from each other?

### CRITICAL THINKING

4. **Apply** Suppose you cut DNA. You know that you should find four DNA fragments on a gel, but only three appear, and one fragment is very large. Explain what happened.
5. **Synthesize** What is the relationship between restriction sites and a **restriction map**?

### CONNECT TO

**MUTATIONS**

6. Would a mutation in a gene always be detectable by using restriction maps? Why or why not?

# Organs-on-a-Chip

Researching human diseases and the drugs that could possibly treat these diseases can be tough to do. Ethics and regulations strictly limit using humans as subjects. Using other animals for testing is also not ideal, as the physiology of a rat or dog does not always react the same way that a human body does. Human cells can be cultured in a petri dish, but they grow into a flat layer that also may not respond the way they would as part of an entire body.

A new technology called an organ-on-a-chip may solve some of these issues and reduce the amount of time it takes to develop a new treatment for a disease. Cells are grown on a membrane within a small, three-dimensional plastic "chip." The membrane can be hooked up to a device that pulls it and then allows it to contract, simulating the movement of cells within the body. Different types of cells can be grown on each side of the membrane, and air or liquids such as blood can be sent flowing above and below the membrane. Cells live longer in this arrangement than in a petri dish culture, making longer-term studies possible.

Like DNA microarrays, in which many genes are placed on a chip for study, cellular microarrays miniaturize the scale of research. Fewer materials and less space are needed with chip biotechnology, and at a lower cost than similar research on a larger scale. Organs that have been studied using this method include the heart, kidneys, liver, and lungs.

Based on the lung-on-a-chip technology, scientists at Harvard University recently developed an airway-on-a-chip to study inflammation caused by common disorders such as asthma. Airway cells on one side of the membrane are exposed to air, and capillary cells on the other side are exposed to blood cells. Adding a factor that triggers asthma allows researchers to study how the cells become inflamed and what treatments are effective to reduce the inflammation. While many diseases can affect people as they age, asthma is a condition that affects millions of children as well as adults. Asthma is one of the most common causes of missed school days, and severe attacks can be life-threatening.

Because diseases such as asthma affect each individual differently, using one person's cells on a chip can potentially offer that individual personalized treatment in less time than it takes new pharmaceuticals to reach the market. While it may be too early to rely solely on this new biotechnology for disease and treatment research, it is a tool that someday might be available in a doctor's office near you.

## Questions

1. How might organs-on-a-chip be able to replace animal testing in the future?

2. Some researchers are investigating a "human-on-a-chip" model that connects the various organ chips. What do you think would be the benefits of linking chips with different types of cells?

# 9.2 Copying DNA

**KEY CONCEPT** **The polymerase chain reaction rapidly copies segments of DNA.**

### VOCABULARY

polymerase chain reaction (PCR)

primer

**MAIN IDEAS**

- ○ PCR uses polymerases to copy DNA segments.
- ○ PCR is a three-step process.

**SC.912.L.16.10** Evaluate the impact of biotechnology on the individual, society and the environment, including medical and ethical issues.

## Connect to Your World

Forensic scientists use DNA from cells in a single hair at a crime scene to identify a criminal. Doctors test a patient's blood to quickly detect the presence of bacteria that cause Lyme disease. Scientists compare DNA from different species to determine how closely the species are related. However, the original amount of DNA from any of these sources is far too small to accurately study. Samples of DNA must be increased, or amplified, so that they can be analyzed.

## ○ MAIN IDEA

## PCR uses polymerases to copy DNA segments.

How do scientists get an amount of DNA that is large enough to be studied and manipulated? They copy the same segment of DNA over and over again. **Polymerase chain reaction (PCR)** is a technique that produces millions—or even billions—of copies of a specific DNA sequence in just a few hours. As the name indicates, the DNA polymerase enzymes that help copy DNA play key roles in this process.

Kary Mullis, who invented PCR, is shown in **FIGURE 2.1.** While working for a California biotechnology company in 1983, Mullis had an insight about how to copy DNA segments. He adapted the process of DNA replication that occurs in every living cell into a method for copying DNA in a test tube. Under the right set of conditions, DNA polymerases copy DNA in a test tube just as they do inside cells. However, in cells several other enzymes are needed before the polymerases can do their job. For example, before a cell can begin to copy its DNA, enzymes called helicases unwind and separate DNA molecules. Instead of using these enzymes, Mullis used heat to separate the DNA strands.

Unfortunately, heat also broke down the *E. coli* polymerases that Mullis first used. Then came Mullis's second stroke of genius: Why not use polymerases from a bacterium that lives in temperatures above 80°C (176°F)? By using this enzyme, Mullis was able to raise the temperature of the DNA to separate the strands without destroying the DNA polymerases. Here again, just as with restriction enzymes that you read about in Section 1, a major advance came from applying an adaptation found in nature to biotechnology. Mullis introduced PCR to the world in 1985, and in 1993 he won the Nobel Prize in chemistry for his revolutionary technique.

**FIGURE 2.1** Kary Mullis came up with the idea for PCR while on a surfing trip in 1983. He won the Nobel Prize in chemistry in 1993.

**Compare and Contrast** How are replication and PCR similar? different? Explain.

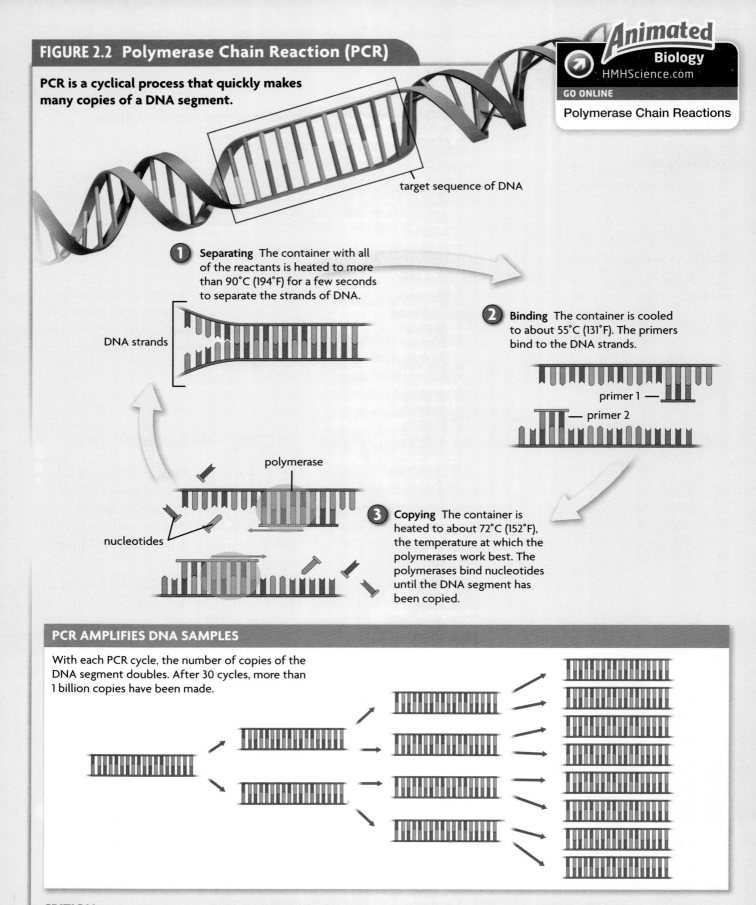

FIGURE 2.2 Polymerase Chain Reaction (PCR)

PCR is a cyclical process that quickly makes many copies of a DNA segment.

**Animated Biology**
HMHScience.com
**GO ONLINE**
Polymerase Chain Reactions

target sequence of DNA

**1** **Separating** The container with all of the reactants is heated to more than 90°C (194°F) for a few seconds to separate the strands of DNA.

DNA strands

**2** **Binding** The container is cooled to about 55°C (131°F). The primers bind to the DNA strands.

primer 1

primer 2

polymerase

nucleotides

**3** **Copying** The container is heated to about 72°C (152°F), the temperature at which the polymerases work best. The polymerases bind nucleotides until the DNA segment has been copied.

## PCR AMPLIFIES DNA SAMPLES

With each PCR cycle, the number of copies of the DNA segment doubles. After 30 cycles, more than 1 billion copies have been made.

**CRITICAL VIEWING** How many copies of DNA will exist after one more PCR cycle? After three more cycles?

## MAIN IDEA
# PCR is a three-step process.

PCR is a surprisingly simple process. It uses just four materials: the DNA to be copied, DNA polymerases, large amounts of each of the four DNA nucleotides (A, T, C, and G), and two primers. A **primer** is a short segment of DNA that acts as the starting point for a new strand. If DNA polymerases build new DNA strands, why are primers needed for PCR? DNA polymerases can add nucleotides to strands that have already been started, but they cannot start the strands. In PCR, two primers are used to start the copying of DNA close to the desired segment. The two primers are like bookends for the DNA strand. They limit the length of the copied DNA to one small segment of the strand.

PCR has three main steps, as shown in **FIGURE 2.2**. All of the steps of the cycle take place in the same container but at different temperatures. The main function of the first two PCR cycles is to produce the small segment of DNA that is desired. By making a copy of the desired segment, many copies of that tiny piece of DNA can be made, rather than copying an entire chromosome.

**1** **Separating** The container with all of the reactants is heated to separate the double-stranded DNA into single strands.

**2** **Binding** The container is cooled and the primers bind to their complementary DNA sequences. One primer binds to each DNA strand. The primers bind on opposite ends of the DNA segment being copied.

**3** **Copying** The container is heated again and the polymerases begin to build new strands of DNA. Added nucleotides bind to the original DNA strands by complementary base pairing. The polymerases continue attaching nucleotides until the entire DNA segment has been copied.

Each PCR cycle doubles the number of DNA copies. The original piece of DNA becomes two copies. Those two copies become four copies. And the cycle is repeated over and over to quickly copy enough DNA for study. After only 30 cycles of PCR, for example, the original DNA sequence is copied more than 1 billion times. This doubling is why the process is called a chain reaction.

**Infer** **Why is it necessary to keep changing the temperature in the PCR process?**

### READING TOOLBOX

**VOCABULARY**
The term *primer* comes from a Latin word that means "first." In PCR, a primer is the starting point for the DNA copying process.

### CONNECT TO
**REPLICATION**
Look back at the process of DNA replication in the chapter **From DNA to Proteins** to compare PCR with replication.

---

## 9.2 Formative Assessment

### REVIEWING ◉ MAIN IDEAS

1. Briefly describe the function of **polymerase chain reaction (PCR)**.

2. Summarize the cycle involved in the PCR process.

### CRITICAL THINKING

3. **Synthesize** Describe how heating double-stranded DNA separates the strands. Why does heating also inactivate DNA polymerases from many organisms?

4. **Analyze** Explain two reasons why **primers** are important in PCR.

### CONNECT TO
**HUMAN GENETICS**

5. Many human genetic diseases are caused by recessive alleles of genes. How might PCR be important in the diagnosis of these illnesses?

SELF-CHECK Online
HMHScience.com
GO ONLINE

# DNA Fingerprinting

SC.912.L.16.10

**KEY CONCEPT** DNA fingerprints identify people at the molecular level.

**VOCABULARY**

DNA fingerprint

**MAIN IDEAS**

- A DNA fingerprint is a type of restriction map.
- DNA fingerprinting is used for identification.

**SC.912.L.16.10** Evaluate the impact of biotechnology on the individual, society and the environment, including medical and ethical issues.

## Connect to Your World

You hear about it in the news all the time. DNA evidence is used to convict a criminal, release an innocent person from prison, or solve a mystery. A couple of decades ago, the lines and swirls of someone's fingertip were a detective's best hope for identifying someone. Now, investigators gather biological samples and analyze DNA for another kind of evidence: a DNA fingerprint.

### ▶ MAIN IDEA

## A DNA fingerprint is a type of restriction map.

Unless you have an identical twin, your complete set of DNA, or your genome, is unique. This variation in DNA among people is the basis of DNA fingerprinting. A **DNA fingerprint** is a representation of parts of an individual's DNA that can be used to identify a person at the molecular level.

A DNA fingerprint is a specific type of restriction map, which you learned about in Section 1. First, a DNA sample is cut with a restriction enzyme. Then the DNA fragments are run through a gel and the pattern of bands on the gel is analyzed. As you can see in **FIGURE 3.1**, a DNA fingerprint can show relationships among family members. The children (C) have similar DNA fingerprints to one another, but they are not identical. Also, their DNA fingerprints are combinations of the DNA fingerprints of the parents (M and F).

The greatest differences in DNA among people are found in regions of the genome that are not parts of genes. As a result, DNA fingerprinting focuses on noncoding regions of DNA, or DNA sequences outside genes. Noncoding DNA sequences often include stretches of nucleotides that repeat several times, one after another, as shown in **FIGURE 3.2**. Each person's DNA differs in the numbers of copies of the repeats. For example, one person may have seven repeats in one location, and another person may have three in the same place. To get to the specific regions of DNA that can be identified through DNA fingerprinting, the DNA is cut in known locations with restriction enzymes.

The differences in the number of repeats are found by separating the DNA fragments with gel electrophoresis. When there are more repeats, a DNA fragment is larger. The pattern of DNA fragments on a gel represents the uniqueness of a person's DNA. Individuals might have some of the fragments in common, but it is very unlikely that all of them would be the same.

**Synthesize** **Does a DNA fingerprint show a person's genotype? Why or why not?**

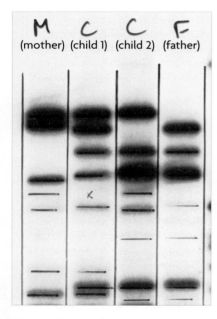

**FIGURE 3.1** DNA fingerprints can be compared to identify people. Both children share some bands with each parent.

## FIGURE 3.2 DNA Fingerprinting

**A DNA fingerprint shows differences in the number of repeats of certain DNA sequences.**

This DNA sequence of 33 bases can be repeated many times in a sample of a person's DNA.

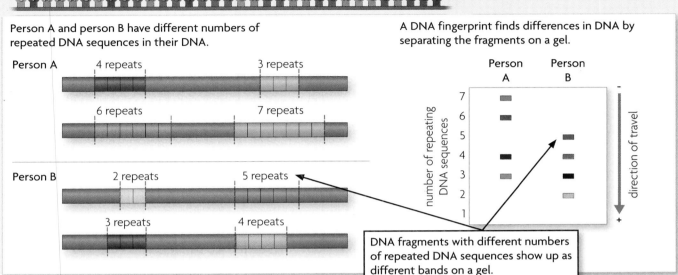

Person A and person B have different numbers of repeated DNA sequences in their DNA.

A DNA fingerprint finds differences in DNA by separating the fragments on a gel.

DNA fragments with different numbers of repeated DNA sequences show up as different bands on a gel.

**Infer** How would the DNA fingerprints change if a different restriction enzyme cut the DNA in the middle of one of the repeated DNA sequences?

## ⏵ MAIN IDEA
# DNA fingerprinting is used for identification.

DNA fingerprinting to identify people has become a reliable and widely used process since the 1990s. Why? The specific nucleotide sequences that are repeated can be found in everyone. More importantly, from one person to another, the number of repeat sequences can differ greatly, even among brothers and sisters.

### DNA Fingerprints and Probability

Identification with DNA fingerprinting depends on probability. Suppose that 1 in every 500 people has three copies of the repeat at location A. This means any person has a 1-in-500 chance of having a matching DNA fingerprint for that region of a chromosome. By itself, the number of repeats in one location cannot be used for identification, because too many people would match.

But then suppose that 1 in every 90 people has six copies of the repeat sequence at location B, and 1 in every 120 people has ten copies of the repeat sequence at location C. Individual probabilities are multiplied by each other to find the total probability. Therefore, when the three separate probabilities are multiplied, suddenly the chance that two people have the same DNA fingerprint is very small.

$$\frac{1}{500} \times \frac{1}{90} \times \frac{1}{120} = \frac{1}{5,400,000} = 1 \text{ chance in } 5.4 \text{ million people}$$

**⚛ CONNECT TO**

**GENOME**

Recall from the chapter **Meiosis and Mendel** that a genome is the entire set of DNA in a cell. You will learn more about genome research in **Section 5**.

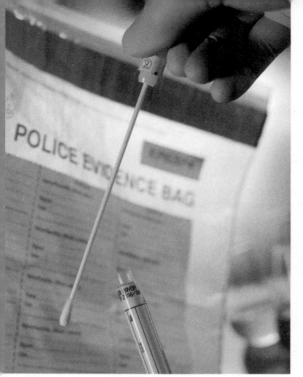

**FIGURE 3.3** DNA collected at crime scenes is used as evidence in many legal cases.

Usually, DNA fingerprinting compares at least five regions of the genome. That way it is more certain that the pattern of DNA fragments in the fingerprint is unique. The more regions of DNA that are studied, the less likely it becomes that another person would have the same DNA fingerprint. For this reason, DNA fingerprinting is considered very reliable for identification purposes.

## Uses of DNA Fingerprinting

DNA fingerprints are often used in legal cases. Because PCR can make a large sample of DNA even when there is a very small sample to start with, DNA fingerprints can be made from a few cells. Evidence, such as that shown in **FIGURE 3.3**, can come from just a single drop of blood.

Sometimes, DNA fingerprints are used against a suspect, but other times they are used to prove someone's innocence. The Innocence Project at Benjamin Cardozo Law School in New York City has used DNA evidence to help free nearly 300 wrongfully convicted people. Through DNA fingerprinting, the Innocence Project showed that DNA from those people did not match DNA from the crime scenes. Proving a person's guilt through DNA fingerprinting is harder than proving a person's innocence. For example, a DNA sample can become contaminated with other DNA if it is not handled carefully. Investigators must also consider the probability that another person has the same DNA fingerprint and what chance is low enough to be acceptable. In fact, there is no legal standard for this probability of a random DNA fingerprint match.

Outside of the courtroom, DNA fingerprints can prove family relationships, such as paternity and the kinship necessary for immigration requests. Small samples and bone fragments can be sequenced to identify victims of catastrophes or resolve historical debates. DNA fingerprinting may also be used to study human migration patterns and genealogy. Genetic comparisons through DNA fingerprinting are used to study biodiversity and to locate genetically engineered crops. And, as you saw at the beginning of the chapter, DNA fingerprinting has even been used in disasters to identify the parents of lost children.

©Tek Image/Photo Researchers, Inc.

**Summarize** How does identification by DNA fingerprinting depend on probability?

---

## 9.3 Formative Assessment

**SELF-CHECK Online**
HMHScience.com
**GO ONLINE**

### REVIEWING ▶ MAIN IDEAS

1. On what, in a person's DNA, is a **DNA fingerprint** based?
2. Describe two ways in which DNA fingerprinting is used.

### CRITICAL THINKING

3. **Compare and Contrast** How are DNA fingerprints and restriction maps similar? different? Explain.
4. **Synthesize** Briefly describe how restriction enzymes, gel electrophoresis, and PCR are used in DNA fingerprinting.

### CONNECT TO

**MUTATIONS**

5. Why might noncoding regions of DNA outside of genes be more variable than coding regions of DNA?

# 9.4 Genetic Engineering

SC.912.L.16.10

| KEY CONCEPT **DNA sequences of organisms can be changed.**

### MAIN IDEAS

- Entire organisms can be cloned.
- New genes can be added to an organism's DNA.
- Genetic engineering produces organisms with new traits.

**SC.912.L.16.10** Evaluate the impact of biotechnology on the individual, society and the environment, including medical and ethical issues.

### VOCABULARY
clone
genetic engineering
recombinant DNA
plasmid
transgenic
gene knockout

---

**Connect to Your World**

Glowing mice are used in cancer research. Glowing plants are used to track genetically modified crops. And, in 1999, British researchers introduced glowing yeast cells that locate water pollution. The scientists put a gene for a fluorescent protein into yeast. Under normal conditions, the yeast cells do not glow. But they do glow when certain chemicals are present. The glow identifies areas that need to be cleaned. New biotechnology applications seem to be developed on a daily basis. What advances will you see during your lifetime?

## MAIN IDEA

## Entire organisms can be cloned.

HMHScience.com

**GO ONLINE**

Animal Cloning

**FIGURE 4.1** The cat named CC—for Copy Cat or Carbon Copy—is the first successful clone of a cat (right). The original cat is on the left.

The term *cloning* might make you think of science fiction and horror movies, but the process is quite common in nature. A **clone** is a genetically identical copy of a gene or of an organism. For example, some plants clone themselves from their roots. Bacteria produce identical genetic copies of themselves through binary fission. And human identical twins are clones of each other.

People have cloned plants for centuries. The process is fairly easy because many plants naturally clone themselves and because plants have stem cell tissues that can develop into many types of cells. Some simple animals, such as sea stars, can essentially clone themselves through a process called regeneration. Mammals, however, cannot clone themselves.

To clone a mammal, scientists swap DNA between cells with a technique called nuclear transfer. First, an unfertilized egg is taken from an animal, and the egg's nucleus is removed. Then the nucleus of a cell from the animal to be cloned is implanted into the egg. The egg is stimulated and, if the procedure is successful, the egg will begin dividing. After the embryo grows for a few days, it is transplanted into a female. In 1996 a sheep named Dolly became the first clone of an adult mammal. The success of Dolly led to the cloning of adult cows, pigs, and mice. Now, a biotechnology company has even said that it can clone people's pets.

But pet owners who expect cloning to produce an exact copy of their furry friend will likely be disappointed. As you can see from the cat called CC in **FIGURE 4.1**, a clone may not look like the original, and it will probably not behave like the original, either. Why? Because, as you have learned, many factors, including environment, affect the expression of genes.

Cloning brings with it some extraordinary opportunities. For example, scientists are studying how to use organs from cloned mammals for transplant into humans. This use of cloning could save an enormous number of lives each year and would not cause rejection problems in the organ recipient. Cloning could even help save endangered species. Cells from endangered species could be taken and used to produce clones that would increase the population of the species.

Cloning is also controversial. Many people think the success rate is too low to be attempted. The success rate in cloning mammals has improved substantially, but it varies widely by species. As cloning has become more common, ecological concerns have been raised. Cloned animals in a wild population would reduce biodiversity because the clones would be genetically identical.

**Apply** **Given the opportunity, would you have a pet cloned? Explain your answer based on your knowledge of genetics, biotechnology, and cloning.**

**CONNECT TO**

**BIODIVERSITY**

In the chapter **Biology in the 21st Century,** you learned that biodiversity can be defined as the number of different species in an area. You will learn much more about genetic diversity within a species in the **Evolution** unit.

▶ **MAIN IDEA**

## New genes can be added to an organism's DNA.

Genetic research relies on cloning, but not the cloning of organisms. Instead, it relies on the cloning of individual genes. A clone of a gene is a copy of that one segment of DNA. In some cases, scientists insert cloned genes from one organism into a different organism. This changing of an organism's DNA to give the organism new traits is called **genetic engineering.** Genetic engineering is possible because the genetic code is shared by all organisms.

Genetic engineering is based on the use of recombinant DNA technology. **Recombinant DNA** (ree-KAHM-buh-nuhnt) is DNA that contains genes from more than one organism. Scientists use recombinant DNA in several ways. For example, recombinant DNA is used to produce crop plants that make medicines and vitamins. Large amounts of medicines are made through this process, which has been called "pharming." Scientists are also studying ways of using recombinant DNA to make vaccines to protect against HIV, the virus that causes AIDS.

Bacteria are commonly used in genetic engineering. One reason is because bacteria have tiny rings of DNA called plasmids. **Plasmids,** as shown in **FIGURE 4.2,** are closed loops of DNA that are separate from the bacterial chromosome and that replicate on their own within the cell. Recombinant DNA is found naturally in bacteria that take in exogenous DNA (or DNA from a different organism) and add it to their own. Scientists adapted what happens in nature to make artificial recombinant DNA. First, a restriction enzyme is used to cut out the desired gene from a strand of DNA. Then plasmids are cut with the same enzyme. The plasmid opens, and when the gene is added to the plasmid, their complementary sticky ends are bonded together by a process called ligation. The resulting plasmid contains recombinant DNA, as shown in **FIGURE 4.3.**

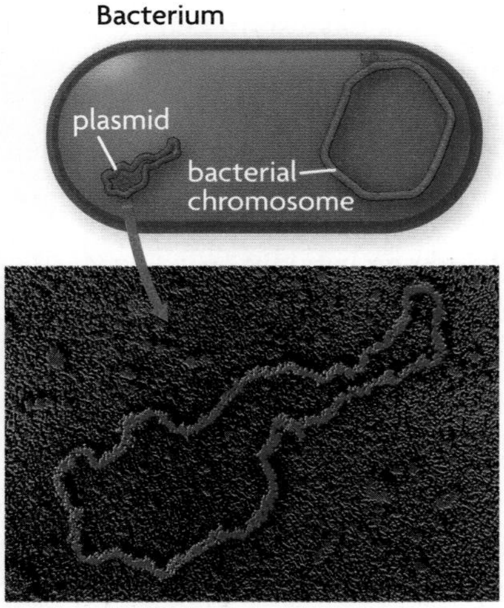

**Summarize** **How does genetic engineering rely on a shared genetic code?**

Bacterium

plasmid
bacterial chromosome

**FIGURE 4.2** A plasmid is a closed loop of DNA in a bacterium that is separate from the bacterial chromosome. (colored TEM; magnification 48,000×)

## FIGURE 4.3 Making Recombinant DNA

**Foreign DNA can be inserted into a plasmid to make recombinant DNA.**

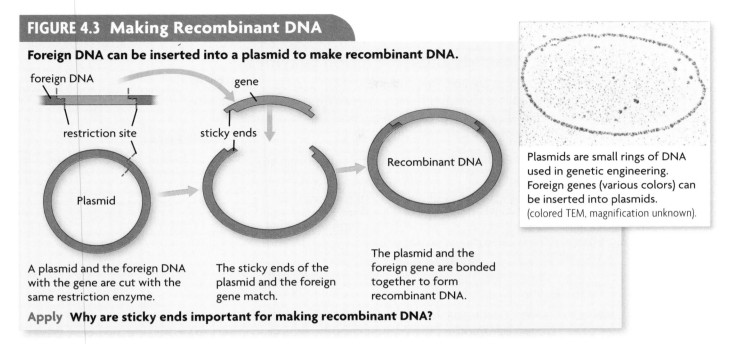

A plasmid and the foreign DNA with the gene are cut with the same restriction enzyme.

The sticky ends of the plasmid and the foreign gene match.

The plasmid and the foreign gene are bonded together to form recombinant DNA.

Plasmids are small rings of DNA used in genetic engineering. Foreign genes (various colors) can be inserted into plasmids. (colored TEM, magnification unknown).

**Apply** Why are sticky ends important for making recombinant DNA?

## ● MAIN IDEA

# Genetic engineering produces organisms with new traits.

After a gene is added to a plasmid, the genetically engineered plasmids can be put into bacteria. In a way, bacteria are turned into tiny gene factories that make copy after copy of the plasmid. As a result, the transformed bacteria make many copies of the new gene. The bacteria will express the new gene and make that gene's product. The bacteria with the recombinant plasmid are described as transgenic. A **transgenic** organism has one or more genes from another organism inserted into its genome. For example, the gene for human insulin can be put into plasmids. The plasmids are inserted into bacteria. The transgenic bacteria make human insulin that is collected and used to treat people with diabetes.

### Genetic Engineering of Plants

Genetic engineering of plants is directly related to genetic engineering of bacteria. To change a plant's DNA, a gene is inserted into a plasmid and the plasmid is inserted into bacteria. After the bacteria infect the plant, the new gene becomes a part of the plant's DNA and is expressed like any other gene.

This technique has allowed scientists to give plants new traits, such as resistance to frost, diseases, and insects. For instance, certain bacteria, called *Bt*, produce a natural protein pesticide. Farmers used to spray their crops with *Bt* bacteria to prevent the crops from being attacked by insects. But by genetically engineering the crop plants, the plants can make the bacterial pesticide themselves. These genetically engineered crops, which are also called genetically modified (GM), are now common in the United States. They include *Bt* potatoes and corn. GM crops are even more important in developing countries because by increasing crop yields, more food is produced quickly and cheaply.

**VIRTUAL Lab**
HMHScience.com
**GO ONLINE**
Bacterial Transformation

### ◉ READING TOOLBOX

**VOCABULARY**

The prefix *trans-* means "across," and the root *genic* means "referring to genes." When genes are transferred across different organisms, transgenic organisms are produced.

## Modeling Plasmids and Restriction Enzymes

Restriction enzymes are enzymes that cut DNA at precise locations. These enzymes allow scientists to move a gene from one organism into another. In this lab, you will use DNA sequences from a datasheet to simulate the use of restriction enzymes.

**PROBLEM** How do different restriction enzymes cut a plasmid?

**PROCEDURE**

1. Make models of 3 plasmids. Cut out the DNA sequences from the copies of Figure 1 on the datasheet. Use tape to attach the appropriate piece of yarn to each end. The yarn represents the entire plasmid. The finished plasmid should be a circle.

2. Use the scissors to cut a plasmid at the correct sites for *Eco*RI.

3. Use the sequences for sites of *Hind*III and *Sma*I to repeat step 2 with the other two plasmids.

**ANALYZE AND CONCLUDE**

1. **Apply** How many DNA fragments would you get if you cut the same plasmid with both *Eco*RI and *Sma*I?

2. **Infer** Why might scientists use different restriction enzymes to cut out different genes from a strand of DNA?

**MATERIALS**

- 3 copies of Plasmid Sequence Datasheet
- scissors
- 10 cm clear tape
- 3 sets of five 5-cm yarn pieces

**FIGURE 4.4** This knockout mouse has been bioengineered so researchers can use it as a model to study obesity.

## Genetic Engineering in Animals

In general, transgenic animals are much harder to produce than GM plants because animals are more resistant to genetic manipulation. To produce a transgenic animal, a researcher must first get a fertilized egg cell. Then the foreign DNA is inserted into the nucleus and the egg is implanted back into a female. However, only a small percentage of the genetically manipulated eggs mature normally. And only a portion of those that develop will be transgenic. That is, only a small number will have the foreign gene as a part of their DNA. But those animals that are transgenic will have the gene in all of their cells—including reproductive cells—and the transgenic trait will be passed on to their offspring.

Transgenic mice are often used as models of human development and disease. The first such animal was called the oncomouse. This mouse is more likely to develop cancer, because a gene that controls cell growth and differentiation was mutated. Researchers use the oncomouse to study both cancer and anti-cancer drugs. Other types of transgenic mice are used to study diabetes, brain function and development, and sex determination.

Some mice have genes that have been purposely "turned off." These mice, called **gene knockout** mice, are very useful for studying a gene's normal function because a researcher can observe specific changes in gene expression and traits. For example, scientists are using a gene knockout mouse to study obesity, as you can see in **FIGURE 4.4**. Other mice, called knockdown mice, are created using RNAi technology to decrease the expression of a specific gene or to silence the expression temporarily. Recall that RNAi technology shuts down expression of a gene by preventing a gene from making its protein. Scientists use knockdown technology to study metabolic pathways in animals.

©Science & Society Picture Library/Getty Images

Scientists are also developing new tools that make it easier to modify the genomes of both plants and animals. One particularly effective tool, called CRISPR (pronounced like *crisper*), is based on a mechanism some bacteria use as a kind of immune defense against viruses that infect them. In bacteria, the CRISPR mechanism identifies viral DNA and directs an enzyme to chop the foreign DNA into pieces. As a tool in biotechnology, CRISPR can be used to target particular DNA sequences with a high degree of precision, allowing researchers to delete, modify, or even replace genes in the cells of any organism, even human cells. CRISPR is proving particularly effective for studying diseases that involve many genes, such as some cancers, because its accuracy and ease of use make it possible to manipulate many genes at once. CRISPR also makes it much more practical for scientists to genetically engineer animal cells as compared with earlier methods.

## Concerns About Genetic Engineering

Scientists have genetically engineered many useful organisms by transferring genes between species to give individuals new traits. At the same time, there are concerns about possible effects of genetically engineered organisms on both human health and the environment. And at an even more basic level, some people wonder whether genetic engineering is ethical in the first place.

Questions have been raised about GM crops, even though scientists have not yet found negative health effects of GM foods. Critics say that not enough research has been done, and that some added genes might cause allergic reactions or have other unknown side effects. Scientists also have concerns about the possible effects of GM plants on the environment and on biodiversity. For example, what would happen if genetically engineered *Bt* plants killed insects that pollinate plants, such as bees and butterflies? In some instances, transgenic plants have cross-pollinated with wild type plants in farming regions. Scientists do not yet know what long-term effect this interbreeding might have on the natural plants. In addition, all organisms in a transgenic population have the same genome. As a result, some scientists worry that a decrease in genetic diversity could leave crops vulnerable to new diseases or pests.

**Infer** **Why is it important that a transgenic trait is passed on to the transgenic organism's offspring?**

---

## 9.4 Formative Assessment

**SELF-CHECK Online**
HMHScience.com
**GO ONLINE**

### REVIEWING ▶ MAIN IDEAS

1. Why is the offspring of asexual reproduction a **clone**?

2. What are **plasmids,** and how are they used in **genetic engineering**?

3. Describe two applications of **transgenic** organisms.

### CRITICAL THINKING

4. **Compare and Contrast** How is the cloning of genes different from the cloning of mammals?

5. **Summarize** How are restriction enzymes used to make both **recombinant DNA** and transgenic organisms?

### CONNECT TO

#### ECOLOGY

6. Do you think cloning endangered species is a good idea? What effect might this have on an ecosystem?

 **9.5**

# Genomics and Bioinformatics

SC.912.L.16.10

**KEY CONCEPT** Entire genomes are sequenced, studied, and compared.

**MAIN IDEAS**

○ Genomics involves the study of genes, gene functions, and entire genomes.

○ Technology allows the study and comparison of both genes and proteins.

**VOCABULARY**

genomics
gene sequencing
Human Genome Project
bioinformatics
DNA microarray
proteomics

**SC.912.L.16.10** Evaluate the impact of biotechnology on the individual, society and the environment, including medical and ethical issues.

### Connect to Your World

Humans and chimpanzees are identical in 98 to 99 percent of their DNA. How do scientists know this? They have sequenced all of the DNA in both species. Recent technologies are allowing scientists to look at huge amounts of genetic information at once. What might tomorrow's discoveries tell us about evolution, gene expression, and medical treatments?

○ **MAIN IDEA**

## Genomics involves the study of genes, gene functions, and entire genomes.

A gene, as you know, is a single stretch of DNA that codes for one or more polypeptides or RNA molecules. A genome is all of an organism's genetic information. **Genomics** is the study of genomes, which can include the sequencing of all of an organism's DNA. Scientists compare genomes both within and across species to find similarities and differences among DNA sequences. Comparing DNA from many people at one time helps researchers to find genes that cause disease and to understand how medications work. Biologists who study evolution can learn when closely related species diverged from each other. Scientists can also learn about interactions among genes and find out how an organism's genome makes the organism unique.

**Video Inquiry**
HMHScience.com
**GO ONLINE**

Coral Colds

### DNA Sequencing

All studies of genomics begin with **gene sequencing,** or determining the order of DNA nucleotides in genes or in genomes. An early sequencing method was developed in the 1970s by British scientist Frederick Sanger. The Sanger method is somewhat similar to PCR, which you read about in Section 2.

A radioactive primer is added to a single strand of DNA. Polymerase then builds a short segment of a new DNA strand. The lengths of the new strands are controlled so that they can be separated by gel electrophoresis. Based on the pattern of DNA fragments on the gel, the DNA sequence of the original strand can be put together like the pieces of a puzzle.

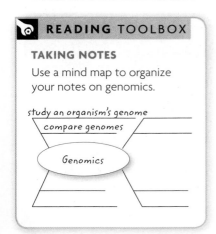

**READING TOOLBOX**

**TAKING NOTES**

Use a mind map to organize your notes on genomics.

study an organism's genome
compare genomes
Genomics

You might be surprised to learn that humans do not have the largest genome—the most DNA—among organisms. Scientists have determined the DNA sequences for the genomes of several species, including the ones listed in **FIGURE 5.1**. In some cases, the genomes are used to study basic questions about genes and genetics. In other cases, a genome is sequenced because that organism is used as a model in medical research. In all cases, the genomes of organisms that have been sequenced, including bacteria, insects, plants, and mammals, give us important clues toward finding out how genes function.

Yeast, for example, are very useful for scientists who study gene regulation. Genes that control development in the fruit fly are very similar to those genes in humans. The genomes of several plants have been sequenced so that scientists can learn ways to improve crop yields and to increase the resistance of those crops to disease and weather extremes. The genomes of rats and mice are quite similar to the human genome. As a result, both of these species are used as models for human diseases and gene function.

| **FIGURE 5.1 COMPARING GENOME SIZES** | |
| --- | --- |
| Organism | Approximate Total DNA (millions of base pairs) |
| E. coli | 5 |
| Yeast | 12 |
| Fruit fly | 165 |
| Banana | 873 |
| Chicken | 1200 |
| Human | 3000 |
| Vanilla | 7672 |
| Crested newt | 18,600 |
| Lungfish | 139,000 |

Source: University of Nebraska

## The Human Genome Project

The genomes of yeast and fruit flies are easier to sequence than the human genome. This difficulty is not due to the number of genes that humans have. In fact, while there is still a debate about the exact number of human genes, scientists agree it is surprisingly small. It is estimated that there are between 20,000 and 25,000 protein-coding genes in the human genome. But think about the amount of DNA that each of us has in our cells. The human genome has at least 3 billion base pairs. This means that there is an average of about one gene in each sequence of "120,000 to 150,000" bases. Now just try to imagine the huge task of finding out the exact order of all of those DNA bases. In 1990, an international effort began to do exactly that.

The two main goals of the **Human Genome Project** were (1) to map and sequence all of the DNA base pairs of the human chromosomes and (2) to identify all of the genes within the sequence. The first goal was accomplished in 2003 when scientists announced that they had sequenced the human genome. However, the Human Genome Project only analyzed the DNA from a few people. Knowing those few complete DNA sequences was only the first step in understanding the human genome.

Today scientists continue to work on determining the roles of genes and other functional elements. Some scientists are studying how DNA sequences vary among people in a project called HapMap. The goal of the HapMap is to develop a method that will quickly identify genetic differences that may play a part in human diseases. By identifying and studying the estimated 10 million single-base differences that occur in the human genome, scientists hope to learn what makes different populations of humans similar, and yet different, and use that knowledge to customize the treatment of diseases.

**FIGURE 5.2** Computer analysis of DNA was necessary in sequencing the human genome.

**Synthesize** **How is genomics related to genes and DNA?**

## CONSTRUCTING HISTOGRAMS

To construct a histogram a scientist will count the number of data points in each category and then graph the number of times that category occurs. The categories are shown on the x-axis and the frequencies are shown on the y-axis. The data table to the right shows the ranges of base pair lengths for the 24 human chromosomes (chromosomes 1–22, the X chromosome, and the Y chromosome). The data are organized by these ranges.

| TABLE 1. HUMAN CHROMOSOME SIZES | |
|---|---|
| Millions of Base Pairs | Number of Human Chromosomes |
| 0–50 | 2 |
| 51–100 | 6 |
| 101–150 | 8 |
| 151–200 | 6 |
| 201–250 | 2 |

Source: U.S. Department of Energy Office of Science

1. **Graph Data** Construct a histogram that shows the frequency of base pair lengths for the 24 human chromosomes.

2. **Interpret** Which range of base pair length is most common for human chromosomes?

3. **Analyze** Summarize the overall trend for human chromosome length shown in the histogram.

## ⊙ MAIN IDEA

# Technology allows the study and comparison of both genes and proteins.

You have learned about specific genes that produce specific traits. But you also know that genes act as more than simple, separate units. They interact and affect each other's expression. Most biological processes and physical traits are the result of the interactions among many different genes.

### Bioinformatics

Genes are sequenced, genomes are compared, and proteins are analyzed. What happens to the huge amounts of data that are produced? These data can be analyzed only if they are organized and searchable. **Bioinformatics** is the use of computer databases to organize and analyze biological data. Powerful computer programs are needed to compare genomes that are billions of base pairs in length, especially if the genomes differ by only a small amount.

Bioinformatics gives scientists a way to store, share, and find data. It also lets researchers predict and model the functions of genes and proteins. A scientist can now search databases to find the gene that is the code for a known protein. Bioinformatics can help researchers find the genetic basis of some diseases and the causes of molecular diseases.

### DNA Microarrays

**DNA microarrays** are tools that allow scientists to study many genes, and their expression, at once. A microarray is a small chip that is dotted with all of the genes being studied. The genes are laid out in a grid pattern. Each block of the grid is so small that a one-square-inch chip can hold thousands of genes.

> ⚡ **CONNECT TO**
>
> **COMPUTER MODELS**
>
> Recall from **Biology in the 21st Century** how computer models are used to investigate biological systems that cannot be studied directly. Computer models are often used in genetics and genomics.

Virtual
INVESTIGATION
HMHScience.com
GO ONLINE
Gene Technologies

Complementary DNA (cDNA) labeled with a fluorescent dye is added to the microarray. A cDNA molecule is a single-stranded DNA molecule that is made from an mRNA molecule. The mRNA acts as a template for the cDNA. Therefore, a cDNA molecule is complementary to an mRNA molecule and is identical to a gene's DNA sequence. The cDNA binds to its complementary DNA strand in the microarray by the same base pairing that you learned about previously.

Anywhere cDNA binds to DNA in the microarray shows up as a glowing dot because of the dye. A glowing dot in the microarray is a match between a cDNA molecule and the DNA on the chip. Therefore, a glowing dot shows which genes are expressed and how much they are expressed. Microarrays, as shown in **FIGURE 5.3**, help researchers find which genes are expressed in which tissues, and under what conditions. For example, DNA microarrays can compare gene expression in cancer cells with gene expression in healthy cells. Scientists hope that this method will lead to cancer treatments that target the faulty genes.

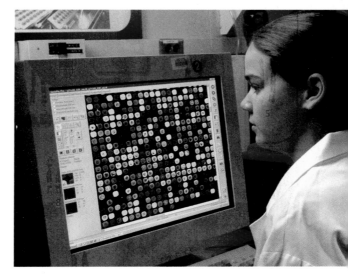

**FIGURE 5.3** Gene expression can be studied with microarrays. The red dots show genes that are expressed after exposure to a toxic chemical.

## Proteomics

You have read how genomics is the study of genomes. **Proteomics** (PROH-tee-AH-mihks) is the study and comparison of all the proteins that result from an organism's genome. Proteomics also includes the study of the functions and interactions of proteins. Identifying and studying proteins is more difficult than identifying and studying genes. A single gene, depending on how its mRNA is edited, can code for more than one polypeptide. Different proteins are found in different tissues, depending on gene expression. And, often, the functions of proteins have to be studied within a biological system.

Proteomics has potential benefits for many areas of biology. Shared evolutionary histories among organisms are studied by comparing proteins across species. Proteomics allows scientists to learn about proteins involved in human diseases. By better understanding the proteins that might play a part in cancer, arthritis, or heart disease, scientists might be able to develop new treatments that target the proteins. Proteomics even has the potential to help doctors match medical treatments to a patient's unique body chemistry.

Apply  **How is bioinformatics a form of data analysis?**

**SELF-CHECK Online**
HMHScience.com
GO ONLINE

## 9.5 Formative Assessment

### REVIEWING ▶ MAIN IDEAS

1. Describe the goals of the **Human Genome Project.**

2. Why is **bioinformatics** important in genetic research?

### CRITICAL THINKING

3. **Apply** Describe the difference between **gene sequencing** and DNA fingerprinting.

4. **Compare and Contrast** How is the study of specific genes different from the study of a genome?

### CONNECT TO

### CELL BIOLOGY

5. How might **genomics** and **proteomics** help researchers predict how a medical treatment might affect cells in different tissues?

# Genetic Screening and Gene Therapy

**KEY CONCEPT** **Genetics provides a basis for new medical treatments.**

**MAIN IDEAS**

○ Genetic screening can detect genetic disorders.
○ Gene therapy is the replacement of faulty genes.

## Connect to Your World

Anyone could be a carrier of a genetic disorder. Genetic screening is used to help people figure out whether they are at risk for passing on that disorder. If they are at risk, what do they do? Do they not have children? Do they have children and hope that a child does not get the disorder? What would you do?

### ○ MAIN IDEA
## Genetic screening can detect genetic disorders.

Every one of us carries alleles that produce defective proteins. Usually, these genes do not affect us in a significant way because we have other alleles that make up for the deficiency. But about 10 percent of people will find themselves dealing with an illness related to their genes at some point in their lives.

**Genetic screening** is the process of testing DNA to determine a person's risk of having or passing on a genetic disorder. Recall that genetic screening often involves both pedigree analysis and DNA tests. Because our knowledge of the human genome is still limited, it is not yet possible to test for every possible defect. Often, genetic screening is used to look for specific genes or proteins that indicate a particular disorder. Some tests can detect genes that are related to an increased risk of developing a disease, such as a gene called BRCA1 that has been linked to breast cancer. There are also tests for more than 1000 genetic disorders, including cystic fibrosis and Duchenne's muscular dystrophy (DMD). In DMD, it is quite easy to see differences in DNA tests between people with and without the disorder, as shown in **FIGURE 6.1**.

Genetic screening can help save lives. It can also lead to some difficult choices. Suppose a person has a family history of cancer and tests positive for a gene that may lead to an increased risk of cancer. Is that information helpful or harmful? If a person has a chance of being a carrier of a genetic disorder, should screening be required? As genetic screening becomes more common, more questions like these will need to be answered.

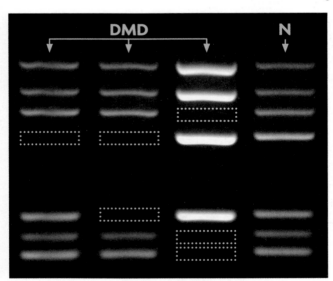

**FIGURE 6.1** Genetic screening can be used to detect Duchenne's muscular dystrophy (DMD). Notice the missing bands on the gel (boxes) for three people with DMD as compared with a person without the disorder (N).

**Infer** **Why might genetic screening raise ethical concerns about privacy?**

©National Centre for Medical Genetics, Dublin, Ireland

## ▶ MAIN IDEA

# Gene therapy is the replacement of faulty genes.

A defective part in a car or in a computer can be easily replaced. If someone has a faulty gene that causes a disorder, is it possible to replace the gene? The goal of gene therapy is to do exactly that. **Gene therapy** is the replacement of a defective or missing gene, or the addition of a new gene, into a person's genome to treat a disease. If the gene is replaced in a somatic cell, the change in the genome will affect only the individual and cannot be inherited by the patient's offspring. Scientists are trying to make the change in the patient's gametes as well so the change will be inherited.

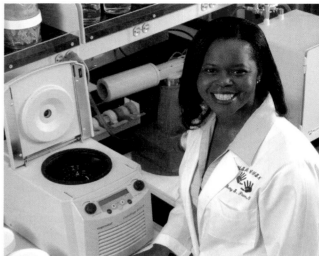

For any type of gene therapy to work, researchers such as Dr. Betty Pace, shown in **FIGURE 6.2**, must first get the new gene into the correct cells of a patient's body. Once in the body, the gene has to become a part of the cells' DNA. One method of gene therapy that scientists have tried is to take a sample of bone marrow stem cells and "infect" them with a virus that has been genetically engineered with the new gene. Then the stem cells are put back into the patient's bone marrow. Because they are stem cells, they divide and make more blood cells with the normal gene.

**FIGURE 6.2** Dr. Betty Pace, a molecular and cell biologist, is studying potential gene therapy treatments for sickle cell disease.

The first successful trial of gene therapy took place in 1990. The treatment was used on two children with a genetic autoimmune disorder, and the children are now adults leading normal lives. However, much of gene therapy is still experimental. For example, researchers are studying several methods to treat cancer with gene therapy. One experimental approach involves inserting a gene that stimulates a person's immune system to attack cancer cells. Another method is to insert "suicide" genes into cancer cells. These genes activate a drug inside those cells so that only the cancer cells are killed.

Gene therapy has many technical challenges. First, the correct gene has to be added to the correct cells. And even after researchers have figured out how to transfer the desired gene, the gene's expression has to be regulated so that it does not make too much or too little protein. Scientists must also determine if the new gene will affect other genes. The many trials have produced long-lasting positive results in only a few diseases. But because of its great potential, research on gene therapy continues.

Synthesize **How does gene therapy rely on genetic screening?**

---

**SELF-CHECK Online**
HMHScience.com
**GO ONLINE**

## 9.6 | Formative Assessment

### REVIEWING ▶ MAIN IDEAS

1. How does **genetic screening** use both old and new methods of studying human genetics?

2. Briefly describe the goals and methods of **gene therapy.**

### CRITICAL THINKING

3. **Compare and Contrast** How is gene therapy similar to, and different from, making a transgenic organism?

4. **Synthesize** How are restriction enzymes and recombinant DNA important for gene therapy?

### ⊙ CONNECT TO

**CELL SPECIALIZATION**

5. How is the type of cell into which a new gene is inserted important in gene therapy?

©John Scott Glass

CHAPTER

# 9 Summary

**BIG IDEA** Advances in biotechnology and the study of genomes allow scientists to manipulate DNA and combine the genes of multiple organisms, and may provide new medical treatments in the future.

## KEY CONCEPTS

### 9.1 Manipulating DNA

**Biotechnology relies on cutting DNA at specific places.** Bacterial enzymes called restriction enzymes are used to cut DNA. Each restriction enzyme cuts DNA at a specific DNA sequence. After DNA is cut with a restriction enzyme, the fragments of DNA can be separated using gel electrophoresis. A restriction map of the DNA is made based on the lengths of the fragments.

### 9.2 Copying DNA

**The polymerase chain reaction rapidly copies segments of DNA.** The polymerase chain reaction (PCR) is based on the process of DNA replication. By combining the DNA to be copied, DNA nucleotides, primers, and specific polymerase enzymes, a desired segment of DNA can be copied in the laboratory.

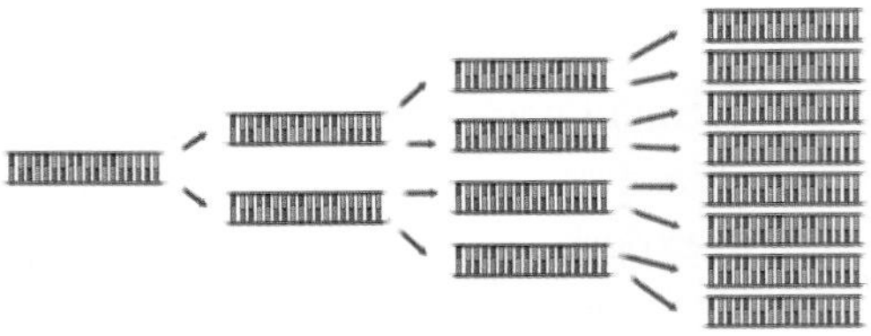

### 9.3 DNA Fingerprinting

**DNA fingerprints identify people at the molecular level.** DNA has many repeating base sequences. The number of repeats differs from person to person. DNA fingerprinting uses restriction enzymes and gel electrophoresis to detect these differences. By using DNA fingerprinting on several regions of DNA, one particular person can be identified.

### 9.4 Genetic Engineering

**DNA sequences of organisms can be changed.** Clones, or identical genetic copies, of many organisms can be made. Organisms can also be implanted with genes that give them new traits. Often, genes are inserted into plasmids to make recombinant DNA. Genetically engineered plasmids are inserted into bacteria, producing a transgenic organism. Transgenic bacteria, plants, and animals are used in many ways.

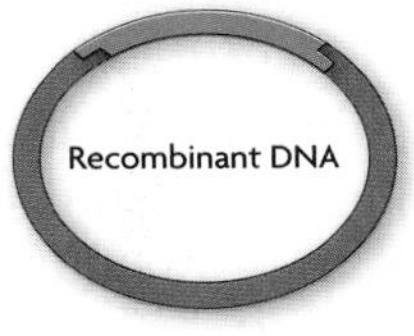


### 9.5 Genomics and Bioinformatics

**Entire genomes are sequenced, studied, and compared.** Through DNA sequencing, the genomes of several organisms, including humans, have been found and studied. Genomic data are organized and analyzed through bioinformatics. DNA microarrays are used to study interactions among genes in a genome. In addition, genomics has led to the study and comparison of proteins through proteomics.

### 9.6 Genetic Screening and Gene Therapy

**Genetics provides a basis for new medical treatments.** Genetic screening is used to test people for genes that are linked to genetic disorders. One method to correct these faulty genes or to replace missing genes is gene therapy. Gene therapy is experimental, but has the potential to cure many diseases.

## READING TOOLBOX SYNTHESIZE YOUR NOTES

**Two-Column Chart** Use your notes to make two-column charts for the processes described in the chapter. On one side of the chart, define and explain the process. On the other side, draw a sketch of the process

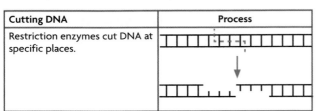

| Cutting DNA | Process |
|---|---|
| Restriction enzymes cut DNA at specific places. | 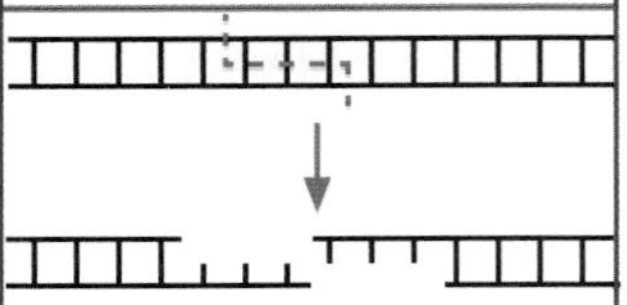 |

**Concept Map** Use concept maps like the one below to visualize the relationships among different biotechnologies.

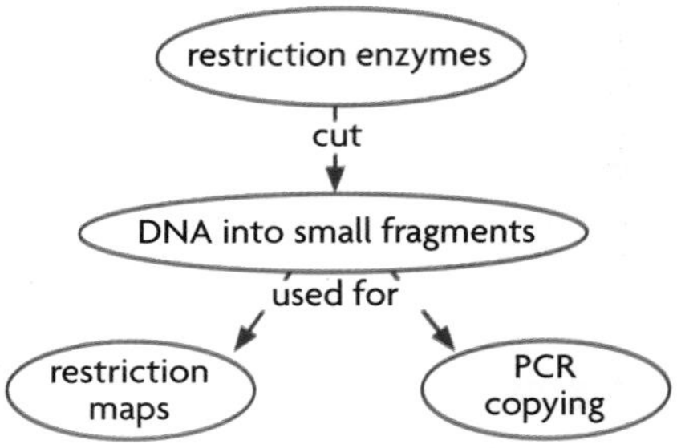

CHAPTER

9 Review

INTERACTIVE Review
HMHScience.com

GO ONLINE
Review Games • Concept Map • Section Self-Checks

## CHAPTER VOCABULARY

**9.1** restriction enzyme
gel electrophoresis
restriction map
**9.2** polymerase chain reaction (PCR)
primer

**9.3** DNA fingerprint
**9.4** clone
genetic engineering
recombinant DNA
plasmid
transgenic
gene knockout

**9.5** genomics
gene sequencing
Human Genome Project
bioinformatics
DNA microarray
proteomics
**9.6** genetic screening
gene therapy

## Reviewing Vocabulary

### Label Diagrams

In your science notebook, write the vocabulary term that matches each item that is pointed out below.

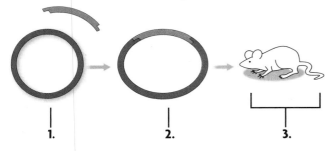

1. _____  2. _____  3. _____

### Keep It Short

For each vocabulary term below, write a short, precise phrase that describes its meaning. For example, a short phrase to describe *PCR* could be "DNA copying tool."

4. genetic screening
5. genomics
6. DNA fingerprint
7. clone

### READING TOOLBOX  WORD ORIGINS

8. The prefix *electro-* means "electricity." The suffix *-phoresis* means "transmission" or "carrying." How do these meanings relate to the meaning of the term *electrophoresis*?

9. The suffix *-ics* means "science or study of." What is studied in *genomics*? in *proteomics*? in *bioinformatics*?

## Reviewing MAIN IDEAS

10. Why can restriction enzymes be thought of as molecular "scissors"?

11. Explain what gel electrophoresis shows about DNA, and how it is used to separate DNA.

12. PCR requires DNA polymerase from bacteria that live in hot springs. Why can't DNA polymerase from organisms that live in cooler temperatures be used in PCR?

13. Briefly describe the three main steps of PCR.

14. What parts of DNA molecules are the basis of the differences detected by DNA fingerprinting?

15. Why is probability important in DNA fingerprinting?

16. What is the role of nuclear transfer in the process of cloning an animal?

17. Describe the general process used to make bacteria that have recombinant DNA. Include the terms *restriction enzyme* and *plasmid* in your answer.

18. How are gene knockout mice useful in determining the function of genes?

19. How does genomics rely on DNA sequencing?

20. Explain why computer databases are important in genomics and proteomics.

21. How are pedigree analysis and DNA testing used together in genetic screening?

22. What is gene therapy, and how might it be used as a treatment for cancer or for genetic disorders?

# Critical Thinking

23. **Analyze** How are DNA microarrays related to genomics?

24. **Compare and Contrast** How are restriction maps and DNA fingerprints similar? How are they different? Explain your answers.

25. **Compare and Contrast** A plant can send out a runner that will sprout a new plant that is a clone of the "parent." Single-celled organisms divide in two, forming two clones. How is the cloning of an animal similar to and different from the cloning that happens in nature?

26. **Synthesize** Some fruits and vegetables are the result of crossing different species. A tangelo, for example, results from crossing a tangerine with a grapefruit. How are the genetic engineering processes of making transgenic organisms similar to and different from crossbreeding?

27. **Apply** Identical twins are technically clones of each other but can differ in both appearance and behavior. How is it possible that two people with the same genome could be different?

28. **Synthesize** Transgenic bacteria can be used to make human insulin. Explain how bacteria can produce a human protein.

## Interpreting Visuals

The gel below shows two different restriction maps for the same segment of DNA. One of the maps is for a normal gene (N) and the other is for a disease gene (D). Use the information in the gel to answer the next two questions.

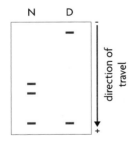

29. **Analyze** Which restriction map (N or D) has the smallest fragment of DNA? Which has the largest fragment? Explain your answers.

30. **Interpret** What do the restriction maps tell you about differences between a normal allele (N) and a disease (D) allele? Explain.

## Analyzing Data    Construct a Histogram

Ten of the most commonly modified crops include rice, potatoes, maize, papayas, tomatoes, corn, soybeans, wheat, alfalfa, and sugar cane. The histogram below shows how many times these crops have been modified. Among the 15 countries studied from 2001 through 2003, for example, different researchers modified rice a total of 37 times. Use the data to answer the next two questions.

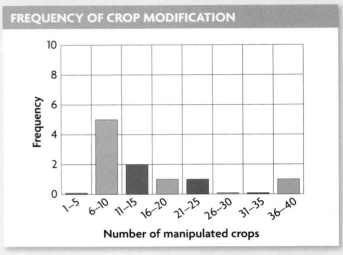

**FREQUENCY OF CROP MODIFICATION**

Source: Cohen, *Nature Biotechnology*, 23:1.

31. **Analyze** What is the most common range of genetic modifications for crop plants? The least common?

32. **Calculate** What percentage of crop types fall in the range of 11–15 genetic modifications?

## Making Connections

33. **Write an Informational Pamphlet** Suppose that you work for a biotechnology company that specializes in DNA fingerprinting to help reunite families that have been separated. Write a pamphlet that describes how DNA fingerprinting works. Explain why the results of DNA fingerprinting can be trusted.

34. **Synthesize** Look again at the picture of Baby 81 on the chapter opener. After reading this chapter, you know that DNA fingerprinting is just one part of biotechnology. Choose a topic from the chapter, such as genetic engineering or PCR. Discuss how that topic is related to Mendel's work on heredity, and how it is related to the structure and function of DNA.

**How could evolution lead to this?**

The star-nosed mole has a pink snout that is especially good at finding food. The snout's 22 fingerlike rays can touch up to 12 objects in just one second. The mole also uses strong paddle-shaped feet for burrowing, and its large ear openings give it excellent hearing. These special traits make up for its poor vision—which it doesn't really need underground.

---

 **READING TOOLBOX**  **This reading tool can help you learn the material in the following pages.**

### USING LANGUAGE

**Hypothesis or Theory?** In everyday language, there is little difference between a *hypothesis* and a *theory*. But in science, the meanings of these words are more distinct. A *hypothesis* is a specific, testable prediction for a limited set of conditions. A *theory* is a general explanation for a broad range of data. A theory can include hypotheses that have been tested and can also be used to generate new hypotheses. The strongest scientific theories explain the broadest range of data and incorporate many well-tested hypotheses.

### YOUR TURN

Use what you have learned about a hypothesis and a theory to answer the following questions.

1. List some scientific theories that you have heard of.
2. Make a simple concept map or Venn diagram to show the relationship between hypotheses and theories.
3. The word *theory* may also be used to describe general trends and areas of active investigation in a scientific field. In this context, what does the term *evolutionary theory* mean?

**Chapter 10:** Principles of Evolution  **285**

# 10.1 Early Ideas About Evolution

SC.912.N.1.3

SC.912.N.1.3 Recognize that the strength or usefulness of a scientific claim is evaluated through scientific argumentation, which depends on critical and logical thinking, and the active consideration of alternative scientific explanations to explain the data presented.

**KEY CONCEPT** **There were theories of biological and geologic change before Darwin.**

**MAIN IDEAS**
○ Early scientists proposed ideas about evolution.
○ Theories of geologic change set the stage for Darwin's theory.

**VOCABULARY**
- evolution
- species
- fossil
- catastrophism
- gradualism
- uniformitarianism

## Connect to Your World

Why are there so many kinds of living things, such as the strange looking star-nosed mole? Earth is home to millions of species, from bacteria to plants to ocean organisms that look like they came from science fiction. The search for reasons for Earth's great biological diversity was aided in the 1800s, when Charles Darwin proposed his theory of evolution by natural selection. But long before Darwin, evolution had been the focus of talk among scholars.

## ○ MAIN IDEA

## Early scientists proposed ideas about evolution.

Although Darwin rightly deserves much of the credit for evolutionary theory as we know it today, he was not the first person to come up with the idea. **Evolution** is the process of biological change by which descendants come to differ from their ancestors. This concept had been discussed for more than 100 years when Darwin proposed his theory of the way evolution works. Today, evolution is a central theme in all fields of biology.

The 1700s were a time of great advances in intellectual thought. Many fields of science developed new ways of looking at the world during that century. Four scientists in particular are important. They not only made valuable contributions to biology in general, but they also laid the foundations upon which Darwin would later build his ideas. **FIGURE 1.1** highlights the work of some of these early scientists.

**Carolus Linnaeus** In the 1700s, the Swedish botanist Carolus Linnaeus developed a classification system for all types of organisms known at the time. Although Linnaeus used his system to group organisms by their similarities, the system also reflects evolutionary relationships. This system is still in use by scientists today. Years into his career, Linnaeus abandoned the common belief of the time that organisms were fixed and did not change. He proposed instead that some might have arisen through hybridization—a crossing that he could observe through experiments with varieties, or species, of plants. A **species** is a group of organisms that are closely related and can mate to reproduce fertile offspring.

### READING TOOLBOX

**TAKING NOTES**
Create a chart with a column for the scientists mentioned in this section and a second column for their contributions to evolutionary theory.

| Scientist | Contribution |
|-----------|-------------|
| Linnaeus | |
| Buffon | |

**Georges-Louis Leclerc de Buffon**  Buffon, a French naturalist of the 1700s, challenged many of the accepted ideas of the day. Based on evidence of past life on Earth, he proposed that species shared ancestors instead of arising separately. Buffon also rejected the common idea of the time that Earth was only 6000 years old. He suggested that it was much older. This argument was similar to that of Charles Lyell, a geologist whose work helped inspire Darwin's writings. You will read more about Lyell later in this section.

**Erasmus Darwin**  Born in 1731, Charles Darwin's grandfather was a respected English doctor and a poet. He proposed that all living things were descended from a common ancestor and that more-complex forms of life arose from less-complex forms. This idea was expanded upon 65 years later by his grandson.

**Jean-Baptiste Lamarck**  In 1809, the year of Darwin's birth, a French naturalist named Lamarck proposed that all organisms evolved toward perfection and complexity. Like other scientists of the time, he did not think that species became extinct. Instead, he reasoned that they must have evolved into different forms.

Lamarck proposed that changes in an environment caused an organism's behavior to change, leading to greater use or disuse of a structure or organ. The structure would become larger or smaller as a result. The organism would pass on these changes to its offspring. For example, Lamarck thought that the long necks of giraffes evolved as generations of giraffes reached for leaves higher in the trees. Lamarck's idea is known as the inheritance of acquired characteristics.

CONNECT TO

**SCIENTIFIC PROCESS**
Recall from the chapter **Biology in the 21st Century** that in every scientific field, knowledge is built upon evidence gathered by earlier scientists.

## FIGURE 1.1  Early Naturalists

**Evolutionary thought, like all scientific inquiry, draws heavily upon its history. The published works of these scientists contributed important ideas prior to Darwin's theory.**

| 1735 *Systema Naturae* | 1749 *Histoire Naturelle* | 1794–1796 *Zoonomia* | 1809 *Philosophie Zoologique* |
|---|---|---|---|
| **Carolus Linnaeus** proposed a new system of organization for plants, animals, and minerals based upon their similarities. | **Georges Buffon** discussed important ideas about relationships among organisms, sources of biological variation, and the possibility of evolution. | **Erasmus Darwin** considered how organisms could evolve through mechanisms such as competition. | **Jean-Baptiste Lamarck** presented evolution as occurring due to environmental change over long periods of time. |
| 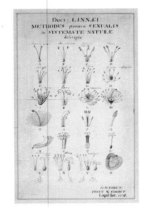 |  |  |  |

**Summarize**  Explain why Darwin was not the first scientist to consider evolution.

Lamarck did not propose how traits were passed on to offspring, and his explanation of how organisms evolve was flawed. However, Darwin was influenced by Lamarck's ideas that changes in physical characteristics could be inherited and were driven by environmental changes over time.

**Compare** **What common idea about organisms did these scientists share?**

### ▶ MAIN IDEA
## Theories of geologic change set the stage for Darwin's theory.

The age of Earth was a key issue in the early debates over evolution. The common view was that Earth was created about 6000 years earlier, and that since that time, neither Earth nor the species that lived on it had changed.

French zoologist Georges Cuvier did not think that species could change. However, he did think that they could become extinct, an idea considered radical by many of his peers. Cuvier had observed that each stratum, or rock layer, held its own specific type of fossils. **Fossils** are traces of organisms that existed in the past. He found that the fossils in the deepest layers were quite different from those in the upper layers, which were formed by more recent deposits of sediment. Cuvier explained his observations in the early 1800s with the theory now known as catastrophism, shown in **FIGURE 1.2.**

**⁑ CONNECT TO**

**EARTH SCIENCE**

Cuvier based his thinking on what we know as the law of superposition. It states that in a sequence of layered rocks, a given layer was deposited before any layer above it.

### FIGURE 1.2 Principles of Geologic Change

**Ideas from geology played a role in the development of Darwin's theory.**

| CATASTROPHISM | GRADUALISM | UNIFORMITARIANISM |
|---|---|---|
| Volcanoes, floods, and earthquakes are examples of catastrophic events that were once believed responsible for mass extinctions and the formation of all landforms. | Canyons carved by rivers show gradual change. Gradualism is the idea that changes on Earth occurred by small steps over long periods of time. | Rock strata demonstrate that geologic processes, which are still occurring today, add up over long periods of time to cause great change. |

**Compare and Contrast** **How are these three theories similar, and what are their differences?**

The theory of **catastrophism** (kuh-TAS-truh-FIHZ-uhm) states that natural disasters such as floods and volcanic eruptions have happened often during Earth's long history. These events shaped landforms and caused species to become extinct in the process. Cuvier argued that the appearance of new species in each rock layer resulted from other species moving into the area from elsewhere after each catastrophic event.

In the late 1700s, the Scottish geologist James Hutton proposed that the changes he observed in landforms resulted from slow changes over a long period of time, a principle that became known as **gradualism** (GRAJ-oo-uh-LIHZ-uhm). He argued that the laying down of soil or the creation of canyons by rivers cutting through rock was not the result of large-scale events. He believed, rather, that they resulted from slow processes that had happened in the past. This idea has become so important to evolution that today the term gradualism is often used to mean the gradual change of a species through evolution.

One of the leading supporters of the argument for an ancient Earth was the English geologist Charles Lyell. In *Principles of Geology*, published in the 1830s, Lyell expanded Hutton's theory of gradualism into the theory of **uniformitarianism** (YOO-nuh-FAWR-mih-TAIR-ee-uh-NIHZ-uhm). This theory states that the geologic processes that shape Earth are uniform through time. Lyell observed processes that made small changes in Earth's features. He inferred that similar changes had happened in the past. Uniformitarianism combines Hutton's idea of gradual change over time with Lyell's observations that such changes have occurred at a constant rate and are ongoing. Uniformitarianism soon replaced catastrophism as the favored theory of geologic change. Lyell's theory greatly affected the scientific community—particularly a young English naturalist named Charles Darwin.

**Compare** What important concepts about Earth did Hutton and Lyell agree upon?

**READING** TOOLBOX

**VOCABULARY**
The names of these geologic theories can be broken down into familiar words.
- *Catastrophe* means "sudden disaster."
- *Gradual* means "moving or changing slowly."
- *Uniform* means "always staying the same."

**VISUAL VOCAB**

**Uniformitarianism** proposes that present geologic processes are the key to the past.

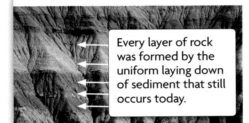

Every layer of rock was formed by the uniform laying down of sediment that still occurs today.

**CONNECT TO**

**SCIENTIFIC PROCESS**
Recall from the chapter **Biology in the 21st Century** that in science, the term theory describes a well-supported explanation that incorporates observations, inferences, and tested hypotheses.

---

## 10.1 Formative Assessment

**SELF-CHECK Online**
HMHScience.com
**GO ONLINE**

### REVIEWING ● MAIN IDEAS

1. Briefly describe two ideas about **evolution** that were proposed by scientists in the 18th century.

2. What ideas in Lyell's theory of **uniformitarianism** were important for evolutionary theory?

### CRITICAL THINKING

3. **Contrast** What are the key differences between the theories of **gradualism** and **catastrophism**?

4. **Apply** Why are the ideas that Earth undergoes change and is billions of years old important for evolutionary theory?

**CONNECT TO**

**GENETICS**

5. How can you use the concept of genetic inheritance to disprove Lamarck's idea of the inheritance of acquired characteristics?

# 10.2 Darwin's Observations

SC.912.N.1.6,
SC.912.L.15.15

| KEY CONCEPT **Darwin's voyage provided insights into evolution.**

**MAIN IDEAS**

- ◯ Darwin observed differences in appearance among island species.
- ◯ Darwin observed fossil and geologic evidence supporting an ancient Earth.

**VOCABULARY**

variation
adaptation

**SC.912.N.1.6** Describe how scientific inferences are drawn from scientific observations and provide examples from the content being studied.

**SC.912.L.15.15** Describe how mutation and genetic recombination increase genetic variation.

### Connect to Your World

Maybe you would love the chance to sail around the world. Or maybe just the thought of it makes you seasick! In 1831, the ship HMS *Beagle* set sail from England on a five-year journey to map the coast of South America and the Pacific islands. Hired at first to keep the captain company, Darwin was interested in observing the land and its inhabitants. During the voyage, he read Lyell's *Principles of Geology*. When the ship reached South America, Darwin spent most of his time ashore, where he found much evidence supporting Lyell's views.

### ◯ MAIN IDEA

## Darwin observed differences in appearance among island species.

Darwin, shown in **FIGURE 2.1,** was struck by the variation of traits among similar species that he observed in all his travels. In biology, **variation** is the difference in the physical traits of an individual from those of other individuals in the group to which it belongs. Variation can occur either among members of different species (*inter*specific variation) or among individuals of the same species (*intra*specific variation). Darwin noted that the species found on one island looked different from those on nearby islands and that many of the islands' species looked different from those on the nearest mainland.

The differences between species on different islands was especially noticeable in the Galápagos Islands, an island chain off the coast of Ecuador in South America. Some differences seemed well suited to the animals' environments and diets, as shown in **FIGURE 2.2.** For example, saddle-backed tortoises, which have long necks and legs, lived in areas with a lot of tall plants. Domed tortoises, with their shorter necks and legs, lived in wet areas rich in mosses and short plants. Similarly, finches with strong, thick beaks lived in areas with a lot of large, hard-shelled nuts, while those species of finch with more delicate beaks were found where insects or fruits were widely available.

These observations led Darwin to realize that species may somehow be able to adapt to their surroundings. An **adaptation** is a feature that allows an organism to better survive and reproduce in its environment. Adaptations can lead to genetic change in a population over time.

**Connect** **What adaptations did Darwin see in the finches of the Galápagos Islands?**

**FIGURE 2.1** Darwin spent more than 20 years compiling evidence before publishing in 1859 his ideas on how evolution works.

©The Granger Collection, New York

## FIGURE 2.2 Adaptations Within Species

Galápagos tortoises (*Geochelone elephantopus*) are evidence that species can adapt to their environments.

Domed tortoises have a short neck and short legs, and live in areas with low vegetation.

Saddle-backed tortoises have a high shell edge, allowing them to stretch their long necks.

Galápagos Islands

**Explain** Why do these tortoises of the same species look different?

▶ MAIN IDEA

# Darwin observed fossil and geologic evidence supporting an ancient Earth.

On his voyage, Darwin found fossil evidence of species changing over time. In Argentina, he found fossils of huge animals, such as *Glyptodon,* a giant armadillo. The fact that these fossils looked like living species suggested that modern animals might have some relationship to fossil forms. These fossils suggested that, in order for such changes to occur, Earth must be much more than 6000 years old.

During his voyage, Darwin also found fossil shells of marine organisms high up in the Andes mountains. Darwin later experienced an earthquake during his voyage and saw firsthand the result: land that had been underwater was moved above sea level. This experience explained what he saw in the Andes. Darwin's observations on his voyage supported Lyell's theory that daily geologic processes can add up to great change over a long period of time. Darwin later extended the ideas of an old Earth and slow, gradual change to the evolution of organisms. This became known as evolutionary gradualism.

**Infer** What could account for fossils of marine organisms being found on top of modern-day mountain ranges?

**SELF-CHECK** Online
HMHScience.com
GO ONLINE

## 10.2 Formative Assessment

### REVIEWING ▶ MAIN IDEAS

1. What accounts for the **variation** Darwin observed among island species?

2. What did Darwin learn from the fossils that he observed on his voyage?

### CRITICAL THINKING

3. **Apply** Explain how wings are an **adaptation** for birds.

4. **Synthesize** How did Darwin's observations support Lyell's theory of an ancient Earth undergoing continual geologic change?

### ✴ CONNECT TO

### ECOLOGY

5. Some birds in the Galápagos Islands build nests in trees, while others hide eggs in rock crevices. What could account for this difference in nesting behaviors?

# 10.3 Theory of Natural Selection

SC.912.L.15.13

**KEY CONCEPT** Darwin proposed natural selection as a mechanism for evolution.

**MAIN IDEAS**

- Several key insights led to Darwin's idea for natural selection.
- Natural selection explains how evolution can occur.
- Natural selection acts on existing variation.

**VOCABULARY**

artificial selection
heritability
natural selection
population
fitness

**SC.912.L.15.13** Describe the conditions required for natural selection, including: overproduction of offspring, inherited variation, and the struggle to survive, which result in differential reproductive success.

## Connect to Your World

Have you ever had an experience that changed your outlook or your opinion about an issue? Darwin began his voyage thinking that species could not change. However, his experiences during the five-year journey changed the way he thought about life and evolution. He became convinced that evolution occurs. But he had yet to determine how it could happen.

### ▶ MAIN IDEA

## Several key insights led to Darwin's idea for natural selection.

After his voyage, Darwin spent more than 20 years conducting research while thinking about the way evolution occurs. Although he had traveled the world, Darwin also found great insight in his home country of England. One important influence on Darwin's research was the work of farmers and breeders.

### Artificial Selection

Darwin noticed a lot of variation in domesticated plants and animals. The populations of domesticated species seemed to show variation in traits that were not shown in their wild relatives. Through selection of certain traits, breeders could produce a great amount of diversity. The process by which humans change a species by breeding it for certain traits is called **artificial selection.** In this process, humans make use of the genetic variation in plants and animals by acting as the selective agent. That is, humans determine which traits are favorable and then breed individuals that show those traits.

To explore this idea, Darwin turned to the hobby of breeding pigeons. Although Darwin had no knowledge of genetics, he had noticed certain traits being selected in animals such as livestock and pets. For thousands of years, humans had been breeding pigeons that showed many different traits, such as those in **FIGURE 3.1**. In order for artificial—or natural—selection to occur, the trait must be heritable. **Heritability** (HER-ih-tuh-BIHL-uh-tee) is the ability of a trait to be passed down from one generation to the next.

Darwin compared what he learned about breeding to his ideas on adaptation. In artificial selection, features such as reversed neck feathers, large crops, or extra tail feathers are favored over generations only if these traits are liked by breeders. However, breeders might also select against features that are not desirable or "useful." During artificial selection, humans act as the selective agent. In nature, however, the environment creates the selective pressure that determines if a trait is passed on or not.

Darwin used this line of thinking for his theory of natural selection. **Natural selection** is a mechanism by which individuals that have inherited beneficial adaptations show differential reproductive success. In other words—they tend to produce more offspring on average than do other individuals. In nature, the environment is the selective agent. Therefore, in nature, characteristics are selected only if they give advantages to individuals in the environment as it is right now. Furthermore, Darwin reasoned, desirable breeds are not produced immediately. He knew that it sometimes took many generations for breeders to produce the varieties he had observed.

## Struggle for Survival

Another important idea came from English economist Thomas Malthus. Malthus had proposed that resources such as food, water, and shelter were natural limits to population growth. That is, human populations would grow geometrically if resources were unlimited. Instead, disease and a limited food

**FIGURE 3.1 Artificial Selection of Pigeon Traits**

For thousands of years, new varieties of organisms, such as pigeons, have resulted from selective breeding for particular traits.

neck feathers

crop

tail feathers

SELECTIVELY BRED PIGEONS

Jacobins are bred for their reversed neck feathers.

Croppers are bred for their inflatable crop.

Fantails are bred to have many tail feathers.

**Connect** What other species of organisms are often subjects of artificial selection?

**READING** TOOLBOX

**VOCABULARY**
The term *descent* is used in evolution to mean the passing of genetic information from generation to generation.

supply kept the population smaller. Darwin reasoned that a similar struggle took place in nature. If resources are limited and organisms have more offspring than could survive, why do some individuals, and not others, survive?

Darwin found his answer in the variation he had seen within populations. A **population** is all the individuals of a species that live in an area. Darwin had noticed in the Galápagos Islands that in any population, such as the tortoises or the finches, some individuals had variations that were particularly well-suited to their environment. He proposed that these adaptations arose over many generations. Darwin called this process of evolution "descent with modification."

**Explain   How did Malthus's economic theory influence Darwin?**

## ▶ MAIN IDEA
# Natural selection explains how evolution can occur.

Charles Darwin was not the only person to develop a theory to explain how evolution may take place. An English naturalist named Alfred Russel Wallace independently developed a theory very similar to Darwin's. Both Darwin and Wallace had studied the huge diversity of plants and animals in the tropics, and both had studied the fossil record. In 1858, the ideas of Darwin and Wallace were presented to an important group of scientists in London. The next year, Darwin published his ideas in the book *On the Origin of Species by Means of Natural Selection.*

There are four main principles to the theory of natural selection: variation, overproduction, adaptation, and descent with modification.

**READING** TOOLBOX

**TAKING NOTES**
Write a sentence in your own words that summarizes each of the four principles of natural selection.

| variation |
| overproduction |
| adaptation |
| descent with modification |

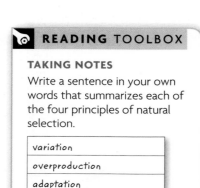

- **Variation**  The heritable differences, or variations, that exist in every population are the basis for natural selection. The differences among individuals result from differences in the genetic material of the organisms, whether inherited from a parent or resulting from a genetic mutation.
- **Overproduction**  While having many offspring raises the chance that some will survive, it also results in competition between offspring for resources.
- **Adaptation**  Sometimes a certain variation allows an individual to survive better than other individuals it competes against in its environment. More successful individuals are "naturally selected" to live longer and to produce more offspring that share those adaptations for their environment.
- **Descent with modification**  Over time, natural selection will result in species with adaptations that are well suited for survival and reproduction in an environment. More individuals will have the trait in every following generation, as long as the environmental conditions continue to remain beneficial for that trait.

A well-studied example of natural selection in jaguars is shown in **FIGURE 3.2.** About 11,000 years ago, many species faced extinction. Large cats, including jaguars, faced a shortage of food due to the changing climate of that time. There were fewer mammals to eat, so the jaguars had to eat reptiles. In the jaguar population, there were variations of jaw and tooth size that became important for survival. Like many other species, jaguars can produce more offspring than can be supported by the environment. Jaguars with the biggest jaws and teeth could prey more easily on the shelled reptiles. Because jaw size and tooth size are heritable traits and were beneficial, large jaws and teeth became adaptations for this population. The jaguars' descendants showed modifications, or changes, over time.

In biology, the term **fitness** is a measure of the ability to survive and produce more offspring relative to other members of the population in a given environment. After the change in climate, jaguars that had larger teeth and jaws had a higher fitness than other jaguars in the population. Jaguars that ate less didn't necessarily all die or stop producing altogether; they just reproduced a little less. Today, large teeth and jaws are considered typical traits of jaguars.

**READING TOOLBOX**

**VOCABULARY**

In everyday language, *fitness* means "physically fit." In biology, however, fitness is related to reproductive success.

**Compare and Contrast** What are the similarities and differences between natural selection and artificial selection?

## FIGURE 3.2 The Principles of Natural Selection

**Animated**
**Biology**
HMHScience.com

**GO ONLINE**

Principles of Natural Selection

Certain traits become more common in a population through the process of natural selection.

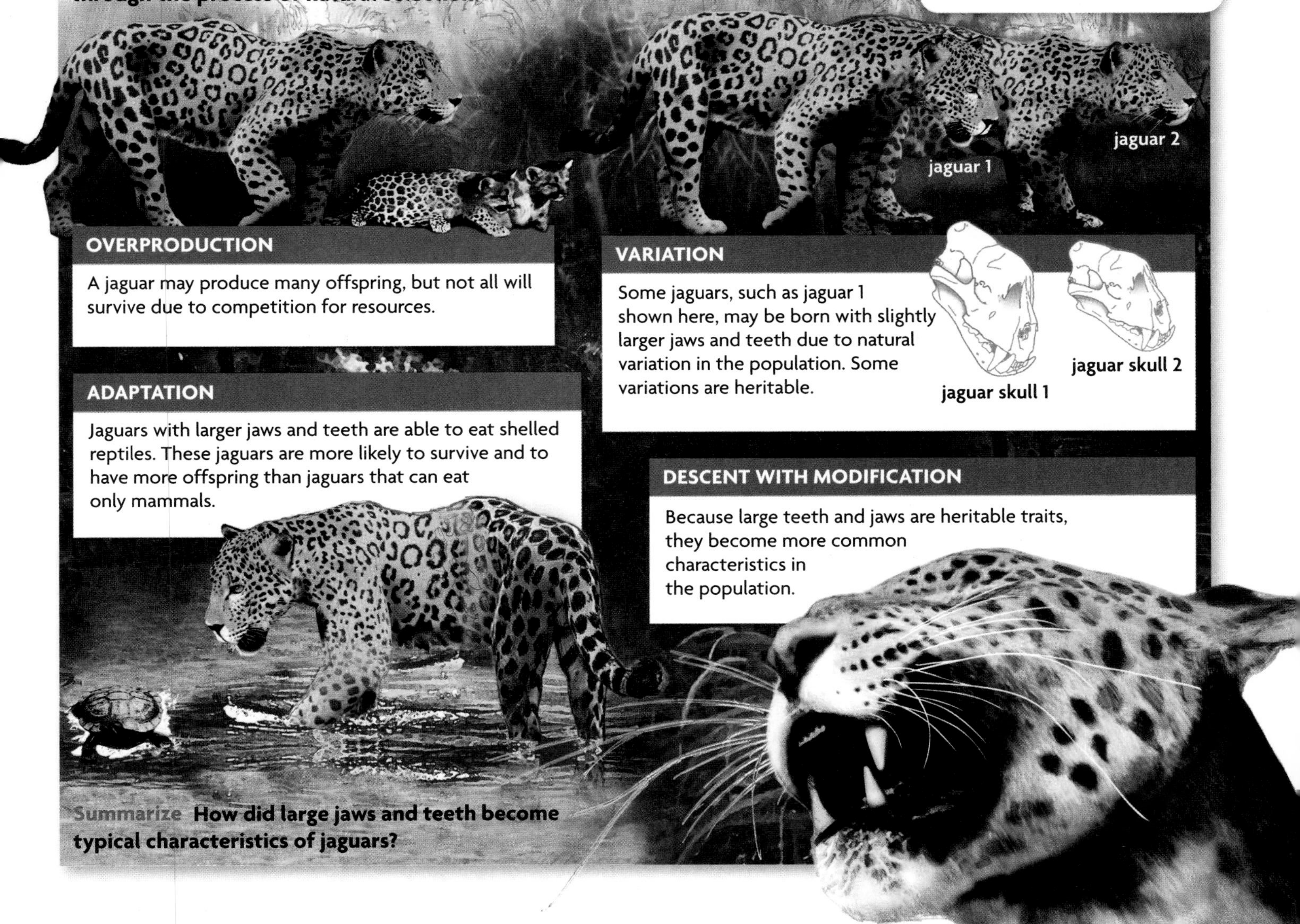

jaguar 1

jaguar 2

**OVERPRODUCTION**

A jaguar may produce many offspring, but not all will survive due to competition for resources.

**VARIATION**

Some jaguars, such as jaguar 1 shown here, may be born with slightly larger jaws and teeth due to natural variation in the population. Some variations are heritable.

jaguar skull 1    jaguar skull 2

**ADAPTATION**

Jaguars with larger jaws and teeth are able to eat shelled reptiles. These jaguars are more likely to survive and to have more offspring than jaguars that can eat only mammals.

**DESCENT WITH MODIFICATION**

Because large teeth and jaws are heritable traits, they become more common characteristics in the population.

Summarize How did large jaws and teeth become typical characteristics of jaguars?

## INTERPRETING LINE GRAPHS

Scientists used mice to study whether exercise ability can improve in animals over several generations. In this experiment, mice were artificially selected for increased wheel-running behavior. The mice that were able to do the most wheel running were selected to breed the next generation. The control group represents generations of mice that were allowed to breed randomly.

- The *x*-axis shows different generations of mice, from Generation 1 to Generation 9.
- The *y*-axis shows the number of revolutions the mice ran on the wheel per day.
- The solid blue line represents the control group, in which generations of mice were allowed to breed randomly.
- The dotted orange line represents the generations of mice that were artificially selected based on their wheel-running ability. This is the experimental group.

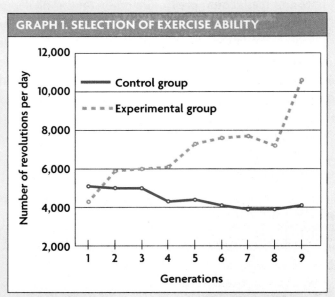

GRAPH 1. SELECTION OF EXERCISE ABILITY

Source: Swallow et. al, *Behavior Genetics* 28:3.

1. **Interpret** What is the difference in results between the mice in the control group and the mice in the experimental group?

2. **Predict** Use the trend in the data to make a general prediction about the number of revolutions on the wheel per day for mice in Generation 10 of the experimental group.

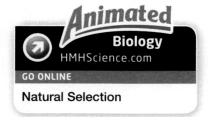

**Animated**
**Biology**
HMHScience.com

GO ONLINE

Natural Selection

○ **MAIN IDEA**

# Natural selection acts on existing variation.

Natural selection acts on phenotypes, or physical traits, rather than on genetic material itself. New alleles are not made by natural selection—they occur by genetic mutations. Natural selection can act only on traits that already exist.

## Changing Environments

Ecologists Peter and Rosemary Grant observed an example of natural selection acting on existing traits within a population of medium ground finches on one of the Galápagos Islands. A drought in 1977 suddenly reduced the amount of small, soft seeds that the finches preferred. However, there were still plenty of large, tough-shelled seeds. Because the large-beaked finches in the population were able to crack the large, tough seeds, they did not starve. The next year, the Grants noted a big increase of large-beaked hatchlings. In contrast, most of the finches with small beaks had died.

Darwin's theory predicted exactly what the Grants observed. A trait that was already in the population became favorable for survival because of a change in the environment, and thus was passed on to future generations.

As an environment changes, different traits will become beneficial. The numbers of large-beaked finches on this Galápagos Island kept rising until 1984, when the supply of large seeds went down after an unusually wet period. These conditions favored production of small, soft seeds and small-beaked birds. With evolution, a trait that is an advantage today may be a disadvantage in the future.

## Adaptations as Compromises

One mistake people make about natural selection is to think that adaptive characteristics passed down over a long time result in individuals that are perfectly suited to their surroundings. This is not the case. For example, some structures may take on new functions. Pandas have a structure in their wrist that acts like a thumb. As pandas eat bamboo shoots, they hold the shoots as you would hold a carrot. However, a close look at the paw reveals that it has six digits: five digits that resemble your fingers, plus a small thumblike structure. The panda's "thumb," shown in **FIGURE 3.3**, is actually an enlarged wrist bone. The ancestors of today's pandas had five full digits like today's bears, but those early pandas with bigger wrist bones had an advantage in eating bamboo. Because of its size and position, this bone functions like a human thumb. It is not considered a true thumb, because it does not have separate bones and joints as a human thumb does. It is also not a typical wrist bone, as the bone is clearly longer than needed to function for the wrist. Instead, it functions both as a wrist bone and a thumb.

five digits    wrist bone

**FIGURE 3.3** A panda's wrist bone also functions like a thumb.

**Explain** **Why is the panda's "thumb" considered an adaptive compromise?**

## 10.3 Formative Assessment

**SELF-CHECK** Online
HMHScience.com
**GO ONLINE**

### REVIEWING ▶ MAIN IDEAS

1. What did Darwin hope to learn about **artificial selection** by studying pigeons?

2. What are the four principles of **natural selection**?

3. Why must there be variation in the **population** in order for natural selection to occur?

### CRITICAL THINKING

4. **Evaluate** Explain why there was an increase in large-beaked finch hatchlings following a drought that left a finite amount of the small, soft seeds the birds preferred.

5. **Synthesize** Why is it said that natural selection acts on phenotypes rather than on the genetic material of organisms?

### CONNECT TO

#### ECOLOGY

6. You have learned that the environment affects how organisms change over generations. How would you explain a species that remains the same for millions of years?

(tr) ©AP/Wide World Photos; (br) ©Keren Su/Corbis

# Evidence of Evolution

SC.912.L.15.1

## KEY CONCEPT   Evidence of common ancestry among species comes from many sources.

**MAIN IDEAS**

- Evidence for evolution in Darwin's time came from several sources.
- Structural patterns are clues to the history of a species.

**SC.912.L.15.1** Explain how the scientific theory of evolution is supported by the fossil record, comparative anatomy, comparative embryology, biogeography, molecular biology, and observed evolutionary change.

### Connect to Your World

Whenever you need to complete an assignment on an unfamiliar topic, you first need to gather information. The different pieces of information might come from the library, the Internet, your teachers, or maybe even your friends. Together, all these pieces help you to understand the topic. Darwin also drew information from many sources, all of which helped to strengthen his understanding of evolution.

## ▶ MAIN IDEA

## Evidence for evolution in Darwin's time came from several sources.

Darwin found evidence from a wide range of sources to support his argument for evolution. The most important and convincing support came from fossils, geography, developmental similarities, and anatomy.

### Fossils

Even before Darwin, scholars studying fossils knew that organisms changed over time. Scientists who study fossils focus on more than just the fossil itself. They also think about its age, its location, and what the environment was like when the organism it came from was alive.

In the late 1700s, geologists wondered why certain types of fossils were found in some layers of rock and not others. Later studies suggested that the fossil organisms in the bottom, or older, layers were more primitive than those in the upper, or newer, layers. Geologists during this time were mostly interested in the order in which fossils were found within rock strata as a record of natural events such as earthquakes, not as proof of evolution. However, the sequential nature of fossil groups and other findings in the fossil record supported Darwin's concept of descent with modification.

### Geography

Recall that during the *Beagle* expedition Darwin saw that island plants and animals looked like, but were not identical to, species on the South American continent. He extended this observation, proposing that island species most closely resemble species on the nearest mainland.

**FIGURE 4.1** This trilobite, an early marine invertebrate that is now extinct, was found in this loose rock bed in Ohio. Although far from modern-day oceans, this site is actually the floor of an ancient sea.

(both) ©AP/Wide World Photos

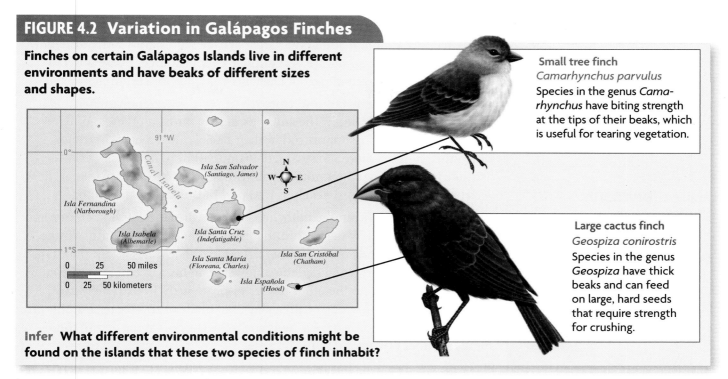

## FIGURE 4.2 Variation in Galápagos Finches

Finches on certain Galápagos Islands live in different environments and have beaks of different sizes and shapes.

**Small tree finch**
*Camarhynchus parvulus*
Species in the genus *Camarhynchus* have biting strength at the tips of their beaks, which is useful for tearing vegetation.

**Large cactus finch**
*Geospiza conirostris*
Species in the genus *Geospiza* have thick beaks and can feed on large, hard seeds that require strength for crushing.

**Infer** What different environmental conditions might be found on the islands that these two species of finch inhabit?

Darwin hypothesized that at some point in the past, some individuals from the South American mainland had migrated to the islands. This relationship between island and mainland species is today an important principle of **biogeography**, the study of the distribution of organisms around the world.

Different ecosystems on each island—with different plants, climates, and predators—had favored different traits in these migrants. Over time, these new traits became well established in the separate island populations, since the islands were too far apart for mating to occur.

One clear example of local adaptation is found in what are now known as Darwin's finches. The finches from the Galápagos Islands, shown in **FIGURE 4.2,** have distinct-looking beaks, as well as different habits, diets, and behaviors that evolved after generations of adaptation to specific island habitats. However, they all share a common ancestor from the South American mainland.

Since Darwin's time, the same pattern of evolution on islands has been studied in many living things, such as fruit flies and honeycreepers found among the Hawaiian Islands. A 2011 study analyzing DNA from all living species of Hawaiian honeycreepers indicated that they are all likely descended from a population of rosefinches that arrived in Hawaii from Asia sometime between 7.2 million and 5.8 million years ago. The evidence from this study also indicated that nearly all species of honeycreepers likely diverged between 5.8 million and 2.4 million years ago, the same period during which the island of Oahu first appeared. Like the honeycreepers, most species of plants and animals on the Hawaiian Islands are not found anywhere else on Earth, and the age of these species is close to the age of the islands on which they live.

## Developmental Similarities

A study proposing a relationship between barnacles, which are fixed in place as adults, and crabs, which are mobile at all stages in their life cycles, fascinated Darwin. Darwin collected specimens of barnacles over many years of research.

In making his observations of these crustaceans, he noticed, as shown in **FIGURE 4.3**, that although adult crabs and barnacles are significantly different, their free-swimming larvae are very similar in appearance. These observations formed an important part of Darwin's evidence for common descent.

**Notochord** In the same fashion, embryos of vertebrates share many similar characteristics. For example, the embryos of fish, birds, reptiles, and mammals all have a flexible support rod in their backs called a notochord, for which the phylum Chordata is named. Primitive chordates, such as the fish-like lancelet, keep their notochords throughout their lives, while in the vertebrates, the notochord develops into part of the vertebral column.

**Dorsal nerve cord** Within the notochord of both the lancelets and embryonic vertebrates lies a hollow nerve cord that runs along the dorsal, or back side, of the animal and extends into a flexible tail. Many vertebrates retain their tails as they develop a bony axial skeleton. However, in human embryos, the tail is generally absorbed into the other tissues prior to birth. In extremely rare cases, human babies are born with a short tail made of soft tissue, but the vast majority of humans only have a "tailbone" (the coccyx) at the end of the spine that does not extend to the outside.

**Pharyngeal arches** All chordate embryos have six structures known as pharyngeal arches, separated by slits. The upper arches develop into structures of the face, ears, and jaws. In adult fish, the two lower arches become the gills. However, in humans, the fifth arch disappears and the third, fourth, and sixth arches develop into the nerves, bones, and other structures of the throat.

The similarity of features in vertebrate embryos, shown in **FIGURE 4.4**, has been the subject of controversy since the late 1800s, when *Natural History of Creation (Natürliche Schöpfungsgeschichte)* was published by German scientist Ernst Haeckel. A great follower of Darwin's theory, Haeckel maintained that

**CONNECT TO**

**ANIMAL DIVERSITY**

Refer to sections 1 and 2 of the chapter **Invertebrate Diversity** to find out more about how members of the animal kingdom are alike and different.

**FIGURE 4.3** Although adult crabs and barnacles look and behave very differently, they can look very similar as larvae. This suggested to Darwin that they share a common ancestor.

Larva

Adult crab

Adult barnacles

the stages of development found in vertebrate embryos reflected the stages of evolution for each of those organisms. This became known as the recapitulation theory and was stated as "ontogeny recapitulates phylogeny."

His book and its accompanying drawings, which were borrowed and adapted from vertebrate anatomy experts of the time, immediately drew criticism from those who disputed evolutionary theory. Despite this, for many years, Haeckel's drawings commonly appeared in textbooks throughout the world. When photography became more widely used, some scientists pointed out discrepancies in size and scale between Haeckel's drawings and photographs. Other scientists argued that Haeckel openly stated in the captions of his drawings that he deliberately reduced them to similar sizes to enable observers to make comparisons. Although Haeckel revised and added new evidence with each of the five editions of his book, his reputation never recovered from the accusations of fraud. His recapitulation theory is no longer under serious consideration by scientists.

With today's technology, scientists have shown that all vertebrates have a set of very similar genes that direct the development of body structures from a basic body plan. These genes, the *Hox* genes, are discussed in more detail in the chapter Invertebrate Diversity. Evidence such as this suggests that vertebrates and other organisms evolved from distant common ancestors.

**Evaluate** What aspects of Ernst Haeckel's book led to criticism by his peers?

## FIGURE 4.4 Developmental Homologies

**Although humans, pigs, and chickens appear different from each other as adults, several of the same structures can be seen at various stages in their developing embryos.**

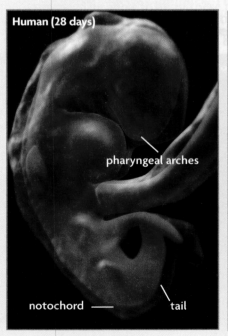
Human (28 days)
pharyngeal arches
notochord —— tail

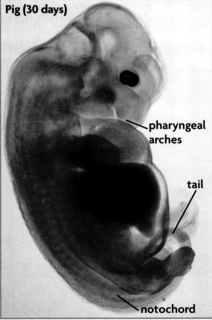
Pig (30 days)
pharyngeal arches
tail
notochord

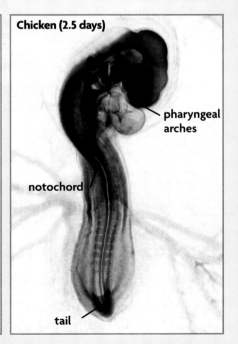
Chicken (2.5 days)
pharyngeal arches
notochord
tail

**Analyze** How would these similar structures provide evidence of a common vertebrate ancestor?

**WebQuest**

HMHScience.com

GO ONLINE

Dinosaur Descendants

**READING TOOLBOX**

**VOCABULARY**

A tetrapod is a four-limbed animal. *Tetra-* means "four," and *-pod* means "foot."

## Anatomy

Some of Darwin's best evidence came from comparing the body parts of different species. Chief among such evidence were homologous structures. **Homologous structures** (huh-MAHL-uh-guhs) are features that are similar in structure but appear in different organisms and have different functions. Their appearance across different species offers strong evidence for common descent. It would be unlikely for many species to have such similar anatomy if each species evolved independently.

The most common examples of homologous structures are the forelimbs of tetrapod vertebrates. The forelimbs of humans, bats, and moles are compared in **FIGURE 4.5.** In all of these animals, and indeed in every tetrapod, the forelimbs have several bones that are very similar to each other despite their different functions. Notice also how the same bones vary in different animals. In addition to this, all tetrapods, including birds, will have five digits on their limbs at some point in their development. Homologous structures are different in detail but similar in structure and relation to each other.

In using homologous structures as evidence of evolution, Darwin posed a logical question: If each of these groups descended from a different ancestor, why would they share these homologous structures? A simple answer is that they share a common ancestor.

The idea of common descent provides a logical explanation for how homologous structures appeared in diverse groups. Having similar structures doesn't always mean two species are closely related, however. Some structures found in different species have the same functions but did not evolve from a common ancestor.

## FIGURE 4.5 Homologous Structures

**Homologous structures, though they often have differing functions, are the result of a common ancestor.**

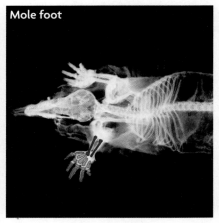

Human hand

Bat wing

Mole foot

Notice that each of these homologous structures uses the same bones in relation to the others.

**Apply** **What body part of a dolphin is homologous to the structures shown above?**

Suppose two organisms have similar needs caused by the environment. For example, two different organisms benefit from the ability to fly. Both can develop similar adaptations using different body parts. Think about the wings of bats and the wings of flying insects. Clearly these organisms differ in more ways than they are similar. Insects are arthropods, while bats are mammals. The wings of bats and insects are called analogous structures, as shown in **FIGURE 4.6. Analogous structures** (uh-NAL-uh-guhs) are structures that perform a similar function—in this case, flight—but are not similar in origin. This means that in each of the organisms, the analogous structures did not derive from the same original structure. Bat wings, when examined closely, have the same bone structure as an elongated hand, connected by thin skin. In contrast, insect wings do not have bones, only membranes that are supported by a series of long veins with cross-connections for strength. The similar function of wings in bats and flying insects evolved separately. Their ancestors faced similar environmental challenges and evolved similar adaptations to overcome those challenges.

**FIGURE 4.6 ANALOGOUS STRUCTURES**

Analogous structures evolved separately and are not evidence of a common ancestor. Bat wings and insect wings are derived from different structures.

**Analyze** Using the terms *homologous* and *analogous,* identify which group of structures provides evidence for a common ancestor. Explain.

## QUICKLAB    INFERRING

### Piecing Together Evidence

Evolutionary biologists and paleontologists rarely get all of the pieces of what they are studying. In this activity, you will receive pieces of "evidence" about a picture in order to make observations, inferences, and predictions about it.

**PROBLEM** How are inferences modified when new information is obtained?

**MATERIALS**
picture cut into strips

**PROCEDURE**

1. Using the three strips that your teacher has provided, write down all observations and inferences that you can make about this picture.

2. Make a prediction about the picture's topic, using your observations as supporting evidence for your prediction.

3. Record observations, inferences, and a prediction for each remaining strip of "evidence" that you receive from your teacher.

**ANALYZE AND CONCLUDE**

1. **Analyze** What inferences did you modify as you gathered more evidence from your teacher?

2. **Provide Examples** What type of evidence might paleontologists find that would allow them to see the big picture of a species' evolutionary past?

**FIGURE 4.7** Vestigial structures, such as the wings of an ostrich, are organs or structures that are greatly reduced from the original ancestral form and have little or no current use.

▶ **MAIN IDEA**

# Structural patterns are clues to the history of a species.

Some organisms have structures or organs that seem to lack any useful function, or at least are no longer used for their original purpose. For example, snakes have tiny pelvic bones and stumplike limbs, even though snakes don't walk. Underdeveloped or unused features are called vestigial structures. **Vestigial structures** (veh-STIHJ-ee-uhl) are remnants of organs or structures found in an early ancestor that no longer serve a useful function or may now serve a different function. As vertebrates, snakes share a common ancestor with tetrapods such as lizards and dogs. The tiny pelvic bones and hind limbs in many snakes are homologous to the pelvic bones of tetrapods.

The wings of ostriches are another example of vestigial structures. Ostriches use wings for balance but not to fly, as shown in **FIGURE 4.7**. Over generations, their increasingly large bodies and powerful long legs may have been enough to avoid predators. If ancient ostriches could escape by running or by kicking viciously, their large wings would no longer have been useful. Thus, the genes coding for large wings were not preserved over generations.

Examples of vestigial structures are found in many organisms. In humans, the appendix is often cited as an example of a vestigial structure. The appendix is a remnant of the cecum, a major part of the large intestine in plant-eating mammals. It helps to digest the cellulose in plants. As omnivores, humans do not eat much cellulose and the appendix cannot digest cellulose. Whether or not the appendix retains any function is still not certain.

Vestigial structures did not get smaller in one individual organism. It took many generations for those organs to shrink. Today, biologists consider vestigial structures among the most important examples demonstrating how evolution works.

**Summarize** **What are vestigial structures, and how do they demonstrate common ancestry?**

---

**SELF-CHECK Online**
HMHScience.com
**GO ONLINE**

## 10.4 Formative Assessment

**REVIEWING ▶ MAIN IDEAS**

1. Describe the four sources of evidence for evolution upon which Darwin based his ideas on common ancestry.

2. Why are **vestigial structures** considered critical evidence of evolution?

**CRITICAL THINKING**

3. **Evaluate** How would you assess the biogeographic evidence used to explain the divergence of Hawaiian honeycreeper species?

4. **Apply** How can a bat's wing be considered both a **homologous structure** and an **analogous structure**?

▷ **CONNECT TO**

**HUMAN BIOLOGY**

5. Wisdom teeth are a third set of molars that usually appear in humans between the ages of 17 and 25, and often need removing because they crowd out other teeth. Explain why wisdom teeth are vestigial structures.

# The Uses of Stable Isotopes

You may have heard about radiometric dating, in which radioactive isotopes are used to determine the age of objects such as fossils and rocks. Radioactive isotopes, or radioisotopes, are naturally occurring elements that have unstable nuclei, and so they decay. As a radioisotope's neutrons change into protons and electrons, it emits radiation and eventually becomes another element. Because radioisotopes decay at a constant rate, they are useful for determining the age of rocks and fossils. But not all isotopes are radioactive.

Stable isotopes are isotopes that do not decay over time. Because the ratios of stable isotopes typical for a certain environment remain constant, stable isotopes are useful for tracking objects and organisms. Analysis of stable isotopes can be used for a variety of purposes, such as authenticating that a cheese labeled as Parmesan was truly produced in Parma, Italy.

Stable isotopes of four elements are commonly used to authenticate a biological product, such as a type of food. Hydrogen exists as the isotopes $^1H$ and $^2H$. Oxygen exists as $^{16}O$, $^{17}O$, and $^{18}O$. Carbon exists as $^{12}C$ and $^{13}C$ ($^{14}C$ is a radioactive isotope). Nitrogen exists as $^{14}N$ and $^{15}N$.

Stable isotope analysis can tell scientists whether this wedge of cheese was made in Parma, Italy, or Hoboken, New Jersey.

Stable isotopes can be used to identify the geographic origins of water and test whether the bottled water you're drinking is from Fiji, a spring in France, or the local municipal water supply. How is this possible? Oceans show only small variations in isotopic abundance. Therefore, ocean water is typically used as a standard, where both the H and O isotope ratios are deemed to be 0 percent. However, as water evaporates from the ocean and condenses into clouds, the isotopic ratios differ significantly, depending on cloud temperature and the amount of leftover moisture in the cloud mass. Bodies of water, such as lakes and rivers, reflect these isotopic ratios from the input of precipitation. These isotopic abundances can further change as evaporation occurs over these bodies of water. Through the water and oxygen cycles, plants and animals incorporate hydrogen and oxygen isotopes from local water sources into their bodies. The isotopic analysis of water samples collected from locations all across the United States, as well as from locations around the world, has allowed scientists to create a map that indicates the expected isotopic ratios in a substance from a given area. Thus, when testing a bottled water sample, scientists can determine if the water's source is correctly labeled.

## Measuring Stable Isotopes

To determine the stable isotope ratio in a sample, whether it is a drop of water or a piece of meat, the sample is placed into a machine called a mass spectrometer. The sample is converted to a gaseous form and then bombarded with ions to scatter the sample's atoms. A strong magnet is used to pull the sample's atoms through a flight tube. Because the different isotopes vary in mass, it takes longer for the more massive atoms to travel through the flight tube, thereby separating the different isotopes in flight. A detector at the end of the flight tube counts the number of atoms for each specific atomic mass. The counts of each isotope are added and calculated as a ratio. It is the ratios of heavy to light isotopes that convey the important information to scientists.

**Question**
Stable isotopes are also used from ice cores, tree rings, or ocean sediments as evidence about past climate conditions. Why could this information be beneficial to future generations?

# Evolutionary Biology Today

**SC.912.N.3.1,**
**SC.912.L.15.1**

**KEY CONCEPT** New technology is furthering our understanding of evolution.

**MAIN IDEAS**

- Fossils provide a record of evolution.
- Molecular and genetic evidence support fossil and anatomical evidence.
- Evolution unites all fields of biology.

**SC.912.N.3.1** Explain that a scientific theory is the culmination of many scientific investigations drawing together all the current evidence concerning a substantial range of phenomena; thus, a scientific theory represents the most powerful explanation scientists have to offer.

**SC.912.L.15.1** Explain how the scientific theory of evolution is supported by the fossil record, comparative anatomy, comparative embryology, biogeography, molecular biology, and observed evolutionary change.

**READING TOOLBOX**

**VOCABULARY**

Paleontology is the study of prehistoric life forms. *Paleo-* means "ancient," and *-ology* means "the study of."

## ☀️ Connect to Your World

Darwin had spent many years collecting evidence of evolution from different fields of science before publishing his results. Since that time, technology has advanced greatly. Scientists can now share information and examine evidence that was only dreamed about in the 1800s. In particular, the relatively new fields of genetics and molecular biology have added strong support to Darwin's theory of natural selection. They have shown how hereditary variation occurs.

### ▶ MAIN IDEA

## Fossils provide a record of evolution.

**Paleontology** (PAY-lee-ahn-TAHL-uh-jee), the study of fossils or extinct organisms, continues to provide new information and support current hypotheses about how evolution occurs. The fossil record is not complete, because most living things do not form into fossils after they die, and because fossils have not been looked for in many areas of the world. However, no fossil evidence that contradicts evolution has ever been found.

In Darwin's time, paleontology was still a new science. Darwin worried about the lack of transitional fossils between groups of organisms. Since Darwin's time, however, many transitional forms between species have been discovered, filling in large gaps in the fossil record. The fossil record today includes many thousands of species that show the change in forms over time that Darwin outlined in his theory. These "missing links" demonstrate the evolution of traits within groups as well as the common ancestors between groups.

Although scientists classify organisms into groups, the mix of traits in transitional species often makes it difficult to tell where one group ends and another begins. One example of transitional species in the evolution of whales is shown in **FIGURE 5.1**. *Basilosaurus isis* had a whalelike body, but it still had the limbs of land animals.

**Infer** Why are fossils such as *Basilosaurus isis* considered transitional fossils?

**FIGURE 5.1** This spinal column of a 40-million-year-old whale was found in a desert in Egypt.

Mike Nelson/EPA/NewsCom

## MAIN IDEA
# Molecular and genetic evidence support fossil and anatomical evidence.

As with homologous traits, very different species have similar molecular and genetic mechanisms. Because all living things have DNA, they share the same genetic code and make most of the same proteins from the same 20 amino acids. DNA or protein sequence comparisons can be used to show probable evolutionary relationships between species.

**DNA sequence analysis** Recall that the sequences of nucleotides in a gene change over time due to mutations. DNA sequence analysis depends on the fact that the more related two organisms are, the more similar their DNA will be. Because there are thousands of genes in most organisms, DNA contains a huge amount of information on evolutionary history.

Because all living organisms share the same genetic code and use the same 20 amino acids, it has been possible to determine that organisms share a remarkable number of proteins that are similar to one another. Due to mutations, the sequences of nucleotides change over time. Thus, comparing the sequences of DNA in organisms can show evolutionary relationships among the organisms. Scientists hope to eventually be able to correlate changes in DNA sequences with past geological events.

**Pseudogenes** Sequences of DNA nucleotides known as pseudogenes also provide evidence of evolution. Pseudogenes are like vestigial structures. They no longer function but are still carried along with functional DNA. They can also change as they are passed on through generations, so they provide another way to figure out evolutionary relationships. Functioning genes may be similar in organisms with similar lifestyles, such as a wolf and a coyote, due to natural selection. Similarities between pseudogenes, however, must reflect a common ancestor.

**Protein comparisons** Similarities among cell types across organisms can be revealed by comparing their proteins, a technique called molecular finger-printing. A unique set of proteins are found in specific types of cells, such as liver or muscle cells. Computers are used to search databases of protein sequences and look for homologous sequences in different species. Cells from different species that have the same proteins most likely come from a common ancestor. For example, the proteins of light-sensitive cells in the brainlike structure of an ancient marine worm, as shown in **FIGURE 5.2**, were found to closely resemble those of cells found in the vertebrate eye. This resemblance shows a shared ancestry between worms and vertebrates. It also shows that the cells of the vertebrate eye originally came from cells in the brain.

**Homeobox genes** As you will learn in the chapter Invertebrate Diversity, homeobox genes control the development of specific structures. These sequences of genes are found in many organisms, from fruit flies to humans. They also indicate a very distant common ancestor. Evidence of homeobox gene clusters are found in organisms that lived as far back as 600 million years ago.

**Explain** **How have protein comparisons helped determine ancestral relationships between organisms?**

### READING TOOLBOX

**VOCABULARY**
A pseudogene is a DNA sequence that resembles a gene but seems to have no function. *Pseudo-* means "false" or "deceptive."

**FIGURE 5.2** The eye spots of this ragworm have light-sensitive cells with a molecular fingerprint similar to that of a vertebrate eye.

## FIGURE 5.3 Evidence of Whale Evolution

The evidence that whales descended from hoofed mammals is supported by scientific research in several different fields of biology.

Modern-day whale

### Vestigial Evidence

Many modern whale species have vestigial pelvic and leg bones. They also have vestigial nerves for the sense of smell, and small muscles devoted to external ears that no longer exist.

### Embryological Evidence

Whale embryos have features such as hind leg buds and nostrils that resemble those of land animals. Nostrils are at the end of the whale's snout early in development but travel to the top of the head to form one or more blowholes before birth.

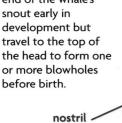

nostril

hind leg bud

### Molecular Evidence

The DNA sequences of milk protein genes in whales and hoofed mammals are very similar, as demonstrated by the DNA fragments below.

| Hippopotamus | TCC TGGCA GTCCA GTGGT |
| Humpback whale | CCC TGGCA GTGCA GTGCT |

### Fossil Evidence

There are many transitional fossils that have characteristics of both land mammals and whales. These are a few examples.

*Dorudon*  about 40 million years ago

Tiny hind legs were useless on land, and a shorter neck and longer tail makes *Dorudon* similar to modern-day whales. Its ankle joints closely resemble those of modern ungulates.

*Ambulocetus natans*  about 50 million years ago

With a name that means "the walking whale that swims," *Ambulocetus natans* was an amphibious fish eater the size of a sea lion.

*Pakicetus*  about 50 million years ago

*Pakicetus* had a whale-shaped skull and teeth adapted for hunting fish. However, with ear bones that are in between those of land and aquatic mammals, it could not hear well underwater or make deep dives.

CRITICAL VIEWING  Whales are divided into two groups: toothed whales, such as the orca pictured above, and baleen whales, such as the humpback whale pictured on the next page. Which would you predict is most closely related to *Dorudon*? Explain.

## ► MAIN IDEA
# Evolution unites all fields of biology.

Scientists are still actively studying evolution through natural selection. The 21st century is an exciting time to study evolutionary biology. New tools are providing more data than ever before. Considering the number of proteins in a single organism, the amount of data gathered through molecular evidence alone is overwhelming.

Scientists from many fields of science are shedding new light on the mechanisms and patterns of evolution. In some cases, the use of modern technology has supported fossil evidence. For example, you have read that fossil evidence suggests that early ancestors of whales were hoofed land mammals. Comparing the examples from the fossil record shown in **FIGURE 5.3** highlights the transitional characteristics between land mammals and whales. Shifts in skull shape, modified limb structures, and changes in tail length provide evidence for the descent of modern whales from a common ancestor with the group of hoofed mammals that includes deer, antelope, and hippopotamuses. Comparisons of milk protein genes confirm this relationship and even provide evidence that the hippopotamus is the closest living land animal related to whales.

The basic principles of evolution are used in fields such as medicine, geology, geography, chemistry, and ecology. The idea of common descent helps biologists understand where new diseases come from, as well as how to best manage endangered species. There is so much more waiting to be discovered about life on Earth. As the great geneticist Theodosius Dobzhansky (1900–1975) once noted, "Nothing in biology makes sense except in the light of evolution."

**FIGURE 5.4** Baleen whales, such as this humpback whale, have evolved a highly specialized adaptation for catching microscopic food. Molecular techniques have allowed scientists to discover the whale's relationship with hoofed animals.

**Evaluate** How would you rate the strength of the support provided by fossil evidence for common ancestry among groups such as land mammals and whales? Explain.

## 10.5 Formative Assessment

**SELF-CHECK** Online
HMHScience.com
**GO ONLINE**

### REVIEWING ► MAIN IDEAS

1. How has our knowledge of the fossil record changed since Darwin proposed his theory of natural selection?

2. How has molecular genetics, combined with **paleontology,** added to our understanding of evolution?

3. What are some of the fields of science to which evolutionary biology contributes?

### CRITICAL THINKING

4. **Apply** Describe how similar protein comparisons of cells in two species can suggest a close evolutionary relationship.

5. **Synthesize** You have discovered the fossil remains of three organisms. One is mammalian, one is reptilian, and the third has both mammalian and reptilian features. What techniques could you apply to determine possible relationships among these organisms?

### CONNECT TO
### GENETICS

6. Researchers have found that a gene controlling reproduction is linked to the gene for the number of digits an organism has. How does this help explain why many vertebrates have five digits per limb, despite the fact that there is no fitness benefit in having five rather than six or four?

©Paul A. Souders/Corbis

# 10 Summary

Many different forms of evidence support the theory that Earth is ancient and that species can change over time.

## KEY CONCEPTS

### 10.1 Early Ideas About Evolution

**There were theories of biological and geologic change before Darwin.** Early biologists suggested that different species might have shared ancestors, and geologists observed that new species appeared in the fossil record. Charles Lyell proposed the theory of uniformitarianism to explain how present-day observations explain past events.

### 10.2 Darwin's Observations

**Darwin's voyage provided insights into evolution.** Darwin observed variations between island species on his voyage, such as with the Galápagos tortoises. He noticed that species have adaptations that allow them to better survive in their environments. He also observed fossil evidence of species changing over time.

### 10.3 Theory of Natural Selection

**Darwin proposed natural selection as a mechanism for evolution.** Natural selection is a mechanism by which individuals that have inherited beneficial adaptations produce more offspring on average than do other individuals. Natural selection is based upon four principles: overproduction, variation, adaptation, and descent with modification.

### 10.4 Evidence of Evolution

**Evidence of common ancestry among species comes from many sources.** Fossil evidence is a record of change in a species over time. The study of biogeography showed that species could adapt to different environments. Two species that exhibit similar traits during development likely have a common ancestor. Vestigial and homologous structures also point to a shared ancestry.

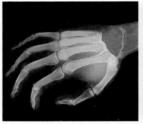 

### 10.5 Evolutionary Biology Today

**New technology is furthering our understanding of evolution.** Modern techniques, such as DNA sequence analysis and molecular fingerprinting, continue to provide new information about the way evolution occurs. Evolution is a unifying theme of all the fields of biology today.

---

🐌 **READING TOOLBOX**    SYNTHESIZE YOUR NOTES

**Main Idea Web** Use a main idea web to summarize the four principles of natural selection.

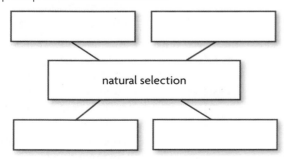

**Concept Map** Use a concept map like the one below to summarize what you know about evolutionary evidence.

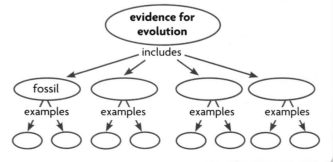

# 10 Review

**INTERACTIVE Review**
HMHScience.com
**GO ONLINE**
Review Games • Concept Map • Section Self-Checks

## CHAPTER VOCABULARY

**10.1**
evolution
species
fossil
catastrophism
gradualism
uniformitarianism

**10.2**
variation
adaptation

**10.3**
artificial selection
heritability
natural selection
population
fitness

**10.4**
biogeography
homologous structure
analogous structure
vestigial structure

**10.5**
paleontology

## Reviewing Vocabulary

### Vocabulary Connections

The vocabulary terms in this chapter are related to each other in various ways. For each group of words below, write a sentence or two to clearly explain how the terms are connected. For example, for the terms *variation* and *natural selection*, you could write "Natural selection depends on heritable variations."

**1.** catastrophism, gradualism

**2.** population, variation

**3.** adaptation, evolution

**4.** vestigial structure, analogous structure

**5.** fossil, paleontology

### READING TOOLBOX  GREEK AND LATIN WORD ORIGINS

**6.** The term *homologous* comes from the Greek word *homos*, which means "the same". Explain how this meaning relates to *homologous* structures.

**7.** The term *vestigial* comes from the Latin word *vestigium*, which means "track or footprint". Explain how this meaning relates to *vestigial* structures.

## Reviewing MAIN IDEAS

**8.** Describe one idea about evolution that was proposed before Darwin published his theory of natural selection.

**9.** Briefly explain how the geologist Charles Lyell influenced Darwin's ideas about how evolution works.

**10.** What insights did Darwin gain from observing island organisms such as the Galápagos tortoises and finches?

**11.** On his voyage, Darwin found fossils of extinct organisms that resembled living organisms and shells of marine organisms high up in the mountains. How did these observations provide evidence that Earth is very old?

**12.** Thomas Malthus was an economist who proposed that resources such as food, water, and shelter are natural limits to human population growth. Explain how Darwin extended this idea in his theory of natural selection.

**13.** Why is heritability important for both natural and artificial selection?

**14.** Natural selection is based on four main principles: variation, overproduction, adaptation, and descent with modification. Briefly explain how each of these principles is necessary for natural selection to occur.

**15.** Explain how the sequential nature of fossil groups found in rock strata supports Darwin's principle of "descent with modification".

**16.** Embryology provides evidence of evolution by revealing developmental homologies among species. Analyze and evaluate one example of such embryological evidence.

**17.** Give an example of a vestigial structure and explain how vestigial structures are significant to evolution.

**18.** Paleontology is the study of fossils or extinct organisms. Explain how this field is important to evolutionary biology.

**19.** How are genes and proteins similar to homologous structures when determining evolutionary relationships among species?

**20.** Explain what the following quote by Theodosius Dobzhansky means: "Nothing in biology makes sense except in the light of evolution."

# Critical Thinking

**21. Compare** Jean-Baptiste Lamarck hypothesized that changes in an environment led to an organism's greater or lesser use of a body part. Although his hypothesis was incomplete, what ideas related to evolution did Lamarck and Charles Darwin share?

**22. Evaluate** What types of scientific evidence provide support for common ancestry among groups such as land mammals and whales? How would you assess the relative strength of these different types of evidence?

**23. Analyze** The turkey vulture and the California condor both feed upon dead animals, known as carrion. Neither species of bird has feathers on its head. Explain how natural selection may have played a role in the featherless heads of these carrion eaters.

**24. Analyze** What are three trends that biologists have identified in the transitional characteristics of different groups in the whale fossil record?

## Interpreting Visuals

Use the following diagram, which shows the evolution of the wild mustard plant, to answer the next three questions.

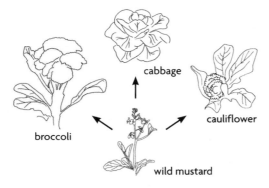

cabbage

cauliflower

broccoli

wild mustard

**25. Infer** Traits of the wild mustard plant have been emphasized by artificial selection to produce different vegetables. In some varieties, the flower heads were emphasized. In other vegetables, it was the leaves or the stems that were to be eaten. Which traits were emphasized to produce cauliflower? Cabbage?

**26. Apply** Describe a procedure humans may have used to produce broccoli, which has small flowers and thick stems.

**27. Predict** What would a protein comparison of broccoli, cabbage, and cauliflower confirm about their relationships to each other?

## Analyzing Data Interpret Line Graphs

One hundred million seabirds use the island of Gaugh, in the South Atlantic Ocean, as a critical nesting ground. Non-native carnivorous mice eat the helpless seabird chicks at a rate of about 1 million per year. Prior to the arrival of the mice, no natural predators existed on the island, so the birds did not evolve any defense mechanisms. Scientists estimate the current population of the mice at 700,000. The graph below displays a projection of seabird casualties and changes in the size of the mouse population.

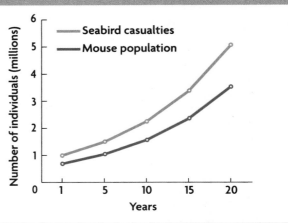

**SEABIRD CASUALTIES AND MOUSE POPULATION**

**28. Interpret** What does the graph show about seabird casualties and the mouse population over a 20-year period?

**29. Predict** Imagine that some seabirds began defending their nests from the mice, and that this behavior is heritable. What changes might such a graph show over the next 20 years? Explain.

## Making Connections

**30. Write a Scenario** Imagine a way in which seabirds could adapt to the mouse population and avoid predation of their chicks. Then consider how, after many generations, the mouse population could counter this defense and again limit the seabird population. What are possible adaptations that could lead to this co-evolution of mice and seabirds?

**31. Synthesize** Look again at the picture of the star-nosed mole. Its claws are well adapted for breaking through soil. How could natural selection have played a role in this trait becoming common among star-nosed moles?

# Standards-Based Assessment

Record your answers on a separate piece of paper.

## MULTIPLE CHOICE

1  As developing embryos, some organisms appear to have features that are similar in structure. As these organisms continue their development, features that were similar in the embryonic stage develop into different structures that have different functions. What type of evidence of common ancestry do these features represent?

A  vestigial structures

B  homologous structures

C  analogous structures

D  fossil structures

2  Although the fossil record is incomplete, paleontologists continue to search for fossils that are commonly referred to as "missing links." What evidence of evolution do discoveries of fossil evidence known as "missing links" provide to scientists?

A  Discoveries of "missing links" provide fossil evidence that contradicts the theory of evolution.

B  Discoveries of "missing links" show that organisms once thought to be related are not.

C  Discoveries of "missing links" serve as transitional species that show the evolution within and between related groups.

D  Discoveries of "missing links" serve as additional evidence that organisms do not change or evolve.

3  All vertebrates have very similar *Hox* genes. How does this provide evidence suggesting vertebrates evolved from a common ancestor?

A  Greater similarity of genes indicates closer evolutionary relationships among species.

B  Species with major differences in *Hox* genes would have gone extinct.

C  The greater the number of *Hox* genes present, the greater the relationship among species.

D  *Hox* genes control the same genes in all species of vertebrates.

4  The diagram below represents several sedimentary rock layers in which fossils of different organisms have been found. The rock layers show no evidence of having been disturbed since their formation.

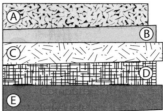

What information about the ages of the fossils relative to each other can be explained by their positions in these rock layers?

A  The rock layers do not provide any information about the ages of the fossils relative to each other.

B  The rock layers suggest that the fossils in layer A are much older than those in layers B, C, D, and E.

C  The rock layers suggest that the oldest fossils are in layer E and the youngest are in layer A.

D  The rock layers suggest that all of the fossils found in the rocks will be of the same age regardless of the type of organism the fossil represents.

5  An herbicide killed 99% of a weed population. Which of the following is the **best** biological explanation for some weeds being able to survive?

A  Some individuals were able to evolve before the spraying.

B  The spray caused some individuals to mutate, and they were able to survive and reproduce.

C  Each individual occupied a different ecological niche and so some were unaffected.

D  Genetic variation in the population allowed some weeds to survive.

### THINK THROUGH THE QUESTION

Consider what conditions must be present for natural selection to occur.

# 11 The Evolution of Populations

**BIG IDEA** The genetic composition of populations evolves through natural selection as species adapt to changes in their environment.

## ⊘ ONLINE BIOLOGY  HMHScience.com

**ONLINE** Labs
- Natural Selection in African Swallowtails
- **QuickLab** Genetic Drift
- Investigating an Anole Lizard Population
- Exploring Adaptations
- **S.T.E.M. Lab** Population Genetics
- Microevolution and Antibiotic-Resistant Bacteria

- Exploring Dog Genetics and Evolution
- Modeling Alleles
- Investigating Plant Adaptations
- **Video Lab** Genetic Drift
- **S.T.E.M. Lab** Hardy-Weinberg Equation

Every year, king penguins return to breed in the same colony in which they were born. These colonies help penguins to guard, protect, and defend their young. By ensuring the success of their young, penguins pass on their genes to future generations. Variation in these genes is the basis for the evolution of populations.

---

◉ **READING** TOOLBOX    **This reading tool can help you learn the material in the following pages.**

## USING LANGUAGE

**General Statements**  A general statement often summarizes the features of a group or describes an average or typical feature of members of the group. But if many features are summarized, some individual members in the group probably do not share all of those features. And if an average feature is described, some members of the group will not match the average. So, general statements may be true most of the time, but not always.

## YOUR TURN

Use what you know about general statements to complete the following tasks.

1. Write a general statement about apples, bananas, tomatoes, and peanuts.
2. List exceptions to the statement "Humans are bigger than monkeys."

# Genetic Variation Within Populations

**SC.912.L.15.15**

| KEY CONCEPT **A population shares a common gene pool.**

**MAIN IDEAS**

- Genetic variation in a population increases the chance that some individuals will survive.
- Genetic variation comes from several sources.

**VOCABULARY**

gene pool
allele frequency

**SC.912.L.15.15** Describe how mutation and genetic recombination increase genetic variation.

## Connect to Your World

You may think that if you've seen one penguin, you've seen them all. However, penguins can differ in body size, feather patterns, and many other traits. Just like humans, penguins are genetically different from one another. What causes genetic variation in populations of organisms? And what methods do biologists use to measure this variation?

**Video Inquiry**
HMHScience.com
**GO ONLINE**
Shark Trails

### READING TOOLBOX

**TAKING NOTES**
Use mind maps to show relationships among related terms and concepts.

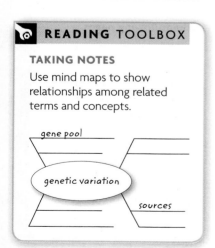

## ▶ MAIN IDEA

# Genetic variation in a population increases the chance that some individuals will survive.

Body size and feather patterns in penguins are each examples of phenotypes. A phenotype is a trait produced by one or more genes. In a population, there may be a wide range of phenotypes. For example, some penguins may be short and rounded. Others could be tall and slim.

Natural selection acts on different phenotypes in a population. The expression of different phenotypes, however, depends on genetic variation in a population. A population with a lot of genetic variation likely has a wide range of phenotypes. The greater the variation in phenotypes, the more likely it is that some individuals can survive in a changing environment. For example, in an unusually cold winter, short, rounded penguins might be better able to stay warm than tall, slim penguins. But if there is a shortage of food, tall, slim penguins might be better divers, allowing them to catch more fish.

Genetic variation is stored in a population's **gene pool**—the combined alleles of all of the individuals in a population. Different combinations of alleles in a gene pool can be formed when organisms mate and have offspring. Each allele exists at a certain rate, or frequency. An **allele frequency** is a measure of how common a certain allele is in the population. As shown in **FIGURE 1.1,** you can calculate allele frequencies. First, count the number of times an allele occurs in a gene pool. Then, divide by the total number of alleles for that gene in the gene pool.

**Analyze** **What is the relationship between allele frequencies and a gene pool?**

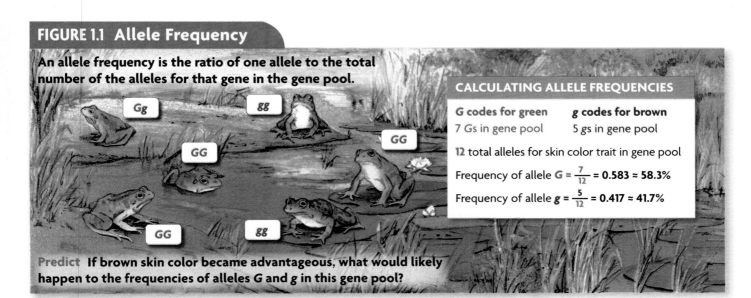

## FIGURE 1.1 Allele Frequency

An allele frequency is the ratio of one allele to the total number of the alleles for that gene in the gene pool.

Gg
gg
GG
GG
GG
gg

**CALCULATING ALLELE FREQUENCIES**

G codes for green    g codes for brown
7 Gs in gene pool    5 gs in gene pool

12 total alleles for skin color trait in gene pool

Frequency of allele $G = \frac{7}{12} = 0.583 \approx 58.3\%$

Frequency of allele $g = \frac{5}{12} = 0.417 \approx 41.7\%$

**Predict** If brown skin color became advantageous, what would likely happen to the frequencies of alleles *G* and *g* in this gene pool?

## ▶ MAIN IDEA
# Genetic variation comes from several sources.

Genetic variation comes from two main sources: mutation and recombination.

- **Mutation** A mutation is a random change in the DNA of a gene. This change can form a new allele. Mutations in reproductive cells can be passed on to offspring. This increases the genetic variation in the gene pool. Because there are many genes in each individual and many individuals in a population, new mutations form frequently in gene pools.

- **Recombination** New allele combinations form in offspring through a process called recombination. Most recombination occurs during meiosis—the type of cell division needed for sexual reproduction. When gametes are made, each parent's alleles are arranged in new ways. This shuffling of alleles results in many different genetic combinations.

Some biologists are studying hybridization as another source of genetic variation. Hybridization is the crossing of two different species that share common genes. Research suggests that this process occurs within many groups of animals, including birds and mammals, when similar species live in the same area and individuals cannot easily find mates of their own species.

**Infer** Why aren't mutations in nonreproductive cells sources of genetic variation?

**CONNECT TO**

**GENETICS**

As you learned in the chapter **From DNA to Proteins,** mutations on noncoding regions of DNA do not affect phenotypes. Only mutations on coding regions of DNA can affect an organism's phenotype.

**SELF-CHECK Online**
HMHScience.com
**GO ONLINE**

## 11.1 Formative Assessment

### REVIEWING ▶ MAIN IDEAS

1. Why does genetic variation increase the chance that some individuals in a population will survive?

2. Describe two main sources of genetic variation.

### CRITICAL THINKING

3. **Analyze** In what way is a **gene pool** representative of a population?

4. **Apply** If a certain trait's **allele frequency** is 100%, describe the genetic variation for that trait in the population.

**CONNECT TO**

**GENETICS**

5. How does crossing over during meiosis provide a source of genetic variation? Draw a diagram to show this process.

# Natural Selection in Populations

SC.912.L.15.13

## VOCABULARY

normal distribution
microevolution
directional selection
stabilizing selection
disruptive selection

**SC.912.L.15.13** Describe the conditions required for natural selection, including: overproduction of offspring, inherited variation, and the struggle to survive, which result in differential reproductive success.

**KEY CONCEPT** **Populations, not individuals, evolve.**

### MAIN IDEAS

▶ Natural selection acts on distributions of traits.
▶ Natural selection can change the distribution of a trait in one of three ways.

### Connect to Your World

How do you describe a person's appearance? Perhaps you use height, hair color, and eye color. These traits are often used in descriptions because these traits vary widely among humans. In this section, you will learn about the way natural selection can act on such variation.

## CONNECT TO

### GENETICS

As you learned in the chapter **Extending Mendelian Genetics,** single-gene traits are expressed in either one distinct form or another. However, the range of phenotypes common for most traits is the result of polygenic traits, which are controlled by multiple genes.

## ▶ MAIN IDEA

## Natural selection acts on distributions of traits.

Any time you stand in a large crowd of people, you are likely to observe a wide range of heights. Imagine organizing this crowd across a football field according to each individual's height, with very short people at one end, people of average height in the middle, and very tall people at the other end. You would soon notice a pattern in distribution of the human height trait. Relatively few people would be at each extreme height, very short or very tall. A majority of people of medium height would be in the middle.

This type of distribution, in which the frequency is highest near the mean value and decreases toward each extreme end of the range, is called a **normal distribution.** When these frequency values are graphed, the result is a bell-shaped curve like the one you see in **FIGURE 2.1.**

For some traits, all phenotypes provide an equal chance of survival. The distribution for these traits generally shows a normal distribution. Phenotypes near the middle of the range tend to be most common, while the extremes are less common. However, environmental conditions can change, and a certain phenotype may become an advantage. Natural selection favors individuals with this phenotype. These individuals are able to survive and reproduce at higher rates than individuals with less favorable phenotypes. Therefore, alleles associated with favorable phenotypes increase in frequency through differential reproductive success.

**Synthesize** **What other types of data might follow a normal distribution?**

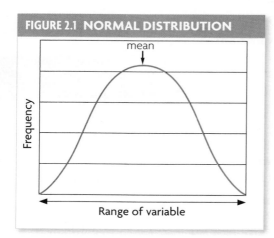

FIGURE 2.1 NORMAL DISTRIBUTION

mean

Frequency

Range of variable

## MAIN IDEA

# Natural selection can change the distribution of a trait in one of three ways.

**Microevolution** is the observable change in the allele frequencies of a population over time. Microevolution occurs on a small scale—within a single population. One process that can lead to microevolution is natural selection. Natural selection can change the distribution of a trait along one of three paths: directional, stabilizing, or disruptive selection. Such changes can have major effects on how a population looks and behaves.

## Directional Selection

A type of selection that favors phenotypes at one extreme of a trait's range is called **directional selection.** Directional selection causes a shift in a population's phenotypic distribution. An extreme phenotype that was once rare in a population becomes more common. As shown in **FIGURE 2.2**, during directional selection, the mean value of a trait shifts in the direction of the more advantageous phenotype.

The rise of drug-resistant bacteria provides a classic example of this type of selection. Before antibiotics were developed in the 1940s, a trait for varying levels of drug resistance existed among bacteria. At the time, there was no advantage to having drug resistance. But once antibiotics came into use, the resistant bacteria had a great advantage.

The early success of antibiotics in controlling infectious diseases led to overuse of these drugs. This overuse favored even more resistant phenotypes. New drugs were then developed to fight the resistant bacteria. This resulted in the evolution of "superbugs" that are highly resistant to many drugs. Today, over 200 types of bacteria show some degree of antibiotic resistance.

### ⊙ CONNECT TO

**BACTERIA**

Although many bacteria are helpful to other organisms, some do cause disease. You will learn more about how bacteria can evolve and become resistant to antibiotics in the chapter **Viruses and Prokaryotes.**

## FIGURE 2.2 Directional Selection

**Directional selection occurs when one extreme phenotype is favored by natural selection.**

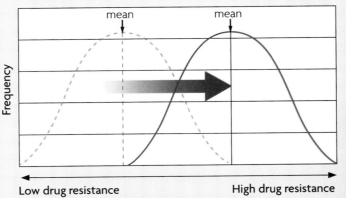

- - - - - Original distribution

→ Antibiotic drugs put pressure on bacteria populations.

——— Distribution after directional selection

Today, scientists continue to research new drugs developed to treat infection-causing bacteria such as *Enterococcus faecalis*, which is resistant to many antibiotics.

**FIGURE 2.3** The gall fly and the goldenrod plant have a parasitic relationship. The fly benefits by receiving shelter and food during its larval stage, while the goldenrod is harmed, growing more slowly than a gall-free goldenrod.

## Stabilizing Selection

The gall fly and its predators provide an excellent example of stabilizing selection. During **stabilizing selection,** the intermediate phenotype is favored and becomes more common in the population. That is, the distribution becomes stable at the intermediate phenotype rather than shifting toward one of the extremes. In the case of gall flies, something in nature selects against phenotypes at both extremes of the trait's range.

Gall flies lay their eggs in developing shoots of the tall goldenrod plant. The fly larvae produce a chemical that causes the plant tissue to swell around them. **FIGURE 2.3** shows the resulting mass of plant tissue, called a gall. The gall serves as a home where the larvae can develop. There is a range of phenotypes for body size in gall-fly larvae. Each body size causes a certain size gall to form, and each of the two main predators of gall flies specializes on a specific gall size.

- Downy woodpeckers attack larger galls and feed on the larvae inside.
- The parasitic wasp lays its own eggs inside small galls. After the wasp larvae emerge from the eggs, they eat the gall-fly larvae.

In this situation, selective pressure from predators works against fly phenotypes that produce galls at both extremes, large and small. As a result, flies that produce middle-sized galls become more common. As you can see in **FIGURE 2.4,** over time, stabilizing selection results in a higher frequency of flies that produce middle-sized galls.

Stabilizing selection increases the number of individuals with intermediate phenotypes. Notice, however, that selection against both extremes decreases the genetic diversity of the gall-fly population. Flies that produce small and large galls become less common. In some populations, these extreme phenotypes may be lost altogether.

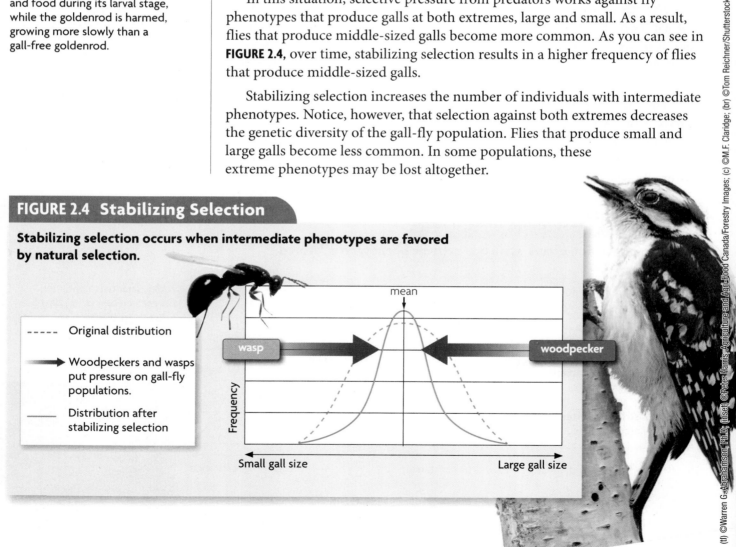

### FIGURE 2.4 Stabilizing Selection

Stabilizing selection occurs when intermediate phenotypes are favored by natural selection.

- - - - - Original distribution

→ Woodpeckers and wasps put pressure on gall-fly populations.

⎯⎯ Distribution after stabilizing selection

wasp → woodpecker

mean

Frequency

Small gall size ⟷ Large gall size

## Disruptive Selection

**Disruptive selection** occurs when both extreme phenotypes are favored, while individuals with intermediate phenotypes are selected against by something in nature. As you can see in **FIGURE 2.5**, the middle of the distribution is disrupted. One example of this type of selection involves feather color in male lazuli buntings, a bird species native to North America.

Young male lazuli buntings vary widely in the brightness of their feathers, ranging from dull brown to bright blue. Dominant adult males are those with the brightest blue feathers on their heads and backs. These birds have their pick of the best territories. They also are most successful at attracting females. However, for young buntings, the brightest blue and dullest brown males are more likely to win mates than males with bluish brown feathers.

Research suggests that dominant adult males are aggressive toward young buntings that they see as a threat, including bright blue and bluish brown males. The dullest brown birds can therefore win a mate because the adult males leave them alone. Meanwhile, the bright blue birds attract mates simply because of their color.

Both extreme phenotypes are favored in this situation, while intermediate forms are selected against. The bluish brown males are not as well adapted to compete for mates because they are too blue to be left alone by adult males, but not blue enough to win a mate based on color alone. By favoring both extreme phenotypes, disruptive selection can lead to the formation of new species.

**Apply** **If bluish brown coloring became advantageous for young males, what type of selection would likely occur in a lazuli bunting population?**

## FIGURE 2.5 Disruptive Selection

Disruptive selection occurs when both extreme phenotypes are favored by selection.

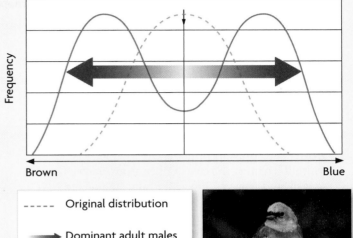

----- Original distribution

→ Dominant adult males put pressure on young males in the bunting population.

—— Distribution after disruptive selection

Adult male lazuli bunting

**SELF-CHECK Online**
HMHScience.com
**GO ONLINE**

## 11.2 Formative Assessment

### REVIEWING ▶ MAIN IDEAS

1. In terms of phenotypes, describe what is meant by the phrase "distribution of traits."

2. What are the three ways in which natural selection can change a distribution of traits?

### CRITICAL THINKING

3. **Analyze** How might the extinction of downy woodpeckers affect the phenotypic distribution within a population of gall flies?

4. **Analyze** How might overfishing of large pink salmon select for smaller body size in subsequent generations?

### CONNECT TO

**GENETICS**

5. For polygenic traits, a smooth curve results when the range of phenotypes is plotted against frequency. If you were to plot the frequencies of two phenotypes of a single-gene trait, you would end up with a double bar graph. Explain why.

©C. Allan Morgan/Peter Arnold, Inc.

# Crossbreeding: Genetically Modified Organisms

Today there are many types of agricultural crops that are genetically engineered (GE), often referred to as genetically modified organisms (GMOs). The crops have been genetically engineered to resist herbicides, insect pests, viruses, and cold temperatures, among other harmful conditions. These traits are beneficial to both the plants and the growers. If a crop is herbicide resistant, such as GE cotton or soybeans, it means a grower can spray his or her entire field for weeds without harming the crop. Other crops, such as corn, squash, and papayas, are genetically engineered to resist insect pests or viruses. Some crops, such as GE strawberries, are more resistant to cold temperatures. All of these genetically engineered traits can help increase crop yields.

Scientists who study plants and ecosystems have investigated what effects, if any, the introduction of GE plants into human-made ecosystems (agricultural operations) would have on natural ecosystems. Over the last decade, research in both laboratory and natural settings has shown that GE plants can successfully crossbreed with related wild plants and that the GE traits are passed on to the hybrid offspring. In a laboratory experiment, rice genetically engineered to be resistant to a common herbicide easily crossbred with a weed relative. The resulting hybrid did contain the GE trait and had higher rates of photosynthesis and produced more flowers and seeds than non-GE hybrids. Another study, conducted under controlled conditions, found that sunflowers that were genetically engineered to be resistant to a moth pest crossbred with wild sunflowers. The hybrid offspring had the GE trait. As a result, the hybrids were more fit and produced 50 percent more seeds than nonhybrid wild sunflowers. The hybrids also showed less physical damage due to insects.

In a natural setting, genetically engineered creeping bentgrass, a grass commonly planted on golf courses, crossbred with related wild grasses through wind pollination. The hybrid offspring contained the GE trait, resistance to a common herbicide. A similar situation occurred with GE rapeseed (canola), which naturally crossbred with wild relatives, producing hybrids that contained the GE trait of herbicide resistance.

Some scientists are concerned that transgenic hybrids may be able to outcompete native plants in natural ecosystems. In the case of the weedy rice, scientists are concerned that the transgenic hybrid could even outcompete the cultivated rice that is its parent. With creeping bentgrass, scientists are concerned that the transgenic bentgrass could outcompete native grasses. Also, if the hybrid grass grew in an area where it needed to be controlled, such as a waterway, it could not be eradicated through the traditional method of spraying with a common herbicide that is safe to use in a water environment. The general concern of some scientists is that in any natural setting, a hybrid with increased fitness due to inheriting a GE trait could cause an imbalance in an ecosystem.

## S.T.E.M. Activity

Research more about proposed methods to prevent GE plants from producing viable hybrids if they were to crossbreed with related native plants. How are scientists using the technology behind genetic engineering to help prevent such occurrences?

Genetically engineered creeping bentgrass can crossbreed with wild grasses through wind pollination.

# Other Mechanisms of Evolution

**SC.912.L.15.14**

**KEY CONCEPT** **Natural selection is not the only mechanism through which populations evolve.**

**MAIN IDEAS**

◯ Gene flow is the movement of alleles between populations.
◯ Genetic drift is a change in allele frequencies due to chance.
◯ Sexual selection occurs when certain traits increase mating success.

**SC.912.L.15.14** Discuss mechanisms of evolutionary change other than natural selection such as genetic drift and gene flow.

### Connect to Your World

Have you ever wondered why many male birds, such as cardinals, are brightly colored while females of the same species are dull brown? Such bright coloring may not make sense in terms of natural selection, since the male birds are more likely to be seen by predators. However, natural selection is not the whole story. There are other factors that can lead to the evolution of populations.

◯ **MAIN IDEA**

## Gene flow is the movement of alleles between populations.

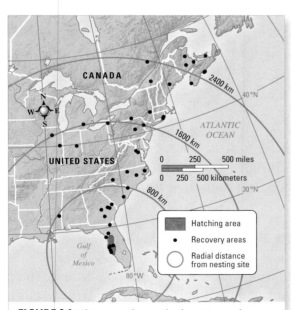

**FIGURE 3.1** This map shows the locations where banded bald eagles were found during the first summer after hatching.

Bird-banding studies have shown that certain birds leave their nesting areas once they are able to fly. As shown in **FIGURE 3.1,** bald eagles that were banded as nestlings have been tracked during the same summer more than 2500 kilometers away. These eagles have possibly joined a new population.

When an organism joins a new population and reproduces, its alleles become part of that population's gene pool. At the same time, these alleles are removed from the gene pool of its former population. The movement of alleles from one population to another is called **gene flow.** For many animals, gene flow occurs when individuals move between populations. Gene flow can occur in fungi and plant populations when spores or seeds are spread to new areas.

Gene flow increases the genetic variation of the receiving population. Gene flow between neighboring populations keeps their gene pools similar. However, the less gene flow that occurs between two populations, the more genetically different the two populations can become. A lack of gene flow also increases the chance that the two populations will evolve into different species.

**Evaluate** **How does gene flow affect neighboring populations?**

## ▶ MAIN IDEA
# Genetic drift is a change in allele frequencies due to chance.

Imagine a patch of 100 flowers growing in a field. Fifty are white, and fifty are purple. If you randomly pick flowers from this patch to create a bouquet, you would expect about half white and half purple flowers. The more flowers you randomly pick, the more likely you are to get these proportions. However, the fewer flowers you pick, the more likely you are to have a bouquet that is not representative of the patch. It might even be all one color.

A similar situation can occur in small populations. Small populations, like small sample sizes, are more likely to be affected by chance. Due to chance alone, some alleles are likely to decrease in frequency and become eliminated. Other alleles are likely to increase in frequency and become fixed. These changes in allele frequencies that are due to chance are called **genetic drift.** Genetic drift causes a loss of genetic diversity in a population.

Two processes commonly cause populations to become small enough for genetic drift to occur. Each of these processes results in a population with different allele frequencies than existed in the original population.

### READING TOOLBOX

**VOCABULARY**
The word *fixed* means "not subject to change." If an allele increases to a frequency of 1.0 (100%), it is said to be fixed in the population.

## Bottleneck Effect
The **bottleneck effect** is genetic drift that occurs after an event greatly reduces the size of a population. One example of the bottleneck effect is the overhunting of northern elephant seals during the 1800s. By the 1890s, the population was reduced to about 20 individuals. These 20 seals did not represent the genetic diversity of the original population. Since hunting has ended, the population has grown to over 100,000 individuals. However, it has very little genetic variation. Through genetic drift, certain alleles have become fixed, while others have been lost completely from the gene pool.

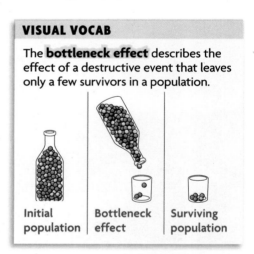

**VISUAL VOCAB**

The **bottleneck effect** describes the effect of a destructive event that leaves only a few survivors in a population.

Initial population | Bottleneck effect | Surviving population

## Founder Effect
As shown in **FIGURE 3.2**, the **founder effect** is genetic drift that occurs after a small number of individuals colonize a new area. The gene pools of these populations are often very different from those of the larger populations. The founder effect can be studied in human populations, such as Old Order Amish communities. These communities were founded in North America by small numbers of migrants from Europe. For example, the Amish of Lancaster County, Pennsylvania, have a high rate of Ellis–van Creveld syndrome. Although this form of dwarfism is rare in other human populations, it has become common in this Amish population through genetic drift. Geneticists have traced this syndrome back to one of the community's founding couples.

## ▶ MAIN IDEA

# The Hardy-Weinberg equation is used to predict genotype frequencies in a population.

For traits in simple dominant-recessive systems, biologists can predict genotype frequencies by using the Hardy-Weinberg equation, as seen in **FIGURE 4.1**. Values predicted by the equation are those that would be present if the population were in equilibrium. If $p$ equals the frequency of the dominant allele, and $q$ equals the frequency of the recessive allele, the equation can be written as follows:

$$p^2 + 2pq + q^2 = 1$$

Population biologists compare predicted genotype frequencies with actual frequencies. If they are the same, the population is in Hardy-Weinberg equilibrium for that trait. If the genetic data do not match the equation, the population is not in equilibrium; it is evolving.

## FIGURE 4.1  Using the Hardy-Weinberg Equation

**Use the Hardy-Weinberg equation to calculate predicted genotype frequencies for this population.**

In a population of 1000 fish, 640 have forked tail fins and 360 have smooth tail fins. Tail fin shape is determined by two alleles: $T$ is dominant for forked, and $t$ is recessive for smooth.

**1** Find $q^2$, the frequency of smooth-finned fish (recessive homozygotes).

$$q^2 = \frac{360 \text{ smooth-finned fish}}{1000 \text{ fish in population}} = 0.36$$

**2** To find the predicted value of $q$, take the square root of $q^2$.

$$q = \sqrt{0.36} = 0.6$$

**3** Use the equation $p + q = 1$ to find the predicted value of $p$. Rearrange the equation to solve for $p$.

$$p = 1 - q$$

$$p = 1 - 0.6 = 0.4$$

> These are the predicted allele frequencies: $p = 0.4$ and $q = 0.6$.

**4** Calculate the predicted genotype frequencies from the predicted allele frequencies.

$$p^2 = 0.4^2 = 0.16 \longrightarrow \text{16\% of fish have forked fins } (TT)$$

$$2pq = 2 \times (0.4) \times (0.6) = 0.48 \longrightarrow \text{48\% of fish have forked fins } (Tt)$$

$$q^2 = 0.6^2 = 0.36 \longrightarrow \text{36\% of fish have smooth fins } (tt)$$

### VARIABLES

- $p$ = **frequency of allele $T$** (dominant allele)
- $q$ = **frequency of allele $t$** (recessive allele)
- $p^2$ = **frequency of fish with $TT$** (homozygous dominant genotype)
- $2pq$ = **frequency of fish with $Tt$** (heterozygous genotype)
- $q^2$ = **frequency of fish with $tt$** (homozygous recessive genotype)

**Analyze  Through genetic analysis, scientists have found the genotype frequencies of the same fish population to be $TT = 0.50$, $Tt = 0.14$, and $tt = 0.36$. What can you infer by comparing these data with the values predicted by the Hardy-Weinberg equation?**

# FIGURE 4.2 Factors That Can Lead to Evolution

**There are five factors that can lead to evolution at the population level.**

## INITIAL POPULATION

Here are the alleles associated with body color in a hypothetical population.

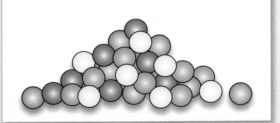

## GENETIC DRIFT

After a bottleneck event, only orange and blue alleles remained in the small population. Through genetic drift, orange alleles increase in frequency.

## GENE FLOW

Green alleles increase in frequency because of immigration; orange alleles decrease in frequency because of emigration.

arriving

leaving

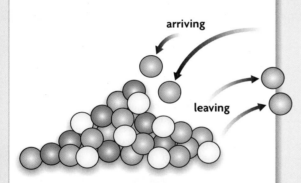

## MUTATION

A new allele, associated with red body color, is formed through mutation. This could affect sexual selection if red body color improves mating success. It could affect natural selection if red body color increases the chance for survival.

new allele

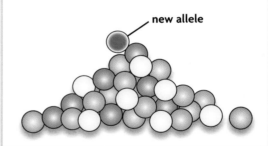

## SEXUAL SELECTION

Blue alleles are associated with blue body color, which improves mating success. Blue alleles, therefore, increase in frequency.

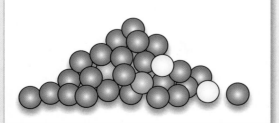

## NATURAL SELECTION

White alleles are associated with white body color, which allows individuals to blend in with their environment and avoid predation. White alleles, therefore, increase in frequency.

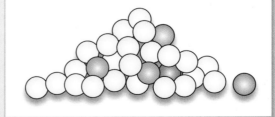

**CRITICAL VIEWING** Describe a scenario in which more than one factor could influence this population at the same time.

## MAIN IDEA

# There are five factors that can lead to evolution.

The conditions needed for Hardy-Weinberg equilibrium are not common in nature. Some parts of a population's environment may stay the same over time. However, other things are likely to change. Perhaps a flood carries part of a population to a new place. This population may then go through genetic drift. A mutation may create a new allele that allows some individuals to run faster and get away from predators. The frequency of this allele may then increase in the gene pool as it is passed on to future generations.

In nature, populations evolve, or change, in response to their environments. Populations that are not in Hardy-Weinberg equilibrium are evolving. In their studies, Hardy and Weinberg concluded that evolution should be expected in all populations almost all of the time. Their model shows that there are five factors that can lead to evolution. These factors are illustrated in **FIGURE 4.2.**

- **Genetic drift**  Allele frequencies can change due to chance alone.
- **Gene flow**  The movement of alleles from one population to another changes the allele frequencies in each population.
- **Mutation**  New alleles can form through mutation. Mutations create the genetic variation needed for evolution.
- **Sexual selection**  Certain traits may improve mating success. Alleles for these traits increase in frequency.
- **Natural selection**  Certain traits may be an advantage for survival. Alleles for these traits increase in frequency.

Evolution is continuous. Environments are always changing, though often very slowly relative to a human's lifetime. Evolution is a response to these changes. As environments change, populations either adapt or go extinct. When a population becomes extinct, a different species can take its place, and the cycle continues.

**Infer**  **Why do real populations rarely reach Hardy-Weinberg equilibrium?**

---

## 11.4  Formative Assessment

### REVIEWING ◉ MAIN IDEAS

1. What conditions are necessary for populations to remain in **Hardy-Weinberg equilibrium**?

2. What can be predicted by using the Hardy-Weinberg equation?

3. What are the five factors that can lead to evolution?

### CRITICAL THINKING

4. **Analyze**  Why is phenotypic variation necessary for natural selection and sexual selection?

5. **Evaluate**  Based on what you read in Section 3, is it likely that a population of peacocks would be in Hardy-Weinberg equilibrium? Why or why not?

### CONNECT TO

**GENETICS**

6. How are the concepts of dominant, recessive, heterozygous, and homozygous related to the Hardy-Weinberg equation?

# Speciation Through Isolation

SC.912.L.15.14,
SC.912.L.15.15

**KEY CONCEPT** New species can arise when populations are isolated.

**MAIN IDEAS**

○ The isolation of populations can lead to speciation.
○ Populations can become isolated in several ways.

**SC.912.L.15.14** Discuss mechanisms of evolutionary change other than natural selection such as genetic drift and gene flow.

**SC.912.L.15.15** Describe how mutation and genetic recombination increase genetic variation.

### Connect to Your World

If you travel through two different cities, towns, or even neighborhoods, you'll notice differences in the way people live. When groups of people are separated, ideas and resources are not shared, and so these groups of people may become more different. Similarly, genes cannot flow between populations that are isolated from each other, and they are more likely to become different. What happens if no gene flow occurs between two populations? This is one way that new species can arise.

## ○ MAIN IDEA

## The isolation of populations can lead to speciation.

If gene flow between two populations stops for any reason, the populations are said to be isolated. As these populations adapt to their environments, their gene pools may change. Random processes such as mutation and genetic drift can also change gene pools. All of these changes add up over many generations. With time, the two isolated populations become more and more genetically different. Individuals in one population may also begin to look and behave differently from individuals in the other population.

**Reproductive isolation** occurs when members of different populations can no longer mate successfully. Sometimes members of the two populations are not physically able to mate with each other. In other cases, they cannot produce offspring that survive and reproduce. Reproductive isolation between populations is the final step of becoming separate species. The rise of two or more species from one existing species is called **speciation.**

**FIGURE 5.1** illustrates a recent experiment that shows how one mutation can result in reproductive isolation. Scientists studied the *ds2* gene of fruit flies. This gene affects how well fruit flies can deal with cold temperatures. Fruit flies living in tropical areas, where competition for food is high, have a tropical allele. Fruit flies living in cooler regions, where there is less competition for food, have a temperate allele. The *ds2* gene also affects chemical scents called pheromones. Fruit flies use these scents to attract mates of their own species.

**CONNECT TO**

**GENETICS**

Fruit flies *(Drosophila melanogaster)* are very common in genetic research, as you may recall from the **Genetics** unit. Their popularity is based on several factors: they are easy to obtain, they reproduce easily and quickly, and they have well-understood genetic structures.

## FIGURE 5.1 Reproductive Isolation

Reproductive isolation occurs when members of isolated populations are no longer able to mate with each other successfully.

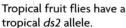
Tropical fruit flies have a tropical *ds2* allele.

Temperate fruit flies have a temperate *ds2* allele.

1 Scientists used lab fruit flies that are genetically similar. They developed a technique that allowed them to replace the *ds2* gene in each lab fruit fly with either the tropical or temperate allele.

2 Laboratory males that received the tropical allele were attracted to females that received the tropical allele. Males that received the temperate allele were attracted to females that received the temperate allele.

**Synthesize** Explain why fruit flies with a specific *ds2* allele prefer to mate with fruit flies that have the same allele.

This experiment shows how speciation may have occurred in natural fruit fly populations. Fruit flies migrating north from Africa to areas where there is less competition for food faced colder temperatures. A mutation in the *ds2* gene may have produced the temperate allele. This allele allows fruit flies to survive in cooler climates. Because the *ds2* gene also affects pheromones, mating behaviors changed. Fruit flies with the temperate allele and fruit flies with the tropical allele mated together less and less often. Eventually, these populations became reproductively isolated.

**Summarize** Why is reproductive isolation considered to be the final stage in speciation?

### ▶ MAIN IDEA

# Populations can become isolated in several ways.

Several kinds of barriers can prevent mating between populations, leading to reproductive isolation. These include behavioral, geographic, and temporal barriers.

**WebQuest**
HMHScience.com
**GO ONLINE**
Speciation in Action

## Behavioral Barriers

Chemical scents, courtship dances of birds, and courtship songs of frogs are examples of sexual signals used to attract mates. Changes in these signals can prevent mating between populations. **Behavioral isolation** is isolation caused by differences in courtship or mating behaviors. Over 2000 species of fireflies are isolated in this way. Male and female fireflies produce patterns of flashes that attract mates of their own species. For example, *Photuris frontalis* emits one flash every second, *P. hebes* emits one flash every 2 seconds, and *P. fairchildi* produces a double flash every 5.5 seconds.

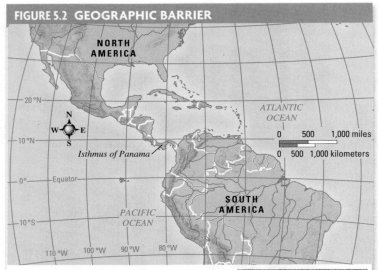

## FIGURE 5.2 GEOGRAPHIC BARRIER

NORTH AMERICA

20°N

ATLANTIC OCEAN

10°N

Isthmus of Panama

0 500 1,000 miles

0 500 1,000 kilometers

0° Equator

PACIFIC OCEAN

SOUTH AMERICA

10°S

110°W 100°W 90°W 80°W

Although snapping shrimp in the Atlantic and Pacific Oceans look similar, they are distinct species that have evolved through geographic isolation.

## Geographic Barriers

The most commonly studied type of isolation is geographic isolation. **Geographic isolation** involves physical barriers that divide a population into two or more groups. These barriers can include rivers, mountains, and dried lakebeds. As shown in **FIGURE 5.2**, the formation of the Isthmus of Panama created a barrier for many marine species. Marine organisms could no longer easily cross between the Atlantic and Pacific Oceans. Over time, the isolated populations became genetically different. Several species of snapping shrimp have evolved through geographic isolation. These species appear almost identical to one another. However, when males and females from opposite sides of the isthmus are placed together, they snap at each other instead of courting. Because they will no longer mate, these shrimp are classified as different species.

## Temporal Barriers

Barriers can also involve timing. **Temporal isolation** exists when timing prevents reproduction between populations. Some members of a population may show signs of courtship at different times if there is a lot of competition for mates. Reproductive periods may change to a different time of the year or a different part of the day. These differences in timing can lead to speciation. For example, two tree species that grow on the Monterey Peninsula in California are very closely related. However, they have different pollination periods. The Monterey pine sheds its pollen in February, while the Bishop pine sheds its pollen in April. These pine species have likely evolved through temporal isolation.

**Compare and Contrast** What are the differences and similarities between behavioral isolation and temporal isolation?

### READING TOOLBOX

**VOCABULARY**
The word *temporal* comes from the Latin word *tempus*, meaning "time."

©Science Source/Getty Images

**SELF-CHECK Online**
HMHScience.com
**GO ONLINE**

## 11.5 Formative Assessment

### REVIEWING ▶ MAIN IDEAS

1. How can **reproductive isolation** lead to **speciation**?

2. What are three types of barriers that can lead to reproductive isolation?

### CRITICAL THINKING

3. **Apply** Why are the flash patterns of fireflies considered to be **behavioral isolation**?

4. **Analyze** How did **geographic isolation** affect the diversity Darwin observed in Galápagos finches?

### CONNECT TO

**SCIENTIFIC PROCESS**

5. What could have been used as a control group in the fruit fly experiment described in Figure 5.1?

# 11.6 Patterns in Evolution

SC.912.L.15.14

SC.912.L.15.14 Discuss mechanisms of evolutionary change other than natural selection such as genetic drift and gene flow.

## VOCABULARY

convergent evolution
divergent evolution
coevolution
extinction
punctuated equilibrium
adaptive radiation

| KEY CONCEPT  **Evolution occurs in patterns.**

**MAIN IDEAS**

- Evolution through natural selection is not random.
- Species can shape each other over time.
- Species can become extinct.
- Speciation often occurs in patterns.

### ☼ *Connect to Your World*

People adapt their behavior to their situation. As you go through school, you are likely to change how you dress, talk, and study. When you learn something that makes your life better, you hold on to that new skill. On a genetic level and over multiple generations, species hold onto traits that benefit them in their environment. Natural selection is the process that preserves these adaptive traits in a population. However, sudden changes in an environment can wipe out a species quickly. The rise and fall of species over time reveal clear evolutionary patterns.

### ● MAIN IDEA

## Evolution through natural selection is not random.

In science, the terms *chance* and *random* relate to how easily an outcome can be predicted. Because mutations and genetic drift cannot be predicted, they are called random events. These random events are sources of genetic diversity. However, natural selection, which acts on this diversity, is not random. Individuals with traits that are better adapted for their environment have a better chance of surviving and reproducing than do individuals without these traits.

You have learned about directional, stabilizing, and disruptive selection. In each of these modes of selection, the effects of natural selection add up over many generations. In other words, natural selection pushes a population's traits in an advantageous direction. As you can see in **FIGURE 6.1,** alleles associated with these traits add up in the population's gene pool.

Remember, however, that having direction is not the same as having purpose or intent. The environment controls the direction of natural selection. When the environment changes, different traits may become advantageous. The response of species to environmental challenges and opportunities is not random.

### FIGURE 6.1 PATTERNS IN NATURAL SELECTION

In this hypothetical population, green body color is favored by natural selection. With each generation, alleles associated with green body color increase in frequency. Over time, more and more individuals in the population will have the advantageous phenotype.

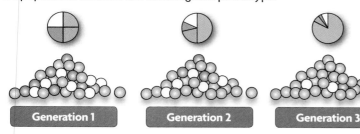

Generation 1    Generation 2    Generation 3

## Convergent Evolution

Different species often must adapt to similar environments. Evolution toward similar characteristics in unrelated species is called **convergent evolution.** Analogous structures, such as wings on birds and insects, are common examples of convergent evolution. Another example is the tail fin of fish and marine mammals, as shown in **FIGURE 6.2**. Sharks, which are fish, and dolphins, which are mammals, are separated by about 300 million years of evolution. Separately, they have both evolved similar tail fins to propel themselves through the water. However, the tail fins of sharks and other fish are vertical, while those of dolphins are horizontal.

## Divergent Evolution

When closely related species evolve in different directions, they become increasingly different through **divergent evolution.** The evolution of the red fox and the kit fox is an example of this trend. Though closely related, the two species have different appearances that are the result of adapting to different environments. The red fox lives in temperate regions, usually in forests. Its dark reddish coat helps it to hide from predators. The sandy-colored coat of the kit fox allows it to blend in with its desert surroundings. Kit foxes also have large ears relative to their body size. This adaptation helps them to keep cool in the desert heat.

**Infer** Are the shells of turtles and snails examples of convergent or divergent evolution? Explain.

---

## FIGURE 6.2 Convergent and Divergent Evolution

Natural selection is not random. It can have direction, and its effects are cumulative through generations.

### CONVERGENT EVOLUTION

Dolphins, which are mammals, and sharks, which are fish, have evolved similar tail fins, as each has adapted to similar environmental conditions.

Dolphin                    Shark

### DIVERGENT EVOLUTION

The kit fox and the red fox evolved from a common ancestor while adapting to different environments.

Kit fox        Red fox

Ancestor

**Analyze** How do convergent and divergent evolution illustrate the directional nature of natural selection?

## ○ MAIN IDEA
# Species can shape each other over time.

Species interact with each other in many different ways. For example, they may compete for the same food source or be involved in a predator-prey relationship. Most of these interactions do not involve evolutionary changes. However, sometimes the evolutionary paths of two species become connected.

### Beneficial Relationships Through Coevolution

The bull-thorn acacia is a plant species with branches covered in hollow thorns. Although the thorns protect the plant from being eaten by large animals, small herbivores such as caterpillars can fit between them. To the rescue comes *Pseudomyrmex ferrugineus,* a species of stinging ants. As shown in **FIGURE 6.3**, these ants live inside the thorns and feed on the plant's nectar. The ants protect the plant by stinging animals that try to eat the leaves.

This relationship is much more than a simple cooperation between two species. The acacia and the ants share an evolutionary history. The hollow thorns and nectar-producing leaves of the acacia and the stinging of the ants have evolved due to the relationship between the two species. Relatives of these species that are not involved in this type of relationship do not have these traits. Such relationships form through **coevolution,** the process in which two or more species evolve in response to changes in each other.

### Evolutionary Arms Races

Coevolution can also occur in competitive relationships. These interactions can lead to "evolutionary arms races," in which each species responds to pressure from the other through better adaptations over many generations.

For example, many plants produce defense chemicals in the soil to discourage other plants from growing nearby and competing for resources. Natural selection then favors competing plants that can overcome the effects of the chemicals. After many generations, most competitors have some level of resistance and are again able to grow near the defensive plant. Natural selection then favors plants that have evolved even more potent chemicals. In another case, the thick shells and spines of murex snails are an adaptive response to predation by crabs. In turn, crabs have evolved powerful claws that are strong enough to crack the snails' shells.

**FIGURE 6.3** The relationship between this ant and the acacia plant has developed through coevolution. The ant lives inside the hollow thorn and protects the acacia by stinging any potential predators.

**Predict  What do you think will happen in future generations of crabs and snails?**

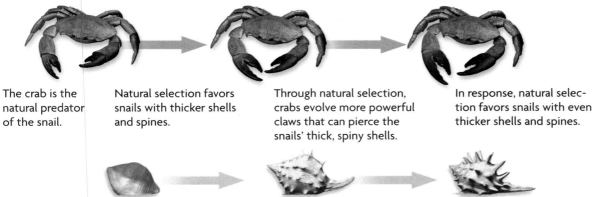

The crab is the natural predator of the snail.

Natural selection favors snails with thicker shells and spines.

Through natural selection, crabs evolve more powerful claws that can pierce the snails' thick, spiny shells.

In response, natural selection favors snails with even thicker shells and spines.

**FIGURE 6.4** Native to Portugal and Spain, the Iberian lynx is the world's most endangered feline. The World Wildlife Federation estimates that there are only 84 to 143 adult individuals remaining in the wild.

# Species can become extinct.

Just as birth and death are natural events in the life of an individual, the rise and fall of species are natural processes of evolution. The elimination of a species from Earth is called **extinction.** Extinction often occurs when a species as a whole is unable to adapt to a change in its environment. Biologists divide extinction events into two categories—background extinctions and mass extinctions. Although they differ in degree, the effect of both is the same: the permanent loss of species from Earth.

## Background Extinctions

Extinctions that occur continuously but at a very low rate are called background extinctions. They are part of the cycle of life on Earth. Background extinctions occur at roughly the same rate as speciation. Unlike catastrophic mass extinctions, background extinction events usually affect only one or a few species in a relatively small area, such as a rain forest or a mountain range. They can be caused by local changes in the environment, such as the introduction of a new predator species or a decrease in food supply. From a human perspective, such extinctions seem to occur randomly but at a fairly constant rate.

## Mass Extinctions

Mass extinctions are much more rare than background extinctions. However, as illustrated in **FIGURE 6.5,** they are much more intense. These events often occur at the global level. Therefore, they destroy many species—even entire orders or families. Mass extinctions are thought to occur suddenly in geologic time, usually because of a catastrophic event such as an ice age or asteroid impact. The fossil record confirms that there have been at least five mass extinctions in the past 600 million years. Some scientists also think that we are in the midst of a sixth mass extinction that has been caused by human impact on the biosphere.

**Compare and Contrast** What are the differences and similarities between background extinctions and mass extinctions?

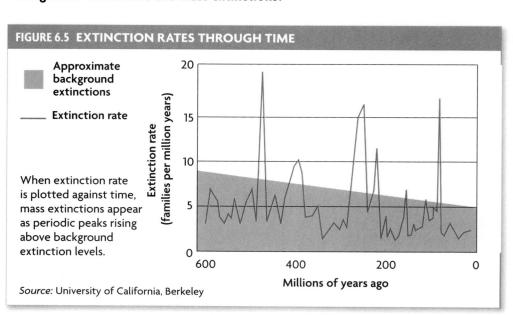

**FIGURE 6.5 EXTINCTION RATES THROUGH TIME**

Approximate background extinctions

Extinction rate

When extinction rate is plotted against time, mass extinctions appear as periodic peaks rising above background extinction levels.

Extinction rate (families per million years)

Millions of years ago

*Source:* University of California, Berkeley

# Speciation often occurs in patterns.

Paleontologists have long noticed repeating patterns in the history of life, reflected in the fossil record. Among these patterns, two stand out from the rest. In evolutionary gradualism, discussed in Section 2 of the chapter Principles of Evolution, evolutionary changes are thought to occur over long periods of time. For many years, advocates of evolution adhered to this idea.

In the second of the two patterns, bursts of evolutionary activity are followed by long periods of stability. This pattern is described by the theory of **punctuated equilibrium,** which states that episodes of speciation occur suddenly in geologic time and are followed by long periods of little evolutionary change, or stasis. Paleontologist Niles Eldredge, a curator at The American Museum of Natural History in New York, and evolutionary biologist Stephen Jay Gould originally proposed the theory of punctuated equilbrium in 1972. Both men were graduate students at Columbia University, studying fossils of four closely related species of trilobite. The fossils showed evidence of the sudden appearance of a new form of eye. This new trilobite eye appears to be linked to an increased ability to roll into a protective ball, allowing for better defense against predators.

The theory of punctuated equilibrium was written as a revision of Darwin's idea that new species arise through gradual transformations of ancestral species. It must be noted that in the sixth edition of his book *On the Origin of Species,* Darwin wrote that "the periods, during which species have undergone modification, though long as measured by years, have probably been short in comparison with the periods during which they retained the same form."

CONNECT TO

**GEOLOGY**

Refer back to Section 1 of the chapter **Principles of Evolution** to review James Hutton's theory that led to the concept of evolutionary gradualism.

## FIGURE 6.6 Evolutionary Gradualism and Punctuated Equilibrium

**The concept that species evolve slowly, over long periods of time, is known as evolutionary gradualism.**

**Punctuated equilibrium proposes that species show little evolutionary change for millions of years, followed by periods of rapid speciation.**

Modern studies show us that in stable ecosystems, most species are well adapted and generally resistant to change, unless some outside force causes disruption. In the case of punctuated equilibrium, this is believed to occur because a portion of a population becomes isolated and undergoes a speciation event. This isolation may be due to some sort of catastrophe, after which those organisms able to evolve quickly are more likely to survive. Isolation may also occur as a result of long-term environmental changes, like the formation of mountains or deserts, or due to a mutation that gives the organism a significant survival advantage over competitors.

When an ecosystem is greatly damaged, such as after the 1980 volcanic eruption of Mt. Saint Helens, in Washington state, other organisms will rapidly move into the area to fill empty niches. Although rapid evolutionary bursts can be compared in some ways to what is seen when such modern ecosystems are seriously disturbed, there is a distinct difference between the two. Rather than existing species moving in to fill vacancies in a changed ecosystem, in punctuated equilibrium, new speciation occurs suddenly following a long interval of stasis. Both evolutionary gradualism and punctuated equilibrium are viable scientific theories, and both are supported by evidence found in the fossil record. Although scientists still debate which of these two ideas best accounts for observed patterns of evolutionary change, most accept that it is likely that evolution occurs by a combination of these two major theories.

The process involving the diversification of one ancestral species into many descendent species is referred to as **adaptive radiation.** These descendent species are usually adapted to a wide range of environments. One example of adaptive radiation is the variation found in Galápagos finches, which were discussed in the chapter Principles of Evolution. Another rather dramatic example is seen in the radiation of mammals following the mass extinction at the end of the Cretaceous period about 65 million years ago.

According to the fossils that have been found thus far, the earliest mammals were tiny, mostly nocturnal, and probably insect eaters, such as the shrew-like *Leptictidium,* seen in **FIGURE 6.7,** allowing them to coexist with the dinosaurs for about 150 million years.

## VISUAL VOCAB

**Adaptive radiation** is the rapid evolution of many diverse species from ancestral species.

descendent species

time

ancestral species

### FIGURE 6.7  LEPTICTIDIUM

This model of *Leptictidium* was made based on the bone structures found in fossil specimens.

## FIGURE 6.8 The K-T Boundary

The K-T boundary layer is marked clearly in rock layers in many places around the world. It is linked to the collision of an asteroid with Earth around 65 million years ago. The layer contains high concentrations of the element Iridium. Iridium is very rare on Earth, but is found in much greater abundance in objects from space.

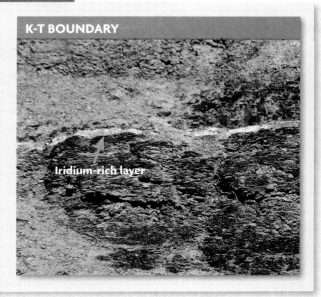

K-T BOUNDARY

Iridium-rich layer

The extinction of the dinosaurs about 65 million years ago left environments full of open niches for other types of animals. In the first 10 million years of the Tertiary period following the mass extinction event, more than 4000 mammal species had evolved, including the ancestors of modern whales, bats, rodents, and primates. Evidence of this mass extinction, known as the Cretaceous-Tertiary (K-T) boundary, can be seen in **FIGURE 6.8.**

The fossil record indicates that there have been at least five mass extinctions in the past 600 million years, where large percentages of global populations were decimated. Studying these extinctions reveals that following each was a period of rapid evolutionary changes and the appearance of new species.

**Synthesize** **The adaptive radiation of mammals followed the extinction of the dinosaurs. How do these events support the theory of punctuated equilibrium?**

**SELF-CHECK** Online
HMHScience.com

**GO ONLINE**

## 11.6 Formative Assessment

### REVIEWING ▶ MAIN IDEAS

1. Explain what it means to say that natural selection is not random.

2. How does **coevolution** shape two species over time?

3. How can mass **extinctions** lead to the sudden appearance of new species?

4. What pattern is described by the theory of **punctuated equilibrium**?

### CRITICAL THINKING

5. **Synthesize** Defensive chemicals are usually found in unripe fruit, but not in ripe fruit. In terms of coevolution, why might this be?

6. **Infer** Analogous structures are often examples of **convergent evolution.** What types of structures would likely be examples of **divergent evolution**?

### CONNECT TO

#### HUMAN BIOLOGY

7. Through mutation, HIV can accumulate resistance to drugs developed for treatment. Describe the relationship between HIV and the humans who develop these drugs in terms of an evolutionary arms race.

# 11 Summary

**BIG IDEA** The genetic composition of populations evolves through natural selection as species adapt to changes in their environment.

## KEY CONCEPTS

### 11.1 Genetic Variation Within Populations

**A population shares a common gene pool.** Genetic variation in a gene pool can be measured through allele frequencies. Genetic variation increases the chance that some members of a population will be able to adapt to their environment.

### 11.2 Natural Selection in Populations

**Populations, not individuals, evolve.** Natural selection acts on distributions of traits in a population. Directional selection occurs when one extreme phenotype is advantageous for survival. If intermediate phenotypes are advantageous, they become more common through stabilizing selection. In the process of disruptive selection, extreme phenotypes are selected.

### 11.3 Other Mechanisms of Evolution

**Natural selection is not the only mechanism through which populations evolve.** Gene flow is the movement of alleles between populations. Changes in allele frequencies due to chance alone can occur through genetic drift. If certain traits increase mating success, those traits can become more common through sexual selection.

### 11.4 Hardy-Weinberg Equilibrium

**Hardy-Weinberg equilibrium provides a framework for understanding how populations evolve.** A population in Hardy-Weinberg equilibrium is not evolving. The conditions required for this equilibrium are rarely met in nature. However, Hardy-Weinberg equilibrium provides a framework for understanding the factors that can lead to evolution. It is therefore very useful to population biologists.

### 11.5 Speciation Through Isolation

**New species can arise when populations are isolated.** Reproductive isolation occurs when members of two populations are no longer able to mate successfully. It is the final stage in speciation—the rise of two or more species from one existing species. Behavioral, geographic, or temporal barriers can lead to isolation.

### 11.6 Patterns in Evolution

**Evolution occurs in patterns.** Evolution through natural selection can have direction, and its effects add up over many generations. The evolutionary paths of two or more species can become connected through the process of coevolution. Extinction and speciation events also appear in patterns in the fossil record.

---

### 🔎 READING TOOLBOX — SYNTHESIZE YOUR NOTES

**Two-Column Chart** Make a two-column chart to synthesize your notes about the three modes of natural selection.

| Type of Selection | Graph |
|---|---|
| Directional Selection<br><br>    Cause:<br><br><br>    Result: | |

**Concept Map** Use a concept map to summarize factors that can lead to evolution.

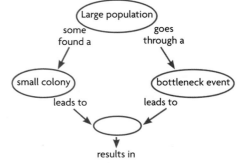

---

CHAPTER
# 11 Review

INTERACTIVE Review
HMHScience.com

GO ONLINE

Review Games • Concept Map • Section Self-Checks

## CHAPTER VOCABULARY

**11.1**   gene pool
allele frequency

**11.2**   normal distribution
microevolution
directional selection
stabilizing selection
disruptive selection

**11.3**   gene flow
genetic drift
bottleneck effect
founder effect
sexual selection

**11.4**   Hardy-Weinberg equilibrium

**11.5**   reproductive isolation
speciation
behavioral isolation

geographic isolation
temporal isolation

**11.6**   convergent evolution
divergent evolution
coevolution
extinction
punctuated equilibrium
adaptive radiation

## Reviewing Vocabulary

**READING TOOLBOX   VISUALIZING VOCABULARY**

For each term below, use simple shapes, lines, or arrows to illustrate their meaning. Below each picture, write a short caption. Here's an example for the term *founder effect*.

*A small group of individuals starts a population that is subject to genetic drift.*

**1.** gene flow
**2.** geographic isolation
**3.** divergent evolution
**4.** punctuated equilibrium

### Keep It Short

For each vocabulary word below, write a short, precise phrase that describes its meaning. For example, a short phrase to describe the word *extinction* could be "gone forever."

**5.** gene pool
**6.** reproductive isolation
**7.** speciation
**8.** convergent evolution
**9.** coevolution
**10.** adaptive radiation

## Reviewing MAIN IDEAS

**11.** Would a population with a lot of genetic variation or little genetic variation be more likely to have individuals that can adapt to a changing environment? Explain your answer.

**12.** Describe two major sources of genetic variation.

**13.** A certain trait in a population is not under any selective pressure. Draw a curve showing the likely phenotypic distribution for this trait.

**14.** Over many generations, certain insect species have become more and more resistant to insecticides. What type of natural selection does this show, and how does it differ from the other types?

**15.** Describe how gene flow can increase genetic variation within two neighboring populations.

**16.** How are the effects of genetic drift similar to the effects of having a small sample size in a scientific experiment?

**17.** Give an example of the way sexual selection can cause extreme phenotypes in a population.

**18.** What are the conditions necessary for a population to stay in Hardy-Weinberg equilibrium?

**19.** How can a lack of gene flow between populations lead to speciation?

**20.** Describe three types of barriers that can cause populations to become reproductively isolated from each other.

**21.** Explain why mutation and genetic drift are random events, while natural selection is not.

**22.** Speciation is the rise of two or more species from one existing species. What process keeps the number of total species on Earth from growing exponentially through speciation?

**23.** What is the relationship between speciation and the theory of punctuated equilibrium?

# Critical Thinking

**24. Evaluate** Biogeographic and genetic evidence indicates that more than 50 species of Hawaiian honeycreeper birds have likely descended from a common ancestor. The 18 surviving species occupy many different niches and exhibit a variety of beak types, songs, and nesting behaviors. What role do the concepts of reproductive isolation and adaptive radiation play in interpreting the evidence for the speciation of Hawaiian honeycreepers?

**25. Apply** How could gene flow affect a population that was founded by a small number of individuals?

**26. Analyze** What type of selection produces a distribution of phenotypes opposite to that produced by stabilizing selection? Explain your answer.

**27. Analyze** Explain how the process of genetic drift occurs completely by chance.

**28. Analyze** Why must allele frequencies in a gene pool always add up to 100%?

**29. Compare and Contrast** What are the differences and similarities between natural selection and sexual selection?

## Interpreting Visuals

Below is a frequency distribution for beak size in a hypothetical population of birds. Use this graph to answer the next three questions.

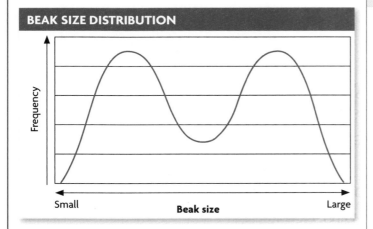

BEAK SIZE DISTRIBUTION

**30. Analyze** What type of selection is demonstrated by the data in this graph? Explain your answer.

**31. Analyze** Which phenotypes are the most common in this population?

**32. Synthesize** Describe a scenario that could realistically lead to this pattern of selection in a bird population.

**Identify Patterns**

Below is a graph showing the relationship between female chimpanzee rank and the survival of offspring. Use the graph to answer the next three questions.

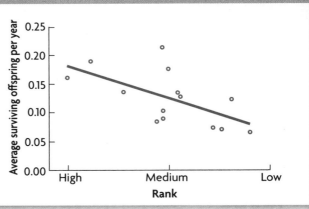

SURVIVAL OF CHIMPANZEE OFFSPRING

Source: Jane Goodall Institute

**33. Analyze** What is the relationship between female rank and the survival of her offspring?

**34. Analyze** Is there a level of rank that prevents a female chimp from reproducing? Explain.

**35. Infer** What can you infer by studying the scale of the y-axis on this graph?

## Making Connections

**36. Write a Proposal** The explosive growth of nonnative species is a major global issue. A few individuals from one area act as founders of new populations on other continents or in other oceans. This is causing many native populations to decline. Human activities such as global commerce and travel are directly causing these destructive founding populations. Write a proposal to an international committee on the environment regarding this issue. Include in your proposal the significance of the changes to native populations, using terms and concepts from the chapter.

**37. Infer** Hemoglobin, an oxygen-carrying protein found in the red blood cells of vertebrates, helps to circulate oxygen from the lungs to all parts of the body. In penguins, the blood has a very high concentration of hemoglobin. Penguin muscles have a high concentration of myoglobin, which also stores oxygen. What might be a reason for these adaptations?

# Standards-Based Assessment

Record your answers on a separate piece of paper.

**MULTIPLE CHOICE**

**1** Which explanation describes how natural selection produces changes in organisms?

 A Natural selection enables a trait of an individual to be expressed.

 B Natural selection occurs when a favorable phenotype allows for differential reproductive success in a population of organisms.

 C Natural selection occurs when individuals that develop disease die.

 D Natural selection occurs when neutral phenotypes become common in a population.

**2** A drought occurs in an environment with a large plant population. Which element of natural selection is *most likely* to enable part of the population to survive and reproduce?

 A the potential for the plant population to produce more offspring than can survive

 B a change in climate conditions

 C competition with other plant and animal populations for finite water resources

 D some individual plants inherited traits that enable them to survive a drought

> **THINK THROUGH THE QUESTION**
>
> Read each of the answer choices carefully. Which of these choices would make a population more likely to survive in a changing environment?

**3** In the 1800s, Georges Cuvier proposed the theory of catastrophism to explain how some species disappear from the fossil record by going extinct and new species appear in the fossil record through immigration. How could Cuvier's theory be used to explain periods of stasis?

 A Periods of stasis would result when organisms were not subject to the effects of natural disasters for extended periods of time.

 B Periods of stasis would appear in the fossil record when regions of Earth were subject to frequent natural disasters.

 C Periods of stasis would result only if an area was completely destroyed by a natural disaster.

 D Periods of stasis would result from slow and steady changes that were constantly occurring on Earth.

**4** Scientists often use the relative positions of fossils in sedimentary rock layers to draw conclusions about the sequential nature of groups of organisms in the fossil record. Why are scientists able to use such observations as a key to the relative ages of fossils?

 A Sedimentary rocks are laid down in layers, so the oldest layers in an undisturbed rock bed will be located beneath upper layers.

 B Even when sedimentary rock layers are disturbed, the oldest layer is always deposited on top of the youngest rock layer.

 C Younger rock layers are always deposited under older layers.

 D Weathering and erosion expose fossils making them easier to examine.

**5**

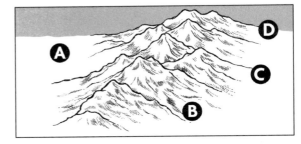

The map above shows the location of four populations of a bee species. Over time, Population A is *most likely* to evolve into a new species due to—

 A geographic isolation

 B temporal isolation

 C convergent evolution

 D adaptive radiation

# 12 The History of Life

**BIG IDEA** Scientists use many types of data collection and experimentation to form hypotheses and theories about how life formed on Earth.

**ONLINE BIOLOGY** HMHScience.com

**ONLINE** Labs
- Radioactive Decay
- **QuickLab** Geologic Clock
- Stride Inferences
- Understanding Geologic Time
- Comparing Indexes Among Primates
- **Virtual Lab** Comparing Hominoid Skulls

- **Video Lab** Model of Rock Strata

©Richard Ashworth/robertharding/Getty Images

# Q What can fossils teach us about the past?

This man, known only as Tollund Man, died about 2200 years ago in what is now Denmark. Details such as his skin and hair were preserved by the acid of the bog in which he was found. A bog is a type of wetland that accumulates peat, the deposits of dead plant material. Older remains from bogs can add information to the fossil record, which tends to consist mostly of hard shells, teeth, and bones.

---

**READING TOOLBOX**    This reading tool can help you learn the material in the following pages.

## USING LANGUAGE

**Describing Time**  Certain words and phrases can help you get an idea of a past event's time frame (when it happened) and duration (for how long it happened). These phrases are called *specific time markers*. Specific time markers include phrases such as 1 hour, yesterday, the 20th century, and 30 years later.

## YOUR TURN

Read the sentences below, and write the specific time markers.

1. Jennifer celebrated her 16th birthday on Saturday two weeks ago.
2. Dinosaurs became extinct about 65 million years ago, at the end of the Cretaceous Period.

# The Fossil Record

**SC.912.L.15.1**

SC.912.L.15.1 Explain how the scientific theory of evolution is supported by the fossil record, comparative anatomy, comparative embryology, biogeography, molecular biology, and observed evolutionary change.

**KEY CONCEPT** **Fossils are a record of life that existed in the past.**

### MAIN IDEAS
- Fossils can form in several ways.
- Radiometric dating provides a close estimate of a fossil's age.

**VOCABULARY**
relative dating
radiometric dating
isotope
half-life

### ☀ *Connect to Your World*

Do you ever consider how much the world and its inhabitants have changed in the past 15, 50, or 100 years? Have you studied ancient civilizations that existed thousands of years ago? These time frames are tiny blips on the scale of time revealed by the fossil record. Some of the world's oldest fossils, found at the Burgess Shale site in Canada, offer a glimpse of what life was like 500 million years before Tollund Man lived. These specimens are keys to understanding the history of life on Earth.

### ▶ MAIN IDEA

## Fossils can form in several ways.

Fossils are far more diverse than the giant dinosaur skeletons we see in museums. The following processes are some of the ways fossils form. **FIGURE 1.1** shows examples of fossils produced in these different ways.

- **Permineralization** occurs when minerals carried by water are deposited around a hard structure. They may also replace the hard structure itself.
- **Natural casts** form when flowing water removes all of the original bone or tissue, leaving just an impression in sediment. Minerals fill in the mold, recreating the original shape of the organism.
- **Trace fossils** record the activity of an organism. They include nests, burrows, imprints of leaves, and footprints.
- **Amber-preserved fossils** are organisms that become trapped in tree resin that hardens into amber after the tree gets buried underground.
- **Preserved remains** form when an entire organism becomes encased in material such as ice or volcanic ash or immersed in bogs.

**FIGURE 1.1** The fossil record includes fossils that formed in many different ways.

Permineralized skeleton of a *Velociraptor* dinosaur

Natural cast of a crinoid, a marine animal

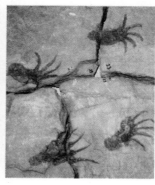

Trace fossils of footprints from a *Dimetrodon* dinosaur

Amber-preserved spider

Ice-preserved 5000-year-old remains of a man found in the Italian Alps

## FIGURE 1.2 The Process of Permineralization

**The process of permineralization requires rapid burial in an area with water and continuous sedimentation.**

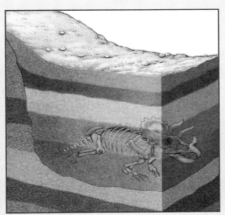

An organism dies in a location, such as a riverbed, where sediments can rapidly cover its body.

Over time, pressure from additional sediment compresses the body, and minerals slowly replace all hard structures, such as bone.

Earthquakes or erosion may expose the fossil millions of years after formation, or it may be uncovered by paleontologists, hikers, or road-building crews.

**Infer** What conditions could occur that would prevent an organism from being preserved through permineralization?

Most fossils form in sedimentary rock, which is made by many layers of sediment or small rock particles. The best environments for any type of fossilization include wetlands, bogs, and areas where sediment is continuously deposited, such as river mouths, lakebeds, and floodplains.

The most common fossils result from permineralization. Several circumstances are critical for this process, as shown in **FIGURE 1.2**. The organism must be buried or encased in some type of material—such as sand, sediment, mud, or tar—very soon after death, while the organism's features are still intact. After burial, groundwater trickles into tiny pores and spaces in plants, bones, and shells. During this process, the excess minerals in the water are deposited on the remaining cells and tissues. Many layers of mineral deposits are left behind, creating a fossilized record by replacing organic tissues with hard minerals. The resulting fossil has the same shape as the original structure and may contain some original tissue.

With such specific conditions needed for fossilization, it is easy to see why only a tiny percentage of living things that ever existed became fossils. Most remains decompose or are destroyed before they can be preserved. Even successful fossilization is no guarantee that an organism's remains will be added to the fossil record. Natural events such as earthquakes and the recycling of rock into magma can destroy fossils that took thousands of years to form.

**Summarize** Why are so few complete fossils discovered?

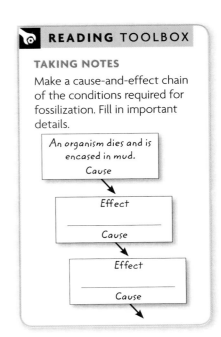

**READING TOOLBOX**

**TAKING NOTES**

Make a cause-and-effect chain of the conditions required for fossilization. Fill in important details.

An organism dies and is encased in mud.
Cause

Effect
_____
Cause

Effect
_____
Cause

## MAIN IDEA
# Radiometric dating provides a close estimate of a fossil's age.

**CONNECT TO**

**CHEMISTRY OF LIFE**

Recall from the chapter **Chemistry of Life** that all atoms of a given element have the same number of protons. Isotopes are named for the total number of protons and neutrons in their nuclei.

● neutrons   ● protons

CARBON-12
NUCLEUS
6 protons
6 neutrons

CARBON-14
NUCLEUS
6 protons
8 neutrons

Recall that geologists in the 1700s had realized that rock layers at the bottom of an undisturbed sequence of rocks were deposited before those at the top, and therefore are older. The same logic holds true for the fossils found in rock layers. **Relative dating** estimates the time during which an organism lived by comparing the placement of fossils of that organism with the placement of fossils in other layers of rock. Relative dating allows scientists to infer the order in which groups of species existed, although it does not provide the actual ages of fossils.

To estimate a fossil's actual, or absolute, age, scientists use **radiometric dating**—a technique that uses the natural decay rate of unstable isotopes found in materials in order to calculate the age of that material. **Isotopes** are atoms of an element that have the same number of protons but a different number of neutrons. Most elements have several isotopes. For example, the element carbon (C) has three naturally occurring isotopes. All carbon isotopes have six protons. Isotopes are named, however, by their number of protons plus their number of neutrons. Thus, carbon-12 ($^{12}$C) has six neutrons, carbon-13 ($^{13}$C) has seven neutrons, and carbon-14 ($^{14}$C) has eight neutrons. More than 98 percent of the carbon in a living organism is $^{12}$C.

Some isotopes have unstable nuclei. As a result, their nuclei undergo radioactive decay—they break down—over time. This releases radiation in the form of particles and energy. As an isotope decays, it can transform into a different element. The decay rate of many radioactive isotopes has been measured and is expressed as the isotope's half-life, as shown in **FIGURE 1.3**. A **half-life** is the amount of time it takes for half of the isotope in a sample to decay into a different element, or its product isotope. An element's half-life is not affected by environmental conditions such as temperature or pressure. Both $^{12}$C and $^{13}$C are stable, but $^{14}$C decays into nitrogen-14 ($^{14}$N), with a half-life of roughly 5700 years.

## Radiocarbon Dating

The isotope $^{14}$C is used commonly for radiometric dating of recent remains, such as those of Tollund Man shown at the beginning of this chapter. Organisms absorb carbon through eating and breathing, so $^{14}$C is constantly being resupplied. When an organism dies, its intake of carbon stops, but the decay of $^{14}$C continues. The fossil's age can be estimated by comparing the ratio of a stable isotope, such as $^{12}$C, to $^{14}$C. The longer the organism has been dead, the larger the difference between the amounts of $^{12}$C and $^{14}$C there will be. The half-life of carbon-14 is roughly 5700 years, which means that after 5700 years, half of the $^{14}$C in a fossil will have decayed into $^{14}$N, its decay product. The other half remains as $^{14}$C. After 11,400 years, or two half-lives, 75 percent of the $^{14}$C will have decayed.

| FIGURE 1.3  DECAY OF ISOTOPES | | |
| --- | --- | --- |
| **Isotope (parent)** | **Product (daughter)** | **Half-life (years)** |
| **rubidium-87** | strontium-87 | 48.8 billion |
| **uranium-238** | lead-206 | 4.5 billion |
| **chlorine-36** | argon-36 | 300,000 |
| **carbon-14** | nitrogen-14 | 5730 |

## FIGURE 1.4 Radiometric Dating Using Carbon-14

**Radiometric dating uses the natural decay rate of unstable isotopes to calculate the age of a fossil.**

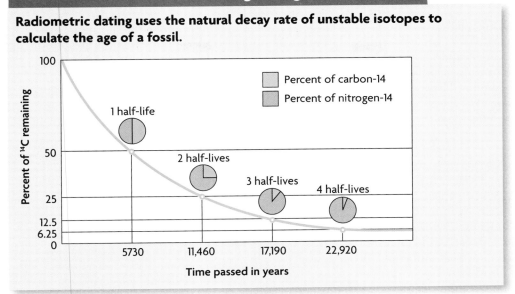

One-quarter of the original $^{14}$C remains. Radioactive decay of $^{14}$C is shown in **FIGURE 1.4.** Carbon-14 dating can be used to date objects only up to about 45,000 years old. If the objects are older than that, the fraction of $^{14}$C will be too small to measure accurately. Older objects can be dated by using an isotope that has a longer half-life, such as uranium.

**Web Quest**
HMHScience.com
**GO ONLINE**
Geologic Dating

### Determining Earth's Age

Scientists have used radiometric dating to determine the age of Earth. Because Earth constantly undergoes erosion and rock recycling, rocks on Earth do not remain in their original state. Unlike Earth's rocks, meteorites—which are mostly pieces of rock and iron that have fallen to Earth's surface from space—do not get recycled or undergo erosion. Meteorites are thought to have formed at about the same time as Earth. Therefore, meteorites provide an unspoiled sample for radiometric dating. Uranium-to-lead isotope ratios in many meteorite samples consistently estimate Earth's age at about 4.5 billion years.

Summarize **Why are meteorites helpful for determining the age of Earth?**

**SELF-CHECK Online**
HMHScience.com
**GO ONLINE**

## 12.1 Formative Assessment

### REVIEWING ▶ MAIN IDEAS

1. What types of evidence of ancient life can be preserved as fossils?

2. In **radiometric dating,** why is a uranium **isotope** often used instead of $^{14}$C to determine the age of Earth?

### CRITICAL THINKING

3. **Apply** Considering that millions of species have lived on Earth, why are there relatively few fossils?

4. **Contrast** Explain the difference between **relative dating** and absolute dating.

### CONNECT TO

### EARTH SCIENCE

5. When mountains form, the order of rock layers can be disturbed. How could radiometric dating be used to sort out the relative ages of such rock layers?

# Effects of Melatonin

Until recently in evolutionary history, humans went to sleep when the sun went down and awoke when the sun rose. This daily light-induced sleeping and waking cycle is known as a circadian rhythm or biological clock and is regulated by the hormone melatonin. These days, with artificial lighting and airplane travel across time zones, our daily activities are no longer tied to our biological clocks.

Scientists have recently discovered that the same melatonin that regulates the human sleep cycle is found in microscopic marine worm larvae, organisms that are part of the huge mass of plankton living in the ocean. Plankton are composed of drifting microscopic algae, protozoans, and larvae that fish and marine mammals feed on. Worm larvae do not sleep, so what function could their melatonin possibly have? Why did melatonin production evolve in these animals?

Worm larvae make a daily vertical migration. Organisms deep in the ocean swim upward during daytime by beating their cilia, microscopic hairlike projections on their outer surface. The larvae arrive at the surface as the sun goes down. Then, during the night, they gradually drift back down to deeper water. The cycle is repeated every day.

When scientists studied the larvae's simple brains, they discovered a group of nerve cells that were light-sensitive. These brain cells produce melatonin at night. Other nerve cells connected to the larvae's cilia respond to the melatonin by causing the cilia to beat less often. During the pauses between beats, the larvae slowly sink into deeper water. No melatonin is produced during the day. The cilia begin to beat without pauses, causing the organisms to swim upward. When the scientists exposed worm larvae to melatonin in the lab during daytime hours, the cilia beat in their typical paused nighttime pattern.

Almost all animals make melatonin, the "hormone of darkness." Because melatonin production is widespread in the animal kingdom, scientists think the ability of light-sensing brain cells to make the hormone arose early in the evolutionary history of animals, hundreds of millions of years ago. Melatonin production may have first evolved in marine organisms as a way to avoid the damaging ultraviolet (UV) radiation in sunlight. In humans and other mammals, it may have further evolved as a way to induce sleep by blocking sensory information from the environment.

## S.T.E.M. Activity

Research the role of melatonin in jet lag. Write a short paper explaining what causes jet lag, how flying across time zones disrupts the circadian rhythms in humans, and how the production of melatonin affects jet lag. Does the direction in which a person travels affect the symptoms of jet lag? Why might that happen?

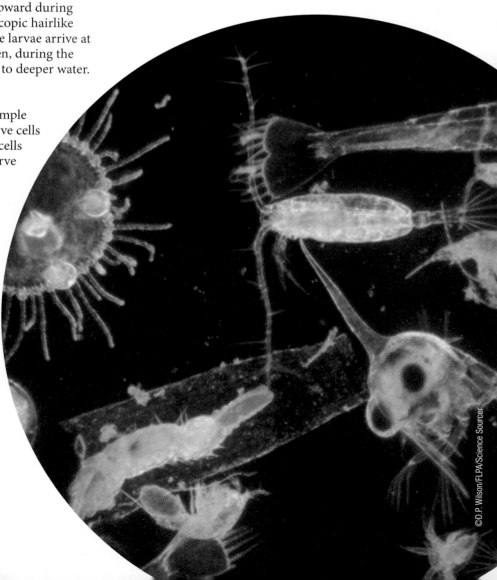

Marine zooplankton, including copepods, cladocerans, barnacle nauplius larvae, and a zoea larva of a crab

©D. P. Wilson/FLPA/Science Sourcer

# 12.2 The Geologic Time Scale

SC.912.L.15.1

**SC.912.L.15.1** Explain how the scientific theory of evolution is supported by the fossil record, comparative anatomy, comparative embryology, biogeography, molecular biology, and observed evolutionary change.

**KEY CONCEPT** **The geologic time scale divides Earth's history based on major past events.**

**MAIN IDEAS**

- ◯ Index fossils are another tool to determine the age of rock layers.
- ◯ The geologic time scale organizes Earth's history.

### Connect to Your World

Life is marked by increments of progress. From your first year of school through high school graduation, each new year is a step in your life development. Earth's life spans about 4.5 billion years. Scientists have divided the Earth's progress into manageable units based on the occurrence of major geologic changes.

### ▶ MAIN IDEA

## Index fossils are another tool to determine the age of rock layers.

You have learned that both relative dating and radiometric dating can help scientists determine the age of rock layers. Scientists who are trying to determine the age of a rock layer almost always use two or more methods to confirm results. Index fossils provide an additional tool for determining the age of fossils or the strata in which they are found. **Index fossils** are fossils of organisms that existed only during specific spans of time over large geographic areas.

Using index fossils for age estimates of rock layers is not a new idea. In the late 1700s, English geologist William Smith discovered that certain rock layers contained fossils unlike those in other layers. Using these key fossils as markers, Smith could identify a particular layer of rock wherever it was exposed.

The shorter the life span of a species, the more precisely the different strata can be correlated. The best index fossils are common, easy to identify, found widely around the world, and existed only for a relatively brief time. The extinct marine invertebrates known as ammonites, shown in **FIGURE 2.1**, are one example of an index fossil. They were at one time very common, but disappeared after a mass extinction event about 251 million years ago. The presence of ammonites indicates that a rock layer must be between 251 million and 359 million years old. Ammonite fossils are useful for dating fossils of other organisms in strata, because the presence of both organisms in one layer shows that they lived during the same time period.

**FIGURE 2.1** Ammonites, marine fossils that range from 1 millimeter to 1 meter in size, are good index fossils. They are abundant in marine sediment, widely distributed, and representative of a specific period of time.

**Apply** **Could a rock layer with ammonite fossils be 100 million years old? Explain.**

©Francois Gohier/Science Source

# FIGURE 2.2 Geologic Time Scale

**X** = Major extinction

## CENOZOIC ERA

### QUATERNARY PERIOD

**1.8 mya–present** This period continues today and includes all modern forms of life.

### TERTIARY PERIOD (PALEOGENE AND NEOGENE)

**65–1.8 mya** Mammals, flowering plants, grasslands, insects, fish, and birds diversified. Primates evolved.

*Primate*

## MESOZOIC ERA

### CRETACEOUS PERIOD

**145–65 mya** Dinosaur populations peaked and then went extinct. Birds survived to radiate in the Tertiary period. Flowering plants arose.

### JURASSIC PERIOD

**200–145 mya** Dinosaurs diversified, as did early trees that are common today. Oceans were full of fish and squid. First birds arose.

### TRIASSIC PERIOD

**251–200 mya** Following the largest mass extinction to date, dinosaurs evolved, as did plants such as ferns and cycads. Mammals and flying reptiles (pterosaurs) arose.

*Mononykus*

## PALEOZOIC ERA

### PERMIAN PERIOD

**299–251 mya** Modern pine trees first appeared, and Pangaea supercontinent was formed as major landmasses joined together.

### CARBONIFEROUS PERIOD

**359–299 mya** Coal-forming sediments were laid down in vast swamps. Fish continued to diversify. Life forms included amphibians, winged insects, early conifers, and small reptiles.

*Pine tree*

### DEVONIAN PERIOD

**416–359 mya** Fish diversified. First sharks, amphibians, and insects appeared. First ferns, trees, and forests arose.

### SILURIAN PERIOD

**444–416 mya** Earliest land plants arose. Melting of glaciers allowed seas to form. Jawless and freshwater fishes evolved.

*Jawless fish*

### ORDOVICIAN PERIOD

**488–444 mya** Diverse marine invertebrates evolved, as did the earliest vertebrates. Massive glaciers formed, causing sea levels to drop and a mass extinction of marine life to occur.

### CAMBRIAN PERIOD

**542–488 mya** All existing animal phyla developed over a relatively short period of time known as the Cambrian Explosion.

*Trilobite*

Millions of years ago (mya)

100
250
550
1000
2000

## PRECAMBRIAN TIME

This time span makes up the vast majority of Earth's history. It includes the oldest known rocks and fossils, the origin of eukaryotes, and the oldest animal fossils. (colored SEM; magnification 50×)

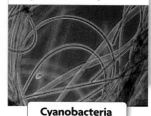
**Cyanobacteria**

# The geologic time scale organizes Earth's history.

The **geologic time scale,** shown in **FIGURE 2.2,** is a representation of the history of Earth. It organizes Earth's development by major changes or events that have occurred, using evidence from the fossil and geologic records. Scientists worked out the entire geologic time scale during the 1800s and early 1900s. Although the scale is still being changed a little bit here and there, the main divisions of geologic time have stayed the same for over a hundred years.

The time scale is divided into a series of units based on the order in which different groups of rocks and fossils were formed. The geologic time scale consists of three basic units of time.

- **Eras** last tens to hundreds of millions of years and consist of two or more periods.
- **Periods** are the most commonly used units of time on the geologic time scale, lasting tens of millions of years. Each period is associated with a particular type of rock system.
- **Epochs** (EHP-uhks) are the smallest units of geologic time and last several million years.

The names of the eras came from early ideas about life forms preserved as fossils. *Paleozoic* means "ancient life," *Mesozoic* means "middle life," and *Cenozoic* means "recent life." Within the eras, the boundaries between many of the geologic periods are defined by mass extinction events. These events help to define when one period ends and another begins. The largest adaptive radiations tend to follow large mass extinctions. Recall that adaptive radiation happens when a group of organisms diversifies into several species. Those species adapt to different ecological niches because mass extinctions make many niches available. Over generations, the adaptive traits favored within these newly opened niches may become common for that population of organisms, and speciation may occur.

**Summarize** Why do adaptive radiations often occur after mass extinctions?

❋ CONNECT TO

**ADAPTIVE RADIATION**

Recall from the chapter **The Evolution of Populations** that *adaptive radiation* refers to the change of a single species into several forms that are each adapted to a specific environmental niche.

SELF-CHECK Online
HMHScience.com
GO ONLINE

## 12.2 Formative Assessment

### REVIEWING ● MAIN IDEAS

1. How are **index fossils** used to date rock layers?

2. What is the usefulness of categorizing Earth's history into the **geologic time scale**?

### CRITICAL THINKING

3. **Infer** The most common index fossils are shells of invertebrates. Give two reasons why this is so.

4. **Analyze** Scientists have inferred that there have been at least five mass extinctions in Earth's history. How would fossil evidence support this inference?

❋ CONNECT TO

**SCIENTIFIC PROCESS**

5. French physicist Henri Becquerel discovered radioactivity in 1896, after geologists had developed the geologic time scale. How did Becquerel's discovery help later geologists as they refined the time scale?

# 12.3 Origin of Life

SC.912.L.15.8

**VOCABULARY**
nebula
ribozyme

SC.912.L.15.8 Describe the scientific explanations of the origin of life on Earth.

| KEY CONCEPT **The origin of life on Earth remains a puzzle.**

**MAIN IDEAS**
- Earth was very different billions of years ago.
- Several sets of hypotheses propose how life began on Earth.

### Connect to Your World

By studying the geologic time scale, it is clear that the farther back in Earth's history we go, the tougher it is to piece together what life was like at that time. Hypotheses about the way Earth formed and life began have been proposed and researched. But as with any branch of science, questions still remain.

### ▶ MAIN IDEA

## Earth was very different billions of years ago.

For centuries, many of history's greatest minds have wondered about the origin of Earth and its living things. Despite differences over the details of Earth's origins, most scientists agree on two key points: (1) Earth is billions of years old, and (2) the conditions of the early planet and its atmosphere were very different from those of today.

Today, the most widely accepted hypothesis of Earth's origins suggests that the solar system was formed by a condensing **nebula,** a cloud of gas and dust in space, as shown in **FIGURE 3.1**. This hypothesis is supported by computer models and observations made with the Hubble Space Telescope. It suggests that about 4.6 billion years ago, the sun formed from a nebula. Over time, most of the material in the nebula pulled together because of gravity. Materials that remained in the nebula's disk circled the newly formed sun. Over millions of years, repeated collisions of this space debris built up into the planets of our solar system.

Earth was most likely violent and very hot for its first 700 million years, a time now called the Hadean eon. Many asteroids, meteorites, and comets struck the planet, releasing enormous amounts of heat. Meanwhile, the radioactive decay of elements trapped deep within Earth released heat as well. This intense heat kept the materials making up Earth in a molten state. Over time, these materials separated into Earth's layers. Hydrogen, carbon monoxide, and nitrogen gas were released from the interior. They combined to form an atmosphere containing compounds such as ammonia, water vapor, methane, and carbon dioxide. Most scientists agree that free oxygen was not abundant until about 2 billion years ago, after the first forms of life had begun to evolve.

Toward the end of the Hadean eon, between 4 and 3.8 billion years ago, impacts became less frequent. That allowed Earth to cool down. Solar radiation and lightning produced energy for reactions on Earth and in the early atmosphere. The continents began to form. Water vapor condensed and fell as rain that collected in pools and larger bodies of water.

**FIGURE 3.1** One hypothesis proposes that the Sun and planets formed from a rotating disk of gas and dust about 4.6 billion years ago.

©David A. Hardy/Photo Researchers, Inc.

Once liquid water was present, organic compounds could be formed from inorganic materials. All living matter is organic, as are the building blocks of life, such as sugars and amino acids. However, you'll see below that the leap that resulted in life on Earth required conditions other than just the presence of water.

**Summarize** Describe the nebular hypothesis of Earth's origin.

## ● MAIN IDEA
## Several sets of hypotheses propose how life began on Earth.

Since the 1950s, scientists have proposed several hypotheses to explain how life began on Earth. These hypotheses have taken into consideration early organic molecules, the formation of organic polymers from these organic building blocks, the evolution of cell structures, and early genetic material.

### Organic Molecule Hypotheses
There are two general hypotheses about the way life-supporting molecules appeared on early Earth.

**Miller-Urey experiment** In 1953 Stanley Miller and Harold Urey designed an experiment to test a hypothesis first proposed by Alexander Oparin in the 1920s. Earlier scientists had proposed that an input of energy from lightning led to the formation of organic molecules from inorganic molecules present in the atmosphere of early Earth. Miller and Urey built a system to model conditions they thought existed on early Earth, as shown in **FIGURE 3.2**. They demonstrated that organic compounds could be made by heating and passing an electrical current, to simulate lightning, through a mixture of gases. These gases—methane ($CH_4$), ammonia ($NH_3$), hydrogen ($H_2$), and water vapor ($H_2O$)—were thought to be present in the early atmosphere. The Miller-Urey experiment produced a variety of organic compounds, such as amino acids.

After Miller's death in 2007, scientists found sealed vials from his early experiments that when tested, proved that more than 20 different amino acids had been formed. Since Miller's experiments occurred, it has been suggested by some scientists that due to volcanic eruptions more than 4 billion years ago, different compounds were present in the early atmosphere. Experiments using more recent estimates of conditions on early Earth have also produced organic molecules, including amino acids and nucleotides.

### FIGURE 3.2 Miller-Urey Experiment

**A laboratory model was used to represent the conditions of early Earth. This experiment demonstrated that organic molecules can be made from inorganic molecules.**

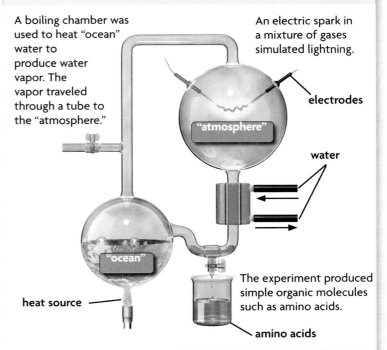

A boiling chamber was used to heat "ocean" water to produce water vapor. The vapor traveled through a tube to the "atmosphere."

An electric spark in a mixture of gases simulated lightning.

electrodes

"atmosphere"

water

"ocean"

heat source

The experiment produced simple organic molecules such as amino acids.

amino acids

**Meteorite hypothesis** Analysis of a meteorite that fell near Murchison, Australia, in 1969 revealed that organic molecules can be found in space. More than 90 amino acids have been identified from this meteorite. Nineteen of these amino acids are found on Earth, and many others have been made in experiments similar to the Miller-Urey study. This evidence suggests that amino acids could have been present when Earth formed, or that these organic molecules may have arrived on Earth through meteorite or asteroid impacts.

## Organic Polymer Hypotheses

Once amino acids and other organic building blocks existed on early Earth, certain requirements would have to have been met in order for more complex organic polymers to form. Planetary conditions were still extreme, ranging from ice sheets to areas having high temperatures and extensive volcanic activity. Since there was no ozone layer at that time, high levels of ultraviolet radiation would have permeated the atmosphere. All of these factors would have contributed to breaking apart the chemical bonds of organic molecules unless they were protected in some way. The survival of organic molecules would have depended on them either dissolving in water or adsorbing to some type of mineral.

**Frozen seawater hypothesis** If you fill a container to the top and place it into your freezer, the ice that forms will expand beyond the rim of the container. This occurs as water molecules form into rigid crystals. Because of this, a solution that is water-based will push any dissolved materials into the spaces between the crystals as it freezes. Recent research has shown that when solutions containing nucleotides are frozen, the nucleotides are pushed into the spaces between the water crystals. As **FIGURE 3.3** illustrates, when nucleotides are concentrated into a tiny area, they can bind together and form long, complex molecules that can carry information. On the basis of these experiments, Scripps Oceanographic scientist Jeffrey Bada proposed in 2004 that biological polymers may have formed in sea ice on the early planet.

**Clay adsorption hypothesis** In the late 1950s and early 1960s, Florida State University scientist Sidney Fox found that when dilute solutions of amino acids and cyanide were dripped onto hot, dry sand, rock, or clay, polymers that he called "proteinoids" were formed spontaneously. The metallic ions on the particles of clay acted as catalysts, binding to the monomers and concentrating them closely enough for the molecules to join together, forming more-complex organic polymers similar to proteins.

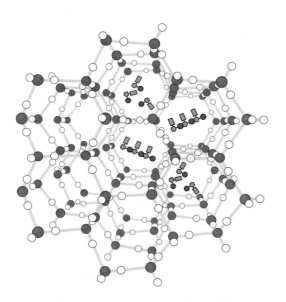

**FIGURE 3.3 Frozen Seawater Hypothesis**
Nucleotides trapped within the spaces between ice crystals and kept in close proximity to one another may have combined to form more-complex polymers.

**Implications of polymer formation** Many hypotheses describing the origin of life on Earth rely on the formation of self-replicating polymers—made from either amino acid or nucleic acid monomers—on early Earth. Once a molecule capable of replication formed, the sequence information contained in the molecule, as well as any variation introduced during replication, would have been inherited by each new generation of molecules. In successive generations, molecules with variations that improved replication efficiency or added other advantageous functions may have been selected, leading to more-complex molecules that carried more information.

## Early Cell Formation Hypotheses

There are several hypotheses about the formation of the first cells. One focuses on the way organic molecules could have been brought together, and others addresses the way cell membranes may have formed.

**Iron-sulfide bubbles hypothesis** In the 1990s, biologists William Martin and Michael Russell noted that hot iron sulfide rising from below the ocean floor reacts with the cooler ocean water to form chimneylike structures with many compartments, such as those shown in **FIGURE 3.4**. Russell modeled this in the laboratory by injecting warm sodium sulfide into a cool, iron-rich solution. Iron sulfide bubbles quickly formed, making a chimney structure within minutes. Russell proposed that, around 4 billion years ago, biological molecules combined in the compartments of these chimneys. The compartment walls concentrated the basic organic molecules in a small space. The walls of the compartments, Russell proposed, acted as the first cell membranes. Once the right ingredients combined, the first organic cell membranes could form. These membranes would have let early microbes leave their rocky compartments and spread out into other environments.

> **CONNECT TO**
>
> ### CELLS
>
> Recall from the chapter **Cell Structure and Function** that most cell membranes are composed of two layers of lipids, or fats. The cell membrane maintains a boundary between the environments inside and outside the cell.

## FIGURE 3.4  Iron–Sulfide Bubbles Hypothesis

Hydrothermal vents produce sulfur that mixes with ocean water to make compartments of rock. These structures may have created conditions necessary for early life to form.

**Lipid membrane hypothesis** Several scientists have proposed that the evolution of lipid membranes was a crucial step for the origin of life. Lipid molecules spontaneously form membrane-enclosed spheres, called liposomes, shown in **FIGURE 3.5**. In 1992 biochemist Harold Morowitz tested the idea that at some point liposomes were formed with a double, or bilayer, lipid membrane. These liposomes could then form around a variety of organic molecules, such as amino acids, fatty acids, sugars, and nucleotides. The liposomes would act as membranes that separated these organic molecules from the environment. These cell-like structures may have later given rise to the first true cells.

**Coacervate hypothesis** In the 1930s, long before Morowitz proposed that cell-like structures formed from liposomes, Alexander Oparin found that by adding a substance called gum arabic into a water-based solution of gelatin, then cooling it down, tiny capsules that he called "coacervates" were produced. These coacervates, when surrounded by water, could absorb and release some compounds in a way that was similar to how bacteria feed and then excrete wastes.

**Proteinoid microsphere hypothesis** In the late 1950s, Sydney Fox, working with Kaoru Harada, took his previous work with the clay adsorption hypotheses a step further. The two scientists discovered that when the proteinoids, produced in hot conditions, were cooled by dropping them into water, they spontaneously formed into microspheres. The proteinoids had a water-soluble chemical group attached to a water-insoluble group. The parts that were water-soluble turned inwards and the insoluble group outwards, forming a bilayer similar to the structure of cell membranes. Under certain laboratory conditions, these proteinoid microspheres would slowly grow larger and eventually bud, forming new spheres.

Liposomes, coacervates, and microspheres were not capable of genetic coding or true replication. In other words—none of them were alive. However, the research of these scientists into how cells originally formed provided the foundations upon which current research is based.

## RNA as Early Genetic Material

A hypothesis that has gained much support in recent years proposes that RNA, rather than DNA, was the genetic material that stored information in living things on early Earth. In the 1980s, Thomas Cech from the University of Colorado and Sidney Altman from Yale University independently discovered that RNA can catalyze reactions. **Ribozymes** are RNA molecules that can catalyze specific chemical reactions. As **FIGURE 3.6** shows, ribozymes can catalyze their own replication and synthesis. RNA can copy itself, chop itself into pieces, and from these pieces make even more RNA. Unlike RNA, DNA needs enzymes to replicate itself.

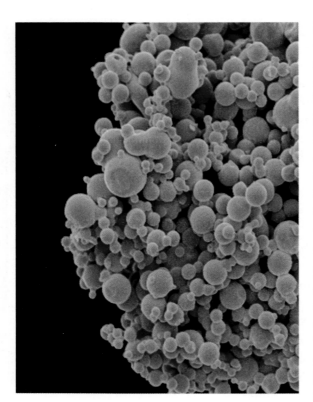

**FIGURE 3.5** Liposomes have a lipid membrane that is similar to the membrane of a living cell.
(colored SEM; magnification 1500×)

FIGURE 3.6 RNA AND DNA

RNA, in the form of a ribozyme, is able to replicate itself without the help of additional enzymes.

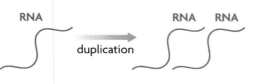

DNA requires many enzymes to replicate. Helicase enzymes separate the DNA strands and polymerase enzymes add nucleotides to the DNA strands.

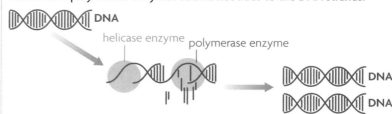

Along with the discovery of ribozymes, several other types of evidence support the RNA hypothesis. Short chains of RNA will form from inorganic materials in a test tube. If zinc is added as a catalyst, longer chains will grow. Also, RNA will fold into different shapes depending upon its sequence of nucleotides. Thus, it can perform more functions than DNA. But RNA does not catalyze chemical reactions as well as proteins do, nor does it store genetic information as well as DNA does. Over time, RNA may have become less important for these functions.

Perhaps the earliest replicating RNA molecule gained simple membranes over many generations through natural selection. Membranes might protect chemical reactions and make them work more efficiently. RNA molecules that made copies of themselves in a double-stranded form, similar to DNA, might eventually have been selected because fewer mutations would occur. Because DNA is more stable than RNA, it could reliably store more sequence information for a longer period of time. This may have led to DNA replacing RNA as the primary genetic material. Currently, there are several hypotheses about how RNA could have led to life as we know it today. Laboratory experiments in which RNA molecules survive and self-replicate support the idea of early cells being based on RNA. This model of the origins of life on Earth is sometimes called the RNA world.

**Synthesize** **Could cell structures or RNA have been present before organic molecules existed on Earth? Explain.**

 **SELF-CHECK** Online
HMHScience.com
**GO ONLINE**

# 12.3 Formative Assessment

## REVIEWING ▶ MAIN IDEAS

1. Describe the environmental conditions that are thought to have existed during the Hadean eon.

2. What evidence do the two organic molecule hypotheses provide regarding the formation of simple organic molecules?

## CRITICAL THINKING

3. **Analyze** What factors do the two organic polymer hypotheses have in common regarding how more-complex organic polymers originated?

4. **Compare and Contrast** Choose two of the early cell formation hypotheses and discuss their differences.

## CONNECT TO

### PROTEIN SYNTHESIS

5. RNA is hypothesized to be the earliest form of genetic material because it can store information, catalyze its own replication, and catalyze other reactions. Which two of these functions can DNA not do? Which two can proteins not do?

# Early Single-Celled Organisms

**KEY CONCEPT** Single-celled organisms existed 3.8 billion years ago.

**VOCABULARY**
cyanobacteria
endosymbiosis

**MAIN IDEAS**
- Microbes have changed the physical and chemical composition of Earth.
- Several theories have been proposed for how eukaryotic cells evolved from prokaryotic cells.
- The evolution of sexual reproduction led to increased diversity.

**SC.912.L.15.8** Describe the scientific explanations of the origin of life on Earth.

## Connect to Your World

If you have ever assembled a complicated model or worked on a car, you know that putting the parts together to get a working result can be very difficult. Billions of years ago, organic molecules were everywhere. However, they didn't yet fully work together. Once the first cells arose from these molecules, the steps toward even more complicated organisms, such as humans, truly began.

## ▶ MAIN IDEA

# Microbes have changed the physical and chemical composition of Earth.

Single-celled organisms changed Earth's surface by depositing minerals. These organisms changed the atmosphere by giving off oxygen as a byproduct of photosynthesis. Before photosynthesis evolved, however, the first prokaryotes would have been anaerobic, or living without oxygen. Many of these early prokaryotes probably got their energy from organic molecules.

Scientists have found evidence that photosynthetic life evolved around 3.5 billion years ago, since that is the age of the oldest known fossils. These fossils are of a group of marine **cyanobacteria** (sy-ah-noh-bak-TEER-ee-uh), which are bacteria that can carry out photosynthesis. Like all early life forms, each cyanobacterium was a single prokaryotic cell. Recall that prokaryotic cells have no membrane-bound organelles.

Some cyanobacteria live in colonies and form stromatolites (stroh-MAT-l-yts). Stromatolites are domed, rocky structures made of layers of cyanobacteria and sediment. There are many stromatolite fossils, but some are living communities, as shown in **FIGURE 4.1.** Fossils of stromatolites as old as 3.5 billion years have been found. Communities of photosynthesizing cyanobacteria in stromatolites released oxygen as a byproduct. Higher oxygen levels in the atmosphere and the ocean allowed the evolution of aerobic prokaryotes, which need oxygen to live.

**FIGURE 4.1** Stromatolites, like these found in Australia, are made by cyanobacteria. Cyanobacteria are considered to have been among the first organisms on early Earth.

**Apply** How are stromatolites evidence of Earth's early life?

## ▶ MAIN IDEA

# Several theories have been proposed for how eukaryotic cells evolved from prokaryotic cells.

The fossil record shows that eukaryotic organisms had evolved by 1.5 billion years ago. A eukaryote is more complex than a prokaryote, having a nucleus and other membrane-bound organelles. While the first eukaryotes were made of only one cell, later eukaryotic organisms became multicellular. Bacterial, plant, and animal cells share certain complex traits, including specific enzymes, metabolic pathways, ribosomes, cell membranes, and the genetic code carried in DNA. While these traits originated in prokaryotes, other eukaryotic traits such as organelles arose through the processes of evolution.

**Endosymbiont theory** One hypothesis of eukaryote evolution did not get much attention until the 1970s. Biologist Lynn Margulis found evidence to support the endosymbiont theory. **Endosymbiosis** (EHN-doh-SIHM-bee-OH-sihs) is a relationship in which one organism lives within the body of another—with both organisms benefitting.

The endosymbiont theory suggests that mitochondria and chloroplasts were once simple prokaryotic cells that were engulfed by larger prokaryotes around 1.5 billion years ago. Instead of being digested, some of the smaller prokaryotes may have survived inside the larger ones as illustrated in **FIGURE 4.2**. If it took in a prokaryote that acted as a mitochondrion, the larger cell got energy in the form of ATP. If it took in a prokaryote that acted as a chloroplast, the larger cell could use photosynthesis to make sugars. In exchange, the mitochondria and the chloroplasts found a stable environment and nutrients.

Margulis based her theory on several factors. Unlike other organelles, mitochondria and chloroplasts have their own DNA and ribosomes. They can copy themselves within the cell in which they are found. Mitochondria and chloroplasts are also about the same size as prokaryotes, their DNA forms a circle, and their gene structures are similar to those of prokaryotes.

**Analyze** What evidence supports the theory of endosymbiosis?

## READING TOOLBOX

**VOCABULARY**
*Endosymbiosis* can be broken down into *endo-*, meaning "within," *sym-*, meaning "together," and *biosis*, meaning "way of life."

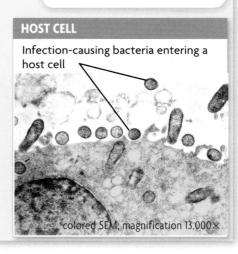

*Animated* **Biology**
HMHScience.com
GO ONLINE
Endosymbiosis

## FIGURE 4.2 Endosymbiosis

The theory of endosymbiosis proposes that the mitochondria found in eukaryotic cells descended from ancestors of infection-causing bacteria. Likewise, chloroplasts are considered descendants of cyanobacteria.

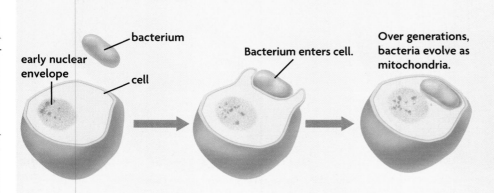

bacterium
early nuclear envelope
cell

Bacterium enters cell.

Over generations, bacteria evolve as mitochondria.

HOST CELL
Infection-causing bacteria entering a host cell

colored SEM; magnification 13,000×

**Autogenous theory** In 1976 botanist F.J.R. Taylor proposed an alternative to the endosymbiont theory. Taylor's theory, known as autogeny, is based upon the extensive folding of the internal membranes found within chloroplasts and mitochondria, as seen in **FIGURE 4.3.**

You may recall that one of the major differences between prokaryotes and eukaryotes is that eukaryotes have membrane-bound organelles and prokaryotes do not. This provides eukaryotes with a distinct adaptive advantage. Since prokaryotic metabolic reactions all occur in the cytoplasm, it is possible for them to interfere with one another. Eukaryotes, on the other hand, have the specialized chemical reactions involved in metabolism separated by the membranes surrounding each organelle.

The autogenous theory proposes that eukaryotic organelles evolved from infoldings of the plasma membrane, creating pockets that eventually pinched off. When they pinched off into separate structures, small sections of nucleic acids and ribosomes were trapped inside. These new structures became specialized in performing different metabolic processes. Having these reactions isolated from one another is much more efficient, allowing eukaryotic cells to evolve even greater complexity. According to the autogenous theory, those organelles that performed photosynthesis eventually developed into chloroplasts. The theory also proposes that those new structures that specialized in providing energy to the other organelles through cellular respiration evolved into mitochondria.

**Analyze** Why do membrane-bound organelles give eukaryotes an adaptive advantage over prokaryotes?

## FIGURE 4.3 Autogenous Theory

**According to the autogenous theory, eukaryotes arose directly from a single prokaryotic ancestor through isolation of metabolic functions by infoldings of the plasma membrane. Such infoldings and pockets can be seen in chloroplasts and in mitochondria.**

**CHLOROPLAST**

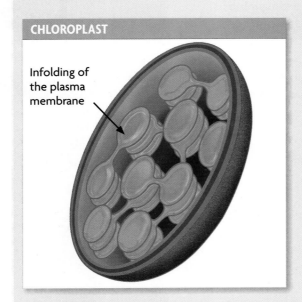

Infolding of the plasma membrane

**MITOCHONDRIA**

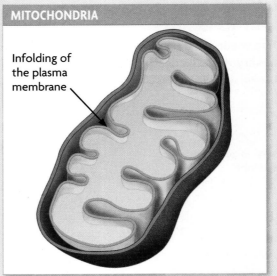

Infolding of the plasma membrane

The middle of the Paleozoic era was a time of great diversity as life moved onto land. The number and variety of plant groups greatly increased. Four-legged vertebrates, such as amphibians, became common. Most of the coal used in the United States formed during the Carboniferous period of this era, illustrated in **FIGURE 5.1**. The decomposed remains of millions of organisms were buried in sediment. Over time they changed into coal and the petroleum that fuels our cars today.

**Summarize** Why is part of the Cambrian period also called the Cambrian explosion?

## ● MAIN IDEA
# Reptiles radiated during the Mesozoic era.

The **Mesozoic** (MEHZ-uh-ZOH-ihk) era began 251 million years ago and ended 65 million years ago. Called the Age of Reptiles because the dinosaurs roamed Earth during this era, the Mesozoic also featured birds and flowering plants. The oldest direct ancestor of mammals first appeared during this era. By the era's end, mammals—particularly marsupials, whose young develop in a pouch—had evolved numerous key traits that improved their chances of survival during the mass extinction at the end of the era.

The Mesozoic era is divided into three periods: the Triassic, the Jurassic, and the Cretaceous. Life took off slowly in the early Triassic. On land, the earliest crocodiles and dinosaurs arose. The fossil record shows that the first mammals also evolved during this time. An extinction event near the end of the Triassic destroyed many types of animals. This mass extinction allowed the radiation of the dinosaurs in the Jurassic period, illustrated in **FIGURE 5.2.**

Although life had moved onto land, it was still abundant underwater. Ichthyosaurs (IK-thee-uh-SAWRZ), a group of predatory marine reptiles, dominated the oceans. Sharks and bony fishes continued to evolve more complex forms.

The Cretaceous period also ended in a mass extinction—the cause of which is still debated. Evidence shows that a massive asteroid struck Earth. The most accepted hypothesis is that this impact sent enormous amounts of dust and debris into the atmosphere, blocking much of the Sun's light. As a result, the climate changed, and plants were unable to perform photosynthesis. Without sufficient plants to eat, herbivorous dinosaurs and many other animal species became extinct. The loss of these herbivorous animals reduced the food supply of meat-eating dinosaurs, contributing to the meat eaters' extinction.

**Analyze** How did life on Earth change from the beginning of the Paleozoic era to the end of the Mesozoic?

**FOSSIL PTEROSAUR (206–144 MYA)**

**FIGURE 5.2** The illustration below depicts a scene from the Jurassic period of the Mesozoic era. Fossils of pterosaurs (above) have been found in groups, suggesting that they may have lived in colonies.

## ▶ MAIN IDEA

# Mammals radiated during the Cenozoic era.

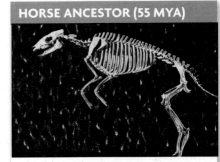

**HORSE ANCESTOR (55 MYA)**

**FIGURE 5.3** The illustration below depicts a scene from the Tertiary period of the Cenozoic era. This ancestor of modern-day horses (above) was the size of a small dog.

The **Cenozoic** era (SEH-nuh-ZOH-ihk) began 65 million years ago and continues today. It is divided into two periods, the Tertiary (65–1.8 million years ago), illustrated in **FIGURE 5.3**, and the Quaternary (1.8 million years ago until today). During the Tertiary, placental mammals and monotremes—a small group of mammals that lay eggs—evolved and diversified. Their adaptive radiation rivaled that of the marsupials in the Mesozoic. The most dramatic radiation of the mammals, however, occurred with the placentals. Today, this group numbers roughly 4000 species. During the Tertiary period, birds, ray-finned fishes, and flowering plants also underwent dramatic radiations.

The earliest ancestors of modern humans evolved near the end of the Tertiary. However, anatomically modern humans did not appear until very recently in Earth's history, nearly 200,000 years ago. The evolution of primates is covered in the next section.

**Infer** Why is the Cenozoic era sometimes referred to as the Age of Mammals?

© Chip Clark/National Museum of Natural History/Smithsonian Institution

**⊰⊱ CONNECT TO**

**MAMMALS**

Placental mammals include all mammals except monotremes, which lay eggs, and marsupials, which rear their underdeveloped young in a pouch. You will learn more about animal classification in the chapter **The Tree of Life.**

---

**SELF-CHECK Online**
HMHScience.com
**GO ONLINE**

## 12.5 Formative Assessment

### REVIEWING ▶ MAIN IDEAS

1. What important events occurred during the **Paleozoic** era?

2. What were some of the key appearances and radiations in the **Mesozoic** era?

3. What two groups of mammals evolved during the **Cenozoic** era?

### CRITICAL THINKING

4. **Evaluate** Explain how natural selection related to the development of diversity in and among species during the **Mesozoic** era.

5. **Infer** How does a great diversity of organisms increase the chances that some will survive a major change in the environment?

### ⊰⊱ CONNECT TO

**ECOLOGY**

6. How do you think the evolution of flowering plants affected the evolution and radiation of birds?

# 12.6 Primate Evolution

SC.912.L.15.10

SC.912.L.15.10 Identify basic trends in hominid evolution from early ancestors six million years ago to modern humans, including brain size, jaw size, language, and manufacture of tools.

## VOCABULARY

primate
prosimian
anthropoid
hominid
bipedal

| KEY CONCEPT **Humans appeared late in Earth's history.**

### MAIN IDEAS
- Humans share a common ancestor with other primates.
- There are many fossils of extinct hominins.
- Modern humans arose nearly 200,000 years ago.

### *Connect to Your World*

In terms of the geologic time scale, the evolution of humans has occurred only very recently. Many fossils of our early ancestors consist of partial skeletons from which details must be inferred through careful study. Though far from complete, this fossil record offers a fascinating glimpse of our past.

### ▶ MAIN IDEA

## Humans share a common ancestor with other primates.

The common ancestor of all primates probably arose before the mass extinction that closed the Cretaceous period 65 million years ago. **Primates** make up a category of mammals with flexible hands and feet, forward-looking eyes—which allow for excellent three-dimensional vision—and enlarged brains relative to body size. Primates also have arms that can rotate in a circle around their shoulder joint, and many primates have thumbs that can move against their fingers. Primates include lemurs, monkeys, apes, and humans. In addition to sharing similar physical traits, primates share strong molecular similarities.

### Primate Evolution

Similar to other groups of related organisms, the relationship among the primate groups forms a many-branched tree. At the tree's base is the common ancestor of all primates. Just above this base, the tree splits into two main subgroups: the prosimians and the anthropoids.

**Prosimians** (proh-SIHM-ee-uhnz) are the oldest living primate group, and most are small and active at night. This group of nocturnal animals includes the lemurs, the lorises, and the tarsiers, like the ones shown in **FIGURE 6.1**. Prosimians are differentiated from anthropoids by smaller size and skull plates that are not fused together when mature.

**FIGURE 6.1** Prosimians, such as these tarsiers, are the oldest living primate group. They are active at night and have large eyes and ears.

### READING TOOLBOX

**TAKING NOTES**
Make a concept map of primate classification. Add more shapes as needed.

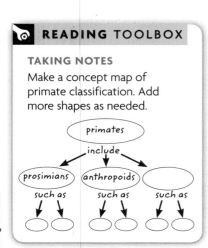

Further distinguishing the prosimians is a single, long grooming claw on the second toe of their hind feet and a unique type of horizontal tooth structure known as a grooming comb. Tarsiers have been called living fossils, as their physical traits have changed little since their appearance in the fossil record more than 40 million years ago.

**Anthropoids** (AN-thruh-POYDZ), the humanlike primates, are further subdivided into the New World monkeys, Old World monkeys, and hominoids, as shown in **FIGURE 6.2.** New World monkeys, which are native to the Americas, all live in trees. Many species have prehensile, or grasping, tails, an adaptation that allows them to hang by their tails from tree branches while feeding. Some Old World monkeys also spend time in trees, but most travel and forage on the ground as well. They have larger brains than do New World monkeys and a greater ability to manipulate objects.

Classification of organisms will be covered in much more detail in the Tree of Life chapter. You will then learn more about how scientists determine how to categorize and name an organism. However, to reduce confusion, it is necessary to show the difference between some of the terms used to classify anthropoids. The terms *hominoid, hominid,* and a third term, *hominin,* all sound very similar because they all originate from the same Latin root word, *homo,* meaning "man."

Hominoids include gibbons and the great apes (orangutans, chimpanzees, and gorillas) as well as humans. **Hominids** include orangutans, chimpanzees, gorillas, and humans, but not gibbons. The term *hominin* refers only to modern humans and their immediate ancestors.

Among primates, hominids are particularly known for using opposable thumbs to their advantage. Because their thumbs are placed in opposition to the four fingers, this allows the hominids to manipulate objects and adapt them. This trait enables hominids not only to pick up and grasp an object but also to use it for multiple purposes. For example, wild chimpanzees in Tanzania have been observed adapting grass and sticks to remove honey from beehives, as well as to dig up roots to eat, and to pry open boxes of bananas left for them by scientists. The chimpanzees also use leaves for collecting water and for wiping mud and sticky fruit from their bodies. Young chimps in Gombe learn how to "fish" for termites by observing adults as they demonstrate the steps involved. Without these observations, it is unlikely that the youngsters would become successful at obtaining termites for food.

**READING TOOLBOX**

VOCABULARY
The term *anthropoid* comes from the word root *anthropo,* which means "human."

**FIGURE 6.3** Opposable thumbs gave hominids the ability to grasp, manipulate, and adapt objects for use as tools or weapons.

**Interpret** How did the ability to manipulate objects, as well as adapt them for use as tools or weapons, give hominids an evolutionary advantage over other primates?

©Thomas Marent/Getty Images

# FIGURE 6.2 Evolutionary Relationships of Primates

Phylogenetic trees, or cladograms, that depict evolutionary relationships between primate groups can be constructed by scientists using karyotype analysis of chromosomes.

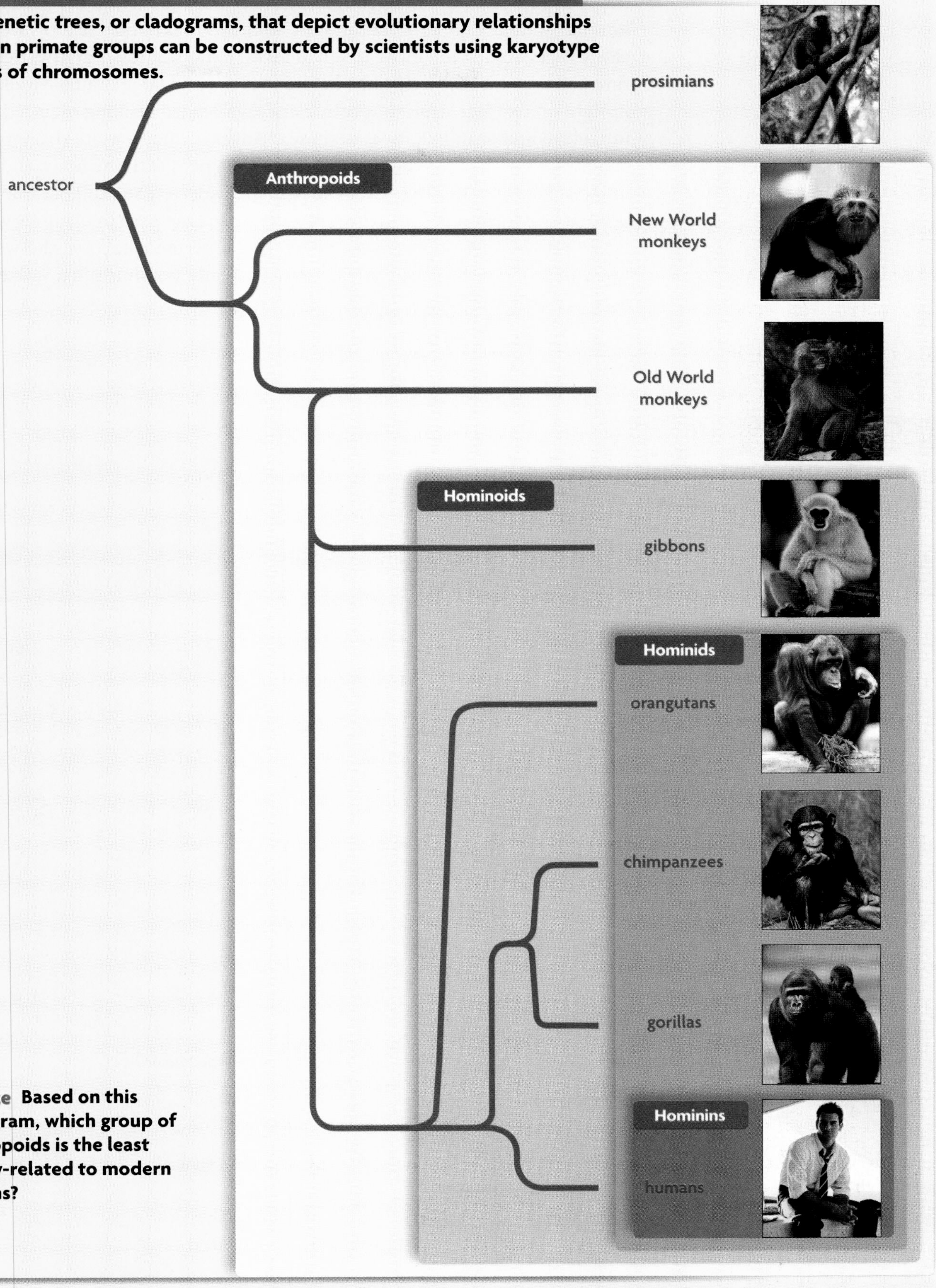

ancestor

Anthropoids

prosimians

New World monkeys

Old World monkeys

Hominoids

gibbons

Hominids

orangutans

chimpanzees

gorillas

Hominins

humans

**Analyze** Based on this cladogram, which group of anthropoids is the least closely-related to modern humans?

## Walking Upright

Many hypotheses have been proposed to explain the evolutionary success of the hominins. Enlarged brain size and the ability to make and use tools were for many years among the most accepted ideas. However, fossil discoveries have revealed that another trait came before tool use and large brains—walking upright on two legs. Upright posture and two-legged walking required changes in skeletal anatomy. Examples of these changes include a more strongly curved, cuplike pelvis, the increased alignment of the knees with the body, and a change in the spine from arch-shaped to an S-shaped curve. The skull became more centered on the top of the spine, allowing for greater ease in using forward-facing vision. These changes can be found in intermediate fossils between hominoids that walked only on all fours and early hominins that walked on two legs, as seen in **FIGURE 6.4**.

## FIGURE 6.4  Walking Upright

**Changes in the skeletal structure of primates were necessary before bipedalism was possible.**

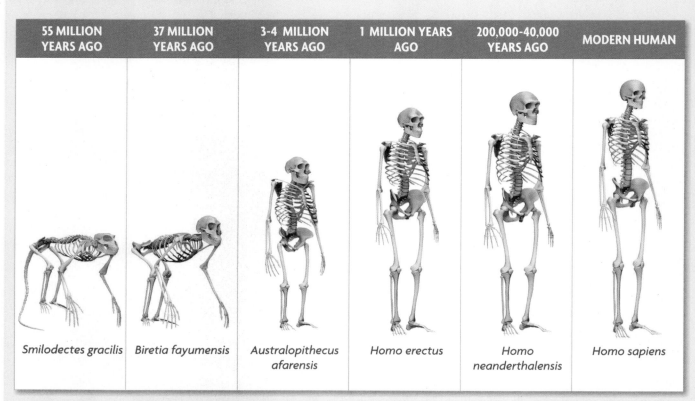

| 55 MILLION YEARS AGO | 37 MILLION YEARS AGO | 3-4 MILLION YEARS AGO | 1 MILLION YEARS AGO | 200,000-40,000 YEARS AGO | MODERN HUMAN |
|---|---|---|---|---|---|
| *Smilodectes gracilis* | *Biretia fayumensis* | *Australopithecus afarensis* | *Homo erectus* | *Homo neanderthalensis* | *Homo sapiens* |

**Analyze** Give a brief summary of the skeletal changes that occurred through time that allowed for an upright posture and bipedal stance in higher primates.

Animals that can walk on two legs are called **bipedal** (BY-PEHD-l). This trait has important adaptive advantages for higher primates. It allows higher reach into tree branches while foraging, and perhaps most importantly, it frees the hands for foraging, carrying infants and food, and using tools. As the landscapes where ancestral humans evolved gradually shifted from heavily forested areas to vast grasslands, food would have become more scarce. Hunter-gatherers would have had to travel farther in order to find enough sources of nutrition for survival. The ability to travel upright on two feet would have enabled them to travel farther while expending less energy than animals that walked on their hind feet and their front knuckles.

In addition to tool usage, bipedal hominins would have been able to fashion weapons to kill prey or to protect themselves, their mates, and their offspring. The higher vantage point provided by their upright posture would have enabled them to better see over obstacles to observe approaching threats.

**Connect** **What is another common animal that is bipedal? Why did this organism need its forelimbs to be free from providing support for its body?**

## QUICKLAB    MODELING

### Geologic Clock

One way to understand the relative length of time in Earth's history is to compare its age to a clock face. Precambrian time goes from 12 noon to about 10:30 P.M. The time span from early human ancestors—more than 5 million years ago—to *Homo sapiens* covers less than a second on our 12-hour clock!

**PROBLEM** How do different geologic time periods compare?

**PROCEDURE**

1. Draw a large circle and mark the 12, 3, 6, and 9 positions of a clock face. Use the scale 1 hour = 400 million years ago, and label the four positions with the appropriate number of years, starting with 12 o'clock = 4800 million years ago. (Example: the three o'clock position = 3600 million years ago.)

2. Using the geological time scale, label Precambrian time and the three eras on your clock, along with the approximate time frames in which they occurred.

3. Label the following events on your clock in the appropriate positions, also filling in the approximate time frames they occurred: formation of Earth, oldest rocks, first stromatolites, first aerobic prokaryotes, first eukaryotes, first fishes, first flowering plants, first dinosaurs, first birds, and earliest hominids.

**MATERIALS**
- paper
- pencil

Clock diagram:
12 — 4600 MYA
9 – ?
? – 3
6
?

**ANALYZE AND CONCLUDE**

1. **Synthesize** How are eras and periods related? Where would the periods fit in this diagram?

2. **Calculate** Using your scale of 1 hour = 400 million years, how many millions of years in Earth's history would 1 minute represent?

**FIGURE 6.5** Computer technology allowed scientists to piece together 7-million-year-old skull fragments found in Africa. The three-dimensional reconstruction suggests that this may be the oldest known hominin ancestor of *Homo sapiens*; it has been named *Sahelanthropus tchadensis*.

**Video Inquiry**
HMHScience.com

**GO ONLINE**

Crafty Cavemen

▶ MAIN IDEA

# There are many fossils of extinct hominins.

Hominins are classified into several groups. Two important groups are the genus *Homo* and the older genus *Australopithecus* (aw-STRAY-loh-PIHTH-ih-kuhs). *Australopithecus* was a long-lived and successful genus. *Australopithecus afarensis* (AF-uh-REHN-sihs), which lived 3 to 4 million years ago in Africa, is one of the better known species of early hominins. Although its brain was much smaller than that of a modern human—about the size of a modern-day chimpanzee's brain—*A. afarensis* had very humanlike limbs.

The earliest member of the genus *Homo* was *Homo habilis*. Nicknamed "handy man" because of the crude stone tools associated with its skeletons, *H. habilis* lived 2.4–1.5 million years ago in what are now Kenya and Tanzania. This species may have lived alongside the australopithecine species for about 1 million years. *H. habilis* is the earliest known hominin to make stone tools. The brain of *H. habilis* was much larger than that of any of the australopithecines, and it more closely resembled the modern human brain in shape.

Another hominin species was *H. neanderthalensis,* commonly called Neanderthals for the Neander Valley in Germany, where their fossils were first found. This group lived from 200,000 to around 40,000 years ago in Europe and the Middle East. Evidence suggests that *H. neanderthalensis* coexisted with modern *Homo sapiens* for approximately 5,000 years, possibly even exchanging ideas and culture. The extinction of *H. neanderthalensis* was most likely caused by a period of extreme cold, inbreeding due to low numbers, and economic competition with *H. sapiens.*

Observations from the fossil record, such as the fossil seen in **FIGURE 6.5**, demonstrate a trend toward increased brain size in the human lineage. Although brain size can only be loosely related to intelligence, the combination of modern-day humans' physical and cultural adaptations has no doubt contributed to our success as a species.

**Hypothesize** **What type of evidence could indicate that *H. sapiens* and *H. neanderthalensis* coexisted?**

▶ MAIN IDEA

# Modern humans arose nearly 200,000 years ago.

Fossil evidence reveals that *Homo sapiens* evolved nearly 200,000 years ago in what is now Ethiopia. However, many of their features were different than those of humans today. After becoming a distinct species, *H. sapiens* clearly did not stop evolving.

## The Role of Culture

Human evolution is influenced by culture. Tools are among key markers of culture in human evolution, although they are used by some other animals as well. A comparison of tools from their first appearance some 2.5 million years ago, through their association with later *Homo* fossil sites, shows a steady trend of increasing sophistication and usefulness.

## FIGURE 6.6 Examples of Hominin Skulls

**Hominin evolution shows changes in brain size.**

| 4–3 MILLION YEARS AGO | 2.4–1.5 MILLION YEARS AGO | 200,000–40,000 YEARS AGO | 200,000 YEARS AGO–PRESENT |
|---|---|---|---|
| *Australopithecus afarensis* | *Homo habilis* | *Homo neanderthalensis* | *Homo sapiens* |
| 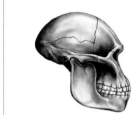 | 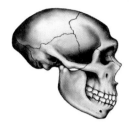 | 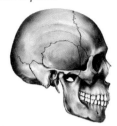 | |
| *Australopithecus afarensis* had a brain volume of 430 cm³. | *Homo habilis* had a brain volume of about 700 cm³. | *Homo neanderthalensis'* brain volume may have reached 1500 cm³. | Modern *Homo sapiens* have a brain volume average of about 1350 cm³. |

**Contrast** What characteristics besides brain size differ among the species shown?

**VIRTUAL Lab**
HMHScience.com
**GO ONLINE**
Comparing Hominoid Skulls

## The Evolution of the Human Brain

Human evolution would not have advanced as it did without an enlarging skull and brain size, as shown in **FIGURE 6.6**. One recent study has demonstrated that genes controlling the size and complexity of the human brain evolved faster than analogous genes in nonhuman primates. Researchers compared the DNA sequences for more than 200 genes affecting brain development in humans, Old World monkeys, rats, and mice. They found that these genes evolved at a much faster rate in the two primates than in the two rodents and that brain-related genes in humans evolved faster than did those in the monkeys. The results of the study support the hypothesis that the rapid evolution of large brain size posed an especially strong selective advantage among the hominids.

**CONNECT TO**

**CLASSIFICATION**
A genus is a closely related group of species. You will learn more about categories for classification in **The Tree of Life.**

**Synthesize** When might having an increasingly larger brain size no longer be a selective advantage?

 **SELF-CHECK** Online
HMHScience.com
**GO ONLINE**

# 12.6 Formative Assessment

### REVIEWING ▶ MAIN IDEAS

1. What characteristics shared by humans and other **primates** suggest that they have a common ancestor?

2. According to the fossil record, what other *Homo* species was present when modern humans arose?

3. From the hominin fossils described, what common trends can be found?

### CRITICAL THINKING

4. **Apply** Explain why, according to the fossil record, it is not correct to say that humans evolved from chimpanzees.

5. **Infer** Scientists can often identify whether a fossil skull was from a **bipedal** primate. What characteristics of a skull might help them make this determination?

**CONNECT TO**

**ANATOMY**

6. Consider the skull illustrations above. Besides size, how did skull structure change as hominins evolved? What features are considered more apelike than humanlike?

# 12 Summary

Scientists use many types of data collection and experimentation to form hypotheses and theories about how life formed on Earth..

## KEY CONCEPTS

### 12.1 The Fossil Record

**Fossils are a record of life that existed in the past.** Fossils can form in several different ways. The age of a fossil or rock can be determined by radiometric dating, which uses radioactive isotopes to determine the age of a fossil or the rock in which it is found. Through radiometric dating, scientists estimate that Earth is about 4.5 billion years old.

### 12.2 The Geologic Time Scale

**The geologic time scale divides Earth's history based on major past events.** Index fossils can be used along with radiometric dating to determine the age of a fossil or rock.

### 12.3 Origin of Life

**The origin of life on Earth remains a puzzle.** There are several hypotheses about the way early organic molecules appeared on Earth and about the way early cells may have formed. The discovery of ribozymes, RNA molecules that can catalyze reactions without the help of proteins, led to the hypothesis that RNA arose before DNA as the first genetic material on Earth.

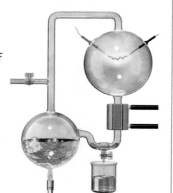

### 12.4 Early Single-Celled Organisms

**Single-celled organisms existed 3.8 billion years ago.** The first organisms on Earth were most likely anaerobic prokaryotes. The theory of endosymbiosis proposes that the first eukaryotic cells arose from a large prokaryote engulfing a smaller prokaryote.

The theories of autogeny and horizontal gene transfer provide alternate ideas of how more complex cell structure arose.

### 12.5 Radiation of Multicellular Life

**Multicellular life evolved in distinct phases.** During the Paleozoic era, members of every major animal group evolved within only a few million years. During the Mesozoic era, dinosaurs, flowering plants, birds, and mammals inhabited Earth. During the Cenozoic era, mammals, birds, fishes, and flowering plants diversified and flourished. Modern humans did not appear until 200,000 years ago.

### 12.6 Primate Evolution

**Humans appeared late in Earth's history.** Humans share a common ancestor with other primates. Primates include all mammals with flexible hands and feet, forward-looking eyes, and enlarged brains relative to their body size. The hominins include all species in the human lineage, both modern and extinct.

## READING TOOLBOX    SYNTHESIZE YOUR NOTES

**Timeline** Make a timeline noting the history of hominid evolution. Add details about characteristics of each hominid that is on your diagram.

**Concept Map** Use a concept map to summarize hypotheses about the origin of life on Earth.

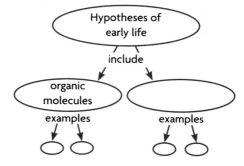

CHAPTER

# 12 Review

INTERACTIVE Review
HMHScience.com

GO ONLINE

Review Games • Concept Map • Section Self-Checks

## CHAPTER VOCABULARY

**12.1**  relative dating
      radiometric dating
      isotope
      half-life

**12.2**  index fossil
      geologic time scale
      era
      period
      epoch

**12.3**  nebula
      ribozyme

**12.4**  cyanobacteria
      endosymbiosis

**12.5**  Paleozoic
      Cambrian explosion
      Mesozoic
      Cenozoic

**12.6**  primate
      prosimian
      anthropoid
      hominid
      bipedal

## Reviewing Vocabulary

**Compare and Contrast**

Describe one similarity and one difference between the two terms in each of the following pairs.

1. relative dating, radiometric dating
2. isotope, half-life
3. era, period
4. cyanobacteria, endosymbiosis
5. Paleozoic, Cambrian explosion
6. primate, hominid

**Keep It Short**

Write a short, precise phrase that describes the meaning of each vocabulary term below. For example, a short phrase to describe *geologic time scale* could be "organizes life's history."

7. index fossil
8. epoch
9. ribozyme
10. bipedal

**READING TOOLBOX**   GREEK AND LATIN WORD ORIGINS

11. *Nebula* is a Latin word that means "cloud." Why do you think astronomers chose this word as a name for what they were observing in outer space?

12. The prefix *iso-* means "the same." How does this meaning relate to the definition of *isotope*?

## Reviewing MAIN IDEAS

13. Fossils can form in several ways, one of which is by permineralization. Describe the process of permineralization and give an example of the type of fossil that may result.

14. Give an example of the way the concept of half-life is used in radiometric dating.

15. How are index fossils used in relative dating?

16. The geologic time scale organizes the history of Earth into eras, periods, and epochs. How are these units of time related to one another?

17. Compare and contrast the evidence that supports the two hypotheses describing how long, complex molecules that carry information, such as DNA, might have formed on early Earth.

18. What are two ways that cyanobacteria have changed the physical or chemical composition of Earth?

19. Summarize the evidence supporting each of the theories describing the origins of eukaryotic cells.

20. One evolutionary advantage of sexual reproduction is that it creates more genetic variation in a population than asexual reproduction. Why might this be an advantage?.

21. What are some criteria by which we can evaluate the relative complexity of a cell?

22. In which era did mammals, dinosaurs, and birds appear on Earth? What happened to these groups in the following era?

23. Humans, apes, monkeys, and lemurs are all examples of primates. What characteristics do all primates share?

# Critical Thinking

24. **Analyze** Some scientists propose that more than one of the theories given in Section 4 may be involved in the evolution of the eukaryotic cell. Explain how this might be possible.

25. **Apply** Why is it likely that autotrophs appeared on Earth before any aerobes, organisms that depended on oxygen?

26. **Evaluate** How does the frozen seawater hypothesis suggest that complex molecules that contain information, such as DNA, could have formed in spite of conditions on early Earth that would have inhibited their formation? How persuasive do you find the evidence supporting this hypothesis?

27. **Evaluate** Thirteen of the 20 amino acids used to make proteins in modern-day cells were made by Miller-Urey's simulation of early Earth's conditions. Do the results support Miller and Urey's hypothesis? Why or Why not?

## Interpreting Visuals

The chart below shows when some human ancestors lived and traits that they had. Use the chart to answer the next three questions.

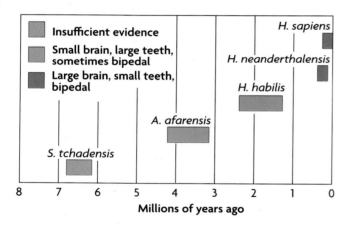

28. **Summarize** In one or two sentences, summarize the information in the chart.

29. **Infer** *Sahelanthropus tchadensis* was pictured in **FIGURE 6.5** of Section 6 as a three-dimensional computer reconstruction. Although skull fragments of this species have been found, the chart above shows that there is not enough evidence to describe the traits of *S. tchadensis*. Explain why this might be so. Consider the scientific process in your explanation.

30. **Analyze** Some scientists suggest that *Homo habilis* should be classified as *Australopithecus habilis*. Based upon the information in the chart, explain why this might be the case.

## Analyzing Data  Calculate Intervals

Both graphs show the rate of decay of chlorine-36, which changes into argon-36. Use the graphs to answer the next two questions.

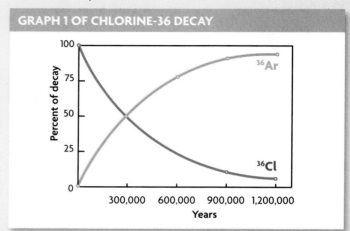

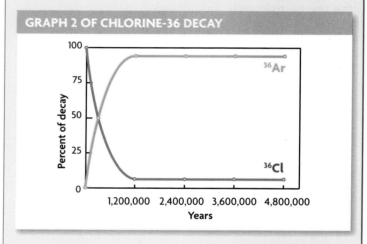

31. **Analyze** Which graph better shows the concept that the percentage change of $^{36}Cl$ and $^{36}Ar$ slows down dramatically over time? Explain.

32. **Analyze** From which graph can you more accurately determine the half-life in years of $^{36}Cl$? Explain.

## Making Connections

33. **Write a Detailed Description** Choose one of the periods in geological time and describe it in detail. Be sure to include vivid details about the organisms of the period.

34. **Connect** The time that the Tollund Man on the chapter opener lived was determined by radiocarbon dating. Why can't $^{14}C$ be used to date Burgess Shale fossils from the Cambrian period?

# Standards-Based Assessment

Record your answers on a separate piece of paper.

## MULTIPLE CHOICE

1 Sexual reproduction and mutation provides means for genetic variation in a population. Why is genetic variation an important element of natural selection?

A It ensures that all members of a population receive only traits that provide them with a survival advantage in their environment.

B It may provide an individual with traits that do not provide any survival advantage.

C It increases the chances that some individuals in a population will gain genes for traits that provide a survival advantage in a changing environment, enabling them to pass these genes to future generations.

D It increases the likelihood that a population will go extinct, providing more resources for other, stronger populations.

2

### Percent of Native Bird Fossils in Hawaii

| Excavated Section | ¹⁴C Dating (years before present) | % Bones from Non-native Species | % Bones from Native Species |
|---|---|---|---|
| I | 390 | 100.0 | 0.0 |
| II | 770 | 98.8 | 1.2 |
| III | 4340 | 9.2 | 90.8 |
| IV | 7750 | 0.0 | 100.0 |

The table above shows the fossil evidence of birds in a section of cave wall in Hawaii. What can be determined from the data presented?

A A catastrophic event occurred between 770 and 4340 years ago.

B Native species out-competed non-native species.

C Most native species died out over 800 years ago.

D The disappearance of non-native species is a function of time.

3 In the evolution of eukaryotes, cells that contained mitochondria-like organelles had an advantage because they—

A could make use of photosynthesis

B could make use of more available energy

C had more DNA

D were protected from bacterial invasion

### THINK THROUGH THE QUESTION

This question is really just asking about the way mitochondria can help a cell.

4 Many scientists believe that the cell parts that are now known as mitochondria and chloroplasts were early types of prokaryote cells. The theory of endosymbiosis suggests that early eukaryote cells formed when large prokaryote cells took in mitochondria or chloroplasts, enabling them to live inside the larger cell without harm. What advantage would the larger host prokaryote cell provide to the chloroplast?

A a stable, protected environment

B the ability to carry out photosynthesis

C access to sunlight

D ability to reproduce

5 The theory of endosymbiosis proposes that the chloroplasts present in some of today's eukaryotic cells descended from ancient cyanobacteria. Which piece of evidence supports this theory?

A Cyanobacteria are single-celled heterotrophs.

B Chloroplasts are much larger than today's prokaryotes.

C Chloroplasts are able to copy themselves independently of the cell.

D Chloroplasts help eukaryotic cells process energy more efficiently.

# BIOZINE
## *at* HMHSCIENCE.COM
### INTERNET MAGAZINE

Go online for the latest biology news and updates on all BioZine articles.

**Expanding the Textbook**

**News Feeds**

- Science Daily
- CNN
- BBC

**Careers**

**Bio Bytes**

**Opinion Poll**

**Strange Biology**

Could a scraped knee land you in the hospital?

# Drug-Resistant Bacteria— A Global Health Issue

A bicyclist falls, scrapes his knees, and within a few days is unable to walk. Soccer players with turf burns suddenly find themselves in the hospital with skin infections that require intravenous antibiotics. Why are these young, healthy athletes developing such serious infections?

## Staph Infections

These athletes were infected by *Staphylococcus aureus*, or "staph." Staph is a common bacteria that most people carry on the surface of their skin and in their nose. To cause an infection, staph bacteria must get inside your body. The scrapes athletes commonly get provide an ideal entrance.

Serious problems due to staph infections used to be rare. Doctors would prescribe antibiotics, such as penicillin, to kill the staph bacteria. Ordinary staph infections can still be treated this way. The athletes in our examples did not have ordinary infections. These athletes' scrapes were infected by methicillin-resistant *Staphylococcus aureus* (MRSA). This bacteria strain is one of many that has evolved resistance to antibiotics.

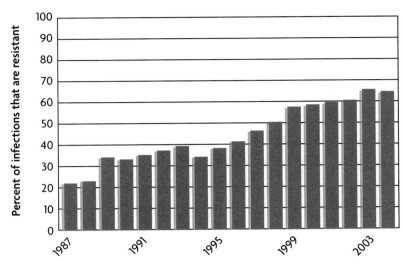

**MRSA on the Rise**

Source: NNIS System and Centers for Disease Control and Prevention

## Drug-Resistant Bacteria

**This petri dish contains** *Staphylococcus aureus* **bacteria.**

Bacteria that can survive antibiotic treatment are called drug-resistant bacteria. Some bacteria have resistance for one particular antibiotic, some have resistance for several, and a few cannot be treated with any known antibiotic.

MRSA can resist an entire class of antibiotics. Patients with an MRSA infection must often be treated with what doctors call "the drug of last resort," vancomycin. Vancomycin is a drug that must be given intravenously. Not surprisingly, doctors began to see cases of vancomycin-resistant *Staphylococcus aureus* (VRSA) in 1997. By 2010, vancomycin-resistant bacteria were being discovered in the droppings of one out of ten seagulls, leading scientists to postulate that migrating birds may play a role in spreading drug-resistant "superbugs."

Staph isn't the only type of bacteria that is making a comeback with drug-resistant strains. In the mid-twentieth century, antibiotics nearly wiped out tuberculosis (TB). But in the 1990s, TB began to approach epidemic numbers again, and now it kills more than 2 million people every year. Drug-resistant TB kills thousands. Drug-resistant strains of cholera and bubonic plague also have been reported.

## How Does Drug Resistance Evolve?

When you take antibiotics for a bacterial infection, most bacteria may be killed right away, but a few will likely survive. Antibiotics leave behind the more resistant bacteria to survive and reproduce. When they reproduce, the genes that make them resistant are passed on to their offspring. Some bacteria reproduce rapidly—*E. coli*, for example, doubles its population every 20 minutes.

In addition to their ability to reproduce quickly, populations of bacteria evolve rapidly. Bacteria use plasmids—small loops of DNA—to transfer genetic material between individual cells. This process is called conjugation. Some plasmids pass on resistance for one particular antibiotic. Others can transfer resistance for several antibiotics at once.

What characteristics do resistant bacteria pass on to their offspring? Some have cell membranes through which antibiotics cannot easily pass. Others have pumps that remove antibiotics once they enter the cell. Some can even produce enzymes that attack the antibiotic drugs themselves.

## Fighting Back

Some scientists are trying to develop ways to treat patients without killing the bacteria that are making them sick. Instead, they target the toxins produced by bacteria. If the bacteria are not harmed by the treatment, no selective pressure is produced. Scientists hope that by using this approach, bacteria will be slower to evolve defense mechanisms against the antibiotics. Other scientists hope to fight back by using bacteria's ancient rival, bacteriophages, which are viruses that infect bacteria.

## CAREERS

### Evolutionary Biologist in Action

| **DR. RICHARD LENSKI** | |
|---|---|
| **TITLE** Professor, Microbial Ecology, Michigan State University | |
| **EDUCATION** Ph.D., Zoology, University of North Carolina, Chapel Hill | |

If you want to observe evolution in action, you must find populations that reproduce quickly. Dr. Richard Lenski, a professor at Michigan State University, has done just that. Dr. Lenski studies populations of *E. coli* bacteria, which he grows in flasks filled with a sugary broth. These bacteria produce about seven generations each day. Dr. Lenski has now observed more than 30,000 generations of *E. coli.*

The rapid rate of *E. coli* reproduction allows Dr. Lenski to watch evolution take place. Dr. Lenski can subject each generation of bacteria to the same environmental stresses, such as food shortages or antibiotics. He then can compare individuals from more recent generations with their ancestors, which he keeps in his laboratory freezer. By comparing generations in this way, Dr. Lenski can study how the population has evolved.

When Dr. Lenski began his research in 1988, watching evolution in action was still new. Now, many evolutionary biologists are following in his footsteps.

**Read More >>** *at* **HMHScience.com**

## TECHNOLOGY S.T.E.M.

### New Drug Delivery System

Researchers at Yeshiva University decided to take on one of the most difficult bacterial infections of all, methicillin-resistant staph. They have developed a treatment using nanoparticles that can be delivered directly to a wound on the skin.

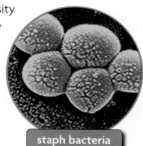

staph bacteria

- Tiny nanoparticles carry nitric oxide (NO), which helps the immune system respond to infection.
- The nanoparticles are applied topically, to deep, infected skin abscesses.
- The nanoparticles absorb water, swell, and release NO. NO kills bacteria and dilates blood vessels, to speed healing.

Because the bacteria are "eating" the nanoballs, cell wall adaptations that once kept antibiotics out are no longer an obstacle.

**Read More >>** *at* **HMHScience.com**

## Unanswered Questions

Some important research questions involving drug-resistant bacteria include the following:

- Can plasmids or bacteriophages be used in vaccines to fight bacteria?
- Are bacteria being exposed to antibiotics in sewage systems and evolving resistant strains there?
- How do antibacterial soaps and household cleaners contribute to the evolution of drug-resistant bacteria?
- Can drug-resistant bacteria be transferred from domestic animals to humans through food?

**Read More >>** *at* **HMHScience.com**

UNIT **5**

# Ecology

 **BIOZINE**
HMHScience.com

**Climate Change—
Changing the Planet**
**TECHNOLOGY** Deep Sea
Sediment Coring
**CAREER** Oceanographer

(t13) ©www.richardettinger.com; (t14) ©Albie Venter/Shutterstock; (t15) ©Andrew Brown/Photo Researchers, Inc.; (t16) ©Simon Fraser/Photo Researchers, Inc.; (t17) ©Adrian Warren/ardea.com; (bg) *gulls, waves* ©PhotoDisc/Getty Images; *lichen, forest, sand dollar, tree rings* ©Getty Images; (br) ©Thomas Nilsen/Science Photo Library/Photo Researchers, Inc.

**BIG IDEA** Living things interact with other organisms and with their environment.

⊘ **ONLINE BIOLOGY**  HMHScience.com

**ONLINE** Labs
- **QuickLab** Quadrat Sampling
- Abiotic Factors and Plant Growth
- Random Sampling
- Build a Terrarium
- Nitrogen Fixation
- Interdependence of Plants and Animals

- **Virtual Lab** Estimating Population Size
- **Video Lab** Ecosystem Change

©www.richardettlinger.com

**Q How does this bird interact with its ecosystem?**

Anhingas live in freshwater marshes and swamps of the southeastern United States. While they are primarily consumers of fish, an anhinga's diet may also include aquatic insects and invertebrates. The anhinga and the fish are just two of the many organisms that interact in this complex wetland ecosystem.

---

**READING TOOLBOX** This reading tool can help you learn the material in the following pages.

**USING LANGUAGE**

**Word Problems** Read word problems several times before trying to solve them. After you understand what the problems are asking, write down all of the relevant information on a piece of paper. Then, use the mathematical processes that apply to the situation.

**YOUR TURN**

Solve the following word problem about energy.

1. When a snake eats a mouse, only about 10% of the energy stored in the mouse's body is stored in the snake. If the body of a mouse contains 2000 kcal of energy, how much energy is stored in the snake?

# Ecologists Study Relationships

SC.912.L.17.5

**KEY CONCEPT** Ecology is the study of the relationships among organisms and their environment.

**VOCABULARY**

ecology
community
ecosystem
biome

**MAIN IDEAS**

- Ecologists study environments at different levels of organization.
- Ecological research methods include observation, experimentation, and modeling.

**SC.912.L.17.5** Analyze how population size is determined by births, deaths, immigration, emigration, and limiting factors (biotic and abiotic) that determine carrying capacity.

### ☀ *Connect to Your World*

Water birds such as anhingas, along with a variety of other plants and animals, rely on the presence of wetlands for their survival. How might the loss of wetland areas affect these aquatic species? Learning about organisms and how they interact with one another, with other species, and with their environment is what the study of ecology is all about.

### ▶ MAIN IDEA

## Ecologists study environments at different levels of organization.

Over their life cycle, Pacific salmon are the main food source for more than 140 species of wildlife, including grizzly bears, as shown in **FIGURE 1.1**. If they are not eaten, their bodies return vital nutrients back into the river system, some of which are used by plants to grow. In addition to their role in the health of river systems, salmon are also important to the Pacific Northwest's economy. Today, many species of wild Pacific salmon are threatened with extinction due to competition from hatchery fish, blocked river paths, and loss of spawning grounds. As salmon populations decline, how are other species affected? What effect would the loss of salmon have on a local and a global scale? These are the types of questions ecologists are trying to answer.

**FIGURE 1.1** Salmon are a primary food source for many species, including grizzly bears. If salmon disappeared, species dependent on them would also suffer.

### What Is Ecology?

**Ecology** is the study of the interactions among living things, and between living things and their surroundings. The word *ecology* comes from the Greek word *oikos,* which means "house." This word origin makes sense if you think of Earth as home and all organisms as members of Earth's household. Ernst Haeckel, a German biologist, coined the term *ecology* in 1866 to encourage biologists to consider the ways organisms interact. Until that time, most scientists studied a plant or an animal as though it existed in isolation—as if it did not affect its surroundings, and its surroundings did not affect it.

©Hal Beral/Corbis

## Levels of Organization

Ecologists study nature on different levels, from a local to a global scale. These levels, shown in **FIGURE 1.2**, reveal the complex relationships found in nature.

- **Organism** An organism is an individual living thing, such as an alligator.
- **Population** A population is a group of the same species that lives in one area, such as all the alligators that live in a swamp.
- **Community** A **community** is a group of different species that live together in one area, such as groups of alligators, turtles, birds, fish, and plants that live together in the Florida Everglades.
- **Ecosystem** An **ecosystem** includes all of the organisms as well as the climate, soil, water, rocks, and other nonliving things in a given area. Ecosystems can vary in size. An entire ecosystem may exist within a decaying log, which in turn may be part of a larger wetland ecosystem.
- **Biome** A **biome** (BY-ohm) is a major regional or global community of organisms. Biomes are usually characterized by the climate conditions and plant communities that thrive there.

Ecologists study relationships within each level of organization and also between levels. For example, researchers may study the relationships within a population of alligators, as well as the relationships between alligators and turtles in a community.

**Apply** **What level of organization describes a flock of pigeons in a park?**

**READING TOOLBOX**

**TAKING NOTES**

Use a diagram to take notes on the levels of organization.

Levels of Organization
- organism
- population
- community
- ecosystem
- biome

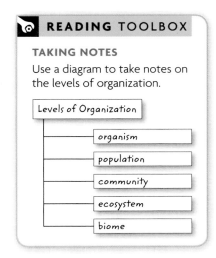

Biome

Savanna

## FIGURE 1.2  Levels of Organization

The Florida Everglades is an example of the subtropical savanna biome. Many organisms live in this aquatic ecosystem.

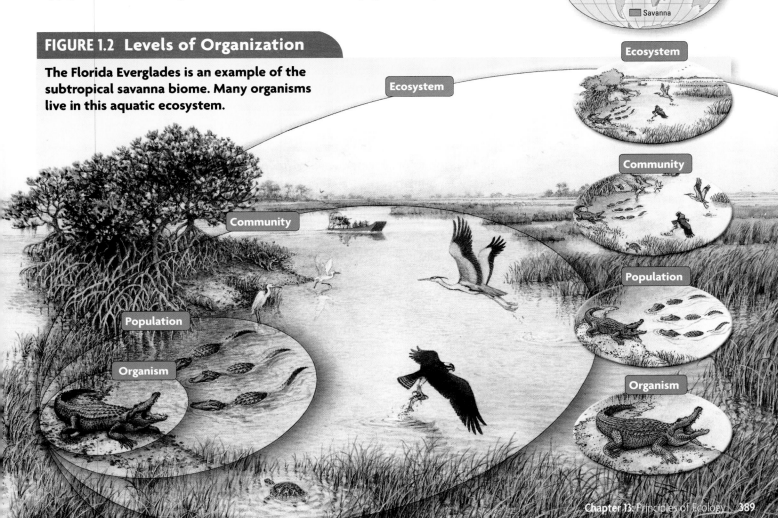

## ▶ MAIN IDEA

# Ecological research methods include observation, experimentation, and modeling.

Scientists rely on a variety of methods and tools to conduct research. Tools can range from a simple tape measure used to find an organism's size to a sophisticated computer system used to create a model of an entire ecosystem.

## Observation

Observation is the act of carefully watching something over time. Such observations may occur over short or long periods of time. Long-term studies are a key part of a scientist's toolkit because most environmental changes happen over a long period of time. For example, studies of prairie-dog populations are helping scientists to determine which locations are most appropriate for the reintroduction of the black-footed ferret. The black-footed ferret is an endangered species that relies on the prairie dog as its main food source.

One way that scientists monitor and observe populations is by conducting surveys. Visual surveys may be direct or indirect.

- Direct surveys are used for species that are easy to follow. In these surveys, scientists watch animals either with the naked eye or with tools such as binoculars or scopes.
- Indirect surveys are used for species that are difficult to track. In these surveys, scientists search for other signs of its presence, such as feces or a recent kill.

Radio telemetry is another method used by scientists to monitor populations. Scientists fit an animal with a radio collar that emits a signal and then use the signal to track the animal's movement, as shown in **FIGURE 1.3**. This practice is especially useful when studying a species that has a broad range, such as the gray wolf.

In addition to observing the activities of a species, scientists often determine the species' population size. Rather than count every individual organism in a large study area, scientists can sample the population instead. Mark-recapture is a method used by scientists to estimate the population size of mobile organisms. For example, to monitor prairie-dog populations, scientists capture and mark prairie dogs with ear tags and then release them back into the wild. When scientists later repeat the survey, the captured prairie dogs will include both marked and unmarked animals. Scientists calculate the ratio of marked to unmarked animals and use this value to estimate the total population size.

To monitor plant populations, scientists use a method called quadrat sampling. In this method, quadrats, or rectangular frames, are randomly placed on the study site. To determine plant population numbers, scientists identify and count the number of plants within each randomly selected plot. The total number of counted plants is then plugged into a mathematical formula to determine the plant population of the entire study site.

**Apply** How might a scientist use observation to study a population of mountain goats? Explain your answer.

**FIGURE 1.3** Much of the data gathered by ecologists results from long hours of observation in the field. This ecologist is using radio telemetry to track gray wolves.

©Jim West/Alamy Ltd

# Changing one factor in an ecosystem can affect many other factors.

An ecosystem is a complex web of connected biotic and abiotic factors. You may not always think of yourself as part of the ecosystem, but humans, like other species, rely on the environment for survival. All species are affected by changes to the biotic and abiotic factors in an ecosystem.

## Biodiversity

The relationships within an ecosystem are very complicated. If you attached a separate string between a forest tree and each of the living and nonliving things in the ecosystem that influenced it, and did the same for each of those living and nonliving things, the forest would quickly become a huge web of strings. The web would also reveal the biodiversity in the forest. **Biodiversity** (by-oh-dih-VUR-sih-tee) is the assortment, or variety, of living things in an ecosystem. An area with a high level of biodiversity, such as a rain forest, has a large assortment of species living near one another. The amount of biodiversity found in an area depends on many factors, including moisture and temperature.

Some areas of the world have an unusually large amount of biodiversity in comparison to other locations. For example, tropical rain forests, which are moist and warm environments, cover less than 7 percent of Earth's ground surface. However, they account for over 50 percent of the planet's plant and animal species. This large amount of biodiversity emphasizes the importance of conserving such areas. Tropical rain forests and coral reefs are two of several areas referred to as hot spots. These hot spots, located across the globe, are areas that are rich in biodiversity, but are threatened by human activities.

## Keystone Species

The complex relationships in ecosystems mean that a change in a single biotic or abiotic factor—a few broken strings in the web—can have a variety of effects. The change may barely be noticed, or it may have a deep impact. In some cases, the loss of a single species may cause a ripple effect felt across an entire ecosystem. Such an organism is called a keystone species. A **keystone species** is a species that has an unusually large effect on its ecosystem.

One example of a keystone species is the beaver. By felling trees to construct dams, beavers change free-flowing stream habitats into ponds, wetlands, and meadows. This modification leads to a cascade of changes within their ecosystem.

> **CONNECT TO**
>
> **BIODIVERSITY**
>
> The discovery of potential medicines and new species are two reasons why it is important to maintain biodiversity. In the chapter **Human Impact on Ecosystems,** you will learn how human activities impact biodiversity and how the loss of biodiversity affects us all.

**VISUAL VOCAB**

Like a keystone that holds up an arch, a **keystone species** holds together a dynamic ecosystem.

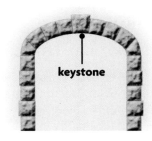

keystone

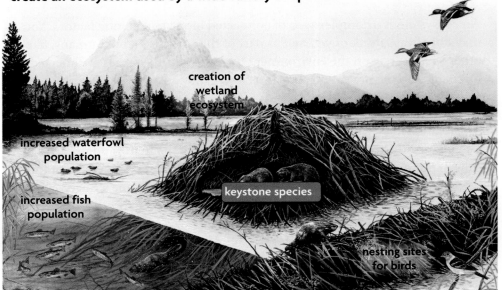

## FIGURE 2.2 Keystone Species

Beavers are a keystone species. By constructing dams, beavers create an ecosystem used by a wide variety of species.

creation of wetland ecosystem

increased waterfowl population

increased fish population

keystone species

nesting sites for birds

**WebQuest**
HMHScience.com
**GO ONLINE**
Keystone Species

As **FIGURE 2.2** shows, beavers cause changes that create an ecosystem used by a variety of species, leading to an overall increase in biodiversity.

- A greater number and wider variety of fish are able to live in the still waters of the pond.
- The fish attract fish-eating birds, such as herons and kingfishers.
- Insects inhabit the pond and the dead trees along the shore, attracting insect-eating birds, such as great-crested flycatchers, that nest in the tree cavities.
- Waterfowl nest among the shrubs and grasses along the pond's edge.
- Animals that prey on birds or their eggs are also attracted to the pond.

Keystone species form and maintain a complex web of life. Whatever happens to that species affects all the other species connected to it.

**Connect** Explain why the Pacific salmon, introduced in Section 1, could be considered a keystone species.

**SELF-CHECK Online**
HMHScience.com
**GO ONLINE**

## 13.2 Formative Assessment

### REVIEWING ▶ MAIN IDEAS

1. Select an ecosystem that is familiar to you and describe the biotic and abiotic factors that exist there.

2. How would the removal of a keystone species affect an ecosystem's biodiversity?

### CRITICAL THINKING

3. **Predict** Explain how a change in an abiotic factor such as sunlight would affect biodiversity.

4. **Analyze** Humans are sometimes described as being a keystone species. Does this label fit? Why or why not?

### CONNECT TO
**EVOLUTION**

5. What role might an abiotic factor such as temperature play in the evolution of a species?

# Algae Farms—Producing a Fuel of the Future?

When you think of farms, you probably picture fields of wheat, corn, or other agricultural crops, or perhaps cattle, chickens, or hogs grazing. But can you imagine a farm that grows microscopic algae to be used as a biofuel? Compared with other sources of biofuels, such as corn, algae can produce more fuel in a smaller amount of space.

A biofuel is any fuel that contains energy from recently living organisms, such as peanut oil from peanuts and ethanol from corn. Biofuels are produced by subjecting biomass (plant or animal material) to heat, chemicals, or bacteria to break down the material. Dwindling petroleum resources, the unstable prices of fossil fuel resources, and the inability to exploit potential new resources have steadily increased the demand for alternative fuel sources such as those derived from plant and animal materials. One of those potential sources is algae, which produce oil that can be used as biodiesel in cars, trucks, and airplanes.

Some scientists are working with businesses to determine the best ways to grow and process algae. At one type of algae farm, microscopic green algae are grown in large open ponds, called raceways. Each raceway has a specially designed paddle wheel that continuously moves the water, mixing the algae so that it does not settle on the bottom of the pond.

After the algae are collected and processed, the cell walls of the algae must be broken down to extract the oil. One way to do this is through the use of ultrasound, sound waves with frequencies too high for humans to hear.

When algae cells are exposed to ultrasound, the cell wall breaks apart. Then the oil is extracted and processed at a biorefinery, in much the same way that petroleum is processed in a traditional oil refinery.

Scientists are researching different ways of growing algae, such as vertically in large plastic sheets like the ones below. The clear plastic exposes the algae to sunlight while the algae are provided the carbon dioxide, oxygen, and nutrients they need. Other studies are being conducted to modify plant cells genetically to make it easier to extract the oil from algae.

As with any fuel source, there are advantages and disadvantages to the production of biofuel from algae. Algae use carbon dioxide as they carry out photosynthesis, so most algae farms could be carbon-neutral operations. Also, algae can produce up to 60 times the amount of oil as land-based plants used to produce biofuels do.

Disadvantages to using algae as a biofuel include the expense of production and the use of water. Current processes use about 350 gallons of water to produce one barrel of algae oil. It costs more to produce oil from algae than it does to produce petroleum. As with most innovations, however, continued research and improved methods of production will lower costs.

## S.T.E.M. Activity

Research more about new designs and technologies being developed for algae farms. What are the latest designs for different types of algae farms? What are some of the advantages and disadvantages of each design?

(bl) ©Hank Morgan/Science Source/Getty Images; (cr) ©Sam Hodgson/Bloomberg/Getty Images

SC.912.L.17.9

**SC.912.L.17.9** Use a food web to identify and distinguish producers, consumers, and decomposers. Explain the pathway of energy transfer through trophic levels and the reduction of available energy at successive trophic levels.

**VOCABULARY**

producer
autotroph
consumer
heterotroph
chemosynthesis

**KEY CONCEPT** **Life in an ecosystem requires a source of energy.**

**MAIN IDEAS**

- Producers provide energy for other organisms in an ecosystem.
- Almost all producers obtain energy from sunlight.

☀ *Connect to Your World* ─────────────

You play an important role in the cycling of energy on Earth, as do the plants and animals you eat. This energy that cycles through Earth's ecosystems is needed to fuel your life processes, such as breathing and growing. Where does this energy come from, and what role does it play in an ecosystem?

▶ **MAIN IDEA**

## Producers provide energy for other organisms in an ecosystem.

All organisms must have a source of energy in order to survive. However, not all organisms obtain their energy by eating other organisms.

- **Producers** are organisms that get their energy from nonliving resources, meaning they make their own food. Their distribution is shown in **FIGURE 3.1.** Producers are also called **autotrophs** (AW-tuh-TRAHFS). In the word *autotroph*, the suffix *-troph* comes from a Greek word meaning "nourishment." The prefix *auto-* means "self."

- **Consumers** are organisms that get their energy by eating other living or once-living resources, such as plants and animals. Consumers are also called **heterotrophs** (HEHT-uhr-uh-TRAHFS). In the word *heterotroph*, the prefix *hetero-* means "different."

All ecosystems depend on producers, because they provide the basis for the ecosystem's energy. Even animals that eat only meat rely on producers. One such species is the gray wolf. Gray wolves are consumers that eat elk and moose. Elk and moose are consumers that eat plants, such as grasses and shrubs. Plants are producers that make their own food. If the grasses and shrubs disappeared, the elk and moose would either have to find some other producer to eat or they would starve. The wolves would also be affected because they eat elk and moose. Although the wolves do not eat plants, their lives are tied to the grasses and shrubs that feed their prey. Likewise, all consumers are connected in some way to producers.

Most producers need sunlight to make food. These producers depend directly on the sun as their source of energy. For this reason, all the consumers connected to these producers depend indirectly on the sun for their energy.

**FIGURE 3.1** This satellite image uses chlorophyll abundance to show the distribution of producers in the Western Hemisphere. Dark green areas are heavily forested, while yellow areas have limited vegetation.

**Predict** How would a long-term drought affect producers and consumers?

NASA

# Almost all producers obtain energy from sunlight.

Most producers on Earth use sunlight as their energy source. Photosynthesis is the two-stage process that green plants, cyanobacteria, and some protists use to produce energy. Chemical reactions form carbohydrates from carbon dioxide and water. Oxygen is released as a waste product.

Photosynthesis in plants begins when energy from the sun hits chloroplasts and is absorbed by chlorophyll. In the first stage of photosynthesis, energy from sunlight is converted to chemical energy. In the second stage, this chemical energy is used to change carbon dioxide into carbohydrates, such as glucose. Plants use these carbohydrates as an energy source to fuel cellular respiration.

Not all producers depend on sunlight for their energy. Scientists were stunned in 1977 when they first visited deep-sea vents on the bottom of the ocean. There they found thriving ecosystems in places where super-heated water shoots up from the ocean floor. Studies showed that tiny prokaryotes were making their own food from minerals in the water. They had no need for sunlight. **Chemosynthesis** (KEE-moh-SIHN-thih-sihs) is the process by which an organism forms carbohydrates using chemicals, rather than light, as an energy source. A series of reactions changes the chemicals into a usable energy form. Different reactions occur depending on which chemicals are present.

In addition to deep-sea vents, chemosynthetic organisms are also found in sulfur-rich salt marsh flats and in hydrothermal pools, such as those in Yellowstone National Park, shown in **FIGURE 3.2**. In this case, chemical energy is used to change carbon dioxide ($CO_2$), water ($H_2O$), hydrogen sulfide ($H_2S$), and oxygen ($O_2$) into an energy-rich sugar molecule. Sulfuric acid ($H_2SO_4$) is released as a waste product.

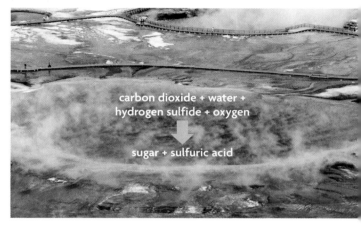

carbon dioxide + water + hydrogen sulfide + oxygen

↓

sugar + sulfuric acid

**FIGURE 3.2** Chemosynthetic bacteria thrive in many of Yellowstone National Park's hydrothermal pools.

©Dennis Frates/Alamy

**Contrast** How do photosynthesis and chemosynthesis differ?

## 13.3 Formative Assessment

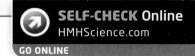
**SELF-CHECK Online**
HMHScience.com
**GO ONLINE**

### REVIEWING ▶ MAIN IDEAS

1. How does the stability of an ecosystem depend on its **producers**?
2. What are the two processes used by producers to obtain energy?

### CRITICAL THINKING

3. **Hypothesize** Few producers live deep below a lake's surface. Suggest an explanation for this pattern.
4. **Infer** Could producers survive without **consumers**? Explain why or why not.

### ⟩⟨ CONNECT TO

**HISTORY OF LIFE**

5. How might chemosynthetic organisms help scientists to understand how life developed on Earth?

# Food Chains and Food Webs

**KEY CONCEPT** Food chains and food webs model the flow of energy in an ecosystem.

## VOCABULARY

| | |
|---|---|
| food chain | herbivore |
| carnivore | omnivore |
| detritivore | decomposer |
| specialist | generalist |
| trophic level | food web |

**SC.912.L.17.9** Use a food web to identify and distinguish producers, consumers, and decomposers. Explain the pathway of energy transfer through trophic levels and the reduction of available energy at successive trophic levels.

### MAIN IDEAS

- A food chain is a model that shows a sequence of feeding relationships.
- A food web shows a complex network of feeding relationships.

### ☀ Connect to Your World

What if you were to write down the names of ten people you know, and then each of them wrote down ten more people, and so on? Very quickly a complex web of relationships would form. Like those in human communities, relationships among organisms in an ecosystem are very complex. These relationships are often described as chains or webs, connecting many species together.

▶ MAIN IDEA

## A food chain is a model that shows a sequence of feeding relationships.

The simplest way to look at energy flow in an ecosystem is through a food chain. A **food chain** is a sequence that links species by their feeding relationships. Rather than describe every potential relationship, this model chain only follows the connection between one producer and a single chain of consumers within an ecosystem. For example, in a desert ecosystem, a desert cottontail eats grass. The food chain is, therefore, grass–desert cottontail. If another consumer such as a Harris's hawk eats a desert cottontail, the food chain gets longer: grass–desert cottontail–Harris's hawk, as shown in **FIGURE 4.1**.

### FIGURE 4.1 Food Chain

**Energy flows through a food chain.**

| GRAMA GRASS | DESERT COTTONTAIL | HARRIS'S HAWK |
|---|---|---|

Grama grass, a producer, obtains its energy through photosynthesis.

The desert cottontail, a consumer, obtains its energy by eating the seeds of plants, such as grama grass.

The Harris's hawk, a consumer, obtains its energy by eating other animals, such as desert cottontails.

## FIGURE 5.1 Hydrologic Cycle

**The hydrologic cycle is the circular pathway of water on Earth.**

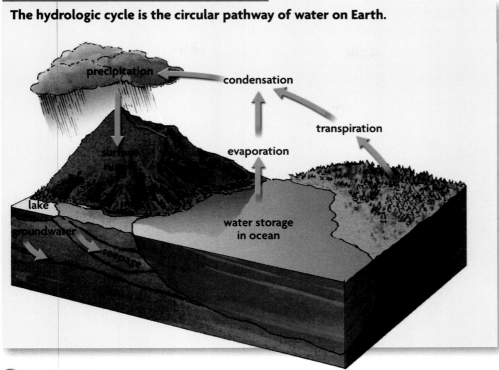

## ▶ MAIN IDEA

# Elements essential for life also cycle through ecosystems.

Many elements are essential to the structure and function of organisms. Elements are basic chemical substances, such as the oxygen and hydrogen found in the chemical compound of water. Additional elements important to life include carbon, nitrogen, phosphorus, and sulfur. As you learned in Chemistry of Life, oxygen, carbon, nitrogen, and hydrogen make up 96 percent of the mass of the human body. This is just one reason why the cycling of these elements is important. All of these elements cycle through ecosystems, as water does.

A **biogeochemical cycle** (BY-oh-JEE-oh-KEHM-ih-kuhl) is the movement of a particular chemical through the biological and geological, or living and nonliving, parts of an ecosystem. Just as water changes from solid form (ice or snow) to liquid form (rain) or gaseous form (water vapor), other substances may also change state as they move through their cycles.

### The Oxygen Cycle

Plants, animals, and most other organisms need oxygen for cellular respiration. As shown in **FIGURE 5.2**, plants release oxygen as a waste product during photosynthesis. In turn, humans and other organisms take in this oxygen and release it as carbon dioxide through respiration. Oxygen is also indirectly transferred through an ecosystem by the cycling of other nutrients, including carbon, nitrogen, and phosphorus.

**Apply** **Explain how deforestation might affect the oxygen cycle.**

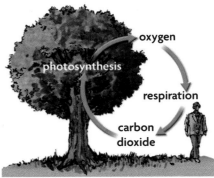

**FIGURE 5.2** In the oxygen cycle, oxygen flows into the atmosphere as a byproduct of photosynthesis. Organisms take in this oxygen and release it as carbon dioxide through respiration.

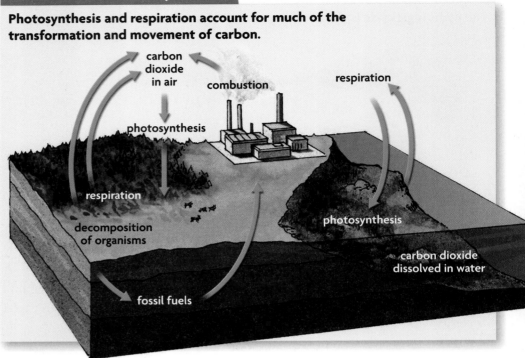

## FIGURE 5.3 Carbon Cycle

Photosynthesis and respiration account for much of the transformation and movement of carbon.

- carbon dioxide in air
- combustion
- respiration
- photosynthesis
- respiration
- decomposition of organisms
- photosynthesis
- carbon dioxide dissolved in water
- fossil fuels

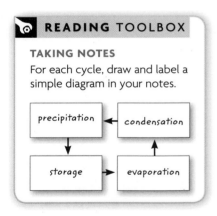
## The Carbon Cycle

Carbon is the building block of life—it is key to the structure of all organisms on our planet. It is an essential component of carbohydrates, proteins, fats, and all the other organic molecules that make up your body. Carbon continually flows from the environment to living organisms and back again in the carbon cycle, shown in **FIGURE 5.3**.

Carbon exists in the abiotic world in several forms. Carbon can be found in solid, liquid, and gaseous states. Sources of carbon include

- carbon dioxide ($CO_2$) gas in the atmosphere
- bicarbonate ($HCO_3^-$) dissolved in water
- fossil fuels, which are underground deposits of oil, natural gas, and coal
- carbonate rocks, such as limestone
- dead organic matter, such as humus, in the soil

The simplest transfer of carbon occurs between plants and animals. Plants use energy from the sun to convert carbon dioxide from the air into organic material that becomes a part of the plant's structure. The carbon then moves through the biotic world as one organism eats another.

Carbon is returned to the atmosphere as carbon dioxide by respiration or through the decomposition of dead organisms. The burning of fossil fuels and wood, as well as emissions from factories and automobiles, adds to carbon dioxide in the atmosphere. Another source of atmospheric carbon is methane, which is emitted from wetlands, landfills, and livestock.

Not all carbon molecules move freely through the cycle. Areas that store carbon over a long period of time are called carbon sinks. One example is forest land, where large amounts of carbon are stored in the cellulose of wood.

## The Nitrogen Cycle

About 78 percent of Earth's atmosphere is made of nitrogen gas. However, most organisms can use nitrogen only in the form of ions such as ammonium ($NH_4^+$) or nitrate ($NO_3^-$). As shown in **FIGURE 5.4**, much of the nitrogen cycle takes place underground.

Certain types of bacteria convert gaseous nitrogen into ammonia ($NH_3$) through a process called **nitrogen fixation.** A few types of cyanobacteria fix nitrogen in aquatic ecosystems. On land, some nitrogen-fixing bacteria live in small outgrowths, called nodules, on the roots of plants such as beans and peas. Other nitrogen-fixing bacteria live freely in the soil. The ammonia released by these bacteria is transformed into ammonium by the addition of hydrogen ions found in acidic soil. Some ammonium is taken up by plants, but most is used by nitrifying bacteria as an energy source. Through the process called nitrification, these bacteria change ammonium into nitrate.

Nitrates released by soil bacteria are taken up by plants, which convert them into organic compounds such as amino acids and proteins. Nitrogen continues along the cycle as animals eat plant or animal matter. When decomposers break down animal excretions or dead animal and plant matter, nitrogen is returned to the soil as ammonium, in a process called ammonification.

Denitrifying bacteria use nitrate as an oxygen source, releasing nitrogen gas into the atmosphere as a waste product. Some nitrogen also enters the soil as a result of atmospheric fixation by lightning. Lightning's energy breaks apart nitrogen molecules in the atmosphere. Nitrogen recombines with oxygen in the air, forming nitrogen oxide. The combination of nitrogen oxide with rainwater forms nitrates, which are absorbed by the soil.

## FIGURE 5.4  Nitrogen Cycle

Much of the nitrogen cycle occurs underground, where bacteria transform ammonium into nitrates, which are used by plants to make amino acids.

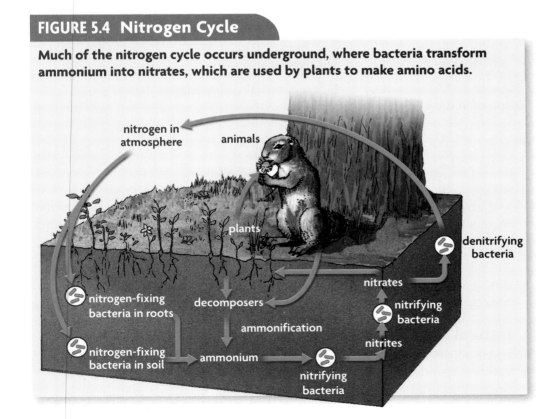

## The Phosphorus Cycle

Unlike the other cycles, the phosphorus cycle does not include an atmospheric portion. Instead, most of the cycle takes place at and below ground level, as shown in **FIGURE 5.5**.

### FIGURE 5.5 Phosphorus Cycle

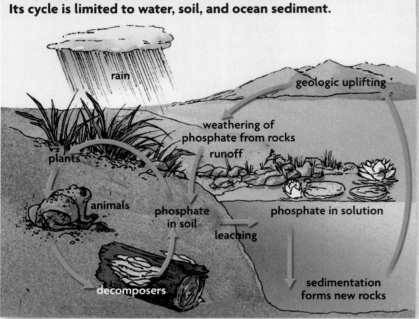

The phosphorus cycle occurs on a local, rather than global, scale. Its cycle is limited to water, soil, and ocean sediment.

The phosphorus cycle begins when phosphate is released by the weathering of rocks. Plants and some fungi found near plant roots are able to take up phosphate. Phosphorus moves from producers to consumers through the food web. When the producers and consumers die, decomposers break down the organisms. This process releases phosphorus back into the soil or water for use by producers. Some phosphorus may leach into groundwater from the soil. This groundwater may flow into a lake or other body of water, where the phosphorus becomes locked in sediments at the bottom. Over many thousands of years, these sediments eventually become rock again, and the cycle starts again as phosphate is released by the weathering of these newly formed rocks.

Mining and agricultural runoff also add to the overall amount of phosphorus in the environment. The excessive flow of phosphorus into an aquatic ecosystem from sewage and agricultural runoff can cause significant problems. Phosphorus is a limiting factor for the growth of plants. Large amounts of phosphorus within an aquatic environment can lead to algal blooms. These blooms crowd out other plant species and negatively impact wildlife populations as well.

**Summarize  Choose one of the biogeochemical cycles, and list the key processes involved in the cycling of the element.**

### ⦿ MAIN IDEA
## Natural and human activities can disrupt biogeochemical cycles and ecosystems.

As you have learned, matter moves through biogeochemical cycles throughout the Earth's ecosystems. But disruptions can occur due to natural events and the actions of humans. The consequences of disruptions include interrupting the flow of elements that serve as chemical building blocks for living systems, altering the balance of nutrients available for organisms, and climate change.

### Natural Disruptions

Natural disruptions occur without direct human causation. Earthquakes, volcanic eruptions, variations in weather, and changes to water movement in oceans and in lakes, rivers, and streams are examples of natural disruptions.

## FIGURE 5.6 Natural Disruptions to Biogeochemical Cycles

**Natural disruptions have occurred throughout the history of Earth and will continue.**

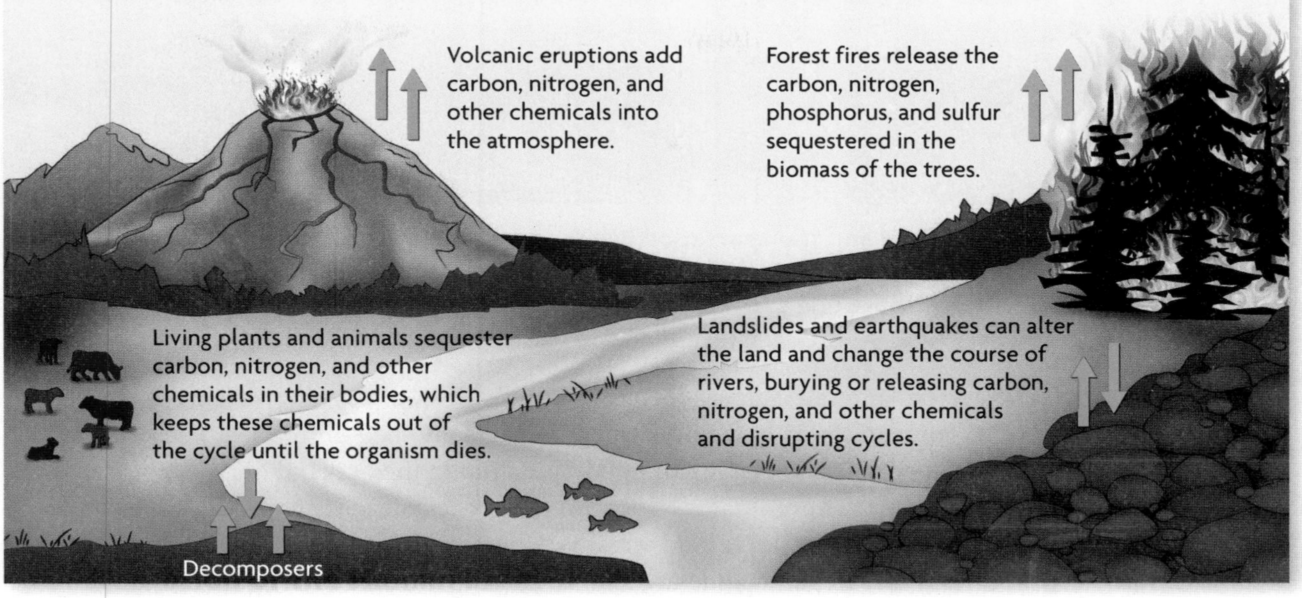

Volcanic eruptions add carbon, nitrogen, and other chemicals into the atmosphere.

Forest fires release the carbon, nitrogen, phosphorus, and sulfur sequestered in the biomass of the trees.

Living plants and animals sequester carbon, nitrogen, and other chemicals in their bodies, which keeps these chemicals out of the cycle until the organism dies.

Landslides and earthquakes can alter the land and change the course of rivers, burying or releasing carbon, nitrogen, and other chemicals and disrupting cycles.

Decomposers

The history of Earth includes many examples of significant natural disruptions, such as a series of volcanic eruptions about 250 million years ago. The consequences of the eruptions and other natural disruptions included the Permian mass extinction and the end of the Paleozoic Era. As shown in **FIGURE 5.6**, volcanic eruptions release gases, ash, and other substances into the atmosphere. The carbon dioxide and nitrogen gases released may overload normal cycles. Also, particles released can block and reduce the amount of sunlight that reaches Earth for several years. When less sunlight reaches Earth, the process of photosynthesis is adversely affected, which in turn, disrupts biogeochemical cycles.

Natural disruptions take place all the time, and most do not lead to mass extinctions. Variations in conditions are normal and disruptions of biogeochemical cycles are compensated for by other events. For example, the growth of forested areas sequesters carbon by taking it out of the carbon cycle and locking it into organisms. However, forest fires, another natural disruption, release the carbon tied up in forest plants back into the atmosphere.

Other natural disruptions include earthquakes, landslides, and changes in water movement. Such disruptions may bury or release materials used in biogeochemical cycles and ecosystems. For example, when a river changes course, the flowing water causes erosion to the land in the river's new path. Phosphorus within the eroded land is released and enters the water phase of the phosphorus cycle.

## Disruptions Caused by Humans

Human actions disrupt both biogeochemical cycles and ecosystems. As the human population grows, so do our needs. Agriculture is responsible for growing most of the foods that humans eat and many products needed for many industries. But poor farming practices cause disruptions to the cycles.

## FIGURE 5.7 Disruptions Caused by Humans

**Some of the methods used to meet food and transportation needs of humans, such as raising herds of livestock and driving vehicles, have consequences for biogeochemical cycles and ecosystems. Algal blooms, which crowd out aquatic plants and cause fish death, are one such consequence.**

Herd animals, such as the water buffalo in **FIGURE 5.7**, may live in dense populations or in feedlots where they are fattened for market. Feedlots can support a much larger animal population than wild land of the same size can support. The animal wastes from feedlots can leach into groundwater or run off into rivers, lakes, and streams. Contamination of water with fecal matter can spread pathogenic organisms, causing illness and death in humans and other organisms.

Poor farming practices can also lead to depletion of soil nutrients, such as nitrogen and phosphorus. Replacing these nutrients through man-made fertilizers can lead to contaminated runoff. When fertilizer-contaminated runoff enters bodies of water, the nutrients promote the overgrowth of algae populations and can cause algal blooms . The algae crowd out aquatic plants and may release harmful toxins. As the algae die and decay, the decomposition process uses up oxygen in the water, causing fish and other organisms to die.

Agricultural practices are not the only ways that humans disrupt biogeochemical cycles and ecosystems. Cars, factories, and power plants burn fossil fuels and release carbon into the atmosphere as carbon dioxide. As a result, the amount of carbon dioxide in the atmosphere has steadily increased, which in turn contributes to climate change. Climate change is an overall increase in the temperature of the Earth, which further disrupts cycles and ecosystems.

**Describe Choose one way that humans disrupt biogeochemical cycles and describe the consequences of the disruption.**

**SELF-CHECK Online**
HMHScience.com
**GO ONLINE**

# 13.5 Formative Assessment

## REVIEWING ▶ MAIN IDEAS

1. How does the **hydrologic cycle** move water through the environment?

2. Describe a human activity that disrupts the carbon cycle and the consequences of that disruption.

## CRITICAL THINKING

3. **Summarize** How can microorganisms, such as some green algae, affect the health of organisms in aquatic ecosystems?

4. **Synthesize** Explain the importance of decomposers to the overall **biogeochemical cycle**.

## CONNECT TO

### EVOLUTION

5. How might Earth's biogeochemical cycles help scientists to understand the early history of life on Earth?

# 13.6 Pyramid Models

SC.912.L.17.9

**KEY CONCEPT** **Pyramids model the distribution of energy and matter in an ecosystem.**

### MAIN IDEAS

○ An energy pyramid shows the distribution of energy among trophic levels.

○ Other pyramid models illustrate an ecosystem's biomass and distribution of organisms.

**VOCABULARY**

biomass
energy pyramid

**SC.912.L.17.9** Use a food web to identify and distinguish producers, consumers, and decomposers. Explain the pathway of energy transfer through trophic levels and the reduction of available energy at successive trophic levels.

### Connect to Your World

You have likely seen pictures of the pyramids of Ancient Egypt. Each level of a pyramid requires a larger level below it for support. Similarly, each trophic level requires a larger level beneath it to support its energy needs. Ecologists use the structure of a pyramid as a model to describe trophic levels in ecosystems. Pyramids can represent the general flow of energy in an ecosystem or the mass or number of organisms at each trophic level.

### ○ MAIN IDEA

## An energy pyramid shows the distribution of energy among trophic levels.

Nearly all ecosystems get their energy from sunlight. Sunlight provides the energy for photosynthesis, and that energy flows up the food chain. However, along the way, some of the energy is dissipated, or lost. Recall that when energy changes form, the total amount of energy is conserved, but some of the energy is no longer useful for doing work. For instance, producers use energy from sunlight to make food. Herbivores eat the plants, but in the process, some energy is given off as heat. Carnivores then eat the herbivores, but again lose energy as heat. In other words, each level in the food chain contains much less useful energy than the level below it.

### Loss of Available Energy

Each meal that you consume is packed with energy in the form of proteins, fats, and carbohydrates. Your body uses this energy for many purposes such as movement and growth. The majority of the food you consume is used to keep your body at its normal temperature. Your body is very inefficient at converting what you consume into useful energy, so there will always be some material that is not used. Unused material is simply excreted as waste.

Energy in an ecosystem works in much the same way, only on a larger scale. **Biomass** is a measure of the total dry mass of organisms in a given area. When a consumer incorporates the biomass of a producer into its own biomass, a great deal of energy is lost in the process as heat and waste. The conversion of biomass from a producer into biomass of the consumer is inefficient.

Consider the simple producer-to-consumer food chain of grass–prairie dog. Photosynthesis stores energy as carbohydrates, which can be thought of as a high-quality form of energy. A hungry prairie dog then eats the grass.

**CONNECT TO**

**CELLULAR RESPIRATION**

As you learned in the chapter **Cells and Energy**, the processes of cellular respiration use ATP to maintain your body's functions. While the chemical reactions of metabolism are relatively efficient, there will always be some loss of available energy.

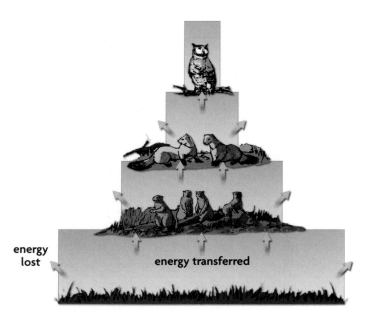

**FIGURE 6.1** An energy pyramid illustrates the energy flow between trophic levels in an ecosystem. Between each tier, up to 90 percent of the energy is lost as heat into the atmosphere.

Some of the energy is used by the animal to grow. The remaining energy may be used to fuel cellular respiration or remains undigested. The dissipation, or loss, of energy between trophic levels may be as much as 90 percent, meaning that only 10 percent of the available energy is left to transfer from one trophic level to another.

### Energy Pyramids

Because energy is lost at each stage of a food chain, the longer the chain is, the more energy is lost overall. The total energy used by producers far exceeds the energy used by the consumers they support. This concept can be illustrated with an energy pyramid. An **energy pyramid** is a diagram that compares energy used by producers, primary consumers, and other trophic levels. The pyramid, therefore, illustrates how available energy is distributed among trophic levels in an ecosystem. The unit of measurement used to describe the amount of energy at each trophic level in an energy pyramid is the kilocalorie (kcal).

A typical energy pyramid has a very large section at the base for the producers, and sections that become progressively smaller above. For example, in a prairie ecosystem, as illustrated in **FIGURE 6.1**, energy flows from grass at the producer level, to prairie dogs at the primary consumer level, to black-footed ferrets at the secondary consumer level, to a great horned owl at the tertiary consumer level.

**Connect** Draw an energy pyramid for the desert food chain introduced in Section 4. Use arrows to illustrate the flow of energy.

**FIGURE 6.2** The biomass pyramid depicts the total dry mass of organisms found at each trophic level.

## ▶ MAIN IDEA
# Other pyramid models illustrate an ecosystem's biomass and distribution of organisms.

A biomass pyramid is a diagram that compares the biomass of different trophic levels within an ecosystem. Unlike an energy pyramid, which represents energy use, a biomass pyramid provides a picture of the mass of producers needed to support primary consumers, the mass of primary consumers required to support secondary consumers, and so on.

In a pond ecosystem, such as the one illustrated in **FIGURE 6.2**, a biomass pyramid shows that the total dry mass (given in grams per square meter, or g/m²) of algae within the pond is far greater than the dry mass of fish. This example illustrates yet again the important role producers play in maintaining a stable ecosystem.

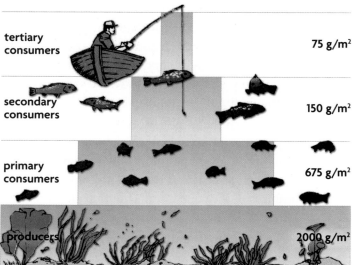

tertiary consumers — 75 g/m²

secondary consumers — 150 g/m²

primary consumers — 675 g/m²

producers — 2000 g/m²

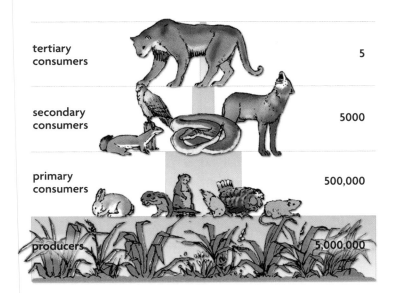

tertiary
consumers — 5

secondary
consumers — 5000

primary
consumers — 500,000

producers — 5,000,000

**FIGURE 6.3** In a pyramid of numbers, each tier represents the actual number of individual organisms present in each trophic level.

A pyramid of numbers shows the number of individual organisms at each trophic level in an ecosystem. For example, a pyramid of numbers depicting a mountainous habitat, as shown in **FIGURE 6.3,** might include organisms such as grasses, snowshoe hares, gophers, coyotes, snakes, and mountain lions. This type of pyramid is particularly effective in showing the vast number of producers required to support even a few top level consumers.

In certain situations, both biomass pyramids and pyramids of numbers may occur in an inverted, or upside down, formation. Consider, for example, a pyramid of numbers based on a single tree. This single tree would be greatly outnumbered by the primary and secondary consumers, such as insects and birds, that live within it. In this case, the upper tiers of the pyramid of numbers would be much larger than the bottom tier representing the single tree.

**Apply** **If a scientist wanted to compare the exact number of organisms at each trophic level within a desert ecosystem, which pyramid model would he or she use?**

**That's Amazing!**

**Video Inquiry**
HMHScience.com

**GO ONLINE**

**Vegetarian Alligators**

**SELF-CHECK Online**
HMHScience.com

**GO ONLINE**

# 13.6 Formative Assessment

## REVIEWING ▸ MAIN IDEAS

1. How does an **energy pyramid** help to describe energy flow in a food web?

2. What is the difference between a **biomass** pyramid and a pyramid of numbers?

## CRITICAL THINKING

3. **Apply** How would you draw a pyramid of numbers for a dog with fleas? What shape would the pyramid take?

4. **Calculate** If each level in a food chain typically loses 90 percent of the energy it takes in, and the producer level uses 1000 kcal of energy, how much of that energy is left after the third trophic level?

## CONNECT TO

### NUTRITION

5. Why is an herbivorous diet more energy efficient than a carnivorous diet? Explain your answer.

# 13 Summary

## KEY CONCEPTS

### 13.1 Ecologists Study Relationships

**Ecology is the study of the relationships among organisms and their environment.** Ecologists study environments at different levels of organization. Ecologists use methods such as observation, experimentation, and modeling to study ecological principles.

### 13.2 Biotic and Abiotic Factors

keystone

**Every ecosystem includes both living and nonliving factors.** Changing one factor in an ecosystem can affect many other factors. The removal of a keystone species may lead to changes in an ecosystem's biodiversity.

### 13.3 Energy in Ecosystems

**Life in an ecosystem requires a source of energy.** Producers provide energy for other organisms in an ecosystem. Most producers obtain their energy from sunlight through photosynthesis. Other producers obtain their energy through a process called chemosynthesis.

### 13.4 Food Chains and Food Webs

**Food chains and food webs model the flow of energy in an ecosystem.** A food chain is a simple model that shows a sequence of feeding relationships. A food web provides a more complex picture of the network of feeding relationships among organisms in an ecosystem.

### 13.5 Cycling of Matter

**Matter cycles in and out of an ecosystem.** Elements essential for life on Earth, such as water, oxygen, carbon, nitrogen, and phosphorus, also cycle through ecosystems. Disruptions in biogeochemical cycles have consequences for organisms and ecosystems.

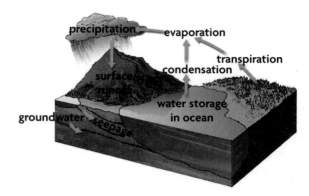

precipitation · evaporation · transpiration · condensation · surface runoff · water storage in ocean · groundwater · seepage

### 13.6 Pyramid Models

**Pyramids model the distribution of energy and matter in an ecosystem.** An energy pyramid shows the distribution of energy in a food chain. Energy flows upward from producers to consumers. Between each tier of the energy pyramid, energy is lost as heat. Sometimes only 10 percent of the original energy is transferred to the next trophic level. A biomass pyramid shows the total mass of organisms at each trophic level, while a pyramid of numbers shows the actual number of organisms present in each trophic level.

energy lost

energy transferred

---

## READING TOOLBOX    SYNTHESIZE YOUR NOTES

**Energy Pyramid** Add labels and organisms that belong in each trophic level to this energy pyramid.

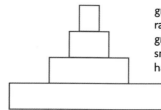

| grass | producer |
| rabbit | primary consumer |
| grasshopper | secondary consumer |
| snake | tertiary consumer |
| hawk | |

**Concept Map** Use a concept map to summarize what you know about food webs.

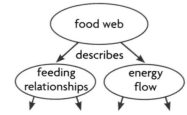

food web
describes
feeding relationships · energy flow

# 13 Review

## CHAPTER VOCABULARY

**13.1**
ecology
community
ecosystem
biome

**13.2** biotic
abiotic
biodiversity
keystone species

**13.3** producer
autotroph

consumer
heterotroph
chemosynthesis

**13.4** food chain
herbivore
carnivore
omnivore
detritivore
decomposer
specialist
generalist

trophic level
food web

**13.5** hydrologic cycle
biogeochemical cycle
nitrogen fixation

**13.6** biomass
energy pyramid

## Reviewing Vocabulary

**Find an Opposite**

Pair each of the words listed below with a different vocabulary term that has an opposing definition. Then, write one sentence describing a difference.

**1.** abiotic factor
**2.** producer
**3.** heterotroph
**4.** carnivore
**5.** specialist

### READING TOOLBOX    GREEK AND LATIN WORD ORIGINS

Use the definitions of the word parts to answer the following questions.

| Part | Meaning |
|------|---------|
| *bio-* | life |
| *eco-* | home |
| *syn-* | together, joined |
| *vore* | eat |

**6.** Explain why the root *vore* is used in the appropriate vocabulary terms.

**7.** Six vocabulary terms include the prefix *bio-*. Describe how they are all related.

**8.** Use the meaning of *eco-* to write your own definition of *ecosystem*.

**9.** *Photo-* means "light," and *chemo-* means "chemical." Explain why *photosynthesis* and *chemosynthesis* both include the prefix *syn-*.

## Reviewing MAIN IDEAS

**10.** How can an individual organism simultaneously be part of a population, community, ecosystem, and biome?

**11.** What are the major differences between observation, experimentation, and modeling?

**12.** A biomass pyramid and a pyramid of numbers are two ways of modeling the flow of matter in an ecosystem. What is the main difference between the two?

**13.** What is a keystone species and how might the removal of it affect the stability of and biodiversity within its ecosystem?

**14.** What would happen to a forest ecosystem if a fire killed most of its producers?

**15.** Describe one similarity and one difference between photosynthesis and chemosynthesis.

**16.** An acorn is eaten by a squirrel, which is eaten by an owl. What model best describes this simple relationship, and how does it show energy flow?

**17.** How is a food web related to energy flow within an ecosystem?

**18.** Describe the main processes involved in the hydrologic cycle.

**19.** Give an example of one biogeochemical cycle and explain how it is important to living things.

**20.** How does a biomass pyramid show the flow of matter in an ecosystem?

# Critical Thinking

**21. Apply** At what level of organization would a scientist study the interaction between seals and polar bears in the Arctic? Explain your answer.

**22. Apply** Explain which biotic factors used by the beaver are related to its role as a keystone species.

**23. Evaluate** Scientists used to say that all living things depend on the sun. Explain why this statement is no longer valid.

**24. Analyze** How might a drought affect a grassland food web? Which trophic level would the drought affect the most? Explain your answer.

**25. Synthesize** Humans have changed many ecosystems on Earth. Compare different types of consumers, and predict which types would be more likely to adapt to these changes and which would not. Explain your answers.

**26. Synthesize** Use the information you learned about carbon-based molecules to explain a human's need to participate in the biogeochemical cycles.

**27. Connect** What role do decomposers play in the nitrogen cycle?

**28. Predict** In a pyramid of numbers, the highest organism has the smallest number of individuals in a community. What might happen if this organism increased its numbers significantly? Explain the effect this increase would have on the other members of the community.

## Interpreting Visuals

Use the energy pyramid below to answer the following questions.

10,000 kcal energy

**29. Apply** Use the energy pyramid to describe the flow of energy within an ecosystem. Identify which tier represents producers, primary consumers, and so on.

**30. Calculate** If 90 percent of the energy is lost as heat between trophic levels, approximately how much energy is available to the secondary consumers in this energy pyramid? Show your calculations.

**Estimate Population Size**

Use the equation $T = N \times A$ to estimate the population size in questions 31–32. Show all of your work.

**31. Calculate** A scientist wants to estimate the population of mushrooms on a forest floor with an area of 300 $m^2$. Each quadrat is 2 $m^2$. She counts 13 mushrooms in 20 quadrats. What is the population of mushrooms in the forest?

**32. Calculate** A scientist uses quadrats to sample the population of strawberry cactus plants in a section of the Chihuahuan desert that is 150 $m^2$. He counts 5 cacti in 10 quadrats. Each quadrat is 2 $m^2$. What is the population of strawberry cacti in the desert?

**33. Analyze** What are the advantages and disadvantages of using random sampling to obtain an estimate of the population size?

**34. Evaluate** A scientist uses quadrats to determine the population size of lupines in a field 500 $m^2$ in size. She uses ten 1 $m^2$ quadrats. Is this an adequate sample size? Explain your answer.

**35. Apply** Scientists often use tables of random numbers to determine where to place quadrats on their study site. Why might they do this? Why can't they choose where to place the quadrats?

**36. Apply** A scientist wants to determine the population size of whiptail lizards within a 15-acre area. What sampling method should she use? How can she ensure that she obtains an accurate estimate of the lizard population? Explain your answer.

## Making Connections

**37. Write About Your Own Ecosystem** Imagine you built a large greenhouse in your home to create your own ecosystem. What types of organisms would you include? How would you ensure that the biogeochemical cycles were in place? Describe in detail an ecosystem you would like to have in your home. Be sure to include the biotic and abiotic factors in your explanation of how the ecosystem would sustain itself.

**38. Make a Food Web** Read the description of anhingas on the chapter opener and draw a partial food web of a freshwater marsh ecosystem. Include producers and consumers in your web.

# Standards-Based Assessment

Record your answers on a separate piece of paper.

## MULTIPLE CHOICE

**1** The nitrogen cycle relies on various organisms carrying out very specific functions. One vital group is that of nitrogen-fixing bacteria. Which of the following explains how the nitrogen cycle would be disrupted if there was a sudden population explosion of nitrogen-fixing bacteria in an aquatic ecosystem?

**A** A population explosion of nitrogen-fixing bacteria would lead to a decrease in ammonium levels in the water, which will cause the water to become very acidic.

**B** A population explosion of nitrogen-fixing bacteria will cause dissolved nitrogen levels in the water to increase.

**C** A population explosion of nitrogen-fixing bacteria will cause dissolved oxygen and dissolved carbon dioxide levels to decrease.

**D** A population explosion of nitrogen-fixing bacteria will cause ammonia levels to rise, which can be detected by testing the ammonia levels in the water.

**2**

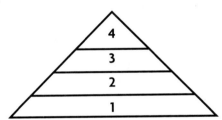

The food web above shows the relationships between organisms in an ecosystem. Which type of organism not shown in this food web is important to the stability of the ecosystem?

**A** producer

**B** consumer

**C** herbivore

**D** decomposer

**3** Several types of plant species grew in an empty lot. The city council decided to turn the lot into a park and planted grass alone to create a playing field. The ecological factor that was *most likely* affected by the change was the lot's —

**A** biomass

**B** carbon cycle

**C** biodiversity

**D** hydrologic cycle

**4** In the carbon cycle, through what process does carbon move from an abiotic resource into organic matter?

**A** deforestation

**B** combustion

**C** respiration

**D** photosynthesis

**5**

```
      /\
     /4 \
    /----\
   /  3   \
  /--------\
 /    2     \
/------------\
|     1      |
```

In which direction does energy flow through the energy pyramid shown above?

**A** 4, 3, 2, 1

**B** 1, 2, 3, 4

**C** 2, 1, 3, 4

**D** 3, 4, 2, 1

**THINK THROUGH THE QUESTION**

Remember that an energy pyramid shows the amount of energy in each trophic level, with producers at the bottom of the pyramid, and consumers at the top.

# 14 Interactions in Ecosystems

**BIG IDEA** Individual organisms and populations of organisms interact with each other and with the environment.

## ⊙ ONLINE BIOLOGY  HMHScience.com

**ONLINE** Labs
- Modeling Predation
- **QuickLab** Survivorship Curves
- Limiting Nutrients for Algae
- Making a Local Field Guide
- Predator-Prey Interactions
- Monitoring Bird Populations

- Using GPS in Ecological Surveys
- Population Dynamics
- **Video Lab** Yeast Population Growth

©Alisha Venter/Shutterstock

# Q Why are these zebras fighting?

For the zebra, life on the African savannah is about survival. Whether escaping the ambush of a pride of lions, walking vast distances to drink fresh water, or competing for the right to mate with females, only the best adapted zebras will survive and pass on their genes. The interactions among organisms, and between organisms and their environment, make ecosystems function.

## READING TOOLBOX

This reading tool can help you learn the material in the following pages.

### USING LANGUAGE

**Predictions** Some predictions are conditional: Something might happen, but only if something else happens first. For example, if the temperature drops below freezing, snow might fall. The prediction is that snow might fall tonight. But snow might fall under one condition. First, the temperature has to drop below freezing.

### YOUR TURN

In the following sentences, identify the condition and the prediction.

1. After the deer population reaches 600 individuals on the island, the deer will eat most of the vegetation, and the number of deer will decrease.
2. If the otters are removed from the ecosystem, the sea urchins will eat all of the kelp.

# Habitat and Niche

| KEY CONCEPT  **Every organism has a habitat and a niche.**

**MAIN IDEAS**
- A habitat differs from a niche.
- Resource availability gives structure to a community.

### Connect to Your World

The ways in which a zebra or a lion interacts with its environment and other organisms are only a small part of the ecology of the African plains. To understand what individuals, populations, and communities need to survive, ecologists study the interactions among species and between species and their environment. Why does a lion fit so well into the African savannah?

## MAIN IDEA

# A habitat differs from a niche.

On the vast plains of Africa, tall grasses grow among trees and shrubs, and small pools of water surrounded by thirsty animals dot the landscape. This challenging environment is the home of the African lion, shown in **FIGURE 1.1**. Here, lions stalk through tall grass to hunt zebras and antelope, find places to rest in the shade of trees, and never stray far from valuable pools of water. These are just a few of the environmental features that make up the lion's habitat. A **habitat** can be described as all of the biotic and abiotic factors in the area where an organism lives. These factors include all aspects of the environment, including the grass, the trees, and the watering holes.

Each species interacts with its environment in a different way. Within an ecosystem, each species has an ecological niche. An **ecological niche** (nihch) is composed of all of the physical, chemical, and biological factors that a species needs to survive, stay healthy, and reproduce.

You can think of a habitat as *where* a species lives and a niche as *how* it lives within its habitat. A niche includes

- **Food**  The type of food a species eats, how a species competes with others for food, and where it fits in the food web are all part of its niche.
- **Abiotic conditions**  A niche includes the range of conditions, such as air temperature and amount of water, that a species can tolerate.
- **Behavior**  The time of day a species is active as well as where and when it reproduces are factors in the niche of a species.

**FIGURE 1.1**  A lion must hunt and kill its prey in order to survive on the African savannah. Its role as a top predator is part of the lion's niche.

©Paul A. Souders/Corbis

Looking closely at all of these factors, we can see that while an antelope may use the tall grasses of the African plains as a food resource, a lion may use the same grasses as camouflage for hunting. A lion uses the antelope as a food resource and hunts primarily during low-light times, such as dawn or dusk. In order to avoid the intense heat of the savannah, lions often spend afternoons in the shade. These examples are only a few parts of the lion's ecological niche, but they help to give a picture of how a lion fits into the African savannah.

**Connect** **What are some of the abiotic and biotic factors of your habitat?**

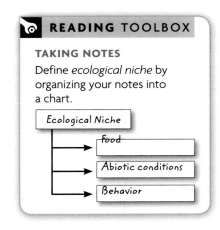

**READING TOOLBOX**

**TAKING NOTES**
Define *ecological niche* by organizing your notes into a chart.

Ecological Niche
→ Food
→ Abiotic conditions
→ Behavior

> MAIN IDEA
# Resource availability gives structure to a community.

You have learned that the ability of an individual to survive and reproduce is the driving force behind natural selection. A species needs resources such as food, water, and shelter to be successful in its habitat. The organism that is best suited to obtain these resources is most likely to survive and reproduce. But what if two species are competing over limited resources?

**Virtual INVESTIGATION**
HMHScience.com
**GO ONLINE**
Population Niches and Competition

## Competitive Exclusion
We have already seen that many species can share similar habitats and that they may use some of the same resources, as shown in **FIGURE 1.2**. But when two species use the same resources in the same ways, one species will always be better adapted to the environment. The principle of **competitive exclusion** states that when two species are competing for the same resources, one species will be better suited to the niche, and the other species will be pushed into another niche or become extinct.

The North American gray squirrel was introduced to Great Britain in the late 1800s. The native European red squirrel was forced to compete with the newcomer for the same food resources, habitat, and space. In this case the gray squirrel was better adapted to the niche and pushed out its smaller competitor. Currently, the red squirrel population is declining due to competition with its larger, more aggressive cousin. But competitive exclusion can also result in other outcomes.

**FIGURE 1.2** Even though bees and butterflies both use these flowers for food, they occupy different niches. Many species with similar niches can coexist.

- **Niche partitioning** The two squirrel species could have naturally divided different resources based on competitive advantages. If one type of squirrel ate nuts from the tops of trees while others ate nuts from the ground, the niche would have been divided.

- **Evolutionary response** The two species of squirrel could have experienced divergent evolution. Selection for larger teeth might have allowed one type of squirrel to become better at cracking large nuts, while selection for smaller teeth might have allowed the other to eat small seeds.

## FIGURE 1.3 Ecological Equivalents

**Ecological equivalents are two species that occupy similar niches in geographically separate areas.**

Madagascar

South America

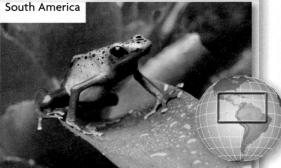

The mantella frog (left) and the poison dart frog (right) have evolved similar defense mechanisms. The bright coloration of each is a warning to predators. Each frog secretes a highly poisonous toxin through its skin that makes it an unpleasant meal for a predator.

**Synthesize** **Explain how natural selection resulted in the evolution of two similar frog species in two similar niches.**

**CONNECT TO**

### AMPHIBIANS

Amphibians were the first vertebrates to move out of the water and onto land. In the chapter **Vertebrate Diversity,** you will learn more about amphibians.

## Ecological Equivalents

The competitive exclusion principle involves species competing for resources in the same community. In different communities, ecological equivalents occur in very similar niches. In mathematics, numbers that are equal are called equivalents. Similarly, **ecological equivalents** are species that occupy similar niches but live in different geographical regions. Pictured in **FIGURE 1.3,** the mantella frog of Madagascar and the poison dart frog of South America have similar niches in similar habitats. They both have brightly colored skin that secretes a highly poisonous toxin to ward off predators. Both prey on similar insects and live in a similar habitat, but because they live in different regions of the world, they never compete for the same resources.

**Apply** **Are these frogs experiencing competitive exclusion? Explain.**

(tl), (tr) ©Chris Mattison/age fotostock

---

## 14.1 Formative Assessment

### REVIEWING ▶ MAIN IDEAS

1. What are the three parts of an organism's **ecological niche**?

2. What does the principle of **competitive exclusion** say will happen when two species compete for the same resource?

### CRITICAL THINKING

3. **Predict** If a group of mantella frogs were transported to the ecosystem of the poison dart frogs, what might happen to the two species' populations?

4. **Analyze** A bison and an elk live in the same **habitat** and feed on the same grasses. Does this mean that the competitive exclusion principle does not apply? Explain.

**CONNECT TO**

### EXOTIC SPECIES

5. Considering the competitive exclusion principle, why may it be harmful to transport a species, such as a rabbit, to another habitat where it currently does not exist?

# Community Interactions

**KEY CONCEPT** Organisms interact as individuals and as populations.

## MAIN IDEAS

○ Competition and predation are two important ways in which organisms interact.

○ Symbiosis is a close relationship between species.

### Connect to Your World

Each day, two hot dog vendors sell virtually identical products to anyone who is hungry. They may be on different sides of the street, but they are still trying to sell hot dogs to the same hungry consumers. A vendor selling hot pretzels may also be trying to sell to the same customers, but with a slightly varied product. Just like these vendors, organisms constantly compete with one another.

## ○ MAIN IDEA

# Competition and predation are two important ways in which organisms interact.

Two birds may fight over territories. A fish may prey on insects floating on the water. These are just two examples of the many interactions within and between species in an ecosystem.

### Competition

**Competition** occurs when two organisms fight for the same limited resources. There are two different types of competition: interspecific competition and intraspecific competition.

Even though they may have different niches, two species may still use similar resources. Interspecific competition occurs when two different species compete for a limited resource, such as space. In a lawn, for example, grass, dandelions, and many other plants all compete for nutrients and water.

Competition also occurs among members of the same species. This is known as intraspecific competition. Individuals of a particular species struggle against one another for limited resources. You can observe intraspecific competition during the spring breeding season of birds. A typical male will share a particular territory with males of different bird species but will not tolerate another male of its own species in the same area.

### Predation

Another way species interact with one another is through predation. **Predation** is the process by which one organism captures and feeds upon another organism. Many organisms, such as the snake in **FIGURE 2.1**, have become highly adapted to hunting and killing their prey.

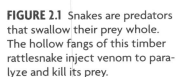

**FIGURE 2.1** Snakes are predators that swallow their prey whole. The hollow fangs of this timber rattlesnake inject venom to paralyze and kill its prey.

The timber rattlesnake, for example, is a predator that preys on small animals such as mice, voles, rabbits, and squirrels. Lying silently, hidden among leaf litter on the forest floor, the rattlesnake has found a niche as an ambush predator. A swift bite from the snake's fangs injects its venom. The venom attacks the nervous system and eventually paralyzes the prey. The snake swallows the paralyzed animal whole.

Herbivores can also be considered predators. The deer that eats grass in fields and leaves from trees is preying on the plants.

**Evaluate** **How does natural selection shape predator–prey relationships?**

## ▶ MAIN IDEA

# Symbiosis is a close relationship between species.

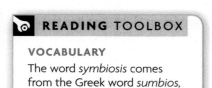
A honeybee buzzes away from a flower with its reward of nectar. Small pollen grains have become attached to the bee's back. When the bee arrives at the next flower, the pollen fertilizes the egg of the next plant. In this way, a relationship, or symbiosis, between the bee and the flower has evolved. **Symbiosis** is a close ecological relationship between two or more organisms of different species that live in direct contact with one another. There are three major types of symbiosis: mutualism, commensalism, and parasitism.

## Mutualism

**Mutualism** is an interspecies interaction in which both organisms benefit from one another. The relationship between the lesser long-nosed bat and the saguaro cactus is an example of mutualism. During the spring, the bats help pollinate the cacti through the indirect transfer of pollen as they fly from one cactus to another to feed on flower nectar. When the fruit ripens in the summer, the bats become fruit eaters, as shown in **FIGURE 2.2.** The cactus benefits when the bat spreads its indigestible seeds across the desert.

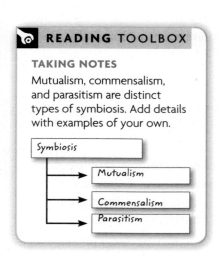
## Commensalism

Another type of symbiotic relationship is commensalism. **Commensalism** is a relationship between two organisms in which one receives an ecological benefit from another, while the other neither benefits nor is harmed. Right now you may be a part of a commensal relationship. Buried deep in the hair follicles of your eyelashes are microscopic mites that feed on the secretions and dead skin cells of your body. These harmless organisms are called demodicids, and they have found their highly specialized niche in your hair follicles.

## Parasitism

Parasitism is a symbiotic relationship involving a species that directly harms its host. **Parasitism** is a relationship similar to predation in that one organism benefits while the other is harmed. But unlike a predator, which quickly kills and eats its prey, a parasite benefits by keeping its host alive for days or years. For example, the braconid wasp lays its eggs inside a caterpillar. When the larvae hatch, they eat the caterpillar from the inside out, consuming the nutrients they need to grow into adults.

The interactions between species in an ecosystem can take many forms. A symbiotic relationship involves interactions between organisms of different species that live in direct contact.

— Organism is harmed

0 Organism is not affe...

+ Organism benefits

## Parasitism

**—** **Hornworm caterpillar** The host hornworm will eventually die as its organs are consumed by wasp larvae.

**+** **Braconid wasp** Braconid larvae feed on their host and release themselves shortly before reaching the pupae stage of development.

## Commensalism

**0** **Human** Our eyelashes are home to tiny mites that feast on oil secretions and dead skin. Without harming us, up to 20 mites may be living in one eyelash follicle.

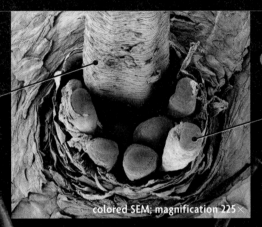

colored SEM; magnification 225×

**+** **Demodicids** Eyelash mites find all they need to survive in the tiny follicles of eyelashes. Magnified here 225 times, these creatures measure 0.4 mm in length and can be seen only with a microscope.

## Mutualism

**+** **Lesser long-nosed bat** The bat depends on night-blooming cacti as its primary source of food. Cacti are a rich source of fruit and nectar, staples of the bat's diet.

**+** **Saguaro cactus** As the bat feeds on the cactus' fruit, it also ingests the seeds. These indigestible seeds are dispersed to new locations as the bat flies across the desert.

**CRITICAL VIEWING** How might the symbiotic relationship change if eyelash mites destroyed hair follicles?

## FIGURE 2.3 Human Parasites: Inside and Out

Humans can get parasites in many ways. Leeches attach to the exposed skin of humans. By penetrating human skin, hookworms find their home in the digestive tract.

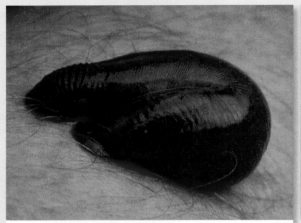

Many leeches feed on the blood of a host organism. Freshwater leeches such as this one can grow to lengths of 12 cm or more.

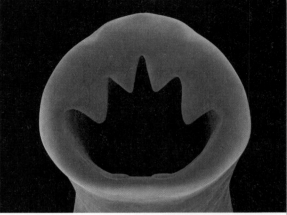

Hookworms are endoparasites with sharp teeth that attach to the intestinal wall of a host organism and absorb nutrients for food.

**Hypothesize** Why is it important for ectoparasites to stay undetected by their hosts?

(tl) ©Martin Dohrn/Photo Researchers, Inc.; (tr) ©Sebastian Kaulitzki/Alamy Images

**CONNECT TO**

**INVERTEBRATES**

Leeches and hookworms are classified as invertebrates. In the chapter **Invertebrate Diversity,** you will learn more about the diversity of invertebrates.

The needs of a parasite are met by a host—the victim of the parasite. There are two ways that parasites can use their host. An ectoparasite makes its home on the exterior of an organism, attaching itself to the outside of the host and usually feeding on its fluids. Common ectoparasites include fleas, ticks, and leeches, such as the one seen in **FIGURE 2.3.** Many types of ectoparasites are also known to carry a wide variety of diseases that can affect their host. Parasites can also be found inside of living organisms. Endoparasites live in the tissues and organs of a host where, safely hidden, they feed on the nutrients ingested by their host. Large endoparasites, such as tapeworms and hookworms, and smaller protozoan endoparasites can kill their host if not treated.

**Connect** What type of symbiosis is the relationship between a dog and its owner?

**SELF-CHECK Online**
HMHScience.com
**GO ONLINE**

## 14.2 Formative Assessment

### REVIEWING ▶ MAIN IDEAS

1. During the fall spawning of salmon, grizzly bears fight over space on the banks of a river. What type of **competition** is this?

2. Describe and give examples of the three types of **symbiosis**.

### CRITICAL THINKING

3. **Compare and Contrast** How are **predation** and **parasitism** similar? How do they differ?

4. **Synthesize** After a lion has made a kill, birds will sometimes arrive to pick at the leftover carcass. Which are the predators: the birds, the lion, or both? Why?

**CONNECT TO**

**ANIMAL BEHAVIOR**

5. You have probably heard the saying "There is safety in numbers." Why might traveling in a large group be beneficial to prey species?

# Sharks and Increased CO$_2$

The ocean and the atmosphere naturally interact. Gases, including oxygen and carbon dioxide (CO$_2$), are exchanged because of wind and wave action, evaporation, and biological processes. Over the last century, the concentration of CO$_2$ in the atmosphere has increased, leading to increased surface temperatures, melting ice sheets and glaciers, and rising sea levels. The increase in CO$_2$ in the atmosphere has also led to an increase in CO$_2$ in ocean water. Carbon dioxide is a normal part of ocean processes and the chemical reactions that occur in seawater. However, an excess of CO$_2$ has thrown off the balance of certain reactions, resulting in more acid being produced in the ocean, lowering the pH. The acidity of ocean water has increased by about 30 percent over the last 250 years. Scientists predict that the acidity of ocean water will increase even more by the year 2100, with pH lowering by 0.3 units.

The effects of increased acidity of ocean water are already evident in some organisms, including certain species of sharks. Researchers from the University of Adelaide in Australia tested the effects of increased carbon dioxide in ocean water on the ability of Port Jackson sharks to hunt for prey. The increased carbon dioxide may interfere with the sharks' ability to smell, one of the main senses sharks use to locate prey.

In a laboratory setting, the researchers kept the sharks in tanks of ocean water with normal levels of CO$_2$ and in tanks with increased levels of CO$_2$. After keeping the sharks an average of 56 days in each tank (the control tank and the experimental tank), the researchers tested the sharks' hunting ability. The test was conducted by hiding the same food in the same way in each tank. The researchers measured how long it took sharks in both

tanks to find the food. The graph on the left below shows the results of the experiment. Sharks in the tank with increased CO$_2$ took about 4 times longer to find food than the control group did.

Other studies have found that increased levels of CO$_2$ in ocean water can interfere with the smooth dogfish's sense of smell. The smooth dogfish is another type of shark. Similar results have been found in experiments conducted on bony fish, such as damselfish and clownfish. Scientists have determined that the increased levels of CO$_2$ in the water interfere with the fishes' nervous system, causing the impairment of nerves involved in the senses of smell and hearing. Scientists are concerned about the broader effects of this discovery on a fish's ability to detect predators and escape. There also may be changes to the food web as a result of changes in predator-prey interactions.

## S.T.E.M. Activity

The researchers from the University of Adelaide also measured the effect of increased CO$_2$ on the growth rate of the Port Jackson sharks. This graph shows their results.

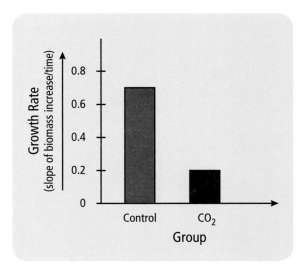

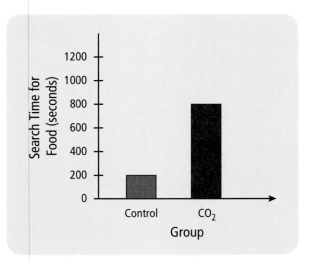

1. What is the relationship between increased CO$_2$ and growth rate in the sharks that were tested?
2. How is the growth rate under increased CO$_2$ conditions likely related to the sharks' ability to find prey in those conditions?
3. How could increased CO$_2$ affect an ocean food web overall?

# 14.3 Population Density and Distribution

SC.912.L.17.5

SC.912.L.17.5 Analyze how population size is determined by births, deaths, immigration, emigration, and limiting factors (biotic and abiotic) that determine carrying capacity.

**VOCABULARY**

population density
population dispersion
survivorship curve

**KEY CONCEPT** Each population has a density, a dispersion, and a reproductive strategy.

**MAIN IDEAS**

○ Population density is the number of individuals that live in a defined area.

○ Geographic dispersion of a population shows how individuals in a population are spaced.

○ Survivorship curves help to describe the reproductive strategy of a species.

### Connect to Your World

If you have ever traveled from a rural area into a city, you may have noticed a change in population density. Cities have more dense populations, while rural areas have more widely dispersed populations. Scientists measure species populations in a similar way. What can we learn from population data?

### ○ MAIN IDEA

## Population density is the number of individuals that live in a defined area.

The wandering albatross may fly over open ocean waters for days or weeks at a time without ever encountering another bird. In contrast to this solitary lifestyle, elephant seals may gather in groups of a thousand or more on California beaches. By collecting data about a population in a particular area, scientists can calculate the density of a population. **Population density** is a measurement of the number of individuals living in a defined space.

Calculating an accurate population density can tell scientists a great deal about a species. When scientists notice changes in population densities over time, they work to determine whether the changes are the result of environmental factors or are simply due to normal variation in the life history of a species. In this way a wildlife biologist can work to make changes that will help to keep the population healthy. One way to calculate population density is to create a ratio of the number of individuals that live in a particular area to the size of the area. This formula is simplified as follows:

$$\frac{\text{\# of individuals}}{\text{area (units}^2)} = \text{population density}$$

For example, if scientists sampling a population of deer counted 200 individuals in an area of 10 square kilometers, the density of this deer population would be 20 deer per square kilometer.

**Connect** What might a decrease in the density of a deer population over a specific time period tell scientists about the habitat in the area?

**CONNECT TO**

**GENE FLOW**

Recall that in the chapter **The Evolution of Populations** you learned about gene flow and geographic isolation. Population dispersion patterns influence the rate of gene flow among and between species.

# Population growth is based on available resources.

⦿ MAIN IDEA

Population growth is a function of the environment. The rate of growth for a population is directly determined by the amount of resources available. A population may grow very rapidly, or it may take a bit of time to grow. There are two distinct types of population growth.

## Exponential Growth

When resources are abundant, a population has the opportunity to grow rapidly. This type of growth, called **exponential growth,** occurs when a population size increases dramatically over a period of time. In **FIGURE 4.1,** you can see that exponential growth appears as a J-shaped curve.

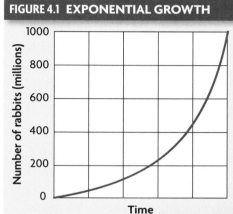

FIGURE 4.1 EXPONENTIAL GROWTH

FIGURE 4.2 In Australia during the early 1900s, the introduced European rabbit population exhibited exponential growth.

Exponential growth may occur when a species moves to a previously uninhabited area. For example, in 1859 an Australian landowner returning home from England brought 24 European rabbits to the country for the purpose of sport hunting. The rabbits were introduced into an environment that had abundant space and food and no predators fast enough to catch them. The initial population of 24 rabbits grew exponentially and spread across the country. After many attempts to control the population, today there are between 200 million and 300 million rabbits in Australia.

## Logistic Growth

Most populations face limited resources and thus show a logistic growth rate. During **logistic growth,** a population begins with a period of slow growth followed by a brief period of exponential growth before leveling off at a stable size. A graph of logistic growth takes the form of an S-shaped curve and can be seen in **FIGURE 4.3,** which models a population's change in size over time. During initial growth, resources are abundant, and

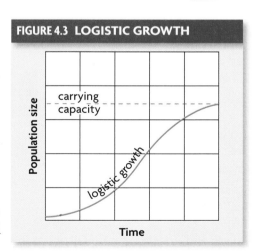

FIGURE 4.3 LOGISTIC GROWTH

the population is able to grow. Over time, resources begin to deplete, and growth starts to slow. As resources become limited, the population levels off at a size the environment can support.

©John Carnemolla/Corbis

**GO ONLINE**

What Limits Population Growth?

## Carrying Capacity

The environment determines how many individuals of the species can be supported based on natural cycles and species diversity. An environment, therefore, has a carrying capacity for each species living in it. The **carrying capacity** of an environment is the maximum number of individuals of a particular species that the environment can normally and consistently support.

In nature, a carrying capacity can change when the environment changes. Consider a population of grasshoppers that feed on meadow grasses. If a fire burns part of the meadow, the insects' food resources diminish, and the carrying capacity declines. But during years with plentiful rain, the meadow grasses flourish, and the carrying capacity rises.

The actual size of the population usually is higher or lower than the carrying capacity. Populations will rise and fall as a result of natural changes in the supply of resources. In this way, the environment naturally controls the size of a population.

## Population Crash

When the carrying capacity for a population suddenly drops, the population experiences a crash. A **population crash** is a dramatic decline in the size of a population over a short period of time. There are many reasons why a population might experience a crash.

## DATA ANALYSIS

### READING COMBINATION GRAPHS

**Combination graphs** show two sets of data on the same graph. One set of data may be shown as a bar graph, while the other set may be shown as a line graph. The two data sets must share the same independent variable on the *x*-axis. Scientists can then interpret the data to determine if a relationship exists between the variables.

This combination graph displays data about fish kill events, during which many fish died at once, and average monthly rainfall in Florida from 1991–2001.

• The *y*-axis on the left side represents the total number of fish kill events.
• The *y*-axis on the right side represents average monthly rainfall during that time.
• The *x*-axis shows the month of data collection.

The graph shows that in January there were four fish kill events and an average of 2.7 inches of rain.

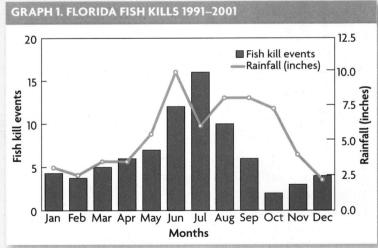

Source: The University of Florida Extension Information Circular 107. Used by permission.

1. **Analyze** An increase in fish kills and a decrease in rainfall occurs in what months?
2. **Analyze** Describe the trend in the fish kill events throughout the year. Describe the trend in rainfall data throughout the year.
3. **Hypothesize** What relationship might exist between fish kill events and rainfall?

For example, in 1944, 29 reindeer were introduced to St. Matthew Island off the coast of Alaska. At the time of the introduction, the entire island was covered with a rich mat of lichens. Plenty of good food allowed the reindeer herd to grow at an exponential rate. By the summer of 1963, the island population had grown to 6000 reindeer. However, over the winter, large amounts of snow fell on food resources that had already become greatly depleted by the large herd. By the spring of 1964, only 50 reindeer remained. The population crash on St. Matthew Island came as the result of two factors that limited resources: the harsh winter and the scarcity of food.

**Predict** **What would have eventually happened to the reindeer herd if the winter had not made foraging so difficult? Explain.**

## ▶ MAIN IDEA

# Ecological factors limit population growth.

Many factors can affect the carrying capacity of an environment for a population of organisms. The factor that has the greatest effect in keeping down the size of a population is called the **limiting factor.** There are two categories of limiting factors—density dependent and density independent.

### Density-Dependent Limiting Factors

**Density-dependent limiting factors** are limiting factors that are affected by the number of individuals in a given area. Density-dependent limiting factors include many types of species interactions.

**Competition** Members of populations compete with one another for resources such as food and shelter. As a population becomes denser, the resources are used up, limiting how large the population can grow.

**Predation** The population of a predator can be limited by the available prey, and the population of prey can be limited by being caught for food. On Isle Royale in Michigan, changes in wolf and moose populations, shown in **FIGURE 4.5,** provide an example. As the moose population grows, so does the wolf population. But at a certain point, the wolves eat so many moose that there are not enough left to feed all the wolves. The result is a decrease in the wolf population. Over time, the two populations rise and fall in a pattern, shown in **FIGURE 4.5**.

**Parasitism and disease** Parasites and diseases can spread more quickly through dense populations. The more crowded an area becomes, the easier it is for parasites or diseases to spread. The parasites or diseases can then cause the size of the population to decrease.

**Analyze** **How does the wolf population on Isle Royale affect the carrying capacity of the moose population?**

**FIGURE 4.4** Taking down prey as large as a moose requires that the members of a pack work together. As many as ten wolves may take hours or even days to wear down this moose.

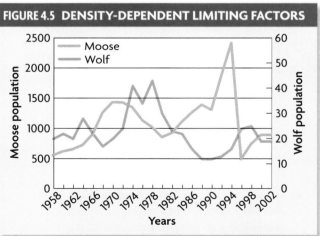

FIGURE 4.5 DENSITY-DEPENDENT LIMITING FACTORS

Source: Isle Royale Research Data

©Rolf O. Peterson

**FIGURE 4.6** The storm surge accompanying a hurricane can cause dangerous flooding.

## Density-Independent Limiting Factors

**Density-independent limiting factors** are the aspects of the environment that limit a population's growth regardless of the density of the population.

**Unusual weather** Weather can affect the size of a population regardless of its density. For example, along the western coast of the United States, a lack of southerly winds can prevent nutrient-poor warm water from being replaced, as it normally is, with nutrient-rich cold water. The lack of nutrients in the water along the coast can prevent phytoplankton, which form the base of the marine ecosystem, from growing in their usual large numbers. In turn, zooplankton, tiny organisms that feed on phytoplankton, have smaller populations. The effects are felt all the way up the food chain, with smaller populations of fish and birds.

**Natural disasters** Volcanoes, tsunamis, tornados, and hurricanes, shown in **FIGURE 4.6**, can wipe out populations regardless of density. For example, the large wave of a tsunami can damage fragile coral reefs, knock down entire mangrove forests, and destroy sea turtle nesting beaches.

**Human activities** Destruction of a wetland habitat along the Platte River in Nebraska has threatened an important feeding ground for the sandhill crane. Urbanization in this area is depleting the resources these migratory birds need during their trek to nesting grounds in northern Canada and in Alaska. By clearing forests, filling wetlands, and polluting the air, land, and water, humans threaten habitats and the organisms that live in them. As we will discuss in Human Impact on Ecosystems, human influence as a limiting factor has had a profound effect on populations. For example, the introduction of nonnative species has caused population crashes in many parts of the world where biodiversity is an important part of the ecosystem's functioning.

**Apply** A population of algae in a pond is limited in size by the amount of sunlight that strikes the pond's surface. Is sunlight a density-dependent or density-independent limiting factor for the algae population?

## 14.4 Formative Assessment

### REVIEWING ▶ MAIN IDEAS

1. What four factors determine the growth rate of a population?

2. How does **carrying capacity** affect the size of a population?

3. What is the main difference between a **density-dependent limiting factor** and a **density-independent limiting factor**? Give examples of each.

### CRITICAL THINKING

4. **Apply** What might cause **exponential growth** to occur only for a short period when a new species is introduced to a resource-filled environment?

5. **Synthesize** How might density-dependent limiting factors be affected by a flood or some other natural disaster?

**SELF-CHECK Online**
HMHScience.com
GO ONLINE

**CONNECT TO**

**SYMBIOSIS**

6. Give an example of how a symbiotic relationship could cause a population crash.

# 14.5 Ecological Succession

SC.912.L.17.4

SC.912.L.17.4 Describe changes in ecosystems resulting from seasonal variations, climate change and succession.

**VOCABULARY**

succession
primary succession
pioneer species
secondary succession

**KEY CONCEPT** Ecological succession is a process of change in the species that make up a community.

**MAIN IDEAS**

○ Succession occurs following a disturbance in an ecosystem.

### ☀ Connect to Your World

It begins with a dirty sock. Then a discarded homework assignment. But this is only the start. If you have ever spent a Saturday afternoon cleaning your bedroom, you may have wondered how a perfectly clean room could manage to become such a cluttered mess. A clean room becoming cluttered is a gradual process much like the process that rebuilds damaged ecosystems.

## ▶ MAIN IDEA

## Succession occurs following a disturbance in an ecosystem.

After an ecosystem experiences a devastating catastrophe and begins to regrow, the space re-forms itself through a process known as succession. **Succession** is the sequence of biotic changes that regenerate a damaged community or create a community in a previously uninhabited area.

The Hawaiian Islands began to form more than 70 million years ago. Over time, volcanic eruptions such as the one shown in **FIGURE 5.1** created these islands in the middle of the Pacific Ocean. Eventually, the bare volcanic rock began to break down into soil, which provided a place for plants to grow. As time passed, the process of succession created unique tropical ecosystems. Succession from bare rock to such highly diverse vegetation takes a great deal of time.

**FIGURE 5.1** The path of a lava flow, such as this one on the island of Hawaii (left), leaves behind nothing but solid rock. Over time, primary succession will turn this harsh landscape into a fertile ecosystem (right).

## FIGURE 5.2 Primary Succession

**Melting glaciers, volcanic eruptions, landslides, and strip mines can all begin the process of primary succession.**

| 0–15 years Moss, lichens, grasses | 15–80 years Shrubs, cottonwoods, alder thicket | 80–115 years Transition to forest, alder, spruce | 115–200 years Hemlock-spruce forest |

Glacier Bay National Park in Alaska has given scientists an opportunity to witness primary succession as the glacier recedes.

**Apply** What function might the mosses and lichens serve in primary succession?

## Primary Succession

One of the best ways to understand succession is to watch it progress. **Primary succession** is the establishment and development of an ecosystem in an area that was previously uninhabited. The first organisms that live in a previously uninhabited area are called **pioneer species.** Typical examples of pioneer species are lichens and some mosses, which can break down solid rock into smaller pieces. The process of primary succession, which is illustrated in **FIGURE 5.2,** follows this basic pattern:

- Bare rock is exposed by a retreating glacier or is created when lava cools. Wind, rain, and ice begin to break down the surface of the rock, forming cracks and breaking the rock into smaller pieces.
- Lichen and moss spores are blown in by wind. As they grow, they break up the rock further. When they die, their remains mix with the rock pieces to form a thin layer of soil.
- Over time, seeds are blown into the area or are dropped by birds. Small flowers and hardy shrubs grow from these seeds. These new plants provide a habitat for small animals, break up the rock with their roots, and add material to the soil when they die.
- As the soil continues to grow thicker, small trees take root, and different animals move into the area. These trees provide shade.
- Different tree species take root in the shade and eventually replace the original trees, which need direct sunlight to thrive.

**CONNECT TO**

**SYMBIOSIS**

A lichen is actually two completely different species. Fungi and algae form a symbiotic relationship in which the fungi collect water, while the algae use chlorophyll to conduct photosynthesis and synthesize food for the lichen community.

(tr) ©Getty Images

## FIGURE 5.3 Secondary Succession

Following a flood or a fire, a community is given a chance for new life. Plants remaining after the disturbance reestablish the ecosystem.

| 0–2 years Horse-weed, crabgrass, asters | 2–18 years Grass, shrubs, pine seedlings | 18–70 years Pine forest and young hardwood seedlings | 70–100 years Oak-hickory forest |

Fire is important in helping forests return nutrients to the soil. Secondary succession uses these nutrients to grow.

**Analyze** Why does secondary succession take less time than primary succession?

(tr) ©Raymond Gehman/National Geographic Image Collection

## Secondary Succession

Succession does not always begin from bare rock. More often, a disturbance, such as a fire or hurricane, halts the progress of succession or destroys an established community. **Secondary succession,** which is illustrated in **FIGURE 5.3,** is the reestablishment of a damaged ecosystem in an area where the soil was left intact. Plants and other organisms that remain start the process of regrowth. There is no end to secondary succession. Small disturbances, such as a tree falling, start the process again and again. The dynamic processes of succession are always changing the face of an ecosystem.

**Connect** Where might succession occur in the ocean?

**SELF-CHECK Online**
HMHScience.com
GO ONLINE

# 14.5 Formative Assessment

## REVIEWING ◉ MAIN IDEAS

1. How is **primary succession** different from **secondary succession**?

2. Why are **pioneer species** so important for primary succession?

## CRITICAL THINKING

3. **Infer** Does the process of primary succession take longer in tropical or arctic areas? Explain.

4. **Predict** During **succession,** what might become the limiting factor for sun-loving mosses as taller plants begin to grow?

## CONNECT TO

### BIOLOGICAL NICHE

5. At what point during primary succession does an ecosystem provide the fewest habitats for organisms? Explain your reasoning.

# 14 Summary

## KEY CONCEPTS

### 14.1 Habitat and Niche

**Every organism has a habitat and a niche.** Each organism in an ecosystem has an ecological niche, which includes the type of food it consumes, its behavior, and its habitat—the place where it lives. Competitive exclusion prevents two species from sharing the same niche. In different geographical regions, ecological equivalents may have similar ecological niches.

### 14.2 Community Interactions

**Organisms interact as individuals and as populations.** Interactions between species include competition and predation. Interactions shape ecosystem dynamics. Parasitism, commensalism, and mutualism are symbiotic relationships involving two species living in direct contact with one another.

### 14.3 Population Density and Distribution

**Each population has a density, a dispersion, and a reproductive strategy.** The distribution of a population can be measured by population density. Species can have clumped, uniform, or random dispersion patterns. Survivorship curves describe the reproductive strategies of different species.

| Clumped dispersion | Uniform dispersion | Random dispersion |
|---|---|---|

### 14.4 Population Growth Patterns

**Populations grow in predictable patterns.** Population growth accommodates changes in population size due to births and deaths as well as immigration and emigration. Populations experiencing exponential growth increase dramatically over time. When resources become a limiting factor, a population will grow logistically until it reaches the environmental carrying capacity, or the maximum population size the environment can support.

Density-dependent limiting factors affect dense populations, but density-independent limiting factors affect populations regardless of density.

### 14.5 Ecological Succession

**Ecological succession is a process of change in the species that make up a community.** Succession refers to the progression of plants and animals that repopulate a region after an ecological disturbance. Primary succession begins in a previously uninhabited area, such as bare rock exposed by the receding of a glacier or created by a volcanic eruption. Secondary succession occurs in a previously inhabited area that is damaged by an ecological disturbance, such as a fire or a flood.

## READING TOOLBOX    SYNTHESIZE YOUR NOTES

**Concept Map** Use a concept map to display the differences between exponential and logistic growth.

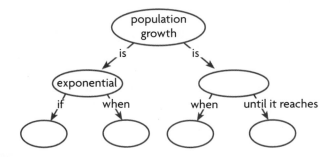

**Main Idea Chart** Use the main idea chart to explain and give examples of density-independent and density-dependent limiting factors.

| Density-Independent | Density-Dependent |
|---|---|
| | |

CHAPTER

# 14 Review

**INTERACTIVE Review**
HMHScience.com

**GO ONLINE**

Review Games • Concept Map • Section Self-Checks

## CHAPTER VOCABULARY

**14.1** habitat
ecological niche
competitive exclusion
ecological equivalent

**14.2** competition
predation
symbiosis
mutualism
commensalism
parasitism

**14.3** population density
population dispersion
survivorship curve

**14.4** immigration
emigration
exponential growth
logistic growth
carrying capacity
population crash
limiting factor

density-dependent limiting
factor
density-independent limiting
factor

**14.5** succession
primary succession
pioneer species
secondary succession

## Reviewing Vocabulary

**Category Clues**

For each clue in the category group, list the appropriate vocabulary words from the chapter.

**Category: Types of Symbiosis**

1. two-way benefit
2. host is harmed
3. no effect on host

**Category: Types of Dispersion**

4. a herd
5. no pattern
6. territories

**Category: Population Growth**

7. quick growth
8. sudden decrease in size
9. number environment can sustain

### READING TOOLBOX  WORD ORIGINS

10. *Niche* is an English word with a French origin. In general, it means "a special place." How does this meaning relate to the ecological definition of the word?

11. *Habitat* comes from a Latin word meaning "it inhabits." Connect this meaning with the definition in Section 1.

## Reviewing MAIN IDEAS

12. A deer is a large herbivore that usually lives in a forest. What is the deer's habitat, and what is its niche?

13. How does competitive exclusion differ from ecological equivalents?

14. A brown bear is an omnivore. Explain how a brown bear and a squirrel can be in interspecific competition and have a predatory–prey relationship.

15. The remora fish has an adaptation that allows it to attach to a shark, and it feeds on scraps of food left over from the shark's meal. What type of symbiotic relationship is this? Explain.

16. If you were to add two goldfish into a fish tank that already contains three goldfish, explain what happens to the population density of the fish tank.

17. Explain how the three types of survivorship curves align with different reproductive strategies.

18. If a large number of individuals immigrated into a population of bison, what two things could happen to return the population to its original size?

19. Why does a population that experiences exponential growth have a high chance of having a population crash?

20. How might the carrying capacity of an environment for a particular species change in response to an unusually long and harsh winter? Why?

21. Describe and give examples of two limiting factors that affect a dense population.

22. Why is succession considered an ongoing process?

# Critical Thinking

23. **Apply**  A bee gathers nectar from a flower by using a strawlike appendage called a proboscis. While on the flower, grains of pollen attach to the bee's back. When the bee travels to another flower, the pollen fertilizes the new plant. What type of symbiosis is this?

24. **Predict**  A population of prairie dogs is experiencing high immigration and birthrates, but resources are beginning to deplete. What could eventually happen to this population? Give two possibilities.

25. **Synthesize**  A species of beetle is in a period of exponential growth, but a competing species has started sharing the same space. Is the competing species an example of a density-dependent or a density-independent limiting factor? Explain.

26. **Evaluate**  Imagine that scientists introduced a disease into the rabbit population of Australia, and the rabbit population crashed. Was the crash caused by a density-dependent or density-independent limiting factor? Justify your answer.

27. **Describe**  How can the process of ecological succession change populations and affect species diversity within an ecosystem?

28. **Describe**  How can environmental change impact ecosystem stability?

## Analyzing a Diagram
Use the diagram below to answer the next two questions.

29. **Apply**  What part of the diagram depicts pioneer species? Explain your answer.

30. **Infer**  What could happen in the ecosystem shown that could make it revert to an earlier stage of succession?

## Analyzing Data   Read a Combination Graph
Use the graph to answer the next three questions.

The combination graph below shows changes in the sizes of bee and mite populations in one area of the Midwest. The mites live as parasites on the bees.

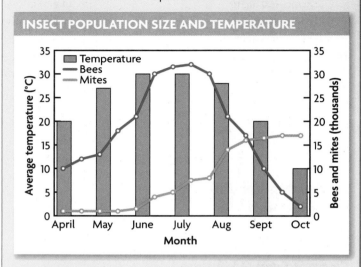

31. **Interpret**  A decrease in the number of bees occurs during which months?

32. **Analyze**  Describe the trends in the bee and mite populations from April through October.

33. **Hypothesize**  What might explain the relationship between the bee and mite population numbers?

## Making Connections

34. **Write Ad Copy**  Imagine that you are an advertising agent trying to encourage a new species to move into an environment. Design an advertisement using the concepts from the chapter. Keep in mind that a population will not want to move to a new area without abundant resources. Choose a target species and make sure that your advertisement answers the following questions: What resources and environmental factors would make this species want to move? What abiotic and biotic factors does it need? Include several vocabulary terms from the chapter.

35. **Apply**  The two zebras on the chapter opener are competing for the right to mate with females. Are they engaging in intraspecific or interspecific competition? Explain your answer.

# Standards-Based Assessment

Record your answers on a separate piece of paper.

## MULTIPLE CHOICE

**1** How do lichens and mosses make an ecosystem suitable for colonization by plant populations?

  **A** They serve as a food source to new plant populations that colonize an ecosystem.

  **B** They provide a suitable shelter for plant populations.

  **C** They break down rock to help form organically rich soil that can support plant growth.

  **D** They filter pollutants from air and water to make them suitable for use by plants.

**2** A lava flow from a volcanic eruption destroys a forest and leaves behind a layer of rock. Before plants can begin to grow again, what event must occur as a part of primary succession?

  **A** Large trees that provide shade must take root.

  **B** Animals must return to the area.

  **C** Lichens and mosses must be blown into the environment.

  **D** Heavy rain must wash pollutants from the area.

**3**

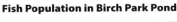

Which of the following **best** completes the concept map shown above?

  **A** volcanic eruption

  **B** toxic spill

  **C** earthquake

  **D** extended drought

| THINK THROUGH THE QUESTION |
| --- |
| Keep in mind that unusual weather is a natural part of ecosystem function. |

**4** Over many years, a diverse hardwood tree population formed a dense forest ecosystem in a region that was previously a meadow. As the population of hardwood trees increased, the species diversity of the grasses and other plants decreased. What event led to the decrease in diversity of the meadow plants as the populations of hardwood trees increased?

  **A** As more trees began growing, animals ate all of the grasses and small plants.

  **B** Many species of low-growing plants died out as the hardwood trees prevented them from getting enough sunlight, water, and soil nutrients to sustain their growth.

  **C** A change in the species diversity of the animal populations corresponded with a change in the diversity of the tree population.

  **D** Decomposition improved soil fertility for tree growth.

**5**

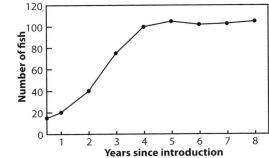

A fish species is introduced to a park pond. Which statement **best** describes the population growth of these fish shown in the graph?

  **A** The population stopped growing because the fish stopped reproducing.

  **B** The population stopped growing because this species of fish lives less than one year.

  **C** The population grew until disease caused the population to level off.

  **D** The population grew until it reached the pond's carrying capacity.

A BOOK EXPLAINING COMPLEX IDEAS USING ONLY THE 1,000 MOST COMMON WORDS

RANDALL MUNROE
XKCD.COM

# TREE
## A tree and the living and not living things around it

You know that a tree is a complex living thing. Trees also provide important habitats for a large variety of other living things, a biotic community. These symbiotic components make up the ecosystem in a tree. Here's an overview in simple terms.

## THE STORY OF A TREE AND ITS NEIGHBORS

A TREE IS A LIVING THING THAT GROWS BOTH UP AND DOWN. MOST TREES LIVE AS LONG AS US, BUT SOME OF THEM CAN LIVE MUCH LONGER.

TREES GIVE FOOD, AIR, AND A LOT OF OTHER STUFF TO LIVING THINGS.

PEOPLE USE TREES TO BUILD HOUSES OUT OF THE WOOD.

THEY ALSO BURN WOOD TO HEAT THOSE HOUSES.

YOU KNOW, I DON'T THINK WE REALLY THOUGHT THIS THROUGH.

THIS IS HOTTER THAN I EXPECTED!

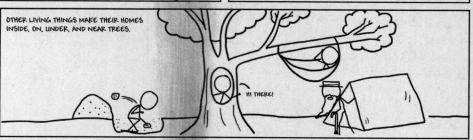

OTHER LIVING THINGS MAKE THEIR HOMES INSIDE, ON, UNDER, AND NEAR TREES.

HI THERE!

**GROWING UP**
Trees grow taller only by making the ends of their branches longer. The spot where a branch joins the main part of the tree is never lifted higher.

**LEAVES**
Trees make power from the Sun's light using leaves. The green stuff in leaves eats light (and the kind of air we breathe out) and turns it into power (and the kind of air we breathe in).

**POINTY CAT**
This animal walks around slowly, climbing trees and eating leaves and sticks. It's covered in sharp points that can stick in your skin, so most animals don't bother it.

**GRAY TREE-JUMPER**
These little animals sleep in big round houses made of sticks and leaves high up in the branches.

**QUIET NIGHT CATCHER**
These birds fly very quietly and have big eyes to catch animals on the ground in the dark.
People think of them as knowing a lot of things, although that may just be because they're quiet and have big eyes.

**BIRD HOLES**
Some birds make holes, but a lot of them just use holes other birds make.

**DRINK HOLES**
These were made by a head-hitting bird looking for tree blood to drink.

**TREE-EATING FLOWERS**
This flower makes holes in trees and steals food and water from inside them. If the flowers get big, they can kill the branches they're growing on, or even kill the whole tree.
When people stand under this flower at a party, other people tell them to kiss.

**LOUD JUMPERS**
These two kinds of tiny animals make loud noises and are known for jumping. One has bones.

**HEAD-HITTING BIRD**
This kind of bird hits trees with its head, making holes in the wood with its sharp mouth. They make holes to find things to eat, and some also make holes to live in.

**STORM BURN**
When flashes of power from storms hit a tree, they can burn a line in the wood.

# TREE

## SKIN BURNER
These leaves have stuff on them that makes your skin turn red. It gives you a really bad feeling, like you need to rub your skin with something sharp, but doing that only makes it worse.

This leaf-flower grows in long lines across the ground or up trees. Sometimes it grows into the air like a small tree of its own. Like many things, its leaves come in groups of three.

## ANIMAL HILL
This is the dirt the walking flies took out of the ground while making their holes.

## DOOR

## BROKEN BRANCH HOLE
When a tree gets hurt, like if a branch breaks off, the place where it got hurt grows differently, just like when skin gets cut. Sometimes animals get in through these spots and make the hole bigger.

## DIRT BRANCHES
Trees grow branches down into the ground, like the ones in the air. The air branches get light from the Sun, while the ground branches get water and food from the dirt. They spread way out—often farther than the air branches—but usually not very deep.

## BIRD HOUSE

## FIRE HOLE
These holes are from fires long ago. The leaves and sticks on the ground burned, and the wind blew the fire against this side of the tree. The burned spot grows in a different way and can sometimes turn into a large hole.

## TINY DOG

## LONG-EAR JUMPERS

## LONG-HOLE MAKERS

## WALKING FLIES
These tiny animals live in big groups and make holes. Most of them don't have babies; each family has one mother who makes all the new animals for the house.

They usually don't fly, and they're not much like house flies. They're in the same group with the kinds of flies whose back end has a sharp point that can hurt you.

## LONG BITERS WITHOUT ARMS OR LEGS (SLEEPING)
These long thin cold-blooded animals don't usually hang out together, and sometimes eat each other.

During the winter, though, lots of different kinds come together and sleep all wrapped up together in big holes under the ground where it's warmer.

## SKIN

The outer skin of trees is where growing happens and where they carry food up and down. Cutting off a ring of skin all the way around a tree will kill it.

Trees grow by adding new layers, and grow differently in different parts of the year. If you cut open a tree, you can see old layers, and count them to tell how many years old the tree is.

## OLD METAL

When people use metal to stick signs to trees, sometimes the tree grows around the metal and eats it up.

Then, many years later, if someone needs to cut down the tree, their saw can hit the metal and send tiny sharp pieces flying everywhere.

## TREE-FOOD STEALER

Instead of growing dirt branches of their own, these flowers grow onto the dirt branches of other trees and steal food from them.

Some of these little flowers don't even have green leaves and can't make their own food from light.

## TALL AND WIDE TREES

The same kind of tree can grow tall or wide. If there are other trees around, they'll grow mostly up, each one trying to get above the others to reach the Sun's light. If a tree is growing alone in a field, it will spread branches out to the sides so it can catch more light.

## FIELD TURNING INTO FOREST

When people cut down a forest, sometimes they leave a few trees—to make a cool shadow area, or because the tree looks nice—and those trees will grow out into the new space.

If the forest grows back, the new trees—fighting with each other as they grow—will be tall and thin.

If you find a forest of tall thin trees with one wide tree with low branches in the middle, it might mean the forest you're in was someone's field a hundred years ago.

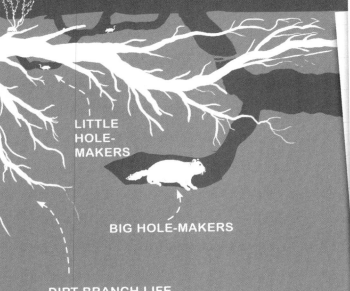

LITTLE HOLE-MAKERS

BIG HOLE-MAKERS

FOREST ABOVE WATER

DIRT BRANCHES

## DIRT-BRANCH LIFE

Most trees and flowers have life growing on their dirt branches. This life helps them talk to the other trees and flowers around them. They can even use this life to share food or attack each other.

If something tries to eat one tree, it can tell other trees through messages carried by this ground life, and the other trees can start making bad water and other things to make themselves harder to eat.

**BIG IDEA** Climate and the distribution of land and water play a role in shaping ecosystems and influencing the distribution of organisms on Earth.

## ⊙ ONLINE BIOLOGY    HMHScience.com

**ONLINE** Labs

- **QuickLab** Microclimates
- Winter Water Chemistry
- Modeling Biomes
- Heating and Cooling Rates of Water and Soil
- Modeling the Water Cycle
- **Open Inquiry Lab** Aquatic Primary Productivity

**Q What species would you expect to find in a rain forest?**

Not all rain forests are teeming with monkeys and macaws. The temperate rain forest of the Pacific Northwest is inhabited by an entirely different community of plants and animals than is found in tropical rain forests. Location, climatic conditions, and other abiotic factors determine what species you will find in a particular area.

---

**READING TOOLBOX**    This reading tool can help you learn the material in the following pages.

**USING LANGUAGE**

**Hypothesis or Theory?** To scientists, a theory is a well-supported scientific explanation that makes useful predictions. The main difference between a theory and hypothesis is that a hypothesis has not been tested, and a theory has been tested repeatedly and seems to correctly explain all the available data.

**YOUR TURN**

Use information from the chapter to complete the following tasks.

1. Is the greenhouse effect a hypothesis? Explain.
2. Write your own hypothesis that explains the increase in global temperatures.

## 15.1 Life in the Earth System

SC.912.L.17.5

**KEY CONCEPT** **The biosphere is one of Earth's four interconnected systems.**

**SC.912.L.17.5** Analyze how population size is determined by births, deaths, immigration, emigration, and limiting factors (biotic and abiotic) that determine carrying capacity.

**MAIN IDEAS**

- The biosphere is the portion of Earth that is inhabited by life.
- Biotic and abiotic factors interact in the biosphere.

### Connect to Your World

You've probably seen many photos of tropical rain forests, complete with monkeys and brightly colored frogs. But did you know that there are also temperate rain forests? They get just as much rain but have cooler temperatures and different types of plants and animals. These are just two of the biomes found within the biosphere.

### ▶ MAIN IDEA
## The biosphere is the portion of Earth that is inhabited by life.

The **biosphere** is the part of Earth where life exists. All of Earth's ecosystems, taken together, form the biosphere. If you could remove all the nonliving parts of the biosphere—all the water, air, rocks, and so on—you would be left with the biota. The **biota** are the living things within the biosphere.

The biosphere is one of Earth's four major interconnected systems. The other three Earth systems are

- the **hydrosphere,** all of Earth's water, ice, and water vapor
- the **atmosphere,** the air blanketing Earth's solid and liquid surface
- the **geosphere,** the features of Earth's surface—such as the continents, rocks, and the sea floor—and everything below Earth's surface

You need to look at how all four Earth systems interact to really understand how an ecosystem works. For example, a plant growing in a swamp depends on the soil in which it grows just as much as on the water in the swamp. It uses carbon dioxide from the atmosphere to make sugars, and it gives off excess oxygen, slightly changing the air around it. One plant growing in one swamp has a small effect on the Earth system as a whole. But all living things together throughout the planet's history have had a vast effect.

**Connect** **Is the air in your classroom part of the biosphere or the biota? Explain.**

**VISUAL VOCAB**

The **biosphere** includes living organisms and the land, air, and water on Earth where living things reside.

biosphere

biota

The collection of living things in the biosphere may also be called the **biota.**

### READING TOOLBOX

**TAKING NOTES**

Use a diagram to take notes on the biosphere.

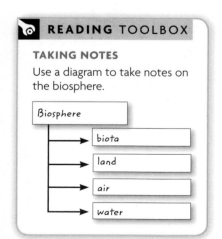

## ▶ MAIN IDEA
# Biotic and abiotic factors interact in the biosphere.

Just as one ecosystem is connected to another, all four Earth systems are also connected. A change in one sphere can affect the others. If plants are removed from a riverbank, for example, rain may flow more easily from the land to the water. This increased flow would likely carry more sediment and therefore make the river water murkier, as shown in **FIGURE 1.1**. The murky water might block sunlight, affecting the growth of aquatic plants. This change might in turn prevent these plants from taking up carbon dioxide and releasing oxygen.

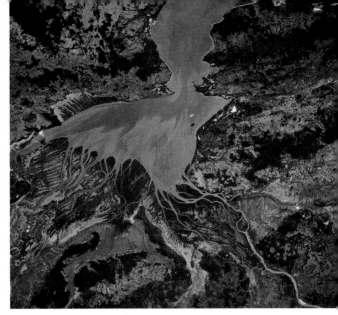

**FIGURE 1.1** Deforestation, or the removal of forests, along the Mahajamba Bay in Madagascar has led to erosion along the waterway, clogging the water with silt and soil.

James Lovelock, an atmospheric scientist from the United Kingdom, proposed the Gaia hypothesis to explain how biotic and abiotic factors interact in the biosphere. This hypothesis considers Earth itself a kind of living organism. Its atmosphere, geosphere, and hydrosphere are cooperating systems that yield a biosphere full of life. He called this living planet Gaia after the Greek goddess of Earth. In the early 1970s, Lynn Margulis, a microbiologist from the United States, added to the hypothesis, specifically noting the ties between the biosphere and other Earth systems. For example, when carbon dioxide levels increase in the atmosphere, plants grow more quickly. As their growth continues, they remove more and more carbon dioxide from the atmosphere. The atmospheric carbon dioxide level drops, and plant growth slows. This give-and-take, known as a feedback loop, helps maintain a fairly constant level of carbon dioxide in the atmosphere.

Sometimes, people mistakenly believe that the Gaia hypothesis suggests that Earth is a thinking being that regulates the geosphere, the atmosphere, and the hydrosphere. This is obviously not the case. Rather, the Gaia hypothesis recognizes the extensive connections and feedback loops between the living and nonliving parts of the planet. Many scientists are now devoting their careers to organizing new fields of study, such as geobiology and geomicrobiology, to examine these intriguing relationships.

**Summarize** **Explain the Gaia hypothesis in your own words.**

©NASA/Corbis

**SELF-CHECK Online**
HMHScience.com
**GO ONLINE**

## 15.1 Formative Assessment

### REVIEWING ▶ MAIN IDEAS

1. What is the relationship between the **biota** and the **biosphere**?

2. How does the Gaia hypothesis explain the interaction between biotic and abiotic factors in the biosphere?

### CRITICAL THINKING

3. **Apply** A frog jumps into a pond and its skin absorbs water. What spheres has the water moved through?

4. **Predict** How might a rise in global temperatures affect the biosphere?

### ❖ CONNECT TO

#### PREDATOR-PREY

5. Explain how feedback loops, such as those described in the Gaia hypothesis, might apply to predator-prey relationships.

# Climate

**SC.912.L.17.4**

**KEY CONCEPT** **Climate is a key abiotic factor that affects the biosphere.**

## MAIN IDEAS

- Climate is the prevailing weather of a region.
- Earth has three main climate zones.

**SC.912.L.17.4** Describe changes in ecosystems resulting from seasonal variations, climate change and succession.

## Connect to Your World

Although you might sometimes check the local weather report to see if you'll need an umbrella, you are already familiar with the general climate where you live. If you live in the Midwest, you know that winter means cold temperatures, while in the Southwest, winter temperatures are much milder. The long-term weather patterns of an area help determine which plants and animals you will find living there.

### ▶ MAIN IDEA
## Climate is the prevailing weather of a region.

The weather of an area may change from day to day, and even from hour to hour. In contrast, the **climate** is the long-term pattern of weather conditions in a region. Climate includes factors such as average temperature and precipitation and relative humidity. It also includes the seasonal variations an area experiences, such as rainy or dry seasons, cold winters, or hot summers.

The key factors that shape an area's climate include temperature, sunlight, water, and wind. Among these abiotic factors, temperature and moisture play a large role in the shaping of ecosystems. Descriptions of a specific region's climate take these abiotic factors into consideration. For example, a specific region such as a desert may be described as hot and dry, while a rain forest may be described as warm and moist.

Even within a specific region, climate conditions may vary dramatically. A **microclimate** is the climate of a small specific place within a larger area. A microclimate may be as small as a hole in a decaying log where mushrooms grow, as pictured in **FIGURE 2.1**, or as large as a city neighborhood. San Francisco, for example, is characterized by frequent fog and cool temperatures. However, not far beyond the city limits, and even within other sections of the city itself, the weather may be quite different.

Microclimates can be very important to living things. The same grassy meadow, for example, may be home to both frogs and grasshoppers. The frogs may tend toward areas that are moist, often at the base of the grasses, while the grasshoppers may prefer drier sites and cling to the tops of the grass blades. Each of these locations is a microclimate.

**Analyze** **Where in a forest might you find different microclimates?**

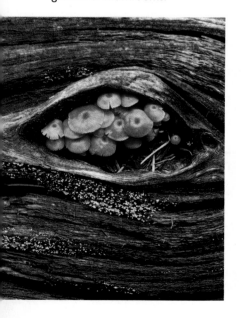

**FIGURE 2.1** The cavity in this log provides a humid microclimate that supports the growth of mushrooms.

©Frank Zullo/Photo Researchers, Inc.

## ▶ MAIN IDEA

# Earth has three main climate zones.

Scientists use average temperature and precipitation levels to categorize a region's climate. Using this system, Earth can be divided into three main climate zones, as shown in **FIGURE 2.2**. These three zones are the polar, tropical, and temperate climates. The polar climate is found at the far northern and southern regions of Earth. The tropical zone surrounds the equator. The temperate zone is the wide area in between the polar and tropical zones.

## Influence of Sunlight

What determines an area's climate? The answer begins with the sun. The sun's rays are most intense, and therefore hottest, on the portion of the planet that sunlight strikes most directly. Earth's surface is heated unevenly due to its curved shape. The area of Earth that receives the most direct radiation from the sun all year is the region at and around the equator, where the tropical climate zone is found. Near the North and South poles, or polar climate zones, the sun's rays strike Earth's surface at a lower angle, diffusing their heat over a larger area.

Earth's tilt on its axis also plays a role in seasonal change. As Earth orbits the sun, different regions of the planet receive higher or lower amounts of sunlight. When the North Pole is at its maximum tilt away from the sun, it is winter in the Northern Hemisphere and summer in the Southern Hemisphere. When the North Pole reaches its maximum tilt toward the sun, the opposite is true.

> ☼ CONNECT TO
>
> ### SEASONS
>
> At the March and September equinoxes, both hemispheres receive equal amounts of sunlight. At the June solstice, the Northern Hemisphere enters summer and the Southern Hemisphere enters winter. The opposite is true at the December solstice.

## FIGURE 2.2  Climate Zones

**The uneven heating of Earth by the sun results in three different climate zones.**

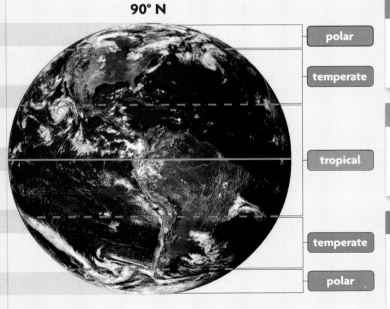

90° N

polar

temperate

tropical

temperate

polar

**POLAR CLIMATE**

The polar climate zone is located in far northern and far southern reaches of the planet, where the temperature is typically cold and often below freezing.

**TROPICAL CLIMATE**

The tropical climate zone, which surrounds the equator, runs from the Tropic of Cancer to the Tropic of Capricorn and is characterized by warm, moist conditions.

**TEMPERATE CLIMATE**

The temperate climate zone is located in the broad area lying between the polar and tropical climate zones. This zone experiences summer and winter seasons of about equal length.

**Apply   What is the relationship between sunlight and climate zone?**

NASA

## Microclimates

Determine the temperature of inside and outside areas of your school to identify different microclimates.

**PROBLEM** Where are different microclimates in and around your school grounds?

**PROCEDURE**

1. Identify one place inside and one place outside your school where microclimates may exist.

2. Place a thermometer at each location. Wait at least five minutes before recording the temperature.

**MATERIALS**
- thermometer
- stopwatch

**ANALYZE AND CONCLUDE**

Compare the temperatures you collected with those recorded by your classmates at different locations.

Western slope

Eastern slope

**FIGURE 2.3** The western slope of the Sierra Nevada, which faces the prevailing winds, receives precipitation throughout the year. Due to the rain shadow, the eastern slope of the Sierras is much drier.

## Air and Water Movement

When the sun heats Earth, it warms not only the land and the rocks but also the water and the air. This heating causes movements in both water and air. Warm air and warm water are less dense than cooler air and water, and therefore they rise. Because the tropics near the equator are especially warm, the warm air here rises and the cooler air from areas to the north or south moves in to take its place. As the warm air rises, it cools. Since cold air holds less moisture than warm air does, a large amount of precipitation drops as rain. This large amount of precipitation, along with warm temperatures, defines the tropical rain forest regions found near the equator. The movement of air also leads to movement in water, forming currents. The rotation of Earth, water temperatures, and salinity levels also interact to form currents.

## Landmasses

Landmasses also shape climates. For example, areas closer to bodies of water have a different climate from areas farther away because land tends to heat and cool more quickly than water. Thus, coastal areas tend to have smaller changes in temperature than areas farther inland. Farther inland, areas experience a much larger range of seasonal high and low temperatures.

Water evaporates from open bodies such as lakes or oceans faster than it does from soil or through plant transpiration. As a result, coastal sites in general have higher humidity and receive more precipitation than inland areas.

Mountains may also have a large effect on an area's climate. As warm, moist air nears a mountain, it rises and cools. This cooling of air results in precipitation on the side of the mountain range facing the wind. On the downwind side of the mountain, drier and cooler air produces a rain shadow, or area of decreased precipitation. The Sierra Nevada mountain range in California, shown in **FIGURE 2.3,** is one example of this phenomenon. While the western slope receives a large amount of precipitation, the Great Basin to the east of the mountains is dry.

| TABLE 1. AVERAGE CLIMATE IN ALBUQUERQUE, NM | | |
| --- | --- | --- |
| **Month** | **Precipitation (mm)** | **Temperature (°C)** |
| January | 12.4 | 2.1 |
| February | 11.2 | 5.2 |
| March | 15.5 | 8.9 |
| April | 12.7 | 13.1 |
| May | 15.2 | 18.2 |
| June | 16.5 | 23.8 |
| July | 32.3 | 25.8 |
| August | 43.9 | 24.5 |
| September | 27.2 | 20.6 |
| October | 25.4 | 14.1 |
| November | 15.7 | 6.9 |
| December | 12.4 | 2.3 |

Source: National Oceanic and Atmospheric Administration

## Adaptations to Climate

Many organisms have adaptations that allow them to survive in a specific climate. The water-holding frog shown in **FIGURE 2.4** is a dramatic example. It lives in the dry grasslands and deserts of inland Australia, where the rainy season comes only once a year. Dry periods can last 10 months or more. The frog survives the dry season by burrowing underground, where water evaporates more slowly. Moisture loss is further reduced by a cocoonlike structure formed from the frog's shed skin. When rains soak the ground, the frogs crawl out of their burrows to mate, and the females lay eggs in water puddles that form in depressions along the ground. Within a matter of weeks, the eggs hatch into tadpoles, and the tadpoles develop into frogs. This frog must move through its life cycle very quickly because the water evaporates quickly once the rains end. If the tadpoles are not ready to leave the ponds, they will die.

**Connect** **Describe the climate where you live.**

**FIGURE 2.4** Water-holding frogs crawl out of their burrows to mate during the rainy season.

©Jason Edwards/Getty Images

## 15.2 Formative Assessment

**SELF-CHECK Online**
HMHScience.com
**GO ONLINE**

### REVIEWING ○ MAIN IDEAS

1. What is the difference between **climate** and weather?

2. What are the three different climate zones, and where are they located?

### CRITICAL THINKING

3. **Connect** Where might there be **microclimates** in your area?

4. **Infer** Would areas along the shores of the Great Lakes have warmer summers and colder winters than other inland areas? Explain.

### ⚙ CONNECT TO

#### NICHES

5. Would you expect an area with several microclimates to have more or fewer ecological niches? Explain your answer.

# 15.3 | Biomes

SC.912.L.17.4

SC.912.L.17.4 Describe changes in ecosystems resulting from seasonal variations, climate change and succession.

**VOCABULARY**

canopy
grassland
desert
deciduous
coniferous
taiga
tundra
chaparral

**KEY CONCEPT** **Biomes are land-based, global communities of organisms.**

**MAIN IDEAS**

- Earth has six major biomes.
- Polar ice caps and mountains are not considered biomes.

⋇ *Connect to Your World* —————————

Have you ever seen a cactus in a tropical rain forest or a penguin in a desert? Individual plant and animal species have adaptations that let them thrive only in certain biomes. In this section, you will learn about the major biomes of the world and the characteristics of each.

⋇ **CONNECT TO**

**LEVELS OF ORGANIZATION**

Recall from the chapter **Principles of Ecology** that a biome is a major community of organisms, usually characterized by the climate conditions and plant communities that live there.

▶ **MAIN IDEA**

## Earth has six major biomes.

The global distribution of biomes is shown in **FIGURE 3.1.** Characteristics of each biome are given in **FIGURE 3.2.** As you will see, these broad biome types can be divided into even more specific zones. For example, the grassland biome can be further separated into zones of temperate and tropical grassland.

A variety of ecosystems are found within a biome. However, because a biome is characterized by a certain set of abiotic factors, ecosystems located across the globe in the same biome—the tropical rain forest of Brazil or Madagascar, for example—tend to have similar plant and animal species.

**FIGURE 3.1  World Biomes**

**A biome is defined by its climate and by the plant communities that live there.**

**Biomes**

- Tropical rain forest
- Grassland
- Desert
- Temperate forest
- Taiga
- Tundra

**Non-Biome Areas**

- Mountain zones
- Polar ice

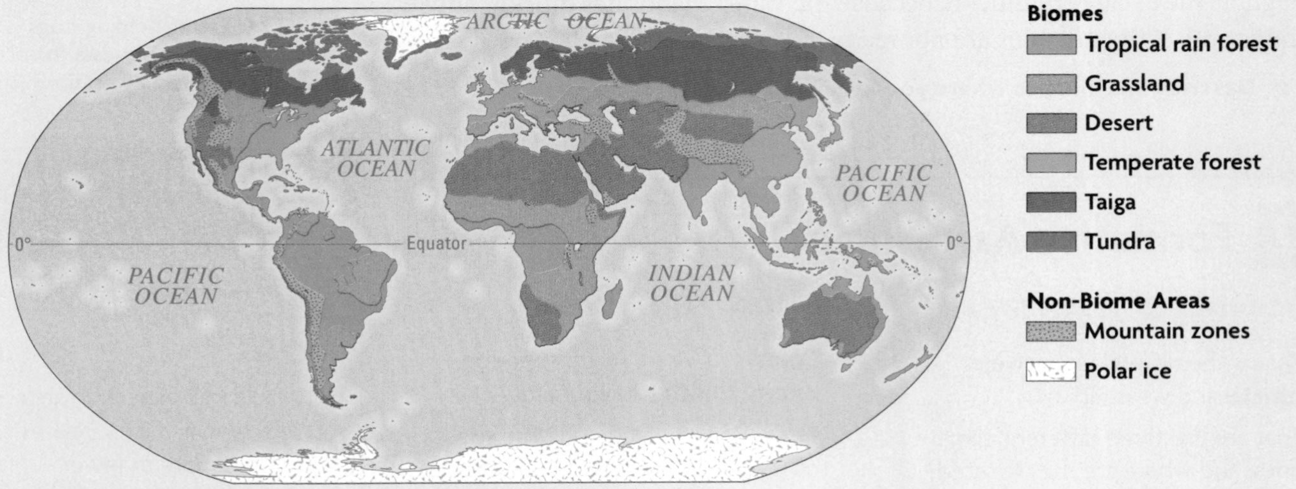

**Identify**  Which biomes are found in North America?

# FIGURE 3.2 Biomes

## TROPICAL

**Tropical rain forest**
- Warm temperatures and abundant rainfall occur all year.
- Vegetation includes lush thick forests.
- Animals that live within the thick cover of the uppermost branches of rain forest trees use loud vocalizations to defend their territory and attract mates.

## GRASSLAND

**Tropical grassland**
- Temperatures are warm throughout the year, with definite dry and rainy seasons.
- Vegetation includes tall grasses with scattered trees and shrubs.
- Hoofed animals, such as gazelles and other herbivores, dominate this biome.

**Temperate grassland**
- This biome is dry and warm during the summer; most precipitation falls as snow during the winter.
- Vegetation includes short or tall grasses, depending on the amount of precipitation.
- Many animals live below ground to survive the dry and windy conditions in this biome.

## DESERT

**Desert**
- This biome has a very dry climate.
- Plants, such as cacti, store water or have deep root systems.
- Many animals are nocturnal; they limit their activities during the day.

## TEMPERATE

**Temperate deciduous forest**
- Temperatures are hot in the summer and cold in the winter; precipitation is spaced evenly over the year.
- Broadleaf forest dominates this biome, and deciduous trees lose their leaves in the winter.

**Temperate rain forest**
- This biome has one long wet season and a relatively dry summer.
- Evergreen conifers, which retain their leaves (needles) year-round, dominate this biome.
- While some species remain active in the winter, others migrate to warmer climates or hibernate.

## TAIGA

**Taiga**
- This biome has long, cold winters and short, warm, humid summers.
- Coniferous trees dominate this biome.
- Mammals have heavy fur coats to withstand the cold winters.

## TUNDRA

**Tundra**
- Subzero temperatures are the norm during the long winter, and there is little precipitation.
- The ground is permanently frozen; only mosses and other low-lying plants survive.
- Animal diversity is low.

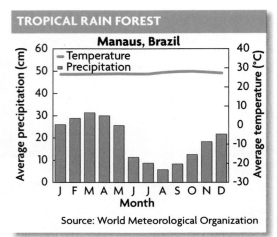

**TROPICAL RAIN FOREST**

**Manaus, Brazil**
— Temperature
▢ Precipitation

Average precipitation (cm) / Average temperature (°C)

Month: J F M A M J J A S O N D

Source: World Meteorological Organization

## Tropical Rain Forest Biome

A tropical rain forest has warm temperatures and abundant precipitation throughout most, if not all, of the year. This climate typically produces lush, thick forests that can completely shade the forest floor. The limiting factor for plants that live on the forest floor is sunlight. In fact, as little as 1 percent of the sunlight that strikes the uppermost branches of the trees, called the **canopy,** may make it through to the ground. The soil is very thin and low in nutrients. Most organisms that live in this biome inhabit branches of the upper canopy. Some plants, called epiphytes, grow above the ground on the branches of trees. A few of these, such as some figs, sprout and develop on branches and then send down long lengths of roots that grow into the ground below.

## Grassland Biomes

Grassland biomes occur in a variety of climates. A **grassland** is an area where the primary plant life is grass. Tropical grasslands are found in the tropical climate zones of South America, Africa, and Australia. Temperate grasslands are found in the temperate climate zones of South Africa, eastern Europe, and central North America.

**Tropical grasslands,** also called savannas, are covered with grass plants that may stand 1–2 meters (3–7 ft) in height. Some grasslands have scattered trees or shrubs, but the trees are never as thick and lush as in the tropical rain forests. The limiting factor in the savanna is rainfall. For five months or more each year, precipitation averages at most 10 centimeters (4 in.) a month; often there is much less. During the rainy season, however, water can replenish lakes, rivers, streams, and wetlands and form temporary ponds. This biome is home to plants and animals that have adapted to the extreme shifts in moisture.

**Temperate grasslands** receive 50–90 centimeters (20–35 in.) of annual precipitation, most occurring as rain in the late spring and early summer. Summers may be warm or quite hot, depending on the latitude of the grassland. Under such arid conditions, fast-spreading fires are common. Some plants in temperate grasslands have adapted to fire by producing fire-resistant seeds that require the fire's heat to start germination.

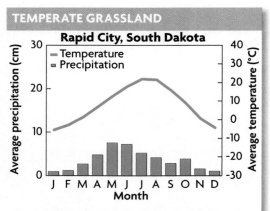

**TEMPERATE GRASSLAND**

**Rapid City, South Dakota**
— Temperature
▢ Precipitation

Average precipitation (cm) / Average temperature (°C)

Month: J F M A M J J A S O N D

Source: National Oceanic Atmospheric Administration

## Desert Biome

**Desert** biomes receive less than 25 centimeters (10 in.) of precipitation annually, and are always characterized by a very dry, or arid, climate. There are four types of deserts: hot, semiarid, coastal, and cold.

In hot deserts, such as the Sonoran Desert in Arizona, the daily summer temperature may easily top 38°C (100°F). At night, however, the temperature can drop by 10 degrees Celsius or more. During the winter, the temperature may be as low as 0°C (32°F). The precipitation falls as rain in hot deserts.

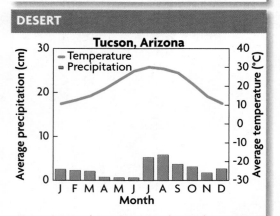

**DESERT**

**Tucson, Arizona**
— Temperature
▢ Precipitation

Average precipitation (cm) / Average temperature (°C)

Month: J F M A M J J A S O N D

Source: National Oceanic Atmospheric Administration

Semiarid deserts, like hot deserts, have long and dry summers and low amounts of rain in the winter. In comparison with hot deserts, however, temperatures are cooler and rarely exceed 38°C. Coastal deserts are characterized by cool winters followed by relatively long, warm summers. Temperatures range from a maximum of 35°C (95°F) in the summer to –4°C (25°F) in the winter. In cold deserts, such as the Great Basin of the western United States, precipitation falls evenly throughout the year and often occurs as snow in the winter. Summer temperatures range between 10°C (50°F) at night to 24°C (75°F) during the day, and winter temperatures can drop below freezing.

Plants use a variety of strategies to survive a desert's heat and lack of moisture. The reduced surface area of a cactus's spines helps it to retain more water by avoiding moisture loss from transpiration. Many desert plants have the ability to conserve or store water over a long period of time. Some desert plants, such as mesquite, have extremely long root systems that absorb water by reaching down to the water table. Desert plants also have heat- and drought-resistant seeds.

**Contrast** **How do rainfall amounts differ in deserts and in tropical rain forests?**

## Temperate Forest Biomes
A key feature of temperate biomes is their distinguishable seasons. The growing season occurs during the warmer temperatures from mid-spring to mid-fall and depends upon the availability of water.

The **temperate deciduous forest** typically receives about 75–150 centimeters (30–59 in.) of precipitation spread over the entire year as rain or snow. This biome is characterized by hot summers and cold winters. **Deciduous** trees have adapted to winter temperatures by dropping their leaves and going dormant during the cold season. Trees, such as oaks, beeches, and maples, along with shrubs, lichens, and mosses, make up the main vegetation.

The **temperate rain forest** does not receive precipitation evenly spaced across the year. Instead, it has one long wet season and a relatively dry summer, during which fog and low-lying clouds provide the needed moisture. Precipitation in the temperate rain forest averages over 250 centimeters (98 in.) per year. Evergreen conifers, such as spruces, Douglas firs, and redwoods, dominate this biome. **Coniferous** trees retain their needles all year. Mosses, lichens, and ferns are plant species found on the forest floor.

## Taiga Biome
The **taiga** (TY-guh), also known as the boreal forest, is located in cooler climates. Winters are long and cold, often lasting six months or more. The average winter temperature is below freezing. Summers are short, typically with only two to three months of frost-free days. However, they may be quite humid and warm, sometimes reaching 21°C (70°F). Precipitation in the taiga is 30–85 centimeters (12–33 in.) per year, which is similar to that in the arid temperate grasslands. Coniferous forest is dominant in the taiga.

**GO ONLINE**

Ecosystems and Energy Pyramids

**CONNECT TO**

**LOCAL ECOSYSTEMS**

See **Appendix D** for information about local ecosystems and guidelines for analyzing an ecosystem.

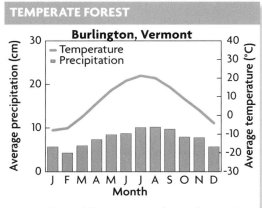

Source: National Oceanic Atmospheric Administration

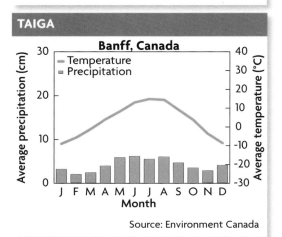

Source: Environment Canada

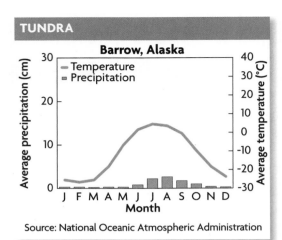

**TUNDRA**

**Barrow, Alaska**

— Temperature
■ Precipitation

Source: National Oceanic Atmospheric Administration

## Tundra Biome

Often described as bleak, the **tundra** is located beyond the taiga in far northern latitudes. Winter lasts as long as 10 months a year. The average winter temperature is below freezing. The ground below the surface is always frozen. This frozen ground is known as permafrost. Summers last just 6 to 10 weeks. Precipitation is meager, averaging less than 13 centimeters (5 in.) annually.

In addition to limited precipitation, permafrost captures and holds moisture, making very little available to plants. Therefore, the tundra is quite barren. Only mosses, other tiny, low-lying plants, and a few scattered shrubs are able to survive. Trees and most flowering plants do not grow here.

## Minor Biomes

In addition to the six major biomes, there are also some other biomes that occur globally, but on a smaller scale. One example is chaparral, shown in **FIGURE 3.3**. **Chaparral** (SHAP-uh-RAL), also called Mediterranean shrubland, is characterized by its hot, dry summers and cool, moist winters. Over the year, temperatures in the chaparral range from 10°C (50°F) to 40°C (104°F). Annual precipitation ranges from 38–102 centimeters (15–40 in.), and occurs mostly during the winter as rain. The dominant plants in the chaparral are small-leaved evergreen shrubs. This biome is found in small areas across the globe, including the central and southern coast of California in the western United States, the coast of Chile in South America, the Mediterranean Sea coast in Europe, the southern and western coasts of Australia, and the southwestern tip of South Africa. Because of the fairly hot climate, the plants in this biome exhibit some of the same adaptations to heat as those found in the desert biome. Many plants have shallow root systems that let them take in as much water as possible when it rains. The leaves of shrubs have thick cuticles that help in water retention. Many plant species, such as sage and rosemary, give off a strong smell. These aromatic oils are also highly flammable, and promote fire. As in temperate grasslands, chaparral plants have adapted to the presence of fire, and some plants need fire in order for their seeds to germinate.

**Connect   What biome includes the area where you live?**

**FIGURE 3.3** In the United States, chaparral is found along the central and southern coasts of California. This biome is characterized by hot, dry summers and cool, moist winters.

©Andrew Brown; Ecoscene/Corbis

## ◎ MAIN IDEA
# Polar ice caps and mountains are not considered biomes.

Polar ice caps are ice-covered areas that have no soil and do not have a specific plant community. In mountains, the climate and the animal and plant communities change depending on elevation. Because of these characteristics, polar caps and mountains are not categorized as biomes.

Polar ice caps occur around the poles at the top and bottom of Earth. In the Northern Hemisphere, the polar ice cap includes parts of Greenland and permanently frozen portions of the Arctic Ocean and surrounding islands. In the Southern Hemisphere, the polar ice cap includes the glacier-covered continent of Antarctica. At the ice caps, ice and snow cover the surface all year. Very few plants or fungi are able to survive the harsh conditions found in the polar regions. Some species found in Antarctica include mosses and lichens. Most animals in this region depend on the sea for their food. Animals such as polar bears, shown in **FIGURE 3.4**, have layers of fat that keep them warm in the cold polar conditions. Different animals are found in the northern and southern polar regions. For example, polar bears are found only in the north, while penguins are found only in the south.

Mountains are often rich with life. Different communities of species have adapted to the variety of ecosystems found at different mountain elevations. As you move up a mountain, the different communities that you see are similar to the biomes found in different latitudes across the globe. For example, you may begin a hike in a grassland at the base of the mountain, continue upward through a coniferous forest, and finally reach a desolate tundralike zone at the mountain's top. While the life zones found on mountains are similar across biomes, their species of plants and animals differ as a result of the different abiotic factors that shape each biome.

**Summarize** **Explain why neither polar ice caps nor mountains are considered biomes.**

**FIGURE 3.4** A polar bear's thick layer of fat, or blubber, keeps it well insulated from the cold as it rests on an ice floe or swims in Arctic waters to catch food.

©Norbert Rosing/National Geographic Image Collection

# 15.3 Formative Assessment

**SELF-CHECK Online**
HMHScience.com
**GO ONLINE**

## REVIEWING ◎ MAIN IDEAS

1. List and describe the six major biome types.

2. What are some characteristics of mountains and polar ice caps?

3. Compare variations and adaptations of desert organisms with organisms in the tundra.

## CRITICAL THINKING

4. **Predict** How might stopping fires change a temperate **grassland**?

5. **Infer** Polar bears have white fur but black skin underneath. Consider the climate in which the bears live. What might be the adaptive advantage of the bears' black skin?

### ⟶ CONNECT TO

### ANIMAL BEHAVIOR

6. Male birds that migrate the earliest to their summer nesting sites can usually secure the best territories. What limiting factor keeps birds from arriving too early in the **taiga**?

# Marine Ecosystems

SC.912.L.17.2

| KEY CONCEPT **Marine ecosystems are global.**

**MAIN IDEAS**

- The ocean can be divided into zones.
- Coastal waters contain unique habitats.

## VOCABULARY

intertidal zone
neritic zone
bathyal zone
abyssal zone
plankton
zooplankton
phytoplankton
coral reef
kelp forest

**SC.912.L.17.2** Explain the general distribution of life in aquatic systems as a function of chemistry, geography, light, depth, salinity, and temperature.

### Connect to Your World

If you've ever been to the ocean, you are already familiar with some ocean zones. If you walked on the beach at the edge of the surf, you were in the intertidal zone. If you went into the water, you were swimming in the neritic zone. In this section, you will learn about these and other zones that divide the ocean. You will also read about the unique habitats found along the ocean's coasts.

## MAIN IDEA

# The ocean can be divided into zones.

The oceans are a global expanse of water containing a large variety of living things that dwell from coastal shallows to the great depths of the deep-sea vents.

## Ocean Zones

Scientists use several systems to divide the ocean into different zones. The simplest division of the ocean separates the water of the open sea, or pelagic zone, from the ocean floor, which is called the benthic zone.

The presence of light is also used to differentiate between areas of the ocean. The photic zone is the portion of the ocean that receives plentiful sunlight. In contrast, the aphotic zone refers to the depths of the ocean where sunlight does not reach.

In a third system, as shown in **FIGURE 4.2,** the ocean is separated into zones using distance from the shoreline and water depth as dividing factors.

The **intertidal zone** is the strip of land between the high and low tide lines. Organisms in this zone, such as those that inhabit tidal pools, must tolerate a variety of conditions that result from changing water levels. Organisms must contend with changes in temperature, amount of moisture, and salinity. The sea anemone, for example, opens up when underwater during high tide. It avoids drying out during low tide by closing up.

The **neritic zone** (nuh-RIHT-ihk) extends from the intertidal zone out to the edge of the continental shelf. The depth of the neritic zone may range from a few centimeters at low tide to more than 200 meters deep.

**FIGURE 4.1** Organisms that live in tidal pools, such as this one off the Washington coast, are adapted to habitats with constantly changing salt and moisture levels.

©Don Geyer/Alamy Images

## FIGURE 4.2 Ocean Zones

The ocean is divided into four major zones.

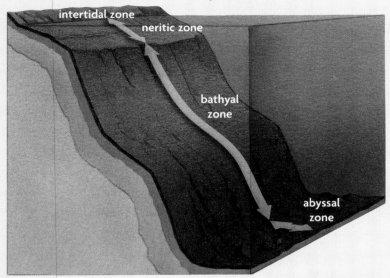

The **bathyal zone** (BATH-ee-uhl) extends from the edge of the neritic zone to the base of the continental shelf. The bathyal zone lies between the depths of 200 and 2000 meters. This zone is characterized by water that is turbid, or murky, due to the accumulation of silt. Fish that have adapted to living in areas of high pressure live in the bathyal zone. Burrowing animals thrive in this zone.

The **abyssal zone** (uh-BIHS-uhl) lies below 2000 meters and is in complete darkness. While deep-sea vents support a large number of organisms, the total number of species found in this zone is much smaller than the number found in the neritic zone. Because there is no light, photosynthetic organisms do not exist. Chemosynthetic organisms are the base of the food webs at the deep-sea vents. Many organisms that live in the abyssal zone make their own light, much as a firefly produces its glow. This light is often used to attract mates and prey.

## Life in the Neritic Zone

Although the neritic zone represents less than one-tenth of the total ocean area, it contains 40 times more biomass than the rest of the ocean. Much of the biomass consists of organisms called plankton. **Plankton** are tiny free-floating organisms that live in the water. These organisms include both animals and protists. **Zooplankton** is another term for animal plankton. **Phytoplankton** are photosynthetic plankton, which include microscopic protists such as algae.

Marine phytoplankton, especially blue-green algae and other types of algae, are critical to life on the planet. These organisms carry out the bulk of photosynthesis on Earth, and therefore provide most of the oxygen. According to many estimates, 70 percent or more of the oxygen in every breath you take can be traced back to marine phytoplankton. In addition to their role in oxygen production, phytoplankton also form the base of the oceanic food web.

**Hypothesize** **What other adaptations might organisms have in the abyssal zone?**

 **READING TOOLBOX**

**VOCABULARY**

In the word *bathyal*, the prefix *bathy-* comes from a Greek word meaning "deep." In the word *abyssal*, the word part *abyss* comes from a Greek word meaning "bottomless."

**CONNECT TO**

**INVERTEBRATES**

Some invertebrates, such as sea stars and lobsters, are plankton during their larval stage. You will learn more about the life stages of invertebrates in the chapter **Invertebrate Diversity.**

# Coastal waters contain unique habitats.

**FIGURE 4.3** Ecologists are working to rebuild coral reef ecosystems by building artificial reefs like this one.

The shallow, coastal waters that make up the neritic zone contain much more than plankton. Two highly diverse habitats found within these coastal waters are coral reefs and kelp forests.

**Coral reefs** are found within the tropical climate zone. In this area, water temperatures remain warm all year. A single coral reef may be home to 50 to 400 species of corals, along with hundreds of other species, including fishes, sponges, and sea urchins. Studies indicate that the biomass in coral reefs may be up to 1000 times greater than the biomass in a similar area of ocean that does not contain a reef.

Corals are animals that have a mutualistic relationship with algae. The coral provides a home for the algae, and algae provide nutrients for the coral as a byproduct of photosynthesis. Coral reefs are made mostly of coral skeletal material, which packs together over thousands of years into solid structures. Coral reefs are delicate. A change in conditions, such as increased water temperature or pollution, can kill the algae, which then starves the coral. With global ocean temperatures on the rise, coral reefs are in decline around the world.

Ecologists are trying to reintroduce these diverse communities in some areas by making artificial reefs, shown in **FIGURE 4.3,** where organisms can find shelter. In addition, some shipwrecks and sunken oil rigs have become artificial reefs that can support fishes and other species associated with coral reefs.

In contrast to coral reefs, **kelp forests** exist in cold, nutrient-rich waters, such as those found in California's Monterey Bay. These forests are composed of large communities of kelp, a seaweed. Kelp grows from the ocean floor up to the water's surface, sometimes extending up to a height of over 30 meters (about 100 ft). Kelp forests are areas of high productivity that provide habitat and food sources to many marine species ranging from tiny invertebrates to large mammals, such as sea lions.

**Compare** What are the similarities between coral reefs and kelp forests?

©Tim Laman/National Geographic/Getty Images

**SELF-CHECK Online**
HMHScience.com
**GO ONLINE**

## 15.4 Formative Assessment

### REVIEWING ▶ MAIN IDEAS

1. What criteria do scientists use to divide the ocean into different zones?

2. What conditions account for the development of highly diverse habitats in coastal waters?

### CRITICAL THINKING

3. **Connect** A red tide occurs when a bloom of **plankton** causes discoloration of ocean waters. What causes this increase in plankton populations?

4. **Predict** What might organisms that inhabit the **abyssal zone** eat?

### CONNECT TO

**FOOD WEBS**

5. How might the disappearance of coastal habitats affect an oceanic food web?

# 15.5 Estuaries and Freshwater Ecosystems

SC.912.L.17.2

**KEY CONCEPT** Freshwater ecosystems include estuaries as well as flowing and standing water.

## VOCABULARY

estuary
watershed
littoral zone
limnetic zone
benthic zone

### MAIN IDEAS

◉ Estuaries are dynamic environments where rivers flow into the ocean.
◉ Freshwater ecosystems include moving and standing water.
◉ Ponds and lakes share common features.

**SC.912.L.17.2** Explain the general distribution of life in aquatic systems as a function of chemistry, geography, light, depth, salinity, and temperature.

─∶- *Connect to Your World* ──────────

You rely on aquatic ecosystems more than you might realize. Many of the fish and shellfish that you might eat depend, at least for a part of their lives, on estuaries. But more importantly for you, freshwater ecosystems provide the water that you need to survive.

## ▶ MAIN IDEA

# Estuaries are dynamic environments where rivers flow into the ocean.

An **estuary** is a partially enclosed body of water formed where a river flows into an ocean. The San Francisco and Chesapeake bays are estuaries. So are the Louisiana bayous, Florida Bay in the Everglades, and many other harbors, sounds, and inlets around the world.

The distinctive feature of an estuary is the mixture of fresh water from a river with salt water from the ocean. The river carries high levels of nutrients from inland areas. The tidal movements of water in the ocean also bring in large volumes of organic matter and a variety of marine species from the ocean. Large numbers of species thrive in this rich mixture of fresh water and salt water.

Estuaries are highly productive ecosystems, on a level comparable to tropical rain forests and coral reefs. Photosynthetic organisms thrive in estuaries throughout the year, providing the basis for the aquatic food web. Estuaries also have thriving detritivore communities that decompose the enormous amounts of dead plant and animal matter that build up in the estuary's waters. These decomposers return vital nutrients back to the ecosystem. Estuaries also provide the necessary habitat for a number of endangered and threatened species. For example, the brown pelican, the Morro Bay kangaroo rat, and a plant called the Morro manzanita are all threatened or endangered species that depend on the Morro Bay estuary in California, shown in **FIGURE 5.1**.

**FIGURE 5.1** An estuary occurs where a river flows into the ocean. Estuaries are high in biodiversity and provide habitat for a number of species.

©RbbrDckyBK/Fotolia

FIGURE 5.2 The Tejo Estuary in Portugal is an important stop-over point for migratory birds such as these greater flamingos.

### CONNECT TO

**KEYSTONE SPECIES**

Recall from the chapter **Principles of Ecology** that a keystone species is a species that has a large effect on its ecosystem. Migratory birds in the Delaware Bay depend on horseshoe crab eggs as a main food source. This dependence illustrates the importance of the horseshoe crab in its estuarine ecosystem.

## Estuary Characteristics

The large number of phytoplankton and zooplankton in an estuary support a variety of species. Populations of fish and crustaceans depend on plankton as their primary food source. In turn, birds and other secondary consumers eat fish and crustaceans. Humans also rely on estuaries as a food source. In fact, 75 percent of the fish we eat depend on estuary ecosystems, making estuaries an important resource for the commercial fishing industry.

Estuaries provide a protected refuge for many species. Reefs and barrier islands along an estuary's boundary with the ocean protect estuary species from storms and the ocean's strong currents and waves. In an estuary's calm waters, many aquatic species lay eggs, and their young mature there before venturing into the ocean. The use of estuaries as spawning grounds explains why these areas are often called nurseries of the sea. Estuaries are also a key part of the migration paths of many bird species, as shown in **FIGURE 5.2**. Birds rely on estuaries as a refuge from the cold weather that occurs in the northern parts of their range during certain parts of the year.

Changing conditions in estuaries present challenges for species that live there. For example, in order to withstand changing salinities, some organisms have glands that remove the excess salt that builds up in their bodies. This adaptation helps organisms cope with an estuary's changing salinity level. Salt levels may lower with the tide and during periods of drought or heavy rainfall.

## Threats to Estuary Ecosystems

Estuaries are made up of a variety of ecosystems, including salt marshes, mud flats, open water, mangrove forests, and tidal pools. When estuaries are lost to land development and other human activities, these ecosystems and the organisms that live within them are also lost.

The removal of estuaries also makes coastal areas more vulnerable to flood damage from catastrophic storms such as hurricanes. Estuaries act as a buffer between the ocean and coastal land. In some coastal areas of the United States, over 80 percent of the original estuary habitat has been lost to land development.

**Analyze** **What characteristics make an estuary such a productive ecosystem?**

# Freshwater ecosystems include moving and standing water.

Rivers and streams are the flowing bodies of fresh water that serve as paths through many kinds of ecosystems. Rivers and streams, along with lakes and ponds, originate from watersheds. A **watershed** is a region of land that drains into a river, a river system, or another body of water.

## Freshwater Ecosystems

If you have ever paddled down a river in a canoe, you have probably witnessed the change in shoreline ecosystems, perhaps with a forest along one stretch and sand dunes along another. Along its course, a river may vary in many ways. For example, the speed of its flow is greater in narrow areas than in wide ones. The river bottom may be alternately sandy, gravel-covered, or rock-strewn. The water level may differ across seasons. In some areas, spring brings about the melting of snow and causes river water levels to rise. Humans also affect water levels by damming rivers or by draining water for irrigation or drinking water.

Unlike rivers and streams, wetlands have very little water flowing through them. A wetland is an area of land that is saturated by ground or surface water for at least part of the year. Bogs, marshes, and swamps are different types of wetlands that are identified by their plant communities. Common wetland plants include cattails, duckweed, and sedges.

Like estuaries, wetlands are among the most productive ecosystems on Earth. They provide a home for a large number of species, some of which are only found in wetlands. Wetlands also help maintain a clean water supply. A wetland filters dirty water and renews underground stores of water.

**FIGURE 5.3** As the Colorado River travels southward from Colorado to Mexico, it flows through different ecosystems, including forests and deserts.

## Adaptations of Freshwater Organisms

The particular variety of freshwater organisms found in a body of water depends on a number of factors. These factors include water temperature, oxygen levels, pH, and the water flow rate. Each type of freshwater ecosystem is home to species with adaptations suited to its conditions. In fast-moving rivers, for example, trout are adapted to swim against the current. They have streamlined bodies that can slice through the water easily. Some aquatic insects, such as the stonefly, have hooks on their bodies. The stonefly uses the hooks to attach itself to a solid surface in fast-running water to avoid being swept away. Similarly, tadpoles that live in fast-running water often have sucker mouths that they use to attach to a surface while feeding. These tadpoles also have streamlined bodies with long tails and low fins that help them to move in the fast water. Tadpoles that live in pools or in slower moving water often lack sucker mouths and have more rounded bodies and higher fins.

**Predict** **What effect would the construction of a dam have on a river ecosystem?**

(t) ©John Kelly/The Image Bank/Getty Images; (b) ©Corbis

**Animated**
**Biology**
HMHScience.com

GO ONLINE

Lake Turnover

**FIGURE 5.4** In the spring and fall, the water in a lake turns over, bringing nutrients from the bottom of the lake to the top.

**Web***Quest*
HMHScience.com

GO ONLINE

Explore an Ecosystem

▶ **MAIN IDEA**

# Ponds and lakes share common features.

Although they are much smaller in size than oceans, freshwater ponds and lakes are also divided into zones. Scientists use the terms *littoral, limnetic,* and *benthic* to identify and separate these zones.

- The freshwater **littoral zone** is similar to the oceanic intertidal zone, and it is located between the high and low water marks along the shoreline. The waters of the littoral zone are well-lit, warm, and shallow. A diverse set of organisms, including water lilies, dragonflies, and snails, live in this zone.
- The **limnetic zone** (also called the pelagic zone) refers to the open water located farther out from shore. This zone is characterized by an abundance of plankton communities, which support populations of fish.
- The **benthic zone** is the lake or pond bottom, where less sunlight reaches. Decomposers, such as bacteria, live in the mud and sand of the benthic zone.

During the summer and the winter, the water temperature within a lake is stratified, which means that different layers of the lake have different temperatures. In the summer, water is warmer near the surface and colder at the bottom of the lake. These warm and cold regions are separated by a thin zone called the thermocline.

All of the water within a lake "turns over" periodically. This happens because water is most dense at 4°C (39°F). When water reaches this temperature, it will sink beneath water that is either warmer or cooler. In autumn, colder air temperatures cool the surface layer of water to 4°C, causing it to sink and mix with the water underneath. During the winter, the surface layer of water cools to less than 4°C. In the spring, when the surface water warms to 4°C, it sinks and mixes with the layers of water below. In both autumn and spring, the underlying water flows upward and switches places with the surface water. This upwelling brings nutrients such as bits of decaying plants and animals from the benthic zone to the surface, where they are eaten by surface-dwelling organisms.

**Analyze** **What is the significance of lake turnover to the lake ecosystem?**

**SELF-CHECK Online**
HMHScience.com

GO ONLINE

## 15.5 Formative Assessment

**REVIEWING ▶ MAIN IDEAS**

1. What are the characteristics of an **estuary** ecosystem?

2. What abiotic factors might affect a river ecosystem?

3. How is a lake different from the ocean? How is it the same?

**CRITICAL THINKING**

4. **Compare and Contrast** How are coastal wetlands different from and similar to estuaries?

5. **Connect** What adaptation do some organisms living in estuaries have in order to survive the changing water conditions?

**CONNECT TO**

**ADAPTATION**

6. Many fish species and other aquatic animals have colorations that closely resemble the rocks or silt found on the bottom of their aquatic habitat. What types of ecological advantages might such an adaptation give an aquatic species?

©HMH

# New Designs for Artificial Coral Reefs

According to the International Maritime Organization, an artificial reef refers to any "submerged structure deliberately constructed or placed on the seabed to emulate some functions of a natural reef such as protecting, regenerating, concentrating, and/or enhancing populations of living marine resources." Some marine scientists also consider structures that are designed for other purposes—such as bridges, piers, and docks—to have the potential to be artificial reefs as well.

In past years, artificial reefs were constructed of concrete slabs, sunken ships, and old aircraft, subway cars, and tanks. Recent artificial reefs are not made up of these repurposed materials but are instead constructed especially for use as an artificial reef. Several companies make specialized structures for use as an artificial reef. These structures vary in shape and size.

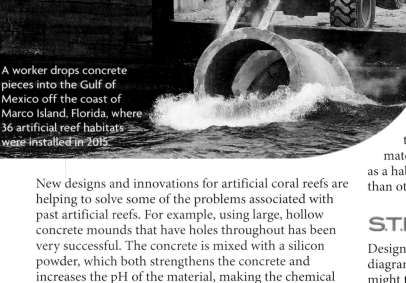

A worker drops concrete pieces into the Gulf of Mexico off the coast of Marco Island, Florida, where 36 artificial reef habitats were installed in 2015.

©Naples Daily News/Corey Perrine/AP Images

New designs and innovations for artificial coral reefs are helping to solve some of the problems associated with past artificial reefs. For example, using large, hollow concrete mounds that have holes throughout has been very successful. The concrete is mixed with a silicon powder, which both strengthens the concrete and increases the pH of the material, making the chemical composition more attractive to organisms. In the past designers of artificial reefs encountered problems because corals cannot settle on certain metals. Materials that are made of or contain paint, plastic, and rubber have also discouraged organisms from settling on an artificial reef. The holes in the concrete mounds help prevent the concrete from moving during strong wave motion from heavy storms, another problem faced by designers of previous artificial reefs. In addition, the mounds can be strategically placed to increase the chances of organisms settling on the concrete and creating a natural habitat.

A large artificial reef is being constructed in Puerto Morelos, in Mexico's Yucatán Peninsula. The reef will be made of concrete as described above, except it will be made up of pyramid shapes. More than 1,000 hollow concrete pyramids containing silicon powder will be lowered by a crane onto a concrete base to create almost 2 kilometers of habitat along the Yucatán coastline.

Another new design for artificial reefs involves using electricity to hold a frame in place on the ocean floor. The frame is made from steel bars. When electricity runs through the metal, minerals in saltwater crystallize on the metal. As a result, the metal thickens a few centimeters every year. The material formed is stronger than concrete. More than 400 reefs have been successfully constructed using this method. Nearby buoys can generate electricity from wave action, while solar panels or a wind turbine can be mounted on a raft to produce electricity—all from renewable energy sources. The electricity does not harm the organisms that settle on the reef because it is weak.

Another intriguing development in the creation of artificial reefs is the use of 3D printers to print out pieces of reefs made from a sandstone material that is not toxic to living organisms. The designers add bumps to the normally smooth surface of the sandstone material to encourage corals and fish to use the reef as a habitat. Producing reefs with a 3D printer is faster than other methods of creating artificial reefs.

## S.T.E.M. Activity

Design an artificial coral reef, including a labeled diagram. Explain the problem your reef solves, how you might test your design, the criteria you can use to evaluate it, and how you might refine it.

# 15 Summary

**BIG IDEA** Climate and the distribution of land and water play a role in shaping ecosystems and influencing the distribution of organisms on Earth.

## KEY CONCEPTS

### 15.1 Life in the Earth System

**The biosphere is one of Earth's four interconnected systems.** The biosphere includes living organisms, called the biota, and the land, air, and water on Earth where the biota live. Biotic and abiotic factors interact in the biosphere, and a change in one Earth system can affect the others.

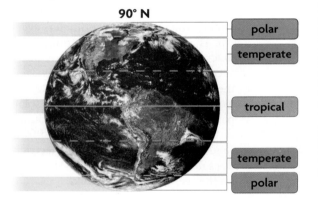

### 15.2 Climate

**Climate is a key abiotic factor that affects the biosphere.** Factors that influence an area's climate include temperature, sunlight, water, and wind. The three main climate zones on Earth are polar, tropical, and temperate. The polar zone is located at the far northern and far southern reaches of the planet. The tropical zone surrounds the equator. The temperate zone is located in the broad area between the polar and tropical zones.

**90° N**

polar
temperate
tropical
temperate
polar

### 15.3 Biomes

**Biomes are land-based, global communities of organisms.** Earth has six major biomes. These biomes include tropical rain forest, grassland, desert, temperate forest, taiga, and tundra. Polar ice caps and mountains are not considered biomes.

### 15.4 Marine Ecosystems

**Marine ecosystems are global.** Scientists use different criteria to separate the ocean into different zones. One system separates the ocean into zones using distance from the shoreline and water depth as dividing factors. The neritic zone contains 40 times more biomass than the open ocean. Coral reefs are found in the warm, shallow waters of the tropical climate zone. Kelp forests thrive in cold, nutrient-rich waters.

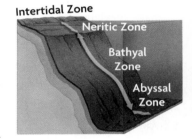

**Intertidal Zone**
Neritic Zone
Bathyal Zone
Abyssal Zone

### 15.5 Estuaries and Freshwater Ecosystems

**Freshwater ecosystems include estuaries as well as flowing and standing water.** An estuary is a partially enclosed body of water that exists where a river flows into an ocean. A variety of organisms are adapted to the constant change in salinity found in an estuarine ecosystem. Freshwater ecosystems include rivers and streams, wetlands, and lakes and ponds.

---

## READING TOOLBOX  SYNTHESIZE YOUR NOTES

**Concept Map** Use a concept map to summarize what you know about climate zones.

**Supporting Main Ideas** Use a diagram like the one below to summarize what you know about biomes.

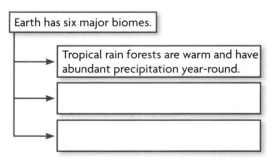

NASA

# 15 Review

**INTERACTIVE Review**
HMHScience.com

**GO ONLINE**
Review Games • Concept Map • Section Self-Checks

## CHAPTER VOCABULARY

**15.1** biosphere
biota
hydrosphere
atmosphere
geosphere

**15.2** climate
microclimate

**15.3** canopy
grassland
desert

deciduous
coniferous
taiga
tundra
chaparral

**15.4** intertidal zone
neritic zone
bathyal zone
abyssal zone
plankton

zooplankton
phytoplankton
coral reef
kelp forest

**15.5** estuary
watershed
littoral zone
limnetic zone
benthic zone

## Reviewing Vocabulary

**Compare and Contrast**

Describe one similarity and one difference between the two terms in each of the following pairs.

1. biosphere, biota
2. zooplankton, phytoplankton
3. hydrosphere, atmosphere
4. climate, microclimate
5. taiga, tundra
6. neritic, intertidal
7. kelp forest, coral reef

**READING TOOLBOX**    **GREEK AND LATIN WORD ORIGINS**

8. The term *plankton* comes from the Greek word *planktos*, which means "wandering." Explain how this meaning relates to plankton.

9. The term *climate* comes from the Greek word *klima*, which means "surface of the earth." Explain how this meaning relates to the definition of *climate*.

10. The term *estuary* comes from the Latin word *æstus*, which means "tide" or "surges." Using this meaning, explain how it relates to what an estuary is.

11. The term *littoral* comes from the Latin word *litoralis*, meaning "shore." Explain how this meaning relates to the definition of *littoral zone*.

12. The term *deciduous* comes from the Latin word *decidere*, which means "to fall off." How is this meaning related to the definition of *deciduous*?

## Reviewing MAIN IDEAS

13. Explain the difference between the terms *biota*, *biosphere*, and *biome*.

14. After a forest fire wipes out plants growing on a hill, rainwater washes soil down into a stream, and the stream fills with silt. In this example, what are the interactions between biotic and abiotic factors?

15. If the temperature in an area drops five degrees between one day and the next, has the climate of the area changed? Explain.

16. What is the connection between sunlight, the curved shape of Earth, and Earth's three main climate zones?

17. Why are two different deserts, each on a separate continent, considered to be the same biome?

18. Why are polar caps and mountains not considered biomes?

19. Briefly compare the four ocean zones—intertidal, neritic, bathyal, and abyssal—based on their distance from the shoreline and their water depth.

20. Where, in terms of water depth, would you expect to find a coral reef? a kelp forest?

21. Estuaries occur where rivers flow into the ocean. What conditions in estuaries make them suitable as nurseries for organisms that live out in the open ocean as adults?

22. The ecosystem of a river upstream in the mountains and downstream in a valley can be very different. Describe the adaptations of an upstream organism and an organism that lives downstream in the same river.

# Critical Thinking

23. **Apply** A deer drinks water from a stream, and then later it breathes out some of the water as vapor into the air. Through which three Earth spheres has this water moved?

24. **Infer** How would Earth's three main climate zones be different if Earth's axis were not tilted in relation to the Sun? (Hint: The tropical climate zone would likely be the most similar to how it is now.)

25. **Infer** Do you think it is possible for a biome to change from one type into another? Explain a situation in which this might happen.

26. **Connect** Why does the health of an entire coral reef ecosystem depend on algae?

27. **Analyze** Describe two reasons why it is critical to protect estuary ecosystems.

## Interpreting Visuals

Use the diagram of a rocky intertidal zone to answer the next three questions.

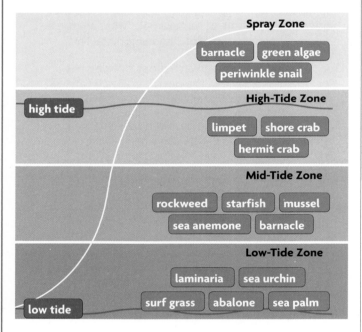

28. **Predict** How do you think the organisms above the high-tide mark are able to obtain the water they need to survive?

29. **Compare** What adaptations are necessary for a species to survive in the spray zone compared with a species in the low-tide zone?

30. **Hypothesize** Why do you think there aren't any fish shown in the diagram? Why wouldn't fish be a major part of the rocky intertidal zone?

## Analyzing Data  Construct a Combination Graph

Below is a climatogram for the city of Portland, Oregon. Use the graph to answer the next four questions.

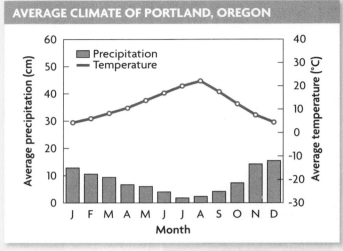

**AVERAGE CLIMATE OF PORTLAND, OREGON**

Source: National Oceanic Atmospheric Administration

31. **Analyze** Which month receives the highest amount of rain? the highest temperature?

32. **Summarize** Describe in one or two sentences the climate of Portland throughout the year.

33. **Analyze** A family is planning to vacation in Portland. Many of their planned activities occur outdoors. If they wish to avoid rain, in which month should they travel?

34. **Connect** Based on the data in the graph, which biome is Portland a part of? Explain your choice.

## Making Connections

35. **Write a Policy** The majority of the wetlands in the United States have been drained and used for development. A company has submitted a proposal to purchase an area of 100 acres of wetland that it plans to develop. If you were an official in the area, how would you respond to this proposal? What would you say to a local environmental group that opposes the proposal? What might be a possible compromise? Use information from the chapter to convince your fellow elected officials to take your position.

36. **Synthesize** Reread the information about the temperate rain forest at the beginning of the chapter. Using your knowledge of climate, biomes, and evolution, explain why different species are found in temperate and tropical rain forests.

## Technology and Human Population

Recall that the carrying capacity of an environment can change as the environment changes. As humans have modified their environment through agriculture, transportation, medical advances, and sanitation, the carrying capacity of Earth has greatly increased.

Technologies developed by humans have allowed Earth to support more people than Malthus could ever have imagined. Motorized farm equipment made possible the production of much more food than could be produced by human and animal power. Medical advances have also contributed to population growth. For example, infant mortality rates in the United States have dropped steadily over the last 70 years. In 1940, more than 40 infants died for every 1000 births. In 2002, only 7 infants died per 1000 births. Antibiotics and antiseptics have lowered infant mortality and the spread of diseases.

For a moment, think about how much we depend on technology. How have human lives changed with the help of plumbing to bring fresh water into homes and to take human waste out of homes? What if there were no transportation to move food and materials around the globe? What if there were no medicines? How many people could Earth support without electricity or gas, or if all construction had to be done by hand? Technological advances have allowed for continued human population growth.

**Connect** **What technologies do you depend on each day?**

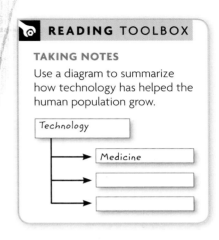

### READING TOOLBOX

**TAKING NOTES**

Use a diagram to summarize how technology has helped the human population grow.

Technology
→ Medicine

## ▶ MAIN IDEA

# The growing human population exerts pressure on Earth's natural resources.

Two resources, oil and coal, currently support the majority of our country's energy use. Oil and coal are the result of natural processes. Over millions of years, natural processes transformed dead organisms into the concentrated carbon substances we use today as oil and coal. Oil and coal are **nonrenewable resources** because they are used faster than the rate at which they form. In 2006, the human population was using oil at a rate of about 77 million barrels per day, and world oil use continues to rise. The growing use of this limited resource will lead to energy crises in the decades ahead unless technologies are developed to use other forms of energy.

Not all resources are nonrenewable. A natural resource that can be replaced at the same rate at which it is used is called a **renewable resource.** For example, wind energy—captured by wind turbines such as those shown in **FIGURE 1.2**—and solar energy are renewable resources because they cannot be used up by humans. Other resources, such as those that come from plants and animals, can be used up, but because they could last indefinitely through regrowth and reproduction, they are renewable. As long as these resources are replenished faster than they are used, they are considered renewable. But if renewable resources are not used carefully, they can become nonrenewable.

**FIGURE 1.2** Giant wind turbines such as these capture renewable energy from Earth's natural processes.

Drinking water is a renewable resource, but pollution and overuse threaten its supply. Pesticides, industrial waste, and other contaminants have been found in water sources that supply tens of millions of people across the United States with fresh water. Groundwater is also being extracted from aquifers faster than it is replaced.

As Earth's human population continues to grow, the management of renewable and nonrenewable resources will become increasingly important. Today, the United States uses more resources and produces more waste than any other country on Earth. Each year, the United States generates about 254 million tons of garbage. That is about 4.3 pounds per day per person, or almost 1 ton per year. What would happen if each of Earth's 7 billion humans generated 1 ton of garbage each year?

**Analyze** **Explain how a renewable resource such as water could become a nonrenewable resource.**

### CONNECT TO

**HYDROLOGIC CYCLE**

In the chapter **Principles of Ecology,** you learned how the hydrologic cycle moves water through Earth's atmosphere and back to Earth's surface. This cycling of water from resources such as lakes, rivers, and aquifers sustains the needs of the surrounding ecosystem.

## ▶ MAIN IDEA

# Effective management of Earth's resources will help meet the needs of the future.

Management of Earth's resources affects both current and future generations. The responsible use of Earth's resources can help to maintain these resources for future generations.

The story of Easter Island is a cautionary tale of destruction caused by careless use of resources. When humans first landed on Easter Island between 400 CE and 700 CE, it was thickly forested on rich soil, with many bird species. The human colony grew quickly over the next 1000 years, building the stone monuments for which the island is now famous. The inhabitants cut down the forests for lumber and for building boats. The trees were cut down faster than they could grow back. Eventually, Easter Island was left with no trees, as shown in **FIGURE 1.3.** Without trees, there was no wood for shelter or boats, the rich soil washed away, and habitat for the island's animal populations was lost. Without boats, there was no offshore fishing. Without food and island resources nearly gone, the Easter Island human population crashed and the Easter Islanders disappeared.

The Easter Islanders' use of trees was unsustainable. In other words, the islanders used trees to meet their short-term needs. But this resource could not be maintained into the future, and its use had negative long-term effects. In contrast, sustainable use of resources means using resources in such a way that they will be available for future generations.

**FIGURE 1.3** Today, the barren landscapes of Easter Island are an eerie reminder of the fate of the island's ancient inhabitants.

©Photodisc/Getty Images

## Ecological Footprint

Humans need natural resources to survive, but the way resources are used threatens the welfare of the human population. Earth's carrying capacity depends on how much land is needed to support each person on Earth. The amount of land necessary to produce and maintain enough food and water, shelter, energy, and waste is called an **ecological footprint.** The size of an ecological footprint depends on a number of factors. These include the amount and efficiency of resource use, and the amount and toxicity of waste produced.

As shown in **FIGURE 1.4,** individuals and populations vary in their use of resources and production of waste, and therefore in the size of their ecological footprints. The average U.S. citizen's ecological footprint covers an area larger than 15 football fields (6.8 hectares) and is one of the largest in the world. But the ecological footprint of individuals in developing nations is growing, and nations such as China and India have populations that are more than three times the size of the U.S. population. Individuals in the United States may have a large footprint, but other nations have a lot more "feet."

As the world population continues to grow, we face many challenging decisions. Waste production and management is an issue that will become more important as we move into the future. Should we have rules to regulate resource use and waste production? If so, how much resource use and waste production should individuals and populations be allowed? How much land needs to be maintained for agriculture, how much for living space, and how much for other uses? How much fresh water should be used for crop irrigation and how much reserved for humans to drink? Our welfare, and the welfare of future generations, depends on sustainable management of Earth's resources.

**Analyze** Why is our ecological footprint related to an area of land?

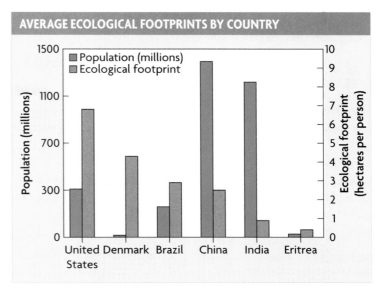

Source: Global Footprint Network

**FIGURE 1.4** Different countries of the world have varying levels of impact on their environment. This graph shows the average ecological footprint of individuals around the world.

**SELF-CHECK** Online
HMHScience.com
**GO ONLINE**

## 16.1 Formative Assessment

### REVIEWING ❍ MAIN IDEAS

1. Give three examples of how technology has influenced human population growth.

2. What is the difference between **renewable** and **nonrenewable resources**?

3. Describe how a population can use resources in a sustainable way.

### CRITICAL THINKING

4. **Connect** What factors can limit the growth of the human population?

5. **Synthesize** How could the Easter Islanders have prevented their population crash?

### CONNECT TO

### CARRYING CAPACITY

6. The progressive increase in Earth's human carrying capacity came from advances in technology. What density-independent and density-dependent limiting factors may prevent the human population from continued growth?

SC.912.L.17.11,
SC.912.L.17.20

VOCABULARY

pollution
smog
particulate
acid rain
greenhouse effect
global warming

SC.912.L.17.11 Evaluate the costs
and benefits of renewable and
nonrenewable resources, such as
water, energy, fossil fuels, wildlife,
and forests.

SC.912.L.17.20 Predict the impact
of individuals on environmental
systems and examine how human
lifestyles affect sustainability.

| KEY CONCEPT **Fossil fuel emissions affect the biosphere.**

MAIN IDEAS
- ◗ Pollutants accumulate in the air.
- ◗ Air pollution is changing Earth's biosphere.

### ☼ Connect to Your World

Fossil fuels are an important part of modern society. Consider that every time you ride in a car, you are being transported by energy that originally came from the sun. This energy was absorbed by ancient organisms and stored in their biomass. Today, as humans burn these fuels in the form of gas and oil, we are creating compounds that pollute Earth's biosphere. Without this energy our lives would be very different, but how does air pollution from fossil fuels affect the biosphere?

### ◗ MAIN IDEA

## Pollutants accumulate in the air.

Although it is sometimes easy to forget, humans are an important part of the biosphere. Our actions have direct and indirect effects on Earth's natural cycles. Each year humans add synthetic chemicals and materials to the Earth. Many of them cannot be integrated into normal ecosystem functions. The addition of these materials to the environment is called pollution. **Pollution** describes any undesirable factor, or pollutant, that is added to the air, water, or soil. Pollution can take the form of microscopic air particles, or waste products from factories and sewers, or household chemicals that are poured down the kitchen sink. The harmful effects of pollutants can be immediate or delayed, but these effects may add up over time and can disrupt the function of ecosystems.

### Smog and Ozone

The most common air pollution comes from the waste products produced by burning fossil fuels such as gas and oil. Chemical compounds released through this process can combine to form a haze of matter called smog, shown in **FIGURE 2.1. Smog** is a type of air pollution caused by the interaction of sunlight with pollutants produced by fossil fuel emissions. There are several components of smog, including particulate matter and ground-level ozone. **Particulates** are microscopic bits of dust, metal, and unburned fuel, 1–10 microns in size, that are produced by many industrial processes. Once in the air, some particulates may stay in the atmosphere for weeks before they settle to the ground. Fine particulates can be inhaled and can cause many types of health problems.

**FIGURE 2.1** The hazy fog over the city of Los Angeles is largely produced by automobile emissions and industrial processes. Smog is a growing problem in many areas of the United States.

©Nik Wheeler/Corbis

# Digitizing Life on Earth

How do biologists study biosphere-level concerns such as climate change, the spread of disease, the resiliency of crops, and patterns of extinction? Researching questions on a global scale is complicated. It usually can't be done in a laboratory, and developing computer models takes an enormous amount of data on past events to make accurate predictions of future changes. Increasingly, scientists are turning to natural history collections.

If you have ever been to a museum or botanic garden, you know there are not only many specimens or artifacts on display but also detailed information about each one. A plaque may state where or how long ago that organism was found, along with facts about its diet, method of reproduction, or requirements for survival. Usually the specimens on display at a museum represent only a portion of the museum's collection. It's likely that hundreds, thousands, or even millions of other specimens are in storage.

Where do all these specimens come from? Natural history collections can come from museum researchers for whom collecting is their job, from other scientists, or from donations by amateur collectors. Some collections are well documented and well preserved, while others may have lost information or are slowly deteriorating. Taken together, the collections reach back for centuries, providing a treasure trove of data on billions of animals,

plants, fungi, and even bacteria. Using the specimens and other historical artifacts of the time, such as diaries, ship logs, photographs, and paintings, researchers are piecing together often fragmented information from multiple sources into a comprehensive look at Earth's past.

Among the world's biggest natural history museums are the Smithsonian in Washington, D.C., the Natural History Museum in London, England, and the Muséum National d'Histoire Naturelle in Paris, France. There are also thousands of smaller museums with collections, including in the world's most biodiverse and remote areas. It would take a lot of time and money to visit all the locations. Instead, researchers are calling for a digitization of all the information that these museums hold, making the information easily accessible to anyone who wants it. Taking digital photographs, transcribing handwritten field notes into computer programs, and recording entire collections as video makes the information searchable and machine-readable and provides billions of potential data points for scientists. The increasing collaboration between museums, botanic gardens, and researchers studying the biosphere is promising to provide new insights into the future of life on Earth.

A collection of beetles from around the world
(Oxford University Museum of Natural History)

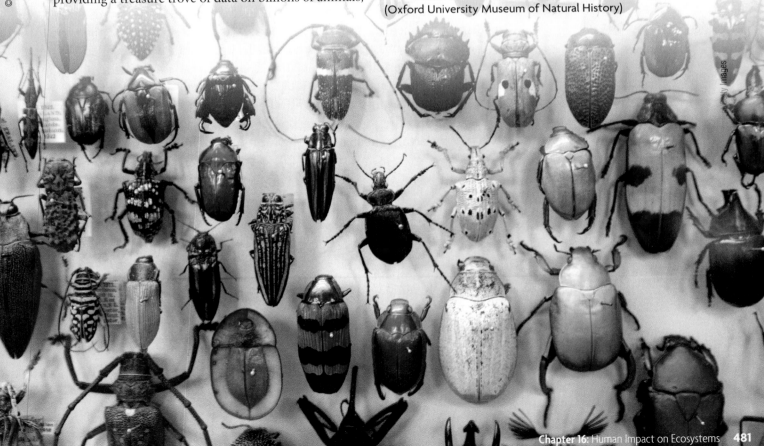

©Jochen Tack/Alamy

# 16.3 | Water Quality

SC.912.L.17.11

**KEY CONCEPT** Pollution of Earth's freshwater supply threatens habitat and health.

**VOCABULARY**

indicator species
biomagnification

**MAIN IDEAS**

- Water pollution affects ecosystems.
- Biomagnification causes accumulation of toxins in the food chain.

**SC.912.L.17.11** Evaluate the costs and benefits of renewable and nonrenewable resources, such as water, energy, fossil fuels, wildlife, and forests.

 **Connect to Your World**

When you swallow a pill, your body only uses a part of the medicine in the pill and gets rid of the rest as waste, which is flushed away. Scientists have detected traces of many prescription drugs in freshwater supplies. Several fish species that live in fresh waters have been exposed to the female hormone estrogen. Some of the male fish have begun showing female characteristics. These "gender-bending" fish are only one effect of water pollution. What other pollutants can be found in our water?

> **MAIN IDEA**

## Water pollution affects ecosystems.

Pollution can have a major impact on water ecosystems. Chemical contaminants, raw sewage, trash, and other waste products are only a few pollutants that make their way into rivers, lakes, and aquifers all over the world.

Runoff from farms and cities may contain toxic chemicals and debris that can disrupt the chemical balance of freshwater lakes and streams and put entire freshwater ecosystems at risk. For example, detergents and fertilizers used in fields can affect a lake ecosystem by stimulating plant and algae overgrowth. A buildup of algae, such as the one shown in **FIGURE 3.1**, can drastically lower the levels of dissolved oxygen, leading to the dying off of fish populations. A lack of oxygen can also keep detritivores from breaking down waste materials. Over time, lakes and ponds slowly begin to fill in through a process called eutrophication.

**FIGURE 3.1** A buildup of algae in lakes such as this one is the direct result of pollution. Eventually, the process of eutrophication will lead to the disappearance of the lake.

One way in which scientists can determine the health of an ecosystem is through the study of natural indicator species. An **indicator species,** also known as a bioindicator, is a species that provides a sign, or indication, of the quality of the ecosystem's environmental conditions. The gender-bending fish discussed above is an example of an aquatic indicator species. Frogs are sometimes considered an indicator species for water quality. Because the skin of tadpoles and adults is water-permeable, they come into direct contact with pollutants that can cause deformities such as extra arms and legs, as well as body tumors. Terrestrial ecosystems have indicator species as well, but the environmental impacts on these species are shown in different ways. Aquatic indicator species show the direct effects of pollution.

©Chris Howes/Wild Places Photography/Alamy Images

For example, as the nation of Sri Lanka has modernized, the natural resources of the island have become increasingly depleted. Ninety-five percent of the island's rain forests have been lost, and with them more than 19 different frog species have gone extinct. In addition, numerous other species, such as the rare frog species shown in **FIGURE 4.1,** are endangered. The loss of even a single species can harm the overall stability of an ecosystem.

Biodiversity is highest in the rain forest biomes of the world, and these are the areas that are most threatened. Currently, about 1 percent of this biome is lost each year to logging or to clearing for agricultural use. Preserving the rain forests of the world will do a great deal to protect and preserve the biodiversity of our planet.

**Connect** **Why is biodiversity highest in tropical rain forests?**

**CONNECT TO**

**CARBON CYCLE**

Rain forests around the world play an integral role in Earth's carbon cycle, storing large amounts of carbon in their structures.

### ▶ MAIN IDEA
# Loss of habitat eliminates species.

One way to protect species is to monitor and manage their numbers, and to ensure they have adequate habitat for survival. Governments and organizations around the world are developing programs to protect species that are threatened by overhunting, overcollecting, and habitat loss.

As the human population moves into what was formerly wilderness, people are moving into the territory of many species of wildlife. In many parts of the world, the loss of habitat can put species in danger of becoming extinct. Historically, for example, wetland habitats were viewed as breeding grounds for disease and as "wasted land." Between the 1780s and the 1980s, more than 53 percent of wetland habitat in the United States was eliminated. This destruction displaced large numbers of wildlife and disrupted migration patterns for many species of water birds.

Efforts to ensure adequate habitat must take into account the life history of the organism, including mating habits and migration patterns. Ecologists have become particularly worried about habitat fragmentation. **Habitat fragmentation** occurs when a barrier forms that prevents an organism from accessing its entire home range. Often, habitat fragmentation is caused by the building of roadways or the harvesting of forests. Bears, deer, raccoons, and opossums are just a few of the animals that find their home ranges fragmented as urban sprawl increases. To try to fix this growing problem, some states are building underpasses and overpasses so that wildlife can avoid busy roadways. Corridors such as the one shown in **FIGURE 4.2** help to maintain continuous tracts of habitat for those species that move between different areas.

**Connect** **Why is wetland habitat important for migrating birds?**

**FIGURE 4.2** By providing a safe way to cross barriers such as roads and highways, land bridges such as this one in Canada allow animals to move safely from one part of their habitat to the next.

©Joel Sartore

FIGURE 4.3 Rodent plagues in India, Australia, and China can cost farmers millions of dollars in lost crops.

### WebQuest

HMHScience.com

GO ONLINE

Invasive Species

## MAIN IDEA

# Introduced species can disrupt stable relationships in an ecosystem.

Introduced species have a direct impact on the biodiversity and natural flow of energy in an ecosystem. An **introduced species** is any organism that was brought to an ecosystem as the result of human actions. Introduced species can pose a great threat to the stability of an ecosystem if they prey on or crowd out native species. In some instances, introduced species can cause economic damage. Just as native species interact with one another and their habitat, nonnative or introduced species are active and sometimes disruptive in their new ecosystems. Invasive species are successful in environments under many circumstances. If an environment has a niche that the invasive species can exploit, or if the invasive species is a better competitor in a particular niche, native species may be pushed out. Invasive species are also successful if there is a lack of predators to keep the population stable.

## Effect on Native Species

The Florida Everglades is a dynamic ecosystem where unique plants and animals have evolved for tens of thousands of years. The climate is similar to that of a tropical jungle, and the Everglades can support a great diversity of organisms. One species that has been introduced to this region originally came from the tropical jungles of Southeastern Asia. The Burmese python, shown in **FIGURE 4.4,** came to the United States as a pet species. Growing more than 6 meters (20 ft) in length, this massive snake can be difficult to care for. Irresponsible owners have released many of the snakes back into the wild. A large number of Burmese pythons have been captured and removed from Everglades National Park, and officials say that there is a good chance that a breeding population is present. As a constrictor species, the Burmese python feeds on small animals such as rats, birds, raccoons, and even dogs. Threats to endangered bird species in the park worry officials. As the python population begins to grow, endangered species protected in the Everglades could be affected.

FIGURE 4.4 Introduced species such as the Burmese python are growing in numbers in places like the Florida Everglades.

Introduced animals are not the only problem. Plant species such as kudzu, another native of southeastern Asia, are invasive in the United States and are choking out native species of plants across the southeastern United States. The kudzu plant, shown in **FIGURE 4.5**, was introduced in 1876 as an ornamental tropical houseplant enjoyed for its fragrant flowers and large leaves. It was planted as field cover to prevent soil loss from erosion, but it rapidly began to spread out of the fields. Currently, kudzu is a classified as a problematic weed species in much of the eastern United States. Kudzu is a hardy plant, at home in virtually any soil, and it can grow up to 18 meters (60 ft) in a single growing season. This growth rate makes it difficult to control. Very few plant species can survive in an environment once kudzu is introduced. By blanketing trees and shrubs with its large leaves, kudzu deprives other plants of the sunlight they need to survive. The plant is resistant to most types of herbicides and can live for many years.

**FIGURE 4.5** After a few months of being left in a single place, these cars have become covered with kudzu. Fast-growing kudzu can destroy natural habitats in just a few years.

### Economic Damage

Invasive species can have a major impact on humans as well as ecosystems. The common house mouse is an introduced species to the Australian continent. During the late 1700s, mice came from Europe as stowaways on British cargo ships. Today, mice are considered a major pest species in Australia and have caused widespread economic damage. Every four or five years, mice populations increase exponentially. Seasons of heavy rainfall lead to bumper crops of corn and grain, causing a dramatic rise in mouse populations and leading to huge numbers of mice moving from one food source to another. It was estimated that during the 1993–1994 season, the mouse population in Australia cost farmers about $65 million in lost revenue. Mice continue to be a problem throughout the region.

**Video Inquiry**
HMHScience.com
**GO ONLINE**

Killer Kitties

**Predict How might a species of carnivorous fish introduced into a lake have a negative impact on the lake ecosystem?**

**SELF-CHECK Online**
HMHScience.com
**GO ONLINE**

## 16.4 Formative Assessment

### REVIEWING ⏵ MAIN IDEAS

1. Give two reasons why biodiversity is important to humans.

2. How does **habitat fragmentation** affect migrating bird populations?

3. What types of damage can **introduced species** cause?

### CRITICAL THINKING

4. **Analyze** How could continued habitat fragmentation reduce biodiversity?

5. **Connect** How might the introduction of a mouse predator help with the mouse problem in Australia? What problems might it cause?

### CONNECT TO

**POPULATION GROWTH**

6. Using your knowledge of populations, describe what will eventually happen to mouse populations in Australia as they run out of food.

# 16.5 Conservation

SC.912.L.17.13,
SC.912.L.17.20

**VOCABULARY**

sustainable development
umbrella species

**KEY CONCEPT** Conservation methods can help protect and restore ecosystems.

**MAIN IDEAS**

- Sustainable development manages resources for present and future generations.
- Conservation practices focus on a few species but benefit entire ecosystems.
- Protecting Earth's resources helps protect our future.

**SC.912.L.17.13** Discuss the need for adequate monitoring of environmental parameters when making policy decisions.

**SC.912.L.17.20** Predict the impact of individuals on environmental systems and examine how human lifestyles affect sustainability.

### Connect to Your World

When Rachel Carson's book *Silent Spring* was published in 1962, the wheels were set in motion for the creation of the modern environmental movement. The book, which described how the pesticide DDT was affecting wildlife, brought about a public uproar and helped lead to a ban on the use of DDT in the United States. Since then, a variety of measures have been put into place, both to restore Earth's biosphere and to protect it from further degradation.

### MAIN IDEA

## Sustainable development manages resources for present and future generations.

To ensure that Earth can continue to support, or sustain, a growing human population, it is important to secure the future of the Earth's ecosystems. This way of thinking is known as sustainable development. **Sustainable development** is a practice in which natural resources are used and managed in a way that meets current needs without hurting future generations.

Sustainable development covers a wide range of resource management methods. Concerns about the condition of the environment have led to changes in methods of harvesting natural resources. In the timber industry, for example, old growth forests are being lost at a fast rate due to a method called clear cutting. By cutting down large sections of wooded areas and removing entire forest ecosystems, lumber companies serve a growing need for building supplies. Today, with the raised awareness of forest ecosystem

**FIGURE 5.1** Forests of bamboo in China grow quickly and can provide an abundant supply of wood to support the growing demand for building materials.

©China Tourism Press/Getty Images

safety, several companies are choosing to cut selected trees rather than clear-cutting forests. This practice encourages rapid regrowth of trees, and makes sure there is only minimal impact to the forest ecosystem. When choosing where and when to harvest trees, foresters must consider how the soil, water, and wildlife of the area will be affected and change their harvest strategy accordingly to protect them.

Global fisheries are also in need of sustainable development practices. Overfishing has depleted fish populations worldwide. Fish stocks are not as hardy as they once were. One reason for this is that the fish that are caught represent the healthy, reproducing age groups of the fish population. By removing the reproducing individuals from the population, the fishing industry is actually hurting itself. Without fish to reproduce now, there will be no fish for the future. In addition, unsustainable fishing techniques damage marine and coastal environments. A number of techniques can be adopted by fisheries to make the industry sustainable:

- **Rotation**  Rotating catches between different species gives the "off" species time to recover their numbers following a harvest.
- **Fishing gear review**  The gear used to catch fish can damage the sea floor and often unintentionally catches other species. Reviewing and possibly banning certain fishing gear could help avoid damaging the sea floor and prevent ecologically important organisms from being killed.
- **Harvest reduction**  Slowing the harvests of deep-water species that grow very slowly allows them more time to recover their populations.
- **Fishing bans**  Creating and enforcing fishing bans in certain areas helps to replenish populations within that area, which may lead to greater fish numbers in nearby locations.

**Connect**  **What important services do forests provide? How might their destruction have an effect on humans?**

### ● MAIN IDEA
## Conservation practices focus on a few species but benefit entire ecosystems.

Laws written to protect individual species also help to protect their habitats. The Endangered Species Act in the United States, for example, is designed to protect individual species that are near extinction by establishing protection for the organism and its environment. When a single species within an ecosystem is placed on a list of endangered species, many other species within the ecosystem also benefit. The listed species is often called an **umbrella species** because its protection means a wide range of other species will also be protected. Such is the case with the West Indian manatee. This aquatic mammal, shown in **FIGURE 5.2**, lives in the waters of the Gulf of Mexico and Atlantic Ocean along the coast of the southeastern United States. Their range extends as far west as Texas and as far north as Virginia.

**☼ CONNECT TO**

**NATURAL SELECTION**
Recall from the chapter **The Evolution of Populations** that in natural selection the environment favors certain traits over others. In a fish's environment, nets used by humans catch fish that are large and slow. Fish that may be smaller and faster have a distinct advantage, thus leading to a genetic shift in the population.

**FIGURE 5.2**  The West Indian manatee is an umbrella species whose protection helps to re-establish marine habitats.

The manatee was placed on the endangered species list in 1967. Its listing resulted from a variety of factors including loss of habitat, overhunting, and deaths due to collisions with powerboats. Today, the situation for manatees is difficult, and fewer than 3000 manatees remain in the United States. To promote their survival, local, state, and federal agencies are working to develop policies to protect their habitat. When developing recovery plans for an endangered species, scientists must consider many factors. For example, because manatees rely on seagrass as their main food source, areas rich in this resource must also be protected. By protecting waterways from pollution, restoring damaged areas, and limiting boating, the marine ecosystem that is the natural habitat for manatees is also protected. As a result, entire ecosystems can benefit from efforts to save a single species from extinction.

**Apply** What factors might scientists consider when developing a recovery plan for the endangered grizzly bear of western North America?

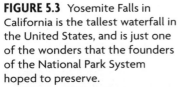

## MAIN IDEA

# Protecting Earth's resources helps protect our future.

All living things, including humans, share Earth and its resources, and the value of the services our planet provides is priceless. The cycling of nutrients and the regulation of water provide essential resources that are almost impossible for humans to manufacture. If we were to put a human economic value on it, the total value of the services Earth's natural ecosystems provide has been estimated to be over $30 trillion a year.

Climate change, pollution, and the loss of biodiversity are only a few of the direct threats our planet is facing. To prevent further loss of the valuable resources of Earth, public actions are helping to preserve and protect the future of our planet.

### Protecting Natural Resources

The Environmental Protection Agency was created as part of the National Environmental Policy Act in 1970. Its creation paved the way for the development of policies and regulations to protect the environment across the United States. Laws such as the Clean Air Act, Clean Water Act, and Endangered Species Act have had a major impact on the environment. The Clean Air Act, signed into law in 1970, has helped to increase air quality across the nation. It regulates emissions from industrial factories and automobiles. In 1970, only 36 percent of the lakes and waterways in the United States were considered safe for swimming. Since the Clean Water Act was signed in 1972, regulations against pollution and an increased public awareness have helped to double the number of waterways that are safe today. Since 1973, when the Endangered Species Act was signed, breeding pairs of the bald eagle, once in danger of extinction, grew from 791 pairs to almost 6500 pairs in 2000.

**FIGURE 5.3** Yosemite Falls in California is the tallest waterfall in the United States, and is just one of the wonders that the founders of the National Park System hoped to preserve.

©Susan Berg/SJB Photography

Setting aside areas as public land is another way that governments can protect ecosystems. The Yosemite Grant of 1864 was the United States' first step to protect nature from development. This grant established what would eventually become Yosemite National Park, part of which is shown in **FIGURE 5.3**. The success of this grant eventually led to the formation of the National Park Service. The management of multiple-use areas and wilderness areas balances recreation for visitors with protection of the natural ecosystem. Today, grassroots environmental organizations are working with local governments and private citizens to purchase and restore areas of land across the country to increase the amount of suitable habitat for wildlife.

## A Sustainable Earth

Humans represent an integral part of Earth's ecosystems and are subject to the same limitations as other species living on the planet. However, unlike other organisms, we have a much larger impact on our environment because of our population size and the fact that we are found over the entire globe. At the same time, we have the ability and technology to change the extent of our impact on Earth's biosphere and ultimately control our destiny.

**FIGURE 5.4** Each year on Arbor Day, people around the world plant trees and play an important role in rebuilding ecosystems for future generations.

- We have the ability to control how fast our population grows by controlling birth rates.
- We can develop technology to produce more food and produce less waste.
- We have the ability to change our practices and take action to protect and maintain ecosystems. In some cases, we can reduce or even eliminate the pressures we place on the planet's biogeochemical processes.

No places on Earth are untouched by humans. While we may not have directly visited each square inch of the planet, human-caused pollutants, invasive species, or ecosystem alterations have reached the world over. Yet our economies, and our very lives, depend on a healthy, thriving, sustainable Earth.

**Connect** How could you reduce the amount of waste produced by your school?

©Raymond Gehman/Corbis

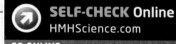

**SELF-CHECK Online**
HMHScience.com
**GO ONLINE**

# 16.5 Formative Assessment

## REVIEWING ▶ MAIN IDEAS

1. Give two examples of **sustainable development**.

2. Describe how the protection of an **umbrella species** can be beneficial to an ecosystem.

3. How do governmental actions help to preserve natural habitats and protect resources?

## CRITICAL THINKING

4. **Connect** What can humans do to minimize the impact of urban sprawl on wildlife?

5. **Evaluate** Could the West Indian manatee be considered a keystone species? Justify your answer.

## CONNECT TO

### NUTRIENT CYCLING

6. Natural ecosystems provide important cleansing and recycling functions to humans. What specific products do Earth's natural cycles provide for humans?

# 16 Summary

Human population growth threatens environmental quality and biodiversity, so conservation methods are necessary to preserve Earth's natural resources.

## KEY CONCEPTS

### 16.1 Human Population Growth and Natural Resources

**As the human population grows, the demand for Earth's resources increases.** The human population has grown tremendously due to advancements in technology. But a large population puts pressure on nonrenewable resources such as fossil fuels as well as on renewable resources such as water. Balancing the needs of our population with the resources of our environments will help to reduce our ecological footprint to sustainable levels.

### 16.2 Air Quality

**Fossil fuel emissions affect the biosphere.** Pollution is the addition of undesirable factors to the air, water, and soil. Fossil fuel emissions from industrial processes are causing an increase in smog and acid rain, which both threaten Earth's ecosystems. Carbon dioxide, methane, and other greenhouse gases slow the release of energy from Earth's atmosphere. But increased fossil fuel emissions appear to be contributing to rapid climate change, increasing global warming.

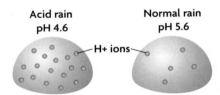

Acid rain
pH 4.6

Normal rain
pH 5.6

H+ ions

### 16.3 Water Quality

**Pollution of Earth's freshwater supply threatens habitat and health.** Indicator species help us understand the effects of pollution on an ecosystem. The process of biomagnification is a threat to both humans and ecosystems, as toxins accumulate at the top of food chains.

### 16.4 Threats to Biodiversity

**The impact of a growing human population threatens biodiversity.** The biodiversity of a region helps keep ecosystems stable. Habitat fragmentation and destruction are threatening biodiversity. Nonnative species can have a negative effect on ecosystems by pushing out native species and using up resources.

### 16.5 Conservation

**Conservation methods can help protect and restore ecosystems.** To protect Earth's natural resources for future generations, we need to plan for sustainable development. In addition, the protection of umbrella species and the positive support of government and industry can help to ensure Earth is protected for future generations.

---

### 🔷 READING TOOLBOX    SYNTHESIZE YOUR NOTES

**Concept Map** Use a concept map like the one below to display the effects of pollution.

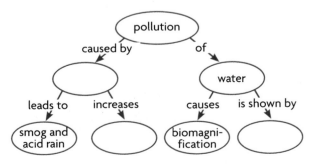

pollution

caused by      of

water

leads to    increases     causes    is shown by

smog and
acid rain

biomagni-
fication

**Process Diagram** Use a process diagram like the one below to explain the greenhouse effect.

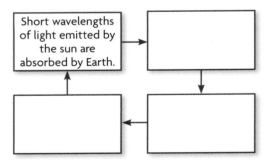

Short wavelengths of light emitted by the sun are absorbed by Earth.

---

# 16 Review

**INTERACTIVE** Review
HMHScience.com

**GO ONLINE**

Review Games • Concept Map • Section Self-Checks

## CHAPTER VOCABULARY

**16.1**  nonrenewable resource
renewable resource
ecological footprint

**16.2**  pollution
smog
particulate
acid rain
greenhouse effect
global warming

**16.3**  indicator species
biomagnification

**16.4**  habitat fragmentation
introduced species

**16.5**  sustainable development
umbrella species

## Reviewing Vocabulary

### Compare and Contrast

Describe one similarity and one difference between the two terms in each of the following pairs.

1. renewable resource, nonrenewable resource
2. smog, acid rain
3. greenhouse effect, global warming
4. indicator species, umbrella species

**READING** TOOLBOX   WORD ORIGINS

5. The word *sustain* comes from the Latin words *sub-*, which means "below," and *tenere*, which means "to hold." Explain how these meanings relate to the term *sustainable development*.

6. The term *biomagnification* is comprised of the prefix *bio-*, which means "life," and the word *magnify*, which comes from a Latin word meaning "great" or "large." Explain how the meanings of the word parts make up the meaning of the term.

7. The word *umbrella* comes from the Latin word *umbra*, which means "shadow." How does the everyday meaning of the word *umbrella* relate to the ecological meaning of the term *umbrella species*?

### Draw Cartoons

For each vocabulary term below, draw a cartoon that will best summarize the definition.

8. ecological footprint
9. global warming
10. introduced species

## Reviewing MAIN IDEAS

11. Earth's human carrying capacity has exceeded many earlier predictions. How has technology affected human population growth?

12. The United States uses more resources and produces more waste than any other country. How is this resource use reflected in the ecological footprint of the United States?

13. What are the major causes of smog and acid rain? What are the effects of each type of pollution?

14. Since the 1970s, human activity has released approximately 150 billion tons of carbon dioxide into the atmosphere. How could the increase in atmospheric carbon dioxide impact the greenhouse effect?

15. Which organism is most likely to have accumulated toxins through biomagnification: plankton, a small plankton-eating fish, or a large fish that eats smaller fish? Explain.

16. How could the extinction of a single species, such as a predatory bird, affect an entire ecosystem?

17. In what ways can an introduced species impact an ecosystem it has colonized?

18. The North American grizzly bear is considered an umbrella species. Explain how the protection of the grizzly bear may affect the larger ecosystem to which the bear belongs.

# Critical Thinking

**19. Analyze** Assuming all other factors are the same, the more meat in a person's diet, the larger that person's ecological footprint. Why might this be the case?

**20. Connect** Nationwide, automobiles are the major source of carbon monoxide, carbon dioxide, nitrogen oxides, particulate matter, and cancer-causing toxins. What can you do to decrease your fossil fuel use?

**21. Evaluate** An ecological footprint is a measure of the impact of the resources we use on the environment. Explain how buying a carton of milk relates to your ecological footprint.

**22. Infer** Frogs are commonly used as an indicator species in aquatic habitats. Could a large predator such as a bear or an eagle be used as an indicator species? Explain.

**23. Synthesize** Explain how a predator insect species, introduced to help control insect pests, could become a threat to an ecosystem.

## Interpreting Visuals

Use the simple food web outlined below to answer the next three questions.

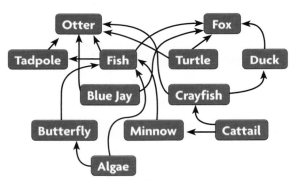

**24. Apply** Which of these organisms is likely to be most affected by biomagnification of toxins? Explain your answer.

**25. Predict** This food web includes both aquatic and terrestrial organisms. Imagine that a new road separates the aquatic environment from the nearby terrestrial environment. Do you think the turtle or the duck would be more affected by this habitat fragmentation? Explain.

**26. Predict** Imagine that an introduced species results in the local extermination of crayfish. How might this change affect the larger ecosystem?

## Analyzing Data   Identify Discrete and Continuous Data

This circle graph shows the components of the ecological footprint for a resident of a North American city. Use the graph to answer the next two questions.

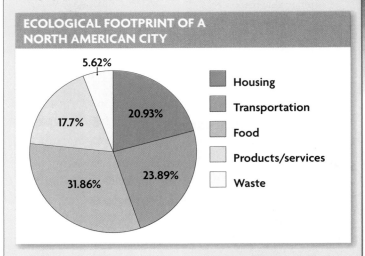

**ECOLOGICAL FOOTPRINT OF A NORTH AMERICAN CITY**

- Housing
- Transportation
- Food
- Products/services
- Waste

**27. Apply** Does the circle graph show discrete or continuous data? Explain.

**28. Analyze** In order of biggest to smallest impact, list the components of human activity that make up the average ecological footprint, according to this graph.

## Making Connections

**29. Write a Scenario** Imagine that successful efforts in sustainable development have made global resource use and waste production fully sustainable by the year 2099. Write a few paragraphs that describe what a sustainable world might look like in 2099. Include information about resource use, waste production, pollution, biodiversity, and conservation.

**30. Connect** Look again at the damaged forest ecosystem on the chapter opener. The emissions produced in this region have led to the rapid decline in the biodiversity of this area. How might this decline affect the resources of local animal populations?

# Standards-Based Assessment

Record your answers on a separate piece of paper.

## MULTIPLE CHOICE

**1**

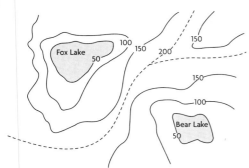

The topographic map above shows the watersheds, or regions that drain into Fox Lake and Bear Lake. The watershed boundary, shown with a dashed line, determines which lake water will flow into. According to the map above, this boundary follows —

A the highest elevation points between the lakes

B the lowest elevation points between the lakes

C a river that likely flows between the lakes

D a path exactly halfway between the two lakes

**2**

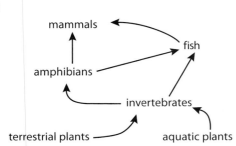

A farmer sprays his crops with pesticide. The runoff enters a nearby lake. Based on the food web above, in which of the following organisms would the pesticide concentration be the highest?

A cattail

B largemouth bass

C water striders

D river otters

**3** Which situation would ***most efficiently*** decrease the size of a field mouse population?

A decreased death rates and emigration

B decreased birth rates and immigration

C increased death rates and immigration

D increased death rates and emigration

> **THINK THROUGH THE QUESTION**
>
> As you look at the answer choices, think carefully about how each factor—birth rates, death rates, immigration, and emigration—affect population size.

**4** $CO_2$ is important in our atmosphere because it is required for photosynthesis and it traps some heat, keeping Earth warm. However, scientists speculate that excessive $CO_2$ production is a problem because it —

A leads to higher global temperatures

B disrupts the natural cycling of other greenhouse gases

C adds too much $CO_2$ to the oceans

D leads to uncontrolled photosynthesis

**5** The nonnative zebra mussel was first found in a lake near Detroit in 1988. By 1989, it had colonized all Great Lakes waterways. Which scenario is ***most likely*** true regarding the introduction of this species?

A Native fish naturally eat zebra mussels.

B The higher biodiversity leads to healthier lakes.

C They compete with native mussels for food and other resources.

D Native mussel populations are growing rapidly.

**BIG IDEA** Organisms use instinctive behaviors and learned behaviors to quickly adapt to their environment.

**ONLINE BIOLOGY** HMHScience.com

**ONLINE** Labs
- **QuickLab** Human Behavior
- Using an Ethogram to Describe Animal Behavior
- Pill Bug Behavior
- Animal Cognition
- Investigating Behavior
- **Virtual Lab** Interpreting Bird Response

- **Video Lab** Territorial Behavior

©Adrian Warren/ardea.com

**Q** # What can be learned from this chimpanzee's behavior?

This chimpanzee is using a twig to dig safari ants out of their anthill. Chimpanzees use a variety of tools. Bunched-up leaves might serve as a sponge to sop up water for drinking or for cleaning themselves. Some chimpanzees also use leaves to scoop up water to drink and rocks to crack open hard-shelled nuts or fruits. Tool use is considered an example of complex behavior.

## READING TOOLBOX

**This reading tool can help you learn the material in the following pages.**

### USING LANGUAGE

**Predictions** You are probably familiar with the phrase "It might rain today." There are many words that are used to make predictions. In science, words such as *rarely, often,* and *always* can offer clues about the likelihood that an event will happen. Analyze the statement "Cats rarely enjoy getting a bath." The statement tells you that most cats, but maybe not all cats, dislike baths.

### YOUR TURN

After reading your text, use *never, rarely, often,* or *always* to fill in the blank in the following sentences.

1. New male lions _____ kill all the young cubs in the pride.
2. Territorial behavior _____ results in serious injuries.

# Adaptive Value of Behavior

**KEY CONCEPT** **Behavior lets organisms respond rapidly and adaptively to their environment.**

**MAIN IDEAS**

- ◐ Behavioral responses to stimuli may be adaptive.
- ◐ Internal and external stimuli usually interact to trigger specific behaviors.
- ◐ Some behaviors occur in cycles.

☼ *Connect to Your World*

Animal behavior can be simple, such as a moth flying toward a light, or it can be complex, such as a chimpanzee using a leaf as a tool to drink water from a stream. At its most basic level, however, every animal behavior demonstrates the adaptive advantage of an organism's ability to detect and respond to stimuli.

**◐ MAIN IDEA**

## Behavioral responses to stimuli may be adaptive.

A houseplant bends its leaves toward a sunny window. A lizard moves into the shade on a hot day. A pufferfish inflates when threatened by a predator, as shown in **FIGURE 1.1.** Your cat comes running when it hears a can opener. What do these four observations have in common? They are all examples of organisms responding to stimuli in a beneficial way. A plant can only bend toward light by growing in its direction, but organisms such as the lizard, the pufferfish, or your cat have mechanisms that let them gather and actively respond to information. Behavior can be quite complex, especially in animals with complex nervous systems, but the adaptive nature of behavior can be seen in the relationship between a stimulus and a response.

### Stimulus and Response

A **stimulus** (plural, *stimuli*) is a type of information that has the potential to make an organism change its behavior. Internal stimuli tell an animal what is occurring in its own body. For example,

- Hunger signals a need for more energy and causes an animal to search for food.
- Thirst signals a loss of internal fluid and causes an animal to look for water.
- Pain warns an animal that some part of its body may be subject to injury and causes it to take some action to avoid injury.

External stimuli give an animal information about its surroundings. For example,

- The sound of a predator can cause an animal to hide or run away to avoid being caught.
- The sight of a potential mate can trigger courtship behaviors.
- Changes in day length can trigger reproductive behaviors or migration.

**FIGURE 1.1** When threatened, a pufferfish responds by inflating itself with water until its spines stick out from its rounded body.

Animals detect sensory information with specialized cells that are sensitive to changes in specific kinds of physical or chemical stimuli. These sensory cells may detect things such as light, sound, or chemicals. They transfer information to an animal's nervous system. The nervous system, in turn, may activate other systems in the animal's body that generate a response to the stimulus. For example, a stimulus may cause a gland to increase or decrease its production of a hormone. When you are startled or scared, your adrenal glands release a hormone called epinephrine that causes many other systems in your body to react in what is known as the "fight-or-flight" response. The most obvious organs activated in response to nervous activity are muscles. An animal's ability to move is what lets it behave in response to stimuli.

**FIGURE 1.2** Being chased by a lioness activates the "flight" response in this zebra, helping it try to evade its predator.

## The Function of Behavior

One way to look at an animal's behavior is to consider it as a kind of high-level homeostatic mechanism. Recall that homeostasis refers to the maintenance of constant internal conditions. Many animal behaviors are responses to stimuli—both internal and external—that affect an individual's well-being. For example, temperature receptors cause a lizard to move to a sunnier spot if it is too cold, or to a shadier spot if it becomes too warm. The lizard's body has an ideal temperature, and when its actual temperature differs from its ideal temperature, the lizard behaves in a way that returns its body to its ideal temperature.

Kinesis and taxis are two simple types of movement-related behaviors that illustrate behavior's adaptive nature. Both behaviors cause an animal to go from a less desirable location to a more desirable location. **Kinesis** is an increase in random movement that lasts until a favorable environment is reached. For example, when a pill bug begins to dry out, its activity increases until it happens upon a moist area, after which its activity decreases again. **Taxis** is a movement in a specific direction, either toward or away from a stimulus. For example, *Euglena* are light-sensitive and will move toward a light source.

**VISUAL VOCAB**

**Kinesis** is an increase in random movement.

Like a taxi that takes you directly from one location to another, **taxis** is a movement in a particular direction induced by a stimulus.

Like any trait, the way an animal behaves can vary from individual to individual. A zebra that waits too long to run may wind up being a lion's dinner, as shown in **FIGURE 1.2.** A male mockingbird with a weak repertoire of songs may not attract a mate. Animals with more successful behaviors tend to have more offspring. If the behaviors are heritable, their offspring will likely behave in similar ways. Just like any of an animal's characteristics, behaviors can evolve by natural selection.

**Analyze** How is taxis or kinesis an example of the adaptive nature of behavior?

(tr) ©S. Purdy Matthews/Stone/Getty Images; (b) ©Alan Schein Photography/Corbis; (c) ©Guy Jarvis/HMH

**FIGURE 1.3** The extended red dewlap of this male green anole announces to females that it is ready to mate. The dewlap is also used in territorial defense as a "keep out" signal to other males.

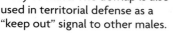
▶ MAIN IDEA

# Internal and external stimuli usually interact to trigger specific behaviors.

Some behaviors can be triggered by a single stimulus, but most behaviors occur in response to a variety of internal and external stimuli. For example, an external signal, such as a change in day length, might cause an animal to secrete specific hormones. These hormones act as internal signals that cause other physiological changes. These changes, in turn, make the animal more likely to respond to another external stimulus, such as the mating display of an individual of the opposite sex. This kind of interaction can be seen in the reproductive behavior of green anoles.

Green anoles are small lizards that live in the woodlands of the southeastern United States. During most of the year, female anoles ignore males. However, their behavior changes each spring, when males begin to aggressively guard territories and court females. Two external stimuli trigger the females' change in behavior. First, females must be exposed to long days and short nights. Females must also see reproductively active males.

To court females, males that are ready to mate bob their bodies up and down while extending their dewlap. The dewlap, shown in **FIGURE 1.3**, is a flap of bright red skin under the lizard's chin. Seeing the red dewlap during the spring makes females release sex hormones into their bloodstream. Sex hormones are an internal signal that make females reproductively receptive.

Experiments with female anoles have shown that their reproductive behavior depends on the presence of both external and internal signals. Females that do not have sex hormones do not respond to courtship. And hormones are not released unless females are exposed to both external stimuli.

**Connect** **What might be internal and external stimuli that cause you to wake up in the morning?**

▶ MAIN IDEA

# Some behaviors occur in cycles.

Many environmental changes are predictable, especially those that occur on a daily, monthly, or yearly basis. Animals often use cues such as differences in day length to keep track of these changes, triggering adaptive changes in their behavior. For example, in order to be active during the day, your body requires a period of sleep every night. This daily pattern of activity and sleep is an example of a circadian rhythm. A **circadian rhythm** (suhr-KAY-dee-uhn) is the daily cycle of activity that occurs over a 24-hour period of time.

These activity patterns are controlled by an internal mechanism called a **biological clock.** Evidence indicates that an organism's biological clock is run by a combination of melatonin secretions by the pineal gland in the brain and proteins in the body that can detect changes in light.

©Max Feken

## Hibernation

Hibernation is a behavior in which an animal avoids cold winter temperatures by entering into a dormant state. During hibernation, an animal, such as the dormouse shown in **FIGURE 1.4,** has a lower body temperature, reduced heartbeat, and a slowed breathing rate. Hibernating animals prepare for the winter by eating large amounts of food and storing it as fat. This layer of fat not only provides a food source for the animal but also provides additional insulation from the cold.

External factors such as light intensity and temperature determine when an animal enters and leaves hibernation. Shorter days and cooler temperatures cause animals to enter hibernation in the fall. In the spring, increasing day length and warmer temperatures cause the secretion of hormones that awaken the animal out of its dormant state.

**FIGURE 1.4** During hibernation, the dormouse's blood temperature drops from 36°C (97°F) to just above 0°C (32°F).

## Migration

Many kinds of animals migrate, but you are probably most familiar with bird migration. If you've ever seen—or heard—a flock of geese flying southward during the fall, you've seen bird migration in action. Migratory Canada geese typically spend the spring and summer in Canada and the northern United States. They spend the winter in the southern United States and northern portions of Mexico. Like hibernation, migratory behavior allows animals to avoid harsh conditions in their home range for a part of the year.

Migration is set in motion by a variety of internal and external stimuli. A change in day length during the spring and fall stimulates a change in the portion of the bird's brain that controls hunger. This change causes birds to gain weight. An increase in fat storage is needed to fuel the bird's long-distance migration.

**Infer** **How might climate change affect animal migration patterns?**

# 17.1 Formative Assessment

SELF-CHECK Online
HMHScience.com
GO ONLINE

### REVIEWING ▶ MAIN IDEAS

1. Why are behavioral responses to **stimuli** considered to be adaptive?

2. What internal and external stimuli might signal to Alaskan caribou that it is time to migrate?

3. What is the connection between a **circadian rhythm** and the **biological clock**?

### CRITICAL THINKING

4. **Relate** What is the relationship between an animal's behavior and homeostasis?

5. **Analyze** Why is it important for animals to respond to external factors?

### CONNECT TO

#### SEXUAL SELECTION

6. A peacock uses its colorful train of feathers to attract a mate. What factors might control how large a peacock's train of feathers may grow to be?

## 17.2 | Instinct and Learning

**KEY CONCEPT** Both genes and environment affect an animal's behavior.

**VOCABULARY**

instinct
innate
releaser
habituation
imprinting
imitation
classical conditioning
operant conditioning

**MAIN IDEAS**

- Innate behaviors are triggered by specific internal and external stimuli.
- Many behaviors have both innate and learned components.
- Learning is adaptive.

### Connect to Your World

Why are some families filled with good athletes? Is athleticism passed on from parent to child? Or are younger generations repeating behaviors they watched while they were growing up? You may have heard this "nature versus nurture" debate about many human behaviors, including musical ability, addiction, and thrill seeking. But research shows that genetic and environmental factors interact in most behaviors. "Nature versus nurture" is a false division. Most behaviors represent a mixture of both nature *and* nurture.

### MAIN IDEA
## Innate behaviors are triggered by specific internal and external stimuli.

Nothing teaches a spider to build a web. It builds it correctly the first time it tries. This kind of complex inborn behavior is called an **instinct.** Instinctive behavior is characterized as being innate and relatively inflexible. An **innate** behavior is performed correctly the first time an animal tries it, even when the animal has never been exposed to the stimulus that triggers the behavior. An inflexible behavior is performed in a similar way each time.

Instinctive behaviors are typically found where mistakes can have severe consequences. Baby mammals that do not suckle die of starvation. Newly hatched sea turtles, such as the one shown in **FIGURE 2.1,** that do not race to the ocean will be eaten by predators. By having set reactions to particular stimuli, animals can automatically respond correctly in a life-or-death situation.

Instinctive behavior is especially important in newborns, who have had no time to learn any behaviors. Performing certain innate behaviors is key to both the animal's survival and its ability to pass its genes on to future generations. Animals that do not perform a necessary innate behavior will likely die.

Many innate behaviors are triggered by a simple signal. The signal is called a **releaser** because it makes the animal run through a behavior. Releasers can be any kind of stimulus: a visual sign, a sound, a scent, or a touch. When a releaser signal has been detected, the animal's nervous system triggers the expression of a specific behavior. Sometimes the triggered behavior is fixed, and the animal runs through a set sequence of movements each time the behavior is performed.

**FIGURE 2.1** After hatching from its egg, a leatherback sea turtle hatchling instinctively makes its way to the ocean, where it will remain until maturity.

©Joel Sartore/National Geographic/Getty Images

Dutch zoologist Niko Tinbergen's experiments with herring gulls showed how simple releasers can be. Hungry herring gull chicks will peck at a red spot at the tip of a parent's bill. The parent usually responds by coughing up a bit of half-digested fish for the chick to eat. Very young chicks do not actually recognize their parent when they beg for food. Instead, the behavior is triggered simply by the sight of a long bill with a red dot near its tip. The chicks will beg from any long object with a red dot, including cardboard cutouts of a herring gull head and the end of a painted stick. Other gull species, such as the lesser black-backed gull shown in **FIGURE 2.2,** also have red-dotted bills.

Biologists think that innate behaviors are hard-wired into an animal's nervous system, but they have studied the details for only a few invertebrate species. Innate behaviors are heritable and are strongly affected by gene expression. But they can also be changed by environmental factors. For example, during its lifetime, a honeybee moves through a sequence of innate behaviors that help to maintain the hive. The behaviors are regulated by different sets of genes. As a bee ages, its brain cells express different genes and its behavior changes. But gene expression is also affected by the hive's social environment. If a hive has few older foragers, some of the younger bees will mature faster. Even the bill-pecking behavior of gulls has been shown to improve with age, as young herring gulls become more accurate in their ability to aim their pecks at the red spot on their parent's bill.

**Apply** **Why is behavior considered to be a mixture of both nature and nurture?**

**FIGURE 2.2** Some gull species, such as this lesser black-backed gull, have a red-dotted bill. The red dot is the releaser that causes the gull chick to beg for food.

## ⏵ MAIN IDEA
# Many behaviors have both innate and learned components.

Animals often change their behavior as they gain real-world experience. In other words, animals learn. Learning takes many forms, ranging from simple changes in an innate behavior to problem-solving in new situations. In each case, learning involves the strengthening of nerve pathways. Most animal behaviors are not simple reactions to stimuli using preset pathways in the animal's brain. Instead, they represent a combination of innate tendencies influenced by learning and experience.

### Habituation
Garden shops sell plastic owls that are supposed to frighten away birds. But a gardener who doesn't move the owls every few days may soon see birds sitting on top of them. This is an example of habituation. **Habituation** occurs when an animal's behavioral response decreases due to a repeated stimulus, even if it has features that trigger innate behaviors. The habit of seeing owls in the exact same place in the garden every day causes the birds to get used to, and basically ignore, the stimulus.

> **CONNECT TO**
>
> **ECOLOGY**
> As you learned in the chapter **Interactions in Ecosystems,** organisms interact with their environment to get what they need to survive. The goal of animals' behaviors is to increase their chances of survival.

## Human Behavior

Have you ever wondered what might explain a particular kind of behavior you observe in people? In this lab, you will observe some aspect of human behavior and form a hypothesis that explains the behavior.

**PROBLEM** What is the behavior of people in certain situations?

**MATERIALS**
- paper
- pencil

**PROCEDURE**

1. Choose a question that you have about human behavior that can be answered by observing people. For instance, you could ask, "Where do people sit in a cafeteria?"

2. Determine which behavior you will observe.

3. Determine how you will quantitatively measure the behavior. For example, you may record how many people are in the cafeteria, where people are sitting, and the number of full, partially full, and empty tables.

4. Make your observations and record your data.

**ANALYZE AND CONCLUDE**

1. **Analyze** Present your results in a table or graph. What can you conclude?

2. **Hypothesize** Form a hypothesis that could explain the behavior pattern you saw.

3. **Extend** Create an experiment to test your hypothesis.

## Imprinting

**Imprinting** is a rapid and irreversible learning process that only occurs during a short time in an animal's life. During this critical period the animal may, for example, learn to identify its parents, its siblings, its offspring, characteristics of its own species, or the place it was born.

Austrian zoologist Konrad Lorenz's studies with graylag geese are among the most famous studies of imprinting. Newly hatched graylag geese normally imprint on their mother during the first two days after hatching. After this period, the goslings will follow their mother and eventually grow up to mate with other graylag geese. Lorenz divided a clutch of goose eggs in half, leaving some with the mother and raising the rest himself. The goslings that stayed with their mother behaved normally. Their siblings, which stayed with Lorenz during their critical period, did not recognize other geese as members of their own species. They followed Lorenz as goslings, and tried to mate with humans when they matured. This experiment showed that imprinting is an innate and automatic process, even though the behavior's stimulus is learned.

When working to reintroduce species into the wild, it is important to avoid having the animals imprint on their human handlers. For example, when working with endangered wattled cranes, scientists try to minimize the birds' contact with humans. When humans need to interact with the cranes, they wear costumes that cover their entire bodies. They use puppets painted to look like adult cranes to feed the young, as shown in **FIGURE 2.3**.

**FIGURE 2.3** To avoid having cranes imprint on their human handlers, biologists use puppets painted to resemble the head of an adult crane to feed young birds raised in captivity.

©Denis Farrell/AP Images

## Optimal Foraging

When animals search for food, they must make decisions about what they should eat. The benefits of foraging are measured in the amount of energy gained. The costs of foraging include the energy used to search for, catch, and eat food; the risk of capture by a predator while foraging; and the loss of time to spend on other activities. The theory of **optimal foraging** states that natural selection should favor behaviors that get animals the most, or optimal amount of, calories for the cost.

The foraging methods of oystercatchers, a type of shorebird shown in **FIGURE 3.3**, have been the subject of many studies. As the birds' name suggests, they eat bivalves such as oysters and mussels. Some birds sneak up on relaxed bivalves and quickly stab out the meat. Others use their chisel-shaped beak to hammer a hole through the shells.

Hammering oystercatchers get a benefit from eating the mollusks, but at the cost of the time and energy it takes to break open their shells. Small mussels are easy to open, but don't contain much meat. Larger mussels are meatier but harder to open. Scientists first hypothesized that oystercatchers would prefer to eat the largest mussels they could find. These mussels contained the most meat for the time the birds spent opening them.

When the biologists observed oystercatchers in the wild, they found that the birds did not eat the largest mussels they could find. Their experiment showed that there was another cost to eating mussels. Their first model assumed that the birds could open any mussel given enough time. However, their experiment showed them that the birds also faced a "handling cost" when they hunted. Birds that picked very large mussels lost time handling bivalves they could not open. They actually got less meat on average than birds that ate smaller mussels. Oystercatchers that learn to hunt medium-sized mussels get the most food for their efforts. Better-fed birds have higher survivorship so they reproduce more and their chicks, in turn, learn this behavior.

**Apply** How does optimal foraging improve an individual's overall fitness?

**FIGURE 3.3** The oystercatcher uses its long, sharp beak to break open the shells of bivalves such as oysters.

**Behavioral Costs and Benefits**

**Sharks Vs. Dolphins**

*©Mike Powles/Oxford Scientific/Getty Images*

# 17.3 Formative Assessment

## REVIEWING ▶ MAIN IDEAS

1. Compare the three categories of behavior costs.

2. Any animal behavior has a cost and a benefit. Explain this statement using **optimal foraging** as an example.

## CRITICAL THINKING

3. **Infer** What might be a stimulus that triggers a songbird's **territorial** behaviors?

4. **Analyze** Some species of cichlid fish hold their fertilized eggs inside their mouths until they hatch. What might be the costs and benefits of this behavior?

## ⋇ CONNECT TO

### SCIENTIFIC PROCESS

5. Some spiders build webs that include visible zigzag lines of silk. But more visible webs catch fewer insects than do less visible webs. Hypothesize what benefits the spider gets by building such a visible web.

# Drones and Wildlife Research

Unmanned aerial vehicles (UAVs)—more familiarly known as drones—are quickly becoming a key piece of equipment for wildlife researchers. UAV technology offers safer, less costly, more efficient, and more precise data collection than traditional research methods. According to a 2003 study published in the *Wildlife Society Bulletin*, between the years 1937 and 2000, light aircraft crashes were the number-one cause of death for wildlife biologists in the field. During this time, 91 biologists and other scientists died while conducting fieldwork. Of these deaths, 60 resulted from plane or helicopter crashes. More significantly, these fatal crashes took place while the aircraft were flying at the low altitudes required to track and observe wildlife accurately.

Drones used by wildlife biologists are equipped with cameras and sensors. Digital photos taken from these drones, typically geotagged with the GPS coordinates of where they were taken, can provide a more accurate and permanent record of observations than those that rely on human eyes alone. Photos taken by the drone cameras can be fed into image-recognition programs to help improve population-count accuracy. UAVs used for wildlife research are relatively economical, typically priced between $1,000 and $2,000, depending on the number of cameras and sensors onboard.

A NOAA drone is used for monitoring environmental conditions and wildlife in a marine sanctuary off the Florida Keys.

Lian Pin Koh, a conservation ecologist, and Serge Wich, a primate biologist, cofounded ConservationDrones.org in 2012. The goal of their nonprofit organization is to "share knowledge of building and using low-cost unmanned aerial vehicles for conservation-related applications with conservation workers and researchers worldwide, especially those in developing countries." Koh and Wich first met in early 2011 to discuss the challenges related to wildlife conservation in Southeast Asia. They came up with the concept of using UAVs for conservation project-related research. However, they quickly determined that commercially available UAVs were far too expensive to be practical for use by conservation groups, particularly those in developing countries. So they decided to design their own low-cost UAV.

In early 2012, Koh and Wich tested their prototype UAV (which cost less than $2,000 to build) in North Sumatra, Indonesia. Over a four-day period, their prototype flew more than 30 missions and collected thousands of aerial images and many hours of video footage of the region's tropical rainforests. Following this successful test run, Koh and Wich cofounded ConservationDrones.org as a way to encourage other wildlife conservationists to build and use UAVs for conservation research.

While observation has long been an important part of wildlife research, a major downside is that watching wildlife up close can change the animals' behavior, and this is particularly true for marine animals. Research on penguins and leopard seals in Antarctica conducted by scientists with the National Oceanic and Atmospheric Administration (NOAA) showed that UAVs are less obtrusive and stressful to marine animals than boats are. The researchers noted that the UAVs were "so quiet in flight that we saw no response from the [seals] or penguins at altitudes of around 100 feet." Another project conducted by the NOAA Southwest Fisheries Center noted that marine animals showed no reaction to UAVs flown as low as 30 feet above sea level.

As UAV technology continues to improve, so too will the potential benefits to wildlife scientists in the field.

## S.T.E.M. Activity

Research how animals interact with UAVs and the possible effects of these instruments on animals. Then consider ways in which drone design could be further improved to be even less obtrusive. Design a drone for wildlife research, or improve an existing design. Present your design to the class.

# Social Behavior

**KEY CONCEPT** **Social behaviors enhance the benefits of living in a group.**

**VOCABULARY**

pheromone
altruism
inclusive fitness
kin selection
eusocial

**MAIN IDEAS**

▷ Living in groups also has benefits and costs.
▷ Social behaviors are interactions between members of the same or different species.
▷ Some behaviors benefit other group members at a cost to the individual performing them.
▷ Eusocial behavior is an example of extreme altruism.

## Connect to Your World

Many factors determine if a species lives alone or in a group. Even closely related species have different living patterns. Such is the case with marmots. Woodchucks (*Marmota monax*), found in the eastern United States, live alone. Yellow-bellied marmots (*Marmota flaviventris*), which live out west, live in colonies.

▷ **MAIN IDEA**

## Living in groups also has benefits and costs.

**CONNECT TO**

**TAKING NOTES**

Use a two-column chart to take notes on the costs and benefits of social behavior.

| costs | benefits |
|-------|----------|
|       |          |
|       |          |
|       |          |

Some species, such as the emperor penguins shown in **FIGURE 4.1,** live together in groups. These groups may have a definite social structure or they may have a constantly changing membership. Social behaviors evolve in species in which the benefits of group living outweigh its costs.

### Benefits of Social Behavior

Living in a social group provides significant benefits to individuals within the group. Living in a group may lead to improved foraging, as an individual can follow other members of the group to good feeding sites. Immature or non-reproductive members of the group can provide assistance to those who do reproduce by helping to gather food for or protecting newborn members. Living in a group increases the chances of reproductive success. Having more eyes and ears in the group helps in detecting predators. Although groups of animals are easier for predators to spot, a predator can usually capture only one member of a group in any attack, letting the others escape.

**FIGURE 4.1** During the breeding season, emperor penguins live in huge colonies made up of between 200 and 50,000 pairs.

### Costs of Social Behavior

Living in a group also comes at some cost to an individual. Living together in large groups leads to increased visibility. A group of animals cannot hide from predators as easily as an individual can. Group living also leads to increased competition. A limited amount of resources, such as food or mates, can lead to conflicts between group members. Animals that live together in groups also have an increased chance of contracting diseases or passing parasites to each other. As group size increases, so does the risk.

**Connect** **What is the benefit of doing group work in class? Are there any drawbacks?**

©BMJ/Shutterstock

**FIGURE 4.2** Male satin bower-birds decorate their bowers with shiny and brightly colored objects (including human-made items) to attract a mate.

**CONNECT TO**

**EVOLUTION**

Recall from **The Evolution of Populations** that sexual selection is a factor that violates Hardy-Weinberg equilibrium. When certain traits improve mating success, alleles for these traits increase in frequency within a population, causing the population to evolve over time.

▶ **MAIN IDEA**

# Social behaviors are interactions between members of the same or different species.

Social behaviors are behaviors animals use when interacting with members of their own or other species. These behaviors help to make interactions such as mate selection easier, and they often involve specialized signals.

## Communication

Animals use communication as a way to keep in contact with one another, raise alarm in the presence of danger, and attract a mate.

**Visual** Gestures or postures, such as the submissive posture of a dog with its tail between its legs, may help to identify an animal's status in the group.

**Sound** Animals often use calls to identify offspring, such as the specific call shared between a young penguin and its parents. Alarm calls and distress calls alert others to the presence of a threat. Mating calls are also used to advertise an animal's readiness to mate, increasing reproductive success.

**Touch** Bees use their antennae, for example, to interpret the waggle dance performed by a scout bee in order to locate a food source outside the hive.

**Chemical** Some animals communicate by using pheromones. **Pheromones** are chemicals released by an animal that affect the behavior of other individuals of the same species. Often, these chemicals announce an animal's readiness to mate. Odors are also used to identify group members and mark territory.

## Mate Selection

Courtship displays are behaviors most often used by male members of a species to attract females. Scientists theorize that females use courtship displays to judge the condition of their potential mate or the quality of his genes. By being choosy about a mate, a female can help ensure that her off-spring have the best chance of survival. While some behaviors may be simple in nature, such as the leg-waving dance display of the jumping spider, other behaviors are more elaborate. For example, as shown in **FIGURE 4.2,** the male satin bowerbird of Australia constructs a nest site, called a bower, that is decorated with brightly colored and shiny objects. Females inspect the bowers when choosing a mate.

## Defense

Defensive behaviors include aggressive actions to protect both the individual and the group. For example, when threatened, an elephant herd will form a protective circle surrounding the younger members of the family group. Another defensive behavior is mobbing by birds. When a predator is spotted, flocks of birds, sometimes of different species, will join together to harass the intruder to force it to leave. Keeping watch is another defense tactic. For example, while foraging, one or more members of a giraffe herd will serve as a lookout for the group. While vigilant individuals forage less, they also benefit themselves and their group by keeping an eye out for predators.

**Infer  How might the size of a group affect its defense?**

©Staffan Widstrand/Nature Picture Library

## ▶ MAIN IDEA

# Some behaviors benefit other group members at a cost to the individual performing them.

Individuals that live in a social group often help one another. They may share food or warmth or warn others about an approaching predator. But remember that animals typically perform behaviors that aid their own fitness. In some cases, however, social behaviors seem to reduce the fitness of the individuals that perform them. How could such behaviors evolve?

## Types of Helpful Social Behavior

Most social interactions between animals improve the survival and reproduction of both individuals. The three kinds of helpful social behavior are cooperation, reciprocity, and altruism.

Cooperation involves behaviors that improve the fitness of both individuals. For example, lionesses hunt in a group and share the prey they catch, even though only one member of the pride may have made the kill.

Reciprocity involves behaviors in which individuals help other group members with the expectation that they will be helped in return. For example, vampire bats form feeding relationships with one another. Bats that have fed will regurgitate blood for other bats that are hungry. The cost to the donor bat is small. But there is a large benefit for the hungry bat, because vampire bats starve if they do not eat every few nights. By giving up some food, the donor ensures that it will be fed when it is hungry.

**Altruism** is a kind of behavior in which an animal reduces its own fitness to help other members of its social group. In other words, the animal appears to sacrifice itself for the good of the group. Consider the behavior of Belding's ground squirrels. A Belding's ground squirrel, shown in **FIGURE 4.3**, is a small rodent that lives in large colonies on open grasslands such as the alpine grasslands surrounding the Sierra Nevada mountains in California. When ground squirrels are active during the late spring and summer, they are hunted by predators from the air and on the ground. When an individual spots a predator, it may give an alarm call to alert the rest of the colony. But alarm calls are costly. A calling ground squirrel is twice as likely to be killed as a ground squirrel that does not call. Calling benefits other colony members because it gives them time to escape, but it is harmful to the caller.

## Evolution of Altruism

How can we explain the evolution of altruism if behavior is supposed to increase fitness? British evolutionary biologist William Hamilton addressed this puzzle by asking how alleles involved in altruistic behavior could spread through a population. He realized that alleles can be transmitted and therefore spread in a population two ways, either directly from an individual to its offspring or indirectly by helping close relatives survive.

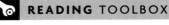

### ▶ READING TOOLBOX

**VOCABULARY**

Reciprocity can be thought of in a "You scratch my back, I'll scratch yours" kind of way. Each animal performing the behavior will eventually benefit when another animal performs it in return.

**FIGURE 4.3** An adult female Belding's ground squirrel gives an alarm call to alert her relatives to the presence of a predator.

©Marie Read

When an animal reproduces, its offspring gets half of its alleles. But its relatives also share some of the same alleles, in the following proportions:

- Parents and siblings share 50 percent of the animal's alleles.
- Nephews and nieces share 25 percent of its alleles.
- First cousins share 12.5 percent of its alleles.

The total number of genes an animal and its relatives contribute to the next generation is called its **inclusive fitness.** It includes both direct fitness from reproduction and indirect fitness from helping kin survive. When natural selection acts on alleles that favor the survival of close relatives, it is called **kin selection.**

If kin selection explains the squirrels' altruism, callers should be closely related to others in the group. Ground squirrel colonies are made up of closely related females and unrelated males. Males do not call much. Nor do adult females foraging alone. The ones that risk their lives are adult females foraging near their daughters, siblings, and nieces. They are warning their relatives.

**Infer** **Why is altruistic behavior not very common?**

 MAIN IDEA

# Eusocial behavior is an example of extreme altruism.

Relationships within populations of some social animals are very specialized. **Eusocial** species live in large groups made up of many individuals, most of whom are members of nonreproductive castes such as workers or soldiers. All of the young in the colony are the offspring of one female, called the queen. Other adults look for food, defend the colony, care for the queen, and raise her offspring. Eusocial behaviors likely evolve by kin selection.

## Social Insects

Many social insects, such as bees, ants, and wasps, are haplodiploid, which means their sex is determined by the number of chromosome sets in an individual. Males are haploid and females are diploid. Female social insects produce daughters through eggs fertilized by sperm. Unfertilized eggs produce sons. In these animals, daughters share half of their mother's alleles but all of their father's alleles. Sisters therefore share up to 75 percent of their alleles overall with one another, compared with 50 percent in humans and most other animals. The very close relationship between sisters in a colony may influence the evolution of eusociality in these insects.

As shown in **FIGURE 4.4,** weaver ants are one example of a eusocial insect species. The three main castes of this species are a queen, major workers, and minor workers. The worker ants work together to weave their nests from leaves that hang from branches throughout one tree or several trees located next to one another. The ants communicate by secreting pheromones. For example, the queen secretes pheromones that induce workers to groom or feed her. If threatened, major worker ants may release pheromones to call in reinforcements to help protect the nest.

# FIGURE 4.4  Social Behavior of Ants

**Ants live together in colonies. Each ant has an important part to play within the colony.**

## COOPERATION

After pulling together two leaves, weaver ants attach one leaf to another by using their mandibles to gently squeeze a larva, which produces a silk that glues the leaf edges to each other.

## ANT CASTES

**Queen**  The queen lays eggs inside the nest.

**Minor worker**  The smaller minor worker spends most of its time within the nest tending the larvae and egg chambers.

**Major worker**  The larger major worker defends the territory surrounding the nest, tends the queen, and forages for food.

**CRITICAL VIEWING**  What genetic benefit does a worker ant receive by taking care of its siblings?

## CONSTRUCTING BAR GRAPHS

An ethogram is a catalogue of the types of behaviors an animal may perform. A time budget shows how much time organisms spend engaged in each type of behavior. Scientists can use these time budgets to compare patterns of behavior between different species, or between different sexes or age groups of the same species.

Table 1 contains data that were recorded through observations of male and female black-shouldered kites, a type of hawk, during the summer.

1. **Graph Data** Construct a time budget that shows the percent of time (per 24-hour period) the hawks spent in each behavior. (**Hint:** Remember to convert the amount of time to a percent before graphing.)

2. **Analyze** What behavior did the hawks spend the most time engaged in? Why do you think this behavior was most common?

| TABLE 1. KITE BEHAVIOR | |
|---|---|
| **Behavior** | **Time (min)** |
| Active perching | 162 |
| Hunting flight | 194 |
| Cruising flight | 4 |
| Other flight | 7 |
| Feeding nestlings | 26 |

Source: Jaksic et al. *The Condor* 89:4.

## Other Eusocial Animals

Eusocial termites, snapping shrimp, and naked mole rats are all normal, diploid animals. But their colonies are still made up of closely related animals. These animals often live in areas where it is difficult for individuals to survive on their own. For example, naked mole rats live in colonies of 70 to 80 individuals dominated by a single queen and a few fertile male "kings." Most of the colony are the queen's siblings or offspring. Nonreproducing adults are either soldiers or workers. Soldiers defend the colony, while workers work together as a chain gang to dig through the soil to find edible tubers. This eusocial behavior may have evolved due to the amount of work needed to find food. If leaving the colony leads to starvation, kin selection may favor staying in the burrow to work together as a group instead.

**Apply** How are eusocial behavior and a species' level of relatedness connected?

# 17.4 Formative Assessment

SELF-CHECK Online
HMHScience.com
GO ONLINE

### REVIEWING ▶ MAIN IDEAS

1. Outline the costs and benefits of living in a group.

2. Use an example to explain what social behavior is.

3. What are the three types of helpful behavior?

4. What characteristic makes a social group **eusocial**?

### CRITICAL THINKING

5. **Connect** Give an example of reciprocal behavior from everyday life.

6. **Analyze** Why might a juvenile scrub jay help its parents raise a new brood of chicks instead of building its own nest?

### CONNECT TO
#### GENETICS

7. How is a haplodiploid species different from a diploid species?

# Animal Cognition

**KEY CONCEPT** Some animals other than humans exhibit behaviors requiring complex cognitive abilities.

**MAIN IDEAS**

- Animal intelligence is difficult to define.
- Some animals can solve problems.
- Cognitive ability may provide an adaptive advantage for living in social groups.

## Connect to Your World

No one would deny that humans are intelligent animals. We surround ourselves with invented objects, from the clothes we wear to the buildings in which we live. But from where did human cognition come? And do other animals share aspects of this ability to think about the world?

### ▶ MAIN IDEA
## Animal intelligence is difficult to define.

In the first half of the 20th century, the focus of many animal intelligence studies was determining whether a certain animal was "intelligent" according to human standards. Today, learning how an animal's level of intelligence compares with a human's is no longer a focus of research. Instead, as shown in **FIGURE 5.1**, scientists study an animal's cognitive abilities. **Cognition** is the mental process of knowing through perception or reasoning. Cognitive behavior also includes awareness and the ability to judge. Animals with a higher level of cognition can solve more complex problems.

In contrast to intelligence, which is difficult to define and measure, cognitive abilities can be more objectively described and measured. However, even an animal's cognitive abilities can be difficult to distinguish from other factors that might be affecting an animal's behavior.

For example, in the early 1900s, a horse in Germany nicknamed Clever Hans seemed to be able to solve math questions by using its hoof to tap out the correct answer. However, upon closer inspection it was found that the horse's ability to tap out the correct answer had nothing to do with mathematical skills. Instead, it was relying on changes in the posture or facial expressions of its trainer. The horse was able to perceive the increased tension in its trainer when it neared the correct answer, and would stop tapping its hoof. This example illustrates how difficult it can be to determine the cognitive abilities of animals. While the horse was unable to solve mathematical problems, it can be argued that its ability to perceive changes in its trainer's posture is an example of cognition on a different level.

**Analyze** Why do scientists focus on an animal's cognitive abilities rather than its "intelligence" when studying animal behavior?

**FIGURE 5.1** While considered to have fewer cognitive abilities than other primates, studies have shown that lemurs have the ability to remember long sequences of images and can place images in the correct order.

©Jim Wallace/Duke University Photography

## ▶ MAIN IDEA

# Some animals can solve problems.

Scientists sometimes study how animals think by giving them problems to solve. If cognition involves the ability to invent new behaviors in new situations, then animals with cognitive abilities should be able to solve problems they have never encountered before. Different species react to new situations with varying amounts of success.

### Problem-Solving Behavior

Researchers have observed extremely complex problem-solving behavior in primates, dolphins, and the corvids—a group of birds that includes crows, ravens, and jays. In one classic study, a chimpanzee was placed in a room containing boxes, sticks, and a banana hung out of reach. At first, the chimp sat around and did nothing. But after a while it suddenly piled up the boxes and climbed up to knock down the fruit with a stick. This ability to solve a problem mentally without repeated trial and error is called **insight.**

### Tool Use

Tools are inanimate objects that help an animal accomplish a task, such as collecting hard-to-reach foods. A number of different animals use tools. For example, Australian bottlenose dolphins use pieces of sponge to cover their snouts when foraging. In addition to protecting their noses from stonefish stings, this method also helps to scare up fish from the ocean floor. Some primates and New Caledonian crows have been observed making tools. Chimpanzees trim sticks to make termite probes. As shown in **FIGURE 5.2**, brown capuchin monkeys use rocks to crack open palm nuts. In one experiment, crows given straight wires bent the wire to make a hook and then used it to fish food out of a tube. Tool use itself is not a sign of cognitive ability. But making tools suggests that an animal can understand cause and effect, and can make predictions about its own behavior.

**Contrast** **What is the difference between insight and associative learning?**

**FIGURE 5.2** Brown capuchin monkeys use a rock to crack open the hard shells of palm nuts.

## ▶ MAIN IDEA

# Cognitive ability may provide an adaptive advantage for living in social groups.

Animals we recognize as the most "intelligent" often have two things in common. They have relatively large brains for their body size, and they live in complex social groups. More neurons may mean more interconnections and greater opportunities for complex behaviors to emerge. But evidence suggests that it is just as important to live in a group with a complex social system.

FIGURE 5.3 Elephants are social animals that form close bonds within their group.

Animals that live in large groups with a definite social structure, such as the elephants shown in **FIGURE 5.3,** are surrounded by politics. Surviving and reproducing depend on remembering and being able to use a vast amount of information to the individual's advantage. These animals must be able to

- identify other individuals in the group
- remember which individuals are their allies and rivals
- keep track of the constantly changing state of affairs among individuals
- use this information to their own advantage

**Cultural behavior** is behavior that is spread through a population by learning, rather than by selection. The key to cultural behavior is that the behavior is taught to one generation by another. The development of cultural behavior does not require living in complex societies. For example, some scientists would argue that the transmission of birdsong is an example of cultural behavior. However, living close together in social groups may help to enhance the transmission and expression of cultural behaviors.

**Connect** **What is an example of cultural behavior from your life?**

©paul hampton/Fotolia

## 17.5 Formative Assessment

**SELF-CHECK** Online
HMHScience.com
**GO ONLINE**

### REVIEWING ▶ MAIN IDEAS

1. Why is animal intelligence difficult to define?

2. Use an example to explain what solving a problem by using **insight** means.

3. Explain how living in a complex social group might select for increased cognitive abilities.

### CRITICAL THINKING

4. **Apply** In Section 2, you learned about the potato-washing behavior of snow monkeys. Is this an example of **cultural behavior**? Explain your reasoning.

5. **Analyze** There are three keys on a table. How might you use insight to determine which key opens a nearby door?

### CONNECT TO

#### SCIENTIFIC PROCESS

6. Why are scientists so interested in studying primate behavior? What might scientists learn about human behavior?

# 17 Summary

Organisms use instinctive behaviors and learned behaviors to quickly adapt to their environment.

## KEY CONCEPTS

### 17.1 Adaptive Value of Behavior

**Behavior lets organisms respond rapidly and adaptively to their environment.** A stimulus is a type of information that has the potential to make an organism change its behavior. An animal's behavior can be considered as a way of maintaining homeostasis. Many animal behaviors are responses to stimuli that affect an individual's well-being. Internal and external stimuli interact to trigger specific behaviors. Some behaviors occur in cycles. Hibernation and migration are two behaviors that are controlled by an animal's biological clock.

### 17.2 Instinct and Learning

**Both genes and environment affect an animal's behavior.** Innate behaviors are inborn instinctive behaviors. Many behaviors have both innate and learned components. Animals that are able to learn can modify their behavior to adapt to new situations. Classical conditioning and operant conditioning are two examples of associative learning.

### 17.3 Evolution of Behavior

**Every behavior has costs and benefits.** Benefits of certain behaviors include increased survivorship and rates of reproduction. Three categories of behavioral costs include energy costs, opportunity costs, and risk costs. Animals perform behaviors for which the benefits outweigh the costs.

### 17.4 Social Behavior

**Social behaviors enhance the benefits of living in a group.** Social behaviors are interactions between members of the same species. Altruistic behaviors benefit other group members at the cost of the individual performing them. Eusocial behaviors are an example of extreme altruism.

### 17.5 Animal Cognition

**Some animals other than humans exhibit behaviors requiring complex cognitive abilities.** Even though animal intelligence is difficult to define, animal behavior scientists are able to study the cognitive abilities of animals. Characteristics of animal cognition include awareness, perception, reasoning, and judgment. Some animals can solve problems through the use of insight. Cultural behavior is behavior that is spread through a population by learning rather than by selection.

---

**🐚 READING TOOLBOX** SYNTHESIZE YOUR NOTES

**Concept Map** Use a concept map like the one below to summarize your notes on cyclical behaviors.

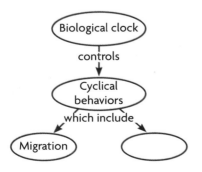

**Process Diagram** Use a process diagram like the one below to summarize your notes on an animal's response to a stimulus.

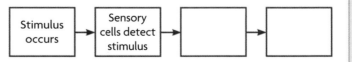

## CHAPTER VOCABULARY

**17.1**
stimulus
kinesis
taxis
circadian rhythm
biological clock

**17.2**
instinct
innate
releaser

habituation
imprinting
imitation
classical conditioning
operant conditioning

**17.3**
survivorship
territoriality
optimal foraging

**17.4**
pheromone
altruism
inclusive fitness
kin selection
eusocial

**17.5**
cognition
insight
cultural behavior

## Reviewing Vocabulary

### Compare and Contrast

Describe one similarity and one difference between the two terms in each of the following pairs.

1. classical conditioning, operant conditioning
2. cultural behavior, imitation
3. territoriality, optimal foraging

### Vocabulary Connections

The vocabulary terms in this chapter are related to each other in various ways. For each group of words below, write a sentence or two to clearly explain how the terms are connected.

4. stimulus, taxis
5. survivorship, territoriality
6. altruism, eusocial
7. instinct, innate

**READING TOOLBOX** GREEK AND LATIN WORD ORIGINS

8. The term *stimulus* comes from a Latin word, *stimulare*, which means "to goad, prod, or urge." Explain how this meaning relates to *stimulus*.

9. The term *habituation* comes from the Latin word *habitus*, which means "condition or habit." Explain how this meaning relates to *habituation*.

10. The term *pheromone* comes from a combination of the Greek words *pherein*, meaning "to carry," and *horme*, meaning "impulse." How do these words relate to the meaning of *pheromone*?

11. The term *altruism* comes from the Latin word *alter*, meaning "other." How is this meaning related to the definition of an altruistic individual?

12. The term *kinesis* comes from the Greek word *kinein*, meaning "to move." Explain this connection.

## Reviewing MAIN IDEAS

13. What is the role of the nervous system in an animal's response to a stimulus?

14. Identify the internal and external factors that are likely to lead to migration in songbirds.

15. What are some of the characteristics of innate behaviors?

16. When does habituation occur?

17. How is the ability to adapt behaviors to new situations important for an animal's survival?

18. Describe the benefits and costs of migratory behavior.

19. The territory of a pack of gray wolves can be more than 3000 square kilometers. The alpha male marks the boundaries of the territory with urine. Explain why this time-consuming behavior is important.

20. Groups of small songbirds will often mob an owl or a hawk. They fly around it and call loudly. What is the cost and benefit of this behavior to the songbirds? Explain your answer.

21. Arctic ground squirrels live in groups and forage for food during daylight. What is the cost of foraging in a group?

22. What information might be provided to potential mates by a courtship display such as the competitive performances of sage grouses?

23. In the meerkat group, one animal always stands guard and sounds an alarm call if a bird of prey is sighted. Why is this an altruistic behavior?

24. What are the characteristics of eusocial behavior?

25. What is the connection between cognitive ability and insight?

# Critical Thinking

**26. Connect** Your alarm clock wakes you up, and you get ready for school. You eat breakfast but then eat one more slice of toast. After stepping outside, you go back in to get a lighter jacket. Identify all the stimuli in this scene and whether they are internal or external.

**27. Apply** A zookeeper needs to use a scale to measure the weight of an otter. How might she use operant conditioning to get the otter onto the scale?

**28. Analyze** Gray wolves live in packs with about 6 to 15 members. Young pups remain behind while the older animals hunt for prey as a group. They often seek out old, sick, and slower prey animals. All of the adults regurgitate food for the pups. Suggest two costs and two benefits of gray wolf feeding behavior.

**29. Infer** The unison call is performed by a pair of whooping cranes. The male and female each have their own notes and perform this call often when they arrive at their nesting area. Suggest some reasons why the birds perform this call.

**30. Apply** You buy a bag of raisins. There are no directions on how to open it. There is no tab to pull. You do not have scissors to cut the bag open. You examine the bag for a few seconds and then pull the seams of the sealed top apart to open it. What type of problem-solving behavior did you demonstrate? Explain your answer.

## Interpreting Visuals

Use the photograph to answer the next three questions.

**31. Infer** Why do you think the baby elephants are traveling between the adults?

**32. Analyze** For which elephants might there be a benefit for this type of behavior and for which elephants might there be a cost?

**33. Evaluate** If there is a benefit, does it outweigh the cost? Explain your answer.

## Analyzing Data Construct a Bar Graph

The graph below shows a time budget for different behaviors exhibited by grizzly bears in a national park in the Yukon Territory, Canada. Use the data to answer the next three questions.

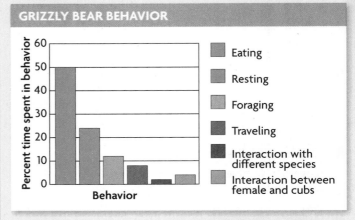

Source: MacHutchon Ursus 12:2001.

**34. Analyze** What behavior did the bears engage in most of the time?

**35. Analyze** Do the bears interact more often with other bears or with other species in this park?

**36. Infer** What can you infer about the habitat based on the data for foraging and eating?

## Making Connections

**37. Write a Fable** You may remember reading Aesop's fables as a child. A fable is a story that ends with a moral, or lesson, such as "the early bird gets the worm." This chapter described reasons for animal behaviors, various types of responses, and the situations in which behaviors might occur. Write a short fable about an animal's behavior, in which the moral of the story illustrates the adaptive value of the behavior.

**38. Analyze** Consider again the chimpanzee shown on the chapter opener. Why might scientists be interested in studying tool use in primates such as chimpanzees?

# Standards-Based Assessment

Record your answers on a separate piece of paper.

## MULTIPLE CHOICE

1 Students plan an experiment to determine whether fish exhibit different feeding behaviors when presented with food flakes of different colors. The students predict that fish will be able to see brightly colored flakes more easily and will therefore eat more of these flakes. This prediction *most closely* resembles a scientific —

A theory

B hypothesis

C conclusion

D law

2 A female ground squirrel may send out a call warning her offspring that a predator is near. Often, the mother sacrifices her own life since the predator can more easily locate her from the call. Even though this behavior results in death, it is beneficial to her in that —

A half of her alleles are preserved in each offspring

B all of her alleles are preserved in each offspring

C the predator may be less likely to attack the population again

D the alleles that caused her behavior will no longer be in the gene pool

3 When a frog hunts, it catches its prey with flicks of its long, sticky tongue. Energy obtained from eating the insect that is not used or stored in the body is —

A passed on to offspring

B recycled within the frog

C lost to the environment as heat

D available to organisms that eat the frog

> **THINK THROUGH THE QUESTION**
>
> Consider the flow of energy through an energy pyramid. In which directions does energy flow?

4

The action illustrated above will *most likely* result in a response produced by the —

A nervous system

B respiratory system

C endocrine system

D immune system

5

**Alleles for Rabbit Fur Color and Nose Color**

| Allele | Trait |
|--------|-------|
| F | Gray Fur |
| f | Brown Fur |
| N | Pink Nose |
| n | Black Nose |

In a hypothetical rabbit species, fur color and nose color are traits that are each controlled by one gene that can occur in a dominant form or a recessive form. Females of the species prefer to mate with gray males with pink noses over brown males with black noses. A gray female (*Ff*) with a black nose (nn) mates with a gray male (*Ff*) with a pink nose (Nn) and produces a litter of eight rabbits. Theoretically, how many of the offspring will have brown fur and black noses?

A 0

B 1

C 2

D 4

# BIOZINE

*at* **HMHSCIENCE.COM**

## INTERNET MAGAZINE

*Go online for the latest biology news and updates on all BioZine articles.*

**Expanding the Textbook**

**News Feeds**

 Science Daily

CNN

BBC

**Careers**

**Bio Bytes**

**Opinion Poll**

**Strange Biology**

As global temperatures rise and arctic ice melts, polar bears are losing important hunting grounds.

## Climate Change— Changing the Planet

*Polar bears are on the move. The area of arctic sea ice on which these carnivores hunt seals has declined 34 percent as worldwide temperatures rise. As this ice is lost, polar bears must swim as far as 100 kilometers (about 60 mi) to find their prey. Some of these polar bears cannot make it, and they drown. Now polar bears must compete with grizzly bears. If climate change is changing the shape of one of Earth's coldest regions, how will it affect the rest of our planet?*

## Q How would you classify this organism?

Pangolins, native to Africa and Asia, are not closely related to any other living mammals. Their backs and tails are covered with large scales similar in arrangement to dinosaur bone plates. Pangolins do not have teeth. Instead, they have an organ similar to a bird's gizzard. Due to these unique traits, pangolins are classified into their own group within class Mammalia.

 **READING TOOLBOX**     **This reading tool can help you learn the material in the following pages.**

### USING LANGUAGE

**Mnemonics** Mnemonic devices are tools that help you remember lists or parts in their proper order. Use the first letter of every word that you want to remember as the first letter of a new word in a memorable sentence. You may be more likely to remember the sentence if the sentence is funny.

### YOUR TURN

Create mnemonic devices that could help you remember all of the parts of the following groups of items.

1. the names of all of your teachers
2. the 12 months of the year

# 18.1 The Linnaean System of Classification

**SC.912.L.15.4**

**KEY CONCEPT** Organisms can be classified based on physical similarities.

SC.912.L.15.4 Describe how and why organisms are hierarchically classified and based on evolutionary relationships.

### VOCABULARY

taxonomy
taxon
binomial nomenclature
genus

### MAIN IDEAS

○ Linnaeus developed the scientific naming system still used today.
○ Linnaeus's classification system has seven levels.
○ The Linnaean classification system has limitations.

☀ *Connect to Your World*

The pangolin shown on the previous page may not look like any other animal that you are familiar with. However, scientists classify pangolins as mammals—the same group of animals that includes dogs, cats, mice, and humans. All female mammals have the ability to produce milk. Unlike pangolins, most mammals have hair. Scientists use key characteristics such as these to classify all living things.

## ▶ MAIN IDEA

# Linnaeus developed the scientific naming system still used today.

### READING TOOLBOX

**TAKING NOTES**
Use a main idea web to take notes about the Linnaean system of classification.

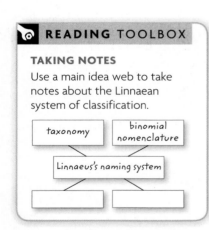

### READING TOOLBOX

**VOCABULARY**
*Taxonomy* comes from the Greek *taxis*, which means "arrangement," and *nomie*, which means "method."

Before Swedish botanist Carolus Linnaeus introduced his scientific naming system, naturalists named newly discovered organisms however they wanted. In fact, they often named organisms after themselves. Because they had no agreed-upon way to name living things, it was difficult for naturalists to talk about their findings with one another. This all changed in the 1750s, when Linnaeus devised a system that standardized the way organisms are classified and named.

### Taxonomy

**Taxonomy** is the science of naming and classifying organisms. Taxonomy gives scientists a standard way to refer to species and organize the diversity of living things. Linnaean taxonomy classifies organisms based on their physical and structural similarities. Organisms are placed into different levels in a hierarchy—a multilevel scale in which each level is "nested" in the next-higher level. In other words, each level is included in a larger, more general level, which in turn is included in an even larger, more general level.

A group of organisms in a classification system is called a **taxon** (plural, *taxa*). The basic taxon in the Linnaean system is the species. In this system, species are most commonly defined as a group of organisms that can breed and produce offspring that can reproduce. Linnaeus's system gives each species a scientific name. With few changes, this method of naming is still used today.

## Scientific Names

**Binomial nomenclature** (by-NOH-mee-uhl NOH-muhn-KLAY-chuhr) is a system that gives each species a two-part scientific name using Latin roots. The first part of the name is the genus. A **genus** (plural, *genera*) includes one or more physically similar species that are thought to be closely related. For example, the genus *Quercus* includes more than 500 species of oak trees. Genus names are always capitalized. They are written in italics or underlined.

### VISUAL VOCAB

**Binomial nomenclature** is a standard naming system that gives each species a two-part name using Latin roots.

| two | name | | naming | system |
|-----|------|--|--------|--------|
| **bi** | **nomial** | | **nomen** | **clature** |

(1) *Genus* (2) *species*

The second part of the name is the species descriptor. It can refer to a trait of the species, the scientist who first described it, or its native location. Like the genus, the species descriptor is written in italics or underlined. However, it is always lowercase. The species descriptor is never written alone because, as **FIGURE 1.1** shows, the same word may be used in different genera. *Quercus alba* is the scientific name for white oak trees (*alba* means "white"), but *Tyto alba* is the scientific name for barn owls.

You may wonder why biologists use scientific names. It may seem easier to use terms such as *white oak* instead of remembering two-part Latin names, as seen in **FIGURE 1.2**. However, scientific names are helpful in many ways. First, genera such as *Quercus* contain hundreds of species. Many of these species have similar common names. Scientific names allow scientists to talk about particular species without confusion. Also, remember that biology is studied all over the world. One species may have several different common names, even within a single country. *Armadillidium vulgare* is the scientific name for pill bugs. However, this species is also called roly-poly, sow bug, and potato bug. Scientific names allow scientists around the world to communicate clearly about living things.

**Contrast** **Describe the difference between a genus and a species.**

**FIGURE 1.1** The white oak (*Quercus alba*) and the barn owl (*Tyto alba*) belong to different genera. The parts of their scientific names signifying species are both *alba*, meaning "white."

### FIGURE 1.2 SCIENTIFIC AND COMMON NAMES

| COMMON NAMES | SCIENTIFIC NAME | |
|--------------|-----------------|--|
| | Genus | species |
| Roly-poly, pill bug, sow bug, potato bug | *Armadillidium* | *vulgare* |
| Dandelion, Irish daisy, lion's tooth | *Taraxacum* | *officinale* |
| House sparrow, English sparrow | *Passer* | *domesticus* |
| Mountain lion, cougar, puma | *Puma* | *concolor* |
| Red maple, scarlet maple, swamp maple | *Acer* | *rubrum* |

(tr) ©Larry Michael/Nature Picture Library; (br) ©Digital Vision/Robert Harding

## MAIN IDEA
# Linnaeus's classification system has seven levels.

**CONNECT TO**

### DOMAINS

The tree of life has been updated since Linnaeus's time. Scientists now classify organisms into an even broader category, called the domain, above the kingdom level. You will learn more about domains and kingdoms in **Section 4.**

The Linnaean system of classification has seven levels, or taxa. From the most general to the most specific, these levels are kingdom, phylum (the term *division* is often used instead of *phylum* for plants and fungi), class, order, family, genus, and species. Each level in Linnaeus's system is nested, or included, in the level above it. A kingdom contains one or more phyla, a phylum contains one or more classes, and so forth. The classification of the gray wolf, *Canis lupus,* is shown in **FIGURE 1.3.** Moving down, the levels represent taxa that become more and more specific, until you reach the species level at the bottom.

## FIGURE 1.3  The Linnaean Classification System

Linnaean taxonomy classifies living things into a hierarchy of groups called taxa. The classification of the gray wolf is illustrated here.

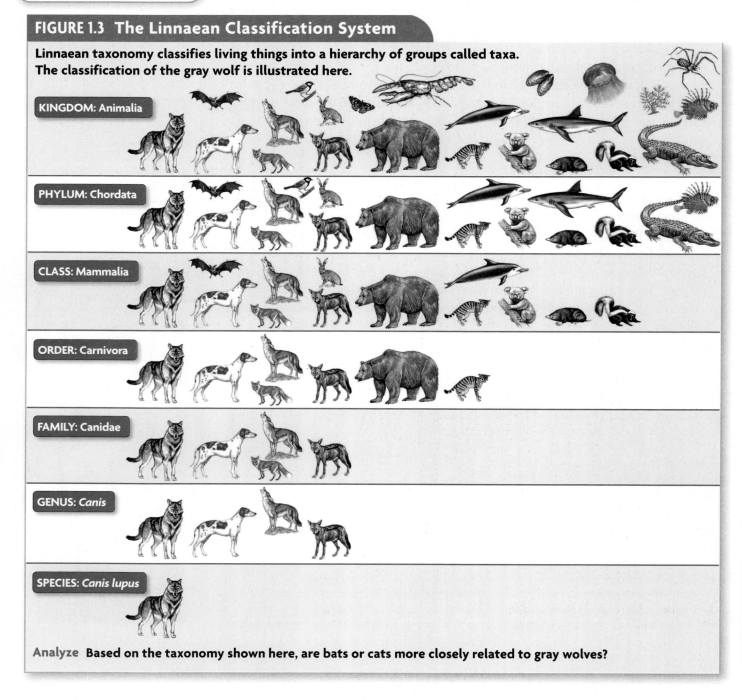

**Analyze**  Based on the taxonomy shown here, are bats or cats more closely related to gray wolves?

The top level represents all of the species in kingdom Animalia. As you move down, the levels show examples of species from phylum Chordata, class Mammalia, order Carnivora, family Canidae, genus *Canis,* and the species *Canis lupis.* Each level is included in all of the more general levels above it.

Notice that gray wolves are in the same genus, *Canis,* as dogs and coyotes. Because the Linnaean system is a nested hierarchy, wolves, dogs, and coyotes also belong to the same family, order, class, phylum, and kingdom. Foxes do not belong to the *Canis* genus, but they do belong to Canidae—the same family as wolves, dogs, and coyotes. Therefore, foxes also belong to the same order, class, phylum, and kingdom as wolves, dogs, and coyotes.

**Apply** **If two species belong to the same order, what other levels in the Linnaean system must they have in common?**

**FIGURE 1.4** This red panda (*Ailurus fulgens*) is more closely related to raccoons than to giant pandas.

MAIN IDEA
# The Linnaean classification system has limitations.

Linnaeus created his classification system before technology allowed us to study organisms at the molecular level. His system focuses on physical similarities alone. Remember that physical similarities between two species are not always a result of close relation between species. Unrelated species can evolve similar traits through convergent evolution. Linnaeus's system does not account for similarities that evolved this way. So today, scientists use genetic research to help classify living things. Genetic similarities between two species are more likely than physical similarities to be due to a common ancestor.

For example, the giant panda and the raccoon have similar ears and snouts. Because of these similarities, they have been placed in the same family in the Linnaean system. However, molecular biologists have found that the giant panda is more closely related to members of the bear family than it is to raccoons. Furthermore, the red panda, shown in **FIGURE 1.4,** is more closely related to the raccoon than to the giant panda.

**Infer** **Why is the common name *red panda* misleading in terms of classification based on relatedness?**

> **CONNECT TO**
> **CLASSIFICATION**
> Refer to **Appendix A** for a complete list of the kingdoms and their phyla.

**SELF-CHECK Online**
HMHScience.com
**GO ONLINE**

## 18.1 Formative Assessment

### REVIEWING ▶ MAIN IDEAS

1. What is **binomial nomenclature**?
2. Name each **taxon** in the Linnaean system of classification, from most general to most specific.
3. What are some limitations of the Linnaean classification system?

### CRITICAL THINKING

4. **Compare** How is a scientific name similar to an address that includes city and state?
5. **Recognize** Why is a standardized taxonomic system important to the scientific community?

> **CONNECT TO**
> **HISTORY OF SCIENCE**
> 6. During his voyages, Darwin collected thousands of organisms, which he classified using the Linnaean classification system. How did this system help him share his findings with other naturalists?

# Cybertaxonomy

Technology affects just about every facet of our lives, including how we do schoolwork, how we entertain ourselves, and how we communicate with friends and family. Even the centuries-old field of taxonomy, the study of biological classification, is being revolutionized by technology and emerging as the new field of cybertaxonomy.

Cybertaxonomy encompasses any way that technology is used to create, access, store, or share taxonomic information. Taxonomy strives to group living things in ways that make sense, so that we can better understand them. Early on, organisms were grouped as either plants or animals. As our understanding of the diversity of Earth's inhabitants has grown, so has the classification system. New species are being named and classified every day, requiring taxonomists to research literature to see if the organism has been previously identified elsewhere, photograph and describe specimens at museum collections around the world, and perform

DNA analyses. Cybertaxonomy makes it possible for this and other information to be updated and communicated at a moment's notice.

Species collection and identification are easier than ever, with remotely operated instruments and interactive dichotomous keys and field guides. Researchers can easily share information in real time with the public. For example, they can show migration routes or geographic ranges of tracked bird, butterfly, and whale species as the tracking occurs. Experts on a particular species can be consulted via Skype™ or another video-based calling service, and high-resolution photos of a new discovery can be shared worldwide within seconds. Data collected from researchers in different fields on a single species—fragmented information that may include physical appearance, fossil findings, molecular analysis, ecological relationships and more—can all be stored in one place, in multiple, clickable layers.

©Jupiterimages/Getty Images

Estimates indicate that millions of species remain to be discovered and named, particularly in remote areas on land and deep in the oceans, and there is a decreasing number of taxonomists to do the work. Loss of habitat and increasing pollution have made identifying and sharing species information more important than ever. By increasing access to updated information about a species' range, population size, and overall health in an area, researchers can better evaluate methods for protecting that species. Cybertaxonomy may ultimately become a vital tool not just in classifying species, but also in protecting them.

# Cybertaxonomy and Butterflies

One species that may benefit from cybertaxonomy is the monarch butterfly (*Danaus plexippus*). Cybertaxonomy is used to help map the monarch's geographic ranges and ecological interactions. Although researchers have been monitoring monarchs for more than 70 years, recent technology is revealing new insights.

There are two North American populations of monarchs. One lives west of the Rocky Mountains, where the monarchs spend their winters along the California coastline near San Diego. A much larger population lives east of the Rockies and overwinters in Mexico. The eastern population migrates between Canada and Mexico, a distance of more than 3,000 miles and the longest migration of any insect. Research on monarchs is especially important now because the monarch population has drastically decreased over the last 20 years, mostly as a result of habitat loss.

Monarchs are monitored and tracked largely through the use of tagging and with the cooperation of citizens who get involved in tagging programs. A participant captures a butterfly, carefully sticks a polypropylene waterproofed tag onto the butterfly wing in a way that does not impede flight, and releases the butterfly. When citizens find a tagged butterfly, they contact the organization that provided the tag.

Participants submit a variety of observations, such as the first monarch they see of the season, the first milkweed shoot (the caterpillars' only food source and where the butterfly lays her eggs), the first monarch eggs found on the back of the milkweed leaf, and the first larva (caterpillar) they find. The submitted information is used in research and becomes data points for interactive migration maps online.

## S.T.E.M. Activity

Research more about how monarch butterflies are tracked and studied. In your research, focus on the following tasks and questions.
- How do researchers track monarchs along their migration?
- How do different generations of monarchs complete different sections of the journey?
- How do you think technology available today has changed how the monarch butterfly is studied?
- Create maps showing the migration routes of the monarchs.
- Find out how you and others can participate in the tracking and monitoring of monarchs. Research Monarch Watch or another tagging organization.

# 18.2

**SC.912.L.15.4**

# Classification Based on Evolutionary Relationships

**KEY CONCEPT** Modern classification is based on evolutionary relationships.

**MAIN IDEAS**

▸ Cladistics is classification based on common ancestry.
▸ Molecular evidence reveals species' relatedness.

**VOCABULARY**

phylogeny
cladistics
cladogram
derived character

**SC.912.L.15.4** Describe how and why organisms are hierarchically classified and based on evolutionary relationships.

## ☀ *Connect to Your World*

If you've ever observed bats in a zoo or in the night sky, you've likely noticed that they have several features in common with birds, such as wings. However, bats are actually more closely related to rodents and primates than they are to birds. Today, scientists agree that species should be classified based on evolutionary relationships rather than just physical similarities.

## ▸ MAIN IDEA

# Cladistics is classification based on common ancestry.

Similar traits between species are often the result of sharing a common ancestor, such as the ancestor shared by dogs and wolves. However, scientists now know that similar traits, such as the wings of bats and birds, can also evolve in species that are adapting to similar environmental conditions. As you have learned, this process is called convergent evolution.

To classify species according to how they are related, scientists must look at more than just physical traits. Modern classification is based on identifying evolutionary relationships using evidence from living species, the fossil record, and molecular data. The evolutionary history for a group of species is called a **phylogeny** (fy-LAHJ-uh-nee).

Phylogenies can be shown as branching tree diagrams. In a way, these diagrams are like family trees. The branches of a family tree show how family members are related to each other. The branches of an evolutionary tree show how different groups of species are related to each other.

**FIGURE 2.1** The glyptodon (*Glyptotherium arizonae*), illustrated here, was the size of a small car and lived more than 10,000 years ago. It is the common ancestor to about 20 modern armadillo species, including the nine-banded armadillo (*Dasypus novemcinctus*).

Glyptodon

Armadillo

(bl) ©The Natural History Museum; (br) ©Pontier, John/Animals Animals - Earth Scenes

## Cladistics

The most common method used to make evolutionary trees is called cladistics. **Cladistics** (kluh-DIHS-tihks) is classification based on common ancestry. The goal of cladistics is to place species in the order in which they descended from a common ancestor. A **cladogram** is a diagram based on patterns of shared, derived traits that shows the evolutionary relationships between groups of organisms.

At the root of the words *cladistics* and *cladogram* is the word *clade*. A clade is a group of species that shares a common ancestor. For example, the glyptodon in **FIGURE 2.1** is the common ancestor of about 20 modern species of armadillos. Together, the glyptodon and all of its descendants form a clade.

Through the course of evolution, certain traits change in some species of a clade but stay the same in other species. Therefore, each species in a clade has some traits from its ancestors that have not changed, such as the similar shells of glyptodons and modern armadillos. Organisms that do not share a common trait with the rest of the group are branched off into their own clade.

The traits that can be used to figure out evolutionary relationships among a group of species are those that are shared by some species but are not present in others. These traits are called **derived characters.** As you will soon see, cladograms are made by figuring out which derived characters are shared by which species. The more closely related species are, the more derived characters they will share. A group of species that shares no derived characters with the other groups being studied is called an outgroup.

**READING TOOLBOX**

**VOCABULARY**
The word *derived* comes from the Latin *de-*, meaning "from," and *rivus*, meaning "stream." Therefore, *derived* refers to something that has "flowed" from a source. The term *derived characters* refers to characters that have evolved in a species since sharing a common ancestor.

---

**QUICKLAB**    CLASSIFYING

### Construct a Cladogram

You can think of a cladogram as an evolutionary family tree in which things that are more closely related share more characteristics. As an analogy, processes that have evolved due to new technologies can be organized using cladistics. In this lab, you will fill in a cladogram for methods of transportation.

**PROBLEM** How can methods of transportation be organized using a cladogram?

**PROCEDURE**
1. Copy the cladogram axes on the right into your notebook.
2. Think about the characteristics of the following methods of transportation: bicycle, car, motorcycle, airplane, and on foot.
3. Complete your cladogram by filling in each method of transportation listed in step 2 on the appropriate line at the top.

**ANALYZE AND CONCLUDE**
1. **Identify** What "derived characters" are used in this cladogram?
2. **Analyze** Which mode of transportation may be considered an "outgroup"—a group that has none of the characteristics labeled on the cladogram?
3. **Connect** A species that has evolved a new trait is not better than a species without that trait. Each species is just adapted to a certain way of life. When might riding a bike have an advantage over flying in an airplane?

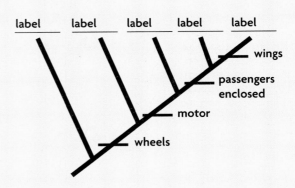

## Interpreting a Cladogram

The main features of a cladogram are shown in **FIGURE 2.2**. Tetrapods are vertebrates that have four limbs—amphibians, reptiles, birds, and mammals. Some tetrapods, such as snakes and marine mammals, no longer have the four limbs that their known ancestors had. However, they are still members of the tetrapoda clade because they share a common ancestor.

**Derived characters** In a cladogram, groups of species are placed in order by the derived characters that have added up in their lineage over time. This order is hypothesized to be the order in which they descended from their common ancestor. Derived characters are shown as hash marks between the branches of the cladogram. All species above a hash mark share the derived character it represents.

**Nodes** Each place where a branch splits is called a node. There are five nodes on the tetrapod cladogram. The first node is where the amphibian branch splits off from the rest of the cladogram. Nodes represent the most recent common ancestor shared by a clade. Therefore, the first node of the tetrapod cladogram represents a common ancestor for the whole tetrapod clade.

**Identifying clades** You can identify clades by using the "snip rule." Whenever you "snip" a branch under a node, a clade falls off. In this cladogram, if you were to "snip" below the node where turtles and tortoises branch off, you would be left with the reptilia clade. This clade includes turtles and tortoises, lizards and snakes, crocodiles and alligators, and birds. As you can see, each clade is nested within the clade that forms just before it. There are five clades in the tetrapod cladogram. Crocodiles, alligators, and birds belong to all five clades.

① All of the organisms in this cladogram belong to the tetrapoda clade (brown). They all share the derived character of four limbs.

② An embryo protected by a fluid-filled sac is a derived character for all organisms in the amniota clade (blue). Because amphibians do not produce an amniotic sac, the amphibian branch splits off from the rest of the branches before the mark that represents this trait.

③ Organisms in the reptilia clade (yellow) have a common ancestor that had four limbs, produced protected eggs, and had a skull with openings behind the eyes. The third node in the cladogram represents this common ancestor. Because mammal skulls do not have these openings, they are not part of the reptilia clade.

④ Organisms in the diapsida clade (green) have openings in the side of the skull. The skulls of turtles and tortoises do not have these openings, so they are not part of the diapsida clade.

⑤ Lizards and snakes branch off of the cladogram next. Their skulls do not have certain openings in the jaw that are found in crocodiles, alligators, and birds. This is the derived character shared by all organisms in the archosauria clade (pink). Feathers and toothless beaks separate crocodiles and alligators from birds within the archosauria clade.

**Contrast** **What is the difference between a clade and a taxon?**

# FIGURE 2.2 Cladogram for Tetrapods

A cladogram presents hypothesized evolutionary relationships among a group of species based on common ancestry and derived characters.

**CLADE**

A clade is a group of organisms that share certain traits derived from a common ancestor. In this cladogram, a clade looks like the letter V, including all the branches that extend from the right end of the V. The diapsida clade includes lizards and snakes, crocodiles and alligators, and birds.

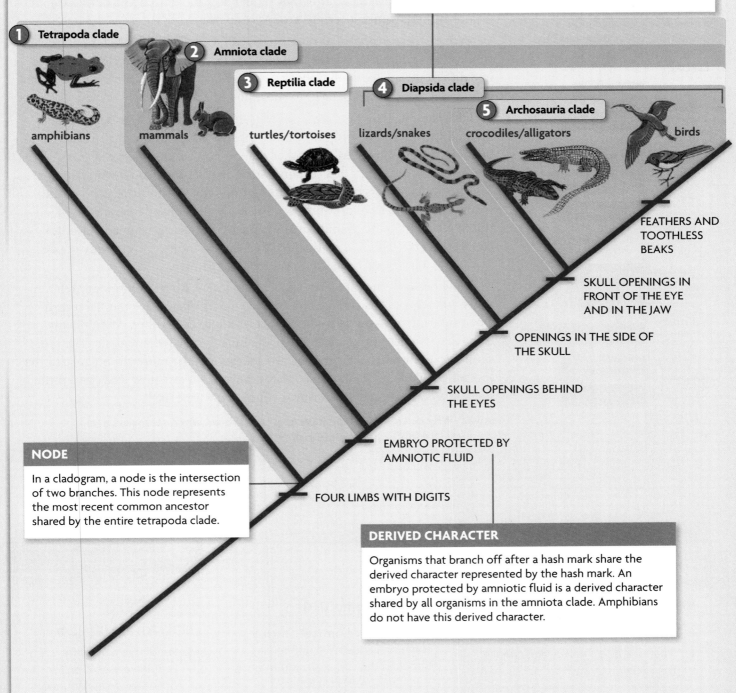

**1** Tetrapoda clade

**2** Amniota clade

**3** Reptilia clade

**4** Diapsida clade

**5** Archosauria clade

amphibians

mammals

turtles/tortoises

lizards/snakes

crocodiles/alligators

birds

FEATHERS AND TOOTHLESS BEAKS

SKULL OPENINGS IN FRONT OF THE EYE AND IN THE JAW

OPENINGS IN THE SIDE OF THE SKULL

SKULL OPENINGS BEHIND THE EYES

EMBRYO PROTECTED BY AMNIOTIC FLUID

FOUR LIMBS WITH DIGITS

**NODE**

In a cladogram, a node is the intersection of two branches. This node represents the most recent common ancestor shared by the entire tetrapoda clade.

**DERIVED CHARACTER**

Organisms that branch off after a hash mark share the derived character represented by the hash mark. An embryo protected by amniotic fluid is a derived character shared by all organisms in the amniota clade. Amphibians do not have this derived character.

CRITICAL VIEWING  Which groups of animals belong to the amniota clade? Which belong to the archosauria clade?

## ▶ MAIN IDEA
# Molecular evidence reveals species' relatedness.

**FIGURE 2.3** Based on structural similarities, scientists previously classified segmented worms and arthropods as sister taxa. The discovery of a hormone found only in roundworms and arthropods has led scientists to propose a new phylogeny for these taxa.

**BEFORE**

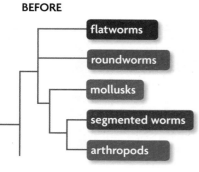

**AFTER**

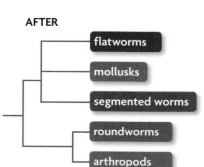

You have learned how physical characteristics, such as protected eggs, can be used to build evolutionary trees. In this example, a protected egg is a derived character shared by all species in the amniota clade. Today, new technology allows biologists to compare groups of species at the molecular level. Molecular evidence, such as a certain DNA sequence, can be used as a derived character if it is shared among certain groups of species.

In many cases, molecular data agree with classification based on physical similarities. In other cases, this type of data leads scientists to classify species in a different way. An evolutionary tree is always a work in progress. With new evidence, trees can be changed to show how species are likely related.

For example, based on physical traits, most biologists considered segmented worms and arthropods (crabs, lobsters, insects, and their relatives) to be more closely related to each other than to any other group of species. However, the discovery of a certain hormone has provided new information. This hormone affects molting, and it is found only in arthropods and roundworms. Biologists have now proposed a new evolutionary tree, shown in **FIGURE 2.3**. In this tree, roundworms and arthropods are grouped closer together. This tree is based on the idea that the hormone evolved only once, in an ancestor shared by arthropods and roundworms.

Proteins and genes are also used to help learn about evolutionary relationships. In fact, DNA is considered by many scientists to have the "last word" when figuring out how related two species are to each other. After all, any traits that can get passed on to offspring must have a genetic basis. The more similar to each other the genes of two species are, the more closely related the species are likely to be. In the next section, you will see how DNA and protein sequences can be used to measure evolutionary time itself.

**Analyze** Why does DNA often have the "last word" when scientists are constructing evolutionary relationships?

---

## 18.2 Formative Assessment

SELF-CHECK Online
HMHScience.com
**GO ONLINE**

### REVIEWING ▶ MAIN IDEAS

1. What is the goal of **cladistics**?
2. What role does molecular evidence play in determining how closely two species are related to each other?

### CRITICAL THINKING

3. **Compare and Contrast** Discuss some similarities and differences between the Linnaean system of classification and cladistics.
4. **Analyze** Describe the relationship between clades and shared **derived characters**.

### ⊹ CONNECT TO

**SCIENTIFIC METHOD**

5. Recall that a hypothesis is a possible explanation for a set of observations. Why are **cladograms** considered to be hypotheses?

# Transforming Data

**Smart** ⊕ **Grapher**
HMHScience.com
**GO ONLINE**
Create animated charts and graphs using Smart Grapher.

Researchers rarely publish raw data alone. Instead, data are usually analyzed in some way. This is because certain types of observations and patterns can be made clearer when data are presented in different ways. For example, data that show change or difference may be best represented as percentage difference.

## Model

Cytochrome C is a protein that functions in cellular respiration. A sequence of 104 amino acids makes up the cytochrome C protein. Scientists have compared this sequence of amino acids in humans with the sequence in a variety of other species. The number of amino acid differences between cytochrome C in humans and in other species has been used to determine relatedness between species.

Look at the data table at the right. Notice that the cytochrome C of chimpanzees most closely resembles that of humans, while the cytochrome C of lampreys, a type of jawless fish, has more differences. To more clearly represent how different they are, these data can be transformed into percentage differences. To calculate the percentage difference of cytochrome C between humans and lampreys, follow this procedure.

1. First, transform the number of amino acid differences into a fraction of the total number of amino acids that make up the cytochrome C protein (104).

$$\frac{20 \text{ differences}}{104 \text{ total amino acids}}$$

2. Next, perform the division.

**20 ÷ 104 = 0.1923**

3. Transform this number into a percentage by multiplying by 100.

**0.1923 × 100 = 19.23% difference**

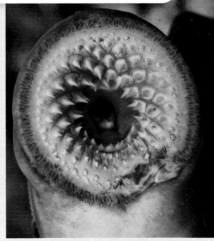

Lampreys such as this one are jawless fish with a round, sucking mouth.

| TABLE 1. AMINO ACID DIFFERENCES COMPARED WITH HUMAN CYTOCHROME C | |
|---|---|
| **Organism** | **Number of Differences** |
| **Chimpanzee** | 0 |
| **Rhesus monkey** | 1 |
| **Whale** | 10 |
| **Turtle** | 15 |
| **Bullfrog** | 18 |
| **Lamprey** | 20 |
| **Tuna** | 21 |

Source: M. Dayhoff, *Atlas of Protein Sequence and Structure*

## Practice  Transform Data

1. **Calculate** Use the procedure outlined above to find percentage differences in cytochrome C between humans and the following animals: tunas, bullfrogs, turtles, whales, rhesus monkeys, and chimpanzees.

2. **Apply** What do the transformed data suggest about how related each type of animal is to humans?

3. **Infer** What percentage of the human cytochrome C protein is the same as that of whales? Hint: 100 percent − percentage difference = percentage similarity.

# 18.3 Molecular Clocks

SC.912.L.15.4

**VOCABULARY**

molecular clock
mitochondrial DNA
ribosomal RNA

**SC.912.L.15.4** Describe how and why organisms are hierarchically classified and based on evolutionary relationships.

**KEY CONCEPT** Molecular clocks provide clues to evolutionary history.

**MAIN IDEAS**

▷ Molecular clocks use mutations to estimate evolutionary time.
▷ Mitochondrial DNA and ribosomal RNA provide two types of molecular clocks.

### Connect to Your World

Have you ever played the game "Telephone?" One person whispers a message to another person, who repeats it to yet another person, and so on. By the time it reaches the final person, the message has changed. In a similar way, DNA changes slightly each time it is passed from generation to generation.

### ▶ MAIN IDEA

## Molecular clocks use mutations to estimate evolutionary time.

In the early 1960s, biochemists Linus Pauling and Emile Zuckerkandl proposed a new way to measure evolutionary time. They compared the amino acid sequences of hemoglobin from a wide range of species. Their findings show that the more distantly related two species are, the more amino acid differences there are in their hemoglobin. Using these data, they were able to calculate a mutation rate for part of the hemoglobin protein.

### Molecular Evolution

**Molecular clocks** are models that use mutation rates to measure evolutionary time. Recall that mutations are nucleotide substitutions in DNA, some of which cause amino acid substitutions in proteins. Pauling and Zuckerkandl found that mutations tend to add up at a constant rate for a group of related species. As shown in **FIGURE 3.1**, the rate of mutations is the "ticking" that powers a molecular clock. The more time that has passed since two species have diverged from a common ancestor, the more mutations that will have built up in each lineage, and the greater the differences between the two species at the molecular level.

### CONNECT TO

**NATURAL SELECTION**

In the chapter **Principles of Evolution,** you learned about the relationship between mutation and natural selection, the force behind evolution.

---

### FIGURE 3.1 MOLECULAR EVOLUTION

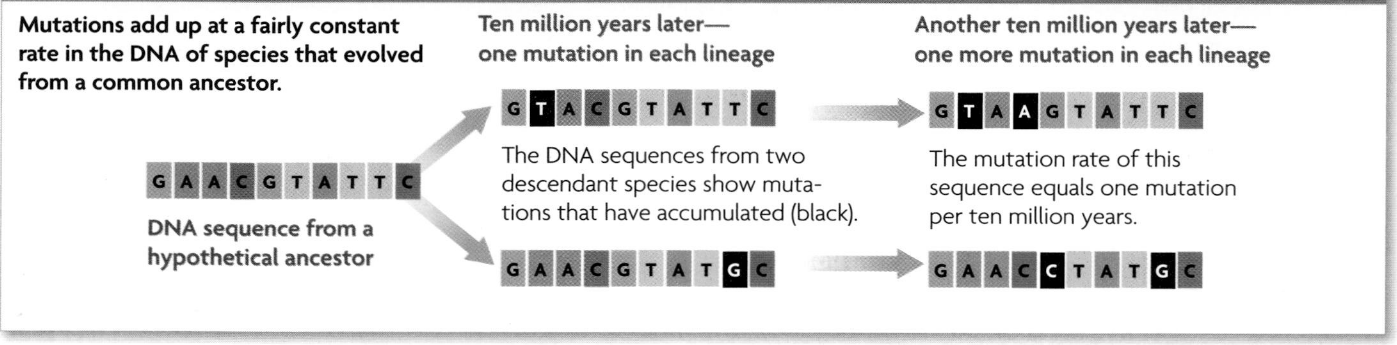

Mutations add up at a fairly constant rate in the DNA of species that evolved from a common ancestor.

G A A C G T A T T C

DNA sequence from a hypothetical ancestor

Ten million years later—
one mutation in each lineage

G T A C G T A T T C

The DNA sequences from two descendant species show mutations that have accumulated (black).

G A A C G T A T G C

Another ten million years later—
one more mutation in each lineage

G T A A G T A T T C

The mutation rate of this sequence equals one mutation per ten million years.

G A A C C T A T G C

**INTERACTIVE** Review
HMHScience.com

**GO ONLINE**

Review Games • Concept Map • Section Self-Checks

## CHAPTER VOCABULARY

**18.1** taxonomy
taxon
binomial nomenclature
genus

**18.2** phylogeny
cladistics
cladogram
derived character

**18.3** molecular clock
mitochondrial DNA
ribosomal RNA

**18.4** Bacteria
Archaea
Eukarya

## Reviewing Vocabulary

**Vocabulary Connections**

For each group of words below, write a sentence or two to explain clearly how the terms are connected. For example, for the terms *taxonomy* and *taxon*, you could write "In Linnaean taxonomy, each level of classification is called a taxon."

1. binomial nomenclature, genus, species
2. Bacteria, Archaea, Eukarya
3. molecular clock, mitochondrial DNA, ribosomal RNA

**Write Your Own Questions**

Think about the relationship between each pair of terms below. Then write a question about the first term that uses the second term as the answer. For the pair *taxonomy*, *taxon*, the question could be "In Linnaean taxonomy, what is each level of classification called?" Answer: taxon

4. phylogeny, cladistics
5. cladogram, derived characters

**READING TOOLBOX** **GREEK AND LATIN WORD ORIGINS**

6. *Klados* is Greek for "branch," and *-gram* is a suffix meaning "something written or drawn." Explain how this meaning relates to *cladogram*.

7. The prefix *archaeo-* comes from the Greek word *arkhaio*, which means "ancient" or "primitive." Explain how this meaning relates to *Archaea*.

## Reviewing MAIN IDEAS

8. The scientific name for humans is *Homo sapiens*. What genus do humans belong to?

9. Why is it important for biologists to include scientific names when reporting their research to other biologists around the world?

10. Name the seven levels of organization in Linnaean taxonomy, from the most general to the most specific.

11. Current technology allows scientists to examine organisms at the molecular level. How has this technology exposed limitations in Linnaean taxonomy?

12. What basic idea does cladistics use to classify groups of organisms?

13. Two species with similar adaptations are found to have key differences at the molecular level. Scientists conclude that these species are not as closely related as previously thought. Why should the molecular evidence outweigh physical similarities that the species share?

14. A particular DNA sequence accumulated three mutations over 10,000 years. After how much time would you expect this sequence to have accumulated six more mutations? Explain.

15. Mutations accumulate more slowly in ribosomal RNA than in mitochondrial DNA. Which of these molecules would provide a better molecular clock for studying the evolution of species from different kingdoms?

16. The original Linnaean system of classification had two kingdoms. Biologists now use six kingdoms. What does this change suggest about the nature of classification?

17. What distinguishes the three domains in the tree of life from one another?

# Critical Thinking

18. **Apply** Are species in the same family more or less closely related than species in the same class? Explain your answer.

19. **Evaluate** Scientists have used mtDNA as a molecular clock to trace human evolution and early migration routes. Explain why mtDNA would be more useful in this research than rRNA.

20. **Apply** Refer to the cladogram in **FIGURE 2.2** of Section 2. Are crocodiles and alligators more closely related to snakes or to birds? Explain your answer using the terms *common ancestor* and *derived characters*.

21. **Compare and Contrast** What types of evidence are used for classifying organisms in the Linnaean classification system? What types of evidence are used for classifying organisms based on evolutionary relationships?

22. **Evaluate** What is the significance of grouping the six kingdoms into three domains? How does the domain model more clearly represent the diversity of prokaryotes than a system with the six kingdoms as its broadest divisions?

## Interpreting Visuals
Use the cladogram, which classifies species A, B, C, and D, to answer the next three questions.

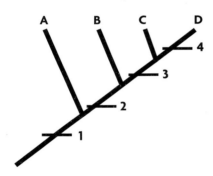

23. **Apply** What represents the derived characters that were used to construct this cladogram?

24. **Analyze** Where are the nodes in this cladogram, and what do they represent?

25. **Analyze** How many clades are represented in this cladogram?

## Analyzing Data  Transform Data
The family Ursidae contains all bear species. The data below show the number of species in each of the five genera of this family. Use these data to answer the next three questions.

| GENERA OF THE FAMILY URSIDAE | |
| --- | --- |
| **Genus Names** | **Number of Species** |
| *Ailuropoda* | 1 |
| *Helarctos* | 1 |
| *Melursus* | 1 |
| *Tremarctos* | 1 |
| *Ursus* | 4 |

Source: University of Michigan Museum of Zoology

26. **Analyze** How many species belong to family *Ursidae*?

27. **Transform Data** Transform the number of species in each genus to a percent of the total number of bear species in family Ursidae.

28. **Analyze** What do the transformed data show that raw data do not show?

## Making Connections

29. **Write a Letter** Imagine that you are a modern-day molecular biologist. Write a letter to Linnaeus explaining how advances in technology have affected the way that scientists classify living organisms. Describe the parts of his classification system that are still used in the same way today. Also describe the aspects of his system that have changed over the years.

30. **Compare and Contrast** The pangolin on the chapter opener shares many physical traits, such as a long snout, with anteaters and aardvarks. However, these traits are known to have evolved separately in each of these groups of species. Write a paragraph that compares how Linnaeus and a modern taxonomist would likely classify pangolins. Include in your paragraph the kinds of additional information that a modern taxonomist might look for in order to classify the pangolin.

# Standards-Based Assessment

Record your answers on a separate piece of paper.

## MULTIPLE CHOICE

**1** Taxonomy can *best* be defined as a —

  **A** standardized means of referring to organisms using a two-part Latin name

  **B** means of grouping organisms based solely upon cell structure

  **C** hierarchal grouping of organisms based upon differences among them

  **D** branching classification system based on the shared characteristics of organisms

**2** In the past 150 years, the classification of life has changed through the addition and restructuring of kingdoms and domains. This system is always changing because —

  **A** genetic research provides more accurate data

  **B** scientific theories never change

  **C** extinctions change evolutionary relationships

  **D** humans increase the rate of speciation

**3** Birds and snakes share a common ancestor from over 250 million years ago, but now they show many physical differences. These differences are most directly the result of —

  **A** coevolution between species

  **B** molecular clocks ticking at different rates

  **C** the long-term accumulation of mutations

  **D** differences in the alleles of the ancestor

**4** Scientists notice very few differences in the DNA sequences of individual cheetahs. This indicates that modern cheetahs likely descended from only a few individuals because —

  **A** smaller populations have less genetic variation

  **B** genetically different individuals are less fit

  **C** the mutation rate depends on population size

  **D** mutations do not affect small populations

**5** Mammals are multicellular organisms with about 3 billion base pairs in their genome. Yeasts are single-celled organisms with about 13 million base pairs in their genome. Both of these groups are classified as eukaryotes because they —

  **A** have over one million base pairs

  **B** can reproduce sexually

  **C** utilize aerobic respiration

  **D** have a similar basic cellular structure

> **THINK THROUGH THE QUESTION**
>
> Do not get confused by extra information provided in this question. Focus on the definition of eukaryotes. The number of base pairs is not relevant to this question.

**6**

| ginger | atgcgccgatccttacgtcgaatcggaac |
|--------|--------------------------------|
| corn | acgcaccgatacttacgtcgattcgggac |
| orchid | acgcgccgatacttacgtcgaatcgggac |
| lily | acgcgccgatacttccgtcgaatctggac |

The DNA sequences above show a conserved, or essentially unchanged, gene among four related plants. The highlighted parts are *most directly* the result of —

  **A** crossing over

  **B** adaptation

  **C** mutation

  **D** meiosis

RANDALL MUNROE
XKCD.COM

# TREE OF LIFE
## All living things as part of the same family

You've learned that organisms can be classified based on physical and genetic characteristics, which reveal their evolutionary relationships. Tree diagrams are used to describe the relationships between organisms, both living and extinct. Here's one that uses easy-to-understand language.

## THE STORY OF LIVING THINGS, FROM THE BEGINNING

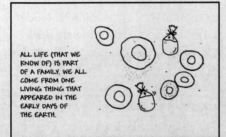

ALL LIFE (THAT WE KNOW OF) IS PART OF A FAMILY. WE ALL COME FROM ONE LIVING THING THAT APPEARED IN THE EARLY DAYS OF THE EARTH.

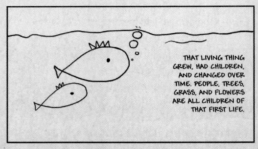

THAT LIVING THING GREW, HAD CHILDREN, AND CHANGED OVER TIME. PEOPLE, TREES, GRASS, AND FLOWERS ARE ALL CHILDREN OF THAT FIRST LIFE.

AS LIVING THINGS MAKE MORE LIVING THINGS, THE INFORMATION THEY PASS TO THEM CHANGES, MAKING THE NEW THINGS A LITTLE DIFFERENT FROM THE OLD.

OVER TIME, THESE SMALL CHANGES CAN LEAD TO VERY DIFFERENT KINDS OF LIVING THINGS GROWING FROM ONE.

FAMILY GET-TOGETHER!

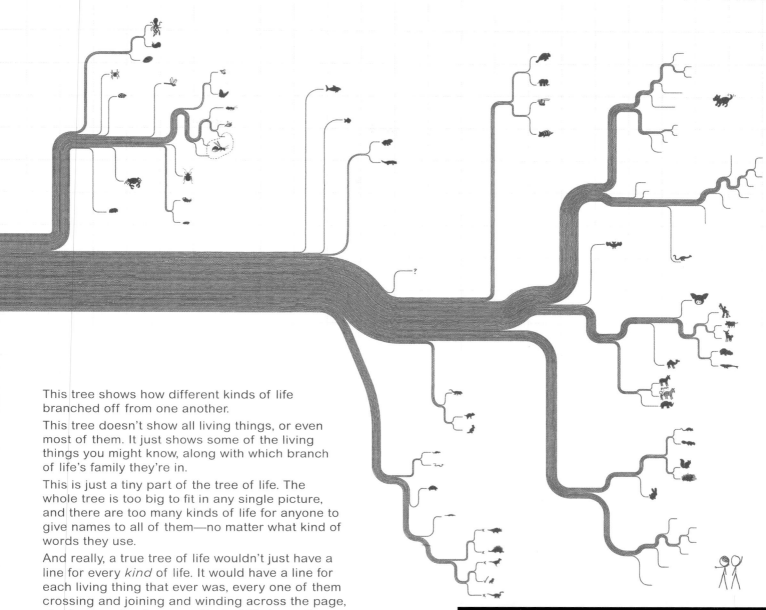

This tree shows how different kinds of life branched off from one another.

This tree doesn't show all living things, or even most of them. It just shows some of the living things you might know, along with which branch of life's family they're in.

This is just a tiny part of the tree of life. The whole tree is too big to fit in any single picture, and there are too many kinds of life for anyone to give names to all of them—no matter what kind of words they use.

And really, a true tree of life wouldn't just have a line for every *kind* of life. It would have a line for each living thing that ever was, every one of them crossing and joining and winding across the page, slowly changing from one kind of life to another, in a path that reaches all the way back, without a single break, to that very first life.

No one really knows how many living things there are in the world, but we can make some guesses, and they're big. Not only can we never find enough words to talk about all those lives, we have a hard time talking about the number itself.

Here's one way to think about how many things have lived on Earth: The world is covered in seas that are ringed with beaches of sand. One day, when you're walking on a beach, pick up some sand and look at it. Imagine that every tiny piece of sand under your feet is a whole world of its own, each one with its own seas and beaches, just like Earth.

The full tree of life has as many living things as there are bits of sand on all those beaches on all those tiny sand worlds put together.

Next to the world we're talking about, all our words are small.

ANIMAL THAT LIVES DEEP IN THE SEA AND HAS BEEN ON EARTH FOR A VERY LONG TIME

# TREE OF LIFE

## WHAT THIS TREE IS GOOD FOR

You can use the tree to tell how much one creature is like another by following their paths. An animal whose path broke off from ours earlier is different from us in more ways than one whose path broke off later, like how an aunt or uncle is different in more ways than a brother or sister.

Sometimes, these families can be a little surprising. Birds and humans are closer to one another than we are to the fish we keep in our houses, which makes sense. But those fish are closer to humans than to the big bitey fish that sometimes eat people, which is strange!

## THE START

This is the start of all known life. Here, pieces that send information from parents to children somehow ended up together in a bag of water, and the bag started making more of itself.

We don't know exactly how that happened; that's one of the biggest questions humans are working on answering.

**???—**
We're still figuring out exactly which things came together here and when.

## TWO GROUPS

Early on, life broke into two big branches. The things in both branches were made of single bags of water and were pretty simple.

The things in these branches look a lot like each other—it took us a while to figure out that they were from such different parts of life's family tree.

## HOW THE THIRD GROUP STARTED

At some point, probably when the Earth was about half as old as it is now, some of those bags ate other bags, and the eaten bags started living inside them.

Those new living things, made from the two groups put together, formed a third group. After a while, the little living things in that group started sticking together to make bigger living things. All living things made from more than one bag of water—like trees, flies, and humans—come from this group.

The other two groups are still around, and in many ways they're much bigger than our group. The creatures in those groups are very small, but there are so many different kinds of them that no one has come close to counting them all. They live everywhere, from seas to the air to inside our bodies and our food. Some of them are even found far below the land's surface, where they live by eating rocks and metal. (Until we found those, we didn't know living things could do that.)

**FIRST GROUP**
(Tiny living things)

**THIRD GROUP**
(Big living things, and some tiny ones, too)

**SECOND GROUP**
(Tiny living things)

## STRANGE GROWING THINGS

These look like tiny trees, but are closer to animals than trees. Some of them are good on food, but some can make you sick.

- PLATE WASHERS
- CLEAR SEA BAGS
- LAND BUILDERS

**GROWING THINGS**
This group is made of growing things like trees and flowers. Most of them are green.

- ANIMALS
- STUFF YOU WON'T FIND ON A ROLLING STONE
- COOL-SHAPED LEAVES
- THINGS WITH FLOWERS

BIG BRAINS WITH LOTS OF ARMS (WRITING WATER ANIMALS)
STOMACHS WITH HOUSES
FLAT STONES THAT BREATHE WATER

BITERS WITH EIGHT LEGS
FAST FLYING STICKS
HOUSE FLIES
DANCING PAPER COLOR FLIES
HILL MAKERS
YELLOW-AND-BLACK FLOWER HELPERS
FLIES WITH POINTY BURNING ENDS
This is a big group of animals from several parts of the tree.

LUCKY RED ANIMALS

ANIMALS WITH CUTTING HANDS

LITTLE ANIMALS
This is a very big group of very small animals.

GRASS JUMPERS

WATER BEARS

HOUSE EATERS
These like to eat the wood under houses, which can make them fall down.

- ROUND FOOD
which shares its name with a round bird
- LIGHT DRINK THAT WAKES YOU UP
- LITTLE ROUND BLUE THINGS
- DARK DRINK THAT WAKES YOU UP
- SOFT RED GARDEN FOOD
- BROWN ROCK FOOD
This food looks like a brown rock, but is white inside.

- TREE THAT STOPS HEAD PAIN
- CRYING TREE
- JUMPS
(flowers used to make beer)
- TIRE TREE
- SWEET THINGS
This group has a lot of the sweet round colorful things we eat.

- TINY TREES
- CLOTHES
- SMALL FOOD THEY SAY BIG GRAY ANIMALS LIKE
- FOOD OFTEN IN CANS
- THE STUFF IN DARK SWEETS
- TREES WITH SWEET BLOOD
- YELLOWS AND YELLOW-REDS

- PRETTY FLOWERS
- FOOD FIXERS
- FOOD THAT MAKES YOU CRY WHEN YOU CUT IT

- BENT YELLOW FOOD
- SWEET POINTY FOOD
- BEACH TREES

*IF YOU GET THIS FOOD WET AND THEN HEAT IT (IN AIR) WHILE STILL IN ITS LEAVES, IT TASTES REALLY GOOD.*

- YELLOW FOOD WRAPPED IN LEAVES
- SWEET STICK GRASS
- WHITE FOOD
- GOLD FOOD GRASS
- FAST-GROWING STICK GRASS
- YARD GRASS

- OLD TREES
- TREES THAT KEEP THEIR POINTY LEAVES IN WINTER
- FLOWERS THAT EAT TREES

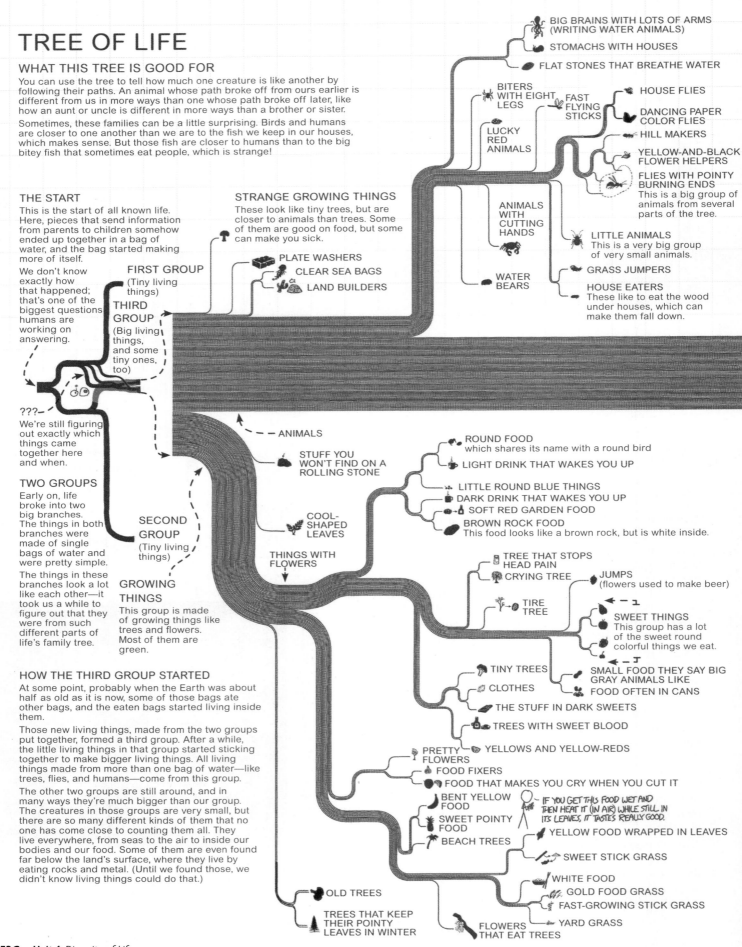

## FIGURE 1.2  Relative Sizes of Cells and Infectious Particles

Although eukaryotic and prokaryotic cells can be microscopic, they are large in comparison to viruses, viroids, and prions.

1 nanometer (nm) = one billionth of a meter

100 nm

eukaryotic cells
10,000–100,000 nm

prokaryotic cells
200–10,000 nm

viruses
50–200 nm

viroids
5–150 nm

prion
2–10 nm

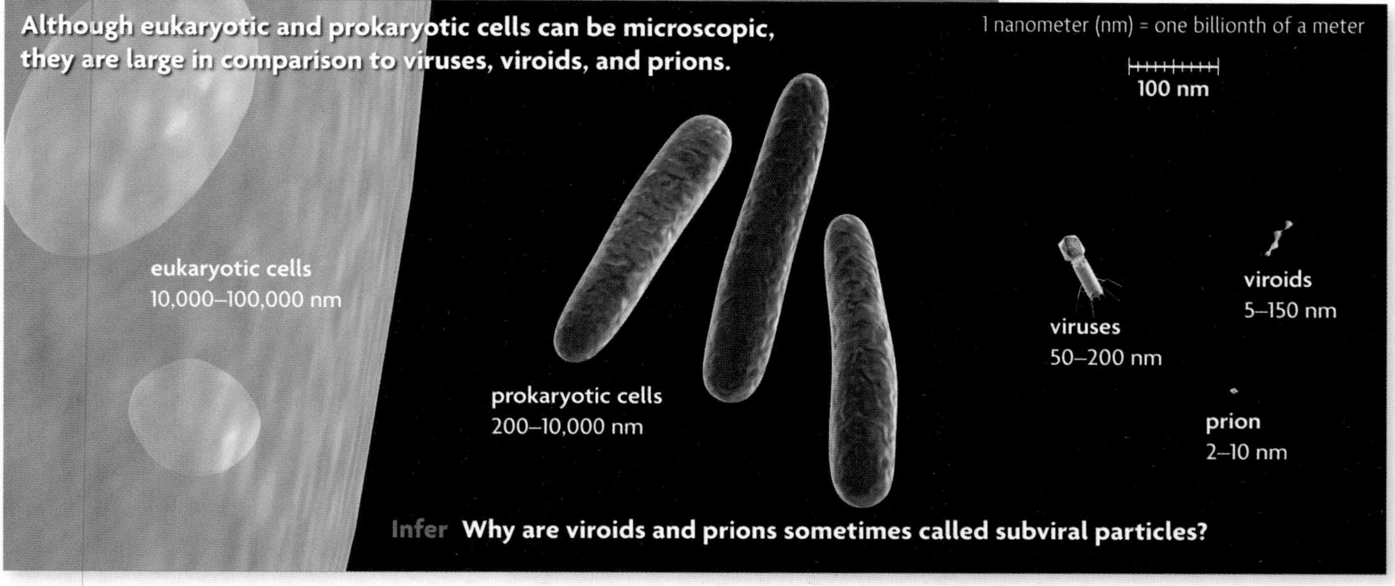

**Infer** Why are viroids and prions sometimes called subviral particles?

At the boundary between living and nonliving, perhaps the strangest entity of all is the prion. A **prion** (PREE-ahn) is an infectious particle made only of proteins that can cause other proteins to fold incorrectly. When proteins misfold, the protein will not work properly. Prions are unusual in that they are infectious yet have no genetic material. They play a part in certain diseases of the brain such as mad cow disease, known to scientists as bovine spongiform encephalopathy, or BSE. Humans may become infected with BSE when they eat meat from animals that are infected. Food safety laws in the United States, however, try to reduce the risk of infection. Creutzfeld-Jakob (KROYTS-fehlt YAH-kawp) disease (CJD), another brain disease that affects humans, is also associated with prions. Prion diseases can incubate for a long time with no effect on their host. However, once symptoms appear, they worsen quickly and are always fatal, because the body has no immune response against a protein.

**Synthesize** Why are viruses, viroids, and prions not included in the Linnaean system of biological classification?

### READING TOOLBOX

**TAKING NOTES**

Use a two-column chart to take notes on viruses, viroids, and prions.

| Main Idea | Detail |
|-----------|--------|
| Virus | |
| Viroid | |
| Prion | |

**SELF-CHECK Online**
HMHScience.com
**GO ONLINE**

# 19.1  Formative Assessment

**REVIEWING ▶ MAIN IDEAS**

1. What are the main differences between living cells and **viruses**?

2. Viruses, **viroids, prions,** and some bacteria can all be considered **pathogens.** What do all pathogens have in common?

**CRITICAL THINKING**

3. **Infer** Prions were not widely known to be infectious agents until the 1980s. Give two reasons why this might be so.

4. **Apply** An RNA-based disease spreads through pollen. Is it likely due to a virus, viroid, or prion? Explain.

**CONNECT TO**

**MEDICINE**

5. To multiply, viruses must take over the functions of the cells they infect. Why does this make it difficult to make effective antiviral drugs?

# Choosing Data Representation

Collecting data on the spread of infectious disease in a population is an important part of monitoring trends and determining a course of treatment. Different methods of displaying data, such as bar graphs or line graphs, often convey different information. Recall from the Data Analysis activity, "Discrete and Continuous Data," the difference between these two data types.

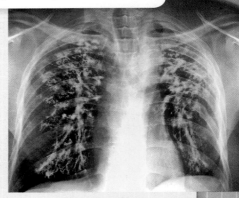

Lungs infected by tuberculosis

| TABLE 1. STATES WITH MOST TB CASES IN 2005 | |
|---|---|
| **State** | **Number of Cases** |
| California | 2900 |
| Texas | 1535 |
| New York | 1294 |
| Florida | 1094 |
| Illinois | 596 |
| Georgia | 510 |
| New Jersey | 485 |
| Virginia | 355 |
| North Carolina | 329 |
| Pennsylvania | 325 |

| TABLE 2. RATE OF TB FOR U.S. RESIDENTS | |
|---|---|
| **Year** | **TB Cases per 100,000 Persons** |
| 1955 | 46.6 |
| 1960 | 30.7 |
| 1965 | 25.2 |
| 1970 | 18.1 |
| 1975 | 15.7 |
| 1980 | 12.2 |
| 1985 | 9.3 |
| 1990 | 10.3 |
| 1995 | 8.7 |
| 2000 | 5.8 |
| 2005 | 4.8 |

Source: Centers for Disease Control and Prevention

## Practice  Choose Data Representation

The tables above show two sets of data describing tuberculosis (TB) infection in the United States.

1. **Connect**  For each of the tables above, identify whether the data are continuous or discrete.

2. **Graph Data**  Determine which type of graph would best represent each set of data and construct the graph for each set.

3. **Analyze**  What trend did your graph show in rates of tuberculosis cases in the United States between the years 1955 and 2005?

4. **Analyze**  Which table gives a more complete picture of TB infection in the United States? Explain.

5. **Predict**  What trend do you expect the rate of TB cases to show in 2010?

## 19.2 Viral Structure and Reproduction

| KEY CONCEPT **Viruses exist in a variety of shapes and sizes.**

**MAIN IDEAS**

- Viruses differ in shape and in ways of entering host cells.
- Viruses cause two types of infections.

**VOCABULARY**

capsid
bacteriophage
lytic infection
lysogenic infection
prophage

### Connect to Your World

Just like the computer viruses that you hear about in the news, viruses that affect living things pass from one host to the next. While computer viruses pass through networks from one computer to another, human viruses pass from person to person. Also like computer viruses, viruses of living things can be simple or complex in structure, and have several different ways to get into their hosts.

### ▶ MAIN IDEA

## Viruses differ in shape and in ways of entering host cells.

The idea that infectious agents cause certain diseases was a fairly new concept in 1892 when Russian scientist Dmitri Ivanovsky made a surprising observation. He was studying tobacco mosaic disease, named for the scar pattern left on affected leaves of tobacco or tomato plants. Mosaic disease, shown in **FIGURE 2.1,** was thought to be caused by a bacterium. But so far no one had been able to prove it. Ivanovsky passed extracts of diseased tobacco leaves through filter pores small enough to strain out bacteria and found that the extracts could still pass on the disease. Was this a new bacterium? Or was it some unknown type of organism?

In 1898, Dutch microbiologist Martinus Beijerinck built upon Ivanovsky's work. He showed that the disease agent passed through agar gel. He proposed that tiny particles within the extracts caused infection, and he called the particles *viruses,* from the Latin for "poison." The observations of Ivanovsky and Beijerinck laid the groundwork for more discoveries. Scientists began finding that many diseases of unknown causes could be explained by viruses.

### The Structure of Viruses

Viruses have an amazingly simple basic structure. A single viral particle, called a *virion,* is made up of genetic material surrounded by a protein shell called a **capsid.** Capsids can have different shapes. In some viruses, the capsid itself is surrounded by a lipid envelope. A lipid envelope is the protective outer coat of a virus, from which spiky structures of proteins and sugars may stick out.

Healthy leaf

Infected leaf

**FIGURE 2.1** These pictures compare a healthy leaf and a leaf infected by tobacco mosaic virus (TMV). TMV was the first virus identified by scientists.

(t) ©Duncan Smith/Photo Researchers, Inc.; (b) ©Norm Thomas/Photo Researchers, Inc.

Some viruses attach to host cells by these spikes. The spikes are such an obvious trait of some viruses that they can be used for identification.

Viruses can only reproduce after they have infected host cells. Viruses are simply packaged sets of genes that move from one host cell to another. Unlike bacteria and other living parasites, a virus has no structures to maintain—no membranes or organelles needing ATP, oxygen, or glucose. All it carries into the cell is what it needs to reproduce—its genes.

The structure and shape of viruses play an important role in how they work. Each type of virus can infect only certain hosts. A virus identifies its host by fitting its surface proteins to receptor molecules on the surface of the host cell, like a key fitting a lock. Some viruses are able to infect several species, while other viruses can infect only a single species. Common viral shapes are shown in **FIGURE 2.2**.

## FIGURE 2.2 Viral Shapes

**The different proteins that make up a viral capsid give viruses a variety of shapes.**

### ENVELOPED

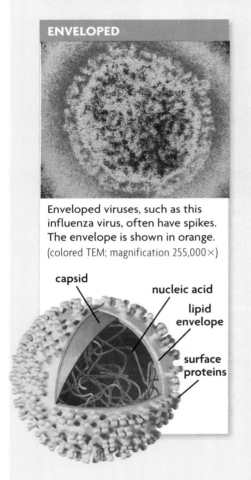

Enveloped viruses, such as this influenza virus, often have spikes. The envelope is shown in orange. (colored TEM; magnification 255,000×)

capsid
nucleic acid
lipid envelope
surface proteins

### HELICAL

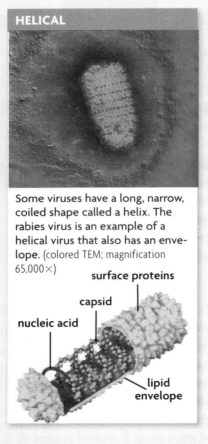

Some viruses have a long, narrow, coiled shape called a helix. The rabies virus is an example of a helical virus that also has an envelope. (colored TEM; magnification 65,000×)

surface proteins
capsid
nucleic acid
lipid envelope

### POLYHEDRAL

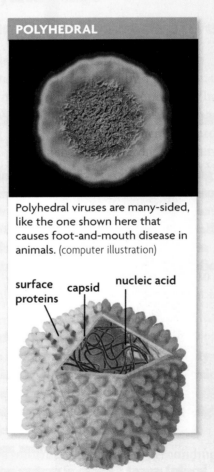

Polyhedral viruses are many-sided, like the one shown here that causes foot-and-mouth disease in animals. (computer illustration)

surface proteins
capsid
nucleic acid

**Compare and Contrast** What are the similarities and differences between the three types of viruses shown above?

In some viruses, capsids form a 20-sided polyhedral. Rod-shaped and strandlike viruses often have capsids shaped in coils, like a spring or helix.

In contrast to prokaryotes and eukaryotes, in which DNA is always the main genetic material, a virus can have either DNA or RNA but never both. The genetic material of viruses can be single-stranded or double-stranded, and linear, circular, or segmented.

### Viruses that Infect Bacteria

One group of viruses is the bacteriophages, often called simply "phages." **Bacteriophages** (bak-TEER-ee-uh-FAYJ-ihz) are viruses that infect bacteria. One example is the T-bacteriophage that infects *Escherichia coli,* the bacteria commonly found in the intestines of mammals. The T-bacteriophage shown in **FIGURE 2.3** has a 20-sided capsid connected to a long protein tail with spiky footlike fibers. The capsid contains the genetic material. The tail and its spikes help attach the virus to the host cell. After attachment, the bacteriophage's tail releases an enzyme that breaks down part of the bacterial cell wall. The tail sheath contracts, and the tail core punches through the cell wall, injecting the phage's DNA. The phage works like a syringe, injecting its genes into the host cell's cytoplasm, where its DNA is found.

### Viruses that Infect Eukaryotes

Viruses that infect eukaryotes differ from bacteriophages in their methods of entering the host cell. For example, these viruses may enter the cells by endocytosis. Recall that endocytosis is an active method of bringing molecules into a cell by forming vesicles, or membrane-bound sacs, around the molecules. If the viruses are enveloped, they can also enter a host cell by fusing with the plasma membrane of the host cell and releasing the capsid into the cell's cytoplasm. HIV is a virus that enters cells in this way. Once inside the cell, eukaryotic viruses target the nucleus of the cell.

**Summarize** **Describe how the structures of a bacteriophage are well-suited for their functions.**

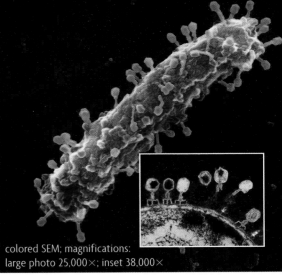

colored SEM; magnifications: large photo 25,000×; inset 38,000×

**FIGURE 2.3** The SEM above shows bacteriophages attacking an *E. coli* bacterium. While injecting their genetic material into the bacterium, the protein coats remain outside the cell (inset). The unique structure of a bacteriophage is shown below.

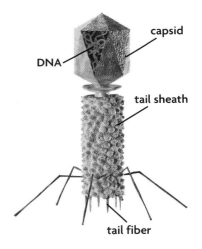

capsid

DNA

tail sheath

tail fiber

### ▶ MAIN IDEA
# Viruses cause two types of infections.

The ways in which viruses enter and leave a cell may vary, but two basic pathways of infection are similar for all viruses. These pathways are shown for the most studied viruses, the bacteriophages, in **FIGURE 2.4.**

Once inside the host cell, phages follow one of two general paths in causing disease. In one path, the phage behaves like a bad houseguest. It takes over the household, eats all of the food in the refrigerator, and then blows up the house when it leaves. The other path of infection is somewhat more subtle. Instead of destroying the house, the phage becomes a permanent houseguest. Neither path is good for the host.

 (t), (inset) ©Eye of Science/Photo Researchers, Inc.

# FIGURE 2.4  General Pathways of Viral Infection

A lytic infection results in the lysis, or breaking apart, of the host cell and release of new viral particles. A lysogenic infection does not destroy the host cell.

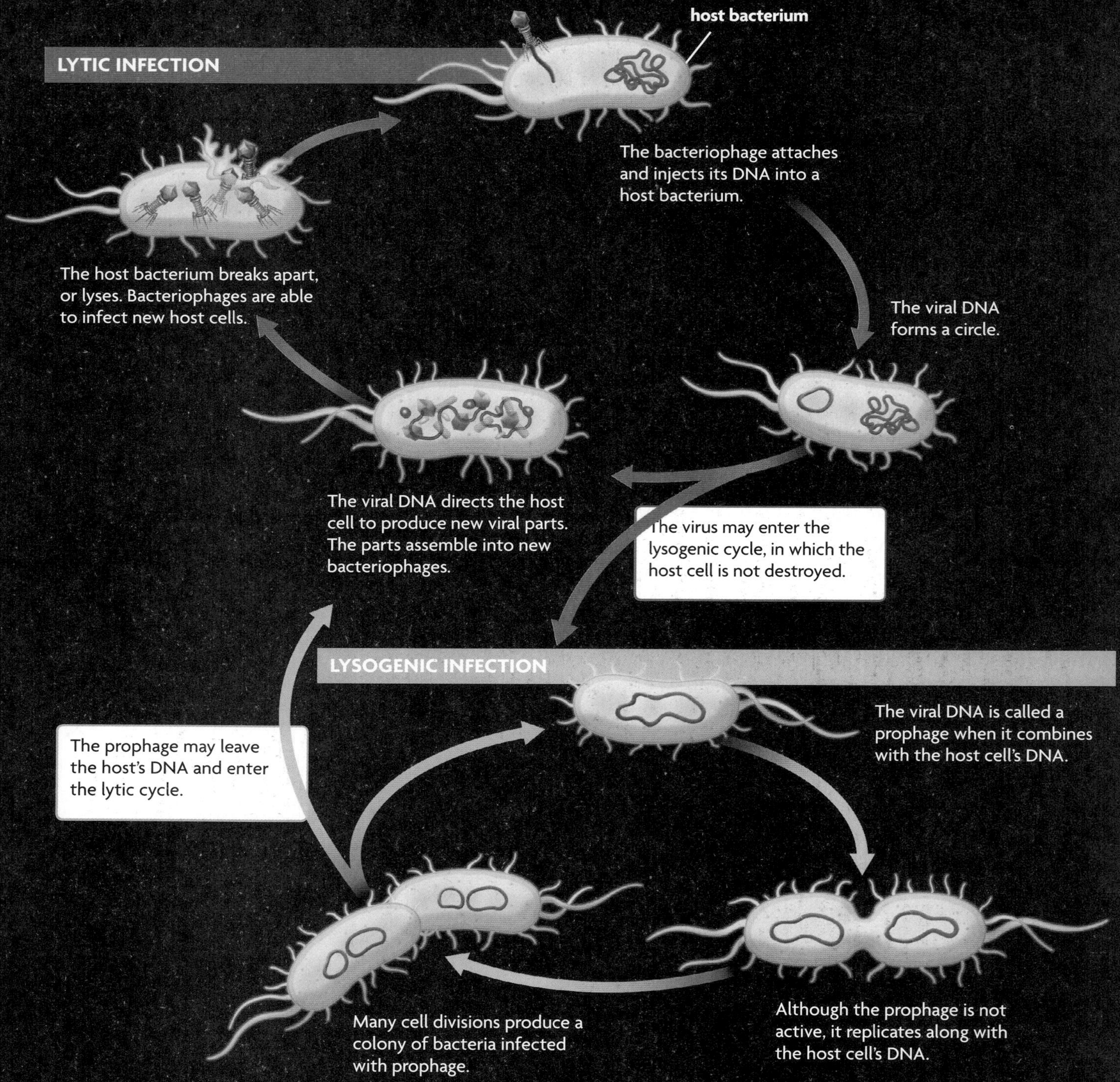

**host bacterium**

**LYTIC INFECTION**

The bacteriophage attaches and injects its DNA into a host bacterium.

The host bacterium breaks apart, or lyses. Bacteriophages are able to infect new host cells.

The viral DNA forms a circle.

The viral DNA directs the host cell to produce new viral parts. The parts assemble into new bacteriophages.

The virus may enter the lysogenic cycle, in which the host cell is not destroyed.

**LYSOGENIC INFECTION**

The viral DNA is called a prophage when it combines with the host cell's DNA.

The prophage may leave the host's DNA and enter the lytic cycle.

Although the prophage is not active, it replicates along with the host cell's DNA.

Many cell divisions produce a colony of bacteria infected with prophage.

CRITICAL VIEWING   Why are no capsids or tail sheaths made during a lysogenic infection?

## Lytic Infection

A **lytic infection** (LIHT-ihk) is an infection pathway in which the host cell bursts, releasing the new viral offspring into the host's system, where each then infects another cell.

- When the viral DNA enters the host cell, it takes over control of the host's own DNA, turning on the genes necessary to copy the viral genes.
- Under direction of the viral genes, the host's DNA undergoes transcription and translation, and produces capsids and enzymes. The enzymes then help in the copying of the virus's DNA.
- Using energy from the host cell, the capsids and viral DNA assemble into new virions. Viral enzymes dissolve the host cell membrane, releasing the new virus particles into the host's bloodstream or tissues—and destroying the host cell in the process.

 **READING TOOLBOX**

**VOCABULARY**

The term *lytic* comes from the Greek word *lutikos*, meaning "able to loosen." The word *lysis* is often used in biology to describe a cell breaking apart.

## Lysogenic Infection

In a **lysogenic infection** (LY-suh-JEHN-ihk), a phage combines its DNA into the host cell's DNA.

- After entering the host cell, the viral DNA combines with the host's DNA, forming a new set of genes called a prophage. A **prophage** is the phage DNA inserted into the host cell's DNA. In organisms other than bacteria, this stage is called a provirus.
- The prophage is copied and passed to daughter cells, with the host's own DNA, when the host cell undergoes mitosis. Although this process doesn't destroy the cell, it can change some of the cell's traits.
- After the cell has been copied, the prophage faces two possible paths. A trigger, such as stress, can activate the prophage, which then uses the cell to produce new viruses. Or the prophage can remain as a permanent gene.

**Connect** Using the analogy of viral infections resembling houseguests, explain which describes a lytic and which describes a lysogenic infection.

 **SELF-CHECK Online**
HMHScience.com
**GO ONLINE**

## 19.2 Formative Assessment

**REVIEWING ▶ MAIN IDEAS**

1. Name and describe the main parts of a typical virus.
2. What are the differences between a **lytic infection** and a **lysogenic infection**? Include the effects of each type of infection on the cells of the host organism in your answer.

**CRITICAL THINKING**

3. **Apply** Researchers studying infection can often grow bacteria more easily than they can grow viruses. What conditions must scientists provide for viruses to multiply?
4. **Classify** A wart is caused by a virus that may lie dormant for years before any symptoms appear. Does this resemble a lytic or lysogenic infection? Explain.

**CONNECT TO**

**EVOLUTION**

5. If the virus is a foreign invader, how is it possible for the proteins of its **capsid** to match the receptors on the host cell's surface? Consider natural selection in your answer.

# 19.3 Viral Diseases

SC.912.L.14.6

SC.912.L.14.6 Explain the significance of genetic factors, environmental factors, and pathogenic agents to health from the perspectives of both individual and public health.

**KEY CONCEPT** **Some viral diseases can be prevented with vaccines.**

## VOCABULARY
epidemic
vaccine
retrovirus

### MAIN IDEAS
○ Viruses cause many infectious diseases.
○ Vaccines are made from weakened pathogens.

### Connect to Your World

Why do we worry about catching a cold or the flu every winter? Cold weather itself does not cause us to get sick, but spending time close to other people can. For most people, winter means spending more time indoors. Cold and flu viruses then easily transfer to hands from doorknobs and other objects. That's why frequently washing your hands can help keep you healthy.

### ○ MAIN IDEA

## Viruses cause many infectious diseases.

As you have read, viruses follow two pathways of infection once they encounter their target cells. But to enter the host's body in the first place, the virus must first pass a major obstacle.

### First Defenses

In vertebrates, the first obstacle a virus must pass is the skin, but in other organisms it might be an outer skeleton or a tough cell wall. Viruses can penetrate the skin only through an opening such as a cut or scrape. Or they can take another route—the mucous membranes and body openings. It's no accident that some of the most common points of entry for infection are the mouth, nose, genital area, eyes, and ears.

Once inside the body, the virus finds its way to its target organ or tissue. However, the targeted cells don't just open the door to this unwanted guest. Body cells have receptors that guard against foreign intruders. These receptors act almost like locks. When the virus arrives at the host cell, it uses its own surface proteins as keys to trick the cell into allowing it to enter.

### Examples of Viral Infections

Viruses can cause symptoms that range from merely bothersome to life-threatening. Below are a few of the many human illnesses caused by viruses.

**The common cold** The most familiar viral disease is the common cold. More than 200 viruses are known to cause this seasonal nuisance. One such cold virus is shown in **FIGURE 3.1**. With so many viruses, it's not easy to find a cure. In fact, cold viruses can mutate as they move from one person to another. Although they're unpleasant to have, colds usually last only about one week.

### CONNECT TO

#### CELLS

Recall from **Cell Structure and Function** that receptors are proteins that detect chemical signals and perform an action in response. In the case of a host-specific infection, these normally helpful receptors provide little protection to the cell.

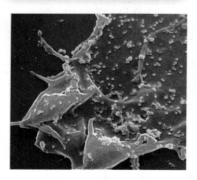

**FIGURE 3.1** Cold virus particles (yellow) on the surface of a cell culture (blue). (colored SEM; magnification 10,000×)

©Dr. Steve Patterson/Photo Researchers, Inc.

**Influenza** Winter usually causes concern about the influenza, or "flu" virus—and with good reason. The flu spreads quickly and can result in frequent local epidemics. An **epidemic** is a rapid outbreak of an infection that affects many people. In the United States, up to 20 percent of the population is infected with the flu each year.

At this time, only three influenza subtypes usually infect humans; other subtypes may infect horses, pigs, whales, and seals. More than fifteen subtypes infect birds, and are all referred to as avian influenza, or bird flu. Sometimes a mutation enables a virus to jump from one species to another, making the spread of infection difficult to control. The high mutation rate of surface proteins on viral capsids makes it necessary for a new influenza vaccine to be made every year. A **vaccine** (vak-SEEN) is a substance that stimulates the body's own immune response against invasion by microbes.

**SARS** Severe acute respiratory syndrome (SARS) is another viral respiratory disease. It has symptoms similar to influenza, such as fever and coughing or difficulty in breathing. SARS first appeared in Asia in late 2002. It spread throughout the world, quickly becoming pandemic. Although it seemed to disappear by the middle of 2003, SARS is still monitored globally.

**HIV** Human immunodeficiency virus, or HIV, is a retrovirus. *Retro-* means "backward," which describes how retroviruses work. Usually, DNA is used to make an RNA copy in a cell, but a **retrovirus** is a virus that contains RNA and uses an enzyme called *reverse transcriptase* to make a DNA copy. Double-stranded DNA then enters the nucleus and combines with the host's genes as a lysogenic infection. The viral DNA can remain dormant for years as a provirus, causing no symptoms to its human host.

When the virus becomes active, it directs the formation of new viral parts. The new viruses leave, either by budding or bursting through cell membranes, and infect new cells. This stage of the disease is a lytic infection that destroys white blood cells of the host's immune system, as shown in **FIGURE 3.3.** The loss of white blood cells ultimately causes AIDS, acquired immune deficiency syndrome. Once a person's immune system is affected, he or she may be unable to fight off even the common microorganisms that humans encounter every day. HIV's unusually high mutation rate has made it a challenge to treat. The combined use of several antiviral drugs—medications that treat viral infection—has proved somewhat effective in slowing the spread of the virus once a person is infected.

**Analyze** **How do retroviruses work differently from other viruses?**

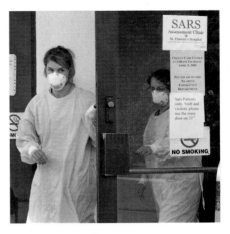

**FIGURE 3.2** Nurses in Canada walk outside an emergency SARS clinic, which was opened to deal with an outbreak.

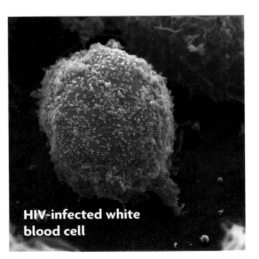

HIV-infected white blood cell

**FIGURE 3.3** This scanning electron micrograph (SEM) shows the HIV virus as purple dots on an infected white blood cell. Destruction of white blood cells weakens the immune system and causes AIDS. (colored SEM; magnification: 3500×)

## FIGURE 3.4 Viral Diseases

| VIRAL INFECTION | SYMPTOMS OF DISEASE | TRANSMISSION OF DISEASE | U.S. VACCINE RECOMMENDATION |
|---|---|---|---|
| Chickenpox | rash, itchy skin, fever, fatigue | contact with rash, droplet inhalation | for children between 12 and 18 months |
| Hepatitis A | yellow skin, fatigue, abdominal pain | contact with contaminated feces | for people traveling to infected locations and protection during outbreaks |
| Mumps | painful swelling in salivary glands, fever | droplet inhalation | for children between 12 and 15 months and again at 4 to 6 years |
| Rabies | anxiety, paralysis, fear of water | bite from infected animal | for veterinarians and biologists in contact with wildlife |
| West Nile | fever, headache, body ache | bite from infected mosquito | no available vaccine |

▶ MAIN IDEA

## Vaccines are made from weakened pathogens.

Chances are good that you have had vaccinations. In the United States, children are vaccinated at an early age against diseases such as measles, mumps, rubella (MMR), and chickenpox. Every year, millions of people are vaccinated against influenza. How does a simple shot provide protection against disease?

A vaccine is made from the same pathogen—disease-causing agent—that it is supposed to protect against. Vaccines consist of weakened versions of the virus, or parts of the virus, that will cause the body to produce a response. The immune system is triggered by the surface proteins of a pathogen. In the host's body, the vaccine works by preparing the host's immune system for a future attack. Vaccines can prevent some bacterial and some viral infections, as shown in **FIGURE 3.4**. Whereas bacterial diseases can also be treated with medicine once they occur, viral diseases are not easily treated. Vaccination is often the only way of controlling the spread of viral disease.

Vaccines cause a mild immune response. If the body is invaded again, it will be able to start an immune defense before the virus can cause damage.

**Apply** Before the chickenpox vaccination was available, children were often purposely exposed to the virus at a young age. What was the reason for doing this?

SELF-CHECK Online
HMHScience.com
GO ONLINE

## 19.3 Formative Assessment

### REVIEWING ▶ MAIN IDEAS

1. Name and describe two infectious viruses and a body's first defense against infection.

2. Briefly describe how a **vaccine** can prevent some viral infections.

### CRITICAL THINKING

3. **Infer** If a vaccine is in short supply, why is it often recommended that older adults and children get vaccinated first?

4. **Apply** Why might getting a flu vaccination sometimes cause you to get a mild case of the flu?

### CONNECT TO

#### HUMAN BIOLOGY

5. People infected with HIV, the virus that causes the disease AIDS, can become unable to fight off infections by organisms that normally do not harm people. Why is this so?

# Bacteria and Archaea

**KEY CONCEPT** **Bacteria and archaea are both single-celled prokaryotes.**

**MAIN IDEAS**

- Prokaryotes are widespread on Earth.
- Bacteria and archaea are structurally similar but have different molecular characteristics.
- Bacteria have various strategies for survival.

### Connect to Your World

Humans not only share the environment with prokaryotes—for many species, we are the environment. Up to 500 types of prokaryotes can live in the human mouth. In fact, you may have as many as 25 different types in your mouth right now. One milliliter of saliva can contain up to 40 million bacterial cells.

### ◉ MAIN IDEA

## Prokaryotes are widespread on Earth.

Prokaryotes, which include bacteria and archaea, are the most widespread and abundant organisms on Earth. Consider that humans are one species with about 7 billion individuals. In contrast, scientists estimate there are more than 1 billion ($10^9$) types of bacteria and more than $10^{30}$ individual prokaryotic cells on, above, and under Earth's surface. Bacteria and archaea are an important part of every community they inhabit. These tiny organisms live in just about every habitat on Earth, including the air we breathe. Prokaryotes have been found living inside rocks, in deserts, and in polar ice caps. One gram of soil may contain as many as 5 billion bacterial cells from up to 10,000 types of bacteria.

Prokaryotes can be grouped based on their need for oxygen. Prokaryotes that cannot live in the presence of oxygen are called obligate anaerobes. An **obligate anaerobe** (AHB-lih-giht AN-uh-ROHB) is actually poisoned by oxygen. As you have learned, archaea are prokaryotes that can live in extreme environments. The archaea that produce methane gas are obligate anaerobes. They live in marshes, at the bottom of lakes, and in the digestive tracts of herbivores such as deer, sheep, and cows, as shown in **FIGURE 4.1**. These microorganisms release nutrients from plants that animals are unable to digest on their own.

In contrast, some prokaryotes need the presence of oxygen in their environment. Organisms that need oxygen in their environment are called **obligate aerobes** (AHB-lih-giht AIR-OHBZ). This group includes several familiar pathogens, such as those that cause the diseases tuberculosis and leprosy. There are also prokaryotes that can survive whether oxygen is present in the environment or not. This type of prokaryote is called a **facultative aerobe** (FAK-uhl-TAY-tihv AIR-OHB).

**Evaluate** **Bacteria are often associated with illness. Why is this a misconception?**

**FIGURE 4.1** A "window" made into a cow's rumen, the first of its four stomachs, allows scientists to study digestion. Anaerobic bacteria live mutualistically within a cow's stomach. The bacteria have shelter and nutrients, and break down plant material for the cow to digest.

# Bacteria and archaea are structurally similar but have different molecular characteristics.

**CONNECT TO**

**CLASSIFICATION**

Recall from the chapter **The Tree of Life** that archaea and bacteria are in separate kingdoms and in separate domains as well. Both their kingdoms and their domains have the same names, Archaea and Bacteria.

**READING** TOOLBOX

**TAKING NOTES**

Create a Venn diagram to compare bacteria and archaea using information from this section.

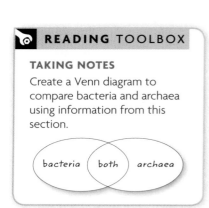

Members of domain Bacteria and domain Archaea comprise all of Earth's prokaryotes. Domain Bacteria is the more diverse and widespread of the two domains, while many archaea are found in Earth's extreme environments. Some archaea are even able to grow at temperatures greater than 100°C (212°F). Bacteria and archaea have many structural similarities but important genetic and biochemical differences.

## Structural Comparisons

Even under the microscope, archaea look very similar to bacteria. For example, both archaea and bacteria are small, single-celled organisms that have cell walls and plasma membranes. Archaea come in many shapes, while the three most common forms of bacteria are shown in **FIGURE 4.2**. Bacteria are often named based upon their shapes. Rod-shaped bacteria are called *bacilli*. Spiral-shaped bacteria are called *spirilla* or *spirochetes*, and spherical bacteria are called *cocci*.

Prokaryotes do not have any membrane-bound organelles, such as a nucleus containing double-stranded DNA. Instead, their DNA is in the form of a circle and is surrounded by cytoplasm. Prokaryotes may also have plasmids. A **plasmid** is a small piece of genetic material that can replicate separately from the prokaryote's main chromosome.

Most prokaryotes can move on their own. Many bacteria and archaea move by gliding or using flagella. A **flagellum** (fluh-JEHL-uhm) is a long, whiplike structure outside of a cell that is used for movement. The flagella of prokaryotes are attached to the plasma membrane and cell wall. They may be at one end of an organism, or they may have different arrangements over the entire cell. Although similar in appearance, the flagella of bacteria and archaea are structurally different from each other. In addition, their flagella are both structurally different from the flagella of eukaryotes.

Many prokaryotes also contain structures called pili that are thinner, shorter, and often more numerous than flagella. Pili help prokaryotes stick to surfaces and to other prokaryotes. A typical prokaryote is shown in **FIGURE 4.3**.

**FIGURE 4.2** The most common shapes of bacteria are rods, spirals, and spheres. Many bacteria are named after these shapes. Some examples are shown at right. (colored SEMs; magnifications: *lactobacilli* magnification unknown; *spirochaeta* 5000×; *enterococci* 7000×)

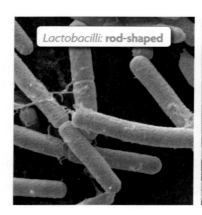

*Lactobacilli:* **rod-shaped**

*Spirochaeta:* **spiral**

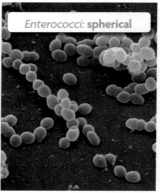

*Enterococci:* **spherical**

**INTERACTIVE Review**
HMHScience.com
**GO ONLINE**
Review Games • Concept Map • Section Self-Checks

## CHAPTER VOCABULARY

**19.1** virus
pathogen
viroid
prion
**19.2** capsid
bacteriophage
lytic infection
lysogenic infection
prophage

**19.3** epidemic
vaccine
retrovirus
**19.4** obligate anaerobe
obligate aerobe
facultative aerobe
plasmid
flagellum

conjugation
endospore
**19.5** bioremediation
**19.6** toxin
antibiotic

## Reviewing Vocabulary

### Category Clues

For each clue, list the appropriate vocabulary term from the chapter.

#### Category: Viral Infection

1. protects against infection
2. plant virus
3. host and viral DNA

#### Category: Bacteria

4. virus of bacteria
5. fights bacterial infection
6. pollution digestion

**READING TOOLBOX** GREEK AND LATIN WORD ORIGINS

7. The term *flagellum* comes from the Latin word *flagrum*, which means "whip." Explain how this meaning relates to flagellum.

8. The term *conjugation* comes from the Latin word *conjugare*, which means "to join together." Using this meaning, explain how it relates to what conjugation is.

9. The term *epidemic* comes from the Greek words *epi-*, which means "upon," and *demos*, which means "people." Explain how these meanings relate to an epidemic.

10. The term *aerobe* means "an organism that requires oxygen to live." The prefixes *a-* or *an-* mean "without, or not." How do these meanings relate to the term *anaerobe*?

## Reviewing MAIN IDEAS

11. Viruses, viroids, and prions are not considered to be living things. Which of their traits resemble living organisms, and which traits do not?

12. The flu virus has an envelope with surface proteins that allow it to infect its host cells. What structures help viruses infect bacterial cells? Explain.

13. Explain the differences between the two ways viruses infect their host cells.

14. Children across the United States get "shots," or injections, during their physical exams. Explain what these shots are and why they are recommended for all children.

15. The success of prokaryotes is due to special characteristics they have, such as the ability to form endospores and perform conjugation. Explain how each of these abilities helps prokaryotes survive changing environments.

16. It surprises most people to learn that their lives depend on bacteria. Describe three roles bacteria play in human health and survival.

17. Due to their unique ability to break down an enormous array of substances, prokaryotes play critical roles in ecosystems. Summarize two of these roles.

18. Doctors recommend washing hands before eating to prevent the spread of disease. What is the connection between bacteria and disease?

19. Prokaryotes have the ability to carry genes other than their own. How is this trait important for genetic engineering?

20. Recently, doctors have been advised to limit the use of antibiotics whenever possible. Why is this recommendation important?

# Critical Thinking

**21. Apply** Many bacteria cause food spoilage because they have dietary needs similar to humans. However, some bacteria consume chemicals such as heavy metals, sulfur, petroleum, and mercury. How are these bacteria being used to help humans?

**22. Compare and Contrast** In a lysogenic infection, viral genes can become a part of the host's cell. In a lytic infection, the host cell is destroyed. What might be the benefit of each type of infection to the virus?

**23. Infer** New viruses may quickly kill their host after infection, but after many generations viruses tend to weaken and cause fewer deaths. Why might it be a disadvantage for a virus to quickly kill its host?

**24. Synthesize** Endospore-forming bacteria include those that cause the diseases tetanus, botulism, and anthrax. Endospores themselves, however, do not cause illness and cannot reproduce. Why, then, are endospores such a concern to the food and healthcare industries?

## Interpreting Visuals

Use the diagram below to answer the next three questions.

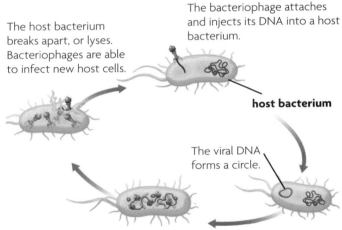

The host bacterium breaks apart, or lyses. Bacteriophages are able to infect new host cells.

The bacteriophage attaches and injects its DNA into a host bacterium.

**host bacterium**

The viral DNA forms a circle.

The viral DNA directs the host cell to produce new viral parts. The parts assemble into new bacteriophages.

**25. Apply** What type of viral infection is shown above? Explain your answer.

**26. Apply** Why is it necessary for the viral genes to enter the host cell?

**27. Analyze** How would the way that the virion enters the host cell change if the virus were a type that infected animals, and the host cell were eukaryotic rather than prokaryotic?

## Analyzing Data  Choose Data Representation

Use the hypothetical data below to answer the next questions.

| TYPE OF BACTERIA AND LENGTH | |
|---|---|
| **Type of bacteria** | **Average length (nm)** |
| Streptococcus | 500 |
| Staphylococcus | 900 |
| Vibrio | 2600 |
| Aquaspirillum | 2800 |

| REPLICATION TIME OF STREPTOCOCCUS | |
|---|---|
| **Time (min)** | **Number of streptococcus cells** |
| 0 | 1 |
| 28 | 2 |
| 56 | 4 |
| 84 | 8 |

**28. Connect** For each of the tables above, identify whether the data are continuous or discrete. Explain.

**29. Calculate** Assuming that nutrients are unlimited, how many *Streptococcus* cells will there be after 112 minutes? Explain.

## Making Connections

**30. Writing a Pamphlet** Scientists agree that a form of the avian flu virus has the potential to cause a worldwide flu epidemic. This type of virus is known to mutate easily and adapt quickly to host changes. Imagine you are a representative from the Centers for Disease Control and are writing a pamphlet to educate citizens about the virus and how it actually causes infection. Using your knowledge of cells and viruses, make a detailed pamphlet that the general public could understand.

**31. Synthesize** The bacteria in the esophagus shown on the chapter opener are one of the many types of symbiotic prokaryotes living within our bodies. How might these types of mutualistic relationships have arisen? Consider natural selection in your answer.

# Standards-Based Assessment

Record your answers on a separate piece of paper.

## MULTIPLE CHOICE

**1**

| The Effects of Antibiotics on Infected Mice | | | |
|---|---|---|---|
| Antibiotic | A | B | C |
| Infected mice tested | 30 | 15 | 15 |
| % Effectiveness | 83% | 25% | 100% |

Scientists are testing three antibiotics—A, B, and C—on 60 mice with bacterial infections. Based on the table above, what is the *most likely* reason why the scientists concluded that they needed to do more testing on antibiotic C?

A They did not test the side effects of antibiotic C.

B Antibiotic C worked better than A and B.

C Antibiotic C had 100% effectiveness.

D The sample size was too small.

**2** Impetigo is a highly contagious skin infection caused by staph or strep bacteria that are normally found on the skin, where they are harmless. This infection is *most likely* to occur when —

A the bacteria gain access to the body through scraped skin

B an uninfected person comes in contact with an infected person

C the infected person did not receive regularly scheduled vaccinations

D the bacteria release endospores on the surface of the skin

**3** Hepatitis B is a viral disease that attacks cells in the liver. When should a person receive a vaccination against hepatitis B?

A before being exposed to the virus

B as soon as viral symptoms begin to appear

C after being diagnosed with the disease

D never; the overuse of vaccines has lead to viral resistance

**4** Some scientists think that measures of an ecosystem's health—such as usable nitrogen levels in the soil—may become more variable as the diversity of organisms on Earth declines. This is because usable soil nitrogen depends on a variety of —

A animals that return nitrogen to the soil through respiration

B animals that return nitrogen to the soil after they die

C bacteria and other decomposers that fix nitrogen into a usable form

D plants, which produce nitrogen as a byproduct of photosynthesis

**5** The main reason that viruses are not considered to be living things is because —

A they are not affected by antibiotics

B they cannot reproduce on their own

C they do not contain a nucleus

D they do not contain any nucleic acids

> **THINK THROUGH THE QUESTION**
>
> All of these answer choices correctly describe viruses, so do not be tricked! Look at each answer choice and try to think of a living organism that fits the characteristic described, making that answer choice wrong.

**6**

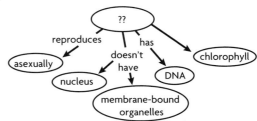

Which of the following can be described by the concept map above?

A an earthworm's muscle cell

B an oak tree's leaf cell

C a bacterium

D a human immunodeficiency virus (HIV)

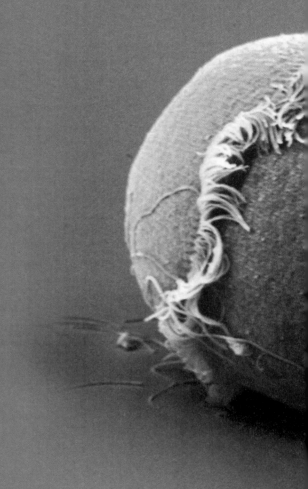

CHAPTER

# 20 Protists and Fungi

**BIG IDEA** Protists and fungi are highly diverse organisms that have both beneficial and detrimental impacts on human health and the environment.

**20.1 Diversity of Protists**

**20.2 Animal-like Protists**

**20.3 Plantlike Protists**

**Data Analysis**
**ANALYZING EXPERIMENTAL DESIGN**

**20.4 Funguslike Protists**

**20.5 Diversity of Fungi**

**20.6 Ecology of Fungi**

---

## ⊘ ONLINE BIOLOGY   HMHScience.com

**ONLINE** Labs
- **QuickLab** Investigating Motion in Protists
- Exploring Mushroom Anatomy
- Quantifying Mold Growth
- Algae in Products
- Investigating Meiosis in *Sordaria fimicola*
- Chemotaxis in *Physarum*

- Exploring Bioluminescence
- **Video Lab** Protistan Response to Light
- **Video Lab** Yeast and Fermentation

(t) ©Eye of Science/Photo Researchers, Inc.

# When these two protists meet, who is the prey?

Although they are both protists, the round *Didinium* hunts live paramecia almost exclusively. Paramecia are much longer than this predator, but that doesn't stop *Didinium*. It captures, paralyzes, and reels in paramecia like fish on a line. It then eats its prey whole, expanding its own body just so that its meal will fit.

colored SEM; magnification 2000×

---

 **READING** TOOLBOX    **This reading tool can help you learn the material in the following pages.**

### USING LANGUAGE

**General Statements**  A general statement summarizes the features of a group or describes an average feature of the members of the group. Some individuals in the group may not share all of the features. So, general statements may be true most of the time, but not always.

### YOUR TURN

Use what you know about general statements to answer the following questions.

1.  Write a general statement that summarizes the features of baseballs, basketballs, tennis balls, soccer balls, and footballs.

2.  Brainstorm exceptions to the general statement "In general, dogs have four legs, fur, and a tail and can bark."

# 20.1 Diversity of Protists

SC.912.L.15.6

**SC.912.L.15.6** Discuss distinguishing characteristics of the domains and kingdoms of living organisms.

**VOCABULARY**

protist

**KEY CONCEPT** Kingdom Protista is the most diverse of all the kingdoms.

**MAIN IDEAS**

○ Protists are difficult to classify.

○ Protists can be informally grouped into three categories.

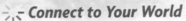

## Connect to Your World

If you looked at a drop of water from a pond, a roadside puddle, or a bird bath, you might find specimens of both *Didinium* and *Paramecium*. Despite their unique appearances, they are single-celled. That is what makes single-celled protists so amazing—they can carry out all life functions within just one cell. As you will see, one cell can be quite complex.

○ **MAIN IDEA**

## Protists are difficult to classify.

Large yellow globs of slime seemed to come out of nowhere. They were spreading across lawns and pulsing up telephone poles. Afraid that this was an alien invasion, residents of a Dallas neighborhood called police and firefighters. The firefighters turned their hoses on the blobs, but water only made the invaders grow.

Scientists came to the rescue. What the people in the Dallas neighborhood were seeing on this sunny day in 1973 wasn't an alien life form, but a slime mold. Specifically, it was *Fuligo septica*, shown in **FIGURE 1.1**, a species commonly called dog-vomit slime mold because of its resemblance to—well, dog vomit.

**FIGURE 1.1** *Fuligo septica*, commonly known as the dog-vomit slime mold, is just one member of the diverse kingdom Protista.

Slime molds usually don't grow large enough to scare a neighborhood, but they are unusual. They are protists. A **protist** is a eukaryote that is not an animal, a plant, or a fungus. In the past, protists were generally grouped together because, although they share some features with animals, plants, and fungi, they also lack one or more traits that these organisms possess. Protists may be single-celled or multicellular, microscopic or very large. Some can make their own food, while others feed on other organisms. Some are parasites. Many protists have structures that allow them to move. All respond to the environment in some way. Some protists reproduce asexually, whereas others reproduce both asexually and sexually. Even among the many species of slime molds, there are significant differences.

 **READING TOOLBOX**

**VOCABULARY**

The word *protist* comes from the Greek word *prōtista*, which means "the very first."

# FIGURE 1.2  Relationships of Protists to Other Eukaryotes

This phylogenetic tree shows one currently proposed system for classifying protists into four superclasses along with the other eukaryotes.

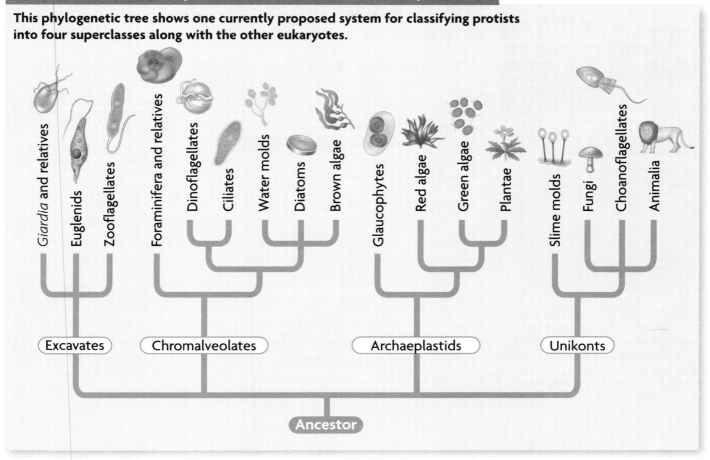

In the past, scientists classified protists in kingdom Protista, a very diverse kingdom that included hundreds of phyla. Kingdom Protista could be considered the "junk drawer" for all the eukaryotes that didn't seem to fit the animal, plant, or fungi definitions. Then, research made possible by new technology revealed the sometimes surprising genetic and genomic relationships between groups of organisms. Scientists began to realize that it was not useful to try to classify all of these organisms in kingdom Protista. The word *protist* itself has been called into question, because the organisms that were once classified under this umbrella term are so diverse and are sometimes more like plants, animals, or fungi than they are like each other.

Today, scientists are rethinking the way they classify not just protists but all eukaryotes. There is an emerging consensus that a more accurate way to classify eukaryotes is in "supergroups." **FIGURE 1.2** shows a way of classifying eukaryotes into four supergroups. Two of these supergroups—Excavata and Chromalveolata—contain only protists. A third supergroup, called Archaeplastida, includes plants, and a fourth, called Unikonta, includes animals and fungi. This proposal for a new way of classifying eukaryotes is a very active field of research. As of yet, there is no one universally accepted set of supergroups.

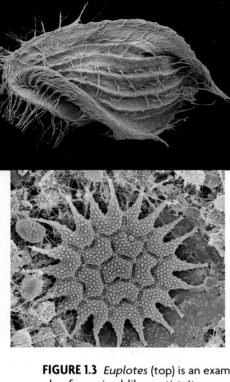

**FIGURE 1.3** *Euplotes* (top) is an example of an animal-like protist. It can move around quickly to find its food. *Pediastrum* (bottom) are algae that live in colonies. Like plants, they use sunlight to make food. (colored SEMs; magnifications unknown)

▶ MAIN IDEA

# Protists can be informally grouped into three categories.

Protists can be divided informally into three broad categories based on how they get their food. Categorizing protists in this way does not reflect evolutionary relationships, but it is a convenient way to study their diversity.

- **Animal-like protists** Animal-like protists, such as the *Euplotes* in **FIGURE 1.3**, are heterotrophs—organisms that consume other organisms. However, all animal-like protists are single-celled, while all animals—no matter how simple—are multicellular.

- **Plantlike protists** Plantlike protists, such as the algae *Pediastrum* in **FIGURE 1.3**, make their own food by photosynthesis just as plants do. Although these protists may have chloroplasts, they do not have roots, stems, or leaves. And while all plants are multicellular, plantlike protists may be either single-celled, colonial, or multicellular.

- **Funguslike protists** Funguslike protists, such as slime molds, decompose dead organisms. Because of this trait, these protists were once classified in kingdom Fungi. However, funguslike protists can move during part of their life cycle, whereas fungi cannot. You will learn about fungi later in this chapter.

**Apply** **What one characteristic do all protists share?**

---

| 20.1 | **Formative Assessment** |

**SELF-CHECK Online**
HMHScience.com
**GO ONLINE**

### REVIEWING ▶ MAIN IDEAS

1. Name the proposed supergroups for the classification of eukaryotes. Are protists classified in a supergroup or supergroups that include plants, animals, and fungi? Why or why not?

2. Give two reasons why **protists** are difficult to classify.

### CRITICAL THINKING

3. **Infer** What observable traits might green algae and plants share that support the molecular evidence that these two groups are closely related?

4. **Contrast** At one time, scientists grouped all single-celled organisms together. What are the main differences between single-celled protists and bacteria or archaea?

### CONNECT TO

**ECOLOGY**

5. Organisms that get their food by ingesting it are called heterotrophs, while those that make their own food are called autotrophs. Categorize animal-like, plantlike, and funguslike protists using these two terms.

# 20.2 Animal-like Protists

**KEY CONCEPT** Animal-like protists are single-celled heterotrophs that can move.

## VOCABULARY

protozoa
pseudopod
cilia

## MAIN IDEAS

- Animal-like protists move in various ways.
- Some animal-like protists cause disease.

### Connect to Your World

Think of all the ways that different animals move. Some walk on two legs, while others walk on four. Some spend most of their time flying, while others can only swim. Just like animals, animal-like protists use different ways to get around.

### ▶ MAIN IDEA

## Animal-like protists move in various ways.

The animal-like protists represent the largest number of protist species. In the early two-kingdom classification system, some protists were classified as animals because they had many animal-like traits. Like animals, they can move around, they consume other organisms, and their cells lack chloroplasts. The key difference between animal-like protists and animals is their body organization: all animal-like protists are unicellular, while animals are multicellular. The term **protozoa** is often used informally to describe the many phyla of animal-like protists. A few common protozoan groups are described below.

### Protozoa with Flagella

The zooflagellates (zoh-uh-FLAJ-uh-lihts) are animal-like protists that have one or more flagella at some point in their life cycle. Recall that flagella are tail-like structures that help unicellular organisms swim. Although the flagella of zooflagellates look like the flagella of prokaryotes, they are structurally very different. Prokaryotic flagella attach to the surface of the cell. In contrast, eukaryotic flagella, such as those of the zooflagellate shown in **FIGURE 2.1,** are extensions of the cytoplasm. They are made of bundles of small tubes called microtubules and are enclosed by the plasma membrane. Prokaryotic flagella are also much smaller than the flagella of protists. You can easily see protist flagella with the aid of a light microscope, but prokaryotic flagella are invisible at the same magnification.

More than 2000 species of zooflagellates exist. All free-living zooflagellates are heterotrophs. For example, some zooflagellates eat prokaryotes that feed on dissolved organic matter, thereby playing an important role in recycling nutrients through aquatic ecosystems. Other zooflagellates are pathogens, or disease-causing parasites of humans and other animals. Some zooflagellates live inside other organisms in mutualism—a relationship in which both organisms benefit.

**FIGURE 2.1** Zooflagellates have flagella that help them move through water. (colored SEM; magnification unknown)

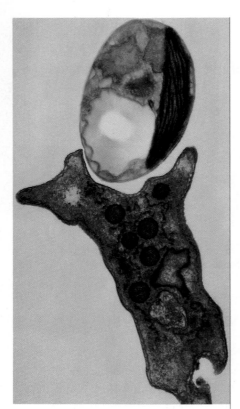

**FIGURE 2.2** An amoeba extends a pseudopod to surround and ingest an algal cell. (LM; magnification 4,200×)

**CONNECT TO**

**CELL ORGANELLES**

Recall from the chapter **Cell Structure and Function** that a vacuole is a fluid-filled sac used for the temporary storage of materials needed by the cell.

Sometimes zooflagellates play a crucial role in another organism's life. For example, termites cannot digest the wood they eat. Inside the gut of a termite is a complex community made of zooflagellates and bacteria that *can* digest wood. The termites get nutrition from the zooflagellate's activity, and the zooflagellates get free meals and a place to live.

## Protozoa with Pseudopods

Two groups of protozoa that can easily change shape as they move are the amoebas and the foraminifera.

**Amoebas**  The amoebas (uh-MEE-buhz) are very flexible. Amoebas form pseudopods to move. A **pseudopod** (SOO-duh-PAHD), which means "false foot," is a temporary extension of cytoplasm and plasma membrane that helps protozoa move and feed. To form a pseudopod, the cell cytoplasm flows outward, forming a bulge. This bulge spreads, anchors itself to the surface it is on, and pulls the rest of the cell toward it. Pseudopod formation uses energy. When the amoeba is not moving or feeding, it does not form pseudopods.

An amoeba's method of getting food is shown in **FIGURE 2.2**. Ingestion takes place by the process of phagocytosis. Recall that phagocytosis is the engulfing of solid material by a cell. The amoeba surrounds the food with its pseudopod, and the outer membrane of the amoeba then forms a food vacuole, or sac. Digestive enzymes enter the food vacuole from the surrounding cytoplasm, and digestion takes place.

Amoebas live in fresh water, salt water, and soil. The majority of amoebas are free-living, but some species are parasites. Most amoebas are microscopic. However, *Pelomyxa palustris* is an amoeba that can grow as large as five millimeters in diameter—a huge size for a single-celled organism—and can be seen without a microscope.

**Foraminifera**  Another group of protozoa with pseudopods are the foraminifera (fuh-RAM-uh-NIHF-uhr-uh). Foraminifera, sometimes simply called forams, are named for their multichambered shell, shown in **FIGURE 2.3**. The Latin word *foramen* means "little hole." Their shells are made of organic matter, sand, or other materials, depending on the species. Forams make up a large group of marine protozoa that, like amoeba, use pseudopods to move.

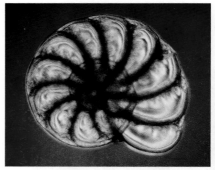

**FIGURE 2.3** Pseudopods can extend from pores in a foraminifera's multichambered shell. This shell is smaller than the head of a matchstick.

## Protozoa with Cilia

This group's name, ciliates, comes from its most obvious feature—cilia. **Cilia** are short, hairlike structures that cover some or all of the cell surface and help the organism swim and capture food. Cilia are usually much shorter than flagella and found in much greater numbers. Some ciliates have many rows of cilia all over their surface, whereas other ciliates just have clusters of cilia.

Certain other photosynthetic dinoflagellates help build coral reefs through their symbiotic partnership with corals. These dinoflagellates live in the inner tissues of the corals. In return for shelter from the corals, the dinoflagellates provide the corals with nutrients in tropical waters that are usually nutrient-poor.

Some species of dinoflagellates produce toxins. A large population of these dinoflagellates can create what is known as a red tide, due to the reddish color produced by a high density of these species. Red tides, shown in **FIGURE 3.3**, occur when changes in ocean currents bring up nutrients from far below the ocean surface. The higher nutrient levels produce a rapid increase, or bloom, in the dino-flagellate population. A toxic bloom in the waters can kill large numbers of fish. The toxins can also build up in the tissues of shellfish, which then can be dangerous to humans who eat the contaminated seafood.

**Diatoms** Most diatoms are easy to recognize when viewed through a microscope. These tiny single-celled algae are covered with delicately patterned glasslike shells. The shells of diatoms serve almost as an external skeleton, helping the cell to hold a rigid shape. Diatom shells, such as those shown in **FIGURE 3.4**, are made of silica, the same brittle substance that is used to make glass. The silica shell is divided into two parts that overlap each other, like the lid of a box.

Like other autotrophs, all diatoms release oxygen into the environment. In fact, diatoms could be considered the world champions of photosynthesis. They play a critical role in the uptake of carbon dioxide on Earth and produce about half of the oxygen we breathe. Diatoms may be freshwater or marine. Many species are phytoplankton. Others live clinging to rocks, plants, soil, and even animals—diatoms have been found growing on crustaceans, turtles, and even whales. Because of their glassy, mineralized shells, diatoms have been well preserved in the fossil record. Some fossil rocks consist almost entirely of diatoms. These diatom skeletons have many industrial uses, such as an ingredient in scrubbing products, because of their rough texture.

Dinoflagellates

**FIGURE 3.3** A high density of dinoflagellates causes reddish coloration of ocean waters, called a red tide. The toxins produced during a red tide can kill sea life and cause illness in humans. (colored SEM; magnification about 850×)

**READING TOOLBOX**

**VOCABULARY**

The name *diatom* comes from the Greek term *diatomos*, meaning "cut in half." This refers to the appearance of the diatom's overlapping shell.

**FIGURE 3.4 DIATOMS**

Diatoms are known for their delicate glasslike cell walls, or shells, that can have many shapes. They are common in both freshwater and marine environments.

(all colored SEMs; magnification 750×; magnification 250×; magnification unknown)

**FIGURE 3.5** Giant kelp are a type of brown algae that form underwater forests. The forests are home to a large variety of marine organisms.

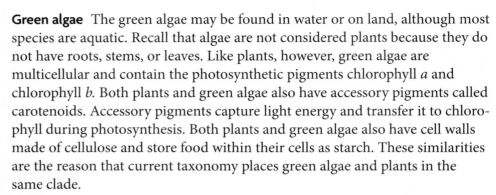

**Green algae** The green algae may be found in water or on land, although most species are aquatic. Recall that algae are not considered plants because they do not have roots, stems, or leaves. Like plants, however, green algae are multicellular and contain the photosynthetic pigments chlorophyll *a* and chlorophyll *b*. Both plants and green algae also have accessory pigments called carotenoids. Accessory pigments capture light energy and transfer it to chlorophyll during photosynthesis. Both plants and green algae also have cell walls made of cellulose and store food within their cells as starch. These similarities are the reason that current taxonomy places green algae and plants in the same clade.

**Brown algae** The brown algae include the giant kelp, shown in **FIGURE 3.5,** that form thick underwater forests. Brown algae are multicellular and can grow to be extremely large. Some giant kelp can grow up to 100 meters high (about 330 ft). Most brown algae live in marine environments. Brown algae are photosynthetic but have a different form of chlorophyll—chlorophyll *c*—than do plants or green algae. Brown algae share this trait with the diatoms. This observation is why brown algae and diatoms are classified together within the chromalveolates supergroup.

**Red algae** Most red algae are found in the ocean, though a few live in freshwater habitats. Red algae use chlorophyll *a* for photosynthesis, but they get their color from the pigment phycoerythrin. Red algae can grow at deeper depths than other algae because the red pigments allow red algae to absorb the blue light that reaches deepest into the ocean. Some species secrete calcium carbonate, forming thick crusts that look like corals and provide habitats for tiny invertebrates. Red algae provide many products for the food industry. Carrageenan and agar, thickening agents used in products such as ice cream, come from red algae. In Japan, red algae is dried to make nori, a seaweed wrap used for sushi.

**Compare and Contrast** What are the similarities and differences between green, brown, and red algae?

▶ **MAIN IDEA**

## Many plantlike protists can reproduce both sexually and asexually.

Most protists can undergo both sexual and asexual reproduction. All algae can reproduce asexually. Multicellular algae can fragment; each piece is capable of forming a new body. When a single-celled alga, such as the green alga *Chlamydomonas* shown in **FIGURE 3.6,** reproduces asexually, its life cycle is a bit more complex. The dominant phase of the life cycle for this species is haploid. Before reproducing asexually, the haploid parent alga absorbs its flagella and then divides by mitosis. This division may occur two or more times, producing up to eight cells. The daughter cells develop flagella and cell walls. These daughter cells, called zoospores, leave the parent cell, disperse, and grow. The zoospores then grow into mature haploid cells.

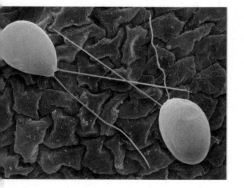

**FIGURE 3.6** *Chlamydomonas* are single-celled green algae with two flagella. (colored SEM; magnification 1600×)

## 20.5 | Diversity of Fungi

SC.912.L.15.6

**SC.912.L.15.6** Discuss distinguishing characteristics of the domains and kingdoms of living organisms.

| KEY CONCEPT **Fungi are heterotrophs that absorb their food.**

**MAIN IDEAS**

- Fungi are adapted to absorb their food from the environment.
- Fungi come in many shapes and sizes.
- Fungi reproduce sexually and asexually.

### Connect to Your World

What is the largest living thing in the world? The blue whale? A giant redwood tree? Although they are big, both species are tiny compared with a fungus growing in Oregon—a single honey mushroom, *Armillaria ostoyae*. Most of it is underground, but this mushroom could cover more than 1500 football fields. It is thought to be at least 2400 years old. As amazing as it sounds, there are other fungi throughout the world nearly as large.

### ⬤ MAIN IDEA

## Fungi are adapted to absorb their food from the environment.

Despite how little most people know about fungi, they are all around us—in soil, water, and even in the air. Many forms live in and on plants and animals. Scientists have named about 70,000 species but estimate there may be a total of 1.5 million fungi species in the world.

### Comparing Fungi and Plants

Members of the kingdom Fungi fall into one of three groups—the single-celled yeasts, the molds, and the true fungi. For many years, biologists classified fungi as plants. But there are a few traits that separate these two kingdoms.

- Plants contain chlorophyll and photosynthesize. Fungi do not have chlorophyll and get food by absorbing it from their environment.
- Plants have true roots, leaves, and stems, but fungi do not.
- Plant cell walls are made of the polysaccharide cellulose. Fungal cell walls are made of **chitin** (KYT-uhn), a tough polysaccharide that is also found in the shells of insects and their close relatives.

### Anatomy of Fungi

With the exception of the yeasts, fungi are multicellular organisms. The bodies of multicellular fungi are made of long strands called **hyphae** (HY-fee). Hyphae (singular, *hypha*) are shown in **FIGURE 5.1**. Depending on the species, each hypha may consist of a chain of cells or may contain one large, long cell with many nuclei. In both cases, cytoplasm can flow freely throughout the hyphae, and each hypha is surrounded by a plasma membrane and a cell wall of chitin.

**FIGURE 5.1** A mushroom is actually just the reproductive, or fruiting, body of a fungus. Most of the fungus grows in the ground, as a mycelium.

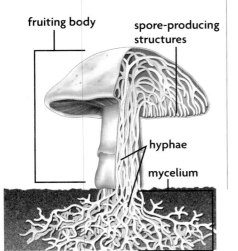

fruiting body

spore-producing structures

hyphae

mycelium

Hyphae often group together in long tangled masses to form a mycelium. A **mycelium** (my-SEE-lee-uhm) is an underground network of hyphae. Under certain conditions, such as a moist environment, a mycelium (plural, *mycelia*) can grow quickly to cover a large area. Mycelia may produce fruiting bodies. A **fruiting body** is a reproductive structure of a fungus that grows above ground. Mushrooms are one type of fruiting body.

Fungi absorb their food from their environment. The food can be from a wide variety of food sources—including tree bark, bread, cheese, and even flesh. As fungi grow, hyphae extend into the food source and release enzymes. These enzymes break down their food so that it can be absorbed across their cell walls. Fungi can take in large amounts of nutrients due to their mycelia, which in turn allows mycelia to grow very quickly.

**Contrast** How is the way that fungi get their food different from that of any other group of organisms?

## ▶ MAIN IDEA
# Fungi come in many shapes and sizes.

The kingdom Fungi is diverse, and it is commonly divided into four main groups—primitive fungi (phylum Chytridiomycota), sac fungi (phylum Ascomycota), bread molds (phylum Zygomycota), and club fungi (phylum Basidiomycota).

### Primitive Fungi
The primitive fungi, or chytrids, are the smallest and simplest group of fungi. They are mostly aquatic, and their spores have flagella, which help propel them through the water. They are the only fungi with flagellated spores. Some primitive fungi are decomposers, while others are parasites of protists, plants, or animals. One explanation for the global decrease of amphibians such as frogs is that a parasitic type of chytrid fungi is attacking them.

### Sac Fungi
Yeasts, certain molds such as *Penicillium,* and morels and truffles—which many people consider delicious to eat—are all sac fungi. The sac fungi are a diverse group, but they have one key trait in common. They all form a sac, called an ascus, that contains spores for reproduction. Some examples of sac fungi are shown in **FIGURE 5.2**

The yeast that makes bread rise is *Saccharomyces cerevisiae*. This yeast is also an important model organism used in molecular biology. As a eukaryote, it has many of the same genes as humans. Because it is single-celled, it is easy to work with in a laboratory.

If you've ever let an orange grow moldy, you've seen *Penicillium chrysogenum*. This mold is usually a deep green color and appears fuzzy. *Penicillium* is also the source for the antibiotic penicillin. In contrast, one dangerous sac fungus is *Aspergillis flavus,* a mold that makes a poison called aflatoxin that can contaminate cereals, nuts, and milk.

**FIGURE 5.2** Many sac fungi are sac- or cup-shaped or have cup-shaped indentations. Sac fungi include morels (top), which are prized for their tastiness, and moss cup fungi (bottom), also known as scarlet elf cups.

## Bread Molds

The bread molds range from the molds you see on spoiled foods to fungi used to ferment certain foods such as soy sauce. Most members of this phylum get food by decomposing dead or decaying matter. At least one group of symbiotic fungi belongs to this group. **Mycorrhizae** (MY-kuh-RY-zuh) are mutualistic partnerships between fungi and the roots of certain plants. Mycorrhizae help these plants to fix nitrogen—that is, they take inorganic nitrogen from the soil and convert it to nitrates and ammonia, which the plants use.

## Club Fungi

The club fungi get their name because their fruiting bodies are club-shaped. This phylum includes mushrooms, puffballs, and bracket, or shelf, fungi. It also includes the rusts and smuts, which are two types of fungi that cause diseases in plants. Puffballs, shown in **FIGURE 5.3**, form dry-looking structures that release their spores when someone or something strikes the mature fruiting body. Bracket fungi are a common sight in forests, where they grow outward from tree trunks, forming a little shelf.

**Identify** What two organisms share a mutualistic partnership in the formation of mycorrhizae?

**FIGURE 5.3** Puffballs release a cloud of spores when the fruiting body matures and bursts.

## ● MAIN IDEA
# Fungi reproduce sexually and asexually.

Most fungi reproduce both sexually and asexually through a wide variety of strategies.

## Reproduction in Single-Celled Fungi

Yeasts are single-celled fungi. They reproduce asexually, either through simple fission or through a process called budding, shown in **FIGURE 5.4**. Fission is identical to mitosis—the cell's DNA is copied and the nucleus and cytoplasm divide, making two identical daughter cells. During budding, the parent cell forms a small bud of cytoplasm that also contains a copy of the nucleus. When these buds reach a certain size, they detach and form a cell.

Some yeasts undergo sexual reproduction. A diploid yeast cell undergoes meiosis, producing four haploid nuclei. However, the parent cell's cytoplasm does not divide. Recall that a yeast is a type of sac fungi. Instead of the cytoplasm dividing, it produces the characteristic saclike structure of this phylum called an ascus. The haploid nuclei it contains are actually a type of spore. The ascus undergoes budding, releasing each of the haploid spores. Some spores may then reproduce more haploid spores through budding. Others may fuse with other haploid spores to form diploid yeast cells.

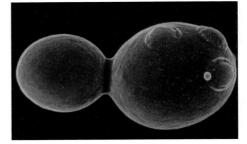

**FIGURE 5.4** Yeast can reproduce by budding, the pinching of small cells off the parent cell. (colored SEM; magnification 6000×)

## FIGURE 5.5 REPRODUCTIVE STRUCTURES OF FUNGI

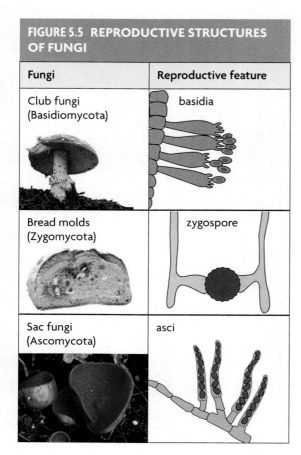

| Fungi | Reproductive feature |
|---|---|
| Club fungi (Basidiomycota) | basidia |
| Bread molds (Zygomycota) | zygospore |
| Sac fungi (Ascomycota) | asci |

## CONNECT TO

### ASEXUAL REPRODUCTION

Recall from the chapter **Cell Growth and Division** that asexual reproduction is the creation of offspring from a single parent that does not involve the joining of gametes. The offspring are genetically identical to each other and to the parent.

## Animated Biology
HMHScience.com

GO ONLINE

Life Cycle of Zygote Fungus

## Reproduction in Multicellular Fungi

The multicellular fungi have complex reproductive cycles. Examples of life cycles for two phyla of fungi are shown in **FIGURE 5.6**.

**Club fungi** Basidiomycota are named for their club-shaped structures called basidia, where spores are produced during sexual reproduction. Basidia are found on the undersides of mushrooms. They form within the leaflike gills that you can easily see. In club fungi, unlike the other phyla, spores are most often formed by sexual reproduction.

- Nuclei within the basidia fuse to form diploid zygotes.
- The zygotes undergo meiosis to form haploid spores.
- The spores drop from the gills and are carried away by wind or by contact with animals.
- If the spores land in a favorable environment, they grow and form haploid hyphae.
- Some cells of the haploid mycelium may fuse with the cells of another haploid mycelium, producing a diploid mycelium underground.
- An environmental cue, such as rain or change in temperature, can trigger the formation of aboveground fruiting bodies such as mushrooms.

**Bread molds** Members of Zygomycota are also known as zygote fungi because of the structures they form during sexual reproduction. Bread molds reproduce sexually when the food supply is low but can also reproduce asexually when there is plenty of food. They reproduce asexually by producing spores in **sporangia,** spore-forming structures at the tips of their hyphae. The term *sporangium* is used to describe similar reproductive structures of a variety of organisms, including some fungi, mosses, algae, and ferns.

### VISUAL VOCAB

**Sporangia** are structures that produce spores.

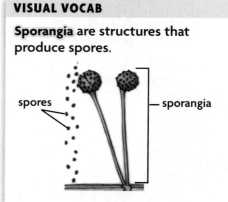

spores

sporangia

- As in the club fungi, sexual reproduction in zygote fungi involves hyphae that look alike but are different mating types.
- The two types of hyphae fuse their nuclei to produce a diploid zygospore that can tolerate long periods of extreme conditions.
- When the conditions become favorable, a sporangium grows and produces haploid spores.
- The spores are released and can grow into new hyphae.
- The new hyphae in turn may reproduce asexually, by forming haploid spores in sporangia. Or they may reproduce sexually, by fusing hyphae to produce more zygospores.

(t) ©Orla/ShutterStock; (c) ©Ocean/Corbis; (b) ©Vaughan Fleming/Photo Researchers, Inc.

# FIGURE 5.6 Typical Life Cycles of Fungi

Reproduction in fungi can occur in several ways. Although most club fungi reproduce sexually, bread molds can reproduce both sexually and asexually.

## LIFE CYCLE OF CLUB FUNGI

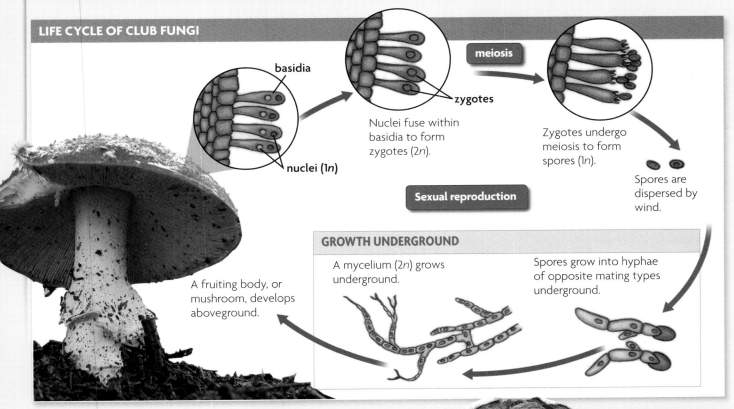

basidia

nuclei (1n)

meiosis

zygotes

Nuclei fuse within basidia to form zygotes (2n).

Zygotes undergo meiosis to form spores (1n).

Spores are dispersed by wind.

Sexual reproduction

**GROWTH UNDERGROUND**

A mycelium (2n) grows underground.

Spores grow into hyphae of opposite mating types underground.

A fruiting body, or mushroom, develops aboveground.

## LIFE CYCLE OF BREAD MOLDS

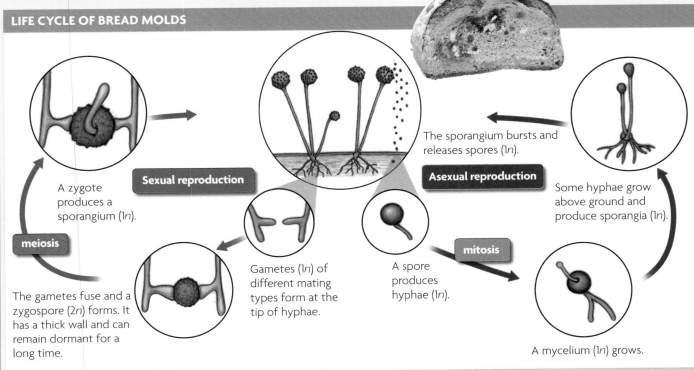

A zygote produces a sporangium (1n).

Sexual reproduction

meiosis

The gametes fuse and a zygospore (2n) forms. It has a thick wall and can remain dormant for a long time.

Gametes (1n) of different mating types form at the tip of hyphae.

The sporangium bursts and releases spores (1n).

Asexual reproduction

A spore produces hyphae (1n).

mitosis

Some hyphae grow above ground and produce sporangia (1n).

A mycelium (1n) grows.

**CRITICAL VIEWING** How are the life cycles of club fungi and bread molds similar? How are they different?

(tl) ©Orla/ShutterStock; (c) ©Ocean/Corbis

**ascospore**

**ascus**

**FIGURE 5.7** A cross-section of the cup-shaped fruiting body of a sac fungus shows spores encased in an ascus. (magnification 400×)

**Sac fungi** Members of Ascomycota are called the sac fungi due to the saclike case, or ascus (plural, *asci*), that forms during sexual reproduction. These reproductive structures are shown in **FIGURE 5.7.** Most asci are found within the fungi's cup-shaped fruiting body. As in club fungi and bread molds, sexual reproduction in multicellular sac fungi involves the joining of two mycelia that are different mating types. The joined hyphae grow into the aboveground fruiting body. An ascus, or sac, develops at the tip of each hypha within the fruiting body. Inside the ascus, haploid spores form. When mature, the cup-shaped fruiting body collapses, and releases the spores.

Like the bread molds, sac fungi usually reproduce asexually when conditions are favorable and reproduce sexually when conditions are harsh. They produce different types of spores during asexual reproduction than they do during sexual reproduction. Spores produced during asexual reproduction are called conidia, which means "dust," because they travel easily through air.

## Release of Spores

Fungi release their spores at the tips of their hyphae, high above their food source. This strategy allows the small spores to be carried in air currents to a new location. Some species of fungi go even further and use unusual strategies in releasing their spores. For example, members of the fungal genus *Cordyceps* grow on insects. In some species, the fungi penetrate the insect's brain, causing the insect to climb high into a tree or other vegetation. Eventually, the insect stops climbing and remains fixed in place. The fungus then releases its spores from this greater height.

Spores of fungi are everywhere, and have even been found in the air more than 150 kilometers (93 mi) above the surface of Earth. The great number of spores in the air at any given time is the reason that the growth of mold on our leftover food cannot be avoided, even if the food is refrigerated. Fungal spores are also a source of allergies for many people worldwide.

**Hypothesize  How might producing spores benefit an organism?**

## 20.5 Formative Assessment

### REVIEWING ▶ MAIN IDEAS

1. Describe how fungi use **hyphae** to obtain their food.

2. Describe a typical **fruiting body** of sac fungi, bread mold, and club fungi.

3. **Sporangia** are formed during the life cycle of a typical bread mold. At what stage are they formed?

### CRITICAL THINKING

4. **Summarize**  Draw a flowchart showing the sequence of steps in the reproduction of yeast, a single-celled fungus.

5. **Infer**  The **mycelium** of a fungus grows underground. In what ways might this be helpful for the fungus?

### ⁂ CONNECT TO

### ECOLOGY

6. Some scientists support using fungi such as *Cordyceps* instead of pesticides to control insect pests in agriculture. What might be some pros and cons of such a plan?

(inset) ©Ed Reschke/Peter Arnold, Inc.; (tl) ©pupunkkop/Shutterstock

# White-Nose Syndrome

Bat with white-nose syndrome

A lethal visitor arrived in New York from Europe in the winter of 2006–2007, a fungus known as *Pseudogymnoascus destructans* (Pd). As the fungus spread westward through the United States and Canada, it killed millions of bats that were hibernating in caves and abandoned mines. When bats hibernate, their metabolism slows and body temperature drops. They survive on fat reserves stored in their bodies. The fungus, which grows on the noses, wings, and other hairless parts of bats' bodies, causes a disease called white-nose syndrome (WNS). Infection causes bats to come out of hibernation temporarily during the cold winter. The normal diets of these bats are insects or fruit, which are not available in winter, so the bats must deplete their fat reserves and they starve to death.

The Pd fungus thrives in cold, humid conditions. It attacks the bats while they hibernate but not during summer months, when they are active and their body temperature is warmer. Infected bats that manage to survive the winter seem to recover from the disease when their bodies warm up in the spring, creating suboptimal growing conditions for the fungus. However, these survivors are usually reinfected the following winter by fungi that live on cave or mine walls.

Scientists are searching for ways to control the fungus and fight the disease. They hope to save as many bats as possible until a long-term cure is found. One group of scientists has discovered that bacteria growing on bats' wings can kill the Pd fungus—at least in the laboratory, but they haven't tested the bacteria in the wild yet. Other scientists have discovered a soil bacterium that produces chemicals capable of killing Pd fungal spores in the lab. The scientists isolated the chemicals and applied them to hibernating bats, which emerged disease-free from their hibernation four months later. But scientists are cautious people. Instead of declaring success, they continued to analyze their data. They realized that the bats did not develop immunity to the fungus after being treated with chemicals. Surviving bats could very well become reinfected winter after winter. A vaccine would be longer lasting, if one could be developed. But how would workers vaccinate millions of bats?

Some scientists are starting to think outside the box. They hypothesize that changing the airflow in the caves where bats hibernate might make living conditions unfavorable for the fungus. By opening new routes for air to move in and out of a cave, the scientists hope to warm the air enough to drive out the fungus, which cannot grow at temperatures above 20°C. They are concerned, though, that the bats also might be driven out of their usual hibernation sites if conditions change. Still, the situation is so serious that scientists think it is worth a try. Until a breakthrough occurs, scientists and government agencies in the United States and Canada are trying to coordinate their work to save bats and permanently cure white-nose syndrome.

## S.T.E.M. Activity

Choose one of the stopgap measures discussed in the article. Make a hypothesis explaining how that measure might cure WNS or increase the survival of bats during hibernation. Alternatively, suggest a different treatment that might be successful. Design an experiment that tests your hypothesis either in a lab or in a field study.

Consider the challenge of changing the airflow in a bat cave from the perspective of an engineering design problem. What would be the criteria for a successful solution? What constraints must be considered in designing a solution?

## 20.6 Ecology of Fungi

| KEY CONCEPT **Fungi recycle nutrients in the environment.**

**MAIN IDEAS**
- Fungi may be decomposers, pathogens, or mutualists.
- Fungi are studied for many purposes.

**VOCABULARY**

lichen

### Connect to Your World

Fungi just might be the most overlooked and unappreciated organisms on Earth. Fungi grow on shower curtains, spoil food, and cause illnesses in humans. But humans also eat some fungi and use them to make things that range from bread to antibiotics. Perhaps most importantly, these unusual organisms play a major role in every ecosystem on Earth.

### ▶ MAIN IDEA

## Fungi may be decomposers, pathogens, or mutualists.

| Some fungi act as decomposers in the environment. Others act as either pathogens or mutualists to other organisms—including humans.

**FIGURE 6.1** Fungi produce enzymes that help break down the complex molecules in wood to simpler molecules that fungi can absorb and use.

### Fungi as Decomposers

Fungi and bacteria are the main decomposers in any ecosystem. Fungi, such as those shown in **FIGURE 6.1,** decompose dead and decaying organic matter such as leaves, twigs, logs, and animals. They return nutrients such as carbon, nitrogen, and minerals back into the soil. Because of the large surface area of their mycelia, fungi are well adapted for absorbing their food and can recycle nutrients quickly. This constant cycling of nutrients helps enrich soil with organic compounds. The nutrients can then be taken up by other organisms.

Plants and animals could not survive without the activity of decomposers. The ability of fungi to break down tough plant materials such as lignin and cellulose is especially important in woodland ecosystems. Fungi are the main decomposers of these hard parts of plants, which cannot be used by animals without being first broken down by decomposers.

The decomposing activity of fungi is not always helpful to humans, however. Fungi can damage fruit trees, and they can also cause damage inside wooden houses and boats. Molds and other fungi inside a house can weaken its walls, and their spores can cause respiratory illness. Homeowners should check for and remove molds that are established in their homes.

©Merryl Brackstone/ShutterStock

## Fungi as Pathogens

Like bacteria, some fungi can be pathogenic, or disease-causing. A few pathogenic fungi always cause disease. These fungi are called obligate pathogens—the term *obligate* means necessary or obliged. Other fungi are normally harmless, coexisting with other organisms in a delicate ecological balance. However, changes in environmental circumstances can upset this balance and lead to disease. Organisms that normally don't cause a problem until there is a change in the host's homeostasis are called opportunistic pathogens. A change in the host's body provides them an opportunity to grow unchecked and cause infection.

**Fungi and humans** The overuse and incorrect use of antibiotics is one example of how humans allow pathogens an opportunity to cause infection. Antibiotics can destroy certain beneficial bacteria in the human digestive system, allowing other organisms such as fungi to thrive. Typically harmless fungi also cause disease when the immune system is not functioning at its best. For instance, all healthy humans have populations of the yeast *Candida* that occupy certain parts of the body, such as the skin and mouth. If a human's immune system is damaged, populations may grow and cause disease.

Some fungal pathogens, such as those that cause ringworm and athlete's foot, have fairly mild effects. But several fungi cause severe diseases, such as some lung illnesses, that are hard to cure and can even cause death. Fungal infections are hard to treat because fungi are eukaryotes, and so their cellular structure is very similar to ours. It is difficult to develop medicine that will harm fungal cells but not damage human cells.

**Fungi and plants** Fungal diseases also affect plants, and they can be especially devastating in agriculture and horticulture. Dutch elm disease is caused by a fungus that is transmitted by elm bark beetles, shown in **FIGURE 6.2**. In the United States, the first cases of Dutch elm disease were reported in Ohio in 1930. Today, the disease has destroyed more than half of the elms in the northern United States. Fungi also destroy a large portion of the world's fruit crops. A disease of peaches called peach scab is caused by a fungus and results in millions of dollars in losses to growers each year. Gray mold is a disease of produce such as strawberries. This fungus can grow even in refrigerated fruit and is a major cause of fruit spoilage during shipment and storage.

Fungal diseases in agriculture are often treated with chemical sprays called fungicides. Today, however, crops that are genetically engineered to resist fungi are becoming more common. Fungal diseases in animals, including those in humans, are usually treated with antifungal medications. These treatments usually come from fungi themselves, which produce them as a defense against other fungi. Like bacteria and protists, however, fungi can develop resistance to treatments if they are overused. These products should be used carefully.

⚡ **CONNECT TO**

**PROKARYOTES**

In biology, the term obligate means requiring a particular environment to survive. Recall from the chapter **Viruses and Prokaryotes** that prokaryotes can be obligate anaerobes, meaning they cannot have oxygen in their environment. Some bacteria, protists, and fungi can also be obligate pathogens or obligate parasites.

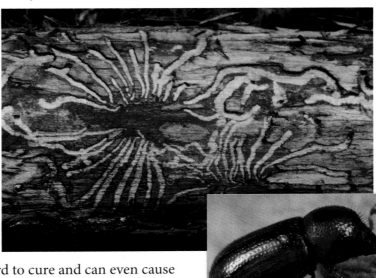

**FIGURE 6.2** A fungus is responsible for Dutch elm disease. Adult elm bark beetles tunnel into the bark of elms to lay their eggs. If the trees are diseased, fungus spores stick to the adults as they visit new trees.

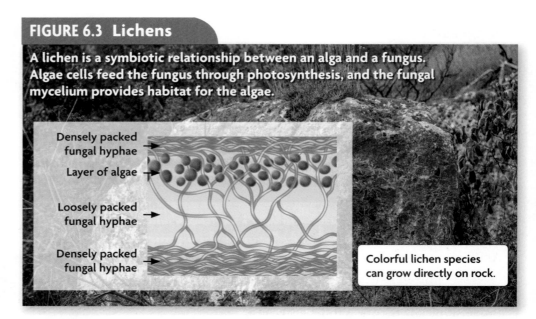

## FIGURE 6.3  Lichens

A lichen is a symbiotic relationship between an alga and a fungus. Algae cells feed the fungus through photosynthesis, and the fungal mycelium provides habitat for the algae.

Densely packed fungal hyphae

Layer of algae

Loosely packed fungal hyphae

Densely packed fungal hyphae

Colorful lichen species can grow directly on rock.

## Fungi as Mutualists

Mutualism is a symbiotic relationship in which both organisms benefit. Fungi form mutualistic relationships with several types of organisms.

**Lichens**  A **lichen** (LY-kuhn) is a mutualistic relationship between a fungus and algae or photosynthetic bacteria. Only certain fungi, algae, or cyanobacteria can combine to form a lichen body. The body itself consists mainly of fungal hyphae that surround and grow into the algal cells, as shown in **FIGURE 6.3.** The algal part of the lichen carries out photosynthesis, making sugars that feed both the alga and the fungus. Lichens (phylum Mycomycota) can grow on almost any solid surface, from tree trunks to soil to rocks. They are common in cool, dry environments. They can also withstand severe temperatures. This characteristic of lichens allows them to live in habitats such as tundra, where fungi could not survive alone.

Lichens play several roles in the environment and in the lives of humans. For example, they are extremely important during primary succession, because they can live on bare rock. Many species of lichens are sensitive to air pollution and can be used as indicators of air quality. Lichens are also important in nutrient cycling, because they function as both a decomposer and a producer. Lichens produce hundreds of unique chemicals, including pigments used as dyes in traditional cultures and compounds that have antibiotic properties.

**Mycorrhizae**  Mutualistic associations between plant roots and soil fungi are called mycorrhizae. More than 80 percent of the world's plants have mycorrhizae on their roots. Mycorrhizae form when the hyphae of a fungus colonize the roots of a nearby plant. The huge surface area of the fungal mycelium is much larger than the root surface area of the plants, so the mycelium can absorb soil nutrients and water faster than the plant's roots could alone. In return, the fungus benefits because it gets sugars and other nutrients from the plant. Mycorrhizae can boost plant growth and reduce the need for fertilizers, which can cause soil and water pollution. Mycorrhizae also produce chemicals with antibiotic properties that help fight harmful bacteria.

> **CONNECT TO**
>
> ### ECOLOGY
>
> Recall from the chapter **Interactions in Ecosystems** that primary succession occurs after disruptive events such as fires and volcanic eruptions. The first organisms to recolonize an area, such as lichens, are called pioneer species.

**Fungal gardens and insects** Some insects also live as partners in a mutualistic symbiosis with fungi. The leafcutter ants of Central and South America, shown in **FIGURE 6.4,** don't just use fungi—they actually grow them. These ants cut tiny pieces of leaf from plants with their jaws. They carry these leaf pieces back to an underground nest area, where they build a garden of leaf pieces. Next, the ants add pieces of the fungus. The fungus breaks down the leaf pieces and absorbs nutrients from them. The ants in turn feed on the fungal mycelium.

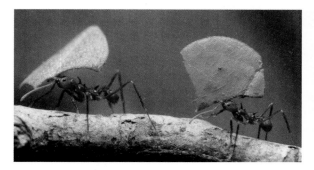

**FIGURE 6.4** Leafcutter ants carry leaves back to their nests to provide food for fungi. The ants then eat the growing fungal mycelium.

**Summarize** **Describe three ways that fungi are important to the environment.**

## ▶ MAIN IDEA
# Fungi are studied for many purposes.

Many species of fungi are edible, such as the mushrooms we eat on pizza and the yeast we use to bake bread. In addition, fungi make citric acid, which is used in soft drinks and some candy. Fungi are also useful in the health care industry. Since the discovery of antibiotics in the 1900s, scientists have been researching how pathogens interact with their natural environments. This knowledge is then applied to develop useful medicines. For example, in their natural habitats fungi and bacteria compete for similar resources, such as space and nutrients. This is true whether they live on a forest floor or in a human digestive tract. Over time, fungi have evolved natural defenses against bacteria.

Studies of yeast have produced equally valuable insights. These tiny single-celled organisms are among the most important model systems used in molecular biology. Most yeasts have many of the same genes and proteins found in plants and animals. Insights gained from studies of a yeast's genome can often be applied to multicellular organisms. Yeast are small, grow quickly, and are easy to culture, or raise, in the laboratory.

**Summarize** **What are three ways that fungi benefit humans?**

**CONNECT TO**

**ANTIBIOTICS**

Recall from the chapter **Viruses and Prokaryotes** that an antibiotic is a chemical that kills or slows the growth of bacteria.

**SELF-CHECK Online**
HMHScience.com
**GO ONLINE**

# 20.6 Formative Assessment

## REVIEWING ▶ MAIN IDEAS

1. How do fungi contribute to the balance of an ecosystem?

2. What are three reasons **lichens** are useful to humans?

## CRITICAL THINKING

3. **Compare** Draw a Venn diagram comparing lichens and mycorrhizae. Include terms such as *roots, photosynthesis,* and *mutualism.*

4. **Analyze** Some antifungal medications can damage the patient's own tissues. Why doesn't this problem occur with antibiotics?

**CONNECT TO**

**NATURAL SELECTION**

5. A peach farmer is faced every year with an outbreak of peach scab, a fungal disease of peaches. Every year he sprays his crop carefully with fungicides, but each time these seem less effective than the year before. Why might this be?

©Mark Bowler/Science Source/Getty Images

CHAPTER
20 **Summary**

**BIG IDEA**  Protists and fungi are highly diverse organisms that have both beneficial and detrimental impacts on human health and the environment.

## KEY CONCEPTS

### 20.1 Diversity of Protists

**Kingdom Protista is the most diverse of all the kingdoms.** It includes organisms that are animal-like, plantlike, and funguslike. Protists may be single-celled or multicellular, and may be microscopic or very large. Protist classification is likely to change in the future, as some protists are more closely related to members of other kingdoms than they are to other protists.

### 20.2 Animal-like Protists

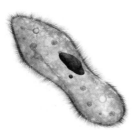

**Animal-like protists are single-celled heterotrophs that can move.** Commonly known as protozoa, animal-like protists have various structures that help them move, such as flagella, pseudopods, or cilia. Some animal-like protists can cause diseases such as malaria and sleeping sickness.

### 20.3 Plantlike Protists

**Algae are plantlike protists.** Unlike animal-like protists, which are all single-celled, plantlike protists can be either single-celled or multicellular. Most plantlike protists can make their own food through photosynthesis. Plantlike protists are not classified as plants because they do not have roots, stems, leaves, or the specialized tissues and reproductive structures that plants have. However, like many plants, most plantlike protists can reproduce both sexually and asexually.

### 20.4 Funguslike Protists

**Funguslike protists decompose organic matter.** These protists have an important role in recycling nutrients through ecosystems. Unlike fungi, funguslike protists can move during part of their life cycle. Funguslike protists include slime molds and water molds.

### 20.5 Diversity of Fungi

**Fungi are heterotrophs that absorb their food.** Their bodies are made of long strands, called hyphae, which grow underground in a tangled mass called a mycelium. The parts of fungi that humans normally recognize, such as mushrooms, are actually only the reproductive structures of the fungi, called fruiting bodies.

### 20.6 Ecology of Fungi

**Fungi recycle nutrients in the environment.** Some fungi cause illness in humans, such as those that cause athlete's foot and ringworm. Other fungi, such as those that cause Dutch elm disease, cause illness to plants or other organisms. Some fungi share a mutualistic relationship with organisms such as algae to form lichens, or plant roots, which form mycorrhizae. Humans use fungi for foods, medicine, and as model organisms in scientific research.

---

🔎 **READING TOOLBOX**   SYNTHESIZE YOUR NOTES

**Supporting Main Ideas**  Use a supporting main ideas diagram to summarize how the three groups of protists get their food.

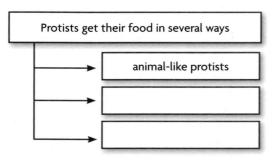

**Concept Map**  Use a concept map like the one below to summarize what you know about the roles of fungi in the environment.

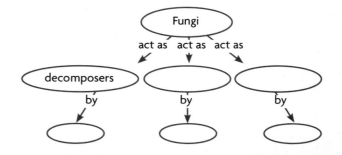

©Orla/ShutterStock

# 20 Review

INTERACTIVE Review
HMHScience.com

GO ONLINE

Review Games • Concept Map • Section Self-Checks

## CHAPTER VOCABULARY

**20.1** protist

**20.2** protozoa
pseudopod
cilia

**20.3** algae

**20.4** slime mold
water mold

**20.5** chitin
hyphae
mycelium

fruiting body
mycorrhizae
sporangia

**20.6** lichen

## Reviewing Vocabulary

### Compare and Contrast

Describe one similarity and one difference between the two terms in each of the following pairs.

1. pseudopod, cilia
2. slime mold, water mold
3. mycorrhizae, lichen
4. protozoa, algae
5. fruiting body, sporangia
6. hyphae, mycelium

### READING TOOLBOX   GREEK AND LATIN WORD ORIGINS

7. The term *hyphae* comes from the Greek word *huphe*, which means "web." Explain how this meaning relates to hyphae.

8. The term *mycorrhizae* comes from the Greek words *mukes*, which means "fungus," and *rhiza*, which means "root." Explain how these meanings relate to mycor-rhizae.

### Labeling Diagrams

In your notebook, write the vocabulary term that matches each numbered item below.

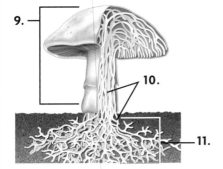

9.
10.
11.

## Reviewing MAIN IDEAS

12. Give one characteristic of each type of protist that explains why it is animal-like, plantlike, or funguslike.

13. Explain why the phyla of the kingdom Protista might be regrouped into several kingdoms and what would likely be the basis for this reclassification.

14. What are three types of structures that help some protists move?

15. When does an amoeba form a pseudopod?

16. Name two animal-like protists that cause disease and briefly describe the diseases they cause.

17. Are protists classified on the basis of being single-celled or multicellular? Give an example to support your answer.

18. How do multicellular algae reproduce asexually?

19. Slime molds have animal-like traits. What might be one reason they are classified with water molds as funguslike protists?

20. Explain how hyphae help a fungus absorb food.

21. The phyla Ascomycota and Basidiomycota are both in the kingdom Fungi. What structures are the basis for placing organisms in one or the other of these phyla?

22. Describe sexual reproduction in yeast, or single-celled fungi.

23. How can the hyphae of bread molds be involved in both asexual and sexual reproduction?

24. Why are yeasts useful to scientific research?

25. How is the decomposing activity of fungi both beneficial and harmful?

# Critical Thinking

**26. Analyze** What characteristics of protists prevent them from being classified as animals, plants, or fungi?

**27. Analyze** Amoebas have pseudopods, zooflagellates have flagella, and ciliates have cilia to help them move. Would you expect to find each of these types of protists on land or water? Explain your answer.

**28. Classify** A new plantlike protist has been discovered. It has the following characteristics: two flagella, found in a marine environment, body covering made of cellulose. What phylum would it likely be placed in?

**29. Describe** The prefix *pseudo-* means "false" or "fake." Why is the term *pseudoplasmodium* used to describe one form of a cellular slime mold?

**30. Predict** A grape crop is infected with a fungus. There is a fungicide that targets only this kind of fungus and kills it. But a broad-spectrum fungicide that kills many kinds of fungi is cheaper, and the farmer decides to use it instead. Explain why the farmer's crops may actually become less healthy.

## Interpreting Visuals

Use the diagram below to answer the next two questions.

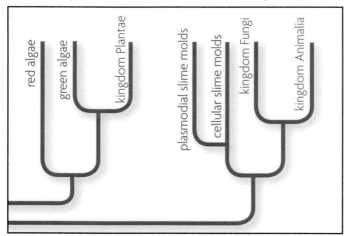

**31. Analyze** What does this diagram suggest about the relationship between fungi and animals, as compared with fungi and plants?

**32. Interpret** Are green algae more closely related to red algae or plants? Explain your answer.

## Analyzing Data  Analyze Experimental Design

Use the text and the data below to answer the next two questions. The following experiment was conducted by two students to determine if adding yeast to a decomposing fruit would speed up the rate of decomposition.

Two 3-cm² pieces of banana were cut. Each was placed in a different plastic bag and the bags were sealed. Each student took one of the banana pieces home.

- Student A placed her banana piece on a bookshelf.

- Student B put some dry yeast on his banana and resealed the bag. He also put his banana piece on a bookshelf.

Both students looked at the banana pieces every day for the next four days and recorded their observations.

| PERCENT DECOMPOSITION | | | | |
|---|---|---|---|---|
| **Organism** | **Day 1** | **Day 2** | **Day 3** | **Day 4** |
| **Student A's banana** | 1% | 5% | 7% | 10% |
| **Student B's banana** | 0% | 4% | 7% | 10% |

**33. Experimental Design** What is the main design flaw in this experiment?

**34. Analyze** Does the experimental design clearly support the question that the students were trying to answer? Explain.

## Making Connections

**35. Write an Argument** Write an imaginary argument between two euglenoids in which one wants to be placed with animals and the other wants to be placed with plants. Include the decision of the referee who explains why they can be neither plants nor animals.

**36. Evaluate** Look again at the picture of *Didinium* eating the *Paramecium* on the chapter opener. What might be one advantage and disadvantage of having a specialist feeding strategy? a generalist feeding strategy? Explain your answer.

# Standards-Based Assessment

Record your answers on a separate piece of paper.

## MULTIPLE CHOICE

1  When scientists first observed protists with chlorophyll, they thought the protists were actually single-celled plants. By using more recent molecular techniques, scientists have determined that these organisms are genetically different from plants. This is an example of —

A  how scientific theories can change with the development of new technologies

B  why scientific theories should not be influenced by new scientific evidence

C  why all scientific investigations should involve genetic analysis

D  why protists should be classified as plants

2

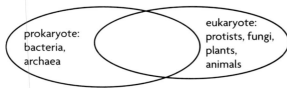

The grouping of kingdoms into prokaryotes and eukaryotes is shown in the Venn diagram above. One cellular characteristic that could be placed in the area that overlaps both groups is —

A  nucleus

B  organelles

C  chloroplasts

D  cell membrane

3  Diatoms carry out a large portion of the photosynthesis that occurs on Earth. In which biogeochemical cycle do diatoms probably have the greatest effect?

A  phosphorus cycle

B  nitrogen cycle

C  carbon cycle

D  water cycle

4  Most fungi are decomposers. How do their life processes affect other organisms in the community?

A  Fungi keep other populations under control by preying on weak organisms.

B  Fungi make stored nutrients available to other organisms.

C  Fungi compete with plants for soil nutrients.

D  Fungi compete with plants and animals for space.

> **THINK THROUGH THE QUESTION**
>
> If you are having a hard time answering this question in terms of fungi, try to consider it based on the role of decomposers in general.

5

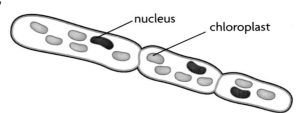

A researcher discovers a new type of organism. Only some structures, labeled above, can be seen clearly. Based on this information, the researcher is able to conclude that the organism —

A  is a protist that lives in colonies

B  is a multicellular protist

C  can capture energy from the sun

D  will not prey upon other organisms

6  Yeast is a single-celled fungus that can reproduce both asexually and sexually. How is sexual reproduction in a yeast cell different from sexual reproduction in animals?

A  In a yeast cell, the DNA is not copied.

B  The yeast cell does not undergo meiosis.

C  During meiosis, a yeast cell produces only two haploid nuclei.

D  During meiosis in a yeast cell, the cytoplasm does not divide.

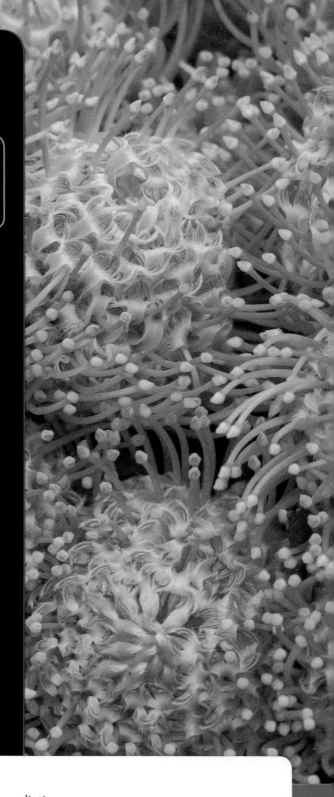

# 21 Plant Diversity

**BIG IDEA** Many organisms on Earth, including humans, depend on the diversity of plants and their traits for survival.

## ⊙ ONLINE BIOLOGY  HMHScience.com

**ONLINE** Labs
- **QuickLab** Classifying Plants as Vascular or Nonvascular
- Habitat Clues
- Comparing Monocots and Dicots
- Investigating Medicinal Plants
- Plants and Pollinators

- Phytoremediation
- **Video Lab** Plant Diversity
- **Video Lab** Monocot and Dicot Seeds

©Helmut Meyer zur Capellen/Alamy

# How have flowering plants come to dominate Earth's landscapes?

From the mosses that live in Antarctica to these flowering protea plants of South Africa, the plant kingdom is diverse. Proteas are native to one region of South Africa, called the Cape floristic region, which can go through long periods of drought. This small region is home to over 9000 plant species, including at least 6000 that are found nowhere else on Earth.

---

 **READING** TOOLBOX    **This reading tool can help you learn the material in the following pages.**

## USING LANGUAGE

**Classification** As you read the chapter, make distinctions between general words that describe categories and specific words that describe individuals within a category. Words that name categories are more general than words that describe individuals.

## YOUR TURN

Use information that you read in the chapter to answer the following questions.

1.  What are two types of seedless vascular plants?
2.  What is the general term identifying the category that includes mosses, liverworts, and hornworts?

# Origins of Plant Life

SC.912.L.14.7

**SC.912.L.14.7** Relate the structure of each of the major plant organs and tissues to physiological processes.

**VOCABULARY**

plant
cuticle
stomata
vascular system
lignin
pollen grain
seed

**KEY CONCEPT** **Plant life began in the water and became adapted to land.**

**MAIN IDEAS**

- Land plants evolved from green algae.
- Plants have adaptations that allow them to live on land.
- Plants evolve with other organisms in their environment.

☀️ *Connect to Your World*

The flowering proteas shown on the previous page are not just plants with beautiful flowers. Various birds, rodents, and insects rely on protea nectar and pollen as food sources. Green protea beetles even live inside of protea flowers. Without plants, animal life as we know it would not exist on land.

▶ **MAIN IDEA**

## Land plants evolved from green algae.

All green algae share certain characteristics with plants. **Plants** are multicellular eukaryotes, most of which produce their own food through photosynthesis and have adapted to life on land. Like plants, green algae are photosynthetic eukaryotes. They have chlorophyll that captures energy from sunlight during photosynthesis. Chlorophyll is what makes these algae—and most of the plants that we are familiar with—green. Green algae and plants have the same types of chlorophyll. Another feature both green algae and plants share is that they use starch as a storage product. Most green algae also have cell walls that contain cellulose, a complex carbohydrate that is found in the cell walls of all plants.

Evidence from genetic analysis points to one ancient species of green algae that is the common ancestor of all plants. If it were alive today, this species would be classified as a member of the class Charophyceae, like the algae in **FIGURE 1.1**. Several other important plant characteristics likely originated in charophyceans.

- A multicellular body, which led to the specialization of cells and tissues
- A method of cell division that produces cells with small channels in their walls, which allows cells to communicate with each other chemically
- Reproduction that involves sperm traveling to and fertilizing an egg cell

Today, charophyceans are common in freshwater habitats. Scientists hypothesize that the ancestral charophycean species may have grown in areas of shallow water that dried out from time to time. Natural selection likely favored individuals that could withstand longer dry periods. Eventually, the first true plant species evolved, as shown in **FIGURE 1.2**. True plants have multicellular embryos that remain attached to the female parent as they develop.

**FIGURE 1.1** Multicellular green algae of the genus *Chara* can be found in many lakes and ponds. They are called charophyceans and are thought to be the closest living relatives of the common ancestor of all plants.

## FIGURE 1.2 Evolution of Plants

**Plants have evolved from green algae. An extinct charophycean species is the common ancestor of all plants.**

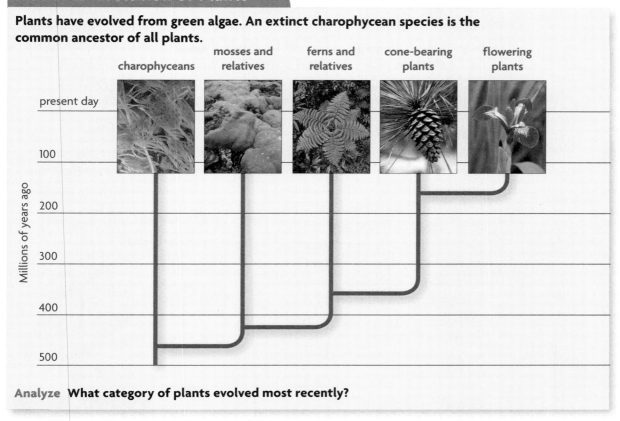

charophyceans | mosses and relatives | ferns and relatives | cone-bearing plants | flowering plants

Millions of years ago

present day
100
200
300
400
500

**Analyze** What category of plants evolved most recently?

The earliest plant fossils date to more than 450 million years ago. The first true plants probably grew on the edges of lakes and streams. Like modern-day mosses, they relied on droplets of water that brought sperm to eggs to produce the next generation of plants. They also had a fairly simple structure similar to that of moss, keeping low to the ground to retain moisture. Over time, the descendants of these plants were able to live in even drier areas.

**Apply** What evidence suggests that green algae are close relatives of land plants?

### ▶ MAIN IDEA
# Plants have adaptations that allow them to live on land.

Life on land presents different challenges than does life in the water. Unlike land plants, algae are constantly surrounded by water, which is needed for photosynthesis. The buoyancy of water supports the weight of most algae. For algae, water provides a medium through which sperm and spores can travel, allowing for reproduction and dispersal. Finally, water prevents sperm, eggs, and developing offspring from drying out.

The challenges of living on drier land have acted as selective pressures for plant life on Earth. In turn, many land plants have evolved adaptations that allow them to retain moisture, transport water and other resources between plant parts, grow upright, and reproduce without free-standing water.

**CONNECT TO**

**ALGAE**

Recall from the chapter **Protists and Fungi** that algae are plantlike protists. Photosynthetic pigments give various types of algae their distinct colors.

**READING TOOLBOX**

**TAKING NOTES**
Use a main idea web to take notes about the challenges of life on land and plants' adaptations to these challenges.

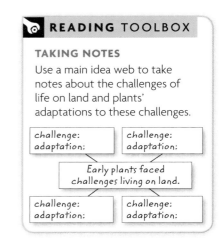

challenge: adaptation: | challenge: adaptation:

Early plants faced challenges living on land.

challenge: adaptation: | challenge: adaptation:

### Retaining Moisture

Plants will die if they dry out from exposure to air and sunlight. The surfaces of plants are covered with a cuticle. A **cuticle** is a waxy, waterproof layer that helps hold in moisture. As **FIGURE 1.3** shows, there are tiny holes in the cuticle, called **stomata** (singular, *stoma*). Special cells allow stomata to close to prevent water loss, or to open to allow air to move in and out. Without stomata, the movement of air would be prevented by the cuticle.

### Transporting Resources

Taller plants often have more access to sunlight than do shorter plants, but growing tall presents another challenge. While plants must get sunlight and carbon dioxide from the air, they must also get water and nutrients from the soil. A structure for moving these resources to different parts of the plant evolved in the form of a vascular system. A **vascular system** is a collection of specialized tissues that bring water and mineral nutrients up from the roots and disperse sugars down from the leaves. A vascular system allows a plant to grow higher off the ground.

**VISUAL VOCAB**

A **vascular system** allows water, mineral nutrients, and sugars to be transported to various parts of a plant.

water and mineral nutrients

sugars

### Growing Upright

Plant height is also limited by the ability of a plant to support its own weight. Plants need structure to support their weight and provide space for vascular tissues. This support comes from a material called **lignin** (LIHG-nihn), which hardens the cell walls of some vascular tissues. Lignin is also responsible for the strength of wood and provides stiffness to the stems of other plants. As a result, plants can retain their upright structure as they grow toward the sun.

### Reproducing on Land

In all plants, eggs are fertilized within the tissue of the parent plant. There, the fertilized egg develops into an embryo, the earliest stage of growth and development for a plant. Some plants reproduce with the help of rainwater or dew, while others do not need free-standing water to reproduce. Pollen and seeds are adaptations that allow seed plants to reproduce completely free of water.

A **pollen grain** is a two-celled structure that contains a cell that will divide to form sperm. Pollen can be carried by wind or animals to female reproductive structures. A **seed** is a storage device for a plant embryo. A seed has a hard coat that protects the embryo from drying wind and sunlight. Once a seed encounters the right conditions, the embryo can develop into an adult plant.

**Analyze  Discuss why the four challenges on this page do not apply to most algae.**

# FIGURE 1.3 Adaptations of Land Plants

**Land plants have evolved to adapt to the challenges of life on land.**

## POLLEN AND SEEDS

Pollen can be carried by wind or animals. Each pollen grain contains one cell that will divide to form sperm.

Seeds protect and provide nutrients for developing embryos.

pollen          seeds

## STOMATA AND CUTICLES

Stomata are small openings in the cuticle that allow for gas exchange between the plant and the atmosphere.

A cuticle is a waxy coating that protects plant leaves from drying out.

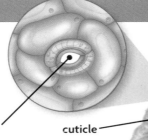

stoma          cuticle

## LIGNIN

Tough lignin is found in the cell walls of plant tissues that provide support and conduct fluids.

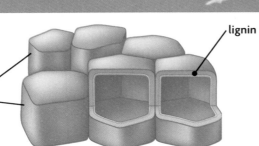

lignin

plant cells

## VASCULAR SYSTEM

Vascular tissues form "pipelines" that carry resources up and down to different parts of the plant. A vascular system allows plants to grow higher off the ground.

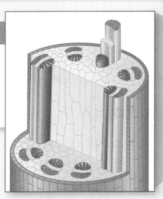

<u>CRITICAL VIEWING</u>   **Why is lignin especially important in the cell walls of vascular tissues?**

## MAIN IDEA

# Plants evolve with other organisms in their environment.

Plants have coevolved with other terrestrial organisms for millions of years. Some of these relationships are cooperative, while others have evolved between plant species and the animal species that eat them.

## Mutualisms

Mutualism describes an interaction between two species in which both species benefit. Mutualistic relationships exist between plant roots and certain types of fungi and bacteria. Roots provide a habitat for these fungi and bacteria, while the fungi and bacteria help the plant get mineral nutrients from the soil.

Many flowering plants depend on specific animal species for pollination or seed dispersal. In turn, these animals are fed by the plant's pollen, nectar, or fruit. For example, in Madagascar, Darwin noticed a variety of orchids with long, tubular flower parts. He predicted that a nocturnal moth with a tongue 30 and 35 cm (10–14 in.) long must be the pollinator. That very moth, shown in **FIGURE 1.4**, was discovered 40 years after Darwin's prediction.

## Plant-Herbivore Interactions

Plants have a variety of adaptations that discourage animals from eating them. The spines on a cactus and the thorns on a rose stem are examples. Other plants produce defensive chemicals that act as pesticides against plant-eating predators. Natural selection favors herbivores that can overcome the effects of defensive plant adaptations. In turn, natural selection favors plants that produce even sharper spines or thorns or even more toxic chemicals.

Some insects use defensive chemicals produced by plants to their advantage. The larvae of monarch butterflies, for example, feed exclusively on milkweed species. Milkweed plants produce a chemical that makes monarch larvae, adults, and even eggs taste bad to potential predators. In this way, the butterfly has a type of chemical protection as a result of eating milkweed leaves during its development.

**Synthesize** Describe how defensive chemicals in plant leaves may have evolved.

**FIGURE 1.4** The hawk moth has a tongue that measures between 30 and 35 cm (10–14 in.). It is the pollinator of a night-blooming orchid whose nectar is produced 30 cm down inside the flower.

(tl) ©Colin Keates/Dorling Kindersley, Courtesy of the Natural History Museum, London; (cl) ©Paul Harcourt Davies/Photo Researchers, Inc.

---

## 21.1 Formative Assessment

**SELF-CHECK Online**
HMHScience.com
**GO ONLINE**

### REVIEWING ▶ MAIN IDEAS

1. What characteristics do land **plants** share with green algae?

2. What adaptations allow plants to thrive on dry land?

3. Describe two ways in which plants evolve with other organisms.

### CRITICAL THINKING

4. **Synthesize** Describe how a **cuticle** could have evolved through natural selection.

5. **Evaluate** For plants, what are the advantages and disadvantages of growing tall?

### ☀ CONNECT TO

#### CLASSIFICATION

6. Some scientists think that certain species of green algae should be in the kingdom Plantae. What reasons might these scientists use to defend their position?

## 21.2 Classification of Plants

SC.912.L.15.4,
SC.912.L.15.6

| KEY CONCEPTS **Plants can be classified into nine phyla.**

### MAIN IDEAS

- Mosses and their relatives are seedless nonvascular plants.
- Club mosses and ferns are seedless vascular plants.
- Seed plants include cone-bearing plants and flowering plants.

**VOCABULARY**

pollination
gymnosperm
angiosperm
cone
flower
fruit

**SC.912.L.15.4** Describe how and why organisms are hierarchically classified and based on evolutionary relationships.

**SC.912.L.15.6** Discuss distinguishing characteristics of the domains and kingdoms of living organisms.

### Connect to Your World

How many different types of plants can you think of? You are probably familiar with the plants that grow in your neighborhood and in places you regularly visit. Scientists have described about 300,000 plant species, and many more probably remain to be found. All plants belong to the kingdom Plantae. However, DNA analysis continues to reveal new relationships that keep taxonomists updating the plant family tree.

### ○ MAIN IDEA

## Mosses and their relatives are seedless nonvascular plants.

In a damp forest, mosses lend an emerald green color to the landscape. These plants do not produce seeds. They have no vascular systems. Instead, they grow close to the ground or on surfaces such as tree trunks, where they can absorb water and nutrients directly. They also rely on free-standing water to allow their sperm to swim to and fertilize eggs. Mosses belong to Bryophyta, one of the three phyla of nonvascular plants. The other phyla in this category are Hepatophyta, the liverworts, and Anthocerophyta, the hornworts.

### CONNECT TO

**CLASSIFICATION**

Recall from the chapter **The Tree of Life** that the term *division* is sometimes used instead of the term *phylum* for the classification of plants and fungi.

### Liverworts

Most liverworts live in damp environments and get moisture directly from the surface of the soil. They are often found growing on wet rocks, in greenhouse flowerpots, and in other areas with plenty of moisture. Liverworts can have one of two basic forms: thallose or leafy. The name *liverwort* refers to thallose liverworts, which look like the lobes of a liver flat on the ground. Eggs are produced on umbrella-like structures of the thallose liverwort, shown in **FIGURE 2.1**. Though thallose liverworts may be easier to recognize, leafy liverworts are much more common. Leafy liverworts have stemlike and leaflike structures. These leaflike structures are most often arranged in three rows.

**FIGURE 2.1** Thallose liverworts, like the one shown here, can grow from 2 mm to 25 cm in length.

©Harold Taylor/Getty Images

## Hornworts

Hornworts are a widespread group of plants that are found in tropical forests and along streams around the world. Hornworts grow low to the ground, and the main plant body has a flat, lobed appearance similar to that of thallose liverworts. Little green horns rising above the flat plant body, as shown in **FIGURE 2.2**, produce spores.

## Mosses

Mosses are the most common nonvascular plants. Some look like clumps of grass, others look like tiny trees, and still others look like strands of green yarn. Mosses do not have true leaves. Instead, they have leaflike structures that are just one cell thick. While they lack vascular systems, some moss species do have cuticles, and most of them have stomata. Mosses can anchor themselves to surfaces such as soil, rocks, or tree trunks, as shown in **FIGURE 2.3**, with structures called rhizoids (RY-zoyDz).

Mosses are often tolerant of harsh weather conditions and nutrient-poor soils. They can grow in many places where other plants are unable to grow. Some mosses can survive in deserts and tundras by entering a stage of dormancy until water is available. In fact, mosses are often among the first plants to colonize bare land and begin the soil-making process in the early stages of primary succession.

One moss that is commonly used by humans is sphagnum (SFAG-nuhm), which grows in acidic bogs. Sphagnum does not decay when it dies, so thick deposits of this dead moss, called peat, build up over time. Peat can be cut from the ground and burned as fuel. Dried peat can absorb water, and it has antibacterial properties. In fact, dried peat has been used in products such as diapers and bandages. Peat also has an important role in the carbon cycle, as a reservoir that holds carbon in an organic form.

**Apply** Why can't nonvascular plants grow tall?

**FIGURE 2.2** The stalks of these hornworts are 2 to 5 cm long.

**CONNECT TO**

**ECOLOGY**

Recall from the chapter **Interactions in Ecosystems** that primary succession is the establishment of an ecosystem in an area that was previously uninhabited. Mosses are common pioneer species that help to break down solid rock into smaller pieces—one of the first steps in producing soil.

**FIGURE 2.3** Like all nonvascular plants, mosses need to live in moist environments.

## MAIN IDEA
# Club mosses and ferns are seedless vascular plants.

About 300 million years ago, during the Carboniferous period, shallow swamps were home to enormous seedless vascular plants. Over time, the dead remains of these plants were pressed and heated underground, where they gradually turned into coal. This is why we call coal a fossil fuel.

Club mosses (phylum Lycophyta) and ferns (phylum Pterophyta) are modern seedless vascular plants. Like nonvascular plants, they depend on water for reproduction. However, a vascular system allows these plants to grow higher above the ground and still get materials they need from the soil.

**FIGURE 2.4** Club mosses, such as this *Lycopodium* species, are able to grow up off of the ground because they have vascular systems.

## Club Mosses

Club mosses, which are not true mosses, belong to the oldest living group of vascular plants. Some ancient species looked like modern trees, growing more than ten stories tall. These giant plants were wiped out when the Carboniferous climate cooled, but some of the smaller species survived. One common living genus of club moss is *Lycopodium*. Some *Lycopodium* species, such as the one shown in **FIGURE 2.4**, look like tiny pine trees and are sometimes called "ground pines."

## Whisk Ferns, Horsetails, and Ferns

Ferns and their relatives, whisk ferns and horsetails, can be grouped together in one phylum. Whisk ferns grow mostly in the tropics and subtropics. Although they lack true roots and leaves, DNA analysis indicates that whisk ferns are closely related to ferns.

Horsetails grow in wetland areas and along rivers and streams. They have tan, scalelike leaves that grow in whorls around a tubular stem. Like club mosses, horsetails were much larger and more common in the Carboniferous period. Because horsetails' cell walls contain a rough compound called silica, colonial settlers used the plant, also called "scouring rush," to scrub pots.

Ferns are the most successful survivors of the Carboniferous period, with about 12,000 species alive today. Most ferns grow from underground stems called rhizomes (RY-zohmz). Their large leaves, shown in **FIGURE 2.5**, are called fronds. Newly-forming fronds, called fiddleheads, uncurl as they grow. Some ferns are grown as houseplants. Others, called tree ferns, live in the tropics and can grow over three stories tall.

**FIGURE 2.5  FERNS**

frond

fiddlehead

Fern leaves are called fronds. Newly-forming fronds, called fiddleheads, uncurl as they grow.

**Infer  Why do most seedless vascular plants live in moist areas?**

## Classifying Plants as Vascular or Nonvascular

In this lab, you will examine tissues from several plants to determine whether they are vascular or nonvascular. This is the first step in classifying plants into one of the nine phyla.

**PROBLEM**  Are the plants vascular or nonvascular?

**PROCEDURE**

1. Observe each slide under the microscope.
2. Make a sketch of each plant tissue you examine.

**MATERIALS**
- prepared slides of plant tissue
- microscope

**ANALYZE AND CONCLUDE**

1. **Analyze**  In what ways are the plant tissues similar? In what ways are they different?
2. **Analyze**  Based on your observations, are the plants vascular or nonvascular? What evidence did you use to determine their identity?
3. **Apply**  How does the absence of vascular tissue affect the size (height) of nonvascular plants?

▶ **MAIN IDEA**

# Seed plants include cone-bearing plants and flowering plants.

You may be familiar with seeds as the small plant parts that, when sown and tended, will produce another plant. From an evolutionary viewpoint, seed plants have several great advantages over their ancestors.

- **Seed plants can reproduce without free-standing water.**  Seedless plants depend on water through which sperm swim to fertilize an egg. However, seed plants do not depend on water in this way. Seed plants, such as the pine tree in **FIGURE 2.6,** produce pollen. Pollen can be carried by the wind or on the body of an animal pollinator, such as a bee. **Pollination** occurs when pollen meets female reproductive parts of the same plant species. Each pollen grain has a cell that will then divide to form sperm. Fertilization occurs when a sperm meets an egg. The ability to reproduce without free-standing water allows many seed plants to live in drier climates.

- **Seeds nourish and protect plant embryos.**  A seed consists of a protective coat that contains a plant embryo and a food supply. A seed can survive for many months, or even years, in a dormant state. During this time, the seed can withstand harsh conditions, such as drought or cold, that might kill an adult plant. When conditions are right, the embryo will begin growing, using the food supply provided by the seed.

- **Seeds allow plants to disperse to new places.**  Wind, water, or animals often carry seeds far from the individual plant that produced them. In fact, many seed plants have adaptations that aid in the dispersal of seeds, such as the "wings" that carry maple seeds in the wind. Because seeds can remain dormant, the embryo will not begin to develop until it reaches a suitable environment.

**FIGURE 2.6**  Seed plants produce pollen. In pine trees such as the one shown here, clouds of pollen are released from male pine cones.

©James Zipp/Science Source/Getty Images

Scientists hypothesize that seed plants evolved as Earth's climate changed from warm and moist to hot and dry during the Devonian period, 410 to 360 million years ago. Fossil evidence suggests that seed plants evolved about 360 million years ago. Seed plants can be grouped according to whether their seeds are enclosed in fruit.

- A **gymnosperm** (JIHM-nuh-SPURM) is a seed plant whose seeds are not enclosed in fruit.
- An **angiosperm** (AN-jee-uh-SPURM) is a seed plant that has seeds enclosed in some type of fruit.

Most gymnosperms are cone-bearing and evergreen, such as pine trees. A woody **cone** is the reproductive structure of most gymnosperms. It contains hard protective scales. Pollen is produced in male cones, while eggs are produced in female cones. Seeds also develop on the scales of female cones, which protect fertilized eggs. There are three living phyla of gymnosperms: cycads (phylum Cycadophyta), *Ginkgo biloba* (phylum Ginkgophyta), and conifers (phylum Coniferophyta).

**FIGURE 2.7** Cycads, such as the one shown here, produce seeds on large, protective, female cones.

 **READING TOOLBOX**

**VOCABULARY**

*Gymnosperm* comes from the Greek words *gumnos*, which means "naked," and *sperma*, which means "seed." *Angiosperm* comes from the Greek words *angos*, which means "vessel," and *sperma*, which means "seed."

## Cycads

Cycads look like palm trees with large cones, as shown in **FIGURE 2.7**. Huge forests of cycads grew during the Mesozoic era, 248 million to 65 million years ago. These plants provided food for dinosaurs. In fact, the Jurassic period of this era is commonly called the Age of the Cycads. Today, cycads grow in tropical areas in the Americas, Asia, Africa, and Australia. Many cycad species are endangered because of their slow growth and loss of habitat in these tropical areas.

## Ginkgo

Like cycads, ginkgoes were abundant while the dinosaurs lived. Only one species lives today, *Ginkgo biloba*, shown in **FIGURE 2.8**. This species is native to China, and it has survived in part due to its cultivation by Buddhist monks since the year 1100. Because it so closely resembles its fossil ancestors, Darwin called this species a living fossil. In fact, the ginkgo may be the oldest living species of seed plants. Today, it is grown around the world in gardens and used in urban landscaping.

**FIGURE 2.8** The name *Ginkgo biloba* refers to the two-lobed leaves of this plant. Ginkgo trees are used commonly in garden landscapes.

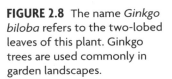

FIGURE 2.9 This Ponderosa pine is a typical evergreen conifer with needlelike leaves.

## Conifers

By far, the most diverse and common gymnosperms alive today are the conifers—familiar trees with needlelike leaves, such as those in **FIGURE 2.9**. Pines, redwood, spruce, cedar, fir, and juniper all belong to this phylum. Conifers supply most of the timber used for paper, cardboard, housing lumber, and plywood. They grow quickly, and large tree farms help produce enough wood to meet demand.

Many conifers are evergreen, or green all year-round. However, a few lose their needles in the winter. Conifers are well adapted to high altitudes, sloping hillsides, and poor soil. These characteristics allow conifers to thrive in mountainous regions.

Conifers tend to grow old and grow tall. Two known conifers hold world records. At more than 9550 years of age, one spruce tree in the Dalarna province of Sweden is the oldest known living tree. And a giant sequoia tree in Sequoia National Park in California is the world's most massive living thing. It has a mass of 1.2 million kilograms, which is about the mass of 40 buses.

## Flowering Plants

Angiosperms belong to a phylum of their own (phylum Anthophyta) and are commonly called flowering plants. A **flower** is the reproductive structure of flowering plants. Flowers protect a plant's gametes and fertilized eggs, as woody cones do for most gymnosperms. A **fruit** is the mature ovary of a flower. Fruit can take the form of a juicy peach, the wings attached to a maple seed, or the fluff surrounding dandelion seeds. As you will learn in the next section, flowers and fruits have played a large role in the dominance and diversity of flowering plants today.

**Apply** What adaptation of seed plants allows sperm to reach and fertilize an egg in the absence of water?

## 21.2 Formative Assessment

### REVIEWING ▶ MAIN IDEAS

1. What are the habitat requirements for seedless nonvascular plants?
2. What are the evolutionary advantages of a vascular system?
3. What are the evolutionary advantages of seeds?

### CRITICAL THINKING

4. **Infer** In what type of environment might you find nonvascular plants, seedless vascular plants, and seed plants growing together? Explain.
5. **Apply** Consider the characteristics of pollen grains. Why do people with pollen allergies find it difficult to avoid exposure to pollen?

### ▸ CONNECT TO

**HISTORY OF LIFE**

6. According to the fossil record, seed plants date back to 360 million years ago, when Earth's climate was becoming hotter and drier. What role did this global climate change likely play in the evolution of seed plants?

# Engineering the Vault: Protecting Seed Diversity

For centuries, human beings have looked for ways to prepare for natural or human-made catastrophes. Today, people have the knowledge—and the technology—to implement plans our ancestors could only dream of. The construction of seed vaults is one of humanity's most practical precautions against disaster.

A seed vault is, quite simply, a building for storing seeds for future use. Such storage helps preserve the genetic diversity of the world's plants and protects against the extinction of plant species due to climate change, habitat destruction, disease, natural disasters, and industrial agriculture's overreliance on just a few species of plants. There are approximately 1,700 seed vaults located across the world. Some vaults store varieties of one type of staple plant, such as beans, potatoes, wheat, or rice. Others store seeds from a particular region or country.

Still other seed vaults, such as the Svalbard Global Seed Vault (SGSV), store seeds from all over the globe. The SGSV, which was established in 2008 on a Norwegian island in the Arctic Ocean, is a backup for other seed banks around the world that are in locations more susceptible to damage by climate change or war. The SGSV has room for up to 4.5 million samples of seeds. Because each sample contains 500 seeds, potentially 2.5 billion seeds can be stored there. More than 860,000 seed samples, sent from most of the world's countries, are currently stored in the SGSV.

The SGSV's location on the island of Spitsbergen is ideal for several reasons. First, Spitsbergen is very remote, far from the possibility of damage by war or civil unrest. Second, it is well above sea level, which protects against sea-level rise due to climate change. Third, the island has low humidity and is in an area not prone to earthquakes. Finally, the facility was built into the side of a mountain, and the low temperatures and thick rock keep the seeds inside frozen at −18°C.

Several natural and technological elements work in tandem to keep the seeds in the SGSV frozen. Refrigeration units in the facility keep the seeds at the required temperature. The units are powered by a local power grid, with a backup generator for extra security. But if both the local power grid and the backup generator should fail, the island's low temperatures and permafrost—and the mountain's thick rock—will keep temperatures inside the facility low.

The SGSV has been opened once already. War and civil unrest in the Syrian city of Aleppo forced scientists there to flee the violence, leaving behind the seeds at a nearby seed vault. In 2015 barley, wheat, and grass seeds were withdrawn from the SGSV to allow the relocated scientists to continue their work in safe locations in other countries.

The future is always shrouded in uncertainty, but the construction of seed vaults around the world helps ensure that humankind will be able to feed itself in the face of disaster.

## S.T.E.M. Activity

Research another seed vault in a location of your choice. Learn about the vault's focus and the technology used there to store seeds safely. Then pick a location elsewhere in the world that doesn't have a seed vault. Design a seed vault that will take advantage of the area's natural and human-made characteristics. Decide what technology will be needed in the seed vault and indicate that technology in a labeled diagram.

Entrance to the Svalbard Global Seed Vault

© Sergio Pitamitz/National Geographic Magazines/Getty Images

# 21.3 Diversity of Flowering Plants

**SC.912.L.15.6**

**KEY CONCEPT** The largest phylum in the plant kingdom is the flowering plants.

**SC.912.L.15.6** Discuss distinguishing characteristics of the domains and kingdoms of living organisms.

## VOCABULARY

cotyledon
monocot
dicot
wood

## MAIN IDEAS

- Flowering plants have unique adaptations that allow them to dominate in today's world.
- Flowering plants can be categorized based on seed type.
- Flowering plants are also categorized by stem type and lifespan.

 **Connect to Your World**

Sunflower seeds in the shell aren't just a tasty snack. They are an example of one of the great adaptations of flowering plants. Like all flowering plants, sunflowers produce fruits. Technically, the fruit is the shell surrounding the sunflower seed. As you will soon learn, fruits can take many forms beyond the juicy apple or peach that may first come to mind.

## ▶ MAIN IDEA

# Flowering plants have unique adaptations that allow them to dominate in today's world.

Up until about 65 million years ago, there were far fewer flowering plants than there are today. After the mass extinction event that ended the Cretaceous period, the fossil record reveals that a major shift took place in species that dominated Earth. Dinosaurs disappeared, as did many seedless plant species. These plant extinctions left open niches into which flowering plants, such as the dogwoods in **FIGURE 3.1,** could radiate and prosper. Their diversification happened quickly in geologic terms and was closely tied to the diversification of land animals such as insects and birds. The same adaptations that were important to the success of flowering plants long ago continue to be important today.

### CONNECT TO

### EVOLUTION

Recall from the chapter **The Evolution of Populations** that mammals also went through a period of adaptive radiation after the mass extinction that killed the dinosaurs 65 million years ago.

**FIGURE 3.1** Many trees, including dogwoods, are flowering plants.

### Flowers and Pollination

Flowers allow for more efficient pollination than occurs in most gymnosperms, which rely on wind for pollination. You have probably observed a bee or a butterfly hovering around the center of a flower. These insects and other animals feed on pollen, which is high in protein, or on nectar, a sugary solution produced in the flowers of some plant species. As an animal feeds from a flower, it gets pollen on itself. Then, when it moves to another flower for more food, some of the pollen brushes off onto the new flower. Thus, animal pollinators transfer pollen from flower to flower in a very targeted way. For this reason, flowering plants pollinated by animals don't need to produce nearly as much pollen as do plants that rely on the wind to randomly transfer their pollen.

©Royalty-Free/Corbis

## FIGURE 3.2  Adaptations of Flowering Plants

**Flowers and fruits are unique adaptations of all flowering plants.**

Many flowering plants are pollinated by animals.

Fruits protect the seeds of flowering plants and often play a role in seed dispersal.

**Synthesize  How is each photograph showing a coevolutionary relationship?**

### Fruits and Seed Dispersal

The many types of fruits include some very unlike the kinds you see in a grocery store. In biological terms, a fruit is a flower's ripened ovary, which surrounds and protects the seed or seeds. For example, the shells of sunflower seeds and peanuts are fruits. Fruits play an important role in seed dispersal. As shown in **FIGURE 3.2**, the more familiar fleshy fruits are tasty food sources for animals, which digest the fruit tissue but not the seeds. Seeds pass through the animal and are deposited along with a convenient supply of fecal fertilizer that is helpful during germination. Others take the form of burrs that cling to passing wildlife, or fibers that help spread seeds by wind.

**Infer  Why is pollination by animals more efficient than wind pollination?**

That's Amazing!

**Video Inquiry**
HMHScience.com
**GO ONLINE**

Cotton-Ball Bats

## ▶ MAIN IDEA
# Flowering plants can be categorized based on seed type.

There are at least 300,000 identified flowering plant species. Compared with other living plant phyla—the three gymnosperm phyla have a total of 720 species—the number of flowering plants is impressive.

Botanists used to classify flowering plants into two groups based on two basic kinds of seeds: seeds with one or two cotyledons. A **cotyledon** (KAHT-uhl-EED-uhn), or seed leaf, is an embryonic leaf inside a seed. However, scientists now know that the classification of flowering plants is more complex. Based on genetic and fossil evidence, current taxonomy places plants with one cotyledon into a single group but classifies plants with two cotyledons into several diverse groups. Nevertheless, a categorization into two main groups remains useful for understanding plant structure.

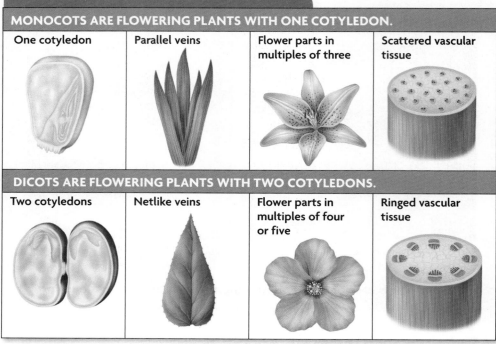

## FIGURE 3.3 Monocots and Dicots

**MONOCOTS ARE FLOWERING PLANTS WITH ONE COTYLEDON.**

| One cotyledon | Parallel veins | Flower parts in multiples of three | Scattered vascular tissue |

**DICOTS ARE FLOWERING PLANTS WITH TWO COTYLEDONS.**

| Two cotyledons | Netlike veins | Flower parts in multiples of four or five | Ringed vascular tissue |

### Monocots

Flowering plants whose embryos have one seed leaf are called monocotyledons, or **monocots** (MAHN-uh-кαнтs). As **FIGURE 3.3** shows, monocot plants generally have parallel veins in long, narrow leaves, such as those of an iris or lily. Their flower parts usually occur in multiples of three, and bundles of vascular tissues are scattered throughout the stem. The cereal plants we depend on—corn, wheat, rice—are monocots, as are all other grasses, irises, and lilies.

### Dicots

Dicotyledons, or **dicots** (DY-кαнтs), are flowering plants whose embryos have two seed leaves. In contrast to monocots, dicots have leaves with netlike veins. Flower parts in dicots usually occur in multiples of four or five, and bundles of vascular tissue are arranged in rings. Most deciduous trees, which lose their leaves in the fall, are dicots. Peanuts are also dicots. Each "half" of a peanut that has been removed from its shell is a cotyledon.

**Predict** **Would you expect that cotyledons are green inside a seed? Explain.**

▶ MAIN IDEA

## Flowering plants are also categorized by stem type and lifespan.

Flowering plants can also be categorized by stem type and lifespan, as shown in **FIGURE 3.4**. These characteristics help describe mature flowering plants and are commonly used by botanists, gardeners, landscape designers, and horticulturists.

**Iris** Monocot, herbaceous, perennial

**Wheat** Monocot, herbaceous, annual

**Foxglove** Dicot, herbaceous, biennial

**Oak** Dicot, woody, perennial

**Big bluestem** Monocot, herbaceous, perennial

## Herbaceous or Woody Stems

Some flowering plants develop woody stems, while others do not. **Wood** is a fibrous material made up of dead cells that are part of the vascular system of some plants. High concentrations of lignin and cellulose make the cell walls of these cells thick and stiff. Woody plants therefore have stiff stems and branches. Wood also accounts for the thickness of many woody plant stems. Trees, shrubs, and most vines have woody stems. Plants that do not produce wood, such as cucumbers, cacti, and marigolds, are called herbaceous plants.

## Three Types of Lifespans

It is helpful for biologists to classify plants in terms of their lifespans, since lifespan is an important life history trait.

- **Annual** Flowering plants that mature from seeds, produce flowers, and die all in one year are called annuals. Corn and lettuce are common annuals, as are some garden flowers such as zinnias.
- **Biennial** Flowering plants that take two years to complete their life cycle are called biennials. During the first year, a biennial produces a short stem, leaves that grow close to the ground, and underground food reserves. During the second year, these reserves are used to produce a taller stem, leaves, flowers, and seeds. Carrots are common biennial garden plants.
- **Perennial** Any flowering plant that lives for more than two years is a perennial. Most woody plants, including trees, are perennials. The stems and leaves of some herbaceous perennials, such as some grasses and dandelions, die at the end of the fall and grow back in the spring.

**Contrast** How do the lifespans of annuals, biennials, and perennials differ?

**FIGURE 3.4** Flowering plants are the largest and most diverse of the plant phyla. They are commonly categorized according to seed type, stem type, and lifespan.

# 21.3 Formative Assessment

 **SELF-CHECK Online**
HMHScience.com
**GO ONLINE**

## REVIEWING ▶ MAIN IDEAS

1. What adaptations give flowering plants a reproductive advantage over gymnosperms?

2. What are the primary differences between **monocots** and **dicots**?

3. Name three ways in which flowering plants can be categorized.

## CRITICAL THINKING

4. **Contrast** In what ways does pollination in gymnosperms differ from pollination in angiosperms?

5. **Apply** How would you take plant lifespan type into account when planning a garden?

### ☼ CONNECT TO

## MASS EXTINCTIONS

6. The fossil record reveals a mass extinction at the end of the Cretaceous period. Discuss why mass extinctions are commonly followed by a period of adaptive radiation, in this case, of flowering plants.

# Mean, Median, and Mode

One way to analyze data is to use measures of **central tendency,** which are measures that indicate the center of a data set. The three most common measures of central tendency are the mean, median, and mode. It is often helpful to look at all three of these measures because they may each point out different characteristics of a data set.

The **mean** is calculated by adding all of the data points together and dividing by the number of data points. The mean considers the full range of data and is therefore affected by outliers—data points that vary greatly from all of the other points in the data set.

The **median** is the data point that falls in the middle when all of the data points are ordered from least to greatest. If there is an even number of data points, the median is the average of the two middle numbers. Since outliers do not affect the median, this may be a good measure to use with a data set that includes outliers.

The **mode** is the value that occurs most frequently. It is not affected by outliers. Some data sets have more than one mode. If there are several modes that dominate the data set, it is a good idea to study these data points more closely.

## Model

A class counted the number of seeds found in some common fruits. These data are shown in Table 1.

- **Oranges** The mean is an appropriate measure to use for this data set because there are no obvious outliers.
- **Watermelons** The mean is affected by an outlier, 582 seeds. The median is a good measure to represent this data set.
- **Apples** The two modes represent a trend in these results that the students may want to investigate further.

| TABLE 1. NUMBER OF SEEDS IN VARIOUS FRUIT | | | | |
|---|---|---|---|---|
| **Fruit** | **Number of Seeds per Fruit** | **Mean** | **Median** | **Mode** |
| **Apples** | 6, 7, 6, 4, 4, 4, 3, 6, 4, 6 | 5 | 5 | 4 and 6 |
| **Oranges** | 14, 6, 10, 8, 4, 11, 6, 3, 5, 13 | 8 | 7 | 6 |
| **Strawberries** | 171, 208, 230, 171, 159, 182, 217, 238, 165, 179 | ? | ? | ? |
| **Watermelons** | 582, 133, 207, 87, 164, 290, 98, 155, 196, 278 | 219 | 180 | none |

## Practice Choose an Appropriate Measure of Central Tendency

Use the data for the number of seeds counted in each of ten strawberries to answer the questions below.

1. **Calculate** Find the mean, median, and mode for this set of data.

2. **Evaluate** Which measure of central tendency best represents this data set? Why?

# 21.4 Plants in Human Culture

**VOCABULARY**

botany
ethnobotany
pharmacology
alkaloid

**MAIN IDEAS**

- Agriculture provides stable food supplies for people in permanent settlements.
- Plant products are important economic resources.
- Plant compounds are essential to modern medicine.

## Connect to Your World

Books are made from plants. The pages are pulverized wood from trees, the ink contains plant oil, and the glue that binds them together is made from petroleum—the ancient leftovers of algae and plants. Humans rely on plants for nearly everything in daily life. Today, crop plants are so important to our economy that their changing prices are reported in the media alongside those of stocks and bonds.

## ◉ MAIN IDEA

# Agriculture provides stable food supplies for people in permanent settlements.

**READING TOOLBOX**

**VOCABULARY**
The word *ethnobotany* comes from the Greek words *ethnos,* which means "people," and *botane–* which means "plants."

Some of the plants that are considered important by humans have changed over time, but plants have always been used to fill the basic needs of our species: food, shelter, clothing, and medicine. While **botany** is the study of plants, **ethnobotany** explores how people in different cultures use plants.

For most of human history, people survived by hunting and gathering. This requires a very thorough understanding of local botany—plant locations, life cycles, and characteristics. Hunting and gathering also requires people to change locations if resources are diminished by weather, disease, or overuse. People then must become familiar with the resources of the new area.

©Charles O'Rear/Corbis

**FIGURE 4.1** Agriculture has become an important part of our global economy. Many river deltas, such as the Sacramento River delta in California, are used for farmland because of their nutrient-rich soils and water.

Teosinte

Modern corn

**FIGURE 4.2** Teosinte (top) is the ancestor of modern corn. Modern corn evolved through artificial selection. Humans likely selected individual plants that had the most numerous and accessible seeds.

Archaeological evidence suggests that people started intentionally planting for harvest about 10,000 years ago. Over the centuries, ancient farmers "tamed" wild species by a process of artificial selection, as shown in **FIGURE 4.2.** They chose plants with the best traits, saved their seeds, and planted them the next year. Most of the world's staple foods—corn, rice, and wheat—were developed from wild grasses in this way. These farmers became more closely tied to particular areas.

Because farming requires people to stay in one place, agriculture gave rise to more socially complex centers of human populations. A benefit of farming was a more reliable source of food that could support a growing population. Eventually, farmers grew enough excess food to sell it to neighbors as a cash crop. In this way, farming became part of a culture's economy.

**Summarize** What does an ethnobotanist study?

▶ **MAIN IDEA**

## Plant products are important economic resources.

Plant products have been traded among various regions for thousands of years. Spices such as pepper, cinnamon, and cloves were so valuable that they were commonly used as a form of currency during the early Middle Ages. In fact, many of the seafaring explorations to Asia and the Americas during the 1400s and 1500s were prompted by the value of spices, like those shown in **FIGURE 4.3.** Columbus, Magellan, and da Gama were all in search of a new route to the valuable commodities of the East.

Today, plants are important economic resources on a global scale. The values of rice, grains, soybeans, coffee, sugar, and cotton traded in world markets every year are each billions of dollars. Paper, textiles, and lumber are just a few of the plant-derived products that contribute to our economy.

**Connect** What plants were used to make the clothes that you are wearing and the contents of your backpack?

**FIGURE 4.3** Spices have been an economically important resource for at least 4000 years.

# Plant compounds are essential to modern medicine.

The study of drugs and their effects on the body is called **pharmacology.** Many of the drugs used today are derived from plants, and much of the knowledge of these plants comes from traditional cultures. We still use some plants medicinally in the same way they have been used for thousands of years. For instance, the aloe vera gel you can buy to soothe sunburn was used for the same purpose by the Egyptians 3500 years ago.

As shown in **FIGURE 4.4**, scientists continue to look for and find new uses for plants that have been used medicinally for centuries. For example, Native Americans have long used the Pacific yew to treat a variety of conditions. In the 1960s, scientists isolated a compound called taxol from the tree, which has been used as a cancer treatment since 1993. Salicin, which comes from willow trees, is another plant compound that you are likely familiar with. It is the active ingredient in aspirin, the most widely used medicine in the world.

While plant oils and resins are common in traditional medicines, other plant compounds, including gums, steroids, and alkaloids, have found their way into modern medicines. **Alkaloids** are potent plant chemicals that contain nitrogen. In small amounts, many alkaloids are medicinal. By interfering with cell division, some alkaloids—such as taxol—have anti-cancer properties. Two alkaloids produced by the Madagascar periwinkle are used to treat childhood leukemia and Hodgkin's disease. Other alkaloids have been identified to treat conditions ranging from a nasty cough to high blood pressure.

Today, much medical research focuses on the chemical properties of various plant compounds—especially compounds from plants that have been used medicinally in traditional cultures. Chemists also work to develop synthetic drugs based on the structure of these natural compounds, often changing the structures slightly to increase effectiveness and reduce side effects.

**Infer** Why might certain plant compounds have healing effects in small quantities but be dangerous in larger doses?

**FIGURE 4.4** This scientist, standing waist-high in water, is studying a mangrove forest in Thailand. Mangrove forests grow in intertidal zones in the tropics. These diverse ecosystems may hold treatments for a variety of medical conditions.

---

**CONNECT TO**

**CELLS**

Some alkaloids help stop the spread of cancer by interfering with mitosis. Recall from the chapter **Cell Growth and Division** that mitosis is the phase of the cell cycle when the duplicated chromosomes separate so that two new cells form.

©Bojan Brecelj/Corbis

---

**SELF-CHECK Online**
HMHScience.com
**GO ONLINE**

# 21.4 Formative Assessment

## REVIEWING ▶ MAIN IDEAS

1. How has agriculture affected the day-to-day life of humans?

2. In what ways are plants an important part of our culture today?

3. Why is a knowledge of plants so important to **pharmacology**?

## CRITICAL THINKING

4. **Analyze** How did the average person's knowledge of plants change in societies that adopted agriculture? Explain your answer.

5. **Connect** Aside from food and medicine, in what ways are plants used in your life?

**CONNECT TO**

**HUMAN IMPACT ON ECOSYSTEMS**

6. Many plants harvested for medicinal purposes grow in rain forests of developing countries. How might this fact affect the ecosystems and economies of these countries?

# 21 Summary

## KEY CONCEPTS

### 21.1 Origins of Plant Life

**Plant life began in the water and became adapted to land.** The common ancestor of plants is an ancient species of green algae. Green algae called charophyceans are the closest living relatives to this common ancestor. Over time, the first true plant species evolved as they adapted to life on land. Land plants have evolved mechanisms to retain moisture, transport resources, grow upright, and reproduce on land. They have also coevolved with other organisms that inhabit dry land.

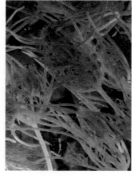

### 21.2 Classification of Plants

**Plants can be classified into nine phyla.** Mosses and their relatives make up three phyla of seedless nonvascular plants. These plants rely on water for reproduction and must grow low to the ground to absorb water and nutrients. Club mosses and ferns make up two phyla of seedless vascular plants. Vascular tissue allows these plants to grow higher above the ground. Seed plants, which include three phyla of cone-bearing plants and one phylum of flowering plants, do not rely on water for reproduction. Sperm of seed plants are produced by pollen grains. Seeds nourish and protect the embryos of these plants.

### 21.3 Diversity of Flowering Plants

**The largest phylum in the plant kingdom is the flowering plants.** Flowers and fruit are two adaptations that have allowed flowering plants to become the dominant plant group on Earth today. Flowers often allow for more efficient pollination by animals, while fruit can aid in seed dispersal. Flowering plants can be categorized into two groups based on the number of cotyledons inside the seed. Flowering plants can also be categorized based on stem type and lifespan.

### 21.4 Plants in Human Culture

**Humans rely on plants in many ways.** Plants are essential to human existence. All of the food that we eat comes either directly or indirectly from plant life. Agriculture provides stable food supplies for most people today. Many agricultural products are important economic resources on a global scale. Plants also provide us with clothing, paper, textiles, lumber, and medicines.

---

## READING TOOLBOX     SYNTHESIZE YOUR NOTES

**Three-Column Chart** Use a three-column chart to take notes about the nine divisions of plants. Use the columns to write the scientific names of each division, the common names, and details about the plants.

| Scientific Name | Common Name | Details |
|---|---|---|
|  |  |  |

**Concept Map** Use a concept map to review how flowering plants can be categorized.

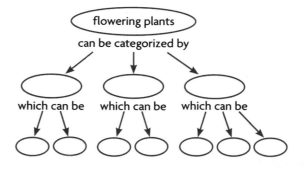

## CHAPTER VOCABULARY

**21.1**
plant
cuticle
stomata
vascular system
lignin
pollen grain
seed

**21.2**
pollination
gymnosperm
angiosperm
cone
flower
fruit

**21.3**
cotyledon
monocot
dicot
wood

**21.4**
botany
ethnobotany
pharmacology
alkaloid

## Reviewing Vocabulary

### Vocabulary Connections

For each group of words below, write a sentence or two to clearly explain how the terms are connected. For example, for the terms *cuticle* and *stomata,* you could write "Together, the cuticle and stomata prevent water loss while allowing for gas exchange."

1. lignin, wood
2. pollen grain, pollination
3. gymnosperm, seed, cone
4. angiosperm, seed, flower, fruit
5. cotyledon, monocot, dicot
6. pharmacology, alkaloid

### READING TOOLBOX    GREEK AND LATIN WORD ORIGINS

7. *Cuticula* is the Latin word for "skin." How does this meaning relate to the definition of the word *cuticle*?

8. In Greek, the word *stoma* means "mouth." How does this meaning relate to its botanical meaning?

9. In Latin, the word *pollen* means "dust" or "fine flour." How does this meaning relate to its botanical meaning?

10. The word *conus* is a Latin word that means "wedge" or "peak." How does this meaning relate to the definition of the word *cone*?

11. *Fruï* is a Latin verb meaning "to enjoy." How does this meaning relate to the role that various fruits play in human culture?

12. The prefix *mono-* means "one" in Latin, while the prefix *di-* means "two." How do these meanings relate to the words *monocot* and *dicot*?

## Reviewing MAIN IDEAS

13. Summarize the evidence supporting the statement that modern plants evolved from an ancient species of green algae.

14. Discuss four major challenges that early plants faced while adapting to life on dry land.

15. The 30-centimeter tongue of the hawk moth is long enough to reach the nectar—and reproductive organs—of the night-blooming orchid. What can be concluded about the evolution of plants from these types of relationships? Explain.

16. Describe the structural features that limit the height of mosses and their relatives.

17. Explain why most seedless vascular plants live in moist environments.

18. What is the main difference between the seeds of cone-bearing plants and the seeds of flowering plants?

19. Summarize two of the adaptations of flowering plants that allow them to flourish in today's world.

20. Describe how the number of cotyledons a plant has is useful in categorizing plants.

21. Compare and contrast annual, biennial, and perennial lifespans.

22. What role does agriculture play in the stability and survival of modern human populations?

23. How can plants play a role in developing modern medicines, even if they are not used as ingredients?

# Critical Thinking

**24. Analyze** Aquatic plants, which evolved from land plants, have adaptations that allow them to live in the water. Some aquatic plants grow completely submerged in water. What challenges might these plants face that do not apply to plants that live entirely on land?

**25. Analyze** The sperm of seedless plants are flagellated, while those of seed plants are not. How do the sperm of seed plants reach eggs without flagella?

**26. Compare** When a plant reproduces, it is important for its offspring to disperse so that they do not compete directly with the parent plant. Compare the structures that allow seedless plants and seed plants to disperse to new locations.

**27. Synthesize** Some experts predict that the Amazon rain forest will be completely destroyed within the next century due to human activities. What resources would potentially be lost along with this ecosystem?

**28. Infer** Some types of flowers have special markings on their petals that act as guides to the pollen or nectar for their pollinators. How could such markings have evolved through natural selection?

**29. Analyze** What evolutionary advantage do the seeds of dandelions have over the seeds of pine trees?

**30. Synthesize** How might an increase in the use of insecticides affect flowering-plant populations in the area?

## Interpreting Visuals

Use the illustration below to answer the next two questions.

**31. Analyze** What parts of this plant could you examine to determine whether it is a monocot or a dicot?

**32. Apply** Is this plant likely a monocot or a dicot? Explain your reasoning.

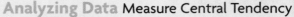

## Analyzing Data Measure Central Tendency

Valencia oranges, which likely originated in Spain or Portugal, are now the most widely planted orange variety in the world. Use the data below on the number of California Valencia oranges per tree to answer the next three questions.

| CALIFORNIA VALENCIA ORANGES PER TREE |
| --- |
| 596,  402,  489,  708,  374,  548,  640,  585,  518,  450 |

Source: *California Agricultural Statistics Service*

**33. Calculate** What are the mean, median, and mode for this data set? Round the mean to the nearest whole number.

**34. Analyze** Does this data set contain outliers? Explain your answer.

**35. Evaluate** Which measure of central tendency best represents this data set? Explain your answer.

## Making Connections

**36. Write About Seeds** From the viewpoint of a plant embryo, write about the importance of a seed. What does the seed provide for you? In what ways does it help you? What advantages do you have over nonseed plants?

**37. Synthesize** The flowering proteas of South Africa are adapted to a dry climate that receives as little as 600 mm (23.6 in) of rain each year. However, plants must retain moisture in order for photosynthesis to occur. Describe the adaptations that allow these plants to retain moisture in their leaves while still allowing for air to move in and out.

# Standards-Based Assessment

Record your answers on a separate piece of paper.

## MULTIPLE CHOICE

**1** In the 1940s, Barbara McClintock observed patterns of inheritance in corn plants that could not be explained by the current gene theory. The conclusions of her work were not widely accepted for years until further supported by the work of other scientists. What does this scenario demonstrate about science?

    **A** Data that are more than 50 years old should be discarded.

    **B** Data that do not fit a scientific theory should be discarded.

    **C** Theories may be modified as additional data leads to new conclusions.

    **D** The repetition of results by many scientists is not necessary to validate a theory.

**2**

| Tomato Plant Growth Per Week (cm) | | |
|---|---|---|
| **Plot** | **Condition** | **Average Growth** |
| 1 | full sun | 9 cm |
| 2 | part sun | 7 cm |
| 3 | full shade | 2 cm |

Gardeners are testing three plots of land with similar soil to find out which is **best** for growing tomato plants. Which of the following conclusions is best supported by their data?

    **A** Plot 1 received the most nutrients.

    **B** Tomato plants grow best in full sun.

    **C** Tomato plants cannot grow in the shade.

    **D** The data are not reliable because there is no control.

**3** The sugar in corn quickly converts to starch after the corn has been picked. After picking, corn that has the *Sh2* gene in its DNA was found to have more sugar and less starch than corn without this gene. Which of the following statements is **most likely** true about corn with this gene?

    **A** Corn that expresses this gene cannot convert sugar to starch.

    **B** This gene causes corn to convert sugar to starch when picked.

    **C** Plants with this gene produce less sugar.

    **D** This gene works in conjunction with other genes to convert sugar to starch.

> **THINK THROUGH THE QUESTION**
>
> Think about the process by which plants produce sugars. You can eliminate any answer choices that would result in plants with less sugar.

**4** The beak shape shown below likely evolved as a result of the birds that could get food most efficiently with this adaptation —

    **A** dying in the absence of long, tubular flowers

    **B** not attracting a mate

    **C** being able to eat a wide variety of food, such as nuts, insects, and berries

    **D** being more likely to survive and reproduce

**5** Rock from the Cretaceous period contains the fossils of a variety of dinosaurs and seedless plants. The fossil record afterwards includes the fossils of many flowering plants and smaller animals, but no dinosaurs. Which of the following statements is supported by this evidence?

    **A** Dinosaurs had begun to die out during the Cretaceous period.

    **B** A mass extinction at the end of the Cretaceous period made new niches available for flowering plants.

    **C** The Cretaceous environment was less favorable to seedless plants than to flowering plants.

    **D** Dinosaurs evolved around the end of the Cretaceous period.

# ONLINE BIOLOGY
HMDScience.com

**ONLINE** Labs
- Density of Stomata
- **QuickLab** Chlorophyll Fluorescence
- Photosynthesis and Red Leaves
- Connecting Form to Function
- Comparing Plant Structures
- Absorption Spectra of Plant Pigments
- Virtual Lab Plant Transpiration

**BIOLOGY**

PREMIUM CONTENT

**Pressure-Flow Model** Organic compounds move in a plant from a source, such as a leaf, to a sink, or an area of low concentration. Learn more about the pressure-flow model of water movement in plants in this interactive activity.

# Q How would this tree compete with other species?

Fig trees (*Ficus*) have a unique way of growing. Many trees of this genus are called strangler figs because their aggressive growth actually strangles other trees. Strangler figs can also wrap around unmoving objects such as these temple walls. Their seeds germinate easily in tree branches or building cracks, and then snakelike roots grow down to the ground.

## READING TOOLBOX    This reading tool can help you learn the material in the following pages.

### USING LANGUAGE

**Cause and Effect**  In biological processes, one step leads to another step. When reading, you can recognize cause-and-effect relationships by words that indicate a result, such as *so, consequently, next, then,* and *as a result.*

### YOUR TURN

Identify the cause and the effect in the following sentences.

1. Some seeds float on the wind, so they are often found far from the parent plant.
2. The substance that makes up plant cell walls is very strong. As a result, trees are able to grow very tall without breaking.

# Plant Cells and Tissues

SC.912.L.14.7

### VOCABULARY

parenchyma cell
collenchyma cell
sclerenchyma cell
dermal tissue
ground tissue
vascular tissue
xylem
phloem

**SC.912.L.14.7** Relate the structure of each of the major plant organs and tissues to physiological processes.

**KEY CONCEPT** Plants have specialized cells and tissue systems.

### MAIN IDEAS
- Plant tissues are made of three basic cell types.
- Plant organs are made of three tissue systems.

---

**Connect to Your World**

You already know that besides roots, plants have stems (or trunks) and leaves. But did you know that these parts are considered the organs of the plant? Just like other organisms, plants have organs that are made of tissues, and tissues that are made of cells. It is easy to remember: plants have three main organs, made up of three tissue systems, mostly made up of three basic cell types.

> **MAIN IDEA**
## Plant tissues are made of three basic cell types.

Plant cells are quite different from animal cells. In addition to all of the structures that animal cells have, plant cells have cell walls, plastids, and a large vacuole. Just as with animals, plants are made up of many types of cells that are organized into tissues. Three basic types of plant cells, shown in **FIGURE 1.1**, are parenchyma cells, collenchyma cells, and sclerenchyma cells.

### Parenchyma Cells

A **parenchyma cell** (puh-REHNG-kuh-muh)—the most common type of plant cell—stores starch, oils, and water for the plant. You can find parenchyma cells throughout a plant. These cells have thin walls and large water-filled vacuoles in the middle. Photosynthesis occurs in green chloroplasts within parenchyma cells in leaves. Both chloroplasts and colorless plastids in parenchyma cells within roots and stems store starch. The flesh of many fruits we eat is also made of parenchyma cells. Parenchyma cells are sometimes thought of as the least specialized of plant cells, but they have one very special trait. They have the ability to divide throughout their entire lives, so they are important in healing wounds to the plant and regenerating parts. For example, parenchyma cells let you place stem cuttings of many types of plants in water to grow into a complete, new plant.

### Collenchyma Cells

A **collenchyma cell** (kuh-LEHNG-kuh-muh) has cell walls that range from thin to thick, providing support while still allowing the plant to grow. These cells are most common in the younger tissues of leaves and shoots. They often form into strands. For example, celery strings are strands of collenchyma cells.

### CONNECT TO

#### CELLS

Recall from **Cell Structure and Function** that plant cells differ from animal cells in having cell walls, chloroplasts, and large vacuoles. Like animals, plants have different cell types.

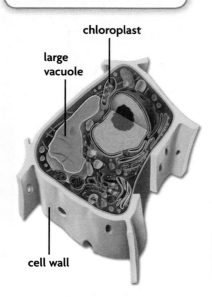

chloroplast

large vacuole

cell wall

## FIGURE 1.1 Basic Plant Cell Types

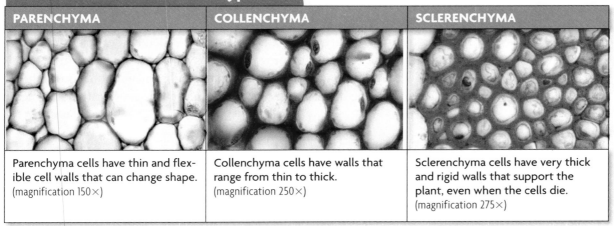

| PARENCHYMA | COLLENCHYMA | SCLERENCHYMA |
| --- | --- | --- |
| Parenchyma cells have thin and flexible cell walls that can change shape. (magnification 150×) | Collenchyma cells have walls that range from thin to thick. (magnification 250×) | Sclerenchyma cells have very thick and rigid walls that support the plant, even when the cells die. (magnification 275×) |

The unique feature of collenchyma cells is that they are flexible. Their cell walls don't contain lignin, so they are stretchy and can change size. As a young leaf grows, collenchyma cells can elongate and still give the leaf structure.

### Sclerenchyma Cells

Of the three basic plant cell types, a **sclerenchyma cell** (skluh-REHNG-kuh-muh) is the strongest. These cells have a second cell wall that is hardened by lignin, which makes these cells very tough and durable. But the lignin also makes these cells very rigid. Unlike collenchyma cells, they can't grow with the plant. Therefore, sclerenchyma cells are found in parts of the plant that aren't lengthening anymore. Many sclerenchyma cells, such as those within the vascular system, die when they reach maturity. The cytoplasm and organelles of these dead cells disintegrate, but the rigid cell walls are left behind as skeletal support for the water-conducting tissues or for the plant itself. Sclerenchyma cells form a major part of fruit pits and the hard outer shells of nuts. They are also found in stems and leaf veins and are responsible for the gritty texture of pears. Humans use sclerenchyma cell fibers to make linen and rope.

**Contrast** **How are the cell walls of parenchyma, collenchyma, and sclerenchyma cells different from one another?**

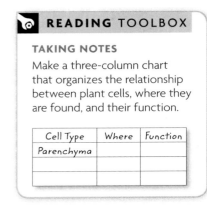

**READING TOOLBOX**

**TAKING NOTES**
Make a three-column chart that organizes the relationship between plant cells, where they are found, and their function.

| Cell Type | Where | Function |
| --- | --- | --- |
| Parenchyma | | |
| | | |
| | | |

### ▶ MAIN IDEA
## Plant organs are made of three tissue systems.

Just as there are three basic types of plant cells, there are three groups of tissue systems in plants: dermal, ground, and vascular tissue systems. Recall that a tissue is a group of cells working together to perform a certain function. The tissue systems of plants may consist of simple tissues from the basic cell types: parenchyma, collenchyma, and sclerenchyma. They may also be made of complex tissues that have additional types of cells. Neighboring cells are often connected by plasmodesmata (PLAZ-muh-DEHZ-muh-tuh), strands of cytoplasm that pass through openings in cell walls and connect living cells. Through the plasmodesmata, cells of a plant tissue can share water, nutrients, and chemical signals.

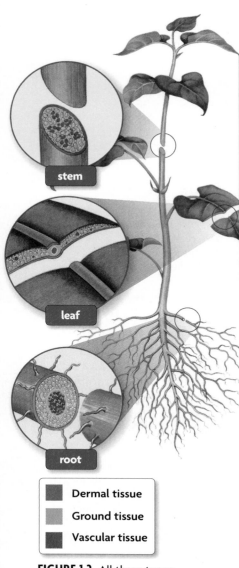

stem

leaf

root

■ Dermal tissue
■ Ground tissue
■ Vascular tissue

**FIGURE 1.2** All three types of tissue systems are found throughout a plant.

## Dermal Tissue System

Your body is covered with skin. Plants don't have skin, but they do have a system of **dermal tissue,** shown in **FIGURE 1.2,** that covers the outside of a plant and protects it in a variety of ways. Dermal tissue called epidermis is made up of live parenchyma cells in the nonwoody parts of plants. On leaves and some stems, epidermal cells may secrete a wax-coated substance that becomes the cuticle. Dermal tissue made of dead parenchyma cells makes up the outer bark of woody plants.

## Ground Tissue System

Dermal tissue surrounds the system of **ground tissue,** which makes up much of the inside of a plant. Ground tissue provides support and stores materials in roots and stems. In leaves, ground tissue is packed with chloroplasts, where photosynthesis makes food for the plant. The ground tissue system consists of all three of the simple tissues—parenchyma tissue, collenchyma tissue, and sclerenchyma tissue—but parenchyma is by far the most common of the ground tissues. The ground tissue of cacti has many parenchyma cells that store water. However, the spines of cacti—which are actually modified leaves—contain mostly rigid sclerenchyma cells in their ground tissue.

## Vascular Tissue System

Surrounded by ground tissue, the system of **vascular tissue** transports water, mineral nutrients, and organic compounds to all parts of the plant. Plants can transport necessary fluids and nutrients throughout their systems. A plant's vascular system is made up of two networks of hollow tubes somewhat like our veins and arteries. Each network consists of a different type of vascular tissue that works to move different resources throughout the plant. **Xylem** (ZY-luhm) is the vascular tissue that carries water and dissolved mineral nutrients up from the roots to the rest of the plant. **Phloem** (FLOH-ehm) is the vascular tissue that carries the products of photosynthesis through the plant. You will learn more about the vascular system in the next section.

**Identify** **What tissue system contains the most photosynthesizing cells?**

## 22.1 Formative Assessment

SELF-CHECK **Online**
HMDScience.com
PREMIUM CONTENT

### REVIEWING ▶ MAIN IDEAS

1. Describe three basic types of cells found within plants.

2. List two functions for each type of tissue system found in plants.

### CRITICAL THINKING

3. **Connect** The **dermal tissue** system has been compared to human skin. In what ways does this analogy hold true?

4. **Compare** What structures in the human body provide a function similar to that of **sclerenchyma cells** in plants? Explain.

### CONNECT TO

#### CELL BIOLOGY

5. Plant cells have distinct differences from animal cells, such as cell walls, large vacuoles, and chloroplasts. How are these differences useful for a plant?

## 22.2 The Vascular System

**SC.912.L.14.7**

**SC.912.L.14.7** Relate the structure of each of the major plant organs and tissues to physiological processes.

**KEY CONCEPT** **The vascular system allows for the transport of water, minerals, and sugars.**

### MAIN IDEAS
- Water and dissolved minerals move through xylem.
- Phloem carries sugars from photosynthesis throughout the plant.

**VOCABULARY**

cohesion-tension theory
transpiration
pressure-flow model

### Connect to Your World

As you read this, your heart is pumping blood, which carries nutrients to your cells and removes wastes from them. In the world outside, fluids are also moving from tree roots all the way up to the highest leaves. But a tree has no heart to act as a pump. How can it move water up to a height of two, three, or even ten stories?

▶ **MAIN IDEA**

## Water and dissolved minerals move through xylem.

Recall that xylem is one of the two types of vascular tissue. Water and dissolved minerals move up from the roots to the rest of the plant through xylem. Xylem contains other types of cells besides the basic cell types. Because it contains other types of cells, xylem tissue is called a complex tissue.

One type of specialized cell in xylem is called a tracheid (TRAY-kee-ihd). Tracheid cells, shown in **FIGURE 2.1,** are long and narrow. Water can flow from cell to cell in tracheids through openings in the thick cell walls. Some types of vascular plants, including most flowering plants, have an additional kind of xylem cell called a vessel element. Vessel elements are shorter and wider than tracheids. Both types of cells mature and die before water moves through them. When a vessel element dies, the cell wall disintegrates at both ends. The cells then connect end to end, forming long tubes.

Amazingly, plants don't use any metabolic energy to move water through xylem. So how do they do it? The **cohesion-tension theory** proposes that the physical properties of water allow the rise of water through a plant. This well-supported theory is based on the strong attraction of water molecules to one another and to other surfaces. The tendency of hydrogen bonds to form between water molecules creates a force called cohesion. However, water molecules are also attracted to the xylem wall due to adhesion, a force made by hydrogen bonds forming between water molecules and other substances. Cohesion and adhesion create tension that moves water upward in xylem.

**vessel element**

**tracheid**

**FIGURE 2.1** Xylem tissue consists of tracheids and vessel elements, conducting and supporting cells that lie end-to-end throughout xylem. Tracheid cells are narrow and long, while vessel elements are wider and shorter. (colored SEM; magnification unknown)

**CONNECT TO**

### HYDROGEN BONDING

Recall from **Chemistry of Life** that a hydrogen bond is an attraction between a slightly positive hydrogen atom and a slightly negative atom. Hydrogen bonds between water molecules produce a force called cohesion that helps water move through a plant.

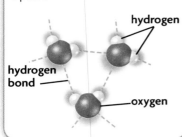

hydrogen

hydrogen bond

oxygen

FIGURE 2.2 Movement of Fluids Through Xylem

Forces responsible for the movement of fluids through xylem are transpiration, cohesion, adhesion, and absorption.

Animated
**Biology**
HMDScience.com
**PREMIUM CONTENT**
Movement Through a Plant

## TRANSPIRATION

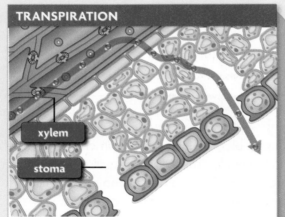

xylem

stoma

Transpiration is the evaporation of water through leaf stomata. It is the major force moving water through plants.

## COHESION AND ADHESION

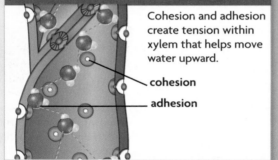

Cohesion and adhesion create tension within xylem that helps move water upward.

cohesion

adhesion

## ABSORPTION

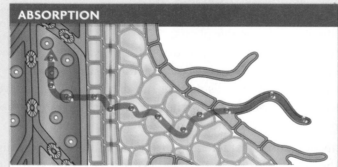

Water and dissolved minerals in the soil are pulled into roots through cell walls, through plasmodesmata (channels), or from cell to cell through their vacuoles.

water vapor

water

**CRITICAL VIEWING** What process is the main force for the movement of fluids through xylem? Explain.

To understand how cohesion and adhesion affect xylem flow, imagine you are inside the cylinder of a xylem vessel. In the middle, the water molecules float freely, attracted to each other. Toward the edges, though, the molecules are also drawn to the xylem wall. Where the water meets the wall, this attraction draws it upward a bit so that the actual shape of the water surface is slightly concave. You can see this shape if you fill a test tube with water. The tendency of water to rise in a hollow tube is known as capillary action. Capillary action causes water to rise above ground level in the xylem of plants.

For most plants, capillary action is not enough force to lift water to the top branches. Upward force is also provided by the evaporation of water from leaves. The loss of water vapor from plants is called **transpiration.** As leaves transpire, the outward flow of water lowers the pressure in the leaf xylem, creating a vacuum that pulls water upward. This force is responsible for most of the water flow in plants, including lifting water to the tops of trees. The movement of water through xylem is shown in **FIGURE 2.2.**

**Apply** **How does transpiration affect water movement through a plant?**

**READING TOOLBOX**

**VOCABULARY**

The term *cohesion* comes from the Latin prefix *co-*, which means "together," and the term *haerere*, which means "to cling."

**VIRTUAL Lab**
HMDScience.com
**PREMIUM CONTENT**

**Plant Transpiration**

## ● MAIN IDEA
# Phloem carries sugars from photosynthesis throughout the plant.

The second tissue in a plant's vascular system is phloem tissue, shown in **FIGURE 2.3.** Phloem carries plant nutrients, including minerals and sugars, throughout the plant. Phloem moves the products of photosynthesis out of the leaves to stems and roots. Minerals that travel up the xylem can also move into the phloem through specialized parenchyma transfer cells in the leaves.

Unlike xylem, phloem tissue is alive. Phloem is a complex tissue made mostly of cells called sieve tube elements. Their name comes from the small holes in the end walls of their cells. These holes let the phloem fluids, or sap, flow through the plant. As they form, sieve tube elements lose their nuclei and ribosomes. Nutrients can then move from cell to cell. Each sieve tube element is next to a companion cell, and the two cells are connected by many plasmodesmata, or small channels. Because the companion cells keep all their organelles, they perform some functions for the mature sieve tube cells. In some plants, the companion cells help load sugars into the sieve tube cells.

Recall that fluids in xylem always flow away from the roots toward the rest of the plant. In contrast, phloem sap can move in any direction, depending on the plant's need. The **pressure-flow model** is a well-supported theory that explains how food, or sap, moves through a plant. Phloem sap moves from a sugar source to a sugar sink. A source is any part of the plant that has a high concentration of sugars. Most commonly this source is the leaves, but it can also be a place where the sugars have been stored, such as the roots. A sink is a part of the plant using or storing the sugar, such as growing shoots and stems, a fruit, or even the storage roots that will be a sugar source later in the season. The locations of sugar sources and sinks in a plant can change as the plant grows and as the seasons change.

**FIGURE 2.3** Fluids move from the roots to the rest of the tree through the xylem. Phloem carries the sugars produced by photosynthesis.

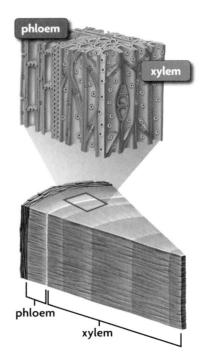

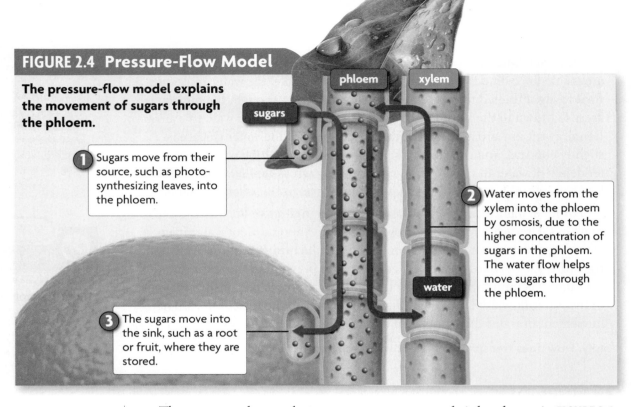

## FIGURE 2.4 Pressure-Flow Model

The pressure-flow model explains the movement of sugars through the phloem.

phloem

xylem

sugars

**1** Sugars move from their source, such as photosynthesizing leaves, into the phloem.

**2** Water moves from the xylem into the phloem by osmosis, due to the higher concentration of sugars in the phloem. The water flow helps move sugars through the phloem.

water

**3** The sugars move into the sink, such as a root or fruit, where they are stored.

The pressure changes between sugar sources and sinks, shown in **FIGURE 2.4**, keep nutrients moving through phloem. At a source, many plants use ATP to pump or load sugar into phloem at a high concentration. Therefore, at a source, there is a low concentration of water relative to sugars. Water then flows into the phloem through osmosis, due to the high concentration of sugars. Osmosis requires no energy on the part of the plant. This active loading of sugars and passive flow of water creates high pressure at the sugar source. At the same time, the sugar concentration of the sink end is lessened as sugar is unloaded into the sink. Unloading sugars also uses ATP from the plant. The overall result is higher pressure at the source end and lower pressure at the sink end. This difference in pressure keeps the sugary sap flowing in the direction of the sink.

**Apply** What are two plant parts that can be sugar sources?

### CONNECT TO

**OSMOSIS**

Recall from **Cell Structure and Function** that osmosis is the diffusion of water molecules across a semipermeable membrane from an area of high concentration to an area of lower concentration.

---

## 22.2 Formative Assessment

**SELF-CHECK Online**
HMDScience.com
PREMIUM CONTENT

### REVIEWING ◉ MAIN IDEAS

1. How are absorption and **transpiration** involved in the movement of water through the xylem of a plant?

2. Describe how nutrients are moved through the phloem according to the **pressure-flow model.**

### CRITICAL THINKING

3. **Infer** Suppose that xylem were located only in the roots and stems of a plant. Would fluids in the xylem still move? Why or why not?

4. **Analyze** How are the specialized cells of xylem and phloem suited for their functions?

### CONNECT TO

**CELL FUNCTION**

5. Which process requires more energy from the plant, moving water up through the xylem or moving nutrients down through the phloem? Explain.

# GO Online!

## REACH

for the Sky!

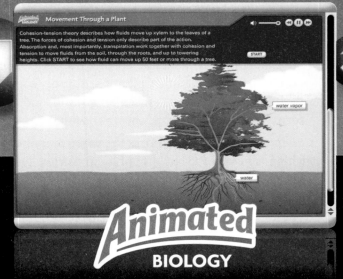

**Movement Through a Plant**

Cohesion-tension theory describes how fluids move up xylem to the leaves of a tree. The forces of cohesion and tension only describe part of the action. Absorption and, most importantly, transpiration work together with cohesion and tension to move fluids from the soil, through the roots, and up to towering heights. Click START to see how fluid can move up 50 feet or more through a tree.

START

water vapor

water

*Animated* BIOLOGY

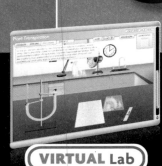

Plant Transpiration

**VIRTUAL Lab**

**WebQuest**

**Plant Transpiration**
Determine how different environmental conditions affect the rate of transpiration.

**Movement Through a Plant**
See how different materials move through a plant.

**Plant Adaptations** Learn about adaptations that help plants to survive in their specific environments.

## 22.3 Roots and Stems

SC.912.L.14.7

SC.912.L.14.7 Relate the structure of each of the major plant organs and tissues to physiological processes.

**VOCABULARY**

vascular cylinder
root hair
root cap
meristem
fibrous root
taproot
primary growth
secondary growth

**KEY CONCEPT** **Roots and stems form the support system of vascular plants.**

**MAIN IDEAS**

○ Roots anchor plants and absorb mineral nutrients from soil.

○ Stems support plants, transport materials, and provide storage.

*Connect to Your World*

Humans reach a certain height and stop growing. Plants, however, can continue growing their entire lives. Woody plants in particular can keep growing in both height and width. Each part of a plant grows in the direction that allows it to reach the resources the plant needs, and each part plays a role in the plant's survival.

▶ **MAIN IDEA**

## Roots anchor plants and absorb mineral nutrients from soil.

Why are roots important? Roots may make up over half of the body of a plant. They anchor the plant to the ground, and from the soil they absorb water and minerals the plant needs.

### Parts of a Root

Roots support the plant and absorb, transport, and store nutrients. Like other plant parts, roots contain all three tissue systems—vascular, ground, and dermal. Parts of a root are shown in **FIGURE 3.1**.

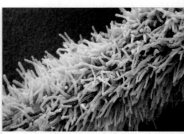

**FIGURE 3.2** Root hairs are located above the root tip. (colored SEM; magnification 80×)

In the center of the root is the **vascular cylinder,** which is made of xylem and phloem tissues. The vascular cylinder is surrounded by ground tissue, covered by dermal tissue. A plant absorbs most of its water in the dermal tissue just above the root tips. These cells have tiny projections called **root hairs,** shown in **FIGURE 3.2**. Root hairs find their way through the spaces between soil particles, greatly adding to the surface area available to take up water. Covering the tip of the root is the **root cap,** a small cone of cells that protects the growing part of the root as it pushes through the soil.

Just behind the root cap is where most of the root's growth occurs. Groups of cells that are the source of new cells form tissue called **meristem.** Meristem cells aren't specialized, but when they divide, some of the new cells specialize into tissues. Areas of growth that lengthen the tips of roots and stems are called apical (AY-pik-kul) meristems. Lateral meristems, found all along woody roots and stems, increase the thickness of these plant parts.

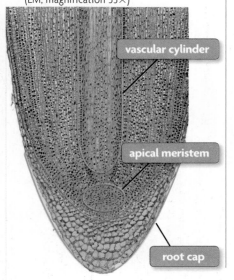

**FIGURE 3.1** This light micrograph of a root tip cross-section shows some of the parts of a root. (LM; magnification 35×)

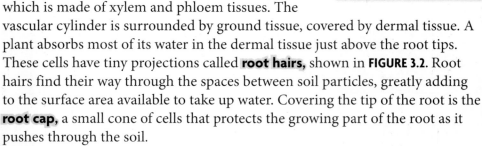

vascular cylinder

apical meristem

root cap

## Types of Roots

Roots take one of two basic forms, as shown in **FIGURE 3.3**. **Fibrous root** systems make fine branches in which most of the roots are the same size. These roots spread like a mat beneath the soil surface, and firmly anchor the plant to the ground. **Taproot** systems have a long, thick, vertical root with smaller branches. Long taproots allow plants to get water from deep in the ground. The thick taproot can also sometimes store food. Radishes, carrots, and beets are examples of taproots that we eat.

## Water and Mineral Uptake

All plants require water and certain mineral nutrients for growth, development, and function. Their roots take up nutrients in a process that also results in water absorption. Mineral nutrients are usually dissolved in soil water as ions. For example, nitrogen is often taken up as $NO_3^-$ ions, and iron can be taken up as $Fe^{2+}$ ions. Plants use energy to transport nutrient ions into the roots through active transport. The increased concentration of ions within root cells also causes water to move into the root tip by osmosis.

Some minerals are needed in large amounts. Nitrogen, for example, is an essential mineral needed for nucleic acids, proteins, and chlorophyll. Other minerals serve mostly to catalyze reactions and are needed only in tiny amounts. Magnesium is a mineral involved in the production of chlorophyll. Even though only tiny amounts are needed, these minerals are also necessary for plant health.

**Explain** **How do root hairs help roots absorb water?**

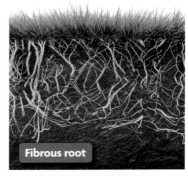
Fibrous root

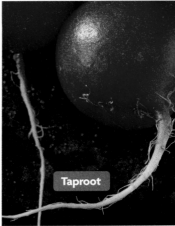
Taproot

**FIGURE 3.3** Grass plants have fibrous root systems. Radishes have one large taproot from which much smaller roots may branch.

## DATA ANALYSIS

### IDENTIFYING THE IMPORTANCE OF REPEATED TRIALS

Scientists need to include repeated trials in experiments in order to draw reliable conclusions. One factor to consider when determining the number of trials in an experiment is how much variation there is among the organisms being tested.

A group of students collected data on the effect of water on the root densities of bean plants. They planted three bean seeds of the same species, each in the same size pot. They used the same type and amount of soil for each plant. Each plant received the same amount of sunlight.

- Plant A received 30 mL of water every day.
- Plant B received 30 mL of water every other day.
- Plant C received 30 mL of water once a week.

Root density, the number of roots per $cm^2$, was measured in all three plants after 30 days. The graph shows the results of the experiment. The students conclude that this species of bean plant should receive 30 mL of water every other day in order to produce the most roots.

1. **Analyze** Did the students reach a valid conclusion? Why or why not?

2. **Experimental Design** How would you change the experiment to improve the experimental design?

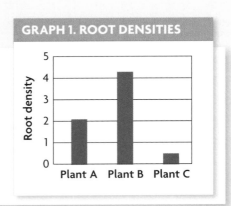
**GRAPH 1. ROOT DENSITIES**

Baobab trees

Cactus

Strawberry stolons

Ginger rhizomes

Potato tubers

**FIGURE 3.4** Stems take various forms. Baobab tree trunks store water, as do the fleshy stems of cacti; potato tubers store starch; ginger rhizomes are underground stems; and strawberry stolons, or runners, form new plants.

*baobab tree* ©Pierre-Yves Babelon/age fotostock; *cactus* ©B.S.P.I./Corbis; *strawberry stolons* ©Alan & Linda Detrick/Science Source; *ginger* ©Ron Chapple/Alamy Images; *potato tubers* ©TPH/Alamy Images; *monocot* ©Ed Reschke/Peter Arnold, Inc.; *dicot* ©Dr. Keith Wheeler/Science Photo Library/Science Source

### ▶ MAIN IDEA

## Stems support plants, transport materials, and provide storage.

You may know that stems support flowers and leaves, giving them better access to pollinators and sunlight. But stems have other functions as well, as you can see in **FIGURE 3.4**. Stems often house a majority of the vascular system and can store food or water. The green stems of cacti, for example, can both photosynthesize and store water. Although most stems grow above ground, potatoes and ginger are examples of stems that can grow underground.

Some stems are herbaceous. Herbaceous plants produce little or no wood. They are usually soft because they do not have many rigid xylem cells. Herbaceous plants may be monocots, such as corn, or dicots, such as beans, and most do not grow taller than two meters. Herbaceous stems are often green and may conduct photosynthesis.

Stems can also be woody. Most plants with woody stems are dicots, such as many broadleaf trees or gymnosperms—pines or fir trees. Tree trunks are an example of woody stems. The oldest part of the xylem, the heartwood, is in the center of a tree trunk. Heartwood no longer conducts water but still provides structure. Sapwood, which is xylem and conducts water, surrounds the heartwood. Phloem produced near the outside of the trunk forms the inner layer of bark. An outer layer of bark provides a protective covering.

### Stem Growth

For as long as a plant survives, it is capable of growth. The continued growth of plants is possible because meristems are active throughout the life of the plant. Meristem cells divide to create more cells. Some of the divided cells remain meristem cells for future divisions, while the others become specialized and end up as part of the tissues and organs of a plant.

**⊹ CONNECT TO**

## MONOCOTS AND DICOTS

Recall from **Plant Diversity** that the pattern of vascular tissue in dicots differs from that in monocots. The cross-section of a monocot stem shows ground tissue with bundles of vascular tissue scattered through it. The cross-section of a herbaceous dicot shows vascular bundles forming a ring.

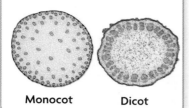

Monocot          Dicot

The pattern of plant growth depends on the location of the meristems within the plant. Growth that increases a plant's length—makes stems grow taller or roots grow longer—is called **primary growth.** This type of growth takes place in apical meristems found at the ends of stems and roots. **Secondary growth** adds to the width in the stems and roots of woody plants. Dicot trees, such as oak and maple, produce a lot of secondary growth over their lifetimes. Secondary growth takes place in lateral meristems in the outer trunk layers.

**VISUAL VOCAB**

**Primary growth** lengthens roots and stems.

**Secondary growth** widens roots and stems.

## Tree Rings

Secondary growth is also responsible for the formation of tree rings, shown in **FIGURE 3.5.** Tree rings form due to uneven growth over the seasons. In spring, if water is plentiful, new xylem cells are wide and have thin walls. These cells appear light in color. When water becomes more limited in the following months, xylem cells are smaller and have thicker walls, so they appear darker in color.

The age of a tree can be determined by counting these annual rings. One ring represents one year of growth. Each ring includes both the larger, lighter cell bands of spring growth and the smaller, darker cell bands of later season growth. Climate, too, can be inferred from the rings since the rings will be thicker if there were good growing conditions. Some trees live thousands of years and can provide climate data that are not available from any other scientific records.

**Summarize** **How are tree rings formed?**

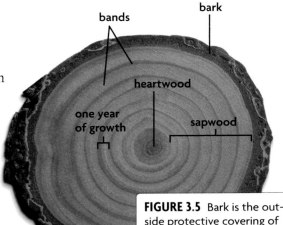

**FIGURE 3.5** Bark is the outside protective covering of woody plants. The light-colored wood, sapwood, conducts water and grows in bands. One year of growth is represented by a light and a dark band. Heartwood is the non-functional dark-colored wood in the center.

©Alan Linn/ShutterStock

## 22.3 Formative Assessment

**SELF-CHECK Online**
HMDScience.com

**PREMIUM CONTENT**

### REVIEWING ▶ MAIN IDEAS

1. Describe two major functions of roots. Explain why these functions are important to the plant.

2. How do the functions of stems differ from those of roots? How are they similar?

### CRITICAL THINKING

3. **Analyze** Some stems, such as ginger rhizomes, grow underground. Why are they considered stems rather than roots?

4. **Apply** What effect could a cold winter with little precipitation have on the **primary growth** and **secondary growth** of a tree?

### CONNECT TO

#### EARTH'S HISTORY

5. The principle of uniformitarianism states that processes that can be observed today can be used to explain events that occurred in the past, or "The present is the key to the past." How does this principle relate to tree ring dating?

SC.912.L.14.7

SC.912.L.14.7 Relate the structure of each of the major plant organs and tissues to physiological processes.

## VOCABULARY

blade
petiole
mesophyll
guard cell

| KEY CONCEPT **Leaves absorb light and carry out photosynthesis.**

**MAIN IDEAS**

◉ Most leaves share some similar structures.

◉ Most leaves are specialized systems for photosynthesis.

### Connect to Your World

"Leaves of three, let it be." This is a saying of many experienced hikers who know how to avoid poison ivy. Hikers can identify poisonous plants in the same way that people can identify many plants that are safe to eat—by the shapes of their leaves. Plant species have their own unique leaf shapes, specially adapted for light gathering and retaining water in their particular environment.

◉ MAIN IDEA

# Most leaves share some similar structures.

Leaves of different species don't all look the same, but most leaves do share some common parts. Leaves grow out from a plant's stem, and they are made up of a few basic parts. The **blade** is usually broad and flat, and it collects the sunlight for the plant. The blade connects to the stem by a thin stalk called the **petiole** (PEHT-ee-ohl). A bud that grows between the petiole and the stem of a plant, called an axillary bud, marks where a leaf ends.

### Leaf Tissues

Like roots and stems, leaves have an outer covering of dermal tissue and an internal system of vascular tissue surrounded by ground tissue. The dermal tissue of many leaves is covered by a waxy cuticle that forms a water resistant covering. The cuticle protects the inner tissues and limits evaporation from the plant. Between the two dermal layers of a leaf is parenchyma tissue called **mesophyll** (MEHZ-uh-FIHL). The vascular tissues of xylem and phloem make up the veins that run throughout the mesophyll.

### VISUAL VOCAB

The blade of a leaf collects sunlight for photosynthesis. It connects to the plant's stem by a petiole.

blade

petiole

### Stomata and Guard Cells

In most plants, the top and undersides of leaves have different functions. The upper portion of the mesophyll has most of the chloroplasts and is where most photosynthesis takes place. The underside portion of a leaf has stomata and is the site of transpiration and gas exchange.

©Photodisc/Getty Images

A pair of **guard cells,** shown in **FIGURE 4.1,** surround each stoma, and can open and close by changing shape. During the day, the stomata of most plants are open, allowing the carbon dioxide ($CO_2$) necessary for photosynthesis to enter. Potassium ions ($K^+$) from neighboring cells accumulate in the guard cells. A high concentration of $K^+$ causes water to flow into the guard cells as well. When the plant is full of water, the two guard cells plump up into a semicircle shape, opening the stoma.

When the stomata are open, water evaporates from the leaves. When the plant is losing water from transpiration faster than it is gaining water at its roots, the guard cells deflate and close the stomata. With the stomata closed, the plant may run low on $CO_2$ for photosynthesis. The stomata also close at night. Factors such as temperature, humidity, hormonal response, and the amount of $CO_2$ in the leaves signal the guard cells to open or close.

guard cell, stoma ©Dr. Jeremy Burgess/Photo Researchers, Inc.; *simple leaf, compound leaf* ©Melba Photo Agency/Alamy Ltd; *double compound leaf* ©Dorling Kindersley/Getty Images; *parallel veins* ©Brian Tan/ShutterStock; *pinnate veins* ©Adam Hart-Davis/ Photo Researchers, Inc.; *toothed margin, entire margin* ©Melba Photo Agency; *lobed margin* ©Photodisc/Getty Images

## FIGURE 4.1 GUARD CELLS

Two guard cells help regulate water loss and photosynthesis by opening and closing the stoma. (colored SEMs; magnification 450×)

Open stoma          Closed stoma

guard cells          stoma

## Leaf Characteristics

It is not always obvious what part of a plant is actually a leaf. As shown in **FIGURE 4.2,** leaves may be simple, with just one blade connected to the petiole, or they may be compound, with many blades on one petiole. The multiple blades are called leaflets. All of the leaflets and their petiole together are actually a single leaf because the axillary bud is at the base of the petiole. There are no buds at the bases of the leaflets. Besides leaf shape, other traits of leaves used to identify plants include the pattern of veins and the leaf edge, or margin.

**Summarize** **What is the function of the guard cells of a plant?**

## FIGURE 4.2 Leaf Characteristics

**Certain leaf characteristics—such as the leaf type, the vein pattern, and the shape of the leaf margin—can be used to identify plants.**

LEAF TYPE

Compound leaf

Simple leaf

Double compound leaf

LEAF VEINS

Parallel veins

Pinnate veins

LEAF MARGIN

Toothed margin          Entire margin

Lobed margin

**Infer** **How might compound leaves and leaves with lobed margins be well-suited to windy environments?**

## Chlorophyll Fluorescence

If you remove chlorophyll molecules from their cells and then expose them to bright light, the energy absorbed from the excited electrons in the chlorophyll will be either lost as heat or released as a dull-colored light as the electrons return to their normal state. This is an example of fluorescence: the absorption of light at one wavelength, and its release at a longer—and lower-energy—wavelength.

**PROBLEM** How can fluorescence be used to study photosynthesis?

**PROCEDURE**

1. Use the mortar and pestle to crush a handful of spinach leaves, adding enough methanol to make 10 mL of extract. Use a graduated cylinder to collect and measure the extract.

2. Place the filter paper in the funnel, and hold the funnel over a beaker. A second person should pour the extract through the funnel to filter the extract.

3. Carefully transfer the extract to a test tube, and hold it in front of a lit flashlight. Observe the fluorescence that occurs at a 90-degree angle from the beam of light.

**ANALYZE AND CONCLUDE**

1. **Identify** What color does the fluorescence appear?

2. **Analyze** Why did the chlorophyll have to be extracted before the fluorescence could be observed?

### MATERIALS

- mortar
- pestle
- handful spinach leaves
- 10 mL methanol
- graduated cylinder
- filter paper
- funnel
- beaker
- eyedropper or pipette
- test tube
- test tube rack
- flashlight

▶ MAIN IDEA

## Most leaves are specialized systems for photosynthesis.

The leaves of a plant are the main sites for photosynthesis. The broad, flat shape of many leaves allows for light gathering on the upper surface and gas exchange on the underside. Since the undersides of leaves are not exposed to direct sunlight, the plant loses less water while the stomata are open.

### Photosynthetic Structures

There are two types of mesophyll cells in leaves, shown in **FIGURE 4.3**. Mesophyll is the photosynthetic tissue of a leaf. Both types of cells in mesophyll have chloroplasts. Just under the dermal layer is a layer of tall, rectangular cells called the palisade mesophyll. These cells absorb much of the light that enters the leaf. Beneath this layer is the spongy mesophyll. Spongy mesophyll has cells that are loosely packed, creating many air spaces. These air spaces connect with the outside of the plant through the stomata, allowing carbon dioxide and oxygen to diffuse in and out of the leaf. Carbohydrates that the plant makes move from mesophyll cells into phloem vessels, which carry the products to tissues throughout the plant.

**READING** TOOLBOX

**TAKING NOTES**

Use combination notes to describe and sketch each leaf structure mentioned here.

| Notes | Sketch |
|-------|--------|
| stomata mesophyll | |

## Leaf Adaptations

Not all leaves are "leafy." Leaves are adapted for photosynthesis in the plant's particular environment. For example, cacti leaves are actually the sharp spines that protect them from predators and help minimize water loss due to transpiration. Other desert plants, such as agave, store water in their leaves. The leaves and stems of many desert plants are protected by very thick cuticles, which minimize the loss of water from the plant.

Similar adaptations are common in coniferous trees in cold, dry climates. Pine needles, for example, are leaves with a small surface area and a thick, waxy epidermis that protects them from cold damage. Tiny sunken areas for the stomata help reduce water loss.

In comparison, water loss is not a problem for aquatic plants. The undersides of a water lily's leaves are below the water surface. To accommodate gas exchange in an aquatic environment, the water lily has stomata on the upper surface of its leaves. Many aquatic plants also have flexible petioles adapted to wave action.

Many tropical plants have very large, broad leaves. In the crowded rain forest, the challenge is to get enough light and space among all the other plants. Larger leaves mean more light-gathering surface.

A few plants are actually predators. The pitcher plant, for example, has tall, tubular leaves that help lure, trap, and digest insects. These insects provide extra nitrogen for the plant, which is needed because there is little of it in the soil where the plant grows.

**Infer** **Flower petals are also an adaptation of leaves. Their bright colors and fragrance attract animals and insects. Why is attracting other organisms important for some plants?**

### FIGURE 4.3 LEAF CROSS-SECTION

This cross-section of a leaf shows the cuticle, dermal tissue, leaf veins made up of xylem and phloem, and palisade and spongy mesophyll.

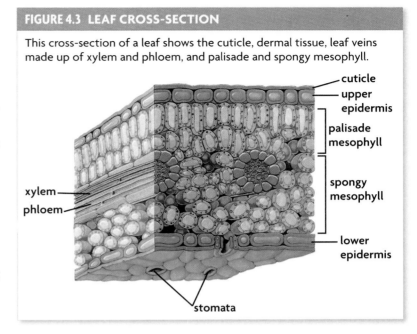

WebQuest
HMDScience.com
PREMIUM CONTENT
Plant Adaptations

SELF-CHECK Online
HMDScience.com
PREMIUM CONTENT

## 22.4 Formative Assessment

### REVIEWING ○ MAIN IDEAS

1. Describe the functions of the **blade** and **petiole** in a leaf.

2. How do the palisade and spongy **mesophyll** layers help a leaf perform photosynthesis?

### CRITICAL THINKING

3. **Infer** The leaves of aquatic plants that are completely underwater have few stomata. Why might this be so?

4. **Apply** Grass blades are leaves that are joined directly to the stem. What structure that is typical of many leaves is missing in grass?

### CONNECT TO

#### ANALOGOUS STRUCTURES

5. The tendrils that allow pea plants to climb up an object are modified leaves, whereas the tendrils of grape vines are modified stems. Explain.

# 22 Summary

**INTERACTIVE** Review
HMDScience.com

**PREMIUM CONTENT**
Review Games • Concept Map • Section Self-Checks

## KEY CONCEPTS

### 22.1 Plant Cells and Tissues

**Plants have specialized cells and tissue systems.** There are three basic types of plant cells that differ in cell wall structure. Each of these cell types can make up simple tissues. These tissues, as well as complex tissues, make up tissue systems. A plant has a dermal tissue system that covers the plant, a ground tissue system that makes up most of the inside of the plant, and a vascular tissue system that transports fluids throughout the plant.

stem

leaf

root

### 22.2 The Vascular System

**The vascular system allows for the transport of water, minerals, and sugars.** Xylem and phloem are the two main tissues of the vascular system. Water and dissolved minerals move through xylem from the roots of a plant up to the leaves, where it evaporates through leaf stomata. This process is called transpiration. The pressure-flow model is a hypothesis of how sugars from photosynthesis move through the plant within the phloem.

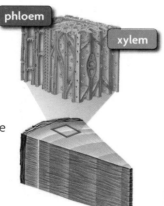
phloem
xylem

### 22.3 Roots and Stems

**Roots and stems form the support system of vascular plants.** Roots anchor plants in the soil and absorb water and mineral nutrients for the plant to use. There are two main types of roots: fibrous roots and taproots. Stems provide support for the plant, and house the vascular systems of the plant. They also give leaves and flowers better access to sunlight and to pollinators. Some stems can store food, while other stems are adapted to store water.

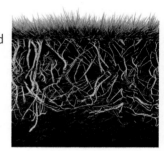

### 22.4 Leaves

**Leaves absorb light and carry out photosyn-thesis.** Most leaves are specialized for photosynthesis, with a broad shape, many chloroplasts, and stomata that allow carbon dioxide and oxygen to move into and out of the plant. Certain leaf characteristics, such as the vein pattern and the shape of the leaf, can be used to help identify plants. There are many adaptations of leaves, such as cactus spines, pine needles, and the tubular leaves of a pitcher plant that are used to lure and trap insects for food.

---

### READING TOOLBOX    SYNTHESIZE YOUR NOTES

**Supporting Main Ideas** Use a main idea diagram to outline the tissue systems in plants.

| Plant organs are made of three tissue systems. |
|---|

→ [ ]
→ [ ]
→ [ ]

**Three-Column Chart** Make a three-column chart to summarize the forces involved in the movement of fluids within xylem.

| Force | Description | Where in Plant |
|---|---|---|
| Transpiration | | |
| Cohesion and adhesion | | |
| Absorption | | |

# 22 Review

## CHAPTER VOCABULARY

| | | |
|---|---|---|
| **22.1** parenchyma cell | **22.2** cohesion-tension theory | taproot |
| collenchyma cell | transpiration | primary growth |
| sclerenchyma cell | pressure-flow model | secondary growth |
| dermal tissue | **22.3** vascular cylinder | **22.4** blade |
| ground tissue | root hair | petiole |
| vascular tissue | root cap | mesophyll |
| xylem | meristem | guard cell |
| phloem | fibrous root | |

## Reviewing Vocabulary

### Compare and Contrast

Describe one similarity and one difference between the two terms in each of the following pairs.

1. parenchyma cell, sclerenchyma cell
2. ground tissue, vascular tissue
3. xylem, phloem
4. fibrous root, taproot
5. primary growth, secondary growth

### READING TOOLBOX    WORD ORIGINS

6. The Greek word *skleros* means "hard" and the suffix *-enchyma* means "cellular tissue." Explain how these word parts relate to characteristics of sclerenchyma.

7. *Derma* is a Greek word meaning "skin." How does this relate to the function of dermal tissue in plants?

8. The Greek verb *merizein* means "to divide." How does this relate to the function of a root's meristem?

9. *Meso-* is a prefix meaning "middle" and *-phyll* is a suffix meaning "leaf." Based on these word parts, explain where you would find a plant's mesophyll.

### Visualize Vocabulary

For each word or pair of words below, use simple shapes, lines, or arrows to illustrate the meaning. Label each picture, and write a short caption.

10. cohesion
11. transpiration
12. blade, petiole
13. guard cell

## Reviewing MAIN IDEAS

14. Name two roles of parenchyma cells, and briefly explain how these cells are specialized for these roles.

15. Both collenchyma and sclerenchyma cells provide support to a plant. But only one of these cell types can exist in plant parts that are still growing. Identify the cell type and explain the traits that make this so.

16. Describe one similarity and one difference between the dermal tissues in nonwoody and woody parts of a plant.

17. Some ground tissue contains many chloroplasts. Where is this tissue located and why does it contain so many chloroplasts?

18. How is the structure of vascular tissue related to its ability to transport materials in the plant?

19. What must happen to tracheids and vessel elements before they can function in xylem?

20. What processes are responsible for water flowing through xylem from the roots to the tips of leaves?

21. Name three substances that are transported by phloem.

22. What can taproots do that fibrous roots cannot do?

23. Describe similarities between herbaceous stems and woody stems.

24. How can xylem and phloem in a plant's leaves be used to help identify the species?

25. Photosynthesis requires carbon dioxide and produces oxygen. How does spongy mesophyll play a role in the diffusion of these gases into and out of the leaves?

# Critical Thinking

**26. Compare** In animals, the term *stem cells* refers to unspecialized or undifferentiated cells that give rise to specialized cells, such as a blood cell. How are meristem cells in plants similar to animal stem cells?

**27. Analyze** A sugar beet plant develops a large root in the first year of growth and stores sugar in it until the second growing season. But, besides sugar, as much as three-fourths of the root's weight can be water. Why is there so much water in the root?

**28. Apply** In 1894, naturalist John Muir wrote about white bark pines he saw at Yosemite National Park in California. At high elevations, where there was snow on the ground for six months each year, he studied a tree only three feet tall and six inches in diameter and determined it was 426 years old. How did he know how old the tree was? Why might it be so small when trees of the same species were much larger down the mountain?

**29. Infer** Many rain forest plants have leaves that taper to tips on the ends. Water from heavy rains drips off the tips of the leaves so that water doesn't collect on the leaves. Why might this be an adaptive advantage for the plant?

**30. Synthesize** Use what you know about cohesion and adhesion to explain why almost an entire sheet of paper towel can become wet even if only a corner of it is placed in water.

## Interpreting Visuals

Use the photograph to answer the next three questions.

**31. Apply** About how many years old was this tree when it was cut down?

**32. Infer** What does the pattern of growth rings indicate about the climate and the rate of growth of this tree over the years?

**33. Predict** Imagine this tree were still growing. If the next year had a spring with much less rain than previous springs and then a summer with a lot of sunshine, what would the next growth ring look like? Explain.

## Analyzing Data Evaluate Repeated Trials

An experiment was designed to test the effect of various environmental factors on the successful germination of grass seed. The control group of seeds was planted according to the directions on the seed packet. Each of three additional groups tested one variable. The experimental design and results are shown in the chart below. Use the chart to answer the next three questions.

| ENVIRONMENTAL FACTORS THAT AFFECT GRASS SEED GERMINATION | | | | |
|---|---|---|---|---|
| Environmental Factor | Control Group | Group A | Group B | Group C |
| Hours daylight | 12 | 6 | 12 | 12 |
| Water | 100% | 100% | 50% | 100% |
| Temperature (°C) | 24 | 24 | 24 | 12 |
| Seeds planted/ seeds germinated | 5/5 | 5/5 | 5/1 | 5/3 |

**34. Infer** What does the data suggest about the conditions under which grass seeds will or will not germinate?

**35. Evaluate** Do the results seem logical? Explain.

**36. Analyze** If you could change anything in this experimental design, what would it be? Give at least two reasons to support your response.

## Making Connections

**37. Write an Instruction Manual** Imagine that you want to sell plant dissection kits. The kits will include instructions on where to find the basic structures of a certain plant, such as the different type of cells and tissues, roots, leaves, stomata, stems, phloem, and xylem. First decide what type of plant will be dissected. Then write a set of instructions to dissect the plant from the bottom up.

**38. Analyze** Strangler figs were transplanted from the tropics to states such as Florida and California because of their unusual growth forms. Considering how they got their common name, why was this perhaps not a good idea?

# Standards-Based Assessment

1.

### Tree Ring Growth from 1955 to 2005

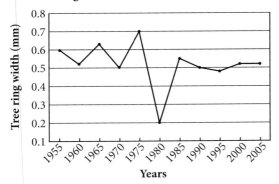

Suppose a tree farmer has collected data about tree ring growth for many years. During that time, only one major drought has occurred. Based on the graph, between which years did the drought *most* likely occur?

A  1955–1960

B  1965–1970

C  1975–1980

D  1990–1995

### THINK THROUGH THE QUESTION

First, eliminate answer choices that list the years where there is no remarkable change in the graph. Then consider the remaining choices. Would drought have a negative or a positive effect on the width of a tree ring?

2. Plant tissues are made of three basic types of cells: parenchyma, collenchyma, and sclerenchyma. Which of the following statements is *true* about all plant cells?

A  They do not have a nucleus.

B  They do not have a cell membrane.

C  They have a cell wall.

D  They have the same function.

3. Plants capture radiant energy from sunlight and convert it into usable energy in the form of

A  carbon dioxide.

B. protein.

C  oxygen.

D  sugar.

4. What two structures do plant cells have that animal cells do not have?

A  ribosomes and mitochondria

B  mitochondria and cell walls

C  chloroplasts and cell walls

D  chloroplasts and ribosomes

5. Which of the following characteristics is shared by both plant cells and photosynthetic bacteria?

A  cell wall of lignin

B  chlorophyll

C  DNA enclosed in a nucleus

D  vacuole for starch storage

6.

| Effect of Nitrogen on Bean Plant Growth | | | | |
|---|---|---|---|---|
| Trial | 0% N | 5% N | 10% N | 15% N |
| 1 | 1.4 cm | 2.2 cm | 2.2 cm | 3.6 cm |
| 2 | 0.5 cm | 2.6 cm | 2.6 cm | 2.6 cm |
| 3 | 1.0 cm | 3.6 cm | 2.9 cm | 3.5 cm |

Students recorded data on the effect of different percentages of nitrogen (N) in fertilizer on the growth of bean plants in centimeters. Fertilizer with no nitrogen was included in this experiment because it served as the

A  model for the experiment.

B  control for the experiment.

C  independent variable for the experiment.

D  dependent variable for the experiment.

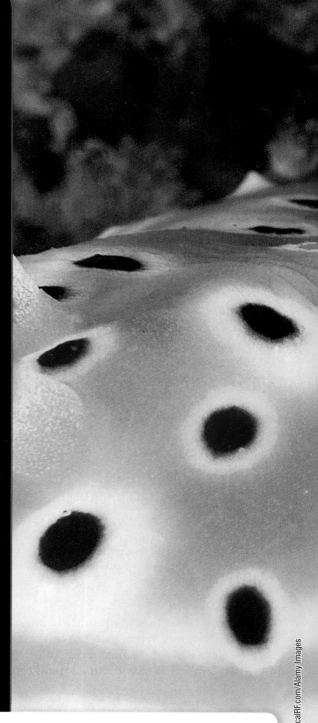

# 23 Invertebrate Diversity

**BIG IDEA** Animals share many characteristics, yet have a variety of shapes, structures and sizes, and most have no backbone.

## ⊙ ONLINE BIOLOGY  HMHScience.com

**ONLINE** Labs
- Feeding *Hydra*
- **QuickLab** Anatomy of a Clam
- Anatomy of a Sea Star
- Anatomy of an Annelid
- Evolution of Coelom
- Cardiovascular System of Mudworms

- **Video Lab** Embryonic Development
- **Video Lab** *Hydra* Behavior
- **Video Lab** Clam Characteristics

**How is this sea slug similar to a spider?**

Both sea slugs and spiders are invertebrates. Invertebrates, which are animals without backbones, account for the vast majority of animals on Earth. You are surrounded by invertebrates on a daily basis, whether you are aware of them or not. Invertebrates exist in a wide variety of shapes and sizes and live in many different habitats, which can include your body!

---

 **READING TOOLBOX**    This reading tool can help you learn the material in the following pages.

**USING LANGUAGE**

**Describing Space** Describing an object accurately is not as easy as it may seem. Certain words, called *spatial* words, can help you describe the shape and position of an object. Spatial words include *perpendicular, parallel, diagonal, horizontal,* and *vertical.*

**YOUR TURN**

Practice using spatial words by completing the activity below.

1. Look around your classroom, and choose an object to describe.
2. Without revealing what the object is, use spatial words to help a partner draw the object you have chosen.

# Animal Characteristics

SC.912.L.15.6

**KEY CONCEPT** Animals are diverse but share common characteristics.

**MAIN IDEAS**

- Animals are the most physically diverse kingdom of organisms.
- All animals share a set of characteristics.

**SC.912.L.15.6** Discuss distinguishing characteristics of the domains and kingdoms of living organisms.

## Connect to Your World

We are animals. So are jellyfish, squid, cockroaches, tapeworms, sea stars, and the family dog. Animals live in nearly every environment on Earth, from high in the atmosphere to the deepest sea trench. While they come in a huge variety of shapes and sizes, they all share a common ancestry and a set of common physical and genetic characteristics.

## ● MAIN IDEA

# Animals are the most physically diverse kingdom of organisms.

More than 1 million species of animals have been described so far, and scientists predict that tens of millions more have yet to be discovered. Animals are a remarkably diverse group of organisms. They range in size from blue whales twice the length of a school bus to rotifers smaller than the period at the end of this sentence. As shown in **FIGURE 1.1**, some look like soft tubes, and others have muscular bodies inside hard shells, or soft tissues over hard internal skeletons. Some animals have many specialized tissues and organs, and others have no distinct tissues at all.

**FIGURE 1.1** Animal body plans vary widely in shape and size, from microscopic rotifers (colored SEM; magnification 170×) to blue whales 24 meters in length.

Rotifer

Giraffe

Red leaf beetle

Steller's jay

Tubeworm

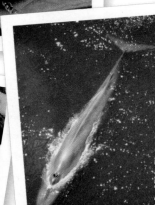

Blue whale

Animals are found nearly everywhere on Earth, including places where plants and fungi do not live. They are the dominant herbivores, predators, and detritivores in most ecosystems. Some walk, burrow, swim, fly, or slide along on mucus trails in search of food. Others spend their whole adult lives fixed to a single spot, endlessly straining water to collect microscopic particles of food.

**Connect** **What ecological factors determine where certain animals are found?**

### CONNECT TO

**NICHES**

Recall from **Interactions in Ecosystems** that an ecological niche includes all of the factors a species needs to survive, thrive, and reproduce.

## ▶ MAIN IDEA
# All animals share a set of characteristics.

Given the huge physical diversity among animals, what characteristics distinguish animals from other organisms? All animals share a set of derived characters, or heritable features, that set them apart from other eukaryotes. These characteristics suggest that all animals are the descendants of a single common ancestor.

### READING TOOLBOX

**TAKING NOTES**
Use a diagram to take notes on the unique characteristics of animals.

Animal characteristics
→ Multicellular heterotroph
→ Collagen
→
→

### All Animals Are Multicellular Heterotrophs
Animals must eat. Their cells lack the chloroplasts that let photosynthetic organisms make their own food. All animals are heterotrophs, meaning they eat other organisms to gain the nutrients they need to survive. Any organic compound an animal uses in cellular respiration has to come from an outside source. Single-celled protists also eat other organisms. But because even the simplest animal is built of many specialized cells, all animals can ingest and process larger food particles than a single cell can engulf.

Animals are not the only eukaryotes that are both heterotrophic and multicellular. Fungi are also multicellular and use organisms for food. But cells of fungi do not have the same diversity of functions that animal cells have. Although animals and fungi share heterotrophic ancestors, it is likely that they evolved the trait of multicellularity independently.

### Animal Cells Are Supported by Collagen
Unlike the cells of plants and fungi, animal cells lack rigid cell walls. Therefore, animals cannot rely on the rigidity of their cells for structural support. What component carries out these functions in animals?

**Collagen** (KAHL-uh-juhn), shown in **FIGURE 1.2**, is a three-stranded protein unique to animals. Animal body parts that contain collagen include skin, bone, ligaments, fingernails, and hair. Individual collagen proteins combine with one another to form ropelike fibers that are both strong and flexible. These fibers form an extracellular network that many animal cells use for support. Unlike a cell wall, the collagen network does not glue cells in place, so it is possible for cells to move within the animal's body. Collagen also forms an integral part of the jointed skeleton that many animals use to move their entire bodies.

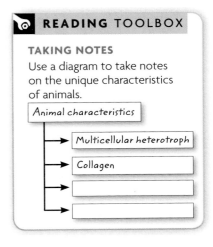
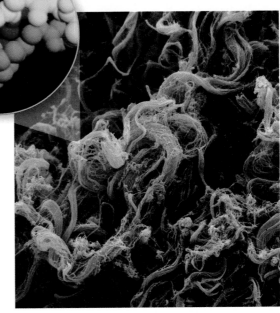

**FIGURE 1.2** This molecular model and SEM show the triple-stranded structure of collagen, a strong and flexible protein that is unique to animals. (colored SEM; magnification 3000×)

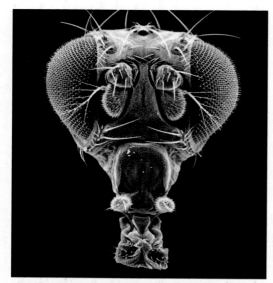

**FIGURE 1.3** In the wild-type fly (top), the antennae develop normally. In the mutant fly (bottom), a mutation causes legs to form in place of the antennae.
(SEMs; magnification 70×)

## Animals Are Diploid and Usually Reproduce Sexually

Animals are the only multicellular organisms that do not alternate between free-living diploid and haploid stages. In all animal species, the individuals that reproduce are diploid and they produce offspring that are also diploid. Some kinds of animals can reproduce both asexually and sexually. For example, a *Hydra* can clone itself by budding. These species have male and female sexual organs and also reproduce sexually. A few animals have become completely asexual. All whiptail lizards, for example, are females and offspring are clones of the mother. But these animals evolved from sexual species, and their asexual habits are derived characters.

## Most Animals Have *Hox* Genes

Most animals that scientists have studied so far share a group of genes called homeotic genes. **Homeotic** (HOH-mee-AH-tihk) genes are a class of genes that control early development. In animals, an important group of homeotic genes called *Hox* genes are defined by a sequence of 180 nucleotides called **homeobox** (HOH-mee-uh-BAHKS) genes. *Hox* genes define the head-to-tail pattern of development in animal embryos. Homeotic genes create segments in a larva or embryo that develop into specific organs and tissues. The *Hox* genes within these segments determine the position of cell differentiation and development by switching certain genes "on" or "off."

A mutation in a homeotic gene can lead to the development of a body structure in the wrong position. For example, the effect of a mutation in the homeotic gene *Antennapedia* determines whether an insect body segment will grow antennae or legs. As shown in **FIGURE 1.3**, in the wild-type fly (top), antennae develop normally. In a fly with a mutation in this gene (bottom), legs develop where the antennae should be, but the rest of the fly develops normally. The misplaced legs look normal in structure, but are not functional for the fly. Flies with homeotic mutations usually do not live very long.

**Analyze** How are homeotic and *Hox* genes related?

(t), (c) ©F. R. Turner, Indiana University

---

**SELF-CHECK Online**
HMHScience.com
**GO ONLINE**

## 23.1 Formative Assessment

### REVIEWING ▶ MAIN IDEAS

1. In what ways are animals physically diverse? Give three examples.

2. List and describe the derived characters that all animals share.

### CRITICAL THINKING

3. **Apply** How does the structure of animal cells allow animals to move?

4. **Hypothesize** Animals are heterotrophs. How might this have contributed to such great animal diversity?

### ✦ CONNECT TO

### GENETICS

5. How does the genome of an offspring resulting from sexual reproduction differ from that of an offspring resulting from asexual reproduction?

# 23.2 Animal Diversity

SC.912.L.15.6

**MAIN IDEAS**
- Each animal phylum has a unique body plan.
- Animals are grouped using a variety of criteria.
- A comparison of structure and genetics reveals the evolutionary history of animals.

### VOCABULARY

vertebrate
invertebrate
phylum
bilateral symmetry
radial symmetry
protostome
deuterostome

**SC.912.L.15.6** Discuss distinguishing characteristics of the domains and kingdoms of living organisms.

## Connect to Your World

When you think of an animal, something familiar such as a dog or a snake probably comes to mind. Both of these animals are vertebrates, a group that represents one small subset of animals. However, most animals are invertebrates and look nothing like your mental picture. To understand the vast diversity of animal life, biologists look for unique characteristics that help them sort animals into distinct groups and arrange those groups into a family tree.

### ▶ MAIN IDEA

## Each animal phylum has a unique body plan.

A **vertebrate** (VUR-tuh-briht) is an animal with an internal segmented backbone. Vertebrates are the most obvious animals around us, and we are vertebrates too. But vertebrates make up less than five percent of all known animal species. All other animals are invertebrates. **Invertebrates** (ihn-VUR-tuh-brihts) are animals without backbones. Early animal classifications divided all animals into vertebrates and invertebrates. But because invertebrates are not defined by a set of shared derived characters, the division is considered outdated. Many invertebrates are not closely related to one another.

### CONNECT TO

**CLASSIFICATION**

Recall from the chapter **The Tree of Life** that in the Linnaean system of classification, phylum is the first level below kingdom. All animals are classified in the kingdom Animalia.

### Animal Phyla

Scientists now use shared characters to divide animals into more than 30 major groups. Each group, or **phylum** (FY-luhm) (plural, *phyla*), of animals is defined by structural and functional characteristics that are different from every other animal group. Each animal phylum has a unique body plan and represents a different way that a multicellular animal is put together.

Every animal phylum has a unique set of anatomical characteristics. These unique characteristics are true of both the largest and smallest phyla. Some phyla, such as mollusks, have tens of thousands of species, ranging from land snails to marine octopuses. Others are much less diverse. Phyla such as Arthropoda contain species that look very different from one another. In other phyla, such as Nematoda, all of the species look very similar. The relative number of invertebrate species per group is shown in **FIGURE 2.1**.

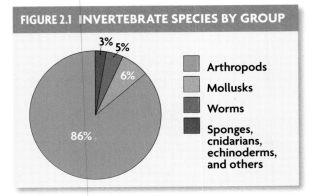

**FIGURE 2.1 INVERTEBRATE SPECIES BY GROUP**

- Arthropods
- Mollusks
- Worms
- Sponges, cnidarians, echinoderms, and others

3% 5% 6% 86%

## Homeobox Genes and Body Plans

If you take a look at the animals that you might see on a walk through a park, you may notice how different their body plans are. The fish swimming in the park's pond have sets of fins, the birds nesting in the trees have pairs of wings, and the squirrels chasing one another have four legs.

Differences in body plans result from differences in the expression of homeobox genes. As shown in **FIGURE 2.2,** homeobox genes tell embryonic cells which part of the body they are going to become, such as the head, midsection, or tail. These instructions start a chain reaction that turns on all other genes that define the adult form—where limbs go, how many eyes will develop, the location of the gut, and so on. For this reason, a mutation in a *Hox* gene can change an animal's entire body plan. Scientists think that mutations in these genes led to the vast diversity of animal species.

All the animal phyla now known first appeared during the Cambrian explosion. How did so many unique body plans appear in such a short time? The trigger may have been an increase in oxygen levels in the atmosphere that began about 700 million years ago. As oxygen levels rose, eukaryotic organisms could become more active and begin to occupy different niches within more complex ecosystems.

The Cambrian explosion was possible only because animals had already evolved *Hox* genes. These genes became a toolkit that changed animal bodies through duplication and loss. For example, a sponge is a simple animal that has at least one *Hox* gene, while an arthropod has eight. This difference suggests that over time, mutations have caused the original *Hox* gene to be copied repeatedly, forming a series of similar genes along a chromosome. Every time a gene is duplicated, one of the copies can keep doing its original job in the organism, leaving the other free to mutate and take on new roles.

**Analyze** How are *Hox* genes related to the diversity of body plans?

### FIGURE 2.2 *Hox* Gene Expression

The genes that determine a fruit fly's body plan are variations of the same genes that determine a human's, but they are expressed in different patterns.

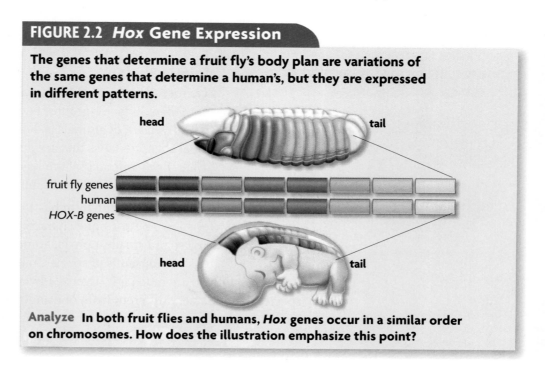

head     tail

fruit fly genes
human
*HOX-B* genes

head     tail

**Analyze** In both fruit flies and humans, *Hox* genes occur in a similar order on chromosomes. How does the illustration emphasize this point?

## ▶ MAIN IDEA
# Animals are grouped using a variety of criteria.

Like other organisms, animals are placed in separate groups based on certain characteristics. Three criteria used to categorize animals are body plan symmetry, number of tissue layers, and developmental patterns.

## Body Plan Symmetry

Symmetry refers to how similar an object is across a central axis. For example, if you draw a line down the middle of a square, both sides are equal in shape and size. An object is asymmetrical if the two sides are not mirror images of each other. Most animal body plans fall into one of two types of symmetry.

- Animals with **bilateral symmetry** can be divided equally along only one plane, which splits an animal into mirror-image sides.
- Animals with **radial symmetry** have body parts arranged in a circle around a central axis.

Bilateral animals have distinct heads and tails, which are called the anterior (head) and posterior (tail) ends. These animals also have distinct backs and bellies, which are called the dorsal (back) and ventral (belly) surfaces. Each of these regions can become specialized. For example, structures that an animal uses to move, such as legs, are usually found on its ventral surface. Active hunters that often travel in one direction in search of food have a head region with a concentration of nervous tissue that forms a brain and with sensory organs such as eyes.

### VISUAL VOCAB

Animals with **bilateral symmetry** can be divided equally along only one plane, which splits an animal into mirror-image sides.

Animals with **radial symmetry** have body parts arranged in a circle around a central axis.

 **READING** TOOLBOX

**TAKING NOTES**

Draw a simple sketch of an animal in your notes. Mark its symmetry, then label its anterior, posterior, dorsal, and ventral areas.

## Tissue Layers

Bilateral animals are triploblastic, that is, they have three distinct layers of tissue. These layers are the ectoderm, endoderm, and mesoderm. The ectoderm is the outer layer that develops into the skin, the brain, and the nervous system. The endoderm is an inner layer that lines the animal's gut. The mesoderm is a middle layer that develops into internal tissues and organs. Complex organ systems resulted from the evolution of this third tissue layer.

Most radial animals have only two distinct layers of tissue. These layers are an inner endoderm and an outer ectoderm. Radial animals do not have a mesoderm layer, and therefore they lack the complex internal tissues and organs found in triploblastic animals.

**READING** TOOLBOX

**VOCABULARY**

The following Greek word parts can help you remember the names of tissue layers.

- *-derm* comes from a word meaning "skin"
- *ecto-* means "outer"
- *endo-* means "inner"
- *meso-* means "middle"

GO ONLINE

Digestive Tract Formation

## Developmental Patterns

Animals are separated into two major divisions: the protostomes and the deuterostomes. As shown in **FIGURE 2.3**, protostome and deuterostome development differs in a number of ways:

- **First opening of the digestive cavity** The major difference between protostomes and deuterostomes is the structure that develops from the first opening of the digestive cavity. In **protostomes** (PROH-tuh-STOHMZ), the mouth is formed first, and the anus second. In **deuterostomes** (DOO-tuh-roh-STOHMZ), the first opening forms the anus, and the mouth is formed second.

- **Gut cavity formation** In protostomes, the gut cavity is formed from separations in the mesoderm. In deuterostomes, the gut cavity forms from pouches created by the folds in the gut tube.

- **Cleavage pattern** In most protostomes, early cell divisions lead to an eight-celled embryo in a twisted arrangement called spiral cleavage. In deuterostomes, cells divide into eight-celled embryos with cells that are lined up one atop the other in an arrangement called radial cleavage.

**Connect  Is the symmetry of the human body bilateral or radial?**

▶ **MAIN IDEA**

# A comparison of structure and genetics reveals the evolutionary history of animals.

Work by the American zoologist Libbie Hyman in the mid-1900s provided the basis for scientists' understanding of the relationships among invertebrate species. Hyman based her phylogeny, or evolutionary history, on major events in development. The ability to compare ribosomal DNA and *Hox* genes has helped to both confirm and rearrange some relationships among invertebrate animal groups.

The presence of tissues is one characteristic that separates one animal group from another. Sponges, which lack tissues, are the simplest members of the animal kingdom, followed by animals with two tissue layers, such as jellyfish and corals. Whether an animal has radial or bilateral symmetry is another defining characteristic. As shown in **FIGURE 2.4,** the two major radiations, or phylogenetic branches, are the protostomes and the deuterostomes.

**Protostomes** Protostomes are further divided into the Lophotrochozoa (flatworms, annelids, and mollusks) and Ecdysozoa (roundworms and arthropods). All members of the Lophotrochozoa have either a specialized feeding structure made of hollow tentacles or a free-swimming ciliated larval form. Members of the Ecdysozoa must shed their outer skin to grow.

**Deuterostomes** Deuterostomes include members of the Echinodermata (such as sea stars and sand dollars) and the Chordata (such as birds, mammals, and all other vertebrates). As a member of the Chordata, you are a deuterostome.

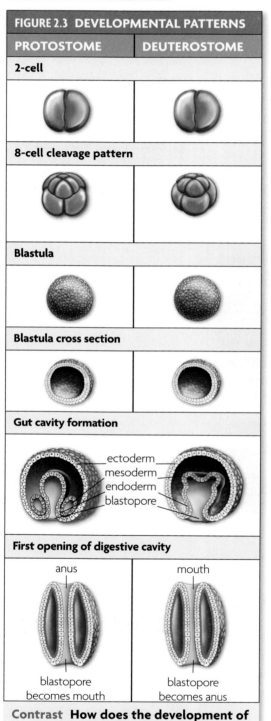

**FIGURE 2.3  DEVELOPMENTAL PATTERNS**

| PROTOSTOME | DEUTEROSTOME |
| --- | --- |

2-cell

8-cell cleavage pattern

Blastula

Blastula cross section

Gut cavity formation

ectoderm
mesoderm
endoderm
blastopore

First opening of digestive cavity

anus          mouth

blastopore          blastopore
becomes mouth      becomes anus

**Contrast  How does the development of protostomes and deuterstomes differ?**

# FIGURE 2.4 Phylogeny of Animals

**Comparisons of genetic sequences were used to modify the phylogenetic tree of animals.**

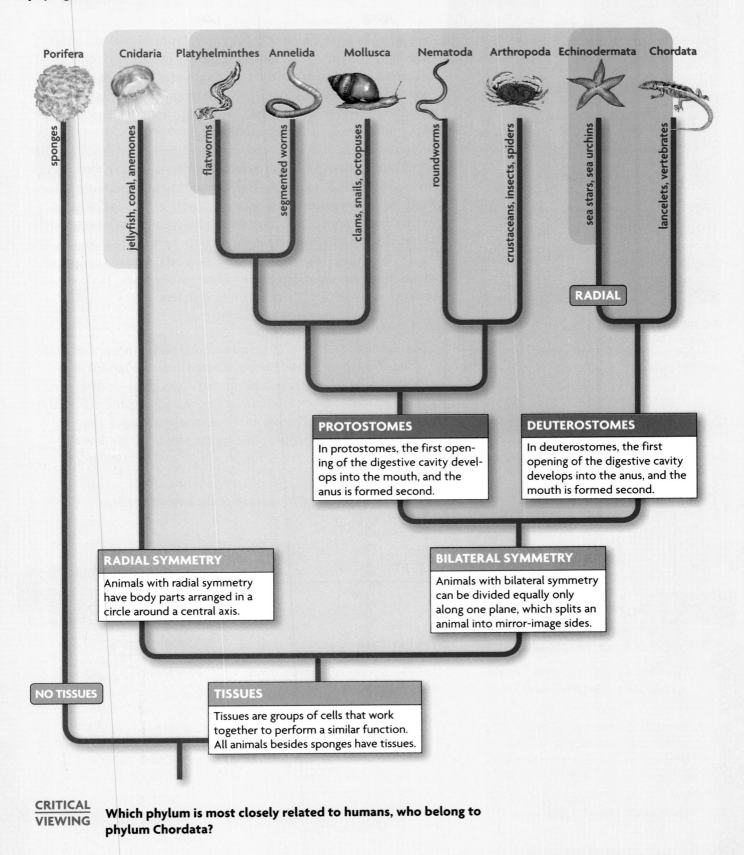

Porifera — sponges

Cnidaria — jellyfish, coral, anemones

Platyhelminthes — flatworms

Annelida — segmented worms

Mollusca — clams, snails, octopuses

Nematoda — roundworms

Arthropoda — crustaceans, insects, spiders

Echinodermata — sea stars, sea urchins

Chordata — lancelets, vertebrates

**RADIAL**

**PROTOSTOMES**
In protostomes, the first opening of the digestive cavity develops into the mouth, and the anus is formed second.

**DEUTEROSTOMES**
In deuterostomes, the first opening of the digestive cavity develops into the anus, and the mouth is formed second.

**RADIAL SYMMETRY**
Animals with radial symmetry have body parts arranged in a circle around a central axis.

**BILATERAL SYMMETRY**
Animals with bilateral symmetry can be divided equally only along one plane, which splits an animal into mirror-image sides.

**NO TISSUES**

**TISSUES**
Tissues are groups of cells that work together to perform a similar function. All animals besides sponges have tissues.

**CRITICAL VIEWING** Which phylum is most closely related to humans, who belong to phylum Chordata?

## Unexpected Evolutionary Relationships

The new organization of the animal kingdom shows previously unexpected relationships between animals. Originally, round-worms and earthworms were grouped together because of their similarity in appearance and simple structure. However, round-worms are actually more closely related to insects and other arthropods than to earthworms. Earthworms and arthropods are not closely related and, in fact, evolved segmentation independently. Flatworms are now split into two groups. One group, the Acoelomorpha (not shown in **FIGURE 2.4**), is thought to be simple in form because it evolved early in the animal radiation. The other, Platyhelminthes, is thought to have evolved its simple form from more complex ancestors. As well as showing unexpected relationships among organisms, the new phylogeny shows that animal forms can change much more dramatically than was once thought. Animals with similar characteristics may have evolved those traits at different times. Genetic evidence supports Hyman's original hypothesis that animal groups evolved by branching from earlier groups, and not directly from a single ancestor.

**FIGURE 2.5** The current animal phylogeny resulted from the comparison of ribosomal DNA and *Hox* genes.

## Unanswered Questions

The current phylogenetic tree for invertebrate animals is in no way considered a finished product. Systematics—the field of science dedicated to the study of the diversity of life and the relationships among organisms—is dynamic, meaning that things constantly change as new knowledge is gathered. A large number of questions still need to be answered. As molecular technologies improve, and an increased number of species are studied, scientists will be able to put together an even more accurate picture of the invertebrate evolutionary tree.

**Summarize** What evidence was used to reorganize the animal kingdom?

©Deco/Alamy Images

**SELF-CHECK Online**
HMHScience.com
**GO ONLINE**

## 23.2 Formative Assessment

### REVIEWING ▶ MAIN IDEAS

1. What is the main difference between **vertebrate** and **invertebrate** body plans?

2. List and describe the differences among the three criteria used to distinguish between different animal groups.

3. What evidence is used to create the phylogenetic tree for animals?

### CRITICAL THINKING

4. **Analyze** Scientists' view of animal relationships has changed since the mid-1900s. What development led to this change in scientists' understanding of the relationships among animals?

5. **Provide Examples** Think again about animals, and list five invertebrates that might live in your neighborhood. To which **phylum** does each invertebrate belong?

### CONNECT TO

### EVOLUTION

6. A phylogeny is a hypothesis of evolutionary relationships. What does the current animal phylogeny say about the relationship of vertebrates to invertebrates?

# Sponges and Cnidarians

| KEY CONCEPT  **Sponges and cnidarians are the simplest animals.**

### MAIN IDEAS

○ Sponges have specialized cells but no tissues.
○ Cnidarians are the oldest existing animals that have specialized tissues.

**VOCABULARY**

sessile
filter feeder
polyp
medusa
mesoglea
nematocyst
gastrovascular cavity

## Connect to Your World

Imagine you are snorkeling beneath the clear blue waters surrounding Australia's Great Barrier Reef. In addition to schools of tropical fish and sharks, covering the ocean floor are brightly colored sponge and coral species. Sponges and corals are members of two of the simplest animal phyla, the Porifera and the Cnidaria.

 **MAIN IDEA**

## Sponges have specialized cells but no tissues.

Sponges have long been considered the most primitive animals on Earth because their body plan is much like what scientists would expect for an early multicellular organism. Two lines of recent evidence have strengthened this hypothesis.

- Sponge fossils more than 570 million years old were found in Australia, making sponges one of the most ancient groups of known animals.
- Molecular evidence confirms that sponges are closely related to a group of protists called choanoflagellates. Choanoflagellates are very similar in size and shape to certain cells found within a sponge. These protists are considered the most likely ancestors of all animals.

**READING TOOLBOX**

**VOCABULARY**

*Sessile* comes from a Latin word meaning "to sit." The opposite of sessile is mobile. *Mobile* comes from a Latin word meaning "to move."

**FIGURE 3.1** Sponges are among the simplest animals that still exist today.

### Sponge Characteristics

Sponges lack muscle and nerve cells. So, not surprisingly, they are **sessile,** meaning they are unable to move from where they are attached. As **FIGURE 3.1** shows, sponges attach to hard surfaces. They secrete toxic substances that prevent other sponges from growing into their area and also protect them from hungry predators and parasites. Some of these chemicals have been used in the development of medicines to treat forms of cancer, such as lymphoma.

### Sponge Reproduction

Sponges reproduce both sexually and asexually. In sexual reproduction, some species release eggs and sperm into the water, and fertilization occurs there. In other species, sperm is released into the water, and the egg is fertilized within the female sponge. The fertilized egg develops into a free-swimming larva that attaches to a surface, where it remains and develops into its adult form.

©Carlos Villoch 2004/Image Quest Marine

Some sponges reproduce asexually by budding. Buds break off from the adult sponge and float in the water until they attach to an underwater surface, where they grow into their adult form.

## Sponge Anatomy

Sponges do not have mouths. As you can see in **FIGURE 3.2**, their cells are arranged around a network of channels that let water flow directly through the sponge's body. Water is pulled into the sponge through tiny pores in its body wall, and used water is ejected from a larger hole at the top of the sponge called the osculum. Of the thousands of known species of sponges, most are marine filter feeders. **Filter feeders** eat by straining particles from the water.

Sponges can be found in many colors and shapes. Some sponges are shaped like tubes, while others lie flat against the ocean floor. Regardless of their shape, all sponge bodies are made up of two layers of cells that cover a framework of collagen-like fibers, called spongin. The skeleton is usually reinforced with hard calcium- or silicon-based crystals called spicules. While sponges do not have tissues, they do have several types of specialized cells.

- **Pinacocytes**  These thin and leathery cells form the sponge's outer layer.
- **Choanocytes**  These cells, also called "collar cells," form the inner layer of the sponge. Each has a long flagellum surrounded by a collar of tiny hairlike structures called microvilli. These cells pull water through the sponge by beating their flagella. As the water passes the choanocytes, tiny food particles are trapped in the mucus on the microvilli.
- **Amoebocytes**  These are mobile cells found in the jellylike material sandwiched between the two cell layers. Amoebocytes absorb and digest the food particles caught by the choanocytes and move the nutrients to other parts of the sponge. They also transport oxygen and wastes in the sponge. Because of their mobility, amoebocytes are important to a sponge's growth and repair of injuries.

**Summarize** **What characteristics make sponges the simplest animals?**

**FIGURE 3.2** Sponges are animals that have specialized cells but lack tissues. This cutaway shows the internal organization of a sponge.

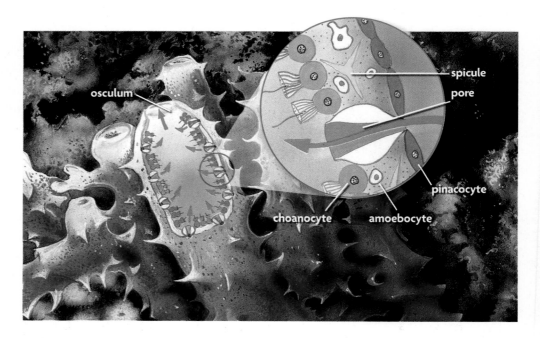

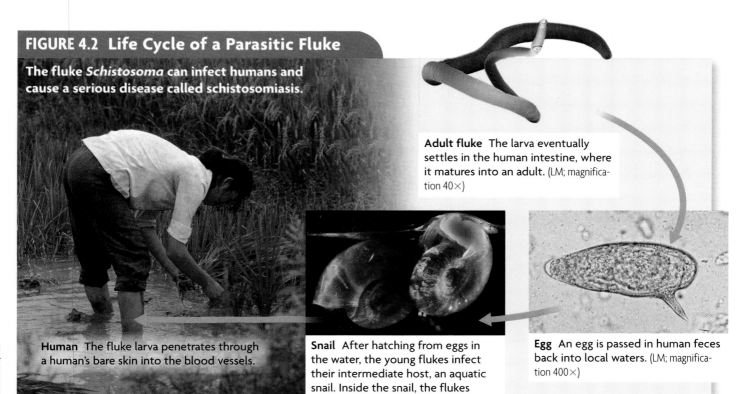

## FIGURE 4.2 Life Cycle of a Parasitic Fluke

The fluke *Schistosoma* can infect humans and cause a serious disease called schistosomiasis.

**Adult fluke** The larva eventually settles in the human intestine, where it matures into an adult. (LM; magnification 40×)

**Human** The fluke larva penetrates through a human's bare skin into the blood vessels.

**Snail** After hatching from eggs in the water, the young flukes infect their intermediate host, an aquatic snail. Inside the snail, the flukes develop into tadpolelike larvae.

**Egg** An egg is passed in human feces back into local waters. (LM; magnification 400×)

## Flukes

Flukes are parasites that feed on the body fluids of other animals. Flukes have a mouth with a pharynx that opens into a gut cavity. They are found in both invertebrate and vertebrate hosts. Many species of flukes have life cycles that involve more than one host. **FIGURE 4.2** shows the life cycle of one fluke, *Schistosoma* (SHIHS-tuh-SOHM-uh), which can infect humans and cause a serious disease called schistosomiasis. This disease affects about 200 million people in areas such as Africa and Southeast Asia. The disease is contracted by wading in or drinking fresh water contaminated with fluke larvae. Symptoms of the disease include the onset of fever and muscle pain within one to two months of infection. The disease is treated by an antiparasitic medicine.

## Tapeworms

Tapeworms are parasites that live in vertebrate guts. They have a small head with suckers or hooks used to attach to the host. Their long, ribbonlike body has no gut. Instead of swallowing food, these animals absorb nutrients from the digested food in which they live. An adult tapeworm's body is made up of segments containing both male and female sexual organs. When these segments fill with fertilized eggs, they break off and are excreted with the host's feces.

Many tapeworms have complex life cycles involving multiple hosts. The life cycle of a dog tapeworm begins when an egg is passed with a dog's feces. A flea eats the egg, and the egg develops into a larva within the flea's body. The tapeworm infects another dog when it accidentally eats the infected flea while licking its fur. The tapeworm develops into an adult within the dog's intestines, and the cycle begins again.

**Contrast** How are planarians different from flukes and tapeworms?

GO ONLINE

Parasites

**CONNECT TO**

**STRUCTURE AND FUNCTION**

The simple structure of a tapeworm reflects that as an adult it does not have to move or digest food. The lack of complex internal systems allows for a simpler body plan.

## ▶ MAIN IDEA

# Mollusks are diverse animals.

While flatworms have a digestive sac with only one opening, mollusks and all other bilateral animals have a complete digestive tract. A **complete digestive tract** consists of two openings—a mouth and an anus—at opposite ends of a continuous tube. Because food moves one way through the gut, animals with complete digestive tracts can turn their guts into disassembly lines for food. As food moves down the gut, it travels through areas that are specialized for digestion or absorption. Animals with complete digestive tracts can eat continuously. This efficient and frequent digestion allows animals to be more active.

## Mollusk Anatomy

Mollusks include animals as different-looking as oysters, garden snails, and giant squid. Mollusks may be sessile filter feeders, herbivores that graze on algae, or predators. Despite this variety of form and lifestyle, all mollusks share at least one of three features, shown in **FIGURE 4.3.**

- **Radula** The **radula** is a filelike feeding organ. Mollusks eat by scraping the radula over their food. The hard teeth of the radula pick up tiny particles that the animal swallows.
- **Mantle** The mantle is an area of tissue covering the internal organs. In most mollusks, the mantle secretes a hard, calcium-based shell that protects the animal from predators.
- **Ctenidia** (tih-NIHD-ee-uh) The ctenidia are flat gills found in a pocket of the mantle tissue called the mantle cavity. The gills absorb oxygen from water that enters this cavity. In the land-dwelling snail shown below, the gills have been lost, and oxygen is absorbed from air rather than from water in the cavity.

While the gills contain blood vessels, blood is also pumped through the hemocoel. The **hemocoel** (HEE-muh-SEEL) consists of spaces between cells within the animal's tissues. This circulatory system extends into a large muscular foot. Snails and slugs crawl on the foot, while clams and scallops dig with the foot. In cephalopods, such as squids and octopuses, the foot forms a muscular siphon, parts of the tentacles, and head.

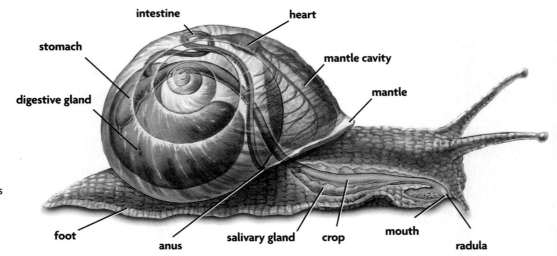

**FIGURE 4.3** The anatomy of a common garden snail includes a radula and a mantle, both of which are features shared by most mollusks.

## Classes of Mollusks

There are seven classes of mollusks. The majority of species, however, are found within three classes: the gastropods, pelecypods (bivalves), and cephalopods.

- **Gastropoda** This class includes snails, nudibranchs, abalones, and limpets. Gastropods make up over half of the species found in the Mollusk phylum. They live in both land and aquatic ecosystems. This class includes species that are herbivores, carnivores, and scavengers.

- **Pelecypoda** This class includes clams, oysters, mussels, and scallops. Pelecypods, which are also called bivalves, have a soft body that is protected by two hard shells that are hinged together. Most bivalves are filter feeders that live in marine ecosystems.

- **Cephalopoda** This class includes squid, as shown in **FIGURE 4.4**, octopuses, nautiluses, and cuttlefish. Among the mollusks, the nervous system and eye of the cephalopod are the most well-developed. Cephalopods are carnivores that eat animals such as crustaceans, fish, and other mollusks.

- **Scaphopoda** This class is also called the tusk shells, so named because their shells resemble the shape of an elephant's tusks. These mollusks live at the bottom of water bodies, where they feed on detritus.

- **Polyplacophora** This class is also called the chitons, which are animals that have a shell with overlapping plates. These marine mollusks spend most of their lifetime clinging to rocks, where they feed by using their radula to scrape algae and plant matter from the rocks.

- **Aplacophora** This class includes small wormlike animals that, unlike most mollusks, do not have shells. These mollusks live in deep water. Some feed on small marine invertebrates, while others are parasites of coral.

- **Tryblidiiae** This class of mollusks was once believed to be extinct, but they were rediscovered in 1952. Little is known about these marine mollusks that live in deep water.

## Mollusk Reproduction

Mollusks use a variety of reproductive strategies. Garden snails, for example, are hermaphrodites. Hermaphrodites are organisms that have both male and female reproductive organs. Reproduction usually involves cross-fertilization. Just before mating, the impregnating snail fires a "love dart" into the other. This calcium-rich, mucus-covered dart causes the recipient snail's reproductive system to store more sperm. During mating, a packet of sperm is transferred into the recipient snail. This packet of sperm is used to fertilize the eggs. These eggs are laid in underground nests. After a period of two to four weeks, juvenile snails hatch from the eggs.

**Summarize** **What common features are shared by mollusks?**

**FIGURE 4.4** The Humboldt, or jumbo, squid may grow to nearly 2 meters (6 ft) in length.

> **CONNECT TO**
>
> **CONVERGENT EVOLUTION**
>
> Much like the human eye, the cephalopod eye is made up of a lens, retina, iris, and pupil. However, the evolution of cephalopod and human eyes occurred independently. Recall from **The Evolution of Populations** that convergent evolution is the evolution of similar structures in unrelated species.

## Anatomy of a Clam

A clam is a bivalve mollusk. In this lab, you will explore the parts and systems of a clam.

**PROBLEM** What are the internal organs and systems of a clam?

**PROCEDURE**

1. Place the clam in the dissecting tray and follow the instructions on the drawing to carefully open the shell.
2. Look for the gills, and use your probe to study them.
3. Observe and note the shape of the foot. Locate the palps.
4. Follow the instructions to peel away the muscle layer to see the internal organs.
5. Locate the reproductive organs, and then find the digestive system.
6. Dispose of your specimen as instructed by your teacher.

**ANALYZE AND CONCLUDE**

1. **Infer** What organ does the clam use to breathe?
2. **Infer** The clam is a filter feeder. Based on your observations of the digestive system, how does the clam eat?
3. **Infer** The arteries and veins are not attached to each other. How might the circulatory system work?

**MATERIALS**

- preserved clam specimen
- dissecting tray
- Anatomical Clam Drawing
- screwdriver
- scalpel
- probe
- scissors
- forceps
- 12 dissecting pins
- hand lens
- paper towels

▶ **MAIN IDEA**

# Annelids have segmented bodies.

All annelids share more similarities in their body plans than mollusks do. Three groups of annelids—earthworms, marine worms, and leeches—are characterized by segmentation. **Segmentation** refers to the division of an organism's body, in this case an annelid's long body, into repeated sections that contain a complex set of body structures.

## Annelid Anatomy

The features of an annelid's segmented body are shown in **FIGURE 4.5.** A typical annelid segment contains part of the digestive tract, nerve cord, and blood vessels that carry blood to the worm's tissues. Annelids have a closed circulatory system, where blood travels in a closed circuit inside blood vessels. Each body segment also contains organs that collect and excrete wastes, bands of longitudinal and circular muscle, and a coelom.

The **coelom** (SEE-luhm) is a fluid-filled space that is completely surrounded by muscle. The coelom is divided by partitions called septa (singular, *septum*). The fluid inside the coelom acts as a hydrostatic skeleton. To understand how a hydrostatic skeleton works, think of a water balloon. When you squeeze one end, the water moves to the opposite end. An annelid uses its hydrostatic skeleton in a similar way to move from one place to another. When the longitudinal muscles contract, the segment shortens. When circular muscles contract, the segment lengthens. Alternating waves of contractions move from head to tail, producing the worm's characteristic crawling motion.

 **READING** TOOLBOX

**VOCABULARY**

*Coelom* comes from a Greek word meaning "cavity." *Septum* comes from a Latin word meaning "partition."

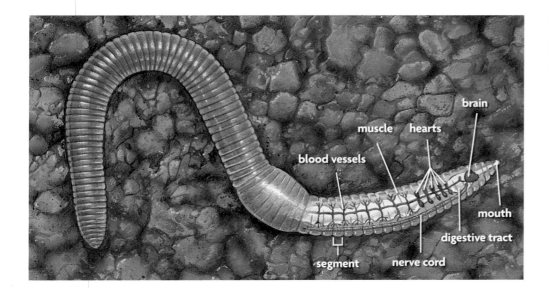

FIGURE 4.5 Annelids, such as earthworms, have similar body plans, characterized by segmentation.

brain

muscle    hearts

blood vessels

mouth

digestive tract

segment    nerve cord

## Annelid Diet

Earthworms and marine worms eat organic waste material. Earthworms excrete digested material, called castings, into the soil. Castings help maintain a nutrient-rich soil. While most people think of leeches as blood-feeders, a number of leech species are actually predators that feed on invertebrates such as snails and aquatic insect larvae.

## Annelid Reproduction

Annelid reproduction may be either asexual or sexual. Asexual reproduction results from fragmentation. In this method, a portion of the posterior end of the annelid breaks off and forms a new individual. Some annelids, such as earthworms, are hermaphrodites. Just as in land snails, reproduction occurs by cross-fertilization. Other annelids, such as marine worms, have separate males and females. Fertilized eggs of marine annelids initially develop into free-swimming larvae. Larvae grow in size by the formation of new segments.

**Contrast  In what ways are annelids different from mollusks?**

# 23.4  Formative Assessment

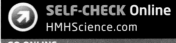

SELF-CHECK Online
HMHScience.com
GO ONLINE

## REVIEWING ▶ MAIN IDEAS

1. Describe the characteristics that separate the three groups of flat-worms.

2. What is the function of a mollusk's **radula**?

3. What are the three groups of anne-lids? Describe their body plan, using the word **coelom.**

## CRITICAL THINKING

4. **Apply**  How might a community prevent *Schistosoma* infections?

5. **Infer**  What adaptations might mollusks without shells use to defend against predators?

## CONNECT TO
### EVOLUTION

6. Free-living flatworms have pairs of sensory organs in their heads. What might make two sense organs set on either side of the head more adaptive than a single central organ?

# 23.5 Roundworms

**KEY CONCEPT** **Roundworms have bilateral symmetry and shed their outer skeleton to grow.**

**MAIN IDEAS**
- Roundworms shed their stiff outer skeleton as they grow.
- Many roundworms are parasites.

### Connect to Your World

Imagine grabbing a handful of soil. In that single handful, there may be thousands of roundworms. These animals are found in nearly every ecosystem on Earth, including mountaintops and deep ocean trenches. They are also found within extreme environments such as hot springs and Arctic ice.

### ▶ MAIN IDEA

## Roundworms shed their stiff outer skeleton as they grow.

Roundworms, also called nematodes, are one of the most numerous kinds of animals, in terms both of numbers and of species diversity. The more than 15,000 species of roundworms vary in size from less than a millimeter to over 10 meters in length.

Roundworms are part of the group Ecdysozoa, which also includes arthropods—crustaceans, spiders, and insects. Like mollusks and annelids, members of the Ecdysozoa are protostomes and have bilateral symmetry. All Ecdysozoans have a tough exoskeleton called a cuticle. The **cuticle** (KYOO-tih-kuhl) is made of chitin, and must be shed whenever the animal grows larger. When the animal sheds its cuticle, its soft body is exposed to predators until its new skeleton hardens.

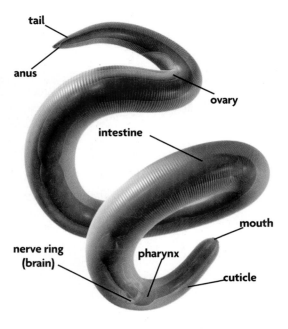

**FIGURE 5.1** Roundworms have a cylindrical shape and must shed their tough outer cuticle to grow in size.

tail
anus
ovary
intestine
mouth
nerve ring (brain)
pharynx
cuticle

### Roundworm Anatomy

As shown in **FIGURE 5.1,** a roundworm is cylindrical, with a blunt head and tapered tail. It is covered with a tough cuticle that lies over a layer of muscle. Muscle in the roundworm is laid out lengthwise. This arrangement means that a roundworm moves by bending its body side-to-side. Rather than crawling like other types of worms, a roundworm's movement is more whiplike.

Muscle within the roundworm is separated from the central gut tube by a fluid-filled space. This fluid-filled space is called a **pseudocoelom** (soo-duh-SEE-luhm) because it is not completely lined by muscle. (The prefix *pseudo-* means "false.") Roundworms do not have circulatory or respiratory systems. However, they do have a digestive system, which includes a mouth, pharynx, intestine, and anus. Food that is eaten, such as plant matter, algae, or bacteria, travels the length of the roundworm, from the mouth at one end to the anus at the other.

### Roundworm Reproduction

Most roundworms reproduce sexually. In some cases, female roundworms bear live young after eggs hatch within the female's reproductive tract. In most cases, however, larvae develop from eggs laid by the female. Roundworms grow into their adult form by molting.

**Contrast** How does growth differ in a roundworm and in a human?

"So much for being the early bird, you've got worms."

### ▶ MAIN IDEA
## Many roundworms are parasites.

Roundworms are parasites of nearly every plant and animal species. These animals cause a lot of damage to the crop species they infect. Such a widespread loss of crops can seriously harm the economy of farming communities. Other roundworms infect humans. These roundworms include hookworms, pinworms, and guinea worms.

- **Hookworms** A hookworm is found within the digestive tract of its host. This parasite feeds on its host's blood. A hookworm infects its human host when a person walks barefoot over contaminated soil. Over 1 billion people are infected with hookworms. Such infections are common in the tropics and subtropics.
- **Pinworms** A pinworm is found in the gut of its host. Pinworm infections often occur when the host accidentally swallows eggs picked up from contaminated surfaces.
- **Guinea worms** Guinea worms are found in the guts and connective tissues of their hosts. Guinea worm infections occur when a person drinks contaminated water. Work by global health organizations has helped to eliminate this disease from most of the world.

**Infer** Why might most parasitic roundworms live in the gut of their host?

## 23.5 Formative Assessment

**SELF-CHECK** Online
HMHScience.com
**GO ONLINE**

**REVIEWING ▶ MAIN IDEAS**

1. Why do roundworms molt? Use the term **cuticle** in your answer.

2. What are three parasitic roundworms that infect human hosts?

**CRITICAL THINKING**

3. **Contrast** How are earthworm and roundworm body cavities different?

4. **Apply** How might Guinea worm infections be prevented?

**CONNECT TO**

**PARASITISM**

5. Many species of roundworms are parasites of plants and animals. How is a roundworm's body plan related to its function as a parasite?

©www.CartoonStock.com

# Echinoderms

**KEY CONCEPT** **Echinoderms are on the same evolutionary branch as vertebrates.**

**VOCABULARY**

ossicle
water vascular system

**MAIN IDEAS**

- Echinoderms have radial symmetry.
- There are five classes of Echinoderms.

## Connect to Your World

If you have ever seen a tide pool, you may have noticed several creatures clinging to the pool's rocky bottom and sides. Brightly colored sea stars and spiky sea urchins are just two of the echinoderms that are often found in these habitats.

## ▶ MAIN IDEA

# Echinoderms have radial symmetry.

Adult echinoderms are slow-moving marine animals that have radial symmetry. In contrast, echinoderm larvae have bilateral symmetry. This difference suggests that echinoderms had bilateral ancestors and that radial symmetry is a derived character.

### Echinoderm Anatomy

The anatomy of a sea star is shown in **FIGURE 6.1.** Note that each arm of a sea star contains both digestive glands and reproductive glands. For clarity, they are shown separately in different arms in the illustration.

All echinoderms have an internal skeleton made up of many tiny interlocking calcium-based plates called **ossicles.** These ossicles are embedded within the skin. The plates are joined together by a unique catch connective tissue with adjustable stiffness. Catch connective tissue allows echinoderms to change their consistency, going from very flexible to very stiff in a matter of seconds. The combination of a firm skeleton and a surface covered with spiny projections (often poisonous) helps to fend off predators.

Echinoderms have a **water vascular system,** which is a series of water-filled radial canals that extend along each arm from the ring canal surrounding the central disk. The radial canals store water that is used for circulation and for filling tiny suckerlike appendages along the arms called tube feet. Changes in water pressure extend and retract the tube feet. On its own, a tube foot is small, but many of them working together can exert large forces. Tube feet are used to grab objects and to move around.

**FIGURE 6.1** Echinoderms, such as sea stars, are radially symmetrical animals with an internal skeleton made of interlocking plates embedded under the skin. Three arms of this sea star have been "cut away" to show internal anatomy.

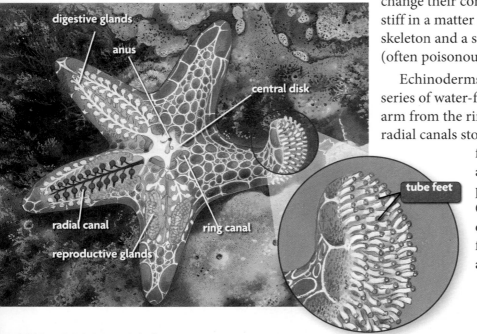

digestive glands
anus
central disk
radial canal
ring canal
reproductive glands
tube feet

A sea star has a complete digestive system made up of a mouth, stomach, a small length of intestine, and an anus. To eat a clam, a sea star grabs hold of the clam with its tube feet and uses pressure to pull apart the clam's shell. Sea stars are able to push their stomach out of their mouths. The stomach enters the narrow space between the two shells of a clam, and digestive juices from the digestive glands dissolve the clam's body. The clam is completely digested in the stomach. Waste material exits out the anus.

Echinoderms such as sea stars can regenerate, or regrow, their limbs, as shown in **FIGURE 6.2**. Sea cucumbers can regenerate a portion of their digestive system, which they sometimes eject when disturbed. For regeneration to occur, certain body parts, such as a portion of a sea star's central disk, must still remain.

**FIGURE 6.2** Sea stars and other echinoderms are able to regenerate, or regrow, limbs.

## Echinoderm Reproduction

Most echinoderms reproduce sexually. Adult sea stars, for example, release sperm and eggs from the reproductive glands in their arms into the water. The fusion of these gametes results in fertilization of the egg. The fertilized egg develops into a free-floating, planktonic larva that matures in the water. As it matures, an echinoderm undergoes a complex series of changes into its adult form. The left side of its body begins to form the tube feet, while the right side forms the ossicle plates that will protect its outer surface. Eventually, the echinoderm settles onto the ocean floor, where it develops into an adult.

**Connect  A sea star specimen has bilateral symmetry. Is it an adult or a larva? Why?**

**FIGURE 6.3** Feather stars are members of the class Crinoidea. These animals are filter feeders.

### ● MAIN IDEA
# There are five classes of Echinoderms.

Echinoderms have a variety of body plans, ranging from the spiny round sea urchin to the oblong and the well-named sea cucumber.

## Feather Stars and Sea Lilies
Feather stars and sea lilies are members of the class Crinoidea (kry-NOY-dee-uh). A feather star, shown in **FIGURE 6.3**, can move with its arms, but it is usually attached to a surface. Sea lilies are sessile. They are attached to the ocean bottom by a stalk on one side of their bodies. These animals filter feed by using the tube foot–like extensions covering their arms to collect and transfer food to the mouth.

## Sea Stars
Sea stars are members of the class Asteroidea (AS-tuh-ROY-dee-uh). Some sea stars are filter feeders, while others are opportunistic feeders, meaning that they will eat whatever food source they happen to come upon. Other sea stars are carnivorous predators.

**FIGURE 6.4** Basket stars (left) use their long, branched arms to capture plankton. Sea urchins (middle) are covered in long, sharp spines that protect them from predators. Sea cucumbers (right) are fleshy animals that live on the ocean floor.

## Brittle Stars and Basket Stars

Brittle stars and basket stars are both members of the class Ophiuroidea (AHF-ee-yuh-ROY-dee-uh). Brittle stars have long spindly arms and are fast movers. Because their tube feet lack suckers, brittle stars use their arms to move. Some brittle stars are scavengers that feed on detritus on the ocean floor. Others are predators. Basket stars, shown in **FIGURE 6.4**, also have long arms, although with many branches. Basket stars filter feed by capturing plankton with their arms.

## Sea Urchins, Sea Biscuits, and Sand Dollars

Sea urchins, sea biscuits, and sand dollars are all members of the class Echinoidea (EHK-uh-NOY-dee-uh). The bodies of sea biscuits and sand dollars are covered with tiny projections, which the animals use for movement and for burrowing on the ocean floor. Sea urchins, which do not burrow, do not have these projections. Instead, these animals are covered in long, sharp spines. Burrowing animals feed on waste matter on the ocean floor. Most sea urchins graze on algae by trapping it on sticky tentacles found on their ventral side.

## Sea Cucumbers

Sea cucumbers are the only members of the class Holothuroidea (HAHL-uh-thu-ROY-dee-uh). Sea cucumbers are fleshy animals that have a long, bilateral shape. Instead of arms, sea cucumbers have thick, fleshy tentacles. These tentacles are used to capture particles of food, which the animal eats by pulling its tentacles through its mouth. Sea cucumbers, which live on the ocean floor, are also sediment feeders. These animals absorb food items in their digestive tract, and eject nonfood particles through their anus.

**Contrast** How do feeding behaviors differ between sea stars and sea cucumbers?

(tl) ©NatureDiver/Shutterstock; (tc) ©Flip Nicklin/Minden Pictures; (tr) ©Fred Bavendam/Minden Pictures

## 23.6 Formative Assessment

**SELF-CHECK Online**
HMHScience.com
GO ONLINE

### REVIEWING ▶ MAIN IDEAS

1. How does the **water vascular system** enable echinoderms to move?

2. Describe the differences in body plans between the five classes of echinoderms.

### CRITICAL THINKING

3. **Contrast** How do the feeding habits of sessile echinoderms differ from those that are mobile?

4. **Infer** How does an echinoderm benefit from the ability to regenerate limbs?

### CONNECT TO

#### BIOINDICATORS

5. Sea urchins live on rock- and sand-covered areas of the ocean floor. What changes in an ocean ecosystem might be indicated by an increase in the sea urchin population?

# Analyzing Scatterplots

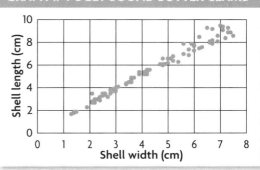

A **scatterplot** is a type of graph used to identify a trend or a correlation between two variables.

- The independent variable is usually graphed on the *x*-axis.
- The dependent variable is usually graphed on the *y*-axis.
- The data points are plotted but not connected.

Three types of correlations between variables can be shown on a scatterplot.

- Positive—as one variable increases or decreases, the other variable increases or decreases respectively.
- Negative (inverse)—as one variable increases, the other decreases.
- No correlation—there is no change in one variable as the other variable either increases or decreases.

## Model

Graph 1, a scatterplot of butter clam shell length and width, shows that as the width of the clam's shell increases, the length of the shell increases as well. This is a positive correlation, because as width increases, length increases. If it were an inverse correlation, one of the variables would increase as the other decreased.

Graph 2, a scatterplot of zooplankton feeding rates, shows no correlation between the feeding rates of zooplankton and the concentration of dinoflagellates. You can infer that there is no correlation from the graph, because the data are scattered across the graph and do not form a pattern.

**GRAPH 1. PUGET SOUND BUTTER CLAMS**

*Source:* Seattle Central Community College

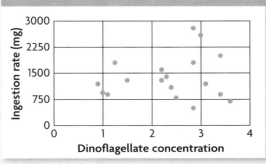

Source: Calbet, A. et al. *Journal of Aquatic Microbial Ecology, 26*

## Practice   Analyze a Scatterplot

Scientists measured the heart rate and shell diameter of snails. These data are shown in the graph at the right. Use the graph to answer the following three questions.

1. **Analyze**  Describe the correlation between the shell diameter and the heart rate in this species of snail.

2. **Predict**  If a snail shell were to grow past 14 mm, what do you think would happen to the snail's heart rate?

3. **Infer**  Suggest a possible explanation for the correlation between heart rate and shell diameter.

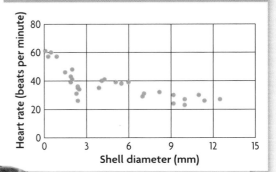

Source: Iowa State University

# 23 Summary

Animals share many characteristics, yet have a variety of shapes, structures, and sizes, and most have no backbone.

## KEY CONCEPTS

### 23.1 Animal Characteristics

**Animals are diverse but share common characteristics.** Animals are the most physically diverse kingdom of organisms. All animals share a set of characteristics.

- All animals are multicellular heterotrophs.
- Animal cells are supported by collagen.
- Animals that reproduce are diploid and usually reproduce sexually.
- Most animals have homeobox, or *Hox*, genes.

### 23.2 Animal Diversity

**More than 95 percent of all animal species are invertebrates.** Each animal phylum has a unique body plan. Scientists have constructed an invertebrate phylogenetic tree supported by anatomy comparisons and molecular evidence.

Bilateral symmetry    Radial symmetry

### 23.3 Sponges and Cnidarians

**Sponges and cnidarians are the simplest animals.** Sponges are aquatic animals that have specialized cells but lack tissues. These animals were among the first to evolve during the Cambrian explosion. Cnidarians, which include jellyfish, corals, and sea anemones, are the most primitive animals with specialized tissues that are still in existence today.

### 23.4 Flatworms, Mollusks, and Annelids

**Flatworms, mollusks, and annelids belong to closely related phyla.** Flatworms are simple bilateral animals. They include planarians, flukes, and tapeworms. Mollusks share at least one feature in common: a radula, a mantle, and ctenidia. Common mollusks include snails, bivalves such as clams, and squids. Annelids have segmented bodies and include earthworms, leeches, and marine polychaete worms.

### 23.5 Roundworms

**Roundworms have bilateral symmetry and shed their outer skeleton to grow.** Roundworms are cylindrical, with a blunt head and tapered tail. They are covered with a tough cuticle that lies over a layer of muscle. Roundworms may be free-living or parasitic. Common human parasites include hookworms, pinworms, and Guinea worms.

### 23.6 Echinoderms

**Echinoderms are on the same evolutionary branch as vertebrates.** Echinoderms and vertebrates are both deuterostomes. Like cnidarians, echinoderms have radial symmetry. These animals have body parts arranged in a circle around a central axis and use a water vascular system to move and transport nutrients. Some echinoderms can regenerate portions of their body, and sometimes they use regeneration as a way to produce offspring.

---

## 🌀 READING TOOLBOX    SYNTHESIZE YOUR NOTES

**Concept Map** Use a concept map to summarize what you know about animal phylogeny.

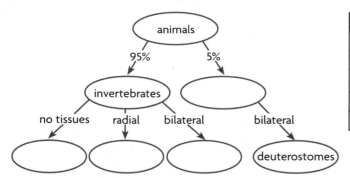

**Content Frame** Use a table to synthesize notes on the characteristics of the different invertebrate phyla.

| Phyla | Features | Symmetry | Examples |
|---|---|---|---|
| Cnidaria | Tissues | Radial | Jellyfish, coral |
| Flatworms | | | |
| | | | |
| | | | |
| | | | |

**INTERACTIVE Review**
HMHScience.com

GO ONLINE
Review Games • Concept Map • Section Self-Checks

## CHAPTER VOCABULARY

**23.1** collagen
homeotic
homeobox

**23.2** vertebrate
invertebrate
phylum
bilateral symmetry
radial symmetry
protostome
deuterostome

**23.3** sessile
filter feeder
polyp
medusa
mesoglea
nematocyst
gastrovascular cavity

**23.4** complete digestive tract
radula

hemocoel
segmentation
coelom

**23.5** cuticle
pseudocoelom

**23.6** ossicle
water vascular system

## Reviewing Vocabulary

### Visualize Vocabulary

For each word or word pair below, use simple shapes, lines, or arrows to illustrate the meaning. Label each picture, and write a short caption.

1. collagen
2. segmentation
3. mesoglea
4. gastrovascular cavity
5. polyp, medusa
6. radial symmetry, bilateral symmetry
7. radula
8. hemocoel

### READING TOOLBOX    GREEK AND LATIN WORD ORIGINS

Using the Greek or Latin word origins of the terms below, explain how the meaning of the root relates to the definition of the term.

9. The word *phylum* comes from the Greek word *phulon*, which means "class."

10. The word *sessile* comes from the Latin word *sedere*, which means "to sit."

11. The word *segment*, as in *segmentation*, comes from *segmentum*, from the Latin word *secare*, which means "to cut."

12. The word *radula* comes from the Latin word *radere*, which means "to scrape."

13. The word *pseudocoelom* comes from the Greek words *pseudes*, which means "false," and *koilos*, which means "hollow."

## Reviewing MAIN IDEAS

14. What four characteristics are common to members of the animal kingdom?

15. What is the difference between an invertebrate and a vertebrate?

16. Describe three different criteria used to classify animals into groups.

17. What types of evidence are used to put together the evolutionary history of the animal kingdom?

18. What characteristic makes sponges the simplest animals?

19. Describe the two general body forms of cnidarians, which include jellyfish and corals.

20. What are the three types of flatworms? Describe the main features of each.

21. Mollusks have a complete digestive tract. What is one benefit of having this feature?

22. Describe what a segmented body plan looks like. Which phylum includes animals with segmented bodies?

23. Why must roundworms shed their outer skeleton?

24. Several species of roundworms are parasites with human hosts. Name one and explain how it affects human health.

25. What is the function of an echinoderm's water vascular system?

26. How does the ability to regenerate help an echinoderm escape from predators?

# Critical Thinking

27. **Analyze** How are the functions of *Hox* genes related to the diversity of body plans and characteristics within the animal kingdom?

28. **Contrast** How is development different between an echinoderm and a mollusk? Use a table to summarize their different development patterns.

29. **Infer** While both sponges and cnidarians are simple animals, cnidarians have specialized tissues. What might be some advantages of having specialized tissues?

30. **Infer** Why is the ability to secrete toxic substances important to the survival of a sponge?

31. **Synthesize** How has molecular biology played a critical role in our understanding of animal relationships and phylogeny?

32. **Infer** Even when an annelid is cut in half, it can often still survive. What anatomical feature enables an annelid to remain alive when half of its body is gone?

33. **Apply** What is the function of an echinoderm's catch connective tissue?

34. **Compare and Contrast** Animals exhibit variety in their digestive systems. What do you think are the advantages and disadvantages of having a gastrovascular cavity compared with a complete digestive tract?

## Interpreting Visuals

Use the *Hox* gene diagram below to answer the next two questions.

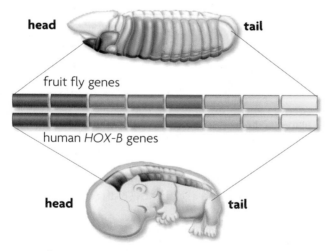

35. **Apply** How do the two organisms above display the pattern seen in all *Hox* genes?

36. **Synthesize** How does the diagram support the idea that all animals share a common ancestor?

## Analyzing Data  Analyze a Scatterplot

Scientists measured the depth and velocity of water in the Columbia River in Washington. These data are shown on the scatterplot graph below. Use the graph to answer the next three questions.

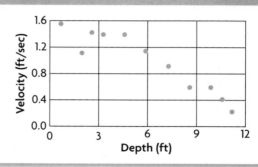

Source: *USGS*

37. **Analyze** What type of relationship exists between the depth and the velocity of the water? Explain your answer.

38. **Predict** Make a prediction about the velocity of the water if the depth were 14 feet.

39. **Infer** In what way might a species adapted to living at lower depths differ from a species adapted to living in shallow water?

## Making Connections

40. **Write a Travel Brochure** Imagine you are an advertising director for a travel agency. Choose an invertebrate from this chapter, and create a brochure to entice your chosen invertebrate to visit a vacation spot. Remember that each invertebrate species has specific requirements for survival. In your brochure, include a description of the location (and why it is the perfect place for your invertebrate), the menu from a local restaurant, and other features that would make your chosen invertebrate feel at home.

41. **Connect** In addition to storing poisonous chemicals from their food, nudibranchs also are very colorful. In other colorful animals, such as birds, fish, and insects, colors are important for a variety of reasons. What might be the adaptive advantage of a nudibranch's bright coloration?

# Standards-Based Assessment

Record your answers on a separate piece of paper.

## MULTIPLE CHOICE

1 The earliest classification system divided all animals into two main groups. Linnaeus's original classification scheme used six major groups of animals. Now, based on hundreds of years of scientific research, over 30 animal groups, or phyla, are recognized. This progression supports the idea that scientific evidence —

A changes frequently

B should be disregarded after 100 years

C is cumulative

D is often incorrect

2

The illustration above shows the chromosomes within the egg cell of a snail. If this egg cell unites with a sperm cell of the same snail species, the offspring will have —

A 6 chromosomes from each parent

B 6 pairs of chromosomes from each parent

C 12 chromosomes from each parent

D 12 pairs of chromosomes from each parent

### THINK THROUGH THE QUESTION

Recall that each egg and sperm cell has a single set of chromosomes.

3 Two roundworms mate and produce offspring. Which of the following *most directly* accounts for each offspring receiving half of its DNA from each parent?

A mutation

B maturation

C mitosis

D meiosis

4

| Appearance of Early Animals in Fossil Record | |
|---|---|
| Organism Type | Appearance in Fossil Record |
| Sponges | 570 million years ago |
| Mollusks | 545 million years ago |
| Echinoderms | 500 million years ago |

Choanoflagellates are animal-like protists that do not leave behind fossil evidence. They are considered the most likely ancestors to sponges and all other animals. Based on the table above, when did choanoflagellates likely evolve?

A less than 500 million years ago

B between 545 and 500 million years ago

C between 570 and 545 million years ago

D more than 570 million years ago

5 Which of the following statements *best* describes the impact that *Hox* genes have on animal diversity?

A Mutations in *Hox* genes lead to greater animal diversity.

B Mutations in *Hox* genes lead to decreases in animal diversity.

C Mutations in *Hox* genes lead to less variability in animal body plans.

D Mutations in *Hox* genes prevent species from occupying new niches when environmental conditions changed.

6 Which of the following provides the *best* evidence that animals and fungi evolved into multicellular organisms independently?

A They are both heterotrophic organisms.

B Animals have eukaryotic cells and fungi have prokaryotic cells.

C Fungal cells do not have the same functions as animal cells.

D Fungi are autotrophic organisms and animals are heterotrophic organisms.

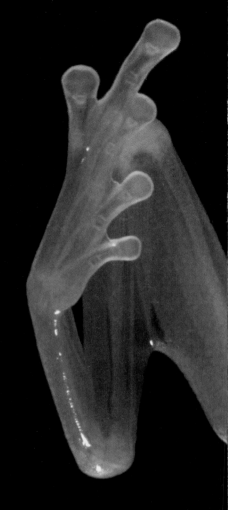

**ONLINE BIOLOGY** HMHScience.com

**ONLINE** Labs
- Fish Reproduction
- **QuickLab** Frog Development
- Anatomy of a Bony Fish
- Vanishing Amphibian—an Indicator Species
- Homologies in Vertebrate Skeletons
- Examining Zebrafish Development

- **Video Lab** Live Frog Observation

(t) ©Gregory C. Dimijian/Photo Researchers, Inc.

# Q Why is this frog see-through?

The Fleischmann's glass frog is one of several members of the family Centrolenidae. Glass frogs lack pigment on their undersides, making their skin transparent. The skin on the top portion of their body has a pigment that reflects the same wavelength of light as plants, helping them to blend in with the green leaves on which they live.

**READING TOOLBOX**    This reading tool can help you learn the material in the following pages.

## USING LANGUAGE

**Comparisons** Comparing is a way of looking for similarities among different things. Contrasting is a way of looking for the differences. Comparison words include *like*, *similar to*, and *also*. Contrast words include *unlike*, *however*, and *although*.

## YOUR TURN

In the following sentences, identify the things that are being compared or contrasted.

1. Like oranges, bananas have a thick peel. However, the seeds of bananas can be eaten easily.
2. Like fish, frogs lay eggs in water. Unlike fish, frogs do not have scales.

# Vertebrate Origins

| KEY CONCEPT **All vertebrates share common characteristics.**

**MAIN IDEAS**

○ The phylum Chordata contains all vertebrates and some invertebrates.

○ All vertebrates share common features.

○ Fossil evidence sheds light on the origins of vertebrates.

**VOCABULARY**

chordate
notochord
endoskeleton

### *Connect to Your World*

Just like the glass frog, you too are a vertebrate. So are birds, tigers, lizards, and squirrels. While the vertebrates you most often see are those that live on land like us, the group first evolved in the ocean. The first vertebrates were fish, and even today the vast majority of vertebrates are still fish.

### ○ MAIN IDEA

## The phylum Chordata contains all vertebrates and some invertebrates.

The phylum Chordata is made up of three groups. One group includes all vertebrates. Vertebrates are large, active animals that have a well-developed brain encased in a hard skull. The other two groups are the tunicates and lancelets, which are both invertebrates. Tunicates, or the urochordates, include both free-swimming and sessile animals such as sea squirts. Lancelets, or the cephalochordates (SEHF-uh-luh-KAWR-DAYTS), are small eel-like animals that are commonly found in shallow, tropical oceans. Although lancelets can swim, they spend most of their lives buried in sand, filtering water for food particles.

Despite their enormous differences in body plans and ways of life, all **chordates** share the four features illustrated in **FIGURE 1.1** at some stage of their development.

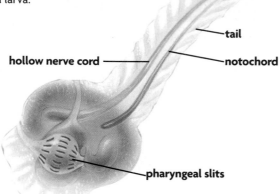

**FIGURE 1.1** A sea squirt shows all four features of a chordate as a larva.

tail
hollow nerve cord
notochord
pharyngeal slits

- **Notochord** A **notochord** is a flexible skeletal support rod embedded in the animal's back.
- **Hollow nerve cord** A hollow nerve cord runs along the animal's back. The nerve cord forms from a section of the ectoderm that rolls up during development.
- **Pharyngeal slits** Pharyngeal (fuh-RIHN-jee-uhl) slits are slits through the body wall in the pharynx, the part of the gut immediately beyond the mouth. Water can enter the mouth and leave the animal through these slits without passing through the entire digestive system.
- **Tail** A tail extends beyond the anal opening. The tail, as well as the rest of the animal, contains segments of muscle tissue used for movement.

Most chordate groups lose some or all of these characteristics in adulthood, but they are present in their larvae and embryos. For example, the larval form of sea squirts have all four chordate characteristics. However, an adult sea squirt, shown in **FIGURE 1.2**, retains only one chordate characteristic, the pharyngeal slits. Adult sea squirts use the pharyngeal slits for filter feeding. Similarly, vertebrate embryos have a notochord that is for the most part replaced by the vertebrae during later development. The fluid-filled disks between adjacent vertebrae are remnants of the notochord.

**Compare and Contrast  How are humans similar to sea squirts? How are they different?**

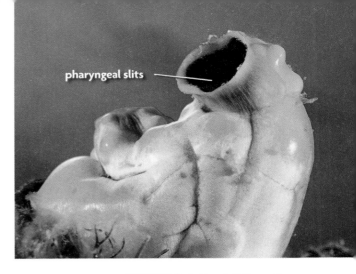

pharyngeal slits

**FIGURE 1.2** In its adult form, the only chordate feature a sea squirt retains is the presence of pharyngeal slits (located within the sea squirt's body).

## All vertebrates share common features.

Vertebrates tend to be large, active animals. Even the smallest living vertebrate, an Indonesian carp smaller than a fingernail, is larger than most invertebrates.

### Vertebrate Endoskeleton

One characteristic that allows vertebrates to grow to large sizes is the endoskeleton. An **endoskeleton** is an internal skeleton built of bone or cartilage. Bone and cartilage are both dense connective tissues. Each tissue is made of collagen fibers that are embedded in a matrix, or combination, of harder materials.

Vertebrate endoskeletons can be divided into distinct parts. Some of these parts are shown on the ape skeleton in **FIGURE 1.3**.

- **Braincase**  A braincase or cranium protects the brain.
- **Vertebrae**  A series of short, stiff vertebrae are separated by joints. This internal backbone protects the spinal cord. It also replaces the notochord with harder material that can resist forces produced by large muscles. Joints between the vertebrae let the backbone bend as the animal moves.
- **Connected bone structure**  Bones support and protect the body's soft tissues and provide points for muscle attachment.

The endoskeleton forms a framework that supports muscles and protects internal organs. It contains cells that can actively break down skeletal material and rebuild it. This characteristic means a vertebrate endoskeleton can slowly change size and shape. It can grow as a vertebrate changes size, unlike arthropod exoskeletons, which must be shed as the animal grows. It can also change shape in response to forces on a vertebrate's body. For example, bones subjected to large forces get thicker.

**FIGURE 1.3** Every vertebrate has an endoskeleton, such as the one you see in this x-ray of a small ape.

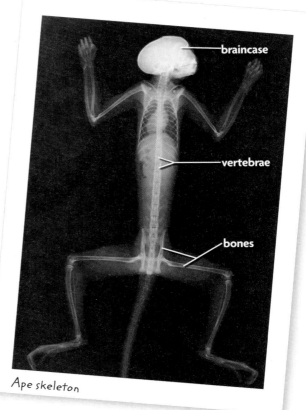

braincase

vertebrae

bones

Ape skeleton

## Vertebrate Classes

The phylogenetic tree shown in **FIGURE 1.5** shows the probable evolutionary relationships among the seven classes of vertebrates.

**Agnatha**  The Agnatha are the oldest class of vertebrates. These jawless animals include lampreys, a type of fish.

**Chondrichthyes**  The Chondrichthyes, or cartilaginous fish, have skeletons made of cartilage. These animals include sharks, rays, and chimeras.

**Osteichthyes**  The Osteichthyes, or bony fish, have skeletons made of bone. Ray-finned fish, a type of bony fish, are the most diverse group of vertebrates.

**Amphibia**  The Amphibia were the first vertebrates adapted to live both in water and on land, although they reproduce in water or on moist land. These animals include salamanders, frogs (including toads), and caecilians.

**Reptilia**  The Reptilia are able to retain moisture, which lets them live exclusively on land. Reptiles produce eggs that do not have to develop in water. Reptiles include snakes, lizards, crocodiles, alligators, and turtles.

**Aves**  The Aves are birds. Aves are distinguished by the presence of feathers, along with other features.

**Mammalia**  The Mammalia are animals that have hair, mammary glands, and three middle ear bones.

**Contrast  How does growth differ between an animal with an endoskeleton and an animal with an exoskeleton?**

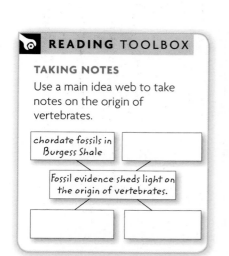

**FIGURE 1.4** Box turtles, members of the class Reptilia, are just one of the many different animals found in the vertebrate subphylum.

## ▶ MAIN IDEA

# Fossil evidence sheds light on the origins of vertebrates.

Much of what we know about early vertebrates comes from fossil evidence found in the Burgess Shale located in the Canadian Rocky Mountains. This fossil site, discovered in the early 1900s, was not fully explored until the late 1960s. Fossils found within the Burgess Shale date from the Cambrian explosion and include preserved exoskeletons, limbs, and in some cases, gut contents and muscles. Fossils of sponges, worms, and arthropods are among the invertebrate remains found at the quarry site. Other fossils with traces of notochords provide evidence of the earliest chordates.

### Closest Relatives of Vertebrates

In the past, scientists thought that lancelets were more closely related to vertebrates than tunicates were. They based this on fossil evidence, along with anatomical comparisons and molecular evidence. However, recent research indicates that tunicates may actually be the closest relatives of vertebrates. All vertebrate embryos have strips of cells called the neural crest, which develops into parts of the nervous system, head, bone, and teeth. Scientists have found that tunicates have cells that resemble the neural crest, but lancelets do not have such cells. This evidence could indicate that either lancelets secondarily lost these cells, or tunicates are indeed the closest relatives to vertebrates.

# FIGURE 1.5 Vertebrate Phylogenetic Tree

**Each vertebrate class has unique characteristics that separate one class from another.**

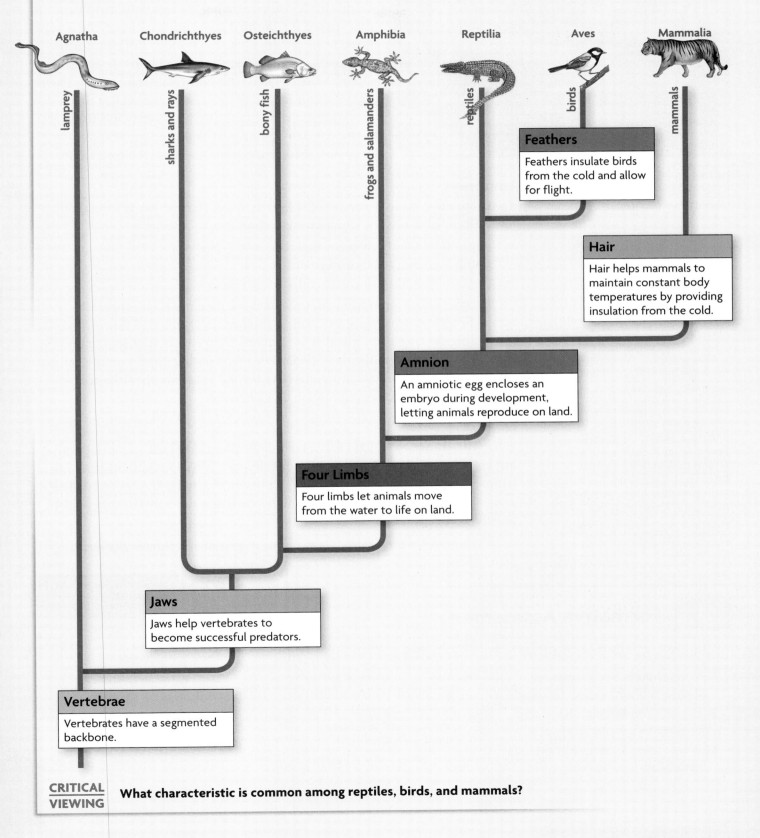

Agnatha — lamprey

Chondrichthyes — sharks and rays

Osteichthyes — bony fish

Amphibia — frogs and salamanders

Reptilia — reptiles

Aves — birds

Mammalia — mammals

**Feathers**
Feathers insulate birds from the cold and allow for flight.

**Hair**
Hair helps mammals to maintain constant body temperatures by providing insulation from the cold.

**Amnion**
An amniotic egg encloses an embryo during development, letting animals reproduce on land.

**Four Limbs**
Four limbs let animals move from the water to life on land.

**Jaws**
Jaws help vertebrates to become successful predators.

**Vertebrae**
Vertebrates have a segmented backbone.

CRITICAL VIEWING    **What characteristic is common among reptiles, birds, and mammals?**

**FIGURE 1.6** Hagfish are thought to be the chordates most closely related to vertebrates.

## Early Vertebrates

The first recognizable vertebrates were fish. The oldest fossil fish are found in 530-million-year-old rocks from China. Early fish were small, jawless bottom-feeders that sucked soft-bodied prey and detritus off the ocean floor. Jawless fish radiated into many different forms during the Paleozoic era. Some had bony head shields. Others were covered with bony plates and scales. Their heavy armor may have been a defense against predators such as giant sea scorpions. Most jawless fish were extinct by 360 million years ago. Today, two groups of jawless fish remain: the lampreys and the hagfish.

## Lampreys

There are more than 35 species of lampreys. Most of these species are highly specialized fish parasites. Their physical characteristics include

- long and slender body plans that lack paired fins
- mouths surrounded by a large sucker
- tongues covered by horny toothlike projections

Lampreys hold on to fish with their suckers, then use their tongues to scrape holes in their prey. Substances in their saliva keep blood flowing by preventing clotting as they feed. The accidental introduction of sea lampreys into the Great Lakes in the early 1900s had a devastating impact on the fishing industry. Ongoing control programs have helped to restore the fisheries by reducing the sea lamprey population by 90 percent.

## Hagfish

A hagfish, shown in **FIGURE 1.6,** is a jawless eel-like animal with a partial skull but no vertebrae. It uses a notochord for support. Although both hagfish and lampreys have primitive characteristics, none of the living species are ancient. They are recent animals that happen to be the living remnants of very ancient, mostly extinct groups.

**Summarize** How have scientists' views on the origins of vertebrates changed?

**SELF-CHECK Online**
HMHScience.com
**GO ONLINE**

## 24.1 Formative Assessment

### REVIEWING ▶ MAIN IDEAS

1. What features are shared by all members of the phylum Chordata?
2. How is an **endoskeleton** involved in an animal's movement?
3. What evidence places fish as the first vertebrates?

### CRITICAL THINKING

4. **Compare and Contrast** What are the advantages of having an endoskeleton instead of an exoskeleton? Are there any disadvantages? Why?
5. **Summarize** Draw a phylogenetic tree that shows the relationships between hagfish, lampreys, and all other fish.

### CONNECT TO

#### ADAPTATIONS

6. How is the structure of a lamprey's body related to the lamprey's function as a parasite?

**CONNECT TO**

**DEFENSE MECHANISMS**

Hagfish secrete massive amounts of slime when disturbed by potential predators. Hagfish rid themselves of their slime cocoon by tying their body into a knot and sliding off the slime. You will learn more about defensive behaviors in **Animal Behavior.**

## 24.2 Fish Diversity

| KEY CONCEPT **The dominant aquatic vertebrates are fish.**

### MAIN IDEAS
- Fish are vertebrates with gills and paired fins.
- Jaws evolved from gill supports.
- Only two groups of jawed fish still exist.

**VOCABULARY**

gill
countercurrent flow
lateral line
operculum

### Connect to Your World

In order to move in a swimming pool, you need to push your body through a thick, heavy blanket of water. Swimming for a long time is tiring. Long-distance swimming requires endurance and a lot of energy. Fish spend their entire lives moving through water, but adaptations to an aquatic environment make their movements through water much more energy-efficient than yours.

### ▶ MAIN IDEA

## Fish are vertebrates with gills and paired fins.

You get the oxygen you need by breathing in the air that surrounds you. Because fish live underwater, the way that they get oxygen is completely different from the way you breathe. Fish use specialized organs called gills to take in the oxygen dissolved in water. **Gills** are large sheets of thin frilly tissue filled with capillaries that take in dissolved oxygen from the water and release carbon dioxide. As shown in **FIGURE 2.1,** gills have a very large surface area, which increases the amount of gases they can exchange with the water. Muscles in the body wall expand and contract, creating a current of water that brings a steady supply of oxygen to the blood.

Just like you, fish have body systems that provide their cells with oxygen and nutrients and also remove waste products. Fish circulatory systems pump blood in a single circulatory loop through a heart with two main chambers. An atrium collects blood returning from the body and moves it into the ventricle. The ventricle pumps blood through the gills, where carbon dioxide is released and oxygen is picked up by the blood. The blood then carries the oxygen directly to the tissues and picks up more carbon dioxide. The blood returns to the heart, and the process begins again.

**Animated Biology**
HMHScience.com

**GO ONLINE**

How Fish Breathe

**FIGURE 2.1** Fish use the large surface area of their gills to exchange carbon dioxide and oxygen with the water in which they live.

water
flow

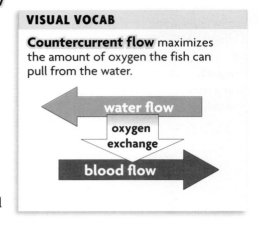
## Countercurrent Flow

Arteries in the gills carry blood to the exchange surfaces. The arteries are arranged so that blood flows in the opposite direction of the current of water entering the gills. **Countercurrent flow** is the opposite movement of water against the flow of blood in the fish's gills. Because oxygen dissolved in the water is at a greater concentration than the oxygen in the fish's blood, countercurrent flow maximizes the amount of oxygen the fish can pull from the water by diffusion. In countercurrent flow, blood is always passing by water that contains more oxygen than it does. Both well-aerated water entering the gills and depleted water leaving the gills pass by blood with an even lower oxygen load. Oxygen diffuses into the blood along the entire length of the gill.

## Swimming and Maneuvering

Most fish swim by contracting large segmented muscles on either side of their vertebral column from the head to the tail. These muscle segments power the contractions that produce a series of S-shaped waves that move down the fish's body and push it through the water. These waves also tend to nudge the fish from side to side. Such horizontal movements waste energy, so fish counteract them with their fins.

As you can see in **FIGURE 2.2,** fins are surfaces that project from a fish's body. Most fish have dorsal fins on their backs and anal fins on their bellies. Most fish also have two sets of lateral paired fins. One set, the pectoral fins, are found just behind the head. The other set, the pelvic fins, are often found near the middle of the belly. The caudal fin is another name for the tail fin. Fin tissue is supported by part of the endoskeleton, and its associated muscles let fish actively move their fins as they swim.

Fins keep fish stable. Their movements redirect water around the fish as it swims, producing forces that keep it from rolling, pitching up and down, and moving from side to side. The dorsal and anal fins keep the fish from rolling over. The caudal fin moves the fish in a forward direction. The pectoral and pelvic paired fins help the fish to maneuver, stop, and hover in the water.

**Infer** **What is the connection between countercurrent flow and a fish's movement in the water?**

**FIGURE 2.2** This clown anemone fish shows the main types of fins commonly found in fish.

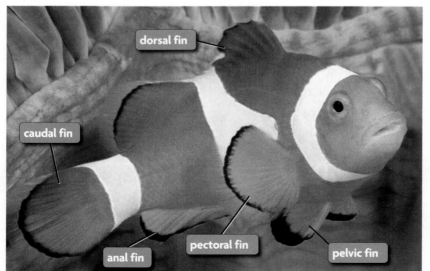

dorsal fin

caudal fin

anal fin

pectoral fin

pelvic fin

©David Fleetham/Bluegreen

- Flatfish, such as the plaice shown in **FIGURE 3.2**, are flat-shaped and lie on the sea floor waiting for their prey to swim by. During development into its adult form, one eye migrates to the top of its head as its body flattens out.
- Some slow-swimming fish use camouflage to hide from predators or prey. For example, a leafy sea dragon has dozens of fleshy flaps on its body that make it look like the seaweed it lives in.

## Staying Afloat

Most ray-finned fish have lungs modified into a buoyancy organ called a **swim bladder.** The swim bladder, shown in **FIGURE 3.3**, helps a fish float higher or lower in the water. The swim bladder lets the fish save energy because a neutrally buoyant fish does not have to swim to keep from sinking or floating toward the surface. But if the fish changes depth, it must either add or remove air from the swim bladder to maintain neutral buoyancy. Adding oxygen from the bloodstream increases buoyancy the same way inflating a life vest makes you more buoyant. Reabsorbing oxygen into the bloodstream reduces buoyancy. Some species' swim bladders are adapted for use as an amplifier, picking up sound waves and transmitting them to the inner ear through a series of bones. A few fish even use the swim bladder to make sounds by vibrating it like a loudspeaker.

Some ray-finned fish still have lungs. One example is the bichir, which lives in stagnant streams in West Africa. These fish have gills, but can also breathe air and survive out of water for several hours at a time.

**Explain** What is a swim bladder, and how does it work?

**FIGURE 3.2** A plaice's flat-shaped body helps it to blend in with the sea floor, where it lies and waits for prey to swim by.

**CONNECT TO**

### BUOYANCY

You may recall from physical science that buoyancy is the upward force that a fluid exerts on an object. To rise to the surface, a fish fills its swim bladder with oxygen, increasing its volume but not its mass, causing it to float upwards.

## FIGURE 3.3  Bony Fish Anatomy

The unique features of the anatomy of a bony fish include a swim bladder that maintains buoyancy and gills used to breathe.

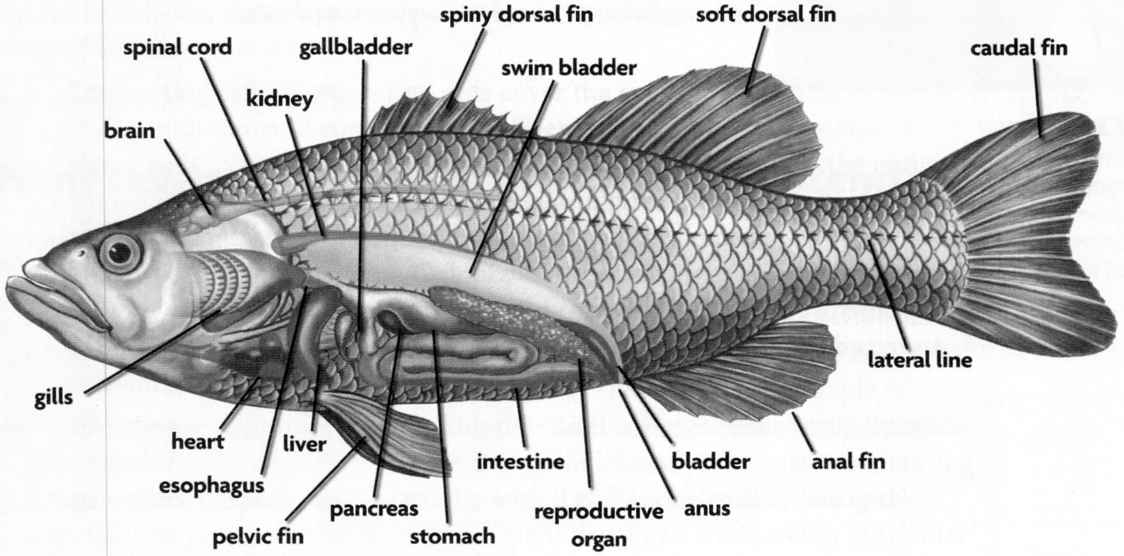

spinal cord
gallbladder
spiny dorsal fin
soft dorsal fin
caudal fin
kidney
swim bladder
brain
lateral line
gills
heart
liver
intestine
bladder
anal fin
esophagus
reproductive organ
anus
pelvic fin
pancreas
stomach

©2006 Kare Telnes/Image Quest Marine

## CONSTRUCTING SCATTERPLOTS

In order to analyze the relationship between two variables, scientists graph their data. The table below contains data about the length and age of largemouth bass in two lakes in Washington state.

1. **Graph** Construct a graph of the data in the table. Remember, for scatterplots you do not connect the data points.
2. **Analyze** What is the relationship between length and age in largemouth bass?
3. **Infer** An additional fish is measured with a length of 250 millimeters (mm). What might be the age of this fish? Explain your answer.

### TABLE 1. LARGEMOUTH BASS LENGTH AND AGE

| Length (mm) | 295 | 310 | 310 | 355 | 365 | 405 | 390 | 400 | 410 | 430 | 470 | 450 | 442 |
|---|---|---|---|---|---|---|---|---|---|---|---|---|---|
| Age (years) | 5 | 4 | 3 | 5 | 5 | 8 | 8 | 7 | 8 | 9 | 11 | 12 | 12 |

Source: *Washington State Department of Ecology*

▶ MAIN IDEA

# Lobe-finned fish have paired rounded fins supported by a single bone.

The lobe-finned fish include the ancestors of all terrestrial vertebrates. But most species of lobe-finned fish are extinct. Only seven species remain today. These fish first appeared about 400 million years ago in the Devonian period. Despite their early presence in the fossil record, the lobe-finned fish have never been as diverse as the ray-finned fish, which first appeared in the Devonian period as well.

**Lobe-fins** are paired pectoral and pelvic fins that are round in shape. These fins are arranged around a branching series of bony struts, like the limb of a land vertebrate. There is always one bone at the base of the fin. It is attached to a pair of bones, which are attached to a fan of smaller bones. Muscles extend into the fin and stretch across the bones, making the fin thick and fleshy. Lobe-fins cannot change shape as quickly as ray-fins can, and they provide less maneuverability in the water. But they are excellent at supporting weight, a feature that eventually let some of these fish walk out of the water onto land.

**Animated Biology**
HMHScience.com

**GO ONLINE**

What Type of Fish Is It?

**VISUAL VOCAB**

**Lobe-fins** are paired limblike fins that are round in shape.

lobe-fins

©Steve Maslowski/Photo Researchers, Inc.

## Coelacanths

Coelacanths (SEE-luh-ᴋᴀɴᴛʜs) are distinctive-looking fish with thick, fleshy fins and a tail with three lobes. They breathe with gills. Their swim bladders are filled with fat and provide buoyancy. There are two species of coelacanth. Both live in deep water in the Indian Ocean.

Coelacanths were first known from fossils. They are found in freshwater and shallow marine deposits from the Devonian until the late Cretaceous periods (410 to 65 million years ago), and then completely disappear from the fossil record. Before 1938, scientists assumed that they had gone extinct at the same time as the dinosaurs. In 1938, a modern coelacanth was caught off the coast of South Africa. Another was discovered near Indonesia in 1997.

## Lungfish

Lungfish, such as the one shown in **FIGURE 3.4,** live in streams and swamps in Australia, South America, and Africa. They can breathe with either gills or lungs. This characteristic means that they can live in stagnant, oxygen-poor water that other fish cannot tolerate. Lungs even keep some species alive when their ponds dry up. They make burrows in the mud, which hardens as the water dries up. Then they breathe air until the next rain refills their pond.

The relationships between lungfish, coelacanths, and the terrestrial vertebrates are controversial. Recent studies of mitochondrial DNA suggest that lungfish are the closest living relatives of terrestrial vertebrates. Anatomical evidence also supports this idea. For example, lungfish and terrestrial vertebrates are the only animals with separate blood circuits for the lungs and the rest of the body. However, this characteristic does not mean that modern lungfish are the direct ancestors of terrestrial vertebrates. Both groups are descended from ancient lungfish, and they have changed in different ways over time.

**Identify** **What are two examples of living lobe-finned fish?**

©Reg Morrison/Auscape/Minden Pictures

**READING** TOOLBOX

**VOCABULARY**

The name *coelacanth* comes from the combination of the Greek word *koilos,* which means "hollow," and the Greek word *akantha,* which means "spine."

**FIGURE 3.4** Lungfish are lobe-finned fish that are able to breathe with either gills or lungs.

---

# 24.3 Formative Assessment

**SELF-CHECK Online**
HMHScience.com
**GO ONLINE**

### REVIEWING ◉ MAIN IDEAS

1. How are the bones arranged in a **ray-fin**? How is the arrangement related to the fin's function?

2. How are **lobe-finned** fish different from ray-finned fish?

3. How are lobe-fins related to vertebrate evolution?

### CRITICAL THINKING

4. **Infer** You are looking at a long, torpedo-shaped fish with a flat head and a mouth that points upward. What do you predict about the hunting style of this fish?

5. **Predict** Any animal that is underwater is under pressure. Diving exposes animals to higher pressures. How would this affect a fish's **swim bladder**?

### CONNECT TO

#### GENETICS

6. Early coelacanth fossils have single dorsal and anal fins. Second sets of dorsal and anal fins appear suddenly in the fossil record and persist in modern species. Explain how *Hox* genes could be responsible for the sudden appearance of this novel feature.

# Biodiversity Hotspots and Other Ecosystem Services

New ways of thinking about the benefits of ecosystems are both challenging and reinforcing a decades-old reliance on biodiversity hotspots as the gold standard of conservation efforts. Scientists and governmental regulating agencies are rethinking their previous view that biodiversity is the only important conservation consideration—while at the same time confirming that biodiversity is a good indicator of which areas of the world most need to be protected.

The concept of biodiversity hotspots emerged in 1988, championed by British ecologist Norman Myers. Biodiversity hotspots are areas of the world that contain thousands of plant and animal species that are endemic, or found only in that area, and that also have lost at least 70 percent of their original habitat to human development. Today, the number of hotspots—found on every continent except Antarctica—has grown to 35, including the island of Madagascar and a large area of Central America.

Once these areas were identified, governments and nonprofit organizations around the world began focusing their conservation efforts on the hotspots, reasoning that they were the most important. If the endemic species of plants and animals that live in the hotspots became eradicated by development, they would become extinct, because they live nowhere else in the world.

However, today conservationists are recognizing that considerations besides biodiversity are also important in conservation and land-planning strategies. Over the past few decades, scientists have developed the concept of "ecosystem services," or benefits that people receive from ecosystems. These benefits include materials (such as food, materials for clothes and construction, and fuel), biodiversity conservation, carbon storage, water conservation, and scenic beauty. Although biodiversity is very important, these other ecosystem benefits are important as well.

A 2013 study done in Costa Rica found that conservationists must consider environmental tradeoffs carefully when deciding which areas to protect. The study's findings are good news for biodiversity hotspots, because scientists found that these areas are also high in value in other ecosystem services, such as carbon storage, water conservation, and scenic beauty. The study found that this correlation doesn't always hold true for other ecosystem services, though. If conservationists choose to preserve an area solely because it provides carbon storage, it will have lower value for other ecosystem services.

The authors of the study acknowledge that more research on ecosystem services needs to be done before scientists have a clear picture that will help governments and nonprofit organizations make decisions about conservation. However, the study's findings provide environmental decision makers with an important mission: When they map areas, they must map information on all of the area's ecosystem services. In this way, they can make informed decisions about which areas are most important to protect.

Lemurs in Madagascar

©KarstinKiehne/Fotolia

# 24.4 Amphibians

| KEY CONCEPT **Amphibians evolved from lobe-finned fish.**

**MAIN IDEAS**

- Amphibians were the first animals with four limbs.
- Amphibians return to the water to reproduce.
- Modern amphibians can be divided into three groups.

## Connect to Your World

What would it really be like to be a "fish out of water"? On shore, the air does not support your body. Gravity pulls on you and makes it hard to move. Your lateral line does not work. You are deaf because your body absorbs sound waves before they reach your ear. The air is too thin to let you suck food into your mouth, and it is so dry that you start losing water through your skin. These are just a few of the conditions animals faced when they first moved onto land.

## MAIN IDEA

## Amphibians were the first animals with four limbs.

One of the oldest known fossils of a four-limbed vertebrate was found in 360-million-year-old rocks from Greenland. We know that *Acanthostega* had lungs and eight-toed legs. But it also had gills and a lateral line system, neither of which work in air. These features suggest that the earliest animals with four limbs were aquatic and used their limbs to paddle underwater.

All of the vertebrates that live on land, as well as their descendants that have returned to aquatic environments, are tetrapods. A **tetrapod** is a vertebrate that has four limbs. Each limb evolved from a lobe-fin. Tetrapod legs contain bones arranged in the same branching pattern as lobe-fins, except that the fan of bones at the end of the fin is replaced by a set of jointed fingers, wings, or toes. Animals such as snakes, which do not have four limbs, are still considered to be tetrapods because they evolved from limbed ancestors.

Limbs and lungs were features that made these animals successful in an oxygen-poor, debris-filled underwater environment. But, over time, these adaptations let tetrapods climb out of the water to search for food or escape predators. These animals gave rise to the first amphibians. **Amphibians** are animals that can live both on land and in water. In the word *amphibian,* the root *amphi* comes from a Greek word meaning "on both sides," while the suffix *-bian* comes from a Greek word meaning "life."

A number of adaptations help amphibians to live on land. Large shoulder and hip bones help support more weight, while interlocking projections on the vertebrae help keep the backbone from twisting and sagging. A mobile, muscular tongue allows amphibians to capture and manipulate food. Development of a middle ear helps some amphibians to hear out of the water.

CONNECT TO

### HISTORY OF LIFE

In 2006, scientists uncovered the fossil remains of a transitional species between fish and tetrapods. *Tiktaalik roseae* has fins and scales like a fish. However, it also has the beginnings of limbs, including digits, proto-wrists, elbows, and shoulders, along with a functional neck and ribs similar to a tetrapod's.

Some amphibians can hear sound due to the development of a tympanic membrane attached to a bone called the stapes. The stapes evolved from the top part of the second gill arch. Sound waves moving through the air vibrate the tympanic membrane, or eardrum, which transfers the sound waves further into the ear cavity to the middle and inner ear.

Depending on the species, amphibians breathe through their skin or with the use of gills or lungs. The balloonlike lungs of an amphibian are simple in structure. An amphibian uses its lungs to breathe by changing the amount and pressure of air in its mouth. Unlike fish, which have a two-chambered heart, amphibians have a three-chambered heart. An amphibian heart is made up of two atria and one ventricle. Oxygenated and deoxygenated blood are partially separated by the two atria. Blood is pumped through the heart on a double circuit. Blood pumped through the pulmonary circuit goes to the skin and lungs. Blood pumped through the systemic circuit brings oxygen-rich blood to the organs and returns oxygen-poor blood to the heart.

Over time, amphibian species evolved with adaptations that allowed them to live on land. But they did not evolve ways to keep themselves or their eggs from drying out in the air.

**Analyze** **What adaptations helped amphibians move from water to live on land?**

▶ MAIN IDEA
## Amphibians return to the water to reproduce.

An amphibian's skin is thin and wet. Water constantly evaporates from it, and amphibians risk drying out if they move too far from a source of water. This need for moisture is why you rarely find an amphibian in arid habitats. A few species live in deserts, where they burrow underground, emerging only during the brief rainy season. Desert-living species can absorb large amounts of water through their skin when it is available and store it for the dry season.

**FIGURE 4.1** This female pygmy marsupial frog keeps her eggs moist by tucking them into a pouch under the skin of her back.

### Reproduction Strategies

Amphibians need a source of water to reproduce. Their eggs do not have a shell, and the embryos will dry out and die without a source of moisture. Amphibians use many strategies to keep their eggs wet, including

- laying eggs directly in water
- laying eggs on moist ground
- wrapping eggs in leaves
- brooding eggs in pockets on the female's back, as shown in **FIGURE 4.1**

Some frogs start their lives as tadpoles. **Tadpoles** are aquatic larvae of frogs. Tadpoles have gills and a broad-finned tail, and they swim by wiggling their limbless bodies like fish. They typically eat algae, but some may eat small invertebrates or even other tadpoles.

**INTERACTIVE** Review
HMHScience.com

**GO ONLINE**

Review Games • Concept Map • Section Self-Checks

## CHAPTER VOCABULARY

**24.1**  chordate
notochord
endoskeleton

**24.2**  gill
countercurrent flow
lateral line
operculum

**24.3**  ray-fin
swim bladder
lobe-fin

**24.4**  tetrapod
amphibian
tadpole

**24.5**  amniote
keratin
amniotic egg
placenta

## Reviewing Vocabulary

### Compare and Contrast

Describe one similarity and one difference between the two terms in each of the following pairs.

1. invertebrate, vertebrate
2. endoskeleton, exoskeleton
3. gill, lung
4. ray-fin, lobe-fin
5. tetrapod, amphibian
6. amniotic egg, placenta

### READING TOOLBOX    GREEK AND LATIN WORD ORIGINS

Using the Greek or Latin word origins of the terms below, explain how the meaning of the root relates to the definition of the term.

7. The word *operculum* comes from the Latin word *operire,* which means "to cover."
8. The term *caecilian* comes from the Latin word *caecus,* meaning "blind." (Hint: Consider where a caecilian lives.)
9. The word *notochord* comes from a combination of the Greek words meaning "back" and "gut or string."
10. In the term *tetrapod,* the prefix *tetra-* means "four."
11. In the term *chondrichthyes,* the word part *chondr-* comes from a Greek word meaning "cartilage." Why is a shark a member of the group Chondrichthyes?

### Visualize Vocabulary

For each term below, use simple shapes, lines or arrows to illustrate their meaning. Below each picture, write a caption. Here's an example for the term *operculum*.

An operculum is a protective plate that covers the gills of a bony fish.

12. countercurrent flow
13. lateral line

## Reviewing MAIN IDEAS

14. Sea squirts and dogs are both chordates, but they are very different kinds of animals. What four features do these animals share at some point in their development?
15. All vertebrates have an endoskeleton. What are the main parts of an endoskeleton?
16. Name the seven classes of living vertebrates.
17. How does countercurrent flow contribute to the function of a fish's gills?
18. What evidence indicates that the jaws of fish were once gill arches?
19. Barracuda and flatfish have very different body shapes and methods of finding food, yet both have ray-fins. How does the structure of their fins help them to survive?
20. What is the function of the swim bladder in a ray-finned fish?
21. What feature of a lobe-fin fish makes it the closest relative to terrestrial vertebrates?
22. List two adaptations of amphibians, and briefly describe why each is important for life on land.
23. Why does amphibian reproduction require a moist environment?
24. What are the three types of modern amphibians?
25. How does the presence of keratin in skin cells affect where an amniote can live?
26. Mammals and birds have very different methods of reproduction, but both are able to reproduce on land. Explain why amniotes do not need to return to water to reproduce.

# Critical Thinking

**27. Analyze** Describe the structure and function of the notochord and the internal backbone of an endoskeleton.

**28. Analyze** Gas exchange in fish occurs in the gills using a countercurrent flow. Imagine that there are five stations in a gill at which gas exchange takes place. Describe what happens and why as the water and blood pass each other at each station.

**29. Apply** Submarines rise and sink using a mechanical system that works much like a swim bladder. Use your knowledge of how a swim bladder works to explain how submarines use these systems to rise and descend in the water.

**30. Infer** Frogs have bodies that are specialized for jumping, yet they have webbed feet. How are webbed feet beneficial for frogs?

**31. Connect** Why would your kidneys help you survive for a couple of days without water better than the type of kidneys that frogs have?

## Interpreting Visuals

Use the image below to answer the next three questions.

**32. Classify** This mudskipper has climbed out of the water and is resting on a rock. Based on the physical characteristics of the mudskipper's fin shape, to which group of fish does the mudskipper belong? Explain your reasoning.

**33. Analyze** When it is out of the water, how might the lungless mudskipper breathe?

**34. Apply** If mudskippers were to evolve into a terrestrial animal, what body part might function as a limb?

## Analyzing Data Construct a Scatterplot

Use the data below to answer the next three questions. The calling activity, body size, and body temperature were recorded for a population of Fowler's toads. Below is a scatterplot that shows the relationship between a male toad's body temperature and calling effort, measured as the number of seconds the male called per minute of time.

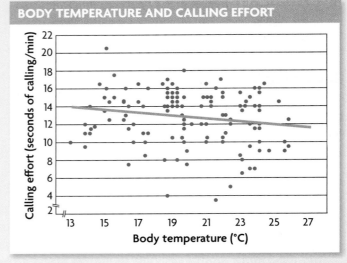

**BODY TEMPERATURE AND CALLING EFFORT**

Source: *Given, M. Copeia 2002:04.*

**35. Analyze** What is the relationship between the body temperature of the Fowler's toad and calling efforts?

**36. Analyze** Is this data an example of positive correlation, negative correlation, or no relationship?

**37. Predict** Would you expect a toad with a body temperature of 15° Celsius to have a higher or lower calling effort than a toad with a body temperature of 21° Celsius? Explain.

## Making Connections

**38. Write a Letter** Imagine you are a green frog, adapted to life both in water and on land, and one of your best friends is a fish that lives in a nearby lake. Write a letter to the fish, explaining what adaptations he would need to survive outside of the water on land. In the letter, be sure to compare any similar characteristics and contrast differing characteristics.

**39. Connect** Take another look at the glass frog on the chapter opener. Its translucent skin helps it to blend in with the green leaves on which it lives. How could natural selection have played a role in the development of this trait common among all glass frogs?

# Standards-Based Assessment

Record your answers on a separate piece of paper.

## MULTIPLE CHOICE

**1** A scientist discovers a new type of organism in the deep ocean. Because this organism was found in the water, the scientist suspects it may be related to fish. This idea *most closely* resembles a scientific —

  **A** theory

  **B** hypothesis

  **C** suggestion

  **D** experiment

**2** Fossils found in New Zealand suggest that as many as 2,000 frog species lived there in the past. Today, there are fewer than 300 frog species. What conclusion can be drawn from this information?

  **A** The climate conditions in New Zealand have changed over time.

  **B** The species alive today are more specialized to a particular niche than the species of the past.

  **C** Biological diversity of frogs in New Zealand has decreased.

  **D** There are fewer frog species today because a mass extinction occurred.

**3**

After studying fossils of prehistoric fish in one region, scientists developed this family tree to describe how the various species they found are related. Which of the following is *true* with regard to the diagram above?

  **A** The Ancestor species has gone extinct.

  **B** Species A and Species C are not related.

  **C** Species D evolved before Species A, B, and C.

  **D** Species C evolved before Species A and B.

**4**

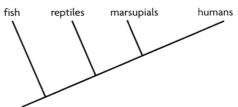

According to the cladogram above, which of the following statements is *true*?

  **A** Fish are more closely related to humans than reptiles.

  **B** Reptiles are more closely related to marsupials than fish.

  **C** Marsupials and fish do not share a common ancestor.

  **D** Marsupials and humans share a common ancestor.

### THINK THROUGH THE QUESTION

Recall that cladograms are based on common ancestry, and that they are read from left to right.

**5** Countercurrent flow in a fish's gills allows blood to efficiently release carbon dioxide into the water and absorb oxygen from the water. Which of the following *best* describes why this process is referred to as "countercurrent flow"?

  **A** Oxygen and carbon dioxide flow in opposite directions.

  **B** Fish need to swim backwards in order for gas exchange to take place.

  **C** The movement of the water flows in the opposite direction as the blood.

  **D** Fish need to swim against the current in order for gas exchange to take place.

**6** About 245 million years ago, at the boundary of the Permian and Triassic periods, 95 percent of all species died out. This event is referred to as a(n) —

  **A** episode of speciation

  **B** population explosion

  **C** mass extinction

  **D** intense adaptation

# BIOZINE

## *at* HMHSCIENCE.COM

### INTERNET MAGAZINE

*Go online for the latest biology news and updates on all BioZine articles.*

Expanding the Textbook

News Feeds

🔊 Science Daily

🔊 CNN

🔊 BBC

Careers

Bio Bytes

Opinion Poll

Strange Biology

Could one of these travelers be carrying a virus that will cause the next pandemic?

# Pandemics— Is the Next One on the Way?

*Imagine that a new virus emerges and people have no immunity. There is no vaccine. If this were to happen, there could be mandatory travel restrictions, quarantines, and social distancing—including staying out of all crowded places. In the United States alone, such an outbreak could kill up to 2 million people. But how can such a virus emerge, and how can we prepare for it?*

## Pandemics

When a new virus emerges, it infects organisms that have not developed immunity, or resistance, to the virus. If a new virus infects humans, it may spread easily from person to person before a vaccine can be produced. A disease outbreak that affects large areas of the world and has a high fatality rate is called a pandemic. The disease is spread very quickly through infection—for example, by sneezing or coughing—to a great number of people.

The 1918 flu pandemic was the most devastating pandemic recorded in world history. This virus infected nearly one-fifth of the world's population, killing about 50 million people worldwide. It spread mainly along global trade routes and with the movement of soldiers during World War I.

If a new and deadly disease emerges today, a pandemic could rapidly result. A carrier could travel around the world in 24 hours. Several million people travel internationally by plane every year, easily reaching their destinations before they show any symptoms of carrying a disease.

## The "Perfect" Virus

Not every virus is well suited to cause massive human casualties. For many viruses, humans represent a dead-end infection because they cannot be passed from human to human. For other viruses, victims die too quickly for the virus to reproduce. Quarantines can contain this type of virus relatively easily.

What characteristics would make an emerging virus likely to cause a pandemic? The virus would need to be adapted to humans as hosts and easily spread through casual contact. Victims would also have to survive infection long enough without symptoms to go about their daily business and infect other people. Finally, the most deadly virus would mutate rapidly, foiling the attempts of scientists to develop a vaccine or a drug that targets it.

# TECHNOLOGY S.T.E.M.

## Dissecting a Virus

Scientists have long debated how the genetic material of influenza A viruses, RNA, is likely arranged. In 2005 virologist Yoshihiro Kawaoka and his team of researchers at the University of Wisconsin unraveled the mystery using a technique called electron tomography.

Electron tomography is a way to construct a three-dimensional image from a series of electron microscope images taken at different angles. By making slices along flu virus particles that cut them into "top" and "bottom" halves, researchers found that all influenza A viruses have a total of eight RNA strands. Seven strands form a circle just inside the edge of the virus particle, surrounding an eighth strand in the center.

Based on this similarity in structure, the researchers concluded that all influenza A viruses must share a specific mechanism for packaging their genetic material. This knowledge may make it possible to engineer viruses that can be used to mass produce vaccines to defend against these viruses, which are responsible for regular seasonal outbreaks as well as the avian flu.

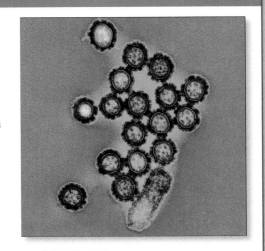

Read More >> *at* HMHScience.com

# CAREERS

## Epidemiologist in Action

| **DR. BEN MUNETA** | |
|---|---|
| **TITLE** Medical Epidemiologist, Indian Health Service |  |
| **EDUCATION** M.D., Stanford University | |

In 1993, a mystery disease began to kill people in the southwestern United States. One of the experts that the Centers for Disease Control (CDC) consulted was Dr. Ben Muneta. Dr. Muneta is an epidemiologist, a scientist who studies the causes, transmission, and control of diseases within a population. He works at the Indian Health Service National Epidemiology Program in Albuquerque, New Mexico.

Dr. Muneta consulted a traditional Navajo healer. From him, Dr. Muneta learned that the disease was associated with extra rainfall, which had caused the pinon trees to produce more nuts than usual. This in turn had led to a population explosion among mice that feed on these nuts.

Using this lead, CDC researchers determined that the disease was caused by hantavirus, a virus spread through the droppings of deer mice. With further research, Dr. Muneta confirmed that some Navajo healers had even predicted the 1993 outbreak.

**Read More >>** *at* **HMHScience.com**

## Diseases That Jump to New Species

A zoonosis is a disease that can jump between species. A virus that evolves the ability to jump from a nonhuman animal species to humans will spread very quickly in the human body, which has not yet developed defenses. If this virus exchanges genetic material with another human virus, the virus may become capable of spreading from person to person.

The swine flu pandemic was caused by the H1N1 virus that originated in pigs. In 2009, it was estimated that 22 million people were infected with the H1N1 virus! World health officials urged individuals to get vaccinated and educated people on its symptoms. A year later, the swine flu was officially contained.

China, Thailand, Russia, Turkey, and Pakistan are among the countries that have confirmed cases of avian flu in poultry farms. Here, a Pakistani health worker vaccinates a healthy chicken.

## Avian Flu H5N1

Perhaps the most familiar zoonosis is the avian flu virus. Sometimes called the bird flu, this virus normally infects wild birds such as ducks and geese as well as domestic birds such as chickens. Migrating birds can carry it to other continents.

Researchers have been tracking a form of avian flu called H5N1. Like other flu viruses, H5N1 mutates rapidly. Random mutations may or may not help the virus adapt to new host species. However, viruses can mutate in a faster, less random way. If an animal becomes infected with viruses from two different species at the same time, the viruses can exchange genetic information. If this happens, the avian flu can jump the species barrier, becoming a flu virus that can be transmitted from one human to another.

## Unanswered Questions

Despite the danger that a new virus represents, no one knows how the virus may mutate or whether it will cause a pandemic. Some of the most important questions include the following:

- How can vaccines be developed quickly enough to stop a disease that can spread in hours or days?
- Can a broad-spectrum antiviral drug be developed that could target more than one flu virus?
- What specific molecular factors allow a virus to jump from one species to another?

**Read More >>** *at* **HMHScience.com**

## UNIT 7

# Human Biology

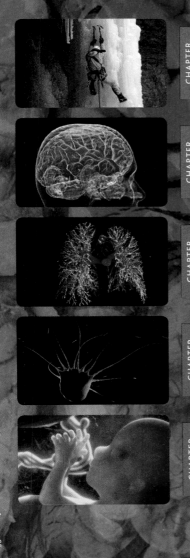

**BIOZINE**
HMDScience.com

**Brain Science—We Are Wired to Learn!**
**TECHNOLOGY** Scanning the Brain
**CAREER** Neuroscientist

**BIG IDEA** The human body is organized into different systems that interact in a coordinated way to maintain homeostasis.

## ⊘ ONLINE BIOLOGY    HMHScience.com

**ONLINE** Labs

- Homeostasis and Exercise
- **QuickLab** Negative Feedback Loop
- Examining Human Cells
- Hormones and Homeostasis
- Negative and Positive Feedback
- **Open Inquiry Lab** Interactions Among Systems

(t) © Ken Redding/Corbis

**Q How does this ice climber hang on to his body temperature?**

This climber has to concentrate on every move—one slip could mean serious injury or even death. His body is working just as hard on the inside to provide energy and to maintain a stable body temperature. The climber's clothes help prevent heat loss, while his body's internal systems increase his body heat.

---

**READING TOOLBOX**    **This reading tool can help you learn the material in the following pages.**

### USING LANGUAGE

**Analogies** Analogies compare words that have similar relationships. You can write analogies with words or with colons. For example, the analogy "up is related to down in the same way that top is related to bottom" can be written "up : down :: top : bottom." To answer an analogy problem, you must figure out how the words are related. In the example given, up is above down and top is above bottom.

### YOUR TURN

Use information found in the chapter to complete the following analogies.

1. heart : pump :: kidney : _____
2. nervous system : nerves :: endocrine system : _____

# Levels of Organization

| **KEY CONCEPT** **The human body has five levels of organization.**

**MAIN IDEAS**

- Specialized cells develop from a single zygote.
- Specialized cells function together in tissues, organs, organ systems, and the whole organism.

**VOCABULARY**

determination
cell differentiation
tissue
organ
organ system

### Connect to Your World

Climbing a wall of ice requires careful interaction among all parts of the body. You probably know that the brain and muscles work together to coordinate the climber's movements. The heart and lungs also have to work together to help provide energy for the climb. Yet every human body starts out as a single cell, a fertilized zygote. How does a single cell give rise to all the different types of cells, tissues, and organs in the human body? Further, how do such different parts coordinate their activities to keep the body functioning?

## ▶ MAIN IDEA

# Specialized cells develop from a single zygote.

If you were to watch an emergency medical team in action, you would quickly notice that each person has a special job. One keeps in radio contact with the main hospital. Another monitors the patient's vital signs. Still others perform life-saving procedures. All emergency teams are made up of people, but each person within the group has a different job.

Likewise, multicellular organisms are made up of cells, but different cells in the organism have different functions. Take a moment to study the images of the blood cells and nerve cells, or neurons, in **FIGURE 1.1.** You will notice that the red blood cells are round with a concave center. This structure gives them more surface area to help deliver oxygen to all parts of the body. In contrast, neurons develop extensions that transmit and receive messages from other neurons.

Humans, like almost all multicellular organisms, are collections of specialized cells that work together. These cells arise from a single cell, the zygote, which is formed by the union of an egg and sperm. The zygote divides and differentiates into more than 200 different types of human cells. These cells allow you to do everything from lifting a glass, to learning people's names, to maintaining your body temperature on a cold day. Cell specialization involves two main steps: determination and differentiation.

## Determination

The cells produced during the first few divisions of the zygote are known as embryonic stem cells. These cells have the potential to become any type of specialized cell in the body. Within a few weeks, however, a process called **determination** occurs, in which most stem cells become committed to develop

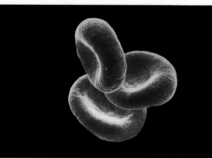
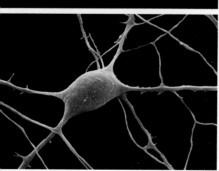

**FIGURE 1.1** The disk-shaped red blood cells (top) carry oxygen to all parts of the body. The neuron (bottom), through its extensions, receives and transmits messages from and to other neurons. (colored SEMs; magnifications: blood cells 2800×; neuron about 1600×)

into only one type of cell. For instance, a stem cell might become a cardiac muscle cell or a spinal neuron. These committed cells still retain all of the genetic information needed to build an entire organism. However, during determination, they lose their ability to express some of this information.

Once a cell is committed to becoming a specialized cell, it will develop into only that type of cell. For instance, a cell that will become a neuron can only be a neuron, even if it is transplanted into another part of the body. During normal development, determination cannot be reversed.

## Differentiation

**Cell differentiation** is the process by which committed cells acquire the structures and functions of highly specialized cells. Cell differentiation occurs because specific genes in each cell are turned on and off in a complex, regulated pattern. The different structures of these specialized cells, such as those shown in **FIGURE 1.2,** allow them to perform specific functions within the body.

The specialization enabled by differentiation is what allows different types of cells to have different functions. The function of muscle cells, for example, is to produce movement by contracting and relaxing. However, skeletal muscle and smooth muscle cells have different structures. Skeletal muscle cells align in bands of orderly rows and contain many nuclei. They are responsible for nearly all voluntary muscle movements, such as lifting your foot to kick a ball. In contrast, smooth muscle cells are shorter and have only one nucleus. They perform involuntary movements, such as raising the hairs on your arm.

Other cells have even more specialized structures and functions. Sperm cells, for instance, develop whiplike tails that enable them to swim. Cells lining the gut are elongated and tightly packed to provide more surface area for the absorption of nutrients.

Not all cells continue to develop into specialized cells. The process of programmed cell death, called apoptosis (AP-uhp-TOH-sihs), is also a normal part of development. For example, when your hands first formed, your fingers resembled a mitten. The death of cells between the fingers allowed individual fingers to develop.

**Analyze** Why do multicellular organisms need specialized cells?

skeletal muscle tissue, smooth muscle, stratified epithelium, columnar epithelium, ©Ed Reschke/Peter Arnold, Inc.; zygote ©Dr. Yorgos Nikas/Photo Researchers, Inc.; group of sperm ©CNRI/Photo Researchers, Inc.; New–Human bone marrow cells ©Carolina Biological Supply company/Phototake Inc./Alamy Ltd; areolar tissue ©Educational Images/Custom Medical Stock Photos

### READING TOOLBOX

**TAKING NOTES**

Use a supporting main ideas strategy to take notes about processes such as cell specialization.

Specialized cells develop from embryonic stem cells.

→ determination—cells are committed to be one type of cell

→ cell differentiation

→ supporting detail

## FIGURE 1.2 Cell Differentiation

**Cells develop specialized structures and functions during differentiation.**

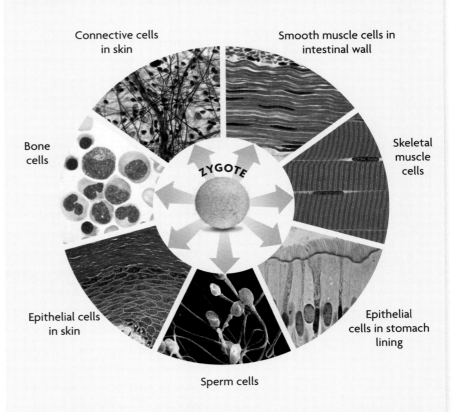

Connective cells in skin

Smooth muscle cells in intestinal wall

Bone cells

ZYGOTE

Skeletal muscle cells

Epithelial cells in skin

Sperm cells

Epithelial cells in stomach lining

**Contrast** How do the structures of sperm cells and epithelial cells in the stomach differ?

## ► MAIN IDEA

# Specialized cells function together in tissues, organs, organ systems, and the whole organism.

Specialized, or differentiated, cells are only the first level of organization in a multicellular organism. Scientists organize multicellular structures into five basic levels, beginning with cells and moving to increasingly complex levels—tissues, organs, organ systems, and the whole organism. These five levels in the human body are shown in **FIGURE 1.3.**

**1** **Cells** Each type of specialized cell has a particular structure and a chemical makeup that enable it to perform a specific task. Some cells in the lungs, for instance, are involved in the exchange of gases. Others secrete mucus that helps to trap foreign particles and to protect the lungs from pathogens, such as bacteria and viruses.

**2** **Tissues** A group of similar cells that work together to perform a specialized function are known as **tissue.** The human body is made up of four general types of tissues.

- Epithelial tissue consists of protective sheets of tightly packed cells connected by special junctions. The skin and the membranes that line the stomach, the lungs, and other organs are epithelial tissues.

- Connective tissue serves to support, bind together, and protect other tissues and organs. Tendons, ligaments, bone, and cartilage are all connective tissues.

- Muscle tissue is capable of contracting to produce movement. The human body contains skeletal, cardiac, and smooth muscle tissues.

- Nervous tissue transmits and receives impulses in response to stimuli, processes information, and regulates the body's response to its environment.

**3** **Organs** A group of tissues that carry out a specialized function of the body form an **organ.** For example, the lungs are composed of all four types of tissues. Muscle and connective tissues expand and contract the lungs. Nervous tissue sends and receives messages that help regulate gas exchange in the lungs and the rate at which a person breathes. Epithelial tissue forms the inner lining of the lungs.

**4** **Organ systems** Two or more organs that work together to perform body functions form an **organ system.** The organ system that allows you to breathe includes not only the lungs but also the sinuses, the nasal passages, the pharynx, and the larynx (the voice box). Organ systems perform the most complex activities in the body.

**5** **Organism** Together, the organ systems make up the entire organism. For you or any other organism to stay alive, all of the systems must interact and work together. As a result, anything that harms one organ or organ system will affect the health of the entire body.

### CONNECT TO

### PLANT BIOLOGY

Animals are not the only organisms with levels of organization that start with cells. Refer to the chapter **Plant Diversity** to review cells, tissues, organs, and organ systems of plants.

# FIGURE 1.3 Five Levels of Organization

**All levels of organization interact and work together to maintain the body's health.**

**1 CELLS**

**Epithelial lung cell**
These cells have tiny hairlike structures (cilia) at the top.

**2 TISSUES**

**Epithelial lung tissue**
Cells with cilia are packed together in the lung's inner lining. They act like a conveyor belt to move foreign particles and pathogens out of the lungs.

**3 ORGANS**

**Lungs**
The lungs are composed of four types of tissue. The lungs are the site where gases are exchanged.

**4 ORGAN SYSTEMS**

**Respiratory system**
This system includes the lungs, trachea, larynx, pharynx, sinuses, and nose. The nose and sinuses filter, moisten, and warm the air before it enters the lungs.

**5 ORGANISM**

**Human**
The respiratory system is one of several organ systems that work together to keep the human body functioning properly.

CRITICAL VIEWING How might a sinus infection affect the rest of the respiratory system?

## FIGURE 1.4  Major Organ Systems

| SYSTEM | MAJOR TISSUES AND ORGANS | PRIMARY FUNCTION |
|---|---|---|
| **Circulatory** | heart, blood vessels, blood, lymph nodes, lymphatic vessels | transports oxygen, nutrients, wastes; helps regulate body temperature; collects fluid lost from blood vessels and returns it to the circulatory system |
| **Digestive** | mouth, pharynx, esophagus, stomach, small/large intestines, pancreas, gallbladder, liver | breaks down and absorbs nutrients, salts, and water; eliminates some wastes |
| **Endocrine** | hypothalamus, pituitary, thyroid, parathyroid, adrenal glands, pancreas, ovaries, testes | influences growth, development, metabolism; helps maintain homeostasis |
| **Excretory** | skin, lungs, kidneys, bladder | eliminates waste products; helps maintain homeostasis |
| **Immune** | white blood cells, thymus, spleen | protects against disease; stores and generates white blood cells |
| **Integumentary** | skin, hair, nails, sweat and oil glands | acts as a barrier against infection, injury, UV radiation; helps regulate body temperature |
| **Muscular** | skeletal, smooth, and cardiac muscles | produces voluntary and involuntary movements; helps to circulate blood and move food through the digestive system |
| **Nervous** | brain, spinal cord, peripheral nerves | regulates body's response to changes in internal and external environment; processes information |
| **Reproductive** | *male:* testes, penis, associated ducts and glands *female:* ovaries, fallopian tubes, uterus, vagina | produces reproductive cells; in females, provides environment for embryo |
| **Respiratory** | nose, sinuses, pharynx, larynx, trachea, lungs | brings in $O_2$ for cells; expels $CO_2$ and water vapor |
| **Skeletal** | bones, cartilage, ligaments, tendons | supports and protects vital organs; allows movement; stores minerals; serves as the site for red blood cell production |

The major organ systems in the human body, including their main parts and primary functions, are listed in **FIGURE 1.4**. Keep in mind that all of the organs in these systems developed from specialized cells and tissues that arose from a single cell, the zygote. The major parts and functions of each organ system are examined in greater detail in the following chapters on human body systems.

How do these complex organs and organ systems keep functioning and working together properly? As you will read in Section 2, the body has sophisticated mechanisms for maintaining a stable internal environment.

**Compare and Contrast**  How do tissues differ from organs and organ systems?

## 25.1  Formative Assessment

**SELF-CHECK** Online
HMHScience.com
**GO ONLINE**

### REVIEWING ▶ MAIN IDEAS

1. How does the process of cell **determination** differ from the process of cell differentiation?

2. Relate the levels of organization to each other and to the whole human body system.

### CRITICAL THINKING

3. **Apply**  What **organ systems** must work together to bring oxygen to the body's cells?

4. **Predict**  A cell has undergone determination to become an endocrine gland cell. If it is transplanted to a leg muscle, what do you think will happen to this cell?

### CONNECT TO

**CELL CYCLE**

5. In the spring, tadpoles lose their tails as part of their life cycle. At a certain stage in development, the human fetus acquires individual fingers and toes. What occurs in some cells of both species to explain these changes?

# Electric Skin

The science and engineering of making prosthetic limbs has advanced greatly since the days of arms and legs molded of solid wood or metal. Today, some prostheses contain microprocessors and are connected directly to the nerves. However, there is one area in which prostheses have always been lacking: They do not have skin that can function in the same way as human skin. With the recent development of "electric skin," though, change is on its way.

In recent years, scientists have developed skinlike devices that could do one—but just one—of the things that human skin does, such as feel pressure or temperature. However, no one had been able to develop a skin that could perform more than one of these functions at the same time.

Now, scientists have finally reached that milestone with the development of "e-skin" that can feel both static and dynamic pressure, temperature, and even sound. The e-skin was modeled on the ridged skin of human fingertips, which is very sensitive to external stimuli. Mimicking the way the dermis and epidermis of human skin fit together, e-skin is made of a ridged film layered over ridged plastic and graphene sheets.

When pressure is applied to the e-skin, the ridges of the film and the ridges of the sheets are pressed together, and an electric current is generated.

The e-skin also produces an electric current when it is exposed to something hot or cold, when touching different textures causes different vibrations in the ridges, and when sound waves cause the ridges to vibrate.

So could human brain cells actually sense those electric currents? Another recently developed e-skin that senses pressure has been successful in this area. When tested, the e-skin proved capable of sending electric impulses, caused by pressure applied to the e-skin, to the brain cells of a mouse.

Scientists see multiple uses for e-skin. Because of their flexibility, e-skins could be used in hearing aids that are much more comfortable than the rigid ones available today. They also could be used as wearable medical and diagnostic devices, capable of taking temperature and measuring pulse and blood pressure. Prostheses that are covered in humanlike skin are still in the future, but recent progress in e-skin development provides hope that the technology will one day be available.

## S.T.E.M. Activity

In a group, brainstorm possible uses of e-skin. Identify a need that an application of e-skin could fill. Draw a diagram of the application and write several paragraphs that explain the need, how the e-skin application could fill it, and any possible constraints on the application.

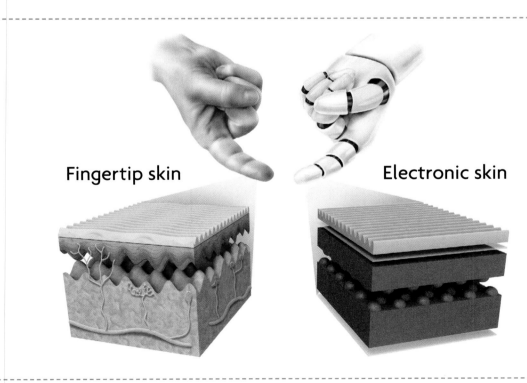

Fingertip skin          Electronic skin

# Mechanisms of Homeostasis

**KEY CONCEPT** **Homeostasis is the regulation and maintenance of the internal environment.**

**MAIN IDEAS**

◗ Conditions within the body must remain within a narrow range.
◗ Negative feedback loops are necessary for homeostasis.

## Connect to Your World

The complex tissues, organs, and organ systems in your body must respond to a wide variety of conditions. For instance, during the summer, you might walk out of a cold, air-conditioned store into a stifling hot, summer day. Your body temperature has to remain the same under both conditions in order for you to survive. In fact, your life depends on your body's ability to maintain the delicate balance of your internal chemistry.

## ▶ MAIN IDEA

# Conditions within the body must remain within a narrow range.

During every moment of your life, trillions of chemical reactions are taking place in your body. The enzymes that control these reactions work best within a narrow range of conditions. One of these conditions is your internal body temperature, which should remain between 36.7°C and 37.1°C (98.2°F and 98.8°F). If it rises only a few degrees, you could easily die from overheating. At temperatures over 41°C (106°F), many enzymes stop functioning. If your internal temperature falls below 27°C (80°F), your heart may fail.

Likewise, the levels of trace minerals in your body must stay within strict limits. For instance, if calcium levels are too high, you can slip into a coma. If they are too low, your heartbeat becomes irregular.

You live in a constantly changing environment. Your body must cope not only with temperature changes but also with pollution, infection, stress, and many other conditions. Every change is a challenge to your body. What keeps the human body from breaking down every time the internal or external environment changes?

### Homeostasis and the Internal Environment

Fortunately, the body has many control systems that keep its internal environment stable. Together, these control systems are responsible for maintaining homeostasis. **Homeostasis** (HO-mee-oh-STAY-sihs) is the regulation and maintenance of the internal environment—temperature, fluids, salts, pH, nutrients, and gases—within the narrow ranges that support human life. Your internal control systems respond quickly to environmental change, whether from outside conditions or internal ones, as shown in **FIGURE 2.1**.

**Biology**
HMHScience.com
**GO ONLINE**

Keep an Athlete Running

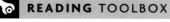

### READING TOOLBOX

**VOCABULARY**

The word *homeostasis* is formed from two Greek words: *homos*, meaning "similar," and *stasis*, meaning "standing" or "stopping."

## Control Systems in the Body

Internal control systems require sensors, a control center, communication systems, and targets.

**Sensors** Sensors, also called receptors, gather information about conditions inside and outside of the body. In cold or hot weather, for instance, sensors in your skin and nasal passages gather data about air temperatures. The body has thousands of internal sensors and other specialized sensors that detect changes in the outside world.

**Control center** A control center, often the brain, receives information from the sensors. It then compares this information to the set points, or ideal values, at which the body functions best. When conditions move above or below a set point, the control center responds by sending messages through a communication system.

**Communication systems** Communication is controlled by the nervous system and the endocrine system, which carry messages to all parts of the body. These messages, in the form of nerve impulses or hormones, tell targets in the body how to respond to internal or external changes.

### FIGURE 2.1 Homeostasis and Change

Control systems in the skin help reduce or conserve body heat.

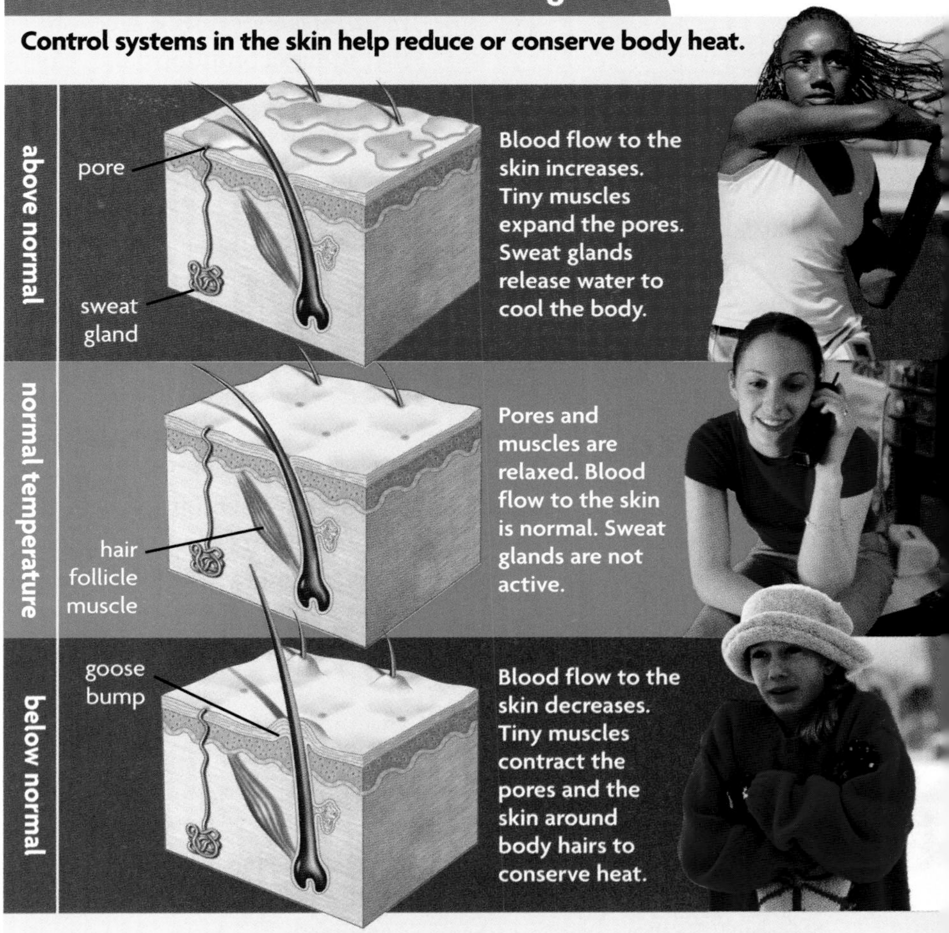

**above normal**
pore
sweat gland

Blood flow to the skin increases. Tiny muscles expand the pores. Sweat glands release water to cool the body.

**normal temperature**
hair follicle muscle

Pores and muscles are relaxed. Blood flow to the skin is normal. Sweat glands are not active.

**below normal**
goose bump

Blood flow to the skin decreases. Tiny muscles contract the pores and the skin around body hairs to conserve heat.

**Apply** If the girl in cold temperature starts jogging, how would the control mechanisms in her skin respond as she runs?

**Targets** A target is any organ, tissue, or cell that changes its level of activity in response to a message. For instance, in a cold environment, a message might cause the muscles to start shivering to generate more body heat.

**Explain** Why is it so important to maintain homeostasis within the body?

## ▶ MAIN IDEA
# Negative feedback loops are necessary for homeostasis.

Sensors, control centers, communication systems, and targets work together in what is known as a feedback loop. **Feedback** is information from sensors that allows a control center to compare current conditions to a set of ideal values. In a feedback loop, information moves continuously among sensors, a control center, and a target. Most functions in the body are regulated by negative feedback loops.

## Negative Feedback

In **negative feedback,** a control system counteracts any change in the body that moves conditions above or below a set point. Negative feedback loops help maintain homeostasis. A thermostat is a good example of how a negative feedback loop works. A sensor in the thermostat continuously measures air temperature in a room. A control mechanism then compares the current room temperature to a set point, say 21°C (69.8°F). When the temperature falls below 21°C, the thermostat sends an electronic message that turns on the furnace. When the air temperature is at or just above 21°C, the thermostat sends another message that turns off the furnace. As a result, the room always stays within a few degrees of the desired temperature.

Negative feedback loops are the reason why you cannot hold your breath for a long time. The control systems involved in this feedback loop are shown in **FIGURE 2.2.** As you hold your breath, sensors in the circulatory and respiratory systems send information to the brain stem, the body's respiratory control center. Sensors signal a gradual increase in carbon dioxide ($CO_2$) and a decrease in oxygen ($O_2$). The control center compares this information with the set points for these gases. When the change becomes too great, the control center takes steps to counteract it. Messages are sent to the muscles of the diaphragm and the rib cage to relax and then contract, forcing you to exhale and then inhale deeply. At this point, you cannot stop these muscles from moving. You will continue to breathe rapidly and deeply until the gas levels return to their set points.

⁎⁙ CONNECT TO

**BIOCHEMISTRY**

As you read in **Cells and Energy,** cells require a constant supply of oxygen to maintain cell metabolism. Oxygen is not stored in the human body in any great amounts. Once oxygen reserves have been used up, the body must have a fresh supply of oxygen to prevent cell death.

## FIGURE 2.2 Negative Feedback Loop

**Negative feedback counteracts any change in the body that moves conditions away from a set point.**

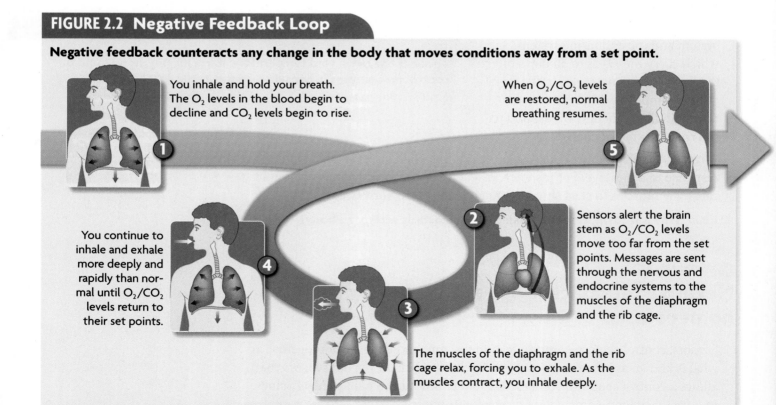

You inhale and hold your breath. The $O_2$ levels in the blood begin to decline and $CO_2$ levels begin to rise.

When $O_2$/$CO_2$ levels are restored, normal breathing resumes.

You continue to inhale and exhale more deeply and rapidly than normal until $O_2$/$CO_2$ levels return to their set points.

Sensors alert the brain stem as $O_2$/$CO_2$ levels move too far from the set points. Messages are sent through the nervous and endocrine systems to the muscles of the diaphragm and the rib cage.

The muscles of the diaphragm and the rib cage relax, forcing you to exhale. As the muscles contract, you inhale deeply.

**Infer** If you continued to breathe rapidly and deeply for too long in Step 4, how would this affect the negative feedback loop?

MODELING

## Negative Feedback Loop

You can experience a negative feedback loop by doing a simple demonstration.

**MATERIALS**
hardcover book at least 6" × 9"

**PROBLEM** How does a negative feedback loop work?

**PROCEDURE**

1. Balance the hardcover book on your head.
2. Walk 3 meters forward and backward—once with eyes open, then with eyes closed.

**ANALYZE AND CONCLUDE**

1. **Analyze** Summarize the negative feedback loop that helped keep the book balanced on your head. How did closing your eyes affect your ability to balance the book?
2. **Connect** Describe the role of internal feedback mechanisms in the maintenance of homeostasis.

### Positive Feedback

Negative feedback loops maintain homeostasis by counteracting, or reversing, change to return conditions to their set points. In some cases, however, the body actually needs change to accomplish a specific task. In **positive feedback,** a control center uses information from sensors to increase the rate of change away from the set points. Though not as common in the body, this type of feedback is important whenever rapid change is needed.

If you cut your finger, positive feedback mechanisms increase the rate of change in clotting factors in the blood until the wound is sealed. Once the injury heals, another positive feedback loop occurs as chemicals are released to dissolve the clot. Positive feedback also occurs in the release of certain growth hormones during puberty. Your body needs higher levels of these hormones to accomplish all of the changes that take place at this time.

**Infer  Why are most of the functions of the body regulated by negative, rather than by positive, feedback mechanisms?**

---

**SELF-CHECK Online**
HMHScience.com
GO ONLINE

## 25.2 Formative Assessment

**REVIEWING ▶ MAIN IDEAS**

1. A system to maintain **homeostasis** must have at least four parts that function together. Name these parts, and briefly explain what each one does.

2. What is the main difference between the way **negative feedback** and **positive feedback** loops regulate change in the body?

**CRITICAL THINKING**

3. **Predict** When a newborn baby nurses, the mother's body is stimulated to produce milk. What would happen to the milk supply if the mother chose to bottle feed rather than breast feed? Why?

4. **Sequence** Suppose you go on a long hike in hot weather. Describe a possible negative feedback loop that would keep your body from overheating.

**CONNECT TO**

**ZOOLOGY**

5. Reptiles regulate their body temperature by changing their environment. A snake, for instance, must lie in sunlight to warm its body. Mammals can regulate their internal environment to gain or lose body heat. How might this ability give mammals an advantage over reptiles?

# Interactions Among Systems

| **KEY CONCEPT** **Systems interact to maintain homeostasis.**

**MAIN IDEAS**

○ Each organ system affects other organ systems.

○ A disruption of homeostasis can be harmful.

**VOCABULARY**

thermoregulation

*·ᚷᚷ·- Connect to Your World* ———————————————

The moment a racecar pulls in for a pit stop, the pit crew springs into action. Each person has a special role that must be coordinated with the efforts of the team. As one member jacks up the car, others are changing the tires, putting in fuel, and checking the engine. If anyone fails to do a job properly, it affects the entire team and places the driver at serious risk.

## ○ MAIN IDEA

# Each organ system affects other organ systems.

At its most basic level, the body is a community of specialized cells that interact with one another. On a larger scale, all of the organ systems form a type of community regulated by feedback mechanisms. This interaction among organ systems means that what affects a single organ system affects the entire body.

Like the highly trained crew members in **FIGURE 3.1**, each organ system in your body must do its own special job. But for you to remain healthy, each system also must coordinate with other organ systems through chemical messages and nerve impulses. The relationship among your organs and organ systems is not always obvious—for example, when the body produces a substance such as vitamin D. In other cases, you are more aware that some organs are affecting others, as in the regulation of your body temperature in hot or cold weather.

**FIGURE 3.1** Precision teamwork is the secret to a pit crew's success. Likewise, your life depends on every organ system doing its job at the right time and in the right order.

### Vitamin D Production

You may know that sunlight plays a part in the production of vitamin D in your body. You may not know that the liver, kidneys, circulatory system, and endocrine system are necessary for this process as well. The skin contains a substance that in the presence of ultraviolet light is changed into an inactive form of vitamin D. As **FIGURE 3.2** shows, this form enters the blood and is carried to the liver. The liver changes the inactive form of vitamin D into another compound, which is then carried to the kidneys. Here, this compound is converted into active vitamin D.

The blood transports active vitamin D throughout the body, where it interacts with hormones that regulate the amount of calcium and phosphorus in the body. These two minerals are essential for building strong bones. If any organ along this path fails to do its job, the level of vitamin D in the body decreases. Without enough vitamin D, children's bones do not develop normally. Adults lose bone mass, which means their bones break more easily.

©Kevin Fleming/Corbis

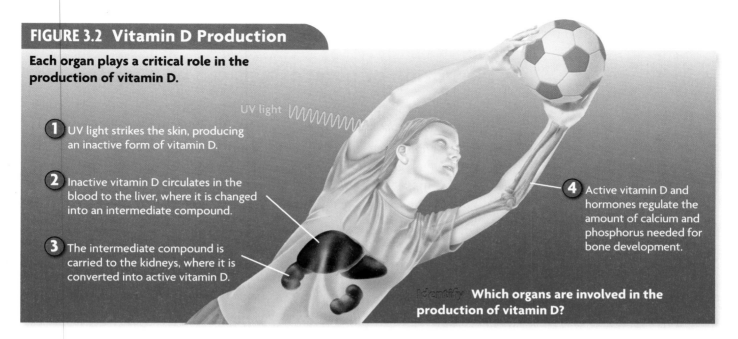

## FIGURE 3.2  Vitamin D Production

**Each organ plays a critical role in the production of vitamin D.**

UV light

**1** UV light strikes the skin, producing an inactive form of vitamin D.

**2** Inactive vitamin D circulates in the blood to the liver, where it is changed into an intermediate compound.

**3** The intermediate compound is carried to the kidneys, where it is converted into active vitamin D.

**4** Active vitamin D and hormones regulate the amount of calcium and phosphorus needed for bone development.

**Identify**  **Which organs are involved in the production of vitamin D?**

## Regulation of Body Temperature

The process by which the body regulates its internal temperature under a variety of conditions is known as **thermoregulation** (THUR-moh-REHG-yoo-LAY-shuhn). The most obvious organ systems involved in maintaining body temperature are the skin and muscles. You sweat in hot weather and shiver when you are cold. However, far more is going on than what you can see on the surface. Thermoregulation requires the close interaction of the respiratory, circulatory, nervous, and endocrine systems.

Sensors in the skin and blood vessels provide information about body temperature to a control center in the brain called the hypothalamus. The hypothalamus protects the body's internal organs by monitoring temperature. When the hypothalamus receives information that the temperature of the blood is rising, it sends messages through the nervous and endocrine systems. These messages activate the sweat glands, dilate, or widen, blood vessels in the skin, and increase both heart and breathing rates. All of these activities carry heat away from the center of the body to the surface, where excess heat can escape.

When the temperature of the blood falls too low, the hypothalamus sends another set of signals to the skin and to the muscular, respiratory, and circulatory systems. Blood vessels in the skin constrict, reducing blood flow to prevent loss of heat. Muscles in the skin contract around the pores, reducing their size. Rapid, small contractions of skeletal muscles cause shivering. The thyroid gland releases hormones that increase metabolism. All of these activities increase body heat production and reduce the loss of heat to the environment.

### VISUAL VOCAB

**Thermoregulation** maintains a stable body temperature under a variety of conditions, just as a thermostat regulates a furnace. Both mechanisms use feedback to keep temperatures within set ranges.

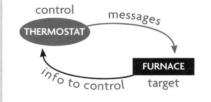

control

messages

THERMOSTAT

info to control

FURNACE

target

**Web** *Quest*

HMHScience.com

**GO ONLINE**

Hypothermia

**Infer**  **If a person's circulatory system does not function well, how might thermoregulation in his or her body be affected?**

## ▶ MAIN IDEA

# A disruption of homeostasis can be harmful.

Some changes may be too great or too rapid for your body to control through feedback mechanisms. Homeostasis can be disrupted for several reasons.

- Sensors fail to detect changes in the internal or external environment.
- Wrong messages may be sent or the correct ones fail to reach their targets.
- Serious injuries can overwhelm the homeostatic mechanisms.
- Viruses or bacteria can change the body's internal chemistry.

Disruption of homeostasis can begin in one organ or organ system and result in a chain reaction that affects other organs and organ systems. These effects can be harmful to your body over the short or long term.

## Short-Term Effects

Short-term effects usually last a few days or weeks. For example, when a cold virus first enters your body, your immune system may not be able to prevent the virus from multiplying. As a result, you develop a sore throat, runny nose, and dry cough, and your muscles and joints become inflamed. However, within a few days, your body's immune system begins to kill the virus and to restore homeostasis. Usually, there is no lasting harm to your body.

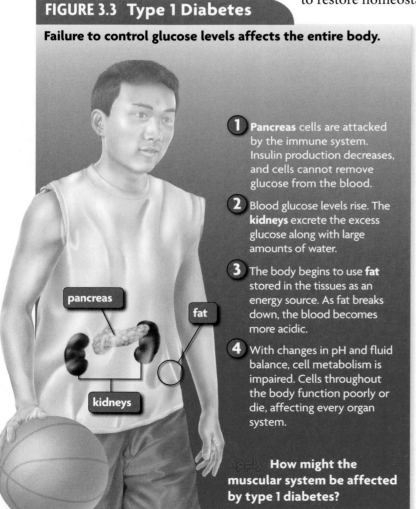

### FIGURE 3.3 Type 1 Diabetes

**Failure to control glucose levels affects the entire body.**

1. **Pancreas** cells are attacked by the immune system. Insulin production decreases, and cells cannot remove glucose from the blood.

2. Blood glucose levels rise. The **kidneys** excrete the excess glucose along with large amounts of water.

3. The body begins to use **fat** stored in the tissues as an energy source. As fat breaks down, the blood becomes more acidic.

4. With changes in pH and fluid balance, cell metabolism is impaired. Cells throughout the body function poorly or die, affecting every organ system.

pancreas

fat

kidneys

Apply **How might the muscular system be affected by type 1 diabetes?**

## Long-Term Effects

A long-term disruption of homeostasis, as in the case of diabetes, can cause more damage. Diabetes occurs when the body fails to control the amount of glucose circulating in the blood.

**Normal glucose control** Glucose levels are controlled by two hormones—insulin and glucagon—which are released by the pancreas. When glucose in the blood rises above a set point, beta cells in the pancreas release insulin. Insulin causes cells to take in more glucose from the blood and causes the liver to store glucose as glycogen. When blood glucose levels fall below the set point, alpha cells in the pancreas release glucagon. This hormone stimulates the liver to break down stored glycogen into glucose and release it until levels in the blood rise to the set point.

**Type 1 and type 2 diabetes** What if the pancreas fails to do its job? The result can be diabetes mellitus, a condition in which the body can no longer regulate glucose levels. There are two types of diabetes. Type 1 occurs when the body's immune system destroys the ability of beta cells to produce insulin. Type 2 is caused when insulin production decreases or when insulin cannot move glucose into cells.

## DATA ANALYSIS

### INTERPRETING INVERSE RELATIONSHIPS

Two variables are inversely related if an increase in the value of one variable is associated with a decrease in the value of the other variable. For example, the level of insulin decreases the longer a person exercises. Therefore, insulin levels have an inverse relationship with exercise time. The graphs at right show the levels of insulin, glucose, and glucagon during moderate exercise over 250 minutes. Use the graphs to answer the questions.

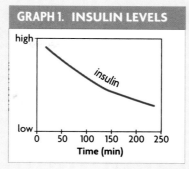

GRAPH 1. INSULIN LEVELS

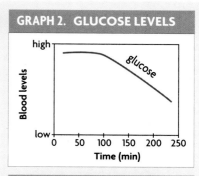

GRAPH 2. GLUCOSE LEVELS

GRAPH 3. GLUCAGON LEVELS

1. **Analyze** Which variable(s) has/have an inverse relationship with time?

2. **Conclude** What relationship exists between glucagon and the other two variables (insulin and glucose)? Explain.

In type 1 diabetes, the failure of the pancreas sets up a destructive chain reaction in other organ systems, as shown in **FIGURE 3.3**. As glucose builds up in the blood, the kidneys must remove it along with large amounts of water. Also, since the body is unable to use glucose as an energy source, it must use stored fat instead. As the fat breaks down, the blood becomes more acidic. This altered pH disrupts the metabolism of the cells in every organ and every system in the body. The long-term effects can result in heart disease, blindness, nerve damage, kidney damage, and even coma and death.

In type 2 diabetes, the pancreas cannot produce enough insulin, or the insulin cannot be used to move glucose into the cells. As a result, blood glucose levels rise, and the cells starve. Risk factors for developing type 2 diabetes include chronic obesity, a family history of diabetes, and aging.

**Connect** **Why might diabetes be a particular problem for an athlete?**

# 25.3 Formative Assessment

**SELF-CHECK** Online
HMHScience.com
**GO ONLINE**

### REVIEWING ▶ MAIN IDEAS

1. Why do the organ systems in the body need to work so closely together?

2. Explain why a long-term disruption of homeostasis can often be more damaging to the body than a short-term disruption.

### CRITICAL THINKING

3. **Analyze** Why would giving synthetic insulin to people with type 1 diabetes restore their glucose homeostasis?

4. **Predict** If you lived in Alaska for the whole year, what changes might occur in your calcium and phosphorus levels during the winter versus the summer? Explain.

### ☼ CONNECT TO

**EVOLUTION**

5. Some animals can store more glucose—in the form of glycogen—in their bodies than can other animals. What might be the evolutionary advantage of having these extra energy stores?

# 25 Summary

The human body is organized into different systems that interact in a coordinated way to maintain homeostasis.

## KEY CONCEPTS

### 25.1 Levels of Organization

**The human body has five levels of organization.** Specialized cells in multicellular organisms arise from the zygote. Most embryonic stem cells go through determination, during which they are committed to becoming specialized cells. During cell differentiation, cells develop specialized structures and functions.

A group of similar specialized cells form tissue. A collection of tissues with the same function form an organ, and various specialized organs together form an organ system. All of the organ systems together make up an entire organism.

**Differentiated Cells**

### 25.2 Mechanisms of Homeostasis

**Homeostasis is the regulation and maintenance of the internal environment.** Conditions within the body must remain within the narrow ranges that support human life. Homeostasis is maintained by internal control systems composed of sensors, a control center, communication systems, and target tissues or organs. The control centers use feedback to keep the internal environment stable. In a negative feedback loop, control systems counteract change to maintain conditions within a narrow range. In a positive feedback loop, control systems increase change away from set points.

### 25.3 Interactions Among Systems

**Systems interact to maintain homeostasis.** Each organ system affects other organ systems. For example, thermoregulation depends on the interaction of the circulatory, respiratory, endocrine, and skin systems. If one organ system fails, it can affect other systems in a chain reaction. Long-term disruptions of homeostasis, as in diabetes, are more serious than temporary, short-term disruptions because more organ systems can be damaged over time.

---

## READING TOOLBOX    SYNTHESIZE YOUR NOTES

**Cycle Diagram** Use this note-taking strategy to summarize what you know about how control systems work to maintain homeostasis.

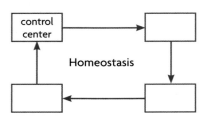

**Concept Map** Draw a concept map to help you remember the developmental steps of cells.

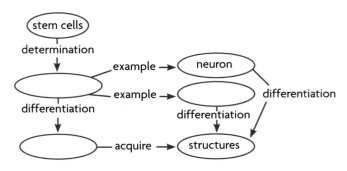

# 25 Review

**INTERACTIVE Review**
HMHScience.com

**GO ONLINE**

Review Games • Concept Map • Section Self-Checks

## CHAPTER VOCABULARY

**25.1** determination
differentiation
tissue
organ
organ system

**25.2** homeostasis
feedback
negative feedback
positive feedback

**25.3** thermoregulation

## Reviewing Vocabulary

**Keep It Short**

For each vocabulary word that follows, write a short phrase that defines its meaning. For example: *cell—the basic unit of life.*

1. tissue
2. organ
3. organ system
4. determination
5. differentiation
6. negative feedback
7. positive feedback
8. thermoregulation

**READING TOOLBOX** GREEK AND LATIN WORD ORIGINS

9. The word *organ* comes from the Latin word *organum,* meaning "instrument" or "implement." Describe how this meaning relates to the definition of a living organ.

10. The word *homeostasis* can be broken into two parts: *homos,* meaning "similar," and *stasis,* meaning "standing" or "stopping." Write a brief definition of *homeostasis* based on the meaning of these two parts.

11. A thermos is a container for keeping liquids hot. The word comes from the Greek *thermos,* which means "hot" or "warm." How does this meaning relate to the term *thermoregulation*?

12. The word *feedback* originally comes from the field of electrical engineering. Feedback occurs when part of a signal put out by an amplifier returns to its source. It's that loud squeal you sometimes hear when someone is using a microphone. Explain how this meaning of feedback relates to what happens in a feedback loop.

## Reviewing MAIN IDEAS

13. Embryonic stem cells have the potential to become any type of cell in the body. What happens to these cells during the process of determination?

14. Once a cell goes through the process of determination, what happens next as the cells develop in the embryo?

15. Briefly explain how cell differentiation and cell death are both needed to develop such structures as human hands and feet.

16. Humans are composed of five levels of organization. Name each of the levels of organization, and describe how each level relates to the next using an example.

17. Organs have many specialized cells and tissues that enable them to carry out their functions. Describe two specialized cells in the respiratory system that enable the lungs to function well.

18. Your body has control systems that keep its internal conditions within the narrow ranges that support life. On a hot day, how do your body's control center and sensors work together to help you stay cool?

19. Describe the role of internal feedback mechanisms in the maintenance of homeostasis.

20. Explain how the failure of one organ can lead to the failure of other organs or of an entire organ system.

21. When glucose levels in the blood rise above a set point, hormones are released that cause the glucose levels to decline. Is this process an example of a positive or a negative feedback loop? Explain your answer.

22. Give two examples of what can happen to a person if the body's homeostasis is not maintained.

# Critical Thinking

**23. Compare** Explain how the cells in the human body might be similar to various building materials in a house.

**24. Infer** Scientists are investigating methods to use embryonic stem cells to repair any tissue in the human body. What characteristic of embryonic stem cells could make this type of treatment possible?

**25. Analyze** Review the chart of organ systems on the last page of Section 1. Identify some interconnections between the immune system and the circulatory system.

**26. Apply** Describe which organ systems you think would be involved in maintaining homeostasis when a person gives a major speech or presentation. Include what may be happening within the person just before, during, and after the speech.

**27. Explain** For various specialized cells to work together, they must communicate with one another. Use the information you learned in the chapter Cell Structure and Function about cell parts to describe how you think a neuron might communicate with a muscle cell.

**28. Compare and Contrast** Explain how the difference between negative and positive feedback makes negative feedback more effective in maintaining homeostasis in the body.

**29. Describe** People with weak or damaged hearts often have trouble regulating their body temperatures in a hot or a cold environment. Explain why an impaired heart might make a person less able to maintain homeostasis.

## Analyzing Visuals

Use the diagram of the digestive system to answer the next three questions.

**30. Analyze** Why is this considered an organ system?

**31. Infer** How do you think the nutrients released from food leave the digestive system and travel throughout the body?

**32. Relate** When a person is sick and is vomiting, how does this condition affect the organ system and its ability to provide nutrients to the body?

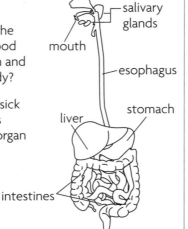

salivary glands

mouth

esophagus

liver

stomach

intestines

## Analyzing Data Interpret an Inverse Relationship

The graph below shows the relationship between different types of energy yield during exercise. Use the graph to answer the next three questions.

**EXERCISE AND ENERGY YIELD**

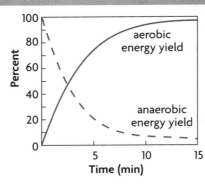

**33. Compare and Contrast** Within what time period does the greatest amount of change occur in both variables?

**34. Analyze** Which variable is inversely related to time? Explain.

**35. Conclude** What relationship do the two variables have to each other at the beginning and at the end of the exercise period?

## Making Connections

**36. Communicate** Blogs have become a popular form of communicating personal experiences online. Think about the changes that occur in your body when you wake up in the morning—changes in your heart rate, in your breathing, and in the movements of your arms and legs. Describe in a blog entry some of the environmental and physical changes that you experience. Which organ systems seem to be involved? What feedback loops might be working to make sure such changes do not become too great?

**37. Interpret** Extreme sports test the limits of the human body. Describe one extreme condition, other than temperature, facing the ice climber in the photograph on the chapter opener. Explain how feedback mechanisms in the climber's body can maintain homeostasis under the extreme condition you choose to describe.

# Standards-Based Assessment

Record your answers on a separate piece of paper.

**MULTIPLE CHOICE**

**1** A group of scientists investigates how the blood pressure of students changes while taking an exam. To properly control their experiment, the scientists must first select the appropriate equipment and measure the —

   A number of questions on the exam

   B students' grade point averages

   C temperature and humidity of the exam room

   D students' blood pressure before the exam

**2** The hormone glucagon increases blood sugar levels while the hormone insulin reduces blood sugar levels. When blood sugar becomes too high, what is *most likely* to happen to insulin and glucagon levels for the body to maintain homeostasis?

   A Insulin levels increase and glucagon levels decrease.

   B Insulin and glucagon levels remain the same.

   C Glucagon levels increase and insulin levels decrease.

   D Insulin and glucagon levels decrease.

**3** Why is it important that oxygen and carbon dioxide levels be closely regulated in the human body?

   A Both gases are needed for the proper functioning of cell processes.

   B Oxygen is needed for cell processes and carbon dioxide is a waste product.

   C Both gases are waste products that need to be removed from cells.

   D The carbon and oxygen from the gases are needed to build new molecules.

**4** No matter what the temperature is outside, the human body temperature stays relatively constant at about 98.6°F. This is part of the body's ability to maintain —

   A osmoregulation

   B homeostasis

   C negative feedback loops

   D positive feedback loops

**5** The kidneys filter wastes and excess salts from the blood. If salt concentrations are low, negative feedback mechanisms would most likely —

   A decrease the amount of salts removed

   B increase the amount of salts removed

   C slow down overall kidney function

   D increase the rate of kidney function

**THINK THROUGH THE QUESTION**

Think about what the body needs to do to maintain homeostasis in this situation. Remember, the feedback mechanism should affect only salt concentration.

**6** Which characteristic *best* fits in the overlapping area of the Venn diagram below?

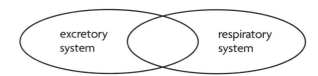

   A absorbs nutrients

   B brings in oxygen

   C transports oxygen

   D removes wastes

# 26 Nervous and Endocrine Systems

## ONLINE BIOLOGY
HMDScience.com

**ONLINE** Labs
- The Stroop Effect
- **QuickLab** The Primary Sensory Cortex
- Reaction Time
- Brain-Based Disorders
- Smell and Olfactory Fatigue
- Investigating the Photic Sneeze Reflex
- Investigating Eye Anatomy
- **Video Lab** Reaction Times
- **Video Lab** Epinephrine and Heart Rate

VIDEO INQUIRY          PREMIUM CONTENT

**Monkey Megaphone** Find out how howler monkeys can damage your hearing.

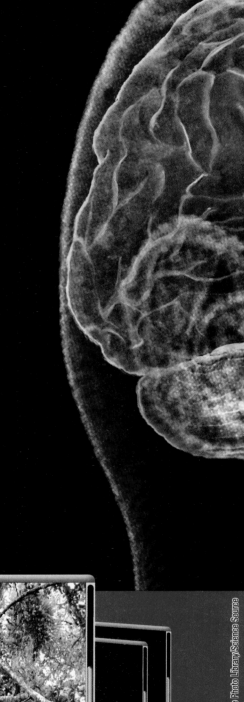

(t) ©Zephyr/Science Photo Library/Science Source

# What happens when you think?

Some technology allows researchers to look into the body of a living person. As recently as the 1970s, there was no way for doctors and scientists to see inside of the body without putting a patient through surgery. Today, researchers and others use magnets and computer technology, such as the MRI scan here, to look at the internal organs of live patients.

 **READING** TOOLBOX   **This reading tool can help you learn the material in the following pages.**

## USING LANGUAGE

**Cause and Effect**  In biological processes, one step leads to another step. When reading, you can often recognize these cause-and-effect relationships by words that indicate a result, such as *so, consequently, next, then,* and *as a result*.

## YOUR TURN

Identify the cause and the effect in the following sentences.

1. Some hormones cause growth. So a person will be very tall if his or her body produces large amounts of these hormones.

2. Fear causes the production of adrenaline. As a result of the adrenaline, the heart beats faster and the body is prepared to run away.

# How Organ Systems Communicate

**SC.912.L.14.26**

**KEY CONCEPT** The nervous system and the endocrine system provide the means by which organ systems communicate.

**MAIN IDEAS**

- The body's communication systems help maintain homeostasis.
- The nervous and endocrine systems have different methods and rates of communication.

### VOCABULARY

nervous system
endocrine system
stimulus
central nervous system (CNS)
peripheral nervous
 system (PNS)

**SC.912.L.14.26** Identify the major parts of the brain on diagrams or models.

 **Connect to Your World**

Scientists try to find new ways, such as MRI scans, to study the brain because the brain is so important. Your brain lets you think and move. It controls digestion, heart rate, and body temperature. Your brain does these things with help from the endocrine system and the rest of the nervous system.

**MAIN IDEA**

## The body's communication systems help maintain homeostasis.

Homeostasis depends on the ability of different systems in your body to communicate with one another. To maintain homeostasis, messages must be generated, delivered, interpreted, and acted upon by your body. The nervous system and the endocrine system are the communication networks that allow you to respond to changes in your environment countless times each day.

- The **nervous system** is a physically connected network of cells, tissues, and organs that controls thoughts, movements, and simpler life processes such as swallowing. For example, when you walk outside without sunglasses on a sunny day, your nervous system senses the bright light coming into your eyes. It sends a message that tells your pupils to shrink and let in less light.
- The **endocrine system** (EHN-duh-krihn) is a collection of physically disconnected organs that helps to control growth, development, and responses to your environment, such as body temperature. For example, when you are outside on a hot day or you exercise, your body starts to feel warm. Your endocrine system responds by producing messages that tell your body to sweat more so that you can cool down.

Both of these systems, which are shown in **FIGURE 1.1,** let you respond to a stimulus in your environment and maintain homeostasis. A **stimulus** (STIHM-yuh-luhs) is defined most broadly as something that causes a response. In living systems, a stimulus is anything that triggers a change in an organism. Changes can be chemical, cellular, or behavioral.

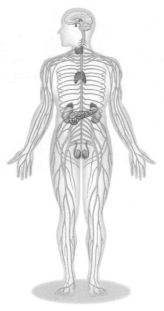

**FIGURE 1.1** The nervous system (yellow) is a physically connected network, while the endocrine system (red) is made up of physically separated organs.

**Analyze** What stimuli cause you to sweat and cause your pupils to shrink?

## ▶ MAIN IDEA
# The nervous and endocrine systems have different methods and rates of communication.

You can think about your endocrine system as working like a satellite television system. A satellite sends signals in all directions, but only televisions that have special receivers can get those signals. Your endocrine system's chemical signals are carried by the bloodstream throughout the body, and only cells with certain receptors can receive the signals. On the other hand, your nervous system is like cable television. A physical wire connects your television to the cable provider. Similarly, your nervous system sends its signals through a network of specialized tissues.

The nervous and endocrine systems also have different rates of communication. Your endocrine system works slowly and controls processes that occur over long periods of time, such as hair growth, aging, and sleep patterns. The endocrine system also helps regulate homeostatic functions such as body temperature and blood chemistry. For example, as the day gradually warms, your endocrine system responds by releasing chemicals that stimulate sweat glands. The change in the temperature over the course of a day is slow so you do not need a rapid response from your body.

Your nervous system works quickly and controls immediate processes, such as heart rate and breathing. If you touch your hand to a hot stove, an immediate response from the nervous system causes you to jerk your hand away. Without a quick reaction, your hand would be badly burned.

Signals move from the skin on your hand to the muscles in your arm by passing through the two parts of the nervous system: the central and the peripheral. The **central nervous system (CNS)** includes the brain and spinal cord. The CNS interprets messages from other nerves in the body and stores some of these messages for later use. The **peripheral nervous system (PNS)** is a network of nerves that transmits messages to the CNS and from the CNS to other organs in the body. You can see some of the nerves of the PNS extending from the spinal cord toward the neck and shoulders in **FIGURE 1.2.**

**Infer  Which system controls the rate at which your fingernails grow?**

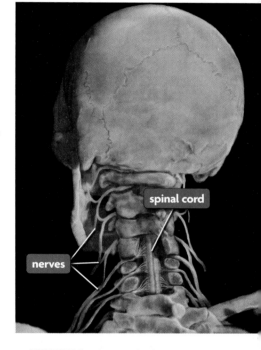

**FIGURE 1.2**  This medical illustration shows how the spinal cord connects the brain to the nerves that run throughout the body.

---

## 26.1  Formative Assessment

### REVIEWING ▶ MAIN IDEAS

1. Why does your body need a communication system?

2. What are three differences between the ways in which the **endocrine system** and the **nervous system** work?

### CRITICAL THINKING

3. **Apply**  Which system, the endocrine or the nervous, controls the rate at which you blink? Explain.

4. **Predict**  How might a clogged blood vessel affect the nervous system's and the endocrine system's abilities to deliver signals?

**SELF-CHECK Online**
HMDScience.com
PREMIUM CONTENT

### CONNECT TO

#### CELL STRUCTURE

5. What structures on a cell membrane might ensure that the endocrine system's signals only affect the cells for which they are intended?

# 26.2 Neurons

**VOCABULARY**

neuron
dendrite
axon
resting potential
sodium-potassium pump
action potential
synapse
terminal
neurotransmitter

**KEY CONCEPT** The nervous system is composed of highly specialized cells.

**MAIN IDEAS**

○ Neurons are highly specialized cells.
○ Neurons receive and transmit signals.

## Connect to Your World

When you eat a snack, you might flick crumbs off of your fingers without giving it much thought. The specialized cells of your nervous system, however, are hard at work carrying the messages between your fingers and your brain.

### ○ MAIN IDEA

## Neurons are highly specialized cells.

A **neuron** is a specialized cell that stores information and carries messages within the nervous system and between other body systems. Most neurons have three main parts, as shown in **FIGURE 2.1**.

**1** The cell body is the part of the neuron that contains the nucleus and organelles.

**2** **Dendrites** are branchlike extensions of the cytoplasm and the cell membrane that receive messages from neighboring cells. Neurons can have more than one dendrite, and each dendrite can have many branches.

**3** Each neuron has one axon. An **axon** is a long extension that carries electrical messages away from the cell body and passes them to other cells.

## FIGURE 2.1 Structure of a Neuron

**A neuron is a specialized cell of the nervous system that produces and transmits signals.**

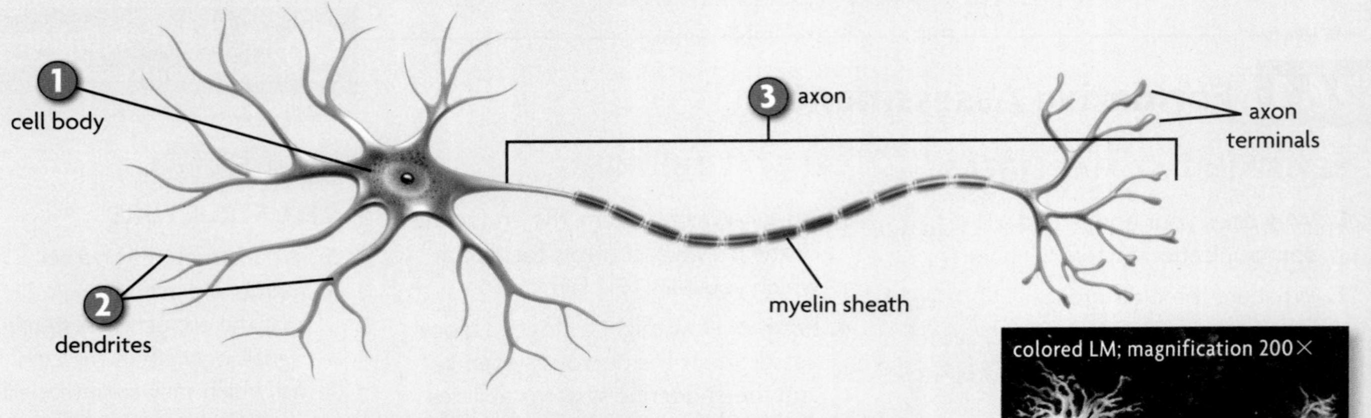

1 cell body

3 axon

axon terminals

myelin sheath

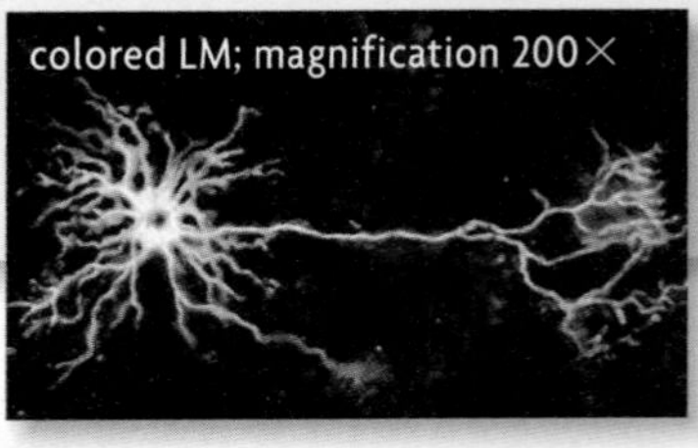

2 dendrites

colored LM; magnification 200×

©James Cavallini/Photo Researchers, Inc.

**Infer** Why might it be beneficial for a neuron to have more than one dendrite?

There are three types of neurons: (1) sensory neurons, (2) interneurons, and (3) motor neurons. Sensory neurons detect stimuli and transmit signals to the brain and the spinal cord, which are both made up of interneurons. Interneurons receive signals from sensory neurons and relay them within the brain and the spinal cord. They process information and pass signals to motor neurons. Motor neurons pass messages from the nervous system to other tissues in the body, such as muscles.

The nervous system also relies on specialized support cells. For example, Schwann cells cover axons. A collection of Schwann cells, called the myelin sheath, insulates neurons' axons and helps them to send messages.

**Analyze** **How does a neuron's shape allow it to send signals across long distances?**

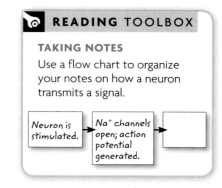
## ● MAIN IDEA
# Neurons receive and transmit signals.

When your alarm clock buzzes in the morning, the sound stimulates neurons in your ear. The neurons send signals to your brain, which prompt you to either get out of bed or hit the snooze button. Neurons transmit information in the form of electrical and chemical impulses. When a neuron is stimulated, it produces an electrical impulse that travels only within that neuron. Before the signal can move to the next cell, it changes into a chemical signal.

### Before a Neuron Is Stimulated

When a neuron is not transmitting a signal, it is said to be "at rest." However, this does not mean that the neuron is inactive. Neurons work to maintain a charge difference across their membranes, which keeps them ready to transmit impulses when they become stimulated.

While a neuron is at rest, the inside of its cell membrane is more negatively charged than the outside. The difference in charge across the membrane is called the **resting potential,** because it contains the potential energy needed to transmit an impulse. The resting potential occurs because there are unequal concentrations of ions inside and outside the neuron.

Two types of ions—sodium ions ($Na^+$) and potassium ions ($K^+$)—cause the resting potential. More $Na^+$ ions are present outside the cell than inside it. On the other hand, there are fewer $K^+$ ions outside the cell than inside it. Notice that both ions are positively charged. The neuron is negative compared with its surroundings because there are fewer positive ions inside the neuron.

Proteins in the cell membrane of the neuron maintain the resting potential. Some are protein channels that allow ions to diffuse across the membrane— $Na^+$ ions diffuse into the cell and $K^+$ ions diffuse out. However, the membrane has many more channels for $K^+$ than for $Na^+$, so positive charges leave the cell much faster than they enter. This unequal diffusion of ions is the main reason for the resting potential. In addition, the membrane also has a protein called the **sodium-potassium pump,** which uses energy to actively transport $Na^+$ ions out of the cell and bring $K^+$ ions into the cell. This process also helps maintain the resting potential.

**CONNECT TO**

**ACTIVE TRANSPORT**

Recall from **Cell Structure and Function** that energy and specialized membrane proteins are required to move molecules and ions against the concentration gradient.

outside          inside

energy

## FIGURE 2.2  Transmission Through and Between Neurons

Once a neuron is stimulated, a portion of the inner membrane becomes positively charged. This electrical impulse, or **action potential**, moves down the axon. Before it can move to the next neuron, it must become a chemical signal.

area of detail

### ACTION POTENTIAL

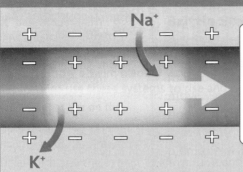

Na⁺

K⁺

- Na⁺ channels open quickly. Na⁺ rushes into the cell, and it becomes positive.
- The next Na⁺ channels down the axon spring open, and more Na⁺ rushes into the cell. The impulse moves forward.
- K⁺ channels open slowly. K⁺ flows out of the cell, and it becomes negative again.

impulse

impulse

### CHEMICAL SYNAPSE

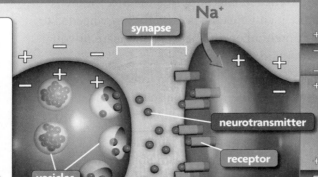

synapse

Na⁺

neurotransmitter

receptor

vesicles

Na⁺

impulse

- When the impulse reaches the axon terminal, vesicles in the terminal fuse to the neuron's membrane.
- The fusing releases neurotransmitters into the synapse.
- The neurotransmitters bind to the receptors on the next neuron, stimulating the neuron to open its Na⁺ channels.

impulse

### ACTION POTENTIAL

- Na⁺ channels in the second neuron open quickly. Na⁺ rushes into the cell.
- A new impulse is generated.

**CRITICAL VIEWING**  How is an action potential generated, and how does it move down the axon?

## Transmission Within a Neuron

As you tap your finger on a desk, pressure receptors in your fingers stretch. The stretching causes a change in charge distribution that triggers a moving electrical impulse called an **action potential,** shown in **FIGURE 2.2.**

An action potential requires ion channels in the membrane that have gates that open and close. When a neuron is stimulated, gated channels for $Na^+$ open quickly, and $Na^+$ ions rush into the cell. This stimulates adjacent $Na^+$ channels down the axon to spring open. $Na^+$ ions rush into the cell, and then those ion channels snap shut. In this way, the area of positively charged membrane moves down the axon.

At the same time $Na^+$ channels are springing open and snapping shut, $K^+$ ion channels are opening and closing more slowly. $K^+$ ions diffuse out of the axon and cause part of the membrane to return to resting potential. Because $K^+$ channels are slow to respond to the change in axon's charge, they appear to open and close behind the moving impulse.

## Transmission Between Neurons

Before an action potential moves into the next neuron, it crosses a tiny gap between the neurons called a **synapse.** The axon **terminal,** the part of the axon through which the impulse leaves that neuron, contains chemical-filled vesicles. When an impulse reaches the terminal, vesicles bind to the terminal's membrane and release their chemicals into the synapse. **Neurotransmitters** (NUR-oh-TRANS-miht-urz) are the chemical signals of the nervous system. They bind to receptor proteins on the adjacent neuron and cause $Na^+$ channels in that neuron to open, generating an action potential.

Typically, many synapses connect neurons. Before the adjacent neuron generates an action potential, it usually needs to be stimulated at more than one synapse. The amount a neuron needs to be stimulated before it produces an action potential is called a threshold.

Once neurotransmitters have triggered a new action potential, they must be removed from the synapse so that ion channels on the second neuron will close again. These neurotransmitters will be broken down by enzymes in the synapse, or they are transported back into the terminal that released them.

**Contrast   How does signal transmission within and between neurons differ?**

**Virtual INVESTIGATION**
HMDScience.com
PREMIUM CONTENT
Responses in the Human Nervous System

**SELF-CHECK Online**
HMDScience.com
PREMIUM CONTENT

## 26.2   Formative Assessment

### REVIEWING ▶ MAIN IDEAS

1. What are the roles of the three types of **neurons**?

2. Draw a picture to illustrate **resting potential,** and explain how it helps transmit signals in neurons.

### CRITICAL THINKING

3. **Infer**  How does a threshold prevent a neuron from generating too many **action potentials**?

4. **Predict**  What might happen if a drug blocked **neurotransmitter** receptors?

### CONNECT TO

**CELL CHEMISTRY**

5. Hyponatremia occurs when people have very low amounts of sodium in their body. How might the nervous system be affected if a person had this condition?

# 26.3 The Senses

**VOCABULARY**

rod cell
cone cell
hair cell

**KEY CONCEPT** **The senses detect the internal and external environments.**

### MAIN IDEAS
- The senses help to maintain homeostasis.
- The senses detect physical and chemical stimuli.

---

## Connect to Your World

You may think that you hear sounds with your ear, smell with your nose, or taste with your tongue, but that is not true. Your sensory organs only collect stimuli and send signals to your brain. Your brain interprets these signals. Together, your sensory organs and your brain allow you to perceive stimuli as various sounds, sights, smells, tastes, and so forth.

### ▶ MAIN IDEA

## The senses help to maintain homeostasis.

You rely on your sensory organs to collect information about the world around you. Once your brain has information from sensory organs, it triggers a response that will maintain homeostasis. For example, eyes adjust to bright and dim light by changing the size of your pupils, as shown in **FIGURE 3.1**. If your skin feels cold, you might shiver. You might get goose bumps, or your arm hairs might stand up, trapping the heat that would otherwise escape from your skin.

Your sensory organs also influence your behavior. Although homeostasis is strictly defined as the regulation and maintenance of the body's internal condition, you could also think of behaviors that prevent death or injury as a kind of homeostatic mechanism.

Imagine that you are getting ready to cross a street, and you look both ways to see if it is safe. Light enters your eyes and the light receptors in your eyes are stimulated to produce impulses. The impulses travel down bundles of axons to your brain. Your brain filters these impulses and forwards some of them to the specific area of your brain that interprets visual information. Your brain then combines this information with that from your other sense organs. Your brain interprets the light that entered your eyes as a large truck speeding your way. With the help of your eyes, you will wait for the truck to pass before walking into the street.

Your senses influence many other behaviors that help protect your tissues from damage. For example, if automatic responses such as shivering and goose bumps don't warm you up, you might decide to put on a jacket. If the sun is too bright, you might decide to put on sunglasses. If a room is too dark, you might decide to turn on a light.

**Summarize** **How do your sensory organs help you to maintain homeostasis?**

**FIGURE 3.1** The size of your pupil changes depending on the amount of light around you. In bright light, your pupil constricts. In dim light, the pupil expands.

# MAIN IDEA
# The senses detect physical and chemical stimuli.

Humans have specialized sensory organs that detect external stimuli. The information these organs collect helps to make up the five senses: vision, hearing, touch, taste, and smell. Five different types of sensory receptors help humans to detect different stimuli.

- Photoreceptors sense light.
- Mechanoreceptors respond to pressure, movement, and tension.
- Thermoreceptors monitor temperature.
- Chemoreceptors detect chemicals that are dissolved in fluid.
- Pain receptors respond to extreme heat, cold, and pressure, and to chemicals that are released by damaged tissues.

**READING TOOLBOX**

**VOCABULARY**
You can remember what kind of stimuli each receptor receives by remembering what their prefixes mean:
*photo-* = light
*mechano-* = machine, movement
*thermo-* = heat
*chemo-* = chemical

## Vision

Humans rely on vision more than any of the other senses. In fact, the eye contains about 70 percent of all the sensory receptors in the body. Most of these are photoreceptors on the back inside wall of the eye. This layer of tissue, called the retina, is shown in **FIGURE 3.2**. Specialized cells called rods and cones are the photoreceptors. **Rod cells** detect light intensity and are used in black and white vision. **Cone cells** detect color. Rod cells are sensitive to low amounts of light, and cone cells need bright light to function. This is why you have difficulty seeing color when it is dark.

Because sight depends on the amount of light available, the eye must have a way to limit the amount of light from a bright source or allow more light to enter from a dim light source. Muscles around the iris—the colored part of the eye—control the size of the hole at its center, the pupil. The eye adjusts the amount of light that enters it by changing the size of the pupil. The larger the pupil, the more light that can enter.

Before light can stimulate the rod and cone cells in the retina, it must pass through structures at the front of the eye. Light enters the eye through a protective transparent layer called the cornea and moves through the pupil. After the pupil, light passes through the lens. The lens is behind the iris, and it focuses the light onto the retina. The light stimulates the rod and cone cells, which generate nerve impulses. The impulses travel along the bundle of axons that form the optic nerve. The nerve carries the impulses to the brain, where they are interpreted as images.

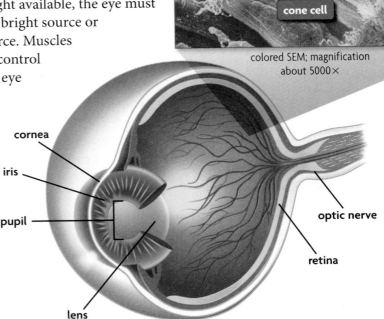

colored SEM; magnification about 5000×

**FIGURE 3.2** Light is focused by the lens onto the retina, where rod and cone cells generate impulses. These impulses travel through your optic nerve to your brain, where they are interpreted as images.

©Omikron/Photo Researchers, Inc.

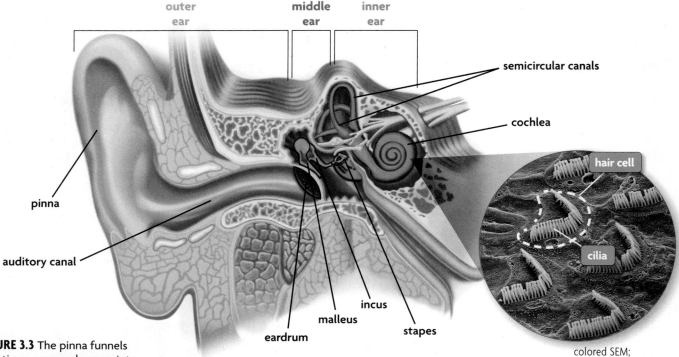

outer ear • middle ear • inner ear

semicircular canals

cochlea

hair cell

cilia

pinna

auditory canal

incus

malleus

eardrum

stapes

colored SEM; magnification 3400×

**FIGURE 3.3** The pinna funnels vibrations, or sound waves, into the ear. Hair cells convert vibrations into impulses that are sent to the brain for interpretation.

**CONNECT TO**

**ANIMAL BEHAVIOR**

Sensory organs collect stimuli that influence human and animal behavior, as you read in **Animal Behavior**.

THAT'S **Amazing!**

**Video Inquiry**
HMDScience.com

**PREMIUM CONTENT**

Monkey Megaphone

## Hearing

The ear collects vibrations—sound waves—from the air, amplifies them, and converts them into nerve impulses that are interpreted in the brain as sounds. **Hair cells** are specialized cells in the inner ear that contain mechanoreceptors that detect vibrations. Hair cells produce action potentials when their cilia are bent.

Sound waves enter the body through the outer ear. The pinna, the part of the ear you can see, collects sound and funnels it into the auditory canal. Sound waves in the auditory canal hit the eardrum, or tympanic membrane, causing it to vibrate like the head of a drum. The vibrations are amplified by three small bones in the middle ear—the malleus, the incus, and the stapes.

As **FIGURE 3.3** shows, the amplified vibrations are transferred to the cochlea. The cochlea is a structure of fluid-filled canals in the inner ear where hair cells are located. The fluid in the cochlea moves in response to vibrations. This movement causes the cilia on the hair cells to bend, producing an impulse. The impulse is carried by the auditory nerve to the brain, where it is perceived as a sound.

The ear also has organs that regulate balance. Balance is controlled by an organ in the inner ear called the semicircular canals. When your head moves, fluid inside the semicircular canals moves. The movement bends the cilia on the hair cells in the canals. As the cilia bend, they generate impulses that are transmitted to the brain.

## Smell and Taste

You may have noticed that food seems to have less flavor when you have a cold. If you haven't, you can try holding your nose the next time you eat. It will have a similar effect. Your sense of taste is less sensitive when your nose is stuffed up because your smell and taste senses are closely related. Both the nose, which senses odors, and the tongue, which senses flavors, have chemoreceptors. These receptors detect molecules that are dissolved in liquid.

©Steve Gschmeissner/Photo Researchers, Inc.

In smell, small airborne chemicals enter the nose. These chemicals dissolve in mucus in the nose, and they are detected by olfactory cells, which generate impulses. The olfactory nerve takes impulses to the brain.

Taste buds are chemoreceptors that detect tastes. They are found in bumps on the tongue called papillae. As in the nose, chemicals must be dissolved before they can be detected. The chemoreceptors generate impulses that are sent to the brain. Although your tongue can only detect five basic tastes—sweet, sour, salty, bitter, and savory—your brain interprets combinations of these as complex flavors.

### Touch, Temperature, and Pain

Your skin contains receptors that sense touch, temperature, and pain. Touch is sensed by mechanoreceptors that detect pressure, movement, and tension. The skin has two general types of mechanoreceptors. Mechanoreceptors that detect gentle touch are located in the upper layer of the skin. Some of these are wrapped around hair follicles. They help you feel when these hairs move, as they might when a small fly lands on your arm. Mechanoreceptors that recognize heavy pressure are found deeper within the skin, as you can see in **FIGURE 3.4.**

Temperature and pain are sensed by thermoreceptors and pain receptors. Thermoreceptors detect heat and cold. Pain receptors detect chemicals that are released by damaged cells. Some pain receptors detect sharp pains, such as the pain you would feel by stepping on a nail. Other pain receptors sense blunt or throbbing pain, such as that caused by a bruise.

**Summarize** To which senses do mechanoreceptors contribute?

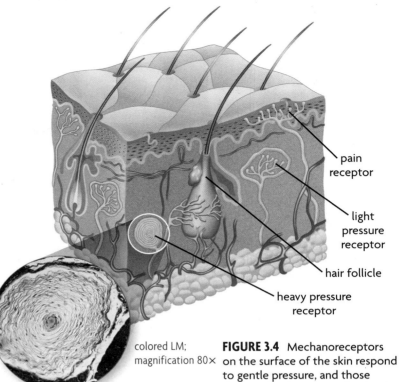

colored LM; magnification 80×

**FIGURE 3.4** Mechanoreceptors on the surface of the skin respond to gentle pressure, and those deep in the skin respond to hard pressure. Pain receptors are close to the skin's surface.

pain receptor
light pressure receptor
hair follicle
heavy pressure receptor

**Biology VIDEO CLIP**
HMDScience.com
PREMIUM CONTENT
Blocking Pain Sensors

**SELF-CHECK Online**
HMDScience.com
PREMIUM CONTENT

## 26.3 Formative Assessment

### REVIEWING ▶ MAIN IDEAS

1. How do your sensory organs work with your brain to help you perceive the world around you?

2. What kinds of receptors are **hair cells, rod cells,** and **cone cells,** and to which of your senses do these cells contribute?

### CRITICAL THINKING

3. **Connect** Why do you think that you can perceive some sounds as loud and others as very soft?

4. **Predict** In the human eye, there are 20 rod cells for every 1 cone cell. How would your vision be different if you had 5 rod cells for every 20 cone cells?

### CONNECT TO

### EVOLUTION

5. For some invertebrates that live in water, the sense of taste and the sense of smell are identical. Why do you think separate organs for taste and smell might have evolved in animals that live on land but not in some animals that live exclusively in water?

# GO Online!

## The **I**nformation Highway

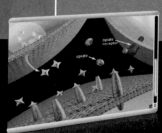

### WebQuest

**Drug Addictions** Find out how different drugs affect neurons and neurotransmitters, altering your brain and creating dependency.

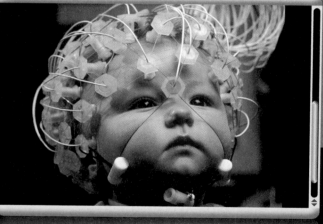

### BIOZINE

**Brain Science—We Are Wired to Learn!**

Catch the latest headlines about human biology, such as stories about brain development and what happens to your brain while playing video

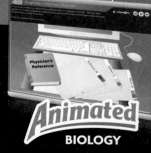

### Animated BIOLOGY

**Diagnose a Hormone Disorder** Review patient histories and compare each to a set of hormone disorders. Then diagnose your patients and get their

# 26.4 Central and Peripheral Nervous Systems

## VOCABULARY

cerebrum
cerebral cortex
cerebellum
brain stem
reflex arc
somatic nervous system
autonomic nervous system
sympathetic nervous system
parasympathetic
  nervous system

**KEY CONCEPT** The central nervous system interprets information, and the peripheral nervous system gathers and transmits information.

### MAIN IDEAS

- The nervous system's two parts work together.
- The CNS processes information.
- The PNS links the CNS to muscles and other organs.

### ☼ Connect to Your World

Imagine that you're watching television, and you want to turn up the volume. Without taking your eyes off the screen, you reach for the remote control on a table next to you. When you touch a glass of water or your homework that is sitting on the table, you will not pick it up because you know that it does not feel like the remote. Your brain is interpreting the stimuli gathered by your sense of touch. If you had no way to interpret each stimulus, you might pick up every item on the table before finding the remote.

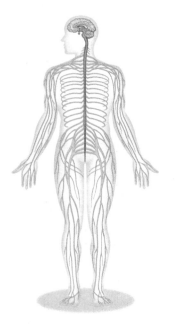

**FIGURE 4.1** Your central nervous system (orange) and peripheral nervous system (yellow) are connected.

### ◉ MAIN IDEA

## The nervous system's two parts work together.

Earlier in this chapter you read that your nervous system is divided into two parts—the central nervous system and the peripheral nervous system—which are shown in **FIGURE 4.1**.

- The central nervous system (CNS) includes the brain and spinal cord. The CNS is composed of interneurons that interact with other nerves in the body. The CNS receives, interprets, and sends signals to the PNS.

- The peripheral nervous system (PNS) is the collection of nerves that connects the CNS to all of your organ systems. The PNS uses sensory neurons to detect stimuli from inside and outside your body, and it uses motor neurons to carry signals from the CNS to other parts of the body and stimulate your muscles or other target organs.

Both the CNS and the PNS are made of several smaller parts. For example, the brain has several areas that control different functions. Divisions of the PNS influence voluntary responses, such as muscle contractions that occur while you walk, and involuntary responses, such as those that occur during digestion.

**Summarize** How do the neurons of the CNS and PNS work together to produce responses to stimuli?

## The Primary Sensory Cortex

The primary sensory cortex is the part of your cerebrum that receives information about your sense of touch from different parts of your body. Each body part sends information to a different place in your primary sensory cortex. In this lab, you will determine the relationship between different body parts and the amount of space the brain devotes to receiving touch information from those body parts.

**MATERIALS**
- 3 toothpicks
- soft blindfold/bandana

**PROBLEM** Does your finger or your forearm have more space devoted to it in the primary sensory cortex?

### PROCEDURE

1. Hypothesize which area will be more sensitive. Make a data table to record the information you gather during the lab.

2. Have your partner close his or her eyes. Gently, touch the tip of your partner's index finger with the tip(s) of one, two, or three toothpicks at the same time.

3. Ask your partner how many points he or she feels. Write down the number your partner says next to the number of toothpicks you used. Repeat three more times, varying the number of toothpicks used.

4. Repeat steps 2 and 3 on your partner's forearm.

### ANALYZE AND CONCLUDE

1. **Analyze** Did your partner's finger or forearm receive more sensory information? Do your data support your hypothesis? Why or why not?

2. **Infer** Which area likely has more space in the primary sensory cortex?

| TABLE 1. PRIMARY SENSORY CORTEX DATA | | |
|---|---|---|
| Area Tested | Number of Toothpicks | |
| | Used | Reported |
| | | |
| | | |
| | | |

---

▶ MAIN IDEA
# The CNS processes information.

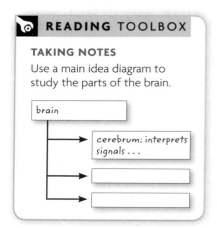

**READING TOOLBOX**

**TAKING NOTES**
Use a main idea diagram to study the parts of the brain.

The interneurons of the brain and spinal cord are arranged in a particular way. All of the neuron cell bodies are clustered together, and all of the axons are clustered together. The collection of neuron cell bodies is called gray matter because of its dark gray color. The collection of axons is called white matter because the myelin sheath on the axons give them a white appearance. In the brain, the gray matter is on the outside, and the white matter is on the inside. The spinal cord has the opposite arrangement.

## The Brain

The entire brain weighs about half as much as a textbook and has more than 100 billion neurons. The brain is protected by three layers of connective tissue, called meninges (muh-NIHN-jeez), that surround it. Between the layers of meninges is a fluid. The fluid cushions the brain so that the brain will not bang up against the skull. The brain itself has three main structures: the cerebrum, the cerebellum, and the brainstem.

The **cerebrum** (SEHR-uh-bruhm) is the part of the brain that interprets signals from your body and forms responses such as hunger, thirst, emotions, motion, and pain. The cerebrum has right and left halves, or hemispheres.

Each hemisphere controls the opposite side of the body. For example, the right hemisphere of your brain processes all of the stimuli received by your left hand. Similarly, the left side of your brain controls the muscles that kick your right leg. When the spinal cord brings a signal from the body, the signal crosses over to the opposite hemisphere in the corpus callosum. The corpus callosum is a thick band of nerves that connects the two hemispheres.

The outer layer of the cerebrum, called the **cerebral cortex,** interprets information from your sensory organs and generates responses. The cerebral cortex is about as thick as a pencil. Yet its size is deceptive because its folds give it a larger surface area than you might expect. If the cerebral cortex were unfolded, it would cover a typical classroom desk. This surface area is large enough to hold more than 10 billion neurons.

The neurons in the cerebral cortex are arranged in groups that work together to perform specific tasks. For example, movement is initiated by an area of the brain called the motor cortex, and the sense of touch is received by the sensory cortex. Scientists divide the cerebral cortex into different areas, or lobes, based on function. Each hemisphere of the human brain can be divided into four lobes—frontal, parietal, occipital, and temporal. The lobes and the cortical areas they contain are shown in **FIGURE 4.2.**

## FIGURE 4.2  Lobes of the Brain

**The various areas of the cerebral cortex process different types of information.**

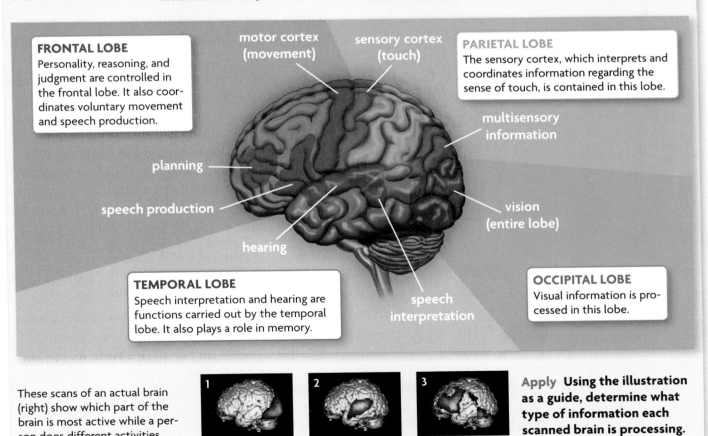

**FRONTAL LOBE**
Personality, reasoning, and judgment are controlled in the frontal lobe. It also coordinates voluntary movement and speech production.

motor cortex (movement)

sensory cortex (touch)

**PARIETAL LOBE**
The sensory cortex, which interprets and coordinates information regarding the sense of touch, is contained in this lobe.

multisensory information

planning

speech production

vision (entire lobe)

hearing

**TEMPORAL LOBE**
Speech interpretation and hearing are functions carried out by the temporal lobe. It also plays a role in memory.

speech interpretation

**OCCIPITAL LOBE**
Visual information is processed in this lobe.

These scans of an actual brain (right) show which part of the brain is most active while a person does different activities.

1   2   3

**Apply** Using the illustration as a guide, determine what type of information each scanned brain is processing.

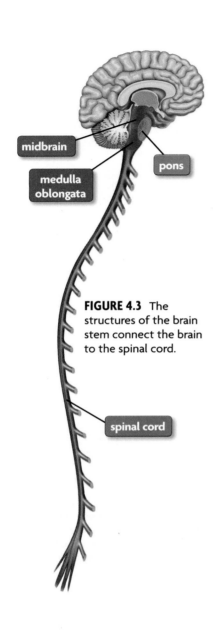

**FIGURE 4.3** The structures of the brain stem connect the brain to the spinal cord.

Underneath the cerebral cortex are many smaller areas with different functions. The limbic system, for example, is involved in learning and emotions and includes the hippocampus and the amygdala. The thalamus sorts information from your sensory organs and passes signals between the spinal cord and other parts of the brain. The hypothalamus gathers information about body temperature, hunger, and thirst. Then it sends signals that help the body adjust and maintain homeostasis, as you will see in Section 6.

The **cerebellum** (sehr-uh-BEHL-uhm) is the part of the brain that coordinates your movements. It helps you maintain your posture and balance, and it automatically adjusts your body to help you move smoothly. For example, when you brush your teeth, your cerebellum gets information about where your arm is positioned compared with the rest of your body. Your cerebellum plans how much your arm would need to move in order to brush your teeth. It sends this information to the motor cortex in your cerebrum, which signals your arm to move.

**VISUAL VOCAB**

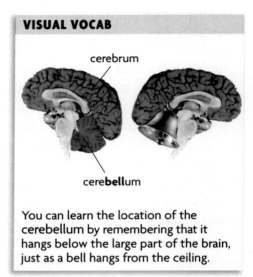

You can learn the location of the cerebellum by remembering that it hangs below the large part of the brain, just as a bell hangs from the ceiling.

The **brain stem** connects the brain to the spinal cord and controls the most basic activities required for life, such as breathing and heartbeat. The brain stem has three major parts—midbrain, pons, and medulla oblongata—which are shown in **FIGURE 4.3.**

- The midbrain controls some reflexes, such as changing the size of the pupil to control the amount of light entering the eye.
- The pons regulates breathing and passes signals between the brain and the spinal cord.
- The medulla oblongata connects the brain to the spinal cord. It controls basic life-sustaining functions, such as heart function, vomiting, swallowing, and coughing.

## The Spinal Cord

The spinal column consists of vertebrae, fluid, meninges, and the spinal cord. The spinal cord is a ropelike bundle of neurons that is about as wide as your thumb. It connects the brain to the nerves that are found throughout the body. All signals that go to or from the brain pass through the spinal cord.

Although movement is controlled by your cerebrum and cerebellum, your brain depends on your spinal cord to deliver messages to the proper muscles. When you are brushing your teeth, and you want to move your arm, the cerebrum sends an impulse down the spinal cord. The impulse is directed by an interneuron to the motor neuron that connects to the arm muscles. The motor neuron then carries the impulse to receptors in the arm muscle. When the receptors are stimulated by the impulse, your arm moves. If the spinal cord

**CONNECT TO**

**CHORDATES**

The spinal cord is one anatomical feature that defines the phylum Chordata, which includes humans and many other animals. You can read more about chordates in **Vertebrate Diversity**.

is damaged, messages cannot move between the brain and the rest of the body. This results in paralysis.

The spinal cord also controls involuntary movements called reflexes. **Reflex arcs,** as shown in **FIGURE 4.4**, are nerve pathways that need to cross only two synapses before producing a response. Because the signal never has to travel up the spinal cord to the brain, you react quickly.

For example, when the doctor taps your knee, tissues that connect your kneecap to your leg muscles stretch and stimulate a sensory neuron in your leg. The sensory neuron sends an impulse to your spinal cord. An interneuron in the spinal cord directs the impulse into motor neurons that cause your leg to jerk.

Reflex arcs play an important role in protecting your body from injury. When you put your hand on a hot stove, for example, you will jerk your hand away before you even have the chance to say "Ouch!" You do not feel the pain until moments after you jerk your hand away. If you did not have reflex arcs, your hand would remain on the stove until your brain interpreted the heat detected by thermoreceptors in your skin. Your hand would be badly burned before you ever reacted.

**Summarize  How is a muscle movement caused by a reflex arc different from a voluntary muscle movement?**

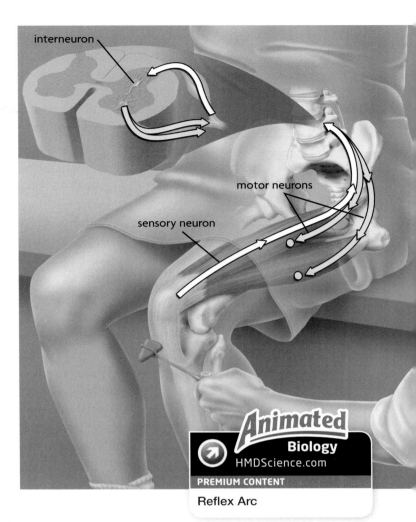

**FIGURE 4.4**  Reflex arcs allow your body to respond quickly and without thinking, as when your leg jerks after your doctor taps your knee with a mallet.

> **MAIN IDEA**
# The PNS links the CNS to muscles and other organs.

The peripheral nervous system (PNS) includes 12 pairs of nerves in the head, such as the facial and olfactory nerves, and 31 pairs of spinal nerves. Most nerves contain axons from both sensory and motor neurons that carry information to and from the CNS. In general, the PNS is made up of a sensory system and a motor system. The system of sensory nerves collects information about the body and its surroundings. The system of motor nerves triggers voluntary and involuntary responses within the body.

When you are running, walking, or even sitting, you rely on your somatic nervous system to stimulate your muscles to maintain your movement, posture, and balance. The **somatic nervous system** is the division of the PNS that regulates all of the movements over which you have voluntary control. It connects the CNS to target organs.

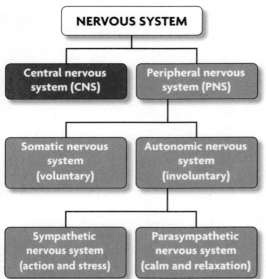

**FIGURE 4.5** The nervous system can be divided into subsystems based on their functions.

The **autonomic nervous system** is the division of the PNS that controls automatic functions that you do not have to think about. For example, involuntary muscles help you to digest food by pushing it through your intestines. The autonomic nervous system is also important in maintaining homeostasis. It takes messages from the hypothalamus to organs in the circulatory, digestive, and endocrine systems.

Within the autonomic nervous system are two subdivisions: the sympathetic nervous system and the parasympathetic nervous system. **FIGURE 4.5** shows how these two systems relate to the rest of the nervous system. Although the two systems have opposite effects on the body, they both function continuously. If something happens to cause one system to produce more signals, the other system will become more active to balance the effects of the first. Together, the sympathetic and parasympathetic nervous systems help your body to maintain homeostasis.

The **sympathetic nervous system** is the part of the autonomic nervous system that prepares the body for action and stress. This is called the "fight or flight" response. When you become frightened or you are preparing to compete in a sport, your sympathetic nervous system is stimulated. Blood vessels going to the skin and internal organs contract, which reduces blood flow to those areas. Meanwhile, blood vessels going to the heart, brain, lungs, and skeletal muscles expand, increasing the blood supply in those areas. Heart rate increases. Airways enlarge, and breathing becomes more efficient. These changes improve your physical abilities and allow you to think quickly.

If something frightens you, your sympathetic nervous system activates. When the danger passes, the parasympathetic nervous system takes over to bring your body back to normal. The **parasympathetic nervous system** is the division of the autonomic nervous system that calms the body and helps the body to conserve energy. It does this by lowering blood pressure and heart rate. It is active when the body is relaxed.

**Analyze** Are reflex arcs part of the somatic or autonomic nervous system? Explain.

# 26.4 Formative Assessment

## REVIEWING ▶ MAIN IDEAS

1. How do the types of neurons found in the CNS and PNS differ in their functions?

2. How does the **cerebral cortex** differ from the rest of the **cerebrum**?

3. What are some similarities and differences between the **somatic nervous system** and **autonomic nervous system**?

## CRITICAL THINKING

4. **Apply** Why might a person with a brain injury be able to understand the speech of others but not be able to speak?

5. **Synthesize** You step on a sharp rock, your leg jerks upward, and a moment later you feel pain in your foot. Use the words *motor neuron, sensory neuron,* and *interneuron* to explain what happened.

## CONNECT TO

### EVOLUTION

6. Which part of the brain—the cerebrum, **cerebellum,** or **brain stem**—probably evolved first? (Hint: Consider which part is most important for basic life processes.)

# 26.5 Brain Function and Chemistry

VOCABULARY

addiction
desensitization
tolerance
sensitization
stimulant
depressant

**KEY CONCEPT** **Scientists study the functions and chemistry of the brain.**

### MAIN IDEAS
- New techniques improve our understanding of the brain.
- Changes in brain chemistry can cause illness.
- Drugs alter brain chemistry.

## Connect to Your World

When you take medicine for a headache, the drug alters your brain's chemistry. Aspirin, for example, stops your brain from making certain chemicals. In small amounts, it is beneficial to your health. However, even nonprescription drugs can cause permanent damage to your nervous system if taken incorrectly.

## MAIN IDEA
# New techniques improve our understanding of the brain.

For many years, the only way scientists could study brain function was by observing changes that occurred in people who had accidental brain injuries or by dissecting the brains of people who had died. A live patient would have to undergo surgery in order for scientists to learn about brain function.

Today, scientists use imaging technologies such as CT, MRI, and PET scans to study the brain in living patients without the need for surgery. These methods use x-rays, magnetic fields, or radioactive sensors and computer programs to form images of the brain, as shown in **FIGURE 5.1**.

Computerized tomography (CT) scans use x-rays to view the brain. Magnetic resonance imaging (MRI) uses magnetic fields and radio waves. Both CT and MRI scans make images that show the structure of the brain. These scans are used to examine the brain's physical condition.

Positron emission tomography (PET) scans show which areas of the brain are most active. During PET scans, a person is injected with radioactive glucose. Recall that cells use glucose for energy. By measuring where the radioactive glucose collects in the brain, scientists can see which areas of the brain are using the most energy. In the image shown above, the bright red and yellow areas are the most active, and the dark blue areas are the least active.

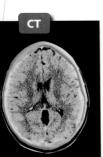
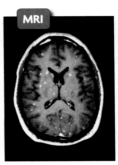
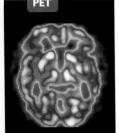

**FIGURE 5.1** Modern technologies use computers and sensing devices to observe the brain without the need for surgery.

**Infer** Why are modern technologies for studying the brain safer for the patients being studied?

# Changes in brain chemistry can cause illness.

**⚡ CONNECT TO**

**ENZYMES**

In **Chemistry of Life** you read that enzymes are like locks because only certain shaped molecules can fit into them. Neurotransmitters only affect certain areas of the brain because they are like keys that can only fit into certain neurons' receptors.

In Section 2, you learned that your nervous system cannot work without neurotransmitters. These chemicals regulate different functions in different areas of the brain. Neurotransmitters are specific to some areas of the brain because, like hormones, they only affect cells that have specific receptors. The function of neurotransmitters relates to the functions of the cells they stimulate.

- Acetylcholine is involved in learning and memory.
- Dopamine primarily influences your emotional behavior, but it also plays some role in stress and voluntary muscles.
- Serotonin is mainly found in the hypothalamus and midbrain. It also influences mood, some muscle functions, and hunger.
- Glutamate affects learning, memory, and brain development.
- Gamma amino butyric acid (GABA) is found throughout the brain. Unlike other neurotransmitters, when GABA binds to a neuron's membrane, it prevents the neuron from generating an impulse.

When your brain produces the correct amount of these neurotransmitters, homeostasis is maintained. If your body produces too much or too little of a neurotransmitter, the areas of your brain that are targeted by that chemical will be more or less active than normal. Because all of the areas of your brain work together, abnormal activity in one part of the brain can affect the whole brain and change the way you move, behave, and think. **FIGURE 5.2** shows that the brain activity of a healthy patient differs from that of patients with depression or schizophrenia, which are associated with chemical imbalances in the brain.

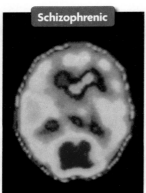
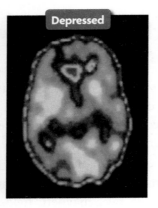

Normal  Schizophrenic  Depressed

**FIGURE 5.2** These PET images show the activity of a normal, a schizophrenic, and a depressed brain. Blue and green areas have low activity, and red areas are the most active.

Illnesses such as Parkinson's disease and schizophrenia are linked to abnormal amounts of dopamine. Parkinson's disease is caused by low amounts of dopamine in certain areas of the brain. People with Parkinson's disease have difficulty controlling their movements, maintaining their balance, and starting movements. Many patients with Parkinson's take drugs that increase the amount of dopamine in the brain. On the other hand, schizophrenia sometimes occurs when a person has too much dopamine. Schizophrenia is a mental disorder that causes hallucinations, irrational behavior, and illogical speech. It is treated with drugs that block dopamine receptors in the brain.

Depression is linked to low amounts of serotonin in parts of the brain. Depression causes extended periods of intense sadness, inability to sleep, and feelings of helplessness. One treatment for clinical depression uses drugs that extend the time that serotonin remains active in nerve synapses.

**Summarize** How do treatments for neurological illnesses alter brain chemistry?

(cl), (c), (r) ©Science Source/Photo Researchers, Inc.

## MAIN IDEA
# Drugs alter brain chemistry.

You may have noticed that some medicines come with warnings that say they may cause drowsiness so they should only be taken at night. People who use prescription, illegal, or other types of drugs can experience behavioral changes, such as changes in appetite, aggression, or sleep cycles. Drugs also cause changes in coordination or sensitivity to pain. Drugs might return one system in the body to homeostasis while pushing another system further out of balance. These changes occur because drugs change the way the brain works.

Many drugs affect the amount of neurotransmitter in synapses. Remember from Section 2 that a certain amount of neurotransmitter must be in the synapse before the threshold is reached and an action potential is generated. If a drug increases the amount of neurotransmitter released, impulses are more likely to occur. If a drug decreases the amount of neurotransmitter, action potentials are less likely to occur.

### Some Drugs Cause Addiction
Many illegal, recreational, and prescription drugs can lead to addiction. **Addiction** is the physiological need for a substance. Through feedback loops, a person becomes addicted to a substance when the body changes the way it works so that it needs the drug in order to function normally. The brain adapts to drug exposure so that neurons will generate normal amounts of impulses despite abnormal levels of neurotransmitter.

Brain cells undergo **desensitization** when there is more neurotransmitter present in the synapse than usual. When a drug increases the amount of neurotransmitter in the synapses, the neuron generates more impulses than normal. The neuron responds by reducing the number of receptors on its cell membrane, as shown in **FIGURE 5.3**. With fewer receptors, less neurotransmitter can bind to the cell membrane and impulses are less likely to generate. Desensitization builds a person's tolerance. When someone has a **tolerance,** it takes larger doses of the drug to produce the same effect.

**Sensitization** occurs when low amounts of a neurotransmitter are in the synapses. When drugs lower the amount of a neurotransmitter, fewer action potentials are generated than normal. With less neurotransmitter than normal, brain cells adapt by increasing the number of receptors for them, also shown in **FIGURE 5.3**. By producing more receptors, cells increase the amount of neurotransmitter that bind to the cell. This causes the cell to generate more action potentials, just as if the normal amount of neurotransmitter were in the synapse.

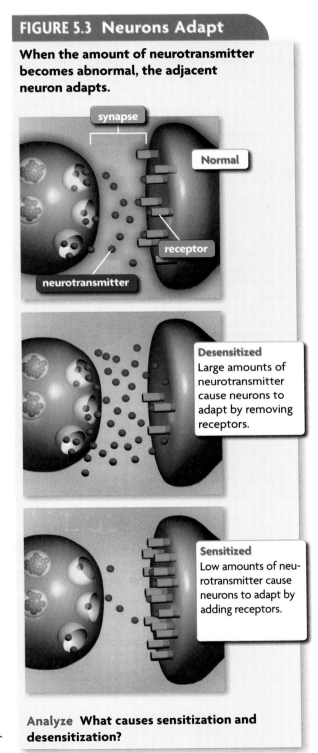

### FIGURE 5.3 Neurons Adapt

When the amount of neurotransmitter becomes abnormal, the adjacent neuron adapts.

synapse

Normal

receptor

neurotransmitter

**Desensitized**
Large amounts of neurotransmitter cause neurons to adapt by removing receptors.

**Sensitized**
Low amounts of neurotransmitter cause neurons to adapt by adding receptors.

**Analyze** What causes sensitization and desensitization?

## How Drugs Work

In order for drugs to have an effect on your behavior, they must change the number of action potentials your neurons generate.

Some drugs make a person feel happy, energetic, and alert. **Stimulants** are drugs that increase the number of action potentials that neurons generate by increasing the amounts of neurotransmitter in the synapses. Methamphetamine, for example, causes neurons to produce and release more neurotransmitters, especially serotonin and dopamine. However, there are other ways that stimulants can increase the amount of neurotransmitter.

Some drugs have almost the same chemistry as neurotransmitters, and they bind directly to the receptors on neuron membranes. Other drugs slow the removal of neurotransmitters from the synapses. These drugs can bind to enzymes that break down the neurotransmitters and make them unable to work. Drugs such as cocaine, however, bind to transport proteins on the axon terminal, as shown in **FIGURE 5.4**. Normally, these proteins would allow neurotransmitters to flow back into the cell that released them. If a drug is blocking the protein, the neurotransmitter remains in the synapse and an action potential is more likely to occur.

**Depressants** are drugs that make a person feel relaxed and tired. The person may react slowly or seem out of touch with the world around them. Depressants reduce the ability of neurons to generate impulses. Some depressants block neuron receptors so that neurotransmitters cannot produce an impulse. Other depressants, such as methaqualone, can make a person feel relaxed or sleepy by increasing in the synapses the amount of GABA, which prevents neurons from generating impulses.

Analyze **How do stimulants and depressants affect a neuron's ability to generate impulses?**

### FIGURE 5.4 How Cocaine Works

Cocaine keeps neurotransmitters in the synapse.

Normally, extra neurotransmitters go back into the cell that released them.

cocaine

neurotransmitter

receptor

When cocaine is present, neurotransmitters cannot be reabsorbed.

Then more neurotransmitters are available to stimulate the next neuron.

synapse

Analyze **How does cocaine act as a stimulant?**

## 26.5 Formative Assessment

### REVIEWING ▶ MAIN IDEAS

1. How are CT and MRI scans different from PET scans?

2. Why is it important that neurotransmitters are balanced in the brain?

3. How do **sensitization** and **desensitization** differ?

### CRITICAL THINKING

4. **Synthesize** Draw before and after pictures to explain why a person whose neurons were sensitized by drug use experiences opposite symptoms when they quit.

5. **Analyze** How does desensitization relate to drug **tolerance**?

### CONNECT TO

**FEEDBACK LOOPS**

6. What kind of feedback loops are sensitization and desensitization? Explain. (Hint: What causes these processes to begin and end?)

# Correlation or Causation?

When scientists analyze their data, they must remember that just because two variables are related, it does not mean that one caused the other to change. A **causation** occurs when a change in one variable was caused by the other. Sometimes the cause of change in a variable may be the result of a third, unknown variable. A **correlation** occurs when scientists find that two variables are closely related, but the change in one variable did not definitely cause the change in the other. When a strong correlation exists between two variables, scientists will conduct other experiments to discover exactly how the variables are related.

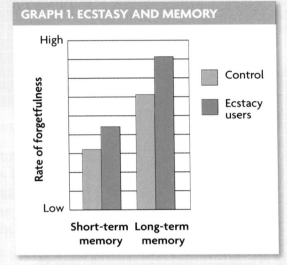

**GRAPH 1. ECSTASY AND MEMORY**

Rate of forgetfulness (High / Low)

Short-term memory   Long-term memory

Control
Ecstacy users

Source: T. M. Heffernan, et al., *Human Psychopharmacol Clinical Experiments* 2001:16.

## Model

Scientists studied the memory of people who regularly used the illegal drug ecstasy. They found that ecstasy users were more forgetful than people who didn't use ecstasy. Therefore, ecstasy use and memory loss are correlated. However, scientists do not know that ecstasy causes forgetfulness. It could be that people who are forgetful use ecstasy.

## Practice Determine Correlation or Causation

A panic attack is characterized by a sudden increase in pulse and anxiety. The graph on the right shows hypothetical data for the incidence of panic attacks in the general population and in a population of people who have a disorder called mitral valve prolapse, in which a heart valve does not work properly.

1. **Analyze** Does a correlation or a causation exist between mitral valve prolapse and panic attacks? How do you know?

2. **Evaluate** Can you conclude that mitral valve prolapse causes panic attacks? Why or why not?

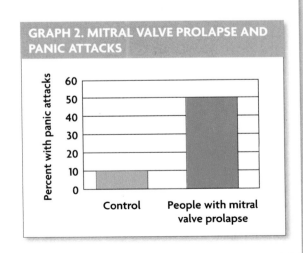

**GRAPH 2. MITRAL VALVE PROLAPSE AND PANIC ATTACKS**

Percent with panic attacks: 60, 50, 40, 30, 20, 10, 0

Control   People with mitral valve prolapse

# The Endocrine System and Hormones

**VOCABULARY**

hormone
gland
hypothalamus
pituitary gland
releasing hormones

**KEY CONCEPT** **The endocrine system produces hormones that affect growth, development, and homeostasis.**

**MAIN IDEAS**

- ▶ Hormones influence a cell's activities by entering the cell or binding to its membrane.
- ▶ Endocrine glands secrete hormones that act throughout the body.
- ▶ The hypothalamus interacts with the nervous and endocrine systems.
- ▶ Hormonal imbalances can cause serious illness.

## Connect to Your World

If you hear a loud BANG, your brain tells your body that you could be in danger. You might need to run away or defend yourself. Your brain alerts your endocrine system to send out chemicals that will speed up your heart rate, increase blood flow to your muscles, and get you ready for action.

### ▶ MAIN IDEA
## Hormones influence a cell's activities by entering the cell or binding to its membrane.

The endocrine system makes chemical signals that help the body grow, develop, and maintain homeostasis. Some of these chemicals control processes such as cell division, cell death, and sexual development. Others help you maintain homeostasis by affecting body temperature, alertness, or salt levels.

The chemical signals made by the endocrine system are called **hormones.** Hormones are made in organs called **glands,** which are found in many different areas of the body. Glands release hormones into the bloodstream, as shown in **FIGURE 6.1.** As a hormone moves through the body, it comes into contact with many different cells. But it will interact only with a cell that has specific membrane receptors. If the hormone touches a cell that does not have a matching receptor, nothing happens. If it touches a cell that has the correct receptors, it binds to the cell and prompts the cell to make certain proteins or enzymes. Cells that have receptors for a hormone are called the target cells of that hormone.

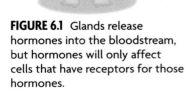

**FIGURE 6.1** Glands release hormones into the bloodstream, but hormones will only affect cells that have receptors for those hormones.

All hormones belong to one of two categories: steroid hormones and nonsteroid hormones. All steroid hormones are made of cholesterol, a type of lipid. On the other hand, there are three types of nonsteroid hormones that are made up of one or more amino acids.

As **FIGURE 6.2** shows, steroid hormones and nonsteroid hormones influence cells' activities in different ways. A steroid hormone can enter its target cells by diffusing through the cell membrane. Once inside, the steroid hormone attaches to a receptor protein, which transports the protein into the nucleus. After it is inside, the steroid hormone binds to the cell's DNA. This binding causes the cell to produce the proteins that are coded by that portion of DNA.

Nonsteroid hormones do not enter their target cells. These hormones bind to protein receptors on a cell's membrane and cause chemical reactions to take place inside the cell. When nonsteroid hormones bind to receptors, the receptors change chemically. This change activates molecules inside the cell. These molecules, called second messengers, react with still other molecules inside the cell. The products of these reactions might initiate other chemical reactions in the cell or activate a gene in the nucleus.

**Apply**  **Why do hormones only affect some cells?**

**⇄ CONNECT TO**

**CELL MEMBRANE**

Recall from **Cell Structure and Function** that cell membranes are made of a phospholipid bilayer. Only some molecules, such as steroid hormones, can diffuse through it.

## FIGURE 6.2  Hormone Action

**Steroid hormones enter the cell, but nonsteroid hormones do not.**

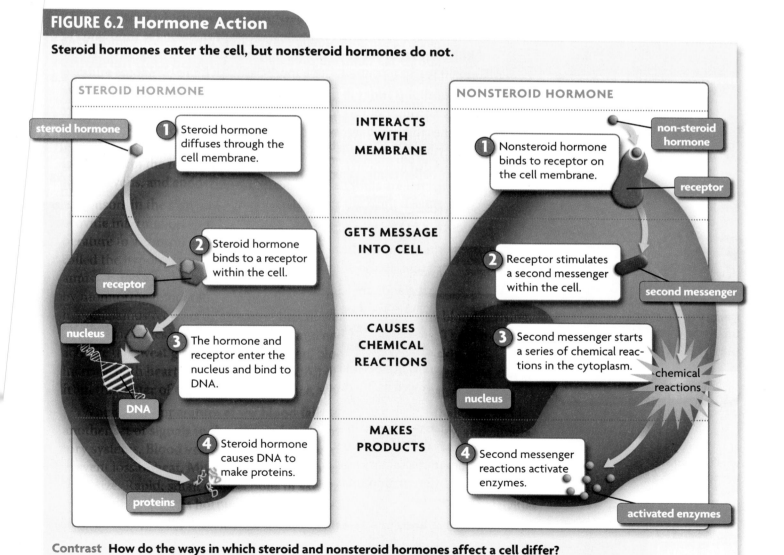

**Contrast  How do the ways in which steroid and nonsteroid hormones affect a cell differ?**

▶ MAIN IDEA

# Endocrine glands secrete hormones that act throughout the body.

Unlike the nervous system, the endocrine system does not have its own connected network of tissues. However, its chemical messages can still travel where they need to go. Hormones travel in the bloodstream to all areas of the body to find target cells.

The endocrine system has many glands. Each gland makes hormones that have target cells in many areas of the body. Some of these glands make hormones that prompt other endocrine glands to make and release their hormones. Other glands affect different body systems. Their hormones prompt cells to divide or to take up nutrients. Other hormones keep the body's blood pressure within a set limit. Some of the major glands, along with a few of the hormones that they make, are described below and in **FIGURE 6.3.**

1. The **hypothalamus** is a small area of the middle of the brain, as you might recall from Section 4. It makes hormones that stimulate the pituitary gland to release hormones. It also stimulates the production of hormones that control growth, reproduction, and body temperature. You will read more about the hypothalamus later in this section.

2. The **pituitary gland** is also in the middle of the brain. It makes and releases hormones that control cell growth as well as osmoregulatory hormones that regulate the concentration of water in the blood. Some pituitary hormones stimulate the adrenals, thyroid, and gonads. The pituitary also acts as a gateway through which hypothalamus hormones pass before they enter the bloodstream.

3. The **thyroid gland** wraps around the windpipe on three sides. Its hormones regulate metabolism, growth, and development.

4. The **thymus** is in the chest. It makes hormones that cause white blood cells to mature. It also stimulates white blood cells to fight off infection.

5. The **adrenal glands** are above the kidneys. The adrenals secrete hormones that control the "fight or flight" response when stimulated by the parasympathetic nervous system. Adrenal hormones increase breathing rate, blood pressure, and alertness.

6. The **pancreas** lies between the stomach and intestines. It makes digestive enzymes as well as hormones that regulate how much glucose the body stores and uses.

7. The **gonads**—ovaries in women and testes in men—make steroid hormones that influence sexual development and functions. Gonads of men and women make the same hormones. However, men and women make them in different amounts, which gives men and women different sexual characteristics.

**Summarize** **What body processes do each of the main endocrine glands influence?**

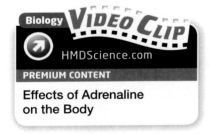

Biology VIDEO CLIP
HMDScience.com
PREMIUM CONTENT
Effects of Adrenaline on the Body

⊹ CONNECT TO

**REPRODUCTION**

You can read more about how chemical signals in the body affect growth, development, and reproduction in **Reproduction and Development**.

# FIGURE 6.3  Glands and Some of the Major Hormones

Endocrine glands are found throughout the body, and they influence whole-body processes. Some of the hormones they make are listed here.

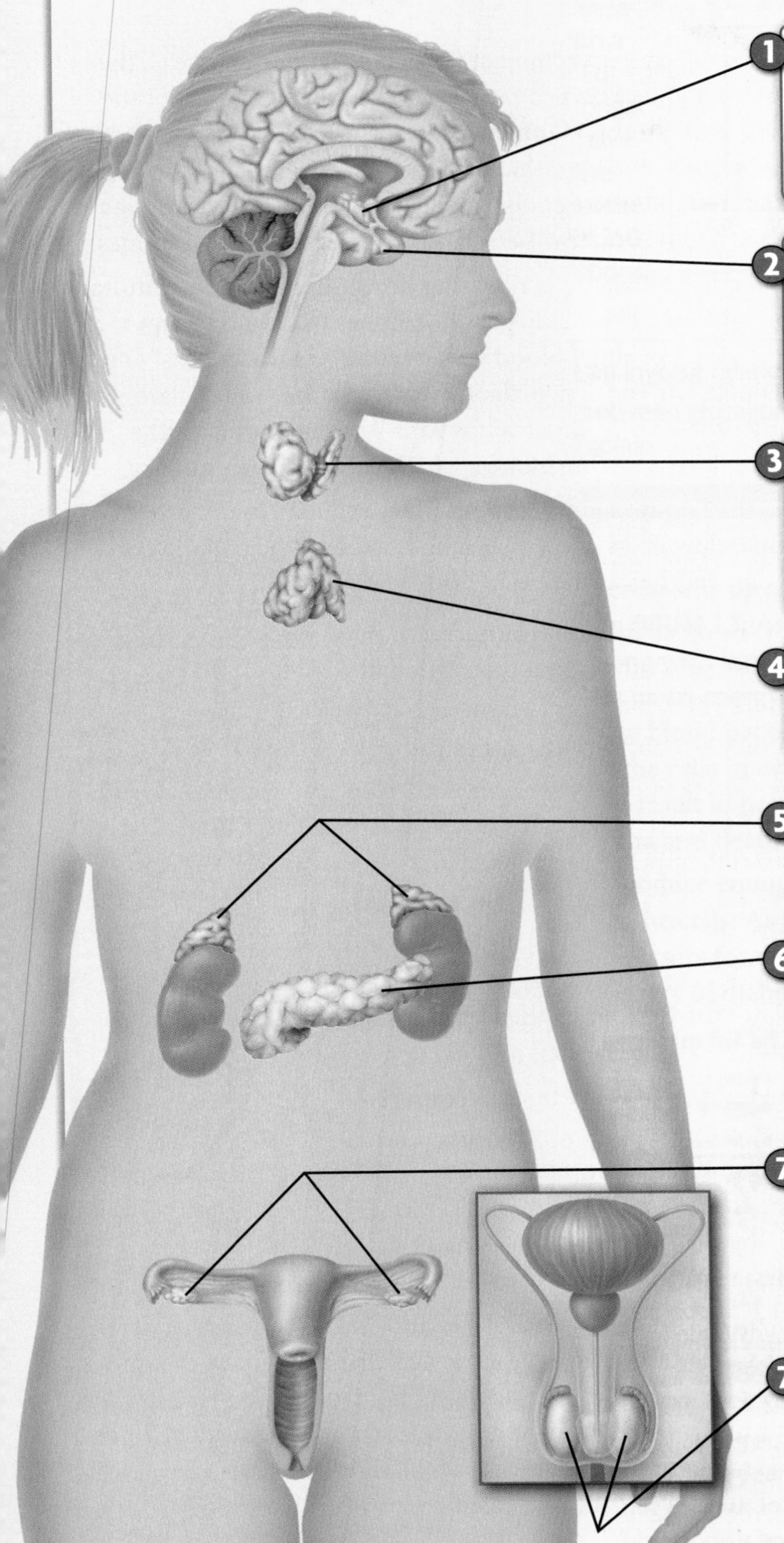

**1 HYPOTHALAMUS**
- **Growth hormone–releasing hormone (GHRH)** causes the pituitary to release growth hormone.
- **Gonadotropin-releasing hormone (GnRH)** causes gonads to release hormones that control the reproductive system.

**2 PITUITARY**
- **Growth hormone (GH)** stimulates cell division, protein synthesis, and bone growth in multiple tissues.
- **Antidiuretic hormone (ADH)** causes the blood to absorb water from the kidneys.

**3 THYROID**
- **Thyroxin (T4)** and **Triiodothyronine (T3)** increase metabolism, digestion, and a person's energy levels.
- **Calcitonin** causes the body to remove calcium from the blood and increase bone formation.

**4 THYMUS**
- **Thymosin** causes white blood cells to reproduce and mature.

**5 ADRENAL GLANDS**
- **Epinephrine** causes the heart to increase its strength and number of contractions, circulating blood more quickly.

**6 PANCREAS**
- **Insulin** removes sugar from the bloodstream and increases sugar metabolism.
- **Glucagon** increases sugar production and adds sugar to the bloodstream.

**7 FEMALE GONADS: OVARIES**
- **Estrogen** causes sexual maturation, including egg production, and influences female characteristics, such as fat distribution and widening of the hips.
- **Progesterone** causes menstruation.

**7 MALE GONADS: TESTES**
- **Testosterone** causes sexual maturation, including sperm production, and male characteristics, such as facial hair and a deep voice.

CRITICAL VIEWING  Why is the bloodstream a good means for transporting hormones such as growth hormone and calcitonin?

## ▶ MAIN IDEA

# The hypothalamus interacts with the nervous and endocrine systems.

The nervous and endocrine systems connect to each other at the base of the brain, where the hypothalamus acts as a part of both systems. As part of the CNS, it receives, sorts, and interprets information from sensory organs. As part of the endocrine system, the hypothalamus produces releasing hormones that affect tissues and other endocrine glands. **Releasing hormones** are hormones that stimulate other glands to release their hormones.

Many of the hypothalamus's releasing hormones affect the pituitary gland. These glands can quickly pass hormones back and forth to each other. A series of short blood vessels connects the two, as you can see in **FIGURE 6.4.** These two glands work together to regulate various body processes. When the nervous system stimulates the hypothalamus, it releases hormones, which travel to the pituitary.

Together, the hypothalamus and pituitary regulate many processes. The diagram below shows how releasing hormones help glands to "talk with" one another to maintain body temperature.

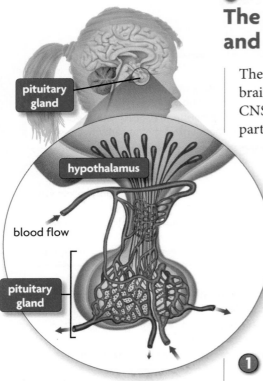

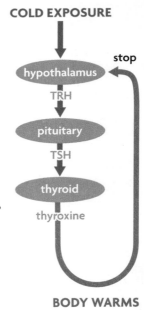

**1** When the body becomes cold, thermoreceptors in the nervous system send a signal that stimulates the hypothalamus.

**2** The hypothalamus responds to this stimulus by secreting a releasing hormone called TRH (TSH-releasing hormone).

**3** TRH travels through a short blood vessel and stimulates the pituitary to release TSH (thyroid-stimulating hormone).

**4** TSH travels through the bloodstream to the neck, where it stimulates the thyroid to release thyroxine, a hormone that increases cells' activity.

**5** As cells become more active, the body's temperature increases. Thermoreceptors signal the hypothalamus to stop releasing TRH. In the absence of TRH, the other glands are no longer stimulated. One by one, they stop releasing their hormones, and the cycle is turned off.

FIGURE 6.4 The hypothalamus stimulates the pituitary to secrete hormones into the bloodstream.

**Animated Biology**
HMDScience.com

**PREMIUM CONTENT**

Diagnose a Hormone Disorder

Notice that releasing hormones, such as TRH and TSH, act as a type of feedback on the glands they target. You have learned that a feedback is something that stimulates a change. As long as releasing hormones are present, each target gland will continue to make more and more hormones. However, when the body reaches its ideal temperature, the hypothalamus stops releasing TRH. Then the pituitary and the thyroid stop releasing their hormones too.

**Analyze** How does the hypothalamus connect the nervous and endocrine systems?

## MAIN IDEA

# Hormonal imbalances can cause severe illness.

Because hormones play an important role in maintaining homeostasis, too much or too little of a hormone will affect the entire body. You have learned that diabetes occurs when the pancreas does not make the right amounts of insulin and glucagon, hormones that regulate sugar concentration in the blood. When other glands do not function properly, a person may get other diseases. For example, if the thyroid does not make enough hormones, a person will develop hypothyroidism. In children, this condition slows growth and mental development. In adults, hypothyroidism causes weakness, sensitivity to cold, weight gain, and depression. Hyperthyroidism, or the condition of having too many thyroid hormones, produces opposite symptoms.

The wrong amount of adrenal hormones also affects the entire body. Cortisol is an adrenal hormone that helps the body break down and use sugars and control blood flow and pressure. If the adrenal glands produce too much cortisol, the body cannot metabolize sugars properly, and a person can develop Cushing's syndrome. This syndrome causes obesity, high blood pressure, diabetes, and muscle weakness. It occurs when the pituitary, which releases hormones that stimulate the adrenal glands, is not working the way it should. Steroids, a pituitary tumor, or some prescription drugs can make the pituitary overactive and indirectly cause Cushing's syndrome.

On the other hand, in Addison's disease the adrenal glands do not make enough cortisol. Usually, Addison's disease occurs because the immune system attacks the adrenal glands. The disease causes loss of appetite, weight loss, and low blood pressure. Although hormonal imbalances can cause serious illnesses and may even be fatal, many hormonal imbalances can be treated with surgery or medicine.

**Infer** Why might a problem with a person's pituitary gland lead to problems in other body systems?

Biology **VIDEO CLIP**

HMDScience.com

**PREMIUM CONTENT**

Replacement Hormone Therapy

---

**SELF-CHECK Online**
HMDScience.com
**PREMIUM CONTENT**

# 26.6 Formative Assessment

### REVIEWING ▶ MAIN IDEAS

1. What determines whether a particular **hormone** will act on a target cell?

2. What two main hormones does the **pituitary gland** produce?

3. How do **releasing hormones** of the **hypothalamus** connect the nervous and endocrine systems?

4. Why do hormonal imbalances affect the entire body?

### CRITICAL THINKING

5. **Predict** How might your body be affected if a certain **gland** made too much releasing hormone that stimulates the thyroid? What if it made too little releasing hormone?

6. **Apply** What two body systems does the endocrine system rely on to generate and transport signals?

### CONNECT TO

#### CELL BIOLOGY

7. Steroid hormones are made of cholesterol, which is a type of lipid. Using what you know about cell membranes, why do you think steroids can diffuse into a cell, while non-steroid hormones cannot?

# 26 Summary

## KEY CONCEPTS

### 26.1 How Organ Systems Communicate

**The nervous system and the endocrine system provide the means by which organ systems communicate.** The body's nervous system and endocrine system generate, interpret, and deliver messages that help to maintain homeostasis. The two systems have different rates of communication because they send their signals by different methods.

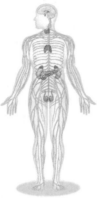

### 26.2 Neurons

**The nervous system is composed of highly specialized cells.** Neurons are specialized cells of the nervous system that have long extensions for transmitting signals over long distances. These cells produce, receive, and transmit impulses called action potentials.

### 26.3 The Senses

**The senses detect the internal and external environments.** The senses gather information about the body's internal and external environments. The senses use five types of receptors and many specialized cells, including rod, cone, and hair cells, that detect physical and chemical stimuli.

### 26.4 Central and Peripheral Nervous Systems

**The central nervous system interprets information, and the peripheral nervous system gathers and transmits information.** The CNS and PNS work together. In the CNS, the cerebrum controls conscious thought and interprets sensory signals from throughout the body. The PNS delivers messages from the body toward and away from the CNS.

### 26.5 Brain Function and Chemistry

**Scientists study the function and chemistry of the brain.** Imaging techniques allow scientists to look at the brain without having to have a patient undergo surgery. This technology can show chemical and physical changes in brains that have severe illnesses. Both prescription drugs and illegal drugs alter brain chemistry and neuron structure.

### 26.6 Endocrine System and Hormones

**The endocrine system produces hormones that affect growth, development, and homeostasis.** The glands of the endocrine system produce chemical signals called hormones that act throughout the body. The hypothalamus is a gland that interacts with the nervous and endocrine systems. Hormone imbalances can cause severe illnesses, such as hypothyroidism, diabetes, and Addison's disease.

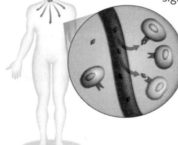

---

### READING TOOLBOX    SYNTHESIZE YOUR NOTES

**Concept Map** Summarize your notes about the nervous system by drawing a concept map.

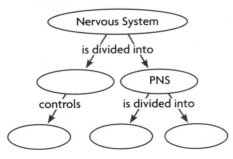

**Three-Column Chart** Make a chart to organize the information you learned about the senses.

| Sense | Receptor Type | Receptor Name |
|-------|---------------|---------------|
| sight | photoreceptor | |
| | | |
| | | |
| | | |
| | | |

# 26 Review

## CHAPTER VOCABULARY

**26.1** nervous system
endocrine system
stimulus
central nervous
system (CNS)
peripheral nervous
system (PNS)

**26.2** neuron
dendrite
axon
resting potential
sodium-potassium pump
action potential

synapse
terminal
neurotransmitter

**26.3** rod cell
cone cell
hair cell

**26.4** cerebrum
cerebral cortex
cerebellum
brain stem
reflex arc
somatic nervous system
autonomic nervous system

sympathetic nervous system
parasympathetic nervous system

**26.5** addiction
desensitization
tolerance
sensitization
stimulant
depressant

**26.6** hormone
gland
hypothalamus
pituitary gland
releasing hormones

## Reviewing Vocabulary

### Compare and Contrast

Describe one similarity and one difference between the two terms in each of the following pairs.

**1.** somatic nervous system, autonomic nervous system

**2.** rod cell, cone cell

**3.** sensitization, desensitization

### READING TOOLBOX  GREEK AND LATIN WORD ORIGINS

**4.** *Dendrite* comes from the Greek word dendron, which means "tree." Explain how the root word relates to the meaning of *dendrite*.

**5.** *Addiction* comes from the Latin word *addicere*, which means "deliver, yield, devote." How does this meaning relate to addiction?

**6.** *Endocrine* comes from the Greek word *krinein*, which means "to distinguish, separate." Explain how the root word relates to the meaning of *endocrine*.

### Keep It Short

For each vocabulary term below, write a short, precise phrase that describes its meaning. For example, a short phrase to describe stimulus could be "causes change."

**7.** action potential

**8.** reflex arc

**9.** hormone

**10.** axon

## Reviewing  MAIN IDEAS

**11.** Name two differences between the way in which the nervous and endocrine systems communicate.

**12.** How does the structure of a neuron make it effective in carrying out the functions of the nervous system?

**13.** Draw pictures to show how Na⁺ ions, K⁺ ions, and electrical charges are distributed across a neuron's membrane during resting and action potential.

**14.** What type of receptor do each of your five senses have?

**15.** If you have a question, you will raise your hand to ask it. How do your CNS and PNS work together to allow you to raise your hand?

**16.** What types of information do the occipital lobe and the temporal lobe process?

**17.** What are the differences between the sympathetic and the parasympathetic nervous systems?

**18.** How can a PET scan give clues about the activity of different neurotransmitters in the brain?

**19.** Why do hormones act only on some cells?

**20.** How do releasing hormones help glands to communicate with one another?

**21.** How are a target cell's activities changed if a gland produces too much of a particular hormone?

# Critical Thinking

**22. Apply** You wake up at night and turn on the light next to your bed. The light seems very bright at first, but soon your eyes adjust. Describe how your senses and your brain interact to let your eyes adjust to the light level.

**23. Infer** Research on babies shows that a certain part of a neuron gets longer as the babies interact with more stimuli. Which part do you think it is? Why?

**24. Analyze** How does the inside of a neuron become positively charged during an action potential, even though both potassium ($K^+$) and sodium ($Na^+$) ions are positively charged?

**25. Predict** An eye disease called macular degeneration damages the light-sensitive cells in the eye. How might this disease affect the ability of the eye to communicate with the brain?

**26. Compare** What are three similarities between neurotransmitters, used in the nervous system, and hormones, which are used in the endocrine system?

**27. Apply** The part of your brain that processes touch devotes more space to interpreting signals from your hands than from other parts of your body. Why might this be beneficial?

## Interpreting Visuals

The toxin in the diagram is commonly known as botox. It is a cosmetic treatment used on the muscles under skin to reduce wrinkles. Use the diagram below to answer the next two questions.

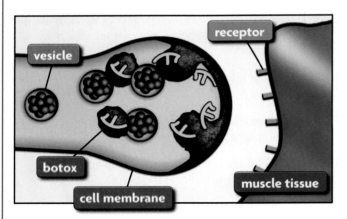

**28. Apply** What structures of the nervous system are being shown in the diagram?

**29. Analyze** Botox affects the normal functioning of nerve cells. According to the diagram, what part of the normal process is botox affecting?

## Analyzing Data Determine Correlation or Causation

Cataracts can impair a person's vision, making objects appear fuzzy. Cataracts occur when the lens in a person's eye becomes cloudy, or less transparent. This happens when the proteins that make up the lens clump. Use the graph below to answer the next three questions.

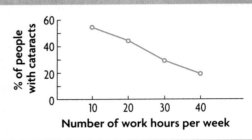

**CATARACTS AND WORK HOURS**

(y-axis: % of people with cataracts; x-axis: Number of work hours per week)

**30. Analyze** Does a correlation exist between incidents of cataracts and work hours? Explain.

**31. Evaluate** Can you conclude for sure that the number of hours worked causes cataracts? Explain your reasoning.

**32. Infer** If a correlation exists between cataracts and work hours, what might explain it?

## Making Connections

**33. Write a Script** Imagine you have a friend who wanted to try drugs, and you wanted to tell your friend about the effects that drugs have on the nervous system. Write a conversation that you could have about addiction and the negative effects of drug use.

**34. Connect** The image on the chapter opener shows some of a person's internal organs. Write a paragraph that discusses which division of the nervous system is shown in this picture. Also, discuss how the cells of this body system allow you to rapidly pull your hand off of a hot pan before your hand is burned.

# Standards-Based Assessment

1. A scientist investigates the toxic effects of a chemical on the brain. Which of the following experimental design elements would *most* likely lead to inconsistent results?

   A using the same method to measure toxicity

   B having a sample size that is very large

   C keeping the chemical at a constant temperature

   D running the tests in different locations

2. 

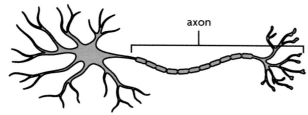

   What is the *main* function of the axon, which is illustrated here?

   A receives signals from neighboring cells

   B regulates nutrient intake within the body

   C increases the cell's surface area

   D transmits messages to neighboring cells

3. The hypothalamus releases antidiuretic hormone, which causes the kidneys to release less water from the body. Under which condition might the hypothalamus produce *more* antidiuretic hormone?

   A having high levels of antidiuretic hormone

   B having excess water in the body

   C drinking a bottle of juice

   D sweating due to exercise

   **THINK THROUGH THE QUESTION**

   Think carefully about each answer choice. Under which condition would the body respond by conserving water?

4. Anabolic steroids are drugs that mimic specific hormones in the body. As athletes abuse anabolic steroids in hopes of becoming stronger, their bodies produce less natural hormone. This effect can be *best* described as a(n)

   A form of negative feedback.

   B reflex arc.

   C conditioned response.

   D osmoregulatory response.

5. In what form does a nerve impulse travel from one neuron to another?

   A electrical signal

   B chemical signal

   C magnetic signal

   D ionic signal

6. 

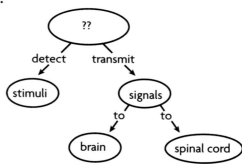

   Which of the following *best* completes this concept map?

   A motor neurons

   B interneurons

   C electric neurons

   D sensory neurons

# 27 Respiratory and Circulatory Systems

## ONLINE BIOLOGY
HMDScience.com

**ONLINE** Labs
- Carbon Dioxide and Exercise
- **QuickLab** Blood Cells
- Making and Using a Respirometer
- Stimuli and Heart Rate
- Monitoring EKG
- Ventilation and Heart Rate
- **Virtual Lab** Blood Typing
- **Video Lab** Lung Capacity

**VIRTUAL Lab**     PREMIUM CONTENT

**Blood Typing** Do you know your blood type? Learn how to identify blood types and then work on your own to identify the blood types of several samples.

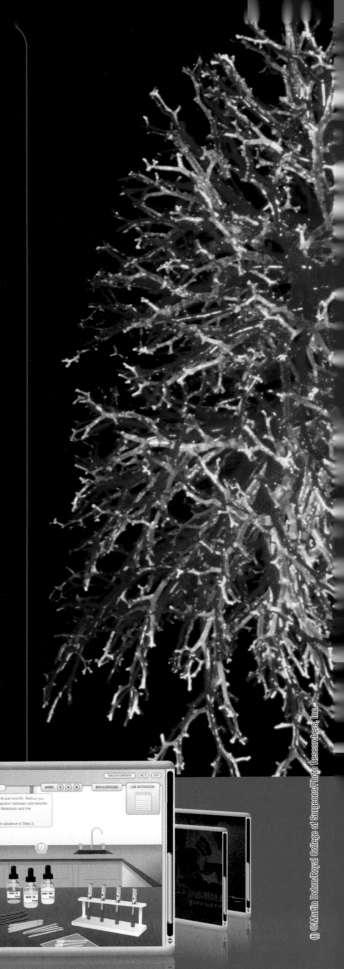

(t) ©Martin Dohrn/Royal College of Surgeons/Photo Researchers, Inc.

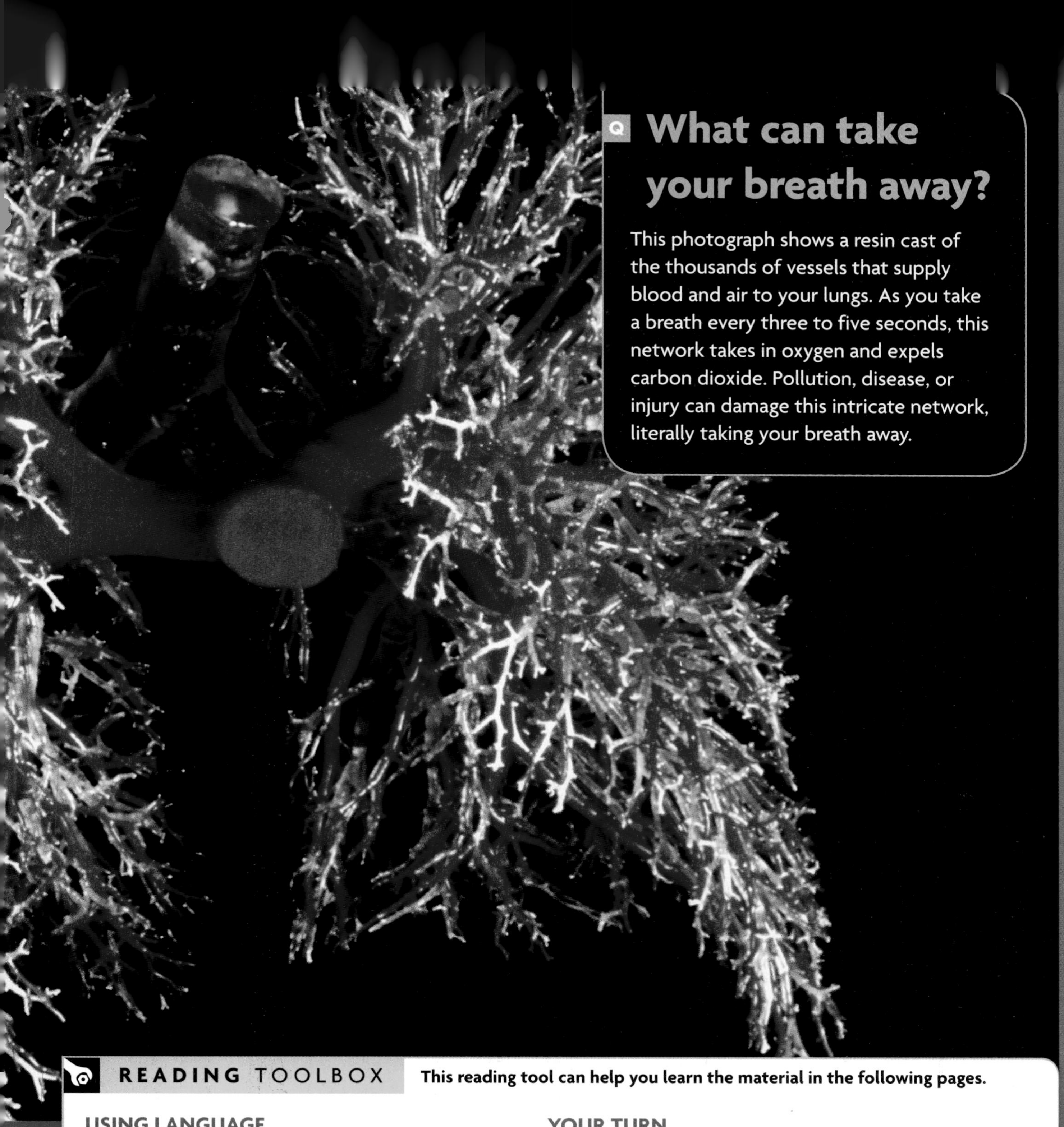

## Q What can take your breath away?

This photograph shows a resin cast of the thousands of vessels that supply blood and air to your lungs. As you take a breath every three to five seconds, this network takes in oxygen and expels carbon dioxide. Pollution, disease, or injury can damage this intricate network, literally taking your breath away.

### 🔊 READING TOOLBOX    This reading tool can help you learn the material in the following pages.

#### USING LANGUAGE

**Recognizing Main Ideas**  A main idea is a statement that tells you about the main point of a paragraph. It summarizes what the paragraph is about. The main idea is often, but not always, one of the first few sentences of a paragraph.

#### YOUR TURN

Find the main idea in the paragraph below.

*Cardiovascular diseases include high blood pressure, clogged and hardened arteries, heart attack, and stroke. High blood pressure causes the heart to work harder than normal, weakening the heart. Clogged and hardened arteries raise blood pressure and can also lead to heart attack and stroke.*

## 27.1 Respiratory and Circulatory Functions

SC.912.L.14.36

**KEY CONCEPT** The respiratory and circulatory systems bring oxygen and nutrients to the cells.

### MAIN IDEAS

- ◗ The respiratory and circulatory systems work together to maintain homeostasis.
- ◗ The respiratory system moves gases into and out of the blood.
- ◗ The circulatory system moves blood to all parts of the body.

**VOCABULARY**

circulatory system
respiratory system
trachea
lung
alveoli
diaphragm
heart
artery
vein
capillary

**SC.912.L.14.36** Describe the factors affecting blood flow through the cardiovascular system.

### ⚬ Connect to Your World

You have thousands of kilometers of blood vessels in your body and several hundred *million* tiny air sacs in your lungs. Blood circulates constantly through the vessels, while air continually fills and empties from the tiny air sacs. Your heart keeps beating and your lungs keep working 24 hours a day, every day of your life. Even more amazing, everything works without your having to think about it.

### ▶ MAIN IDEA

## The respiratory and circulatory systems work together to maintain homeostasis.

Every cell in your body needs nutrients and oxygen to function and needs to get rid of its waste products. The **circulatory system** is the body system that transports blood and other materials. It brings vital supplies to the cells and carries away their wastes. The blood vessels of the circulatory system also keep oxygen-poor blood from mixing with oxygen-rich blood. The **respiratory system** is the body system in which gas exchange takes place. You can think of your respiratory system as a major supply depot where the blood can pick up oxygen ($O_2$) and deposit excess carbon dioxide ($CO_2$). The lungs of the respiratory system are the only place in your body where gases in the blood are exchanged with gases from the atmosphere.

The respiratory and circulatory systems work closely together to maintain homeostasis in the face of constant change. Every time you exercise, lie down to rest, or simply stand up, you change your needs for oxygen and nutrients. As a result, your heart speeds up or slows down and you breathe faster or slower, depending on your activity. This section gives you an overview of the major structures of the respiratory and circulatory systems and their functions. Sections 2 through 5 provide a closer look at the organs of each system, how they work, and what can damage them.

**Apply** When you stand up after lying down, why do your heart rate and breathing rate increase?

### ⚬ READING TOOLBOX

**TAKING NOTES**

Use a supporting main ideas strategy to help you remember the respiratory and circulatory structures and their functions.

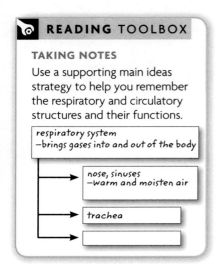

respiratory system
—brings gases into and out of the body

nose, sinuses
—warm and moisten air

trachea

FIGURE 1.1  **Respiratory Organs and Tissues**

**Specialized structures move air into and out of the body.**

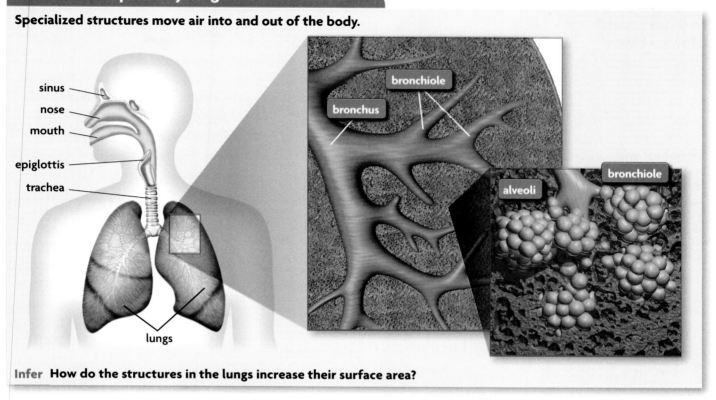

sinus
nose
mouth
epiglottis
trachea
lungs

bronchus
bronchiole
alveoli
bronchiole

**Infer**  **How do the structures in the lungs increase their surface area?**

## ▶ MAIN IDEA
# The respiratory system moves gases into and out of the blood.

The function of the respiratory system is to bring $O_2$ into the body and to expel $CO_2$ and water vapor. The structures of this system bring the gases in close contact with the blood, which absorbs $O_2$. The circulatory system then carries $O_2$ to all of the body's cells and transports $CO_2$ from the rest of the body to the lungs, where it is exhaled.

The specialized structures of the respiratory system are shown in **FIGURE 1.1.** The nose and mouth are the entry points to the system. When air enters the nose, mucus that lines the nasal passages warms and moistens the air. The mucus and tiny hairs called cilia help filter dust and pathogens from the air. At the back of the throat, a small piece of tissue, the epiglottis, regulates airflow into the trachea, or windpipe. The **trachea** (TRAY-kee-uh) is a long structure made of soft tissue reinforced with C-shaped rings of cartilage. It resembles the hose of a vacuum cleaner. When you swallow, the epiglottis closes the entrance to the trachea to keep food or saliva from entering the airways. The trachea divides into the two bronchi, with one branch going to each lung.

The **lungs** are the organs that absorb $O_2$ from the air you inhale. Inside the lungs, the bronchi divide into smaller and smaller branches that resemble the limbs and twigs of a tree. The smallest branches, the bronchioles, end in clusters of tiny air sacs called **alveoli** (al-VEE-uh-ly). One air sac is called an alveolus. The lungs have a huge number of alveoli—from 300 to 600 million.

**CONNECT TO**

**CELLULAR RESPIRATION**
You learned in **Cells and Energy** that eukaryotic cells require a constant supply of oxygen to produce ATP, which is the main energy source for cells.

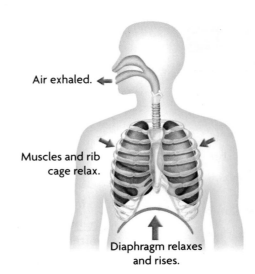

Air inhaled. ►

Muscles contract and rib cage expands.

Diaphragm flattens and moves downward.

Air exhaled. ◄

Muscles and rib cage relax.

Diaphragm relaxes and rises.

**FIGURE 1.2** When you inhale, movements of the rib cage and diaphragm produce lower pressure in the lungs, and air flows in. When you exhale, rib cage and diaphragm movements produce higher pressure in the lungs, and air flows out.

**READING TOOLBOX**

**VOCABULARY**

The word *diaphragm* is based on the Latin *diaphragma,* which means "midriff." The midriff extends from below the breast to the waist. The diaphragm is located in this area.

This huge number of alveoli gives the lungs a massive surface area for absorbing $O_2$ and releasing $CO_2$ and water vapor. Lung tissue is spongy and elastic, which allows the lungs to expand and contract as you breathe. Lung mucus and cilia help trap and remove foreign materials and pathogens.

The mechanics of breathing involve the muscles of the rib cage and the diaphragm, as **FIGURE 1.2** shows. The **diaphragm** is a dome-shaped muscle at the base of the rib cage. When you inhale, the muscles of the rib cage contract, causing the rib cage to expand. The diaphragm then flattens and moves downward. The volume of your lungs increases, and the air pressure decreases, falling below the air pressure outside your body. Gases move from areas of greater pressure to areas of lower pressure, so air flows into the lungs.

When you exhale, the rib cage muscles relax, and the rib cage becomes smaller. The diaphragm also relaxes, causing it to rise and regain its domelike shape. Now the air pressure inside your lungs is greater than the air pressure outside your body, so air flows out.

**Predict   How might damaged alveoli affect the oxygen level in the blood?**

## ▶ MAIN IDEA

# The circulatory system moves blood to all parts of the body.

The function of the circulatory system is to transport $O_2$ and nutrients to body cells and to carry oxygen-poor blood and $CO_2$ back to the heart and lungs. To do its job, the system must keep blood constantly circulating.

The main parts of the circulatory system are the heart, the blood, and the blood vessels. The **heart** is a muscular pump, about the size of your fist, that keeps the blood moving to every part of the body. The blood circulates through a closed system—that is, blood in the circulatory system stays inside the vessels. The average adult body contains about 5 liters (more than 5 qt) of blood. On average, your blood circulates from your heart, throughout your body, and back to your heart about every 60 seconds.

The circulatory system has three types of blood vessels: arteries, veins, and capillaries. **Arteries** are blood vessels that carry blood away from the heart to the rest of the body. **Veins** are blood vessels that carry blood from the rest of the body back to the heart. As illustrated in **FIGURE 1.3**, arteries carry oxygen-rich blood (red) and veins carry oxygen-poor blood (blue). Blue is used for illustration purposes only. In your body, oxygen-poor blood is not actually blue but a darker red color. You can think of arteries and veins as a system of roads. Large arteries and veins are like major highways. Smaller arteries and veins are like streets that route traffic through local neighborhoods.

Arteries and veins are connected by a system of capillaries. **Capillaries** are the tiny blood vessels that transport blood to and from the cells of the body. These vessels are so small that blood cells must move through them in single file. The walls of these tiny blood vessels are only one cell thick. Materials can easily diffuse into and out of them.

In addition to transporting vital supplies to the cells, the circulatory system performs two other important functions that maintain homeostasis.

- The circulatory system collects waste materials produced by digestion and cell metabolism, and delivers them to the liver and kidneys to be filtered out of the body. For example, muscle cell activity produces a waste product known as urea. As blood moves past the muscle cells, urea is moved into the bloodstream and carried to the kidneys to be excreted.
- The circulatory system helps maintain body temperature by distributing the heat that cells produce in the muscles and internal organs. When you are active, your organs and muscles produce more heat. The heart pumps harder, and the blood vessels dilate to bring excess heat to the skin, where it can escape. In cold weather, the blood vessels constrict to conserve heat.

The heart, the blood vessels, and the blood are described in more detail in Sections 3 through 5.

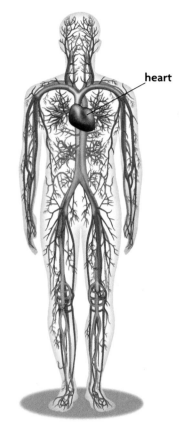

heart

**FIGURE 1.3** The circulatory system is composed of the heart, arteries carrying oxygen-rich blood (red), veins carrying oxygen-poor blood (blue), and capillaries.

**Infer** If a person has a weak heart, how might his or her ability to maintain a stable body temperature be affected?

## 27.1 Formative Assessment

### REVIEWING ▶ MAIN IDEAS

1. How do the **respiratory** and **circulatory systems** help maintain homeostasis in the body?
2. List the main parts and functions of the respiratory system.
3. Describe the basic parts and functions of the circulatory system.

### CRITICAL THINKING

4. **Apply** Why can't you breathe through the mouth while you are swallowing food? What would happen if you could do this?
5. **Infer** **Arteries** and **veins** are equally distributed throughout the body. How does this arrangement help to maintain the functions of each cell?

**SELF-CHECK Online**
HMDScience.com
**PREMIUM CONTENT**

**CONNECT TO**

### SCIENCE AND TECHNOLOGY

6. A mechanical ventilator breathes for a paralyzed person. During inhalation, the machine forces air under pressure into the **lungs**. During exhalation, the pressure drops and air moves out of the lungs. How does this machine compare with natural breathing?

# Respiration and Gas Exchange

SC.912.L.14.36

**SC.912.L.14.36** Describe the factors affecting blood flow through the cardiovascular system.

## VOCABULARY

red blood cell
hemoglobin
emphysema
asthma

**KEY CONCEPT** **The respiratory system exchanges oxygen and carbon dioxide.**

### MAIN IDEAS

○ Gas exchange occurs in the alveoli of the lungs.
○ Respiratory diseases interfere with gas exchange.

### Connect to Your World

Nearly every winter, newspapers carry stories of people killed by carbon monoxide (CO) gas in their homes. This colorless, odorless gas escapes from leaks in furnaces that burn fossil fuels. What makes CO so deadly? Your body readily absorbs it into the blood, which means less $O_2$ is absorbed. Within a short time, your cells become oxygen starved. You must quickly get to an area where you can breathe fresh air.

### ○ MAIN IDEA

## Gas exchange occurs in the alveoli of the lungs.

Recall that the cells in your body carry out cellular respiration, which requires $O_2$ and produces $CO_2$ as a waste product. Thus, every cell in the body needs $O_2$ and must get rid of $CO_2$. However, the alveoli and their capillaries are the only places where gas exchange with the atmosphere occurs. The lungs bring in a steady supply of $O_2$ and expel excess $CO_2$. Gas exchange in the lungs is based on three principles:

- $O_2$ and $CO_2$ are carried by the blood.
- Gases move by diffusion—that is, they move from an area of higher concentration to an area of lower concentration.
- The lining of the alveoli must be moist to help gases diffuse.

### Diffusion of $O_2$ and $CO_2$

In the alveoli, the respiratory and circulatory systems come together in the process of gas exchange. When you inhale, air flows from the bronchi to the bronchioles and finally to the alveoli. A cross-section of a bronchiole and several alveoli is shown in **FIGURE 2.1**. Each alveolus is about the size of a grain of sand, but all of the alveoli together give the lungs a surface area of about 100 square meters. Without this huge area for gas exchange, the lungs would be unable to extract enough $O_2$ from the air to keep you alive.

A complex network of capillaries surrounds and penetrates the alveoli, as shown in **FIGURE 2.2.** Blood entering these capillaries contains a lower concentration of $O_2$ than does the air in the alveoli. As a result, the $O_2$ diffuses from an area of high concentration in the alveoli to an area of low concentration in

**FIGURE 2.1** This micrograph shows a bronchiole and several alveoli. Alveoli walls are about one cell thick, which allows $O_2$ and $CO_2$ to diffuse easily across them. (colored SEM; magnification 150×)

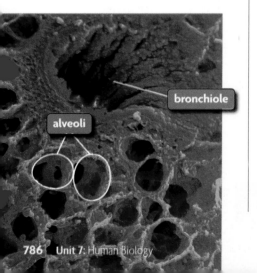

bronchiole

alveoli

## FIGURE 2.2 Gas Exchange in the Alveoli

Diffusion of gases into and out of the alveoli maintains $O_2$ and $CO_2$ homeostasis.

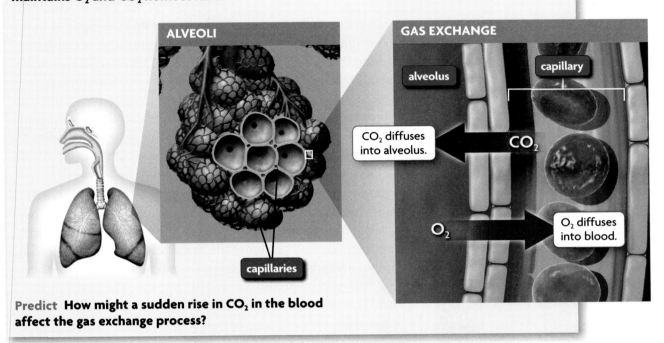

ALVEOLI

capillaries

GAS EXCHANGE

alveolus

capillary

$CO_2$ diffuses into alveolus.

$CO_2$

$O_2$

$O_2$ diffuses into blood.

**Predict** How might a sudden rise in $CO_2$ in the blood affect the gas exchange process?

the capillaries. The blood in the capillaries contain **red blood cells,** a type of cell that picks up oxygen in the lungs and delivers it to all of the body's cells. In red blood cells, most of the $O_2$ molecules bind to an iron-rich protein called **hemoglobin** (HEE-muh-GLOH-bihn). Each molecule of hemoglobin binds with four $O_2$ molecules. The iron in hemoglobin is what gives blood its reddish color. Blood becomes bright red only when it absorbs oxygen. The blood leaving the alveoli carries almost three times the amount of $O_2$ that it had coming into the lungs.

In contrast, $CO_2$ concentrations are higher in the blood than in the alveoli. As a result, $CO_2$ diffuses into the alveoli. The higher concentration of $CO_2$ in the blood is due to the fact that every cell produces $CO_2$ and water as waste products. The $CO_2$ and water combine in the blood to form the compound carbonic acid. The more carbonic acid there is in the blood, the more acidic the blood becomes. When carbonic acid diffuses into the alveoli, the compound separates into $CO_2$ and water, which are exhaled.

## Gas Exchange and the Nervous System

Gas exchange is so critical to the body that it is an autonomic function regulated by the medulla and pons in the brain stem. These centers monitor dissolved gases in the blood, particularly $CO_2$ concentrations. As you become more active, $CO_2$ levels increase and the blood becomes more acidic. Sensors in the respiratory and circulatory systems signal this change to the brain stem. The medulla sends messages through the nervous and endocrine systems that stimulate the diaphragm and rib cage muscles to work harder. The medulla regulates how often and how deeply you breathe based on your activity.

**Analyze** How does the alveoli's structure relate to the function of gas exchange?

**THAT'S** **Amazing!**

**Video Inquiry**
HMDScience.com

PREMIUM CONTENT

**Turtle Breath**

**CONNECT TO**

**NERVOUS SYSTEM**

As you read in **Nervous and Endocrine Systems,** the brain stem is located at the base of the brain. The brain stem is involved in regulating breathing and other autonomic functions that help maintain homeostasis.

## ▶ MAIN IDEA
# Respiratory diseases interfere with gas exchange.

**FIGURE 2.3** Healthy lung tissue is free of any deposits. When a person smokes for several years, black tar deposits first invade and then choke the tissue, and greatly reduce gas exchange. (LM; magnification 250×)

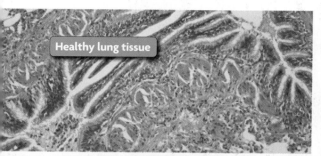
Healthy lung tissue

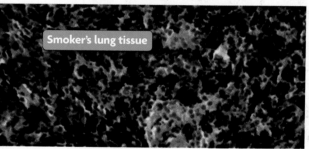
Smoker's lung tissue

## Web *Quest*
HMDScience.com
**PREMIUM CONTENT**
Asthma

Damage to the respiratory system makes gas exchange more difficult, which in turn affects every cell in the body. Smoking is the leading cause of respiratory diseases such as lung cancer and emphysema. Tobacco smoke contains more than 4800 chemicals that can paralyze cilia, damage alveoli, and cause genetic mutations leading to cancer. In **FIGURE 2.3,** you can see the effects of smoking on lung tissue. When a person smokes for several years, the lung tissue is slowly coated by tars and other chemicals. Eventually, the tissue becomes almost solid black. The sooner people stop smoking, the sooner such damage to the lungs can be reversed.

**Emphysema** (EHM-fih-SEE-muh) is a lung disorder caused mainly by smoking. Over time, many alveoli are destroyed. This process gradually reduces the surface area for gas exchange, and not enough oxygen can enter the blood. People with advanced emphysema must use supplemental oxygen, but eventually their lungs fail. At present, this disease has no cure. The best way to prevent emphysema is to refrain from smoking.

**Asthma** (AZ-muh) causes the bronchioles to constrict due to muscle spasms. This condition makes it hard to move air in and out of the lungs. A person having a severe asthma attack can die from lack of oxygen. Attacks may be triggered by allergies, stress, exposure to smoke and chemicals, or exercise. The attacks can be relieved by drugs that relax the bronchioles.

Cystic fibrosis (CF) is a genetic disease that causes the lungs to produce a thick, sticky mucus. This mucus blocks the airways and allows microorganisms to thrive in the lungs. People with CF have frequent, sometimes fatal, lung infections. Treatments focus on preventing the mucus from building up.

**Synthesize  How does smoking affect gas exchange?**

*(t) ©Dachez/Photo Researchers, Inc.; (b) ©Kent Wood/Photo Researchers, Inc.*

## ⟳ SELF-CHECK Online
HMDScience.com
**PREMIUM CONTENT**

## 27.2  Formative Assessment

### REVIEWING ▶ MAIN IDEAS

1. Explain how diffusion allows gases to move into and out of the alveoli of the lungs. Use the term **red blood cell** in your explanation.

2. In what ways can respiratory diseases reduce the level of $O_2$ in the blood?

### CRITICAL THINKING

3. **Synthesize**  Explain how your breathing rate would change if your blood became more acidic.

4. **Apply**  People poisoned by CO are often given 100 percent $O_2$ in a room with two to three times normal atmospheric pressure. Explain why more oxygen would enter their blood under these conditions.

### ✦ CONNECT TO
#### FORENSIC SCIENCE

5. When police find a body in a lake or river, they must determine if the person was drowned or was killed in some other way and then thrown into the water. How would examining the lungs of the person help them to solve the mystery?

# 27.3 The Heart and Circulation

SC.912.L.14.36

**KEY CONCEPT** **The heart is a muscular pump that moves the blood through two pathways.**

## VOCABULARY

atrium
ventricle
valve
pacemaker
pulmonary circulation
systemic circulation

**SC.912.L.14.36** Describe the factors affecting blood flow through the cardiovascular system.

### MAIN IDEAS

- The tissues and structures of the heart make it an efficient pump.
- The heart pumps blood through two main pathways.

### ☀- Connect to Your World

*Lub-dub, lub-dub.* This is the sound of your heart beating. The *lub* sound occurs when the valves between the upper and lower chambers of the heart snap shut. The *dub* sound is made by valves closing the two arteries that carry blood out of the heart. If a valve does not close properly and allows blood to leak backward, the sound of the heart changes. A heart with a leaky valve might sound like this: *Lub-dub-shhh, lub-dub-shhh.* The sounds your heart makes can tell a physician a great deal about how it is performing.

### ◉ MAIN IDEA

## The tissues and structures of the heart make it an efficient pump.

Each day your heart beats about 100,000 times, circulating blood through nearly 96,000 kilometers of blood vessels—roughly one-quarter of the distance to the moon. Over 70 years, your heart will beat about 2.5 *billion* times. How can it keep going? One reason is that cardiac muscle tissue, unlike skeletal muscle tissue, can work continuously without becoming tired. Also, the structures of the heart make this organ an efficient pump.

### Structures of the Heart

The largest structures in your heart are the four chambers. As shown in **FIGURE 3.1,** the two smaller chambers are the right **atrium** and left atrium (plural, *atria*), and the two larger chambers are the right and left **ventricles.** The ventricles are separated by the septum, a thick wall of tissue. The heart **valves** are flaps of tissue that prevent blood from flowing backward. They open when the atria or ventricles contract, and close when the atria or ventricles relax.

After blood fills a chamber, the cardiac muscle contracts and pumps the blood out of the chamber. The heart is an amazingly powerful pump.

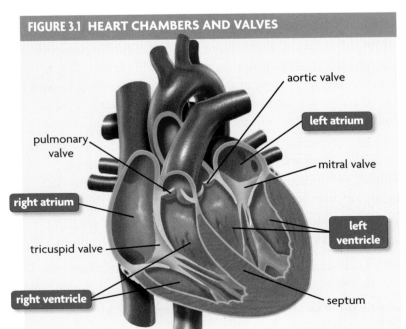

**FIGURE 3.1 HEART CHAMBERS AND VALVES**

aortic valve
left atrium
mitral valve
pulmonary valve
right atrium
left ventricle
tricuspid valve
right ventricle
septum

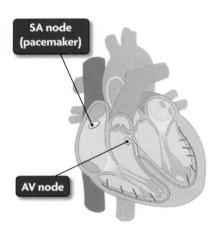

**FIGURE 3.2** An electrical signal from the SA node causes both atria to contract. The AV node then picks up the signal and transmits it to both ventricles, causing them to contract.

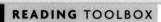

**PREMIUM CONTENT**

**Heart Anatomy and Function**

**READING TOOLBOX**

**VOCABULARY**

The word *pulmonary* comes from the Latin root *pulmo*, meaning "lung." The suffix *-ary* means "belonging to or connected with." Therefore, *pulmonary* means something "belonging to or connected with the lung."

---

The reason has to do with the small size of the heart, which allows the strong cardiac muscles to exert a great deal of force on the chamber. The combination of small size and large force results in a powerful pumping action. The heart is also an efficient, self-regulating pump. It can respond to signals from the nervous system to change the speed and force of its pumping action. For example, if you increase your level of activity, your heart will pump faster.

### The Heartbeat

The heartbeat consists of two contractions: the first takes place in the atria and the second in the ventricles. The contractions occur partly because the cardiac muscle fibers of the chambers have a unique property. Whenever one fiber is stimulated to contract, all of the fibers contract at the same time.

The first contraction of the heart begins in the right atrium at a signal from the sinoatrial (SA) node, shown in **FIGURE 3.2**. The SA node is known as the heart's **pacemaker** because the cells in this node generate an electrical signal that starts the wave of contractions. Once the atria have contracted, the electrical signal spreads through conducting fibers to the atrioventricular (AV) node, located in the wall of the right ventricle. The AV signal stimulates both ventricles to contract at the same time.

If the SA node is seriously damaged by injury or disease, it can be replaced with an artificial pacemaker that is implanted into the heart. This device, like the SA node, sends electrical signals to the muscle fibers of the atria.

### Blood Flow in the Heart

Once you know the basic structures and actions of the heart, you can follow how oxygen-rich and oxygen-poor blood flow through this organ. Study **FIGURE 3.3**, which illustrates this pathway. Notice that blood always enters the heart through an atrium and leaves the heart through a ventricle. The contractions of the atria and then of the ventricles keep blood moving in this sequence.

1. Oxygen-poor blood from the body enters the right atrium. The SA node signals the atria to contract, and blood flows into the right ventricle.

2. When the AV node signals the ventricles to contract, blood is pumped from the right ventricle into the pulmonary artery. This artery, which goes to the lungs, is the only artery in the body that carries oxygen-poor blood. The blood enters the lungs, where $CO_2$ and water vapor diffuse into the alveoli and $O_2$ diffuses into the blood.

3. Oxygen-rich blood returns to the heart through the pulmonary vein and enters the left atrium. This is the only vein in the body that carries oxygen-rich blood. As the atria contract, blood is pumped into the left ventricle, the largest chamber in the heart.

4. When the ventricles contract, blood is pumped from the left ventricle into a large artery, the aorta, and is circulated to the rest of the body.

After oxygen has been delivered to the cells, the oxygen-poor blood returns through the veins to the heart, and the sequence begins again.

**Analyze** **The left ventricle is the largest chamber of the heart. How is its size related to its function?**

# FIGURE 3.3  Blood Flow in the Heart

**The structures of the heart keep oxygen-poor blood separated from oxygen-rich blood.**

Oxygen-poor blood

Oxygen-rich blood

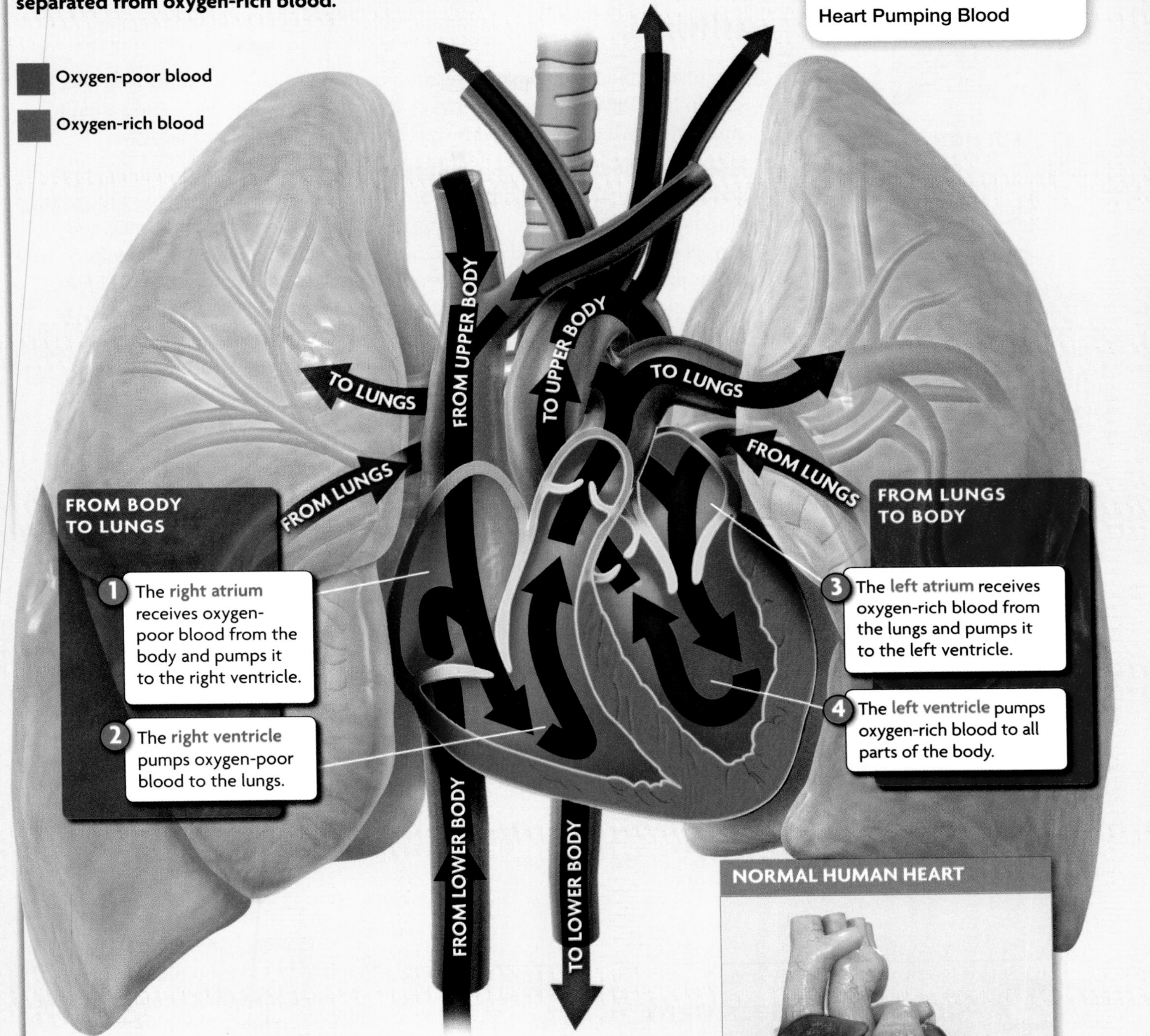

FROM UPPER BODY

TO UPPER BODY

TO LUNGS

FROM LUNGS

TO LUNGS

FROM LUNGS

**FROM BODY TO LUNGS**

1 The right atrium receives oxygen-poor blood from the body and pumps it to the right ventricle.

2 The right ventricle pumps oxygen-poor blood to the lungs.

**FROM LUNGS TO BODY**

3 The left atrium receives oxygen-rich blood from the lungs and pumps it to the left ventricle.

4 The left ventricle pumps oxygen-rich blood to all parts of the body.

FROM LOWER BODY

TO LOWER BODY

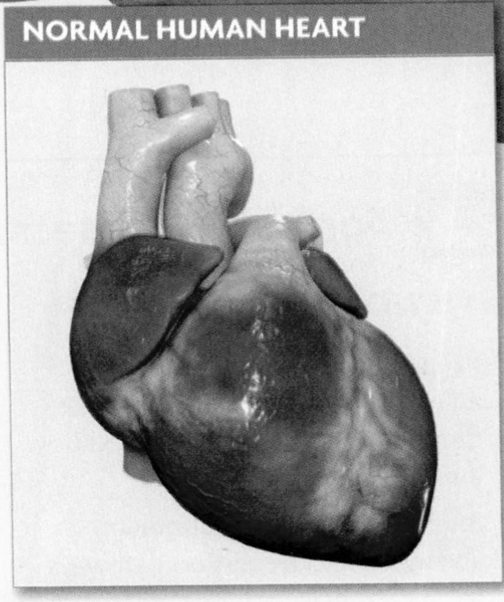

**NORMAL HUMAN HEART**

CRITICAL VIEWING  If the valves in the right ventricle do not close properly, where in the body might circulation be affected the most?

©7activestudio/Getty Images

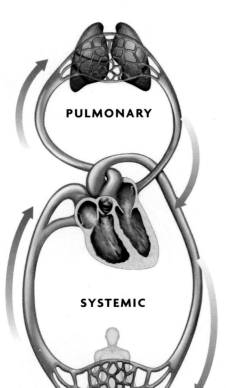

PULMONARY

SYSTEMIC

**FIGURE 3.4** The circulatory system has two general pathways. Pulmonary circulation moves blood between the heart and the lungs. Systemic circulation moves blood between the heart and the rest of the body.

◉ MAIN IDEA
# The heart pumps blood through two main pathways.

Circulating blood follows two separate pathways that meet at the heart, as shown in **FIGURE 3.4**. These pathways are called the pulmonary and systemic circulation. All of your blood travels through both of these pathways.

**Pulmonary circulation** (PUL-muh-NEHR-ee) occurs only between the heart and the lungs. The main function of this circulation is to carry oxygen-poor blood to the lungs, where it picks up $O_2$, expels excess $CO_2$ and water, and carries oxygen-rich blood back to the heart. Each lung is supplied by its own pulmonary artery and pulmonary vein. **Systemic circulation** (sihs-STEHM-ihk) occurs between the heart and the rest of the body, except for the lungs. The main function of this circulation is to carry oxygen-rich blood to all cells and transport oxygen-poor blood back to the heart. Systemic circulation begins when blood leaves the left ventricle, the largest chamber of the heart. The blood then circulates through the torso, arms, legs, and head, and then returns to the heart.

As the body's need for oxygen changes, sensors in the walls of major arteries in the pulmonary and systemic pathways send information to the medulla in the brain stem. The medulla coordinates this information with signals from the respiratory system. Homeostasis is maintained by matching heart rate and respiration rate with the oxygen needs of the body.

In extreme conditions, such as severe cold, the pulmonary and systemic circulation systems serve another vital function—making sure the body's brain, heart, and other major organs remain at a constant temperature. When the body is exposed for any length of time to a cold environment, blood vessels to the arms and legs begin to constrict. The blood flow to the arms and legs is reduced in order to keep the torso and head warm. Once you reach a warmer environment, these blood vessels dilate and normal circulation resumes.

**Infer** **Why is it important to have two separate pathways for circulation?**

**SELF-CHECK Online**
HMDScience.com
**PREMIUM CONTENT**

## 27.3 Formative Assessment

**REVIEWING ◉ MAIN IDEAS**

1. What structures make the heart an efficient pump? In your answer, describe the direction of blood flow into and out of the heart.

2. Briefly describe the **pulmonary** and **systemic circulation** pathways.

**CRITICAL THINKING**

3. **Predict** Explain how leaky heart **valves** might damage the heart over time.

4. **Predict** How might a high fever affect a person's heart and breathing rates? Explain your answer.

**CONNECT TO**

**ANIMALS**

5. Unlike a human heart, an amphibian heart has two **atria** but only a single **ventricle.** How might living in a watery environment help reduce the work that an amphibian heart needs to do?

# GO Online!

## GO with the FLOW

**Biology VIDEO CLIP**

**Body's Blood Usage** Find out which parts of your body use the most blood.

**THAT'S Amazing! VIDEO INQUIRY**

### Turtle Breath

How can sea turtles hold their breaths for so long? Learn more about these fascinating creatures, and analyze data on their diving and breathing patterns to help answer this question.

**WebQuest**

**Asthma** Learn what causes asthma, what triggers an episode, and why people with asthma can still live healthy, active lives.

# 27.4 Blood Vessels and Transport

SC.912.L.14.36

SC.912.L.14.36 Describe the factors affecting blood flow through the cardiovascular system.

**KEY CONCEPT** The circulatory system transports materials throughout the body.

### VOCABULARY
blood pressure
systolic pressure
diastolic pressure

**MAIN IDEAS**
- ◗ Arteries, veins, and capillaries transport blood to all parts of the body.
- ◗ Lifestyle plays a key role in circulatory diseases.

## Connect to Your World

The last time you visited a doctor, you may have had your blood pressure measured. You can feel the pulsing of the blood under the cuff on your arm. Your blood pressure indicates how hard your heart is working. We've come a long way in our understanding of blood flow. In the 1600s, most scientists thought that the lungs were responsible for the movement of blood. William Harvey, court physician to the king of England, changed this perception with his studies. Harvey's work on circulation is regarded as one of the greatest advances in the history of medicine.

## ▶ MAIN IDEA

# Arteries, veins, and capillaries transport blood to all parts of the body.

As you read in Section 1, the circulatory system includes three types of blood vessels—arteries, veins, and capillaries—that act as transportation networks for the blood. Each of the three vessels has its own structure and function, as illustrated in **FIGURE 4.1**.

### Arteries

Arteries need to be strong and flexible because the blood they carry from the heart is under great pressure. An artery's thick wall is composed of three layers. The innermost layer consists of endothelium coated with a protein that prevents blood from clotting. The middle layer is a thick band of smooth muscle and elastic fibers. The outer layer consists of connective tissue and elastic fibers. The elastic fibers allow the arterial walls to expand and contract to help move blood through the arteries. Arterioles, or smaller arteries, contain the same three layers, but the outer and middle layers are much thinner.

### Veins

The structures of veins reflect the fact that blood is under much less pressure when it is returning to the heart. Veins have larger diameters and thinner walls than do arteries and contain valves that prevent blood from flowing backwards. Veins do not have a thick layer that expands and contracts to keep blood moving. Instead, they need the activity of skeletal muscles to help maintain circulation. For example, as you walk, skeletal muscles in your legs push against the veins. The valves open, and blood moves toward the heart. If you sit for too long, the lack of exercise makes it harder for the blood to move upward. Venules are small veins that join larger veins to capillaries.

### READING TOOLBOX

**TAKING NOTES**

A two-column chart can help you organize your notes about different blood vessels and circulatory pathways.

| arteries | - Thicker, more muscular than veins<br>- Blood under greater pressure |
|---|---|
| | |

## FIGURE 4.1 Three Types of Blood Vessels

**Arteries, veins, and capillaries transport the blood to every cell.**

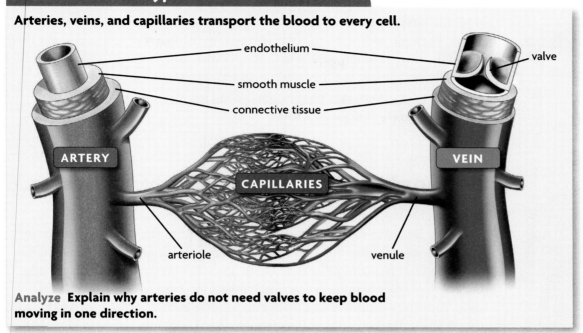

endothelium

smooth muscle

connective tissue

valve

ARTERY

VEIN

CAPILLARIES

arteriole

venule

**Analyze** **Explain why arteries do not need valves to keep blood moving in one direction.**

## Capillaries

Capillary walls are made of epithelium, but they contain no muscle cells or elastic fibers. The thinness of capillary walls allows materials to diffuse into and out of the blood quickly and easily. In areas of high metabolic activity, such as the lungs, kidneys, and liver, capillaries form dense networks called capillary beds. These beds move a great deal of blood into and out of these organs.

## Circulation and Blood Pressure

**Blood pressure** is the force with which blood pushes against the wall of an artery. A healthy resting blood pressure for a young adult is around 120/70 mm Hg (read as "120 over 70 millimeters of mercury"). The top, and higher, number is known as the **systolic pressure** (sih-STAHL-ihk). This is the amount of pressure on the walls of an artery when the left ventricle contracts to pump blood through the body. The bottom, and lower, number is known as the **diastolic pressure** (DY-uh-STAHL-ihk). This is the pressure in the artery when the left ventricle relaxes.

Blood pressure depends on how elastic and unblocked the arteries are and on the strength of the heart contraction. The less elastic the arteries and the more blockages that reduce blood flow, the harder the heart must pump. As a result, blood pressure rises. Blood pressure also rises naturally with activity, stress, and strong emotions, but it should drop again with rest. If the pressure remains high, there could be a problem in the circulatory system.

### VISUAL VOCAB

**Systolic pressure** occurs when the left ventricle contracts. **Diastolic pressure** occurs when the ventricle relaxes. You can write these numbers as a fraction in which systolic pressure is always on top.

$$\frac{120 \quad \textbf{systolic} = \text{numerator}}{70 \quad \textbf{diastolic} = \text{denominator}}$$

### CONNECT TO

**DIFFERENTIATED CELLS**

In **Human Systems and Homeostasis,** you learned that epithelial cells line most organs and structures in the body. These cells provide a protective layer that helps each organ or structure to do its job.

Biology **VIDEO CLIP**

HMDScience.com

PREMIUM CONTENT

**Blood and Blood Vessels**

People with permanently high blood pressure have a condition called hypertension, which can lead to a heart attack or stroke. A heart attack occurs when the arteries to the heart muscle are damaged or blocked. A stroke can occur when blood flow to the brain is interrupted. Most people can lower their blood pressure through weight loss, proper diet, and exercise. If these remedies fail, people can use medications to reduce blood pressure.

**Infer** **Why do you think that blood moving from the heart to the lungs must be carried by an artery and not by a vein?**

## ▶ MAIN IDEA

## Lifestyle plays a key role in circulatory diseases.

Lifestyle choices strongly influence the health of your circulatory system. Smoking, lack of exercise, excessive weight, long-term stress, and a diet low in fruits and vegetables but high in saturated fats are all linked to an increased risk of developing circulatory diseases. These diseases mainly affect the heart and the arteries. For example, in arteriosclerosis (ahr-TEER-ee-oh-skluh-ROH-sihs), the artery walls become thick and inflexible. In atherosclerosis (ATH-uh-roh-skluh-ROH-sihs), blood flow is partially or fully blocked by sticky material, called plaque, that collects on the walls of the arteries, as **FIGURE 4.2** shows. High blood pressure is often the only warning sign of these problems.

Both diseases can lead to a heart attack, stroke, or kidney damage. Some blocked arteries supplying the heart muscle can be opened using a surgical technique known as a balloon angioplasty (AN-jee-uh-PLAS-tee). A device is threaded into the artery and then inflated so that it squeezes the obstruction against the artery wall. If this procedure does not work, bypass surgery may be necessary. In this operation, a healthy blood vessel from another part of the body (usually the leg) is attached to the artery on either side of the blockage. Blood can then bypass the obstruction.

To reduce the risk of circulatory diseases, physicians urge people to not smoke, to maintain a healthy weight, and to exercise regularly. Medications can also help reduce the risks of heart disease.

**Provide Examples** **How can lifestyle choices affect the function of the arteries?**

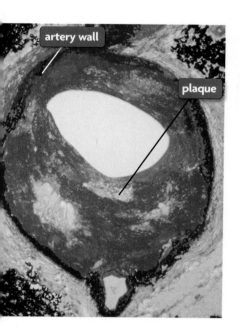

artery wall

plaque

**FIGURE 4.2** This micrograph clearly shows fatty deposits, called plaque, building up on an artery wall. If such deposits block blood flow, they can cause a heart attack or stroke. (LM)

©CMSP/Getty Images

**SELF-CHECK Online**
HMDScience.com
**PREMIUM CONTENT**

# 27.4 **Formative Assessment**

### REVIEWING ▶ MAIN IDEAS

1. How do the structures of arteries, veins, and capillaries relate to their functions?

2. How can lifestyle choices help reduce the risk of heart disease?

### CRITICAL THINKING

3. **Infer** People who smoke often have cold hands and feet. What might explain this condition in terms of blood flow?

4. **Apply** Explain why narrowing of the arteries decreases blood flow but increases **blood pressure**.

### CONNECT TO

**ARTHROPODS**

5. The hard exoskeleton of an arthropod exerts pressure on the animal's circulatory system. In what way does the exoskeleton serve the same function as the heart does in mammals?

# Forming a Null Hypothesis

When scientists investigate some type of phenomenon, such as when they are trying to determine the cause of a disease, they often need to rule out variables that may or may not be important. This is especially helpful when many factors might play some role in the phenomenon, as is often the case, in the causes of disease.

The formation of a null hypothesis is useful during these types of investigations. The null hypothesis states that there is no difference among study groups for the independent variable being tested. The null hypothesis is always stated in the negative: one variable does not have an effect on the other variable. The null hypothesis is accepted or rejected based on the data. If the investigation shows that the one variable does affect the other, the null hypothesis is rejected. If the investigation shows that the one variable does not affect the other, then the null hypothesis is accepted.

## Model

A scientist investigates the rate of death from heart disease among different age groups. The null hypothesis for this investigation would be, "There is no difference in the rate of death from heart disease among different age groups." Consider the results listed below for the rate of death from heart disease per 100,000 people.

- Rate for ages 55–64 is 246.9
- Rate for ages 65–74 is 635.1
- Rate for ages 75–84 is 1725.7

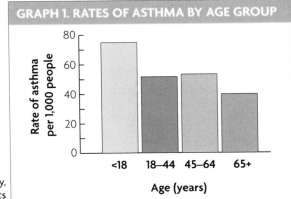

Exercise is an important factor in preventing heart disease.

In this case, the null hypothesis would be rejected because there is an obvious difference in the rate of death due to heart disease among different age groups. As people get older, the rate of death increases.

## Practice Form a Null Hypothesis

The graph at right shows the results of an investigation about differences in the rate of asthma based on age.

1. **Hypothesize** Form a null hypothesis for this investigation.

2. **Evaluate** Explain whether you accept or reject the null hypothesis, based on the data.

**GRAPH 1. RATES OF ASTHMA BY AGE GROUP**

Rate of asthma per 1,000 people (y-axis: 0, 20, 40, 60, 80)

Age (years): <18, 18–44, 45–64, 65+

Source: National Health Interview Survey, National Center for Health Statistics

# 27.5 Blood

**KEY CONCEPT** **Blood is a complex tissue that transports materials.**

**MAIN IDEAS**

○ Blood is composed mainly of cells, cell fragments, and plasma.
○ Platelets and different types of blood cells have different functions.

## ☼ Connect to Your World

The adult human body contains about 5 liters (more than 5 qt) of blood. This fluid supplies your organs with gases and nutrients, helps you keep warm or cool off, and gets rid of waste products from your cells. Blood also has other components that help fight infections and control bleeding from damaged blood vessels. How can one substance accomplish all of these functions?

## ▶ MAIN IDEA

# Blood is composed mainly of cells, cell fragments, and plasma.

When you look at blood with the naked eye, it appears to be a single substance. Whole blood is actually a sticky mixture of cells, cell fragments, and fluid, along with particles of fat, other nutrients, and dissolved gases. If you put blood in a test tube and spin it in a centrifuge, it will separate into two main parts, as shown in **FIGURE 5.1.** At the bottom, a reddish-brown band contains red blood cells, white blood cells, and platelets. **Platelets** are cell fragments, produced in bone marrow, that help in blood clotting.

At the top of the tube is **plasma,** a clear pale-yellow fluid that makes up about 55 percent of the blood. Plasma is roughly 90 percent water. Many types of molecules dissolve in plasma and can be transported throughout the body. These molecules include amino acids, glucose, hormones, vitamins, salts, and waste products.

Why is plasma important? The concentration of molecules dissolved in plasma determines which substances will diffuse into and out of the blood that moves through the capillaries. The movement of water, gases, nutrients, and ions between the capillaries and the cells plays a critical role in maintaining homeostasis. For instance, as the concentration of glucose increases in the capillaries, it moves outward to an area of lower concentration and eventually enters the cells.

Plasma proteins such as albumin, fibrinogen, and immune proteins also help maintain homeostasis. Albumin, the same substance as in egg white, is the most abundant plasma protein. Its main role is to stabilize blood volume so that fluid in the blood does not leak out of the vessels. Fibrinogen is a clotting factor that works with platelets to stop the bleeding after an injury.

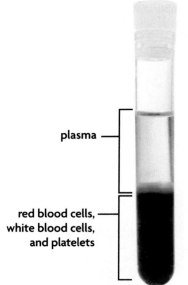

plasma ⎯

red blood cells, ⎯
white blood cells,
and platelets

**FIGURE 5.1** Whole blood is composed of several parts that help to fight infections, control bleeding, and transport gases, nutrients, waste products, and hormones.

©Nixx Photography/Shutterstock

A group of specialized proteins made by the immune system fights infection or attacks foreign materials in the blood. You will learn more about these proteins in the chapter on the immune system and disease.

**Predict** **What do you think might happen to your blood if you become dehydrated?**

⬤ MAIN IDEA
# Platelets and different types of blood cells have different functions.

Blood contains red blood cells, several types of white blood cells, and platelets, as the photograph in **FIGURE 5.2** shows. These three blood components are manufactured mostly in the bone marrow. Each one has a specialized shape and function.

## Red Blood Cells
Red blood cells make up 40 to 45 percent of all cells in the blood. Mature red blood cells are shaped like an inner tube with a solid center. They are produced from stem cells in bone marrow. As these cells mature, they gradually fill with hemoglobin and lose their nuclei and other organelles. Without nuclei, they cannot undergo cell division. Red blood cells circulate through the body for about 120 days before they begin to degrade. Degraded cells are carried to the liver and spleen, which break up the cells and recycle them.

The most important function of red blood cells is to transport $O_2$ to the cells and carry $CO_2$ away from them. As you read in Section 3, $O_2$ binds to the hemoglobin in red blood cells and is transported to all cells. When blood is returning to the heart, it picks up $CO_2$ and carries it to the lungs.

If red blood cells are damaged or misshapen, they cannot transport $O_2$ effectively. In sickle cell disease, for example, red blood cells are distorted into crescent shapes, as shown in **FIGURE 5.3**. They transport less $O_2$, last only 10 to 20 days, and tend to clump in blood vessels. This genetic disorder is most commonly found in people of African descent.

## ABO Blood Group and Rh Factors
Red blood cells have surface protein markers that define your blood type. Blood type is very important when people give or receive blood for transfusions. If you receive blood with a protein marker different from your own, your immune system will attack the foreign blood cells, causing them to clump. The clumped blood can block vital blood vessels and result in death.

Protein markers exist for about 26 different blood types. The most common markers are A and B, which produce four blood types: A, B, AB, and O, also known as the **ABO blood group.** Type O has no protein marker and can be donated to a person with any other blood type. Type AB blood has both protein markers and can accept any type of blood. People with Type A and Type B blood can receive only their own blood type or type O blood.

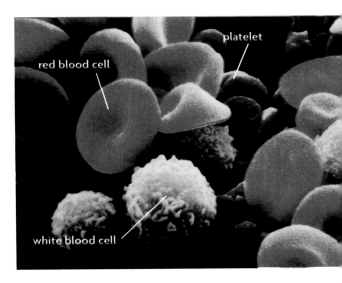

**FIGURE 5.2** Red blood cells transport gases, white blood cells defend the body against pathogens and foreign materials, and platelets help seal wounds. (colored SEM; magnification 3,400×)

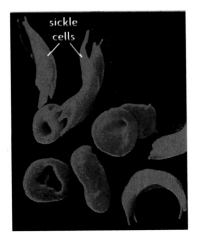

**FIGURE 5.3** Sickle cell anemia is an inherited blood disease in which hemoglobin proteins clump together. This causes red blood cells to stiffen and curl into a crescent shape. (colored SEM)

## Blood Cells

In this lab, you will examine different types of blood cells under the microscope.

**MATERIALS**
- slide of blood cells
- microscope

**PROBLEM**  What are the different characteristics of blood cells?

**PROCEDURE**

1. Examine the slide under low power and high power on the microscope. Identify a red blood cell, a white blood cell, and a platelet. Notice the proportion of each type of cell on your slide.

2. Draw each type of cell and label its structures.

**ANALYZE AND CONCLUDE**

1. **Explain**  What is the general shape of a red blood cell? How is this shape related to the function of a red blood cell?

2. **Infer**  Based on the proportion of each type of cell on your slide, which type of cell is the most numerous in the blood of a healthy person? Which is least numerous?

## CONNECT TO

### GENETICS

In **Extending Mendelian Genetics,** you read about the alleles that produce the different phenotypes in the ABO blood group.

**VIRTUAL Lab**

HMDScience.com

PREMIUM CONTENT

**Blood Typing**

Another blood protein, known as the **Rh factor,** is also critical in making a successful transfusion. People either are Rh positive (Rh⁺) and have this protein or are Rh negative (Rh⁻) and do not have it. Anyone can receive Rh⁻ blood without harm. However, if you are Rh⁻ and receive Rh⁺ blood, your immune system will make proteins that cause the Rh⁺ blood cells to swell and burst. As a result, blood must be matched for both the ABO group and the Rh group. The possible ABO/Rh blood combinations are shown in **FIGURE 5.4**.

| FIGURE 5.4  ABO Rh BLOOD COMBINATIONS | | |
|:---:|:---:|:---:|
| **BLOOD TYPE** | **CAN DONATE TO** | **CAN RECEIVE FROM** |
| **A** | A, AB | A, O |
| **B** | AB, B | B, O |
| **AB** | AB | A, B, AB, O |
| **O** | A, B, AB, O | O |
| **Rh FACTOR** | **CAN DONATE TO** | **CAN RECEIVE FROM** |
| **Rh⁺ factor** | Rh⁺ | Rh⁺, Rh⁻ |
| **Rh⁻ factor** | Rh⁺, Rh⁻ | Rh⁻ |

## White Blood Cells

**White blood cells,** which contain no hemoglobin, are cells that defend the body against infection and that remove foreign material and dead cells. Different kinds of white blood cells defend the body in different ways. Some surround and ingest microorganisms. Others produce proteins that act to destroy pathogens. Unlike red blood cells, white blood cells are not limited to the circulatory system. Some of these cells are able to pass through capillary walls into the lymphatic system and attack pathogens in the body's tissues. For this reason, white blood cells are also considered part of the immune system.

## Platelets and Blood Clotting

Platelets are cell fragments that help form clots that control bleeding. When you cut or tear a blood vessel, platelets quickly cluster around the wound.

**Repairing injuries** At the site of an injury, platelets form spiky extensions that intertwine into a complex net. The platelets then release proteins known as clotting factors, which begin the process of repair. One of the factors converts prothrombin, a plasma protein, into thrombin. Thrombin, in turn, converts fibrinogen into fibrin. Sticky threads of fibrin form a web that traps platelets and white blood cells, as the top photo shows in **FIGURE 5.5.**

The bottom photo shows how the tangle of fibrin, platelets, and blood cells has grown to form a plug, or clot, on the blood vessel. The clot seals the wound and prevents any further loss of blood. The steps in blood clotting are a good example of a positive feedback loop. The body increases the rate of change in clotting until the wound is sealed. Once the injury heals, other chemicals are released that dissolve the clot.

**Blood clotting disorders** Blood clots can also form inside blood vessels and present serious risks to a person's health. For example, clots that block arteries to the heart or brain can cause a heart attack or stroke. Medications that thin the blood or dissolve clots can help prevent these circulatory problems.

The inability to form clots can be equally serious. For example, hemophilia is a genetic disorder in which a key clotting factor is missing in the blood. For people with hemophilia, even a minor cut can cause life-threatening bleeding. As a result, they must guard against the slightest scrape or bruise. When injured, they must have the missing clotting factor injected into their blood to help seal the wound.

**Apply** **Why might it be important for white blood cells to be part of a clot that seals an injury?**

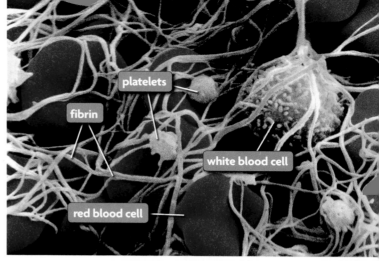
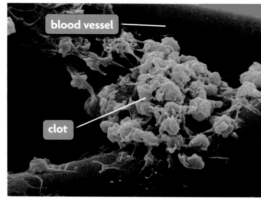

**FIGURE 5.5** The top photograph shows platelets clustering at the site of a wound. Fibrin threads trap more cells until a plug, or clot, forms (bottom) and stops the bleeding from a blood vessel. (colored SEMs; magnifications: platelets and fibrin 6000×; clot 1900×)

*(t) ©Photo Researchers, Inc.; (cr) ©CNRI/Photo Researchers, Inc.*

---

## 27.5 Formative Assessment

**SELF-CHECK Online**
HMDScience.com
**PREMIUM CONTENT**

### REVIEWING ▶ MAIN IDEAS

1. List some of the substances dissolved in **plasma** and describe how they help maintain homeostasis.

2. What are the primary roles of red blood cells, **white blood cells,** and **platelets**?

### CRITICAL THINKING

3. **Apply** What would happen if a person with type A Rh⁻ blood were transfused with type A Rh⁺ blood?

4. **Infer** Some people must take medications that interfere with clotting factors. How might they need to change their activities?

### CONNECT TO

#### CHEMISTRY

5. Water is the most abundant component in human blood. What characteristic of water allows glucose, hormones, and many other materials to dissolve into it?

# Lymphatic System

VOCABULARY

**VOCABULARY**

lymphatic system
lymph
node
lymphocyte

**KEY CONCEPT**  **The lymphatic system provides another type of circulation in the body.**

**MAIN IDEAS**

- Lymph is collected from tissues and returned to the circulatory system.
- The lymphatic system is a major part of the immune system.

## ☀ Connect to Your World

Your body has two transport networks that circulate fluids. The first is the circulatory system, which brings gases and nutrients to every cell. The second is the lymphatic system. While this system also helps to distribute nutrients, its main jobs are to absorb excess fluid, to fight disease, and to carry waste products away from the cells. These two systems work so closely together that almost everywhere there are blood vessels, there are also lymph vessels.

▶ **MAIN IDEA**

## Lymph is collected from tissues and returned to the circulatory system.

The **lymphatic system** (lihm-FAT-ihk) consists of a complex network of organs, vessels, and nodes throughout the body, as shown in **FIGURE 6.1**. The system collects excess fluid that leaks out of the blood capillaries into the area between the cells. This fluid, called interstitial (IHN-tuhr-STIHSH-uhl) fluid, brings nutrients to the cells and removes their wastes.

Although 90 percent of the fluid returns to the capillaries, up to 3 liters (3 qt) per day remain outside the blood vessels. Without the lymphatic system, your body would begin to swell as more fluid becomes trapped in your tissues. The system prevents this problem through a two-step process:

- It collects the fluid and filters it to remove dead cells and microorganisms.
- It returns the cleaned fluid to the circulatory system.

Lymphatic circulation begins when the fluid between the cells enters the lymphatic capillaries, where it becomes known as **lymph.** The lymph then flows into larger vessels within the lymphatic system. Without a heart to pump the fluid, the vessels rely on contractions of skeletal and smooth muscles to circulate the lymph. One-way valves similar to those in veins keep the fluid from flowing backwards.

From the vessels, lymph collects in small rounded structures called lymph **nodes.** The nodes filter the lymph and trap bacteria, viruses, fungi, and cell fragments. Specialized immune cells ingest and destroy this organic material. Vessels then carry the lymph out of the nodes. In the last stage of the journey, the lymph returns to the circulatory system. Two large vessels, one on either side of the body, enter veins located just under the collarbones. The lymph is returned to the blood and becomes part of the circulatory system again.

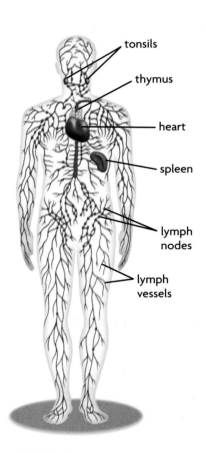

tonsils
thymus
heart
spleen
lymph nodes
lymph vessels

**FIGURE 6.1** The lymphatic system collects fluid that leaks from the blood vessels and returns it to the heart. The spleen recycles old red blood cells; white blood cells mature in the thymus.

When lymphatic tissues and nodes are damaged or removed, lymph cannot drain normally from that area. The result is swelling as fluid accumulates. The swelling can be controlled by exercise, pressure bandages or garments, and massage. These treatments exert pressure on the tissues and nodes to "push" lymph into the vessels.

**Predict  How would sitting for a long time affect the lymphatic circulation?**

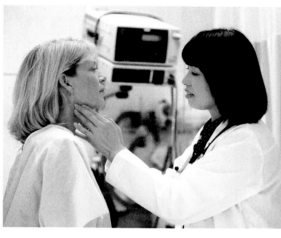

FIGURE 6.2  Doctors check your lymph nodes during a routine physical examination. Enlarged or lumpy nodes might indicate that your body is fighting an infection.

## ◉ MAIN IDEA
# The lymphatic system is a major part of the immune system.

Three structures in the lymphatic system—the tonsils, thymus, and spleen—also function as part of the immune system. Each of these structures has specialized functions that help the body to defend itself. The tonsils are lymph nodes set in the back of the throat on either side. These nodes help to filter out bacteria and viruses that have escaped the body's outer defenses. When too many pathogens collect in the tonsils, these nodes become swollen and infected and may have to be removed.

The thymus, located behind the breastbone, is important in developing certain types of white blood cells known as **lymphocytes** (LIHM-fuh-sYTs). These cells help the body fight pathogens, parasites, and other types of foreign organisms. Some immature lymphocytes migrate from the bone marrow to the thymus, where they develop the ability to recognize specific microorganisms. Most of these cells leave the thymus and circulate through the lymphatic and circulatory systems to protect the body.

The spleen is the largest organ in the lymphatic system. Its main job is to filter and clean the lymph of cell fragments and abnormal tissue. This organ also contains many lymphocytes and other white blood cells that destroy harmful bacteria and foreign organisms.

**Predict  If the spleen is removed, how might the immune and lymphatic systems be affected?**

> **CONNECT TO**
>
> **IMMUNE SYSTEM**
>
> You will read more in **Immune System and Disease** about how the body uses lymphocytes and other types of cells to fight pathogens.

**SELF-CHECK Online**
HMDScience.com
PREMIUM CONTENT

## 27.6  Formative Assessment

### REVIEWING ◉ MAIN IDEAS

1. Describe the main organs and functions of the **lymphatic system.**

2. Give three examples of organs that are part of both the immune and lymphatic systems, and briefly describe their functions.

### CRITICAL THINKING

3. **Compare and Contrast**  How are the structures of an artery and a vein different from or similar to the structure of a **lymph** vessel?

4. **Infer**  The circulatory system of the blood is a closed system. Is the lymphatic system a closed or an open system? Explain your answer.

> **CONNECT TO**
>
> **IMMUNOLOGY**
>
> 5. Mononucleosis is a disease that causes the body to greatly increase the number of **lymphocytes** circulating in the blood and lymph. If you felt the spleen and looked at the tonsils of someone with mononucleosis, what might you observe and why?

©Dynamics Graphics Group/Creatas/Alamy Images

# 27 Summary

**INTERACTIVE Review**
HMDScience.com

**PREMIUM CONTENT**

Review Games • Concept Map • Section Self-Checks

## KEY CONCEPTS

### 27.1 Respiratory and Circulatory Functions

**The respiratory and circulatory systems bring oxygen and nutrients to the cells.** These two systems work together to maintain homeostasis. The respiratory system moves gases into and out of the blood. The circulatory system transports blood to all parts of the body.

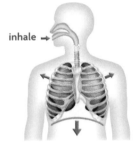 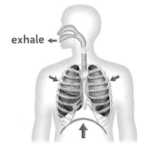

inhale → ← exhale

### 27.2 Respiration and Gas Exchange

**The respiratory system exchanges oxygen and carbon dioxide.** Gas exchange occurs in the alveoli of the lungs, where oxygen and carbon dioxide diffuse into and out of the blood. Respiratory diseases such as emphysema and asthma interfere with gas exchange.

### 27.3 The Heart and Circulation

**The heart is a muscular pump that moves the blood through two pathways.** The tissues and structures of the heart make it an efficient pump and allow it to work continuously. The heartbeat consists of two contractions that move blood from the atria to the ventricles. Blood circulates through the pulmonary and systemic pathways.

### 27.4 Blood Vessels and Transport

**The circulatory system transports materials throughout the body.** Arteries, veins, and capillaries transport blood to all the cells. The force with which blood pushes against the wall of an artery is known as blood pressure. The health of the circulatory system can be supported or harmed by lifestyle choices.

### 27.5 Blood

**Blood is a complex tissue that transports materials.** Blood is composed mainly of cells, platelets, and plasma. Red blood cells transport gases, white blood cells help fight diseases, and platelets help seal wounds. Proteins in blood determine blood type and Rh+ and Rh- factors. The ABO group is the most commonly used of all the blood grouping systems.

### 27.6 Lymphatic System

**The lymphatic system provides another type of circulation in the body.** The lymphatic system collects excess fluid between the cells, filters it, and returns it to the circulatory system. The lymphatic system is also an important part of the immune system.

---

### ⟳ READING TOOLBOX    SYNTHESIZE YOUR NOTES

**Venn Diagram** Use a Venn diagram to help you compare structures in the respiratory and circulatory systems.

arteries                          veins

thicker, more muscular   • same three tissue layers  • part of closed system   thinner, with valves

**Concept Map** A concept map is a good way to organize your notes on topics such as the components of blood.

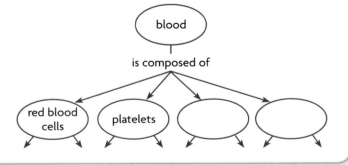

blood

is composed of

red blood cells    platelets

# 27 Review

## CHAPTER VOCABULARY

**27.1**
circulatory systems
respiratory systems
trachea
lung
alveoli
diaphragm
heart
artery
vein
capillaries

**27.2** red blood cell
hemoglobin

emphysema
asthma

**27.3** atrium
ventricle
valve
pacemaker
pulmonary circulation
systemic circulation

**27.4** blood pressure
systolic pressure
diastolic pressure

**27.5** platelet
plasma
ABO blood group
Rh factor
white blood cells

**27.6** lymphatic system
lymph
node
lymphocyte

## Reviewing Vocabulary

### Term Relationships

For each pair of terms below, write a sentence that describes or explains a relationship between the two terms. For example, *oxygen*, *carbon dioxide*: All cells use oxygen and produce carbon dioxide as a waste product.

1. vein, capillary
2. atrium, ventricle
3. artery, heart
4. systemic circulation, pulmonary circulation
5. systolic pressure, diastolic pressure
6. platelet, plasma
7. lung, trachea
8. lymph, lymphocyte

### READING TOOLBOX   GREEK AND LATIN WORD ORIGINS

For each term below, describe how its Latin or Greek meaning relates to its definition.

9. *Alveolus* comes from the Latin term *alveus*, which means "small hollow space."

10. *Emphysema* comes from the Greek term *emphysan*, which means "to inflate."

11. *Hemoglobin* is a combination of the Greek term *haima*, which means "blood," and the word *globin*, which refers to a protein.

12. *Plasma* comes from the Greek term *plassein*, which means "to mold or spread thin."

## Reviewing MAIN IDEAS

13. When you exercise, your need for $O_2$ rises. How do your respiratory and circulatory systems react to maintain homeostasis in your body?

14. Describe how the diaphragm and muscles of the rib cage help bring air into and out of the lungs.

15. Explain how, in normal respiration, $CO_2$ and $O_2$ are able to diffuse in opposite directions through the alveolar and capillary walls.

16. How does damage to the alveoli from injury or disease affect the exchange of gases in the lungs?

17. Describe how the structures of the heart make it an efficient pump.

18. Explain how the circulatory system keeps oxygen-poor blood separate from oxygen-rich blood.

19. Compare the functions of arteries and veins.

20. Advice for maintaining a healthy circulatory system always includes proper diet and exercise. Explain what impact these two factors can have on the arteries.

21. Describe the main components of blood and the function of each component.

22. Explain what happens after a blood vessel is torn.

23. Why might it be important to know your blood type?

24. Explain what the lymphatic system is and why it is considered part of the immune system.

# Critical Thinking

25. **Infer** When people lift or push a heavy weight, their veins often puff up and become visible under their skin. Why do you think this happens?

26. **Synthesize** A person who is exposed to high levels of smoke during a fire may be taken to a hospital for a test to determine whether he or she has enough oxygen in the blood. Would you test the blood from an artery or a vein in this case? Explain your answer.

27. **Analyze** In volcanic areas, certain depressions in the ground are filled with high levels of $CO_2$. Animals wandering into these areas die so quickly that they have no chance of getting out. Use your knowledge of diffusion and circulation to explain why death might occur so quickly.

28. **Apply** If someone has a heavy weight on his or her chest, explain why after a short time it becomes difficult to breathe, even though the person's mouth and nose are not affected.

29. **Predict** A stroke occurs when the blood supply to the brain is interrupted. What immediate impact would this event have on the brain cells?

## Interpreting Visuals

Use the diagram of the heart to answer the next three questions.

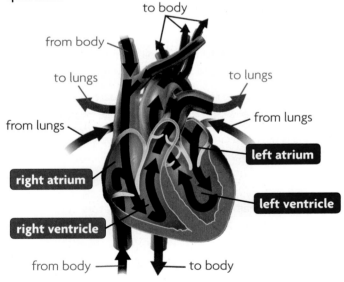

30. **Identify** Describe the path of blood in the heart.

31. **Infer** Why does the heart need two openings leading into the right atrium?

32. **Analyze** Which chamber(s) and valve(s) do you think would be under the most stress from high blood pressure? Explain.

## Analyzing Data Form a Null Hypothesis

A scientist is investigating the relationship between age and rates of smoking—light, medium, or heavy. Use the graph below about age and smoking rates to answer the next two questions about accepting or rejecting a null hypothesis

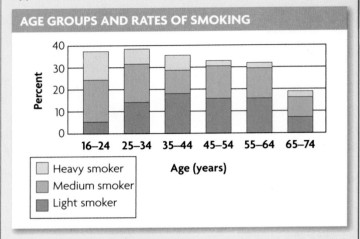

33. **Evaluate** One null hypothesis for this investigation might be: "There is no relationship between age and smoking rates." Based on the data, would you accept or reject this null hypothesis? Explain your answer.

34. **Apply** Form another null hypothesis for this investigation based on age and smoking rates. Explain whether the data would cause you to accept or reject your hypothesis.

## Making Connections

35. **Write a Proposal** Suppose you are asked to make an animated film about the journey of an oxygen molecule from the time it is inhaled until it reaches a cell. Write a proposal describing your concept for the film. Include in your description the names of structures in the circulatory and respiratory systems, such as *trachea, alveoli, atrium, ventricle,* and so on.

36. **Synthesize** The heart and lungs work very efficiently, but they can be strengthened by exercise to work even better. For instance, the heart rate of an athlete at rest is actually lower than the resting heart rate of a person who does not regularly exercise. Why do you think this is so? Use your knowledge of the muscular, circulatory, and respiratory systems in your answer.

# Standards-Based Assessment

**1.**

| Blood Type Compatibility | |
|---|---|
| **Blood Type** | **Can Receive Blood From** |
| A | A or O |
| B | B or O |
| AB | A, B, AB, O |
| O | O |

This chart shows compatibility between different blood types. What would happen if a person with type O blood received a blood transfusion of any other blood type?

A There would be no complications because any blood type can be exchanged for another.

B Complications would result as the immune system attacks the foreign blood cells.

C A larger amount of the different blood type would be needed to supply the missing protein.

D There would be complications only if type AB were given.

**2.** The circulatory and respiratory systems work together to provide cells with oxygen and nutrients and remove waste products such as carbon dioxide. When you need *more* oxygen, how does the circulatory system respond?

A More blood is sent to the lungs and less to the rest of the body.

B The blood vessels to the arms and legs constrict to conserve oxygen.

C The heart beats faster to match the rise in breathing rate.

D Blood moves more slowly through the organs to carry away more wastes.

**3.** In order for the body to maintain homeostasis, the intake of oxygen into the lungs *must* be followed by

A an increase in blood pressure.

B the exhalation of carbon dioxide.

C a decrease in gas exchange.

D a decrease in blood flow.

**4.**

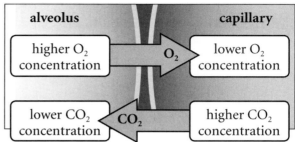

As shown above, gas exchange occurs between the alveoli and the capillaries of the lungs. What process is this diagram illustrating?

A circulation

B absorption

C diffusion

D exhalation

**5.** At higher elevations, the air has a lower concentration of oxygen. What effect would living at higher elevations have on a person's lung capacity?

A It would be larger to take in more oxygen.

B It would be smaller because the lungs need less oxygen.

C It would be larger because there is more carbon dioxide.

D It would be the same regardless of elevation.

> **THINK THROUGH THE QUESTION**
>
> Think about what *concentration* means in this context. At higher elevations, a standard breath of air would contain less oxygen than would the same volume of air at lower elevations.

**6.** The circulatory system helps to maintain a stable body temperature as you exercise. Which statement *best* describes this process?

A Heat produced by the muscles is absorbed by the surrounding blood, where it cools.

B Blood carries excess heat from the muscles to the skin, which allows heat to escape.

C The circulatory and lymphatic systems work together to remove heat from the muscles.

D Excess heat from the muscles is transported to the heart and lungs, where it cools.

## ONLINE BIOLOGY
HMDScience.com

**ONLINE** Labs
- **QuickLab** How Pathogens Spread
- Observing Normal and Diseased Tissue
- Modeling T Cell Activation
- What Is an Autoimmune Disease?
- Simulating Viral Detection with ELISA
- Food Allergies
- **Video Lab** Disease Transmission Model

  PREMIUM CONTENT

**Leukemia and the Immune System**
Meet a leukemia patient who has had a bone marrow transplant and learn about this experience.

(t) ©Saturn/Science Photo Library/Corbis

## Q How do your cells fight off invaders?

You do not get sick every time disease-causing germs invade your body. Sometimes white blood cells, like the one in blue shown here, attack and destroy invaders without your feeling ill. Other times, you get sick because germs, such as these red *E. coli*, start winning. Fortunately, a healthy immune system can overpower many different types of germs—even when the germs temporarily gain the upper hand.

---

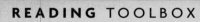

### READING TOOLBOX     This reading tool can help you learn the material in the following pages.

#### USING LANGUAGE

**Mnemonics** Mnemonic devices are tools that can help you memorize words, steps, and concepts that go together. Use the first letter of every word you want to remember as the first letter of a new word, in a sentence that is easy to remember. For example, the trees *maple, dogwood, ash* and *sycamore* can be remembered by the mnemonic "My Dear Aunt Sally."

#### YOUR TURN

Create mnemonic devices to help you remember the following groups of words.

1. The four parts of blood: *red cells, white cells, platelets,* and *plasma*
2. The four major tissue types: *epithelial, nervous, connective,* and *muscle*

# Pathogens and Human Illness

**SC.912.L.14.6**

| **KEY CONCEPT** **Germs cause many diseases in humans.**

**MAIN IDEAS**

- Germ theory states that microscopic particles cause certain diseases.
- There are different types of pathogens.
- Pathogens can enter the body in different ways.

## VOCABULARY

germ theory
pathogen
vector

**SC.912.L.14.6** Explain the significance of genetic factors, environmental factors, and pathogenic agents to health from the perspectives of both individual and public health.

### Connect to Your World

Diseases caused by germs, such as the *E. coli* bacteria on the previous page, can be fatal. From 1330 to 1352, the bacteria that caused the Black Death killed 43 million people worldwide, or 13 percent of the population at the time. In 1918, a viral disease called the Spanish flu killed between 20 and 50 million people worldwide, or as much as 3 percent of the population. Because diseases can have devastating effects, scientists become concerned whenever new diseases appear.

### ▶ MAIN IDEA

## Germ theory states that microscopic particles cause certain diseases.

A disease can be either infectious or noninfectious. Infectious diseases, such as flu and polio, can be passed from one person to another because infectious diseases are caused by germs. In contrast, cancer and heart disease are non-infectious diseases. These diseases are called noninfectious because a sick person cannot pass the disease to, or infect, a healthy person. Noninfectious diseases are not due to germs; they may result from genetic factors or lifestyle.

## FIGURE 1.1 History of Medicine

**Most modern understanding about diseases occurred after Pasteur's germ theory.**

**B.C. 7000**
**Spirits** Ancient societies drill holes in people's heads to release the evil spirits believed to cause disease.

**A.D. 1330–1352**
**Herbal treatments** People use incense in an attempt to cure those with the Black Death, caused by bacteria transmitted by rats' fleas.

(LM; magnification 15×)

**1857**
**Germ theory** Louis Pasteur hypothesizes that disease is caused by small "animals."

B.C. ◆ A.D.      1400    1600      1800

**B.C. 460–B.C. 377**
**Humors** Greek physician Hippocrates hypothesizes that fluids, called humors, cause disease.

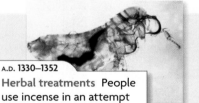

**1400–1600**
**Anatomy** People begin to study anatomy. This drawing was made in the Middle East in 1555.

**1865**
**Antiseptic technique** Joseph Lister finds that cleaning his surgical tools reduces patients' infections.

On the other hand, infectious diseases can be passed from one person to another because infectious diseases are caused by germs.

Today, it seems obvious that some germs cause infectious disease, but this concept is only a little more than 100 years old. It was not until the 1850s that French scientist Louis Pasteur helped make the connection between microorganisms and disease. His theory, called the **germ theory** of disease, proposed that specific microorganisms caused diseases. These disease-causing agents are called **pathogens.** Pasteur hypothesized that if pathogens were eliminated from the body, a person would not get sick.

Pasteur's germ theory led to rapid advances in our understanding of disease, as shown in **FIGURE 1.1.** But at the time, germ theory was not immediately accepted. It took the work of two other scientists to bring about the complete acceptance of Pasteur's germ theory.

Between 1861 and 1865, about half of British surgeon Joseph Lister's patients died from infections after otherwise successful operations. After hearing Pasteur's germ theory, Lister began using a weak acid to clean his operating tools and his patients' wounds before surgery. The number of his patients who died from infection dropped dramatically to near zero.

Meanwhile, German scientist Robert Koch found that he could make a healthy animal sick by injecting it with pathogens from a sick animal. From his experiments, he concluded that four conditions must be met before one can say that a certain pathogen causes a disease. These conditions are called Koch's postulates.

- The pathogen thought to cause the disease must be present in every case in which the disease is found.
- The pathogen must be isolated and grown outside the body in a pure, uncontaminated culture.
- Healthy animals infected with the pure culture must develop the disease.
- The pathogen must be re-isolated and cultured from the newly sick animals and must be identical to the original pathogen.

**Contrast** **How is germ theory different from earlier theories about disease?**

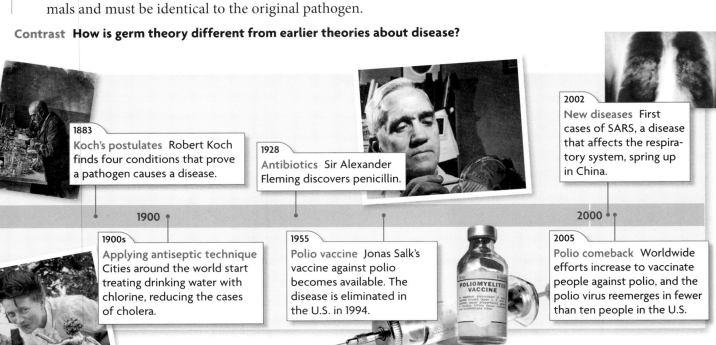

**1883**
**Koch's postulates** Robert Koch finds four conditions that prove a pathogen causes a disease.

**1928**
**Antibiotics** Sir Alexander Fleming discovers penicillin.

**2002**
**New diseases** First cases of SARS, a disease that affects the respiratory system, spring up in China.

**1900**

**2000**

**1900s**
**Applying antiseptic technique** Cities around the world start treating drinking water with chlorine, reducing the cases of cholera.

**1955**
**Polio vaccine** Jonas Salk's vaccine against polio becomes available. The disease is eliminated in the U.S. in 1994.

**2005**
**Polio comeback** Worldwide efforts increase to vaccinate people against polio, and the polio virus reemerges in fewer than ten people in the U.S.

POLIOMYELITIS VACCINE

> MAIN IDEA
# There are different types of pathogens.

Traditionally, bacteria and larger pathogens were isolated by straining them through a ceramic filter with tiny pores. The disease-causing bacteria would remain on the filter, and the solution that passed through the pores was harmless.

Sometimes, however, there were no visible pathogens on the filter, and the solution caused disease. By 1898, scientists had hypothesized that some disease-causing agents must be smaller than bacteria. They called these agents filterable viruses. As better technology was developed, scientists discovered a huge variety of tiny new pathogens, which are outlined below and in **FIGURE 1.2.**

⚡ **CONNECT TO**

**PATHOGENS**
You can read more about microorganisms and viruses that cause disease in **Viruses and Prokaryotes** and **Protists and Fungi**.

- **Bacteria** are single-celled organisms. They can cause illness by releasing chemicals that are toxic to the host or by destroying healthy body cells. Food poisoning, which causes a person to become nauseous, is a sickness caused by bacteria-released toxins.
- **Viruses** are disease-causing strands of DNA or RNA that are surrounded by protein coats. Viruses are so small that they could not be seen until the invention of the electron microscope in the 1930s. These particles enter and take over a healthy cell, forcing it to stop its normal activities and produce more viruses. Viruses cause illnesses such as flus, colds, and AIDS. You will learn more about AIDS in Section 6.
- **Fungi** can be multicellular or single-celled organisms, such as those you read about previously. The fungi that cause disease do so by piercing healthy cells and taking the cell's nutrients. Fungal infections usually occur in places that are warm and damp. Athlete's foot, for example, is a fungus that invades the skin cells between the toes.

## FIGURE 1.2  Common Infectious Diseases Worldwide

| DISEASE | PATHOGEN TYPE | HOW IT SPREADS | AFFECTED BODY SYSTEMS | DEATHS ANNUALLY |
|---|---|---|---|---|
| HIV | virus | body fluids | immune | 3,100,000 |
| Pneumonia | virus, bacteria | airborne | respiratory | 2,000,000 |
| Tuberculosis | bacteria | airborne | respiratory, digestive | 1,800,000 |
| Malaria | protozoa | mosquito bite | digestive, circulatory, muscular | 1,000,000 |
| Hepatitis B | virus | contaminated food/water | digestive, immune | 1,000,000 |
| Measles | virus | airborne | respiratory, nervous | 500,000 |
| Influenza | virus | airborne, direct contact | respiratory | 400,000 |

Source: World Health Organization

- **Protozoa** are single-celled organisms that prey on other cells. Like viruses, protozoa need healthy cells to complete their life cycles. Malaria is a blood disease that is caused by a protozoan. The chapter on protists and fungi includes a description of how the protozoan that causes malaria uses red blood cells to complete its life cycle.
- **Parasites** are organisms that grow and feed on a host. Some parasites kill the host, while others drain the body's resources without killing the host. **FIGURE 1.3** shows a filaria, a parasitic worm found in tropical climates. Filaria will rarely kill its host, although some forms, such as heartworm, can be fatal in mammals. You can read more about parasitic worms in the chapter on invertebrate diversity.

Although each of these pathogens is different, they all cause disease by attacking healthy cells. However, the way by which they attack varies.

**Summarize** **What do all of these pathogens do that makes a person sick?**

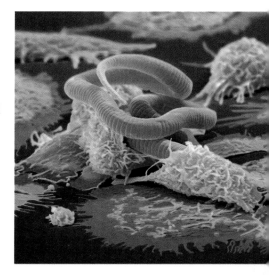

**FIGURE 1.3** Filaria, such as this one, enter the body through contaminated food and can grow to be a meter long. (colored SEM; magnification 2500×)

## ▶ MAIN IDEA

# Pathogens can enter the body in different ways.

Before a pathogen can make a person sick, it must get inside the body. Some pathogens can be transferred by direct or indirect contact. Pathogens that spread by direct contact are those that require an infected person or animal to physically touch a healthy person. Rabies, for example, is transferred when an infected animal bites a healthy animal. HIV is transmitted through an exchange of bodily fluids, such as during sexual intercourse or sharing of infected needles. It can also be transmitted from a mother to her child through the placenta or breast milk.

## QUICK LAB    MODELING

### How Pathogens Spread

Pathogens are disease-causing particles. In this lab, you will model how a pathogen spreads through a population.

**PROBLEM** From whom did the pathogen originate?

**PROCEDURE**

1. Obtain a cup filled with an unknown solution. Pour half your solution into a classmate's cup. Then pour the same amount from your classmate's cup back into your cup. Now your cup contains a mixture of the two solutions.

2. Repeat step 1 two more times with different classmates. Keep a record of with whom you exchanged solutions and in which order.

3. After you have exchanged solutions with three classmates, add three drops of "pathogen"-detecting solution to your cup. If your solution becomes pink, your cup contains the pathogen.

**ANALYZE AND CONCLUDE**

1. **Analyze** If your cup contained the pathogen, can you identify its origin? If your cup did not contain the pathogen, is it possible that any of the other solutions poured into your cup contained the pathogen?

2. **Analyze** Only one person in your class began with the pathogen in his or her cup. How can you determine whose cup had it?

**MATERIALS**

- 8-oz cup
- 100 mL unknown solution
- eyedropper
- 3 drops "pathogen"-detecting solution

**FIGURE 1.4** Sometimes even surfaces that we think are clean are covered with pathogens. Here you can see different types of pathogens clinging to a kitchen sponge. (colored SEM)

Pathogens that are spread by indirect contact can survive on nonliving surfaces, such as tables, door knobs, or kitchen sponges—as shown in **FIGURE 1.4**. Some parasitic worm larvae live in the soil and can burrow through the skin of a victim's bare foot. Once inside the body, the larvae travel into the victim's intestines. Species that remain in the intestines throughout their life cycle can cause discomfort, nausea, and diarrhea.

Other pathogens are spread through the air. When you cough or sneeze, you release droplets into the air around you. When you are sick, these droplets might contain pathogens. Other airborne pathogens are lightweight and hearty enough that they can survive in the air on dry particles. Respiratory diseases such as tuberculosis and SARS are examples of airborne diseases.

Still other pathogens are spread by vectors. A **vector** is anything that carries a pathogen and transmits it into healthy cells. Insects are examples of vectors. Insects can transmit bacteria, viruses, and protozoa. The Black Death, which killed millions of people in the 1300s, is caused by a bacterium that lives in the stomach of a rat's flea. People got sick with the Black Death when they were bitten by a contaminated flea. Mosquitoes can also pass diseases between animals. The protozoan that causes malaria, for example, completes a part of its life cycle in the gut of a mosquito. Mosquitoes can also transmit diseases between species. West Nile virus originally affected birds, but when an infected mosquito bites a person with a weak immune system, the virus can cause the person's brain to swell. However, insects cannot transmit pathogens, such as HIV, that die when the insect digests the infected human blood cells.

Pathogens can also be transmitted through food. Some diseases are caused by pathogens that were alive when the food-animal lived. Mad cow disease, which causes neurological problems in humans, is caused by an abnormal protein that is found in some beef cattle. Salmonella, which causes vomiting, is found in the intestines of some pigs and other animals. Most parasitic worm eggs enter the body through the mouth, as when a person eats contaminated food. Other diseases, such as various types of food poisoning, are caused by bacteria or fungi that decompose food.

**Infer** Why are some diseases only spread by insect bites?

©SCIMAT/Science Photo Library/Science Source

# 28.1 Formative Assessment

## REVIEWING ▶ MAIN IDEAS

1. What conditions must be met before a specific **pathogen** is proved to cause a disease?

2. Name five general types of pathogens.

3. What are some ways in which pathogens spread?

## CRITICAL THINKING

4. **Contrast** How do bacteria and viruses differ in the ways they affect cells in the body?

5. **Synthesize** How did the work of Lister and Koch support Pasteur's **germ theory** of disease?

## CONNECT TO

### VIRUSES

6. Viruses infect healthy cells by injecting their genetic material into them. How are viruses similar to **vectors**? If the virus is the vector, what is the pathogen?

# Immune System

**KEY CONCEPT** The immune system consists of organs, cells, and molecules that fight infections.

## VOCABULARY

immune system
phagocyte
T cell
B cell
antibody
interferon
passive immunity
active immunity

**SC.912.L.14.52** Explain the basic functions of the human immune system, including specific and nonspecific immune response, vaccines, and antibiotics.

### MAIN IDEAS

- Many body systems protect you from pathogens.
- Cells and proteins fight the body's infections.
- Immunity prevents a person from getting sick from a pathogen.

### ☼ Connect to Your World

Think of your body as a heavily guarded castle. When pathogens come to invade, they must first break down the outer wall or find a way around it. If the intruders get past the physical barriers, they must face your body's fighters in hand-to-hand combat. When the invaders gain the upper hand, you become sick. When the body's defenses are winning the war, you remain healthy.

### ⏵ MAIN IDEA

## Many body systems protect you from pathogens.

The **immune system** is the body system that fights off infection and pathogens. Just as a castle has several lines of defense, so does your body's immune system. The immune system relies on physical barriers to keep pathogens out. However, when pathogens get past the physical barriers, the warrior cells of the immune system travel through the lymphatic and circulatory systems to reach the site of infection.

Your skin is your body's first line of defense. Like a castle's outer wall, the skin surrounds and protects your insides. The skin physically blocks invading pathogens. The skin also secretes oil and sweat, which make the skin hypertonic and acidic. Many pathogens cannot survive in this kind of environment.

Just as a castle's walls have doors and windows, your skin also has openings. For example, your eyes, nose, ears, mouth, and excretory organs are open to the environment, and so they need extra protection. Mucous membranes in these organs use hairlike cilia that are covered with a sticky liquid to trap pathogens before they move into the body, as shown in **FIGURE 2.1.**

### ☼ CONNECT TO

#### HYPERTONIC

You learned in **Cell Structure and Function** that when the environment has more solutes than a cell, water will diffuse out of the cell and the cell could die.

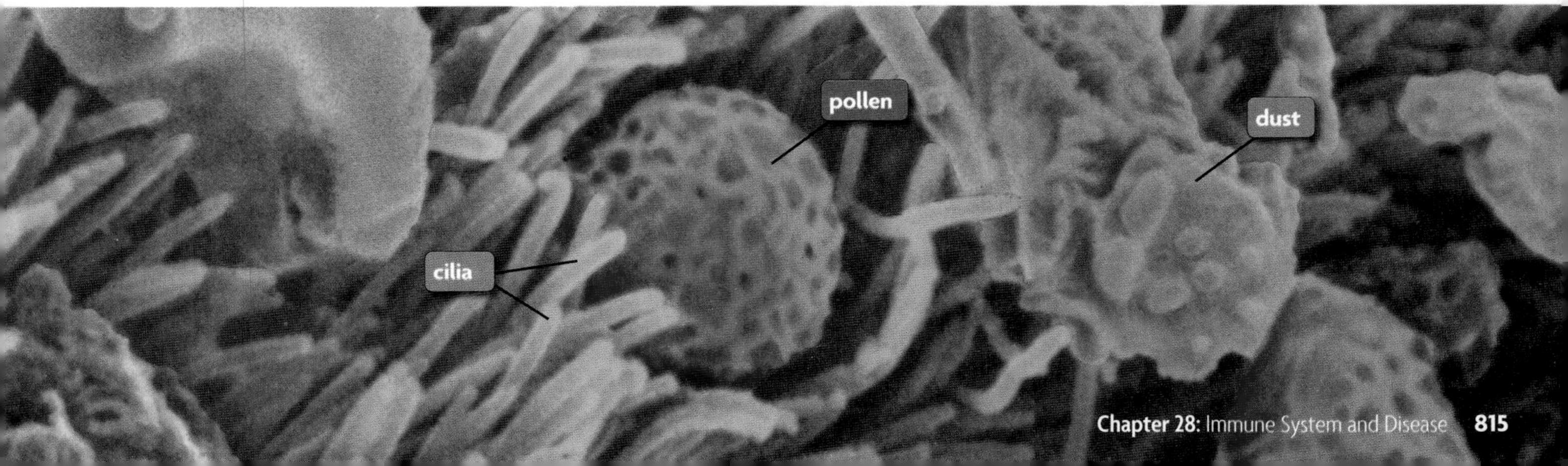

**FIGURE 2.1** Cilia that line the throat (yellow) capture foreign particles. (colored SEM; magnification 7500×)

©E. Gray/Photo Researchers, Inc.

pollen

dust

cilia

Even with skin and mucous membranes to protect you, some pathogens still get into the body. Once pathogens are inside, the immune system relies on the circulatory system to send chemical signals to coordinate an attack and to transport specialized cells to the infection.

**Summarize**  **Name some of the tissues that help to prevent and fight infection.**

## ▶ MAIN IDEA

# Cells and proteins fight the body's infections.

Once pathogens get past all of your outer defenses, the cells of your immune system spring into action. Just as a castle has many fighters and weapons, your immune system has many types of white blood cells and proteins.

### White Blood Cells

White blood cells find and kill pathogens that have gotten past the body's external barriers. The six main types of white blood cells and their roles in fighting infection are summarized in **FIGURE 2.2**.

When a pathogen enters the body, basophils in the blood stream or mast cells found in other tissues release chemical signals. These signals attract other white blood cells to the site of the infection. If the pathogen is a parasite, eosinophils come and spray the parasite with poison. If the pathogen is a virus, bacterium, or fungus, neutrophils and macrophages go to work. These cells are phagocytes. A **phagocyte** (FAG-uh-SYT) is a cell that destroys pathogens by surrounding and engulfing them.

**VISUAL VOCAB**

A **phagocyte** is a cell that engulfs and destroys other cells. It comes from Greek words that translate to mean "cell eater."

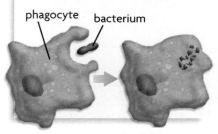

phagocyte          bacterium

After phagocytes, lymphocytes reach the infection. Lymphocytes are white blood cells that initiate the specific immune responses, which you will read about in Section 3. There are two types of lymphocytes: T-lymphocytes and B-lymphocytes, also called T cells and B cells. **T cells** destroy body cells that are infected with pathogens. **B cells** produce proteins that inactivate pathogens that have not yet infected a body cell.

**CONNECT TO**

**LYMPHOCYTES**

Recall from **Respiratory and Circulatory Systems** that lymphocytes are cells of the lymphatic system that attack disease-causing particles.

## FIGURE 2.2  White Blood Cells

| NAME | FUNCTION |
|---|---|
| Basophil | makes chemicals that cause inflammation in the bloodstream |
| Mast cell | makes chemicals that cause inflammation in other body tissues |
| Neutrophil | engulfs pathogens and foreign invaders; phagocyte |
| Macrophage | engulfs dead or damaged body cells and some bacteria; phagocyte |
| Lymphocyte | destroys infected body cells or produces proteins that inactivate pathogens |
| Eosinophil | injects poisonous packets into parasites, such as protozoa |

## IDENTIFYING EXPERIMENTAL DESIGN FLAWS

Sometimes scientific investigations can be flawed as a result of how the experiments were designed. Such design problems could include having a sample that is not representative of the population or one that is too small. This can result in the collection of invalid data, incorrect conclusions, and the release of misleading information.

To study how common certain diseases are in the United States, a student interviews 100 people as they exit a small Midwestern hospital. The student asks them if they have ever had any of five specific infectious diseases. He calculates the percent of people who responded "yes" to each question and puts the data in the graph to the right.

Based on his data, the student concludes that chickenpox is the most contagious disease of the five diseases studied. He also concludes that people in the United States no longer get tuberculosis.

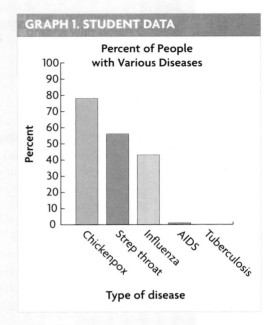

**GRAPH 1. STUDENT DATA**

Percent of People with Various Diseases

*(y-axis: Percent, 0 to 100; x-axis: Type of disease — Chickenpox, Strep throat, Influenza, AIDS, Tuberculosis)*

1. **Evaluate** What problems exist with the sample population in this investigation?

2. **Analyze** Are the conclusions drawn from this data accurate? Why or why not?

3. **Evaluate** How could this investigation be redesigned to produce valid results?

## Proteins

The immune system uses three types of proteins to fight off invading pathogens: complement proteins, antibodies, and interferons.

- Complement proteins are made by white blood cells and by certain organs. Some complement proteins weaken a pathogen's cell membrane, allowing water to enter the cell and cause it to burst. Others attract phagocytes to the infected area. Still others cause microbes to stick to the walls of blood vessels, where they can more easily be found and destroyed by circulating phagocytes.

- **Antibodies** are proteins made by B cells. Antibodies destroy pathogens in one of three ways. Antibodies might make the pathogen ineffective by binding to the pathogen's membrane proteins. As **FIGURE 2.3** shows, antibodies might also cause pathogens to clump, making them easier for phagocytes to engulf and destroy. Other antibodies activate complement proteins that weaken the pathogen's cell membrane.

- **Interferons** (ihn-tuhr-FEER-AHNZ) are proteins produced by body cells that are infected by a virus. Cells release interferons, which stimulate uninfected body cells to produce enzymes that will prevent viruses from entering and infecting them. If viruses cannot enter healthy cells, they cannot reproduce. Other interferons stimulate an inflammation response.

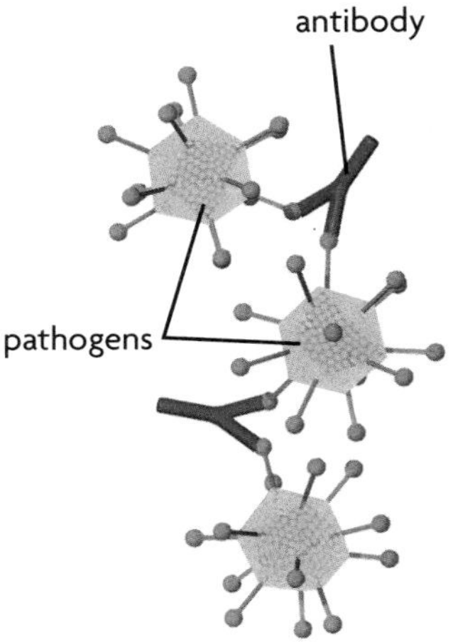

**FIGURE 2.3** Antibodies help the immune system. Some types of antibodies cause pathogens to clump, making them easier to engulf and destroy.

*(labels: antibody, pathogens)*

**Compare and Contrast** **What are some differences between the ways white blood cells and proteins fight infections?**

▶ MAIN IDEA

# Immunity prevents a person from getting sick from a pathogen.

If you are immune to a pathogen, it means that you will not get sick when that pathogen invades your body. There are two types of immunity—passive and active.

## Passive Immunity

**Passive immunity** is immunity that occurs without the body's undergoing an immune response. Passive immunity is transferred between generations through DNA and between mother and child.

Some viruses can be spread between different species. A pathogen that infects a bird might infect a person as well. However, some viruses only make members of a specific species sick. Genetic immunity is immunity that a species has because a pathogen is not specialized to harming that species. Infants have another type of immunity. Inherited immunity occurs when pathogen-fighting antibodies in a mother's immune system are passed to the unborn baby through the umbilical cord or the mother's milk.

## Active Immunity

**Active immunity** is immunity that your body produces in response to a specific pathogen that has infected or is infecting your body. Acquired immunity is a type of active immunity that occurs after your immune system reacts to a pathogen invasion. Acquired immunity keeps you from becoming sick by a particular pathogen more than once. We will look more closely at how the immune system produces acquired immunity in the next section.

Sometimes people get the same colds or flus over and over again throughout their lifetimes. This occurs because the viruses that cause these sicknesses mutate very quickly. Each time a different strain of virus invades, your immune system has to start from the beginning again. On the other hand, your immune system destroys repeat invaders before you get sick.

**Contrast** How do passive and active immunity differ?

---

## 28.2 Formative Assessment

SELF-CHECK Online
HMDScience.com
PREMIUM CONTENT

### REVIEWING ▶ MAIN IDEAS

1. How does the **immune system** work with other body systems to prevent and fight disease?

2. How do **phagocytes** help to fight infections?

3. Which of the two types of immunity requires white blood cells? Explain.

### CRITICAL THINKING

4. **Contrast** How do complement proteins differ from **antibodies**?

5. **Predict** If a person had a disease that prevented lymphocytes from maturing, how would the immune system's response to infection change?

CONNECT TO

#### PROTEIN SYNTHESIS

6. How might a person's immune system be affected if a portion of the DNA that codes for **interferons** has mutated?

# GO Online!

## SHIELDS UP!

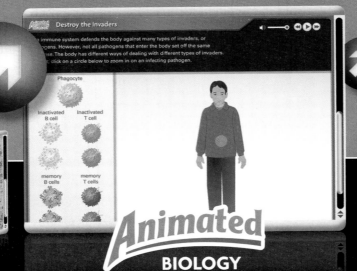

Destroy the Invaders

...e immune system defends the body against many types of invaders, or ...ogens. However, not all pathogens that enter the body set off the same ... The body has different ways of dealing with different types of invaders. ... click on a circle below to zoom in on an infecting pathogen.

Phagocyte

Inactivated B cell   Inactivated T cell

memory B cells   memory T cells

## Animated
### BIOLOGY

**THAT'S Amazing!** VIDEO INQUIRY

### WebQuest

**HIV and AIDS** Learn how HIV works and causes AIDS. Then explore how it is treated and look into ongoing research devoted

### Destroy the Invaders
Can you keep someone from contracting an illness? Use a set of immune cells to mount attacks against a variety of pathogens to keep a person healthy

**Snake Venom** Learn about how antivenom is made and how it can save your life if you are bitten by a snake!

# Immune Responses

SC.912.L.14.52

**SC.912.L.14.52** Explain the basic functions of the human immune system, including specific and nonspecific immune response, vaccines, and antibiotics.

**VOCABULARY**

inflammation
antigen
memory cell
cellular immunity
humoral immunity
tissue rejection

**KEY CONCEPT** **The immune system has many responses to pathogens and foreign cells.**

**MAIN IDEAS**

- Many body systems work to produce nonspecific responses.
- Cells of the immune system produce specific responses.
- The immune system rejects foreign tissues.

## Connect to Your World

Your body responds to pathogens in several different ways. For example, when you get a mosquito bite, your skin might swell and itch. After you are bitten, the skin around the bite becomes swollen, and the cells of your immune system attack the pathogens that entered the skin through the bite.

## ▶ MAIN IDEA

# Many body systems work to produce nonspecific responses.

The body responds to pathogens and foreign particles with specific and nonspecific responses. Responses that occur on the cellular level are called specific defenses. Specific responses are slightly different for each pathogen. Nonspecific immune responses are those that happen in the same way to every pathogen. Some examples of nonspecific defenses are inflammation and fever.

### Inflammation

**Inflammation** is a nonspecific response that is characterized by swelling, redness, pain, itching, and increased warmth at the affected site. Inflammation occurs when a pathogen enters the body or when the body's other tissues become damaged. For example, if you scrape your knee, it swells up. This occurs because the body is trying to head off pathogens that enter the body through the newly broken skin.

An inflammation response begins when mast cells or basophils release chemicals called histamines in response to a pathogen invasion. Histamines cause the cells in blood vessel walls to spread out. When this happens, fluids can move out of the blood vessel and into the surrounding tissues. White blood cells squeeze out of the capillary and move toward the site of infection, as shown in **FIGURE 3.1.** Once outside of the circulatory system, the white blood cells fight off the infection. When the pathogens are defeated, swelling stops, and tissue repair begins. Inflammation is a normal body response, but sometimes it occurs in response to things other than pathogens, as you will read in Section 5.

**FIGURE 3.1** When pathogens invade your body, white blood cells squeeze through the capillary wall and move toward the infection. (magnification unknown)

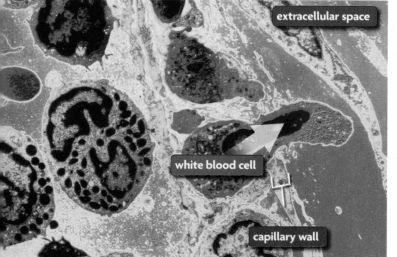

extracellular space

white blood cell

capillary wall

©Joubert/Phanie/Photo Researchers, Inc.

## Fever

Fevers develop when mast cells or macrophages release chemicals that cause the hypothalamus to increase the body's temperature. When the infection is controlled and the mast cell's chemicals are no longer being made, the body temperature returns to normal.

Fever is a response that affects the entire body. Low fevers, around 37.7°C (100°F), stimulate the production of interferons. Recall that interferons are proteins that prevent viruses from reproducing. Low fevers also increase the activity of white blood cells by increasing the rate at which they mature, as shown in **FIGURE 3.2.** Having many mature white blood cells is important because only mature cells can destroy pathogens. The more mature white blood cells in the body, the more quickly the body can fight off an infection.

While low fevers speed up pathogen destruction, high fevers—more than 39°C, or 103°F—are dangerous. Under high fever conditions, the hypothalamus can no longer regulate body temperature. Enzymes that control chemical reactions in the body stop functioning. High fever can cause seizure, brain damage, and even death.

**Connect  What body systems, other than the immune system, help to produce inflammation and fever?**

### FIGURE 3.2  WHITE BLOOD CELL MATURATION

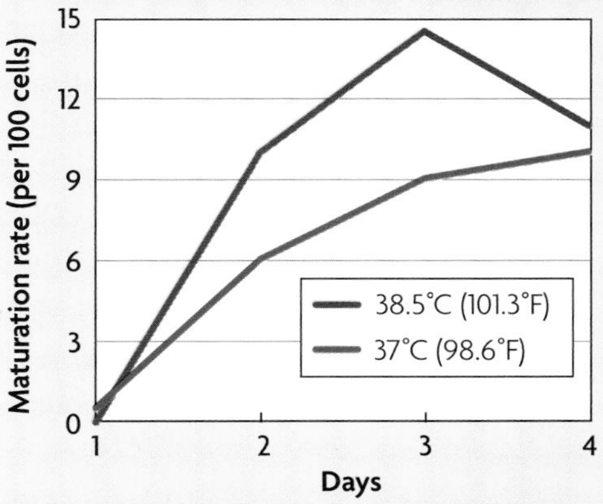

Scientists put immature white blood cells in a nutrient solution and found that they matured faster when the cells were heated as in a low fever (red line).

Source: Roberts, N. J. Jr. and R. T. Stergbigel. *American Society of Microbiology*

## ⊙ MAIN IDEA
# Cells of the immune system produce specific responses.

Specific immune defenses lead to acquired immunity, and they occur on the cellular level. For these specific immune defenses to work, the body must be able to tell the difference between its own healthy cells and foreign or infected cells. **Antigens** (AN-tih-juhnz) are protein markers on the surfaces of cells and viruses that help the immune system identify a foreign cell or virus. If pathogens are the invading army that is waging war on the immune system, then you can think of antigens as the pathogens' uniforms.

When the immune system detects a pathogen, it triggers an immune response. There are two types of specific immune system responses: cellular and humoral immune responses. Although the two responses are different, as you will read on the next page, they both produce acquired immunity. Immunity is acquired when your body produces memory cells after fighting off an infection. **Memory cells** are specialized T and B cells that provide acquired immunity because they "remember" an antigen that has previously invaded your body. So when memory cells come across this antigen a second time, they quickly destroy the pathogen before the body has a chance to get sick. You will learn more about how memory cells work in Section 4, when you read about vaccines. Now, we will discuss how the immune system fights a pathogen that it is encountering for the first time.

### ⊶ CONNECT TO

**T CELLS AND B CELLS**

Recall from Section 2 that T and B cells are lymphocytes that are specialized to fight off pathogens.
- T cells destroy infected body cells.
- B cells produce proteins that inactivate pathogens.

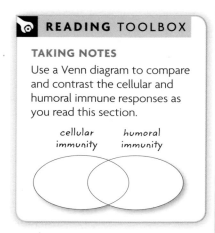

**READING** TOOLBOX

**TAKING NOTES**

Use a Venn diagram to compare and contrast the cellular and humoral immune responses as you read this section.

cellular immunity    humoral immunity

## Cellular Immunity

**Cellular immunity** is an immune response that depends on T cells. As shown in **FIGURE 3.3**, T cells attach to infected body cells and cause them to burst. Before they can do this, however, T cells must become activated.

1. A phagocyte recognizes a foreign invader and engulfs it. Once inside the phagocyte, the invader's antigens are removed, and the phagocyte displays them on its cell membrane. A phagocyte that displays foreign antigens on its membrane is called an antigen-presenting cell.

2. A T cell encounters the antigen-presenting cell and binds to it. The antigen-presenting cell releases proteins that activate the T cell.

3. When a T cell is activated, it begins to divide and differentiate into two different types of T cells: activated and memory. The activated T cells will fight the current infection, but the memory T cells act as reserves that will wait for future invasions.

4. The activated T cells bind to and destroy infected body cells.

## FIGURE 3.3 Cellular Immunity

**In cellular immunity, T cells destroy infected body cells.**

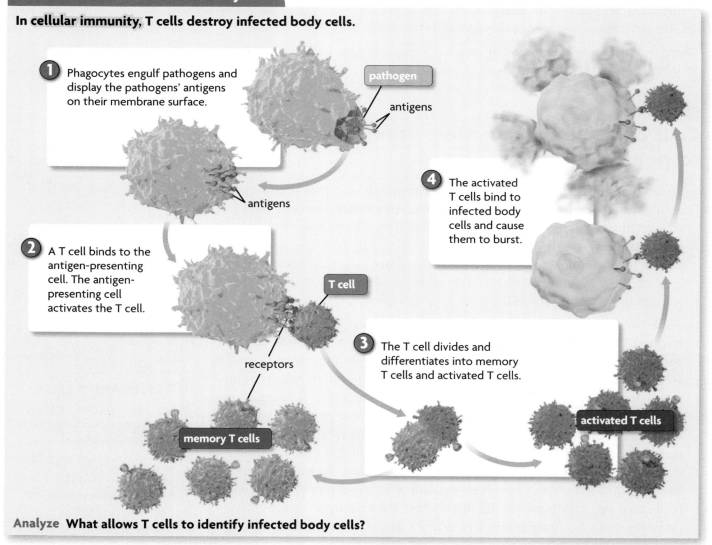

1. Phagocytes engulf pathogens and display the pathogens' antigens on their membrane surface.

pathogen

antigens

antigens

2. A T cell binds to the antigen-presenting cell. The antigen-presenting cell activates the T cell.

T cell

receptors

3. The T cell divides and differentiates into memory T cells and activated T cells.

4. The activated T cells bind to infected body cells and cause them to burst.

memory T cells

activated T cells

**Analyze** **What allows T cells to identify infected body cells?**

## Humoral Immunity

**Humoral immunity** is a type of immune response that depends on antibodies. Different types of antibodies fight pathogens by either causing them to burst, inactivating them, or causing them to clump, as shown in **FIGURE 3.4**.

**1** A pathogen binds to a B cell. The B cell engulfs the pathogen and puts part of the antigen onto its surface.

**2** When a T cell encounters the antigen-presenting B cell, it binds to the antigens. Then the T cell releases proteins that activate the B cell.

**3** Once activated, the B cell divides and differentiates into activated B cells and memory B cells.

**4** Activated B cells produce as many as 2000 pathogen-specific antibodies per second. In some cases, antibodies cause pathogens to clump.

**5** Phagocytes engulf and destroy the pathogen clumps.

**Compare** What are some similarities between the cellular and humoral responses?

**Animated Biology**
HMDScience.com

**PREMIUM CONTENT**

Destroy the Invaders

---

**FIGURE 3.4  Humoral Immunity**

In humoral immunity, B cells produce antibodies that help destroy pathogens.

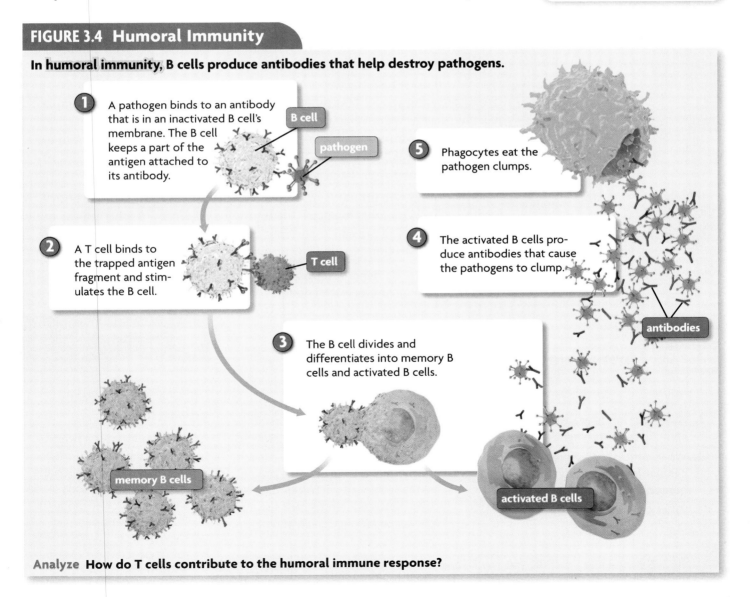

**1** A pathogen binds to an antibody that is in an inactivated B cell's membrane. The B cell keeps a part of the antigen attached to its antibody.

**B cell**

**pathogen**

**5** Phagocytes eat the pathogen clumps.

**2** A T cell binds to the trapped antigen fragment and stimulates the B cell.

**T cell**

**4** The activated B cells produce antibodies that cause the pathogens to clump.

**antibodies**

**3** The B cell divides and differentiates into memory B cells and activated B cells.

**memory B cells**

**activated B cells**

**Analyze** How do T cells contribute to the humoral immune response?

## ▶ MAIN IDEA

# The immune system rejects foreign tissues.

**CONNECT TO**

**BLOOD TYPING**

Blood cells have different proteins, called Rh factors, on their cell walls. Review **Respiratory and Circulatory Systems** for more information on how blood types affect a person's ability to receive blood transfusions.

All cells have protein markers on their surfaces. Your body must constantly decide whether your healthy cells are, in fact, your own or foreign cells. Sometimes you do not want your body to be able to identify foreign tissues and cells. For example, when you receive a blood transfusion or an organ transplant, you want to fool your body into ignoring the foreign tissues' protein markers. If protein markers on donated tissue differ from your cells' proteins, an immune response can occur and the transplanted tissue will be attacked and rejected. **Tissue rejection** occurs when the recipient's immune system makes antibodies against the protein markers on the donor's tissue.

Antigen receptors on the surface of your white blood cells determine whether your immune system will attack or ignore a transplanted tissue. Cells with protein markers that fit into the white blood cells' receptor molecules are foreign. Cells with protein markers that do not interact with white blood cells' receptor molecules are not detected by the immune system.

People have thousands of different combinations of protein markers on their cells. The fewer of these protein markers that differ between a donor's tissue and a recipient's, the better the chance that the recipient's immune system will not attack the donor tissue. For this reason, it is important that tissues are analyzed to determine whether a donor and recipient are compatible. To prevent tissue rejection, recipients must take drugs that decrease the activity of their immune system. These drugs weaken the person's immune response against all pathogens. This leaves the recipient less able to fight off infections from viruses, bacteria, and fungi.

Other times, the immune system loses the ability to recognize the body's healthy cells. When this happens, the immune system attacks the healthy body cells. These diseases are called autoimmune diseases, and you will read more about them in Section 5.

**Infer** Why might it be beneficial for a person to get blood or tissues donated from a relative instead of a non-related donor?

---

**SELF-CHECK Online**
HMDScience.com
PREMIUM CONTENT

## 28.3 Formative Assessment

### REVIEWING ▶ MAIN IDEAS

1. How does **inflammation** help the immune system to fight pathogens?

2. What is the main difference between **cellular immunity** and **humoral immunity**?

3. What is **tissue rejection,** and why does it occur?

### CRITICAL THINKING

4. **Contrast** What are the differences between a specific and a nonspecific immune response?

5. **Synthesize** Explain how the proteins on the surface of white blood cells, pathogens, and transplanted tissues interact to produce an immune response.

**CONNECT TO**

**GENETICS**

6. Doctors can test a person's blood to determine what types of proteins are on the surface of the person's blood cells. This is called blood typing. Why does blood typing reduce the likelihood of tissue rejection in blood transfusions?

# 28.4 Immunity and Technology

SC.912.L.14.52,
HE.912.C.1.7

**SC.912.L.14.52** Explain the basic functions of the human immune system, including specific and nonspecific immune response, vaccines, and antibiotics.

**HE.912.C.1.7** Analyze strategies for prevention, detection, and treatment of communicable and chronic diseases.

**Video Inquiry**
HMDScience.com

**PREMIUM CONTENT**

Snake Venom

**FIGURE 4.1** Antibiotics have killed the bottom cell by weakening its cell wall and causing it to burst. (colored TEM; magnification 55,000×)

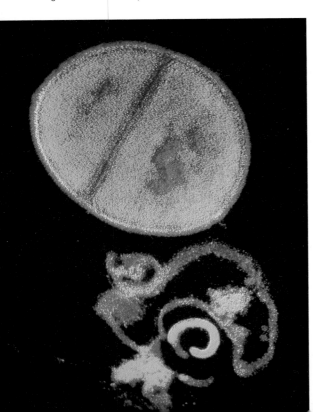

**KEY CONCEPT** **Living in a clean environment and building immunity help keep a person healthy.**

**MAIN IDEAS**

○ Many methods are used to control pathogens.
○ Vaccines artificially produce acquired immunity.

### Connect to Your World

Because infectious diseases are spread from person to person, the risk of getting sick increases when there are many people in one area. Luckily, scientists have developed many different ways to control the spread of disease. Cleaning supplies, medicines, and vaccines are technologies that help to prevent against sickness or treat people who are already sick.

## ○ MAIN IDEA
## Many methods are used to control pathogens.

Because pathogens can have such a negative effect on health, scientists have developed many ways to kill pathogens that our immune system might otherwise have a hard time fighting off. One way to prevent infection is to keep your environment clean. Cleaning can kill pathogens before they ever have a chance to enter your body and make you sick.

Heat and chemicals kill pathogens that are outside of the body. **Antiseptics** (an-tih-SEHP-tihks) are chemicals, such as soap, vinegar, and rubbing alcohol, that kill pathogens. Rubbing alcohol, for example, weakens cell membranes. Without a strong cell membrane, the microbe's nutrients leak out, and the microbe bursts. Antiseptics are not specific, meaning that they can kill many different types of pathogens.

Once pathogens enter the body, sometimes they can be killed with medicines. Antibiotics are medicines that target bacteria or fungi and keep them from growing or reproducing. Antibiotics work in a variety of ways. For example, penicillin makes bacteria unable to form cell walls. The bacteria cannot divide successfully, and they burst, as shown in **FIGURE 4.1**.

Unlike antiseptics, antibiotics target one type of bacterium or fungus. As antibiotic use has become more common, antibiotic-resistant bacteria have evolved. As you read in the chapter on viruses and prokaryotes, **antibiotic resistance** occurs when bacteria mutate so that they are no longer affected by antibiotics. Mutations make the bacteria resistant to the effects of antibiotics. When bacteria become resistant, scientists must find new medicines that can kill these mutant bacteria.

**Compare and Contrast** **What are the similarities and differences between antiseptics and antibiotics?**

▶ **MAIN IDEA**

# Vaccines artificially produce acquired immunity.

Vaccination cannot cure a person who is sick because vaccines only work to prevent infection. Vaccination allows a person to develop memory cells and acquired immunity against an illness without actually contracting the disease.

## FIGURE 4.2 Vaccine Response

**Vaccines stimulate an immune response so that you will not get sick if the real pathogen infects you.**

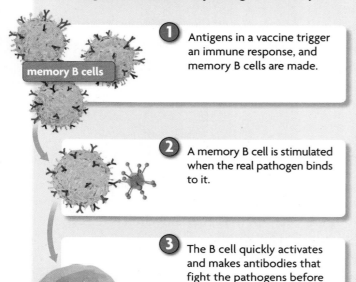

memory B cells

**1** Antigens in a vaccine trigger an immune response, and memory B cells are made.

**2** A memory B cell is stimulated when the real pathogen binds to it.

**3** The B cell quickly activates and makes antibodies that fight the pathogens before you get sick.

**Compare** How do memory cells cause a faster immune response?

A **vaccine** is a substance that contains the antigen of a pathogen. The antigen causes your immune system to produce memory cells, but you will not get sick. You do not get sick because the pathogen is weakened, and it cannot reproduce or attack your cells. When you are exposed to a pathogen and have not been vaccinated, you get sick because the pathogen reproduces faster than your immune system can respond. You stop being sick when your B or T cells win the fight over the infection.

If the pathogen enters your body after you are vaccinated, your memory B cells make antibodies right away, as shown in **FIGURE 4.2**. If you have not been vaccinated, your body must go through the entire humoral immune response, and the pathogen has enough time to make you feel sick.

There are four main types of vaccines.

- Some vaccines contain whole dead bacteria or viruses.
- Live attenuated vaccines contain weak living pathogens.
- Component vaccines use only the parts of the pathogen that contain the antigen, such as the protein coat of a virus that has had its genetic material removed.
- Toxoid vaccines are made from inactivated bacterial toxins, which are chemicals a bacterium produces that causes a person to become ill.

**Apply** Why do you think that some vaccines, such as the flu vaccine, need to be given every year?

## 28.4 Formative Assessment

### REVIEWING ▶ MAIN IDEAS

1. Under what circumstances might antibiotics not be useful in treating a disease caused by a pathogen?

2. How does the immune system respond to a pathogen that the person has been vaccinated against?

### CRITICAL THINKING

3. **Summarize** Write out and describe the steps that your immune system takes when you are vaccinated.

4. **Apply** Why is the immune response faster after vaccination than the response that occurs the first time a pathogen invades?

### ⁙ CONNECT TO

### EVOLUTION

5. Explain why **antibiotic resistance** is considered to be evidence of evolution. (Hint: Review the chapter on viruses and prokaryotes and the information about natural selection.)

However, problems can arise from bone marrow transplants. In graft-versus-host disease (GVHD), the donor marrow makes antibodies against the host's healthy tissues. Chemotherapy and radiation treatments also kill both cancerous cells and healthy cells, leaving the immune system weak and open to opportunistic infections. An **opportunistic infection** is an infection caused by a pathogen that a healthy immune system would normally be able to fight off. When the immune system is weakened, an opportunistic infection can make a person very sick.

**Analyze** **Shortness of breath and inability to form blood clots are common symptoms of leukemia. How does the disease lead to these symptoms?**

**Biology** VIDEO CLIP
HMDScience.com
PREMIUM CONTENT
Leukemia and the Immune System

## ▶ MAIN IDEA

# HIV targets the immune system.

The World Health Organization estimates that more than 30 million people in the world have HIV/AIDS. During the 1980s, fewer than 2 million people had the virus. The **human immunodeficiency virus (HIV),** illustrated in **FIGURE 6.2,** is a retrovirus that attacks and weakens the immune system. A retrovirus is a type of virus that contains RNA instead of DNA. HIV is a retrovirus that has nine genes. HIV weakens the immune system, and the body is likely to get opportunistic infections.

### HIV Transmission

Although HIV is a very dangerous pathogen, it can only live in human blood cells and thus will not survive for long outside of the human body. For this reason, HIV is not transmitted through shaking hands with an infected individual, or swimming in a pool with an infected person. HIV cannot be transmitted through insect bites either. Insects that suck blood, such as ticks or mosquitoes, quickly digest the blood cells in their guts. Once the blood is digested, HIV dies.

A person becomes infected with HIV when the virus enters his or her bloodstream. HIV is passed from person to person through the mixing of blood and other body fluids. HIV is transmitted through sexual intercourse with an infected individual. It can also be passed from mothers to their unborn babies through the umbilical cord. A person might also get HIV if his or her skin is pierced by a needle that an infected individual recently used. Hypodermic needles used for injecting some illegal drugs and needles used for body piercing and tattooing have transmitted HIV between individuals. However, needles that your doctor uses to give shots or take blood do not transmit HIV because doctors use a new needle for every patient.

### HIV Reproduces in T Cells

HIV infects T cells, the white blood cells that trigger the body's immune responses. When HIV enters a T cell, the T cell becomes ineffective and can no longer stimulate an immune response. While the T cell cannot function in the immune system, it remains alive as a host and produces new HIV. A single T cell can give rise to thousands of HIVs before it eventually dies.

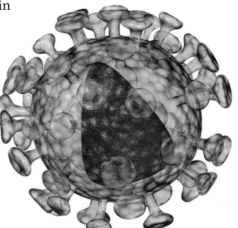

**FIGURE 6.2** HIV is a small retrovirus that is covered with bumps, which are its antigens. This illustration shows an HIV about 500,000 times its actual size.

**Web**Quest
HMDScience.com
PREMIUM CONTENT
HIV and AIDS

# FIGURE 6.3  HIV Destroys T cells

**HIV reproduces within T cells, killing T cells and weakening the immune system.**

**① HIV ENTERS THE BODY**

When HIV first enters the body, T cells activate B cells, and the activated B cells make antibodies against HIV.

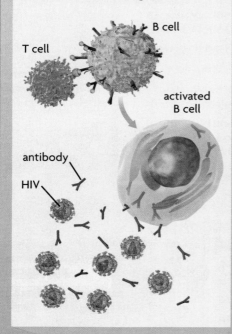

**② HIV DESTROYS T CELLS**

Because HIV kills T cells and reproduces more quickly than T cells, as HIV continues to reproduce, fewer and fewer T cells remain in the body.

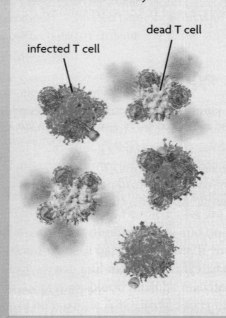

**③ HIV OVERPOWERS THE IMMUNE SYSTEM**

With fewer T cells, B cells cannot be activated to make antibodies. HIV and pathogens that cause opportunistic diseases take over the body.

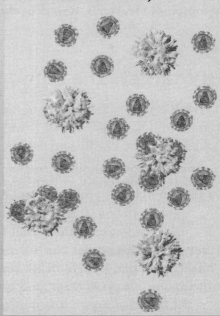

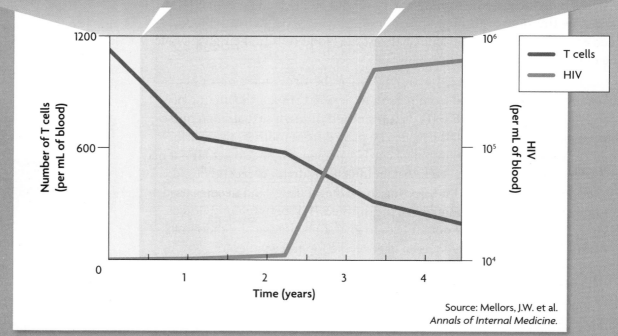

Source: Mellors, J.W. et al. *Annals of Internal Medicine.*

**CRITICAL VIEWING**  Why might a graph comparing HIV and antibodies have a similar shape to the one above, which compares HIV and T cells?

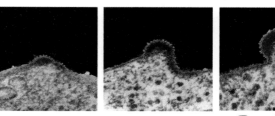

As HIV reproduces, the body cannot make replacement T cells fast enough. As the immune system weakens, opportunistic infections begin to take over.

During the first few weeks of infection, a person usually does not feel sick. Although HIV is infecting some T cells, there are still enough healthy T cells that B cells can be activated to produce antibodies against HIV, as shown in **FIGURE 6.3**. At this stage, HIV is diagnosed by determining whether a person's blood contains antibodies against HIV.

After the initial infection, an infected person can have HIV for ten years or more without experiencing any symptoms. During this stage, more and more T cells become infected, and each cell produces thousands of HIV cells, as shown in **FIGURE 6.4**. Soon, the bone marrow cannot replace dead T cells quickly enough, and the body develops opportunistic infections and AIDS.

## HIV Leads to AIDS

**Acquired immune deficiency syndrome (AIDS)** is the final stage of the immune system's decline due to HIV. Whereas HIV is a virus, AIDS is the condition of having a worn-out immune system. A person with AIDS can have several opportunistic infections—such as fungal infections, tuberculosis, pneumonia, viral infections, and cancers—and very few T cells. AIDS almost always results in death because the body cannot fight many such infections.

Current treatment of an HIV infection is expensive, complicated, and only slows—but does not cure—the disease. Treatment involves a combination of three to four antiviral drugs that are taken as often as five times each day. These drugs can cause many unpleasant side effects and can be very expensive. What's more, as HIV mutates, a patient might need to use many different drug combinations to keep the infection under control. Also, HIV mutates rapidly, and so far no vaccine has provided complete protection against the constantly evolving strains of HIV. However, treatment can enable a person to live for 20 years or more after initial HIV infection.

**Apply** How does destruction of T cells lead to overall immune system failure?

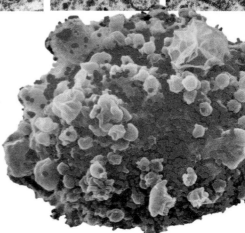

**FIGURE 6.4** Thousands of HIV, shown in red, will bud off a T cell before the T cell dies. (top: colored TEM, magnification 105,000×; bottom: colored SEM, magnification 5000×)

---

**SELF-CHECK Online**
HMDScience.com
**PREMIUM CONTENT**

## 28.6 Formative Assessment

### REVIEWING ◉ MAIN IDEAS

1. How does **leukemia** affect a person's entire body?

2. How do **HIV** and **AIDS** differ?

### CRITICAL THINKING

3. **Analyze** Why is HIV infection difficult to cure, even with treatment with multiple medications?

4. **Compare and Contrast** Which cells of the immune system are affected by HIV and leukemia, and what parts of the immune response do these cells influence?

### ◉ CONNECT TO

**ANTIBIOTICS**

5. You have learned that viruses cannot be treated with antibiotics. Why, then, might doctors prescribe antibiotics to patients with HIV anyway?

# 28 Summary

## KEY CONCEPTS

### 28.1 Pathogens and Human Illness

**Germs cause many diseases in humans.** Germ theory hypothesized that microbes—not spirits—caused disease. Viruses, bacteria, fungi, protozoa, and parasitic worms are examples of pathogens. These pathogens can be spread through physical contact, the air, or vectors.

### 28.2 Immune System

**The immune system consists of organs, cells, and molecules that fight infections.** Skin and mucous membranes work to keep pathogens out of the body. Once a pathogen is inside the body, the circulatory and lymphatic systems transport white blood cells to the infection site. Some microbes and viruses do not cause illness because a person has some type of immunity.

### 28.3 Immune Responses

**The immune system has many responses to pathogens and foreign cells.** Nonspecific responses, such as inflammation and fever, are those that react the same to every pathogen. Specific responses, such as the cellular and humoral responses, are different for every pathogen. The immune system might initiate a specific response against transplanted tissues.

### 28.4 Immunity and Technology

**Living in a clean environment and building immunity help keep a person healthy.** Antiseptics destroy pathogens outside of the body, and antibiotics destroy pathogens inside of the body. Vaccines activate an immune response without getting a person sick. When the pathogen does invade, a vaccinated person's immune response is so quick that the person will not get sick.

### 28.5 Overreactions of the Immune System

**An overactive immune system can make the body very unhealthy.** Allergies occur when the immune system responds to a harmless antigen. In autoimmune diseases, white blood cells attack the body's healthy cells.

### 28.6 Diseases That Weaken the Immune System

**When the immune system is weakened, the body cannot fight off diseases.** Leukemia is characterized by immature white blood cells. HIV attacks T cells so that other pathogens can take over the body. When a person has very few T cells and several opportunistic diseases, the person has a condition called AIDS.

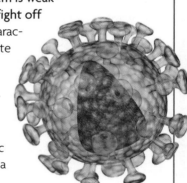

---

## READING TOOLBOX    SYNTHESIZE YOUR NOTES

**Concept Map** Use a concept map to organize your notes about lymphocytes.

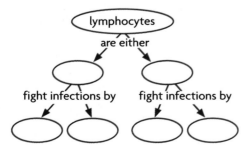

**Chart** Use a three-column chart to compare similar concepts.

| Word | Definition | How It Is Different from Others |
|---|---|---|
| antigen | | |
| allergen | | |
| protein marker | | |

## CHAPTER VOCABULARY

**28.1** germ theory
pathogen
vector

**28.2** immune system
phagocyte
T cell
B cell
antibody
interferon
passive immunity
active immunity

**28.3** inflammation
antigen
memory cell
cellular immunity
humoral immunity
tissue rejection

**28.4** antiseptic
antibiotic resistance
vaccine

**28.5** allergy
allergen
anaphylaxis

**28.6** leukemia
opportunistic infection
human immunodeficiency
  virus (HIV)
acquired immune deficiency
  syndrome (AIDS)

## Reviewing Vocabulary

### Vocabulary Connections

For each group of words below, write a sentence or two to clearly explain how the terms are connected. For example, for the terms *HIV* and *AIDS*, you could write, "HIV weakens the immune system and leads to AIDS."

1. pathogen, vector
2. T cells, B cells
3. antibody, antigen

### Keep It Short

For each vocabulary term below, write a short, precise phrase that describes its meaning. For example, a short phrase to describe *leukemia* could be "cancer of the bone marrow."

4. interferon
5. inflammation
6. cellular immunity
7. antiseptic

**READING** TOOLBOX  **GREEK AND LATIN WORD ORIGINS**

Using the Greek or Latin word origins of the terms below, explain how the meaning of the root relates to the definition of the term.

8. The term *phagocyte* comes from the Greek word *phagos*, meaning "to eat." Explain how this meaning relates to the word *phagocyte*.

9. The word *antibiotic* contains the prefix *anti-*, from a Greek word meaning "opposite," and the Greek word *bios*, meaning "life." Explain how, together, these meanings relate to the term *antibiotic resistance*.

## Reviewing MAIN IDEAS

10. Why do Koch's postulates and germ theory apply to infectious diseases but not noninfectious diseases?

11. What are some types of pathogens, and how do they attack the body?

12. What are some ways that pathogens spread?

13. How do other body systems help the immune system respond to infections?

14. How do phagocytes, antibodies, and interferons help to fight pathogens?

15. How are passive immunity and active immunity similar and different?

16. How does fever help to fight infections?

17. How do specific immune responses lead to active immunity?

18. How might organ transplants, which are meant to save a person's life, endanger the person?

19. People say, "Too much of a good thing can be bad." How does this statement relate to the use of antibiotics?

20. How does a vaccine produce active immunity without making a person sick?

21. How do autoimmune diseases disrupt homeostasis?

22. How does leukemia weaken the immune system?

23. What is the difference between HIV and AIDS?

# Critical Thinking

**24. Apply** In 1918, scientists found a bacterium in the lungs of some people who died of flu. The bacteria were given to healthy volunteers, but only some volunteers developed flulike symptoms. Using germ theory, decide whether this bacterium caused flu.

**25. Connect** How does the evolution of pathogens, specifically bacteria and viruses, negatively affect humans' ability to stay healthy?

**26. Synthesize** If you get stung by a bee, the skin around the bite will swell. Explain the process that produced the swelling. Use and define the terms *vector*, *allergen*, *inflammation*, and *white blood cell* in your answer.

**27. Compare and Contrast** How can the humoral immune response both help and hurt the body?

**28. Analyze** People infected with HIV are said to be HIV-positive because they have the antibodies for the virus. Why don't antibodies, which normally protect the body against pathogens, protect people who are HIV-positive from developing AIDS?

**29. Explain** Summarize the process by which a vaccine helps the body fight off pathogens. Begin with what happens when a person gets vaccinated, and conclude with the destruction of the invading pathogen.

**30. Infer** Compare the normal humoral immune response to the response after someone is vaccinated. Which steps of the humoral response probably take the longest, allowing the pathogen to make the body sick?

## Interpreting Visuals
Use the diagram below to answer the next three questions.

**31. Summarize** What is happening in each numbered part of the process shown above?

**32. Apply** Before this process could take place, one of two events must have occurred. What are the two events?

**33. Analyze** What kind of immunity is shown here?

## Analyzing Data Identify Experimental Design Flaws
Use the graph below to identify data flaws and answer the next two questions.

A researcher designs an experiment to determine what dose of a new antibiotic must be given to patients to kill the bacteria that cause pneumonia. The researcher infects three groups of mice with three different strands of pneumonia bacteria. Group 1 is not given any antibiotic. The researcher gives Groups 2 and 3 different doses of the antibiotic. The results are shown below.

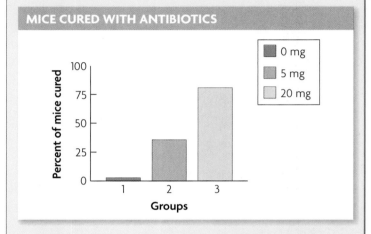

MICE CURED WITH ANTIBIOTICS

**34. Analyze** Can the researcher conclude that the largest dose of antibiotic is necessary to cure pneumonia? Why or why not?

**35. Evaluate** How could this investigation be redesigned to better answer the researcher's question?

## Making Connections

**36. Design a Video Game** Imagine that you are creating a video game in which the player can choose to be a T cell or a B cell. Describe the player's goals for each version of the game. How will the player direct the cells in their mission to seek out and destroy the invading pathogens?

**37. Design an Experiment** One fall, children who live in a wooded area become ill. They develop an itchy rash, a hacking cough, and a sick feeling in their stomachs. One local doctor tells concerned parents that their children had an allergic reaction to something in the woods and advises that the children rest in bed. Another doctor thinks that a bacterium causes the sickness and prescribes medicine for the children. Design an experiment to determine who is correct. (Hint: What evidence do you need to prove a pathogen caused a disease?)

# Standards-Based Assessment

1. In the 1850s, Louis Pasteur conducted many experiments and, based on his results, proposed that specific microorganisms cause disease. This proposal is an example of a scientific

   A hypothesis.

   B guess.

   C theory.

   D experiment.

2.

| Set Up for Chicken Pox Experiment | | |
|---|---|---|
| Volunteer | Injected with Dead Chicken Pox Virus | Injected with Distilled Water |
| A | X | |
| B | X | X |
| C | X | X |

   A scientist studies three volunteers who never had chicken pox by injecting each with a dead virus, distilled water, or a combination of the two. The experimental design is described in the table above. After the injection, whose blood stream would *most* likely contain antibodies for the chicken pox virus?

   A volunteer A only

   B volunteer B only

   C volunteers A and B

   D volunteers A and C

3. A person infected with HIV is *more* likely to become sick with other diseases because

   A people infected with HIV must take drugs to suppress the immune system.

   B pathogens can enter the bodies of people infected with HIV during surgery.

   C HIV mutates quickly into other diseases that affect the immune system.

   D HIV attacks the cells that produce immune responses.

4. Mucous membranes and the skin are nonspecific defenses against infection. The functions of the skin in immunity are to block the entry of pathogens and to

   A release white blood cells.

   B produce antibodies.

   C secrete sweat and oil.

   D activate active immunity.

5.

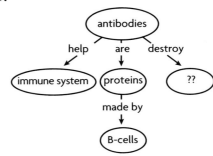

   Which word *best* completes this concept map?

   A white blood cells

   B red blood cells

   C pathogens

   D vectors

6. Some interferons stimulate noninfected cells to produce thick coats that prevent viruses from infecting the cells. Which statement *best* explains why interferons are effective against viruses but not bacteria?

   A Bacteria are living microorganisms, but viruses are not.

   B Interferons affect viral DNA, but do not affect bacterial DNA.

   C Bacteria have a cell wall, but viruses only have a protein coat.

   D Viruses need to enter a cell to reproduce, but bacteria do not.

   **THINK THROUGH THE QUESTION**

   To answer this question, think about how bacteria and viruses are different. Which of these differences is related to the way interferons act?

# 29 Reproduction and Development

## ONLINE BIOLOGY
HMDScience.com

**ONLINE** Labs
- **QuickLab** Human Sex Cells
- Hormones in the Human Menstrual Cycle
- Development of an Embryo
- Effects of Chemicals on Reproductive Organs
- Stages of Human Development
- **Video Lab** Sonography

**PREMIUM CONTENT**

BIOLOGY

**Developmental Timeline** Use an interactive timeline to explore different milestones of fetal development, such as when the heart develops and when fingers form.

(t) © Nestle/Petit Format/Photo Researchers, Inc.

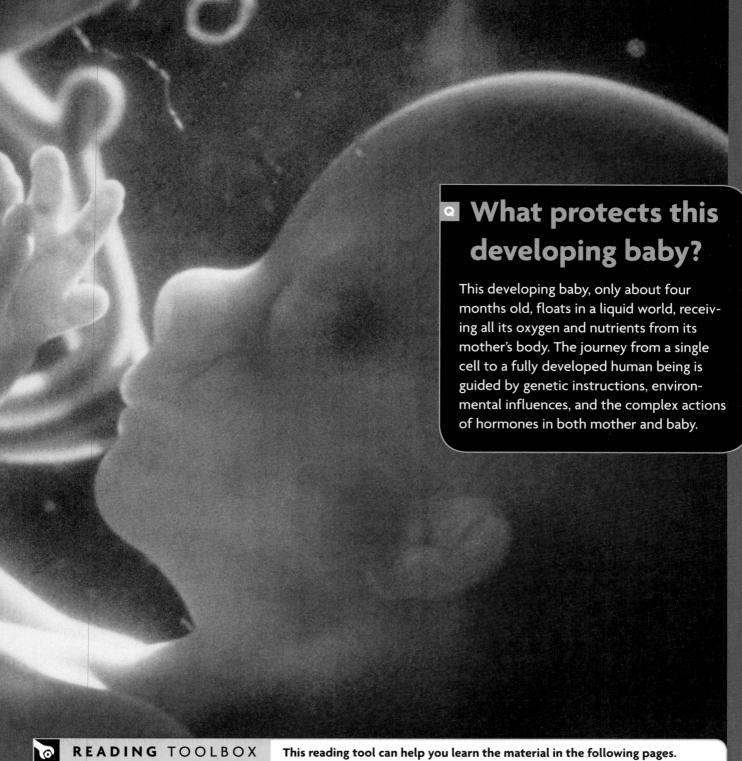

**Q What protects this developing baby?**

This developing baby, only about four months old, floats in a liquid world, receiving all its oxygen and nutrients from its mother's body. The journey from a single cell to a fully developed human being is guided by genetic instructions, environmental influences, and the complex actions of hormones in both mother and baby.

---

**READING TOOLBOX**   **This reading tool can help you learn the material in the following pages.**

### USING LANGUAGE

**Recognizing Main Ideas**  A main idea is a sentence that states the main point of a paragraph. The main idea is often, but not always, one of the first few sentences of a paragraph. All the other sentences of the paragraph give support to the main idea.

### YOUR TURN

Find the main idea in the paragraph below.

*Disease-causing pathogens are transmitted in many ways. Some pathogens can be passed by drinking contaminated water. Other pathogens are present in body fluids such as semen. These pathogens can be passed from one person to another through sexual contact.*

## 29.1 Reproductive Anatomy

SC.912.L.16.13

**SC.912.L.16.13** Describe the basic anatomy and physiology of the human reproductive system. Describe the process of human development from fertilization to birth and major changes that occur in each trimester of pregnancy.

**KEY CONCEPT** Female and male reproductive organs fully develop during puberty.

**MAIN IDEAS**

- The female reproductive system produces ova.
- The male reproductive system produces sperm.

### Connect to Your World

You have something in common with every person ever born. Like everyone else, you began life as a single cell, produced when one male sex cell joined with one female sex cell. Sexual reproduction is the means by which the human species passes on genetic information to each generation.

**CONNECT TO**

**ENDOCRINE SYSTEM**

You read in **Nervous and Endocrine Systems** that the hypothalamus and pituitary glands are part of the endocrine system. These two glands are considered "master" glands because the hormones they secrete affect other glands that play key roles in human reproduction, growth, and development.

### ▶ MAIN IDEA

## The female reproductive system produces ova.

The **reproductive system** is a collection of specialized organs, glands, and hormones that help to produce a new human being. Females and males reach sexual maturity, or the ability to produce offspring, only after puberty. **Puberty** marks a time in your life when your hypothalamus and your pituitary gland release hormones, such as follicle-stimulating hormone (FSH) and luteinizing hormone (LH). Such hormones begin the process of developing your sexual characteristics and reproductive system.

The main functions of the female reproductive system are to produce ova (singular, **ovum**), or egg cells, and to provide a place where a fertilized egg can develop. Unlike males, females have all of their reproductive organs located inside their bodies. This organization helps to protect a fertilized egg while it develops. The egg cells are produced in the ovaries. The **ovaries** are paired organs located on either side of the **uterus,** or womb, as shown in **FIGURE 1.1.** When a female baby is born, she already has about 2 million potential egg cells stored in her ovaries.

In the ovaries, FSH and LH stimulate the release of another important hormone, estrogen. **Estrogen** is a steroid hormone that has three main functions. First, it controls the development of female sexual characteristics, including widening the pelvis, increasing fat deposits and bone mass, and enlarging the breasts. Second, it is needed for egg cells to develop fully before they leave the ovaries. Third, estrogen helps to prepare the uterus for pregnancy every month and helps to maintain a pregnancy when it occurs.

When an egg cell matures each month, it is released from an ovary and enters the fallopian tube. The **fallopian tube** (fuh-LOH-pee-uhn) is an organ about 10 centimeters (4 in.) long that ends in the uterus. An egg takes several days to travel through this tube. During that time, it can be fertilized by sperm

## FIGURE 1.1 FEMALE REPRODUCTIVE ANATOMY

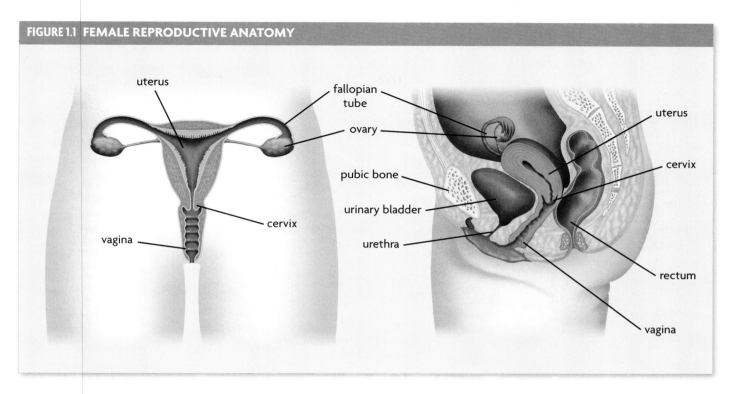

that enter the tube. A fertilized egg will attach to the wall of the uterus, but an unfertilized egg will eventually be broken down and discarded.

The uterus is about the size and shape of a pear. It is composed of three layers: a thin inner layer of epithelial cells, a thick middle layer of muscle, and an outer layer of connective tissue. The lower end of the uterus is called the cervix, which opens into the vagina. In a normal birth, a baby is pushed down the canal of the vagina to exit the mother's body. The complex processes of fertilization and human development are described in Sections 2 and 3.

**Analyze** **How does the release of estrogen affect the female reproductive system during puberty?**

○ MAIN IDEA
# The male reproductive system produces sperm.

The main functions of the male reproductive system are to produce sperm cells and to deliver them to the female reproductive system. The diagram in **FIGURE 1.2**, on the following page, shows the organs in which sperm are produced and stored and the organs that deliver the sperm.

Males do not produce sperm until puberty but afterward can produce sperm all their lives. Sperm production takes place in the testicles, or **testes** (TEHS-teez), which are paired organs. Each testis (singular of *testes*) contains hundreds of tiny tubules where millions of sperm cells are produced. In the testes, LH stimulates the release of testosterone. **Testosterone** (tehs-TAHS-tuh-ROHN) is a steroid hormone that, along with FSH, stimulates the production of sperm cells. Testosterone also controls the development of male sexual characteristics. These include a deeper voice than a female's, more body hair,

### READING TOOLBOX

**TAKING NOTES**
Use a two-column chart to list the major parts and functions of the female and male reproductive anatomy.

| Female | Male |
|---|---|
| Ovaries — Paired organs where eggs are produced | Testes — Paired organs that produce sperm cells |

## FIGURE 1.2 MALE REPRODUCTIVE ANATOMY

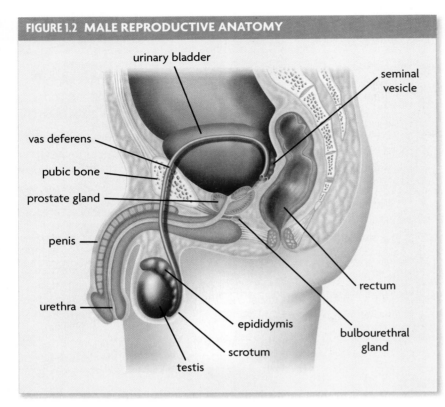

urinary bladder

seminal vesicle

vas deferens

pubic bone

prostate gland

penis

urethra

epididymis

scrotum

testis

rectum

bulbourethral gland

greater bone density, and increased muscle mass.

The testes are enclosed in a pouch, the **scrotum.** It hangs below the pelvis outside of the body, which keeps the testes two to three degrees cooler than the core body temperature. The lower temperature is important because sperm cannot develop if the temperature in the testes is too high. When the immature sperm leave the testes, they travel through a duct to a long, coiled tube known as the **epididymis** (EHP-ih-DIHD-uh-mihs). Here the sperm mature and remain until expelled or reabsorbed.

During sexual stimulation, the sperm travel into another long duct called the **vas deferens** (vas DEHF-uhr-uhnz). Secondary sex glands secrete fluids into the vas deferens to nourish and protect the sperm. The prostate gland, which surrounds the urethra, produces a fluid that helps sperm move more easily. The bulbourethral gland (BUHL-boh-yu-REE-thruhl) and the seminal vesicle secrete basic fluids that help to neutralize the acidity in the urethra and in the female's vagina. The fluids from all three glands, together with the sperm, form a milky white substance known as **semen.**

During sexual arousal, blood flows into the penis, making it rigid. Semen moves from the vas deferens into the urethra, which runs the length of the penis. When ejaculation occurs, a muscle closes off the bladder to prevent urine from mixing with the semen in the urethra. Smooth muscle contractions then propel the semen along the urethra and eject it from the penis.

**Apply** **Why might having a high fever affect sperm production?**

**SELF-CHECK Online**
HMDScience.com
PREMIUM CONTENT

# 29.1 Formative Assessment

## REVIEWING ▶ MAIN IDEAS

1. Explain the function of the following parts of the female reproductive system: **ovary, fallopian tube, uterus.**

2. Explain the function of the following parts of the male reproductive system: **testes, scrotum, epididymis, vas deferens.**

## CRITICAL THINKING

3. **Compare** In what ways are the effects of **testosterone** on males and **estrogen** on females similar?

4. **Infer** Both males and females have paired organs that produce sex cells. What survival advantage for our species might this pairing of organs provide?

### CONNECT TO

## PLANTS

5. Recall that flowering plants reproduce sexually. The stamen produces pollen grains, and the carpel contains an ovary where eggs are produced. How do these structures compare with human reproductive organs?

# 29.2 Reproductive Processes

SC.912.L.16.13

**KEY CONCEPT** **Human reproductive processes depend on cycles of hormones.**

## MAIN IDEAS

- Eggs mature and are released according to hormonal cycles.
- Sperm production in the testes is controlled by hormones.
- Fertilization occurs when a sperm cell joins an egg cell.
- Sexually transmitted diseases affect fertility and overall health.

### VOCABULARY

follicle
ovulation
menstrual cycle
endometrium
corpus luteum
menopause
zygote
infertility
sexually transmitted disease

**SC.912.L.16.13** Describe the basic anatomy and physiology of the human reproductive system. Describe the process of human development from fertilization to birth and major changes that occur in each trimester of pregnancy.

### Connect to Your World

You may have heard the phrase "Timing is everything." In football, for instance, precise timing between players can mean the difference between catching or dropping a key pass. Likewise, timing is everything for the hormones that regulate the reproductive processes in your body. Numerous feedback loops among these hormones help ensure that each process occurs at the right time and in the right order.

### ● MAIN IDEA

## Eggs mature and are released according to hormonal cycles.

A female's reproductive cycle is controlled by hormones released by the hypothalamus, the pituitary gland, and the ovaries. Each month, the levels of these hormones rise and fall in well-timed feedback loops that regulate the development and release of an egg and prepare the uterus to receive it.

### Production of Eggs

The production of eggs, or ova, begins before a female is born, as described in Section 1. Recall that meiosis is a type of cell division that produces sex cells, or gametes. After the chromosomes in each of the cells are duplicated, meiosis I can begin. The potential eggs then enter a resting phase that lasts until puberty. At birth, a female has about 2 million of these partially developed eggs in her ovaries. Before puberty begins, many of these cells break down until only about 400,000 are left.

At puberty, a monthly hormone cycle begins the second stage of egg production. Every 28 days or so, an increase in FSH stimulates a potential egg to complete meiosis I, as shown in **FIGURE 2.1.** The potential egg divides unevenly, producing two sex cells. The larger cell receives most of the organelles, cytoplasm, and nutrients an embryo will need when an egg is fertilized. The smaller cell, or polar body, simply breaks down. The larger sex cell completes meiosis II only after a sperm enters it. The cell divides again to produce an ovum, or egg, and a second polar body that also breaks down. Both the ovum and the second polar body contain 23 chromosomes from the mother.

**FIGURE 2.1** Potential eggs go through meiosis I and II to produce mature ova, or eggs with 23 chromosomes each.

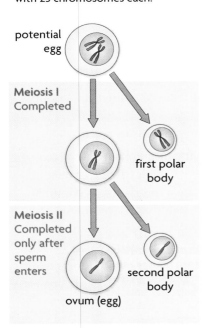

potential egg

Meiosis I Completed

first polar body

Meiosis II Completed only after sperm enters

second polar body

ovum (egg)

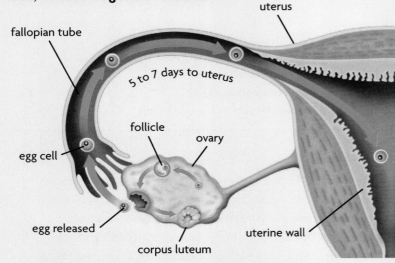

## FIGURE 2.2 Release of Egg

**After an egg is released, it travels through the fallopian tube, where it might be fertilized.**

uterus

fallopian tube

5 to 7 days to uterus

follicle

ovary

egg cell

egg released

corpus luteum

uterine wall

**Infer** Why might it be an advantage that the egg takes several days to travel through the fallopian tube?

Biology **VIDEO CLIP**

HMDScience.com

PREMIUM CONTENT

Ovulation

**CONNECT TO**

**ANIMAL BEHAVIOR**

As you read in **Animal Behavior,** hormone cycles control more than reproduction. Certain glands and proteins in some animals detect seasonal changes in temperature and in the hours of daylight. As a result, the glands secrete hormones that control when an animal will hibernate or migrate.

## Release of Egg

Each developing sex cell, which you can think of as an egg, is surrounded by a group of cells called a **follicle** that helps the egg to mature. When an egg is ready to be released, the follicle ruptures, and the egg breaks through the ovary wall, as shown in **FIGURE 2.2.** The release of an egg from the ovary is called **ovulation.** The egg is swept into the fallopian tube, where it can be fertilized by a sperm. Over the next five to seven days, the egg moves through the tube to the uterus. An unfertilized egg is discarded during menstruation.

In most cases, only one egg is released during ovulation. About 400 to 500 eggs are released over a female's reproductive life. Which ovary releases an egg each month is entirely random. If one ovary is damaged, however, the other may take over and release an egg each month.

## The Menstrual Cycle

The **menstrual cycle** is a series of monthly changes in the reproductive system that include producing and releasing an egg and preparing the uterus to receive it. The length of the cycle is slightly different for each female, but averages about 28 days. The cycle has three main phases—flow phase, follicular phase, and luteal phase, as **FIGURE 2.3** shows. The timing of each phase is regulated by specific hormones.

1. **Flow phase** Day 1 of the menstrual cycle is the first day that the menstrual flow begins. The flow occurs when the lining of the uterus, or **endometrium** (EHN-doh-MEE-tree-uhm), detaches from the uterine wall and passes through the vagina to the outside of the body. Some blood, mucus, and tissue fluid are also expelled. The muscles of the uterus contract to help expel the lining. These contractions, known as "cramps," can be painful for some females. During this phase, the level of FSH starts to rise, and another follicle in the ovaries begins to mature.

2. **Follicular phase** The follicular (fuh-LIHK-yuh-luhr) phase lasts from about day 6 to day 14. At the start of this phase, the level of estrogen in the blood is relatively low. Hormones from the hypothalamus stimulate the pituitary to release more FSH and LH. Recall that a rise in FSH and LH causes the egg and follicle to mature. Ovulation occurs at about day 14. As the egg is developing, the follicle releases estrogen, which steadily increases over the next few days. This hormone causes the endometrium to thicken. Estrogen also stimulates a sharp increase in LH, which causes the follicle to rupture, releasing the egg.

**3** **Luteal phase** In the luteal (LOO-tee-uhl) phase, the release of hormones is now timed to stop egg production and to develop the endometrium to receive a fertilized egg. After ovulation, the empty follicle turns yellow and is called the **corpus luteum** (KAWR-puhs LOO-tee-uhm), or "yellow body." The corpus luteum releases estrogen and another hormone, progesterone, which limits the production of LH. Progesterone and estrogen also increase the number of blood vessels in the endometrium. If the egg is not fertilized, rising levels of estrogen and progesterone cause the hypothalamus to stop releasing FSH and LH. The corpus luteum then breaks down and stops secreting estrogen and progesterone. As a result, the uterus lining begins to shed, and the next flow phase starts.

For most women, the menstrual cycle continues throughout their reproductive years, which may last from preteen years to the late 50s. Eventually, however, the levels of hormones decline with age. This decline disrupts the normal timing of the menstrual cycle. In a process called **menopause,** the cycle gradually becomes more and more irregular and finally stops altogether. Menopause can occur as early as a woman's mid-30s.

**READING TOOLBOX**

**VOCABULARY**
*Menstruation* and *menopause* are based on the Latin word *mensis,* which means "month."

**Summarize** What are the main functions of estrogen and progesterone during the follicular and luteal phases?

## FIGURE 2.3 Menstrual Cycle

Hormones cause changes in the follicle, egg, and lining of the uterus.

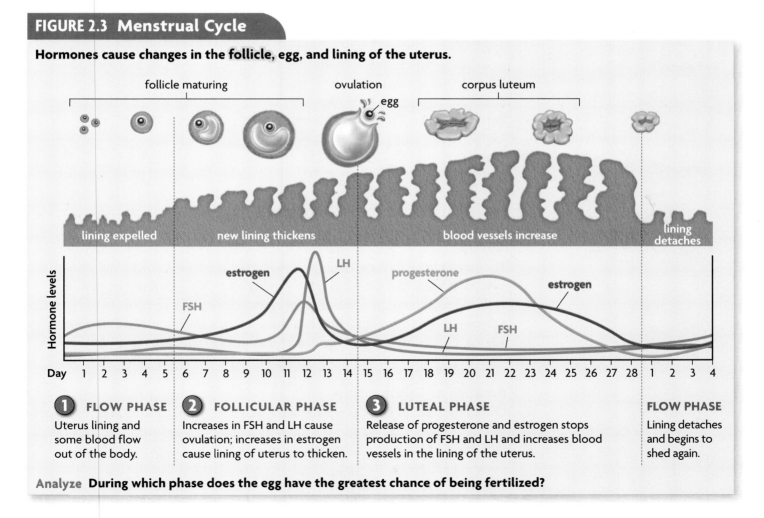

follicle maturing   ovulation   corpus luteum

egg

lining expelled   new lining thickens   blood vessels increase   lining detaches

Hormone levels

estrogen  LH  progesterone  estrogen

FSH   LH  FSH

Day 1 2 3 4 5 6 7 8 9 10 11 12 13 14 15 16 17 18 19 20 21 22 23 24 25 26 27 28 1 2 3 4

**1 FLOW PHASE**
Uterus lining and some blood flow out of the body.

**2 FOLLICULAR PHASE**
Increases in FSH and LH cause ovulation; increases in estrogen cause lining of uterus to thicken.

**3 LUTEAL PHASE**
Release of progesterone and estrogen stops production of FSH and LH and increases blood vessels in the lining of the uterus.

**FLOW PHASE**
Lining detaches and begins to shed again.

**Analyze** During which phase does the egg have the greatest chance of being fertilized?

# Sperm production in the testes is controlled by hormones.

**FIGURE 2.4** Each potential sperm cell that undergoes meiosis produces four mature sperm cells with 23 chromosomes each. A mature sperm has a head, midpiece, and whiplike tail that enables it to move.

**SPERM PRODUCTION**

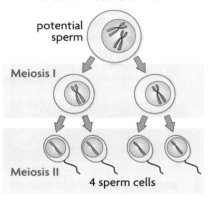

potential sperm

Meiosis I

Meiosis II

4 sperm cells

**SPERM CELL**

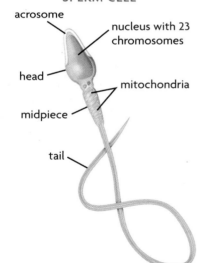

acrosome

nucleus with 23 chromosomes

head

mitochondria

midpiece

tail

The reproductive cycles for males and females are different in two ways. First, females begin to produce eggs before they are born, but males do not produce sperm until they reach puberty. Second, females usually produce only one egg a month to be fertilized, while males produce millions of sperm almost daily.

The production of sperm begins when hormones from the hypothalamus stimulate the pituitary to release FSH and LH, which circulate to the testes. The testes start releasing testosterone, which causes specialized cells to go through meiosis to develop into mature sperm. As the levels of testosterone rise, the levels of FSH and LH begin to decline. This feedback loop among the hormones helps to control the number of sperm that are produced.

Unlike eggs, which produce polar bodies, the developing sperm divide into four equal sperm cells, as shown in **FIGURE 2.4**. Each cell is haploid, with 23 chromosomes. Sperm cells then fully mature in the epididymis. As the diagram shows, each sperm has a head, midpiece, and tail. The head contains a nucleus and a cap region called the acrosome. When a sperm cell contacts an egg, the acrosome releases enzymes that allow the sperm to penetrate the egg's membrane. The midpiece holds the mitochondria that supply the sperm with ATP for the energy it needs. The tail, or flagellum, propels the sperm from the vagina to the fallopian tubes, where fertilization can take place.

After sperm are released through the penis, testosterone levels decline. These low levels stimulate the hypothalamus, and sperm production increases again. Most men can produce sperm throughout their lives, starting in puberty. However, the number of sperm usually declines with age.

**Compare** **How are the structures of the sperm and the egg similar?**

► MAIN IDEA

# Fertilization occurs when a sperm cell joins an egg cell.

For an egg to be fertilized, sperm must be present in the female reproductive system, usually in a fallopian tube. During sexual intercourse, the penis is inserted into the vagina until the tip comes close to the opening of the uterus. When semen is ejaculated through the penis, sperm are released into the vagina. One ejaculation can contain 50 million to 500 million sperm cells. The sperm must swim up through the uterus and into the fallopian tubes.

## Process of Fertilization

Out of millions of sperm cells released, only one will fertilize an egg. Why only one? The answer has to do with the egg's membrane—a protective layer filled with binding sites where the sperm can attach. When a sperm manages to contact and bind to the egg, the sperm's acrosome releases an enzyme that digests the membrane at that spot. The sperm can then enter the egg, as

## QUICK LAB | OBSERVING

### Human Sex Cells

In this lab, you will examine prepared slides of mammalian male and female sex cells.

**PROBLEM** How do male and female sex cells differ?

**PROCEDURE**

1. Examine a slide of sperm cells under low power and high power. Draw a sperm cell and label its structures.

2. Examine a slide of egg cells under low power and high power. Draw an egg cell and label its different structures.

**ANALYZE AND CONCLUDE**

1. **Analyze** Why is the flagellum an important structure in a sperm cell?

2. **Contrast** How is the egg structurally different from the sperm?

**MATERIALS**
- slide of mammalian sperm cells
- slide of mammalian egg cells
- microscope

shown in **FIGURE 2.5**. Once the egg is penetrated, its surface changes to form a barrier that stops other sperm from entering. In effect, the egg lets in one sperm, then closes the door on the others. The egg then completes meiosis II. Then the 23 chromosomes of the sperm join with the 23 chromosomes of the egg to form a fertilized egg called a **zygote.** This combination of chromosomes helps preserve genetic diversity because chromosomes in a pair often have different alleles of genes. This is one reason children are never exact genetic copies of their parents.

In rare cases, more than one egg may be released into the fallopian tubes. If two eggs are fertilized, they will develop into fraternal twins. Fraternal twins are not genetically the same. They are just like any other siblings who are born separately.

Genetically identical twins occur only when a single fertilized egg splits into two zygotes, each one with 46 chromosomes. As a result, two identical but separate embryos develop in the uterus. In even rarer cases, a fertilized egg may split into three, four, or more zygotes. If they all develop, the mother will give birth to several genetically identical babies.

### Problems in Fertilization

**Infertility** refers to any condition that makes reproduction difficult or impossible. In the male, for instance, the vas deferens may be too narrow or blocked, which prevents sperm from leaving the body. If the sperm count is too low or the sperm are weakened or deformed, fertilization may not occur. Certain illnesses, such as mumps in adults, can destroy the testes' ability to produce sperm. In females, diseases that damage the ovaries or fallopian tubes can prevent eggs from being produced or reaching the uterus. The eggs themselves may have defects that keep the sperm from getting through the membrane. Many infertility problems can be corrected through treatments such as medications, surgery, or even dietary changes.

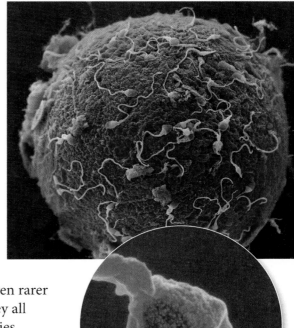

**FIGURE 2.5** In the top image, sperm surround an egg. The bottom image shows one sperm penetrating an egg's membrane. (colored SEM)

**Apply** **If twins are born and one is a boy and one is a girl, are they identical or fraternal siblings? Explain your answer.**

# Sexually transmitted diseases affect fertility and overall health.

Diseases passed from one person to another during sexual contact are called **sexually transmitted diseases,** or STDs. These diseases affect millions of people in their peak reproductive years and cause thousands of deaths. Some STDs in the early stages produce few symptoms. People do not realize they are carrying the disease and continue to infect others through sexual contact.

Bacterial STDs include chlamydia, syphilis, and gonorrhea. Chlamydia is the most common infection in the United States. Bacterial STDs attack the reproductive organs, such as the ovaries, and often cause infertility. In the case of syphilis, an untreated infection can even be fatal. Another infection, trichomoniasis, is caused by a parasite, shown in **FIGURE 2.6**. Trichomoniasis and chlamydia mostly affect young women aged 15 to 24 and can cause a serious condition known as pelvic inflammatory disease. People with these infections show few symptoms at first. This may be one reason why rates for trichomoniasis and chlamydia are increasing. Most parasitic and bacterial STDs can be treated with antibiotics.

Viral STDs include hepatitis B, genital herpes, human papillomavirus (HPV), and human immunodeficiency virus (HIV), which causes AIDS. Although medications can control these diseases, there are no cures. Antibiotics have no effect on viruses. HPV has been linked to cervical cancer, and AIDS has caused millions of deaths worldwide.

People can avoid STDs, just as they avoid other diseases. The surest ways are to abstain from sexual contact before marriage and for partners who do not have STDs to remain faithful in a committed relationship. Using a condom is the next safest choice; however, a condom can break or tear.

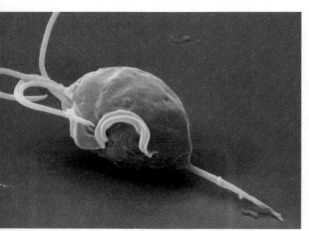

**FIGURE 2.6** The parasite *Trichomonas vaginalis* causes a common STD infection, trichomoniasis, that can affect fertility. (colored SEM; magnification 9000×)

**Infer  How might a bacterial STD infection affect the reproductive cycle of a male or female?**

©Eye of Science/Photo Researchers, Inc.

---

## 29.2 Formative Assessment

SELF-CHECK Online
HMDScience.com
PREMIUM CONTENT

### REVIEWING ▶ MAIN IDEAS

1. What is the main function of each phase in the **menstrual cycle**?

2. How does the structure of the sperm cell aid its function?

3. Describe how an egg is fertilized.

4. **Sexually transmitted diseases** can affect fertility. Explain why.

### CRITICAL THINKING

5. **Contrast**  Name two ways that the production of eggs differs from the production of sperm.

6. **Apply**  A woman gives birth to quadruplets, or four infants. Two of her children are identical twins. The other two are fraternal twins. How could this have happened?

### ⟡ CONNECT TO

#### DEVELOPMENTAL BIOLOGY

7. Every egg contains one X chromosome. Each sperm contains either one X or one Y chromosome. Explain why the sperm always determines a baby's gender.

# GO Online!

# GROW UP!

meals on the go

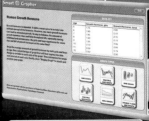

**Biology VIDEO CLIP**

**WebQuest**

**Smart ⊕ Grapher**

**Embryonic Development**
Find out which organs develop in the early stages of pregnancy.

**Healthy Diet, Healthy Body**
Developing fetuses depend on their mothers for nutrition. Explore the foods that a pregnant woman should eat and what she should avoid.

**Human Growth Hormone**
Graph the rise and fall of human growth hormone levels through adolescence for both girls and boys.

# Fetal Development

**KEY CONCEPT** Development progresses in stages from zygote to fetus.

### VOCABULARY

blastocyst
embryo
amniotic sac
placenta
umbilical cord
trimester
fetus

**SC.912.L.16.13** Describe the basic anatomy and physiology of the human reproductive system. Describe the process of human development from fertilization to birth and major changes that occur in each trimester of pregnancy.

### MAIN IDEAS

◗ The fertilized egg implants into the uterus and is nourished by the placenta.
◗ A zygote develops into a fully formed fetus in about 38 weeks.
◗ The mother affects the fetus, and pregnancy affects the mother.

### Connect to Your World

A human zygote develops from a single cell into a fully formed human in about nine months. The rate of growth in the first few weeks is astonishing. If you grew at the same rate after birth, you would be 4 meters (13 ft) tall at one month of age. The zygote's growth is directed by its DNA. However, the environment of the uterus and the mother's overall health also have a strong impact on how well the zygote develops.

### ▶ MAIN IDEA

## The fertilized egg implants into the uterus and is nourished by the placenta.

After fertilization, the zygote begins to divide through mitosis as it travels down the fallopian tube. During this time, the corpus luteum continues to secrete progesterone and some estrogen. These hormones increase the number of blood vessels in the lining of the uterus and prepare it to receive the fertilized egg. After the zygote reaches the uterus, another chain of events takes place that helps it to develop.

### Implantation in the Uterus

The zygote continues to undergo cell division until a hollow ball of cells called the **blastocyst** is formed. Cells on the surface of the blastocyst attach, or implant, into the uterine lining, as shown in **FIGURE 3.1**. Once the blastocyst is implanted, it goes through another stage in which three cell layers develop: the ectoderm, the mesoderm, and the endoderm.

The ectoderm layer develops into the skin and nervous system. The mesoderm layer forms many of the internal tissues and organs. The endoderm layer develops into many of the digestive organs and the lining of the digestive system. Once these structures begin to form, the ball of cells is known as an **embryo.**

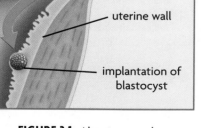

**FIGURE 3.1** About seven days after fertilization, the blastocyst enters the uterus and attaches, or implants, into the uterine wall.

blastocyst
uterine wall
implantation of blastocyst

**VISUAL VOCAB**

The **blastocyst** is a hollow ball of cells that implants in the uterus.

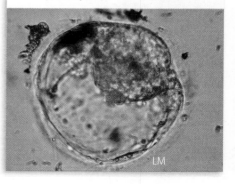

LM

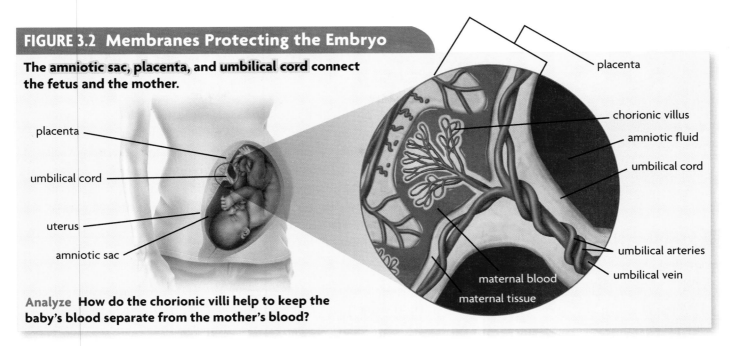

## FIGURE 3.2 Membranes Protecting the Embryo

**The amniotic sac, placenta, and umbilical cord connect the fetus and the mother.**

placenta

umbilical cord

uterus

amniotic sac

placenta

chorionic villus

amniotic fluid

umbilical cord

umbilical arteries

umbilical vein

maternal blood

maternal tissue

**Analyze** How do the chorionic villi help to keep the baby's blood separate from the mother's blood?

## Embryonic Membranes

As the pregnancy continues, membranes form that nourish and protect the developing embryo, as shown in **FIGURE 3.2**. One membrane, the amnion, becomes filled with fluid and is called the **amniotic sac** (AM-nee-AHT-ihk). This sac cushions the embryo within the uterus and protects it from sudden temperature changes. The amniotic sac surrounds the embryo until birth. Another membrane, the chorion (KAWR-ee-AHN), also begins to form. The chorion helps to nourish the embryo as it develops. The outer surface of the chorion has small projections called chorionic villi that extend into the uterine lining.

Together, the chorionic villi and the lining of the uterus form an important organ called the placenta. The **placenta** (pluh-SEHN-tuh) connects the mother and embryo to allow for the exchange of oxygen, nutrients, and wastes between them. Another structure, the **umbilical cord,** consists of two arteries and a vein that are twisted together. This cord connects the embryo inside the amniotic sac to the placenta. Nutrients and oxygen from the mother's blood diffuse into the chorionic villi, which contain blood from the embryo. The nutrients are carried to the embryo along the umbilical cord. In turn, wastes from the embryo are carried back along the umbilical cord to the chorionic villi. From there, the wastes diffuse into the mother's blood and are excreted in her urine.

The blood flows of the mother and the embryo move past each other but never mix. The placenta keeps the two flows separated. If proteins from the embryo leaked into the mother's circulatory system, they might be detected as foreign invaders by her immune system. The mother's immune system would then attack the proteins, which could end the pregnancy. The placenta provides a protective barrier for the embryo as it develops.

**Apply** Why might a pregnant woman need to be concerned about what she eats or drinks during pregnancy?

### CONNECT TO

#### CIRCULATORY SYSTEM

Like the pulmonary arteries and veins that you read about in **Respiratory and Circulatory Systems,** the umbilical arteries carry oxygen-poor blood and the umbilical vein carries oxygen-rich blood. The umbilical arteries carry blood away from the fetus's heart, and the umbilical vein carries blood to the fetus's heart.

Biology **VIDEO CLIP**

HMDScience.com

PREMIUM CONTENT

Fetal Development

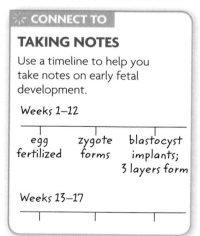

▶ MAIN IDEA

# A zygote develops into a fully formed fetus in about 38 weeks.

Human pregnancies are divided into **trimesters,** or three periods of roughly three months each, as summarized in **FIGURE 3.3.** Put in other terms, human pregnancy averages about 38 weeks from fertilization of the egg, or 40 weeks from the start of the last menstrual cycle. Throughout the nine months, several hormones help to maintain the pregnancy, including estrogen, progesterone, and human chorionic gonadotropin (goh-NAD-uh-TROH-pihn), which is produced by the placenta to help maintain progesterone levels. Thyroid hormones from the mother help to regulate the embryo's development.

## First Trimester

In the first trimester, embryonic stem cells undergo determination and differentiation to form the many specialized tissues and organs that will make up a human body. Recall that stem cells have the potential to become any one of the hundreds of different types of cells in the human body. The embryo can be more easily damaged during this trimester as the result of genetic errors or mutations, nutritional deficiencies in the mother, and any toxic chemicals, such as alcohol or drugs, that the mother may consume.

Even at this early stage, the complete body plan is already becoming visible. The heart begins beating at about five weeks. The early structures for the vertebrae and spinal cord have been formed. The brain is developing, many internal organs have appeared, and the arms and legs are evident. The embryo at nine weeks—now called a **fetus**—is only about 3 centimeters (about 1 in.) long, but is beginning to look like a small human being.

## Second Trimester

The second trimester is a time of continuing development and increased physical activity. The heartbeat can now be heard by placing a stethoscope over the uterus. As the fetus flexes its muscles, the mother can feel movement within her uterus. During these three months, the uterus expands enough to make the mother's pregnancy noticeable. As the fetus develops, the uterus continues to expand until it reaches four to five times its original size. At the end of the second trimester, the fetus may be only 30 centimeters (12 in.) long, but it looks more and more like a full-sized baby. Even its fingers and toes are fully formed, as shown in **FIGURE 3.3**.

## Third Trimester

In the third trimester, the fetus grows to its largest size. At birth, most babies weigh about 3 to 4 kilograms (7 to 9 lb) and are about 50 centimeters (20 in.) long. Babies born prematurely at the beginning of the third trimester have a difficult time surviving. Their organs, especially their lungs, are often too immature to function well. Babies born prematurely toward the middle of the third trimester often survive and thrive. In the last month, the lungs are strengthened as the fetus sucks in and pushes out the amniotic fluid.

**Infer** **Why might a fetus be more easily damaged by genetic errors or toxic chemicals during the first trimester than during any other trimester?**

# FIGURE 3.3  Trimesters of Development

During each trimester, the fetus goes through different stages of growth and development.

**Animated Biology**
HMDScience.com
PREMIUM CONTENT
Developmental Timeline

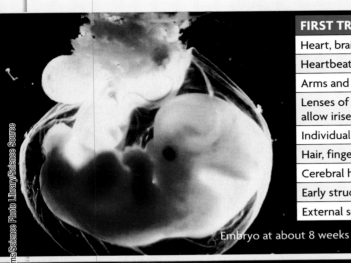

Embryo at about 8 weeks

### FIRST TRIMESTER: WEEKS 1–12

| |
|---|
| Heart, brain, intestines, pancreas, kidneys, liver are forming. |
| Heartbeat can be detected after week 5. |
| Arms and legs begin to develop. |
| Lenses of the eye appear; eyelids will later fuse shut to allow irises to develop. |
| Individual fingers and toes begin to form. |
| Hair, fingernails, and toenails develop. |
| Cerebral hemispheres begin to form. |
| Early structure of bronchi begin to develop. |
| External sex organs show sex of the fetus. |

Hand at week 6

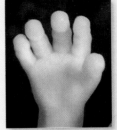

Hand at week 12

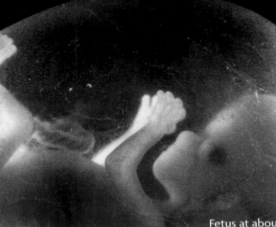

Fetus at about 25 weeks

### SECOND TRIMESTER: WEEKS 13–27

| |
|---|
| Most joints and bones have started to form. |
| Skin is protected by fine hair and waxy substance. |
| First movements are felt by mother. |
| Wake and sleep cycles are more regular. |
| Brain begins a stage of rapid growth. |
| Eyes open and blink; eyebrows and eyelashes have formed. |
| Fetus breathes in amniotic fluid, which strengthens lungs. |
| Fetus swallows amniotic fluid and makes urine. |

Hand at week 20

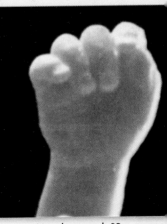

Fetus at about 32 weeks

### THIRD TRIMESTER: WEEKS 28–40

| |
|---|
| Fetus responds more strongly to light and sound outside the uterus. |
| Fetus has periods of dreaming; eyes are open when awake and closed when asleep. |
| Fine body hair thins and scalp hair grows in. |
| Bones are growing and hardening. |
| Synapses between neurons form in huge numbers. |
| Lungs complete development. |
| Fetus turns to head-down position. |

Hand at week 32

**CRITICAL VIEWING** Study the pictures of the embryo and fetus. What are some of the structural changes that have taken place from week 8 to week 32?

## INTERPRETING GRAPHS

Scientists collected data on the amounts of thyroid-stimulating hormone (TSH) in mothers and in their developing fetuses. Researchers wanted to determine the point at which a fetus's own endocrine system begins to work independently of its mother's. The *x*-axis shows the different times during the pregnancy that levels of TSH were measured.

- The *y*-axis shows the amount of TSH in microliters per milliliter ($\mu$L/mL).
- The blue bar represents the fetus's levels of TSH.
- The orange bar represents the mother's levels of TSH.

1. **Analyze** What happens to both the mother's TSH levels and the fetus's TSH levels as the pregnancy progresses?

2. **Analyze** What is the relationship between the week of pregnancy and fetal TSH levels?

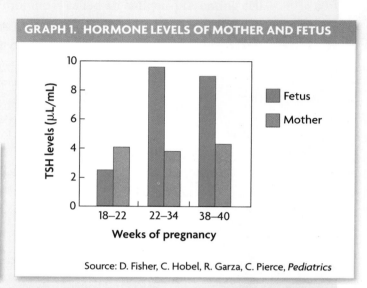

**GRAPH 1. HORMONE LEVELS OF MOTHER AND FETUS**

Source: D. Fisher, C. Hobel, R. Garza, C. Pierce, *Pediatrics*

## ▶ MAIN IDEA

# The mother affects the fetus, and pregnancy affects the mother.

Throughout pregnancy, the mother and the fetus continually affect each other's health. For the most part, whatever the mother eats or drinks, the baby is exposed to through the placenta and the umbilical cord. On the other hand, the hormones released during pregnancy and the nutritional needs of the fetus present their own challenges to the mother's health.

## Health of the Fetus

The fetus depends on the mother for all its nutrition. As a result, it is vitally important that the mother eat well throughout pregnancy. Her diet must include all the essential amino acids, vitamins, minerals, fats, and carbohydrates that the developing fetus needs. Vitamin and mineral supplements can provide extra amounts of these nutrients. For example, folic acid is an important B vitamin that can significantly lower the risk of serious birth defects in a fetus's brain and spinal cord. Folic acid is found in such foods as poultry, oranges, and dark green leafy vegetables. In contrast, toxic chemicals in alcohol, tobacco, and many other drugs can diffuse through the placenta and harm the fetus. These substances often interfere with fetal development and can cause many types of birth defects and produce learning disabilities in a child.

Studies have shown that many of these problems can be completely prevented if the mother avoids alcohol, tobacco, and drugs during the pregnancy. Even some over-the-counter medications can harm the fetus. As a result, the mother must check with a health care provider to be sure any medications she needs to take are safe for the fetus.

## Health of the Mother

The mother's health is affected by pregnancy in a number of ways. To supply enough energy for herself and her baby, the mother must add roughly 300 more Calories a day to her diet after the first trimester. During pregnancy, most women will gain an average of 12 kilograms (26 lb). However, gaining too much or too little weight can affect the fetus. Women who gain too little weight often have underweight babies who may have impaired immune systems, learning disabilities, and delayed development.

Hormone levels also fluctuate, affecting the mother's ability to maintain homeostasis. For example, some pregnant women are unable to control their glucose levels and may develop pregnancy-related diabetes. This type of diabetes normally disappears after the pregnancy is over. Hormones may also affect the digestive tract, causing what is known as morning sickness, or vomiting, for a time. This condition generally clears up as the pregnancy progresses. After the baby is born, some women may experience some depression during the time that their hormone levels are stabilizing. To help ensure a healthy pregnancy, the mother should have regular physical checkups. The normal challenges of pregnancy can be managed through proper diet, exercise, and medical care.

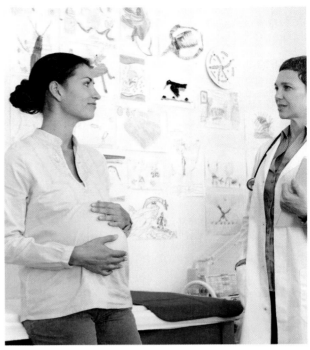

**FIGURE 3.4** Routine medical tests can be used to check the mother's blood pressure, glucose levels, nutrition, and other factors. The baby's growth and development in the uterus can also be monitored.

**Infer  When a woman first learns that she is pregnant, what lifestyle changes might she need to make?**

**SELF-CHECK** Online
HMDScience.com
PREMIUM CONTENT

# 29.3 Formative Assessment

### REVIEWING ▶ MAIN IDEAS

1. Explain the main functions of the **placenta** during a pregnancy.

2. List two milestones of fetal growth and development achieved in each **trimester.**

3. Give two examples of how the mother and **fetus** affect one another during pregnancy.

### CRITICAL THINKING

4. **Apply**  A woman doesn't want to gain more than 6 kg (13 lbs) during her pregnancy. What effects might this decision have on the fetus?

5. **Infer**  A baby is born 12 weeks premature. The organs are developed, but the baby must breathe using a ventilator. Explain why this treatment is necessary.

### CONNECT TO

**TISSUE REJECTION**

6. A woman with type O Rh⁻ blood is pregnant for a second time. During her first pregnancy, she developed antibodies for Rh⁺ factor. Her second baby's blood is type O Rh⁺. What might happen if some fetal blood leaks into the mother's blood?

# 29.4 Birth and Development

SC.912.L.16.13

SC.912.L.16.13 Describe the basic anatomy and physiology of the human reproductive system. Describe the process of human development from fertilization to birth and major changes that occur in each trimester of pregnancy.

**VOCABULARY**

infancy
childhood
adolescence
adulthood

**KEY CONCEPT** Physical development continues through adolescence and declines with age.

**MAIN IDEAS**

◉ Birth occurs in three stages.
◉ Human growth and aging also occur in stages.

### ⋅⋅⋅ Connect to Your World

After birth, you will spend nearly two decades learning how to live on your own. Until recently, scientists thought that the most important learning period happened in the first three years of life. Now they have discovered that in adolescence the brain goes through a second period of development. During this time, you are maturing emotionally and mentally, not just physically. This may be one reason why humans take so long to grow up.

### ► MAIN IDEA

## Birth occurs in three stages.

When the fetus has fully developed, the placenta can no longer provide enough nourishment. The time has come for the baby to be born. The birth process involves three stages: dilation of the cervix, emergence of the baby, and expulsion of the placenta, as shown in **FIGURE 4.1**. The physical changes that the mother's body goes through are known as labor.

### Dilation of the Cervix

Labor begins with regular contractions of the uterus. The hormone oxytocin (AHK-sih-TOH-sihn), released by the mother and the fetus, stimulates the muscles in the wall of the uterus. However, not all contractions mean that the baby is about to be born. Expectant mothers are usually taught to count the number and strength of these contractions. When they become more frequent, intense, and painful over time, then true labor has begun. The amniotic sac usually breaks in the early stages of labor, although it can break earlier. The amniotic fluid is released through the vagina, which is also called the birth canal.

The contractions serve to push the walls of the cervix apart. The baby cannot leave the uterus until the cervix dilates, or widens, to at least 10 centimeters (4 in.). This space allows most babies to pass through. If the cervix does not dilate, the doctor must make an incision through the abdominal wall to remove the baby, a procedure called a cesarean section, or c-section.

### Emergence of the Baby

This stage of the birth process is often the most stressful for the mother and the baby. If everything goes well, the powerful contractions of the uterus help rotate the baby so that its head is toward the cervix. In some cases, the baby

### ⋅⋅⋅ CONNECT TO

#### MARSUPIALS

In **A Closer Look at Amniotes,** you read about marsupial mammals that give birth to young that are little more than embryos. These tiny life forms must then find their way into the mother's pouch to complete their development. In contrast, human babies are born at an advanced stage of development.

FIGURE 4.1 **Three Stages of Birth**

**Birth begins with contractions and continues until the baby and placenta emerge.**

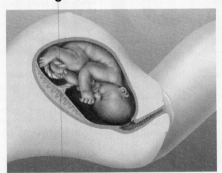

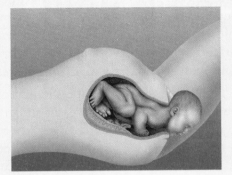

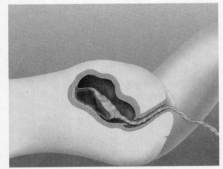

**STAGE 1**
As regular, strong contractions occur, the cervix dilates and the baby turns.

**STAGE 2**
The baby is pushed through the cervix and out of the vaginal canal.

**STAGE 3**
Contractions continue, expelling the placenta and helping to control bleeding.

**Predict** **At what point might the baby begin to breathe on its own?**

does not turn and is born feet first, which is a more difficult birth process. Usually, however, the baby is in the right position. The muscles of the uterus then push the baby into the birth canal. Once the head emerges, the rest of the body usually slips out quickly. Within a short time, the baby is breathing on its own. The hormone oxytocin also stimulates the mother's breasts to produce milk and increases her desire to bond with her infant. This bond helps to ensure that she will care for the baby after it is born.

### Expulsion of the Placenta

The third stage of birth happens soon after the baby emerges. As the uterine contractions continue, the placenta detaches from the wall of the uterus and is expelled. These contractions also help to constrict blood vessels and reduce the amount of bleeding the mother experiences. The baby's umbilical cord is clamped and cut a few inches from the abdomen. This bit of cord eventually dries up and falls away, leaving a scar called the navel, or belly button.

After living in the uterus for nine months, this newborn is breathing air for the first time. From now on it must live outside the protected environment of its mother's body.

**Infer** **Why might a head-first delivery be the safest for both mother and baby?**

### ▶ MAIN IDEA
# Human growth and aging also occur in stages.

Just as hormones regulate human reproduction, they are also involved in human growth after birth. Most children follow the same pattern of growth and development, but each child matures at his or her own pace. Rates of growth are also affected by factors such as genetics, nutrition, and environment.

Key hormones involved in growth include thyroxin, estrogen, testosterone, and human growth hormone (hGH), which is secreted by the pituitary gland. Human growth hormone increases the body's rate of fat metabolism and protein synthesis. These processes cause all body cells to divide, particularly bone and skeletal muscle cells. However, as a person ages, the pituitary secretes less and less hGH.

Smart ⊕ Grapher
HMDScience.com
**PREMIUM CONTENT**
**Human Growth Hormone**

©David Turnley/Corbis

## Infancy and Childhood

**Infancy** lasts from birth to about age 2. When babies are born, their homeostatic mechanisms are not completely developed. As a result, a newborn's body temperature, heart rate, and breathing rate vary more than they do in older children. Also, an infant's kidneys are less efficient at reabsorbing water, which can lead to rapid dehydration. As infancy progresses, homeostatic mechanisms mature and these variations decrease.

The first year of life is a period of rapid growth. Both male and female infants usually triple their weight and grow about 25 centimeters (10 in.) by their first birthday. Other changes are equally dramatic. Rapid development of the brain and nervous system occurs, and vision improves as babies learn to focus their eyes. They begin to coordinate muscle groups to sit, stand, and finally walk. By the end of infancy, children usually have a vocabulary of several words and may even express themselves using short sentences.

**Childhood** begins at age 2 and extends to about age 12. During childhood, physical growth slows down. Each year, most children grow only about 6 centimeters (3 in.) and gain about 4 kilograms (6 lb). Childhood is a time during which muscle skills and coordination improve as the nervous system matures. The continued development of sensory receptors, nerves, and muscles mean that children can learn both fine-motor skills such as writing and large-motor skills such as walking, as shown in **FIGURE 4.2**. Language and abstract reasoning abilities improve. Children begin to express more complex and varied emotions and become better able to understand the emotions of others.

**FIGURE 4.2** The child (top) is learning to control major muscle groups in her legs in order to walk. The adolescent skater (below) is adapting her knowledge of walking to learn a more sophisticated skill.

## Puberty and Adolescence

Puberty marks the beginning of sexual maturity and the development of sexual characteristics. As you read in Section 1, puberty begins when the hormones FSH and LH are released by the pituitary gland. For girls, the average age range for the onset of puberty is 10 to 14. For boys, the average age range is 10 to 16. During this time, young people experience a period of rapid growth stimulated by the release of testosterone and estrogen. Growth averages 5 to 7 centimeters (2 to 3 in.) and can reach up to 15 centimeters (6 in.) in one year. Young people often feel clumsy as they adjust to their changing bodies. They also experience rapid changes in their emotions and in their reasoning abilities as the brain continues to make new neural connections.

**Adolescence** begins at sexual maturity. In girls, sexual maturity is marked by ovulation and the first menstrual cycle. Although boys can ejaculate before sexual maturity, sexual maturity is indicated by the presence of sperm in the semen. During adolescence, bone growth continues until about age 15 in girls and about age 17 in boys. Adolescent boys and girls often experience greater strength and physical endurance in these years, and their coordination often improves. Although the brain stops increasing in size, the rearrangement of neural connections continues. In a very real sense, the adolescent brain is being "rewired" in preparation for adulthood.

## Adulthood and Aging

You might think that **adulthood** marks a time when people reach their peak in terms of skills and abilities. For the most part, you would be right. During these years, most people establish independent lives, and many raise their own families. However, adulthood, like other life stages, also marks a time of distinct physical changes, as you can see in **FIGURE 4.3.**

Scientists are only now beginning to unlock the mysteries of how the body ages. As a person grows older, some of the most important changes include a decline in immune functions and in the production of many key hormones, such as growth hormone, testosterone, and estrogen. Most women around age 50 or so go through menopause. In men, the sperm count gradually decreases. For both sexes, the body's rates of metabolism and digestion slow down. Skin becomes thinner and less elastic, bones lose calcium, and muscle mass decreases and is replaced by fat deposits.

However, scientists are also finding that how one experiences the aging process may depend as much on genetics, lifestyle, and environment as it does on chronological age. In general, those who eat a healthy diet, remain physically active, and keep learning may be able to slow down or even counteract many of the changes that aging brings about. For example, regular weight-bearing exercise such as walking several miles a week can help to maintain bone and muscle mass. Also, studies have shown that if a person keeps learning throughout life, the brain continues to make new neural connections just as it did when the person was younger.

**Compare** **Describe some of the ways that the process of aging is the reverse of the processes that occur during puberty and adolescence.**

FIGURE 4.3 These photos show the changes that occur in the same person's face from childhood to the 70s.

*1 ½ years*
*11 years*
*17 years*
*48 years*
*71 years*

(all) The Peel Family, Chicago, IL.

## 29.4 Formative Assessment

### REVIEWING ▶ MAIN IDEAS

1. Briefly describe the three stages of the birth process. What are the signs that true labor has begun?

2. What are the basic stages of development after birth? During which stage(s) does the greatest amount of physical growth usually occur?

### CRITICAL THINKING

3. **Compare and Contrast** What are some similarities and differences between the first year of life and the first year of puberty?

4. **Connect** Most large prey species, such as elk or antelope, are eutherian (placental), and not marsupial. What survival advantage might this give the offspring of the prey species?

### ✳ CONNECT TO

#### REPRODUCTIVE STRATEGIES

5. Many insects and fish give birth to hundreds of young at one time but do little to care for them. Most birds and mammals give birth to only one or a few young, but care for them until they are independent. What are some advantages and disadvantages to each type of reproduction?

# 29 Summary

**INTERACTIVE Review**
HMDScience.com

**PREMIUM CONTENT**
Review Games • Concept Map • Section Self-Checks

## KEY CONCEPTS

### 29.1 Reproductive Anatomy

**Female and male reproductive organs fully develop during puberty.** Puberty in both males and females begins with the release of two hormones: FSH and LH. These two hormones stimulate the release of estrogen in females and of testosterone in males. The female reproductive system produces ova, or egg cells, and provides an environment for a fertilized egg to develop. The male reproductive system produces sperm cells and delivers sperm to the female reproductive system.

### 29.2 Reproductive Processes

**Human reproductive processes depend on cycles of hormones.** In females, FSH, LH, estrogen, and progesterone control the production of egg cells and the three phases of the menstrual cycle. Females usually release only one egg a month until menopause.

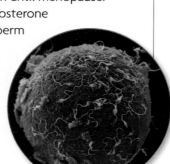

In males, FSH, LH, and testosterone control the production of sperm cells. Males release millions of sperm on ejaculation and can continue to produce sperm all their lives. When a sperm penetrates an egg and the two nuclei fuse, fertilization occurs. Reproductive organs can be damaged or destroyed by STDs.

### 29.3 Fetal Development

**Development progresses in stages from zygote to fetus.** The fetus is nourished and protected by the amniotic fluid, placenta, and umbilical cord, which connect the mother and fetus. Development takes roughly nine months, divided into three trimesters. To ensure the health of her baby, a mother needs to eat well, exercise, and have regular medical checkups.

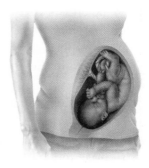

### 29.4 Birth and Development

**Physical development continues through adolescence and declines with age.** The birth process takes place in three stages: dilation of the cervix, emergence of the baby, and expulsion of the placenta. Key hormones regulate human growth and development throughout infancy, childhood, adolescence, and adulthood.

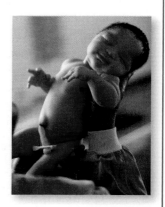

---

### 🔊 READING TOOLBOX    SYNTHESIZE YOUR NOTES

**Concept Map** Use a concept map like the one below to take notes on topics such as puberty.

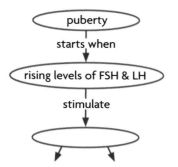

```
        puberty
           │
      starts when
           │
  rising levels of FSH & LH
           │
       stimulate
           │
         (     )
         ╱     ╲
```

**Process Diagram** A process diagram like the one below is a good way to remember the steps in reproductive processes.

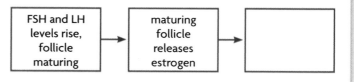

| FSH and LH levels rise, follicle maturing | → | maturing follicle releases estrogen | → | |

# 29 Review

## CHAPTER VOCABULARY

**29.1** reproductive system
puberty
ovum
ovary
uterus
estrogen
fallopian tube
testis
testosterone
scrotum
epididymis

vas deferens
semen
**29.2** follicle
ovulation
menstrual cycle
endometrium
corpus luteum
menopause
zygote
infertility
sexually transmitted disease

**29.3** blastocyst
embryo
amniotic sac
placenta
umbilical cord
trimester
fetus
**29.4** infancy
childhood
adolescence
adulthood

## Reviewing Vocabulary

**READING TOOLBOX** TERM RELATIONSHIPS

For each pair of terms below, write a sentence that contains both terms and shows a relationship between them. For example, *fetus, umbilical cord: The fetus obtains nutrients through the umbilical cord.*

1. puberty, testosterone
2. follicle, ovulation
3. menstrual cycle, endometrium
4. embryo, amniotic sac
5. menopause, adulthood

### Label Diagrams

In your notebook, write the term that matches each item pointed out in the diagrams below.

MALE

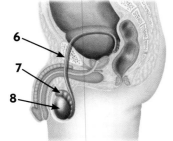

FEMALE

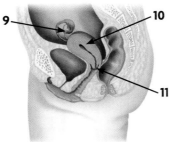

## Reviewing MAIN IDEAS

**12.** Describe the three main functions of estrogen.

**13.** The sperm move from the testes to the epididymis to the vas deferens as they develop. What happens at each location?

**14.** Explain what happens to the endometrium during the three phases of the menstrual cycle.

**15.** What process of cell division do eggs and sperm undergo to become mature sex cells?

**16.** What happens to their chromosomes when one sperm joins with an egg?

**17.** Why can chlamydia and syphilis be cured with antibiotics, but genital herpes and HIV cannot?

**18.** Explain how nutrients and oxygen from the mother's blood are transported to the embryo.

**19.** A premature baby is born near the end of the second trimester. Why would it have a harder time surviving than one born during the middle of the third trimester?

**20.** Discuss two ways in which a fetus's health could be harmed by a mother's actions during pregnancy.

**21.** Describe what marks the beginning of the birth process and what marks the end of the process.

**22.** In what two phases of human development might human growth hormone be the most active? Explain.

# Critical Thinking

**23. Infer** A young woman discovers that she is not ovulating. What endocrine glands might a doctor suspect are not functioning well? Explain your answer.

**24. Analyze** Alcohol and drug abuse can damage the brain, including the hypothalamus. How would this condition affect sperm production?

**25. Synthesize** In a bird egg, the developing embryo is inside the amnion, which contains fluid. The embryo gets nourishment from the yolk. The chorion lines the inside of the shell and helps protect the embryo. What structures in a human provide the same functions as these structures in the bird egg?

**26. Connect** How do you think your ability to express complex emotions and use abstract reasoning changed between the ages of 5 and 15?

## Interpreting Visuals

The structures shown below supply a fetus with oxygen and nutrients and remove its waste products. Use the diagram to answer the next three questions.

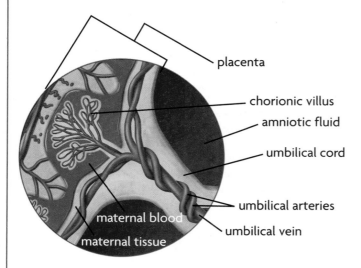

placenta

chorionic villus

amniotic fluid

umbilical cord

umbilical arteries

umbilical vein

maternal blood

maternal tissue

**27. Apply** Explain how the chorionic villi help move nutrients from the maternal blood to the fetus.

**28. Analyze** Look carefully at the umbilical arteries and vein. Which of these carries oxygen to the fetus? Explain.

**29. Predict** Suppose the umbilical arteries became blocked. Describe one way this condition would immediately affect the health of the fetus.

## Analyzing Data Interpret a Graph

Puberty is a time of rapid physical development. The graph below shows average height increases for boys and girls in centimeters per year from ages 8 to 19. Study the data to answer the next two questions.

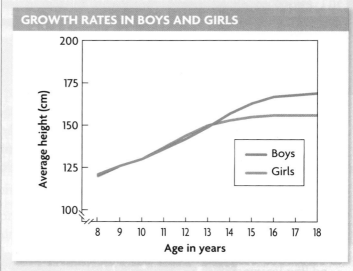

**GROWTH RATES IN BOYS AND GIRLS**

Source: Centers for Disease Control and Prevention

**30. Analyze** What does the graph show about the growth rates of boys and girls?

**31. Analyze** According to the graph, at about what age does the growth rate peak for boys? for girls?

## Making Connections

**32. Write a Brochure** This chapter explained how a pregnant woman can affect the health of her fetus. Write the text for a brochure that gives women information on how to promote their own health and the health of their babies during pregnancy. Include a list of what to do and what to avoid and the reasons why. Be sure to cover the topics of food, checkups, and unhealthy activities.

**33. Synthesize** Look again at the picture of the fetus on the chapter opener. Use what you have learned in this chapter to explain how the fetus can live without breathing while it is in the uterus.

# Standards-Based Assessment

1.

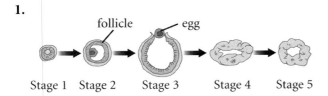

follicle    egg

Stage 1    Stage 2    Stage 3    Stage 4    Stage 5

The release of an egg from the ovary is called ovulation. A female's body temperature typically rises significantly when ovulation occurs. Above is an illustration of the development of the follicle and egg. At which stage would you expect to plot the highest temperature?

A  Stage 2

B  Stage 3

C  Stage 4

D  Stage 5

2. Each month, the levels of hormones in the female's reproductive system rise and fall. The precise coordination of these hormone levels is responsible for the timing and release of an egg. These hormones are coordinated through a series of

A  mitotic divisions.

B  meiotic divisions.

C  feedback loops.

D  fallopian tubes.

3. During most months of a woman's life, no egg is fertilized. Estrogen and progesterone hormone levels then both decline, and the uterus lining is shed in the process of menstruation. If an egg is fertilized, which of the following happens?

A  The levels of these hormones still decline.

B  The levels of these hormones remain high.

C  Another egg will soon be released.

D  Hormones are no longer needed.

**THINK THROUGH THE QUESTION**

Think about the importance of the uterus to a developing embryo. What needs to happen to prevent its lining from being shed?

4. Sex cells are produced during a specific type of cell division known as

A  mitosis.

B  meiosis.

C  ovulation.

D  implantation.

5.

During fertilization, a sperm enters an egg, and the two join to form a zygote. Which statement is *true* regarding the combination of alleles in the zygote?

A  All of the alleles come from the mother's egg.

B  All of the alleles come from the father's sperm.

C  New combinations of alleles are formed.

D  Allele combinations depend on when the egg is fertilized.

6. The placenta is an organ that allows for the exchange of oxygen, nutrients, and wastes between the mother and the developing embryo. In other words, the placenta is responsible for

A  allowing the mother and the embryo to maintain homeostasis at the same time.

B  repairing genetic damage due to mutation in the embryo.

C  ensuring that no fluids leave or enter the uterus.

D  serving as a barrier to keep out all toxic materials.

# BAGS OF STUFF INSIDE YOU

## Parts of your body and how they work together

A BOOK EXPLAINING COMPLEX IDEAS USING ONLY THE 1,000 MOST COMMON WORDS

RANDALL MUNROE
XKCD.COM

You know that an organ system is two or more organs working together to perform body functions. Here's a look at several organ systems in the human torso.

## THE STORY OF WHAT'S INSIDE YOUR BODY

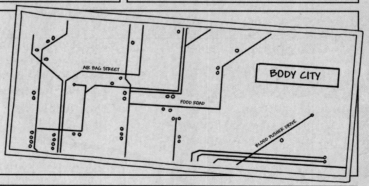

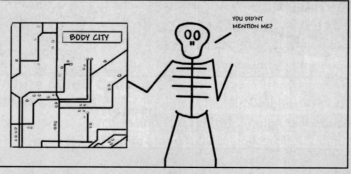

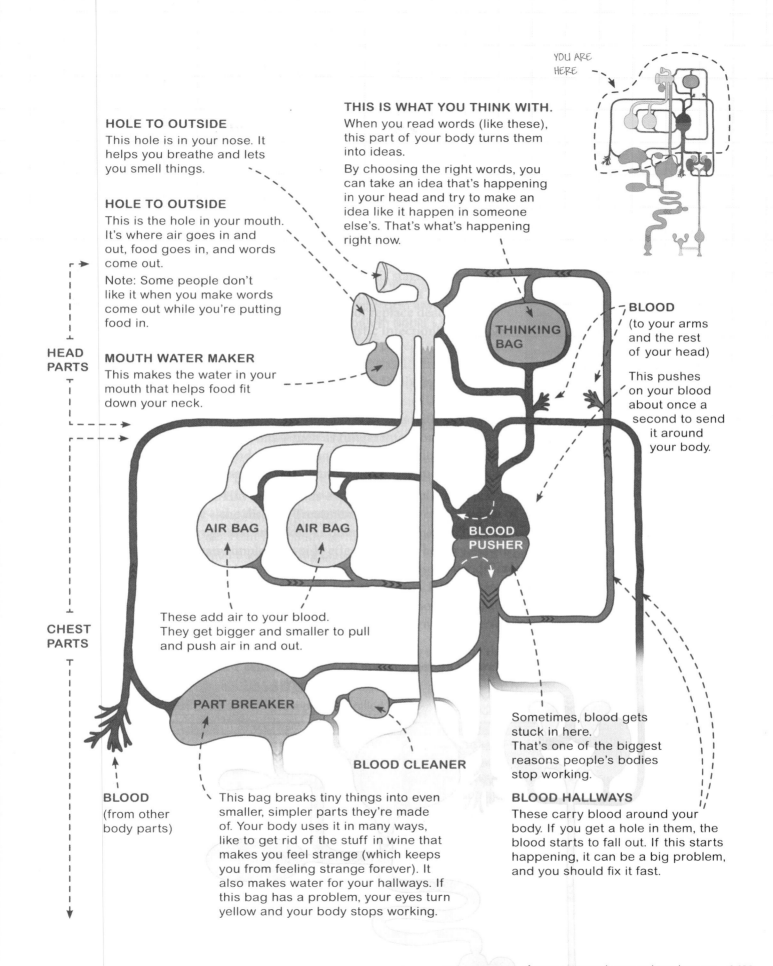

**HOLE TO OUTSIDE**

This hole is in your nose. It helps you breathe and lets you smell things.

**HOLE TO OUTSIDE**

This is the hole in your mouth. It's where air goes in and out, food goes in, and words come out.

Note: Some people don't like it when you make words come out while you're putting food in.

**MOUTH WATER MAKER**

This makes the water in your mouth that helps food fit down your neck.

**THIS IS WHAT YOU THINK WITH.**

When you read words (like these), this part of your body turns them into ideas.

By choosing the right words, you can take an idea that's happening in your head and try to make an idea like it happen in someone else's. That's what's happening right now.

YOU ARE HERE

**HEAD PARTS**

**CHEST PARTS**

**THINKING BAG**

**BLOOD**

(to your arms and the rest of your head)

This pushes on your blood about once a second to send it around your body.

**AIR BAG**

**AIR BAG**

**BLOOD PUSHER**

These add air to your blood. They get bigger and smaller to pull and push air in and out.

**PART BREAKER**

**BLOOD CLEANER**

Sometimes, blood gets stuck in here. That's one of the biggest reasons people's bodies stop working.

**BLOOD**

(from other body parts)

This bag breaks tiny things into even smaller, simpler parts they're made of. Your body uses it in many ways, like to get rid of the stuff in wine that makes you feel strange (which keeps you from feeling strange forever). It also makes water for your hallways. If this bag has a problem, your eyes turn yellow and your body stops working.

**BLOOD HALLWAYS**

These carry blood around your body. If you get a hole in them, the blood starts to fall out. If this starts happening, it can be a big problem, and you should fix it fast.

# BAGS OF STUFF INSIDE YOU

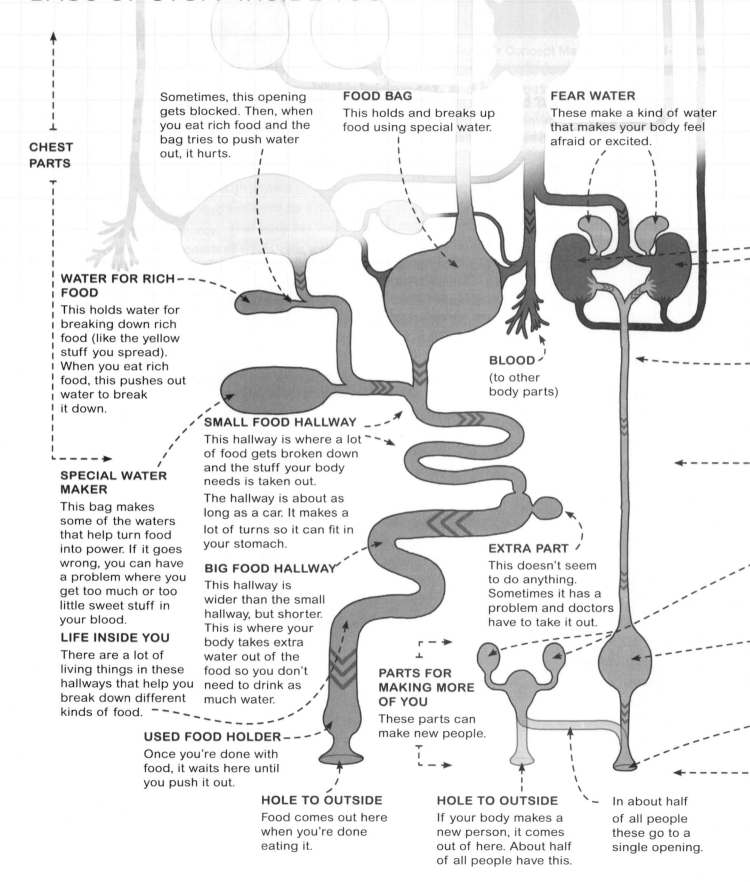

CHEST PARTS

Sometimes, this opening gets blocked. Then, when you eat rich food and the bag tries to push water out, it hurts.

**FOOD BAG**
This holds and breaks up food using special water.

**FEAR WATER**
These make a kind of water that makes your body feel afraid or excited.

**WATER FOR RICH FOOD**
This holds water for breaking down rich food (like the yellow stuff you spread). When you eat rich food, this pushes out water to break it down.

**SPECIAL WATER MAKER**
This bag makes some of the waters that help turn food into power. If it goes wrong, you can have a problem where you get too much or too little sweet stuff in your blood.

**LIFE INSIDE YOU**
There are a lot of living things in these hallways that help you break down different kinds of food.

**SMALL FOOD HALLWAY**
This hallway is where a lot of food gets broken down and the stuff your body needs is taken out.
The hallway is about as long as a car. It makes a lot of turns so it can fit in your stomach.

**BIG FOOD HALLWAY**
This hallway is wider than the small hallway, but shorter. This is where your body takes extra water out of the food so you don't need to drink as much water.

**BLOOD**
(to other body parts)

**EXTRA PART**
This doesn't seem to do anything. Sometimes it has a problem and doctors have to take it out.

**PARTS FOR MAKING MORE OF YOU**
These parts can make new people.

**USED FOOD HOLDER**
Once you're done with food, it waits here until you push it out.

**HOLE TO OUTSIDE**
Food comes out here when you're done eating it.

**HOLE TO OUTSIDE**
If your body makes a new person, it comes out of here. About half of all people have this.

In about half of all people these go to a single opening.

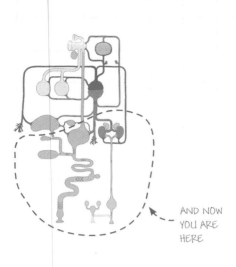

AND NOW
YOU ARE
HERE

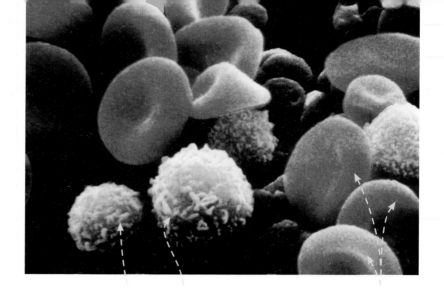

WHITE BLOOD
PIECES

RED BLOOD
PIECES

## BLOOD CLEANERS

These look for stuff in your blood that you're done with or have too much of—like extra sweet stuff, or stuff from the doctor that you ate to feel better—and send it to be pushed out of your body.

## YELLOW WATER HALLWAY

Most of the time, the water from your blood cleaners is yellow, but eating certain colorful foods can make it change color for a while.

(If it turns dark or red, it may mean you're sick.)

## BODY PLAN HOLDERS

These parts hold lots of plans for new people. Each plan is made from pieces of the plans used to make you.

These parts also control how your voice, hair, and body grow.

## YELLOW WATER HOLDER

This holds yellow water until you push it out.

## HOLE TO OUTSIDE

The yellow water from your blood comes out here.

LOWER
PARTS

## PUSHED TOGETHER

In real life, these parts are all pushed together inside your chest like this.

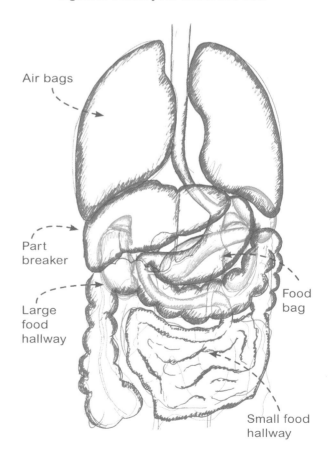

Air bags

Part
breaker

Large
food
hallway

Food
bag

Small food
hallway

©Kenneth Eward/BioGrafx/Science Source

# BIOZINE

*at* **HMDScience.com**

INTERNET MAGAZINE

*Go online for the latest biology news and updates on all BioZine articles.*

## Expanding the Textbook

### News Feeds

- 🔊 Science Daily
- 🔊 CNN
- 🔊 BBC

## Careers

## Bio Bytes

## Opinion Poll

## Strange Biology

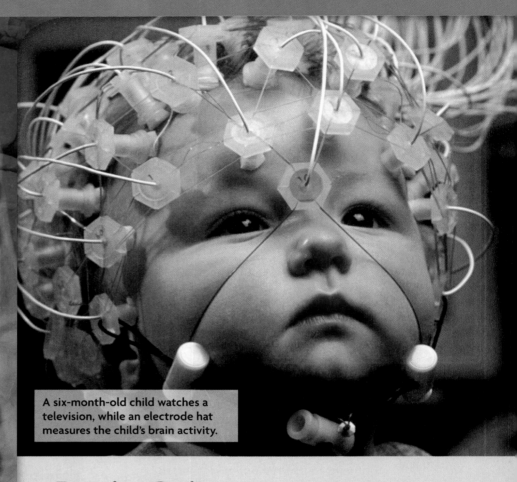

A six-month-old child watches a television, while an electrode hat measures the child's brain activity.

# Brain Science— We Are Wired to Learn!

*Your brain has more than 100 billion cells, called neurons. Together, the neurons in your brain are so powerful that they can process more information than the most powerful existing computer can in the same amount of time. Your brain can accomplish so much because you've spent years— every second of your life—learning from and interpreting the world around you.*

©Cary Wolinsky/National Geographic Image Collection

## Plasticity of the Brain

What factors affect the brain's plasticity, or ability to learn new things? How does the brain change with age? Neuroscientists have been addressing these questions since the early years of brain research.

During the first three years of life, the neurons in the brain rapidly form connections, or synapses, between each other. Neurons and synapses are overproduced in babies' brains because their brains are taking in a lot of new information. At three years old, the brain begins to prune, or reduce the number of, these connections so that only the most used connections are intact. On average, three-year-olds have two times more synapses than adults have.

The brain does not lose all of its plasticity after the age of three. Even adults can learn a new skill, such as speaking a foreign language. Neuroscientists have found a second wave of brain growth and plasticity, similar to that observed in infants, that begins just before puberty. During the teenage years, an intense period of pruning and strengthening begins and continues until the person is about 30. Connections that are used least are pruned away, and connections that are used the most are strengthened.

So how teenagers spend their time can affect their brain's wiring. A teen violinist who stops practicing will see his or her musical skill fade. One researcher says, "If a teen is doing music or sports or academics, those are the cells and connections that will be hard-wired. If they're lying on the couch or playing video games . . . those are the connections that are going to survive."

Although researchers agree that playing video games affects the brain, they do not agree on how the brain is affected. Some studies suggest that video games could strengthen beneficial connections. Other studies imply that some beneficial connections could become weakened.

## TECHNOLOGY S.T.E.M.

### Scanning the Brain

Much of today's research on brain function uses functional magnetic resonance imaging (fMRI). In a traditional MRI, computers use information from a magnetic field to make a three-dimensional cross-sectional image of the brain. An fMRI uses an MRI machine to detect the areas of the brain that are receiving the most oxygenated blood. Computer software analyzes this data to determine which part of the brain is active while a person performs different tasks, such as reading, listening to music, doing math, or even receiving medical treatment.

MRIs and fMRIs, though, are expensive and cumbersome, making it impractical to do brain imaging studies on large groups of people. Some researchers are now experimenting with using portable, weak lasers to scan the brain. This technique is called functional near-infrared spectroscopy, or fNIRS. The weak lasers used in fNIRS can measure changes in blood flow in the front part of the brain. Because it is the size of a headband and easily portable, researchers have used fNIRS to study blood flow to the brain in extreme environments, such as in parabolic flight.

Late in 2010, scientists at the University of Texas in Dallas and Arlington presented a new invention that can take images of a brain without a person's hair getting in the way: a laser hairbrush. Called "the hairbrush that reads your mind," the "brush optrode" slides laser fibers between hair follicles, getting an optical signal that is three to five times stronger than can be generated on the same head by a fNIRS headband.

**Read More >>** *at* **HMDScience.com**

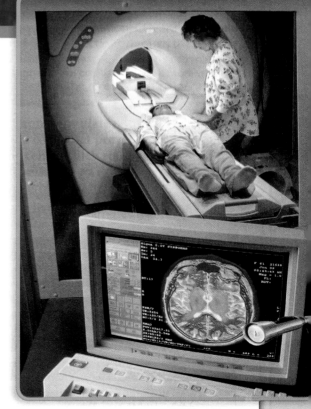

**A patient emerges from an MRI machine as a computer maps oxygen (orange) in the patient's brain.**

## The Multitasking Brain

How might video games strengthen connections in your brain? Some video games present the player with complicated puzzles and patterns. The player must take in visual messages from the video screen while using problem-solving skills to analyze patterns. This multitasking requires the player to use different areas of the brain at the same time. Using language has a similar effect on the brain as playing video games in that both activate many areas of the brain at the same time.

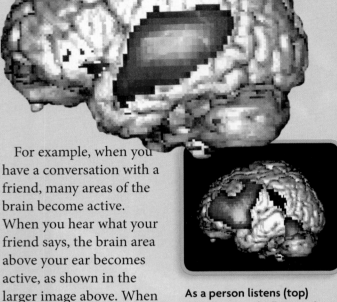

## CAREERS

### Neuroscientist in Action

| DR. RAE NISHI | |
|---|---|
| **TITLE** Director, Neuroscience Graduate Program, University of Vermont | |
| **EDUCATION** Ph. D., Biology, University of California, San Diego | |

Dr. Rae Nishi's research proves that you do not need complicated technology, such as fMRIs, to make discoveries in neuroscience. Through observation and experiment, Dr. Nishi's research tries to answer the question: What causes brain cells to die?

Although the question is too broad to answer completely, Dr. Nishi has discovered a molecule that seems to keep alive brain cells in dying chick embryos. She also found that by blocking a certain receptor on the surface of neurons, dying neurons will stop showing signs of decline. Studies of how and why brain cells might die are important in understanding Alzheimer's and Parkinson's diseases, which cause certain areas of the brain to become inactive.

"There is no profession as exciting as being a scientist," Dr. Nishi says. "You get to learn new things every day. You get to make discoveries. You get to solve puzzles." Dr. Nishi is currently working to determine how the molecules released during one neuron's death might trigger the growth of new, neighboring neurons.

**Read More >>** *at* **HMDScience.com**

For example, when you have a conversation with a friend, many areas of the brain become active. When you hear what your friend says, the brain area above your ear becomes active, as shown in the larger image above. When you form a response and speak, different brain areas become activated, as shown in the smaller image at right. The front of the brain is activated when you interpret your friend's words and form a response. When you begin to respond, an area in the back of the brain becomes active. This area becomes more and more active as you talk.

As a person listens (top) and then speaks (bottom), different areas of the brain become active (red and yellow).

Reading is another complicated activity. The same areas of your brain that are active when you talk to your friend are active when you read. But another area is also activated. This third area is farther back in the brain. It allows you to see and interpret the printed words in front of you. Even people who read Braille use the visual part of their brain to interpret what is on the page.

## Unanswered Questions

Every new discovery in neuroscience brings with it new questions. Some of these include the following:

- Can the plasticity of an adult brain be used to help adults recover from brain injuries and diseases?
- Can neuroscientists find ways to treat, or even cure, disorders such as Alzheimer's disease?
- Why are humans, and not other primates, good at learning words and systems of grammar?

**Read More >>** *at* **HMDScience.com**

# Student Resources

# Lab Handbook

## Safety

Before you work in the laboratory, read these safety rules. Ask your teacher to explain any rules that you do not completely understand. Refer to these rules later on if you have questions about safety in the science classroom.

### Directions

- Know where the fire extinguisher, fire blanket, shower, and eyewash are located in your classroom.
- Read all directions and make sure that you understand them before starting an investigation or lab activity. If you do not understand how to do a procedure or how to use a piece of equipment, ask your teacher.
- Do not begin any investigation or touch any equipment until your teacher has told you to start.
- Never experiment on your own. If you want to try a procedure that the directions do not call for, ask your teacher for permission first.
- If you are hurt or injured in any way, tell your teacher immediately.

### Dress Code

- Wear goggles when using glassware, sharp objects, or chemicals; heating an object; or working with anything that can easily fly up into the air and hurt someone's eye.
- Tie back long hair or hair that hangs in front of your eyes.
- Remove any article of clothing—such as a loose sweater or a scarf—that hangs down and may touch a flame, chemical, or piece of equipment.
- Observe all safety icons calling for the wearing of eye protection, gloves, and aprons.

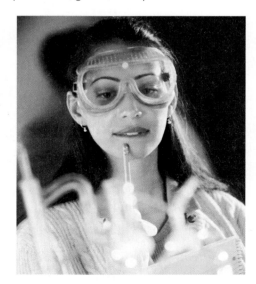

### Heating and Fire Safety

- Keep your work area neat, clean, and free of extra materials.
- Use only borosilicate glass for heating substances.
- Never reach over a flame or heat source.
- Point objects being heated away from you and others.
- Never heat a substance or an object in a closed container.
- Use oven mitts, clamps, tongs, or a test tube holder to hold heated items.
- Never touch an object that has been heated. If you are unsure whether something is hot, treat it as though it is.
- After heating test tubes, place them in a test tube rack.
- Do not throw hot substances into the trash. Wait for them to cool and dispose of them in the container provided by your teacher.

### Chemical Safety

- Always wear goggles when working with any type of chemical, even household items such as baking soda.
- Stand when you are working with chemicals. Pour them over a sink or your work area, not over the floor. If you spill a chemical or get it on your skin, tell your teacher right away.
- If you get a chemical in your eye, use the eyewash immediately.
- Never touch, taste, or sniff any chemicals in the lab. If you need to determine odor, waft. To waft, hold the chemical in its container 15 cm (6 in.) away from your nose, and use your fingers to bring fumes from the container to your nose.
- Keep lids on all chemicals you are not using.
- Use materials only from properly labeled containers.
- Never use more chemicals than the procedure calls for.
- When diluting acid with water, always add acid to water.
- Never put unused chemicals back into the original containers. Dispose of extra chemicals in the container provided by your teacher.
- Always wash your hands after handling chemicals.

## Electrical Safety

- Never use lamps or other electrical equipment with frayed cords.
- Make sure no cord is lying on the floor where someone can trip over it.
- Do not let a cord hang over the side of a counter or table so that the equipment can easily be pulled or knocked to the floor.
- Never let cords hang into sinks or other places where water can be found.
- Turn off all power switches before plugging an appliance into an outlet.
- Never touch electrical equipment with wet hands.
- Never try to fix electrical problems. Immediately inform your teacher of any problems.
- Unplug an electrical cord by pulling on the plug, not the cord.

## Glassware and Sharp-Object Safety

- Use only clean glassware that is free of chips and cracks.
- If you break glassware, tell your teacher right away.
- If you use a microscope that has a mirror, do not aim the mirror directly at the sun as you can damage your eyes.
- Use knives and other cutting instruments carefully. Always wear eye protection and cut away from yourself.
- Clean glassware according to your teacher's instructions after you use it.
- Use an appropriately sized test tube for the quantity of chemicals you are using, and store test tubes in a test tube rack.

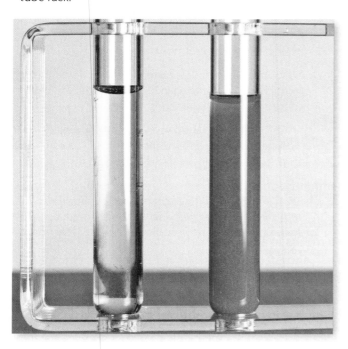

## Animal Safety

- Never hurt an animal.
- Touch animals only when necessary. Follow your teacher's instructions for handling animals.
- Wear gloves when handling animals or preserved specimens.
- Specimens for dissection should be properly mounted and supported.
- Do not cut a specimen while holding it in your hands.
- Do not open containers of live microorganisms unless you are directed to do so.
- Dispose of preserved specimens as directed by your teacher.
- Always wash your hands with soap and water after working with animals or specimens.

## Cleanup

- Follow your teacher's instructions for the disposal, recycling, or storage of supplies.
- Clean your work area and pick up anything that has dropped to the floor.
- Wash your hands.

# Lab Handbook

## Safety Symbols

Safety is the priority in the science classroom. In all of the activities in this textbook, safety symbols are used to alert you to materials, procedures, or situations that could be potentially hazardous if the safety guidelines are not followed. Learn what you need to do when you see these icons, and read all lab procedures before coming to the lab so you are prepared. Always ask your teacher if you have questions.

 **ANIMAL SAFETY** Never injure an animal. Follow your teacher's instructions for handling specific animals or preserved specimens. Wash your hands with soap and water when finished handling animals or preserved specimens.

 **APRON** Wear an apron when using any substance that could cause harm if spilled on you. Stand whenever possible to avoid spilling in your lap.

 **BREAKAGE** Use caution when handling items that may break, such as glassware and thermometers. Always store test tubes in a test tube rack.

 **CHEMICAL SAFETY** Always wear goggles when working with chemicals. Stand whenever possible when working with chemicals to avoid spilling on your lap. Tell your teacher immediately if you spill chemicals on yourself, the table, or floor. Never taste any substance or chemical in the lab. Always wash your hands after working with chemicals.

 **DISPOSAL** Follow your teacher's instructions for disposing of all waste materials, including chemicals, specimens, or broken glass.

 **ELECTRICAL SAFETY** Keep electrical cords away from water to avoid shock. Do not use cords with frayed edges. Unplug all equipment when done.

 **FIRE SAFETY** Put on safety goggles before lighting flames. Remove loose clothing and tie back hair. Never leave a lit object unattended. Extinguish flames as soon as you finish heating.

 **FUMES** Always work in a well-ventilated area. Bring fumes up to your nose by wafting with your fingers instead of sniffing.

 **GENERAL SAFETY** Always follow the safety rules and ask your teacher if you are unsure about something. If you are designing your own experiment, get your teacher's approval on your plan before you start. Think about which safety rules you must follow in your experiment.

 **GLOVES** Always wear gloves to protect your skin from possible injury when working with substances that may be harmful or when working with animals.

 **HAND WASHING** Wash your hands with soap and water after working with soil, chemicals, animals, or preserved specimens.

 **HEATING SAFETY** Wear goggles and never leave any substance while it is being heated. Use tongs, hot pads, or test tube holders to hold hot objects. Point any materials being heated away from you and others. Place hot objects such as test tubes in test tube racks while cooling.

 **HOT/GLOVE** Always wear gloves such as oven mitts when handling larger hot materials.

 **POISON** Never touch, taste, or inhale chemicals. Most chemicals are toxic in high concentrations. Wear goggles and wash your hands.

 **SAFETY GOGGLES** Always wear safety goggles when working with chemicals, heating any substance, or using a sharp object or any material that could fly up and injure you or others.

 **SHARP OBJECTS** Use scissors, knives, or razor tools with care. Wear goggles when cutting something with scalpels, knives, or razor tools. Always cut away from yourself.

# The Metric System and SI Units

Scientists around the world use the metric system of measurement. The official name for the metric system is the International System of Units (SI). The short name SI comes from the French name, Système International d'Unités.

## SI Units

SI includes units for measuring length, mass, volume, temperature, and many other properties. The most commonly used SI units are shown in Table 1.

The relationships between all SI units are based on powers of 10. In most cases, an SI unit has a prefix that shows its relationship to the base unit. For example, 1 kilometer is 1000 meters, and 1 centimeter is one-hundredth of a meter. Table 2 lists the commonly used SI prefixes along with their symbols and values.

### TABLE 1: COMMON SI UNITS

| PROPERTY | NAME |
|---|---|
| Length | meter (m) |
| Volume | liter (L) |
| Mass | kilogram (kg) |
| Temperature | Kelvin (K) |

### TABLE 2: SI PREFIXES

| PREFIX | SYMBOL | VALUE |
|---|---|---|
| giga- | G | 1,000,000,000 |
| mega- | M | 1,000,000 |
| kilo- | k | 1000 |
| hecto- | h | 100 |
| deca- | da | 10 |
| deci- | d | 0.1 |
| centi- | c | 0.01 |
| milli- | m | 0.001 |
| micro- | μ | 0.000001 |
| nano- | n | 0.000000001 |
| pico- | p | 0.000000000001 |

For your reference, the mass of a paper clip is about 1 g. The diameter of a red blood cell is very small—about 10 μm.

## Customary to SI Conversion

Although all scientists use the metric system, in the United States the customary system of measurements is still widely used. Table 3 provides useful equivalents for making conversions between these two systems of measurement.

### TABLE 3: CUSTOMARY AND SI EQUIVALENTS

| U.S. CUSTOMARY | SI |
|---|---|
| 1 inch (in.) | 2.54 centimeters (cm) |
| 39.37 inches (in.) | 1 meter (m) |
| 0.62 miles (mi) | 1 kilometer (km) |
| 1.06 quarts (qt) | 1 liter (L) |
| 1 fluid ounce (oz) | 236 milliliters (mL) |
| 2.2 pounds (lb) | 1 kilogram (kg) |
| 1 ounce (oz) | 28.3 grams (g) |

## Temperature

Use the formulas at right for converting between Celsius and Fahrenheit temperatures.

$$°C = \frac{5}{9} \times (°F - 32)$$

$$°F = \left(\frac{9}{5} \times °C\right) + 32$$

**Mass of paper clip = 1 g**

**Diameter of a red blood cell = 10 μm**

## Measuring in the Lab

Collecting accurate and precise data in the lab requires the skillful use of some basic lab equipment. Be sure that you know how to use all equipment correctly in the lab, not only to obtain accurate results but also to ensure your safety.

### Metric Rulers

- Use metric rulers or meter sticks to measure length.
- Because the end of a meter stick or ruler is often imperfect, begin the measurement from the 1 cm mark.
- Lay a ruler flat on top of the object so that the 1 cm mark lines up with one end. Make sure the ruler and the object do not move between the time you line them up and the time you take the measurement.
- Estimate the reading to one place value beyond what is marked on the ruler. The ruler is marked to the tenths place value, so estimate to the hundredths. The stem of the leaf hits the ruler about halfway between the 4.2 and 4.3 cm marks, so it is estimated at 4.25 cm. However, it is necessary to subtract 1 cm from the edge of the ruler not used in the measurement, so the leaf measures 3.25 cm.

### Graduated Cylinder

- Use a graduated cylinder to measure the volume of a liquid.
- You can use a graduated cylinder to find the volume of a solid object by measuring the increase in a liquid's level after you add the object to the cylinder.
- Be sure that the graduated cylinder is on a flat surface. Your eye level should be even with the surface of the liquid.
- Read the volume of the liquid at the bottom of the curve, or meniscus (muh-NIHS-kuhs).
- The volume of liquid is on the 96 mL mark. Estimate to one place value beyond what is marked on the graduated cylinder. The volume of liquid is 96.0 mL.

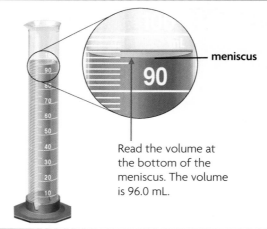

meniscus

Read the volume at the bottom of the meniscus. The volume is 96.0 mL.

### Thermometer

- To measure the temperature of a liquid, place a thermometer into the container without letting the thermometer touch the bottom of the container. Attach a clip to hold the thermometer in place, especially if the liquid is hot.
- As the liquid moves up or down inside the thermometer, rotate the thermometer for more accurate results.
- Record the measurement when the liquid in the thermometer stops moving. Take note of the highest point of liquid by estimating to the nearest tenth of a degree.
- The temperature on this thermometer is 24.5°C.

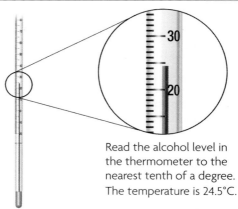

Read the alcohol level in the thermometer to the nearest tenth of a degree. The temperature is 24.5°C.

## Triple-Beam Balance

This balance has a pan and three beams with sliding masses, called riders. Each beam is calibrated to a different level of mass, allowing the balance to be accurate to a tenth of a gram. At one end of the beams, a pointer indicates whether the mass on the pan is equal to the masses shown on the beams.

1. Place the balance on a stable, level surface.

2. Make sure the balance is zeroed before measuring the mass of an object. The balance is zeroed if the pointer is at zero when nothing is on the pan and the riders are at their zero points. Use the adjustment knob under the pan of the balance to zero it.

3. Place the object to be measured on the pan. Do not place a hot object or chemical on the pan. The changing temperature may have a direct impact on your measurement and can also be dangerous.

4. Move the riders one notch at a time away from the pan. Begin with the largest rider. If moving the largest rider one notch brings the pointer below zero, move the mass back and then begin measuring the mass of the object with the next smaller rider.

5. Change the positions of the riders until they balance the mass on the pan and the pointer is at zero. Then add the readings from the three beams to determine the mass of the object.

6. The balance below is being used to measure a beaker of water. To find the mass of the water inside the beaker, a student moved the riders to the positions shown. The total mass of the beaker and water is 163.0 g, but you must also subtract the mass of the empty beaker from the total.

Mass of water = Mass of beaker + water   = 163.0 g
                            − Mass of beaker =   63.0 g
-------------------------------------------------------
Mass of water                                  = 100.0 g

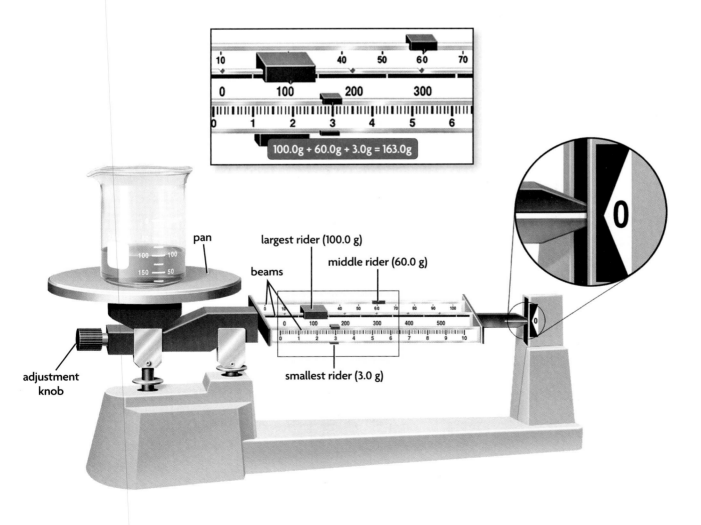

100.0g + 60.0g + 3.0g = 163.0g

pan

largest rider (100.0 g)

middle rider (60.0 g)

beams

smallest rider (3.0 g)

adjustment knob

# Lab Handbook

## Using a Light Microscope

Microscopes are used to view objects too small to be seen with the naked eye.

### Viewing an Object

Use these directions to view your specimen.

1. Use the coarse adjustment to raise the body tube.
2. Adjust the diaphragm so that you can see a bright circle of light through the eyepiece.
3. Place the slide on the stage. Be sure to center it over the hole in the stage and secure it with the stage clips.
4. Turn the nosepiece to click the scanning objective lens into place.
5. Using the coarse adjustment knob, slowly lower the lens and focus on the specimen being viewed. Be sure not to touch the slide or object with the lens.
6. When using the high power lens, use only the fine adjustment knob.
7. Move the slide on the stage with very small movements to view other parts of it. You may need to refocus using the fine adjustment.

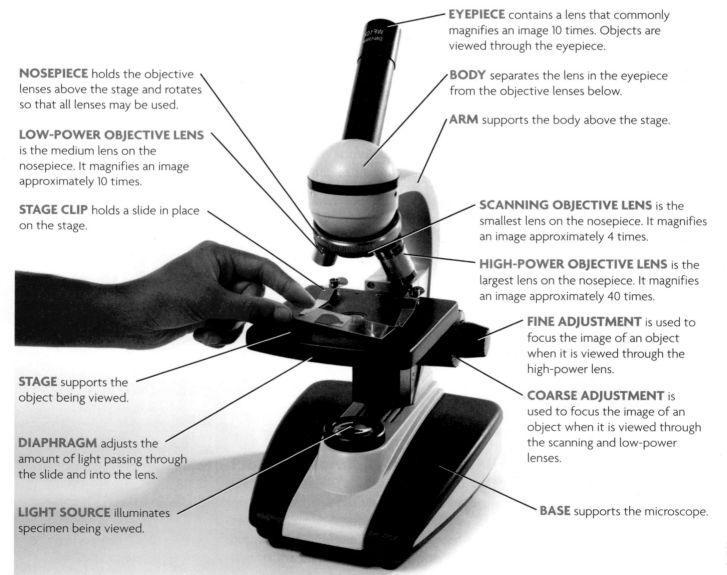

**NOSEPIECE** holds the objective lenses above the stage and rotates so that all lenses may be used.

**LOW-POWER OBJECTIVE LENS** is the medium lens on the nosepiece. It magnifies an image approximately 10 times.

**STAGE CLIP** holds a slide in place on the stage.

**STAGE** supports the object being viewed.

**DIAPHRAGM** adjusts the amount of light passing through the slide and into the lens.

**LIGHT SOURCE** illuminates specimen being viewed.

**EYEPIECE** contains a lens that commonly magnifies an image 10 times. Objects are viewed through the eyepiece.

**BODY** separates the lens in the eyepiece from the objective lenses below.

**ARM** supports the body above the stage.

**SCANNING OBJECTIVE LENS** is the smallest lens on the nosepiece. It magnifies an image approximately 4 times.

**HIGH-POWER OBJECTIVE LENS** is the largest lens on the nosepiece. It magnifies an image approximately 40 times.

**FINE ADJUSTMENT** is used to focus the image of an object when it is viewed through the high-power lens.

**COARSE ADJUSTMENT** is used to focus the image of an object when it is viewed through the scanning and low-power lenses.

**BASE** supports the microscope.

© HMH

## Making a Wet Mount

Use these steps to prepare a specimen to be viewed under a microscope.

Place the specimen in the center of a clean slide.

Place a drop of water on the specimen.

Place a cover slip on the slide. Put one edge of the cover slip into the drop of water, and slowly lower the cover slip over the specimen.

Remove any air bubbles from under the cover slip by gently tapping the cover slip.

Dry any excess water before placing the slide on the microscope stage for viewing.

## Staining a Specimen

After you make a wet mount, use these steps to stain the specimen.

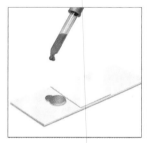 

filter paper

Place a drop of stain at one end of the cover slip.

Hold a piece of filter paper with forceps at the other end of the cover slip. The stain will flow underneath the cover slip and stain the specimen.

# Lab Handbook

## Calculating Magnification

When you look through a microscope, you see a magnified image of the specimen on the slide. Magnification describes how much larger an object appears when viewed through a microscope than its actual size. Calculating the magnification of the image will give you an idea of the sizes of its features.

There are two magnifying features of every microscope: the eyepiece and the objective lens. The **eyepiece** has a lens that magnifies the image 10× (times) its actual size. The objective lenses magnify the image by different levels.

|  |  |  |
|---|---|---|
| | Scanning Objective | 4× |
| Eyepiece 10× • | Low-Power Objective | 10× |
| | High-Power Objective | 40× |

The total magnification of the image is the product of multiplying the eyepiece magnification by the objective lens magnification.

The examples below show how to calculate the total magnification of the daphnia under each lens.

**EXAMPLE**
Eyepiece • Scanning Objective = Total Magnification
  (10×)  •       (4×)       = 40×
This image is magnified 40× its actual size.

**EXAMPLE**
Eyepiece • Low-Power Objective = Total Magnification
  (10×)  •     (10×)     = 100×
The image is magnified 100× its actual size.

**EXAMPLE**
Eyepiece • High-Power Objective = Total Magnification
  (10×)  •     (40×)    = 400×
This image is magnified 400× its actual size.

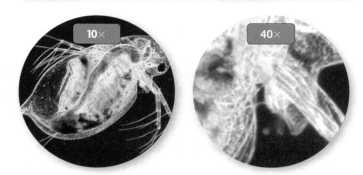

## Calculating Specimen Size

The field of view is the area seen through the microscope eyepiece. You can calculate the estimated size in micrometers (μm) of a specimen or object you are viewing based on the size of the field of view. Since many specimens viewed are smaller than a millimeter, the sizes of specimens are usually written in micrometers. Use these steps to calculate specimen size.

1. Place a ruler on the microscope stage and use the coarse adjustment to focus the image in the 4× objective lens.

2. Look at the markings on a ruler viewed in the eyepiece, as shown in the image below.

3. Estimate the diameter of the field of view to the nearest millimeter, which is approximately 4 mm in this example.

4. Remove the ruler and put the slide specimen on the stage.

5. Adjust the slide so the specimen is at one side of the field of view. Estimate the size of the specimen based on the field of view. The length of the daphnia specimen viewed under the scanning objective lens is about 2 mm.

6. Convert mm to μm.

  **length of specimen** • 1000 μm/mm = ?
       2 mm    •  1000 μm/mm = 2000 μm

# Designing Experiments

Biologists continually make observations about the natural world around them and raise questions about these observations. Designing experiments to answer these questions serves as the basis of scientific discovery.

An **experiment** is a test under controlled conditions that is made to find a cause-and-effect relationship between variables. Every well-designed experiment has a purpose and an organized, step-by-step procedure.

## Determining a Purpose

A simple observation that sparks your interest can lead to a purpose for an experiment. An observation can lead to many questions, but you should choose just one question to study. From that starting point, you can do background research and examine the results of previous experiments.

- Write the purpose of your experiment as a question or problem that you want to investigate.
- Write down specific questions that you will research to find information that will help you design your experiment.

**EXAMPLE**

Suppose you notice that different patches of plants appear to grow better in different areas around your school. How could you use this observation to design an experiment?

Problem: How does fertilizer affect plant growth?

Research Questions
  What nutrients do plants need?
  Which fertilizers contain those nutrients?

©Cathlyn Melloan/Getty Images

## Writing a Hypothesis

A **hypothesis** is a tentative explanation for an observation. A hypothesis leads to testable predictions of what would happen if the hypothesis is valid.

An experiment is designed to test a hypothesis, not to prove that a hypothesis is correct. An experiment cannot prove a hypothesis; data from the experiment can only support it or fail to support it. Keep in mind that there are no "good-or-bad, right-or-wrong" experimental results. Even when results fail to support a hypothesis, they can lead to an idea for another experiment. Hypotheses can be written in several ways.

**EXAMPLE**

Hypothesis: Nitrogen is a nutrient that plants need for growth.

Testable prediction: If plants are given fertilizer that contains nitrogen, plant growth will increase.

Formalized hypothesis: If plants need the nutrient nitrogen to grow, then plants given fertilizer with nitrogen will experience an increase in growth.

## Identifying Variables and Constants

All experiments include constants and variables. **Constants** are all of the factors that are kept the same—held constant—during the entire experiment. A variable is any factor that changes. The **independent variable** is the factor that you are testing and that you manipulate, or change. The **dependent variable** is the factor that you measure. The dependent variable changes, or "depends on," the independent variable. In the example below, plant growth (the dependent variable) is measured and depends on the amount of fertilizer with nitrogen (the independent variable) the plant is given.

**EXAMPLE**

Independent variable: amount of fertilizer with nitrogen

Dependent variable: plant growth

Constants: temperature, amount of light, intensity of light, type of plant, amount of water, frequency and time of watering, time when dependent variable is measured, amount of soil, type of soil

# Lab Handbook

## Determining Experimental and Control Groups

An experiment to determine how two factors are related always has at least two groups—a control group and an experimental group.

- The control group is exactly the same as the experimental group—except for the factor that is being tested.
- An experiment can have one or more experimental groups. With one experimental group, you are testing whether the independent variable has an effect. With more than one experimental group, you are testing the presence of the independent variable and different amounts of it.

### EXAMPLE

In our example, there are three experimental groups—each tests a different amount of fertilizer.

Experimental Groups

    5 g fertilizer
    10 g fertilizer
    15 g fertilizer

Control Group
    0 g fertilizer

## Identifying Types of Data

There are two types of data: qualitative and quantitative.

- **Qualitative data** are descriptions of the dependent variable, such as color, or sound. Qualitative data can also be a simple "yes-or-no" observation about whether something happens, such as whether a plant grows.
- **Quantitative data** are numerical measurements of the dependent variable. Quantitative data include measurements of size, mass, frequency, temperature, rate, and many other factors.

Qualitative data are useful, but they cannot be statistically analyzed. No experiment is based on qualitative data alone.

## Forming Operational Definitions

An **operational definition** is a description of the exact way in which you will measure the dependent variable. Your operational definition will help you determine how you will do your experiment.

### EXAMPLE

Quantitative operational definition: Height of the plant's main stem (in mm) is the operational definition for the effect of fertilizer on plant growth.

## Writing a Procedure

All experiments need a step-by-step written procedure. The procedure should be detailed and clear so that someone else could exactly repeat the experiment. You can think of your procedure as a cookbook recipe that has to be followed exactly. A procedure should include

- a detailed materials list
- how and when to make observations

Even if you are planning to collect only quantitative data, you can still make qualitative observations. These observations may help you to explain your data and can provide clues toward a new experiment.

If something goes wrong during your experiment, make sure you record and report it. Not following the procedure exactly can produce errors in your results that you will need to explain.

© Marilyn Gittmann

## Analyzing Data

You have carried out your experiment and collected data. Do the data support your hypothesis? You cannot answer that question by looking at a list of numbers and making a guess at what they show. Without organizing and analyzing your data, it is difficult to draw conclusions from your experiment.

- Organize all of the individual measurements, or data points, in a table. Data tables provide a person evaluating your experiment with a summary of your data.
- Analyze the raw data that you organized in your table. Calculate the mean, median, mode, and range for each group in the experiment. Use whatever type of statistics are appropriate for your data.

**EXAMPLE**

| TABLE 1. PLANT GROWTH – CONTROL GROUP | | | |
|---|---|---|---|
| Day | Plant 1 Height (cm) | Plant 2 Height (cm) | Plant 3 Height (cm) |
| 0 | 12.40 | 11.30 | 11.90 |
| 3 | 12.45 | 11.40 | 12.20 |
| 6 | 13.25 | 12.00 | 13.10 |
| 9 | 14.75 | 12.75 | 14.25 |
| 12 | 15.35 | 13.40 | 15.65 |
| 15 | 16.85 | 14.95 | 16.95 |
| 18 | 18.00 | 15.90 | 17.25 |
| 21 | 19.75 | 16.50 | 17.80 |
| Total growth | 7.35 | 5.20 | 5.90 |

**Mean Growth = 6.15 cm**

## Presenting Results

To present your results, look at your organized and analyzed data. Look for ways to most accurately and effectively show your results. You might make a graph to show and compare the groups' means. You might make several graphs that show each group separately. When possible, use spreadsheet software to present your data.

**EXAMPLE**

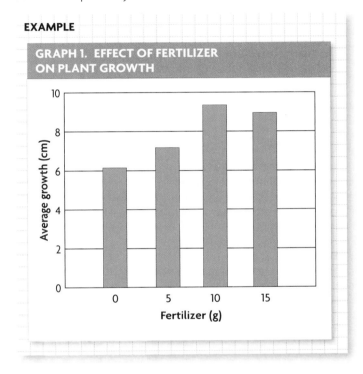

GRAPH 1. EFFECT OF FERTILIZER ON PLANT GROWTH

## Drawing Conclusions

Compare your results with your hypothesis to determine whether your results support your hypothesis. Discuss what your results show about a relationship between the independent variable and the dependent variable. It is important to draw conclusions from your results, but do not make inferences about factors that you did not test.

**EXAMPLE**

Adding a fertilizer with nitrogen to soil tends to increase plant growth. Both high and moderate amounts of fertilizer tend to increase plant growth more than a low amount of fertilizer. However, high and moderate amounts of fertilizer appear to have the same effect on growth.

# Math and Data Analysis Handbook

## Common Math Skills Used in Science

Some math skills that are often used in science are presented below.

### Calculating Mean

The **mean** of a data set is the average: the sum of the values divided by the number of values.

> **EXAMPLE**
>
> To find the mean of the data set {14, 6, 10, 8, 4, 11, 6, 3, 5, 13}, add the values and then divide the sum by the number of values.
>
> ANSWER $\dfrac{14 + 6 + 10 + 8 + 4 + 11 + 6 + 3 + 5 + 13}{10} = \dfrac{80}{10} = 8$

### Calculating Median

The **median** of a data set is the middle value when the values are ranked in numerical order. Half of the values fall above the median value, half below. If a data set has an even number of values, the median is the mean of the two middle values.

> **EXAMPLE**
>
> To find the median value of the data set {582, 133, 207, 87, 164, 290, 98, 155, 196, 278 }, arrange the values in order from least to greatest. The median is the middle value.
>
> 87, 98, 133, 155, 164, 196, 207, 278, 290, 582
>
> ANSWER The median is the mean of the two middle values, $\dfrac{164 + 196}{2} = 180$.

### Finding Mode

The **mode** of a data set is the value that occurs most often. A data set can have more than one mode if two or more values are repeated the same number of times. A data set can have no mode if no values are repeated.

> **EXAMPLE**
>
> To find the mode of the data set {6, 7, 6, 4, 4, 4, 3, 6, 4, 6}, arrange the values in order from least to greatest and determine the value that occurs most often:
>
> 3, 4, 4, 4, 4, 6, 6, 6, 6, 7
>
> ANSWER There are two modes, 4 and 6.

### Using Significant Figures

The number of **significant figures** in a measurement or calculation is equal to the number of digits that are known with some degree of confidence plus the next digit, which is an estimate. When multiplying or dividing measurements, the answer should have only as many significant figures as the value with the fewest significant figures.

> **EXAMPLE**
>
> A density calculation is made in which 5.31 g is divided by 22 mL. The calculator output was 0.2413636 g/mL.
>
> ANSWER There are three significant figures in the mass, but only two in the volume measurement. The density should have two significant figures: 0.24 g/mL.

### Using Scientific Notation

**Scientific notation** is a shorthand way to write very large or very small numbers as a product of a number times a power of 10.

> **EXAMPLE**
>
> To convert from standard form to scientific notation:
>
> | Standard Form | Scientific Notation |
> |---|---|
> | 720,000 | $7.2 \times 10^5$ |
> | 5 decimal places left | Exponent is 5 |
> | 0.000291 | $2.91 \times 10^{-4}$ |
> | 4 decimal places right | Exponent is -4 |
>
> To convert from scientific notation to standard form:
>
> | Scientific Notation | Standard Form |
> |---|---|
> | $4.63 \times 10^7$ | 46,300,000 |
> | Exponent is 7 | 7 decimal places right |
> | $1.08 \times 10^{-6}$ | 0.00000108 |
> | Exponent is -6 | 6 decimal places left |

# Presenting Data

Scientists often communicate results of their experiments through tables and graphs. Tables and graphs organize and display information so that it can be easily interpreted.

## Data Tables

A **data table** is used to organize and record data that are collected. Data tables can also help identify trends in data. Tables are organized according to the independent and dependent variables in the experiment. The **dependent variable** changes as a result of a change in the **independent variable.** The independent variable is listed in rows. The dependent variable is in columns. When repeated trials are conducted, they are recorded in subdivisions of the dependent variable column. When recording data in a table, the values of the independent variable are ordered. Most data are arranged from the smallest to largest.

The information given in each column is identified with a heading at the top of each column. When units are used, they are also included at the top of the column. Data tables should always have a title that clearly communicates what is being shown in the table. The title should make reference to the variables in the experiment.

| TABLE 2. EFFECT OF HORMONES ON CELL GROWTH | | |
| --- | --- | --- |
| Concentration of Hormone Solution (%) | Diameter of Cell Clump After 24 Hours (mm) | |
| | Trial 1 | Trial 2 |
| 0 | 3 | 4 |
| 25 | 4 | 4 |
| 50 | 8 | 7 |
| 75 | 9 | 8 |

**EXAMPLE**

Table 2 shows data from a hypothetical experiment in which growth hormones were added to clumps of cells in a laboratory. The growth of the cell clumps was measured. In this example, the independent variable is the concentration of hormone solution. The values of the independent variable are listed in rows from lowest to highest concentration. The dependent variable, the diameter of the cell clumps after 24 hours, is in columns.

## Line Graphs

A **line graph** is used to show a relationship between two variables. Line graphs are particularly useful for showing changes in variables over time. Line graphs are used when variables are continuous—that is, they can have any value including fractional values. For example, the height of a growing plant changes continuously. As a plant grows from 10 cm to 11 cm, its height can be 10.2 cm, 10.537 cm, or any other value between 10 and 11.

Line graphs are useful for representing trends. Two values are inversely related or have a **negative correlation** if an increase in the value of one variable is associated with a decrease in the value of the other variable. If an increase in one variable is associated with an increase in another variable, there is a **positive correlation** between the two variables. If there is no relationship between the two variables, they are said to have **no correlation.**

**EXAMPLE**

The level of the hormone insulin and length of exercise time have a negative correlation. As length of time increases, levels of insulin decrease.

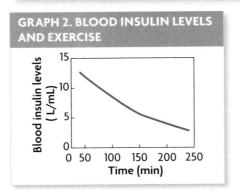

GRAPH 2. BLOOD INSULIN LEVELS AND EXERCISE

# Math and Data Analysis Handbook

The level of the hormone glucagon and length of exercise time have a positive correlation. As length of time increases, levels of glucagon increase.

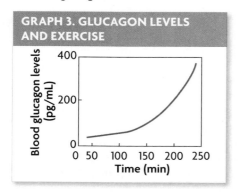

**GRAPH 3. GLUCAGON LEVELS AND EXERCISE**

The level of the hormone ghrelin and length of exercise time have no correlation. The levels of ghrelin do not increase or decrease over time.

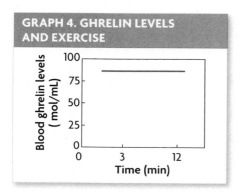

**GRAPH 4. GHRELIN LEVELS AND EXERCISE**

## Bar Graphs

A **bar graph** is a type of graph in which the lengths of the bars are used to represent and compare data. A numerical scale is used to determine the lengths of the bars. Bar graphs can be used with either continuous or discrete data. **Discrete data** can have only whole-number values, such as the number of people or trees in a neighborhood.

**EXAMPLE**
The bar graph at the top of the next column contains data about the frequency of various genetic disorders in the human population. For each syndrome on the *x*-axis, the bar extends vertically on the *y*-axis to represent the incidence per 100,000 births. For example, out of 100,000 births, 111 children are born with Down syndrome.

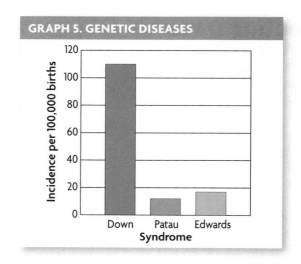

**GRAPH 5. GENETIC DISEASES**

## Combination Graphs

**Combination graphs** show two sets of data on the same graph. One set of data may be shown as a bar graph, and the other set may be shown as a line graph. The two data sets must share the same independent variable on the *x*-axis. Sharing the same independent variable makes it possible to determine if a relationship exists between two dependent variables.

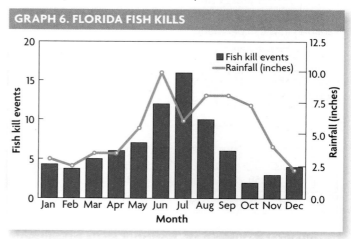

**GRAPH 6. FLORIDA FISH KILLS**

**EXAMPLE**
The combination graph above displays data about fish kill events and monthly rainfall in Florida.
- The *y*-axis on the left side of the graph represents the number of fish kill events.
- The *y*-axis on the right side of the graph represents rainfall amounts.
- The *x*-axis shows the month of data collection.

For example, the graph shows that in January there were four fish kill events and about 2.7 inches of rain.

## Histograms

A **histogram** is a type of bar graph used to show the frequency distribution of data. A **frequency distribution** displays the number of cases that fit into each category of a variable.

### EXAMPLE

The histogram below shows the frequency distribution of body fat in adult men. According to the histogram, the percentage body fat with the greatest frequency is 20 percent. When interpreting histograms, it is important to note that how the histogram is constructed can affect how the data are interpreted.

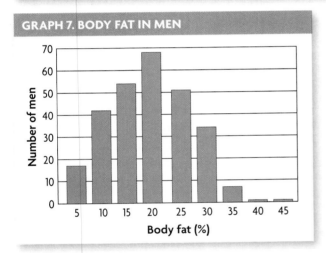

GRAPH 7. BODY FAT IN MEN

## Scatterplots

A **scatterplot** is a type of graph used to identify a trend or correlation between two variables. The origin is usually at zero on both the x-axis and the y-axis. On a scatterplot, the data points are plotted but not joined together as they are on a line graph. Three types of relationships between variables that can be shown on a scatterplot are positive, negative, and no relationship. In a positive relationship, as one variable increases or decreases, the other variable increases or decreases, respectively. In a negative relationship, as one variable increases, the other variable decreases. For some variables, there is no consistent change in one variable as the other variable increases or decreases. Thus, there is no relationship between those two variables.

### EXAMPLE

The scatterplot below of butter clam shell measurements shows that as the width of the clam's shell increases, its length also increases. This is a positive relationship, because as the value of one variable increases, the value of another variable increases. If it were a negative relationship, one of the variables would increase as the other decreased.

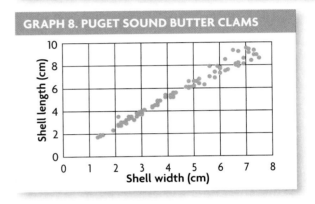

GRAPH 8. PUGET SOUND BUTTER CLAMS

## Circle Graphs

A **circle graph,** or pie chart, is a type of graph used to represent parts of a whole. It is made of a circle divided into sections that represent the frequency of each category's occurrence. To determine how much of the circle each section should cover, divide the number of occurrences for that category by the total number that the circle represents. When the result is multiplied by 100, it gives the percentage of the circle covered by the category.

### EXAMPLE

In the circle graph below, the diversity of invertebrates is illustrated. Notice that all of the percentages for each category of invertebrate can be added together to equal 100. This is always the case in a circle graph, unless the values have been rounded after calculation.

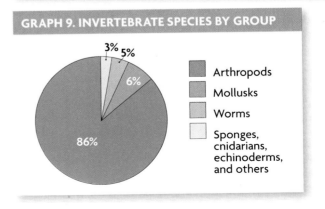

GRAPH 9. INVERTEBRATE SPECIES BY GROUP

# Vocabulary Handbook

## Greek and Latin Word Parts

Many words in the English language developed from Greek and Latin words. If you know some common Greek and Latin word parts, you can decode the meanings of other unknown words.

Suppose you read a magazine article that says, "If you see this plant, don't touch it! It's phototoxic and could cause a skin rash." How can you predict what the word *phototoxic* means without looking it up in a dictionary? To decode a word, follow the steps to the right.

**Break the word into parts.** Try to find the Greek or Latin word parts within the word. In the word *phototoxic,* you can find two word parts: *photo-* and *tox-*.

**Look up the word parts in the table below.** You will find that *photo-* means "light" and *tox-* means "poisonous."

**Analyze the clues to determine a definition.** In this example, your word clues are "light" and "poisonous." But there is also a clue in the sentence, "skin rash." You might guess that a phototoxic plant is one that can poison a person's skin when a chemical in the plant reacts with sunlight, and that's just what it means!

| WORD PART | DEFINITION | EXAMPLE |
|---|---|---|
| a- | not, without | **a**biotic: factor in an ecosystem that is not alive |
| ab- | away, apart | **ab**sorption: movement away from one system and into another |
| ad- | to, toward | **ad**hesion: attraction that pulls molecules of the same substance toward one another |
| anti- | against | **anti**biotic: chemical that acts against bacteria |
| -ase | enzyme | DNA polymer**ase**: enzyme that builds DNA polymers |
| bi- | two | **bi**nary fission: asexual reproduction in which a cell divides into two cells |
| bio- | life | **bio**engineering: process by which life forms are changed using technology |
| cardio- | of or relating to the heart | **cardi**ac muscle: muscle in the heart |
| cerebr- | brain | **cerebr**al cortex: part of the brain that controls voluntary functions |
| chloro- | green | **chloro**phyll: green pigment in photosynthetic organisms that absorbs light |
| -cide | kill | insecti**cide**: chemical that kills insects |
| con-, co-, com- | with, together | **co**dominance: both genes expressed together |
| cyto- | cell | **cyto**plasm: jellylike substance within a cell |
| di- | two | **di**cot: plant whose seeds have two cotyledons |
| diplo- | double | **diplo**id: having double genetic information |
| ecto- | outer, outside | **ecto**therm: organism that uses the outer environment to regulate body temperature |
| endo- | inner, inside | **endo**skeleton: skeleton found inside of the body |
| -gram | write, record | clado**gram**: record of proposed evolutionary relationships |
| hetero- | different | **hetero**zygous: having two different alleles |
| homo-, homeo- | the same | **homo**zygous: having two of the same alleles |
| hydro- | water | **hydro**logic cycle: water cycle |

| WORD PART | DEFINITION | EXAMPLE |
|---|---|---|
| hyper- | above, over | **hyper**tonic: having a concentration above that of another solution |
| hypo- | below, under | **hypo**tonic: having a concentration below that of another solution |
| im-, in- | with, into | **im**migration: movement of individuals into a population |
| iso- | equal | **iso**tonic: having a concentration equal to that of another solution |
| -itis | inflammation | appendic**itis**: inflammation of the appendix |
| -lysis | decomposition, dissolving | glyco**lysis**: breakdown of glucose |
| meso- | middle | **meso**phyll: layer of tissue in the middle of the plant leaf |
| mono- | one | **mono**hybrid cross: mating that examines inheritance of one trait |
| -morph | form | meta**morph**osis: change in body form |
| neuro- | neuron | **neuro**transmitter: chemical that signals neurons |
| -osis | condition or process | mit**osis**: process of cell division |
| path- | disease | **path**ogen: disease-causing agent |
| peri- | around | **peri**pheral nervous system: nerves found around, or outside, the central nervous system |
| phago- | to eat | **phago**cytosis: engulfing, or eating, of bacteria or foreign bodies by phagocytes |
| -philic | having a preference for | hydro**philic**: having an attraction to water |
| -phobic | having an aversion for | hydro**phobic**: having an aversion to water |
| photo- | light | **photo**synthesis: process that uses light to make sugars |
| phyto- | plants | **phyto**plankton: plantlike plankton |
| -pod | foot | pseudo**pod**: fake foot |
| poly- | many | **poly**genic trait: trait resulting from the interaction or many genes |
| re- | again, new | **re**generation: regrowth of lost or destroyed parts or organs |
| sperma- | relating to sperm or seeds | **sperma**togenesis: process that forms sperm |
| tel-, telo- | end | **telo**phase: ending phase of mitosis |
| -therm | heat | endo**therm**: animal that uses its internal tissues to produce its body heat |
| tox- | poisonous | **tox**in: poisonous substance that can destroy cells |
| trans- | across | **trans**genic: an organism that contains a gene from a different species |
| -troph | nutrition | auto**troph**: organism that makes its own source of nutrition |
| -tropism | response | geo**tropism**: growth response to gravity |
| uni- | single, one | **uni**cellular: organism made up of one cell |
| zoo- | animal | **zoo**logy: study of animals |

# Vocabulary Handbook

## Academic Vocabulary

Academic vocabulary words are words that occur frequently in textbooks, instructions, and standardized tests. The words can have many meanings. Some of these words are defined below and grouped into categories. These words appear in all subject areas. The simple definitions below give only one meaning of each word, the way it might be used in this book. Learn to recognize and understand these words.

### Words Used in Lab Instructions

**affect** to produce a change
**alter** to change
**analyze** to study the parts
**assemble** to put together
**characteristic** a distinct part or feature
**component** part
**conduct** to manage or control
**confirm** to use data to support a statement
**consequence** a result
**constraint** a limit
**control** a part of the experiment that keeps all variables constant
**criteria** standards for judging
**demonstrate** to show
**dominant** having the most influence or control
**emerge** to rise from or to come forth
**extract** to draw or pull out
**factor** an individual part of a combination, ingredient
**function** a job, duty, or activity
**indirect** not direct or to the point
**method** a way of doing something
**model** a small object made to look like the real one
**modify** to change
**monitor** to watch closely
**objective** a goal
**obtain** to get

**parameter** a measurable factor that can vary
**potential** possible but does not yet exist
**process** a series of actions
**produce** to bring forth or create
**property** a trait or characteristic
**prove** to show as true by using evidence
**purpose** a reason to do
**represent** to stand for
**restrict** to keep within limits
**reveal** to show, to make known
**signal** a sign for communicating
**source** the origin or place something began
**spatial** having to do with space
**structure** the way the parts are put together
**sufficient** enough, as much as needed
**technique** a procedure, the way something is done
**trace** tiny amount
**trait** a feature
**transfer** to move from one to another
**variation** the result of changing
**vary** to change or to show change

### Words About Math and Measuring

**approximate** nearly
**compile** to put together into one
**convert** to change something to another form
**cumulative** increasing by adding
**derive** to arrive at by reasoning
**dimension** measurement of one part
**diminish** to make less or smaller
**equivalent** equal to
**pace** the rate of speed
**proportion** an equation stating that two ratios are equal
**range** the difference between the smallest and largest amounts
**reduce** to make smaller
**solve** to find the answer to a problem

### Words About Importance

**core** the center part
**crucial** a must-have, extremely important
**essential** necessary or basic
**regular** usual or normal
**requisite** necessary, required
**significance** the importance
**standard** the usual and accepted measure for comparing

## Words Found in Test Directions

**analyze** to study the parts
**apply** to put on; to be relevant
**assess** to figure out the value of
**clarify** to make clear
**compose** to create or write something new
**critique** to judge carefully
**define** to tell what it means
**demonstrate** to show
**develop** to add detail, to fill out
**evaluate** to judge or decide the value of
**exhibit** to show or display
**indicate** to point out
**interpret** to explain the meaning of
**relate** to tell; to hook to something else
**revise** to review and change for the better
**summarize** to reduce to the main points in a few words
**synthesize** to combine parts into a whole

## Other Words Used in Tests

**alternative** another choice
**analogy** a comparison to something similar
**approach** to come near; the way of getting near
**articulate** to say or write clearly
**aspect** appearance from one point of view
**background** the knowledge behind something
**concise** in a few words
**confirm** to make sure it's true
**convey** to communicate or show
**correspond** to be similar in nature
**detail** an individual part
**detect** to discover or learn about
**determine** to learn the facts; to decide
**emphasize** to stress
**establish** to set up
**explicit** fully and clearly expressed
**focus** to direct to one point
**general** about the whole or entire thing
**imply** to express indirectly
**optional** left to a person's choice
**refer** to direct to a source for help
**specific** definite and particular
**succinct** in a few words
**symbolize** to act as a sign that stands for something else
**technical** used in a special job or subject
**topic** a subject
**transition** the words that link one part to the next
**valid** correct or well-grounded
**verify** to prove the truth of

## Words About Organization

**category** a class or special division
**compile** to put together
**consist** to be made up of
**correlate** to put into relation to something else
**differentiate** to separate by differences
**dominant** the strongest
**integrate** to put together
**organize** to put in order
**primary** first or most important
**sequence** order
**series** one after another
**subsequent** ones coming after

## Words About Ideas

**abstract** cannot be touched
**analogy** a comparison to something else
**authentic** real
**claim** a statement that says something is a fact
**complex** not simple
**conceive** to form an idea
**concept** an idea
**concrete** actual or real
**credible** believable
**deduce** to figure out by reasoning
**devise** to form, plan, or design
**discover** to notice or learn; to be the first to learn
**innovation** a new idea or thing
**irrelevant** off the point
**logical** reasoning in a clear manner
**origin** the beginning; where something began to exist
**principle** a basic truth, rule, or standard
**relevant** to the point
**strategy** a plan of action
**subjective** depends on a person's viewpoint
**topic** the subject of writing or speech

## Words About Time

**intermittent** off and on
**invariably** always, every time
**prior** before
**typically** usually

# Note-taking Handbook

Graphic organizers are tools to help you take notes. Some graphic organizers are best used as you read to help you understand concepts. Others are best used to summarize or review information. Using a variety of graphic organizers will help you to understand and remember what you have learned.

## During Reading

Use these graphic organizers while you are reading. They help you organize ideas in paragraphs and sections as you read them.

### Process Diagrams

**What is it?** A process is series of steps that produces a result. Process diagrams show these steps.

**How do you make it?** Start with the first step, and then draw each step, one after the other, and connect them with arrows.

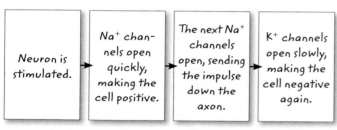

### Cycle Diagrams

**What is it?** A cycle, such as the cell cycle, is a repeating series of events that happen one after another. Cycles do not have a beginning or an end. Cycle diagrams identify the steps in a cycle or process that repeat regularly.

**How do you make it?** Draw a cycle diagram to show processes that repeat without a beginning or ending. Use the arrows between the boxed steps to show the direction or order in which the cycle happens.

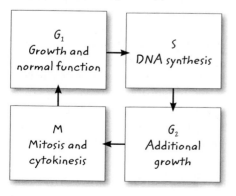

## Supporting Main Ideas Notes

**What is it?** A main idea graphic helps separate and organize reading material into important concepts and related details of support. You can choose the main idea graphic that best fits the material. The first strategy is useful when details follow some type of order.

**How do you make it?** First, find the main idea. The main idea may be the title of the section, it may be labeled "main idea" or "key concept" in your book, or it may be the topic sentence in a paragraph. Write the main idea in the top box. Next, summarize or paraphrase details that help explain that idea in the boxes that follow.

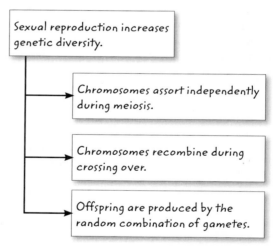

## Main Idea Webs

Another way you can take notes on main ideas is to draw a web. Write the main idea in the center and the details in the web around it. This is useful when the details do not occur in any particular order.

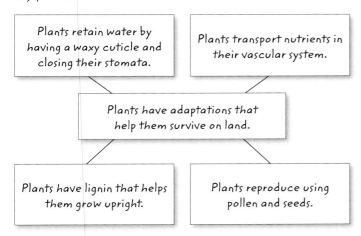

## Two-Column Notes

**What is it?** Two-column notes is a strategy for taking notes to show

- vocabulary and their definitions
- processes or cycles and their steps
- main ideas and supporting details
- questions and possible answers
- causes and effects
- comparisons and contrasts

**How do you make it?** List processes, concepts, main ideas, or vocabulary in the left column of a two-column table. Write the description or explanation of the words or concepts in the right-hand column across from the words in the left column. You can also draw pictures in the right-hand column.

Leave enough space between words or concepts in the left-hand column so that you can write notes in the right column.

To study for quizzes and tests, fold your two-column notes in half vertically so you can only see the left column. Ask yourself to describe and explain the word in the left column.

| Cellular Respiration | produces ATP<br>occurs in mitochondria<br>$C_6H_{12}O_6 + 6O_2 \rightarrow 6CO_2 + 6H_2O$ |
|---|---|
| Photosynthesis | absorbs sunlight<br>occurs in chloroplasts<br>$6CO_2 + 6H_2O \rightarrow C_6H_{12}O_6 + 6O_2$ |

# After Reading

Use these graphic organizers after you have read material and have taken notes on it. These organizers help you summarize the most important concepts and relate them to each other.

## Cause-and-Effect Diagrams

**What is it?** This strategy shows cause-and-effect relationships. In the diagram below, several effects result from a single cause. Those effects can cause more effects. A cause-and-effect diagram can also be drawn to show how multiple causes can produce a single effect.

**How do you make it?** Write the cause in the first box, and write the effects in the boxes connected to the cause. Then think about what effects can result from the first effects, and connect them.

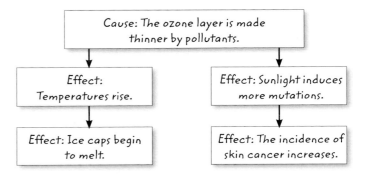

## Content Frames

**What is it?** Content frames are tables that help you organize and condense large amounts of information.

**How do you make it?** To make a content frame, make a table. Label the rows along the side with characteristics. Label the columns with the topics or categories. You can also include a column for drawings or sketches.

| Biome | Tropical | Temperate | Tundra |
|---|---|---|---|
| Climate | Warm and rainy | Hot summers, cold winters | Cold and dry |
| Vegetation | Lush, thick forests | Broadleaf forests | Mosses and similar |
| Example | Manaus, Brazil | Burlington, Vermont | Barrow, Alaska |

# Note-taking Handbook

## Venn Diagrams

**What is it?** Venn diagrams help you show how two processes, ideas, or things are alike and different.

**How do you make it?** Draw two circles that overlap, such as the ones below. Write one of the words or processes that you are going to compare in each circle. For example, the word *arteries* is written in the left circle and the word *veins* is written in the right circle. Under *arteries*, list characteristics or traits that only arteries possess. Under *veins*, list characteristics or traits that only veins possess. In the intersection of the two circles, list the traits that both arteries and veins share.

When you finish the diagram, write a sentence to summarize the similarities and differences: "Both veins and arteries have three-tissue layers and are each part of the closed circulatory system, but arteries are thicker and more muscular, and veins are thinner and have valves."

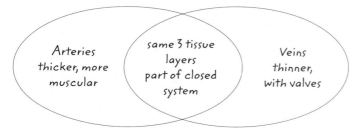

## Y Diagrams

**What is it?** Y diagrams can be used instead of Venn diagrams to show how two processes, ideas, or things are alike and different.

**How do you make it?** On the top parts of the Y, list the characteristics of each topic separately. Then find the characteristics that are the same in both halves. Write them at the bottom part of the Y, and cross them out from the top half. When you finish, the top limbs of the Y show differences, and the bottom part shows similarities between the two topics.

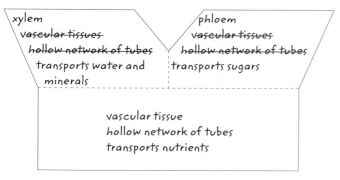

## Concept Maps

**What is it?** A concept map is a diagram that shows the main concepts from a passage you've read as well as the relationships between those concepts. Concept maps are useful tools for organizing and reviewing information.

**How do you make it?** First, identify the concepts in the section you've read. A concept is a single word or short phrase that represents an idea, process, or important characteristic. Next, identify the major concept and place it at the top of your concept map. Then arrange the other concepts from the most general to the most specific. Each concept should be enclosed in an oval or box. Finally, use lines to connect concepts and write linking words on the lines. Linking words are usually verbs, verb phrases, or prepositions that show the relationship between the concepts.

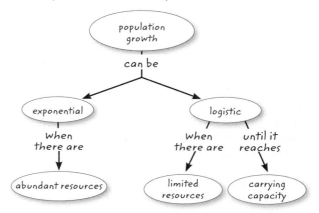

# FoldNotes

FoldNotes are a useful study tool that you can use to organize concepts. One FoldNote focuses on a few main concepts. By using a FoldNote, you can learn how concepts fit together. FoldNotes are designed to make studying concepts easier, so you can remember ideas for tests.

Go to **HMDScience.com** for step-by-step illustrated instructions for how to make these FoldNotes.

## Tri-Fold

A tri-fold is a useful tool that helps you track your progress. By organizing the chapter topic into what you know, what you want to know, and what you learn, you can see how much you have learned after reading a chapter.

## Pyramid

A pyramid provides a unique way for taking notes. The three sides of the pyramid can summarize information into three categories. Use the pyramid as a tool for studying information in a chapter.

## Booklet

A booklet is a useful tool for taking notes as you read a chapter. Each page of the booklet can contain a main topic from the chapter. Write details of each main topic on the appropriate page to create an outline of the chapter.

## Layered Book

A layered book is a useful tool for taking notes as you read a chapter. The four flaps of the layered book can summarize information into four categories. Write details of each category on the appropriate flap to create a summary of the chapter.

## Double-Door Fold

A double-door fold is useful when you want to compare the characteristics of two topics. The double-door fold can organize characteristics of the two topics side by side under the flaps. Similarities and differences between the two topics can then be easily identified.

## Two-Panel Flip Chart

A two-panel flip chart is useful when you want to compare the characteristics of two topics. The two-panel flip chart can organize the characteristics of the two topics side by side under the flaps. Similarities and differences between the two topics can then be easily identified.

## Four-Corner Fold

A four-corner fold is useful when you want to compare the characteristics of four topics. The four-corner fold can organize the characteristics of the four topics side by side under the flaps. Similarities and differences between the four topics can then be easily identified.

## Three-Panel Flip Chart

A three-panel flip chart is useful when you want to compare the characteristics of three topics. The three-panel flip chart can organize the characteristics of the three topics side by side under the flaps. Similarities and differences between the three topics can then be easily identified.

## Table Fold

A table fold is a useful tool for comparing the characteristics of two or three topics. In a table fold, all topics are described in terms of the same characteristics so that you can easily make a thorough comparison.

## Key-Term Fold

A key-term fold is useful for studying definitions of key terms in a chapter. Each tab can contain a key term on one side and its definition on the other. Use the key-term fold to quiz yourself on the definitions of the key terms in a chapter.

# Appendix A: Classification

Living things are classified into three domains. Based on genetic evidence, systems for further classifying Domain Eukarya are changing. This chart presents an approach using four superclasses.

| DOMAIN | COMMON NAME AND DESCRIPTION |
|---|---|
| **DOMAIN ARCHAEA** | |
| **ARCHAEA** *Pyrococcus* | **Archaea** Single-celled prokaryotes (no nucleus or other membrane-bound organelles) with distinct rRNA sequences. Lack peptidoglycan cell walls. Reproduce asexually. Live in some of Earth's most extreme environments, including salty, hot, acidic, and the deep ocean. They are often grouped according to where they live. Examples: *Sulfolobus solfataricus, Pyrococcus*. |
| **DOMAIN BACTERIA** | |
| **BACTERIA** *Escherichia* | **Bacteria** Single-celled prokaryotes (no nucleus or other membrane-bound organelles), most with peptidoglycan cell walls. Live in all types of environments, including the human body. Reproduce by binary fission or budding. Examples: blue-green bacteria (cyanobacteria), *Streptococcus, Bacillus, Escherichia*. |
| **DOMAIN EUKARYA** | |
| **EUKARYA** | **Eukaryotes** Cells are larger than archaea or bacteria and are eukaryotic (have a nucleus containing DNA, as well as other membrane-bound organelles). Can be single-celled, colonial, or multicellular. |

*Superclass Excavata*

| | | |
|---|---|---|
| *Euglena* | Euglenozoa | **Euglenoids** Single-celled, with one or two flagella. Most live in fresh water. Some are heterotrophs, others are photosynthetic autotrophs. Examples: *Euglena, Trypanosoma*. |
| | Zoomastigophora | **Zooflagellates** Have usually one or two long, hairlike extensions called flagella. Sometimes called Zoomastigina. Example: *Trichomonas*. |

# Appendix A: Classification

| DOMAIN | PHYLUM | COMMON NAME AND DESCRIPTION |
|---|---|---|
| Superclass Chromalveolata | | |
| | Apicomplexa | **Sporozoans** Parasites that can move by body flexion or gliding. Cause diseases in animals such as birds and humans. Example: *Plasmodium*. |
| | Foraminifera | **Forams** Use footlike extensions called pseudopods to move. Have multi-chambered shells made of organic material. Most are marine. Example: *Rosalina globularis*. |
| | Ciliophora | **Ciliates** Have many short, hairlike extensions called cilia, which they use for feeding and movement. Example: *Paramecium*. |
| | Dinoflagellata | **Dinoflagellates** Single-celled, with two flagella that allow cell to turn over and change direction. Some species are autotrophic, some are heterotrophic. In great numbers, some species can cause red tides along coastlines. Example: *Noctiluca*. |
| | Chrysophyta | **Chrysophytes** Also called yellow algae or golden-brown algae. Single-celled. Named for the yellow pigments in their chloroplasts (*chrysophyte*, in Greek, means "golden plant"). Example: *Thallasiosira*. |
| | Oomycota | **Water molds and downy mildews** Produce thin, cottonlike extensions called hyphae. Feed from dead or decaying material, often in water. Some are parasites of plants or fish. Example: *Phytophthora infestans* (cause of potato blight). |
| | Bacillariophyta | **Diatoms** Single-celled with glasslike shells made of silica. Shells serve as external skeleton. Example: *Amorpha ovalis*. |
| | Phaeophyta | **Brown algae** Multicellular, photosynthetic. Live mainly in salt water. Contain the pigment fucoxanthin, which is the source of their brown color. Includes kelp. Example: *Sargassum*. |
| Superclass Archaeplastida | | |
| | Rhodophyta | **Red algae** Multicellular, photosynthetic. Most live in salt water. Contain a red pigment called phycoerythrin that makes these organisms red, purple, or reddish-black. Example: coralline algae. |
| | Chlorophyta | **Green algae** May be single-celled, colonial, or multicellular. Contain both chlorophyll-*a* and chlorophyll-*b*, which are the same photosynthetic pigments found in land plants. Examples: *Pediastrum*, *Ulva*, *Spirogyra*. |

*Paramecium*

*Diatom*

*Red Algae*

| KINGDOM | PHYLUM | COMMON NAME AND DESCRIPTION |
|---|---|---|
| Superclass Archaeplastida | | |
| **PLANTAE** | | **Plants** Multicellular photosynthetic autotrophs. Most have adapted to life on land. Cells have thick cell walls made of cellulose. |
| | Bryophyta | **Mosses** Nonvascular plants. Gametophyte generation is a grasslike plant. Most live in moist environments. Example: sphagnum (peat) moss. |
| | Hepatophyta | **Liverworts** Nonvascular plants named for the liver-shaped gametophyte generation. Most live in moist environments. Example: *Marchantia*. |
| | Anthocerotophyta | **Hornworts** Nonvascular plants named for the visible hornlike structures with which they reproduce. Live in moist, cool environments. Example: *Dendroceros*. |
| | Lycophyta | **Club mosses** Seedless vascular plants. Some resemble tiny pine trees. Live in wooded environments. Example: *Lycopodium* (ground pine). |
| | Pterophyta | **Ferns, whisk ferns, and horsetails** Seedless vascular plants. Most have fringed leaves. Whisk ferns sometimes classified in phylum Psilotophyta; horsetails sometimes classified in phylum Sphenophyta. Example: *Psilotum* (whisk fern). |
| | Cycadophyta | **Cycads** Gymnosperms; reproduce with seeds produced in large cones. Slow-growing, palmlike plants that grow in tropical environments. Example: sago palms |
| | Ginkgophyta | **Ginkgo biloba** Only species in phylum, a tree often planted in urban environments. Gymnosperm; reproduces with seeds that hang from branches. |
| | Coniferophyta | **Conifers** Gymnosperms; reproduce with seeds produced in cones. Usually evergreen. Examples: pines, spruces, firs, sequoias. |
| | Anthophyta | **Flowering plants** Also called angiosperms. Reproduce with seeds produced in flowers. Seeds are surrounded by fruit, which is the ripened plant ovary.<br><br>**CLASS: Monocotyledonae** Monocots. Embryos have one cotyledon. Leaves with parallel veins, flower parts in multiples of three, and vascular bundles scattered throughout the stem. Examples: irises, tulips, grasses.<br><br>**CLASS: Dicotyledonae** Dicots. Embryos have two cotyledons. Leaves with netlike veins, flower parts in multiples of four or five, and vascular bundles arranged in rings. Examples: roses, daisies, deciduous trees, foxgloves. |
| Superclass Unikonta | | |
| | Acrasiomycota | **Cellular slime molds** Live partly as free-living single-celled organisms, often in the soil. When food is scarce, they can fuse together to form a many-celled mass that moves as if it's one organism. Example: *Dictyostelium*. |
| | Myxomycota | **Plasmodial slime molds** Live most of their lives as a mass of cytoplasm that is actually one large, slimy cell with many nuclei. Example: *Physarium* (dog-vomit slime mold). |

Sago palm

Foxglove

Slime mold

# Appendix A: Classification

| KINGDOM | PHYLUM | COMMON NAME AND DESCRIPTION |
|---|---|---|
| **FUNGI** | | **Fungi** Eukaryotic, heterotrophic, usually multicellular but some are single-celled. Cells have a thick cell wall usually containing chitin. Obtain nutrients through absorption. Often function as decomposers. |
| | Chytridiomycota | **Chytrids** Oldest and simplest fungi, usually aquatic. Have flagellated spores. Some are decomposers, some are parasitic. Example: chytrid frog fungus. |
| | Ascomycota | **Sac fungi** Reproduce with spores formed in an ascus. Includes single-celled yeasts as well as morels, truffles, and molds. Example: *Penicillium*. |
| | Zygomycota | **Bread molds** Obtain food by decomposing dead or decaying matter. Mold hyphae grow into food source and digest it. Some are parasitic. Example: black bread molds. |
| | Basidiomycota | **Club fungi** Multicellular with club-shaped fruiting bodies. Examples: mushrooms, puffballs, bracket fungi, rusts, smuts. |
| **ANIMALIA** | | **Animals** Multicellular, eukaryotic heterotrophs with cells supported by collagen. Cells lack cell walls. Most have cells that are organized into specialized tissues, which make up organs. Most reproduce sexually. |
| | Porifera | **Sponges** Spend most of their lives fixed to the ocean floor. Feed by filtering water (containing nutrients and small organisms) through their body. Reproduce sexually and asexually. Example: *Euplectella* (Venus's flower basket). |
| | Cnidaria | **Cnidarians** Aquatic animals with a radial (spokelike) body shape; named for their stinging cells (cnidocytes). Have two basic body forms: the polyp and the medusa. May produce sexually and asexually. <br><br> **CLASS: Hydrozoa** Alternate between polyp and medusa stages. Medusas reproduce sexually, polyps reproduce asexually. Example: hydras. <br><br> **CLASS: Scyphozoa** Dominant medusa form. Example: jellyfish. <br><br> **CLASS: Anthozoa** Dominant polyp form; there is no medusa stage. May be colonial or solitary. Central body surrounded by tentacles. Examples: sea anemones, corals. <br><br> **CLASS: Cubozoa** Dominant cube-shaped medusa form with well-developed eyes. Examples: tropical box jellyfish, sea wasps. |

Sac fungus

Toad stool mushroom

Giant anemone

| KINGDOM | PHYLUM | COMMON NAME AND DESCRIPTION |
|---|---|---|
| | Ctenophora | **Comb jellies** Resemble jellyfish; named for the comblike rows of cilia (hairlike extensions) that are used for movement. Example: *Pleurobrachia*. |
| | Platyhelminthes | **Flatworms** Thin, flattened worms with simple tissues and sensory organs. Includes planaria and tapeworms, which cause diseases in humans and other hosts.<br><br>**CLASS: Turbellaria (turbellarians)** Free-living carnivores or scavengers that move with cilia. Example: planarians.<br><br>**CLASS: Trematoda (flukes)** Internal parasites; life cycle often includes alternation of hosts. Example: *Schistosoma*.<br><br>**CLASS: Cestoda (tapeworms)** Internal parasites; segmented body and head with suckers or hooks for attaching to host. Example: dog tapeworm. |
| | Mollusca | **Mollusks** Soft-bodied aquatic animals that usually have an outer shell.<br><br>**CLASS: Gastropoda (gastropods)** Use muscular foot for movement. Have a distinct head and complete digestive tract. Most have a chambered shell. Examples: snails and slugs.<br><br>**CLASS: Pelecypoda (bivalves)** Soft body protected by two hard shells that are hinged together. Most are filter feeders. Examples: clams, oysters, mussels, scallops.<br><br>**CLASS: Cephalopoda (cephalopods)** Carnivores with well-developed eyes and nervous systems. Examples: squids, octopuses, nautiluses. |
| | Annelida | **Segmented worms** Body is made of many similar segments.<br><br>**CLASS: Polychaeta (polychaetes)** Marine worms with a pair of appendages on each segment. Have many setae. Examples: fan worms, featherduster worms.<br><br>**CLASS: Oligochaeta (oligochaetes)** Earthworms; live in soil or fresh water. Have no appendages. Have few setae. Example: *Tubifex tubifex* (sludge worm).<br><br>**CLASS: Hirudinea (leeches)** Most live in fresh water. Have flattened body with no appendages. Suckers at both ends; carnivores or blood-sucking parasites. Example: *Macrobdella decora* (medicinal leech). |
| | Nematoda | **Roundworms** Small, round worms; many species are parasites, causing diseases in humans, such as trichinosis and elephantiasis. Example: *Trichinella*. |

Flatworm

Nautilus

Leeches

(t) ©Gary Bell/oceanwideimages.com; (c) ©Fotolia; (b) ©SeDmi/Shutterstock

# Appendix A: Classification

| KINGDOM | PHYLUM | COMMON NAME AND DESCRIPTION |
|---|---|---|
| **ANIMALIA** (continued) | Arthropoda | Animals with an outer skeleton called an exoskeleton, and jointed appendages such as legs or wings. |
| | | **SUBPHYLUM: Trilobita (trilobites)** Includes the trilobites, which are all extinct. Important part of the Paleozoic marine ecosystems for 300 million years. Bodies divided into three lobes. Bottom feeders. |
| | | **SUBPHYLUM: Crustacea (crustaceans)** Live in all of the oceans, freshwater streams, and on land. Have chewing mouthparts and two pairs of antennae. Examples: crabs, lobsters, copepods, pill bugs. |
| | | **SUBPHYLUM: Chelicerata (chelicerates)** First pair of appendages specialized as daggerlike mouthparts that are used for tearing food; no antennae. Examples: horseshoe crabs, scorpions, spiders, mites, ticks. |
| | | **SUBPHYLUM: Uniramia** Most live on land. Have one pair of antennae and chewing mouthparts. |
| | | **CLASS: Insecta (insects)** Have three body segments with three pairs of legs attached to second segment. Examples: ants, bees, butterflies, cockroaches, flies, mosquitoes, dragonflies. |
| | | **CLASS: Chilopoda (centipedes)** Body divided into many segments with one pair of legs per segment. Carnivores; first pair of legs bears fangs for capturing prey. Example: *Scutigera coleoptrata* (common house centipede). |
| | | **CLASS: Diplopoda (millipedes)** Body divided into many segments with two pairs of legs per segment. Most are herbivores. Example: *Glomeris* (pill millipede). |
| | Echinodermata | Adults are slow-moving marine animals with radial symmetry; larvae have bilateral symmetry. Have an internal skeleton, a water vascular system, and a complete digestive system. Some can regenerate limbs. |
| | | **CLASS: Crinoidea (crinoids)** Filter feeders that remain attached to a surface such as the ocean floor. Examples: feather stars, sea lilies. |
| | | **CLASS: Asteroidea (sea stars)** Star-shaped bottom dwellers that may be suspension feeders, opportunistic feeders, or carnivorous predators. Example: *Acanthaster planci* (crown-of-thorns starfish). |
| | | **CLASS: Ophiuroidea** Most have five long spindly arms that they use to help move and feed; tube feet lack suckers. Examples: brittle stars, basket stars. |
| | | **CLASS: Echinoidea** Have a five-part body plan but no arms; body covered with projections or spines. Most graze for food on ocean floor. Examples: sea urchins, sea biscuits, sand dollars. |
| | | **CLASS: Holothuroidea (sea cucumbers)** Fleshy animals with long, cylindrical shape. Tentacles are used to capture food; also feed on sediment from ocean floor. Example: *Holothuria*. |

Scorpion

Dragonfly

Sea star

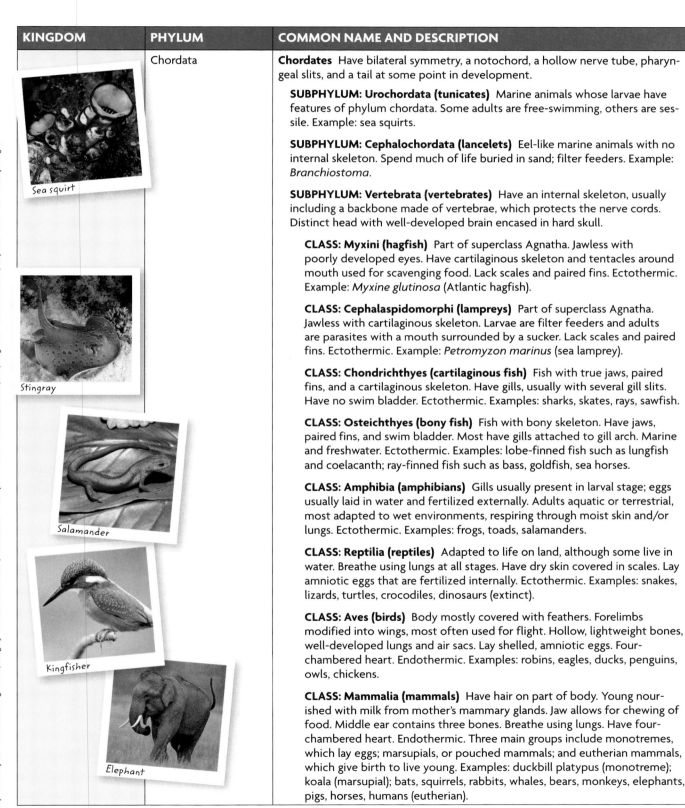

| KINGDOM | PHYLUM | COMMON NAME AND DESCRIPTION |
|---|---|---|
| | Chordata | **Chordates** Have bilateral symmetry, a notochord, a hollow nerve tube, pharyngeal slits, and a tail at some point in development. |

**SUBPHYLUM: Urochordata (tunicates)** Marine animals whose larvae have features of phylum chordata. Some adults are free-swimming, others are sessile. Example: sea squirts.

**SUBPHYLUM: Cephalochordata (lancelets)** Eel-like marine animals with no internal skeleton. Spend much of life buried in sand; filter feeders. Example: *Branchiostoma*.

**SUBPHYLUM: Vertebrata (vertebrates)** Have an internal skeleton, usually including a backbone made of vertebrae, which protects the nerve cords. Distinct head with well-developed brain encased in hard skull.

**CLASS: Myxini (hagfish)** Part of superclass Agnatha. Jawless with poorly developed eyes. Have cartilaginous skeleton and tentacles around mouth used for scavenging food. Lack scales and paired fins. Ectothermic. Example: *Myxine glutinosa* (Atlantic hagfish).

**CLASS: Cephalaspidomorphi (lampreys)** Part of superclass Agnatha. Jawless with cartilaginous skeleton. Larvae are filter feeders and adults are parasites with a mouth surrounded by a sucker. Lack scales and paired fins. Ectothermic. Example: *Petromyzon marinus* (sea lamprey).

**CLASS: Chondrichthyes (cartilaginous fish)** Fish with true jaws, paired fins, and a cartilaginous skeleton. Have gills, usually with several gill slits. Have no swim bladder. Ectothermic. Examples: sharks, skates, rays, sawfish.

**CLASS: Osteichthyes (bony fish)** Fish with bony skeleton. Have jaws, paired fins, and swim bladder. Most have gills attached to gill arch. Marine and freshwater. Ectothermic. Examples: lobe-finned fish such as lungfish and coelacanth; ray-finned fish such as bass, goldfish, sea horses.

**CLASS: Amphibia (amphibians)** Gills usually present in larval stage; eggs usually laid in water and fertilized externally. Adults aquatic or terrestrial, most adapted to wet environments, respiring through moist skin and/or lungs. Ectothermic. Examples: frogs, toads, salamanders.

**CLASS: Reptilia (reptiles)** Adapted to life on land, although some live in water. Breathe using lungs at all stages. Have dry skin covered in scales. Lay amniotic eggs that are fertilized internally. Ectothermic. Examples: snakes, lizards, turtles, crocodiles, dinosaurs (extinct).

**CLASS: Aves (birds)** Body mostly covered with feathers. Forelimbs modified into wings, most often used for flight. Hollow, lightweight bones, well-developed lungs and air sacs. Lay shelled, amniotic eggs. Four-chambered heart. Endothermic. Examples: robins, eagles, ducks, penguins, owls, chickens.

**CLASS: Mammalia (mammals)** Have hair on part of body. Young nourished with milk from mother's mammary glands. Jaw allows for chewing of food. Middle ear contains three bones. Breathe using lungs. Have four-chambered heart. Endothermic. Three main groups include monotremes, which lay eggs; marsupials, or pouched mammals; and eutherian mammals, which give birth to live young. Examples: duckbill platypus (monotreme); koala (marsupial); bats, squirrels, rabbits, whales, bears, monkeys, elephants, pigs, horses, humans (eutherian).

Sea squirt

Stingray

Salamander

Kingfisher

Elephant

## Moss Life Cycle

This diagram illustrates the life cycle of moss in detail. The life cycle of mosses is discussed in Plant Growth, Reproduction, and Response.

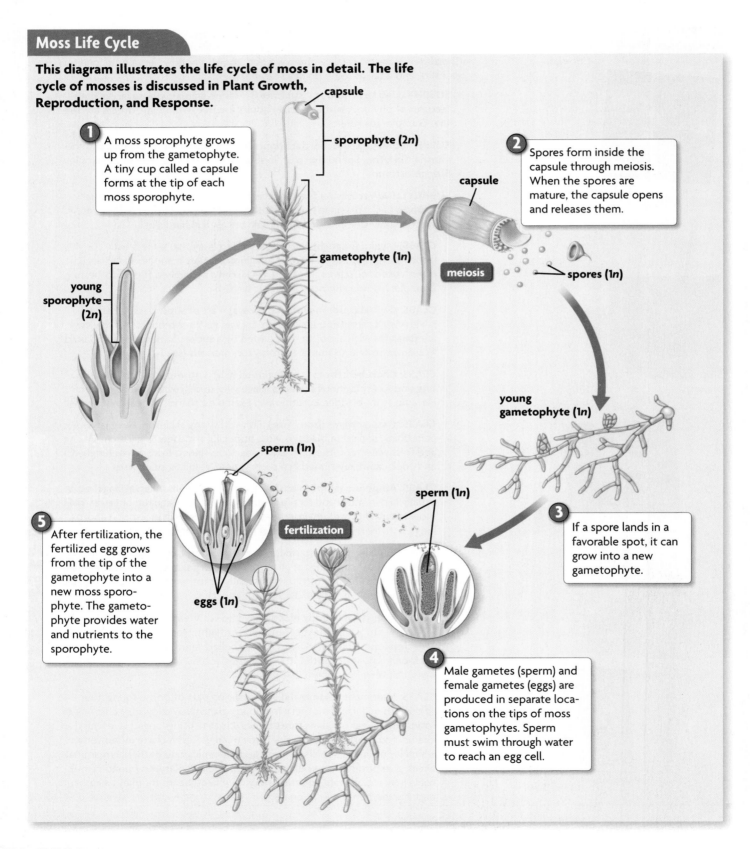

**1** A moss sporophyte grows up from the gametophyte. A tiny cup called a capsule forms at the tip of each moss sporophyte.

capsule

sporophyte (2n)

gametophyte (1n)

young sporophyte (2n)

**2** Spores form inside the capsule through meiosis. When the spores are mature, the capsule opens and releases them.

capsule

meiosis

spores (1n)

young gametophyte (1n)

**3** If a spore lands in a favorable spot, it can grow into a new gametophyte.

sperm (1n)

sperm (1n)

fertilization

eggs (1n)

**5** After fertilization, the fertilized egg grows from the tip of the gametophyte into a new moss sporophyte. The gametophyte provides water and nutrients to the sporophyte.

**4** Male gametes (sperm) and female gametes (eggs) are produced in separate locations on the tips of moss gametophytes. Sperm must swim through water to reach an egg cell.

## Fern Life Cycle

**This diagram illustrates the life cycle of ferns in detail. The life cycle of ferns is discussed in Plant Growth, Reproduction, and Response.**

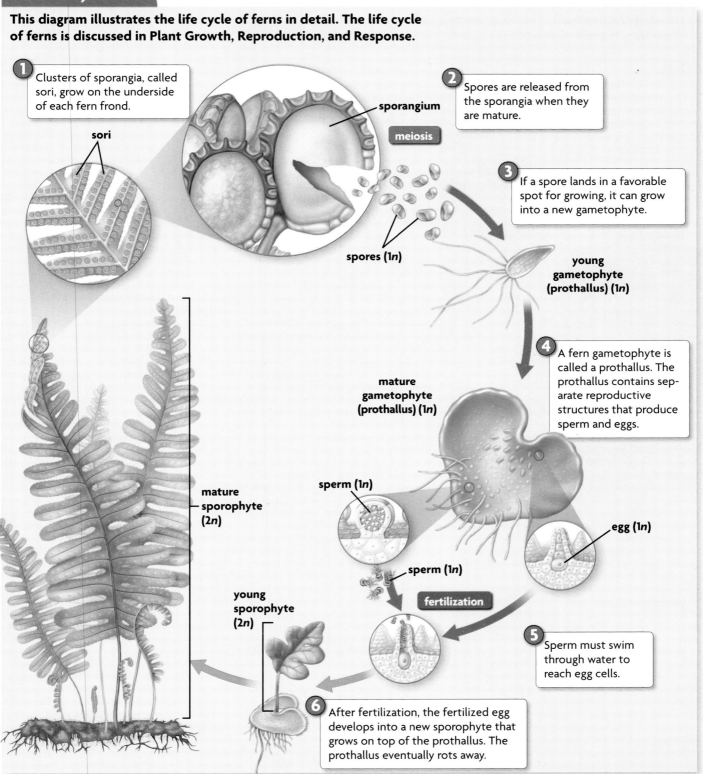

**1** Clusters of sporangia, called sori, grow on the underside of each fern frond.

sori

sporangium

meiosis

**2** Spores are released from the sporangia when they are mature.

spores (1*n*)

**3** If a spore lands in a favorable spot for growing, it can grow into a new gametophyte.

young gametophyte (prothallus) (1*n*)

**4** A fern gametophyte is called a prothallus. The prothallus contains separate reproductive structures that produce sperm and eggs.

mature gametophyte (prothallus) (1*n*)

mature sporophyte (2*n*)

sperm (1*n*)

sperm (1*n*)

egg (1*n*)

fertilization

**5** Sperm must swim through water to reach egg cells.

young sporophyte (2*n*)

**6** After fertilization, the fertilized egg develops into a new sporophyte that grows on top of the prothallus. The prothallus eventually rots away.

## Conifer Life Cycle

This diagram illustrates the life cycle of a conifer in detail. The life cycle of conifers is discussed in Plant Growth, Reproduction, and Response.

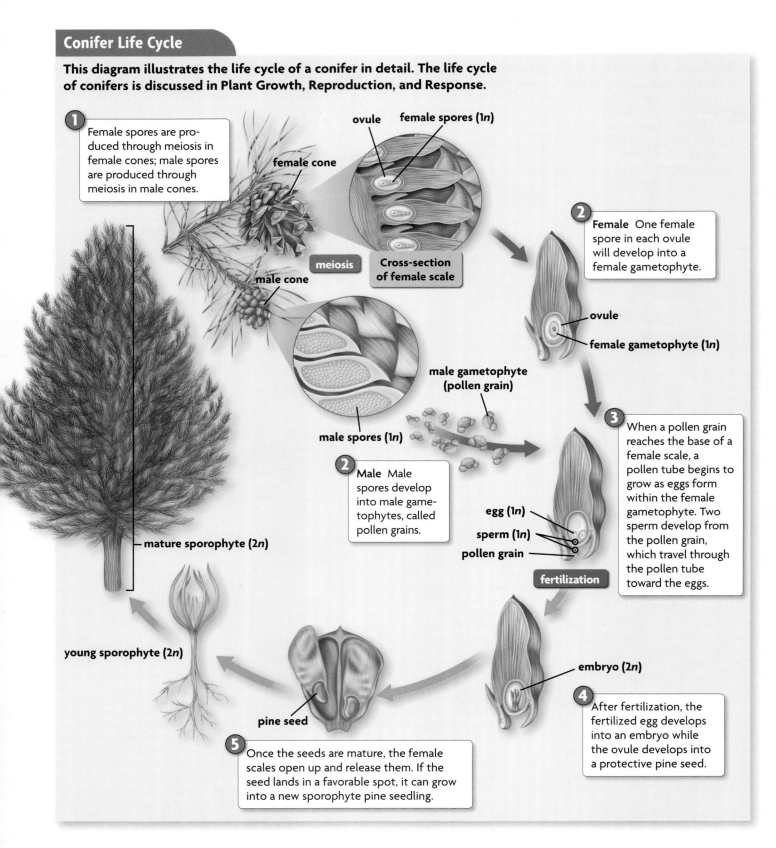

**1** Female spores are produced through meiosis in female cones; male spores are produced through meiosis in male cones.

ovule   female spores (1n)

female cone

meiosis   Cross-section of female scale

male cone

**2** Female One female spore in each ovule will develop into a female gametophyte.

ovule

female gametophyte (1n)

male gametophyte (pollen grain)

male spores (1n)

**2** Male Male spores develop into male gametophytes, called pollen grains.

egg (1n)

sperm (1n)

pollen grain

**3** When a pollen grain reaches the base of a female scale, a pollen tube begins to grow as eggs form within the female gametophyte. Two sperm develop from the pollen grain, which travel through the pollen tube toward the eggs.

fertilization

— mature sporophyte (2n)

young sporophyte (2n)

embryo (2n)

**4** After fertilization, the fertilized egg develops into an embryo while the ovule develops into a protective pine seed.

pine seed

**5** Once the seeds are mature, the female scales open up and release them. If the seed lands in a favorable spot, it can grow into a new sporophyte pine seedling.

# Flowering Plant Life Cycle

This diagram illustrates the life cycle of a flowering plant in detail.
The life cycle of flowering plants is discussed in
Plant Growth, Reproduction, and Response.

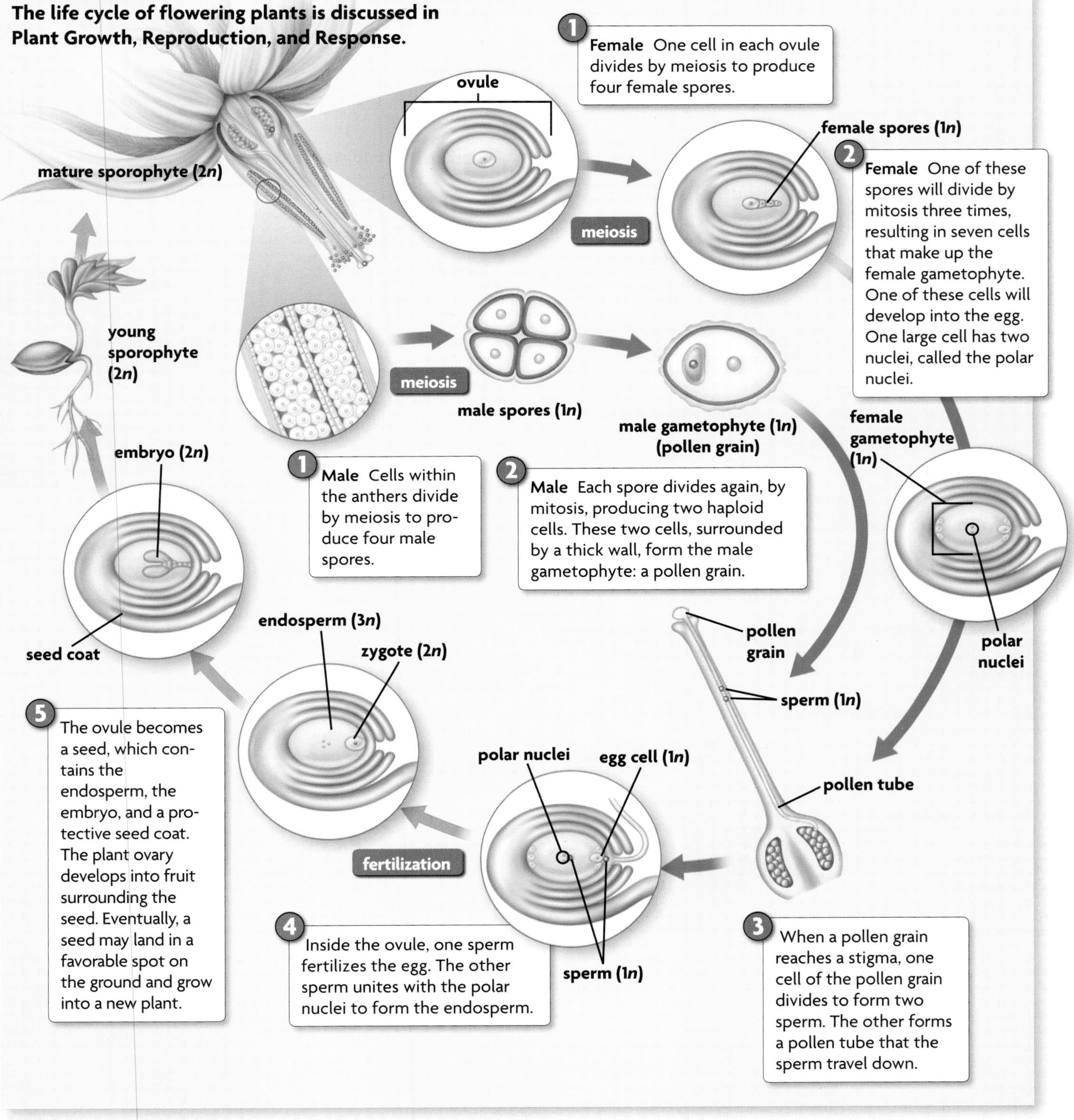

**1** **Female** One cell in each ovule divides by meiosis to produce four female spores.

ovule

mature sporophyte (2n)

female spores (1n)

**2** **Female** One of these spores will divide by mitosis three times, resulting in seven cells that make up the female gametophyte. One of these cells will develop into the egg. One large cell has two nuclei, called the polar nuclei.

meiosis

young sporophyte (2n)

male spores (1n)

male gametophyte (1n) (pollen grain)

female gametophyte (1n)

meiosis

embryo (2n)

**1** **Male** Cells within the anthers divide by meiosis to produce four male spores.

**2** **Male** Each spore divides again, by mitosis, producing two haploid cells. These two cells, surrounded by a thick wall, form the male gametophyte: a pollen grain.

pollen grain

polar nuclei

seed coat

endosperm (3n)

zygote (2n)

sperm (1n)

pollen tube

**5** The ovule becomes a seed, which contains the endosperm, the embryo, and a protective seed coat. The plant ovary develops into fruit surrounding the seed. Eventually, a seed may land in a favorable spot on the ground and grow into a new plant.

polar nuclei

egg cell (1n)

fertilization

**4** Inside the ovule, one sperm fertilizes the egg. The other sperm unites with the polar nuclei to form the endosperm.

sperm (1n)

**3** When a pollen grain reaches a stigma, one cell of the pollen grain divides to form two sperm. The other forms a pollen tube that the sperm travel down.

## Careers in Biology

A number of careers require a background knowledge of biology. Some of these career choices may be more obvious than others, such as that of a biology teacher, doctor, or zookeeper. But there are many more careers that may be less familiar to you. While your image of someone who uses their knowledge of biology might be that of a scientist who works in a laboratory, you just might be surprised to discover what other jobs require a background in the biological sciences.

To learn more about careers in the biological sciences, go to the BioZine at **HMHScience.com**.

**Agronomist** An agronomist is an expert in soil management who advises farmers on how to manage their crops.

**Anthropologist** An anthropologist studies the origin, behavior, and social and cultural development of humans.

**Bioinformatics Professional** A bioinformatics professional uses computers, laboratory robots, and software to develop, manage, and interpret complex biological data.

**Biological Illustrator** A biological illustrator provides scientifically accurate hand-drawn or computer-aided illustrations for clients, ranging from web sites to publications such as textbooks, newspapers, or magazines.

**Biomedical Engineer** A biomedical engineer develops devices and procedures that solve medical and health-related problems.

**Conservation Biologist** A conservation biologist manages, improves, and protects natural resources.

**Ecotourism Guide** An ecotourism guide leads groups of tourists on trips to natural areas to promote conservation and sustain the livelihood of local people.

**Emergency Medical Technician** An emergency medical technician provides emergency medical services to critically ill and injured persons.

**Environmental Economist** An environmental economist uses the principles of economics to determine the impact of such things as species loss, pollution, and climate change.

**Environmental Health Professional** An environmental health professional inspects the health and safety of establishments such as restaurants and housing areas.

**Environmental Journalist** An environmental journalist writes articles or books on environmental topics, frequently in an investigatory manner.

**Epidemiologist** An epidemiologist studies causes and control of diseases.

**Exercise Physiologist** An exercise physiologist develops exercise routines and educates people about the benefits of exercise.

**Ethologist** An ethologist studies animal behavior.

**Farm Manager** A farm manager manages the day-to-day activities of one or more farms, focusing on the business aspects of running a farm.

**Fish and Wildlife Manager** A fish and wildlife manager manages the populations of fish and/or wildlife on public or private lands.

**Forensic Scientist** A forensic scientist analyzes biological, chemical, or physical samples taken as evidence during a criminal investigation.

**Forester** A forester manages and protects forests and supervises tree harvesting.

**Genetic Counselor** A genetic counselor is a health professional who specializes in telling families about the nature and risks of inherited conditions and syndromes.

**Geneticist** A geneticist specializes in the study of genes and their influence on health, as well as the treatment of genetic disorders.

**Immunologist** An immunologist is a medical scientist who studies the immune system.

**Landscape Architect** A landscape architect plans the location of buildings, roads, and walkways along with the placement of plants so that the designs are not only functional but also compatible with the natural environment.

**Medical Transcriptionist** A medical transcriptionist listens to dictated recordings made by doctors and other health care workers and transcribes them into medical reports.

**Medical Device Sales Representative** A medical device sales representative sells medical devices to health professionals.

**Molecular Biologist** A molecular biologist studies the structure and function of biological molecules, such as DNA and proteins.

**Nature Photographer** A nature photographer takes photographs of natural settings and wildlife for publication online and in print material such as books and magazines.

**Neuroscientist** A neuroscientist specializes in the study of the structure and function of the brain and nervous system.

**Nutritionist** A nutritionist plans food and nutrition programs and provides advice to those with food allergies or those seeking weight loss.

**Oceanographer** An oceanographer studies the world's oceans and their inhabitants.

**Park Ranger** A park ranger supervises, manages, and performs work in the conservation and use of resources in national, state, and city parks.

**Pharmacist** A pharmacist distributes drugs prescribed by doctors and other health workers and provides information to patients about medications and their use.

**Phlebotomist** A phlebotomist collects blood samples.

**Physician Assistant** A physician assistant takes medical histories, examines and treats patients, orders and interprets laboratory tests and x-rays, and makes diagnoses, all under the supervision of a doctor.

**Physical Therapist** A physical therapist provides services that help restore function, improve mobility, relieve pain, and prevent or limit permanent physical disabilities of patients suffering from injuries or disease.

**Radiologist** A radiologist is a doctor who specializes in the interpretation of x-rays and other medical images.

**Respiratory Therapist** A respiratory therapist evaluates, treats, and cares for patients with breathing or other cardiopulmonary disorders.

**Science Editor** A science editor edits scientific writing, ranging from academic journals to works meant for a general audience.

**Science Museum Curator** A science museum curator oversees the development and management of museum exhibits.

**Science Patent Lawyer** A science patent lawyer represents clients in legal proceedings, draws up legal documents, and advises clients on legal transactions.

**Science Policy Analyst** A science policy analyst advises lawmakers with regard to legislation focused on scientific issues such as biomedical research or environmental regulations.

**Science Writer** A science writer specializes in writing about scientific topics for both academic and general audiences.

**Speech-Language Pathologist** A speech-language pathologist tests, diagnoses, treats, and helps to prevent speech, language, and other voice-related disorders.

**Sports Trainer** A sports trainer helps athletes in the prevention of injury and provides initial management of a sports-related injury.

**Surgical Technician** A surgical technician assists in surgeries by preparing the surgical room, providing support to surgical workers, and monitoring the patient during surgery.

**Ultrasound Technician** An ultrasound technician operates an ultrasound machine, which collects reflected echoes and forms an image that may be videotaped, transmitted, or photographed for interpretation and diagnosis by a doctor.

**X-Ray Technician** An x-ray technician takes x-rays and administers nonradioactive materials into patients' bloodstreams for diagnostic purposes.

# Investigating Ecosystems

## Types of Ecosystems

An ecosystem contains communities of living organisms (biotic factors) and the nonliving features (abiotic factors) characteristic of an area. Below are descriptions of ecosystems found in the United States.

Deciduous Forests

**Deciduous Forests** grow in drier soils at higher elevations than riparian woodlands. Deciduous hardwood trees, such as oak, walnut, birch, beech, and maple, dominate these forest ecosystems. Birds that make their homes in deciduous forests include woodpeckers, hawks, hummingbirds, songbirds, and ground-dwelling birds such as quail and wild turkey. Mammals include black bears, white-tailed deer, squirrels, coyotes, bobcats, foxes, and raccoons.

Estuaries

**Estuaries** form when fresh water draining from rivers and streams mixes with salt water from the ocean. Microscopic plankton float in open water and form the base of many food chains. They feed small fish and crustaceans which in turn provide food for larger fin fish and marine mammals. Beds of sea grasses and other underwater plants shelter young fish, crabs, and shrimp. Estuaries provide important feeding and nesting habitats for resident and migratory birds. Many species of mammals feed in estuarine waters or along the water's edge, including muskrats, otters, and raccoons.

Boreal Forests

**Boreal Forests** grow in areas with long, cold winters and short summers. The decay of needles and leaves, slowed by cold temperatures, forms a thick layer of peat and moss on the forest floor. Among the billions of birds that nest in the boreal forest during the spring and summer months are loon, grebes, geese, hawks, owls, sandpipers, flycatchers, and sparrows. Mammal species include snowshoe hares, lynx, moose, caribou, and grizzly bears.

Riparian Woodlands

**Riparian Woodlands** grow in moist soil along the edges of streams. These ecosystems are also known as riparian corridors because they feature dense plant growth that provides cover for wildlife traveling from place to place. Riparian trees and shrubs often include willow, birch, and dogwood. Fallen leaves provide habitats for bacteria, fungi, worms, and insects. Animal life also includes snakes, bats, weasels, otters, deer, bobcats, and ground-dwelling birds. Roots and branches that dangle in the water provide shade and protective cover for fish, frogs, and salamanders.

Desert

**Desert** ecosystems are characterized by dry, gravelly soils and infrequent rain. Plants adapted for desert conditions include cacti and desert wildflowers. Many desert animals, from spiders and scorpions to owls and night lizards, are nocturnal, avoiding the intense sunlight and extreme daytime temperatures. Animal life also includes kangaroo rats, jackrabbits, snakes, coyotes, woodpeckers, and roadrunners.

# Analyzing a Local Ecosystem

Use the checklist below to explore and analyze an ecosystem in your area. Example answers for the pond ecosystem shown above are given for each item.

✓ **Define a boundary.** Locate the edges of the ecosystem you're studying. Ecosystems often blend into one another, so boundaries might not be obvious. The pond ecosystem not only includes communities of organisms that live in the pond, but also extends to the communities that live along the water's edge.

✓ **Identify abiotic and biotic components, including a list of species.** A list of the biotic components of this pond ecosystem would include cattails, grasses, plankton, insects, fish, frogs, birds, seeds, mice, snakes, and owls. Abiotic components include water, sunlight, oxygen, and minerals.

✓ **Identify abiotic factors that affect ecosystem health and analyze these factors.** In the pond ecosystem, water is the most important abiotic factor because most species could not survive if the pond dried up. Another important abiotic factor is dissolved oxygen in the water. If oxygen levels get too low, fish could not survive.

✓ **Model the flow of energy through the ecosystem.** Create a food web that describes as many feeding relationships as possible. A food web for the pond ecosystem would show several interrelated food chains, including fish eating plankton and insects, frogs eating insects, and herons eating fish and frogs.

✓ **Model the flow of matter through the ecosystem.** Create diagrams that show how water, carbon, and nitrogen move through the ecosystem. For example, a carbon cycle diagram for the pond ecosystem would show carbon entering the air through respiration, returning to the bodies of plants through photosynthesis, and moving into the bodies of animals via feeding relationships.

✓ **Identify symbiotic relationships among organisms in the ecosystem.** Describe any examples of mutualism, commensalism, or parasitism in the ecosystem. In the pond ecosystem, mosquitoes have a parasitic relationship with mammals and birds because they feed on the blood of these animals.

# Glossary

## A

**abdomen** part of an arthropod's body that is behind the thorax.
**abdomen** parte del cuerpo de un artrópodo situada detrás del tórax.

**abiotic** nonliving factor in an ecosystem, such as moisture, temperature, wind, sunlight, soil, and minerals.
**abiótico** factor inerte de un ecosistema, como la humedad, la temperatura, el viento, la luz solar, el suelo y los minerales.

**ABO blood group** four common blood types (A, B, AB, and O) and the protein markers that distinguish them.
**grupo sanguíneo ABO** sistema que contiene los cuatro tipos de sangre comunes (A, B, AB y O) y los marcadores proteicos que los distinguen.

**absorption** process by which nutrients move out of one system and into another.
**absorción** proceso mediante el cual los nutrientes pasan de un sistema del organismo a otro.

**abyssal zone** (uh-BIHS-uhl) depth of the ocean that lies below 2000 meters and is in complete darkness.
**zona abisal** región del océano por debajo de los 2000 metros de profundidad que se encuentra en total oscuridad.

**accuracy** a description of how close a measurement is to the true value of the quantity measured.
**exactitud** término que describe qué tanto se aproxima una medida al valor verdadero de la cantidad medida.

**acid** compound that donates a proton ($H^+$) when dissolved in a solution.
**ácido** compuesto que cede un protón ($H^+$) al ser disuelto en una solución.

**acid rain** precipitation produced when pollutants in the atmosphere cause the pH of rain to decrease.
**lluvia ácida** precipitación que se produce cuando los contaminantes de la atmósfera hacen que el pH de la lluvia disminuya.

**acquired immune deficiency syndrome (AIDS)** condition characterized by having several infections and very few T cells; caused by HIV.
**síndrome de inmunodeficiencia adquirida (SIDA)** enfermedad caracterizada por falta de defensa contra varias infecciones y muy pocas células T; causada por el VIH.

**actin** filament that is pulled by myosin filaments to cause muscle contraction.
**actina** filamento que al ser accionado por los filamentos de miosina provoca una contracción muscular.

**action potential** fast, moving change in electrical charge across a neuron's membrane; also called an impulse.
**potencial de acción** cambio rápido en la descarga eléctrica a lo largo de la membrana de las neuronas; también llamado impulso.

**activation energy** energy input necessary to initiate a chemical reaction.
**energía de activación** energía necesaria para iniciar una reacción química.

**active immunity** immunity that occurs after the body responds to an antigen.
**inmunidad activa** inmunidad que se produce después de que el cuerpo haya respondido a un antígeno.

**active transport** energy-requiring movement of molecules across a membrane from a region of lower concentration to a region of higher concentration.
**transporte activo** desplazamiento de moléculas a través de una membrana desde un medio de baja concentración a un medio de alta concentración.

**adaptation** inherited trait that is selected for over time because it allows organisms to better survive in their environment.
**adaptación** rasgo heredado durante un periodo de tiempo mediante selección natural, que facilita la supervivencia de los organismos en su medio ambiente.

**adaptive radiation** process by which one species evolves and gives rise to many descendant species that occupy different ecological niches.
**radiación adaptativa** proceso evolutivo mediante el cual una especie da lugar a varias nuevas especies que ocupan distintos nichos ecológicos.

**addiction** uncontrollable physical and mental need for something.
**adicción** necesidad física y mental incontrolable de alguna sustancia o actividad.

**adenosine diphosphate (ADP)** low-energy molecule that can be converted to ATP.
**adenosín difosfato (ADP)** molécula con poca energía que puede convertirse en ATP.

**adenosine triphosphate (ATP)** high-energy molecule that contains, within its bonds, energy that cells can use.
**adenosín trifosfato (ATP)** molécula de alta energía en cuyos enlaces se almacena energía para las células.

**adhesion** attraction between molecules of different substances.
**adhesión** atracción que se produce entre moléculas de diferentes sustancias.

**adolescence** period of life beginning at puberty and ending at adulthood.
**adolescencia** periodo de la vida que comienza en la pubertad y que termina en la edad adulta.

**ADP** *see* adenosine diphosphate.
**ADP** *véase* adenosín difosfato.

**adulthood** period of life when a person is fully developed and physical growth stops.
**edad adulta** período de la vida en el que un individuo alcanza su completo desarrollo y en el que cesa el crecimiento.

**aerobic** (ay-ROH-bihk) process that requires oxygen to occur.
**aeróbico** proceso que requiere la presencia de oxígeno para ocurrir.

**airfoil** surface, such as a bird's wing, whose shape moves air faster over the top than underneath it, allowing for flight.
**superficie aerodinámica** superficie de ala cuya forma, como en el caso de las aves, permite que el aire se mueva más rápido por arriba que por abajo, facilitando así el vuelo.

**air sac** air-filled space that connects to a bird's lungs, aiding in breathing.
**sacos aéreos** órganos llenos de aire conectados a los pulmones de las aves para facilitar la respiración.

**algae** (singular: *alga*) photosynthetic plantlike protists.
**alga** protista fotosintética de aspecto vegetal.

**alkaloid** chemical produced by plants that contains nitrogen, many of which are used in medicines.
**alcaloide** compuesto químico, producido por las plantas, que contiene nitrógeno y es usado en muchos medicamentos.

**allele** (uh-LEEL) any of the alternative forms of a gene that occurs at a specific place on a chromosome.
**alelo** cualquier variante de un gen que ocupa la misma posición en un cromosoma.

**allele frequency** proportion of one allele, compared with all the alleles for that trait, in the gene pool.
**frecuencia alélica** proporción de un alelo determinado con respecto a los demás alelos del mismo rasgo en una misma población.

**allergen** antigen that does not cause disease but still produces an immune response.
**alérgeno** antígeno que, si bien no causa una enfermedad, produce una respuesta inmune.

**allergy** immune response that occurs when the body responds to a nondisease-causing antigen, such as pollen or animal dander.
**alergia** respuesta inmune producida cuando el organismo responde a aquellos antígenos que no causan enfermedades, como el polen o la caspa de ciertos animales.

**alternation of generations** plant life cycle in which the plant alternates between haploid and diploid phases.
**alternancia generacional** ciclo de vida de las plantas en el que la planta alterna fases haploides y diploides.

**altruism** behavior in which an animal reduces its own fitness to help the other members of its social group.
**altruismo** patrón de comportamiento animal, en el cual un individuo sacrifica su integridad para beneficiar a otros miembros de su grupo social.

**alveolus** (al-VEE-uh-luhs) (plural: *alveoli*) tiny, thin-walled structure across which oxygen gas is absorbed and carbon dioxide is released in the lungs.
**alvéolo** pequeña estructura de paredes delgadas a través de la cual se absorbe oxígeno gaseoso y se libera dióxido de carbono en los pulmones.

**amino acid** molecule that makes up proteins; composed of carbon, hydrogen, oxygen, nitrogen, and sometimes sulfur.
**aminoácido** molécula que forma las proteínas; está compuesta de carbono, hidrógeno, oxígeno, nitrógeno y, a veces, de azufre.

**amniote** vertebrate whose embryo or fetus is enclosed by a thin, tough membranous sac.
**amniota** vertebrado cuyo embrión o feto está envuelto en un saco membranoso delgado y resistente.

**amniotic egg** waterproof container that allows an embryo to develop out of water and externally from the mother without drying out.
**huevo amniótico** envoltura impermeable que permite el desarrollo del embrión fuera del agua y de la propia madre sin que éste se deshidrate.

**amniotic sac** fluid-filled organ that cushions and protects the developing embryo of some vertebrates.
**saco amniótico** membrana que contiene líquido y que amortigua y protege el embrión de ciertos vertebrados.

**amphibian** vertebrate that can live on land and in water.
**anfibio** vertebrado que puede vivir en el agua y en tierra firme.

**anaerobic** process that does not require oxygen to occur.
**anaeróbico** proceso que no requiere oxígeno para ocurrir.

**analogous structure** body part that is similar in function as a body part of another organism but is structurally different.
**estructura análoga** parte del cuerpo que cumple una función similar a la parte del cuerpo de un organismo diferente, pero que tiene una estructura diferente.

**anaphase** third phase of mitosis during which chromatids separate and are pulled to opposite sides of the cell.
**anafase** tercera fase de la mitosis, en la cual las cromátidas se separan y se dirigen hacia los polos opuestos de la célula.

**anaphylaxis** (an-uh-fuh-LAK-sihs) severe allergic reaction that causes airways to tighten and blood vessels to leak.
**anafilaxis** reacción alérgica grave que produce rigidez de las vías aéreas y el drenaje de líquido de los vasos sanguíneos.

**angiosperm** (AN-jee-uh-SPURM) seed plant whose embryos are enclosed by fruit.
**angiosperma** planta cuyos embriones se encuentran encerrados en el fruto.

**anthropoid** humanlike primate.
**antropoide** primate semejante al ser humano.

**antibiotic** chemical that kills or slows the growth of bacteria.
**antibiótico** compuesto químico que mata o inhibe el desarrollo de las bacterias.

**antibiotic resistance** process by which bacteria mutate so that they are no longer affected by an antibiotic.
**resistencia antibiótica** proceso mediante el cual una bacteria sufre mutaciones y para hacerse resistente a los antibióticos.

# Glossary

**antibody** protein produced by B cells that aids in the destruction of pathogens.
 **anticuerpo** proteína producida por las células B que contribuye a la destrucción de los patógenos.

**anticodon** set of three nucleotides in a tRNA molecule that binds to a complementary mRNA codon during translation.
 **anticodón** grupo de tres nucleótidos de la molécula de ARNt que se acopla a un codón complementario de ARNm durante la traslación.

**antigen** (AN-tih-juhn) protein marker that helps the immune system identify foreign particles.
 **antígeno** marcador proteico que ayuda al sistema immune a identificar sustancias extrañas tales como los virus.

**antiseptic** (AN-tih-SEHP-tihk) chemical, such as soap, vinegar, or rubbing alcohol, that destroys pathogens outside of the body.
 **antiséptico** compuesto químico, como el jabón, el vinagre o el alcohol, que destruyen los patógenos fuera del cuerpo.

**apoptosis** (AP-uhp-TOH-sihs) programmed cell death.
 **apoptosis** muerte celular programada.

**appendage** extension, such as an antenna or arm, that is attached to the body.
 **apéndice** prolongación del cuerpo, como una antena o un brazo, unida o contigua al mismo.

**appendicular skeleton** part of the skeletal system that allows for most of the body's movements; includes bones of the arms, shoulders, legs, and pelvis.
 **esqueleto apendicular** parte del sistema esquelético que permite la mayor parte de los movimientos del cuerpo; consta, entre otros, de los huesos de los brazos, hombros, piernas y la pelvis.

**arachnid** terrestrial chelicerate, such as a spider.
 **arácnido** quelicerado terrestre, como la araña.

**Archaea** one of the three domains of life, containing single-celled prokaryotes in the kingdom Archaea.
 **Arqueas** uno de los tres dominios de la vida, compuesto de procariontes unicelulares del reino Archaea.

**artery** large blood vessel that carries blood away from the heart.
 **arteria** gran vaso sanguíneo que transporta la sangre desde el corazón.

**arthropod** invertebrate with an exoskeleton, jointed appendages, and a segmented body.
 **artrópodo** invertebrado con exoesqueleto, apéndices articulados y cuerpo segmentado.

**artificial selection** process by which humans modify a species by breeding it for certain traits
 **selección artificial** proceso mediante el cual los seres humanos modifican una especie al criarla para obtener ciertos rasgos.

**asexual reproduction** process by which offspring are produced from a single parent; does not involve the joining of gametes.
 **reproducción asexual** proceso mediante el cual se producen descendientes de un solo progenitor, sin necesidad de la unión de gametos.

**asthma** (AZ-muh) condition in which air pathways in the lungs constrict, making breathing difficult.
 **asma** enfermedad que, al estrechar las vías aéreas de los pulmones, dificulta la respiración.

**atmosphere** air blanketing Earth's solid surface.
 **atmósfera** envoltura de aire que rodea la superficie sólida de la Tierra.

**atom** smallest basic unit of matter.
 **átomo** unidad básica más pequeña de la materia.

**ATP** *see* adenosine triphosphate.
 **ATP** *véase* adenosín trifosfato.

**ATP synthase** enzyme that catalyzes the reaction that adds a high-energy phosphate group to ADP to form ATP.
 **ATP sintetasa** enzima que cataliza la reacción para enlazar un grupo fosfato de alta energía al ADP y formar así el ATP.

**atrium** (plural: *atria*) small chamber in the human heart that receives blood from the veins.
 **aurícula** pequeña cavidad del corazón humano que recibe sangre de las venas.

**autonomic nervous system** division of the peripheral nervous system that controls involuntary functions.
 **sistema nervioso autónomo** parte del sistema nervioso periférico que controla las funciones involuntarias.

**autosome** chromosome that contains genes for characteristics not directly related to the sex of the organism.
 **autosoma** cromosoma cuyos genes no rigen los rasgos relacionados directamente con el sexo del organismo.

**autotroph** organism that obtains its energy from abiotic sources, such as sunlight or inorganic chemicals.
 **autótrofo** organismo que obtiene su energía a partir de fuentes abióticas como, por ejemplo, la luz solar o sustancias inorgánicas.

**auxin** (AWK-sihn) plant hormone that stimulates the lengthening of cells in the growing tip.
 **auxina** hormona vegetal que estimula la elongación de las células y regula el crecimiento de las plantas.

**axial skeleton** part of the skeletal system that supports the body's weight and protects the body's internal tissues; includes the bones of the skull, spinal column, and rib cage.
 **esqueleto axial** parte del sistema esquelético que da soporte al peso corporal y que protege los tejidos internos del organismo; consta de los huesos del cráneo, la columna vertebral y la caja torácica.

**axon** long extension of the neuron membrane that carries impulses from one neuron to another.
 **axón** prolongación de la membrana de la neurona que transmite impulsos eléctricos de una neurona a otra.

# B

**Bacteria** one of the three domains of life, containing single-celled prokaryotes in the kingdom Bacteria.

    **Bacteria** uno de los tres dominios en los que se dividen los seres vivos, que consta de procariontes unicelulares del reino Bacteria.

**bacteriophage** virus that infects bacteria.

    **bacteriófago** virus que infecta a las bacterias.

**bacterium** (plural: *bacteria*) organism that is within the kingdom Bacteria.

    **bacteria** organismo perteneciento al reino Bacteria.

**base** compound that accepts a proton ($H^+$) when dissolved in solution.

    **base** compuesto que al disolverlo en una solución acepta un protón ($H^+$).

**base pairing rules** rule that describes how nucleotides form bonds in DNA; adenine (A) always bonds with thymine (T), and guanine (G) always bonds with cytosine (C).

    **reglas de apareamiento de bases** regla que describe cómo se enlazan los nucleótidos en el ADN; la adenina (A) siempre se enlaza con la timina (T), y la guanina (G) siempre se enlaza con la citosina (C).

**bathyal zone** (BATH-ee-uhl) zone of the ocean that extends from the edge of the neritic zone to the base of the continental shelf.

    **zona batial** region océanica que se extiende desde el límite de la zona nerítica hasta la base de la plataforma continental.

**B cell** white blood cell that matures in the bone marrow and produces antibodies that fight off infection; also called a B-lymphocyte.

    **célula B** glóbulo blanco que madura en la médula osea y que produce los anticuerpos que combaten las infecciones; también se conoce como linfocito B.

**behavioral isolation** isolation between populations due to differences in courtship or mating behavior.

    **aislamiento etológico** aislamiento entre poblaciones debido a diferencias en los rituales de cortejo o apareamiento.

**benign** having no dangerous effect on health, especially referring to an abnormal growth of cells that are not cancerous.

    **benigno** que no tiene efectos graves sobre la salud; se refiere particularmente al crecimiento anormal de células que no son cancerosas.

**benthic zone** lake or pond bottom, where little to no sunlight can reach.

    **zona béntica** fondo de un lago o estanque, adonde llega poca o ninguna luz.

**bilateral symmetry** body plan of some organisms in which the body can be divided equally along only one plane.

    **simetría bilateral** se observa en los organismos que pueden dividirse en partes iguales a lo largo de un plano único.

**bile** fluid released by the liver and gallbladder into the small intestine that aids in the digestion and absorption of fats.

    **bilis** fluido segregado por el hígado y almacenado en la vesícula biliar, y que es liberado al intestino delgado para facilitar la digestión y la absorción de las grasas.

**binary fission** (BY-nuh-ree FIHSH-uhn) asexual reproduction in which a cell divides into two equal parts.

    **fisión binaria** reproducción asexual en la que una célula se divide en dos partes iguales.

**binomial nomenclature** naming system in which each species is given a two-part scientific name (genus and species) using Latin words.

    **nomenclatura binomial** sistema de denominación de especies mediante el cual se les otorga un nombre científico que consta de dos palabras en latín (género y especie).

**biodiversity** variety of life within an area.

    **biodiversidad** variedad de las formas de vida en una zona determinada.

**biogeochemical cycle** movement of a chemical through the biological and geological, or living and nonliving, parts of an ecosystem.

    **ciclo biogeoquímico** movimiento de una sustancia química a través de los componentes biológicos y geológicos, o vivos e inertes, de un ecosistema.

**biogeography** study of the distribution of organisms around the world.

    **biogeografía** estudio de la distribución de los organismos en el mundo.

**bioinformatics** use of computer databases to organize and analyze biological data.

    **bioinformática** utilización de bases de datos de computación para organizar y analizar datos biológicos.

**biological clock** internal mechanism that controls an animal's activity patterns.

    **reloj biológico** mecanismo interno que controla el ritmo de actividad de un animal.

**biology** scientific study of all forms of life.

    **biología** estudio científico de todas las formas de vida.

**biomagnification** condition of toxic substances being more concentrated in tissues of organisms higher on the food chain than ones lower in the food chain.

    **biomagnificación** condición en la cual la concentración de sustancias tóxicas en los tejidos de los organismos que pertenecen a eslabones más altos de la cadena alimentaria es mayor que la concentración en los organismos de los eslabones más bajos.

**biomass** total dry mass of all organisms in a given area.

    **biomasa** masa deshidratada total de todos los organismos de un área determinada.

**biome** regional or global community of organisms characterized by the climate conditions and plant communities that thrive there.
**bioma** comunidad regional o global de organismos caracterizada por las condiciones climáticas y el tipo de vegetación del área.

**bioremediation** process by which humans use living things to break down pollutants.
**biorremediación** proceso mediante el cual los seres humanos emplean organismos vivos para descomponer sustancias contaminantes.

**biosphere** all organisms and the part of Earth where they exist.
**biosfera** todos los seres vivos y las partes de la Tierra en las que existen.

**biota** collection of living things.
**biota** conjunto de seres vivos.

**biotechnology** use and application of living things and biological processes.
**biotecnología** aprovechamiento y aplicación de los seres vivos y de sus procesos biológicos.

**biotic** living things, such as plants, animals, fungi, and bacteria.
**biótico** referente a los seres vivos, tales como las plantas, los animales, los hongos y las bacterias.

**bipedal** animal that walks on two legs.
**bípedo** animal que camina sobre dos patas.

**blade** broad part of a leaf where most of the photosynthesis of a plant takes place.
**lámina** parte ancha de la hoja donde ocurre la mayor parte de la fotosíntesis de una planta.

**blastocyst** stage of development during which the zygote consists of a ball of cells.
**blastocisto** fase de desarrollo en la que el cigoto consta de células apelotonadas.

**blood pressure** force with which blood pushes against the wall of an artery.
**presión sanguínea** fuerza que ejerce la sangre contra las paredes de las arterias.

**bond energy** amount of energy needed to break a bond between two particular atoms; or the amount of energy released when a bond forms between two particular atoms.
**energía de enlace** energía necesaria para romper un enlace entre dos partículas atómicas; energía liberada al formarse un enlace entre dos átomos determinados.

**book lung** respiratory organ that has several membranes that are arranged like the pages in a book.
**pulmón en libro** órgano respiratorio compuesto por una serie de membranas dispuestas como las páginas de un libro.

**botany** study of plants.
**botánica** estudio de las plantas.

**bottleneck effect** genetic drift that results from an event that drastically reduces the size of a population.
**efecto de cuello de botella** deriva genética resultante de un acontecimiento que reduce drásticamente el tamaño de una población.

**brain stem** structure that connects the brain to the spinal cord and controls breathing and heartbeat.
**tronco del encéfalo** estructura que conecta el cerebro con la médula espinal y que controla la respiración y los latidos del corazón.

# C

**calcification** process that hardens bones by adding calcium phosphate and collagen.
**calcificación** proceso que endurece los huesos mediante depósitos de fosfato cálcico y colágeno.

**Calorie** measure of energy released from digesting food; one Calorie equals one kilocalorie of heat.
**caloría** medida de energía liberada al digerir la comida; una caloría equivale a una kilocaloría de calor.

**Calvin cycle** process by which a photosynthetic organism uses energy to synthesize simple sugars from $CO_2$.
**ciclo de Calvin** proceso mediante el cual un organismo fotosintético usa energía para sintetizar monosacáridos a partir del $CO_2$.

**Cambrian explosion** earliest part of the Paleozoic era, when a huge diversity of animal species evolved.
**explosión Cámbrica** periodo inicial de la era paleozoica, en la que surgió una enorme diversidad de especies animales.

**cancer** common name for a class of diseases characterized by uncontrolled cell division.
**cáncer** nombre común de una clase de enfermedades caracterizadas por una división descontrolada de las células.

**canopy** dense covering formed by the uppermost branches of trees.
**cobertura arbórea** tupido entramado formado por las ramas más altas de los árboles.

**capillary** tiny blood vessel that transports blood between larger blood vessels and other tissues in the body.
**capilar** diminuto vaso sanguíneo que transporta la sangre entre vasos sanguíneos más grandes y otros tejidos del cuerpo.

**capsid** protein shell that surrounds a virus.
**cápsida** cubierta proteica que envuelve al virus.

**carapace** (KAR-uh-PAYS) plate of exoskeleton that covers the head and thorax of a crustacean.
**caparazón** parte del exoesqueleto de los crustáceos que cubre la cabeza y el tórax.

**carbohydrate** molecule composed of carbon, hydrogen, and oxygen; includes sugars and starches.
**carbohidrato** molécula compuesta de carbono, hidrógeno y oxígeno; incluye los azúcares y los almidones.

**carcinogen** substance that produces or promotes the development of cancer.
**carcinógeno** sustancia que estimula o contribuye a inducir el cáncer.

**cardiac muscle** muscle tissue that is only found in the heart.
**músculo cardíaco** tejido muscular, también conocido como miocardio, que sólo se halla en el corazón.

**carnivore** organism that obtains energy by eating only animals.
**carnívoro** organismo que obtiene energía al alimentarse únicamente de otros animales.

**carpel** female structure of flowering plants; made of the ovary, style, and stigma.
**carpelo** estructura reproductora femenina de las plantas con flor; consta de ovario, estilo y stigma.

**carrier** organism whose genome contains a gene for a certain trait or disease that is not expressed in the organism's phenotype.
**portador** organismo cuyo genoma contiene un gen de cierto rasgo o enfermedad que no se encuentra expresado en el fenotipo de dicho organismo.

**carrying capacity** number of individuals that the resources of an environment can normally and persistently support.
**capacidad de carga de población** número de individuos que los recursos de un ambiente pueden sustentar normalmente de manera continua.

**cartilage** tough, elastic, and fibrous connective tissue found between bones.
**cartílago** tejido conectivo resistente, fibroso y elástico que se encuentra entre los huesos.

**catalyst** (KAT-uhl-ihst) substance that decreases activation energy and increases reaction rate in a chemical reaction.
**catalizador** sustancia que disminuye la energía de activación y aumenta la tasa de reacción de una reacción química determinada.

**catastrophism** theory that states that natural disasters such as floods and volcanic eruptions shaped Earth's landforms and caused extinction of some species.
**catastrofismo** teoría según la cual la configuración actual de los accidentes geográficos de la Tierra y la extinción de algunas especies se debió a inundaciones, erupciones volcánicas y otras catástrofes naturales.

**cell** basic unit of life.
**célula** unidad básica de la vida.

**cell cycle** pattern of growth, DNA replication, and cell division that occurs in a eukaryotic cell.
**ciclo celular** proceso de crecimiento, replicación de ADN y división celular que ocurre en las células eucarióticas.

**cell differentiation** processes by which unspecialized cells develop into their mature form and function.
**diferenciación celular** proceso mediante el cual las células no especializadas adquieren una forma y una función determinada.

**cell membrane** double-layer of phospholipids that forms a boundary between a cell and the surrounding environment and controls the passage of materials into and out of a cell.
**membrana celular** capa doble de fosfolípidos que forma una barrera entre la célula y el medio que la rodea, y que controla el flujo de materiales hacia dentro y hacia fuera de la célula.

**cell theory** theory that states that all organisms are made of cells, all cells are produced by other living cells, and the cell is the most basic unit of life.
**teoría celular** establece que todos los organismos están formados por células, que todas las células proceden de otras células vivas y que la célula es la unidad básica de la vida.

**cellular immunity** immune response that relies on T cells to destroy infected body cells.
**inmunidad celular** respuesta inmune que depende de las células T para atacar las células infectadas del cuerpo.

**cellular respiration** process of producing ATP by breaking down carbon-based molecules when oxygen is present.
**respiración celular** proceso de producción de ATP mediante la descomposición de moléculas de carbono en presencia de oxígeno.

**cell wall** rigid structure that gives protection, support, and shape to cells in plants, algae, fungi, and bacteria.
**pared celular** estructura rígida que proteje, sustenta y da forma a las células de las plantas, algas, hongos y bacterias.

**Cenozoic** geologic time period that began 65 million years ago and continues today.
**Cenozoico** período geológico que empezó hace 65 millones de años y que se extiende hasta la actualidad.

**central dogma** theory that states that, in cells, information only flows from DNA to RNA to proteins.
**dogma central** teoría que formula que la información en las células siempre fluye del ADN al ARN y luego a las proteínas.

**central nervous system (CNS)** part of the nervous system that interprets messages from other nerves in the body; includes the brain and spinal cord.
**sistema nervioso central** parte del sistema nervioso encargada de interpretar los mensajes recibidos de otros nervios del cuerpo; consta del cerebro y de la médula espinal.

**centriole** (SEHN-tree-OHL) small cylinder-shaped organelle made of protein tubes arranged in a circle; aids mitosis.
**centriolo** orgánulo celular con forma de pequeño cilindro formado por una serie de tubos de proteínas en disposición circular; participa en la reproducción celular.

**centromere** (SEHN-truh-MEER) region of condensed chromosome that looks pinched; where spindle fibers attach during meiosis and mitosis.
**centrómero** región de condensación del cromosoma donde se une el huso durante la meiosis y la mitosis.

# Glossary

**cephalothorax** (SEHF-uh-luh-THAWR-aks) region of a crustacean body where the head and thorax meet.
**cefalotórax** región del cuerpo de los crustáceos donde se unen la cabeza y el tórax.

**cerebellum** (SEHR-uh-BEHL-uhm) part of the brain that coordinates and regulates all voluntary muscle movement and maintains posture and balance.
**cerebelo** parte del encéfalo que coordina y regula todos los movimientos musculares voluntarios, y que permite mantener la postura y el equilibrio.

**cerebral cortex** layer of gray matter on the surface of the cerebrum that receives information and generates responses.
**corteza cerebral** capa de material gris situada en la superficie del cerebro que se encarga de recibir información y de generar respuestas.

**cerebrum** (SEHR-uh-bruhm) largest part of the brain, coordinating movement, thought, reasoning, and memory; includes the cerebral cortex and the white matter beneath it.
**cerebro** la parte más grande del encéfalo que se encarga de coordinar el movimiento, el pensamiento, el razonamiento y la memoria; incluye la corteza cerebral y la materia blanca que se encuentra debajo de ésta.

**chaparral** (SHAP-uh-RAL) biome characterized by hot, dry summers and cool, moist winters; also called Mediterranean shrubland.
**chaparral** bioma caracterizado por veranos secos y calurosos e inviernos frescos y húmedos; también se conoce como matorral mediterráneo.

**chelicerate** arthropod that lacks antennae and has four pairs of walking legs and a pair of fanglike mouth parts.
**quelicerado** artrópodo sin antenas con cuatro pares de patas y una boca de dos piezas en forma de colmillos.

**chemical reaction** process by which substances change into different substances through the breaking and forming of chemical bonds.
**reacción química** proceso mediante el cual una sustancia se transforma en otra sustancia diferente al romperse sus enlaces químicos y formarse otros nuevos.

**chemosynthesis** (KEE-mo-SIHN-thih-sihs) process by which ATP is synthesized by using chemicals as an energy source instead of light.
**quimiosíntesis** proceso de síntesis del ATP cuya fuente de energía no es la luz, sino determinadas sustancias químicas.

**childhood** period of life from age two until puberty.
**infancia** periodo de la vida comprendido entre los dos años y la pubertad.

**chitin** tough, protective polysaccharide that makes up arthropod skeletons and the cell walls of some fungi.
**quitina** polisacárido duro que forma los exoesqueletos de los artrópodos y las paredes celulares de algunos hongos.

**chlorophyll** (KLAWR-uh-fihl) light-absorbing pigment molecule in photosynthetic organisms.
**clorofila** molécula pigmentaria de los organismos fotosintéticos que absorbe la luz.

**chloroplast** (KLAWR-uh-PLAST) organelle composed of numerous membranes that are used to convert solar energy into chemical energy; contains chlorophyll.
**colorplasto** orgánulo compuesto de numerosas membranas cuya funcción es transformer la energía solar en energía química; contiene clorofila.

**chordate** any animal having, at some stage in development, a hollow nerve cord, pharyngeal slits, and tail.
**cordado** todo tipo de animal que en alguna fase de su desarrollo tiene un cordón nervioso dorsal, hendiduras faríngeas y cola.

**chromatid** (KROH-muh-tihd) one half of a duplicated chromosome.
**cromátida** mitad de un cromosoma duplicado.

**chromatin** loose combination of DNA and proteins that is present during interphase.
**cromatina** conjunto de ADN y proteínas que se manifiesta durante la interfase.

**chromosome** long, continuous thread of DNA that consists of numerous genes and regulatory information.
**cromosoma** un largo y continuo filamento de ADN formado por numerosos genes y que almacena información genética.

**chyme** (kym) partially digested, semi-liquid mixture that passes from the stomach to the small intestine.
**quimo** mezcla semi líquida parcialmente digerida que pasa del estómago al intestino delgado.

**cilia** (singular: *cilium*) short hairlike structures that cover some or all of the cell surface and help the organism swim and capture food.
**cilios** estructuras en forma de pelillos cortos que cubren total o parcialmente la superficie de determinadas células y que ayuda a los organismos a nadar y capturar alimentos.

**circadian rhythm** daily cycle of activity that occurs over a 24-hour period of time.
**ritmo circadiano** ciclo diario de actividad que abarca 24 horas.

**circulatory system** body system that transports nutrients and wastes between various body tissues; includes heart, blood, and blood vessels.
**sistema circulatorio** sistema corporal encargado de transportar nutrientes y desechos entre diversos tejidos corporales; consta del corazón, la sangre y los vasos sanguíneos.

**citric acid cycle** *see* Krebs cycle.
**ciclo del ácido cítrico** *véase* ciclo de Krebs.

**cladistics** method of organizing species by evolutionary relationships in which species are grouped according to the order that they diverged from their ancestral line.
**cladismo** método de clasificación de las especies según su parentesco evolutivo en el que las especies son agrupadas en el orden en que se separaron de su linaje ancestral.

**cladogram** diagram that displays proposed evolutionary relationships among a group of species.
**cladograma** diagrama en el que se presentan los parentescos evolutivos propuestos de un grupo determinado de especies.

**classical conditioning** process by which an organism learns to associate a previously neutral stimulus with a reward or punishment.
**condicionamiento clásico** proceso mediante el cual un organismo aprende a asociar un estímulo, que previamente había sido neutro, con un premio o castigo.

**climate** average long-term weather pattern of a region.
**clima** promedio de valores del tiempo en una región a largo plazo.

**clone** genetically identical copy of a single gene or an entire organism.
**clon** copia genéticamente exacta de un gen o de un organismo completo.

**codominance** heterozygous genotype that equally expresses the traits from both alleles.
**codominancia** genotipo heterocigoto que expresa equitativamente los rasgos de ambos alelos.

**codon** sequence of three nucleotides that codes for one amino acid.
**codón** secuencia de tres nucleótidos que codifica un aminoácido.

**coelom** fluid-filled space that is completely covered by muscle.
**celoma** cavidad llena de líquido cubierta enteramente por el músculo.

**coevolution** process in which two or more species evolve in response to changes in each other.
**coevolución** proceso mediante el cual dos o más especies evolucionan a consecuencia de cambios producidos en cada uno de ellas.

**cognition** mental process of knowing, including aspects such as awareness, perception, reasoning, and judgment.
**cognición** conjunto de procesos mentales cuya función es el conocimiento y que incluyen la conciencia, la percepción, el razonamiento y el juicio.

**cohesion** attraction between molecules of the same substance.
**cohesión** atracción entre moléculas de una misma sustancia.

**cohesion tension theory** theory that explains how the physical properties of water allow it to move through the xylem of plants.
**teoría de la tensión-cohesión** teoría que explica el modo en que las propiedades físicas del agua permiten que ésta fluya a través del xilema de las plantas.

**collagen** three-stranded protein, unique to animals, that combines to form strong, flexible fibers.
**colágeno** proteína animal compuesta por tres cadenas que se enlazan para formar fibras resistentes y flexibles.

**collenchyma cell** elongated cells with unevenly thick walls that form a supportive tissue of plants.
**célula del colénquima** célula alargada con paredes de grosor irregular que forma el tejido de sostén de las plantas.

**commensalism** ecological relationship in which one species receives a benefit but the other species is not affected one way or another.
**comensalismo** relación ecológica entre dos especies en la que una se beneficia sin perjudicar ni beneficiar a la otra.

**community** collection of all of the different populations that live in one area.
**comunidad** conjunto de todas las poblaciones que viven en un área determinada.

**competition** ecological relationship in which two organisms attempt to obtain the same resource.
**competencia** relación ecológica en la que dos organismos tratan de obtener el mismo recurso.

**competitive exclusion** theory that states that no two species can occupy the same niche at the same time.
**exclusión competitiva** teoría según la cual dos especies distintas no pueden ocupar el mismo nicho al mismo tiempo.

**complete digestive tract** digestive system that has two openings, a mouth and an anus, that are at opposite ends of a continuous tube.
**tubo digestivo completo** sistema digestivo con dos aperturas, la boca y el ano, situadas en los extremos opuestos de un tubo continuo.

**complete metamorphosis** process by which immature organisms change their body form before becoming an adult.
**metamorfosis completa** proceso mediante el cual se van produciendo cambios en los organismos inmaduros antes de llegar a adultos.

**compound** substance made of atoms of different elements that are bonded together in a particular ratio.
**compuesto** sustancia formada por átomos de diversos elementos combinados en una proporción determinada.

**concentration gradient** difference in the concentration of a substance from one location to another.
**gradiente de concentración** diferencia en la concentración de una sustancia entre un lugar y otro.

**cone** reproductive structure of gymnosperms inside of which the female gamete is fertilized and seeds are produced.
**cono** estructura reproductora de las gimnospermas en cuyo interior se fertiliza el gameto femenino y se producen semillas.

**cone cell** sensory neuron in the eye that detects color.
**cono (célula)** neurona sensorial del ojo que detecta el color.

# Glossary

**coniferous** tree that retains its needles year-round and reproduces with cones.
    **conífera** árbol que mantiene sus hojas durante todo el año y que se reproduce mediante conos.

**conjugation** process by which a prokaryote transfers part of its chromosome to another prokaryote.
    **conjugación** proceso mediante el cual un procarionte transfiere parte de su cromosoma a otro procarionte.

**constant** condition that is controlled so that it does not change during an experiment.
    **constante** condición controlada de un experimento que no varía en el transcurso del mismo.

**consumer** organism that obtains its energy and nutrients by eating other organisms.
    **consumidor** organismo que obtiene su energía y nutrientes mediante la ingestión de otros organismos.

**convergent evolution** evolution toward similar characteristics in unrelated species, resulting from adaptations to similar environmental conditions.
    **evolución convergente** evolución hacia características similares en especies no relacionadas, que resulta de adaptaciones a condiciones ambientales similares.

**coral reef** ocean habitat found in the shallow coastal waters in a tropical climate.
    **arrecife de coral** hábitat oceánico que se encuentra en aguas costeras poco profundas de climas tropicales.

**corpus luteum** (KAWR-puhs LOO-tee-uhm) follicle after ovulation; also called a yellow body because of its yellow color.
    **cuerpo lúteo** folículo que aparece después de la ovulación; se conoce también como cuerpo amarillo a causa de su color.

**cotyledon** (KAHT-uhl-EED-uhn) embryonic leaf inside of a seed.
    **cotiledón** hoja embriónica que se forma en el interior de la semilla.

**countercurrent flow** flow of water opposite that of the flow of blood in a fish's gills.
    **flujo contracorriente** flujo de agua en sentido opuesto al flujo de la sangre en las branquias de los peces.

**covalent bond** chemical bond formed when two atoms share one or more pairs of electrons.
    **enlace covalente** enlace químico que se forma cuando dos átomos comparten uno o más pares de electrones.

**cross** mating of two organisms.
    **cruzamiento** apareamiento de dos organismos.

**crossing over** exchange of chromosome segments between homologous chromosomes during meiosis I.
    **entrecruzamiento** intercambio de segmentos de cromosomas entre cromosomas homólogos durante la meiosis I.

**crustacean** any of the aquatic arthropods, such as lobsters, crabs, and shrimps, that has a segmented body, an exoskeleton, and paired, jointed limbs.
    **crustáceo** artrópodo acuático, como las langostas, los cangrejos y los camarones, que se caracteriza por tener un cuerpo segmentado, un exoesqueleto y pares de extremidades articuladas.

**cultural behavior** behavior that is passed between members of the same population by learning and not natural selection.
    **comportamiento cultural** comportamiento que se transmite entre los miembros de una misma población, no por selección natural, sino mediante un proceso de aprendizaje.

**cuticle** in plants, a waxy layer that holds in moisture; in insects, a tough exoskeleton made of nonliving material.
    **cutícula** en las plantas, es una capa de cera que mantiene la humedad; en los insectos, exoesqueleto duro de material inerte.

**cyanobacteria** (singular: *cyanobaterium*) bacteria that can carry out photosynthesis.
    **cianobacteria** bacteria capaz de realizar la fotosíntesis.

**cytokinesis** (SY-toh-kuh-NEE-sihs) process by which the cell cytoplasm divides.
    **citocinesis** proceso mediante el cual el citoplasma celular se divide.

**cytokinin** (SY-tuh-KY-nihn) plant hormone that stimulates the final stage of cell division, cytokinesis; also involved in the growth of side branches.
    **citoquinina** hormona vegetal que estimula la última fase de la división celular: la citocinesis; también participa en el crecimiento de las ramas laterales.

**cytoplasm** jellylike substance inside cells that contains molecules and in some cells organelles.
    **citoplasma** sustancia gelatinosa del interior de las células que contiene diversos tipos de moléculas y, en algunas células, orgánulos.

**cytoskeleton** network of proteins, such as microtubules and microfilaments, inside a eukaryotic cell that supports and shapes the cell.
    **citoesqueleto** red proteica, como los microtúbulos y los microfilamentos, dentro de una célula eucariótica que da soporte y define la forma de la célula.

# D

**data** (singular: *datum*) observations and measurements recorded during an experiment.
    **datos** observaciones y medidas registrados en el transcurso de un experimento.

**deciduous** tree that has adapted to winter temperatures by dropping its leaves and going dormant during the cold season.
    **caducifolio** árbol que pierde su foliaje y entra en un período de letargo para adaptarse a las temperaturas invernales.

**decomposer** detritivore that breaks down organic matter into simpler compounds, returning nutrients back into an ecosystem.
   **descomponedor** detritívoro que, al descomponer la materia orgánica en compuestos más sencillos, devuelve al ecosistema sus nutrientes básicos.

**dendrite** branchlike extension of a neuron that receives impulses from neighboring neurons.
   **dendrita** prolongación ramificada de la neurona que recibe impulsos eléctricos de las neuronas adyacentes.

**density-dependent limiting factor** environmental resistance that affects a population that has become overly crowded.
   **factor limitativo dependiente de la densidad** resistencia ambiental que afecta a una población sometida a una densidad demográfica excesiva.

**density-independent limiting factor** environmental resistance that affects a population regardless of population density.
   **factor limitativo independiente de la densidad** resistencia ambiental que afecta a una población sin importar su densidad demográfica.

**dependent variable** experimental data collected through observation and measurement.
   **variable dependiente** datos de una investigación recolectados por medio de la observación y de la medición.

**depressant** drug that causes fewer signals to be transmitted between neurons.
   **depresor** medicamento que reduce la transmisión de señales entre las neuronas.

**derived characteristic** trait that differs in structure or function from that found in the ancestral line for a group of species; used in constructing cladograms.
   **caracter derivado** rasgo que difiere, en su estructura o función, del hallado en un linaje ancestral de un grupo de especies; se usa para crear cladogramas.

**dermal tissue** tissue system that covers the outside of plants and animals.
   **tejido dérmico** sistema de tejidos que cubre la superficie de los animales y las plantas.

**dermis** second layer of skin that includes structural proteins, blood vessels, glands, and hair follicles.
   **dermis** segunda capa de piel formada por proteínas estructurales, vasos sanguíneos y folículos capilares.

**desensitization** process by which neurons in the brain break down neurotransmitter receptors in response to a larger amount of neurotransmitter in the synapse than usual.
   **desensibilización** proceso mediante el cual las neuronas del cerebro inactivan los receptores de los neurotransmisores como respuesta a una cantidad de neurotransmisores mayor de lo habitual en la sinapsis.

**desert** biome characterized by a very dry climate.
   **desierto** bioma caracterizado por un clima muy seco.

**determination** process by which stem cells become committed to develop into only one type of cell.
   **determinación celular** proceso mediante el cual las células madre se desarrollan en un tipo específico de célula.

**detritivore** organism that eats dead organic matter.
   **detritívoro** organismo que se alimenta de materia orgánica muerta.

**deuterostome** animal development in which the animal's anus develops before the mouth.
   **deuterostomia** desarrollo animal en el que el ano del animal se desarrolla antes que la boca.

**dialysis** treatment in which a patient's blood is filtered through a machine, the waste is removed, and the cleaned blood is returned to the patient's body.
   **diálisis** tratamiento médico que consiste en filtrar la sangre del paciente mediante una máquina que elimina los desechos y devuelve la sangre purificada al cuerpo del paciente.

**diaphragm** thin muscle below the rib cage that controls the flow of air into and out of the lungs.
   **diafragma** músculo delgado situado debajo de la caja torácica que controla el flujo de aire hacia el interior y el exterior de los pulmones.

**diastolic pressure** (DY-uh-STAHL-ihk) pressure in an artery when the left ventricle relaxes.
   **presión diastólica** presión en la artería en el momento en que se relaja el ventrículo izquierdo.

**dicot** (DY-KAHT) flowering plant whose embryos have two cotyledons.
   **dicotiledónea** planta con flor cuyos embriones tienen dos cotiledones.

**differentiation** process by which committed cells acquire the structures and functions of highly specialized cells.
   **diferenciación celular** proceso mediante el cual ciertas células adquieren estructuras y funciones altamente especializadas.

**diffusion** movement of dissolved molecules in a fluid or gas from a region of higher concentration to a region of lower concentration.
   **difusión** movimiento de las moléculas disueltas en un líquido o gas desde una región de alta concentración a otra región de menor concentración.

**digestion** process by which large, complex molecules are broken down into smaller molecules that can be used by cells.
   **digestión** proceso mediante el cual grandes y complejas moléculas se descomponen en moléculas más pequeñas que pueden ser absorbidas por las células.

# Glossary

**digestive system** body system that digests food; includes mouth, esophagus, stomach, pancreas, intestines, liver, gallbladder, rectum, and anus.
**sistema digestivo** sistema corporal encargado de la digestión de los alimentos; consta de la boca, el esófago, el estómago, el páncreas, los intestinos, el hígado, la vesícula biliar, el recto y el ano.

**dihybrid cross** cross, or mating, between organisms involving two pairs of contrasting traits.
**cruzamiento dihíbrido** cruzamiento o apareamiento entre organismos que tienen dos pares de rasgos opuestos.

**diploid** (DIHP-LOYD) cell that has two copies of each chromosome, one from an egg and one from a sperm.
**diploide** celula que tiene dos copias de cada cromosoma, una proveniente de un óvulo y la otra de un espermatozoide.

**directional selection** pathway of natural selection in which one uncommon phenotype is selected over a more common phenotype.
**selección direccional** proceso de selección natural en el que se favorece un fenotipo menos común sobre un fenotipo más común.

**disruptive selection** pathway of natural selection in which two opposite, but equally uncommon, phenotypes are selected over the most common phenotype.
**selección disruptiva** proceso de selección natural en el que se favorece a dos fenotipos opuestos, pero igualmente poco comunes, sobre el fenotipo común.

**divergent evolution** evolution of one or more closely related species into different species; resulting from adaptations to different environmental conditions.
**evolución divergente** evolución de una o más especies afines que lleva a la formación de especies diferentes como resultado de adaptaciones a diversas condiciones ambientales.

**DNA; deoxyribonucleic acid** (dee-AHK-see-RY-boh-noo-KLEE-ihk) molecule that stores genetic information in all organisms.
**ADN (ácido desoxirribonucleico)** molécula que almacena la información genética de todos los organismos.

**DNA fingerprint** unique sequence of DNA base pairs that can be used to identify a person at the molecular level.
**identificación por ADN** secuencia única de pares de bases de ADN que permite la identificación de una persona a nivel molecular.

**DNA microarray** research tool used to study gene expression.
**micromatriz de material genético (biochip)** instrumento de investigación usado para estudiar la expresión de los genes.

**DNA polymerase** (puh-LIM-muh-rays) enzyme that makes bonds between nucleotides, forming an identical strand of DNA during replication.
**ADN polimerasa** enzima que establece enlaces entre los nucleótidos y que permite la formación de cadenas idénticas de ADN durante el proceso de replicación.

**dominant** allele that is expressed when two different alleles are present in an organism's genotype.
**dominante** el alelo que se expresa de entre dos alelos diferentes que integran el genotipo de un organismo determinado.

**dormancy** state of inactivity during which an organism or embryo is not growing.
**letargo** periodo de inactividad durante el cual un organismo o embrión no crece.

**double fertilization** process by which two sperm of a flowering plant join with an egg and a polar body, forming an embryo and endosperm.
**fertilización doble** proceso mediante el cual dos gametos masculinos de una planta angiosperma se combinan con un óvulo y un núcleo polar para dar lugar al embrión y al endosperma.

**double helix** model that compares the structure of a DNA molecule, in which two strands wind around one another, to that of a twisted ladder.
**doble hélice** modelo mediante el cual se representa la estructura molecular del ADN como dos cadenas que giran sobre sí mismas, como una escalera espiroidal.

# E

**ecological equivalents** organisms that share a similar niche but live in different geographical regions.
**equivalentes ecológicos** organismos que tienen nichos ecológicos similares, pero que viven en diferentes zonas geográficas.

**ecological footprint** amount of land necessary to produce and maintain enough food, water, shelter, energy, and waste.
**huella ecológica** espacio que requiere una población humana para producir y mantener suficiente alimento, agua, alojamiento y energía, y para contener sus desperdicios.

**ecological niche** all of the physical, chemical, and biological factors that a species needs to survive, stay healthy, and reproduce in an ecosystem.
**nicho ecológico** conjunto de factores físicos, químicos y biológicos que una especie requiere para sobrevivir de manera saludable y reproducirse en un ecosistema determinado.

**ecology** study of the interactions among living things and their surroundings.
**ecología** estudio de las interacciones entre los seres vivos y su entorno.

**ecosystem** collection of organisms and nonliving things, such as climate, soil, water, and rocks, in an area.
**ecosistema** conjunto de organismos y factores físicos, como el clima, el suelo, el agua y las rocas, que caracterizan una zona determinada.

**ectotherm** organism that regulates its body temperature by exchanging heat with its environment.
**poiquilotermo** organismo que regula su temperatura corporal mediante el intercambio de calor con el ambiente.

**egg** female gamete.

**óvulo** gameto femenino.

**electron transport chain** series of proteins in the thylakoid and mitochondrial membranes that aid in converting ADP to ATP by transferring electrons.

**cadena de transporte de electrones** serie de proteínas de las membranas de las mitocondrias y los tilacoides que contribuyen a transformar ADP en ATP mediante la transferencia de electrones.

**element** substance made of only one type of atom that cannot be broken down by chemical means.

**elemento** sustancia formada por un solo tipo de átomo que no se puede descomponer por medios químicos.

**embryo** stage of development after the fertilized cell implants into the uterus but before the cells take on a recognizable shape.

**embrión** fase de desarrollo a partir de la implantación del óvulo fertilizado en el útero, anterior a la etapa en que las células adquieren una forma reconocible.

**emigration** movement of individuals out of a population.

**emigración** flujo de individuos que abandonan una población.

**emphysema** (EHM-fih-SEE-muh) condition of the lungs in which the surface area of alveoli decreases, making breathing difficult.

**enfisema** enfermedad de los pulmones que causa una reducción en la superficie de los alvéolos y, en consecuencia, dificulta la respiración.

**endocrine system** (EHN-duh-krihn) body system that controls growth, development, and responses to the environment by releasing chemical signals into the bloodstream.

**sistema endocrino** sistema corporal que controla el crecimiento, el desarrollo y las respuestas al entorno, mediante la liberación de señales químicas al torrente sanguíneo.

**endocytosis** (EHN-doh-sy-TOH-sihs) uptake of liquids or large molecules into a cell by inward folding of the cell membrane.

**endocitosis** captación celular de líquidos o de grandes moléculas mediante una invaginación de la membrana hacia el interior de la célula.

**endometrium** (EHN-doh-MEE-tree-uhm) lining of the uterus.

**endometrio** recubrimiento interior del útero.

**endoplasmic reticulum** (EHN-duh-PLAZ-mihk rih-TIHK-yuh-luhm) interconnected network of thin, folded membranes that produce, process, and distribute proteins.

**retículo endoplasmático** red de finas membranas interconectadas y plegadas que producen, procesan y distribuyen proteínas.

**endoskeleton** internal skeleton built of bone or cartilage.

**endoesqueleto** esqueleto interno formado por huesos y cartílagos.

**endosperm** tissue within seeds of flowering plants that nourishes an embryo.

**endosperma** tejido de reserva dentro de las semillas de las plantas con flor que abastece el embrión.

**endospore** prokaryotic cell with a thick, protective wall surrounding its DNA.

**endospora** célula procariótica cuyo ADN está protegido por una gruesa pared.

**endosymbiosis** ecological relationship in which one organism lives within the body of another.

**endosimbiosis** relación ecológica en la que un organismo vive en el interior de otro.

**endotherm** organism that produces its own heat through metabolic processes.

**endotermo** organismo que regula la temperatura de su cuerpo mediante sus propios procesos metabólicos.

**endothermic** chemical reaction that requires a net input of energy.

**endotérmica** reacción química que requiere un aporte neto de energía.

**energy pyramid** diagram that compares energy used by producers, primary consumers, and other trophic levels.

**pirámide de energía** diagrama mediante el cual se compara la energía usada por los productores, los consumidores primarios y otros niveles tróficos.

**enzyme** protein that catalyzes chemical reactions for organisms.

**enzima** proteína que cataliza reacciones químicas para los organismos.

**epidemic** rapid outbreak of a disease that affects many people.

**epidemia** aparición repentina de una enfermedad que afecta a muchas personas.

**epidermis** outermost layer of skin that consists mainly of dead skin cells, and provides a barrier to pathogens.

**epidermis** primera capa de piel, que consta principalmente de células epiteliales muertas y que constituye una barrera para los patógenos.

**epididymis** coiled tube through which sperm leave the testes and enter the vas deferens.

**epidídimo** tubo enrollado a través del cuál los espermatozoides salen de los testículos y pasan al conducto deferente.

**epoch** smallest unit of geologic time, lasting several million years.

**época** unidad más pequeña de tiempo geológico, que dura varios millones de años.

**equilibrium** (EE-kwuh-LIHB-ree-uhm) condition in which reactants and products of a chemical reaction are formed at the same rate.

**equilibrio químico** estado en el que los reactivos y los productos de una reacción química se forman a la misma velocidad.

# Glossary

**era** second largest unit of geologic time, lasting tens to hundreds of millions of years and consisting of two or more periods.
**era** segunda unidad más amplia de tiempo geológico; que abarca entre decenas y cientos de millones de años y consta de dos o más períodos.

**esophagus** (ih-SAHF-uh-guhs) tube-shaped tissue of the digestive system that connects the mouth to the stomach.
**esófago** tejido en forma de tubo del sistema digestivo que conecta la boca con el estómago.

**estrogen** steroid hormone that is found in greater quantities in women than men and contributes to female sexual characteristics and development.
**estrógeno** hormona esteroide que abunda más en las mujeres que en los hombres, y que contribuye al desarrollo de las características sexuales femeninas.

**estuary** partially enclosed body of water found where a river flows into the ocean.
**estuario** masa de agua parcialmente cerrada donde un río desemboca en el océano.

**ethnobotany** study of how various cultures use plants.
**etnobotánica** estudio del conocimiento que tienen las culturas sobre el uso de las plantas.

**ethylene** (EHTH-uh-LEEN) plant hormone that is produced in fruits and causes them to ripen.
**etileno** hormona vegetal que se produce en las frutas y que las hace madurar.

**Eukarya** one of the three domains of life, contains all eukaryotes in kingdoms Protista, Plantae, Fungi, and Animalia.
**Eukarya** uno de los tres dominios de la vida; consta de todos los eucariotas de los reinos protistas, plantashongos y animales.

**eukaryotic cell** (yoo-KAR-ee-AHT-ihk) cell that has a nucleus and other membrane-bound organelles.
**célula eucariota** célula que consta de un núcleo y de otros orgánulos limitados por una membrana.

**eusocial** organism population in which the role of each organism is specialized and not all of the organisms will reproduce.
**eusocial** población de organismos en la que todos tienen una función especializada y en la que algunos de ellos no se reproducen.

**eutherian** mammal that gives birth to live young that have completed fetal development.
**euterio** mamífero cuyas crías nacen tras un desarrollo fetal completo.

**evolution** change in a species over time; process of biological change by which descendents come to differ from their ancestors.
**evolución** proceso de cambio de las especies a través del tiempo; proceso de cambios biológicos a través del cual los descendientes se diferencian de sus ancestros.

**excretory system** body system that collects and eliminates wastes from the body; includes the kidneys and bladder.
**sistema excretor** sistema corporal que recoge y elimina los desechos del organismo; consta de los riñones y la vejiga urinaria.

**exocytosis** (EHK-soh-sy-TOH-sihs) release of substances out of a cell by the fusion of a vesicle with the membrane.
**exocitosis** expulsión de sustancias de una célula mediante la fusión de una vesícula citoplasmática con la membrana celular.

**exon** sequence of DNA that codes information for protein synthesis.
**exón** secuencia de ADN que codifica la información para la síntesis de las proteínas.

**exoskeleton** hard outer structure, such as the shell of an insect or crustacean, that provides protection and support for the organism.
**exoesqueleto** estructura exterior dura como, por ejemplo, el caparazón de un crustáceo, que protege y sustenta al organismo.

**exothermic** chemical reaction that yields a net release of energy in the form of heat.
**exotérmica** reacción química que, al producirse, libera energía en forma calor.

**experiment** process that tests a hypothesis by collecting information under controlled conditions.
**experimento** procedimiento mediante el cual se trata de comprobar una hipótesis mediante la recolección de datos bajo condiciones controladas.

**exponential growth** dramatic increase in population over a short period of time.
**crecimiento exponencial** intenso incremento de población en un breve espacio de tiempo.

**extinction** elimination of a species from Earth.
**extinción** desaparición de una especie o grupo de especies de la Tierra.

# F

**facilitated diffusion** diffusion of molecules assisted by protein channels that pierce a cell membrane.
**difusión facilitada** difusión de moléculas asistida mediante canales de proteínas que perforan la membrana celular.

**facultative aerobe** organism that can live with or without oxygen.
**aerobio facultativo** organismo capaz de vivir con o sin oxígeno.

**fallopian tube** tube of connective tissue that attaches the ovary to the uterus in the female reproductive system and in which fertilization occurs.
**trompa de Falopio** conducto de tejido conjuntivo que conecta el ovario con el útero en el sistema reproductor femenino, y donde se produce la fertilización.

**fatty acid** hydrocarbon chain often bonded to glycerol in a lipid.
**ácido graso** cadena de hidrocarbono que suele enlazarce con los glicéridos de un lípido.

**feedback** information that is compared with a set of ideal values and aids in maintaining homeostasis.
**retroalimentación** información que se compara con un grupo de valores ideales y que contribuye al mantenimiento de la homeóstasis.

**fermentation** anaerobic process by which ATP is produced by glycolysis.
**fermentación** proceso anaeróbico que da lugar al ATP mediante la glicólisis.

**fertilization** fusion of an egg and sperm cell.
**fertilización** fusión de un gameto masculino y uno femenino.

**fetus** unborn offspring from the end of the eighth week after conception to the moment of birth.
**feto** cría no nacida desde el final de la octava semana después de la concepción hasta el momento del nacimiento.

**fibrous root** root system made up of many threadlike members of more or less equal length.
**raíces fibrosas** sistema radical compuesto de una multitud de filamentos que tienen una longitud aproximadamente igual.

**filter feeder** animal that eats by straining particles from water.
**organismo filtrador** animal que se alimenta mediante la filtración de partículas del agua.

**fitness** measure of an organism's ability to survive and produce offspring relative to other members of a population.
**aptitud biológica** capacidad de un organismo determinado para sobrevivir y producir descendencia en relación con los demás miembros de una población.

**flagellum** (plural: *flagella*) whiplike structure outside of a cell that is used for movement.
**flagelo** estructura en forma de látigo del exterior de determinadas células que les permite moverse en su medio.

**flower** reproductive structure of an angiosperm.
**flor** sistema reproductor de una angiosperma.

**fluid mosaic model** model that describes the arrangement and movement of the molecules that make up a cell membrane.
**modelo de mosaico fluido** modelo que describe la disposición y movimiento de las moléculas que conforman la membrana celular.

**follicle** collection of cells that surrounds and nourishes an egg while it is in the ovary.
**folículo** conjunto de células que rodean y nutren al óvulo mientras éste permanece en el ovario.

**food chain** model that links organisms by their feeding relationships.
**cadena alimentaria** modelo que relaciona los organismos según sus interacciones alimentarias.

**food web** model that shows the complex network of feeding relationships within an ecosystem.
**red alimentaria** modelo que representa una red compleja de relaciones alimentarias en un ecosistema determinado.

**fossil** trace of an organism from the past.
**fósil** huella de un organismo del pasado.

**founder effect** genetic drift that occurs after a small number of individuals colonize a new area.
**efecto fundador** deriva genética que se produce cuando un pequeño número de individuos coloniza una nueva región.

**frameshift mutation** mutation that involves the insertion or deletion of a nucleotide in the DNA sequence.
**mutación del marco de lectura** mutación que implica la incorporación o la eliminación de un nucleótido en una secuencia de ADN.

**fruit** fertilized and mature ovary of a flower.
**fruto** ovario fertilizado y maduro de una flor.

**fruiting body** spore-producing structure of a fungus that grows above ground.
**esporocarpo** estructura productora de esporas de un hongo que crece sobre la tierra.

# G

**gamete** sex cell; an egg or a sperm cell.
**gameto** célula sexual; óvulo o espermatozoide.

**gametogenesis** (guh-MEE-tuh-JEHN-ih-sihs) process by which gametes are produced through the combination of meiosis and other maturational changes.
**gametogénesis** proceso de producción de gametos mediante una combinación de meiosis y otros cambios de maduración.

**gametophyte** (guh-MEE-tuh-FYT) haploid, gamete-producing phase in a plant life cycle.
**gametofito** fase de producción de gametos o células sexuales haploides en el ciclo de vida de las plantas.

**gastrovascular cavity** saclike digestive space.
**cavidad gastrovascular** espacio digestivo en forma de bolsa.

**gel electrophoresis** (ih-LEHK-troh-fuh-REE-sihs) method of separating various lengths of DNA strands by applying an electrical current to a gel.
**electroforesis en gel** método de separación de fragmentos de ADN mediante la aplicación de una corriente eléctrica a un gel.

**gene** specific region of DNA that codes for a particular protein.
**gen** parte específica del ADN con información codificada para sintetizar una proteína.

**gene flow** physical movement of alleles from one population to another.
**flujo génico** desplazamiento físico de alelos de una población a otra.

# Glossary

**gene knockout** genetic manipulation in which one or more of an organism's genes are prevented from being expressed.
**supresión génica** manipulación genética mediante la cual se anula la capacidad de expresarse de uno o más genes de un organismo determinado.

**gene pool** collection of alleles found in all of the individuals of a population.
**acervo genético** colección de alelos de todos los individuos de una población determinada.

**generalist** species that does not rely on a single source of prey.
**generalista** especie que no depende de un solo tipo de presa.

**gene sequencing** process of determining the order of DNA nucleotides in genes and genomes.
**secuenciación génica** proceso de determinación del orden de los nucleótidos de ADN en los genes y en los genomas.

**gene therapy** procedure to treat a disease in which a defective or missing gene is replaced or a new gene is inserted into a patient's genome.
**terapia génica** procedimiento para el tratamiento de una enfermedad en el que un gen defectuoso o ausente se reemplaza por uno sano que se inserta en el genoma del paciente.

**genetic drift** change in allele frequencies due to chance alone, occurring most commonly in small populations.
**deriva genética** cambio en las frecuencias de alelos que se produce, sobre todo, en poblaciones pequeñas.

**genetic engineering** process of changing an organism's DNA to give the organism new traits.
**ingeniería genética** proceso de modifación del ADN de un organismo con el fin de dotarlo de nuevos rasgos.

**genetic linkage** tendency for genes located close together on the same chromosome to be inherited together.
**ligamiento genético** tendencia de los genes que se encuentran muy próximos en un cromosoma a ser transmitidos juntos a la descendencia.

**genetics** study of the heredity patterns and variation of organisms.
**genética** estudio de los patrones hereditarios y de la variación de los organismos.

**genetic screening** process of testing DNA to determine the chance a person has, or might pass on, a genetic disorder.
**análisis genético** proceso de análisis de ADN para determinar las probabilidades que tiene una persona de contraer o transmitir una enfermedad genética.

**genome** all of an organism's genetic material.
**genoma** todo el material genético de un organismo determinado.

**genomics** (juh-NOH-mihks) study and comparison of genomes within a single species or among different species.
**genómica** estudio comparativo de los genomas de una misma especie y de especies diferentes.

**genotype** (JEHN-uh-TYP) collection of all of an organism's genetic information that codes for traits.
**genotipo** conjunto de todos los rasgos codificados en la información genética de un organismo.

**genus** first name in binomial nomenclature; the second-most specific taxon in the Linnaean classification system that includes one or more physically similar species, which are thought to be closely related.
**género** primera palabra de la nomenclatura binomial; segundo taxón más específico del sistema de clasificación de las especies de Linneo, que consta de dos o más especies físicamente semejantes consideradas muy próximas.

**geographic isolation** isolation between populations due to physical barriers.
**aislamiento geográfico** separación entre poblaciones debido a barreras físicas.

**geologic time scale** time scale representing the history of Earth.
**escala de tiempo geológico** escala de tiempo para representar la historia de la Tierra.

**geosphere** features of Earth's surface—such as continents and the sea floor—and everything below Earth's surface.
**geosfera** componentes de la superficie de la Tierra, es decir, los continentes, el suelo oceánico y el interior mismo de la Tierra.

**germination** process by which seeds or spores sprout and begin to grow.
**germinación** proceso mediante el cual las semillas o esporas brotan y empiezan a crecer.

**germ theory** theory that states that diseases are caused by microscopic particles called pathogens.
**teoría de los gérmenes** teoría según la cual las enfermedades son causadas por unas partículas microscópicas llamadas patógenos.

**gibberellin** (JIHB-uh-REHL-ihn) plant hormone that stimulates cell growth.
**giberelina** hormona vegetal que estimula el crecimiento celular.

**gill** respiratory organ of aquatic animals that allows breathing underwater.
**branquia** órgano respiratorio de numerosos animales acuáticos que permite respirar bajo el agua.

**gland** organ that produces and releases chemicals that affect the activities of other tissues.
**glándula** órgano que produce y secreta compuestos químicos que afectan el funcionamiento de otros tejidos.

**global warming** worldwide trend of increasing average temperatures.
**calentamiento global** incremento del promedio de la temperatura en toda la Tierra.

**glomerulus** (gloh-MEHR-yuh-luhs) tangled ball of capillaries that circulates blood in the kidneys.
  **glomérulos** ovillo de vasos capilares por los que circula la sangre en los riñones.

**glycolysis** (gly-KAHL-uh-sihs) anaerobic process in which glucose is broken down into two molecules of pyruvate and two net ATP are produced.
  **glicólisis** proceso anaeróbico en el que la glucosa se descompone en dos moléculas de piruvato y se producen dos moléculas de ATP.

**Golgi apparatus** (GOHL-jee) stack of flat, membrane-enclosed spaces containing enzymes that process, sort, and deliver proteins.
  **aparato de Golgi** conjunto de sacos apilados y aplanados rodeados de una membrana que contienen enzimas que procesan, clasifican y distribuyen proteínas.

**gradualism** principle that states that the changes in landforms result from slow changes over a long period of time.
  **gradualismo** principio que postula que los cambios en los accidentes geográficos resultan de pequeños cambios graduales durante extensos períodos de tiempo.

**grassland** biome in which the primary plant life is grass.
  **pradera** bioma en la que las forma de vida vegetal predominante son las hierbas y los pastos.

**gravitropism** growth of plants in response to gravity; plant stems grow upward, against gravity, and roots grow toward the gravitational pull.
  **gravitropismo** crecimiento de las plantas condicionado por la gravedad; el tallo crece hacia arriba, en sentido inverso a la fuerza de gravedad, y las raíces crecen hacia abajo, en el mismo sentido que la gravedad.

**greenhouse effect** normal warming effect produced when gases, such as carbon dioxide and methane, trap heat in Earth's atmosphere.
  **efecto invernadero** calentamiento producido cuando ciertos gases, como el dióxido de carbono y el metano, atrapan el calor en la atmósfera terrestre.

**ground tissue** tissue system that makes up the majority of a plant.
  **tejido fundamental** sistema de tejidos que comprende la parte principal del cuerpo de la planta.

**growth factor** broad group of proteins that stimulate cell division.
  **factor de crecimiento** grupo numeroso de proteínas que estimulan la división celular.

**guard cell** one of a pair of cells that controls the opening and closing of a stoma in plant tissue.
  **células oclusivas** las dos células que controlan la apertura y cierre de los estomas en el tejido vegetal.

**gymnosperm** (JIHM-nuh-SPURM) seed plant whose seeds are not enclosed by fruit.
  **gimnosperma** planta productora de semillas que no están encerradas en una fruta.

# H

**habitat** combined biotic and abiotic factors found in the area where an organism lives.
  **hábitat** conjunto de factores bióticos y abióticos de la zona donde vive un organismo determinado.

**habitat fragmentation** process by which part of an organism's preferred habitat range becomes inaccessible.
  **fragmentación del hábitat** proceso mediante el cual una parte del hábitat de un organismo se hace inaccesible.

**habituation** process of eventually ignoring a repeated stimulus.
  **habituación** proceso que eventualmente conduce a ignorar un estímulo que se repite.

**hair cell** mechanoreceptor in the inner ear that detects sound waves when bent.
  **célula ciliada** mecanoreceptor del oído interno que detecta las ondas sonoras que lo accionan.

**hair follicle** pit in the dermis of the skin that contains cells that produce hair.
  **folículo piloso** estrecha cavidad de la piel que contiene células que forman el cabello.

**half-life** amount of time it takes for half of the isotope in a sample to decay into its product isotope.
  **vida mitad** intervalo de tiempo necesario para que la mitad de los átomos de una muestra de isótopos se desintegren.

**haploid** (HAP-LOYD) cell that has only one copy of each chromosome.
  **haploide** célula que sólo tiene una copia de cada cromosoma.

**Hardy-Weinberg equilibrium** condition in which a population's allele frequencies for a given trait do not change from generation to generation.
  **equilibrio de Hardy-Weinberg** condición en la que las frecuencias alélicas de un rasgo determinado en una población determinada se mantienen constantes de una generación a otra.

**heart** muscle in the chest that moves blood throughout the body.
  **corazón** músculo situado en el pecho que hace circular la sangre por el cuerpo.

**hemocoel** open space between cells in animal tissues.
  **hemocele** cavidad intracelular de los tejidos animales.

**hemoglobin** (HEE-muh-GLOH-bihn) iron-rich protein in red blood cells that allows the cells to absorb oxygen gas.
  **hemoglobina** proteína rica en hierro de los glóbulos rojos que permite a las células absorber oxígeno gaseoso.

**herbivore** organism that eats only plants.
  **herbívoro** organismo que sólo se alimenta de plantas.

# Glossary

**heritability** ability of a trait to be passed from one generation to the next.
  **heredabilidad** propiedad de un rasgo determinado de ser transmitido de una generación a la siguiente.

**heterotroph** organism that obtains its energy and nutrients by consuming other organisms.
  **heterótrofo** organismo que obtiene su energía y sus nutrientes alimentándose de otros organismos.

**heterozygous** characteristic of having two different alleles that appear at the same locus of sister chromatids.
  **heterocigoto** característica que consiste en tener dos alelos diferentes en el mismo locus de cromátidas hermanas.

**histone** protein that organizes chromosomes and around which DNA wraps.
  **histona** proteína que ordena los cromosomas y alrededor de la cual se enrolla el ADN.

**homeobox** (HOH-mee-uh-BAHKS) genes that define the head-to-tail pattern of development in animal embryos; also called *Hox* genes.
  **homeobox** genes que definen el desarrollo de los embriones animales organizado de cabeza a cola; también se conocen como genes *Hox*.

**homeostasis** (HOH-mee-oh-STAY-sihs) regulation and maintenance of constant internal conditions in an organism.
  **homeostasis** regulación y mantenimiento de condiciones internas constantes en un organismo determinado.

**homeotic** (hoh-mee-AH-tihk) genes that control early development in animals.
  **homeóticos** genes que controlan la primera fase del desarrollo de los animales.

**hominid** primate group that includes orangutans, chimpanzees, gorillas, and humans, as well as their immediate ancestors.
  **homínido** grupo de primates que incluye orangutanes, chimpancés, gorilas, así como humanos y los antepasados inmediatos de éstos.

**homologous chromosomes** chromosomes that have the same length, appearance, and copies of genes, although the alleles may differ.
  **cromosomas homólogos** cromosomas de la misma longitud, aspecto y secuencia de genes, aunque los alelos de uno y otro cromosoma pueden ser distintos.

**homologous structure** body part that is similar in structure on different organisms but performs different functions.
  **estructura homóloga** estructura anatómica similar de organismos diferentes pero que cumplen funciones diferentes.

**homozygous** characteristic of having two of the same alleles at the same locus of sister chromatids.
  **homocigoto** característica que consiste en tener los mismos alelos en el mismo locus de cromátidas hermanas.

**hormone** chemical signal that is produced in one part of an organism and affects cell activity in another part.
  **hormona** señal química producida en una parte del organismo que afecta a la actividad celular en otra parte del cuerpo.

**Human Genome Project** project whose goal is to map, sequence, and identify all of the genes in the human genome.
  **Proyecto Genoma Humano** proyecto cuya meta consiste en cartografiar un mapa, identificar y hallar la secuencia de todos los genes del genoma humano.

**human immunodeficiency virus (HIV)** virus that weakens the immune system by reproducing in and destroying T cells; causes AIDS.
  **virus de inmunodeficiencia humana (VIH)** virus que debilita el sistema inmune al reproducirse en las células T y destruirlas; causa el SIDA.

**humoral immunity** immune response that relies on B cells to produce antibodies to help fight infection.
  **inmunidad humoral** respuesta inmune basada en los anticuerpos producidos por las células B para combatir las infecciones.

**hydrogen bond** attraction between a slightly positive hydrogen atom and a slightly negative atom.
  **enlace de hidrógeno** atracción entre un átomo de hidrógeno con una carga parcial positiva y otro con una carga parcial negativa.

**hydrologic cycle** pathway of water from the atmosphere to Earth's surface, below ground, and back.
  **ciclo hidrológico** movimiento del agua desde la atmósfera hasta la superficie de la Tierra, al subsuelo y de vuelta a la atmósfera.

**hydrosphere** collection of Earth's water bodies, ice, and water vapor.
  **hidrosfera** conjunto de las masas de agua líquida, sólida y gaseosa de la Tierra.

**hypertonic** solution that has a higher concentration of dissolved particles compared with another solution.
  **hipertónica** solución con una concentración mayor de partículas disueltas que otra solución.

**hypha** (plural: *hyphae*) threadlike filament forming the body and mycelium of a fungus.
  **hifa** filamento que forman el cuerpo y el micelio de los hongos.

**hypothalamus** small area of the midbrain that plays a role in the nervous and endocrine systems.
  **hipotálamo** área reducida del cerebro medio que participa en las funciones de los sistemas nervioso y endocrino.

**hypothesis** (plural: *hypotheses*) proposed explanation or answer to a scientific question.
  **hipótesis** proceso de explicación o respuesta a una pregunta científica.

**hypotonic** solution that has a lower concentration of dissolved particles compared with another solution.
**hipotónica** solución con una concentración menor de partículas disueltas que otra solución.

**I**

**imitation** process by which an organism learns a behavior by observing other individuals.
**imitación** proceso mediante el cual un organismo aprende un determinado comportamiento mediante la observación de otros individuos.

**immigration** movement of individuals into a population.
**inmigración** desplazamiento de individuos hacia una población establecida.

**immune system** body system that fights off infections.
**sistema inmune** sistema encargado de combatir las infecciones.

**imprinting** process by which a newborn animal quickly learns to recognize another animal, such as a parent.
**impronta filial** proceso mediante el cual un animal recién nacido aprende rápidamente a reconocer a otro como, por ejemplo, su progenitor.

**inclusive fitness** total number of genes an animal contributes to the next generation.
**aptitud inclusiva** número total de genes que un animal transmite a la siguiente generación.

**incomplete dominance** heterozygous phenotype that is a blend of the two homozygous phenotypes.
**dominancia incompleta** fenotipo heterocigoto que resulta de la mezcla de dos fenotipos homocigotos.

**incomplete metamorphosis** process by which immature arthropods look similar to their adult form.
**metamorfosis incompleta** proceso mediante el cual los especímenes jóvenes de los artrópodos son muy similares en forma a los adultos.

**independent variable** condition or factor that is manipulated by a scientist during an experiment.
**variable independiente** condición o factor que es manipulado en el transcurso de un experimento científico.

**index fossil** fossil of an organism that existed during only specific spans of geologic time across large geographic areas.
**fósil índice** fósil de un organismo que existió en el pasado geológico durante un intervalo corto con una amplia distribución geográfica.

**indicator species** species whose presence in an ecosystem gives clues about the condition of that ecosystem.
**especies indicadoras** especies cuya presencia en un ecosistema proporcionan claves sobre el estado en que se encuentra dicho ecosistema.

**infancy** period of life from birth until the ability to walk has been acquired.
**infancia** periodo de vida comprendido entre el nacimiento y los primeros pasos.

**infertility** persistent condition in which offspring cannot be produced.
**esterilidad** incapacidad recurrente de un individuo para reproducirse.

**inflammation** immune response that is characterized by swelling, redness, pain, and itching.
**inflamación** respuesta inmune caracterizada por hinchazón, rubor, dolor y picazón.

**innate** behavior that is not learned through experience.
**innato** comportamiento que no se aprende a través de la experiencia.

**insecticide** chemical that is used to kill insects.
**insecticida** compuesto químico usado para matar insectos.

**insight** ability to solve a problem without repeated trial and error.
**perspicacia** capacidad para resolver un problema sin necesidad de pasar por procesos reiterados de prueba y error.

**instinct** inborn pattern of behavior that is characteristic of a species.
**instinto** patrón innato de comportamiento característico de cada especie.

**integumentary system** body system that separates the other body systems from the external environment; includes the skin and the tissues found within it.
**sistema tegumentario** sistema que delimita los sistemas corporales del medio exterior; consta de la piel y de los tejidos que la conforman.

**interferon** type of protein, produced by body cells, that prevents viruses from replicating in infected cells.
**interferón** tipo de proteína generada por las células corporales que impide la replicación de los virus en el interior de las células infectadas.

**intertidal zone** strip of land between the high and low tide lines.
**zona intermareal** banda de tierra comprendida entra las líneas de pleamar y de bajamar.

**introduced species** species that is not native and was brought to an area as a result of human activities.
**especie introducida** especie no autóctona que llega a otras regiones como resultado de actividades humanas.

**intron** segment of a gene that does not code for an amino acid.
**intrón** región de un gen que no participa en la codificación de amino ácidos.

**invertebrate** animal without a backbone.
**invertebrado** animal sin columna vertebral.

**ion** atom that has gained or lost one or more electrons.
**ión** átomo que ha ganado o perdido uno o más electrones.

# Glossary

**ionic bond** chemical bond formed through the electrical force between oppositely charged ions.
**enlace iónico** enlace químico que se establece mediante la fuerza eléctrica ejercida entre dos iones de cargas opuestas.

**isotonic** solution that has an equal concentration of dissolved particles compared with another solution.
**isotónica** solución que tiene la misma concentración de partículas disueltas que otra solución.

**isotope** form of an element that has the same number of protons but a different number of neutrons as another element.
**isótopo** átomo de un elemento químico que tiene el mismo número de protones, pero una cantidad diferente de neutrones que otro átomo del mismo elemento.

# J

**joint** location in the body where two bones meet.
**articulación** área del cuerpo en la que se unen dos huesos.

# K

**karyotype** (KAR-ee-uh-TYP) image of all of the chromosomes in a cell.
**cariotipo** imagen de todos los cromosomas de una célula.

**kelp forest** ocean habitat that exists in cold, nutrient-rich, shallow coastal waters, composed of large communities of kelp, a seaweed.
**bosques de quelpo** hábitat oceánico de frías aguas costeras de poca profundidad que son ricas en nutrientes y en las que abundan grandes comunidades de algas pardas llamadas quelpos.

**keratin** protein that binds to lipids inside a skin cell, forming a waterproof layer within the skin.
**queratina** proteína que se enlaza con los lípidos dentro de las células epiteliales creando una capa impermeable en el interior de la piel.

**keystone species** organism that has an unusually large effect on its ecosystem.
**especie clave** organismo que tiene una rol dominante en su ecosistema.

**kidney** organ of the excretory system that removes waste from the blood and helps to maintain stable water levels in the body.
**riñón** órgano del sistema excretor que elimina los desechos de la sangre y contribuye a mantener niveles estables de agua en el organismo.

**kinesis** random movement that results from an increase in activity levels due to a stimulus.
**quinesia** movimiento aleatorio que resulta de un incremento en los niveles de actividad producidos por un estímulo.

**kin selection** when natural selection acts on alleles that favor the survival of close relatives.
**nepotismo** selección natural de los alelos que favorece la supervivencia de los familiares más próximos.

**Krebs cycle** process during cellular respiration that breaks down a carbon molecule to produce molecules that are used in the electron transport chain.
**ciclo de Krebs** proceso de respiración celular en el que se desintegra una molécula de carbono para generar moléculas que intervienen en la cadena de transporte de electrones.

# L

**lactic acid** product of fermentation in many types of cells, including human muscle cells.
**ácido láctico** producto de fermentación de muchos tipos de células como, por ejemplo, las células musculares humanas.

**lateral line** sensory system in fish that allows them to sense distant movements in the water.
**línea lateral** sistema sensorial de los peces que les permite captar movimientos lejanos en el agua.

**law of independent assortment** Mendel's second law, stating that allele pairs separate from one another during gamete formation.
**ley de transmisión independiente** segunda ley de Mendel, según la cual los pares de alelos se separan durante la formación de los gametos.

**law of segregation** Mendel's first law, stating that (1) organisms inherit two copies of genes, one from each parent, and (2) organisms donate only one copy of each gene in their gametes because the genes separate during gamete formation.
**ley de la segregación** primera ley de Mendel, según la cual (1) los organismos heredan dos copias de cada gen, una de cada progenitor, y (2) que los organismos sólo reciben una copia de cada gen de los gametos de sus progenitores ya que los genes se separan durante la formación de gametos.

**leukemia** cancer of the bone marrow that weakens the immune system by preventing white blood cells from maturing.
**leucemia** cáncer de la medula ósea que debilita el sistema inmune al impedir que maduren los glóbulos blancos.

**lichen** fungus that grows symbiotically with algae, resulting in a composite organism that grows on rocks or tree trunks.
**liquen** organismo compuesto por un hongo y una alga que viven en y que crece sobre las rocas y los troncos de los árboles.

**ligament** long, flexible band of connective tissue that joins two bones across a joint.
**ligamento** tira alargada y flexible de tejido conjuntivo que une dos huesos a través de una articulación.

**light-dependent reactions** part of photosynthesis that absorbs energy from sunlight and transfers energy to the light-independent reactions.
**reacciones lumínicas** etapa de la fotosíntesis en la que se absorbe energía solar para luego usarse en las reacciones oscuras.

**light-independent reactions** part of photosynthesis that uses energy absorbed during the light-dependent reactions to synthesize carbohydrates.
**reacciones oscuras** etapa de la fotosíntesis en que se aplica la energía absorbida durante las reacciones lumínicas para la síntesis de carbohidratos.

**lignin** (LIHG-nihn) complex polymer that hardens cell walls of some vascular tissues in plants.
**lignina** polímero complejo que endurece las paredes celulares de determinados tejidos vasculares de las plantas.

**limiting factor** environmental factor that limits the growth and size of a population.
**factor limitante** factor ambiental que limita el crecimiento y tamaño de una población determinada.

**limnetic zone** open water of a lake or pond that is located away from shore.
**zona limnética** aguas abiertas de un lago o estanque alejadas de las orillas.

**linkage map** diagram that shows the relative locations of genes on a chromosome.
**mapa de ligamiento** diagrama que representa la situación relativa de los genes en un cromosoma determinado.

**lipid** nonpolar molecule composed of carbon, hydrogen, and oxygen; includes fats and oils.
**lípido** molécula apolar compuesta de carbono, hidrógeno y oxígeno; las grasas y los aceites son lípidos.

**littoral zone** area between the high and low water marks along the shoreline of a lake or pond.
**zona litoral** área de aguas de profundidad intermedia a lo largo de la orilla de un lago o estanque.

**lobe-fin** paired limblike fin that is round in shape.
**aleta lobulada** tipo de aleta de forma redondeada que se presenta en pares y que se asemeja a una extremidad.

**logistic growth** population growth that is characterized by a period of slow growth, followed by a period of exponential growth, followed by another period of almost no growth.
**crecimiento logístico** crecimiento de población que se caracteriza por un período de crecimiento lento, seguido por un período de crecimiento exponencial al que le sigue un período de crecimiento insignificante.

**lung** organ that absorbs oxygen gas from air that an organism inhales.
**pulmón** órgano que absorbe el oxígeno gaseoso que inhala un organismo.

**lymph** collection of interstitial fluid and white blood cells that flows through the lymphatic system.
**linfa** conjunto de los fluidos intersticiales y de glóbulos blancos que circulan por el sistema linfático.

**lymphatic system** (lihm-FAT-ihk) body system that consists of organs, vessels, and nodes through which lymph circulates.
**sistema linfático** sistema corporal que consta de órganos, vasos y nódulos a través de los cuales circula la linfa.

**lymphocyte** (LIHM-fuh-SYT) white blood cell that plays a role in an immune response; *see* B cell and T cell.
**linfocito** glóbulo blanco que participa en la respuesta inmune; *véanse* célula B y célula T.

**lysogenic infection** infectious pathway of a virus in which host cells are not immediately destroyed.
**infección lisogénica** infección vírica en la que las células huésped no son destruidas de inmediato.

**lysosome** (LY-suh-SOHM) organelle that contains enzymes.
**lisosoma** orgánulo que contiene enzimas.

**lytic infection** infectious pathway of a virus in which host cells are destroyed.
**infección lítica** infección vírica en la que se destruyen las células huésped.

# M

**malignant** cancerous tumor in which cells break away and spread to other parts of the body, causing harm to the organism's health.
**maligno** tumor canceroso en el que las células se desprenden y se diseminan a otras partes del cuerpo provocando daños a la salud del organismo.

**mammal** endothermic organism that has hair, mammary glands, bones in the ear that allow for hearing, and a jaw for chewing food.
**mamífero** organismo endotérmico que tiene pelo y glándulas mamarias, además de huesos en el oído que le permiten oír y una mandíbula para masticar.

**mammary gland** gland that produces milk.
**glándula mamaria** glándula productora de leche.

**mandible** appendage that is used to crush and bite food.
**mandíbula** apéndice empleado para triturar y morder la comida.

**marsupial** mammal whose young complete fetal development in the mother's external pouch.
**marsupial** mamífero cuyas crías terminan su desarrollo fetal en una bolsa exterior de la madre.

**measurement** a determination of the dimensions of something using a standard unit.
**medida** una determinación de las dimensiones de algo por medio del uso de una unidad estándar.

# Glossary

**medusa** umbrella-shaped body form of a cnidarian in which the mouth and tentacles are on the underside.
**medusa** organismo cnidario en forma de paraguas que tiene la boca y los tentáculos en la superficie cóncava.

**meiosis** (my-OH-sihs) form of nuclear division that divides a diploid cell into haploid cells; important in forming gametes for sexual reproduction.
**meiosis** forma de división nuclear en la que una célula diploide se divide en células haploides; importante en la formación de gametos para la reproducción sexual.

**memory cell** specialized white blood cell that contributes to acquired immunity by acting quickly to a foreign substance that infected the body previously.
**célula de memoria** glóbulo blanco que participa en el proceso de inmunización mediante una respuesta rápida ante una sustancia extraña que ya había infectado el organismo anteriormente.

**menopause** period of life when the female reproductive system permanently stops the menstrual cycle.
**menopausia** período de la vida en que el sistema reproductor femenino deja de producir el ciclo menstrual.

**menstrual cycle** series of changes in the female reproductive system that takes place over the course of one month.
**ciclo menstrual** sucesión de cambios en el sistema reproductor femenino que ocurre en el plazo de un mes.

**meristem** undifferentiated plant tissue from which new cells are formed.
**meristemo** tejido indiferenciado de las plantas en el que se forman nuevas células.

**mesoglea** jellylike material that separates the two tissue layers of a cnidarian.
**mesoglea** matriz gelatinosa que separa las dos capas de tejidos de un cnidario.

**mesophyll** photosynthetic tissue of a leaf, located between the upper and lower epidermis.
**mesófilo** tejido fotosintético de la hoja, situado entre la epidermis superior y la epidermis inferior de la hoja.

**Mesozoic** era during which dinosaurs roamed Earth (from 248 million years ago to 65 million years ago).
**Mesozoico** era de la Tierra que se inició hace unos 248 millones de años y que finalizó hace 65 millones de años en la que abundaron los dinosaurios.

**messenger RNA (mRNA)** form of RNA that carries genetic information from the nucleus to the cytoplasm, where it serves as a template for protein synthesis.
**ARN mensajero (ARNm)** forma de ARN que transporta la información genética del núcleo al citoplasma, donde sirve de patrón para la síntesis de las proteínas.

**metabolism** all chemical processes that synthesize or break down materials within an organism.
**metabolismo** conjunto de procesos químicos que sintetizan o descomponen sustancias en el interior de los organismos.

**metaphase** second phase of mitosis when spindle fibers align the chromosomes along the cell equator.
**metafase** segunda fase de la mitosis en la que las fibras de los husos alinean los cromosomas en el plano ecuatorial de la célula.

**metastasize** (mih-TAS-tuh-syz) to spread by transferring a disease-causing agent from the site of the disease to other parts of the body.
**metástasis** diseminación de una enfermedad causada por un agente patógeno del foco en que se origina a otras partes del cuerpo.

**microclimate** climate of a specific location within a larger area.
**microclima** clima de un lugar específico enclavado en un área más extensa.

**microevolution** observable change in the allele frequencies of a population over a few generations.
**microevolución** cambio observable en las frecuencias alélicas de una población en el transcurso de unas pocas generaciones.

**microscope** tool that provides an enlarged image of an object.
**microscopio** instrumento que permite ver una imagen amplificada de un objeto.

**microvillus** (plural: *microvilli*) small hairlike projection on the surface of a villus in the small intestine.
**microvellosidad** proyección pilosa muy pequeña que recubre las vellosidades del intestino delgado.

**mineral** inorganic material, such as calcium, iron, potassium, sodium, or zinc, that is essential to the nutrition of an organism.
**mineral** material inorgánico, como el calcio, el hierro, el potasio, el sodio o el zinc, que resulta esencial en la nutrición de los organismos.

**mitochondrial DNA** DNA found only in mitochondria, often used as a molecular clock.
**ADN mitocondrial** ADN propio de las mitocondrias que suele actuar a modo de reloj molecular.

**mitochondrion** (MY-tuh-KAHN-dree-uhn) (plural: *mitochondria*) bean-shaped organelle that supplies energy to the cell and has its own ribosomes and DNA.
**mitocondria** orgánulo en forma de fríjol que suministra energía a la célula y que tiene sus propios ribosomas y ADN.

**mitosis** (my-TOH-sihs) process by which a cell divides its nucleus and contents.
**mitosis** proceso en el cual tanto el núcleo como los demás elementos de la célula se duplican.

**molecular clock** theoretical clock that uses the rate of mutation to measure evolutionary time.
**reloj molecular** reloj teórico que emplea la tasa de mutación para medir el tiempo evolutivo.

**molecular genetics** study of DNA structure and function on the molecular level.
**genética molecular** estudio de la estructura y función del ADN a nivel molecular.

**molecule** two or more atoms held together by covalent bonds; not necessarily a compound.
**molécula** dos o más átomos unidos mediante enlaces covalentes; no forman necesariamente un compuesto.

**monocot** (MAHN-uh-KAHT) flowering plant whose embryos have one cotyledon.
**monocotiledónea** planta angiosperma cuyos embriones tienen un solo cotiledón.

**monohybrid cross** cross, or mating, between organisms that involves only one pair of contrasting traits.
**cruzamiento monohíbrido** cruzamiento o apareamiento entre dos organismos que sólo involucra un par de rasgos diferentes.

**monomer** molecular subunit of a polymer.
**monómero** subunidad molecular del polímero.

**monotreme** mammal whose offspring complete fetal development in laid eggs.
**monotrema** mamífero que pone huevos donde sus crías completan su desarrollo fetal.

**muscle fiber** cell of the muscular system that shortens when it is stimulated by the nervous system.
**fibra muscular** célula del sistema muscular que se contrae al ser estimulada por el sistema nervioso.

**muscular system** body system that moves bones within and substances throughout the body.
**sistema muscular** sistema corporal que mueve los huesos y que hace circular sustancias a través del cuerpo.

**mutagen** agent that can induce or increase the frequency of mutation in organisms.
**mutágeno** agente que puede inducir mutaciones en un organismo o incrementar la frecuencia de éstas.

**mutation** change in the DNA sequence.
**mutación** cambio en la secuencia de ADN.

**mutualism** ecological relationship between two species in which each species gets a benefit from the interaction.
**mutualismo** relación ecológica entre dos especies que resulta beneficiosa para ambas.

**mycelium** vegetative part of a fungus, consisting of a mass of branching, threadlike hyphae that grows underground.
**micelio** parte vegetativa del hongo compuesta de un entramado de filamentos ramificados, llamados hifas, que crece bajo tierra.

**mycorrhizae** ecological relationship between the mycelium of a fungus and the roots of certain plants.
**micorriza** relación ecológica entre el micelio de un hongo y las raíces de determinadas plantas.

**myofibril** long strand of protein within a muscle fiber.
**miofibrilla** larga cadena proteica dentro de una fibra muscular.

**myosin** filament that pulls actin filaments to cause muscle contraction.
**miosina** filamento que al tensar los filamentos de actina causa la contracción muscular.

# N

**natural selection** mechanism by which individuals that have inherited beneficial adaptations produce more offspring on average than do other individuals.
**selección natural** mecanismo mediante el cual los organismos que han heredado adaptaciones beneficiosas producen un promedio más alto de descendientes que los demás individuos.

**nebula** rotating cloud of gas and dust.
**nebulosa** nube giratoria de polvo y gases.

**negative feedback** control system for homeostasis that adjusts the body's conditions when the conditions vary from the ideal.
**retroalimentación negativa** sistema de control de la homeostasis que regula las condiciones del cuerpo cuando éstas no son óptimas.

**nematocyst** capsule containing a thin, coiled tubule with a poisonous barb at one end.
**nematocisto** cápsula que contiene un fino túbulo enrollado con un aguijón venenoso en la punta.

**nephron** (NEHF-rahn) individual filtering unit of the kidney that removes waste from the blood.
**nefrona** unidad de filtración del riñón que retira los desechos de la sangre.

**neritic zone** zone of the ocean that extends from the intertidal zone out to the edge of the continental shelf.
**zona nerítica** zona del océano que se extiende desde la zona intermareal hasta el límite de la plataforma continental.

**nervous system** body system that controls sensation, interpretation, and response; includes the brain, spinal cord, and nerves.
**sistema nervioso** sistema corporal que controla las sensaciones, las interpretaciones y las respuestas; incluye el encéfalo, la médula espinal y los nervios.

**neuron** cell of the nervous system that transmits impulses between the body systems as well as interprets and stores some messages in the brain.
**neurona** célula del sistema nervioso que transmite impulsos entre los diversos sistemas del organismo y que, además, interpreta y almacena información en el cerebro.

**neurotransmitter** (NUR-oh-TRANS-miht-uhr) chemical that transmits a nervous system's signal across a synapse.
**neurotransmisor** compuesto químico que transmite una señal del sistema nervioso a través de la sinapsis.

# Glossary

**nitrogen fixation** process by which certain types of bacteria convert gaseous nitrogen into nitrogen compounds.
**fijación del nitrógeno** proceso mediante el cual ciertos tipos de bacterias transforman el nitrógeno gaseoso en compuestos nitrogenados.

**node** organ located along the lymphatic vessels that filters bacteria and foreign particles from lymph.
**ganglio linfático** órgano situado a lo largo de los vasos linfáticos encargado de filtrar bacterias y sustancias extrañas de la linfa.

**nonrenewable resource** natural resource that is used more quickly than it can be formed.
**recurso no renovable** recurso natural que se consume con más rapidez de la que se puede reponer.

**normal distribution** distribution in a population in which allele frequency is highest near the mean range value and decreases progressively toward each extreme end.
**distribución normal** distribución de la población en la que la frecuencia alélica es mayor en la zona de valor medio y disminuye progresivamente hacia ambos extremos.

**notochord** flexible skeletal support rod embedded in an animal's back.
**notocordio** bastón esqueletal flexible que proporciona sostén y que está situado en el dorso de los animales.

**nucleic acid** polymer of nucleotides; the genetic material of organisms.
**ácido nucleico** polímero de nucleótidos; material genético de los organismos.

**nucleotide** (NOO-klee-uh-TYD) monomer that forms DNA and has a phosphate group, a sugar, and a nitrogen-containing base.
**nucleótido** monómero que forma el ADN y que tiene un grupo fosfato, un azúcar y una base nitrogenada.

**nucleus** (NOO-klee-uhs) (plural: *nuclei*) organelle composed of a double membrane that acts as the storehouse for most of a cell's DNA.
**núcleo** orgánulo compuesto de una doble membrana que almacena la mayor parte del ADN de la célula.

# O

**obligate aerobe** prokaryote that cannot survive without the presence of oxygen.
**aerobio obligado** procariota que no puede sobrevivir en un entorno sin oxígeno.

**obligate anaerobe** prokaryote that cannot survive in the presence of oxygen.
**anaerobio obligado** procariota que no puede sobrevivir en un entorno oxigenado.

**observation** using the senses to study the world; using tools to collect measurements; examining previous research results.
**observación** utilización de los sentidos para estudiar el mundo; uso de instrumentos de medición; análisis de resultados de investigación.

**omnivore** organism that eats both plants and animals.
**omnívoro** organismo que se alimenta tanto de animales como de plantas.

**operant conditioning** process by which a behavior increases or decreases as the result of a reward or punishment.
**condicionamiento operante** proceso mediante el cual varía la frecuencia de un comportamiento como resultado de un premio o un castigo.

**operculum** protective bony plate that covers a fish's gills.
**opérculo** placa protectora ósea que recubre las branquias de los peces.

**operon** section of DNA that contains all of the code to begin transcription, regulate transcription, and build a protein; includes a promotor, regulatory gene, and structural gene
**operon** sección de ADN que contiene todos los códigos necesarios para iniciar y regular el proceso de transcripción y para sintetizar una proteína: consta de un promotor, de un gen regulador y de un gen estuctural.

**opportunistic infection** infection caused by a pathogen that a healthy immune system would normally be able to fight off.
**infección oportunista** infección causada por un patógeno que un sistema inmune saludable podría combatir con eficacia.

**optimal foraging** theory that states that natural selection will favor organisms that have behaviors that can gather the best food sources.
**abastecimiento óptimo** teoría según la cual la selección natural favorece a aquellos organismos cuyos comportamientos les permiten acceder a las mejores fuentes de alimento.

**organ** group of different types of tissues that work together to perform a specific function or related functions.
**órgano** grupo de diversos tipos de tejidos que funcionan de manera coordinada para desarrollar una función específica o funciones relacionadas.

**organelle** membrane-bound structure that is specialized to perform a distinct process within a cell.
**orgánulo** estructura intracelular que se especializa en una función específica.

**organism** any individual living thing.
**organismo** cualquier ser vivo.

**organ system** two or more organs that work in a coordinated way to carry out similar functions.
**sistema de órganos** dos o más órganos que funcionan de manera coordinada para realizar funciones similares.

**osmosis** diffusion of water molecules across a semipermeable membrane from an area of higher water concentration to an area of lower water concentration.
**ósmosis** difusión de moléculas de agua a través de una membrana semipermeable, desde un área de mayor concentración de agua a otra de menor concentración de agua.

**ossicle** small bone, especially one of the three found in the middle ear of mammals.
**huesecillo** en los mamíferos, cada uno de los tres huesos pequeños que se encuentran en el oído medio.

**ovary** organ in which female gametes develop prior to fertilization.
**ovario** órgano en el que se desarrollan los gametos femeninos antes de la fertilización.

**oviparous** reproductive strategy in which the embryos develop outside of the mother's body.
**ovíparo** organismo que se reproduce mediante un sistema en el que los embriones se desarrollan fuera del cuerpo materno.

**ovulation** process by which an egg is released from the ovary and becomes available for fertilization.
**ovulación** proceso mediante el cual se libera un óvulo del ovario, quedando susceptible a ser fertilizado.

**ovum** (plural: *ova*) egg cell that is produced by the female reproductive system.
**óvulo** ovocito producido en el sistema reproductor femenino.

# P

**pacemaker** collection of cells that stimulates the pumping action of the heart.
**nódulo sinusal** conjunto de células que estimula los latidos del corazón; también conocido como marcapaso natural.

**paleontology** study of fossils or extinct organisms.
**paleontología** estudio de los fósiles o de los organismos extinctos.

**Paleozoic** era of geologic time (from 544 to 248 million years ago) during which members of every major animal group alive today evolved.
**Paleozoico** era geológica (desde hace 544 a 248 millones de años) durante la cual evolucionaron especies de los principales grupos de animales de la actualidad.

**parasitism** ecological relationship in which one organism benefits by harming another organism.
**parasitismo** relación ecológica en la que un organismo se beneficia perjudicando al otro organismo.

**parasympathetic nervous system** division of the peripheral nervous system that calms the body and helps the body to conserve energy.
**sistema nervioso parasimpático** parte del sistema nervioso periférico encargado de mantener un estado corporal de descanso y ayudar al cuerpo a conservar energía.

**parenchyma cell** cell with thin walls that forms tissues within leaves, roots, stems, and fruit of plants.
**célula del parénquima** célula de paredes delgadas que forma tejidos en el interior de las hojas, raíces, tallos y frutas de las plantas.

**particulate** microscopic bits of dust, metal, and unburned fuel produced by industrial processes.
**materia particulada** partículas microscópicas de polvo, metal y combustibles sin quemar, que se generan en los procesos industriales.

**passive immunity** immunity that occurs without the body undergoing an immune response.
**inmunidad pasiva** inmunidad que tiene lugar sin que el cuerpo experimente una reacción inmune.

**passive transport** movement of molecules across the cell membrane without energy input from the cell.
**transporte pasivo** movimiento de moléculas a través de la membrana celular, que se produce sin aporte de energía celular.

**pathogen** agent that causes disease.
**patógeno** agente que causa una enfermedad.

**pedigree** chart of the phenotypes and genotypes in a family that is used to determine whether an individual is a carrier of a recessive allele.
**pedigrí** diagrama de los fenotipos y genotipos de una familia que se emplea para determinar si un individuo es portador de un alelo recesivo.

**period** unit of geologic time that lasts tens of millions of years and is associated with a particular type of rock system.
**periodo** unidad de tiempo geológico que abarca decenas de millones de años y que suele asociarse a tipos determinados de formaciones rocosas.

**peripheral nervous system (PNS)** division of the nervous system that transmits impulses between the central nervous system and other organs in the body.
**sistema nervioso periférico (SNP)** división del sistema nervioso que transmite impulsos entre el sistema nervioso central y otros órganos del cuerpo.

**peristalsis** (PEHR-ih-STAWL-sihs) wavelike involuntary muscle contractions that push food through the organs of the digestive system.
**peristaltismo** contracciones involuntarias en forma de ondas que impulsan los alimentos a través de los órganos del sistema digestivo.

**petal** modified leaf that surrounds a flower's reproductive structures.
**pétalo** hoja modificada que rodea las estructuras reproductivas de la flor.

**petiole** stalk that attaches a leaf blade to a stem.
**peciolo** rabillo que une la lámina de la hoja al tallo.

# Glossary

**pH** measurement of acidity; related to free hydrogen ion concentration in solution.
**pH** medida de acidez; relacionada con la concentración de los iones libres de hidrógeno en una solución.

**phagocyte** cell that destroys other cells by surrounding and engulfing them.
**fagocito** célula que destruye a otras células rodeándolas y engulléndolas.

**phagocytosis** (FAG-uh-sy-TOH-sihs) uptake of a solid particle into a cell by engulfing the particle; *see* endocytosis.
**fagocitosis** absorción de una partícula sólida por parte de una célula que la envuelve: *véase* endocitosis.

**pharmacology** study of drugs and their effects on the body.
**farmacología** estudio de los medicamentos y de los efectos que causan en el cuerpo.

**phenotype** collection of all of an organism's physical characteristics.
**fenotipo** conjunto de todas las características físicas de un organismo determinado.

**pheromone** chemical released by an organism that stimulates a behavior in other organisms of the same species.
**feromona** compuesto químico liberado por un organismo que estimula ciertos comportamientos en otros organismos de la misma especie.

**phloem** tissue that transports sugars in vascular plants.
**floema** tejido transportador de azúcares en las plantas vasculares.

**phospholipid** molecule that forms a double-layered cell membrane; consists of a glycerol, a phosphate group, and two fatty acids.
**fosfolípido** molécula que forma una membrana de capa doble; consta de glicerol, un grupo fosfato y dos ácidos grasos.

**photoperiodism** response of an organism to changes in the length of the day.
**fotoperiodismo** respuesta de un organismo a las variaciones de luz en un período de 24 horas.

**photosynthesis** process by which light energy is converted to chemical energy; produces sugar and oxygen from carbon dioxide and water.
**fotosíntesis** proceso mediante el cual la energía del sol se convierte en energía química; produce azúcar y oxígeno a partir de dióxido de carbono y agua.

**photosystem** series of light-absorbing pigments and proteins that capture and transfer energy in the thylakoid membrane.
**fotosistema** conjunto de pigmentos y proteínas que capturan y transfieren energía en la membrana tilacoide.

**phototropism** growth of a plant toward a light source.
**fototropismo** crecimiento de la planta hacia la luz.

**phylogeny** evolutionary history of a group of related species.
**filogenia** historia evolutiva de un grupo de especies relacionadas.

**phylum** group of animals defined by structural and functional characteristics that are different from every other animal phylum.
**división** grupo de animales definidos por una serie de características estructurales y funcionales que se diferencian de cualquier otra división; también se conoce como filum.

**phytoplankton** photosynthetic microscopic protists, such as algae.
**fitoplancton** colonia de protistas microscópicas fotosintéticas, como las algas.

**pioneer species** organism that is the first to live in a previously uninhabited area.
**especie pionera** primer organismo que vive en una zona hasta entonces deshabitada.

**pituitary gland** area in the middle of the brain that makes and releases hormones that control cell growth and osmoregulation, water levels in the blood.
**glándula pituitaria** zona en el centro del cerebro que produce y segrega hormonas que controlan el crecimiento celular y la osmorregulación, es decir, la regulación de los niveles de líquidos en la sangre.

**placenta** (pluh-SEHN-tuh) organ that develops in female mammals during pregnancy and carries nutrients from the mother to the embryo.
**placenta** órgano que se desarrolla en las hembras de los mamíferos durante la gestación y que lleva nutrientes de la madre al embrión.

**plankton** microscopic, free-floating organisms, which may be animals or protists, that live in the water.
**plancton** organismos microscópicos, animales o protistas, que flotan libremente en el agua.

**plant** multicellular eukaryote that produces its own food through photosynthesis.
**planta** organismo eucariota multicelular que produce su propio alimento mediante la fotosíntesis.

**plasma** clear yellowish fluid, about 90 percent water, that suspends cells in the blood.
**plasma** líquido de color amarillento pálido que consisten en un 90 por ciento deagua en el que están suspendidas las células sanguíneas.

**plasmid** circular piece of genetic material found in bacteria that can replicate separately from the DNA of the main chromosome.
**plásmido** cadena de material genético en forma circular que se encuentra en las bacterias y que se replica independientemente del ADN cromosómico.

**platelet** cell fragment that is produced in the bone marrow and is important for blood clotting.
**plaqueta** fragmento celular que se produce en la médula ósea y que cumple una función importante en la coagulación de la sangre.

**point mutation** mutation that involves a substitution of only one nucleotide.
**mutación puntual** mutación que involucra la sustitución de un solo nucleótido.

**polar body** haploid cell produced during meiosis in the female of many species; these cells have little more than DNA and eventually disintegrate.
**cuerpo polar** célula haploide producida durante la meiosis en las hembras de muchas especies; esta célula tiene poco más que ADN y termina por desintegrarse.

**pollen grain** two-celled structure that contains the male form of the plant's gamete.
**grano de polen** estructura formada por dos células que contiene el gameto masculino de la planta.

**pollination** process by which seed plants become fertilized without the need for free-standing water.
**polinización** proceso mediante el cual las plantas con semillas se fertilizan sin depender del agua del suelo.

**pollution** anything that is added to the environment and has a negative affect on the environment or its organisms.
**contaminación** cualquier sustancia que se libera en el medio ambiente con efectos negativos para los organismos que lo habitan y su entorno.

**polygenic trait** trait that is produced by two or more genes.
**rasgo poligénico** rasgo producido por dos o más genes.

**polymer** large, carbon-based molecule formed by monomers.
**polímero** gran molécula de carbono formada por monómeros.

**polymerase chain reaction (PCR)** method for increasing the quantity of DNA by separating it into two strands and adding primers and enzymes.
**reacción en cadena de la polimerasa (RCP)** método para obtener un gran número de copias de ADN separándolo en dos hebras y añadiendo cebadores y enzimas.

**polyp** tube-shaped body form of a cnidarian in which the mouth and tentacles face upward.
**pólipo** cuerpo de forma tubular de un cnidario con la boca y los tentáculos orientados hacia arriba.

**population** all of the individuals of a species that live in the same area.
**población** conjunto de individuos de la misma especie que viven en la misma zona.

**population crash** dramatic decline in the size of a population over a short period of time.
**colapso poblacional** reducción drástica del tamaño de una población en un breve período de tiempo.

**population density** measure of individuals living in a defined area.
**densidad de población** cantidad de habitantes que viven en un área determinada.

**population dispersion** way in which individuals of a population are spread out over an area or volume.
**dispersión de población** manera en la que los individuos de una población determinada se han distribuido en una área o en un volumen.

**positive feedback** control system in which sensory information causes the body to increase the rate of change away from homeostasis.
**retroalimentación positiva** sistema de control mediante el cual la información sensorial estimula el cuerpo a incrementar la tasa de cambio, alejándola de valores homeostáticos.

**precision** the exactness of a measurement.
**precisión** la exactitud de una medición.

**predation** process by which one organism hunts and kills another organism for food.
**predación** proceso mediante el cual un organismo acecha, mata y se come a otro organismo.

**pressure-flow model** model for predicting how sugars are transported from photosynthetic tissue to the rest of a plant.
**modelo de flujo de presión** modelo para predecir la forma en que los azúcares son transportados del tejido fotosintético al resto de una planta.

**primary growth** growth in vascular plants resulting in elongation of the plant body.
**crecimiento primario** crecimiento de las plantas vasculares que resulta de la elongación del cuerpo de la planta.

**primary succession** establishment and development of an ecosystem in an area that was previously uninhabited.
**sucesión primaria** establecimiento y desarrollo de un ecosistema en una zona hasta entonces deshabitada.

**primate** mammal with flexible hands and feet, forward-looking eyes, and enlarged brains relative to body size.
**primate** mamífero de manos y pies flexibles, mirada frontal y un cerebro grande en relación con el tamaño del cuerpo.

**primer** short segment of DNA that initiates replication by DNA polymerase.
**cebador** pequeño segmento de ADN que inicia la replicación mediante ADN polimerasa.

**prion** infectious agent that consists of a protein fragment that can cause other proteins to fold incorrectly.
**prión** agente infeccioso que consta de una partícula proteica que induce a otras proteínas a plegarse de forma incorrecta.

**probability** likelihood that a particular event will happen.
**probabilidad** posibilidad de que ocurra un suceso en particular.

# Glossary

**producer** organism that obtains its energy from abiotic sources, such as sunlight or inorganic chemicals.
    **productor** organismo que obtiene su alimento de fuentes abióticas, como la luz solar o compuestos inorgánicos.

**product** substance formed by a chemical reaction.
    **producto** sustancia formada por una reacción química.

**prokaryotic cell** (proh-KAR-ee-AHT-ihk) cell that does not have a nucleus or other membrane-bound organelles.
    **célula procarionta** célula que no tiene núcleo ni orgánulos limitados por membranas.

**promoter** section of DNA to which RNA polymerase binds, starting the transcription of mRNA.
    **promotor** sección de ADN a la que se enlaza el ARN polimerasa al inicio del proceso de transcripción de ARNm.

**prophage** DNA of a bacteriophage inserted into a host cell's DNA.
    **profago** ADN de un bacteriófago insertado en el ADN de la célula huésped.

**prophase** first phase of mitosis when chromatin condenses, the nuclear envelope breaks down, the nucleolus disappears, and the centrosomes and centrioles migrate to opposite sides of the cell.
    **profase** primera fase de la mitosis, en la que la cromatina se condensa, la membrana nuclear se desintegra, el nucleolo desaparece y los centrosomas y los centriolos migran a lados opuestos de la célula.

**prosimian** oldest primate group that includes mostly small, nocturnal primates such as lemurs.
    **prosimio** grupo de primates más antiguo que consta, principalmente, de pequeños primates nocturnos, como los lemures.

**protein** polymer composed of amino acids linked by peptide bonds; folds into a particular structure depending on bonds between amino acids.
    **proteína** polímero compuesto de aminoácidos unidos por enlaces peptídicos; se pliega formando una estructura determinada según sean los enlaces que hay entre los aminoácidos.

**proteomics** (PROH-tee-AH-mihks) study and comparison of all the proteins produced by an organism's genome.
    **proteómica** estudio y comparación de todas las proteínas producidas por el genoma de un organismo determinado.

**protist** eukaryote that is not an animal, plant, or fungus.
    **protista** organismo eucariota que no es un animal, una planta, ni un hongo.

**protostome** animal development in which the animal's mouth develops before the anus.
    **protóstomo** animal en el que la boca se desarrolla antes que el ano.

**protozoa** animal-like protist.
    **protozoo** protista con características animales.

**pseudocoelom** fluid-filled space with mesoderm only on one side of the space.
    **pseudoceloma** cavidad llena de fluido que tiene mesodermo en un solo lado de la cavidad.

**pseudopod** temporary extension of cytoplasm and plasma membrane that helps protozoa move and feed.
    **pseudópodo** extensión temporal del citoplasma y de la membrana plasmática que permite a los protozoos moverse y alimentarse.

**puberty** stage of adolescence that is marked by the production of hormones involved in reproduction.
    **pubertad** fase de la adolescencia marcada por la producción de hormonas involucradas en la reproducción.

**pulmonary circuit** (PUL-muh-NEHR-ee) collection of blood vessels that carries blood between the lungs and heart.
    **circuito pulmonar** conjunto de vasos sanguíneos que transporta sangre entre los pulmones y el corazón.

**pulmonary circulation** see pulmonary circuit.
    **circulación pulmonar** *véanse* circuito pulmonar.

**punctuated equilibrium** theory that states that speciation occurs suddenly and rapidly followed by long periods of little evolutionary change.
    **equilibrio puntuado** teoría según la cual la especiación se produce repentinamente y va seguida de largos períodos de escasa actividad evolutiva.

**Punnett square** model for predicting all possible genotypes resulting from a cross, or mating.
    **cuadrado de Punnet** modelo de predicción de todos los genotipos posibles que se pueden obtener a partir de un determinado cruzamiento o apareamiento.

**pupa** stage of metamorphosis in which the organism reorganizes into a completely new body form.
    **pupa** fase de la metamorfosis en la que el organismo adopta una nueva forma corporal.

**purebred** type of organism whose ancestors are genetically uniform.
    **pura raza** organismo de ancestros con uniformidad genética.

# R

**radial symmetry** arrangement of body parts in a circle around a central axis.
    **simetría radial** disposición de las partes del cuerpo en un círculo que rodea un eje central.

**radiometric dating** technique that uses the natural decay rate of isotopes to calculate the age of material.
    **fechado radiométrico** técnica para medir la tasa natural de decaimiento de los isótopos para calcular la edad de los materiales.

**radula** filelike feeding organ found in mollusks.
    **rádula** órgano raspador con el que se alimentan los moluscos.

**ray-fin**  fan-shaped arrangement of bones in a fish's fin.
**aleta radial**  disposición en abanico de las espinas de una aleta de pez.

**reactant**  substance that is changed by a chemical reaction.
**reactante**  sustancia que cambia a consecuencia de una reacción química.

**receptor**  protein that detects a signal molecule and performs an action in response.
**receptor**  proteína que detecta la señal de una molécula y responde con una acción concreta.

**recessive**  allele that is not expressed unless two copies are present in an organism's genotype.
**recesivo**  alelo que no se expresa, a menos que en el genotipo del organismo en cuestión estén presentes dos copias de dicho gen.

**recombinant DNA**  (ree-KAHM-buh-nuhnt) genetically engineered DNA that contains genes from more than one organism or species.
**ADN recombinante**  ADN manipulado geneticamente que contiene genes de más de un organismo o especie.

**red blood cell**  cell that carries oxygen gas from the lungs to the rest of the body.
**glóbulo rojo célula**  encargada de transportar oxígeno gaseoso de los pulmones al resto del cuerpo.

**reflex arc**  nerve pathway in which an impulse crosses only two synapses before producing a response
**arco reflejo**  circuito nervioso en el que un impulso sólo atraviesa dos simpasis antes de producir una respuesta.

**regeneration**  process by which a new plant can grow from a fragment of a nonreproductive structure, such as a root, stem, or leaf.
**regeneración**  proceso mediante el cual una nueva planta puede desarrollarse a partir de un fragmento de una estructura no reproductora, como una raíz, un tallo o una hoja.

**relative dating**  estimate of the age of a fossil based on the location of fossils in strata.
**datación relativa**  estimación de la edad de un fósil según la ubicación de los fósiles en los estratos.

**releaser**  stimulus that triggers a specific behavior.
**estímulo liberador**  que suscita un comportamiento específico.

**releasing hormone**  chemical that stimulates other glands to release their hormones.
**hormona liberadora**  sustancia química que estimula otras glándulas para que secreten hormonas.

**renewable resource**  resource that replenishes itself quickly enough so that it will not be used faster than it can be produced.
**recurso renovable**  recurso natural que se restablece a un ritmo superior del ritmo al que se consume.

**replication**  process by which DNA is copied.
**replicación**  proceso mediante el cual se copian las moléculas de ADN.

**reproductive isolation**  final stage in speciation, in which members of isolated populations are either no longer able to mate or no longer able to produce viable offspring.
**aislamiento reproductor**  fase final de la especiación en la que los miembros de poblaciones aisladas pierden la capacidad de aparearse o no pueden producir crías viables.

**reproductive system**  body system that allows for sexual reproduction; includes testes, ovaries, uterus, and other male and female sex organs.
**sistema reproductor**  sistema corporal que permite la reproducción sexual; consta de testículos, ovarios, útero y otros órganos sexuales masculinos y femeninos.

**reptile**  ectotherm that is covered with dry scales, breathes with lungs, and reproduces by laying eggs.
**reptil**  vertebrado ectotermo con la piel cubierta de escamas, que respira con pulmones y que pone huevos para reproducirse.

**respiratory system**  body system that brings oxygen into the body and removes carbon dioxide; includes the nose, trachea, and lungs.
**sistema respiratorio**  sistema corporal que lleva oxígeno al cuerpo y elimina el dióxido de carbono; consta de nariz, tráquea y pulmones.

**resting potential**  difference in electrical charge between the inside and outside of a neuron; contains the potential energy needed to transmit the impulse.
**potencial de reposo**  diferencia de carga eléctrica entre el interior y el exterior de una neurona; energía potencial necesaria para transmitir un impulso.

**restriction enzyme**  enzyme that cuts DNA molecules at specific nucleotide sequences.
**enzima de restricción**  enzima que fragmenta moléculas de ADN en secuencias específicas de nucleótidos.

**restriction map**  diagram that shows the lengths of fragments between restriction sites in the strand of DNA.
**mapa de restricción**  diagrama que representa las longitudes de los fragmentos entre los sitios de corte de una hebra de ADN.

**retrovirus**  virus that contains RNA and uses the enzyme called reverse transcriptase to make a DNA copy.
**retrovirus**  virus que contiene ARN y que usa una enzima llamada transcriptasa para hacer una copia del ADN.

**Rh factor**  surface protein on red blood cells in the ABO blood group; people can be Rh$^+$ or Rh$^-$.
**factor Rh**  proteína de la superficie de los glóbulos rojos de los grupos sanguíneos ABO; el factor Rh de las personas puede ser Rh$^+$ o Rh$^-$.

# Glossary

**ribosomal RNA (rRNA)** RNA that is in the ribosome and guides the translation of mRNA into a protein; also used as a molecular clock.

**ARN ribosómico (ARNr)** ARN presente en los ribosomas que guía el proceso de síntesis de las proteínas a partir del ARNm; también denominado reloj molecular.

**ribosome** (RY-buh-SOHM) organelle that links amino acids together to form proteins.

**ribosoma** orgánulo que enlaza las moléculas de aminoácidos para formar proteínas.

**ribozyme** RNA molecule that can catalyze specific chemical reactions.

**Ribozima** molécula de ARN que tiene la capacidad de catalizar determinadas reacciones químicas.

**RNA** nucleic acid molecule that allows for the transmission of genetic information and protein synthesis.

**ARN** molécula de ácido nucleico encargada de la transmisión de información genética y de la síntesis de las proteínas.

**RNA polymerase** enzyme that catalyzes the synthesis of a complementary strand of RNA from a DNA template.

**ARN polimerasa** enzima que cataliza la síntesis de una hebra complementaria de ARN a partir de un patrón de ADN.

**rod cell** photoreceptor in the eye that detects light intensity and contributes to black and white vision.

**bastoncillo** célula fotosensible del ojo que detecta la intensidad de la luz y contribuye a la visión en blanco y negro.

**root cap** mass of cells that covers and protects the tips of plant roots.

**ápice de la raíz** masa de células que cubre y protege las puntas de las raíces de las plantas.

**root hair** thin hairlike outgrowth of an epidermal cell of a plant root that absorbs water and minerals from the soil.

**pelos radicales** finas extensiones de la célula epidérmica en las raíces de una planta encargada de absorber agua y minerales del suelo.

## S

**sarcomere** section of a muscle fiber that contains all of the filaments necessary to cause muscle contraction.

**sarcómero** sección de fibra muscular con todos los filamentos necesarios para generar una contracción muscular.

**science** the knowledge obtained by observing natural events and conditions in order to discover facts and formulate laws or principles that can be verified or tested.

**ciencia** el conocimiento que se obtiene por medio de la observación natural de acontecimientos y condiciones con el fin de descubrir hechos y formular leyes o principios que puedan ser verificados o probados.

**sclerenchyma cell** thick-walled, lignin-rich cell that forms a supportive plant tissue.

**esclereida célula** rica en lignina que constituye el esclerénquima, un tejido de sostén de las plantas.

**scrotum** skin that encloses the testes outside of the male body.

**escroto** piel que envuelve las gónadas masculinas en el exterior del cuerpo.

**secondary growth** growth in woody plants resulting in wider roots, branches, and stems.

**crecimiento secundario** crecimiento de las plantas que produce un engrosamiento de las raíces, de las ramas y de los tallos.

**secondary succession** reestablishment of a damaged ecosystem in an area where the soil was left intact.

**sucesión secundaria** desarrollo de un ecosistema dañado en una zona donde el suelo permanece inalterado.

**seed** structure used by some land plants to store and protect the embryo.

**semilla** estructura empleada por algunas plantas para almacenar y proteger al embrión.

**segmentation** repeated sections of an annelid's long body that contain the same set of body structures, apart from its distinct head and tail region.

**segmentación** secciones repetidas del cuerpo alargado de un anélido, cada una de las cueles contiene el mismo conjunto de estructuras corporales, con excepción de la cabeza y de la cola.

**selective permeability** condition or quality of allowing some, but not all, materials to cross a barrier or membrane.

**permeabilidad selectiva** condición o cualidad que permite discriminar el flujo de determinados materiales a través de una membrana o barrera.

**semen** white substance that contains sperm and fluids produced by sex glands of the male reproductive system.

**semen** sustancia blanca que contiene espermatozoides y fluidos generados por las glándulas sexuales del sistema reproductor masculino.

**sepal** modified leaf that covers and protects the flower while it develops.

**sépalo** hoja modificada que cubre la flor durante su desarrollo.

**sensitization** process by which a neuron adds more receptors to its surface in response to consistently lower amounts of a neurotransmitter in the synapse.

**sensibilización** proceso mediante el cual una neurona incorpora a su superficie más receptores en respuesta a una insuficiencia sostenida de neurotransmisores en el espacio sináptico.

**sessile** unable to move from a fixed point.

**sésil** fijo a un punto, que no se mueve.

**sex chromosome** chromosome that directly controls the development of sexual characteristics.

**cromosoma sexual** cromosoma que controla directamente el desarrollo de las características sexuales.

**sex-linked gene** gene that is located on a sex chromosome.

**gen ligado al sexo** gen ubicado en un cromosoma sexual.

**sexually transmitted disease (STD)** disease that is passed from one person to another during sexual contact.
**enfermedad de transmisión sexual (ETS)** enfermedad que se transmite de una persona a otra durante el contacto sexual.

**sexual reproduction** process by which two gametes fuse and offspring that are a genetic mixture of both parents are produced.
**reproducción sexual** proceso mediante el cual se unen dos gametos que dan lugar a crías cuyo genoma es una mezcla del de los dos progenitores.

**sexual selection** selection in which certain traits enhance mating success; traits are, therefore, passed on to offspring.
**selección sexual** selección en la que determinados rasgos incrementan el éxito del apareamiento; en consecuencia, tales rasgos se transmiten a las crías.

**skeletal muscle** muscle tissue that is attached to the skeletal system and, when contracted, moves bones.
**músculo esquelético** tejido muscular adherido al sistema esquelético que, al contraerse, mueve los músculos.

**skeletal system** body system that includes bones and the connective tissues that hold the bones together in the body.
**sistema esquelético** sistema que consta de los huesos y de los tejidos conjuntivos que mantienen unidos a los huesos.

**slime mold** protist with a slimelike amoeboid stage that grows on decaying vegetation and in moist soil.
**moho mucoso** protista de aspecto gelatinoso con una fase ameboide, que crece en material vegetal en descomposición y en la tierra húmeda.

**small intestine** organ of the digestive system that connects the stomach to the large intestine and in which chemical digestion takes place.
**intestino delgado** órgano del sistema digestivo que conecta el estómago al intestino grueso y en el que se produce la digestión química.

**smog** air pollution in which gases released from burning fossil fuels form a fog when they react with sunlight.
**smog** contaminación atmosférica en la que los gases liberados por la combustión de hidrocarburos reaccionan con la luz creando una niebla.

**smooth muscle** muscle tissue that moves substances, such as food and blood, through organs and tissues, such as the digestive system organs and blood vessels.
**músculo liso** tejido muscular que mueve los alimentos y la sangre por los órganos y los tejidos como, por ejemplo, los órganos del sistema digestivo y los vasos sanguíneos.

**sodium potassium pump** active transport protein in neurons that carries sodium ($Na^+$) ions out of the cell and bring potassium ($K^+$) ions into the cell.
**bomba sodio-potasio** transporte activo de proteínas en las neuronas, en el que se extrae de la célula iones de sodio ($Na^+$) y se mete iones de potasio ($K^+$).

**solute** substance that dissolves in a solvent and is present at a lower concentration than the solvent.
**soluto** sustancia que se disuelve en un solvente y que aparece en menor concentración que éste.

**solution** mixture that is consistent throughout; also called a homogeneous mixture.
**solución** mezcla uniforme en toda su extensión; también se conoce como mezcla homogénea.

**solvent** substance in which solutes dissolve and that is present in greatest concentration in a solution.
**solvente** sustancia en la que se disuelve un soluto y que se presenta en mayor concentración que éste.

**somatic cell** (soh-MAT-ihk) cell that makes up all of the body tissues and organs, except gametes.
**célula somática** célula que conforma todos los tejidos y órganos del organismo, excepto los gametos.

**somatic nervous system** division of the peripheral nervous system that transports signals from the brain to the muscles that produce voluntary movements.
**sistema nervioso somático** parte del sistema nervioso periférico que transporta señales del encéfalo a los músculos para producir los movimientos voluntarios.

**specialist** consumer that eats only one type of organism.
**especialista** consumidor que se alimenta de un solo tipo de organismo.

**speciation** evolution of two or more species from one ancestral species.
**especiación** evolución de dos o más especies a partir de una sola especie ancestral.

**species** group of organisms so similar to one another that they can breed and produce fertile offspring.
**especie** grupo de organismos tan semejantes entre sí que pueden reproducirse y tener descendencia fértil.

**sperm** male gamete.
**espermatozoide** gameto masculino.

**sphincter** (SFIHNGK-tuhr) ring of muscle that separates the different organs of the digestive system.
**esfínter** músculo en forma de anillo que separa a los diversos órganos del sistema digestivo.

**spiracle** (SPIHR-uh-kuhl) hole on the body of an insect's exoskeleton through which air can be taken in or released.
**espiráculo** orificio en el cuerpo del exoesqueleto de los insectos a través del cual entra y sale aire.

**sporangia** spore-forming structures found in fungi, algae, and some plants.
**esporangio** estructura que produce esporas y que se encuentra en los hongos, las algas y algunas plantas.

**sporophyte** (SPAWR-uh-FYT) diploid, spore-producing phase of a plant life cycle.
**esporofita** fase diploide de producción de esporas en el ciclo de vida de una planta.

# Glossary

**stabilizing selection** pathway of natural selection in which intermediate phenotypes are selected over phenotypes at both extremes.
**selección estabilizadora** proceso de selección natural en el que se da preferencia a los fenotipos intermedios sobre los fenotipos de ambos extremos.

**stamen** male structure of flowering plants; includes the stalk and anther, which produces pollen.
**estambre** estructura floral masculina de las gimnospermas; consiste de una antera productora de polen unida a un pedicelo.

**start codon** codon that signals to ribosomes to begin translation; codes for the first amino acid in a protein.
**codón de iniciación** codón que da la señal a los ribosomas para que inicien el proceso de traducción; codifica el primer aminoácido de la proteína.

**stem cell** cell that can divide for long periods of time while remaining undifferentiated.
**célula madre** célula capaz de dividirse durante largos periodos de tiempo sin diferenciarse.

**sternum** long, flat bone that connects the ribs in front of the chest and to which the chest muscle attaches.
**esternón** hueso plano y alargado que conecta las costillas a la altura del pecho y al que van adheridos los músculos pectorales.

**stimulant** drug that increases the number of impulses that neurons generate.
**estimulante** droga que incrementa el número de impulsos que generan las neuronas.

**stimulus** (STIHM-yuh-luhs) (plural: *stimuli*) something that causes a physiological response.
**estímulo** cualquier cosa capaz de provocar una respuesta fisiológica.

**stomach** muscular sac in the digestive system that breaks down food into a liquidlike mixture.
**estómago** saco muscular del sistema digestivo donde se descompone la comida en una mezcla líquida.

**stomata** (singular: *stoma*) pores in the cuticle of a plant through which gas exchange occurs.
**estoma** poro en la cutícula de una planta a través del cual se produce el intercambio gaseoso.

**stop codon** codon that signals to ribosomes to stop translation.
**codón de terminación** codón que indica a los ribosomas que detengan el proceso de traducción.

**substrate** reactant in a chemical reaction upon which an enzyme acts.
**sustrato** reactivo de una reacción química sobre el que actúa un enzima.

**succession** sequence of biotic changes that regenerate a damaged community or start a community in a previously uninhabited area.
**sucesión** secuencia de cambios bióticos que regeneran una comunidad dañada o que crean una nueva comunidad en una zona hasta entonces deshabitada.

**survivorship** probability of surviving to a particular age.
**supervivencia** probabilidad de sobrevivir hasta una edad determinada.

**survivorship curve** graph showing the surviving members of each age group of a population over time.
**curva de sobrevivencia** gráfica que representa los sobrevivientes de una población por grupos de edad durante un periodo determinado.

**sustainable development** practice of not using natural resources more quickly than they can be replenished.
**desarrollo sostenible** práctica que consiste en no utilizar los recursos naturales más rápidamente de lo que pueden ser generarlos.

**swim bladder** buoyancy organ that helps fish to swim at different depths in the water.
**vejiga natatoria** órgano de flotación que permite a los peces nadar a diferentes profundidades.

**symbiosis** ecological relationship between members of at least two different species that live in direct contact with one another.
**simbiosis** relación ecológica en la que los miembros de al menos dos especies diferentes viven en contacto directo.

**sympathetic nervous system** part of the autonomic nervous system that prepares the body for action and stress.
**sistema nervioso simpático** sistema que forma parte del sistema nervioso autónomo y que se encarga de preparar el cuerpo para situaciones de acción y de estrés.

**synapse** tiny gap between neurons through which chemical signals are sent.
**sinapsis** pequeño espacio entre las neuronas a través del cual se envían señales químicas.

**system** changing, organized group of related parts that interact to form a whole.
**sistema** conjunto organizado y dinámico de partes que interactúan entre sí para formar un todo.

**systemic circuit** (sihs-STEHM-ihk) collection of blood vessels that carries blood between the heart and the rest of the body, except for the lungs.
**circuito sistémico** conjunto de vasos sanguíneos que transporta la sangre entre el corazón y el resto del cuerpo, excepto los pulmones.

**systemic circulation** *see* systemic circuit.
**circulación sistémica** *véanse* circuito sistémico.

**systolic pressure** (sih-STAHL-ihk) measure of pressure on the walls of an artery when the left ventricle contracts to pump blood through the body.
**presión sistólica** medida de la presión de las paredes arteriales cuando el ventrículo izquierdo se contrae para bombear sangre a través del cuerpo.

# T

**tadpole** aquatic larva of frogs or toads.
**renacuajo** larva acuática de las ranas y los sapos.

**taiga** (TY-guh) biome with long and cold winters, lasting up to six months; also called a boreal forest.
**taiga** bioma propio de zonas de largos y fríos inviernos de hasta seis meses de duración; también se conoce como bosque boreal.

**taproot** main root of some plants, usually larger than other roots and growing straight down from a stem.
**raíz pivotante** raíz principal de determinadas plantas, normalmente más grande que las demás raíces y que crece en en lína recta hacia abajo a partir del tallo.

**taxis** movement in a particular direction, either toward or away from a stimulus.
**taxismo** movimiento en una dirección determinada, ya sea hacia un estímulo o en sentido opuesto a éste; conocido también como taxis.

**taxon** (plural: *taxa*) level within the Linnaean system of classification (kingdom, phylum, class, order, family, genus, or species) that is organized into a nested hierarchy.
**taxón** cualquiera de los niveles del sistema de clasificación jerárquico de Linneo, (reino, división, clase, orden, familia, género o especie).

**taxonomy** science of classifying and naming organisms.
**taxonomía** ciencia dedicada a la clasificación y nomenclatura de los organismos.

**T cell** white blood cell that matures in the thymus and destroys infected body cells by causing them to burst; also called a T-lymphocyte.
**célula T** glóbulo blanco que madura en el timo y que destruye las células infectadas haciéndolas reventar; también se conoce como linfocito T.

**telomere** (TEHL-uh-MEER) repeating nucleotide at the ends of DNA molecules that do not form genes and help prevent the loss of genes.
**telómero** extremo de la molécula de ADN compuesto de nucleótidos repetidos que no producen genes pero que ayudan a prevenir la pérdida de éstos.

**telophase** last phase of mitosis when a complete set of identical chromosomes is positioned at each pole of the cell, the nuclear membranes start to form, the chromosomes begin to uncoil, and the spindle fibers disassemble.
**telofase** última fase de la mitosis en que un conjunto completo de cromosomas idénticos se sitúa en los polos opuestos de la célula; empiezan a formarse las membranas nucleares; los cromosomas empiezan a desenrollarse y el huso mitótico se desintegra.

**temporal isolation** isolation between populations due to barriers related to time, such as differences in mating periods or differences in the time of day that individuals are most active.
**aislamiento temporal** aislamiento entre poblaciones que se produce por motivos de índole temporal como, por ejemplo, diferencias en los períodos de apareamiento o de las horas del día en que los individuos son más activos.

**tendon** band of connective tissue that joins a muscle to the bone that it moves.
**tendón** banda de tejido conjuntivo que conecta cada músculo con el hueso que mueve.

**terminal** end of the neuron's axon from which neurotransmitters are released to stimulate an adjacent cell.
**terminal** extremo del axón de la neurona desde el cual se segregan neurotransmisores para estimular a la célula adyacente.

**territoriality** behavior pattern in which an organism controls and defends a specific area.
**territorialidad** patrón de comportamiento mediante el cual un organismo determinado controla y defiende un área específica.

**testcross** cross between an organism with an unknown genotype and an organism with a recessive phenotype.
**cruzamiento de prueba** cruzamiento entre un organismo de genotipo desconocido y un organismo de fenotipo recesivo.

**testis** (plural: *testes*) organ of the male reproductive system that produces sperm.
**testículo** órgano del sistema reproductor masculino encargado de la producción de espermatozoides.

**testosterone** (tehs-TAHS-tuh-ROHN) steroid hormone that is found in greater quantities in men than women and contributes to male sexual characteristics and development.
**testosterona** hormona esteroide que se encuentra en mayor cantidad en el hombre que en la mujer y que contribuye al desarrollo de las características sexuales masculinas.

**tetrapod** vertebrate with four limbs.
**tetrápodo** vertebrado con cuatro extremidades.

**theory** proposed explanation for a wide variety of observations and experimental results.
**teoría** explicación de un fenómeno a partir de una amplia gama de observaciones y resultados experimentales.

# Glossary

**thermoregulation** (THUR-moh-REHG-yoo-LAY-shuhn) process of the body maintaining a stable internal temperature under various conditions.
**termorregulación** proceso que permite mantener una temperatura interna constante bajo diferentes condiciones.

**thigmotropism** turning or bending of a plant in response to contact with an object.
**tigmotropismo** giro o flexión de una planta como respuesta al contacto con un objeto.

**thylakoid** (THY-luh-KOYD) membrane-bound structure within chloroplasts that contains chlorophyll and other light-absorbing pigments used in the light-dependent reactions of photosynthesis.
**tilacoide** estructura de la membrana interna de los cloroplastos que contiene clorofila y otros pigmentos fotoabsorbentes que intervienen en las reacciones captadoras de luz de la fotosíntesis.

**tissue** group of cells that work together to perform a similar function.
**tejido** grupo de células similares que trabajan juntas para desempeñar la misma función.

**tissue rejection** process by which a transplant recipient's immune system makes antibodies against the protein markers on the donor's tissue; could result in the destruction of the donor tissue.
**rechazo de tejidos** proceso mediante el cual el sistema inmune de un individuo receptor de un transplante genera anticuerpos contra los marcadores proteicos del tejido donante; puede producir la destrucción del tejido donante.

**tolerance** drug resistance that occurs when cells adapt, requiring larger doses of the drug to produce the same effect.
**tolerancia** resistencia a una droga producida cuando las células se adaptan a ella, lo cual requiere un aumento de la dosis para producir el mismo efecto.

**toxin** poison released by an organism.
**toxina** sustancia tóxica producida por un organismo.

**trachea** (TRAY-kee-uh) (plural: *tracheae*) long structure made of soft tissue that connects the mouth and nose to the lungs in human; a system of thin branching tubes in the bodies of insects that allow for breathing.
**tráquea** tubo alargado de tejido blando que conecta la boca y la nariz con los pulmones de los humanos; sistema de finos tubos ramificados en el cuerpo de los insectos que les permite respirar.

**trait** characteristic that is inherited.
**rasgo** característica heredada.

**transcription** process of copying a nucleotide sequence of DNA to form a complementary strand of mRNA.
**transcripción** proceso donde se copia una secuencia de ADN para formar una cadena complementaria de ARNm.

**transfer RNA (tRNA)** form of RNA that brings amino acids to ribosomes during protein synthesis.
**ARN de transferencia (ARNt)** tipo de ARN que transporta aminoácidos a los ribosomas durante el proceso de síntesis proteica.

**transgenic** organism whose genome has been altered to contain one or more genes from another organism or species.
**transgénico** organismo cuyo genoma ha sido alterado mediante la incorporación de uno o más genes de otro organismo o especie.

**translation** process by which mRNA is decoded and a protein is produced.
**traducción** proceso mediante el cual se decodifica el ARNm y se produce una proteína.

**transpiration** release of vapor through the pores of the skin or the stomata of plant tissue.
**transpiración** liberación de vapor a través de los poros de la piel o, en los tejidos vegetales, de los estomas.

**trimester** one of three periods of approximately three months each into which a human pregnancy is divided.
**trimestre** uno de los períodos de aproximadamente tres meses en que se divide la gestación humana.

**trophic level** level of nourishment in a food chain.
**nivel trófico** nivel de alimentación de la cadena trófica.

**tropism** movement or growth of a plant in response to an environmental stimulus.
**tropismo** movimiento o crecimiento determinado por un estímulo ambiental.

**tundra** biome found at far northern latitudes where winters last as long as ten months per year.
**tundra** bioma de latitudes septentrionales extremas donde los inviernos duran hasta diez meses.

# U

**umbilical cord** structure that connects an embryo to its mother and provides the embryo with nourishment and waste removal.
**cordón umbilical** estructura que conecta el embrión con su madre y que le suministra alimento y un sistema de eliminación de residuos.

**umbrella species** species whose being protected under the Endangered Species Act leads to the preservation of its habitat and all of the other organisms in its community.
**especie paraguas** especie protegida por la Ley de Especies en Peligro de Extinción cuya salvaguarda conlleva la protección de su hábitat y la de todos los otros organismos que viven en él.

**uniformitarianism** theory that states that the geologic processes that shape Earth are uniform through time.
**uniformitarismo** teoría según la cual los procesos geológicos que dan forma a la Tierra se producen de manera uniforme a lo largo del tiempo.

**ureter** (yu-REE-tuhr) tube of connective tissue that carries urine from each of the kidneys to the bladder.
**uréter** tubo de tejido conjuntivo que transporta la orina desde los riñones hasta la vejiga.

**urinary bladder** saclike organ that collects and stores urine before it is excreted from the body.
**vejiga urinaria** órgano en forma de bolsa donde se recoge y se almacena la orina antes de ser excretada del cuerpo.

**uterus** organ of the female reproductive system in which a fertilized egg attaches and a fetus develops.
**útero** órgano del sistema reproductor femenino al que se adhiere el huevo fertilizado y dónde se desarrolla el feto.

# V

**vaccine** substance that stimulates an immune response, producing acquired immunity without illness or infection.
**vacuna** sustancia que estimula una respuesta inmune y que proporciona inmunidad ante una enfermedad o infección determinada sin provocarla.

**vacuole** (VAK-yoo-OHL) organelle that is used to store materials, such as water, food, or enzymes, that are needed by the cell.
**vacuola** orgánulo encargado de almacenar diversos materiales necesarios para la célula, como el agua, nutrientes o enzimas.

**valve** flap of tissue that prevents blood from flowing backward into a blood vessel or heart chamber.
**válvula** tejido membranoso encargado de evitar que la sangre refluya por el vaso sanguíneo en que circula o hacia una cavidad del corazón.

**variation** differences in physical traits of an individual from the group to which it belongs.
**variación** diferencia en rasgos físicos que presenta un individuo con respecto al grupo al que pertenece.

**vascular cylinder** center of a root or stem that contains phloem and xylem.
**cilindro vascular** cilindro en el centro de una raíz o tallo que contiene el floema y el xilema.

**vascular system** collection of specialized tissues in some plants that transports mineral nutrients up from the roots and brings sugars down from the leaves.
**sistema vascular** conjunto de tejidos especializados de determinadas plantas que transportan nutrientes minerales desde las raíces hacia arriba y que conducen el azúcar de las hojas hacia abajo.

**vascular tissue** supportive and conductive tissue in plants, consisting of xylem and phloem.
**tejido vascular** tejido conductor y de sostén de las plantas que consta de xilema y de floema.

**vas deferens** duct in which sperm mixes with other fluids before reaching the urethra.
**conducto deferente** conducto en el que el esperma se mezcla con otros fluidos antes de alcanzar la uretra.

**vector** organism, such as a mosquito or tick, that transfers pathogens from one host to another.
**vector** organismo, como o el mosquito o la garrapatas que puede transferir patógenos de un huésped a otro.

**vegetative reproduction** asexual reproduction in which a stem, leaf, or root will produce a new individual when detached from a parent plant.
**reproducción vegetativa** reproducción asexual en la que un tallo, una hoja o una raíz producen un nuevo individuo cuando se separan de la planta de la cual forman parte.

**vein** large blood vessel that carries blood from the rest of the body to the heart.
**vena** vaso sanguíneo de gran caudal que transporta la sangre desde todas las partes del cuerpo hasta el corazón.

**ventricle** large chamber in the heart that receives blood from an atrium and pumps blood to the rest of the body.
**ventrículo** amplia cámara del corazón que recibe sangre de la aurícula y la impulsa al resto del cuerpo.

**vertebra** (plural: *vertebrae*) bone that makes up the spinal column.
**vértebra** hueso que compone la columna vertebral.

**vertebrate** animal with an internal segmented backbone.
**vertebrado** animal con una columna vertebral interna y segmentada.

**vesicle** (VEHS-ih-kuhl) small organelle that contains and transports materials within the cytoplasm.
**vesícula** pequeño orgánulo que contiene y transporta materiales en el interior del citoplasma.

**vestigial structure** remnants of an organ or structure that functioned in an earlier ancestor.
**estructura vestigial** restos de algún órgano o estructura en una especie determinada que cumplieron alguna función en un ancestrode ésta.

**villus** (VIHL-uhs) (plural: *villi*) small fingerlike projection in the small intestine that absorbs nutrients.
**vellosidades** pequeñas proyecciones en forma de dedo del intestino delgado encargadas de absorber los nutrientes.

**viroid** infectious particle made of single-stranded RNA without a protein coat, that almost always uses plants as its host.
**viroide** partícula infecciosa que consta de un solo filamento de ARN sin envoltura de proteínas, que casi siempre se hospeda como parásito en las plantas.

**virus** infectious particle made only of a strand of either DNA or RNA surrounded by a protein coat.
**virus** partícula infecciosa que consta de un sólo filamento de ADN o ARN y rodeado por una envuelta de proteína.

**vitamin** organic molecule that works with enzymes to regulate cell function, growth, and development.
**vitamina** molécula orgánica que funciona con enzimas para regular el funcionamiento, el crecimiento y el desarrollo de las células.

# Glossary

**viviparous** reproductive strategy in which the embryo develops within the mother's body.
    **vivíparo** modalidad de reproducción en la que los embriones se desarrollan en el interior de la madre.

# W

**water mold** fungus that is either a parasite or decomposer and lives in fresh water or moist soil.
    **moho acuático** hongo acuático o de suelos húmedos que actúa como parásito o descomponedor de materia orgánica.

**watershed** region of land that drains into a river, river system, or other body of water.
    **cuenca hidrográfica** área terrestre que vierte sus aguas hacia un río, una red fluvial o cualquier otra masa acuática.

**water vascular system** system of water-filled canals that extend down each arm of a echinoderm, such as a sea star.
    **sistema ambulacral** sistema formado por una serie de tubos llenos de agua que se prolongan por los brazos de los equinodermos como, por ejemplo, la estrella de mar.

**white blood cell** cell that attacks pathogens.
    **glóbulo blanco** célula cuya funcíon es atacar a los patógenos.

**wood** fibrous material made of dead cells that are part of the vascular system in some plants.
    **madera** material fibroso formado por células muertas que forman parte del sistema vascular de algunas plantas.

# X

**X chromosome inactivation** process that occurs in female mammals in which one of the X chromosomes is randomly turned off in each cell.
    **inactivación X** proceso en los mamíferos del sexo femenino en que uno de los cromosomas X de cada célula se desactiva aleatoriamente.

**xylem** tissue that transports water and dissolved minerals in vascular plants.
    **xilema** tejido de las plantas vasculares que transporta agua y sales minerales disueltas.

# Z

**zooplankton** animal plankton.
    **zooplancton** plancton animal.

**zygote** cell that forms when a male gamete fertilizes a female gamete.
    **cigoto** célula formada cuando un gameto masculino fertiliza un gameto femenino.

# Index

*Note:* Page numbers for illustrations, maps, and charts are printed in *italics.* Page numbers for definitions are printed in **boldface** type.

## A

abiotic factor, **394**
  in biomes, 452, R41
  biotic factors and, 445, 447–451, *447*
  of climate, 448
  in niches, 420
ABO blood group, 197–198, *197,*
   799–800, *800*
absorption, *646,* 651
abyssal zone, *459,* **460**
acacia, 337, *337*
academic vocabulary, R20–R21
Acanthodian, 703
*Acanthostega,* 711
accuracy, *22,* **23**
*Acer rubrum,* 533
acetate, 104
acetylcholine, 766
acid, 44–46, **44,** 57, 477, 481
acid rain, *470–471,* 471, **477,** *477*
acne, *576*
Acoelomorpha, 672
acquired characteristics, 287
acquired immune deficiency syndrome
   (AIDS), 266, 565, 812, 830, 833. *See also*
   HIV (human immunodeficiency virus)
acquired immunity, 818, 821
Acrasiomycota (phylum), 597, 598, *598,* R28
acrosome, 846
action potential, *752,* **753,** 756, 767–768
activation energy, *54, 55,* **55,** 56–58, *56*
active immunity, 818, **818**
active site, 58, *58*
active transport, 89–91, **89,** *89, 90, 91, 92, 92,*
   751, *751*
adaptation, **12, 290**
  of animals to biomes, 457, 458, 459
  to climate, 451, *451*
  of cuttlefish, 677
  to estuary conditions, 462
  evolution and, 12–13, *12,* 32, 290, *295*
  of flowering plants, 628–629, *628*
  of freshwater organisms, 463
  to hypotonic environments, 87
  of land plants, 455, 456, 617–618,
   *619,* 620
  learning as, 507–508, *508*
  of leaves, 657
  natural selection and, 12–13,
   294–297, *295*
adaptive radiation, **340,** 355, 628
adaptive value of behavior, 500–501, *500,*
   *501, 502, 503*
addiction, **767**
Addison's disease, 775
adenine (A), 220–221, 222–223, *222, 223,*
   230, 247

adenosine diphosphate (ADP), **99,** *99*
  in cellular respiration, 98–100, *98,*
   *115, 117*
  in fermentation, *121, 122*
  muscle's use of, 121
  photosynthesis and, 108, 110, *110*
adenosine triphosphate (ATP), **98, 99,** 108
  active transport using, 90
  cell production of, 108
  from cellular respiration, 98–100, *98,*
   111–113, *112, 113,* 115–118, *115,*
   *117, 118*
  in fermentation, 120–122, *121, 122*
  photosynthesis and, 103, 106–110,
   *107, 109*
adhesion, **43,** *43,* 645–647, *646*
adolescence, **858**
ADP (adenosine diphosphate), **99,** *99,* 108
  in cellular respiration, 98–100, *98,*
   *115, 117*
  in fermentation, *121, 122*
adrenal gland, 501, **772,** *773,* 775, 863C,
   *863C*
adulthood, **859**
adult stem cell, 150–151
aerobe, obligate, 567
aerobic process, **111**
aflatoxin, 600
agar, 594
agave plant, 657
Age of Cycads, 625
Age of Reptiles, 369
aging, 247, 859
Agnatha, 368, **698,** *699. See also* jawless fish
agriculture
  antibiotic use, 577
  biogeochemical cycles and, 409–410
  carrying capacity increased by, 473
  environmental impact of, 409–410, *410,*
   *482, 482*
  functions of, 633–634
  genetic engineering and, 30, 266, 322
  genetic sequencing and, 271
  history of, 634
  phosphorus cycle and, *408*
agronomist, R38
AIDS (acquired immune deficiency
   syndrome), 266, 565, 812, 830, 833.
   *See also* HIV (human immunodeficiency virus)
*Ailurus fulgens,* 535
aircraft crashes, 512
air movement, 450
air quality
  human impact on, 494
  indicator of, 608
  pollution, 476–478, *476, 477, 478, 479,*
   *480, 480*

alanine (Ala), 234, *234*
albatross, 428
albinism, 199
albumin, 798
alcoholic fermentation, 122–123
aldosterone, 84
algae, **591**
  brown, R28
  cell walls of, 79
  corals and, 460
  as energy source, 30, *30*
  evolution, 617
  in food web, *402, 403*
  green, R28
  kelp, 591, 594, *594*
  in lichens, 608, *608*
  in neritic zone, 460
  photosynthesis by, 97
  as producer, *402*
  red, R28, *R28*
  reproduction, 617
algal bloom, 408, 410, *482*
alkaloid, 635
allele, **174.** *See also* **chromosome; genetics**
  distribution of, 318–319
  dominant, 175–176, 193
  frequency of, 316–317, *317*
  in gene pool, 323–326
  heterozygous, 174
  homozygous, 174
  incomplete dominance of, 196–197
  lethal, 325
  mutations of, 296
  phenotype and, 192–193, 196–198
  recessive, 175, 193
allele frequency, 316–317, **316,** *317*
allergen, 827–828
allergy, 28, 827–828
alligator, 540, *541*
aloe vera, 635
Altman, Sidney, 360
altruism, 515–516, **515,** *515, 517,* 518, 522
Alzheimer's disease, 281–282
amber-preserved fossil, 348, *348*
*Ambulocetus natans,* 308
amino acid, **49**
  estimation of evolutionary time,
   544–545, *544, 545*
  in hormones, 770
  origins of life and, 357
  structure, 49–50, *49*
  translation of RNA, 233–235, *233,*
   *236,* 237
amino group ($NH_2$), 49, *49*
Amish community, 324
ammonia, 356, 357, 407, *407*
ammonification, 407, *407*
amnion, *699,* 851

# Index

Aristotle, 6
*Armadillidium vulgare,* 533, *533*
armadillo, *538,* 539
arms race, evolutionary, 337
arteriole, 794
arteriosclerosis, 796
artery, 785, *785,* 794, *795,* 796
arthropod, 542, *542, 667,* 668, 670, R32
Arthropoda (phylum), 667, *671,* R32
artificial coral reef, 465, *465,* 460, *460*
artificial nucleotide, 254
artificial photosynthesis, 104–105
artificial selection, **292,** 634, *634*
Ascomycota, 600, *602,* 604, R29
ascus, 600, *601, 602,* 604
ASD (Autism Spectrum Disorder), 200
asexual reproduction, 144
    advantages and disadvantages of, 145
    of animals, 666
    of annelids, 683
    binary fission, 144–145, *144, 145,* 152
    of cnidarians, 675
    of fungi, 601, *601, 602, 603*
    of plantlike protists, 594, *595*
    of prokaryotes and eukaryotes, 366
    of sponges, 674
asparagine (Arg), *234*
*Aspergillis flavus,* 600
Assessment, Standards-Based, 35, 63, 95,
    127, 155, 189, 213, 251, 279, 313, 345,
    381, 417, 443, 469, 497, 525, 553, 581,
    613, 639, 661, 693, 721, 745, 779, 807,
    837, 863
associative learning, 507
assortment, independent, **180**
asteroid, 369
Asteroidea, 687, R32
asthma, 258, **788**
athlete's foot, 607, 812
atmosphere, 446, 447
atom, 38–40, **38,** 59–60, 350–351
atomic model, 39
ATP (adenosine triphosphate), **98**
    active transport using, 90
    in cellular respiration, 98–100, 108, *108,*
      111–113, *112, 113,* 115–118, *115, 117,*
      124, 648
    in fermentation, 120–122, *122*
    muscle's use of, 121
    in photosynthesis, 103, 106–108, *107*
    in sperm, 846
ATP synthase, 108, *108,* 119
atrioventricular (AV) node, 790, *790*
atrium, 789–790, **789,** *789,* 791
Australian bottlenose dolphin, 520
Australian redback spider, 510, *510*
*Australopithecus afarensis, 374,*
    *376, 377*
Autism Spectrum Disorder (ASD), 200
autogenous theory, 364
autoimmune disease, 574, 829, *829*
autonomic nervous system, **764**
autosomal disorder, 205

autosome, 163, *163*
    phenotype and, 192–193
    tracing, 206, *207*
autotroph, 101, 398–399, **398**
Avery, Oswald, 217, *217*
Aves, 698, *699,* R33. *See also* **bird**
avian flu (influenza), 565, 724, *724,* 810
avian flu H5N1, 724, *724*
axillary bud, 654
axolotl, 714
axon, 750–751, *750,* 753–754, 760, 763
azalea, 45

## B

Bacillariophyta, 593, R28
*bacilli,* 568
*Bacillus anthracis,* 576
background extinction, 338
bacteria, 812. *See also* **prokaryote**
    abundance and territory of, 567
    aerobes and anaerobes, 567
    antibiotic resistance, 145, 319, 382–384,
      575–578, *577*
    antibiotics produced by, 576
    archaea compared to, 568
    artificial photosynthesis and, 104–105
    asexual reproduction, 144–145, *145*
    beneficial roles of, 571–573, *571, 573,* 578
    in benthic zone of lakes, 464
    body systems providing protection
      from, 69, *69*
    cell division and, 144–145, *145*
    cell wall of, 79
    characteristics of, 13
    classification of, R27, *R27*
    cyanobacteria, *354,* 362, *362,* 363, 407,
      *407,* 572
    in digestive tract, 123, 555, *555,* 571, 574,
      *574,* 607
    diseases caused by, 564–566, *565, 566,*
      575–577, *575, 576, 577,* 578, 812, 816
    DNA of, 568
    effect on homeostasis, 740
    in extreme environments, 21
    fermentation by, 121, 123
    generation time, *367*
    genetic engineering and, 254, 266–268
    gene transfer, 570, *570,* 578
    germ theory, 19, 811
    growth, *80, 145*
    humans and, 13
    in lichens, 608, *608*
    mutualist relationship with plants, 620
    nitrogen-fixing, nitrifying, and
      denitrifying, 407, *407*
    photosynthesis by, 101
    protein production in, 229, 238–239
    species of, 549
    structure of, 568–569, *568, 569,* 578
    survival strategies, 570, *570*
    transforming principle and, 216–217, *216*
    transgenic, 267–268

    ulcers caused by, 19, *19*
    viruses infecting, 218, *218,* 561, *562*
Bacteria (domain), **548,** *549,* 568, 585, R27
Bacteria (kingdom), *547*
bacteriophage, **218,** *218,* 561–562, **561,**
    *561, 562*
Bada, Jeffery, 358
balance, triple-beam, R7, *R7*
bald eagle, 323, 492
baleen whale, *308,* 309
banana, *271*
band 3 protein, 84
bandicoot, 184, *184*
baobab tree, *652*
bar graph, 166, 202, 518, 651, 769, 797, 854,
    R16, *R16*
bark, *443C,* 443D, 652, *653*
barnacle, 299–300, *300*
barn owl, 533
barracuda, 706, *706*
barrier islands, 462
basal cell, 148, 149, *149*
base (chemical), **44**
base of DNA, 220, 256
base of microscope, R8, *R8*
base of nucleotide, 134, *134*
base-pairing rules, 222–223, **222,** *223,* 225
basic solution, 44
basidia, 602, *602*
Basidiomycota, 602, *602,* R29
*Basilosaurus isis,* 306, *306*
basket star, 688, *688*
basophil, 827, *827*
bat
    chromosomes of, *166*
    mutualism with cactus, 424, *425*
    reciprocity among, 515
    white-nose syndrome, 605, *605*
    wings of, 302–303, *302, 303*
Bateson, William, 201
bathyal zone, **459,** *459,* 460
B cell, 132, 816–817, **816,** 821, 823, *823*
Beagle expedition, 298
bear
    grizzly, 388
    polar, 11, 457, *457*
beaver, 395–396, *396*
bee, 5, *5, 421,* 424, 505, 514, 516, 628
beetle, *10,* 11, *664*
behavior. *See* **animal behavior;**
    **human activity**
behavioral isolation, **333**
Beijerinck, Martinus, 559
Belding's ground squirrel, 515, *515*
beluga whale, 484
benign tumor, **142**
bentgrass, 322, *322*
benthic zone, 458, **464**
betta fish, 197, *197*
bicarbonate, 53, 406
bichir, 707
biennial plant, 631
big bluestem, *631*

# Index

# Index

on phospholipids in cell
membranes, 81–82, *81*
on protons and electrons, 38
Charophyceae class, 616
chart, 75, 276, 286, 342, 421
main idea, 440, 729
supporting main idea, 60, 99, 254,
466, R22
three-column chart, 548, 584, 636
timeline, 378
two-column chart, 124, 194,
557, R23
Chase, Martha, 218
cheese, 121, *123*, 571
chelicerate, R32
chemical
gene expression affected by, 243, 247
as plant defense, 620
pollution by, 476, 482, 483
chemical bond
covalent, 41, 46–47, 49, 222–223, *223*
in DNA, 222–223, *223*
hydrogen, 42–43, *43*, 50, 81, 222–223, *223*,
226–227, *247*
ionic, 40, *40*
peptide, 49, *49, 236,* 237
in reactions, 53
chemical energy, *124. See also* **cellular
respiration; photosynthesis**
ATP and, 98–100
cellular respiration releasing, 111–113,
115–119
chemosynthesis using, 100, 399
photosynthesis storing, 101–110
chemical equilibrium, 53
chemical reaction, 52–55, **52**
activation energy, *54*, 55
bond energy, 53
bond formation and breaking, 52–53
equilibrium, 53
exothermic and endothermic, *54*, 55
chemical safety, R2, R4, *R4*
chemical signals, 514
chemiosmotic gradient, 108
chemistry of life
atoms, ions, and molecules, 38–41
carbon-based molecules, 46–50
chemical reactions, 52–55
enzymes, 56–58
water properties, 42–45
chemoreceptor, 678, 755–757
chemosynthesis, **100, 399,** 459
chemotherapy, 143
chicken, *301*
chicken pox, *566*
childhood, **858**
Chilopoda, R32
chimera, 698, 703, 704
chimpanzee, 5, 372, *373,* 499, *499,* 520
chitin, 79, **599,** 684
*Chlamydomonas,* 594, *594,* 595
chloride ion, 40, *40*

chlorophyll, **101**
in algae, 594
of euglenoids, 592
fluorescence, 656
minerals needed for, 651
photosynthesis by, 101–110, *101, 102,
107, 109, 124,* 399
of plants, 616
in producers, 398, *398*
Chlorophyta (phylum), 594, R28
chloroplast, *74,* **79**
autogenous theory and, 364, *364*
DNA of, 363
endosymbiosis theory and, 363, *363*
locations of, 642, *642,* 644, 654
mitochondrion compared to, 112
photosynthesis by, 101–110, *101, 102,
107, 109, 124,* 399
in plantlike protists, *592*
replication of, 144, 363
in specific trees, *80*
structure and function of, 78, 79, *79,* 80
choanocytes, 674, *674*
Choanoflagellate, 673
cholesterol, 49, 82, *82,* 163, 770
Chondrichthyes, 698, *699,* 704–705, *704,* R33
Chordata (phylum), 300, *534,* 670, *671,*
696–697, *696, 697*
chordate, 696–697, **696,** *696, 697,* 762, R33
chorion, 851
Chromalveolata, 585, *585*
chromatid, **135,** *135,* 136, *137,* 167–169,
*167, 169*
chromatin, 135, *135*
chromium (Cr), 39
chromosomal mutation, 245, *245*
chromosome, **134.** *See also* **allele; genetics**
binary fission, 145
crossing over, 184, 201, 202, I184
diversity and, 183–185, *184*
fertilization and, 847
gene linkage, 201–203
homologous, 163, 167–169, *167, 168, 169*
human, *163*
during interphase, 134
karyotypes and, 208–209, *209*
mapping of, 201–203, 210
during meiosis, 164–170, *165, 168, 169,*
177–178, 183–186, *186*
during mitosis, 134, *134,* 136, *136,* 137
mutations of, 244–247, *244, 245*
number of, 162, *166*
phenotype and, 192–195, 210
of prokaryotes, 144
chromosome mapping, 209
Chrysophyta, R28
chytrid, R29
Chytridiomycota, 600, R29
cigarette smoke, 29, *29,* 788
cilia, 78, *589,* 783, 788, 815, *815*
ciliate, *586,* 588–589, *589,* R28
Ciliophora (phylum), 588–589, *589,* R27
circadian rhythm, 352, **502**

circle graph, R17, *R17*
circulatory system, **782,** 784–785, *785,* 863B
of amphibians, 712, 713
of annelids, 682, *683*
blood transport and, 794–796
diseases of, 796
of fish, 701–702
gas exchange and, 786–787, *787*
heart and, 789–792, *791*
of humans, *732*
immune system and, 815–816
lymphatic system and, 802–803, *802*
of mollusks, 680
regulation of body temperature, 739
citric acid, 116–117, *117,* 609
CJD (Creutzfeldt-Jakob disease), 19, 557
clade, 539, *541*
cladistics, 538–539, *539*
cladogram, 539–540, **539,** *539, 541*
clam, *671,* 680, *689*
class, 534–535, *534*
of cnidarians, 676
of echinoderms, 687–688, *688*
of flatworms, 678–679
of mollusks, 681
of vertebrates, 698
classical conditioning, **508**
classification, 377, 584, R27–R33. *See also*
**tree of life**
of amphibians, 714
by ancient Greeks, 6
of animals, *671, 672,* R30–R33
based on evolutionary relationships,
538–540, *538, 541, 542, 542,* 550
domains and kingdoms, R27–R33
early ideas about evolution and, 286–287
of fish, 703–705, *704, 705*
of fungi, R29
of hominoid, hominid, and hominin,
372, *373,* 377
Linnaean system, 286–287, *287,* 532–535,
*534, 535,* 550
of plants, 621–626, *621, 622, 623, 624,
625, 626, 636,* R29–R30
of protists, 585–586, *586,* R27–R29
of vertebrates, 698, *698, 699,* 700
Claudette (hurricane), *20*
clay adsorption hypothesis, 358–359
Clean Air Act (1970), 492
cleaner shrimp, *10*
cleanup, R3
Clean Water Act (1972), 492
clear cutting, 490–491
cleavage pattern, 670, *670*
Clever Hans, 519
climate, 448–451, **448,** *448, 449, 450, 451,*
452, 466
climate change, 104, 410, 478, 479, 480, 481,
492, 526–528
climate zone, 449–450, *449*
cloaca, 713, *713*
cloning, 157, 265–266, *265,* 666
*Clostridium botulinum,* 575, *575,* 576

# Index

# Index

# Index

exclusion, competitive, **421**
excretory system, *732, 863C*
exercise, *120,* 296
exercise physiologist, R38
exocytosis, **91,** *91, 92, 92*
exon, 241
exoskeleton, 697
exothermic reaction, *54,* 55
experiment, 18. *See also* **QuickLabs**
    design of, 596, R11–R13
    field, 391
    hypotheses and, 17–18
    laboratory, 391
experimental group, R12
exponential growth, **433,** *433*
external stimulus, 500–501, 502, 504–505
extinction
    background, **338**
    catastrophism and, 288
    causes of, 409
    effects of, 486–487
    of mammals, 716
    mass, 338, *338,* 340–341, 355, 368–369,
        409, 628
    regularity of, 5, 331
extreme environments, life in, 4
    heat-loving microbes, 21
    hydrothermal vents, 100, 359, *359,*
        *459, 548*
    worms in frozen methane gas, 31, *31*
eye, 242, *242,* 669, 681, 754–755, *754, 755*
eye color, 198, 204, *298*
eyelash, 424, *424,* 425
eyepiece, R8, *R8,* R10
eye spot, *592*

# F

F1 generation, 172
F2 generation, 172
facilitated diffusion, **87,** *87*
facultative aerobe, 567
FADH, 116, 117–118
*Faecalibacterium prausnitzii,* 574
fallopian tube, 840–841, **840,** *841,* 846
family, 534–535, *534*
farming. *See* **agriculture; livestock**
farm manager, R38
fat
    energy in, 48, 100, *100*
    molecular structure of, 48–49, *48, 49*
    as nonpolar solvent, 44
    saturated and unsaturated, 48–49, *48*
fatty acid, 48–49, **48,** *48, 81, 81*
feather, 321, *321,* 699
feather star, 665, *665,* 687, *687*
fecal transplant, 574
feedback, 774
    negative, 11, **735,** *736*
    positive, **737**
feedback loop, 447
feedlot farming, 410
feet, 11

female reproductive system, 840–841, *841.*
    *See also* **human reproduction**
fermentation
    alcoholic, 122–123, *122*
    in the body, 120–123, *120,* 124
    of food, 571
    lactic acid, 116, 121, *121*
fern, 162, 455, 623, *623,* R30, R35
fertilization, **164,** 846–847
    differentiation and, 242
    of human egg, *160–161,* 161
    of seed plants, 624
    of sponges, 673
fertilizer, 573, 608
fetal development, 141, *141,* 850–855
fetal development, apoptosis during, 141, *141*
fetus, 717, **852,** *853*
fibrin, 801, *801*
fibrinogen, 798
fibrous root, **651**
*Ficus,* 641
fiddlehead, 623, *623*
field experiment, 391
field of view, R10, *R10*
fig, 454
fight-or-flight response, 501, *501,* 764, 772
fig tree, 641
filament, 73, *73*
filaria, 813, *813*
filter feeder, **674,** 697, *697*
fin, 701, *701,* 706–707, *707,* 708, *708,* 709
finch, 290, 296–297, 299, *299,* 340
fine adjustment, R8, *R8*
fingernail, 665
fingerprinting, DNA, 253, 262–264, *263,* 276
fire, 409, *409,* 439, 443C, *443C,* 454, 456, 608
firefly, 55, 333
fire-resistant seed, 454, 456
fire safety, R2, *R4*
fish
    anatomy of, 701–702, *701, 702*
    as biotic factor, 394
    body plan, 668
    bony, 369, 698, 700, 703, *705,* 706–709,
        *706, 707, 708, 709,* 718
    buoyancy, 707
    cartilaginous, 698, 703, 704–705, *704*
    classification of, R33
    coelacanth, 709, *709*
    as consumers, *402,* 403, 483
    in estuaries, 462
    evolution of, 369
    as first vertebrates, 700
    genetics of coloration, 197, *197*
    genotype frequencies in population
        of, 329
    global warming and, 527
    jaw development, 703, *703*
    jawless, *354,* 368, 700, *700*
    lamprey, 698
    lobe-finned fish, 708, *708*
    operculum of, 705, *705*
    as prey, 388

ray-finned, 370, 706, *706*
    sustainable harvesting, 491
    swimming and maneuvering of, 702, *702*
    water pollution and, 482
fish and wildlife manager, R38
fisheries, 491
fishing ban, 491
fishing gear review, 491
fishing industry, 491
fission, 144–145, *145*
fitness, 295
flagellum, **568,** 846
    centrioles and, 78
    of dinoflagellates, 592
    of euglenoids, 592
    on primitive fungus spores, 600
    of sperm cell, 170
    of zooflagellates, 587, *587*
flatworm, 146, 670, *671,* 672, 678–679, *678,*
    *679,* 690, *R31*
flea, 814
Fleischmann's glass frog, *694–695,* 695, 696
Fleming, Sir Alexander, 811, *811*
floating, 707
flooding, 289, 436, *436,* 462
Florida Everglades, *389,* 401, 488, *488*
Florida snail kite, 401, *401*
flower, **625**
flower color, 171–173, *172, 173,* 176, 178–179
flowering plant
    adaptations of, 628–629, *628, 629*
    categories of, 629–631, *630, 631*
    classification of, 626, R30, *R30*
    diversity of, *614–615,* 615, 628–631, *628,*
        *629, 630, 631,* 636
    evolution of, 369, 370
    life cycle of, R37, *R37*
    monocots and dicots, 630, *630*
    pollination of, *620*
    in primary succession, 438
    seed dispersal, 629, *629*
flow phase, 844, *845*
fluid mosaic model, 82
fluke, 679, *679,* R31
fluorescence, 656
flu virus, 565, 723–724, *723, 724,* 810, *812*
fly, 590, 666, *666. See also* **fruit fly**
fMRI (functional magnetic resonance
    imaging), 865
FoldNotes, R25–R26, *R25–R26*
folic acid, 854
follicle, **844,** *844*
follicle-stimulating hormone (FSH), 840,
    841, 844–846, 858
follicular phase, 844, *845*
food
    allergen, 828
    allergy to, 28
    calorimetry and, 59
    carbohydrates, 47–48, *47*
    chemosynthesis of, 100
    ecological niches and, 420, 421
    energy in, 98, 99–100, 411–412

# Index

# Index

horizontal gene transfer theory, 365, *365*
hormone, 770–775, **770**, *770, 773*, 859
    cell membrane permeability, 84
    control of homeostasis, 735, 737
    endocrine system and, 770–775, *773*
    fetal development and, 852
    glands and, 772, *773*
    growth and, 857
    growth promotion, 141
    illness and, 775
    menstrual cycle and, 840, 843–845, 849
    nonsteroid, 770–771, *771*
    pregnancy and, 855
    releasing, 774
    response to stimulus, 502
    sperm production and, 846
    steroid, 770–772, *771*
hornworm caterpillar, 425
hornwort, 622, *622*, R29
horse, *370*
horseshoe crab, 462, *462*
horsetail, 623, R30
host-parasite relationship, 424, *425*, 426, *426*
hot desert biome, 454
hotspot, 395, 710, *710*
house sparrow, *533*
*Hox* genes
    body plan determination, 240, 666, 668, *668*
    determining evolutionary descent, 670, *672*
    as evidence of evolution, 307
    mutation of, 666, *666*, 668, *668*
    vertebrates and, 301
HPV (human papillomavirus), 848
human. *See also* hominid; human biology
    air quality, impact on, 476–478
    bacteria's relationship with, 13
    biodiversity, threats to, 486–489
    cells of, 94A–94B, *94A–94B*
    characteristics of, 13
    chromosomes of, 183, *272*
    classification of, 670
    conservation efforts, 490–493
    development of, *301*, 852, *853*, 857–859
    disruption of cycles in ecosystems, *410*
    disruption of homeostasis, 740–741, *740*
    embryo, 839, 850–851, *851*, 853
    evolution of, 370, 372, *373, 374, 375–377*
    evolution of brain, 376–377
    eyelashes of, 424, *425*
    fungal infections, 607
    genome of, *271*
    hand structure, *302*
    hemoglobin of, *545*
    *Hox* gene expression, 668, **668**
    interaction of organ systems, 727, *727*, 728, 738–741, *738, 739, 740, 741,* 863A–863B
    internal body temperature, 734, *735*
    learning, 507

mechanisms of homeostasis, 734–737, *735, 736*
    microbiota of, 574, *574*
    number of chromosomes, 162
    organization of the body, 730, *731*, 732
    parasites of, 426, *426*
    population growth and natural resources, 472–475, *472, 473, 475,* 494
human activity
    air quality affected by, *476, 477, 478, 479,* 480, *480,* 494
    biodiversity threatened by, *486, 487, 488,* 494
    conservation efforts, *490, 491, 492, 493,* 494
    disruption of cycles in ecosystems, 409–410, 462
    natural resource use, 472–475
    population growth affected by, 436
    water quality affected by, 482–484, *482, 483,* 494
human biology
    circulatory system, 782–785, **782**, *785,* 789–796
    endocrine system, 748–749, *748,* 770–775, *773*
    fetal development and birth, 850–857
    immune system, 815–833
    lymphatic system, 802–803, *802*
    nervous system, 748–768, *748*
    reproductive system, 772, 840–848
    respiratory system, 782–784, 786–788
human culture
    plants in, 633–635, *634, 635,* 636
    role in evolution, 376–377
human embryo, 839, 850–851, **850**, *851,* 853
human genetic screening, 30–31
human genome, 175, 208–209, 271–272, *271,* 282
Human Genome Project, 175, 209, 271, **271**, *271,* 282
human growth hormone (hGH), 857
human immunodeficiency virus. *See* HIV (human immunodeficiency virus)
human microbiota, 576, 607
human papillomavirus (HPV), 848
human reproduction, 838–859, **840**
    anatomy of, 840–842, *841, 842*
    birth and development, 856–859
    exposure to chemicals and, 854–855
    fertilization, 846–847
    fetal development, 850–855
    hormones and, 840, 843–845, 846, 849, 852, 855
    menstrual cycle, 844–845, *845*
human systems
    determination and differentiation of cells, 728–729, *729*
    specialized cells, 728–729, *729*
    tissues, organs, organ systems, 730, *731,* 732, *732*
hummingbird, *629*
humoral immunity, **823**, *823*

humour, 6, 19
humus, 406
hunger, 500
hunting and gathering, 375, 633
Huntington's disease, 182, 193, 204
hurricane, *20,* 436, *436,* 462
Hutton, James, 289, 339
hybridization, 286, 317
*Hydra,* 146, *146,* 666
hydrogen (H), 39, 357, 572
hydrogen atom, 38
hydrogen bond
    cohesion and, 645
    in DNA, 222–223, *223*
    DNA replication and, 226
    mutations and, 247
    in phospholipid layers, 81, *81*
    protein folding and, 50
    in water, 42–43, *43*
hydrogen evolution reaction (HER), 104–105, *105*
hydrogen ion (H+), 40
    active transport of, 90
    in cellular respiration, 118, *118*
    pH and, 44–45
    in photosynthesis, 107–108, *107*
    in proton pump, 90, 107
hydrogen sulfide, 399
hydrologic cycle, 404, *405,* 474, 477
hydrologic (water) cycle, 404, *405,* 474, 477
hydrosphere, **446**, 447
hydrostatic skeleton, 682, 715
hydrothermal pool, 399, *399*
hydrothermal vent, 21, 100, 359, *359,* 399, 459, *548*
Hydrozoa, 676, R30
Hyman, Libbie, 670, 672
hypertension, 796
hypertonic solution, 86, **86**
hypha, 599–600, **599**, *599,* 602, *603*
hypothalamus, **772**
    in homeostasis, 764
    hormones from, 772–774, *773, 774*
    in reproduction, 840, 846
    in temperature regulation, 739, 762, 772, 774
hypothesis, **16**, R11
    experimental testing of, 17–18
    forming a null hypothesis, 797
    theory compared to, 3, 19, 285, 445
hypothyroidism, 775
hypotonic solution, 86–87, **86**, *86, 87,* 815

**I**

Iberian lynx, 338
ice cap, 457, *457, 480,* 528
ice climber, 727, *727*
ichthyosaur, 369
identification, 263–264
identifying clade, 540
illustrator, R38
imitation, 507

# Index

kudu, 501, *501*
kudzu, 489, *489*

## L

lab equipment, 7. *See also* **microscope**
    **graduated cylinder**, R6, *R6*
    **metric ruler**, R6, *R6*
    **thermometer**, R6, *R6*
    **triple-beam balance**, R7, *R7*
lab experiment, 391. *See also* **QuickLabs**
labor, birth, 856
laboratory instructions, R20
lab safety, R2–R4, *R4*
    animal, R3
    chemical, R2
    cleanup, R3
    directions, R2
    dress code, R2
    electrical, R3, *R4*
    glassware and sharp-object, R3
    heating and fire, R2
    symbols, R4, *R4*
Lacks, Henrietta, 143
*lac* operon, 238–239, *239*
lactic acid, **121**
lactic acid fermentation, 121, *121*
*Lactobacilli,* 568
lactose, 238–239, *239*
lake, 463, 464, *464,* 482
lake turnover, 464, *464*
Lamarck, Jean-Baptiste, 287–288, *287*
lamprey, *543,* 698, *699,* 700, R33
lancelet, 300, *671,* 696, 698, R33
landmass, 450, *450*
land plant. *See also* **flowering plant;**
    **nonvascular plant; plant**
    adaptations of, 617–618, *619,* 620
    evolution of, 616–617, *616, 617*
    reproduction of, 618, *619*
    transportation in, 618, *619*
landscape architect, R38
landslide, 409, *409*
large intestine, 716, 863C, *863C, 863D*
larva (plural: larvae)
    of annelids, 683
    of chordates, 697
    of cnidarians, 675
    of echinoderms, 686
    of salamanders, 714
    of worms, 352
lateral line, 704–705, **705**
lateral meristem, 650, *653*
Latin word parts, R18–R19
lava, 437
law, scientific, 19
law of independent assortment, **180**
law of segregation, 173, *173,* 177–178, 180
law of superposition, 288
lazuli bunting, 321, *321*
leaf
    adaptations, 657
    characteristics of, 655, *655, 657*

of monocots and dicots, 630, *630*
    photosynthesis in, *101,* 101–110, *102,*
    656–657
    stomata, 102, 147, 618, *619,* 622, 649,
    654–655, *655*
    transpiration, 147, 404, *405,* 646, 647
leafcutter ant, 609, *609*
leaf hair, 8
leaflet, 655
leafy sea dragon, 707
learning, 505–508, *506, 507, 508,* 521, 522
leatherback sea turtle, 504, *504*
leech, *426, 426,* R31
Leeuwenhoek, Anton van, 70, *71*
leg, 669, 711
legume, 573, *573*
length, R5, *R5*
lens, of eye, 755, *755*
Lenski, Richard, 384, *384*
leprosy, 567
*Leptictidium,* 340, *340*
lesser long-nosed bat, 424, *425*
lethal allele, 325
leucine (Leu), 234, *234*
leukemia, 151, 635, 830, *830*
LH (luteinizing hormone), 840–841,
    844–846, 858
lichen, 438, *438,* 455, 608, *608*
life cycle, R34–R37
    of amphibians, 713, *713*
    of cnidarians, 675
    of conifer, R36, *R36*
    of fern, R35, *R35*
    of flowering plants, R37, *R37*
    of fluke, 679, *679*
    of fungi, *603*
    of green algae, *595*
    of moss, R34, *R34*
    of sponges, 673
    of tapeworm, 679
life in Earth system, 446–447, **446,** *446, 447*
ligament, 665
ligand, 84, *84*
ligation, 267, *267*
light, 243. *See also* **sunlight**
    animal behaviors influenced by, 502,
    *502,* 503
    produced by abyssal zone animals, 459
    as stimulus for animal behavior, 500, 501
light-dependent reaction, 102–103, *102,*
    106–108, *107*
light-independent reaction, 103,
    108–110, *109*
light microscope, 23–24, *23, 24,* 70–71, *R8,*
    R8
lightning, 356, 357, 407, *443B*
light source, R8, *R8*
lignin, **618,** *619,* 631, 643
lily, 630, *630*
limbic system, 762
limbs, *699*
limestone, 406
limiting factor, 435, 454

limnetic zone, **464**
line graph, 216, R15, *R15*
linkage, genetic, *185,* **185,** 186, 201–203, 210
linkage map, 202–203, **202,** *203*
Linnaean classification, 286–287, *287,*
    532–535, *533, 534, 535,* 550, 667
Linnaeus, Carolus, 286, *287,* 532
lion, 420–421, *420,* 501, *501,* 515
lion's tooth, *533*
lipid
    of archaea, 569
    in cell membranes, 81–82, *81*
    diffusion into cells, 86
    energy in, 98, 99–100, *100*
    origin of life and, 360, *360*
    structure of, 48–49, *48, 49*
    in viruses, 559
lipid membrane hypothesis, 360, *360*
liposome, 360, *360*
Lister, Joseph, 810–811
littoral zone, **464**
live birth, 717
liver, *132,* 738, 863B, *863D*
liverwort, 621, *621,* R29
livestock, 410, 577
living things, characteristics of, 8–9, 556
lizard, 500, 502, *502,* 540, *541,* 666
lobe, brain, 761, *761*
lobe-finned fish, **708,** *708*
lobster, 459
local ecosystem, 455
lock-and-key model, 58, *58*
logical thinking, 15
logistic growth, **433,** *433*
lophophore, 678
Lophotrochozoa, 670, 678–679, *678, 679. See*
    *also* **flatworm**
Lorenz, Konrad, 506
love dart, 681
Lovelock, James, 447
lumen, 76
lung, **783** , *863D*
    of amniotes, 716
    of amphibians, 711, 712
    blood supply in, *781*
    cancer, 788
    cell replacement in, 132
    diseases of, *788*
    effects of smoking on, 788, *788*
    gas exchange in, 783–784, *783,* 786–788
    in homeostasis, 782
    of lungfish, 709
    as organ, 730
    of the planet, 149
    of ray-finned fish, 707
    research on, 258
lung cancer, *128–129*
lungfish, *271,* 709, *709*
luteal phase, 845, *845*
luteinizing hormone (LH), 840–841,
    844–846, 858
Lycophyta (phylum), 623, R29
*Lycopodium,* 623, *623*

# Index

diagram of, R8, *R8*
discovery of cells and, 70–71, *70*
electron, 23–24, *24*, 723, 812
light, 23–24, *23, 24*, R8, *R8*
scanning electron, 24, *24*
transmission electron, 24, *24*
using, R8–R10
microtubule, 73, *73*, 78, 95C, 136, 587
midbrain, 762, *762*
middle ear, 711–712
migration, 462, 487, 500, 503, 509
migratory bird, 462
milkweed, 620
Miller, Stanley, 357
Miller-Urey experiment, 357, *357*
millipede, R32
mind maps, *28*, 121, 270, 316
mineral control in human body, 734
mineral nutrient, 651
mining, 408
missing link, 306
mite, 828, *828*
mitochondrial DNA (mtDNA), 545–546, **546**, *546*
mitochondrion (plural: mitochondria), *74, 77*
  autogenous theory and, 364, *364*
  cellular respiration in, 111–112, *111, 112, 113*, 115–119, *117, 118*, 124, *124*
  chloroplast compared to, 112
  DNA of, 363
  endosymbiosis theory and, 363, *363*
  functions of, 77, *77*
  in plant cells, 79
  structure of, 112, *112*
mitosis, **131**
  binary fission opposed to, 144
  budding, 146, *146*
  eukaryotic reproduction, 146
  meiosis compared to, 165, *165*, 169, 186, *186*
  of plantlike protists, 595, *595*
  process of, *130*, 131, *131*, 134–136, *135, 136, 137*, 138, *138*, 152
  X chromosome and, 195
mitosis (M) phase, 130–131, *130*
mixture, homogeneous, 44
mnemonics, 531
mocking bird, 501
mode, 632, R14
modeling. *See also* **QuickLabs**
  biomagnification, 484
  of disease, 26, *26*, 813
  in ecological research, 392
  genetic drift, 325
  geologic clock, 375
mold, 123, *123*, 599, 756–757, *757. See also* **fungi; protist**
mole, 285, 302, *302*
molecular biologist, R39
molecular biology
  discovery of DNA, 216–218, 248

gene expression and regulation and, 238–243, *239, 240, 241, 242, 243*, 248
  mutations and, 244–247
  structure of DNA, 220–223, 248
  as tool, 27
  transcription and, 229–230, *231*, 238–239, 248
  translation and, 233–235, *236, 237*, 248
molecular clock, 544–546, **544**, *544, 545, 546*, 550
molecular evidence, *308*, 673
molecular genetics, 27
molecule, **41**
  carbon-based, 46–50, *46*
  passive transport across cell membrane, 85–87, *85, 86*
  polar and nonpolar, 42–44
  transport into cells, 83
  water, 42–43, *42*
Mollusca (phylum), *671*, R31, *R31*
mollusk, 667, *667*, 670, 680–681, *680, 681*, 690
molting, 685
monarch butterfly, 620
Monera (kingdom), 547–548
monkey, 372, *372, 373*, 445, *507*, 520
monoamine oxidase, 29, *29*
monocot, 630, *630, 631*, 652
monocotyledonae, R30, *R30*
monohybrid cross, **178**, *178*
monomer, **47**, *47*
  amino acid, *49*
  fatty acid, *48*
  monosaccharide, *47, 47*
  nucleotide, 50, 220, *220*
*Mononykus*, 354
monosaccharide, *47, 47*
monotreme, 370
Monterey pine, 334
moose, 398, 435, *435*
moray eel, *10*
morel, 600, *600*
Morgan, Thomas Hunt, 201
morning sickness, 855
Morowitz, Harold, 360
morphogenesis, 242, *242*
Morro Bay estuary, 461
mosquito, 3, *3*, 4, *44*, 566, 590, 814
moss
  classification of, R29
  in deciduous forests, 455
  life cycle of, R34, *R34*
  as pioneer species, 438, *438*
  as seedless nonvascular plants, 621–622, *622*
  in tundra, 456
moss cup fungus, *600*
moth, 620, *620*
motor cortex, 761–762, *761*
motor neuron, 751, 759, 762
mountain, 450, *450*
mountain habitat, 457
mountain lion, *533*

mountain zones, *452*
mouse
  classification of, 377
  DNA of, 271
  genetic engineering of, 215, *215*, 268–269, *269*
  hibernation of, 503, *503*
  inherited traits, 198–199
  as invasive species, 488, *489*
  seed dispersal by, *629*
mouth, 783, 863B, *863B*
MRI (magnetic resonance imaging), 25, *25*
MRI scan, 747, 765, *765*, 865
mRNA (messenger RNA), **230**
  function of, 233–235, *233, 234, 236, 237*, 240–241, *241*
  mutation and, 244, *245*
MRSA (methicillin-resistant *Staphylococcus aureus*), 383
mtDNA (mitochondrial DNA), 545–546, **546**, *546*
mucus, 757, 783–784, 788
mudskipper, 706
Mullis, Kary, 259, *259*
multicellular organisms, 8, *9*
  cell growth and division, 147–151, *148, 149, 150, 151*, 152
  organization of, 728–730, *729, 731, 732*
  radiation of, 368–370, *368, 369, 370*
multidrug-resistant bacteria, 145
multiple sclerosis (MS), 829
multipotent stem cell, 150
multitasking, 866
mummification, 6, *6*
Mumps, 566
Muneta, Ben, 724, *724*
murex snail, 337, *337*
muscle
  development of, 149
  lactic acid and, 120, 121
  regulation of body temperature, 739
muscle cell, 729
muscle tissue, 730
muscular dystrophy, 182, 274, *274*
muscular system, *732*
museum curator, R39
Muséum National d'Histoire Naturelle (Paris), 481
mushroom, *599*, 600, *600*, 601, 609
mussel, 486, 511, *511*
mutagen, **247**
mutation, 244–247, **244**
  cancer and, 142
  causes of, 247
  estimation of evolutionary time, 544–546, *545*
  evolution and, 296, 307, *330, 331*
  on fly, 666
  frameshift, 244, *245*
  genetic variation from, 317
  Hardy-Weinberg equilibrium and, 328
  insertion, *245*
  point, 244, *245*

# Index

evolution of, 368–370, 553C, *553C*
fungal infections, 607
fungi compared to, 599
genetic engineering of, *265*, 266–269, *266, 269*
growth of, 652–653
herbaceous, 652
in human culture, 633–635, *633, 634, 635, 636*
introduced species, 489, *489*
leaves (*See* leaf)
life cycles of, R37, *R37*
mutualist relationships, 620
of neritic zone, 459
in nitrogen cycle, 407, *407*
origins of, 616–618, *616, 617*, 620, 636
as producers, 398
of rain forest, 445, *445*
reproduction, 616, 618, *619*, 620–621, 623–625
reproduction of, 616
response to stimulus, 500–501
role in ecosystem, 618
roots, 641, 650–651, *650, 651*
as source of medicine, 486
stems, 652–653, *652*
structure and function, 640–661
succession, 437–439, *437, 438, 439*
systems of, *148*
tetraploidy, 164
tissues, 643–644, *644*
vascular system of, 645–648, 654
vegetative reproduction, 146
wild and engineered cross breeding, 322, *322*
Plantae (kingdom), *547*, 548, 585, *586*, R29–R30
plant-herbivore interactions, 620
plantlike protist, 585, *585*, 591–595, *591, 592, 593, 594, 595*, 610, R28
planula, 675
plaque, 796, *796*
plasma, 44, *53*, **796**, 798, *798*
plasmid, 266–267, **266**, *266, 267*, 383, 568, 577
plasmodesmata, 643, 647
plasmodial slime mold, *586*, 597–598, *597*, R29, *R29*
*Plasmodium*, 590, *590*, 597
platelet, 141, 798–799, **798**, *799*
Platyhelminthes (phylum), *671*, 672, R31
pluripotent stem cell, 150, 151
pneumonia, *812*
PNS (peripheral nervous system), **749**, *759*, 763–764, *764*
point mutation, **244**, *245*
poison, R4, *R4*
poison dart frog, 422, *422*
polar bear, 11, *11*, 457, *457*, 526
polar body, **170**, *170*, 843
polar climate zone, 449, *449*
polar ice cap, *452*, 457, *457*, 480, 528
polar molecule, 42–43, *42*, 44, 81–82, *81*
policy analyst, R39

polio, 810–811, *811*
pollen, 828, *828*
pollen grain, 618, *619*, 624, *624*, 625, 628
pollination
    of flowering plants, 5, *5*, 12, 424, 620, *620*, 624, 628, *629*
    temporal isolation and, 334
pollinator, 620, *620*, 624, 628
pollution, **476**
    air, 476–478, *479*, 480
    bioremediation of, 573
    fossil fuel and, 476–478, *476, 477, 478, 479*, 480, *480*
    global warming from, 478, *479*, 480
    health risks, 29, *29*
    human contribution to, 474
    threat of, 492
    water, 482–484, *482, 483*
Polychaeta, R31
polychlorinated biphenyl (PCB), 483
polydactyly, *175*
polygenic trait, 175, **198**, *198*
polyhedral virus, *560*, 561
polymer, 47
    carbohydrate, 47–48, *47*
    lipid, 48, *48, 49*
    nucleic acid, 50
    origin of life and, 357, 358–359
    protein, 49–50, *49, 50*
polymerase
    DNA, 226–227, *226*, 244, 259–261, *260*, 270
    RNA, 230, *231*, 232, *232*
polymerase chain reaction (PCR), 21, 259–261, *259, 260*, 276
polyp, **675**, *675*
polypeptide, 49–50, *49*, 229
Polyplacophora, 681
pond ecosystem, 412, *412*, 463, 464, 482
Ponderosa pine, 626, *626*
pons, 762, *762*, 787
population, **294**, 389, *389*
    bottleneck effect, 324, *324*
    crash, 434–435, *434*
    density, 428
    dispersion, 429, *429*
    distribution of, 429
    estimating size of, 393
    evolution of, 315–342
    founder effect, 324, *325*
    gene flow, 323, *323*, 342
    genetic drift, 324, 325, 342
    genetic variation within, 316–317, 342
    growth patterns, 432–436, *433, 434, 435, 436*
    Hardy-Weinberg equilibrium in, 328–329, *329, 330*, 331, 342
    human, growth of, 440, 472–475, *472, 473, 475*, 494
    natural selection in, 318–321, *319, 320, 321*, 342
    patterns of evolution in, 335–341, *335, 336, 337, 338, 339, 340, 341*

sexual selection in, 326, *326*, 342
    speciation through isolation, 332–334, *333, 334*, 342
    survivorship curve, 430–431, *431*
    variation within, 315, *315*, 316–317, *317*
population crash, 434
population density, **428**
population dispersion, **429**, *429*
porcupine, 443B, *443B*
pore, *735*
Porifera (phylum), *671*, R30
porpoise, *166*
positive correlation, R15
positive feedback, 737, 801
positron emission tomography (PET), 765–766, *766*
posterior, 669
potassium (K), 39
potato, *166*, 598, *652*
potato blight, 598
potency, 150
prairie dog, 390, 411–412, *411, 412*
Precambrian time, 354
precipitation
    acid rain, 470–471, *471*, 477, *477*
    in biomes, 454–457
    climate and, 448
    in hydrologic cycle, 404, *405*
    land masses and, 450, *450*
    in phosphorus cycle, 408, *408*
precision, *22*, **23**
predation, 423–424, **423**, *423*, 435, *435*, 488
predator, 337, *337*, 483, 513
predictions, 419, 499
prefixes of the metric systems, R5, *R5*
pregnancy, 854–855
preserved remains, 348, *348*
pressure-flow model, 647–648, **647**
primary consumer
    biomagnification and, 483
    in biomass pyramid, 412, *412*
    in food web, 401, *402*, 403
    in numbers pyramid, 413, *413*
primary growth, **653**
primary information source, 20
primary sensory cortex, 760
primary succession, **438**, *438*, 608, 622
primate
    characteristics of, 371
    evolution of, *354*, 370, 371–372, *371, 373*, 374–377, *374*
    problem-solving behavior, 499, *499*, 520
primer, **261**
primitive fungus, 600
*Principles of Geology* (Lyell), 289, 290
prion, 19, *557*
privacy, 66
probability, **181**, *181*, 186, 263–264
probeware, 25
probiotic, 574
problem-solving behavior, 520
procedure writing, R12
process diagram, 494, 522, R22, *R22*

# Index

rain forest, 395, *444–445*, 445, 452, *453, 455*, 487
rain shadow, 450, *450*
random dispersion, 429, *429*
rapeseed, 322
rat, 258, 271, 377
ratfish, 704
rattlesnake, 423–424, *423*
ray, 698, *699*, 703, 704, *704*
ray-fin, **707**
ray-finned fish, 370, 518, 706–707, *706, 707*
reactant, 52
reaction, *54*
reading frame, 234–235, *234*
Reading Toolbox
  analogies, 191, 253, 727
  cause and effect, 641, 747
  cause-and-effect relationships, 129, 349, 500, 555
  charts, 75, 276, 286, 342, 421
  classification, 615
  comparing and contrasting, 161
  comparison, 695
  concept maps, 32, 60, 92, 124, 152, 210, 248, 276, 310, 342, 371, 378, 414, 440, 466, 494, 522, 550, 578, 610, 636, 690, 718, 742, 776, 804, 834, 860
  content frames, 32, 47, 690
  cycle diagrams, 131, 186, 226, 578, 742
  describing space, 97, 663
  describing time, 347
  diagrams, 389, 406, 446, 473, 665, 713, 804
  energy pyramid, 414
  examples, 471
  finding examples, 215
  general statements, 315, 583
  Greek and Latin word origins, 691, 719, 743, 777, 805, 835
  hypothesis compared to theory, 3, 285, 445
  main idea charts, 440
  main idea diagrams, 610
  main ideas, 659, 691, 719, 729, 743, 777, 781, 805, 835, 839, 861
  main idea webs, 38, 92, 135, 210, 310, 532, 550, 617, 698, R23, *R23*
  mind maps, 28, 121, 270, 316
  mnemonics, 531, 809
  outlining, 70
  predictions, 419, 499
  process diagrams, 494, 522, 718, 860
  quantifiers, 37
  sentences, 294
  similes, 69
  sketches, 669, 702
  summarize, 248
  supporting main ideas charts, 60, 99, 254, 466, 610
  synthesize your notes, 658, 776, 804, 834, 860
  tables, 216

  taking notes, 5, 28, 38, 47, 70, 75, 99, 121, 131, 135, 162, 167, 216, 226, 254, 270, 286, 294, 316, 371, 389, 406, 421, 424, 446, 473, 500, 513, 532, 548, 557, 568, 584, 617, 643, 656, 665, 669, 698, 702, 713, 729
  term relationships, 861
  three-column charts, 548, 584, 636, 776, 834
  timelines, 378
  two-column charts, 194, 276, 342, 557
  two-column table, 124, 162
  Venn diagrams, 167, 568
  visualize vocabulary, 659, 719
  vocabulary, 18, 41, 55, 87, 90, 109, 164, 172, 197, 205, 221, 230, 238, 261, 267, 289, 294, 295, 302, 306, 307, 324, 326, 334, 357, 363, 372, 401, 424, 432, 459, 502, 515, 516, 532, 539, 546, 563, 592, 593, 625, 630, 633, 647, 669, 682, 691, 704, 709, 734, 755, 784, 823, 845
  word origins, 659
  word problems, 387
  Y diagrams, 186
recapitulation theory, 300–301
receptor, 735, 749, 753, 754–756, 762, 766–768
  intracellular and membrane, 84, *84*
  viruses and, 564
recessive allele, 175, *175*, 193
recessive disorder, 193, *193*
reciprocity, 515
recombinant DNA, 266–267, **266**, *266, 267*
recombination, 317
red algae, *586*, 594, R28
red blood cell, **787**, 863D
  erythropoietin stimulating increase, 141
  hemoglobin and, *50*
  malaria and, *813*
  replacement of, *132*
  shape of, 728, *728*
  structure and function of, 10–11, 84, 798–799, *799*
red fox, 336, *336*
red leaf beetle, *664*
red-legged frog, 430
red maple, *533*
red panda, 535
red squirrel, 421
red tide, 593, *593*
reduction division, 165
reef, coral, 394, *395*, 403, *403*, 460, *460*, 462, 593
reef shark, *402*, 403
reflex arc, 763, *763*
reforestation, 443D, *443D*
reindeer, 435
rejection, 158
relative dating, 350
relative humidity, 448
releaser, **504**
releasing hormone, 774
remote-sensing technology, 392

renewable resource, 104, **473**, *473*
repetition of tests, 16
replication, **225**
  of chloroplasts, 144, 363
  of DNA, 130–131, *130*, 136, *137*, 168, 225–228, *227, 228*, 248, 361, *361*
  error correction, 228
  mutations during, 244–245, 247
  of prokaryotes, 229, 238
  of RNA, *361*
  transcription compared to, 232
repressor protein, 239, *239*
reproduction, 9, R34–R37. *See also* asexual reproduction; human reproduction; sexual reproduction
  of algae, 617
  of amphibians, 712, *712*
  of annelids, 683
  of cartilaginous fish, 704
  of cnidarians, 675
  of echinoderms, 687
  of flowering plants, 625
  of fungi, 600, 601–602, *601, 603*, 604
  of green algae, 616
  of land plants, 618, *619*, 620, *620*
  of mollusks, 681
  of mosses and ferns, 621, 623
  of plantlike protists, 594–595, *595*
  of plants, 616, 618, *619*, 620–621, 623–625
  of prokaryotes, 570
  of protists, 584
  of roundworms, 685
  of seed plants, 624
  of sponges, 673–674
  survivorship strategy and, 430, *430*
  of viruses, 556, 560
reproductive cost, 326
reproductive gland, 686, *686*
reproductive isolation, **332**
reptile
  classification of, 540, *699*, R33, *R33*
  in Mesozoic era, 369, *369*
  thermoregulation, 11
Reptilia (phylum), 698, *699*, R33
reptilia clade, 540, *541*
research, 21
resource availability
  carrying capacity and, 434–435
  competition for, 423
  competitive exclusion and, 421
  ecological equivalents and, 422, *422*
  as limiting factor, 293–294
  population growth based on, 433
respiration, 405, 406. *See also* cellular respiration
respiratory rate, 739
respiratory system, 782–784, **782**, *783*, 786–788, *787*
respiratory therapist, R39
response to environment, 9
response to stimulus, 500–501, *500*
resting potential, 751

# Index

sedimentation, 408, *408*
sediment coring, 527
seed, 618, *619,* 624
  classification of plants by type of, 629
  dispersal of, 629, *629*
  of gymnosperms, 625
  number in specific fruits, *632*
  protection of diversity, 627
seed leaf, *149,* 629, 630, *630*
seed plant, 624–626, *624, 625, 626*
seed vault, 627
segmentation, 682
segmented worm, *671,* R31
segregation, law of, 173, *173,* 177–178, 180
selection. *See also* natural selection
  directional, 319, *319,* 335
  disruptive, 321, *321,* 335
  sexual, 326, 328, *330,* 331
  stabilizing, 320, *320,* 335
selective permeability, **83,** *83*
SEM (scanning electron microscope), 24, *24*
semen, **842**
semiarid desert biome, 454, 455
seminal vesicle, 842, *842*
semipermeable membrane, 83, *83*
sensitization, **767,** *767*
sensor, 735, *736,* 739, 740
sensory cell, 501
sensory cortex, 761, *761*
sensory neuron, 751, 759–761, 763
sensory organs, 669, 754–757, 761–762
septum, 682
sequencing DNA, 270–271
serine (Ser), 49, *49,* 234
serotonin, 766, 768
sessile animal, **673,** 687, *687*
severe acute respiratory syndrome (SARS),
  565, 810–811, *811*
sex cell, 162
sex chromosome, **163,** *163,* 192, 193, *193,*
  205, 206, 207, 208
sex determination, 199
sex-linked disorder, 205
sex-linked gene, **193**
  expression of, 193–195, *193*
  tracing, 206, *207,* 208
sex-linked traits, 193, *193*
sexually transmitted disease (STD), 811,
  848, **848**
sexual reproduction, **164.** *See also* human
  reproduction
  advantages and disadvantages of, 145
  of animals, 9, 666
  of annelids, 683
  chemical signals and, 772
  chromosomes and, 163
  of cnidarians, 675
  of conifers, R36, *R36*
  diversity and, 183–185, *184,* 366
  of echinoderms, 687
  of ferns, R35, *R35*
  fertilization, 160–161, *161*
  of flowering plants, R37, *R37*

of fungi, 601–602, *603*
  mating success and, *326*
  meiosis and, 164–165, *165*
  of moss, R34
  of plantlike protists, 595, *595*
  recombination of DNA, 317
  of red-legged frog, 430
  of roundworms, 685
  of sponges, 673
  survival and, 430–431
  as unifying theme, 9, *9*
sexual selection, **326,** 327, *327,* 328, *330,* 331,
  514
S form of bacteria, 216–217, *216*
shark
  ability to find food, 481, *481*
  characteristics of, 703, *704*
  classification of, 698, *699*
  electroreception of, 677, *705*
  evolution of, 336, *336,* 369
  in food web, *402,* 403
sharp-object safety, R3, R4, *R4*
shelf fungus, 601
shoot system, *148*
shrimp, *10,* 334, *334,* 402, 518, 674
shrubs, 438
Siberian tiger, 509, *509*
sickle cell anemia, 50, *50,* 182, 275, 799, *799*
side group, 49–50
sieve tube elements, 647
signal molecule, 242
significance, 16
significant figures, R14
silencers, 240
*Silent Spring* (Carson), 490
Silurian period, *354*
similes, 69
simple sugar, 47, *47*
simulation, 26, *26*
single-celled organism, 362–366, 378. *See
  also* archaea; bacteria; cyanobacteria;
  prokaryote
  autogenous theory, 364, *364*
  classification of, 547
  as earliest organisms, 362, *362*
  endosymbiont theory, 363, *363,* 365
  horizontal gene transfer theory,
    365, *365*
single-gene conditions, 182, *182*
sinoatrial (SA) node, 790, *790*
sister chromatid
  in meiosis, 167–169, *167, 169,* 201, 202
  in mitosis, 135, 136, 167
SI unit system, 23, R5, *R5*
size of specimen, R10
skate, 704
skeletal muscle cell, 729, *729*
skeleton
  of amphibians, 711
  of bony fish, 698, 705
  of cartilaginous fish, 704
  collagen in, 665
  of echinoderms, 686

of humans, *732*
  of sponges, 674
skepticism, 15
sketches, 669, 702
skin
  of amniotes, 716
  of amphibians, 712
  as barrier to infection, 564
  cell replacement in, *132*
  collagen in, 665
  development of, 149
  e-skin, 733, *733*
  functions of, 73
  mechanoreceptors in, 757, *757*
  pathogens and, 815
  regulation of body temperature, 739
skin cancer, 142, *142*
Skinner, B. F., 508
Skinner box, 508
skull, 376, 377, *377*
sleeping sickness, 590
slide mount, R9, *R9*
slime cocoon, 700
slime mold, *584,* 597–598, **597,** *597,* R28, *R29*
sloth, *429*
slug, 680
small intestine, *863C, 863C, 863D*
Smart Grapher, 769, 797, 819, 849
smell, 756–757
smelt, *483*
*Smilodectes gracilis,* 374
Smith, William, 353
Smithsonian Museum (Washington, D.C.),
  481
smog, **476,** *476*
smoking, 29, *29,* 142
smooth endoplasmic reticulum, 74, 76, *76*
smooth muscle cell, 729, *729*
smut, 601
snail
  anatomy of, 680, *680*
  classification of, 667, *671,* 681
  evolution and, 337, *337*
  fluke infestation of, *679*
  in food chain, 401, *401*
  in littoral zone of lakes, 464
snake, *443C*
  classification of, 540, *541*
  eggs of, 717
  evolution of, 711
  as introduced species, 488, *488*
  as predator, 423–424, *423*
  vestigial structure of, 304
snapping shrimp, 334, *334,* 518
snip rule, 540
snout beetle, *10,* 11
snow monkey, 507, *507*
social behavior, 522
  altruism, 515–516, *515, 517,* 518
  benefits and costs, 513, *513*
  cognitive ability as advantage to, 520–521
  communication among members, 514
  cooperation, 515

# Index

sugar
  chemosynthesis of, 100, 399, *399*
  in DNA, 220, *220, 223*
  energy in, 99–100
  in nucleotides, 134, *134*
  photosynthesis of, 97, 100, 101–110, *102, 107, 399*
  production in plants, 114
  in RNA, 229–230
suicide gene, 275
sulfide, 100
sulfur (S), 39, 572
sulfuric acid, 100
sunflower, 322
sunlight
  cancer caused by, 142, 247
  in climate, 448, 449, *449*
  environmental impact on, 409
  greenhouse effect, 478, *479*
  in ocean zones, 458
  ozone and, 477
  in photosynthesis, 100, 101–103, *102*, 106–108, *107*, 398–399
  production of vitamin D, 738, *739*
  as source of energy for life, 356, 358
supernatural phenomenon, 19
superposition, law of, 288
supporting main ideas chart, 60, 99, 254, 466, R22, *R22*
surface tension, 43, *43*
surgical technician, R39
survey, 390
survivorship, **509**
survivorship curve, 430–431, **430**, *431*, 434–435
sustainable development, 490–491, **490**, *490*
sustainable Earth, 493
sustainable resource use, 474
Svalbard Global Seed Vault (SGSV), 627
swamp, *443D*, 463
swamp maple, *533*
swan-neck flasks, *7*
sweat gland, *735, 739*
swim bladder, **707**, *707*, 709
symbiosis, **424**, *425*, 571, *573*
  commensalism, 424, *425*
  of fungi, 608–609, *608*
  mutualism, 424, *425*
  parasitism, 424, *425*
  of sponges, 674
symbiotic relationships, R41
symbols, safety, R4, *R4*
sympathetic nervous system, **764**
symposium, 20, *20*
synapse, *752*, **753**, 763, 767–768
synthesis (S) phase, 130–131, *130*
syphilis, 848
system, 9–10, **9**, *148*
*Systema Naturae* (Linnaeus), *287*
systemic circulation, 792, *792*
systolic pressure, **795**

# T

table
  data, 138, 216, R15, *R15*
  two-column, 124, 162
tadpole, 463, 485, *485*, 712, **712**, *713*
taiga, *453*, 455, *455*
taiga biome, *452, 453*, **455**, *455*
tail, *696*
tail fin, 336, *336*, 713
tapeworm, 426, 679, R31
taproot, **651**
*Taq*I enzyme, *256*
*Taraxacum officinale*, *533*
target, 735, 770
tarsus, *10*, 11
taste, *16*, 756–757
TAT box, 240
taxa, 534, *534*
taxis, *501*
taxol, 635
taxon, **532**
taxonomy, **532**
Taylor, F.J.R., 364
TB (tuberculosis), 383, *558*, 567, 575, 812
T-bacteriophage, 561, *561*
T cell, 132, 816, 821–822, *822*, 831–833, *832, 833*
technology
  algae farms, 397, *397*
  artificial coral reef, 465, *465*, 460, *460*
  artificial nucleotide, 254
  artificial photosynthesis, 104–105
  bioinformatics, DNA microarrays, proteomics and, 272–273
  of biology, 23–27, 32
  brain scans, 865
  carrying capacity increased by, **473**
  CRISPR, 269
  digitizing life on Earth, 481, *481*
  electric skin, 733, *733*
  electron microscope, 23–24, *24*, 723, 812
  imaging technology, 25, *25*
  light microscope, 23–24, *23, 24*, 70–71, R8, *R8*
  medical, 280–282
  organ-on-a-chip, 258, *258*
  probewear, 25
  progress of science with, 22–27
  protecting seed diversity, 627
  stable isotopes, 305
  telemetry, 390, *390*
  for wildlife research, 512, *512*
teeth, 703
Tejo estuary, 462
telemetry, 390, *390*
telomere, **135**, *135*
telophase
  in meiosis, 168–169, *169*
  in mitosis, 130, 136, *137*
telophase I, 168, *168*
telophase II, 169, *169*

TEM (transmission electron microscope), 24, *24*
temperate biome
  deciduous forest, *453*, 455, *455*
  grassland, 452, *452, 453*
  rain forest, *444–445*, 445, *453*
temperate climate zone, 449, *449*
temperate deciduous forest, *453*
temperate forest, *452, 455*
temperate grassland, 452, *453*, 454, *454*
temperate rain forest, *453*
temperature, 448
  activation energy and, 57
  enzymes affected by, 56
  gene expression and, 243
  global warming, 478, *478*
  human body, 748–749, 757, 774, 785, 792
  measuring, R6
  regulation in human body, 734, *735, 739*
  sex determination, 199
  as stimulus for animal behavior, 503
  units of, R5, *R5*
temporal isolation, **334**
temporal lobe, 761, *761*
tentacle, 680
teosinte, 634
terminal, **753**
term theory, 289
tern, 483
territoriality, **510**
tertiary consumer
  biomagnification and, 483
  in biomass pyramid, 412, *412*
  in food chain and food web, 401–402, *402*, 403
  in numbers pyramid, 413, *413*
Tertiary period, 341, *354*, 370, *370*
testcross, **179**
testes, 772, *773*, 841–842, **841**, 846, 847
testicle, 841
testing vocabulary, R21
testosterone, 49, **841**, 846, 857, 859
tetanus, *576*
tetraploidy, 164
tetrapod, 540, *541*, 711, **711**
tetrapoda clade, 540, *541*
thalamus, 762
thalidomide, 243
thallose liverwort, 621, *621*
theory, 3, **19**, 285, 445
therapeutic cloning, 157
thermocline, 464
thermometer, R6, *R6*
thermophilic microbe, 21
thermoreceptor, 755, 763, 774
thermoregulation, 11, 734, *735, 739*
*Thermotoga maritima*, 549
*Thermus aquaticus*, 21
Thing Explainer
  Bags of Stuff Inside You, 863A–863D
  Tiny Bags of Water, 95A–95D

# Index

Tree, 443A–443D
Tree of Life, 553A–553D
thirst, 500
thorn bug, 12–13, *12, 32*
three-toed sloth, *429*
threshold, neuron, 753, 767
thumb, 372, *372*
thylakoid, 79, 102–103, **102,** *102,* 106, 107, 108
thymine (T), 220–221, 222–223, *222, 223,* 247
thymus, 772, *773,* 803
thyroid gland, 772–775, *773,* 857
thyroid hormone, 852
thyroxine, 857
tidal pool, *458*
*Tiktaalik roseae,* 712
timber rattlesnake, 423–424, *423*
timelines, 378
timing, **334,** R21
Tinbergen, Niko, 505
tissue, 7, **147,** *148, 671,* **730**
  of animals, 669
  of cnidarians, 675
  epithelial lung tissue, *731*
  leaf, 654
  rejection, 824
  system, 643–644, *644*
T-lymphocyte, **816,** 821–822, *822,* 831–833, *832, 833*
TMV (tobacco mosaic virus), 559, *559*
toad, 715
toad stool mushroom, *R29*
tobacco, 788
tobacco mosaic virus (TMV), 559, *559*
tobacco smoke, 29, *29,* 142
tolerance, **767**
Tollund Man, *346–347, 347*
tongue, 711
tonsils, 803
tool, 7, 23–27, R6–R7, R8
tool use, 372, 375, 499, *499,* 520, *520*
tooth decay, *576*
tornado, 436
tortoise, 290–291, *291, 541*
tortoiseshell cat, *195*
totipotent stem cell, 150
touch, 757
touch signals, 514
toxin, **575**
  bacteria producing, 575–576
  biomagnification of, 483, *483*
  of frogs, 715
  in red tide, 593
  of sponges, 673
toxoid vaccine, 826
TP53 gene, 139
trace element, 39
trace fossil, 348, *348*
trachea, 783, *783*
tracheid cell, *148,* 645, *645*
tracing genes in family, 206, *207,* 208
trait, **171.** *See also* **phenotype**
  behavior, 501

behavioral, 501
chromosomes and phenotype, *190–191, 192–195, 192, 193,* 195
  codominance, 197–198, *197*
  distribution of, 318–319, *318*
  incomplete dominance, 196–197, *197*
  inheritance of, 204
  polygenic, *175,* 175–176, 198, *198*
  probability and, 181, *181*
  sex-linked, 193, *193*
  X-chromosome inactivation and, 195, *195*
transcription, 230
  in eukaryotes, 239–243, *239, 240, 241, 242, 243*
  process of, 229–230, *229, 231, 232,* 238–240, 248
  in prokaryotes, 229, 238
transcription factor, 240, *240*
transdifferentiation, 151
transfer RNA (tRNA), 230
  function of, 232, 235, *235, 236,* 237
  in prokaryotes, 238–239
transforming principle, 216–217, *217*
transgenic organism, 30, 267–269, **267,** *269*
transitional species, 306
translation, **233**
  in eukaryotes, 233–235, *233, 234, 236, 237,* 248
  in prokaryotes, 229, *229,* 238
translocation, 245, *245*
transmission electron microscope (TEM), 24, *24*
transpiration, 404, *405, 646,* **647**
transplantation
  adult stem cells and, 150
  bone marrow, 158
  cloning and, 266
transportation within land plants, 618, *619*
transport protein, 87, *87,* 89–90, *89*
tree
  acid rain's effect on, 477, *477*
  classification of, 533
  conifer, 626, *626*
  deciduous, 630
  in ecosystem, 443A–443D, *443A–443D*
  flowering, 626
  ginkgo, 625, *625*
  pine, *354*
  in primary succession, 438, *438*
  rings, 653, *653*
tree fern, 623
tree finch, *299*
tree of life, 553A–553B, *553A–553B. See also* classification
  domains and kingdoms, 547–549, *547, 548, 549,* 550
  evolutionary relationship classification, 538–540, *538, 541, 542, 542,* 550
  Linnaean classification, 532–535, *533, 534, 535,* 550
  molecular clocks, 544–546, *544, 545, 546,* 550

Trematoda, R31
trematode, 29
trials, repeated, 651
Triassic period, *354, 369*
*Trichomonas vaginalis,* 848, *848*
trichomoniasis, 848
triggerfish, *402, 403*
triglyceride, 48, *49,* 100
trilobite, *298, 354,* 368, R32
trimester, 852, *853*
triple-beam balance, R7, *R7*
triplet code, 233–235, *233, 234, 235, 236,* 237
triploblastic animal, 669
tRNA (transfer RNA)
  in eukaryotes, 230, 232, 235, *235, 236,* 237
  in prokaryotes, 238–239
trochophore, 678
trophic level, **401,** 403
tropical biome, *452, 453,* 454
tropical climate zone, 449, *449*
tropical grassland, *452, 453,* 454
tropical rain forest, 395, 450, *452, 452, 453, 454, 454*
trout, *483*
true fungi, 599
truffle, 600
Tryblidiiae, 681
*Trypanosoma,* 590
tsetse fly, 590
tsunami, 436
tube feet, 686, *686*
tuber, *652*
tuberculosis (TB), 383, *558,* 567, 575, 812
tubeworm, *664*
tumor, 142
tuna, 706
tundra biome, *452, 453,* 456
tunicate, 696, 698, R33
Turbellaria, R31
turnover, 464, *464*
turtle, 199, *402, 504, 541, 698*
twins, 199
two-column notes, 124, 194, 557, R23, *R23*
tympanic membrane, 756
Type 1 diabetes, 740–741, *740*
Type 2 diabetes, 740–741
Type III survivorship, 431, *431*
Type II survivorship, 431, *431*
Type I survivorship, 431, *431*
tyrosine (Tyr), *234*
*Tyto alba,* 533

# U

UAVs (unmanned aerial vehicles), 512, *512*
ulcer, 19, *19*
ultrasound, 397
ultrasound technician, R39
ultraviolet (UV) light, 247, 358
umbilical cord, 851, *851, 854,* 857
umbrella species, 491–492, *491*
unicellular organism. *See* single-celled organism

# Index

# Periodic Table

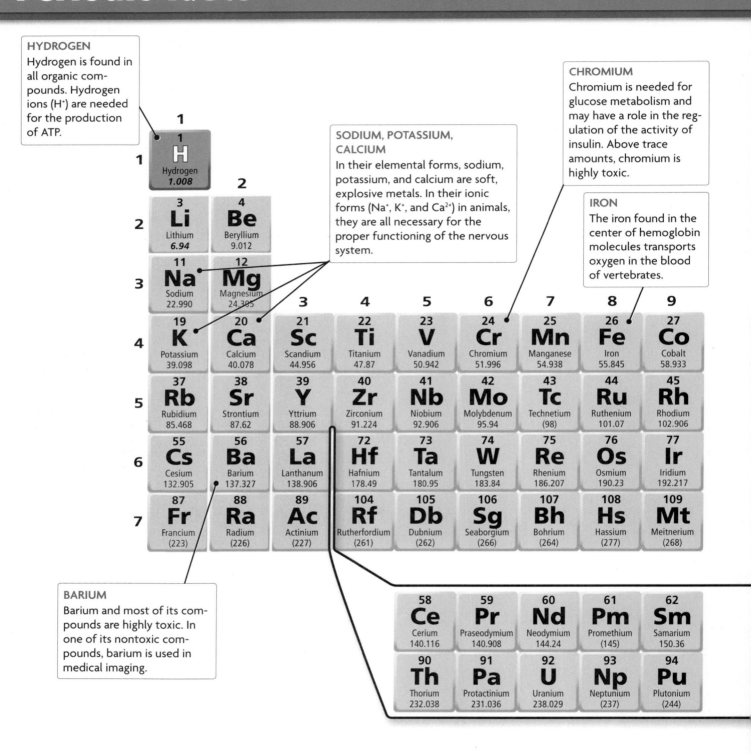

**HYDROGEN**
Hydrogen is found in all organic compounds. Hydrogen ions (H⁺) are needed for the production of ATP.

**SODIUM, POTASSIUM, CALCIUM**
In their elemental forms, sodium, potassium, and calcium are soft, explosive metals. In their ionic forms ($Na^+$, $K^+$, and $Ca^{2+}$) in animals, they are all necessary for the proper functioning of the nervous system.

**CHROMIUM**
Chromium is needed for glucose metabolism and may have a role in the regulation of the activity of insulin. Above trace amounts, chromium is highly toxic.

**IRON**
The iron found in the center of hemoglobin molecules transports oxygen in the blood of vertebrates.

**BARIUM**
Barium and most of its compounds are highly toxic. In one of its nontoxic compounds, barium is used in medical imaging.

| | | | | | | | | |
|---|---|---|---|---|---|---|---|---|
| **1** | | | | | | | | |
| 1 **H** Hydrogen *1.008* | **2** | | | | | | | |
| 3 **Li** Lithium *6.94* | 4 **Be** Beryllium 9.012 | | | | | | | |
| 11 **Na** Sodium 22.990 | 12 **Mg** Magnesium 24.305 | **3** | **4** | **5** | **6** | **7** | **8** | **9** |
| 19 **K** Potassium 39.098 | 20 **Ca** Calcium 40.078 | 21 **Sc** Scandium 44.956 | 22 **Ti** Titanium 47.87 | 23 **V** Vanadium 50.942 | 24 **Cr** Chromium 51.996 | 25 **Mn** Manganese 54.938 | 26 **Fe** Iron 55.845 | 27 **Co** Cobalt 58.933 |
| 37 **Rb** Rubidium 85.468 | 38 **Sr** Strontium 87.62 | 39 **Y** Yttrium 88.906 | 40 **Zr** Zirconium 91.224 | 41 **Nb** Niobium 92.906 | 42 **Mo** Molybdenum 95.94 | 43 **Tc** Technetium (98) | 44 **Ru** Ruthenium 101.07 | 45 **Rh** Rhodium 102.906 |
| 55 **Cs** Cesium 132.905 | 56 **Ba** Barium 137.327 | 57 **La** Lanthanum 138.906 | 72 **Hf** Hafnium 178.49 | 73 **Ta** Tantalum 180.95 | 74 **W** Tungsten 183.84 | 75 **Re** Rhenium 186.207 | 76 **Os** Osmium 190.23 | 77 **Ir** Iridium 192.217 |
| 87 **Fr** Francium (223) | 88 **Ra** Radium (226) | 89 **Ac** Actinium (227) | 104 **Rf** Rutherfordium (261) | 105 **Db** Dubnium (262) | 106 **Sg** Seaborgium (266) | 107 **Bh** Bohrium (264) | 108 **Hs** Hassium (277) | 109 **Mt** Meitnerium (268) |

| | | | | |
|---|---|---|---|---|
| 58 **Ce** Cerium 140.116 | 59 **Pr** Praseodymium 140.908 | 60 **Nd** Neodymium 144.24 | 61 **Pm** Promethium (145) | 62 **Sm** Samarium 150.36 |
| 90 **Th** Thorium 232.038 | 91 **Pa** Protactinium 231.036 | 92 **U** Uranium 238.029 | 93 **Np** Neptunium (237) | 94 **Pu** Plutonium (244) |

Metal    Metalloid    Nonmetal    **Fe** Solid    **Hg** Liquid    Ⓞ Gas

**CARBON**
All organic molecules, which are the basic building blocks of life, contain carbon.

**NITROGEN**
Proteins and nucleic acids both contain nitrogen. Although nitrogen makes up almost 80 percent of Earth's atmosphere, plants and animals cannot directly use nitrogen gas.

**OXYGEN**
Oxygen is found in many organic molecules and is needed for the aerobic stages of cellular respiration. Oxygen also is a waste product of photosynthesis and is in some cases toxic to cells.

**ZINC**
Zinc is found in many enzymes. Zinc is also important for maturation of human reproductive systems.

**CHLORINE**
Chlorine gas is a deadly poison. Chloride ions (Cl⁻) are necessary for the transmission of certain types of signals in the nervous system.

**PHOSPHORUS**
Phosphorus is found in the lipids that make up all cell membranes. It is a part of the "backbone" of both DNA and RNA molecules. On a larger scale, both bones and teeth contain phosphorus.

**18**

| | | | | | 2 |
| | | | | | He |
| | | | | | Helium |
| | | | | | 4.003 |

**13**  **14**  **15**  **16**  **17**

| 5 | 6 | 7 | 8 | 9 | 10 |
| B | C | N | O | F | Ne |
| Boron | Carbon | Nitrogen | Oxygen | Fluorine | Neon |
| 10.81 | 12.01 | 14.007 | 15.999 | 18.998 | 20.180 |

| 13 | 14 | 15 | 16 | 17 | 18 |
| Al | Si | P | S | Cl | Ar |
| Aluminum | Silicon | Phosphorus | Sulfur | Chlorine | Argon |
| 26.982 | 28.085 | 30.974 | 32.06 | 35.45 | 39.948 |

**10**  **11**  **12**

| 28 | 29 | 30 | 31 | 32 | 33 | 34 | 35 | 36 |
| Ni | Cu | Zn | Ga | Ge | As | Se | Br | Kr |
| Nickel | Copper | Zinc | Gallium | Germanium | Arsenic | Selenium | Bromine | Krypton |
| 58.69 | 63.546 | 65.39 | 69.723 | 72.63 | 74.922 | 78.96 | 79.904 | 83.80 |

| 46 | 47 | 48 | 49 | 50 | 51 | 52 | 53 | 54 |
| Pd | Ag | Cd | In | Sn | Sb | Te | I | Xe |
| Palladium | Silver | Cadmium | Indium | Tin | Antimony | Tellurium | Iodine | Xenon |
| 106.42 | 107.868 | 112.4 | 114.818 | 118.710 | 121.760 | 127.60 | 126.904 | 131.29 |

| 78 | 79 | 80 | 81 | 82 | 83 | 84 | 85 | 86 |
| Pt | Au | Hg | Tl | Pb | Bi | Po | At | Rn |
| Platinum | Gold | Mercury | Thallium | Lead | Bismuth | Polonium | Astatine | Radon |
| 195.078 | 196.967 | 200.59 | 204.38 | 207.2 | 208.980 | (209) | (210) | (222) |

| 110 | 111 | 112 | 113 | 114 | 115 | 116 | 117 | 118 |
| Ds | Rg | Cn | Nh | Fl | Mc | Lv | Ts | Og |
| Darmstadtium | Roentgenium | Copernicium | Nihonium | Flerovium | Moscovium | Livermorium | Tennessine | Oganesson |
| (281) | (272) | (285) | (284) | (289) | (288) | (292) | (294) | (294) |

| 63 | 64 | 65 | 66 | 67 | 68 | 69 | 70 | 71 |
| Eu | Gd | Tb | Dy | Ho | Er | Tm | Yb | Lu |
| Europium | Gadolinium | Terbium | Dysprosium | Holmium | Erbium | Thulium | Ytterbium | Lutetium |
| 151.964 | 157.25 | 158.925 | 162.50 | 164.930 | 167.26 | 168.934 | 173.04 | 174.967 |

| 95 | 96 | 97 | 98 | 99 | 100 | 101 | 102 | 103 |
| Am | Cm | Bk | Cf | Es | Fm | Md | No | Lr |
| Americium | Curium | Berkelium | Californium | Einsteinium | Fermium | Mendelevium | Nobelium | Lawrencium |
| (243) | (247) | (247) | (251) | (252) | (257) | (258) | (259) | (262) |

**Atomic number**
Number of protons in the nucleus of the element

1
H
Name — Hydrogen
1.008

**Symbol**
Each element has a symbol. The symbol's color represents the element's state at room temperature.

**Atomic mass**
This value is the average atomic mass of isotopes of this element. Each element for which this value is bolded and italicized has an atomic mass that is officially expressed as a range of values. In nature, the average atomic mass often varies depending on the properties of the material in which the element is found. Values in parentheses indicate the atomic mass of the most stable isotope.